1 MONTH OF
FREE
READING

at

www.ForgottenBooks.com

By purchasing this book you are eligible for one month membership to ForgottenBooks.com, giving you unlimited access to our entire collection of over 700,000 titles via our web site and mobile apps.

To claim your free month visit: www.forgottenbooks.com/free1247341

ISBN 978-0-332-76917-2
PIBN 11247341

Vol. 25—New Series

No. 1

Monday, January 6, 1930

Journal of Proceedings
Board of Supervisors

City and County of San Francisco

The Recorder Printing and Publishing Company
337 Bush Street, S. F.

•352
Sa 52:7 $\underline{25}$

JOURNAL OF PROCEEDINGS
BOARD OF SUPERVISORS

MONDAY, JANUARY 6, 1930, 10 A. M.

In Board of Supervisors, San Francisco, Monday, January 6, 1930, 10 a. m.

The Board of Supervisors met in regular session.

CALLING THE ROLL.

The roll was called and the following Supervisors were noted present:

Supervisors Andriano, Deasy, Colman, Gallagher, Havenner, Hayden, Kent, McGovern, McSheehy, Marks, Powers, Roncovieri, Schmidt, Stanton, Suhr, Toner—16.

Absent—Supervisors Shannon, Todd—2.

Quorum present.

His Honor Mayor Rolph appeared at 10 a. m., was excused, and Supervisor Kent was elected to preside.

APPROVAL OF JOURNALS.

The Journals of Proceedings of the meetings of December 16, 23 and 30, 1929, were considered read and approved.

ROLL CALL FOR PETITIONS AND COMMUNICATIONS.

Relative to Naval Base at Sunnyvale.

The following were presented and read by the Clerk:

House of Representatives, Washington, December 17, 1929.

Mr. J. S. Dunnigan, Clerk, City and County of San Francisco, San Francisco, Calif.

Dear. Mr. Dunnigan: Congressman Lea has directed me to acknowledge with thanks your communication of December 10 containing copy of resolution recently adopted by the Board of Supervisors of the City and County of San Francisco with reference to the selection of Sunnyvale for the proposed dirigible base.

Very truly yours,
M. W. MARTIN, Secretary.

Congress of the United States, House of Representatives.
Washington, D. C., December 19, 1929.

Mr. J. S. Dunnigan, Clerk, Room 235 City Hall, San Francisco, Calif.

My Dear Mr. Dunnigan: I am in receipt of your letter of recent date urging the designation of Sunnyvale, Santa Clara County, California, as the logical and strategic location for the proposed main naval dirigible base. Please be assured of my interest in this matter and that I am using every effort to have this base located at Sunnyvale.

Very sincerely yours,
ALBERT E. CARTER, M. C.

Ordered *filed.*

Congress of the United States, House of Representatives.
Washington, D. C., December 16, 1929.

Mr. John S. Dunnigan, Clerk of Board of Supervisors, San Francisco, Calif.

Dear Mr. Dunnigan: This is to acknowledge receipt of your letter of December 10, containing the Board's recent resolution regarding the Secretary of the Navy's rejection of the Sunnyvale site.

Please assure the Board that the Northern California representatives here are determined to fight this decision to the bitter end and that not a stone will be left unturned in our struggle for what we believe to be justice and fair play.

The Committee on Naval Affairs has decided not to hold any hearings on this matter until after the International Conference on Naval Limitation, which is about to take place in London. That means that these hearings will not be held until some time next spring. Such delay is in our favor because Admiral Moffett, who was chairman of the board of experts that investigated the proposed sites, will have returned from the London conference. He will be our best witness at the hearings.

Sincerely yours,

RICHARD J. WELCH, M. C.

Congress of the United States, House of Representatives.

Washington, D. C., December 17, 1929.

Mr. J. S. Dunnigan, Clerk's Office, Room 235 City Hall, City and County of San Francisco, San Francisco, Calif.

My Dear Mr. Dunnigan: I am in receipt of your letter of December 10 and resolution adopted by the Board of Supervisors of the City and County of San Francisco on December 9, urging the location of the naval dirigible base at Sunnyvale, California.

Let me assure you that I am and will do all possible to secure such location. We have a long, hard fight ahead of us, but I feel that ultimately we will win out.

With kindest regards, I am

Sincerely yours,

A. M. FREE.

United States Senate, Committee on Immigration.

December 14, 1929.

Mr. J. S. Dunnigan, Clerk, Board of Supervisors, Room 235 City Hall, San Francisco, Calif.

My Dear Mr. Dunnigan: I acknowledge receipt of your letter of December 10, advising me of the passage of a resolution adopted by the Board of Supervisors of the City and County of San Francisco on December 9 favoring the location of the proposed naval dirigible base at Sunnyvale, California.

Sincerely yours,

HIRAM W. JOHNSON.

Jesse Lilienthal School Property.

Communication, from Board of Education, advising that resignation of George C. Turner, superintendent of the Lilienthal School, and John D. Mulholland, caretaker, have been received, effective January 1, 1930. This to inform of the necessity of protecting property of the City and County.

Referred to Education, Parks and Playgrounds Committee.

Taxation Exemption, Municipal Employees.

Communication, from Hon. Samuel M. Shortridge, thanking Board for resolution with reference to the matter of exempting from taxation the incomes of certain classes of municipal employees.

Ordered *filed.*

Veterans' Welfare Board Thanks Supervisors.

Communication, from Veterans' Welfare Board, expressing appreciation of Board of Supervisors for its helpfulness and cooperation during past year.

Ordered *filed.*

Joint Highway District Legislation.

Communication, from Legislative Committee on Joint Highway District Laws, inviting cooperation and recommendation of necessary legislation to the 1931 Legislature in the study of joint highway district laws of the State of California and other States.

Ordered *filed*.

Abatement of Hog Ranches.

Communication from Health Officer William C. Hassler, advising that it is the opinion of the Board of Health that no intention exists on the part of the owners of hog ranches in San Francisco to comply with the law and the orders of the Board of Health, and requests that the City Attorney be directed to begin abatement proceedings under Ordinance No. 1410.

Referred to Health Committee.

City to Contract With Serge Prokofieff for Concert at Municipal Auditorium.

The following was read by the Clerk:

January 6, 1930.

Board of Supervisors, City Hall, San Francisco, Calif.

Gentlemen: I herewith transmit to you resolution to be adopted by your Honorable Board authorizing the Mayor to enter into a contract with Serge Prokofieff re concert at the Municipal Auditorium, as per recommendation of the Auditorium Committee.

If the resolution meets with the approval of your Board, I would ask its adoption and that you forward same, with the contracts, to the Mayor for his signature.

Yours very truly,

JOHN J. O'TOOLE,

City Attorney.

Whereupon, the following resolution was *adopted*:

Resolution No. 31870 (New Series), as follows:

Resolved, That the City and County of San Francisco enter into a contract with Serge Prokofieff for a concert to be given by said Prokofieff at the Municipal Auditorium on Tuesday, the 18th day of February, 1930, for which said Prokofieff is to receive from the City and County of San Francisco the sum of eight hundred ($800) dollars; be it

Further Resolved, That the Mayor of the City and County of San Francisco be and is hereby authorized to execute said contract for and on behalf of said City and County.

Ayes—Supervisors Andriano, Colman, Deasy, Gallagher, Havenner, Hayden, Kent, McGovern, McSheehy, Marks, Powers, Roncovieri, Schmidt, Stanton, Suhr, Toner—16.

Absent—Supervisors Shannon, Todd—2.

Opinion of City Attorney on Right of Board of Supervisors to Make Cost of Third Street Bridge a Charge on Surrounding Property.

The following was read by the Clerk:

December 26, 1929.

Dear Sirs: I am in receipt of your letter as to the legality of a plan for the reconstruction of the Third street bridge which would provide for the defraying of the cost thereof, or a part of the cost thereof, by the assessment of property adjacent to the bridge and the channel over which it is constructed.

Opinion.

Bridges over streams, whether navigable or unnavigable, are considered as a part of the highways of which they are the connecting link, and usually the same rules apply to the construction of the bridge as govern the construction of the highway.

Section 2 of the act of the Legislature of the State of California, entitled an act "To provide for work to be done on streets, lanes and alleys, etc.," approved March 18, 1885, and amended from time to time, and which act is commonly known as the "Vrooman Act," provides for the construction of bridges as a part of street improvement work where such construction is necessary. The same section provides that the cost of any work done pursuant to the provision of the act may be made a charge against a district.

In the case of Bailey v. The City of Hermosa Beach, 183 Cal. 757, the Supreme Court of this State upheld the right of a municipality to construct a bridge under the provisions of the Vrooman Act, as long as such bridges were for street purposes. In the same case the Supreme Court has also sustained the right of the legislative body of a city to make the cost of the bridge a charge upon a district, provided that all of the property within the district is benefited by the improvement.

You are, therefore, advised that if the Board of Supervisors should determine that the construction of the Third street bridge will be a benefit to any particular district, that the Board has the right to establish such a district and make the cost of the bridge, or any part thereof, a charge against all of the property within the district.

Your attention is, however, called to the federal law, which requires the consent of the Secretary of War and the Chief of Engineers of the War Department, or of Congress itself, before any bridge can be constructed over navigable waters.

Sincerely,
(Signed)   JNO. J. O'TOOLE,
City Attorney.

Referred to the Committee on Streets and Commercial Development of the Board of Supervisors.

Excessive Switching Charges.

The following, presented by Supervisor Todd at last meeting and inadvertently omitted from the Journal, is here inserted as a matter of record:

The State Board of Harbor Commissioners of the State of California filed with the Interstate Commerce Commission State Belt Railroad Tariff No. 2, Interstate Commerce Commission No. 2 on September 30, 1929, effective November 1, 1929, Item 45 increasing switching charges from $3.50 per car to $4.50 per car, and also increasing car rental charges from $5 per car to $6 per car in Item 125 of the same tariff.

Tariffs were not distributed by the Harbor Commission until after effective date and actual collection of the switching did not commence until November 26, 1929, although switching charges will be retroactive to the effective date of November 1, 1929.

The terminal railroad lines absorb $3.50 per car in San Francisco on shipments moving to and from their lines for a line haul, but they refuse to increase this absorption to cover the increased switching assessed by the Belt Railroad. The terminal switching charges in Oakland are absorbed by the terminal railroads.

As the matter now stands it costs the shippers of goods through the San Francisco docks $1 per car more than shipments going through the East Bay docks, and it also costs the San Francisco industries located on the State Belt Railroad $1 per car more for both their inbound and outbound cars where moving to and from the wharves, or to and from the connecting terminal railroad line than an industry located in the East Bay.

Although protest has been made by the San Francisco Chamber of Commerce to the Harbor Board no action has been taken and the charge remains in effect today.

Switching charges from connecting terminal lines to San Francisco wharves by the State Belt Railroad, $4.50 per car.

Absorbed by terminal railroads, $3.50 per car.

Cost to shipper, $1.

Switching charges from connecting line in Oakland to wharves by railroads serving wharves, $2.70 per car.

Absorbed by railroad receiving line haul, $2.70 per car.

Cost to shipper, nothing.

Switching charges for industry located on State Belt Railroad in San Francisco between industry and wharf, $4.50 per car.

Plus car rental, $6 per car.

Total cost to industry, $10.50 per car.

(Cost before increase, $8.50 per car.)

Switching charges for industry located in East Bay for a comparative distance from wharves. Switching charge between industry and wharf, 34 cents per ton, minimum $7.20 per car.

No car rental—total cost to industry, $7.20 per car.

For longer distances the charge increases to 45 cents per ton, minimum $11 per car.

PRESENTATION OF PROPOSALS.

Laundry Machinery.

Sealed proposals were received between the hours of 10 and 11 a. m. for furnishing laundry machinery and *referred to the Supplies Committee.*

Bathing Suits.

Sealed proposals were received by the Board of Supervisors for furnishing bathing suits for Park Commissioners and *referred to the Supplies Committee.*

HEARING OF APPEAL.

Henry Cowell Lime and Cement Company.

Hearing of appeal of Henry Cowell Lime and Cement Company from the action and decision of the Board of Public Works in overruling the protest of Henry Cowell Lime and Cement Company against the improvement of the north half of Commercial street from the west line of The Embarcadero to a line at right angles with Commercial street and one hundred and twenty-five (125) feet six and three-eighths (6⅜) inches west of the west line of The Embarcadero, by the construction of full width artificial stone sidewalks, where sidewalks are not now to official grade, and the construction of a retaining wall to support this sidewalk, as set forth in Resolution of Intention No. 96689 (Second Series).

Communication from W. H. George, Secretary Henry Cowell Lime and Cement Company, requesting that hearing be deferred until after the first of the year.

Attorney Van Fleet requests a continuance of hearing. He will be unable to attend.

Motion.

Supervisor Gallagher moved that the appeal be denied.

Amendment.

Supervisor Hayden, seconded by Supervisor Colman, moved to lay over one week.

Amendment *carried* by the following vote:

Ayes—Supervisors Deasy, Hayden, Kent, McSheehy, Marks, Schmidt, Suhr, Toner—8.

Noes—Supervisors Andriano, Colman, Gallagher, McGovern, Roncovieri, Stanton—6.

Absent—Supervisors Havenner, Powers, Shannon, Todd—4.

Hearing of Appeal of Property Owners on Kirkham Street Between Sixteenth and Seventeenth Avenues.

Appeal of property owners on Kirkham street between Sixteenth and Seventeenth avenues from the action and decision of the Board of Public Works in overruling the protest of a majority of the property owners against the ordering of the improvement of Kirkham street between Sixteenth and Seventeenth avenues, as set forth in Resolution No. 105862 (Second Series) of the Board of Public Works.

The Clerk read the names of the protestants and asked if any wanted to be heard.

No response.

Appeal Denied, Kirkham Street.

Whereupon, Supervisor Gallagher presented:

Resolution No. 31869 (New Series), as follows:

Resolved, That the appeal of property owners from the action and decision of the Board of Public Works in overruling the objection of property owners against the improvement of Kirkham street between the westerly line of Sixteenth avenue as produced southerly from the northwesterly corner of Sixteenth avenue and Kirkham street and the easterly line of Seventeenth avenue, by the construction of concrete curbs; by the construction of a 12-inch ironstone pipe sewer with accompanying Y branches and side sewers; and by the construction of an asphaltic concrete pavement, consisting of a 6-inch concrete foundation and a 1½-inch asphaltic concrete wearing surface on the roadway thereof, as set forth in Resolution of Intention No. 105862 (Second Series), be and the same is hereby denied and the work ordered.

Adopted by the following vote:

Ayes—Supervisors Andriano, Colman, Deasy, Gallagher, Havenner, Hayden, Kent, McGovern, McSheehy, Marks, Powers, Roncovieri, Schmidt, Stanton, Suhr, Toner—16.

Absent—Supervisors Shannon, Todd—2.

Passed for Printing.

Thereupon, the following bill was *passed for printing*:

Bill No. 9165, Ordinance No. ———— (New Series), as follows:

Ordering the performance of certain street work to be done in the City and County of San Francisco, approving and adopting specifications therefor.

Be it ordained by the People of the City and County of San Francisco as follows:

Section 1. The Board of Public Works in written communication filed in the office of the Clerk of the Board of Supervisors May 7, 1929, having recommended the ordering of the following street work, the same is hereby ordered to be done in the City and County of San Francisco in conformity with the provisions of the Street Improvement Ordinance of 1918 of said City and County of San Francisco, said work to be performed under the direction of the Board of Public Works, and to be done in accordance with the specifications prepared therefor by said Board of Public Works, and on file in its office, which said plans and specifications are hereby approved and adopted.

That said Board of Supervisors, pursuant to the provisions of Part II of the said Street Improvement Ordinance of 1918 of said City and County of San Francisco, does hereby determine and declare that the assessment to be imposed for the said contemplated improvements, respectively, may be paid in ten installments; that the period of time after the time of the payment of the first installment when each of the succeeding installments must be paid is to be one year from the time of the payment of the preceding installment, and that the rate of interest to be charged on all deferred payments shall be seven per centum per annum.

The improvement of Kirkham street between the westerly line of Sixteenth avenue as produced southerly from the northwesterly corner of Sixteenth avenue and Kirkham street and the easterly line of Seventeenth avenue, by the construction of concrete curbs; by the construction of a 12-inch ironstone pipe sewer with accompanying Y branches and side sewers; and by the construction of an asphaltic

concrete pavement, consisting of a 6-inch concrete foundation and a
1½-inch asphaltic concrete wearing surface, on the roadway thereof.
Section 2. This ordinance shall take effect immediately.

UNFINISHED BUSINESS.

Final Passage.

The following matters, heretofore passed for printing, were taken
up and *finally passed* by the following vote:

Authorizations.

On recommendation of Finance Committee.

Resolution No. 31871 (New Series), as follows:

Resolved, That the following amounts be and the same are hereby
authorized to be expended out of the hereinafter mentioned funds in
payment to the following named claimants, to-wit:

Park Fund.

(1) Frank Food Co., foodstuffs for parks (claim dated Dec.
20, 1929) ... .$ 695.09
(2) Granfield, Farrar & Carlin, clay furnished parks (claim
dated Dec. 20, 1929) 2,035.00
(3) Granfield, Farrar & Carlin, clay for parks (claim dated
Dec. 20, 1929) 2,275.50
(4) Industrial and Municipal Supply Co., furnishing and installing pumping plant at Lloyd Lake (claim dated Dec. 20,
1929) 2,002.00
(5) Langendorf United Bakeries, Inc., bread for parks (claim
dated Dec. 20, 1929) 918.21
(6) Meyer Rosenberg, loam furnished parks (claim dated
Dec. 20, 1929) 1,836.00
(7) San Francisco Dairy Co., milk for parks (claim dated
Dec. 20, 1929) 546.00
(8) Sherry Bros., foodstuffs for parks (claim dated Dec. 20,
1929) 528.54

Auditorium Fund.

(9) Musical Association of San Francisco, for services of San
Francisco Symphony Orchestra, performances of "The Messiah," December 18, 1929 (claim dated Dec. 20, 1929)......$ 2,500.00
(10) Louise Bennett, for payment to soloists, etc., performance of "The Messiah," December 18, 1929 (claim dated
Dec. 20, 1929) 904.00

Playground Fund.

(11) J. P. Holland, Inc., grading, etc., for St. Mary's Playground (claim dated Dec. 18, 1929) .. ..$ 1,420.61
(12) Baker, Hamilton & Pacific Co., hardware for playgrounds (claim dated Dec. 18, 1929) 575.60
(13) Michel & Pfeffer, metal fence material for playgrounds
(claim dated Dec. 18, 1929) 541.36
(14) Spring Valley Water Co., water for playgrounds (claim
dated Dec. 18, 1929) 1,248.60
(15) Playground Commission Mather Revolving Fund, reimbursement for account of expenditures, per vouchers
attached (claim dated Dec. 18, 1929) 812.17
(16) A. G. Spalding & Bros., playground recreational supplies (claim dated Dec. 18, 1929) 552.00

School Bond Fund, Issue 1923.

(17) E. P. Finigan, gymnasium equipment for Polytechnic
High School (claim dated Dec. 17, 1929) .. ..$ 2,005.50

Special School Tax.

(18) Edward F. Dowd, first and final payment, electric fixtures for second unit of South Side (Balboa) High School (claim dated Dec. 18, 1929) .. ..$ 1,620.00

(19) Newberry, Pearce Electric Co., final payment, electrical work for second unit, South Side (Balboa) High School (claim dated Dec. 17, 1929) 2,288.67

Municipal Railway Fund.

(20) Emma J. Fish and J. D. Fish, in full settlement of claim by reason of any damage sustained by Emma J. Fish on or about November 30, 1928, while attempting to board Municipal car at Geary and Powell streets (claim dated Dec. 12 1929) .. ..$ 2,500.00

(21) Tansey Crowe Co., tubes and tires for Municipal Railway buses (claim dated Dec. 12, 1929)................... 742.64

(22) Pacific Gas and Electric Co., electric service furnished Municipal Railway (claim dated Dec. 17, 1929)........... 41,931.94

(23) Street Repair Department, Board of Public Works, reimbursement for asphalt repairs to Municipal Railway right of way (claim dated Dec. 17, 1929).................... 1,555.37

County Road Fund.

(24) Pacific Coast Aggregates, Inc., gravel for street reconstruction (claim dated Dec. 13, 1929) ....$ 575.30

(25) Pacific Coast Aggregates, Inc., gravel for street reconstruction (claim dated Dec. 13, 1929)................... 594.98

(26) The Texas Co., gasoline furnished for account of street reconstruction (claim dated Dec. 13, 1929)..............$ 1,219.40

(27) James T. Tobin, wrecking pagoda on Naples street between Geneva avenue and Rolph street, and for paving that portion of the roadway (claim dated Dec. 18, 1929)........ 1,645.00

(28) James T. Tobin, resurfacing of Naples street between Amazon avenue and Munich street (claim dated Dec. 18, 1929).. .. .. 3,066.00

Hetch Hetchy Construction Fund, Bond Issue 1928.

(29) Mine Safety Appliances Co., gas masks (claim dated Dec. 11, 1929) .. ..$ 525.00

(30) Alfred Pereira & Bros., hauling, month of October (claim dated Dec. 11, 1929) .. .' 622.13

(31) Santa Cruz Portland Cement Co., cement (claim dated Dec. 11, 1929) 1,028.00

(32) Thomson, Wood & Hoffman, professional services in re opinion on Hetch Hetchy Water Bonds (claim dated Dec. 12, 1929) 600.00

(33) San Francisco City Employees' Retirement System, to match contributions by employees engaged on Hetch Hetchy construction (claim dated Dec. 13, 1929) 635.16

Auditorium Fund.

(34) Pacific Gas and Electric Co., gas and electricity furnished the Auditorium during November (claim dated Dec. 12, 1929) .. ..$ 842.89

General Fund, 1929-1930.

(35) Children's Agency, maintenance of minors (claim dated Dec. 13, 1929) $30,884.89

(36) Little Children's Aid, maintenance of minors (claim dated Dec. 13, 1929) 12,128.64

(37) Eureka Benevolent Society, maintenance of minors (claim dated Dec. 13, 1929) 3,139.22

(38) St. Vincent's School, maintenance of minors (claim dated Dec. 13, 1929) 1,115.24

(39) The Albertinum Orphanage, maintenance of minors (claim dated Dec. 13, 1929) 702.63

(40) Roman Catholic Orphanage, maintenance of minors (claim dated Dec. 13, 1929) 1,869.70

(41) San Francisco Protestant Orphanage, maintenance of minors (claim dated Dec. 13, 1929).................... 500.00

(42) Preston School of Industry, maintenance of minors (claim dated Dec. 13, 1929) 766.44

(43) Preston School of Industry, maintenance of minors (claim dated Dec. 16, 1929) 780.00

(44) Board of Public Works, reimbursement for expense of repairs to boiler, County Jail No. 2 (claim dated Dec. 16, 1929) 543.79

(45) Old Homestead Bakery, bread for County Jails (claim dated Dec. 16, 1929) 720.00

(46) Hanni & Girard, repairs to Police Department Buick autos (claim dated Dec. 16, 1929) 611.00

(47) Berringer & Russell, hay, etc., furnished Police Department (claim dated Dec. 16, 1929) 1,117.42

(48) James Rolph, Jr., Mayor, for personal and other than personal services, office of the Mayor, months of November and December, 1929 (claim dated Dec. 28, 1929)......... 1,464.16

(49) Elliott Addressing Machine Co., supplies for Elliott addressing machine, office of the Assessor (claim dated Dec. 19, 1929) 1,515.75

(50) Board of Park Commissioners, reimbursement for beautification of Civic Center, month of November (claim dated Dec. 20, 1929) 760.22

(51) A. P. Jacobs, rent of No. 333 Kearny street, December 3, 1929, to January 3, 1930 (claim dated Dec. 23, 1929)........ 1,120.75

(52) T. M. Gallagher, construction of artificial sone sidewalk on Chestnut street between Fillmore and Webster streets (claim dated Dec. 18, 1929) 548.40

(53) Photostat Corporation, Bureau of Engineering (claim dated Dec. 16, 1929) 526.80

(54) Tay-Holbrook, Inc., pipe and fittings, Board of Public Works (claim dated Dec. 16, 1929) 1,059.20

(55) Mack-International Motor Truck Corporation, four Mack tractors for Fire Department (claim dated Nov. 30, 1929).. 30,100.00

(56) E. R. Squibb & Sons, drug sundries, San Francisco Hospital (claim dated Nov. 30, 1929) 531.40

(57) Barnard & Bunker, beans for San Francisco Hospital (claim dated Nov. 30, 1929) 545.00

(58) Kahn & Co., X-Ray fiilms for San Francisco Hospital (claim dated Nov. 30, 1929) 708.00

(59) O'Brien, Spotorno & Mitchell, turkeys furnished San Francisco Hospital (claim dated Nov. 30, 1929).......... 619.44

Ayes—Supervisors Andriano, Colman, Deasy, Gallagher, Havenner, Hayden, Kent, McGovern, McSheehy, Marks, Powers, Roncovieri, Schmidt, Stanton, Suhr, Toner—16.

Absent—Supervisors Shannon, Todd—2.

Payments for Properties Required for Boulevards.

Also, Resolution No. 31872 (New Series), as follows:

Resolved, That the following amounts be and the same are hereby set aside and appropriated out of Boulevard Bond Fund, Issue 1927, and authorized in payment to the hereinafter named; being payments for properties required for the Sunset boulevard, to-wit:

(1) Sterling Realty Company and Title Insurance & Guaranty Co., for the purchase of all of Lots 1, 2, 18, 19, 20, 21,

22, 23, 24, 25, 26, 44, 45, 46, 47, 48, 49, 50 and 51 in Block
1714 as per the Assessor's Block Books; approved by Resolution No. ———, New Series (claim dated Dec. 18, 1929) .$61,000.00
(2) Florence Kustel and City Title Insurance Co., for Lots 25
and 27 in Block 2098, as per the Assessor's Block Books;
approved by Resolution No. ———, New Series (claim
dated Dec. 18, 1929)..................................   1,350.00
(3) Joseph Estate Company and Title Insurance & Guaranty
Co., for Lots 1, 3 and 4 in Block 1791, and Lots 1 and 3 in
Block 1882, as per the Assessor's Block Books; approved by
Resolution No. ———, New Series (claim dated Dec.
18, 1929) 115,000.00
(4) George Neary and Ethel Neary, and City Title Insurance
Co., for the easterly one-half of Lot 1 in Block 2313, as per
the Assessor's Block Books; approved by Resolution No.
———, New Series (claim dated Dec. 19, 1929)......... 18,627.27
(5) William F. Altvater, R. W. Gillogley and R. L. Husted,
and Title Insurance & Guaranty Co., for all of Block 1907,
as per the Assessor's Block Books; approved by Resolution
No. ———, New Series (claim dated Dec. 19, 1929)...... 44,000.00
(6) Karen Eliasen and California Pacific Title & Trust Co.,
for Lot 37 in Block 2389, as per the Assessor's Block Books;
approved by Resolution No. ———, New Series (claim
dated Dec. 20, 1929)..................................   1,500.00

Ayes—Supervisors Andriano, Colman, Deasy, Gallagher, Havenner,
Hayden, Kent, McGovern, McSheehy, Marks, Powers, Roncovieri,
Schmidt, Stanton, Suhr, Toner—16.
Absent—Supervisors Shannon, Todd—2.

Appropriation for Account of School Buildings.

Also, Resolution No. 31873 (New Series), as follows:
Resolved, That the following amounts be and the same are hereby
set aside, appropriated and authorized to be expended out of Special
School Tax for the following purposes, to-wit:
(1) For the cost of installing acoustical material in the Auditorium of the Polytechnic High School (contract awarded
Western Asbestos Magnesia Company)...................$ 4,125.00
(2) For cost of boring test holes to ascertain condition of the
ground on the sites of new school buildings............... 1,500.00

Ayes—Supervisors Andriano, Colman, Deasy, Gallagher, Havenner,
Hayden, Kent, McGovern, McSheehy, Marks, Powers, Roncovieri,
Schmidt, Stanton, Suhr, Toner—16.
Absent—Supervisors Shannon, Todd—2.

Appropriations From General Fund.

Also, Resolution No. 31874 (New Series), as follows:
Resolved, That the following amounts be and the same are hereby
set aside, appropriated and authorized to be expended out of General
Fund, Fiscal Year 1929-1930, for the following purposes, to-wit:
(1) For the printing of 512 copies of the City Engineer's
report on street railway transportation requirements in San
Francisco $1,000.00
(2) For the salary of an additional superintendent in the
Bureau of Sewer Repair, Board of Public Works, for the
six months ending June 30, 1930....................... 1,200.00

Ayes—Supervisors Andriano, Colman, Deasy, Gallagher, Havenner,
Hayden, Kent, McGovern, McSheehy, Marks, Powers, Roncovieri,
Schmidt, Stanton, Suhr, Toner—16.
Absent—Supervisors Shannon, Todd—2.

Appropriations for Account of Street Improvements.

Also, Resolution No. 31875 (New Series), as follows:

Resolved, That the following amounts be and the same are hereby set aside, appropriated and authorized to be expended out of County Road Fund for the following purposes, to-wit:

(1) For the cost of replanking the Evans avenue bridge at Army street, including possible extras, engineering and inspection (M. Bertolino contract) $1,674.00

(2) For the improvement of Laidley street from Thirtieth street to Noe street, including 50 per cent of assessment under public contract................................... 11,100.00

(3) For the painting of traffic lanes on Portola drive, including 60,000 lineal feet of 6-inch and 4-inch, eight "Slow" signs on surface of pavement and eight painted "Pedestrian Crossing" signs on surface of pavement................... 1,272.00

(4) For the cost of the improving of the easterly one-half of Elk street from Bosworth street to Chenery street...... 2,375.00

(5) For cost of rehabilitating of improvements on property at No. 3433 Market street, damage due to the extension of Market street 632.00

(6) Resurfacing and reconstruction of Vallejo street from Van Ness avenue to Pierce street....................... 6,000.00

Ayes—Supervisors Andriano, Colman, Deasy, Gallagher, Havenner, Hayden, Kent, McGovern, McSheehy, Marks, Powers, Roncovieri, Schmidt, Stanton, Suhr, Toner—16.

Absent—Supervisors Shannon, Todd—2.

Appropriation for Emergency Supplies, Direction of Superintendent of Laguna Honda Home.

Also, Resolution No. 31876 (New Series), as follows:

Resolved, That the sum of $7,500 be and the same is hereby set aside, appropriated and authorized to be expended out of "Urgent Necessity," Budget Item No. 24, Fiscal Year 1929-1930, for additional and emergency supplies by the Board of Health under the direction of the Superintendent of the Laguna Honda Home.

Ayes—Supervisors Andriano, Colman, Deasy, Gallagher, Havenner, Hayden, Kent, McGovern, McSheehy, Marks, Powers, Roncovieri, Schmidt, Stanton, Suhr, Toner—16.

Absent—Supervisors Shannon, Todd—2.

Payment to Joseph Harris for School Property.

Also, Resolution No. 31877 (New Series), as follows:

Resolved, That the sum of $4,323.42 be and the same is hereby set aside and appropriated out of School Construction Fund, Bond Issue 1923, and authorized in payment to Jacob Harris and Joseph Harris; being payment for land situate and commencing at a point formed by the intersection of the northerly line of Ulloa street with the easterly line of Thirty-ninth avenue, running thence easterly along said northerly line of Ulloa street 57 feet 6 inches; thence at a right angle northerly 100 feet; thence at a right angle westerly 57 feet 6 inches to the easterly line of Thirty-ninth avenue; thence southerly along the easterly line of Thirty-ninth avenue 100 feet to the northerly line of Ulloa street and point of commencement. Being a portion of O. L. Block 1159; also known as Block 2387 on Assessor's Map Book. Per acceptance of offer by Resolution No. 31804 (New Series), and required for school purposes. (Claim dated Dec. 23, 1929.)

Ayes—Supervisors Andriano, Colman, Deasy, Gallagher, Havenner, Hayden, Kent, McGovern, McSheehy, Marks, Powers, Roncovieri, Schmidt, Stanton, Suhr, Toner—16.

Absent—Supervisors Shannon, Todd—2.

Referred.

The following resolution was, on motion of Supervisor McSheehy, ordered *referred to the Public Health Committee* by the following vote:

Authorization.

Resolution No. ————— (New Series), as follows:

Resolved, That the following amount be and the same is hereby authorized to be expended out of the hereinafter mentioned fund in payment to the following named claimant, to-wit:

Hospital Bond Construction Fund—Issue 1929.

Henry E. Meyers, for architectural services in connection
with building of Tuberculosis Preventorium (claim dated
Dec. 2, 1929).. $9,842.92

Ayes—Supervisors Andriano, Deasy, Hayden, Kent, McGovern, McSheehy, Powers, Roncovieri, Schmidt, Stanton, Suhr, Todd, Toner—13.

Noes—Supervisors Colman, Gallagher, Havenner—3.

Absent—Supervisors Marks, Shannon—2.

Final Passage.

The following matters, heretofore passed for printing, were taken up and *finally passed* by the following vote:

Ordering the Furnishing and Installing of Motor-Driven Centrifugal Pump at Mills Field Municipal Airport and Plans and Specifications.

On recommendation of Finance Committee.

Bill No. 9141, Ordinance No. 8648 (New Series), as follows:

Authorizing the preparation of plans and specifications for the furnishing and installing of motor-driven centrifugal pump with auxiliary engine drive at the Mills Field Municipal Airport of San Francisco; ordering the furnishing and installing of motor-driven centrifugal pump with auxiliary engine drive at the Mills Field Municipal Airport of San Francisco, and authorizing the Board of Works to enter into contract for the said furnishing and installing of said pump in accordance with the plans and specifications prepared therefor.

Be it ordained by the People of the City and County of San Francisco as follows:

Section 1. The furnishing and installing of motor-driven centrifugal pump at the Mills Field Municipal Airport of San Francisco is hereby ordered, and the Board of Public Works is hereby authorized, instructed and empowered to prepare plans and specifications of the said furnishing and installing of said pump, and to enter into contract for the furnishing and installing of said pump in accordance with the plans and specifications prepared therefor.

Section 2. This ordinance shall take effect immediately.

Ayes—Supervisors Andriano, Colman, Deasy, Gallagher, Havenner, Hayden, Kent, McGovern, McSheehy, Marks, Powers, Roncovieri, Schmidt, Stanton, Suhr, Toner—16.

Absent—Supervisors Shannon, Todd—2.

Ordering the Construction of Addition to Roof Wards at the San Francisco Hospital and Authorizing Preparation of Plans and Specifications Therefor.

Also, Bill No. 9142, Ordinance No. 8649 (New Series), as follows:

The construction of an addition to roof wards at the San Francisco Hospital is hereby ordered; authorizing, directing and empowering the Board of Public Works to prepare plans and specifications for said addition to roof wards at the San Francisco Hospital, and to enter into contract for said construction of addition to roof wards at the

San Francisco Hospital in accordance with the plans and specifications prepared therefor.

Be it ordained by the People of the City and County of San Francisco as follows:

Section 1. The construction of an addition to roof wards at the San Francisco Hospital is hereby ordered, and the Board of Public Works is hereby authorized, instructed and empowered to prepare plans and specifications for said construction of addition to roof wards at the San Francisco Hospital, and to enter into contract for said construction of addition to roof wards at the San Francisco Hospital in accordance with the plans and specifications prepared therefor.

Section 2. This ordinance shall take effect immediately.

Ayes—Supervisors Andriano, Colman, Deasy, Gallagher, Havenner, Hayden, Kent, McGovern, McSheehy, Marks, Powers, Roncovieri, Schmidt, Stanton, Suhr, Toner—16.

Absent—Supervisors Shannon, Todd—2.

Authorizing Plans, Specifications and Receipt of Bids for Rehabilitation of Stockton Street Tunnel.

Also, Bill No. 9143, Ordinance No. 8650 (New Series), as follows:

Authorizing and ordering the preparation of plans and specifications for and the rehabilitation of the Stockton Street Tunnel by cleaning, painting and additional lighting in accordance with the plans and specifications prepared therefor. Authorizing and directing the Board of Public Works to enter into contract for said rehibillation of the Stockton Street Tunnel.

Be it ordained by the People of the City and County of San Francisco as follows:

Section 1. The Board of Public Works is hereby authorized, instructed and empowered to prepare plans and specifications for the rehabilitation of the Stockton Street Tunnel by cleaning, painting and additional lighting; and ordering the rehabilitation of the Stockton Street Tunnel by cleaning, painting and additional lighting in accordance with the plans and specifications prepared therefor, and which plans and specifications are hereby approved. The Board of Public Works is hereby authorized, instructed and empowered to enter into contract for the said rehabilitation of the Stockton Street Tunnel in accordance with the plans and specifications prepared therefor.

Section 2. This ordinance shall take effect immediately.

Ayes—Supervisors Andriano, Colman, Deasy, Gallagher, Havenner, Hayden, Kent, McGovern, McSheehy, Marks, Powers, Roncovieri, Schmidt, Stanton, Suhr, Toner—16.

Absent—Supervisors Shannon, Todd—2.

Granting Thomas T. Cox Automobile Supply Station Permit, Southwest Corner of Fulton and Divisadero Streets.

On recommendation of Fire Committee.

Resolution No. 31879 (New Series) as follows:

Resolved, That Thomas T. Cox be and is hereby granted permission, revocable at will of the Board of Supervisors, to maintain and operate an automobile supply station on the southwest corner of Fulton and Divisadero streets.

The rights granted under this resolution shall be exercised within six months, otherwise said permit shall become null and void.

Ayes—Supervisors Andriano, Colman, Deasy, Gallagher, Havenner, Hayden, Kent, McGovern, McSheehy, Marks, Powers, Roncovieri, Schmidt, Stanton, Suhr, Toner—16.

Absent—Supervisors Shannon, Todd—2.

Authorizing Board of Public Works to Terminate the Existing Contract and to Enter Into a New Seven-Year Lease With the R. G. Scott Advertising Company for Advertising Privileges In and Upon the Cars of the Municipal Railway.

On recommendation of Public Utilities Committee.

Bill No. 9144, Ordinance No. 8651 (New Series), as follows:

Authorizing the Board of Public Works to terminate as of the date of December 31, 1929, the existing contract, and as consideration there-for to lease for a period of seven years, commencing the 1st day of January, 1930, the advertising rights and privileges in and upon the cars of the Municipal Railway, and to enter into written contract there-for with the R. C. Scott Advertising Company of California.

Be it ordained by the People of the City and County of San Francisco as follows:

Section 1. The Board of Public Works is hereby authorized to enter into an agreement to terminate the existing contract with the R. C. Scott Advertising Company of California for the advertising rights and privileges in and upon the cars of the Municipal Railway, said agreement to provide for the termination of said existing contract on December 31, 1929, provided the said R. C. Scott Advertising Company of California, in consideration of said termination, executes and enters into a new lease of said advertising rights and privileges for a period of seven years, commencing the 1st day of January, 1930, upon the following rental basis, to-wit: for the first year, a rental of $23,750; for the second and subsequent years, said sum of $23,750 shall be increased or decreased as the car and bus hours for the previous year compare with the total car and bus hours of the entire system for the calendar year 1929, provided that in so determining the rental for the second and subsequent years 60 per cent only of bus hours for each previous year shall be added to the total number of car hours for each such previous year.

Section 2. The Board of Public Works of the City and County of San Francisco is authorized to lease for a period of seven years, commencing on the 1st day of January, 1930, and ending on the 31st day of December, 1936, the advertising rights and privileges in and upon the cars of the Municipal Railways, owned and controlled by the City and County of San Francisco, to the R. C. Scott Advertising Company of California for the consideration or rental hereinabove in Section 1 of this ordinance provided.

Section 3. The Board of Public Works in entering into said contract shall in writing prescribe such conditions and limitations, rules and regulations as shall appear to said Board meet and proper to protect the interests of the City and County of San Francisco. The said Board of Public Works shall also require of the said R. C. Scott Advertising Company of California a written undertaking or bond to protect said lease. Said undertaking or bond shall be of a sum not less than $10,000 per year for each year of said lease, the same to be executed at such time and in such manner as the Board of Public Works may direct.

Ayes—Supervisors Andriano, Colman, Deasy, Gallagher, Havenner, Hayden, Kent, McGovern, McSheehy, Marks, Powers, Roncovieri, Schmidt, Stanton, Suhr, Toner—16.

Absent—Supervisors Shannon, Todd—2.

Condemnation of Land Required for Widening Portola Drive.

On recommendation of Streets Committee.

Resolution No. 31880 (New Series), as follows:

Resolved, by the Board of Supervisors of the City and County of San Francisco, that public interest and necessity require the acquisition by the City and County of San Francisco, a municipal corporation, of the following properties situated in the City and County of San Francisco, State of California, more particularly described as follows, to-wit:

Parcel 1: All that portion of Lot 42, in Block 22, Fairview Terrace, as per map thereof filed April 13, 1909, in Book "G" of Maps, pages 44 and 45, in the office of the Recorder of the City and County of San Francisco, State of California, described as follows:

Beginning at the point of intersection of the easterly line of Burnett avenue (formerly Lincoln avenue) and the southeasterly line of Portola drive (formerly Corbett avenue); running thence northeasterly along the southeasterly line of Portola drive 5.051 feet; thence southwesterly on a curve to the right with a radius of 300 feet, tangent to a line deflected 171 degrees 12 minutes 42 seconds to the right from the preceding course, 5.360 feet to the easterly line of Burnett avenue, and thence northerly thereon 0.813 feet to the point of beginning.

Parcel 2: All of Block 23, Fairview Terrace, as per map thereof filed April 13, 1909, in the office of the Recorder of the City and County of San Francisco, State of California, and recorded in Map Book "G", pages 44 and 45.

Parcel 3: All that portion of Lot 9, in Block 26, of the subdivision of a part of the San Miguel Rancho, as per map thereof filed March 30, 1867, in Book 2 "A and B" of Maps, page 35, in the office of the Recorder of the City and County of San Francisco, State of California, described as follows:

Beginning at the point of intersection of the westerly line of Portola drive (formerly Corbett avenue) and the southerly line of said Lot 9; running thence westerly along the last-mentioned line 30.110 feet; thence deflecting 85 degrees 00 minutes 45 seconds to the right and running northerly 14.800 feet; thence northerly on a curve to the right with a radius of 300 feet, tangent to the preceding course 15.160 feet to the southerly line of the property now or formerly owned by John J. Barrett; thence deflecting 92 degrees 05 minutes 32 seconds to the right from the tangent of the preceding curve and running easterly along the last-mentioned line 29.741 feet to said westerly line of Portola drive, and thence southerly thereon 30 feet to the point of beginning.

Parcel 4: All that portion of Lot 9, in Block 26 of the subdivision of a part of the San Miguel Rancho, as per map thereof filed March 30, 1867, in Book 2 "A and B" of Maps, page 35, in the office of the Recorder of the City and County of San Francisco, State of California, described as follows:

Beginning at a point on the westerly line of Portola drive (formerly Corbett avenue), distant thereon 30 feet northerly from its intersection with the southerly line of said Lot 9; running thence westerly along the northerly line of the property now or formerly belonging to Marvin E. Dowell 29.741 feet; thence northerly on a curve to the right with a radius of 300 feet, tangent to a line deflected 87 degrees 54 minutes 28 seconds to the right from the preceding course, a distance of 29.901 feet to the southerly line of the property now or formerly belonging to August Mund; thence easterly along the last-mentioned line 26.733 feet to the westerly line of Portola drive; and thence southerly thereon 30 feet to the point of beginning.

Parcel 5: All that portion of Lot 9, in Block 26 of the subdivision of a part of the San Miguel Rancho, as per map thereof filed March 30, 1867, in Book 2 "A and B" of Maps, page 35, in the office of the Recorder of the City and County of San Francisco, State of California, described as follows:

Beginning at a point on the westerly line of Portola drive (formerly Corbett avenue), distant thereon 60 feet northerly from its intersection with the southerly line of said Lot 9; running thence westerly along the northerly line of the property now or formerly belonging to John J. Barrett 26.733 feet; thence northerly on a curve to the right with a radius of 300 feet, tangent to a line deflected 93 degrees 37 minutes 08 seconds to the right from the preceding course, a distance of

30.092 feet to the southerly line of the property now or formerly belonging to City Title Insurance Company; thence easterly along the
last-mentioned line 20.723 feet to the westerly line of Portola drive,
and thence southerly thereon 30 feet to the point of beginning.

Parcel 6: All those portions of Lots 8 and 9, in Block 26 of the subdivision of a part of the San Miguel Rancho, as per map thereof filed
March 30, 1867, in Book 2 "A and B" of Maps, page 35, in the office of
the Recorder of the City and County of San Francisco, State of California, described as follows:

Beginning at a point on the westerly line of Portola drive (formerly
Corbett avenue), distant thereon 90 feet northerly from its intersection with the southerly line of Lot 9; running thence westerly along
the northerly line of the property now or formerly belonging to August
Mund 20.723 feet; thence northerly on a curve to the right with a
radius of 300 feet, tangent to a line deflected 99 degrees 21 minutes 57
seconds to the right from the preceding course, a distance of 30.631 feet
to the southerly line of the property now or formerly belonging to
Mary Kelly; thence easterly along the last-mentioned line 12.336 feet
to the westerly curved line of Portola drive, and thence southerly
thereon 30 feet to the point of beginning.

Parcel 7· Lots 32 and 33, in Block 22, Fairview Terrace, as per map
thereof filed April 13, 1909, in Book "G" of Maps, pages 44 and 45, in
the office of the Recorder of the City and County of San Francisco.

Be it Further Resolved, That said property is suitable, adaptable,
necessary and required for the public use of said City and County of
San Francisco, to-wit: For the opening, widening, construction and
maintenance of Portola drive from its point of intersection with
Twenty-fourth street in a southwesterly direction to the point of intersection with Woodside avenue. It is necessary that a fee simple title
be taken for such use.

The City Attorney is hereby ordered and directed to commence proceedings in eminent domain against the owners of said parcel of land
and of any and all interests therein or claims thereto, for the condemnation thereof for the public use of the City and County of San
Francisco as aforesaid.

Ayes—Supervisors Andriano, Colman, Deasy, Gallagher, Havenner,
Hayden, Kent, McGovern, McSheehy, Marks, Powers, Roncovieri,
Schmidt, Stanton, Suhr, Toner—16.

Absent—Supervisors Shannon, Todd—2.

Condemnation of Land Required for the Opening and Widening of Cayuga Avenue.

Also, Resolution No. 31881 (New Series), as follows:

Resolved, by the Board of Supervisors of the City and County of San
Francisco, that public interest and necessity require the acquisition
by the City and County of San Francisco, a municipal corporation, of
the following properties, situated in the City and County of San
Francisco, State of California, more particularly described as follows,
to-wit:

Parcel 1. Beginning at a point on the southwesterly line of Greece
street, distant northwesterly thereon 177.275 feet from the northwesterly line of Knight's place, and running thence in a westerly direction
along a curve to the left tangent to said southwesterly line and having
a radius of 20 feet and a central angle of 67 deg. 17 min. 14 sec., a distance of 23.488 feet; thence southwesterly along a curve to the right
tangent to the preceding course and having a radius of 400 feet and a
central angle of 1 deg. 32 min. 14 sec., a distance of 10.731 feet to a
point on the southeasterly line of the property now or formerly owned
by Richard C. Brodrick; thence northeasterly along said southeasterly line 22.120 feet to the southwesterly line of Greece street; thence

at right angles southeasterly along said southwesterly line 22.725 feet to the point of beginning.

Being a portion of Lot No. 6 in Block No. 11, as per West End Map No. 1, recorded in Map Book "2 A and B," page 45, records of the City and County of San Francisco.

Parcel 2. Beginning at a point on the southwesterly line of Greece street, distant northwesterly thereon 200 feet from the northwesterly line of Knight's place, and running thence southwesterly at right angles to said southwesterly line of Greece street 22.120 feet; thence southwesterly along a curve to the right tangent to a line deflected 24 deg. 15 min. 00 sec. to the right from the preceding course and having a radius of 400 feet and a central angle of 6 deg. 17 min. 55 sec., a distance of 43.973 feet; thence southwesterly along the tangent to the preceding curve, a distance of 20.904 feet, more or less, to the south-easterly line of the property now or formerly owned by Antonio Tis-cornia; thence deflecting 159 deg. 22 min. 40 sec. to the right and running northeasterly along said southeasterly line 80.346 feet to said southwesterly line of Greece street; thence deflecting 80 deg. 04 min. 25 sec. to the right and running southeasterly along said south-westerly line 17 feet to the point of beginning.

Being a portion of Lot No. 6 in Block No. 11, as per West End Map No. 1, recorded in Map Book "2 A and B," page 45, records of the City and County of San Francisco; be it

Further Resolved, That said properties are suitable, adaptable, neces-sary and required for the public use of said City and County of San Francisco, to-wit: For the opening, widening, construction and mainte-nance of Cayuga avenue at its intersection with Greece street. It is necessary that a fee simple title be taken for such use.

The City Attorney is hereby ordered and directed to commenuce pro-ceedings in eminent domain against the owners of said parcels of land and of any and all interests therein, or claims thereto, for the con-demnation thereof for the public use of the City and County of San Francisco, as aforesaid.

Ayes—Supervisors Andriano, Colman, Deasy, Gallagher, Havenner, Hayden, Kent, McGovern, McSheehy, Marks, Powers, Roncovieri, Schmidt, Stanton, Suhr, Toner—16.

Absent—Supervisors Shannon, Todd—2.

Condemnation of Land Required for Widening of Ocean Avenue From San Leandro Way to San Fernando Way.

Also, Resolution No. 31882 (New Series), as follows:

Resolved, by the Board of Supervisors of the City and County of San Francisco, that public interest and necessity require the acquisition by the City and County of San Francisco, a municipal corporation, of the following property, situated in the City and County of San Fran-cisco, State of California, more particularly described as follows, to-wit:

Beginning at the point of intersection of the northeasterly line of Ocean avenue and the northwesterly line of San Leandro way, running thence northwesterly along the northeasterly line of Ocean avenue 90.001 feet to the northwesterly line of Lot 16, Block 3257, of Balboa Terrace Addition, as per map thereof recorded in Map Book "K", pages 4, 5 and 6, records of the City and County of San Francisco; thence deflecting 89 deg. 44 min. 30 sec. to the right and running northeasterly along the northwesterly line of the aforesaid Lot 16 4.000 feet; thence deflecting 90 deg. 15 min. 30 sec. to the right and running southeast-erly along a line parallel with and distant 4.000 feet at right angles northeasterly from the northeasterly line of Ocean avenue 90.019 feet; thence southeasterly, easterly and northeasterly along a curve to the left, tangent to the preceding course, radius 10 feet, central angle 90 deg. 15 min. 30 sec., a distance of 15.753 feet to tangency with the northwesterly line of San Leandro way; thence southwesterly along the northwesterly line of San Leandro way, tangent to the preceding curve, 4.000 feet; thence southwesterly, westerly and northwesterly along a curve to the right, tangent to the preceding course, radius 10 feet, central angle 90 deg. 15 min. 30 sec., a distance of 15.753 feet to tangeney with the northeasterly line of Ocean avenue and to the point of beginning.

Being a portion of Lot 16, Block 3257, of the above mentioned map. Be it

Further Resolved, That said property is suitable, adaptable, necessary and required for the public use of said City and County of San Francisco, to-wit: For the widening, construction and maintenance of Ocean avenue from San Leandro way to San Fernando way. It is necessary that a fee simple title be taken for such use.

The City Attorney is hereby ordered and directed to commence proceedings in eminent domain against the owners of said parcel of land. and of any and all interests therein, or claims thereto, for the condemnation thereof tor the public use of the City and County of San Francisco, as aforesaid.

Ayes—Supervisors Andriano, Colman, Deasy, Gallagher, Havenner, Hayden, Kent, McGovern, McSheehy, Marks, Powers, Roncovieri, Schmidt, Stanton, Suhr, Toner—16.

Absent—Supervisors Shannon, Todd—2.

Ordering the Improvement of Thirty-fourth Avenue and Other Streets and Avenues.

Also, Bill No. 9145, Ordinance No. 8652 (New Series), as follows:

Ordering the performance of certain street work to be done in the City and County of San Francisco, approving and adopting specifications therefor.

Be it ordained by the People of the City and County of San Francisco as follows:

Section 1. The Board of Public Works, in written communication filed in the office of the Clerk of the Board of Supervisors, December 10, 1929, having recommended the ordering of the following street work, the same is hereby ordered to be done in the City and County of San Francisco in conformity with the provisions of the Street Improvement Ordinance of 1918 of said City and County of San Francisco, said work to be performed under the direction of the Board of Public Works, and to be done in accordance with the specifications prepared therefor by said Board of Public Works, and on file in its office, which said plans and specifications are hereby approved and adopted.

That said Board of Supverisors, pursuant to the provision of Part II of the said Street Improvement Ordinance of 1918 of said City and County of San Francisco, does hereby determine and declare that the assessment to be imposed for the said contemplated improvements, respectively, may be paid in three installments; that the period of time after the time of the payment of the first installment when each of the succeeding installments must be paid is to be one year from the time of the payment of the preceding installment, and that the rate of interest to be charged on all deferred payments shall be seven per centum per annum.

The improvement of the east one-half of Thirty-fourth avenue from a line parallel with and 175 feet north of the north line of Anza street to a line parallel with and 225 feet north of the north line of Anza street, by the removal of sand from the roadway and sidewalk area and the construction of a bulkhead, 3 feet in height.

Bidder is to name price per lineal foot of bulkhead for this work.

The improvement of the west one-half of Thirty-seventh avenue from a line parallel with and 75 feet north of the north line of Balboa street to a line parallel with and 221 feet 9 inches north of the north line of Balboa street, by the removal of sand from the roadway and sidewalk area and the construction of a bulkhead, 3 feet in height.

Bidder is to name price per lineal foot of bulkhead for this work.

The improvement of the north one-half of Ulloa street from a line parallel with and 67 feet 3 inches east of the east line of Fifteenth avenue to a line parallel with and 188 feet 5 inches east of the east line of Fifteenth avenue, by the removal of sand from the roadway and sidewalk area and the construction of a bulkhead 3 feet in height.

Bidder is to name price per lineal foot of bulkhead for this work.

The improvement of the west one-half of Forty-eighth avenue from the north line of Irving street to a line parallel with and 150 feet north of the north line of Irving street, by the removal of sand from the roadway and sidewalk area and the construction of a bulkhead.

Bidder is to name price per lineal foot of 2-foot bulkhead for this work.

Section 2.   This ordinance shall take effect immediately.

Ayes—Supervisors Andriano, Colman, Deasy, Gallagher, Havenner, Hayden, Kent, McGovern, McSheehy, Marks, Powers, Roncovieri, Schmidt, Stanton, Suhr, Toner—16.

Absent—Supervisors Shannon, Todd—2.

Ordering the Improvement of Rivera Street Between Thirty-second and Thirty-third Avenues and Twenty-ninth Avenue between Quintara and Rivera Streets, Unfinished Portions.

Also, Bill No. 9146, Ordinance No. 8653 (New Series), as follows:

Ordering the performance of certain street work to be done in the City and County of San Francisco, approving and adopting specifications therefor.

Be it ordained by the People of the City and County of San Francisco as follows:

Section 1.   The Board of Public Works in written communication filed in the office of the Clerk of the Board of Supervisors, December 10, 1929, having recommended the ordering of the following street work, the same is hereby ordered to be done in the City and County of San Francisco in conformity with the provisions of the Street Improvement Ordinance of 1918 of said City and County of San Francisco, said work to be performed under the direction of the Board of Public Works, and to be done in accordance with the specifications prepared therefor by said Board of Public Works, and on file in its office, which said plans and specifications are hereby approved and adopted.

That said Board of Supervisors, pursuant to the provisions of Part II of the said Street Improvement Ordinance of 1918 of said City and County of San Francisco, does hereby determine and declare that the assessment to be imposed for the said contemplated improvements, respectively, may be paid in twenty installments; that the period of time after the time of the payment of the first installment when each of the succeeding installments must be paid is to be six months from the time of the payment of the preceding installment, and that the rate of interest to be charged on all deferred payments shall be seven per centum per annum.

The improvement of the unfinished portions of Rivera street between Thirty-second and Thirty-third avenues, and of the unfinished portions of Twenty-ninth avenue between Quintara and Rivera streets, by the construction of concrete curbs; by the construction of side sewers; by the construction of a concrete strip 7 feet in width adjacent to the center line of Rivera street between Thirty-second and Thirty-third avenues, and by the construction of an asphaltic concrete pavement, consisting of a 6-inch concrete foundation and a 1½-inch asphaltic concrete wearing surface, on the roadways thereof.

Section 2. This ordinance shall take effect immediately.

Ayes—Supervisors Andriano, Colman, Deasy, Gallagher, Havenner, Hayden, Kent, McGovern, McSheehy, Marks, Powers, Roncovieri, Schmidt, Stanton, Suhr, Toner—16.

Absent—Supervisors Shannon, Todd—2.

Ordering the Improvement of Forty-first Avenue Between Kirkham and Lawton Streets, Where Not Already Improved.

Also, Bill No. 9147, Ordinance No. 8654 (New Series), as follows:

Ordering the performance of certain street work to be done in the City and County of San Francisco, approving and adopting specifications therefor.

Be it ordained by the People of the City and County of San Francisco as follows:

Section 1. The Board of Public Works, in written communication filed in the office of the Clerk of the Board of Supervisors, December 10, 1929, having recommended the ordering of the following street work, the same is hereby ordered to be done in the City and County of San Francisco in conformity with the provisions of the Street Improvement Ordinance of 1918 of said City and County of San Francisco, said work to be performed under the direction of the Board of Public Works, and to be done in accordance with the specifications prepared therefor by said Board of Public Works, and on file in its office, which said plans and specifications are hereby approved and adopted.

That said Board of Supervisors, pursuant to the provisions of Part II of the said Street Improvement Ordinance of 1918 of said City and County of San Francisco, does hereby determine and declare that the assessment to be imposed for the said contemplated improvements, respectively, may be paid in ten installments; that the period of time after the time of the payment of the first installment when each of the succeeding installments must be paid is to be one year from the time of the payment of the preceding installment, and that the rate of interest to be charged on all deferred payments shall be seven per centum per annum.

Improvement of Forty-first avenue between Kirkham and Lawton streets, where not already so improved, by the construction of concrete curbs and the construction of asphaltic concrete pavement, consisting of a 6-inch concrete foundation and 1½-inch asphaltic concrete wearing surface, on the roadway thereof.

Section 2. This ordinance shall take effect immediately.

Ayes—Supervisors Andriano, Colman, Deasy, Gallagher, Havenner, Hayden, Kent, McGovern, McSheehy, Marks, Powers, Roncovieri, Schmidt, Stanton, Suhr, Toner—16.

Absent—Supervisors Shannon, Todd—2.

Ordering the Improvement of Capitol Avenue From Lakeview Avenue to Thrift Street and Crossings of Capitol Avenue and Lakeview Avenue and Capitol Avenue and Thrift Street.

Also, Bill No. 9148, Ordinance No. 8655 (New Series), as follows:

Ordering the performance of certain street work to be done in the City and County of San Francisco, approving and adopting specifications therefor.

Be it ordained by the People of the City and County of San Francisco as follows:

Section 1. The Board of Public Works in written communication filed in the office of the Clerk of the Board of Supervisors December 10, 1929, having recommended the ordering of the following street work, the same is hereby ordered to be done in the City and County of San Francisco in conformity with the provisions of the Street Improvement Ordinance of 1918 of said City and County of San Francisco, said work to be performed under the direction of the Board of Public Works, and to be done in accordance with the specifications prepared therefor by said Board of Public Works, and on file in its office, which said plans and specifications are hereby approved and adopted.

That said Board of Supervisors, pursuant to the provisions of Part II of the said Street Improvement Ordinance of 1918 of said City and County of San Francisco, does hereby determine and declare that the assessment to be imposed for the said contemplated improvements, respectively, may be paid in twenty installments; that the period of time after the time of the payment of the first installment when each of the succeeding installments must be paid is to be six months from the time of the payment of the preceding installment, and that the rate of interest to be charged on all deferred payments shall be seven per centum per annum.

The improvement of Capitol avenue from the northerly line of Lakeview avenue to the southerly line of Thrift street, including the crossing of Capitol avenue and Lakeview avenue, and the crossing of Capitol avenue and Thrift street, by grading to official line and grade; by the construction of unarmored concrete curbs; by the construction of one-course concrete sidewalks; by the construction of brick catchbasins with accompanying 10-inch vitrified clay pipe culvert; by the construction of a 6-inch vitrified clay pipe side sewer; by the construction of a concrete pavement, and by the construction of an asphaltic concrete pavement, consisting of a light traffic concrete base and a 2-inch asphaltic concrete wearing surface, on the roadway thereof.

Section 2. This ordinance shall take effect immediately.

Ayes—Supervisors Andriano, Colman, Deasy, Gallagher, Havenner, Hayden, Kent, McGovern, McSheehy, Marks, Powers, Roncovieri, Schmidt, Stanton, Suhr, Toner—16.

Absent—Supervisors Shannon, Todd—2.

Ordering the Improvement of Ortega Street, Somerset Street and Waterville Street.

Also, Bill No. 9149, Ordinance No. 8656 (New Series), as follows:

Ordering the performance of certain street work to be done in the City and County of San Francisco, approving and adopting specifications therefor.

Be it ordained by the People of the City and County of San Francisco as follows:

Section 1. The Board of Public Works, in written communication filed in the office of the Clerk of the Board of Supervisors December 10, 1929, having recommended the ordering of the following street work, the same is hereby ordered to be done in the City and County of San Francisco in conformity with the provisions of the Street Improvement Ordinance of 1918 of said City and County of San Francisco, said work to be performed under the direction of the Board of Public Works, and to be done in accordance with the specifications prepared therefor by said Board of Public Works, and on file in its office, which said plans and specifications are hereby approved and adopted.

That said Board of Supervisors, pursuant to the provisions of Part II of the said Street Improvement Ordinance of 1918 of said City and County of San Francisco, does hereby determine and declare that the assessment to be imposed for the said contemplated improvements, respectively, may be paid in ten installments; that the period of time after the time of the payment of the first installment when each of the succeeding installments must be paid is to be one year from the time of the payment of the preceding installment, and that the rate of interest to be charged on all deferred payments shall be seven per centum per annum.

The improvement of Ortega street between Forty-eighth avenue and the Great Highway, where not already so improved, by the construction of armored concrete curbs; by the construction of one side sewer, and by the construction of an asphaltic concrete pavement, consisting of a 6-inch concrete foundation and a 1½-inch asphaltic concrete wearing surface, on the roadway thereof; the improvement of Somerset street between Silver avenue and Silliman street, where not already so improved, by the construction of a 1½-inch asphaltic concrete wearing surface on the roadway thereof; the improvement of Waterville street between Silver avenue and Augusta street, including the intersections of Waterville street, Silver avenue and Augusta street, where not already so improved; and the improvement of the northerly portion of Silver avenue between Waterville street and Elmira street where not already so improved, by the construction of concrete curbs; by the construction of side sewers; by the construction of brick catchbasins with appurtenances and 10-inch vitrified clay pipe culverts; by the construction of artificial stone sidewalks on the angular corners of the above-mentioned intersections; and by the construction of an asphaltic concrete pavement, consisting of a 6-inch concrete foundation and a 1½-inch asphaltic concrete wearing surface, on the roadway thereof.

Section 2. This ordinance shall take effect immediately.

Ayes—Supervisors Andriano, Colman, Deasy, Gallagher, Havenner, Hayden, Kent, McGovern, McSheehy, Marks, Powers, Roncovieri, Schmidt, Stanton, Suhr, Toner—16.

Absent—Supervisors Shannon, Todd—2.

Fixing Sidewalk Widths on Corbett Avenue.

Also, Bill No. 9150, Ordinance No. 8657 (New Series), as follows:

Amending Ordinance No. 1061, entitled "Regulating the Width of Sidewalks," approved December 18, 1903, by amending Section Six Hundred and Twelve thereof.

Be it ordained by the People of the City and County of San Francisco as follows:

Section 1. Ordinance No. 1061, entitled "Regulating the Width of Sidewalks," approved December 18, 1903, be and is hereby amended in accordance with the communication of the Board of Public Works, filed in this office December 7, 1929, by amending Section Six Hundred and Twelve thereof, to read as follows:

Section 612. The width of sidewalks on Corbett avenue between Clayton street and Twenty-fourth street shall be eight (8) feet.

Section 2. Any expense caused by the above change of walk widths shall be borne by the property owners.

Section 3. This ordinance shall take effect and be in force from and after its passage.

Ayes—Supervisors Andriano, Colman, Deasy, Gallagher, Havenner, Hayden, Kent, McGovern, McSheehy, Marks, Powers, Roncovieri, Schmidt, Stanton, Suhr, Toner—16.

Absent—Supervisors Shannon, Todd—2.

Fixing Sidewalk Widths on Mullen Street.

Also, Bill No. 9151, Ordinance No. 8658 (New Series), as follows:

Amending Ordinance No. 1061, entitled "Regulating the Width of Sidewalks," approved December 18, 1903, by adding thereto new sections to be numbered ten hundred and eighty-six and ten hundred and eighty-seven.

Be it ordained by the People of the City and County of San Francisco as follows:

Section 1. Ordinance No. 1061, entitled "Regulating the Width of Sidewalks," approved December 18, 1903, be and is hereby amended in accordance with the communication of the Board of Public Works, filed in this office December 12, 1929, by adding thereto new sections to be numbered ten hundred and eighty-six and ten hundred and eighty-seven, to read as follows:

Section 1086. The width of sidewalks on Mullen street between Peralta avenue and Wolfe street shall be as shown on that certain map entitled "Map of Mullen street between Peralta avenue and Wolfe street," showing the location of street and curb lines and the width of sidewalks.

Section 1087. The width of sidewalks on Peralta avenue between the northerly line of Mullen avenue and Montcalm street shall be as shown on that certain map entitled "Map of Peralta avenue between the northerly line of Mullen street and Montcalm street," showing the location of street and curb lines and the width of sidewalks.

The width of sidewalks on Peralta avenue between Montcalm street and Esmeralda avenue shall be fifteen (15) feet.

Section 2. Any expense caused by the above change of walk widths shall be borne by the property owners.

Section 3. This ordinance shall take effect and be in force from and after its passage.

Ayes—Supervisors Andriano, Colman, Deasy, Gallagher, Havenner, Hayden, Kent, McGovern, McSheehy, Marks, Powers, Roncovieri, Schmidt, Stanton, Suhr, Toner—16.

Absent—Supervisors Shannon, Todd—2.

Fixing Sidewalk Widths on Wolfe Street.

Also, Bill No. 9152, Ordinance No. 8659 (New Series), as follows:

Amending Ordinance No. 1061, entitled "Regulating the Width of Sidewalks," approved December 18, 1903, by amending Section Six Hundred and Forty-two thereof.

Be it ordained by the People of the City and County of San Francisco as follows:

Section 1. Ordinance No. 1061, entitled "Regulating the Width of Sidewalks," approved December 18, 1903, be and is hereby amended in accordance with the communication of the Board of Public Works, filed in this office December 12, 1929, by amending Section Six Hundred and Forty-two thereof, to read as follows:

Section 642. The width of sidewalks on Wolfe street between Franconia street and Peralta avenue shall be as shown on that certain map entitled "Map of Wolfe street between Franconia street and Peralta avenue," showing the location of street and curb lines and the width of sidewalks.

Section 2. Any expense caused by the above change of walk widths shall be borne by the property owners.

Section 3. This ordinance shall take effect and be in force from and after its passage.

Ayes—Supervisors Andriano, Colman, Deasy, Gallagher, Havenner, Hayden, Kent, McGovern, McSheehy, Marks, Powers, Roncovieri, Schmidt, Stanton, Suhr, Toner—16.

Absent—Supervisors Shannon, Todd—2.

Repealing Ordinances for Sand Removal and Bulkhead Construction.

Also, Bill No. 9153, Ordinance No. 8660 (New Series), as follows:

Repealing Ordinance No. 8601 (New Series), Ordinance No. 8603 (New Series), Ordinance No. 8611 (New Series), Ordinance No. 8618 (New Series), Ordinance No. 8622 (New Series), ordering the removal of sand and the construction of bulkheads.

Be it ordained by the People of the City and County of San Francisco as follows:

Section 1. Ordinance No. 8601 (New Series) ordering the removal of sand and construction of bulkheads west side of Twenty-second avenue between lines 175 feet and 200 feet south of Lawton street;

Ordinance No. 8603 (New Series) ordering the removal of sand and construction of bulkheads on west side of Twentieth avenue between lines 200 feet and 225 feet south of Judah street;

Ordinance No. 8611 (New Series) ordering the removal of sand and construction of bulkheads on south side of Ulloa street from Twenty-first avenue westerly 120 feet, and west side of Twenty-first avenue from Ulloa street southerly thirty feet;

Ordinance No. 8618 (New Series) ordering the removal of sand and construction of bulkheads on west side of Madrid street between lines 175 feet and 225 feet north of Italy avenue;

Ordinance No. 8628 (New Series) ordering the removal of sand and construction of bulkheads on west side of Fortieth avenue from Fulton street northerly 100 feet be and the same are hereby repealed.

Section 2. This ordinance shall take effect immediately.

Ayes—Supervisors Andriano, Colman, Deasy, Gallagher, Havenner, Hayden, Kent, McGovern, McSheehy, Marks, Powers, Roncovieri, Schmidt, Stanton, Suhr, Toner—16.

Absent—Supervisors Shannon, Todd—2.

PRESENTATION OF BILLS AND ACCOUNTS.

Your Finance Committee, having examined miscellaneous demands not required by law to be passed to print, and amounting to $79,018.05, recommends same be allowed and ordered paid.

Approved by the following vote:

Ayes—Supervisors Andriano, Colman, Deasy, Gallagher, Havenner, Hayden, Kent, McGovern, McSheehy, Marks, Powers, Roncovieri, Schmidt, Stanton, Suhr, Toner—16.

Absent—Supervisors Shannon, Todd—2.

NEW BUSINESS.

Passed for Printing.

The following matters were *passed for printing*:

Authorizations.

On recommendation of Finance Committee.

Resolution No. ———— (New Series), as follows:

Resolved, That the following amounts be and the same are hereby authorized to be expended out of the hereinafter mentioned funds in payment to the following named claimants, to-wit:

Aquarium—Appropriation 56.

(1) California Academy of Sciences, maintenance of Steinhart Aquarium, month of December, 1929 (claim dated Jan. 6, 1930) ....$ 4,985.84

Park Fund.

(2) Marine Electric Co., electric installation for parks (claim dated Jan. 3, 1930).....................................$ 682.70

(3) Pacific Gas & Electric Co., gas and electric service for parks, month of November (claim dated Jan. 3, 1930)..... 2,427.27

(4) Spring Valley Water Co., November, water for parks (claim dated Jan. 3, 1930)............................... 3,861.68

(5) State Compensation Insurance Fund, premium covering insurance on park employments (claim dated Jan. 3, 1930) 569.08

(6) Berringer & Russell, hay, etc., for parks (claim dated Jan. 3, 1930) 1,407.02

(7) Henry Cowell Lime & Cement Co., cement for parks (claim dated Jan. 3, 1930) 519.40

(8) Golden State Milk Products Co., ice cream for parks (claim dated Jan. 3, 1930) 1,570.24

(9) J. H. McCallum, lumber for parks (claim dated Jan. 3, 1930) 612.88

Duplicate Tax Fund.

(10) M. Eisenberg, refund of first installment, 1929-1930, taxes paid in duplicate (claim dated Jan. 2, 1930)........$ 992.88

(11) Boyd Investment Co., refund first installment, 1929-1930, taxes paid in duplicate (claim dated Jan. 2, 1930).. 3,006.71

Hetch Hetchy Construction Fund, Bond Issue 1928.

(12) M. D. Jones, truck hire (claim dated Dec. 21, 1929)....$ 537.72

(13) Grier & Mead, rail and angle bars (claim dated Dec. 21, 1929) 3,057.35

(14) Ingersoll-Rand Co. of Calif., machinery parts (claim dated Dec. 21, 1929) 538.69

(15) The Charles Nelson Co., wood wedges (claim dated Dec. 21, 1929) 1,234.00

(16) Santa Cruz Portland Cement Co., cement (claim dated Dec. 21, 1929) 4,073.50

(17) Sherry Bros., Inc., eggs (claim dated Dec. 21, 1929)... 510.60

(18) Wilsey Bennett Co., butter and cheese (claim dated Dec. 21, 1929) 509.90

(19) Challenge Cream & Butter Association, canned milk (claim dated Dec. 24, 1929)............................. 656.25

(20) M. Greenberg's Sons, bronze base plates (claim dated Dec. 24, 1929) 592.20

(21) J. R. Hanify Co., lumber (claim dated Dec. 24, 1929)... 1,113.21

(22) Santa Cruz Portland Cement Co., cement (claim dated Dec. 24, 1929) 1,578.00

(23) State Compensation Insurance Fund, premium on insurance covering Hetch Hetchy employees (claim dated Dec. 24, 1929) 7,671.82

(24) Standard Oil Co. of Calif., gasoline, etc. (claim dated Dec. 24, 1929) 675.42

(25) Standard Oil Co. of Calif., gasoline, grease, etc. (claim dated Dec. 24, 1929) 659.69

(26) Wilsey, Bennett Co., butter and cheese (claim dated Dec. 24, 1929) 836.26

(27) Sherry Bros., Inc., eggs (claim dated Dec. 24, 1929)... 593.40

County Road Fund.

(28) Pacific Coast Aggregates, Inc., gravel for street reconstruction (claim dated Dec. 18, 1929)....................$ 906.56

(29) Pacific Coast Aggregates, Inc., gravel for street reconstruction (claim dated Dec. 19, 1929).................... 847.06

(30) San Francisco Materials Co., cement for street reconstruction (claim dated Dec. 18, 1929).................. 858.00

(31) Santa Cruz Portland Cement Co., cement for street reconstruction (claim dated Dec. 18, 1929) 876.48

(32) Equitable Asphalt Maintenance Co., resurfacing of streets (claim dated Dec. 23, 1929)...................... 1,307.36

(33) Eclipse Lime & Cement Co., cement for reconstruction of streets (claim dated Dec. 23, 1929).................. 881.76

(34) Santa Cruz Portland Cement Co., cement for reconstruction of streets (claim dated Dec. 23, 1929).............. 881.76

(35) Stores & Yards Account, Board of Public Works, reimbursement for account of repairs to equipment (claim dated Dec. 16, 1929) 1,256.00

(36) Pacific Coast Aggregates, Inc., sand and gravel for reconstruction of streets (claim dated Dec. 27, 1929)........ 4,123.43

(37) Sibley Grading & Teaming Co., sand for street reconstruction (claim dated Dec. 27, 1929) 1,076.25

Tax Judgments—Appropriation 57.

(38) Oscar Samuels and J. Samuels, as Attorneys for Judgment Creditors, one-tenth of final judgment, plus interest;
fifth payment (claim dated Dec. 12, 1929) ....$ 1,165.89

General Fund, 1929-1930.

(39) Dudley B. Perkins, Police Dept. motorcycle repairs and
equipment (claim dated Dec. 30, 1929) ....$ 667.21
(40) The Gunn Furniture Co., office equipment for County
Welfare Dept. (claim dated Dec. 30, 1929) 502.00
(41) San Francisco Society for the Prevention of Cruelty to
Animals, impounding, feeding, etc., of animals (claim dated
Jan. 6, 1930) 1,500.00
(42) San Francisco Chronicle, official advertising (claim
dated Jan. 6, 1929) 3,022.68
(43) California Meat Co., meat for San Francisco Hospital
(claim dated Nov. 30, 1929) 1,889.52
(44) Haas Brothers, groceries, S. F. Hospital (claim dated
Nov. 30, 1929) 698.56
(45) Scatena-Galli Fruit Co., fruit and produce, S. F. Hospital (claim dated Nov. 30, 1929) 897.63
(46) Building Supplies Co., soap chips, etc., S. F. Hospital
(claim dated Nov. 30, 1929) 531.99
(47) A. Levy &. J. Zentner Co., fruit and produce, S. F. Hospital (claim dated Nov. 30, 1929) 1,149.78
(48) Richfield Oil Co., fuel oil, S. F. Hospital (claim dated
Nov. 30, 1929) 1,866.87
(49) Western Meat Co., meat, S. F. Hospital (claim dated
Nov. 30, 1929) 639.82
(50) Del Monte Meat Co., meats, S. F. Hospital (claim dated
Nov. 30, 1929) 1,402.61
(51) Fred L. Hilmer Co., butter, etc., S. F. Hospital (claim
dated Nov. 30, 1929) 1,925.32
(52) Wilsey, Bennett Co., eggs, S. F. Hospital (claim dated
Nov. 30, 1929) 2,452.55
(53) San Francisco Dairy Co., milk, S. F. Hospital (claim
dated Nov. 30, 1929) 4,149.14
(54) L. M. Wilbor, M. D., Supt. of San Francisco Hospital,
for January room allowance to Hospital employees (claim
dated Nov. 30, 1929) 3,500.00

Appropriation, County Road Fund, Improvement of Twentieth Street From San Bruno Avenue to Vermont Street.

Also, Resolution No. ——————— (New Series), as follows:

Resolved, That the sum of $2,943.05 be and the same is hereby set
aside, appropriated and authorized to be expended out of County Road
Fund to defray the cost of the improving of Twentieth street between
San Bruno avenue and Vermont street and the crossing of Twentieth
street and San Bruno avenue, at city property.

Adopted.

The following resolution was *adopted:*

Reimbursement of General Fund, 1927-1928, With Amounts Advanced for Expense of Bond Elections.

On recommendation of Finance Committee.

Resolution No. 31883 (New Series), as follows:

Resolved, That the following amounts be and the same are hereby
set aside and appropriated out of the hereinafter mentioned bond funds
and placed to the credit of the General Fund, Fiscal Year 1927-1928, as
reimbursement of said General Fund for amounts advanced for adver-

tising and incidental expenses in connection with the holding of bond elections, to-wit:

From Spring Valley Water Bond Fund......$ 7,255.18
From Hetch Hetchy Bond Fund 7,056.77
Boulevard Bond Fund 7,850.94
Bernal Cut Bond Fund 30,003.65
War Memorial Bond Fund 29,009.65

Ayes—Supervisors Andriano, Colman, Deasy, Gallagher, Havenner, . Hayden, Kent, McGovern, McSheehy, Marks, Powers, Roncovieri, Schmidt, Stanton, Suhr, Toner—16·

Absent—Supervisors Shannon, Todd—2·

Passed for Printing.

The following matters were *passed for printing*:

Authorizations.

On recommendation of Finance Committee.

Resolution No. ——— (New Series), as follows:

Resolved, That the following amounts be and the same are hereby authorized to be expended out of the hereinafter mentioned funds in payment to the following named claimants, to-wit:

Sewer Bond Construction Fund, Issue 1929.

(1) Thomson, Wood & Hoffman, examining proceedings and furnishing opinion approving validity of 1929 Sewer Bonds (claim dated Dec. 19, 1929).............................$ 650.00

Hospital Bond Construction Fund, Issue 1929.

(2) Thomson, Wood & Hoffman, examining proceedings and furnishing opinion approving validity of 1929 Hospital Bonds (claims dated Dec. 19, 1929)....................$ 1,000.00

Hetch Hetchy Water Construction Fund, Bond Issue 1928.

(3) Bald Eagle Market, meat and fish (claim dated Dec. 18, 1929) . . . .$ 679.76
(4) Dr. Paul E. Dolan, medical service rendered Hetch Hetchy employees (claim dated Dec. 18, 1929)............ 777.75
(5) J. H. McCallum, lumber furnished (claim dated Dec. 18, 1929) 1,011.11

School Construction Fund, Bond Issue 1923.

(6) C. F. Weber & Co., gymnasium equipment furnished Polytechnic High School (claim dated Dec. 23, 1929)...........$ 958.97

Hetch Hetchy Power Operative Fund.

(7) Depreciation Fund, Hetch Hetchy Power Operative, reserve for depreciation, per Charter requirement (claim dated Dec. 19, 1929) $14,584.00

Tax Judgments—Appropriation 57.

(8) Brobeck, Phleger & Harrison, as attorneys, for account of judgment holders, seventh installment, per schedule attached (claim dated Dec. 28, 1929)......................$ 800.92
(9) Brobeck, Phleger & Harrison, as attorneys, for account of judgment holders, seventh installment, per schedule attached (claim dated Dec. 28, 1929)...................... 17,615.31

General Fund, 1928-1929.

(10) Frank J. Reilly, seventh payment, general contract, construction of M. H. deYoung Memoriam Museum (claim dated Dec. 27, 1929) ....$ 9,407.25
(11) California Pottery Co., sewer pipe furnished for sewer extension and reconstruction (claim dated Dec. 23, 1929).. 845.10

(12) Richfield Oil Co. of California, fuel oil furnished Civic
 Center powerhouse (claim dated Dec. 21, 1929)..........   840.89
(13) Graybar Electric Co., copper wire, etc., furnished Department of Electricity (claim dated Nov. 30, 1929).......   1,028.36
(14) H. E. Teller Co, coffee furnished San Francisco Hospital
 (claim dated Nov. 30, 1929)..............................   620.00
(15) H. F. Dugan Co., chemical and surgical supplies furnished San Francisco Hospital (claim dated Nov. 30, 1929)   888.17
(16) Seabury & Johnson, gauze, etc., furnished San Francisco
 Hospital (claim dated Nov. 30, 1929)....................   1,524.00
(17) Haas Brothers, groceries furnished San Francisco Hospital (claim dated Nov. 30, 1929)........................   665.95
(18) Western Meat Co., meat furnished San Francisco Hospital (claim dated Nov. 30, 1929)........................   898.48
(19) Spring Valley Water Co., water furnished San Fransico Hospital (claim dated Nov. 30, 1929)................   1,684.13
(20) Seabury & Johnson, gauze, etc., furnished Laguna
 Honda Home (claim dated Nov. 30, 1929)................   795.00

Payment to Crocker First National Bank, Fees as Fiscal Agent.

Also, Resolution No. ———— (New Series), as follows:

Resolved, That the sum of $844.45 be and the same is hereby set
aside and appropriated out of Urgent Necessity, Budget Item No. 24,
and authorized in payment to Crocker First National Bank; being
payment for expenses in connection with payment of interest on San
Francisco bonds, as fiscal agent. Final payment.

Reimbursing Board of Works for Painting Traffic Signs.

Also, Resolution No. ———— (New Series), as follows:

Resolved, That the sum of $1,441.81 be and the same is hereby set
aside and appropriated out of "Traffic Signals, etc.," Budget Item No.
£7, to the credit of Budget Item No. 442, Board of Public Works; being
reimbursement for labor and material expended in the painting of
traffic signs, lines and curbing during the month of November, 1929.

Appropriation, County Road Fund, for Property Required for Widening of Ocean Avenue.

Also, Resolution No. ———— (New Series), as follows:

Resolved, That the sum of $4,050 be and the same is hereby set
aside and appropriated out of County Road Fund, and authorized in
payment to Bernard L. Drake and Cora M. Drake, and City Title Insurance Company; being payment for Lot 16 in Block 3257, as per the
Assessor's Block Books of the City and County of San Francisco, as
per acceptance of offer by Resolution No. 31843 (New Series), and
required for the widening of Ocean avenue. (Claim dated Dec. 10,
1929.)

Appropriations, Boulevard Bonds, Property for Sunset Boulevard.

Also, Resolution No. ———— (New Series), as follows:

Resolved, That the following amounts be and the same are hereby
set aside and appropriated out of Boulevard Bonds, Issue 1927, and
authorized in payment to the hereinafter named persons; being payments for properties required for the Sunset boulevard, to-wit:
(1) To Louise Franz and City Title Insurance Co., for all of
 Lots 14 and 16 in Block 2365, as per the Assessor's Block
 Books, and authorized by Resolution No. ———— (New
 Series) accepting offer (claim dated Dec. 26, 1929).......$ 6,000.00
(2) To E. Sugarman and City Title Insurance Co., for Lot 21
 in Block 2365, as per the Assessor's Block Books, and authorized by Resolution No. ———— (New Series) accept-
 ing offer (claim dated Dec. 26, 1929).....................   1,675.00

Appropriations for Street Improvements, County Road Fund.

Also, Resolution No. ———— (New Series), as follows:

Resolved, That the following amounts be and the same are hereby set aside, appropriated and authorized to be expended out of County Road Fund for the following improvements, to-wit:

(1) For the reconstruction of Broadway between Hyde and Jones streets, by the construction of a concrete pavement..$16,000.00

(2) For the construction of a three-rail fence, 1962 feet, on Geneva avenue from Mission street southerly............ 588.60

Adopted.

The following resolutions were *adopted*:

Appropriations for Properties Required for Widening of Campbell Avenue, County Road Fund.

On recommendation of Finance Committee.

Resolution No. 31908 (New Series), as follows:

Resolved, That the following amounts be and the same are hereby set aside and appropriated out of County Road Fund, and authorized in payment to the following named persons; being payments for properties required for the widening of Campbell avenue and Somerset street, as per acceptances of offers by Resolution No. 31841 (New Series), to-wit:

(1) Edwin P. La Plant and City Title Insurance Co., for portion of Lot 4 in Block 6205, as per the Assessor's Block Books (50 by 85 ft.) (claim dated Dec. 11, 1929)..........$ 439.20

(2) Anthony L. Noriega and City Title Insurance Co., for portion of Lot 13 in Block 6199, as per the Assessor's Block Books (65 by 7¾ ft.) (claim dated Dec. 11, 1929)......... 104.00

(3) Gustave R. Brown and Sarah J. Brown and City Title Insurance Co., for portion of Lot 12 in Block 6199, as per the Assessor's Block Books (27 ft. by 6 ft. 7 in.) (claim dated Dec. 11, 1929).................................... 50.02

(4) Chas. Henrich and Mathilde Henrich and City Title Insurance Co., for portion of Lot 11 in Block 6199, as per the Assessor's Block Books (27 ft. 6 in. by 4 ft.) (claim dated Dec. 11, 1929) 11.10

(5) Mary A. Craig and City Title Insurance Co., for portion of Lot 2 in Block 6205, as per the Assessor's Block Books (35 by 7½ ft.) (claim dated Dec. 11, 1929).............. 32.20

Ayes—Supervisors Andriano, Colman, Deasy, Gallagher, Havenner, Hayden, Kent, McGovern, McSheehy, Marks, Powers, Roncovieri, Schmidt, Stanton, Suhr, Toner—16.

Absent—Supervisors Shannon, Todd—2.

Accepting Offer of Higgins & Sons to Sell for $1,000, Land Required for San Miguel Reservoir.

Also, Resolution No. 31884 (New Series), as follows:

Resolved, That the offer of sale made by the following named corporation to sell to the City and County of San Francisco the following described land, required for the San Miguel Reservoir of the Hetch Hetchy Water Supply Project, for the sum set forth opposite its name be accepted:

Higgins & Sons, a corporation, $1,000—Lot 13, Block 2894, as per the Assessor's Block Books of the City and County of San Francisco. (As per detailed description and written offer on file.)

The City Attorney is hereby authorized to examine the title to said property, and if the same is found satisfactory, to accept on behalf of the City deed conveying said property to the City, free and clear of all encumbrances, and to record said deed, together with copy of this resolution, in the office of the Recorder of the City and County of San Francisco.

Ayes—Supervisors Andriano, Colman, Deasy, Gallagher, Havenner, Hayden, Kent, McGovern, McSheehy, Marks, Powers, Roncovieri, Schmidt, Stanton, Suhr, Toner—16.

Absent—Supervisors Shannon, Todd—2.

Accepting Offers of E. Sugarman and Louise Franz to Sell Land for the Opening of Sunset Boulevard.

Also, Resolution No. 31885 (New Series), as follows:

Resolved, That the offers of sale made by the following named persons to sell to the City and County of San Francisco the following described land, required for the opening of the Sunset boulevard, for the sums set forth opposite their respective names, be accepted:

E. Sugarman, $1,675—All of Lot 21, Block 2365, as per the Assessor's Block Books of the City and County of San Francisco.

Louise Franz, $6,000—All of Lots 14 and 16, Block 2365, as per the Assessor's Block Books of the City and County of San Francisco.

And the City Attorney is hereby authorized to examine the title to said property, and if the same is found satisfactory, to accept on behalf of the City, deeds conveying said property to the City, free and clear of all encumbrances, and to record said deeds, together with copy of this resolution, in the office of the Recorder of the City and County of San Francisco.

Ayes—Supervisors Andriano, Colman, Deasy, Gallagher, Havenner, Hayden, Kent, McGovern, McSheehy, Marks, Powers, Roncovieri, Schmidt, Stanton, Suhr, Toner—16.

Absent—Supervisors Shannon, Todd—2.

Passed for Printing.

The following resolution was *passed for printing*:

Appropriation, Expense of Supervisor Suhr as San Francisco's Official Representative on Good Will Pacific Cruise of San Francisco Chamber of Commerce.

On recommendation of Finance Committee.

Resolution No. ———— (New Series), as follows:

Resolved, That the sum of $5,000 be and the same is hereby set aside and appropriated out of Publicity and Advertising, Appropriation 54, and authorized in payment to Fred Suhr, Supervisor, for his expense as official representative of the City and County of San Francisco in accompanying the San Francisco Chamber of Commerce on its good will Pacific cruise on the steamship "Mololo," as authorized by Resolution No. 31369, New Series. (Claim dated December 30, 1929.)

(Supervisor Suhr was excused from voting on the foregoing.)

Rereferred.

The following resolution was ordered *rereferred to the Fire Committee*:

Granting John W. McCarthy Automobile Supply Station, South Side Twenty-fourth Street, 50 Feet West of Vicksburg Street.

Resolution No. ———— (New Series), as follows:

Resolved, that John W. McCarthy be and is hereby granted permission, revocable at will of the Board of Supervisors, to maintain and operate an automobile supply station on the south side of Twenty-fourth street, 50 feet west of Vicksburg street.

The rights granted under this resolution shall be exercised within six months, otherwise said permit shall become null and void.
Protest filed.
Petition in favor filed.

Passed for Printing.

The following resolution was *passed for printing*:

Oil Tank Permits.

On recommendation of Fire Committee.

Resolution No. ————— (New Series), as follows:

Resolved, That the following revocable permits be and the same are hereby granted:

Eugene Conway, 153 Eighth avenue, 1,500 gallons capacity.

Gray and Danielson, southeast corner of Nineteenth and Bryant streets, 1,500 gallons capacity.

Haley Bros., northeast corner of Turk and Polk streets, 1,500 gallons capacity.

Albert E. Hawley, northeast corner of Jackson and Walnut streets, 1,500 gallons capacity.

Ben Liebman, southwest corner of Fillmore street and Retiro Way, 1,500 gallons capacity.

Marian Realty Company, southwest corner of Pacific and Laguna streets, 1,500 gallons capacity.

C. N. Miller, south side of Marina boulevard, 150 feet east of Avila way, 1,500 gallons capacity.

National Sanitary Rag Company, 148 Townsend street, 1,500 gallons capacity.

New Eureka Laundry, 329 Noe street, 1,500 gallons capacity.

W. W. Nutter, 71 San Felipe avenue, 1,500 gallons capacity.

Sutter Theatre, west side of Steiner street, 120 feet south of Sutter street, 1,500 gallons capacity.

W. R. Voorhies, south side of Washington street, 165 feet west of Locust street, 1,500 gallons capacity.

The rights granted under this resolution shall be exercised within six months, otherwise said permits shall become null and void.

Rereferred.

The following resolution was ordered *rereferred to the Fire Committee*:

Granting Louise Vannucci and Gloria Cheader, Laundry Permit, 405 O'Farrell Street.

Resolution No. ⊢————— (New Series), as follows:

Resolved, That Louise Vannucci and Gloria Cheader be and are hereby granted permission, revocable at will of the Board of Supervisors, to maintain and operate a laundry at 405 O'Farrell street.

The rights granted under this resolution shall be exercised within six months, otherwise said permit shall become null and void.
Protest filed.

Passed for Printing.

The following matters were *passed for printing*:

Reimbursements to Board of Works for Work Done on Public Buildings.

On recommendation of Public Buildings and Lands Committee.

Resolution No. ————— (New Series), as follows:

Resolved, That the following amounts be and the same are hereby set aside and appropriated out of the hereinafter mentioned Budget Items, General Fund, 1929-1930, to the credit of Bureau of Building

Repair, Board of Public Works, Budget Item No. 442; being reimburse-ments for labor and materials furnished for account of work performed on public buildings, to-wit:

From "City Hall Repairs and Painting," Budget Item No. 54,
for the gilding of ornamental iron work, City Hall........$ 2,782.65
From "Repairs to Public Buildings, other than School Build-ings," Budget Item No. 53, for construction of pits at Fire
Department Corporation Yard 4,362.92
For flooring, etc., detective room, Hall of Justice...........   388.41
For miscellaneous carpentry, metal grills, etc., Juvenile De-tention Home 1,367.90
For plumbing, etc., Chemical Engine No. 7..................   675.28
For repairs, plumbing, etc., Engine No. 21.................   725.68
For electrical work, Coroner's office 226.36
For construction of kitchen, Engine No. 6..................   1,106.40
For handball court, Engine House No. 10....................   287.85
For new counter, etc., office of Chief of Police.............   780.00

Total $12,703.45

Blasting Permit, Mount Vernon Avenue.

On recommendation of Streets Committee.

Resolution No. ————— (New Series), as follows:

Resolved, That H. V. Tucker Company, Inc., be and is hereby granted permission, revocable at will of the Board of Supervisors, to explode blasts while grading on Mt. Vernon avenue, between Howth and Getz streets, and on Williar street between Mt. Vernon and Ni-agara streets, provided said permittee shall execute and file a good and sufficient bond in the sum of $5,000 as fixed by the Board of Public Works and approved by his Honor, the Mayor, in accordance with Ordinance No. 1204 (New Series); provided, also, that said blasts shall be exploded only between the hours of 7 a. m. and 6 p. m. and that the work of blasting shall be performed to the satisfac-tion of the Board of Public Works, and that if any of the conditions of this resolution be violated by said H. V. Tucker Company, Inc., then the privileges and all the rights accruing thereunder shall im-mediately become null and void.

Changing Grades on Sanchez Street Between the Southerly Line of Twenty-first Street and the Northerly Curb Line of Hill Street.

Also, Bill No. 9154, Ordinance No. ————— (New Series), as follows:

Changing and reestablishing the official grades on Sanchez street between the southerly curb line of Twenty-first street and the north-erly curb line of Hill street.

Whereas, the Board of Supervisors, on the written recommendation of the Board of Public Works, did on the 18th day of October, 1929, by Resolution No. 31508 (New Series), declare its intention to change and reestablish the grades on Sanchez street between the southerly curb line of Twenty-first street and the northerly curb line of Hill street.

Whereas, said resolution was so published for ten days, and the Board of Public Works within ten days after the first publication of said resolution of intention caused notices of the passage of said resolu-tion to be conspicuously posted along all streets specified in the resolution, in the manner and as provided by law; and

Whereas, more than forty days has elapsed since the first publica-tion of said resolution of intention; therefore,

Be it ordained by the People of the City and County of San Fran-cisco as follows:

Section 1. The grades on the following named streets at the points hereinafter named and at the elevations above City base as herein-after stated are hereby changed and established as follows:

Sanchez Street.

Twenty-first street northerly line 355 feet. (The same being the present official grade.)

Fifteen feet northerly from Twenty-first street southerly line 358.83 feet. (The same being the present official grade.)

Westerly curb line of, 47.91 feet northerly from the end of the arc, 61.55 feet southerly from Twenty-first street 360.30 feet.

Easterly curb line of, at points of reverse curve at Twenty-first street 360.30 feet.

Westerly curb line of, 16.76 feet southerly from the end of the arc, 61.55 feet northerly from Hill street 353.29 feet.

Easterly curb line of, 20.32 feet southerly from the end of the arc, 61.55 feet northerly from Hill street 353.29 feet.

Westerly curb line of, 47.90 feet southerly from the end of the arc, 61.55 feet northerly from Hill street 347.63 feet.

Easterly curb line of, at the point of reverse curve at Hill street 347.63 feet.

Fifteen feet southerly from Hill street northerly line 346.05 feet. (The same being the present official grade.)

Hill street southerly line 343 feet. (The same being the present official grade.)

On Sanchez street between the southerly curb line of Twenty-first street and the northerly curb line of Hill street changed and estab-lished to conform to true gradients between the grade elevations above given therefor.

Section 2. This ordinance shall take effect immediately

Changing Grades on Goettingen Street Between Woolsey and Dwight Streets.

Also, Bill No. 9155, Ordinance No. ———— (New Series), as follows:

Changing and reestablishing the official grades on Goettingen street between Woolsey and Dwight streets.

Whereas, the Board of Supervisors, on the written recommendation of the Board of Public Works, did on the 2nd day of November, 1929, by Resolution No. 31596 (New Series), declare its intention to change and reestablish the grades on Goettingen street between Woolsey and Dwight streets.

Whereas, said resolution was so published for ten days, and the Board of Public Works within ten days after the first publication of said resolution of intention caused notices of the passage of said resolution to be conspicuously posted along all streets specified in the resolution, in the manner and as provided by law; and

Whereas, more than forty days has elapsed since the first publica-tion of said resolution of intention; therefore,

Be it ordained by the People of the City and County of San Fran-cisco as follows:

Section 1. The grades on the following named streets at the points hereinafter named and at the elevations above City base as herein-after stated, are hereby changed and established as follows:

Goettingen Street.

Woolsey street southerly line, 81 feet. (The same being the pres-ent official grade.)

100 feet southerly from Woolsey street, 94.14 feet.

175 feet southerly from Woolsey street, 106.28 feet.

250 feet southerly from Woolsey street, 123 feet.

(Vertical curve passing through the last three described points.)

Dwight street northerly line, 161 feet. (The same being the pres-ent official grade.)

On Goettingen street between Woolsey and Dwight streets changed and established to conform to true gradients between the grade elevations above given therefor.

Section 2. This ordinance shall take effect immediately.

Changing Grades on Corbett Avenue.

Also, Bill No. 9156, Ordinance No. ———— (New Series), as follows:

Changing and reestablishing grades on Corbett avenue from Clayton street to Portola drive, as hereinafter described.

Whereas, the Board of Supervisors, on the written recommendation of the Board of Public Works, did, on the 2d day of November, 1929, by Resolution No. 31594 (New Series), declare its intention to change and reestablish the grades on Corbett avenue from Clayton street to Portola drive, etc., as shown on that certain diagram entitled "Grade Map of Corbett avenue from Clayton street to Portola drive showing the proposed change and establishment of grades on Corbett avenue and adjoining streets."

Whereas, said resolution was so published for ten days, and the Board of Public Works within ten days after the first publication of said resolution of intention caused notices of the passage of said resolution to be conspicuously posted along all streets specified in the resolution, in the manner and as provided by law; and

Whereas, more than forty days has elapsed since the first publication of said resolution of intention; therefore,

Be it ordained by the People of the City and County of San Francisco as follows:

Section 1. The grades on the following named streets, at the points hereinafter named and at the elevations above city base as hereinafter stated, are hereby changed and established as follows:

On Corbett avenue from Clayton street to Portola drive, etc., as shown on that certain diagram entitled "Grade Map of Corbett avenue from Clayton street to Portola drive showing the proposed change and establishment of grades on Corbett avenue and adjoining streets."

Section 2. This ordinance shall take effect immediately.

Amending Section 2, Ordinance No. 6512 (New Series), Spur Track on Twelfth Street.

Also, Bill No. 9157, Ordinance No. ———— (New Series), as follows:

Amending Section 2 of Ordinance No. 6512 (New Series) granting permission, revocable at will of the Board of Supervisors, to the Southern Pacific Company to operate with steam locomotives and cars over the tracks belonging to the City and County of San Francisco, formerly the property of the Ocean Shore Railway Company, as hereinafter described.

Be it ordained by the People of the City and County of San Francisco as follows:

Section 1. Section 2 of Ordinance No. 6512 (New Series), the title of which is above recited, is hereby amended to read as follows:

Section 2. "Provided, that no locomotive, car or cars shall be taken over this spur track on Twelfth street from Harrison street to Howard street, except between the hours of 6 o'clock a. m. and 8 a. m. and 1 p. m. and 4 o'clock p. m., and that the crossings of Harrison street and Folsom street be flagged on the passing of locomotives, car or cars."

Section 2. This ordinance shall take effect immediately.

Adopted.

The following resolution was *adopted*:

Extension of Time to Complete Improvement of Twentieth Street Between Pennsylvania Avenue and Iowa Street.

On recommendation of Streets Committee.

Resolution No. 31886 (New Series), as follows:

Resolved, That E. J. Treacy be and is hereby granted an extension of thirty days' time from and after December 27, 1929, within which to complete the improvement of Thirtieth street between Pennsylvania avenue and Iowa street, under public contract.

This extension of time is granted upon the recommendation of the Board of Public Works for the reason that the contractor has been delayed by inclement weather.

Ayes—Supervisors Andriano, Colman, Deasy, Gallagher, Havenner, Hayden, Kent, McGovern, McSheehy, Marks, Powers, Roncovieri, Schmidt, Stanton, Suhr, Toner—16.

Absent—Supervisors Shannon, Todd—2.

Approving Map Showing the Widening of Laidley Street at Thirtieth Street.

Also, Resolution No. 31887 (New Series), as follows:

Whereas, the Board of Public Works did by Resolution No. 108865 (Second Series) approve a map showing the widening of Laidley street at Thirtieth street; now, therefore, be it

Resolved, That the map showing the widening of Laidley street at Thirtieth street be and the same is hereby approved.

Further Resolved, That the parcel shown hatched on said map is declared an open public street, to be known as Laidley street.

Ayes—Supervisors Andriano, Colman, Deasy, Gallagher, Havenner, Hayden, Kent, McGovern, McSheehy, Marks, Powers, Roncovieri, Schmidt, Stanton, Suhr, Toner—16.

Absent—Supervisors Shannon, Todd—2.

Accepting Quitclaim Deed From Southern Pacific Company to Land for the Opening of Bay Shore Boulevard.

Also, Resolution No. 31888 (New Series), as follows:

Resolved, That the certain quitclaim deed from Southern Pacific Company, a corporation, to City and County of San Francisco, a municipal corporation, quitclaiming unto said City and County (in connection with acquisition of land for opening of Bay Shore boulevard) a portion of Lots 1, 2, 3, 4, 5 and 6, Block 5037, as per the Assessor's Block Books of City and County of San Francisco, be and the same is hereby accepted.

Ayes—Supervisors Andriano, Colman, Deasy, Gallagher, Havenner, Hayden, Kent, McGovern, McSheehy, Marks, Powers, Roncovieri, Schmidt, Stanton, Suhr, Toner—16.

Absent—Supervisors Shannon, Todd—2.

Lot Credits, Grand View Avenue Assessment District.

Also, Resolution No. 31889 (New Series), as follows:

Whereas, the Board of Public Works by Resolution No. 31602 (New Series) was directed to issue a new assessment for the improvement of Grand View avenue between its northerly and southerly intersections with Market street, including the intervening sections of Twenty-first and Worth streets and Twenty-second street and Hoffman avenue; and

Whereas, the sum of $10,042.99 was appropriated by Resolution No. 31668 (New Series) towards the expense of the improvement of said Grand View avenue; now, therefore, be it

Resolved, That the Board of Public Works is hereby directed to credit the following amounts to each lot, as follows:

		Amount
Assessment No.	1	$142.68
Assessment No.	3	249.37
Assessment No.	12	571.49
Assessment No.	13	214.32
Assessment No.	14	226.03
Assessment No.	15	155.24
Assessment No.	21	211.67

Assessment No. 22	127.49
Assessment No. 40	446.70
Assessment No. 41	196.63
Assessment No. 42	191.78
Assessment No. 43	200.19
Assessment No. 44	191.75
Assessment No. 46	92.46
Assessment No. 47	215.48
Assessment No. 48	180.01
Assessment No. 49	368.04
Assessment No. 80	763.29
Assessment No. 81	139.77
Assessment No. 89	211.29
Assessment No. 90	155.32
Assessment No. 93	237.13
Assessment No. 124	481.28
Assessment No. 125	344.92
Assessment No. 126	254.88
Assessment No. 30	121.03
Assessment No. 31	382.45
Assessment No. 32	242.06
Assessment No. 33	363.09
Assessment No. 34	115.37
Assessment No. 35	242.06
Assessment No. 36	128.29
Assessment No. 37	128.29
Assessment No. 38	128.29
Assessment No. 39	152.29
Assessment No. 140	179.55
Assessment No. 141	163.10
Assessment No. 142	193.85
Assessment No. 143	747.15
Assessment No. 144	186.91
	$10,042.99

Ayes—Supervisors Andriano, Colman, Deasy, Gallagher, Havenner, Hayden, Kent, McGovern, McSheehy, Marks, Powers, Roncovieri, Schmidt, Stanton, Suhr, Toner—16.

Absent—Supervisors Shannon, Todd—2.

Extension of Time to Complete the Improvement of Douglass Street Between Army and Twenty-eighth Streets.

Also, Resolution No. 31890 (New Series), as follows:

Resolved, That California Construction Company is hereby granted an extension of sixty days' time from and after January 7, 1930, within which to complete the improvement of Douglass street between Army and Twenty-eighth streets, under public contract.

This extension of time is granted for the reason that the contractor has been delayed by weather conditions.

Ayes—Supervisors Andriano, Colman, Deasy, Gallagher, Havenner, Hayden, Kent, McGovern, McSheehy, Marks, Powers, Roncovieri, Schmidt, Stanton, Suhr, Toner—16.

Absent—Supervisors Shannon, Todd—2.

Extension of Time to Complete Street Signs.

Also, Resolution No. 31891 (New Series), as follows:

Resolved, That M. J. Lynch be and is hereby granted an extension of sixty days' time from and after December 10, 1929, within which to complete the furnishing and erection of street signs under public contract No. 9.

This extension of time is granted upon the recommendation of the

Board of Public Works for the reason that the contractor has been delayed by non-delivery of pipe standards.

Ayes—Supervisors Andriano, Colman, Deasy, Gallagher, Havenner, Hayden, Kent, McGovern, McSheehy, Marks, Powers, Roncovieri, Schmidt, Stanton, Suhr, Toner—16.

Absent—Supervisors Shannon, Todd—2.

Passed for Printing.

The following matters were *passed* for *printing*:

Changing Grades on Olney Avenue.

On recommendation of Streets Committee.

Bill No. 9158, Ordinance No. ———— (New Series), as follows:

Changing and re-establishing the official grades on Olney avenue between Third street and San Bruno avenue.

Whereas, the Board of Supervisors, on the written recommendation of the Board of Public Works, did on the 2nd day of November, 1929, by Resolution No. 31597 (New Series), declare its intention to change and re-establish the grades on Olney avenue between Third street and San Bruno avenue; and

Whereas, said resolution was so published for ten days, and the Board of Public Works within ten days after the first publication of said resolution of intention caused notices of the passage of said resolution to be conspicuously posted along all streets specified in the resolution, in the manner and as provided by law; and

Whereas, more than forty days has elapsed since the first publication of said resolution of intention; therefore,

Be it ordained by the People of the City and County of San Francisco as follows:

Section 1. The grades on the following named streets at the points hereinafter named and at the elevations above city base as hereinafter stated, are hereby changed and established as follows:

Olney Avenue.

Northeasterly line of, at Third street, 141.00 feet. (The same being the present official grade.)

Southwesterly line of, at Third street, 145.00 feet. (The same being the present official grade.)

22.50 feet southwesterly from the northeasterly line of, 60 feet northwesterly from Third street, 143.85 feet.

22.50 feet southwesterly from the northeasterly line of, 100 feet northwesterly from Third street, 146.41 feet.

22.50 feet southwesterly from the northeasterly line of, 140 feet northwesterly from Third street, 151.81 feet.

Vertical curve passing through the last three described points.

22.50 feet southwesterly from the northeasterly line of, 150.45 feet northwesterly from Third street, 153.59 feet.

22.50 feet southwesterly from the northeasterly line of, 170.45 feet northwesterly from Third street, 156.04 feet.

22.50 feet southwesterly from the northeasterly line of, 190.45 feet northwesterly from Third street, 156.60 feet.

Vertical curve passing through the last three described points.

22.50 feet northeasterly from the southwesterly line of, 60 feet northwesterly from Third street, 144.55 feet.

22.50 feet northeasterly from the southwesterly line of, 100 feet northwesterly from Third street, 146.59 feet.

22.50 feet northeasterly from the southwesterly line of, 140 feet northwesterly from Third street, 151.81 feet.

Vertical curve passing through the last three described points.

22.50 feet northeasterly from the southwesterly line of, 170.45 feet northwesterly from Third street, 157.00 feet.

Northeasterly line of, at San Bruno avenue easterly line, 155.40 feet. (The same being the present official grade.)

Southwesterly line of, at San Bruno avenue easterly line, 158.00 feet. (The same being the present official grade.)

On Olney avenue between Third street and San Bruno avenue changed and established to conform to true gradients between the grade elevations above given therefor.

Changing Grades on Margaret Avenue.

Also, Bill No. 9159, Ordinance No. ———— (New Series), as follows:

Changing and reestablishing official grades on Margaret avenue between Lakeview avenue and Ridge lane; on Louisburg street between Ridge lane and a line parallel with Mount Vernon avenue and 200 feet southerly therefrom; on Majestic avenue between Ridge lane and a line parallel with Lakeview avenue and 544.02 feet northerly therefrom; on Tara street between Mount Vernon avenue and Ridge lane; and on Ridge lane between Caine avenue and Howth streets as hereinafter described.

Whereas, the Board of Supervisors, on the written recommendation of the Board of Public Works, did on the 28th day of October, 1929, by Resolution No. 31,595 declare its intention to change and reestablish the grades on Margaret avenue between Lakeview avenue and Ridge lane; on Louisburg street between Ridge lane and a line parallel with Mount Vernon avenue and 200 feet southerly therefrom; on Majestic avenue between Ridge lane and a line parallel with Lakeview avenue and 544.02 feet northerly therefrom; on Tara street between Mount Vernon avenue and Ridge lane; and on Ridge lane between Caine avenue and Howth street as shown on that certain diagram entitled "Grade Map showing the proposed change and establishment of grades on Margaret avenue between Lakeview avenue and Ridge lane; on Louisburg street between Ridge lane and a line parallel with Mount Vernon avenue and 200 feet southerly therefrom; on Majestic avenue between Ridge lane and a line parallel with Lakeview avenue and 544.02 feet northerly therefrom; on Tara street between Mount Vernon avenue and Ridge lane; and on Ridge lane between Caine avenue and Howth street."

Whereas, said resolution was so published for ten days, and the Board of Public Works within ten days after the first publication of said resolution of intention caused notices of the passage of said resolution to be conspicuously posted along all streets specified in the resolution in the manner as provided by law; and

Whereas, more than forty days has elapsed since the first publication of said resolution of intention; therefore

Be it ordained by the People of the City and County of San Francisco as follows:

Section 1. The grades on the following named streets at the points hereinafter named and at the elevations above City base as hereinafter stated, are hereby changed and established as follows:

On Margaret avenue between Lakeview avenue and Ridge lane; on Louisburg street between Ridge lane and a line parallel with Mount Vernon avenue and 200 feet southerly therefrom; on Majestic avenue between Ridge lane and a line parallel with Lakeview avenue and 544.02 feet northerly therefrom; on Tara street between Mount Vernon avenue and Ridge lane; and on Ridge lane between Caine avenue and Howth street as shown on that certain diagram entitled "Grade Map showing the proposed change and establishment of grades on Margaret avenue between Lakeview avenue and Ridge lane; on Louisburg street between Ridge lane and a line parallel with Mount Vernon avenue and 200 feet southerly therefrom; on Majestic avenue

between Ridge lane and a line parallel with Lakeview avenue and
544.02 feet northerly therefrom; on Tara street between Mount Vernon avenue and Ridge lane; and on Ridge lane between Caine avenue
and Howth street."

Section 2. This ordinance shall take effect immediately.

Width of Sidewalks on Campbell Avenue Between San Bruno Avenue and Goettingen Street.

Also, Bill No. 9160, Ordinance No. ——— (New Series), as follows:

Amending Ordinance No. 1061 entitled "Regulating the Width of
Sidewalks," approved December 18, 1903, by amending sections Four-
hundred and ninety-two and Six hundred and fifty-two thereof.

Be it ordained by the People of the City and County of San Francisco as follows:

Section 1. Ordinance No. 1061 entitled "Regulating the Width of
Sidewalks," approved December 18, 1903, be and is hereby amended
in accordance with the communication of the Board of Public Works,
filed in this office December 19, 1929, by amending sections Four
hundred and ninety-two and Six hundred and fifty-two thereof, to
read as follows:

Section 492. The width of sidewalks on Campbell avenue between
San Bruno avenue and Goettingen street shall be ten (10) feet.

The width of sidewalks on Campbell avenue between Goettingen
street and Alpha street shall be as shown on that certain map entitled "Map of Campbell avenue between Goettingen street and Alpha
street," showing the location of street and curb lines and the width
of sidewalks.

Section 652. The width of sidewalks on Campbell avenue, the
northerly side of, between Alpha street and Rutland street shall be
twenty (20) feet.

The width of sidewalks on Campbell, the southerly side of, between
Alpha street and Rutland street shall be ten (10) feet.

The width of sidewalks on Campbell avenue between Rutland street
and Hoyt street shall be twelve (12) feet.

Section 2. Any expense caused by the above change of walk widths
shall be borne by the property owners.

Section 3. This ordinance shall take effect and be in force from
and after its passage.

Width of Sidewalks on Alpha Street Between Goettingen Street and Tucker Avenue, Etc.

Also, Bill No. 9161, Ordinance No. ——— (New Series), as follows:

Amending Ordinance No. 1061 entitled "Regulating the Width of
Sidewalks," approved December 18, 1903, by amending section Six
hundred and fifty-seven thereof.

Be it ordained by the People of the City and County of San Francisco as follows:

Section 1. Ordinance No. 1061 entitled "Regulating the Width of
Sidewalks," approved December 18, 1903, be and is hereby amended
in accordance with the communication of the Board of Public Works,
filed in this office December 19, 1929, by amending section Six hundred and fifty-seven thereof, to read as follows:

Section 657. The width of sidewalks on Alpha street between
Goettingen street and Tucker avenue shall be seven (7) feet.

The width of sidewalks on Alpha street between Tucker avenue
and Campbell avenue shall be ten (10) feet.

The width of sidewalks on Alpha street between Campbell avenue
and Teddy avenue shall be as shown on that certain map entitled
"Map of Alpha street between Campbell avenue and Teddy avenue,"
showing the location of street and curb lines and the width of sidewalks.

The width of sidewalks on Alpha street between Teddy avenue and Leland avenue shall be ten (10) feet.

Section 2. Any expense caused by the above change of walk widths shall be borne by the property owners.

Section 3. This ordinance shall take effect and be in force from and after its passage.

Width of Sidewalks on Somerset Street.

Also, Bill No. 9162, Ordinance No. ———— (New Series), as follows:

Amending Ordinance No. 1061, entitled "Regulating the Width of Sidewalks," approved December 18, 1903, by adding thereto a new section to be numbered Ten hundred and eighty-eight.

Be it ordained by the People of the City and County of San Francisco as follows:

Section 1. Ordinance No. 1061, entitled "Regulating the Width of Sidewalks," approved December 18, 1903, be and is hereby amended in accordance with the communication of the Board of Public Works, filed in this office December 18, 1929, by adding thereto a new section to be numbered Ten hundred and eighty-eight, to read as follows:

Section 1088. The width of sidewalks on Somerset street between Campbell avenue and a point 112 feet northerly from Campbell avenue are hereby dispensed with and abolished.

The width of sidewalks on Somerset street between Campbell avenue and Rodeo avenue shall be as shown on that certain map entitled "Map of Somerset street between Campbell avenue and Rodeo avenue," showing the location of street and curb lines and the width of sidewalks.

Section 2. Any expense caused by the above change of walk widths shall be borne by the property owners.

Section 3. This ordinance shall take effect and be in force from and after its passage.

Ordering the Improvement of Castro Street Between Twenty-ninth and Thirtieth Streets and on Thirtieth Street Easterly to the Existing Pavement.

Also, Bill No. 9163, Ordinance No. ———— (New Series), as follows:

Ordering the performance of certain street work to be done in the City and County of San Francisco, approving and adopting specifications therefor.

Be it ordained by the People of the City and County of San Francisco as follows:

Section 1. The Board of Public Works, in written communication filed in the office of the Clerk of the Board of Supervisors December 10, 1929, having recommended the ordering of the following street work, the same is hereby ordered to be done in the City and County of San Francisco in conformity with the provisions of the Street Improvement Ordinance of 1918 of said City and County of San Francisco, said work to be performed under the direction of the Board of Public Works, and to be done in accordance with the specifications prepared therefor by said Board of Public Works, and on file in its office, which said plans and specifications are hereby approved and adopted.

That said Board of Supervisors, pursuant to the provisions of Part II of the said Street Improvement Ordinance of 1918 of said City and County of San Francisco, does hereby determine and declare that the assessment to be imposed for the said contemplated improvements, respectively, may be paid in twenty installments; that the period of time after the time of the payment of the first installment when each of the succeeding installments must be paid is to be six months from the time of the payment of the preceding installment, and that the rate of interest to be charged on all deferred payments shall be seven per centum per annum.

The improvement of Castro street from the existing pavement at the south line of Twenty-ninth street to Thirtieth street, and of Thirtieth street easterly to the existing pavement on Thirtieth street, by grading to official line and grade; by the construction of reinforced concrete stairways with 2-pipe railing, reinforced concrete wall, curbs, fence, gutters and coping; by the construction of ironstone pipe sewers with accompanying manholes, Y branches and side sewers; by the construction of brick catchbasins with accompanying 10-inch ironstone pipe culverts; by the construction of gutter sump and storm water inlets with accompanying ironstone pipe connections; by performing the necessary conform work at Twenty-ninth, Day and Thirtieth streets; by the construction of red warning lights and reflectors to be furnished and installed on concrete fence; by the construction of an asphaltic concrete pavement, consisting of a 6-inch concrete foundation and a 1½-inch asphaltic concrete wearing surface; and of a concrete pavement; and artificial stone sidewalks, all to conform to Plans A-7491 and A-7492, on file in the office of the City Engineer.

Section 2. This ordinance shall take effect immediately.

Adopted.

The following resolution was *adopted*:

Closing and Abandoning Portions of Rhode Island, De Haro, Carolina, Wisconsin and Arkansas Streets as Hereinafter Described.

On recommendation of Streets Committee.

Resolution No. 31892 (New Series), as follows:

Resolved, That the public interest requires that the certain following described portions of Rhode Island, De Haro, Carolina, Wisconsin and Arkansas streets be closed and abandoned; and be it

Further Resolved, That it is the intention of the Board of Supervisors to close and abandon all those portions of the above-named streets, more particularly described as follows, to-wit:

Portion of Rhode Island Street to Be Closed.

Beginning at the point of intersection of the northerly line of Army street and the westerly line of Rhode Island street, and running thence northerly along said westerly line 373.00 feet; thence at right angles easterly 80 feet to the easterly line of Rhode Island street; thence at right angles southerly along said easterly line 373.00 feet to said northerly line of Army street; thence westerly thereon 80 feet to the point of beginning.

Portion of De Haro Street to Be Closed.

Beginning at the point of intersection of the northerly line of Army street and the westerly line of De Haro street, and running thence northerly along said westerly line 373.00 feet; thence easterly along the arc of a curve to the left, tangent to a line deflected 90 deg. 00 min. 00 sec. to the right, radius 432.726 feet, central angle 10 deg. 39 min. 14 sec., a distance of 80.463 feet to the easterly line of De Haro street; thence deflecting 100 deg. 39 min. 14 sec. to the right from the tangent to the preceding curve and running southerly along said easterly line 380.459 feet to the northerly line of Army street; thence westerly thereon 80 feet to the point of beginning.

Portion of Carolina Street to Be Closed.

Beginning at the point of intersection of the northerly line of Army street and the westerly line of Carolina street, and running thence northerly along said westerly line 452.594 feet; thence easterly along the arc of a curve to the right, tangent to a line deflected 75 deg. 10 min. 41 sec. to the right, radius 312.726 feet, central angle 14 deg. 49 min. 19 sec., a distance of 80.900 feet to the easterly line of Carolina street; thence deflecting 90 deg. 00 min. 00 sec. to the right from the tangent to the preceding curve and running southerly along said easterly line 463.00 feet to the northerly line of Army street; thence westerly thereon 80 feet to the point of beginning.

Portion of Wisconsin Street to Be Closed.

Beginning at the point of intersection of the northerly line of Army street and the westerly line of Wisconsin street, and running thence northerly along said westerly line 463.00 feet; thence at right angles easterly 80 feet to the easterly line of Wisconsin street; thence at right angles southerly along said easterly line 463.00 feet to the northerly line of Army street; thence westerly thereon 80 feet to the point of beginning.

Portion of Arkansas Street to Be Closed.

Beginning at the point of intersection of the northerly line of Army street and the westerly line of Arkansas street, and running thence northerly along said westerly line 463.00 feet; thence at right angles easterly 80 feet to the easterly line of Arkansas street; thence at right angles southerly along said easterly line 303.996 feet; thence southwesterly and southerly along the arc of a curve to the left, tangent to a line deflected 53 deg. 25 min. 02 sec. to the right from the preceding course, radius 198.015 feet, central angle 53 deg. 25 min. 02 sec., a distance of 184.611 feet to the northerly line of Army street and the point of beginning.

Portion of Arkansas Street to Be Closed.

Beginning at the point of intersection of the northerly line of Army street and the easterly line of Arkansas street, and running thence westerly along said northerly line 20.00 feet; thence northerly and northeasterly along the arc of a curve to the right, tangent to a line deflected 90 deg. to the right, radius 138.015 feet, central angle 31 deg. 13 min. 51 sec., a distance of 75.229 feet to the easterly line of Arkansas street at a point distant northerly thereon 71.561 feet from the point of beginning; thence southerly 71.561 feet to the point of beginning.

Said closing and abandonment of said streets shall be done and made in the manner and in accordance with the provisions of Section 2, Chapter 3 of Article VI of the Charter of the City and County of San Francisco, as amended, and the sections of said chapter and article following Section 2; and be it

Further Resolved, That the damage, cost and expense of said closing and abandonment be paid out of the revenue of the City and County of San Francisco.

And the Clerk of this Board is hereby directed to transmit to the Board of Public Works a certified copy of this resolution, and the Board of Public Works is hereby directed to give notice of said contemplated closing and abandonment of said portions of said streets in the manner provided by law, and to cause notice to be published in the official newspaper, as required by law.

Ayes—Supervisors Andriano, Colman, Deasy, Gallagher, Havenner, Hayden, Kent, McGovern, McSheehy, Marks, Powers, Roncovieri, Schmidt, Stanton, Suhr, Toner—16.

Absent—Supervisors Shannon, Todd—2.

Passed for Printing.

The following matters were *passed for priting*:

Plans for Fifteenth Street Sewer Authorized.

On recommendation of Streets Committee.

Bill No. 9164, Ordinance No. ———— (New Series), as follows:

Authorizing the preparation of plans and specifications for the construction of the Fifteenth street sewer, Section "A," Contract No. 3; ordering the construction of said sewer in accordance with said plans and specifications prepared therefor; authorizing and directing the Board of Public Works to enter into contract for the construction of said sewer, and permitting progressive payments to be made during the course of said work, the cost of said work to be borne out of Sewer Bonds, 1929.

Be it ordained by the People of the City and County of San Francisco as follows:

Section 1. The Board of Public Works is hereby authorized, instructed and empowered to prepare plans and specifications for the construction of Fifteenth street sewer, Section "A," Contract No. 3, and to enter into contract for the construction of said sewer, hereinbefore specified, which is hereby ordered, in accordance with said plans and specifications prepared therefor. The cost of said sewer to be borne out of funds of the Sewer Bonds, 1929.

Section 2. The Board of Public Works is hereby authorized and permitted to incorporate in the contract for the construction of said sewer conditions that progressive payments shall be made in the manner set forth in said specifications, on file in the office of the Board of Public Works, and as provided for by the Charter of the City and County of San Francisco.

Section 3. This ordinance shall take effect immediately.

Appropriations for Boulevard Improvements.

Also, Resolution No. ————— (New Series), as follows:

Resolved, That the following amounts be and the same are hereby set aside, appropriated and authorized to be expended out of Boulevard Bond Fund, Issue 1927, for the hereinafter mentioned boulevard improvements, to-wit:

(1) For improvement of Bay Shore boulevard, Section A, Potrero avenue to Silver avenue, Contract 6, to enable final payment $22,500.00

(2) For the improvement of the Sunset boulevard by grading 18,000.00

(3) For the improvement of the Great Highway, upper roadway, between Lincoln way and Sloat boulevard, by the placing of fill (Granfield, Farrar & Carlin contract)........ 37,875.50

Appropriation, County Road Fund, Improvement of Evans Avenue.

Also, Resolution No. ————— (New Series), as follows:

Resolved, That the sum of $3,425.10 be and the same is hereby set aside, appropriated and authorized to be expended out of County Road Fund for the payment of the city's portion of the liability for the paving and sewering of Evans avenue from Marin to Army streets, and the paving of Evans avenue bridge and intersection at Selby street.

Appropriation for Improvement of Miguel Street at Fairmount Park.

Also, Resolution No. ————— (New Series), as follows:

Resolved, That the sum of $1,980 be and the same is hereby set aside, appropriated and authorized to be expended out of "Street Work in Front of City Property," Budget Item No. 34, for the improvement of Miguel street, fronting Fairmount Park, city property.

Appropriation, County Road Fund, for Improvement of Waterville Street Between Silver Avenue and Augusta Street.

Also, Resolution No. ————— (New Series), as follows:

Resolved, That the sum of $665 be and the same is hereby set aside, appropriated and authorized to be expended out of County Road Fund for the sewering and paving of Waterville street between Silver avenue and Augusta street and northerly portion of Silver avenue between Waterville street and Elmira street.

Adopted.

The following resolution was *adopted*:

Appropriations for Sidewalk and Sewer Construction.

On recommendation of Streets Committee.

Resolution No. 31893 (New Series), as follows:

Resolved, That the following amounts be and the same are hereby set aside, appropriated and authorized to be expended out of the hereinafter funds for the following sidewalk and sewer construction, to-wit:

County Road Fund.

(1) For the construction of a temporary crushed rock sidewalk, four feet in width, on Lyell street between Alemany boulevard and Cayuga avenue ....$ 150.00

Extension and Reconstruction of Sewers—Budget Item 37.

(2) For the extending of the sewer in Duncan street between Douglas street and Hoffman avenue, and relocating of manhole . . . .$ 50.00

(3) For reimbursement to Maude M. Harris, for account of construction of three sidesewers in place of the required one, at property on north line of Shields street easterly from Ralston street 54.00

Ayes—Supervisors Andriano, Colman, Deasy, Gallagher, Havenner, Hayden, Kent, McGovern, McSheehy, Marks, Powers, Roncovieri, Schmidt, Stanton, Suhr, Toner—16.

Absent—Supervisors Shannon, Todd—2.

Accepting Offer of Land for Widening of Ord Court.

Also, Resolution No. 31894 (New Series), as follows:

Resolved, That the offer of sale made by the following named persons to sell to the City and County of San Francisco, the following described land, required for the opening, extension and widening of Ord court, for the sums set forth opposite their respective names, be accepted:

Mary A. and Eugene L. Harrington, $1.—Portion of Lot 71, Block 2619, as per the Assessor's Block Books of the City and County of San Francisco (as per detailed description and written offer on file).

And the City Attorney is hereby authorized to examine the title to said property, and if the same is found satisfactory, to accept on behalf of the City a deed conveying said property to the City, free and clear of all encumbrances and to record said deed, together with copy of this resolution, in the office of the Recorder of the City and County of San Francisco.

Ayes—Supervisors Andriano, Colman, Deasy, Gallagher, Havenner, Hayden, Kent, McGovern, McSheehy, Marks, Powers, Roncovieri, Schmidt, Stanton, Suhr, Toner—16.

Absent—Supervisors Shannon, Todd—2.

Accepting Offer of Land for Opening of Alemany Boulevard.

Also, Resolution No. 31895 (New Series), as follows:

Resolved, That the offer of sale made by the following named owner to sell to the City and County of San Francisco the following described land, required for the opening of Alemany boulevard, for the sum set forth opposite her name, be accepted:

Mrs. Ernest Scossa, $1,155.—All of Lots 5 and 6 and portion of Lots 7and 9, in Block 5819, as per the Assessor's Block Books of the City and County of San Francisco (as per detailed description and written offer on file).

And the City Attorney is hereby authorized to examine the title to said property, and if the same is found satisfactory, to accept on behalf of the City a deed conveying said property to the City, free and clear of all encumbrances, and to record said deed, together with a copy of this resolution, in the office of the Recorder of the City and County of San Francisco.

Ayes—Supervisors Andriano, Colman, Deasy, Gallagher, Havenner, Hayden, Kent, McGovern, McSheehy, Marks, Powers, Roncovieri, Schmidt, Stanton, Suhr, Toner—16.

Absent—Supervisors Shannon, Todd—2.

Accepting Offer of Ed. Logue et al. to Sell Land Required for the Opening of Alemany Boulevard.

Also, Resolution No. 31896 (New Series), as follows:

Resolved, That the offer of sale made by the following named owners to sell to the City and County of San Francisco the following described land, required for the opening of Alemany boulevard, for the sum set forth opposite their names, be accepted:

Ed Logue and Catherine Logue, $5,500.—Portion of lots 3 and 4, Block 7140, as per the Assessor's Block Books of the City and County of San Francisco (as per detailed description and written offer on file).

And the City Attorney is hereby authorized to examine the title to said property, and if the same is found satisfactory, to accept on behalf of the City a deed conveying said property to the City, free and clear of all encumbrances, and to record said deed, together with a copy of this resolution, in the office of the Recorder of the City and County of San Francisco.

Ayes—Supervisors Andriano,. Colman, Deasy, Gallagher, Havenner, Hayden, Kent, McGovern, McSheehy, Marks, Powers, Roncovieri, Schmidt, Stanton, Suhr, Toner—16.

Absent—Supervisors Shannon, Todd—2.

Offer of Sale of Land Required for the Opening of Sunset Boulevard.

Also, Resolution No. 31897 (New Series), as follows:

Resolved, That the offer of sale made by the following named person to sell to the City and County of San Francisco the following described land, required for the opening of the Sunset boulevard, for the sum set forth opposite her name, be accepted:

Karen Eliasen, $1,500.—All of Lot 37, Block 2389, as per the Assessor's Block Books of the City and County of San Francisco.

And the City Attorney is hereby authorized to examine the title to said property, and if the same is found satisfactory, to accept on behalf of the City a deed conveying said property to the City, free and clear of all encumbrances, and to record said deed, together with copy of this resolution, in the office of the Recorder of the City and County of San Francisco.

Ayes—Supervisors Andriano, Colman, Deasy, Gallagher, Havenner, Hayden, Kent, McGovern, McSheehy, Marks, Powers, Roncovieri, Schmidt, Stanton, Suhr, Toner—16.

Absent—Supervisors Shannon, Todd—2.

Accepting Offer of Release of Damage, Bernal Cut.

Also, Resolution No. 31898 (New Series), as follows:

Whereas, The following owner of property adjacent to the proposed Bernal Cut has offered to release the City and County of San Francisco, its contractors or agents, from all claim or claims of damages to his property or the buildings thereon caused by the grading and construction of the proposed Bernal Cut to the proposed official grade and the grading and construction of adjacent streets to said proposed Bernal Cut; and

Whereas, the City Attorney has recommended the acceptance of the said offer, as per the following terms, viz.:

M. J. Collonan, $30.—Lot 18, Block 6662, as per the Assessor's Block Books of the City and County of San Francisco, and also known as No. 99 Randall street.

Resolved, that the said offer be accepted and the City Attorney is hereby authorized to close negotiations and superintend the payment of said specified amount to the above mentioned person upon receipt of the proper release.

Ayes—Supervisors Andriano, Colman, Deasy, Gallagher, Havenner, Hayden, Kent, McGovern, McSheehy, Marks, Powers, Roncovieri, Schmidt, Stanton, Suhr, Toner—16.

Absent—Supervisors Shannon, Todd—2.

Offer of James Millar et al. to Release the City and County of San Francisco and Its Contractors or Agents From All Claims of Damages Caused by the Construction of Bernal Cut.

Also, Resolution No. 31899 (New Series), as follows:

Whereas, the following owners of property adjacent to the proposed Bernal Cut have offered to release the City and County of San Francisco, its contractors or agents, from all claim or claims of damages to their property or the buildings thereon caused by the grading and construction of the proposed Bernal Cut to the proposed official grade and the grading and construction of adjacent streets to said proposed Bernal Cut; and

Whereas, the City Attorney has recommended the acceptance of the said offer, as per the following terms, viz.:

James Millar and Jeannetta F. Millar, $1,808.00—Lot 20, Block 6662, as per the Assessor's Blocks Books of the City and County of San Francisco, and also known as No. 71 Randall street.

Resolved, That the said offer be accepted, and the City Attorney is hereby authorized and directed to close negotiations and superintend the payment of said specified amount to the above mentioned persons upon receipt of the proper release.

Ayes—Supervisors Andriano, Colman, Deasy, Gallagher, Havenner, Hayden, Kent, McGovern, McSheehy, Marks, Powers, Roncovieri, Schmidt, Stanton, Suhr, Toner—16.

Absent—Supervisors Shannon, Todd—2.

Mayor to Execute Deed With Southern Pacific Company for Land for Bay Shore Boulevard.

Also, Resolution No. 31900 (New Series), as follows:

Pursuant to the terms of Resolution No. 31555 (New Series), providing for the purchase of certain property from Southern Pacific Company, a corporation,

Resolved, That the Mayor and the Clerk of the Board of Supervisors of the City and County of San Francisco, in the name of said City and County of San Francisco, are hereby authorized and instructed to execute that certain agreement wherein Southern Pacific Company, a corporation, grants to City and County of San Francisco, a municipal corporation, an easement over the following described property:

Parcel 1: Portion of Lots 1 and 21, Block 5477, as per the Assessor's Block Books of the City and County of San Francisco.

Parcel 2: Portion of Lot 7, Block 5476, as per the Assessor's Block Books of the City and County of San Francisco.

Parcel 3: Portion of Lots 10 and 11, Block 5480, as per the Assessor's Block Books of the City and County of San Francisco.

Parcel 4: Portion of Lots 3, 4 and 5, Block 5480, as per the Assessor's Block Books of the City and County of San Francisco.

Said easements are required in connection with the construction of the Bay Shore boulevard.

Ayes—Supervisors Andriano, Colman, Deasy, Gallagher, Havenner, Hayden, Kent, McGovern, McSheehy, Marks, Powers, Roncovieri, Schmidt, Stanton, Suhr, Toner—16.

Absent—Supervisors Shannon, Todd—2.

Extension of Time, California Construction Company.

On recommendation of Public Welfare, Publicity and Airport Committee.

Resolution No. 31901 (New Series), as follows:

Resolved, That the California Construction Company is hereby granted an extension of thirty days' time from and after December 17, 1929, within which to complete the construction of paving of the San Francisco Municipal Airport, Contract No. 13.

This extension is the second, and is granted upon recommendation of the Board of Public Works for the reason that delay was caused by weather conditions.

Ayes—Supervisors Andriano, Colman, Deasy, Gallagher, Havenner, Hayden, Kent, McGovern, McSheehy, Marks, Powers, Roncovieri, Schmidt, Stanton, Suhr, Toner—16.

Absent—Supervisors Shannon, Todd—2.

Taxicab Stand Permits.

On recommendation of Police Committee.

Resolution No. 31902 (New Series) ,as follows:

Resolved, That the following taxicab stand permits be and they are hereby granted:

Red Top Cab Company: 2959 Baker street, one cab; 696 Filbert street, one cab; 3301 Clement street, one cab; 902 Cole street, one cab; 800 Powell street, one cab.

Ayes—Supervisors Andriano, Colman, Deasy, Gallagher, Havenner, Hayden, Kent, McGovern, McSheehy, Marks, Powers, Roncovieri, Schmidt, Stanton, Suhr, Toner—16.

Absent—Supervisors Shannon, Todd—2.

Award of Contract, Standard Fence Company.

On recommendation of Supplies Committee.

Resolution No. 31903 (New Series), as follows:

Resolved, That award of contract be hereby made to Standard Fence Company on bid submitted December 23, 1929 (Proposal No. 547), for furnishing the following, viz.: Wire Fencing for Golden Gate Park.

Item No. 1—88 2½-inch O. D. line posts, 11 feet long, at $2.48 each.

Item No. 2—1 3-inch O. D. corner post, 11 feet long, at $13.

Item No. 3—15 3-inch O. D. three-way posts, 12 feet long, at $14 each.

Item No. 4—17 3-inch O. D. gate posts, 12 feet long, at $10 each.

Item No. 5—6 sets of fittings for 3-inch O. D. gate posts, at $3.95 a set.

Item No. 6—12,500 Lin. feet No. 6 Ga. coil spring wire, at $0.0063 Lin. foot.

Item No. 7—134 turn buckle bands for 3-inch O. D. posts, at $0.06 each.

Item No. 8—134 ⅜-inch turn buckles, at $0.18 each.

Item No. 9—1310 aluminum bands for 2½-inch O. D. posts, at $0.015 each.

Item No. 10—3500 Lin. feet 4 pt. No. 12 Ga. galvanized barbed wire, at $0.008 Lin. foot.

Item No. 11—88 steel outrigger brackets for 3-strand barbed wire, at $0.37 each.

Item No. 12—1 steel bracket as above to fit 3-inch O. D. Post, at $0.98.

Item No. 13—33 ball ornaments for 3-inch O. D. posts, at $0.38 each.

Item No. 14—1100 Lin. feet chain link fabric No. 9 Ga., 2-inch mesh, 48 inches high, at $0.21 Lin. foot.

Item No. 15—1100 Lin. feet 1⅝-inch O. D. top rail with couplings, at $0.14 Lin. foot.

Note: All above material to be made of copper bearing steel and galvanized after fabrication.

Memo.: Total value, $1,224.58.

Resolved, That a bond in the amount of $200 be required for faithful performance of contract.

Resolved, That all other bids submitted thereon be rejected.

Ayes—Supervisors Andriano, Colman, Deasy, Gallagher, Havenner, Hayden, Kent, McGovern, McSheehy, Marks. Powers, Roncovieri, Schmidt, Stanton, Suhr, Toner—16.

Absent—Supervisors Shannon, Todd—2.

Award of Contract, Traffic Buttons, Etc.

Also, Resolution No. 31904 (New Series), as follows:

Resolved, That award of contract be hereby made on bids submitted November 18, 1929 (Proposal No. 533), for furnishing the following, viz.:

For "Traffic"—Board of Supervisors.

Part I—Traffic turning buttons: (a) 100 special buttons at $1.36 each; (b) 900 standard buttons at $1.19 each; to Pacific Malleable Castings Co.

Part II—1000 plain safety zone buttons at $2.67 each; to Pacific Malleable Castings Co.

Part III—Under advisement.

Part IV—Under advisement.

Part V—Lag screws and expansion shields: Item No. 1, length of screws 7 inches, $18 per 100; Item No. 2, length of screws 5 inches, $17.25 per 100; to Payne's Bolt Works.

Resolved, That bonds for faithful performance of contract be required as follows, viz.:

Pacific Malleable Castings Co. in the amount of $500.

Payne's Bolt Works, none.

Resolved, That all other bids submitted thereon be rejected.

Ayes—Supervisors Andriano, Colman, Deasy, Gallagher, Havenner, Hayden, Kent, McGovern, McSheehy, Marks, Powers, Roncovieri, Schmidt, Stanton, Suhr, Toner—16.

Absent—Supervisors Shannon, Todd—2.

Award of Contract, Eggs.

Also, Resolution No. 31905 (New Series), as follows:

Resolved, That award of contract be hereby made to J. T. Freitas Co. on bid submitted December 18, 1929 (Quotation No. 1554), for furnishing the following, viz.:

Eggs—Fresh, that may be ordered from time to time during the 6 months' period commencing January 1 and ending June 30, 1930, for the several public institutions of the City and County of San Francisco, f. o. b. at vendor's establishment.

Eggs—California White Eggs, U. S. No. 1 extras, retail grade.

Note—The inspection fees, if any, will be cared for by the city.

Price—U. S. Government quotation of wholesale prices day of delivery, less 6 per cent.

Resolved, That a bond in the amount of $500.00 be required for faithful performance of contract.

Resolved, That all other bids submited thereon be rejected.

Ayes—Supervisors Andriano, Colman, Deasy, Gallagher, Havenner, Hayden, Kent, McGovern, McSheehy, Marks, Powers, Roncovieri, Schmidt, Stanton, Suhr, Toner—16.

Absent—Supervisors Shannon, Todd—2.

ROLL CALL FOR THE INTRODUCTION OF RESOLUTIONS, BILLS AND COMMUNICATIONS NOT CONSIDERED OR REPORTED UPON BY A COMMITTEE.

Acceptance of Deed to Land, Fleishhacker Pool.

Resolution No. 31878 (New Series), as follows:

Resolved, That the City and County of San Francisco accept the deed and title to those 9.757 acres of land included within the Fleishhacker Pool, and more particularly described in that certain deed dated the 24th day of December, one thousand nine hundred and twenty-nine, between Spring Valley Water Company, a corporation, grantor, and the City and County of San Francisco, grantee; and be it

Further Resolved, That the City Attorney is hereby authorized and directed to place said deed on record.

Adopted by the following vote:

Ayes—Supervisors Andriano, Colman, Deasy, Gallagher, Havenner, Hayden, Kent, McGovern, McSheehy, Marks, Powers, Roncovieri, Schmidt, Stanton, Suhr, Toner—16.

Absent—Supervisors Shannon, Todd—2.

Masquerade Ball Permit, Bohemian Ladies' Benevolent Society.

Resolution No. 31906 (New Series), as follows:

Resolved, That Bohemian Ladies' Benevolent Society be and is hereby granted permission to hold masquerade ball Saturday evening, January 18, 1930, in Sokol Hall, 739 Page street.

Adopted by the following vote:

Ayes—Supervisors Andriano, Colman, Deasy, Gallagher, Havenner, Hayden, Kent, McGovern, McSheehy, Marks, Powers, Roncovieri, Schmidt, Stanton, Suhr, Toner—16.

Absent—Supervisors Shannon, Todd—2.

Passed for Printing.

The following resolution was *passed for printing*:

Appropriation, $7,500, Additional Emergency Supplies, Board of Health.

Resolution No. ———— (New Series), as follows:

Resolved, That the sum of $7,500 be and the same is hereby set aside, appropriated and authorized to be expended out of "Urgent Necessity," Budget Item No. 24, Fiscal Year 1929-1930, for additional and emergency supplies by the Board of Health under the direction of the Superintendent of the Relief Home.

Report of Finance Committee on Financial Condition for First Half of 1929-1930.

The following was presented, read by the Clerk and ordered *filed*:

January 4, 1930.

To the Honorable Board of Supervisors, City and County of San Francisco.

Gentlemen: Your Finance Committee is happy to report that, at the expiration of the first half of the fiscal year 1929-1930, a careful trial balance of all of the municipal funds shows that the financial affairs of our city are in excellent condition. Based upon the expenditures for the half-year which has just ended and making proper allowauces for all future expenditures which were contemplated at the time your Honorable Board adopted the Budget and Tax Rate Ordinances, the bookkeeper for the Board estimates a possible surplus in the General Fund at the end of this fiscal year.

Your Finance Committee is convinced that the estimates upon which this report is based are conservative and that, in the absence of any necessity for large emergency expenditures which cannot be foreseen at this time, the condition of the city's books at the end of the next six months may be even more favorable than we would undertake now to predict.

Our report is predicated upon estimates obtained from the accounting departments of the Board of Public Works and Board of Health

of the amounts of the annual operating deficits which are usually incurred in those two departments. These departmental deficits, which
cannot be accurately estimated at the time of making the Budget and
which are invariably due to emergency requirements for sick relief
and special construction work, will be more than offset by surpluses
which have accrued and are estimated to accrue in the other public
funds.

The Publicity and Advertising Fund, which is raised by special tax
levy under the State law, has in recent years, in accordance with a
policy adopted by your Honorable Board, been budgeted and expended
upon the recommendation of the Public Welfare Committee, and a
special report on the condition of that fund will be rendered to the
Board by the members of that Committee.

The construction and maintenance of our public streets having been
financed almost exclusively out of the Good Roads Fund during the
present fiscal year, and the allocations and expenditures of that fund
have been delegated to the Streets Committee by your Honorable Board,
subject to the approval of the Finance Committee. A special report
on street construction and maintenance will be rendered to the Board
by the Streets Committee.

Four years ago, when the members of the present Finance Committee took office, your Honorable Board found itself confronted with
a deficit of $1,400,000 in the General Fund as budgeted by the former
Finance Committee for the current fiscal year, and was obliged to
make retrenchments to that amount before the fiscal year expired.
At that time the tax rate was $4.13. Today it is $3.91. We take
especial pride in being able to turn over the funds of the City and
County to the new Board of Supervisors with the assurance that,
barring extraordinary and unavoidable demands upon the City Treasury
in the next six months, no deficit will occur in this fiscal year.

Respectfully submitted,
FRANCK R. HAVENNER,
Chairman Finance Committee.

Report of the Streets Committee on Street and Boulevard Work,
1928-1929.

To the Honorable the Board of Supervisors of the City and County of
San Francisco.

Gentlemen: In accordance with promise made upon taking office,
and in the belief that citizens and taxpayers are entitled to and would
welcome this information, your Streets Committee herewith submits
a report of its actions and recommendations for the past twenty-three
months of its existence.

Your Committee has made an effort to reconstruct, resurface and
repair the streets of San Francisco in the order of their importance
and of priority of petition. It has tried to keep as much work as
possible going, to relieve unemployment.

There is offered for your consideration the following:

(1) Detail of work done, number of men employed, costs and mile-
age, out of County Road Fund (State Gas Tax Fund) and the Boulevard Bond Fund.

(2) A survey of work proposed and tentative costs.

Work performed by and under the Board of Public Works and Engineering Department totaled one million and eighty-three thousand
($1,083,000) dollars, allocated exclusively from the Good Roads Fund
(State Gas Tax). The policy of relieving the Budget has resulted in a
saving in the tax rate for the two years of over seventeen ($.17) cents.

There also was inaugurated a new policy in street and road construction by which we recommended sufficient funds for installation of
traffic signal ducts, larger water mains, ducts for light cables, the
cable itself and for light standards. The purpose of this policy was to
avoid the opening of new streets and roads after installation.

Spur Tracks.

Eighteen applications for spur tracks were granted. No application denied.

Summary.

Number of miles of streets resurfaced and reconstructed, 36.
Number of persons employed (average monthly, 23 months), 280.
Amount paid for labor monthly (average), $45,844.71.
Number of requests received for improvements, 1243.
Number of requests complied with, approximately, 861.
Number of inspections made (on ground by Committee), 1062.
Roving gang (patching), 1,100,000 square feet.
Total appropriations for 23 months (for street purposes), $2,549,413.
Total appropriations for boulevard construction, $3,636,796.

Recommendations.

We beg leave to recommend the following for your consideration and approval:

(1) The construction of a major highway along Army street from San Bruno avenue to San Jose avenue, same to be one hundred feet in width.

(2) That the policy of assisting property owners in outlying districts, i. e., by City contribution, be continued at the discretion of the Streets Committee and the Board.

(3) That the boulevard program be rushed to completion, to redeem our promises to the people, and to provide work for the unemployed.

(4) That the Streets Committee, the Industrial Development Committee and your Board continue to give every cooperation toward construction of a new bridge at Third and Channel streets. We deem the construction of this bridge vital to our future industrial growth.

City Contributions.

Another policy inaugurated and permitted by your Board has been assistance to many worthy projects in outlying districts by contributing a part of the cost where property owners were unable to bear the full value of the cost of the improvement. In this way, in the poorer districts, thousands of property owners were encouraged to do work which would have had to wait for more prosperous conditions.

Below are listed a number of neighborhood improvements which have been assisted by City contribution on the recommendation of the Streets Committee and the Board. These projects were such as to demand special treatment through the Bureau of Engineering and requiring the assistance from the City:

Laidley street improvement	$ 11,000.00
Laidley street slide	16,000.00
Eagle street	3,000.00
Relocation of Market street safety stations	17,200.00
Grand View avenue (contribution)	10,200.00
Josiah street	1,762.89
Glen Park Terraces	6,747.05
Cleaning sidewalk area, Geneva avenue	1,460.00
Reconditioning Pacific avenue	10,000.00
Dressing curbs (Board of Public Works)	10,000.00
Test boring, Third street bridge	1,000.00
Conform work, setting curbs, side sewers, catchbasins, incident to Bayshore boulevard, Laguna Honda, Grand View avenue, bridge repairs and numerous other streets, sidewalks, sand removal	25,564.00
Keith street, Newcomb and Oakdale avenues	1,080.00
Lower Terrace, Saturn-Levant streets	1,500.00
Faith street, San Bruno-Holladay avenues, Holladay avenue, Faith-Costa streets	4,241.85
Roosevelt way, Buena Vista Terrace-Seventeenth street	36,600.00

Vermont street, Twentieth-Twenty-second streets, Twenty-
first street, San Bruno avenue to Vermont street......... 10,000.00
Noe street, crossing of Duncan street.................... 307.50
Orizaba avenue, Holloway-Grafton avenues 1,498.86

$169,162.15

Prospective Work.

Below is listed prospective street work on which legal proceedings
are under way or on which plans and specifications are in process.
Commitment has already been made by the City in instances indicated.
In others no commitment has been made because of no estimate being
at hand:

Carolina street between Twenty-third and Twenty-second
streets (commitment pending) .. ..$ 22,000.00
Twentieth street, San Bruno avenue to Vermont street
(completed) 2,943.05
Woodside avenue (commitment made) 16,000.00
Corbett road (commitment made, amount in question)..... ....
Nineteenth street extension (commitment made, amount
in question) .. ..
Clearing spur track, Corporation Yard (no commitment).... 1,500.00
Toland street extended, Oakdale avenue to Industrial (no
commitment) 9,000.00
Alpha street, Tucker street to Wilde avenue (commitment
made, no amount specified) .. ..
Hyde street widening (commitment made) approximately.. 4,400.00
Van Ness avenue, widen (commitment pending), approxi-
mately 75,000.00
Montcalm street (commitment made, amount in question).. 6,000.00
Montgomery street, Union to Greenwich streets (commit-
ment made) 33,000.00
Divisadero extension to Castro street (commitment made).. 50,000.00
Army street, San Bruno avenue to San Jose avenue (major
highway, first allotment, no commitment)............... 100,000.00
Bernal boulevard, land and construction (commitment
made) .. ..: 25,000.00
Market street at Clayton street, relocate switch-back (com-
mitment made) 20,000.00
Harrison street, regrade between Second and Third streets
(commitment made) 25,000.00

Total $389,843.05

Boulevards.

There have been constructed and in process of construction fifteen
miles of boulevards, involving twenty (20) contracts and employing an
average number of 47 men. Total amount involved, $3,636.796.20. There
were six contracts on the Bayshore boulevard, $936,405; four on the
Alemany boulevard, $289,109.27; two on the Esplanade, $428,000; one
on the Great Highway, $239,263.34; one on the Junipero Serra boule-
vard, $374,396.50; one on Nineteenth avenue extension, $257,142.60;
one on the Bernal Cut, $329,598.28; two on the Alemany storm drain,
$397,836; one on the Kezar roadway, $62,294.34; two on the Laguna
Honda boulevard, $158,046.68; one on Junipero Serra boulevard exten-
sion, $101,914.90.

We are glad to report nearly one hundred per cent cooperation of the
Board of Public Works. We are indebted to the Engineering Department for most efficient assistance and full cooperation in the speedy
solution of many vexatious problems. We tender our thanks to the
California State Board of Harbor Commissioners for their spirit of
generous assistance.

We cannot close this report without expressing our unstinted praise
for the valuable help given and the cordial relationship which has

existed between the State Highway Commission and the Streets Committee.

Your Board has been most considerate of our recommendations and has made our work less hard by your generous support.

Mission District.

Coso avenue, Prospect street to Winfield street............$	5,250.00
Twenty-eighth street, Sanchez street to Noe street..........	5,000.00
Oakwood street extension to Nineteenth street.............	9,000.00
Ocean avenue, Keystone way to Hebrew Asylum............	700.00
Valencia street, Market street to Twenty-eighth street......	30,000.00
Nassau street, France avenue to Italy avenue.............	5,401.00
Elk street, resurfacing	705.00
Twentieth street, Church street to Sanchez street..........	6,670.00
Fourteenth street, Castro street to Noe street.............	6,200.00
Harrison street, Fifteenth street to Sixteenth street........	1,600.00
Fourteenth street, Castro street to Alpine Terrace..........	4,000.00
Crossing St. Charles street, San Mateo to Niantic avenues..	1,000.00
Laidley street, Mateo street to Roanoke street.............	16,356.00
Josiah street, Lakeview avenue to Howth street............	1,672.00
Twenty-sixth street, Church street to Sanchez street........	1,550.00
Diamond street, Nineteenth street to Twentieth street......	3,600.00
Virginia avenue, Coleridge street to Winfield street........	2,750.00
Twenty-third street, Noe street to Castro street............	2,450.00
Whitney street, Thirtieth street to Randall street..........	3,900.00
Manchester street, Bessie street to Stoneman street........	4,500.00
Eighteenth street, Potrero avenue to San Bruno avenue....	3,000.00
Day street, Sanchez street to Noe street..................	3,640.00
Thirtieth street, Sanchez street to Noe street.............	3,640.00
Brazil, Persia and Russia avenues between Mission and London streets	2,600.00
Naples street, Amazon street to Munich street.............	3,066.00
Grand View avenue......................................	10,692.00
Widening of Ocean avenue, Fairfield and Keystone ways....	1,000.00
Test boring, Laidley street	2,812.50
Bartlett street, widening.................................	5,000.00
Guerrero street, resurfacing	3,200.00
Twenty-sixth street, Dolores street to Guerrero street........	3,000.00
Twentieth street, Sanchez street to Noe street.............	27,000.00
Valley street, Castro street to Diamond street.............	600.00
Otsego avenue between Onondaga avenue and Seneca way..	6,794.00
Castro street between Market and Sixteenth streets........	17,000.00
Williams avenue between Newhall and Phelps streets......	5,747.00
Douglass street, Seventeenth street to Eighteenth street....	2,100.00
Noe street, Nineteenth street to Twentieth street...........	5,000.00
Fifteenth street, Folsom street to Harrison street..........	3,500.00
Duboce avenue, Castro street to Buena Vista avenue........	7,500.00
Laidley street, Thirtieth street to Noe street..............	475.00
Genesee street, Joost avenue to Mangels avenue............	1,500.00
Guerrero street, Eighteenth street to San Jose avenue, widen	10,800.00
Sixteenth street, Castro street to Flint street.............	3,400.00
Twenty-second street, Vicksburg street to Sanchez street....	2,030.00
Naples street, Geneva avenue to Rolph street.............	1,700.00
Delano avenue, Oneida avenue to Seneca way.............	1,942.00
Richland avenue bridge	28,000.00
Mission street, Fourteenth street to Army street...........	18,965.00
Grand View avenue, Elizabeth street to Stanton street......	7,500.00
Widening and improving San Jose avenue.................	25,000.00
Judson avenue, Foerster street to Phelan avenue..........	4,000.00
Orizaba avenue, Holloway avenue to Grafton avenue........	2,000.00
Jerrold avenue, Third street to Phelps avenue.............	8,000.00

Extension of Nineteenth street to Mono street..............	5,000.00
Duncan street, Sanchez street to Noe street................	3,500.00
	$353,157.50

North Beach and North of Market Street.

Washington street, Powell street to Mason street ....$	4,000.00
Glover street, Jones street to Leavenworth street............	4,500.00
Scott street, Broadway to Vallejo street.....................	2,500.00
Broadway, Scott street to Divisadero street	6,500.00
Gough street, Washington street to Jackson street..........	4,000.00
Jackson street, Taylor street to Jones street...............	4,000.00
Montgomery street, Polk street to Columbus avenue........	5,000.00
Broadway, Larkin street to Van Ness avenue..............	8,000.00
Leavenworth street, California street to Clay street........	5,000.00
Grant avenue, Pine street to Filbert street.................	6,500.00
Pleasant street, Taylor street to Jones street...............	3,500.00
Francisco street, Powell street to Taylor street.............	1,972.00
Jackson street, Hyde street to Larkin street...............	4,318.00
Laguna street from Bay northerly	1,165.00
Green street, Polk street to Van Ness avenue..............	6,500.00
Montgomery street between Green and Union streets.......	3,307.00
Polk street, crossing at Broadway	2,000.00
Taylor street, Columbus avenue to Bay street.............	2,000.00
Widening of Grant avenue, Columbus avenue to Filbert street	5,500.00
Taylor street, Columbus avenue to Bay street.............	2,400.00
Lombard street, Polk street to Van Ness avenue...........	1,500.00
Mason street, Clay street to Washington street.............	4,000.00
Jackson street, Montgomery street to Sansome street........	3,150.00
Scotland street, Columbus avenue to Jones street..........	2,600.00
Broderick street, Vallejo street to Green street...........	3,600.00
Scott street, Filbert street to Greenwich street............	5,000.00
Drum street, Jackson street to Pacific street..............	4,500.00
Larkin street, Pacific street to Union street...............	16,000.00
Montgomery street, Post street to Columbus avenue........	3,035.00
Pine street, Leavenworth street to Taylor street............	7,605.00
Washington street, Leavenworth street to Hyde street......	595.00
Front street, Pacific street to Broadway....................	3,600.00
Sacramento street, Hyde street to Jones street.............	8,100.00
Washington street, Kearny street to Montgomery street.....	1,000.00
Gough street, Jackson street to Pacific avenue.............	1,500.00
Mason street, Post street to Bush street...................	4,500.00
Market street, relocation of curbs and stations..............	17,200.00
Gough street, Turk street to Eddy street.................	3,750.00
Chestnut street, Leavenworth street to Hyde street........	5,500.00
Chestnut street, Jones street to Leavenworth street........	5,000.00
Lombard street, Battery street to Sansome street, resurfacing	776.00
Sutter street, Van Ness avenue to Octavia street...........	10,000.00
Market street, Polk street to Larkin street, resurface.......	541.00
Polk street, Turk street to Eddy street...................	1,850.00
Spofford alley, Clay street to Washington street, resurface..	536.00
Chestnut street, Jones street to Columbus avenue..........	5,500.00
Bernard street, Taylor street to Leavenworth street........	1,300.00
Stockton street, tunnel to Filbert street...................	6,300.00
Broadway	6,000.00
Pacific street, Columbus avenue to The Embarcadero.......	7,350.00
Grant avenue, Columbus avenue to Filbert street, widen....	6,000.00
Filbert street, Grant avenue to Kearny street..............	5,500.00
Pine street, Montgomery street to Sansome street, resurface	1,820.00
Crossing Clay and Mason streets	1,400.00
Powell street, Post street to Sutter street, resurface........	548.00
Green street, Larkin street to Leavenworth street..........	12,000.00
Taylor street, Jackson street to Pacific street..............	1,950.00

Mason street, Sutter street to Bush street, resurface....... 404.00
Vallejo street, east of Kearny street........................ 800.00
Sutter street, Powell street to Stockton street, resurface.... 538.00
Green street, Van Ness avenue to Franklin street.......... 650.00
Post street, Stockton street to Powell street, resurface..... 444.00
Chestn'ut street, Powell street to Taylor street............. 6,200.00
Webster street, Green street to Union street.............. 6,000.00
Jackson and Mason streets, intersection 450.00
John street, Powell street to Mason street................ 1,000.00
Pacific avenue, Larkin westerly 10,000.00
Crossing Kearny and Vallejo streets...................... 1,250.00
Leidesdorff street, California street to Pine street, resurface 443.00
Laguna street, California street to Sacramento street....... 5,000.00
Waverly place, Sacramento street to Washington street, re-
  surface 947.00
Sacramento street, Gough street to Octavia street.......... 4,000.00

                                                          $291,894.00

South of Market Street and Bay View.

Kansas street, Sixteenth street to Division street.........$ 11,000.00
Oakdale avenue, Barneveld street to Selby street........... 1,204.00
Twenty-third street, De Haro street to Carolina street...... 3,000.00
Eighteenth street, Potrero avenue to San Bruno avenue.... 3,000.00
Kirkwood avenue, Mendell street south 1,000.00
Keith street, Oakdale avenue to Newcomb avenue.......... 1,080.00
Vermont street, Twentieth street to Twenty-second street.. 20,000.00
Potrero avenue, Sixteenth street southerly................ 80,000.00
Carolina street, Twenty-second street to Twenty-third street 500.00
Wisconsin street, Twenty-third street to Twenty-fifth street.. 11,500.00
Utah street, Twenty-fifth street southerly................. 1,800.00
Third street and Islais Creek 450.00
Eighth street, Market street to Mission street............. 2,200.00
Eighth street, Brannan street to Townsend street.......... 4,000.00
Harriet street, Harrison street to Bryant street........... 6,000.00
Third street, Brannan street to bridge................... 7,000.00
Clementina street, First street to Second street........... 9,000.00
Ritch street, Brannan street to Townsend street.......... 5,125.00
Essex street, Folsom street to Harrison street............. 1,000.00
Fremont street, Mission street to Howard street........... 4,500.00
Jessie street, Ninth street to Tenth street................ 1,120.00
Natoma street, Fremont street to First street............. 3,250.00
Third street bridge, flooring 5,000.00
Harrison street, Fourteenth street to Twenty-second street.. 476.00
Seventh street, Mission street to Brannan street........... 9,333.00
Steuart street, Market street to Mission street............. 3,420.00
Tehama street, First street to Second street.............. 3,100.00
First street, Folsom street to Harrison street.............. 5.000.00
Armstrong street, Third street to Keith street............. 3,065.00
Mariposa street, Wisconsin street to Arkansas street........ 2,240.00
Kansas street, Army street to Mission street.............. 1,170.00
Mariposa street, Wisconsin street to Carolina street......... 1,320.00
Wisconsin street, Twenty-second street to Twenty-fifth street. 2,000.00
Carolina street, Seventeenth street to Mariposa street...... 3,160.00
Spear street, Mission street to Howard street.............. 3,900.00
Bryant street, Mission street to Alameda street........... 1,500.00
Third street, Mission street to Townsend street............. 16,000.00
Jessie street, Sixth street to Seventh street, resurface........ 1,090.00
Minna street, extension to Eleventh street................. 5,000.00
Fifth street, Harrison street to Bryant street.............. 6,500.00
South Park, Second street to Third street, resurface......... 4,405.00
Fremont street, Folsom street to Harrison street............. 10,500.00
Berry street, Fourth street to Seventh street............... 19,100.00
Alice street, Folsom street to Shipley street, resurface....... 122.00

Fourth street, Mission street to Townsend street.............   16,000.00
Harrison street, The Embarcadero to First street............   6,215.00
Eighteenth street, Howard street to Folsom street, resurface.   2,579.00
Cleveland street, Sherman street to Seventh street..........   2,800.00

                                                              _____
                                                              $312,724.00
Richmond District.
Third avenue, California street to Clement street...........$ 2,400.00
Arguello boulevard, Washington street to Jackson street.....   1,400.00
Palm street, California street to Geary street..............   5,744.00
Thirty-fifth avenue, Balboa street to Cabrillo street.......   3,000.00
Fifteenth avenue, Anza street to Balboa street..............   1,500.00
Clement street, Forty-third avenue to Forty-fourth avenue...   541.00
Eighth avenue, California street to Clement street..........   2,400.00
Eighteenth avenue, Cabrillo street to Fulton street.........   2,300.00
Sixteenth avenue, Cabrillo street to Fulton street..........   3,000.00
Thirtieth avenue, Geary street to Anza street...............   4,930.00
Thirty-second avenue, Anza street to Balboa street..........   4,060.00
Clement street, First avenue to Fifth avenue................   5,760.00
Fulton street, First avenue to Stanyan street...............   3,150.00
Parker avenue, southerly from Cole street...................   4,500.00
Jackson street, Presidio avenue to Walnut street............   6,000.00
Eighteenth avenue, Judah street to Kirkham street...........   3,000.00
Thirtieth avenue, Balboa street to Cabrillo street..........   1,440.00
Twenty-seventh avenue, Fulton street to Cabrillo street.....   1,425.00
Lyon street, Washington street to Jackson street............   3,600.00

                                                              _____
                                                              $ 60,150.00
Upper Market Street and Ashbury Heights.
Frederick street, Masonic avenue to Buena Vista avenue.....$ 3,500.00
Roosevelt way 1,300.00
Construction park Portola drive.............................   8,800.00
Market street, extended Fowler avenue...................... 15,000.00
Seventeenth street, Clayton street to Cole street...........   2,800.00
Fourteenth street, Alpine street to Buena Vista terrace......   2,500.00
Ashbury street, Oak street to Page street, resurface........   897.00
Belvedere street, Seventeenth street to Rivoli street........   2,800.00
Beulah street, Stanyan street to Shrader street, resurface....   1,967.00
Arguello boulevard, to Parnassus avenue.....................   6,000.00
Carl street, Cole street to Clayton street, resurface........   1,090.00
Roosevelt way, Fourteenth street to Buena Vista terrace.... 10,600.00
Parnassus avenue, Cole street to Clayton street, resurface....   1,001.00
Portola drive, Twenty-fourth street to Stanford Heights.....   1,500.00
Shrader street, Waller street to Frederick street, resurface..   2,102.00
Danvers street, Market street to Corbett avenue.............   3,000.00
Piedmont street, Ashbury street to Masonic avenue..........   2,000.00
Delmar street, Waller street to Frederick street............   5,000.00
Second avenue, Carl street to Parnassus avenue.............   5,000.00
Portola drive, Twenty-fourth street to Fowler avenue....... 137,000.00
Masonic avenue, Roosevelt way to Pluto street..............   700.00
Buena Vista terrace, Fourteenth street to Buena Vista avenue   3,300.00
Willard street, Frederick street to Parnassus avenue........   7,000.00
Woodland avenue, Parnassus avenue southerly.............   4,000.00
Fifteenth street, Beaver street to Buena Vista terrace........   4,000.00
Fifteenth street, Castro street to Beaver street.............   6,200.00
Widning of Duboce avenue...................................   3,500.00
Duboce avenue, Divisadero street to Alpine street...........   2,000.00

                                                              _____
                                                              $244,557.00
Western Addition.
Fell street, Fillmore street to Steiner street................$ 2,200.00
Fell street, Pierce street to Scott street....................   2,200.00

Webster street, Sutter street to Pierce street................ 255.00
Presidio avenue, Geary street to California street............ 2,132.00
Haight street, Scott street to Baker street................... 4,587.00
Octavia street, California street to Sacramento street........ 4,500.00
Buchanan street, Bush street to California street............ 8,000.00
Walnut street, Jackson street to Pacific avenue.............. 1,500.00
Turk street, Masonic avenue to Parker avenue............... 1,200.00
Euclid avenue, Parker avenue easterly...................... 2,000.00
Haight street, Scott street to Baker street................. 13,700.00
Lyon street, California street to Sacramento street........... 3,500.00
Page street, Octavia street to Buchanan street.............. 11,500.00
Sutter street, Fillmore street to Divisadero street............ 5,000.00
Oak street, Divisadero street to Baker street................ 7,700.00
Page street, Scott street to Divisadero street................ 3,600.00
Hermann street, Laguna street to Buchanan street.......... 1,800.00
Broderick street, Ellis street to O'Farrell street.............. 3,000.00
Fillmore street, Sutter street to Fulton street.............. 9,000.00
Lyon street, Washington street to Jackson street............ 3,600.00
Geary street, Van Ness avenue westerly.................... 40,000.00
McAllister street, Central avenue to Masonic avenue......... 2,500.00
O'Farrell street, Fillmore street to Steiner street, resurface... 1,005.00
Steiner street, California street to Clay street, resurface..... 1,195.00
Scott street, Golden Gate avenue to Pine street, resurface..... 8,272.00
Bush street, Van Ness avenue to Octavia street, resurface.... 5,450.00
Post street, Van Ness avenue to Divisadero street, resurface.. 14,622.00
Shrader street, Hayes street to Grove street................ 2,000.00
Geary street, Masonic avenue to Presidio avenue, resurface.. 9,359.00
Lyon street, Golden Gate avenue to McAllister street......... 2,000.00
Fell street, Laguna street to Baker street, resurface.......... 5,259.00
Pierce street, Oak street to Fell street..................... 3,750.00
Steiner street, Fulton street to Clay street................. 11,678.00
Pierce street, Ellis street to O'Farrell street................ 3,750.00
Turk street, Central avenue to Broderick street, resurface.... 4,580.00
Larkin street, McAllister street to Post street.............. 12,500.00
O'Farrell street, Octavia street to Fillmore street............ 7,700.00
Fulton street, Masonic avenue westerly.................... 13,000.00
Scott street, Haight street to Page street, resurface......... 1,082.00
Sutter street, Van Ness avenue to Octavia street............ 10,000.00
Masonic avenue, Hayes street to McAllister street, resurface.. 3,208.00
Broderick street, Oak street to Fell street................. 1,200.00
Page street, Pierce street to Scott street, resurface.......... 1,520.00
Pine street, Larkin street to Van Ness avenue.............. 3,500.0u
Masonic avenue, Fell street to Fulton street, resurface........ 5,092.00
Scott street, Fell street to Duboce avenue.................. 12,300.00
Bush street, Steiner street to Divisadero street, resurface.... 3,308.00
Sacramento street, Polk street to Larkin street............. 2,250.00
                                                          _____
                                                          $283,054.00

Sunset District.

La Plaza, Judah street to Kirkham street.................$ 2,688.00
Forty-third avenue, Kirkham street to Lawton street......... 12,000.00
Laguna Honda boulevard, from Noriega street.............. 15,743.00
Wawona street, Nineteenth avenue to Twentieth avenue..... 324.00
Thirty-third avenue, Irving street to Judah street........... 1,500.00
Santiago street, Twenty-second avenue to Twenty-fourth
  avenue 13,500.00
Junipero Serra boulevard.............................. 4,250.00
Golden Gate Heights................................... 16,000.00
Sloat boulevard, Great Highway.......................... 2,730.00
Twenty-second avenue and Santiago street................. 1,192.00
Twenty-second avenue, Rivera street to Santiago street...... 3,000.00
Eighteenth avenue, Quintara street to Rivera street......... 1,000.00

Forty-third avenue, Kirkham street to Lawton street........   1,200.00
Twenty-sixth avenue, Lawton street to Moraga street........   435.00
Golden Gate Heights, City property........................   30,859.00
Tunnel street, Skyline boulevard at Fleishhacker Pool.......   14,500.00
Garfield street at Junipero Serra boulevard.................   5,000.00
Teresita boulevard, Portola drive to Foerster street........   6,000.00
Eighth avenue, Kirkham street to Lawton street.............   3,000.00
Eleventh avenue, Judah street to Krkham street.............   3,000.00
Ninth avenue, Irving street to Judah street................   2,000.00
Widening of Ninth avenue, Irving street to Judah street.....   3,000.00
Laguna Honda boulevard, Lawton street to Plaza...........   157,600.00
Santiago street, Twenty-second avenue to Twenty-fourth
   avenue 1,224.00
Majestic avenue at Taraval street..........................   650.00
Vicente street, Thirty-third avenue to Thirty-fifth avenue....   3,250.00
Thirty-first avenue, Irving street to Judah street..........   3,500.00
Judah street, Eleventh avenue to Twelfth avenue............   2,055.00
Crossings of Noriega street and Twenty-fourth and Forty-
   fourth avenues..   1,330.00
Lincoln way, First avenue westerly........................   10,000.00

                                                            _____
                                                            $322,530.00

Respectfully submitted,
                    STREETS COMMITTEE.
                        ANDREW J. GALLAGHER, Chairman.
                        ALFRED RONCOVIERI.
                        FRED SUHR, JR.

Supervisor Kent Reviews Activities of Committee on Public Welfare, Publicity and Advertising and Airport.

Supervisor Kent reported verbally on the activities of the Committee on Public Welfare, Publicity and Advertising and Airport. He declared that invaluable advertising had been given San Francisco by reason of the money spent by this City sending delegates to and participating in conventions, conferences and tournaments of our neighboring cities and counties and States; that inestimable good had been done in "selling" San Francisco to the rest of the United States. He deprecated the newspaper talk about "junketeering" at the Rose Tournament at Pasadena, and stated that from a publicity standpoint it was money well spent.

Retiring Members.

Supervisor Havenner expressed his personal regrets on the retirement of Supervisors Deasy, Powers, Schmidt, Kent and Todd. He declared that they had been faithful to their pledges to the people to work for economy in the expenditure of public moneys and had always voted consistently on municipal ownership programs.

Supervisor Hayden also addressed the Board, eulogizing the retiring members, wishing them godspeed and good luck in all their future activities.

Reorganization of the Board.

At the hour of 12 o'clock noon, His Honor Mayor Rolph being in the chair, the Board proceeded to reorganize.

CALLING THE ROLL.

The roll was called and the following Supervisors were noted present: Supervisors Andriano, Canepa, Colman, Gallagher, Havenner, Hayden, McGovern, McSheehy, Miles, Power, Roncovieri, Rossi, Shannon, Spaulding, Stanton, Suhr, Toner—17.
Absent—Supervisor Peyser—1.

Message from Supervisor Jefferson E. Peyser.

San Francisco, Cal., January 6, 1930.

Board of Supervisors, City Hall.

Regret that owing to illness I am unable to attend this first meeting. Congratulations to my colleagues and best wishes for a successful term.

JEFFERSON E. PEYSER.

MESSAGE OF HIS HONOR MAYOR ROLPH.

January 6, 1930.

Whereupon, his Honor the Mayor read the following message, which was *ordered spread in the Journal*:

To the Honorable Board of Supervisors of the City and County of San Francisco.

Gentlemen and My Fellow Citizens: The Charter of our City and County under which we officially act provides two-year periods for changes in the personnel of its legislative body, your Honorable Board, and I offer good wishes to the six members who are retiring from the Board to devote themselves to their private affairs, and cordially greet the six new incoming members, whom the people have honored, and with the confidence that they as Supervisors will prove exceedingly useful, optimistic· members of the Board, for the advancement of the City of San Francisco, and with the hope that they will enjoy their public service.

As Mayor, and, I am sure, speaking for the entire Board of Supervisors, I wish good health and success to Messrs. Cornelius J. Deasy, Milo F. Kent, Milton Marks, Charles J. Powers, Walter J. Schmidt and Charles F. Todd, who leave the Board today.

In the same spirit I welcome Supervisors Angelo J. Rossi, James E. Power, Jefferson E. Peyser, Carl W. Miles, E. J. Spaulding and Victor J. Canepa, our new members, and congratulate Supervisors Franck R. Havenner, William P. Stanton and James B. McSheehy upon the approval of their stewardship of the past by our fellow citizens who voted to continue them in office.

I take pleasure in advising you that I have reappointed Doctor Thomas E. Shumate to the Board of Police Commissioners; Mr. Lawrence Arnstein, Jr., to the Department of Public Health; Mr. M. Earl Cummings to the Board of Park Commissioners; Mr. Frederick W. Meyer to the Board of Public Works; Mr. P. W. Meherin to the Board of Fire Commissioners; all of whose terms expired and their faithful services justified recognition in reappointment. Mr. Timothy A. Reardon has been reelected to the presidency of the Board of Public Works.

The past two years have seen San Francisco make very important progress in its municipal affairs. The consolidation of our water supply system and the construction of great traffic arteries have brought the utmost satisfaction to both public officials and to the whole people.

The sale of bonds recently made for the purchase of the Spring Valley Water System concludes years of effort exerted by the forward-looking men and women of the City to acquire the system for the City's good, and takes from the political arena a question which has been used to agitate and confuse the people's minds for the past half century. It now belongs to the City and we should be thankful to have it. It will grow in value and useful necessity as the City grows.

The combined Spring Valley and Hetch Hetchy water systems will give San Francisco the finest water supply of any city in the United States. The City will now own locally 63,000 acres of land tributary to our distributing reservoirs, the largest and most beautiful park system in the world, and a Congressional grant catchment basin of 420,000 acres in the high Sierras, and own dams, tunnels and huge pipes to transport and store these priceless waters, for a population in excess of ten millions of people.

The City Engineer advises me that water on the Skyline boulevard will be obtainable when Hetch Hetchy mountain water reaches the

Peninsula reservoirs of our water system within three years' time. The coast towns are short of water, and the whole territory of beautiful San Mateo County can be served. Santa Clara County can also be served. Water districts are now being formed in both counties, under lawful acts.

I thank Mr. Amadeo P. Giannini and the officials of the Bank of Italy for their public-spirited solution of the problem by purchasing our Spring Valley bonds of forty-one million dollars at 4½ per cent per annum at this time, thus enabling the City to immediately enter into the profitable and highly advisable public business of operating its own water supply for the benefit of the people.

The water problem has been the major project before the people for nearly half a century and has been beset during all that time by the tactics of politicians, obstructionists, theorists, and pessimists. Its solution is cause for general rejoicing. Rapid completion of our Hetch Hetchy water supply is imperative, and I bespeak the heartiest cooperation of your Board with the members of our Board of Public Works and our distinguished City Engineer, M. M. O'Shaughnessy, who has done his work fearlessly, ably, thoroughly, competently, satisfactorily, with prudent economy under great unforeseen handicaps at times and with the honest expenditure of the people's money.

Our Charter, as I have repeatedly pointed out, commits our City to public ownership of public utilities.

Municipal Railways.

Very successfully San Francisco has acquired by purchase, built and operated its municipal railway system, which is a conspicuous example of successful municipal effort. We now have only, in round numbers, $2,800,000 bonds outstanding to redeem on our railway properties, which the balance sheet shows represents a total investment of over $9,700,000. The track and equipment are of the best type and the people take pride in the administration of the lines. The platform men are courteous and attentive. The lines have carried progress and success to the beautiful Marina, Twin Peaks, Parkside, Sunset, Richmond, North Beach, Mission and Ocean Beach districts and other sections which they serve, and all on a five-cent fare, which should be maintained. We must provide transportation for everybody who wants to ride to all sections of the city.

We are confronted with a railway problem of first importance. Several franchises of the Market Street Railway Company, granted to them by the City fifty years ago, have expired. After careful study, a most comprehensive report on transportation has been made under direction of our City Engineer. I respectfully urge your Honorable Board to give prompt, serious attention to reaching a valuation of the Market Street Company's properties that will permit the carrying out of the Charter declaration for municipal ownership of our public utilities under conditions that will justify the unification of street-car transportation in the hands of the City and that the subject be approached with a desire to acquire a system at a price fair to the company and fair to the City. Both systems, for the benefit of the City, must be owned by the City.

Other problems of the past have been solved by the thoughtful and well-considered action of our municipal authorities, and I trust that our street-railway unification problem may be behind us at the earliest possible moment.

There is no problem of human endeavor that cannot be solved. We owe it to ourselves and to our City to solve the railway problem. Fear of criticism of public acts should not deter an honest public official from doing his duty. The people hold in high esteem a fearless, honest, forward-going public official. This is a hard problem to tackle, but the harder it is the more eager you should be to solve it. You are trusted with and have assumed the responsibility. I will continue to help.

Hydro-Electric Disposal.

In connection with the Hetch Hetchy water and electric activities of the City, we are developing hydro-electric energy at the Moccasin power plant from which the city is deriving an annual return of over $2,000,000 on a contract between the City and the Pacific Gas and Electric Company, terminable on one day's written notice by either party. This contract pays the interest charges on $45,000,000 of our Hetch Hetchy total investment.

By direction of the Board of Supervisors; our able City Attorney, Honorable John J. O'Toole, has instituted proceedings before the California State Railroad Commission to acquire the distribution systems and steam electric plants of the Pacific Gas and Electric Company and the Great Western Power Company in San Francisco. These proceedings were begun in February, 1924. This action necessitated a detailed inventory and appraisal of the properties of both systems, and exhaustive studies on the subjects of accrued depreciation, severance damage and going value. These hearings extended over a period of three years and consumed some 12,000 pages of transcript of testimony, supplemented by voluminous technical exhibits. The cases were submitted in the summer of 1928 and the Commission's decisions were handed down in June, 1929.

The results are summarized in the following table:

JUST COMPENSATION AS OF FEBRUARY 11, 1924.

	Company's Claim	City's Claim	California R.R. Commission Allowance
Pacific Gas and Electric Company	$67,000,000	$18,894,005	$26,880,000
Great Western Power Co.	30,000,000	9,306,537	11,815,000
Total	$97,000,000	$28,200,542	$38,695,000

It will be noted that the difference between the Commission's findings and the claims of the City is approximately $10,495,000; whereas the difference between the Commission and the company's claim is $58,300,000; or, in other words, of a total difference between City claims and company claims of $68,800,000. The Commission decided 85 per cent of this difference in favor of the City.

Each of the companies made application to the Railroad Commission for a rehearing and modification of the values fixed, both of which applications were denied, thereby leaving the values as fixed by the respective decisions. As the values were fixed as of February 11, 1924, the date that the proceedings were initiated, and in the interim a great many additions and betterments have been made by each of the companies to their respective properties, it is estimated that the total purchase price of all the properties will be about $55,000,000.

Under the provisions of the Public Utility Act, proceedings for the acquisition of the properties must be initiated within sixty days after the decision of the Commission. This was done on August 17, 1929, when the Board of Supervisors enacted an ordinance directing the Board of Public Works through the City Engineer to furnish plans and estimates of the total cost of the acquisition of both properties. The City Engineer is now working upon these plans and estimates.

The Utility Act further provides that the legislative body of the City must proceed with due diligence to submit to the electors the question of the issuance of bonds for the acquisition of the properties which have been valued. It will therefore be incumbent upon the Board of Supervisors to provide for an election early in 1930, at which the people may determine the matter of the acquisition of both of these companies and enter into the municipal ownership, operation and distribution of the hydro-electric energy it develops from its Hetch Hetchy water project, which is provided for in the grant to the City from the Congress of the United States and is in keeping with the Charter provision of our City government and the declared policy of the people. This matter requires your earnest attention at once.

Telephone Rates.

The majority of the existing telephone rates have been in effect since 1914, at which time they were established by the Board of Supervisors. In June, 1927, the Pacific Telephone and Telegraph Company applied to the California Railroad Commission for a consolidation of the San Francisco and East Bay exchanges and for a revised rate schedule that would have meant an average rate increase of 50 per cent, or an approximate annual increase in the San Francisco area of $5,000,000. The cases were vigorously prosecuted by the municipalities over a two-year period.

The physical properties were inventoried and appraised on both a historical and a reproduction new basis; operating expenses were scrutinized in detail and many technical problems, such as toll-allocation, Western electric cost, depreciation, transition to automatic equipment and the like, were the subjects of exhaustive studies. The cases were submitted in October, 1929, and the Commission decision handed down on November 7, 1929. The effect of the decision was to revise the rate schedules, with a resultant annual increase to both communities of approximately $2,100,000, or, to the City of San Francisco alone, of approximately $1,400,000. This latter figure is to be contrasted with the $5,000,000 heretofore referred to as claimed by the company. The new rates became effective January 1, 1930. While the prosecution of the cases ran over a considerable period, the ratepayers were substantial gainers thereby. Had the new rates been put in effect in June, 1927, the ratepayers of San Francisco would have paid $3,500,000 excess in the two-and-one-half-year interim between that date and January 1, 1930.

Had the company's claims been allowed, the ratepayers of San Francisco would have paid an excess of $12,500,000 in the two-and-one-half-year period.

In the period subsequent to January 1, 1930, the increase in rate will be 28 per cent of the amount claimed by the company.

Our able legal and engineering departments handled these cases admirably and I thank them.

Electric Rates.

Due to the rapidly increasing activities of both the Pacific Gas and Electric Company and the Great Western Power Company, and the succession of mergers of smaller companies with these two corporations, it has been necessary to keep in constant touch with the electric rate situation and carry on numerous studies and presentations before the California Railroad Commission; in March, 1928, a rate cut was effected which resulted in an annual saving to the electric ratepayers of San Francisco of approximately $650,000. The result of studies made during the latter part of 1929 will bring a further rate reduction, effective early in 1930, that should mean an additional annual saving of $625,000 to San Francisco ratepayers, and it is felt that a continuance of the studies during 1930 will effect further marked reductions.

I recommend that the Public Utilities Committee of your Honorable Board be ever alert and diligent in the handling of these problems for the benefit of the people of the City.

Gas Rates.

On May 7, 1929, the Pacific Gas and Electric Company filed an application with the California Railroad Commission to construct a pipeline from the Kettleman Hills, Kern County, California, to San Francisco for the purpose of transporting natural gas.

The natural gas containing 1100 B. T. U.'s was to be mixed with the artificial 550 B. T. U.'s gas, and a mixed gas containing 700 B. T. U.'s was to be served to consumers. The company proposed a new rate which would have increased the gas bills of 65 per cent of the consumers.

City Attorney O'Toole and his staff vigorously protested any increase of rates due to the use of a mixed gas, with the result that the California Railroad Commission on October 28, 1929, ordered the Pacific Gas and Electric Company to serve a gas of not less than 600 B. T. U.'s at the then prevailing rates for 550 B. T. U. gas. During the last two months this has saved the gas consumers of San Francisco over $120,000.

Natural gas is now being served for industrial purposes in San Francisco and will be available for domestic purposes about April 1, 1930. Interim rates will be handed down by the California Railroad Commission in the near future so that the Pacific Gas and Electric Company can build up their domestic load, which will be materially reduced with the advent of natural gas.

The natural gas situation is being closely watched and the activities of other competing companies in the bay area will bring competition which will undoubtedly result in lower gas rates.

A valuation of the Pacific Gas and Electric Company properties has not been made since 1918 and must therefore be thoroughly examined after natural gas has been here a sufficient length of time and more information is available regarding standby requirements, operating expenses and the correctness of prognosticated revenues. Your attention is directed to this important matter, and requires the attention of your Public Utilities Committee.

Highway Construction.

In road construction the past two years have seen the realization of major units of the city traffic plans, of which the Stockton-street tunnel, Twin Peaks tunnel, the Marina and other boulevards were early developments.

During the past two years, with the approval of the voters of our City, we have been extending a series of boulevards in a southerly direction to make contact with San Mateo County. The people very wisely and very generously voted the sum of $10,780,000 to carry through the execution of these projects. I am happy to state that up to the first of January this year about 80 per cent of the projects had been completed, including the Bay Shore boulevard, Junipero Serra boulevard, Nineteenth avenue extension southerly, Ocean Beach esplanade, the Great Highway and the Bernal cut. The ones remaining to be completed from unexpended bond money are Alemany boulevard, Sunset boulevard and Van Ness avenue extension. There should be no delay in these vital improvements.

The automobiles owned in San Francisco have increased tenfold in the last ten years, until at present there are approximately 150,000 motor-driven vehicles. These vehicles need traffic arteries and I am pleased that the City had the vision to carry out this magnificent scheme of boulevards, which will render necessary service to the inhabitants for all time.

We have laid permanent pavements on all these boulevards, consisting of eight.inches of concrete base with asphalt tops, except on softer fills, subject to settlement, where temporary pavements are laid until settlements are final.

Proposed Betterments.

Necessary worthy improvements must be considered by your Honorable Board, the most important of which is the widening of an east-and-west street—Army street—from Bay Shore highway to San Jose avenue, to a width of 100 feet, estimated to cost $1,000,000; the widening of Illinois street from Eighteenth street to Islais Creek channel. This widening is undertaken partially for the purpose of providing an Embarcadero street for the undeveloped commerce on the easterly side of the City.

Your Board may well pay attention to the feasibility of building a tunnel, cost $1,500,000, on Broadway, between Larkin and Mason streets, which would provide a material exit between the downtown business section and the Western Addition.

Harbor Frontage.

The City has developed, under State authority, an intensive commercial frontage along our bay, from Van Ness avenue to Channel street. This occupies practically three miles of City's frontage and provides docking facilities now to deep-sea shipping. The next mile and a half, from Channel street to Islais Creek, is occupied by private enterprises, which are using all this frontage. The undeveloped part, southerly from Islais Creek, has 165 acres under the control of State authorities, and about a thousand acres in the vicinity of Hunters Point, which is submerged land, capable of reclamation. This can only be done by some central authority, capable of issuing bonds to build a sea-wall on the water frontage and dumping mud in behind. In this way commercial property of very great value will be developed and add to the commercial and industrial importance of our City.

I am pleased to see that a public reclamation district, under State laws, is functioning both north and west of Islais Creek to reclaim 280 acres of land, and I hope to see this improvement go through to a successful conclusion this coming year, and in this way, besides removing an existing nuisance, add to our commercial and industrial potentialities.

We must do everything possible to encourage skyscrapers, industrial plants and harbor facilities, and spend money intelligently to accomplish that end.

Schools.

San Francisco may be exceedingly proud of its schools. For many years a carefully considered plan for school extension has been under way, with the result that our new school buildings are considered the finest in the country. There has been a very large increase in the number of pupils in our schools and the building program must be continued without any slackening of pace if the children are to be cared for as San Francisco would have them.

There are more than 100,000 children and adults enrolled during the year in the public schools. The instruction and care for this large number require the services of approximately 2800 teachers, 300 janitors and 150 other employees.

The support of the School Department of necessity requires a large share of the tax money of the municipality. The total expenditures for the current year are estimated at $8,648,000 for operation and $2,100,000 for new buildings, lands and repairs, a total of $10,748,000, including approximately $1,760,000 received from the State. While this may be considered a large sum, the importance of education to the welfare of the City fully justifies the expenditure. We cannot be parsimonious in the education of our children. It is the best and sweetest and most gratifying money we spend.

The pay of teachers should be materially increased. The Board of Education more than a year ago appointed a Citizens' Salary Committee to make a study and report on necessary revisions to the salary schedule for teachers. This report has now been completed and will soon be printed and available for consideration. The report will undoubtedly recommend a substantial increase in the pay of teachers. Additional funds will be required to provide this deserved increase.

The building program of the Board of Education is moving forward in a very satisfactory manner. There are now under construction the following schools and additions to schools:

The Presidio Junior High School, located at Twenty-ninth and Geary street;

The Roosevelt Junior High School, located at Arguello boulevard near Geary street;

An addition to the Francisco Junior High School, on Francisco and Stockton streets;

A second and a part of the third unit of the Balboa High School, located at Cayuga and Onondago streets;

The Geary Elementary School, located on Cook street north of Geary street;

The Winfield Scott Elementary School, located on North Point and Divisadero streets;

The Sunshine School for crippled children, located at Dolores and Dorland streets.

Plans are now being made and it is expected that the contracts will be let during this fiscal year for the following schools:

The Aptos Junior High School, located on Aptos way and Upland drive;

The James Lick Junior High School, located on Twenty-fifth and Noe streets;

The final unit of the Balboa High School, located at Cayuga and Onondago streets.

An architect has been appointed and plans are being prepared for a new high school in the Presidio District, to be erected on a sixteen-acre site already acquired for that purpose between Thirtieth and Thirty-second avenues, Geary and Balboa streets.

A junior high school is to be provided for the Bernal District.

The growth in population west of Twin Peaks and in the Sunset District will require some additional elementary school accommodations in the immediate future.

The Board of Education has adopted the pay-as-you-go plan and expects to continue this plan, which requires the tax rate each year to include an amount sufficient to provide the new buildings required because of the growth of the City and for replacement of old buildings. The Board of Education has found that at least $2,100,000 will be required each year for its annual building program and to cover the cost of maintenance of the existing buildings.

We have placed trusted honor in the hands of our Board of Education to handle our school problems and I am sure they hold the confidence of the people.

Playgrounds.

During the past year the sum of $133,000 was spent under the direction of the Playground Commission for new playground land in six widely separated sections of the City, with $50,000 additional for enlarging old holdings. Attendance has increased many thousands and additional facilities have been provided for both junior and adult recreation.

The imperative need of the year 1930 is more land, and also several new buildings are required. Recreation areas are highly essential as cities become more closely built up, and a liberal policy should be followed at this time in acquiring such areas while lands can still be purchased at reasonable prices.

The Playground Commission handling playground affairs is composed of the Honorable James D. Phelan, president; Miss Alicia Mosgrove, Mr. George Hearst, Mr. Daniel C. Murphy, Mrs. Sigmund Stern and Mr. Constant J. Auger, and I am sure the people have the utmost confidence in them and will entrust them with more needed funds. They give their time and attention without pay.

Zoo.

I am happy to report that a start has been made in this matter through the generosity of President Herbert Fleishhacker of the Park Commission, who has shown his love for the children of the City by contributing some $50,000 for the purchase of animals and birds as a nucleus of a zoological park. We are on the way now to a permanent zoo for San Francisco by his philanthropy, and I know that it will be fully equipped in due time as a place of great interest and education to our citizens and our visitors and keep San Francisco ever forward in attractive places of amusement.

Traffic Survey.

A great deal of attention has been recently devoted to the complicated traffic problems of the City. We have had the benefit of unofficial advisory committees and officials of several departments who have devoted themselves to this work. Boulevard constructions, installation of traffic signals, new parking regulations, careful policy cooperation, public safety propaganda and the work of the Schools Traffic Reserve have vastly improved traffic conditions and have reduced traffic injuries in a most substantial and desirable way. All of these efforts must be continued with even greater energy in the future.

San Francisco holds the record for the minimum death rate per capita for 1929. That record must be maintained.

During the past year the Department of Electricity expended approximately $80,000 for the manufacture and installation of traffic signal equipment, which included a 104-circuit synchronous progressive traffic signal timer, and the installation of approximately 150 traffic signals and 200 pedestrian signals, which necessitated the pulling in and splicing of about 40,000 feet of cable. The signals are of the Wiley type, the product of our able City Electrician, and are a credit to the city; home invented and home manufactured. The traffic signal timer is the largest and most flexible in the United States. The entire down-town district, including Market street, is now being operated on what is known as progressive timing. The effect of the new system was very noticeable this year during the Christmas holidays in that there was an absence of traffic congestion as compared with previous years.

Police Department.

A wonderful record has been made during the past year by the Police Department in crime prevention and suppression, in addition to arresting the perpetrators where crime has been committed.

No major crimes were committed in San Francisco during the past year that have not been solved; the perpetrators were arrested and prosecuted. In most instances all of the loot resulting from these crimes has been recovered.

The year just closing has seen many innovations in the department, foremost of which has been the inauguration of the motorcycle sidecar corps. A corps of young men recruited from within the ranks of the department, who are on duty at the principal stations in the department on each of the three watches, has guaranteed to the people of San Francisco speedy and accurate police service.

The mobilization of these men has been perfected to such a degree that a company of twenty-eight men can be brought together, in any part of San Francisco, fully armed and equipped for any emergency that might arise, within a period of twelve minutes.

The test of the motorcycle sidecars has been thorough and their value thoroughly established in the department. It is desirable to further equip the Police Department with more of these machines, twenty-eight in number, which will mean that the department will then have forty-two motorcycle sidecars to be used in the department in the same manner as is now customary, with the exception that instead of using fourteen cars for twenty-four hours, fourteen cars will be used for eight hours, which will give the crews on each of the three watches an opportunity to have a motorcycle sidecar for the use of each crew.

Police requirements of San Francisco are growing at a rapid pace. More men are required for traffic duty and patrol duty in the daytime as well as at night. Members of the department at the present time, with the exception of the traffic bureau, must serve on night duty for a period of approximately twenty years before they are eligible for day duty.

The school children of San Francisco need the protection of officers in the daytime. At present, with the limited number of men at the disposal of the department, the department is not able to give the service it should in this respect.

With growing requirements of traffic control, provision must be made for additional members of the department in the near future. The Charter demands it and the Charter provisions should be respected.

The latest innovation in police service is the radio. The department is at the present time, in conjunction with the Fire Department and Chief Ralph W. Wiley of the Department of Electricty, studying and planning for the erection of a radio broacasting station to be used exclusively by the Fire and Police departments for broadcasting fire and police news to cars of both departments which will be equipped with radio receiving sets. This is the last word in police administration.

The Police Department will, of necessity, have to appeal to the Board of Supervisors for sufficient funds for the building of this radio broadcasting station and the money necessary to equip its cars with radio receiving sets. The Police Department is giving instructions in aviation to some of its members for immediate use in an emergency where an airplane might be needed for secret service.

The recent resignation, on account of ill health, of Chief of Police Daniel J. O'Brien was deeply deplored by all who knew the efficiency of his service. He had no peer in his ability, responsibility and personality. I had the opportunity of saving his experience for the City by naming him as Police Commissioner, where he now serves. Temporarily, his place was taken by Chief of Police Thomas P. Walsh, one of the oldest and ablest men in the department, long associated with my office. It is now filled by Chief of Police William J. Quinn, whose progressive policies have won general approval, and he has won the confidence of the department and the people.

Fire Department.

The whole City mourned the recent death of the veteran Chief Engineer of the Fire Department, Thomas R. Murphy. He was Chief for nearly twenty years and died in service. The officials of the City and the department paid high tribute to his memory.

Chief Charles J. Brennan has been appointed to the position and already has shown admirable executive ability and has won sincere commendation for his masterly handling of several large fires, and has gained the good will of the men of the service.

The department has extended the high-pressure system just west of the Civic Center. This system has 975 hydrants and 78 miles of high-pressure pipes.

Additional apparatus has recently been installed. Plans for a sixteen-inch main through the Potrero industrial district will be carried out within a few weeks. A new firehouse has been completed at Forty-second avenue and Geary street, and plans for another building are made to house an engine company, a truck company and a battalion chief's headquarters in Eighteenth avenue, between Q and R streets, to replace a temporary building.

The department is actively conducting the work of fire prevention and is achieving admirable results along all lines of its activity. Important improvements have recently been made in the department's system of response to alarms, and special instruction is being given in the handling of unusual fire hazards, especially those involving especial risks to the lives of citizens or firemen.

Building Inspection.

The past two years have seen a major improvement for San Francisco's benefit in the matter of building inspection. The City grows rapidly. Building permits for 1929 were $33,682,025. Let us help to add greatly to this amount during the coming year and cooperate with President Hoover in his construction plan throughout the country. New standards of building construction have been developed. San Francisco must build only upon lines that will establish confidence in the safety of its structures. This is exceedingly important if rates of earthquake insurance are to be tolerable in our City.

With Mr. John B. Leonard as Superintendent of Building Inspection and at my suggestion, we have an Advisory Board of Building Inspection, conducting the department along the most progressive lines under authority of the Board of Public Works. The Advisory Board, serving without pay, consists of Frederick H. Meyer, former Civic Center construction consulting architect, designated by the San Francisco Branch of the American Institute of Architects; Walter L. Huber, a distinguished engineer, named by the San Francisco Section, American Society of Engineers, and A. H. Wilhelm, experienced builder, representing the Builders' Exchange and General Contractors.

Plans, coast-wide in their scope, are being made for the adoption of a new building code. This code is 90 per cent complete, and within a short time your Board will be asked to consider a new building ordinance which will standardize buildings, reduce insurance rates and insure safety of every structure built in San Francisco.

Removal of County Jail.

The removal of this institution from the very center of Balboa Park, which consists of 100 acres, the County Jail and Police Station, occupying 25 acres of it and now brought prominently into sight through the completion of Bernal cut and the Alemany boulevard, should be brought about, because it has outlived its usefulness in its present location and its removal would add to the beauty of Balboa Park, now surrounded by homes of our people.

The Board of Park Commissioners and the City Planning Commission desire its removal and have given their permission for its location at some site to be selected in the Honora Sharp Park property in San Mateo County. I respectfully urge your Honorable Board to make an appropriation in the forthcoming Budget for its removal and reconstruction on the site named and that it be a special item appropriated and not be a special drag on the Park funds, which, of themselves, are not sufficient to properly take care of our park system. I would respectfully recommend that a committee of your Honorable Board wait on the County Supervisors of San Mateo County and get their permission and approval of this suggested improvement. This project has the full indorsement of the City Planning Commission. There should be no time lost in carrying it through. The unfortunate petty offenders who are committed to the County Jail could enjoy good, healthful recreation by planting trees under the direction of the Park Superintendent in the Honora Sharp Park.

Central Warehouse.

The Bureau of Supplies, operating efficiently under the guidance of Mr. Leonard S. Leavy, requires a new central warehouse, to eliminate the decentralized receipt and distribution of stores which now obtain to permit the purchase of commodities in larger quantities, thus getting the benefit of reduced prices and to enable the Purchaser of Supplies to properly care for receipt and inspection of all materials and supplies.

Sewers.

The people voted a bond issue of $2,500,000 for the extension of our much-needed main sewers, and just as soon as the bonds are sold the construction of the sewers will immediately commence.

Public Health.

The Board of Public Health continues its excellent service to the City, and every endeavor must be made at once to sell remaining available health bonds to permit very necessary improvements in the Board's facilities for conducting its service to the sick and needy poor.

Such bond sale, already authorized by the people, will permit the enlargement of our hospital requirements by the erection of cancer and psychopathic units. These are outstanding in importance to the community over 52 per cent of the psychopathic cases handled in the wards in the San Francisco Hospital are returned to their homes without the stigma of confinement in State institutions for the insane.

Much suffering could be relieved and many early cases cured if our cancer unit were in operation. The bonds must be sold as soon as possible, the architectural plans are nearly ready and it should be built at once.

There have been $740,000 health bonds sold of the $3,500,000 authorized. The money in hand from these sales will, during this year, provide approximately 180 beds for patients at the San Francisco Hospital and 150 beds for the aged and infirm at the Laguna Honda Home, but no further expansion can be accomplished until the remaining bonds are sold. I respectfully urge that the Board of Supervisors authorize the Treasurer to offer for sale the balance of the health bonds over his counter. I sincerely hope that some patriotic local bank will find a way to take over the entire issue of health bonds.

An emergency hospital and health center should be established in the Richmond District. Its cost will approximate between $55,000 and $65,000. The service is urgently necessary.

I trust that within the next two years provision will be made for increasing the capacity of the Health Farm Preventorium in San Mateo County as was originally agreed, namely, that the Board of Supervisors would place in the Budget the sum of $200,000 annually for building purposes. The preventorium has fully justified its existence.

War Memorial.

I have completed a fully detailed report on the history of the War Memorial project. I will call a special meeting of your Honorable Board in the near future on the subject. I have promised before submitting same to you that I would call together in a meeting between the Mayor and representatives of the various veteran organizations, with the hope that an amicable understanding may be reached, and thereafter I will present same to your Honorable Board for the confirmation of a Board of Eleven Trustees to handle the project to its completion and administration. I have a public certified accountant's report of the finances of the fund in detail, dated November 5, 1929, which I will submit to you.

Airport.

All progressive cities must have adequate airport facilities.

Stables were necessary in the days of the horse; garages are necessary now for the automobile; airports and hangars are necessary for the new age of the airplane. I recommend that immediate steps be taken to acquire, by purchase, the land now occupied and known as Mills Field, San Francisco Airport, in San Mateo County, and that pending such action the lease between the City and County of San Francisco and the Mills Estate be kept in full force and effect. Within the past few weeks, I have made to your honorable Board a full report on our airport site, following my conference with Honorable Ogden Mills in Washington, D. C., early in October. I attach hereto and make a part hereof a copy of that report for your information so that when this message is printed a copy of said report be printed in full at this point.

"THE MAYOR: Now, I will take up the question of the Mills Field. When I was in Washington I made inquiries as to whether Mr. Ogden Mills was in Washington at the time and I was told he was not. So knowing that I had to go down to New York, and to give your message, which you asked me to give, to Mayor Jimmie Walker of New York City, I tried to find Mr. Ogden Mills in New York, but his office said he was in Washington, and I telephoned him from Doctor Giannini's office in New York to Washington and he said, 'Mayor, I will be very glad to see you on Thursday morning at 10:30 o'clock.' While I was talking to Doctor Giannini, Doctor Giannini told me that Mr. Ogden Mills is the Under-Secretary of the Treasury, under Secretary

Mellon, and Doctor Giannini's opinion of him is that he is one of the ablest financiers in the country, and was selected by Secretary Andrew W. Mellon to be the Under-Secretary of the Treasury. He said he is eligible for the Presidency. He was defeated for the governorship of New York in the Democratic landslide which elected Al Smith governor of New York the last time. He is likely to succeed Secretary Mellon and Doctor Giannini believes that, if he wants to, he can have it, because there is no man better thought of in New York, in every conceivable form, than Mr. Ogden Mills. And with that fine recommendation of him, which I think you all know, I preface the report which I am going to make to you about Mills Field.

"I wrote these notes at Mr. Mills' desk in the Treasury Building at Washington so that I would make no mistakes. I met him there at 10:30 on the morning of October 3rd, and he had brought from New York Mr. Arthur Hartman, Supervisor of all their California properties, and also General Manager of the Mills' Estate of New York, and he is their New York representative. The conversation which took place was between Mr. Mills, Mr. Hartman and myself. Mr. Mills said that he has no personal knowledge in regard to the negotiations regarding Mills Field. His father, Ogden Mills, senior, whom you know was the only son of D. O. Mills, and Ogden Mills, Junior, is the grandson of D. O. Mills. He said that his father, Ogden Mills, Senior, told him that the low lands of the Mills property should be reserved for industrial purposes. Mr. Mills was out here last winter. Everyone out here told him that there was no understanding between his father or anybody else about giving the field to San Francisco. They were very glad, however, to let the City have it for experimental purposes, as he put it, at a nominal rent. He said there is nothing anywhere to show that the Mills Estate ever had any intention whatever of giving this property to the City. No one has ever heard of such a thing or even of intending to sell. He says he did see Mr. Dunnigan last winter and passed the time of day with him. He said he never made any promises to Mr. Dunnigan, never indicated he was prepared to give the property to the City; it is not his to give; it belongs to the Estate of Mills, Incorporated, a California corporation, owned by the Mills Estate of New York, and all of the stock is in trustees, of which he is one. Ogden Mills, Junior, the one I was speaking to, is President of the New York corporation, and is acting for them. His relationship is that of a trustee. They are taking the position, in the absence of convincing evidence, that there was an agreement, or an implied agreement, that it is his duty to administer this property for the benefit of the beneficiaries. If he can find anywhere any evidence that his father, directly or indirectly, had made a promise, why, naturally, it would be the inclination of the family and his aunt, Mrs. Whitelaw Reid, that they would live up to that promise.

"Now, he told me this, not for publication, but to show their keen interest in this matter, he said that, on the deathbed of his father, he indicated he would have liked to have had the opportunity of changing his will to add another one and a half million dollars to the cathedral here and for other benefactions, and that Ogden, Junior, and his sisters have made the request good, although it was not in the will. He says his father, Ogden Mills, never said a word to him about giving this property to San Francisco, neither did Mr. Ogden Mills, Senior, when returning to New York, after making the lease. And everyone who does know something about it tells Mr. Ogden Mills, Junior, that it was never the intention of Mr. Ogden Mills, Senior, to give it to San Francisco, or to sell it to San Francisco for airport purposes; in fact, he never told his son anything about it, except that the land was to be reserved for industrial purposes.

"Now he said, 'Mr. Mayor,' he said, 'My grandfather purchased that property and told his son to keep it for industrial purposes. As the City of San Francisco grew,' he said, 'we believe that the future of San Francisco is going south and we think that the people of San

Francisco will benefit far greater by industrial enterprises down there than by having an airport, because,' he said, 'you have two railroads and possibly another one.' He said, 'We are keeping up those dykes, we are preventing the water from overflowing Mills Field, we are preventing the water from coming across on to the highway, and we intend each year to spend a lot of money developing that property for industrial purposes because we have faith and confidence in the City of San Francisco.'

"I spoke to them about acquiring it. He said, 'Now, the land is not for sale, but,' he said, after I said to him, 'Now, I want you to give thought to the City of San Francisco, which, like every other city, wants an airport and needs an airport. We want you to give thought to this matter, that it was D. O. Mills, your grandfather, that made his fortune out in the West, and that it was he who came to the rescue of the Bank of California when it suspended payment, and took up the presidency. I want to tell you that we have a deep regard for the name of Mills. I want to tell you that I was raised on a salary, my father working under your grandfather in the Bank of California for 50 years; that we all out there have a great regard and admiration for the honorable name and the honored name of D. O. Mills, and I do not want to see you get into any position of dickering with the City about whether the City should acquire it or whether it should be continued or whether it should be reserved for industrial purposes, or whether it should be acquired, as the City wants it, for an airport.' I pointed out to him that we had lost the Zep coming into our City because we did not have the money to put on our own land a mooring mast to have the Zep land in San Francisco, and therefore it went to Los Angeles, and yet Doctor Eckner said that the finest weather he had on the whole trip was the weather he had coming through the Golden Gate and flying over the City of San Francisco. And I said, 'I do not want you to get into any position where anybody can criticise you for handling an estate whereby you are trying to prevent the City acquiring something which we named after the most honored names in the history of the City of San Francisco.' He said, 'I am not committed to sell the property, but I want to think it over a lot more. The City can do one of two things: It can make an offer for the property.' (He has not made up his mind to sell the property for an airport to the City.) 'Or, we might work out an agreement that, if the City takes over the airport, and we agree upon a price, that we can make an agreement that, if the City ever gives up the airport in the future, we will be permitted, in an option, to take the property back at the price the City pays us for the property,' which is only right. And then he said, 'That is, if we reach an agreement.' He said, 'It is difficult to arrive at a figure without condemnation.' And they do not want condemnation because of the difficulty of ascertaining a value. He said they are holding it for the potential values, and as far as he knows it is very valuable for industrial development. I said, 'It has been stated that you were holding the property for a thousand dollars an acre.' He said, 'That is not true.' He said, 'I have never mentioned the price to anyone, certainly not, none of the property is for sale.' I asked him, 'Would you set a price or do you prefer condemnation, and would you feel hurt if the City started condemnation proceedings?' Mr. Mills said he would resent condemnation of anything except the present field and its present area. Then he spoke to me about the dykes and the two railroads that were going in there and its future value to the City, the great payrolls that would come to the City, the great industrial plants that would be there like they are out in New York, fourteen and fifteen miles from the City, and out of New York they run a hundred miles. He pointed out that a great industrial city would make that land far more valuable to him for industrial sites. Of course, that was his opinion, and I was after the airport.

"Now, my summary of the whole thing is that we should have been careful about expending $300,000 on an airport on which we had a lease which expires in March and which will have to be renewed upon

the request of the City. And' we have got a situation there that is
difficult to handle. I am speaking to you frankly now. I see the whole
situation. Now, Mr. Mills said, 'Let me think it over, because I am
not prepared to reach a decision at this time.' He said, 'We have
got two grandchildren in the family now, they were born in Ireland,
two fine little Irish children, and they have to be considered.' He said
if this were his own property he would do everything for San Francisco, but he is a trustee and he must be guided by his associates.
Now, talking informally, he said, 'I want to talk it over with Mrs.
Whitelaw Reid, my aunt, and yet I do not want to make any commitment.' Mr. Ogden Mills' share of the estate is only one-third of one-
half of the entire Mills Estate, Incorporated, of this particular
property. It was first D. O. Mills', it was second, then, the father and
Mrs. Whitelaw Reid, and now it is the grandson of D. O. Mills and
two sisters, and they have got three children on one side and two
on the other, and therefore he has but one-third of one-half interest in
this property. He is simply acting for others in this matter. The
finale was that the present Mills Field, in its present boundaries, that
is, what is included in the lease, under no circumstances will he go
beyond this area.

"Mr. Arthur A. Hartman, General Manager of the Mills Estate,
Incorporated, in New York, which owns the property, comes out here
twice a year. He has never discussed this matter with anybody except
Mr. Ogden Mills, Senior, and said it was only a temporary measure.
He has never met or knows a Supervisor, Mr. Arthur A. Hartman.
He thinks their attorney, Mr. Duncan McLeod, of San Francisco, Mills
Building, made the lease, and the lines were run by the engineer,
A. Torregano, Mills Building, San Francisco. Mr. Mills, Senior,
handled the whole matter in San Francisco himself. Mr. Mills, whom
I spoke to, hopes to get to San Francisco this winter. Mrs. Whitelaw
Reid would be in New York today, or tomorrow, and after talking with
her, he is going to write me. Now, that is the story and the full report
of my interview with Mr. Ogden Mills regarding Mills Field. And I
found him just what Doctor Giannini said he was, a fine genial sterling
gentleman, whom, if it was his, I think would gladly give it to the
City of San Francisco, in the name of his grandfather. I think that
he is impressed with the situation. He knows we have $300,000, or
thereabouts, in that property. He knows we cannot keep on putting
money into a property that we have not a thread on except a lease.
And I really think, from the bigness of the man, that he is going to
try and do something and find some way to help us solve this problem,
and I think he is kindly disposed to do it, if he can, subject to the
other trustees, along those lines. Gentlemen, that is my report to you
about Mills Field."

Underground Railroad Transportation.

This necessity requires your constant attention. Market street is
becoming so congested that street car transportation may have to
give way to underground for busses and auto traffic on the surface.
We must provide rapid transportation down the Peninsula. The City
is rapidly growing that way. In a few years it will be quicker to
reach the homes of our people down the Peninsula by electric car
system than over the crowded auto highways. It is your duty to
solve this problem by taking hold of it now. The City Engineer and
the City Planning Commission have some fine ideas about this problem and they should be consulted. It has been suggested that an
overhead railway be constructed over the Southern Pacific right of way
through Bernal cut and join the surface lines of the United Railways,
to be ultimately owned by the City, at Baden, San Mateo County.

Purchase of Private Property for City Needs.

I respectfully suggest that hereafter, when the city needs private
holdings for its public improvements, that property owners should
be treated fairly and paid promptly for their property, instead of hav-

ing to hold their property for the City until the City makes up its mind as to how to pay for it. The system of offering property owners less for their property than they have paid the City in taxes is not fair nor just. If the City needs the land for improvements it should pay fairly for it. The private property owner having carried the property over a period of years, hoping for the benefit accruing from the City's growth, should get the benefit due him for his foresight in his investment. The John McLaren Park and the Sunset boulevard are evidences of taking people's property without making provision for their payment after notifying the world of their requirements and condemning the property for public use. The City should set the example at all times of doing business in a prompt, business-like way and not take the attitude that, because it is a City, it can do as it pleases by the authority it holds.

The City has condemned approximately thirty-two acres of property owned by one estate, as well as uncounted numerous small property owners, included in the proposed John McLaren Park, that the owners thereof can neither sell nor improve, nor get any interest from and must hold it at their own expense and pay taxes thereon, which the City demands, until the City finds means of paying for it. My office is continually appealed to by irate public citizens, mostly poor people and small home owners, whose property has been purchased by the City, the owners notified to vacate their small homes, titles searched in the title companies, title ready for delivery to the City, and no money for payment, and yet they are called upon to pay the City taxes. This system must be changed and changed immediately. There must be some relief found for such cases. The City should pay for what it wants and what it takes. Legislation, if required, to refund taxes and add interest to the purchase price until the City pays for the property should be perfected at once.

Municipal Railroad Extension.

Continuance and extension of the Taraval street line of the Municipal Railroad system to the terminus of the Ocean Beach esplanade should be solved by your Public Utilities Committee at once.

New Temple of Justice (Courthouse).

The vacant block of our Civic Center, bounded by Larkin, Fulton, Hyde and Grove streets should be determined upon as a site for a new courthouse. Study should be given to its plan and construction, because it is only a matter of a short time when all the operating branches of the City Government, viz.: its railroad, water and electric projects will be located centrally in the City Hall and plans for a beautiful court house should be under way and a financial plan proposed for its construction.

Yacht Harbor.

Our yacht harbor needs more room—there are many applications for space. These should be provided. It is one of San Francisco's great, useful, amusement, recreational show places. We should encourage yachting the same as we do golf.

Garbage Incinerator.

The erection of a new incinerator must receive your prompt action, because the courts have demanded it and the court's orders must be respected. It is only through the consideration of Judge E. P. Mogan of the Superior Court that the City is being permitted temporarily to operate the old incinerator. The people have decided in favor of incineration and no delays will be permitted by court orders.

Completion of Civic Center.

Fulton street and Leavenworth street should be opened immediately and funds therefor, or means of providing for same, should be forthcoming from your Honorable Board. An appropriation of $15,000 which I have appealed for continuously for several years to pay draughtsmen to prepare plans, under the direction of the Board of Architects of the Civic Center, for the decoration of the unfinished, unsightly walls which desecrate our Civic Center, is urgently needed. These plans should be made immediately, so that the owners of said building will complete the facade at their own expense, which they have agreed to do, if the City will advise them what the City wants done.

Ocean Beach Esplanade Extension.

We should extend the Ocean Beach esplanade from the present terminus at Sloat boulevard to Honora Sharp Park of about 444 acres, at Rockaway Beach, in San Mateo Couuty, a distance of approximately 14.4 miles, and on a level below the old Ocean Shore right of way. The government owns with its life saving station considerable property through which the esplanade would traverse and immediate effort should be exerted upon our members in Congress to secure right of way for this worthy project. Your committee through the City Engineer, should study the project, perfect plans and advise your Board the cost thereof. It can be built out of the Good Roads Funds.

Naval Bases at Alameda and Sunnyvale.

Your Honorable Board should delegate to a committee of its members the special duty of watchfully and unceasingly working to bring about the establishment of these two governmental understakings which have received the approval of government commissions.

Public Utilities Commission.

I am firmly convinced of the desirability of a Municipal Public Service Commission, authorized by the people, to have full control and management of the public utilities owned by the people and I respectfully recommend that the creation of such a commission be resubmitted to the voters at an early, opportune time.

Bay Bridges.

Progress may be reported on the exceptionally important subject of Bay bridges across the Golden Gate and San Francisco Bay. The City must continue its efforts in connection with both of these projects in active and whole-hearted co-operation with community and State authorities holding authority in clearing the way for actual construction.

Consolidation of San Mateo and San Francisco Counties.

State legislation has been enacted permitting the consolidation of cities and towns in adjoining counties so that they may annex themselves for their own advancement. Your honorable Board should appoint a special committee to confer with the county officials of San Mateo County and the officials of the cities and towns thereof, to bring about such consolidation as will meet with the approval of our friendly neighbors in San Mateo County and our own people, all of whom must vote on such a consolidation before it can be accomplished.

I am told that there is a growing feeling in San Mateo County in favor of such consolidation, because the people realize that now that San Francisco owns the properties of the Spring Valley Water Company, and is developing its electric energy and Municipal Railway extensions, it will be a great assurance to them to receive water, electric light, power and telephone services, boulevard construction, road construction and improvements in general on the part of the City of San Francisco by money expended in San Mateo County as a part of San Francisco. Also police and fire protection, high schools, parks, playgrounds and in general full services which San Francisco now enjoys and at the same rate for public utility service which the people of San Francisco also enjoy and at a tax rate lower than any city in the United States. Care must be taken that the political life of San Mateo County shall not be jeopardized by a consolidation with San Francisco County. The big City will spend money for the rapid development of San Mateo County under such a consolidation plan. Harbor improvements from the revenues of San Francisco Harbor can be expended for the development of harbor facilities in San Mateo County if it should become a part of San Francisco County.

To erect at the entrance of San Francisco County at San Francisquito Creek, the border line of Santa Clara County at the door of Stanford University, beautiful entrance gates to greater San Francisco County would be a fine thing for both San Mateo County and San Francisco County as one. "Faint heart never won fair lady," is applicable in this marriage plan of the two counties. But we must not press our suit too hard, unless we know that our sweetheart, San Mateo County, is willing to consider the proposal.

Tribute to Commissioners, Appointees and Employees of the City Administration.

"United we stand. Divided we fall." I pay tribute to and in the name of the City thank the Commissioners, the Appointees and all Employees of the City Government to whom credit is due for their loyalty to the City and their contribution to the great accomplishments which have been completed for the advancement of our City. I name herein, for your information and for record in this message, my able Commissioners and splendid Appointees who administer the various branches of government, in all of whom I am sure the people of this City have confidence.

Board of Police Commissioners.

Hon. Theodore J. Roche, President.
Hon. Jesse B. Cook.
Hon. Thomas E. Shumate.
Hon. Daniel J. O'Brien.
Hon. Wm. J. Quinn, Chief of Police.
Mr. Charles F. Skelly, Secretary.

Board of Administration, Retirement System.

Mr. John W. Rogers, President.
Mr. Arthur S. Holman.
Mr. Dewitt C. Treat.
Hon. Franck R. Havenner.
Hon. Thomas F. Boyle.
Mr. William H. Scott.
Mr. John F. Brady.
Mr. Ralph R. Nelson, Secretary-Actuary.

Civil Service Commissioners.

Mr. E. A. Walcott, President.
Mr. Wm. P. McCabe.
Mr. Hugh A. McKevitt.
Mr. James J. Maher, Chief Examiner and Secretary.

Board of Fire Commissioners.

Hon. Wm. A. Sherman, President.
Hon. Alfred Ehrman.
Hon. Cesare Restani.
Hon. P. W. Meherin.
Mr. Frank T. Kennedy, Secretary.
Mr. Charles J. Brennan, Chief Engineer.
Mr. Frank P. Kelly, Fire Marshal.

Department of Electricity.

Mr. Ralph W. Wiley, Chief.

Mr. Gordon C. Osborne, Assistant Chief.
Mr. Joseph P. Murphy, Secretary.

Department of Elections.

Dr. John E. Bohm, President.
Mr. James K. Prior, Jr.
Mr. John Hermann.
Mr. J. W. Jackson.
Mr. Charles J. Collins, Registrar.
Hon. Harry Zemansky.

Department of Public Health.

Mr. Frank J. Klimm, President.
Dr. Alex S. Keenan.
Dr. James W. Ward.
Dr. Wm. W. Wymore.
Mr. Lawrence Arnstein, Jr.
Mr. Arthur H. Barendt.
Mr. Arthur M. Sharp.
Dr. Wm. C. Hassler.
Mr. Edward M. Coffey, Chief Clerk.
Dr. Arthur A. O'Neill, City Physician.
Dr. T. D'Arcy Quinn, City Physician.
Dr. Joseph F. Poheim, City Physician.
Dr. Edmund Butler, Chief Surgeon.
Dr. Leon M. Wilbur, Supt. S. F. Hospital.
Mr. C. M. Wollenberg, Supt. Laguna Honda Home.

Park Commissioners.

Hon. Herbert Fleishhacker, President.
Hon. Wm. Sproule.
Hon. M. Earl Cummings.

Hon. George Tourny.
Hon. Wm. F. Humphrey.
Capt. B. P. Lamb, Secretary.
Mr. John McLaren, Superintendent of Parks.

City Planning Commission.

Hon. Matt I. Sullivan, President.
Major Charles H. Kendrick.
Mrs. Parker S. Maddux.
Mr. W. W. Chapin.
Mr. R. S. Woodard, Secretary and Engineer.

Board of Education.

Mr. Daniel C. Murphy, President.
Mr. Ira W. Coburn.
Mrs. Ernest J. Mott.
Mr. Alfred I. Esberg.
Mrs. Mary Prag.
Miss Alice R. Power.
Mr. Wm. F. Benedict.
Mr. Joseph Marr Gwinn, Superintendent of Schools.
Mr. H. H. Monroe, Secretary.

Board of Trustees California Palace of the Legion of Honor.

Hon. Herbert Fleishhacker, President.
Hon. Wm. F. Humphrey.
Hon. Wm. Sproule.
Mr. M. Earl Cummings.
Hon. Geo. Tourny.
Mrs. A. B. Spreckels.
Hon. Paul Shoup.
Mr. Walter D. K. Gibson.
Mr. W. M. Strother, Secretary.
Mrs. Cornelia B. Sage Quinton, Director.

Public Pound.

Mr. Matthew McCurrie, Secretary.

Horticultural Commissioner.

Hon. Dudley Moulton.

Board of Public Works.

Mr. Timothy A. Reardon, President.
Col. Chas. E. Stanton.
Mr. Frederick W. Meyer.
Mr. Sidney J. Hester, Secretary.
Mr. Horace B. Chaffee, Photographer.

Superintendent of Public Buildings.

Mr. Martin J. Tierney.

Street Repairs.

Mr. Preston W. King.

Playground Commission.

Hon. James D. Phelan, President.

Mrs. Sigmund Stern.
Miss Alicia Mosgrove.
Hon. Constant J. Auger.
Mr. Daniel C. Murphy.
Mr. George Hearst.
Mr. John McLaren.
Miss Josephine Dows Randall, Superintendent.
Miss Veda B. Young, Secretary.

Sealer of Weights and Measures.

Mr. Thomas Flaherty.

Widows' Pension Bureau.

Miss Eugenie Schenk, Director.

San Francisco Municipal Band.

Mr. Philip H. Sapiro, Director.

Public Library Trustees.

Hon. Max C. Sloss, President.
Mr. Eustace Cullinan.
Mr. Albert M. Bender.
Mr. Frank P. Deering.
Mr. R. B. Hale.
Mr. Geo. W. Kelham.
Miss Eugenie Lacoste.
Miss Laura McKinstry.
Hon. James D. Phelan.
Mr. Wm. R. K. Young.
Mr. Geo. A. Mullin, Secretary.
Mr. Leland W. Cutler, Trustee.
Mr. Robert Rea, Librarian.

Board of Trustees, M. H. De Young Memorial Museum.

Mr. Geo. T. Cameron, Honorary President.
Hon. Herbert Fleishhacker, President.
Hon. Wm. F. Humphrey.
Hon. Wm. Sproule.
Mr. M. Earl Cummings.
Hon. Geo. Tourny.
Mr. Joseph O. Tobin.
Mr. Nion R. Tucker.
Mrs. Helen Cameron.
Mr. Geo. Barron, Curator.
Mr. W. M. Strother, Secretary.

Bureau of Supplies.

Mr. Leonard S. Leavy.

Bureau of Engineering.

Hon. M. M. O'Shaughnessy.

Bureau of Architecture.

Mr. Charles H. Sawyer.

Bureau of Building Inspection.

Mr. John B. Leonard.

Sewer Repairs.

Mr. Joseph Linehan, Superintendent.

Street Cleaning.

Mr. Peter J. Owen, Superintendent.

Municipal Railway.

Mr. Fred Boeken, Superintendent.

Police Judges.

Hon. D. S. O'Brien.

Hon. Geo. J. Steiger.

Hon. Joseph M. Golden.

Hon. S. J. Lazarus.

Exposition Auditorium.

Mr. James L. Foley, Superintendent.

Two Beautiful Fountains for the Civic Center.

Our Civic Center for its completed adornment and beautification requires two beautiful monumental fountains with an everlasting abundant flow of water. I hope these will come as a gift to the City from some philanthropic citizen. I hope they will be given shortly and be erected in time to be ready to gush forth the waters of Hetch Hetchy when it leaves the O'Shaughnessy dam about two and a half years hence to flow into Crystal Springs Lake and from there delivered through these fountains to the heart of San Francisco in our Civic Center. They are estimated to cost aproximately $125,000 each and will be the most beautiful fountains in the world. I have hopes of this gift to the City.

Finally: My observation of what the people of this City expect from their legislative branch of government is harmony, progress and the construction of projects for the advancement of this growing City. Everyone profits from such a program. In other words, the people want the small things as well as the big things done in a big way. They expect prompt action. They want positive, constructive, optimistic, service. As one simple example: they want poles and lights on the boulevards. Let us buy the poles and install the lights at once.

Let us buy and blow horns that will be heard the world around of the great, mighty, growing industrial, commercial, financial, prosperous City of San Francisco and the people will boost it with pride. Let us tell everybody that San Francisco is the Capital of the World, and nearly everybody will soon believe it.

Let us erect at all entrances to the City at the County Line imposing electric welcome signs, instead of the City greeting the visitor in darkness as at present. Keep the front doors of the City open and lighted and polished.

Remember the City Hall of San Francisco is the finest, noblest, public building in the United States, and we have the gold medal of honor to prove it, and both the building and its dome are loftier than the building and the dome of the capitol at Washington, D. C., from sidewalk to top of the finial, and we have the elevation plans of both to prove it. I brought the elevation plans of the United States capitol building home with me from Washington and our Acting City Architect. Mr. Charles H. Sawyer, has given me the exact difference in favor of San Francisco's City Hall. That is civic pride and civic spirit. You cannot lose in boosting civic spirit. When you are proud of your home the world admires you. I wish for you a service of progressive action for the City which honors and places faith in you.

Respectfully,

JAMES ROLPH, Jr., Mayor.

Motion.

Supervisor Hayden moved that the Mayor's message be spread at length in the Journal of Proceedings, copies sent to members, and that the Clerk be directed to dissect the message, referring to appropriate committees such recommendations thereof as require legislative action by the Board.

Motion *carried.*

SUPERVISOR HAVENNER said in part: I desire at this time to congratulate my new colleagues on the Board upon their election and welcome them as members of the Board and to express the hope and the sincere desire, on my part, that we will be able to cooperate on all matters of importance for the welfare of the City.

SUPERVISOR ANDRIANO said in part: I desire to avail myself of this opportunity to join my colleagues in extending my cordial good wishes to the retiring members of the Board and to thank them for the many courtesies that they have extended to me during my incumbency on this Board. I also desire to extend my sincere greetings and best wishes to the new members of this Board.

SUPERVISOR ROSSI: Mr. Mayor, members of the Board, ladies and gentlemen: I know that when each and every one of you entered the room and saw before you the array of beautiful flowers that you at once came to the conclusion that holding public office was a bed of roses, but I assure you it is anything but that. In assuming my duties today as a member of this Board I fully realize and appreciate the responsibility that goes with it. I know that the people of San Francisco expect a great deal from this Board. They expect action, and not procrastination. You all have listened attentively to the message of his Honor the Mayor. He has outlined a very constructive program, which will take several years to put through or to accomplish. One of the most important matters that will come before this Board at an early date will be the taking over of the Spring Valley Water Company, which will be on March 2nd. It will be incumbent upon this Board to pass the necessary legislation, with the approval of his Honor the Mayor, in order that that proposition or that utility will be placed in safe hands and will be conducted as a business enterprise and not as a political organization. I also know the urgent necessity of building the Hetch Hetchy at the earliest possible moment. And while it is true that construction has gone over a period of twenty years—and I do not say that by way of reflection upon any one; obstacles have presented themselves and they were all overcome—still, at the same time, I am for the early completion of Hetch Hetchy in order to obviate the periodicals that you see in the paper, that San Francisco is threatened with a water famine. That, in my opinion, is bad publicity for San Francisco. We also have a big transportation problem. Franchises have expired, others will soon expire. What has been done by way of taking over the railroads that are not owned by the City I am not in a position to know at this time, but I do know that that matter is before us and somehing must be done at an early date in order to unify our transportation system and to see that San Francisco gets rapid transportation to all sections of San Francisco and down the Peninsula. That, in my opinion, is the most serious problem that confronts this Board of Supervisors, and I say that for this reason: I know that there are a number of civic organizations that may differ as to how that should be taken over and the price to be paid. I also know that the press is divided on that particular question, and that is why it is going to make it very difficult for this Board to handle that situation. However, we must have courage to do what we think is right and to take it over at the earliest possible moment. And I would suggest to his Honor the Mayor, if it be in order, that various representatives of the newspapers, and likewise these various organizations who are interested in the welfare and progress of San Francisco, to get together and see if this problem could be solved in a way that would benefit the people of San Francisco as a whole. We also have the problem of disposal of garbage. Several propositions were submitted to the people at the last election. Each and every one of them was turned down, which would indicate that the people want this Board of Supervisors to settle that once and for all. I might go on and mention many other problems that are to be solved by this Board. And I know they must be solved, and I know that they will be solved with the able leadership of his Honor the Mayor. And I want to at this time pledge my whole-hearted support to your Honor, to cooperate with you in every possible way to solve these problems.

I have been honored today by this Board by being elected as Chairman of the Finance Committee. No one knows better than myself the responsibility of that particular position. I know it has been said, time and again, that whoever accepted the chairmanship, whoever accepted membership on the Finance Committee, courted political suicide. Well, I do not altogether agree with that, and I say that for this reason: That as long as one does his duty, and does it conscientiously, he never has any fear, he should not have any fear, as to whether he should be reelected or not. What counts is whether he has done his duty the way he should do it, and let the people judge for themselves. It won't be long now but what the Finance Committee will get together and consider the budget for the next fiscal year. I am happy to have on that committee Supervisor Hayden, who has been a member for a good many years and is familiar with the duties of that committee, and I am likewise very happy to have on that committee Supervisor Power, who at one time was chairman of that committee and had experience in that line. And all that we intend to do, having knowledge of what the work of that committee is, is to render a service which we hope will meet with the approval of San Francisco as a whole. I do not believe in being small or niggardly in appropriations; at the same time I am opposed to wastefulness and extravagance. I do not believe in creating positions just to put someone on the payroll. There are certain fixed charges in the making up of a budget to carry on the various departments of this City government, and an adequate sum should be appropriated in order that each department should function properly and efficiently. In addition to that, we have major projects which the Mayor has mentioned here today, all of which cannot be taken care of in any one year or in any two years or three years. The program as outlined by his Honor the Mayor today will take years to carry through, but, nevertheless, they are all very constructive and things that will be done and should be done at the earliest possible time. I am mindful of the fact, and reference has been made to it today, that, after all, we must take into consideration the man or woman that pays the bill, and that is the taxpayer. I know that no one wants to see the tax rate increased. I go back to four years ago, when the tax rate was $4.13, and I want to assure you that I am not here making any apology for that tax rate, because there was not a cent put in that budget that was not necessary. The claim has been made here today that the tax rate has been reduced. In order that there be no mistake about that I want to give you a few facts and tell you how that tax rate was reduced. During the time of my incumbency in office the tax rate was $4.13. We had at that time a very serious problem before us, and that was what disposition to make of the Hetch Hetchy power. I at that time took the position to dispose of it to the only available company in San Francisco until such time as the City and County of San Francisco provided the funds to operate their own distributing system. That was the only thing left for anyone to do, anyone that would use common sense and common judgment; but, on the false issue that was presented to the people of San Francisco, some of the candidates who were then elected made a promise to the people that they were going to give Hetch Hetchy back to the people. Now, I will ask anyone here, or any citizen who follows the political life of San Francisco, what has that Board done by way of giving Hetch Hetchy back to the people? Nothing has been changed, nothing can be changed only to the detriment of San Francisco, until such time as the people vote to take over the existing distributing system, which, I think, or at least I hope, will be presented to the people of San Francisco in due time. At that time your Finance Committee recommended to this Board, or a subcommitte, I believe it was, the temporary disposition of that power. And what was the result? The result was this: That you received upwards of $2,400,000 a year, or a total up to date of $10,000,000, which you would not have received if those who were elected four years ago carried out their pledge to cancel that contract. I did not expect, or rather I did not intend, to bring this matter up, because I never used it during the last campaign. And I made no reference to it whatsoever. And that, ladies and gentlemen, went a long ways to reduce the tax rate. Two million four hundred thousand dollars a year means 25 to 26 cents in your tax rate. And in addition to that, since we were turned out of office, through the legislation at Sacramento, and sponsored or fathered by Senator Breed, the gasoline tax came into existence, and that has turned into the City and County $1,250,000 a year. That, too, reduces your tax rate 10 to 12 cents, because, prior to that, we were obliged, in order to keep our street work up and our streets clean, to place annually in the budget upwards of six to seven hundred thousand dollars. That is not necessary to be done at this time. So that is what reduced your tax rate. So I say that it is unbecoming, indeed, upon the part of any member of this Board to claim credit for the reduction of the tax rate when he is not responsible at all. I believe in giving credit when credit is due, and I would not have mentioned this question today if it were not for the fact that a report has been placed on file of particular members taking credit for the reduction of the tax rate. I know, I repeat again, of the responsibility of being a member of the Finance Committee, and I do not want to start off and be placed in the wrong light. I want to assure the public that I have only one thought in mind, and that is to render the best possible service that is within me, and I, together with other members of the Finance Committee—I know what their feelings are—will not raise that tax rate one cent if it is possible not to do it. But we must, the City must, go ahead, the City must progress, and we must meet our bills as they present themselves. So I want everyone to know that I did not bring up that question by way of casting reflection upon the past Finance Committee, but I want to set myself clear for the future, that in the event that the tax rate is raised—I am not saying that it will be—the reason will be for need improvements, and only for needed improvements. I have talked longer than I expected. I want to take this opportunity of thanking every member of the Board for the great honor which they have bestowed upon me. I want to thank my friends who have seen fit to send flowers expressing their good will and good wishes. I only hope to have their cooperation, and by having that I am sure that, when my term of office comes to an end, I will be able to give a good account of my stewardship.

SUPERVISOR HAVENNER: If I may say, for the information of the Supervisor, there is a report on file for the Finance Committee, and the statement was made, and no claim of any credit whatever, that four years ago the tax rate was $4.13 and that today it is $3.91, and those are the only two statements contained in there. There is no attempt on the part of the Finance Committee to claim all the credit for it. It is the fact, we set it before you for the information of the old Board and the new Board. It is $3.91, and if you have any doubt about it you can consult the attorney for the Golden Gate Bridge District, who made that point before us.

Supervisor Canepa also addressed the Board, thanking his friends for the flowers and declaring that he was sincerely appreciative of the honor the citizens had bestowed on him in electing him to the office of Supervisor. He referred to the big program of public improvements outlined in the Mayor's message and hoped that after this meeting the Board would get down to business and carry the program through.

Supervisor Power thanked his friends and well-wishers and pledged himself to action rather than words. The people of San Francisco, he said, desire action in all these matters. He expressed appreciation for the many beautiful floral tributes and hoped for the harmonious cooperation of all in promoting San Francisco's welfare and progress.

Supervisor Miles and Supervisor Spaulding also addressed the Board, thanking their friends for floral tributes and the citizens of San Francisco for their election. They pledged themselves to deeds rather than words and fullest cooperation in bringing all San Francisco municipal projects to an early completion.

Supervisor Roncovieri also addressed the Board, bespeaking harmony and cooperation in the solution of San Francisco's important public projects and a dignified conduct of the supervisorial proceedings at all times.

Supervisor Stanton also expressed his appreciation for his reelection at the hands of the citizens of San Francisco. He extended his very best wishes to the retiring members and congratulated the newly-elected members whom he hoped would serve the City to the best of their ability.

Supervisor Gallagher also extended his best wishes to the retiring members and his congratulations to the newly-elected.

RULES OF PROCEEDINGS OF THE BOARD OF SUPERVISORS.

Supervisor Andriano presented the following rules, and asked that, inasmuch as the secretary of the Rules Committee, Supervisor Peyser, had not been able to approve them, that they be laid over one week, with the reservation that if any of the rules do not conform to the notes of the secretary that the committee be permitted to amend them.

Resolved, That the rules hereinafter set forth be and the same are hereby adopted as the Rules of Proceedings of this Board of Supervisors, to-wit:

STANDING COMMITTEES.

1. The following shall constitute the standing committees of the Board (the first named member to be chairman thereof):

Airport and Aeronautics—Spaulding, Peyser, Miles.

Auditorium—Hayden, Canepa, Colman.

Civil Service—Havenner, McSheehy, Rossi.

Education, Parks and Playgrounds—McSheehy, Suhr, Andriano.

Finance—Rossi, Power, Hayden.

Fire—Canepa, Peyser, Toner.

Industrial Development and City Planning—Gallagher, Stanton, Hayden.

Judiciary—Suhr, Andriano, Roncovieri.

Lighting, Water and Telephone Service and Electricity—Stanton, McGovern, Shannon.

Municipal Concerts and Public Celebrations—Roncovieri, Colman, Toner.

Police and Licenses—Andriano, Shannon, McGovern.

Public Buildings and Lands—Shannon, Rossi, Suhr.

Public Health—Toner, McSheehy, Roncovieri.

Public Utilities—Colman, Spaulding, Havenner.

Public Welfare and Publicity—Peyser, Spaulding, Miles.

Streets and Tunnels—Power, Canepa, Gallagher.

Supplies—Miles, Stanton, Power.

Traffic—McGovern, Havenner, Gallagher.

(*The foregoing assignments were made in Board of Supervisors by Resolution No. 31907 (New Series), January 6, 1930.*)

Every Committee shall set a stated time of meeting, or the Committee may meet at a time to be set by the chairman, and every member will be expected to attend every meeting of his Committee, and to be present promptly on time. The clerk of each Committee shall keep a record of the attendance of the members, and he shall report such record to the Clerk of the Board, and the Clerk of the Board shall have the report of the attendance of members at committee meetings available at all times for the information of any or all members of the Board.

DUTIES OF COMMITTEES.

2. The respective duties of each of the foregoing Committees and the time of meetings are hereby defined as follows:

AIRPORT AND AERONAUTICS—To have control and management of the Municipal Airport; to report and recommend on applications for leasing of hangars and concessions in said Airport; to consider and report on all matters relating to said Airport.

AUDITORIUM—To have control and management of the Municipal Auditorium and entertainments held therein under the auspices of the City as provided in Ordinance No. 5320 (New Series); to lease said building and the several halls and apartments therein; to report and recommend on applications for leasing of said building for public assemblages and gatherings; to consider and report on all matters relating to the management, conduct and maintenance of said Auditorium.

CIVIL SERVICE AND RETIREMENT SYSTEM—To consider all matters relating to Civil Service in the several departments and to promote efficiency and economy in expenditures; to consider matters relating to the Retirement System, and all reports of the Board of Administration of the Retirement System shall be referred to it for investigation and report thereon.

COMMERCIAL AND INDUSTRIAL DEVELOPMENT AND CITY PLANNING—To assist in promoting the establishment of industries in San Francisco and to cooperate with commercial and industrial organizations in all efforts to establish new industries; to consider measures helpful in developing San Francisco as an industrial center and to encourage delegations to points where needed to bring new industries, and generally to consider manufacturing problems as related to the industrial needs of the community; to cooperate with the United States, State officials and civic organizations in support of national and state legislation designed to promote world trade and the United States Merchant Marine; to bring about the location of a foreign trade zone within the City and County of San Francisco; to inaugurate a movement to the end that the management, control and development of San Francisco's harbor be placed locally, and also to cooperate with the Federal and State authorities on all matters, especially legislation, that tend for the further development and utilization of San Francisco's harbor to meet the needs of the world's commerce; to promote friendly relations between the City and contiguous and neighboring communities, to consider all matters relating to the City's expansion, and to act in an advisory capacity between the City Planning Commission and the Board of Supervisors and to hear such matters concerning city planning as may be referred to it by the Board of Supervisors; to propose measures for developing and accelerating transcontinental railway and inter-urban railroad transportation on this peninsula; to confer with adjacent cities, towns and counties on intercommunity problems and to suggest to the Board in what manner other committees may be of help in peninsula development.

EDUCATION, PARKS AND PLAYGROUNDS—To consider and report upon all matters relating to the Departments of Education, Parks and Playgrounds and recreation centers, including the Aquatic Park, and to cooperate with the Board of Education, Playground Commission and Park Commission regarding the development and increased usefulness of these departments.

FINANCE—To perform all duties required by the Charter; to audit all bills and report on all matters that may be referred to it by the Board of Supervisors; to act as a budget committee for the Board, hold hearings on budget estimates of and with all departments, receive recommendations from all other committees of the Board, and formulate a budget for submission to the Board on or before the second Monday of May. (Meets Fridays at 2:30 p. m.)

FIRE—To consider all matters relating to the Fire Department; to report on all applications for garage, boiler, laundry and other permits referred to it.

JUDICIARY—To consider and report upon Charter amendments and all matters referred to it by the Board.

LIGHTING, WATER SERVICE, TELEPHONE SERVICE AND ELECTRICITY—To attend to the proper lighting of streets, public parks and public buildings; to investigate and correct complaints of water service and extensions thereof, and telephone service; to recommend installation and removal of City telephones; to recommend from time to time extensions of underground wire system, and to have general charge of all matters pertaining to electricity other than public lighting and amendments to the building laws.

MUNICIPAL CONCERTS AND PUBLIC CELEBRATIONS—To have charge of the Municipal Band and conduct all concerts that are given under the auspices of the City and County of San Francisco (except those concerts under the management of the Park Commissioners and the Auditorium Committee of this Board); to assist in promotion of all semi-public celebrations, dedications, etc.

POLICE AND LICENSES—To consider legislation concerning the Police Department; to investigate the management and character of penal institutions; to consider all matters affecting public morals; to report upon applications for permits referred to it by the Board, including free licenses to those deserving them, and report on all licenses, including taxicabs and public conveyances for hire.

PUBLIC BUILDINGS AND LANDS—To consider the erection of all public buildings and the purchase of sites for all public buildings upon recommendation of the respective departments; to consider and report upon the repairs to public buildings, and to recommend as to the janitorial, elevator and other service required for the proper conduct of all buildings of the City and County; also to assign to the various offices and departments the various rooms and places in the City Hall and Hall of Justice; to investigate and report upon proposed purchases of lands; to formulate plans for leasing City lands not needed for public purposes; to consider transfer of lands from one department to another, and all other matters pertaining to the realty of the City other than school property and airport property.

PUBLIC HEALTH—To consider all matters relating to health and sanitation; to see that institutions under the control of the Board of Health are properly conducted; to establish and maintain a high standard of service in public hospitals and Relief Home; to consider and report upon all complaints of nuisances; to make recommendations upon applications for permits which may be referred to it by the Board; also removal and destruction of garbage.

PUBLIC UTILITIES—To consider and pass upon all matters relating to public utilities, their acquisition, construction, control and management, whether municipally or privately owned, including transbay bridges, transportation, lighting, power, water and steam heating.

PUBLIC WELFARE AND PUBLICITY—To consider matters relating to the social well-being of the community other than those heretofore provided for, and generally to act upon all matters of public advertising, and pass on all bills chargeable against the advertising fund; to consider all matters relating to the Bureau of Weights and Measures.

RULES—To consider amendments to the Rules and such other matters as may be referred to it by the Board. To have supervision of and give instructions to the chauffeurs of the Board of Supervisors.

STATE LAWS AND LEGISLATION—To be appointed by the Finance Committee when occasion requires. To consider all matters pending before the Legislature and proposed legislation which affects the City and County of San Francisco, directly or indirectly, and to make such recommendations to the Board as may be deemed advisable, and to appear before the State Legislature in advocacy of any measures or in opposition to measures as the Board may advise.

STREETS AND TUNNELS—To consider all matters relating to the construction, improvement and maintenance of streets and sewers, including highways outside the County, for which the City and County is authorized to appropriate money, the closing, opening and widening of streets and the cleaning of streets; to designate the streets for the improvement and repair of which appropriations may be made in the budget and to allocate the same. Also direct the expenditure of money received from the State for the construction of public highways; to consider and report upon applications for spur and industrial tracks; to consider and report upon all matters relating to tunnels.

SUPPLIES—To consider and have charge of the purchase of all supplies as provided by the Charter; to prepare schedules for general supplies and to recommend award of contracts; to inspect deliveries and quality and quantity of supplies; to pass on all requisitions for non-contract supplies; to supervise the purchase and distribution of all books, stationery, etc.

TRAFFIC AND SAFETY—To investigate and report on matters relative to traffic conditions in the City and propose Ordinances regulating traffic and the promotion of safety in connection therewith.

CONVENING OF BOARD.

3. The Board shall convene at 2 o'clock p. m. on each Monday, and the Clerk shall immediately, after the call to order, which shall be at 2 o'clock p. m., call the roll of the members of the Board and shall record those present and absent. The Clerk shall also record the time of arrival of those members of the Board who arrive after 2 o'clock p. m., and the name of such member and the time of his arrival shall be entered upon the journal.

It shall be the duty of each Committee charged with the duty of cooperating with any particular department to investigate the financial needs of such department to be provided for in the annual budget; to consider such department's budget estimates and to recommend to the Finance Committee such modifications or changes thereof as it may deem proper.

The designations and duties of the foregoing Committees are hereby made part of these rules.

RULES OF ORDER.

4. The Mayor shall be President of the Board of Supervisors. He shall call each regular, adjourned or special meeting to order at the hour appointed and shall proceed with the order of business. In the absence of the Mayor, the Clerk shall call the roll and the Board shall appoint a presiding officer pro tempore from its own members, who shall have the same right to vote as other members.

The presiding officer shall preserve order and decorum.

The Clerk shall, immediately after the call to order, call the roll of members of the Board, and the record of those present and absent shall be entered upon the Journal.

5. Whenever it shall be moved and carried by 12 members that the Board go into Committee of the Whole, the President shall leave the chair and the members shall appoint a chairman of the Committee of the Whole, who shall report the proceedings of said Committee.

6. The rules of the Board shall be observed in the Committee of the Whole.

7. A motion, in Committee of the Whole, to rise and report the question, shall be decided without debate.

8. The Clerk shall have clips, upon which shall be kept all Bills, Ordinances, Resolutions and Reports to be acted upon by the Board, except those not reported upon by a Committee.

9. No Bill, Ordinance or Resolution shall be considered by the Board unless it has been introduced by a member of the Board or by a Committee of the Board, and the Bill, Ordinance or Resolution must be read by the Clerk in open meeting before being referred to Committee. At the time of introduction the presiding officer shall first indicate to what Committee a Bill, Ordinance or Resolution ought to be referred, and it shall be so referred unless, upon majority vote without debate, the Board shall order it referred to some other committee.

Action by the Board shall not be taken upon any Bill, Ordinance or Resolution until it has been referred to and acted upon by a Committee of the Board.

10. The Order of Business, which shall not be departed from except by the consent of twelve members, shall be as follows:
   1. Roll Call.
   2. Approval of Journal.
   3. Calendar Business.
   4. Roll Call for the Introduction of Resolutions, Bills and Communications Not Considered or Reported on by a Committee.
   5. Communications and Reports from City and County Officers.

11. If any question under debate contains several points, any member may have the points segregated and acted upon separately.

12. When a motion has been made and carried or lost, it shall be in order for any member voting with the prevailing side to move to "reconsider the vote" on that question.

A member may change his vote before the result is announced in order to move to "reconsider the vote" on that question. The vote upon such motion to reconsider shall not be taken before the next regular meeting of the Board. No question shall be reconsidered more than once. Motion to reconsider shall have precedence over every other motion. It shall require a majority vote to carry any motion to reconsider the vote by which any Bill, Ordinance or Resolution has been passed or defeated.

13. A motion to refer or lay on the table until decided shall preclude all amendments to the main question. A motion to lay on the table or to postpone indefinitely shall require a majority vote of the members present.

14. It shall be the duty of the Clerk to issue such certificates as may be required by Ordinances or Resolutions and transmit copies of said Ordinances or Resolutions to the various departments affected thereby. It shall also be the duty of the Clerk to cause the publication in the official newspaper of all Bills, Ordinances, proposals and awards as required by the Charter.

15. All accounts and bills shall be referred to the Finance Committee, provided that any Committee having jurisdiction over subject of expenditures may request that bills be first sent to that Committee before being acted upon by the Finance Committee and the Board.

16. The President shall preserve order and decorum, and prevent demonstrations of approval or disapproval on the part of persons in the Chambers of the Board, and shall decide questions of order, subject to an appeal to the Board.

17. When a Supervisor desires to address the Board he shall arise in his place, address the presiding officer, and when recognized he shall proceed to speak. No Supervisor shall be recognized when seated or when away from his seat.

18. No Supervisor shall speak more than twice in any one debate on the same subject, and at the same stage of the Bill, Ordinance, Resolution or Motion without the consent of a majority of the Board,

and Supervisors who have once spoken shall not again be entitled to the floor so long as any Supervisor who has not spoken desires to speak. No Supervisor shall be allowed to speak more than five minutes on any question except by permission of the Board, except that the author shall have five minutes to open and ten minutes to close.

19. No Supervisor shall be interrupted when speaking without his consent.

20. When two or more Supervisors arise at the same time to address the Board, the presiding officer shall designate the Supervisor who is entitled to the floor.

21. No motion shall be debated until the same *has been seconded* and distinctly announced by the presiding officer.

22. After a motion has been stated by the President, it shall be in the possession of the Board. It may be withdrawn by the mover thereof, with the consent of the second, before it is acted upon.

23. Upon a call of the Board the names of the members shall be called by the Clerk, and the absentees noted. Those for whom no excuse or insufficient excuses are made may, by order of those present, be sent for and be brought to the Chambers of the Board by the Sergeant-at-Arms or by special messengers appointed for the purpose.

24. When a question is under debate, no action shall be entertained except:

> To adjourn.
> Call of the Board.
> To lay on the table.
> The previous question.
> To postpone.
> To commit or amend.

which several motions shall have precedence in the order in which they are arranged; provided, however, that during a call of the Board it may consider and transact any matter or business that the Supervisors there present shall unanimously decide to consider.

25. A motion to adjourn is not debatable.

26. The previous question shall be put in the following form: "Shall the previous question be now put?" It shall only be admitted when demanded by three Supervisors, and its effect shall be to put an end to all debate except that the author of the Bill, Ordinance, Resolution or Motion or Amendments shall have the right to close, and the question under discussion shall thereupon be immediately put to a vote. On a motion for the previous question prior to a vote being taken by the Board a call of the Board shall be in order.

27. Every member present when a question is put shall vote for or against it, unless disqualified by the Charter. No member shall be permitted to vote upon a question unless present when his name is called or before the vote is announced. A roll call shall not be interrupted for debate or personal privilege, but a member may file, in writing, an explanation of his vote.

29. After the Board has acted, the names of those who voted for and those who voted against the question shall be entered upon the Journal, not only in cases required by law, but when any member may require it, and on all Bills, Ordinances and Resolutions on final passage the ayes and nays shall be recorded.

30. All appointments of officers and employees shall be made by a majority of the members of the Board. The Clerk shall assign the assistant clerks to their several duties, and shall immediately transmit to the Mayor all Resolutions and Ordinances which, under the law, require executive approval.

31. No member shall leave the Board during its session without permission from the Board.

32. All Committees shall be appointed by the Board unless otherwise ordered by the Board. Committees shall report on any subject referred to them by the Board and their recommendations thereon. *Unless otherwise ordered, a Committee shall report upon all subjects*

referred to it within thirty days thereafter. It shall be the right of any member of a Committee to move a roll call (in Committee), on any pending motion, and the Chairman or Acting Chairman of said Committee shall, with or without debate, order the roll call. In Committees of three members or less a motion by a member thereof shall not require a second.

33. The Clerk shall prepare and cause to be printed and placed on the desks of the members on days of meeting, at least 30 minutes before such a meeting, a calendar of matters to be presented to the Board at said meeting. Every petition or other written instrument intended to be presented to the Board must be delivered to the Clerk not later than 12 o'clock noon on Saturday, or on the day preceding the meeting; upon the request of the President or of any member its contents shall be read in full.

34. All petitions, protests and communications of a routine character shall be referred by the Clerk to the proper Committee.

35. Ten members shall constitute a quorum to transact business, and no Bill, Ordinance, Resolution or Amendment thereto shall pass without the concurrence of at least that number of members, but a smaller number may adjourn from day to day.

36. Except when otherwise provided by these rules, the Charter or law, a majority vote of the members present shall be necessary for the adoption of any motion.

37. The Clerk shall keep a record of all requests and instructions directed by the Board of Supervisors to any officer or board of the City and County and the action thereon of such officer or board. The record of such requests and instructions, until acted upon by such officer or board, shall be read by the Clerk at each regular meeting of the Board of Supervisors.

38. The privilege of the floor shall not be granted to others than members of the Board, except those entitled to the same under the Charter, or public officials or the City and County of San Francisco. This rule shall not be suspended, except by unanimous consent of all members present.

39. In debate a member must confine himself to the question before the Board.

40. On any questions or points of order not embraced in these rules the Board shall be governed by the rules contained in Robert's Rules of Order.

41. No member of the Board of Supervisors, chairman of a Committee, or Committee of said Board, shall employ or engage the services of any person, or authorize or incur any charge, debt or liability against the City and County unless authority therefor shall have been first given by the Board of Supervisors by Resolution or Ordinance, except as otherwise provided by law.

42. No standing rule or order of the Board shall be suspended or amended without the affirmative vote of twelve members, except that the rule as to the privilege of the floor shall require the unanimous consent of all members present.

43. No special order shall be placed on the Calendar except by order of the Board.

MEMORANDUM OF CHARTER PROVISIONS.

Page 4, Section 3, Chapter 1, Article II—Quorum consists of 10 members.

Page 5, Section 8, Chapter 1, Article II—No Bill shall become an Ordinance or Resolution be adopted unless it receives 10 votes.

Page 7, Section 16, Chapter 1, Article II—14 votes necessary to override Mayor's veto of Resolution or Ordinance.

Page 13, Chapter 2, Article II—Lease of City lands requires two-thirds vote of Board (12 votes).

Page 19, Section 6, Chapter 2, Article II—Street railway franchises require three-fourths vote (14 votes) of all the members of the Board,

while five-sixths vote (15 votes) of all the members of the Board is
necessary to pass these ordinances if MAYOR VETOES SAME.

Page 22, Section 9, Chapter 2, Article II—Sale of City lands requires
15 votes.

Page 30, Section 3, Chapter 1, Article III—Budget Ordinance requires
10 votes.

Page 30, Section 4, Chapter 1, Article III—15 votes are necessary
to override Mayor's veto of Budget.

Page 31, Section 8, Chapter 1, Article III—15 votes necessary to
appropriate from Urgent Necessity Fund.

Page 33, Section 13, Chapter 1, Article III—To suspend temporarily
limit of taxation to meet emergency requires unanimous vote of 18
members of the Board and approval of the Mayor.

Page 76, Section 1, Chapter 1, Article VI—Contracts for street work
require 14 votes.

Page 78, Section 2, Chapter 2, Article VI—When cost of sewer or
drain is in excess of $5 per linear front foot of abutting property and
work is disapproved by Board of Works, it requires 14 votes of the
Board of Supervisors to pass ordinance ordering such work done.

If application for work is made, the expense of which is to be paid
by City and County, and work is not recommended by the Board of
Public Works, it requires 14 votes of the Board of Supervisors to order
such work done.

Page 98, Section 33, Chapter 2, Article VI—Ordinance providing for
street improvements in 10-year installments requires 15 votes.

Page 100, Section 1, Chapter 3, Article VI—Opening and improvement of streets, etc., requires 12 votes.

Page 120, Section 17, Chapter 6, Article VI—15 votes are required
to modify or change procedure as provided in the Charter for changing
street grades and the performance of work in connection therewith.

Page 121, Section 1, Chapter 8, Article VI—Ordinance providing for
tunnel, subway and viaduct construction requires 12 votes.

Page 218, Section 19, Article XVI—Suspension of an elected officer
by the Mayor requires approval of 14 votes of the Board of Supervisors to cause removal.

Page 223, Section 35, Article XVI—Appointments of additional
deputies, clerks or employees require 14 votes.

Action Deferred.

Whereupon, the foregoing rules, on motion of Supervisor Power,
were *laid over one week* by the following vote:

Ayes—Supervisors Andriano, Canepa, Colman, Gallagher, Hayden,
McGovern, Miles, Power, Roncovieri, Rossi, Shannon, Spaulding, Stanton, Suhr, Toner—15.

Noes—Supervisors Havenner, McSheehy—2.

Absent—Supervisor Peyser—1.

Standing Committees.

Supervisor Hayden presented:

Resolution No. 21907 (New Series), as follows:

Resolved, That the standing committees of this Board be constituted
as follows, the first-named member to be chairman thereof:

Airport and Aeronautics—Spaulding, Peyser, Miles.

Auditorium—Hayden, Canepa, Colman.

Civil Service—Havenner, McSheehy, Rossi.

Education, Parks and Playgrounds—McSheehy, Suhr, Andriano.

Finance—Rossi, Power, Hayden.

Fire—Canepa, Peyser, Toner.

Industrial Development and City Planning—Gallagher, Stanton,
Hayden.

Judiciary—Suhr, Andriano, Roncovieri.

Lighting, Water and Telephone Service and Electricity—Stanton, McGovern, Shannon.

Municipal Concerts and Public Celebrations—Roncovieri, Colman, Toner.

Police and Licenses—Andriano, Shannon, McGovern.

Public Buildings and Lands—Shannon, Rossi, Suhr.

Public Health—Toner, McSheehy, Roncovieri.

Public Utilities—Colman, Spaulding, Havenner.

Public Welfare and Publicity—Peyser, Spaulding, Miles.

Streets and Tunnels—Power, Canepa, Gallagher.

Supplies—Miles, Stanton, Power.

Traffic—McGovern, Havenner, Gallagher.

Points of Order.

Supervisor McSheehy raised the point of order that on November 26, 1929, two committees were appointed, the Committee on Committees, and the Committee on Rules. The Rules Committee, he contended, should report first.

Supervisor Gallagher moved that his honor the Mayor be allowed to deliver his message as the first order of business.

Supervisor Hayden thereupon temporarily gave way to the message of the Mayor.

Adoption of Standing Committees.

Supervisor Hayden, subsequent to the delivery of the Mayor's inaugural message, moved the suspension of the rules and the adoption of the resolution theretofore presented for the selection of standing committees of the Board of Supervisors.

Supervisor Gallagher asked for a segregation of the questions and a vote on the recommendations separately.

Supervisor Havenner moved as an amendment that the name of Supervisor James E. Power as chairman of the Streets Committee be stricken out and the name of Supervisor Andrew J. Gallagher inserted in lieu thereof.

Amendment *lost* by the following vote:

Ayes—Supervisors Andriano, Gallagher, McSheehy, Roncovieri, Suhr —6.

Noes—Supervisors Canepa, Colman, Hayden, McGovern, Miles, Power, Rossi, Shannon, Spaulding, Stanton, Toner—11.

Absent—Supervisor Peyser—1.

Resolution Adopted.

Whereupon, the roll was called on the resolution as submitted by Supervisor Hayden, providing for standing committee assignments of the Board of Supervisors, and the same was adopted by the following vote:

Ayes—Supervisors Andriano, Canepa, Colman, Hayden, McGovern, Miles, Power, Rossi, Shannon, Spaulding, Stanton, Suhr, Toner—13.

Noes—Supervisors Gallagher, Havenner, McSheehy, Roncovieri—4.

Absent—Supervisor Peyser—1.

Action Deferred.

The following matter was, on motion of Supervisor Shannon, *laid over one week*:

CONFIRMATION OF SALE OF CITY LANDS—3 P. M.

Consideration of the matter of confirming the sale to R. H. Hawkes, for the sum of seventeen thousand ($17,000.00) dollars, the following described City land, to-wit:

Commencing at a point on the easterly line of Nineteenth avenue, distant thereon 255 feet southerly from the present southerly line of Wawona street, running thence southerly along said easterly line of

Nineteenth avenue 150 feet; thence at a right angle easterly 275.26 feet; thence at a right angle northerly 150 feet; thence at a right angle westerly 275.26 feet to the easterly line of Nineteenth avenue and point of commencement. Being a portion of Outside Lands Block No. 1258, also known as Lot No. 2 in Block No. 2540 on Assessor's Map Book.

If at said meeting an offer of 10 per cent more in amount than that hereinabove named shall be made to the Supervisors in writing by a responsible person, the Supervisors will confirm such sale to such person or order a new sale in conformity with the provisions of the Charter; otherwise said sale to R. H. Hawkes will be confirmed for the price hereinabove stated.

Finance and Industrial Development Committee to Consider State Bond Issue for Harbor Improvements, Etc.

Supervisor Gallagher suggested that the Finance Committee and Committee on Industrial Development take into consideration proposed $10,000,000 State bond issue for the improvement of the harbor and make a report thereon as to what activities we can indulge in to make it successful and as to other proposed constitutional amendments as Judiciary Committee might examine.

So ordered.

Illness of Supervisor Peyser.

Supervisor Hayden moved that the Clerk send a telegram to Supervisor Peyser, expressing regret that illness prevented his presence and expressing hope for a speedy recovery.

So ordered.

San Francisco's Showing at Pasadena Rose Tournament Commended.

Communication from Ed. L. Head, congratulating the Mayor and Board of Supervisors and expressing appreciation of the splendid showing made by San Francisco at the Pasadena Tournament of Roses.

In Memoriam.

On motion of Supervisor Gallagher the Board arose and stood in silence for one minute in memory of the departed members of the Board.

Good Wishes From Marina Home Owners' Protective Association.

Miss V. Fowler, representing Marina Home Owners' Protective Association, wished outgoing Supervisors good luck and thanked them for their cooperation in various improvements at Marina. To the incoming Supervisors she wished success.

World-Wide Aeronautical Contests.

Communication, from his Honor Mayor Rolph, transmitting letter of Mr. McAvoy relative to world-wide aeronautical contests, was referred to Airport Committee.

ADJOURNMENT.

Whereupon, there being no further business, the Board at 6:15 p. m., on motion of Supervisor McSheehy, took a recess until 2 p m. Monday, January 13, 1930.

J. S. DUNNIGAN, Clerk.

Approved by the Board of Supervisors January 27, 1930.

Pursuant to Resolution No. 3402 (New Series) of the Board of Supervisors of the City and County of San Francisco, I, John S. Dunnigan, hereby certify that the foregoing are true and correct copies of the Journal of Proceedings of said Board of the dates stated and approved as above recited.

                              JOHN S. DUNNIGAN,
                         Clerk of the Board of Supervisors,
                         City and County of San Francisco.

Monday, January 13, 1930

urnal of Proceedings
Board of Supervisors

City and County of San Francisco

The Recorder Printing and Publishing Company
337 Bush Street, S. F.

JOURNAL OF PROCEEDINGS
BOARD OF SUPERVISORS

MONDAY, JANUARY 13, 1930, 2 P. M.

In Board of Supervisors, San Francisco, Monday, January 13, 1930, 2 p. m.

CALLING THE ROLL.

The roll was called and the following Supervisors were noted present:

Supervisors Canepa, Colman, Hayden, McGovern, McSheehy, Miles, Rossi, Shannon, Spaulding, Stanton, Suhr, Toner—12.

Absent—Supervisors Andriano, Gallagher, Havenner, Peyser, Power, Roncovieri—6.

Quorum present.

His Honor Mayor Rolph presiding.

APPROVAL OF JOURNAL.

The Journal of Proceedings of the previous meeting was laid over for approval until next meeting.

Report of City Attorney, Telephone, Gas and Electric Rates and Evaluation Proceedings.

San Francisco, January 10, 1930.

Board of Supervisors, City Hall, San Francisco, Calif.

Gentlemen: As the membership of the Board of Supervisors has changed since The Pacific Telephone and Telegraph Company instituted its proceeding before the Railroad Commission for increase in telephone rates, I deem it proper that I should render a report concerning the status of this litigation.

Telephone Rate Litigation.

Since 1914 the telephone rates in San Francisco have not been changed, when these rates were established by the then Board of Supervisors. Most communities throughout the system of The Pacific Telephone and Telegraph Company have received substantial increases in rates from 1914 to date.

In June, 1927, The Pacific Telephone and Telegraph Company applied to the Railroad Commission to consolidate San Francisco and the East Bay cities into one exchange, and asked for rates that would have meant an approximate 50 per cent increase over existing rates, or in annual increases to the users in San Francisco of approximately $5,000,000.

Under the authority of your Board, I delegated Mr. Dion R. Holm to represent the City in the litigation, which extended from June, 1927, until the case was submitted in October, 1929.

It was an extremely hard fought case, and the engineers and accountants assigned to this office for the work investigated the physical properties of the company and appraised both on historical and reproduction bases. Operating expenses were scrutinized; technical problems, such as toll allocation, the cost of materials and supplies furnished by the Western Electric Company, relations with the American Telephone and Telegraph Company, depreciation, the effect of changing from manual equipment to automatic, and numerous other topics, were the objects of exhaustive studies.

The Railroad Commission handed down its decision on November 7, 1929, and after careful study of the decision it was determined that it would be useless to apply for a writ to the Supreme Court. This step was taken by the City of Oakland, and within the last few days the petition was denied.

The effect of the decision of the Railroad Commission creates one exchange between San Francisco and the East Bay communities, and resulted in an annual increase between both communities of approximately $2,100,000, and the approximate portion which San Francisco will bear is the sum of $1,400,000 per year. This latter figure is to be compared to the $5,000,000 claimed by the company.

The money expended by the City and the effort put forth by this office were worth while, for if the rates now prescribed by the Commission had been put into effect in June, 1927, the rate-payers during that approximate two and one-half years up to January 1, 1930, would have paid $3,500,000 over their previous rates, and had the company been allowed its claim, the rate-payers would have paid over that period $12,500,000. The net result of the decision of the Commission shows the company was allowed approximately 28 per cent of what it claimed.

As the rate structure has been decidedly changed as compared with the previous schedules, it is important that close scrutiny be kept over the revenues realized by the company, and if they exceed the estimates of what they are supposed to produce, steps should be taken in the near future to have these rates reduced.

There has been formed on the Pacific Coast an organization known as The Telephone Investigation League of America. The cities of Portland, Tacoma, Spokane, Seattle, San Francisco, Oakland and Los Angeles are members of this association, the purpose of which is primarily to bring about a federal investigation of the relations between the American Telephone and Telegraph Company, the Western Electric Company, The Pacific Telephone and Telegraph Company, and all other subsidiaries of the A. T. & T. Last year the Board of Supervisors contributed toward the expenses of the league the sum of $500.

Several bills have been introduced in Congress to bring about such investigation. There is now a bill pending, which was introduced by Senator Couzens, under the terms of which the Interstate Commerce Committee of the United States Senate is to investigate all wire-using companies in the United States, and to recommend to Congress legislation that will prevent abuses in the conduct of these businesses. The Telephone Investigation League of America and Senator Couzens, who is the chairman of the committee above referred to, urge that a representative of each of the principal cities on the Pacific Coast be present before the committee for the purpose of presenting facts to the committee upon which it may make recommendations to Congress to avoid existing abuses. The City of Seattle has appropriated the sum of $1,500 to send Thomas J. L. Kennedy, corporation counsel of Seattle, to Washington for the purpose of appearing before Senator Couzens' Committee on the 20th instant. It has been stated by representatives of The Telephone Investigation League of America that the City of Portland will also appear before the Interstate Commerce Committee.

Some of the bills introduced in Congress for the purpose of causing this investigation were fostered by San Francisco and the East Bay cities, and it would appear proper that San Francisco should be represented in Washington. However, this is a matter of policy for the Board to determine. and is, therefore, left in your hands.

In the event the City should be represented, I delegate Dion R. Holm to go to Washington, as he has had charge of the telephone litigation from its inception and is thoroughly familiar with the facts of the case.

Telephone Tax Suit.

Under the terms of the franchise granted by the Board of Supervisors to the Home Telephone Company, The Pacific Telephone and

Telegraph Company became the assignee, and by virtue of the terms of this franchise the telephone company is presumed to pay 2 per cent of its gross revenue to the City and County of San Francisco annually as its franchise tax.

For some time past the accountant connected with this office has been making a survey of the books of the telephone company and has found that the company has failed in the past to allocate to exchange revenues what properly should have been credited to the San Francisco exchange, with the result that there is due from the company to the City and County, from the figures thus far submitted, in excess of $100,000. The accounting expert of the Finance Committee has been called in recently to cooperate with the representative of this office, and he shares the same views, namely, that there is a very substantial sum of mony due from the company to the City for back taxes. We are in the process of gathering data necessary to the institution of a suit to recover back taxes, and feel that we will be successful when the ultimate facts are presented to us, and will recover for the City and County a considerable amount.

Electric Rates—P. G. & E. and Great Western Power.

Before the Railroad Commission there are several applications asking for reduction of electric rates that have been instituted by the City and County of San Francisco. For the purpose of bringing about this desired result, it has been necessary to investigate a number of mergers of smaller companies with the two corporations. In March, 1928, a rate cut was effective which resulted in an annual saving to the electric rate-payers of San Francisco of approximately $650,000. The result of studies made during the latter part of 1929 will result in a further rate reduction, effective early in 1930, that should mean an additional saving of $625,000 to San Francisco ratepayers.

The Railroad Commission has suggested an interim electric rate, and pending the establishment of a rate base, an investigation of operating expenses, depreciation and kindred subjects will result in a further deduction of electric rates in San Francisco for both companies.

The situation before the Railroad Commission is this, that they intend to put into effect interim rates, as far as electricity is concerned, for both the P. G. & E. and Great Western Power Company, with the right reserved for the cities to restore to the calendar their applications to have the rates reduced. This should be done, and to do so necessitates the establishment of a rate base and all other acts incident to the full prosecution of a rate case.

.I have detailed Dion R. Holm to take charge of these cases and it is his recommendation to me, after many conferences with me, that the applications should be restored to the calendar, a rate base established and a permanent set of rates instituted. In his recommendation I concur.

Gas Rates.

On May 7, 1929, the Pacific Gas and Electric Company filed an application before the Railroad Commission to construct a pipeline from Kern County to San Francisco for the purpose of transporting natural gas. Up to a few months ago San Francisco was supplied with manufactured gas that contained 550 B. T. units, charged for at the then prevailing rates. When natural gas was contemplated being served users in San Francisco, this office insisted before the Railroad Commission that present rates for 550 B. T. unit gas be maintained until the effect of the natural gas, which contained 1100 B. T. units, was served consumers in this City and the effect of it realized. The company proposed serving 700 B. T. unit gas and proposed a schedule which would have increased the gas bills of 63 per cent of the consumers. This move was protested by this office, with the result that an order was made by the Railroad Commission that the company would serve gas of not less than 600 B. T. units at the then prevailing rate of 550 B. T. unit gas, and which order it has been estimated during the last two months of having saved gas consumers of San Francisco over $120,000.

About April 1, 1930, natural gas will be served to domestic consumers in San Francisco and is now being served for industrial purposes. Interim rates have been suggested by the Railroad Commission by which the P. G. & E. may build up a load for industrial purposes and thus give the domestic consumers a lower rate. The rates suggested are not satisfactory from our standpoint and we believe that a very close watch should be made of the revenues realized from the proposed interim rates. It is also felt that a valuation of the Pacific Gas and Electric Company gas properties has not been made since 1918; that they must be gone into thoroughly after natural gas has been here a sufficient length of time, and that the necessity of maintaining the existing steam plants, operating expenses, etc., have been closely scrutinized.

For your information, I beg to advise you that at present there are assigned to this office an attorney, a chief engineer, two assistant engineers, an accountant, a stenographer and a copyist, to carry on the many cases we have before the Railroad Commission. At the outset of the fiscal year we had appropriated for the purpose of carrying to a conclusion the telephone rate litigation the amount of $30,000. At present there is on hand in the General Fund for this purpose the sum of $5,473.02, against the sum of $30,000, appropriated at the outset, and which we advised would be insufficient in the event gas or electric rate cases were to be presecuted. We have charged many and sundry expenses for the prosecution of the gas and electric cases.

We have an organization competent as a nucleus to prosecute all gas and electric cases now pending before the Railroad Commission, although it may be that the force will have to be augmented when detailed studies of the two electric and the gas cases are to be made. As the litigation involves many millions of dollars' savings to the rate-payers in San Francisco, your opinion as to maintaining the existing force is respectfully requested, as it will be difficult in the future to obtain persons who are loyal to the cause of the City and who have the knowledge, qualifications and training to prosecute this technical litigation, who may be employed by the City on a temporary basis as they are needed.

If it is your intention that these matters should be properly presented before the Railroad Commission, it will be necessary, at least 60 days hence, that you make an added appropriation from the General Fund to defray the cost of maintaining this organization.

I submit to you that public service corporations, with whom we are engaged in litigation, maintain a permanent force with a great number of technical men trained for many years with the idea of meeting rate cases, and cities appear at a great disadvantage with an unorganized force to meet well-qualified and long-standing men of an organization, trained specially in the subjects to be presented concerning rates.

Condemnation of the Electric Distribution Systems of the Pacific Gas and Electric Company and the Great Western Power Company in San Francisco.

Proceedings were instituted before the California State Railroad Commission in February, 1924, to acquire the distribution systems and steam electric plants of the Pacific Gas and Electric Company and the Great Western Power Company in San Francisco. This necessitated a detailed inventory and appraisal of the properties of both systems, and exhaustive studies on the subjects of accrued depreciation, severance damage and going value. Actual hearings extended over a period of three years and involved some 12,000 pages of transcript supplemented by voluminous technical exhibits. The cases were submitted in the summer of 1928 and the Commission's decisions were handed down in June, 1929.

The results are summarized in the following table:

Just Compensation as of February 11, 1924

	Company's Claim	City's Claim	Cal. R. R. Com. Allowance
Pac. Gas & Electric Co	$67,000,000	$18,894,005	$26,880,000
Great Western Power Co	30,000,000	9,306,537	11,815,000
Total	$97,000,000	$28,200,542	$38,695,000

It will be noted that the difference between the Commission's findings and the claims of the City is approximately $10,455,000; whereas, the difference between the Commission and the company's claims is $58,300,000; or, in other words, of a total difference between City claims and company claims of $68,800,000. The Commission decided 85 per cent of this difference in favor of the City.

As the valuation of the properties of the respective companies was fixed as of February 11, 1924, there naturally have been many additions and betterments made to the properties of both companies. During the progress of the hearings before the Railroad Commission the value of these additions were kept practically up to date, but since the conclusion of the hearings no computations on them have been made. The engineers of the City are bringing these values to date, and while no definite figure is available at this time, it is estimated that the total cost of the properties of both companies will be about $55,000,000.

The act providing for the fixing of the value of properties by the Railroad Commission provides that it is incumbent upon a municipality desiring to acquire properties of a public service corporation by condemnation, to institute proceedings looking to a bond issue for their acquisition within sixty days after the decision of the Commission. This was done by your Board, when, on August 12 last, you directed the Board of Public Works, through its engineer, to submit plans and estimates of the cost of the properties of these companies. These reports are now in the course of preparation, the delay in submitting them being due to the fact that it was only on December 15th that certain legal proceedings before the Supreme Court were withdrawn by the Great Western Power Company, and we could definitely state that the decision of the Commission was final.

The law further provides that an election to vote the bonds must be held with due diligence. No specific time is fixed within which it must be held. The necessity of complying with the law as to the holding of an election is twofold, first, to avail ourselves of the right to acquire the properties at the evaluated figure, should the people vote bonds to do so, and second, to save the city the costs incurred by the companies in the litigation, for the law provides that if the matter of the issuance of the bonds is submitted to the people with due diligence, costs of litigation shall not be recovered by the companies.

As I have said, the term "due diligence" is not defined in the act, but I believe that a period exceeding one hundred and twenty days after the engineer makes his report would not be considered acting with due diligence.

It has been suggested that if the proposed bond issue for the acquisition of these properties could be submitted to the people on the same date on which the State primary election will be held during the month of August, a considerable saving would result to the City. If the two companies would agree with the City that the deferring of the election until the August primary would not be considered a lack of due diligence, such a course might effected. If your Board should deem it desirable to defer the election until the August primary, I would be very glad to confer with the representatives of the companies and ascertain their views on the matter.

Respectfully submitted,

JOHN J. O'TOOLE,
City Attorney.

Supervisor Shannon, in connection with the foregoing, requested the City Attorney's advice as to the bond election ordinance providing for the insertion of the words "buy or build." a distributing system.

San Francisco, January 11, 1930.

Honorable Board of Supervisors, City Hall, San Francisco, Calif.

Dear Sirs: I herewith transmit to you a report covering the litigation and proceedings relative to the following matters:

(a) Telephone rate litigation;

(b) Electric rate litigation;

(c) Gas rate litigation;

(d) Evaluation proceedings, Pacific Gas and Electric Co. and Great Western Power Co.

The report speaks for itself, but I desire to direct your attention to two matters, one in regard to telephone rate matters, and the other in regard to the bond election to be held for the purpose of acquiring the properties of the Pacific Gas and Electric Company and Great Western Power Company.

If it is the desire of the Board that the City should be represented at the hearing before the Interstate Commerce Committee of the United States Senate upon the bills offered by Senator Couzens, which call for a nationwide investigation of telephone rates, it will be necessary for your Board at once to authorize me to send Mr. Holm to represent the City, for the hearing on the bills will take place some time between the 20th and 25th of the present month. It will be also necessary for your board to make an appropriation and pass a demand covering Mr. Holm's expenses. While the amount of his expenses will be dependent upon the length of his stay in Washington, I would suggest at this time that an allowance of $750 be made to cover this expense, for which amount Mr. Holm will account upon his return from his mission.

In regard to the evaluation proceedings, it is extremely important that your Board should express itself without delay as to the time at which it desires the special election should be held for the purpose of voting bonds for the purchase of these properties, for the reason that if the election is to be deferred until the August primary, the respective companies should be conferred with at once, to the end that their consent may be obtained to the effect that the deferring of the election until that date will not be considered a lack of due diligence in submitting the matter to the people.

I also request that I may be advised at your earliest convenience as to your desires regarding the continuation of investigation in regard to rates charged by the various public service corporations furnishing service in San Francisco, for the reason that if this work is to continue, it will not be possible, under my present appropriation, to hold my rate litigation organization longer than the first of the coming month.

Sincerely yours,

JOHN J. O'TOOLE,

City Attorney.

January 13, 1930—Referred to Public Utilities and Finance Committees jointly.

Motion.

Supervisor Colman moved, under suspension of the rules, that Dion Holm be sent to Washington, D. C., to attend hearing on telephone rates and that the Finance Committee provide for his expenses.

Supervisor Hayden suggested that the Clerk be directed to prepare proper resolution.

Supervisor Power moved as an amendment reference to Joint Committee on Public Utilities and Finance with instructions to report at next meeting.

Amendment *carried.*

Action Deferred.

The following matter was, on motion of Supervisor Power, *laid over one week*:

HEARING OR APPEAL.

Henry Cowell Lime and Cement Company.

Hearing of appeal of Henry Cowell Lime and Cement Company from the action and decision of the Board of Public Works in overruling the protest of Henry Cowell Lime and Cement Company against the improvement of the north half of Commercial street from the west line of The Embarcadero to a line at right angles with Commercial street and one hundred and twenty-five (125) feet six and three-eighths (6⅜) inches west of the west line of The Embarcadero, by the construction of full width artificial stone sidewalks, where sidewalks are not now to official grade, and the construction of a retaining wall to support this sidewalk, as set forth in Resolution of Intention No. 96689 (Second Series).

CONFIRMATION OF SALE OF CITY LANDS—3 P. M.

Consideration of the matter of confirming the sale to R. H. Hawkes, for the sum of seventeen thousand ($17,000.00) dollars, the following described City land, to-wit:

Commencing at a point on the easterly line of Nineteenth avenue, distant thereon 255 feet southerly from the present southerly line of Wawona street, running thence southerly along said easterly line of Nineteenth avenue 150 feet; thence at a right angle easterly 275.26 feet; thence at a right angle northerly 150 feet; thence at a right angle westerly 275.26 feet to the easterly line of Nineteenth avenue and point of commencement. Being a portion of Outside Lands Block No. 1258, also known as Lot No. 2 in Block No. 2540 on Assessor's Map Book.

If at said meeting an offer of 10 per cent more in amount than that hereinabove named shall be made to the Supervisors in writing by a responsible person, the Supervisors will confirm such sale to such person or order a new sale in conformity with the provisions of the Charter; otherwise said sale to R. H. Hawkes will be confirmed for the price hereinabove stated.

His Honor the Mayor asked if there was any one present who wished to increase the bid of R. H. Hawkes.

No response.

Passed for Printing.

Whereupon, the following bill was *passed for printing*:

Confirming Sale of City Land.

Bill No. 8168, Ordinance No. ――――― (New Series), as follows:

Confirming the sale of land owned by the City and County of San Francisco and situate in the City and County of San Francisco, State of California.

Whereas, by Ordinance No. 8544 (New Series), approved October 1, 1929, the Board of Supervisors. determined that public interest and necessity demanded the sale of the land hereinafter described and hereinbefore referred to, and by said ordinance directed the Mayor of the City and County to sell all of said land at public auction, to be held on the 4th day of November, 1929, and directed that notice of said sale be given for three weeks successively next before the sale as required by law; and

Whereas, the Clerk of the Board of Supervisors thereafter proceeded to publish notice of said sale in the official newspaper and one other daily newspaper published in the City and County for three weeks successively next before said sale was directed to be made, describing the land to be sold therein with common certainty and stating the date on or after which said sale would be made, as specified in Ordinance No. 8544 (New Series), and that all bids or offers would be received by the Mayor at the chambers of the Board of Supervisors in the City Hall, City and County of San Francisco, State of California, on or after said date; and

Whereas, the Mayor, the Assessor and the Chairman of the Finance Committee, being the Board of Appraisement constituted by the Charter of the City and County of San Francisco for such purpose, thereafter duly met and made an appraisement of said land and fixed the fair value thereof and reported said appraisement to the Board of Supervisors in writing; and

Whereas, thereafter, and on the 18th day of November, 1929, at public auction the Mayor sold said property to R. H. Hawkes for the sum of $17,000 and accepted from said R. H. Hawkes a deposit, being a certified check in the sum of $1,700, and being 10 per cent or more of the amount bid as aforesaid, and thereupon and on the 5th day of December, 1929, duly notified the Board of Supervisors in writing of the fact of such sale, stating the sum bid, the name of the bidder, and requesting that the Board confirm the sale; and

Whereas, the Clerk of the Board of Supervisors immediately thereupon proceeded to give notice by publication in the official newspaper and one other newspaper in the City and County of San Francisco, for a period of three weeks from and after the 7th day of December, 1929, that at a meeting of the Board of Supervisors to be held on the 30th day of December, 1929, the matter of said sale would come up for confirmation, stating also in said notice the fact of the sale, the amount for which the property had been sold as aforesaid, and the name of the purchaser, and also stating that if at such meeting on the 30th day of December, 1929, an offer of 10 per cent more in amount than that named in said notice should be made to the Supervisors in writing by a responsible person, the Supervisors would confirm such sale to such person, or order a new sale; and

Whereas, the date of confirmation specified in said notice has arrived and action in said matter was deferred for one week, and on the 6th day of January, 1930, the matter was again deferred for one week, and on this, the 13th day of January, 1930, consideration of the matter was had, and a higher bid has not been obtained, and it appearing to the Board of Supervisors that the sum of $17,000 bid as aforesaid by R. H. Hawkes is not disproportionate to the value of the property sold and that a greater sum cannot be obtained; therefore,

Be it ordained by the People of the City and County of San Francisco as follows:

Section 1. The said sale of the said land hereinafter described to R. H. Hawkes for the sum of $17,000 is hereby ratified, approved and confirmed, and the Mayor and the Clerk of the Board of Supervisors are hereby authorized to execute and deliver to said purchaser. upon payment of the balance of the purchase price, a good and sufficient conveyance in the name of the City and County of San Francisco, conveying to R. H. Hawkes all the right, title and interest of the City and County of San Francisco in and to the land sold as aforesaid, and more particularly described as follows, to-wit:

Commencing at a point on the easterly line of Nineteenth avenue, distant thereon 255 feet southerly from the present southerly line of Wawona street, running thence southerly along said easterly line of Nineteenth avenue 150 feet; thence at a right angle easterly 275.26 feet; thence at a right angle northerly 150 feet; thence at a right angle westerly 275.26 feet to the easterly line of Nineteenth avenue and point of commencement. Being a portion of Outside Land Block 1258, also known as Lot 2 in Block No. 2540 on Assessor's Map Book.

Section 2. The City Attorney is hereby directed to prepare the necessary conveyance and supervise the delivery of deed upon payment of purchase price as aforesaid.

Section 3. This ordinance shall take effect immediately.

Action Deferred.

The following matter was *laid over one week*:

RULES OF PROCEEDINGS OF THE BOARD OF SUPERVISORS.

Supervisor Andriano presented the following rules, and asked that, inasmuch as the secretary of the Rules Committee, Supervisor Peyser, had not been able to approve them, that they be laid over one week, with the reservation that if any of the rules do not conform to the notes of the secretary that the committee be permitted to amend them.

Resolved, That the rules hereinafter set forth be and the same are hereby adopted as the Rules of Proceedings of this Board of Supervisors, to-wit:

STANDING COMMITTEES.

1. The following shall constitute the standing committees of the Board (the first named member to be chairman thereof):

Airport and Aeronautics—Spaulding, Peyser, Miles.
Auditorium—Hayden, Canepa, Colman.
Civil Service—Havenner, McSheehy, Rossi.
Education, Parks and Playgrounds—McSheehy, Suhr, Andriano.
Finance—Rossi, Power, Hayden.
Fire—Canepa, Peyser, Toner.
Industrial Development and City Planning—Gallagher, Stanton, Hayden.
Judiciary—Suhr, Andriano, Roncovieri.
Lighting, Water and Telephone Service and Electricity—Stanton, McGovern, Shannon.
Municipal Concerts and Public Celebrations—Roncovieri, Colman, Toner.
Police and Licenses—Andriano, Shannon, McGovern.
Public Buildings and Lands—Shannon, Rossi, Suhr.
Public Health—Toner, McSheehy, Roncovieri.
Public Utilities—Colman, Spaulding, Havenner.
Public Welfare and Publicity—Peyser, Spaulding, Miles.
Streets and Tunnels—Power, Canepa, Gallagher.
Supplies—Miles, Stanton, Power.
Traffic—McGovern, Havenner, Gallagher.

(*The foregoing assignments were made in Board of Supervisors by Resolution No. 31907 (New Series), January 6, 1930.*)

Every Committee shall set a stated time of meeting, or the Committee may meet at a time to be set by the chairman, and every member will be expected to attend every meeting of his Committee, and to be present promptly on time. The clerk of each Committee shall keep a record of the attendance of the members, and he shall report such record to the Clerk of the Board, and the Clerk of the Board shall have the report of the attendance of members at committee meetings available at all times for the information of any or all members of the Board.

DUTIES OF COMMITTEES.

2. The respective duties of each of the foregoing Committees and the time of meetings are hereby defined as follows:

AIRPORT AND AERONAUTICS—To have control and management of the Municipal Airport; to report and recommend on applications for leasing of hangars and concessions in said Airport; to consider and report on all matters relating to said Airport.

AUDITORIUM—To have control and management of the Municipal Auditorium and entertainments held therein under the auspices of the City as provided in Ordinance No. 5320 (New Series); to lease said building and the several halls and apartments therein; to report and recommend on applications for leasing of said building for public assemblages and gatherings; to consider and report on all matters relating to the management, conduct and maintenance of said Auditorium.

CIVIL SERVICE AND RETIREMENT SYSTEM—To consider all matters relating to Civil Service in the several departments and to promote efficiency and economy in expenditures; to consider matters relating to the Retirement System, and all reports of the Board of Administration of the Retirement System shall be referred to it for investigation and report thereon.

COMMERCIAL AND INDUSTRIAL DEVELOPMENT AND CITY PLANNING—To assist in promoting the establishment of industries in San Francisco and to cooperate with commercial and industrial organizations in all efforts to establish new industries; to consider measures helpful in developing San Francisco as an industrial center and to encourage delegations to points where needed to bring new industries, and generally to consider manufacturing problems as related to the industrial needs of the community; to cooperate with the United States, State officials and civic organizations in support of national and state legislation designed to promote world trade and the United States Merchant Marine; to bring about the location of a foreign trade zone within the City and County of San Francisco; to inaugurate a movement to the end that the management, control and development of San Francisco's harbor be placed locally, and also to cooperate with the Federal and State authorities on all matters, especially legislation, that tend for the further development and utilization of San Francisco's harbor to meet the needs of the world's commerce; to promote friendly relations between the City and contiguous and neighboring communities, to consider all matters relating to the City's expansion, and to act in an advisory capacity between the City Planning Commission and the Board of Supervisors and to hear such matters concerning city planning as may be referred to it by the Board of Supervisors; to propose measures for developing and accelerating transcontinental railway and inter-urban railroad transportation on this peninsula; to confer with adjacent cities, towns and counties on intercommunity problems and to suggest to the Board in what manner other committees may be of help in peninsula development.

EDUCATION, PARKS AND PLAYGROUNDS—To consider and report upon all matters relating to the Departments of Education, Parks and Playgrounds and recreation centers, including the Aquatic Park, and to cooperate with the Board of Education, Playground Commission and Park Commission regarding the development and increased usefulness of these departments.

FINANCE—To perform all duties required by the Charter; to audit all bills and report on all matters that may be referred to it by the Board of Supervisors; to act as a budget committee for the Board, hold hearings on budget estimates of and with all departments, receive recommendations from all other committees of the Board, and formulate a budget for submission to the Board on or before the second Monday of May. (Meets Fridays at 2:30 p. m.)

FIRE—To consider all matters relating to the Fire Department; to report on all applications for garage, boiler, laundry and other permits referred to it.

JUDICIARY—To consider and report upon Charter amendments and all matters referred to it by the Board.

LIGHTING, WATER SERVICE, TELEPHONE SERVICE AND ELECTRICITY—To attend to the proper lighting of streets, public parks and public buildings; to investigate and correct complaints of water service and extensions thereof, and telephone service; to recommend installation and removal of City telephones; to recommend from time to time extensions of underground wire system, and to have general charge of all matters pertaining to electricity other than public lighting and amendments to the building laws.

MUNICIPAL CONCERTS AND PUBLIC CELEBRATIONS—To have charge of the Municipal Band and conduct all concerts that are given under the auspices of the City and County of San Francisco (except those concerts under the management of the Park Commissioners and the Auditorium Committee of this Board); to assist in promotion of all semi-public celebrations, dedications, etc.

POLICE AND LICENSES—To consider legislation concerning the Police Department; to investigate the management and character of penal institutions; to consider all matters affecting public morals; to report upon applications for permits referred to it by the Board, including free licenses to those deserving them, and report on all licenses, including taxicabs and public conveyances for hire.

PUBLIC BUILDINGS AND LANDS—To consider the erection of all public buildings and the purchase of sites for all public buildings upon recommendation of the respective departments; to consider and report upon the repairs to public buildings, and to recommend as to the janitorial, elevator and other service required for the proper conduct of all buildings of the City and County; also to assign to the various offices and departments the various rooms and places in the City Hall and Hall of Justice; to investigate and report upon proposed purchases of lands; to formulate plans for leasing City lands not needed for public purposes; to consider transfer of lands from one department to another, and all other matters pertaining to the realty of the City other than school property and airport property.

PUBLIC HEALTH—To consider all matters relating to health and sanitation; to see that institutions under the control of the Board of Health are properly conducted; to establish and maintain a high standard of service in public hospitals and Relief Home; to consider and report upon all complaints of nuisances; to make recommendations upon applications for permits which may be referred to it by the Board; also removal and destruction of garbage.

PUBLIC UTILITIES—To consider and pass upon all matters relating to public utilities, their acquisition, construction, control and management, whether municipally or privately owned, including transbay bridges, transportation, lighting, power, water and steam heating.

PUBLIC WELFARE AND PUBLICITY—To consider matters relating to the social well-being of the community other than those heretofore provided for, and generally to act upon all matters of public advertising, and pass on all bills chargeable against the advertising fund; to consider all matters relating to the Bureau of Weights and Measures.

RULES—To consider amendments to the Rules and such other matters as may be referred to it by the Board. To have supervision of and give instructions to the chauffeurs of the Board of Supervisors.

STATE LAWS AND LEGISLATION—To be appointed by the Finance Committee when occasion requires. To consider all matters pending before the Legislature and proposed legislation which affects the City and County of San Francisco, directly or indirectly, and to make such recommendations to the Board as may be deemed advisable, and to appear before the State Legislature in advocacy of any measures or in opposition to measures as the Board may advise.

STREETS AND TUNNELS—To consider all matters relating to the construction, improvement and maintenance of streets and sewers, including highways outside the County, for which the City and County is authorized to appropriate money, the closing, opening and widening of streets and the cleaning of streets; to designate the streets for the improvement and repair of which appropriations may be made in the budget and to allocate the same. Also direct the expenditure of money received from the State for the construction of public highways; to consider and report upon applications for spur and industrial tracks; to consider and report upon all matters relating to tunnels.

SUPPLIES—To consider and have charge of the purchase of all supplies as provided by the Charter; to prepare schedules for general supplies and to recommend award of contracts; to inspect deliveries and quality and quantity of supplies; to pass on all requisitions for non-contract supplies; to supervise the purchase and distribution of all books, stationery, etc.

TRAFFIC AND SAFETY—To investigate and report on matters relative to traffic conditions in the City and propose Ordinances regulating traffic and the promotion of safety in connection therewith.

CONVENING OF BOARD.

3. The Board shall convene at 2 o'clock p. m. on each Monday, and the Clerk shall immediately, after the call to order, which shall be at 2 o'clock p. m., call the roll of the members of the Board and shall record those present and absent. The Clerk shall also record the time of arrival of those members of the Board who arrive after 2 o'clock p. m., and the name of such member and the time of his arrival shall be entered upon the journal.

It shall be the duty of each Committee charged with the duty of cooperating with any particular department to investigate the financial needs of such department to be provided for in the annual budget; to consider such department's budget estimates and to recommend to the Finance Committee such modifications or changes thereof as it may deem proper.

The designations and duties of the foregoing Committees are hereby made part of these rules.

RULES OF ORDER.

4. The Mayor shall be President of the Board of Supervisors. He shall call each regular, adjourned or special meeting to order at the hour appointed and shall proceed with the order of business. In the absence of the Mayor, the Clerk shall call the roll and the Board shall appoint a presiding officer pro tempore from its own members, who shall have the same right to vote as other members.

The presiding officer shall preserve order and decorum.

The Clerk shall, immediately after the call to order, call the roll of members of the Board, and the record of those present and absent shall be entered upon the Journal.

5. Whenever it shall be moved and carried by 12 members that the Board go into Committee of the Whole, the President shall leave the chair and the members shall appoint a chairman of the Committee of the Whole, who shall report the proceedings of said Committee.

6. The rules of the Board shall be observed in the Committee of the Whole.

7. A motion, in Committee of the Whole, to rise and report the question, shall be decided without debate.

8. The Clerk shall have clips, upon which shall be kept all Bills, Ordinances, Resolutions and Reports to be acted upon by the Board, except those not reported upon by a Committee.

9. No Bill, Ordinance or Resolution shall be considered by the Board unless it has been introduced by a member of the Board or by a Committee of the Board, and the Bill, Ordinance or Resolution must be read by the Clerk in open meeting before being referred to Committee. At the time of introduction the presiding officer shall first indicate to what Committee a Bill, Ordinance or Resolution ought to be referred, and it shall be so referred unless, upon majority vote

without debate, the Board shall order it referred to some other committee.

Action by the Board shall not be taken upon any Bill, Ordinance or Resolution until it has been referred to and acted upon by a Committee of the Board.

10. The Order of Business, which shall not be departed from except by the consent of twelve members, shall be as follows:

1. Roll Call.
2. Approval of Journal.
3. Calendar Business.
4. Roll Call for the Introduction of Resolutions, Bills and Communications Not Considered or Reported on by a Committee.
5. Communications and Reports from City and County Officers.

11. If any question under debate contains several points, any member may have the points segregated and acted upon separately.

12. When a motion has been made and carried or lost, it shall be in order for any member voting with the prevailing side to move to "reconsider the vote" on that question.

A member may change his vote before the result is announced in order to move to "reconsider the vote" on that question. The vote upon such motion to reconsider shall not be taken before the next regular meeting of the Board. No question shall be reconsidered more than once. Motion to reconsider shall have precedence over every other motion. It shall require a majority vote to carry any motion to reconsider the vote by which any Bill, Ordinance or Resolution has been passed or defeated.

13. A motion to refer or lay on the table until decided shall preclude all amendments to the main question. A motion to lay on the table or to postpone indefinitely shall require a majority vote of the members present.

14. It shall be the duty of the Clerk to issue such certificates as may be required by Ordinances or Resolutions and transmit copies of said Ordinances or Resolutions to the various departments affected thereby. It shall also be the duty of the Clerk to cause the publication in the official newspaper of all Bills, Ordinances, proposals and awards as required by the Charter.

15. All accounts and bills shall be referred to the Finance Committee, provided that any Committee having jurisdiction over subject of expenditures may request that bills be first sent to that Committee before being acted upon by the Finance Committee and the Board.

16. The President shall preserve order and decorum, and prevent demonstrations of approval or disapproval on the part of persons in the Chambers of the Board, and shall decide questions of order, subject to an appeal to the Board.

17. When a Supervisor desires to address the Board he shall arise in his place, address the presiding officer, and when recognized he shall proceed to speak. No Supervisor shall be recognized when seated or when away from his seat.

18. No Supervisor shall speak more than twice in any one debate on the same subject, and at the same stage of the Bill, Ordinance, Resolution or Motion without the consent of a majority of the Board, and Supervisors who have once spoken shall not again be entitled to the floor so long as any Supervisor who has not spoken desires to speak. No Supervisor shall be allowed to speak more than five minutes on any question except by permission of the Board, except that the author shall have five minutes to open and ten minutes to close.

19. No Supervisor shall be interrupted when speaking without his consent.

20. When two or more Supervisors arise at the same time to address the Board, the presiding officer shall designate the Supervisor who is entitled to the floor.

21. No motion shall be debated until the same *has been seconded* and distinctly announced by the presiding officer.

22. After a motion has been stated by the President, it shall be in the possession of the Board. It may be withdrawn by the mover thereof, with the consent of the second, before it is acted upon.

23. Upon a call of the Board the names of the members shall be called by the Clerk, and the absentees noted. Those for whom no excuse or insufficient excuses are made may, by order of those present, be sent for and be brought to the Chambers of the Board by the Sergeant-at-Arms or by special messengers appointed for the purpose.

24. When a question is under debate, no action shall be entertained except:

To adjourn.
Call of the Board.
To lay on the table.
The previous question.
To postpone.
To commit or amend.

which several motions shall have precedence in the order in which they are arranged; provided, however, that during a call of the Board it may consider and transact any matter or business that the Supervisors there present shall unanimously decide to consider.

25. A motion to adjourn is not debatable.

26. The previous question shall be put in the following form: "Shall the previous question be now put?" It shall only be admitted when demanded by three Supervisors, and its effect shall be to put an end to all debate except that the author of the Bill, Ordinance, Resolution or Motion or Amendments shall have the right to close, and the question under discussion shall thereupon be immediately put to a vote. On a motion for the previous question prior to a vote being taken by the Board a call of the Board shall be in order.

27. Every member present when a question is put shall vote for or against it, unless disqualified by the Charter. No member shall be permitted to vote upon a question unless present when his name is called or before the vote is announced. A roll call shall not be interrupted for debate or personal privilege, but a member may file, in writing, an explanation of his vote.

29. After the Board has acted, the names of those who voted for and those who voted against the question shall be entered upon the Journal, not only in cases required by law, but when any member may require it, and on all Bills, Ordinances and Resolutions on final passage the ayes and nays shall be recorded.

30. All appointments of officers and employees shall be made by a majority of the members of the Board. The Clerk shall assign the assistant clerks to their several duties, and shall immediately transmit to the Mayor all Resolutions and Ordinances which, under the law, require executive approval.

31. No member shall leave the Board during its session without permission from the Board.

32. All Committees shall be appointed by the Board unless otherwise ordered by the Board. Committees shall report on any subject referred to them by the Board and their recommendations thereon. *Unless otherwise ordered, a Committee shall report upon all subjects referred to it within thirty days thereafter.* It shall be the right of any member of a Committee to move a roll call (in Committee), on any pending motion, and the Chairman or Acting Chairman of said Committee shall, with or without debate, order the roll call. In Committees of three members or less a motion by a member thereof shall not require a second.

33. The Clerk shall prepare and cause to be printed and placed on the desks of the members on days of meeting, at least 30 minutes before such a meeting, a calendar of matters to be presented to the Board at said meeting. Every petition or other written instrument intended to be presented to the Board must be delivered to the Clerk not later than 12 o'clock noon on Saturday, or on the day preceding

the meeting; upon the request of the President or of any member its contents shall be read in full.

34. All petitions, protests and communications of a routine character shall be referred by the Clerk to the proper Committee.

35. Ten members shall constitute a quorum to transact business, and no Bill, Ordinance, Resolution or Amendment thereto shall pass without the concurrence of at least that number of members, but a smaller number may adjourn from day to day.

36. Except when otherwise provided by these rules, the Charter or law, a majority vote of the members present shall be necessary for the adoption of any motion.

37. The Clerk shall keep a record of all requests and instructions directed by the Board of Supervisors to any officer or board of the City and County and the action thereon of such officer or board. The record of such requests and instructions, until acted upon by such officer or board, shall be read by the Clerk at each regular meeting of the Board of Supervisors.

38. The privilege of the floor shall not be granted to others than members of the Board, except those entitled to the same under the Charter, or public officials or the City and County of San Francisco. This rule shall not be suspended, except by unanimous consent of all members present.

39. In debate a member must confine himself to the question before the Board.

40. On any questions or points of order not embraced in these rules the Board shall be governed by the rules contained in Robert's Rules of Order.

41. No member of the Board of Supervisors, chairman of a Committee, or Committee of said Board, shall employ or engage the services of any person, or authorize or incur any charge, debt or liability against the City and County unless authority therefor shall have been first given by the Board of Supervisors by Resolution or Ordinance, except as otherwise provided by law.

42. No standing rule or order of the Board shall be suspended or amended without the affirmative vote of twelve members, except that the rule as to the privilege of the floor shall require the unanimous consent of all members present.

43. No special order shall be placed on the Calendar except by order of the Board.

MEMORANDUM OF CHARTER PROVISIONS.

Page 4, Section 3, Chapter 1, Article II—Quorum consists of 10 members.

Page 5, Section 8, Chapter 1, Article II—No Bill shall become an Ordinance or Resolution be adopted unless it receives 10 votes.

Page 7, Section 16, Chapter 1, Article II—14 votes necessary to override Mayor's veto of Resolution or Ordinance.

Page 13, Chapter 2, Article II—Lease of City lands requires two-thirds vote of Board (12 votes).

Page 19, Section 6, Chapter 2, Article II—Street railway franchises require three-fourths vote (14 votes) of all the members of the Board, while five-sixths vote (15 votes) of all the members of the Board is necessary to pass these ordinances if MAYOR VETOES SAME.

Page 22, Section 9, Chapter 2, Article II—Sale of City lands requires 15 votes.

Page 30, Section 3, Chapter 1, Article III—Budget Ordinance requires 10 votes.

Page 30, Section 4, Chapter 1, Article III—15 votes are necessary to override Mayor's veto of Budget.

Page 31, Section 8, Chapter 1, Article III—15 votes necessary to appropriate from Urgent Necessity Fund.

Page 33, Section 13, Chapter 1, Article III—To suspend temporarily limit of taxation to meet emergency requires unanimous vote of 18 members of the Board and approval of the Mayor.

Page 76, Section 1, Chapter 1, Article VI—Contracts for street work require 14 votes.

Page 78, Section 2, Chapter 2, Article VI—When cost of sewer or drain is in excess of $5 per linear front foot of abutting property and work is disapproved by Board of Works, it requires 14 votes of the Board of Supervisors to pass ordinance ordering such work done.

If application for work is made, the expense of which is to be paid by City and County, and work is not recommended by the Board of Public Works, it requires 14 votes of the Board of Supervisors to order such work done.

Page 98, Section 33, Chapter 2, Article VI—Ordinance providing for street improvements in 10-year installments requires 15 votes.

Page 100, Section 1, Chapter 3, Article VI—Opening and improvement of streets, etc., requires 12 votes.

Page 120, Section 17, Chapter 6, Article VI—15 votes are required to modify or change procedure as provided in the Charter for changing street grades and the performance of work in connection therewith.

Page 121, Section 1, Chapter 8, Article VI—Ordinance providing for tunnel, subway and viaduct construction requires 12 votes.

Page 218, Section 19, Article XVI—Suspension of an elected officer by the Mayor requires approval of 14 votes of the Board of Supervisors to cause removal.

Page 223, Section 35, Article XVI—Appointments of additional deputies, clerks or employees require 14 votes.

UNFINISHED BUSINESS.

Final Passage.

The following matters, heretofore passed for printing, were taken up and *finally passed* by the following vote:

Authorizations.

On recommendation of Finance Committee.

Resolution No. 31909 (New Series), as follows:

Resolved, That the following amounts be and the same are hereby authorized to be expended out of the hereinafter mentioned funds in payment to the following named claimants, to-wit:

Aquarium—Appropriation 56.

(1) California Academy of Sciences, maintenance of Steinhart Aquarium, month of December, 1929 (claim dated Jan. 6, 1930) ....$ 4,985.84

Park Fund.

(2) Marine Electric Co., electric installation for parks (claim dated Jan. 3, 1930)....................................$ 682.70

(3) Pacific Gas & Electric Co., gas and electric service for parks, month of November (claim dated Jan. 3, 1930)..... 2,427.27

(4) Spring Valley Water Co., November, water for parks (claim dated Jan. 3, 1930)........................... 3,861.68

(5) State Compensation Insurance Fund, premium covering insurance on park employments (claim dated Jan. 3, 1930)   569.08

(6) Berringer & Russell, hay, etc., for parks (claim dated Jan. 3, 1930) 1,407.02

(7) Henry Cowell Lime & Cement Co., cement for parks (claim dated Jan. 3, 1930) 519.40

(8) Golden State Milk Products Co., ice cream for parks (claim dated Jan. 3, 1930) 1,570.24

(9) J. H. McCallum, lumber for parks (claim dated Jan. 3, 1930) 612.88

Duplicate Tax Fund.

(10) M. Eisenberg, refund of first installment, 1929-1930, taxes paid in duplicate (claim dated Jan. 2, 1930).........$ 992.88

(11) Boyd Investment Co., refund first installment, 1929-1930, taxes paid in duplicate (claim dated Jan. 2, 1930).. 3,006.71

Hetch Hetchy Construction Fund, Bond Issue 1928.

(12) M. D. Jones, truck hire (claim dated Dec. 21, 1929)....$ 537.72

(13) Grier & Mead, rail and angle bars (claim dated Dec. 21, 1929) 3,057.35

(14) Ingersoll-Rand Co. of Calif., machinery parts (claim dated Dec. 21, 1929) 538.69

(15) The Charles Nelson Co., wood wedges (claim dated Dec. 21, 1929) 1,234.00

(16) Santa Cruz Portland Cement Co., cement (claim dated Dec. 21, 1929) 4,073.50

(17) Sherry Bros., Inc., eggs (claim dated Dec. 21, 1929)... 510.60

(18) Wilsey Bennett Co., butter and cheese (claim dated Dec. 21, 1929) 509.90

(19) Challenge Cream & Butter Association, canned milk (claim dated Dec. 24, 1929)...................... 656.25

(20) M. Greenberg's Sons, bronze base plates (claim dated Dec. 24, 1929) 592.20

(21) J. R. Hanify Co., lumber (claim dated Dec. 24, 1929)... 1,113.21

(22) Santa Cruz Portland Cement Co., cement (claim dated Dec. 24, 1929) 1,578.00

(23) State Compensation Insurance Fund, premium on insurance covering Hetch Hetchy employees (claim dated Dec. 24, 1929) 7,671.82

(24) Standard Oil Co. of Calif., gasoline, etc. (claim dated Dec. 24, 1929) 675.42

(25) Standard Oil Co. of Calif., gasoline, grease, etc. (claim dated Dec. 24, 1929) 659.69

(26) Wilsey, Bennett Co., butter and cheese (claim dated Dec. 24, 1929) 836.26

(27) Sherry Bros., Inc., eggs (claim dated Dec. 24, 1929)... 593.40

County Road Fund.

(28) Pacific Coast Aggregates, Inc., gravel for street reconstruction (claim dated Dec. 18, 1929)....................$ 906.56

(29) Pacific Coast Aggregates, Inc., gravel for street reconstruction (claim dated Dec. 19, 1929)................... 847.06

(30) San Francisco Materials Co., cement for street reconstruction (claim dated Dec. 18, 1929)................... 858.00

(31) Santa Cruz Portland Cement Co., cement for street reconstruction (claim dated Dec. 18, 1929) 876.48

(32) Equitable Asphalt Maintenance Co., resurfacing of streets (claim dated Dec. 23, 1929)...................... 1,307.36

(33) Eclipse Lime & Cement Co., cement for reconstruction of streets (claim dated Dec. 23, 1929)................... 881.76

(34) Santa Cruz Portland Cement Co., cement for reconstruction of streets (claim dated Dec. 23, 1929)............... 881.76

(35) Stores & Yards Account, Board of Public Works, reimbursement for account of repairs to equipment (claim dated Dec. 16, 1929) 1,256.00

(36) Pacific Coast Aggregates, Inc., sand and gravel for reconstruction of streets (claim dated Dec. 27, 1929)........ 4,123.43

(37) Sibley Grading & Teaming Co., sand for street reconstruction (claim dated Dec. 27, 1929) 1,076.25

Tax Judgments—Appropriation 57.

(38) Oscar Samuels and J. Samuels, as Attorneys for Judgment Creditors, one-tenth of final judgment, plus interest; fifth payment (claim dated Dec. 12, 1929)...............$ 1,165.89

General Fund, 1929-1930.

(39) Dudley B. Perkins, Police Dept. motorcycle repairs and
equipment (claim dated Dec. 30, 1929)....................$ 667.21
(40) The Gunn Furniture Co., office equipment for County
Welfare Dept. (claim dated Dec. 30, 1929)...............   502.00
(41) San Francisco Society for the Prevention of Cruelty to
Animals, impounding, feeding, etc., of animals (claim dated
Jan. 6, 1930)......................................   1,500.00
(42) San Francisco Chronicle, official advertising (claim
dated Jan. 6, 1929) 3,022.68
(43) California Meat Co., meat for San Francisco Hospital
(claim dated Nov. 30, 1929) 1,889.52
(44) Haas Brothers, groceries, S. F. Hospital (claim dated
Nov. 30, 1929) 698.56
(45) Scatena-Galli Fruit Co., fruit and produce, S. F. Hospital (claim dated Nov. 30, 1929) 897.63
(46) Building Supplies Co., soap chips, etc., S. F. Hospital
(claim dated Nov. 30, 1929) 531.99
(47) A. Levy &. J. Zentner Co., fruit and produce, S. F. Hospital (claim dated Nov. 30, 1929) 1,149.78
(48) Richfield Oil Co., fuel oil, S. F. Hospital (claim dated
Nov. 30, 1929) 1,866.87
(49) Western Meat Co., meat, S. F. Hospital (claim dated
Nov. 30, 1929) 639.82
(50) Del Monte Meat Co., meats, S. F. Hospital (claim dated
Nov. 30, 1929) 1,402.61
(51) Fred L. Hilmer Co., butter, etc., S. F. Hospital (claim
dated Nov. 30, 1929) 1,925.32
(52) Wilsey, Bennett Co., eggs, S. F. Hospital (claim dated
Nov. 30, 1929) 2,452.55
(53) San Francisco Dairy Co., milk, S. F. Hospital (claim
dated Nov. 30, 1929) 4,149.14
(54) L. M. Wilbor, M. D., Supt. of San Francisco Hospital,
for January room allowance to Hospital employees (claim
dated Nov. 30, 1929) 3,500.00

Ayes—Supervisors Canepa, Colman, Hayden, McGovern, McSheehy,
Miles, Rossi, Shannon, Spaulding, Stanton, Suhr, Toner—12.

Absent—Supervisors Andriano, Gallagher, Havenner, Peyser, Power,
Roncovieri—6.

Authorizations.

Also, Resolution No. 31910 (New Series), as follows:

Resolved, That the following amounts be and the same are hereby
authorized to be expended out of the hereinafter mentioned funds in
payment to the following named claimants, to-wit:

Sewer Bond Construction Fund, Issue 1929.

(1) Thomson, Wood & Hoffman, examining proceedings and
furnishing opinion approving validity of 1929 Sewer Bonds
(claim dated Dec. 19, 1929).............................$ 650.00

Hospital Bond Construction Fund, Issue 1929.

(2) Thomson, Wood & Hoffman, examining proceedings and
furnishing opinion approving validity of 1929 Hospital
Bonds (claims dated Dec. 19, 1929)....................$ 1,000.00

Hetch Hetchy Water Construction Fund, Bond Issue 1928.

(3) Bald Eagle Market, meat and fish (claim dated Dec. 18,
1929) ....$ 679.76
(4) Dr. Paul E. Dolan, medical service rendered Hetch
Hetchy employees (claim dated Dec. 18, 1929)...........   777.75
(5) J. H. McCallum, lumber furnished (claim dated Dec.
18, 1929) 1,011.11

School Construction Fund, Bond Issue 1923.

(6) C. F. Weber & Co., gymnasium equipment furnished Polytechnic High School (claim dated Dec. 23, 1929)...........$ 958.97

Hetch Hetchy Power Operative Fund.

(7) Depreciation Fund, Hetch Hetchy Power Operative, reserve for depreciation, per Charter requirement (claim dated Dec. 19, 1929) $14,584.00

Tax Judgments—Appropriation 57.

(8) Brobeck, Phleger & Harrison, as attorneys, for account of judgment holders, seventh installment, per schedule attached (claim dated Dec. 28, 1929)......................$ 800.92

(9) Brobeck, Phleger & Harrison, as attorneys, for account of judgment holders, seventh installment, per schedule attached (claim dated Dec. 28, 1929)...................... 17,615.31

General Fund, 1928-1929.

(10) Frank J. Reilly, seventh payment, general contract, construction of M. H. deYoung Memoriam Museum (claim dated Dec. 27, 1929) ....$ 9,407.25

(11) California Pottery Co., sewer pipe furnished for sewer extension and reconstruction (claim dated Dec. 23, 1929).. 845.10

(12) Richfield Oil Co. of California, fuel oil furnished Civic Center powerhouse (claim dated Dec. 21, 1929)........... 840.89

(13) Graybar Electric Co., copper wire, etc., furnished Department of Electricity (claim dated Nov. 30, 1929)....... 1,028.36

(14) H. E. Teller Co, coffee furnished San Francisco Hospital (claim dated Nov. 30, 1929)............................ 620.00

(15) H. F. Dugan Co., chemical and surgical supplies furnished San Francisco Hospital (claim dated Nov. 30, 1929) 888.17

(16) Seabury & Johnson, gauze, etc., furnished San Francisco Hospital (claim dated Nov. 30, 1929).................... 1,524.00

(17) Haas Brothers, groceries furnished San Francisco Hospital (claim dated Nov. 30, 1929)....................... 665.95

(18) Western Meat Co., meat furnished San Francisco Hospital (claim dated Nov. 30, 1929)...................... 898.48

(19) Spring Valley Water Co., water furnished San Fransico Hospital (claim dated Nov. 30, 1929)................ 1,684.13

(20) Seabury & Johnson, gauze, etc., furnished Laguna Honda Home (claim dated Nov. 30, 1929)................ 795.00

Ayes—Supervisors Canepa, Colman, Hayden, McGovern, McSheehy, Miles, Rossi, Shannon, Spaulding, Stanton, Suhr, Toner—12.

Absent—Supervisors Andriano, Gallagher, Havenner, Peyser, Power, Roncovieri—6.

Appropriation, County Road Fund, Improvement of Twentieth Street From San Bruno Avenue to Vermont Street.

Also, Resolution No. 31911 (New Series), as follows:

Resolved, That the sum of $2,943.05 be and the same is hereby set aside, appropriated and authorized to be expended out of County Road Fund to defray the cost of the improving of Twentieth street between San Bruno avenue and Vermont street and the crossing of Twentieth street and San Bruno avenue, at city property.

Ayes—Supervisors Canepa, Colman, Hayden, McGovern, McSheehy, Miles, Rossi, Shannon, Spaulding, Stanton, Suhr, Toner—12.

Absent—Supervisors Andriano, Gallagher, Havenner, Peyser, Power, Roncovieri—6.

Payment to Crocker First National Bank, Fees as Fiscal Agent.

Also, Resolution No. 31912 (New Series), as follows:

Resolved, That the sum of $844.45 be and the same is hereby set aside and appropriated out of Urgent Necessity, Budget Item No. 24, and authorized in payment to Crocker First National Bank; being payment for expenses in connection with payment of interest on San Francisco bonds, as fiscal agent.   Final payment.

Ayes—Supervisors Canepa, Colman, Hayden, McGovern, McSheehy, Miles, Rossi, Shannon, Spaulding, Stanton, Suhr, Toner—12.

Absent—Supervisors Andriano, Gallagher, Havenner, Peyser, Power, Roncovieri—6.

Reimbursing Board of Works for Painting Traffic Signs.

Also, Resolution No. 31913 (New Series), as follows:

Resolved, That the sum of $1,441.81 be and the same is hereby set aside and appropriated out of "Traffic Signals, etc.," Budget Item No. 57, to the credit of Budget Item No. 442, Board of Public Works; being reimbursement for labor and material expended in the painting of traffic signs, lines and curbing during the month of November, 1929.

Ayes—Supervisors Canepa, Colman, Hayden, McGovern, McSheehy, Miles, Rossi, Shannon, Spaulding, Stanton, Suhr, Toner—12.

Absent—Supervisors Andriano, Gallagher, Havenner, Peyser, Power, Roncovieri—6.

Appropriation, County Road Fund, for Property Required for Widening of Ocean Avenue.

Also, Resolution No. 31914 (New Series), as follows:

Resolved, That the sum of $4,050 be and the same is hereby set aside and appropriated out of County Road Fund, and authorized in payment to Bernard L. Drake and Cora M. Drake, and City Title Insurance Company; being payment for Lot 16 in Block 3257, as per the Assessor's Block Books of the City and County of San Francisco, as per acceptance of offer by Resolution No. 31843 (New Series), and required for the widening of Ocean avenue.   (Claim dated Dec. 10, 1929.)

Ayes—Supervisors Canepa, Colman, Hayden, McGovern, McSheehy, Miles, Rossi, Shannon, Spaulding, Stanton, Suhr, Toner—12.

Absent—Supervisors Andriano, Gallagher, Havenner, Peyser, Power, Roncovieri—6.

Appropriations, Boulevard Bonds, Property for Sunset Boulevard.

Also, Resolution No. 31915 (New Series), as follows:

Resolved, That the following amounts be and the same are hereby set aside and appropriated out of Boulevard Bonds, Issue 1927, and authorized in payment to the hereinafter named persons; being payments for properties required for the Sunset boulevard, to-wit:

(1) To Louise Franz and City Title Insurance Co., for all of Lots 14 and 16 in Block 2365, as per the Assessor's Block Books, and authorized by Resolution No. ———— (New Series) accepting offer (claim dated Dec. 26, 1929).......$ 6,000.00

(2) To E. Sugarman and City Title Insurance Co., for Lot 21 in Block 2365, as per the Assessor's Block Books, and authorized by Resolution No. ———— (New Series) accepting offer (claim dated Dec. 26, 1929).................... 1,675.00

Ayes—Supervisors Canepa, Colman, Hayden, McGovern, McSheehy, Miles, Rossi, Shannon, Spaulding, Stanton, Suhr, Toner—12.

Absent—Supervisors Andriano, Gallagher, Havenner, Peyser, Power, Roncovieri—6.

Appropriations for Street Improvements, County Road Fund.

Also, Resolution No. 31916 (New Series), as follows:

Resolved, That the following amounts be and the same are hereby set aside, appropriated and authorized to be expended out of County Road Fund for the following improvements, to-wit:

(1) For the reconstruction of Broadway between Hyde and Jones streets, by the construction of a concrete pavement..$16,000.00
(2) For the construction of a three-rail fence, 1962 feet, on Geneva avenue from Mission street southerly............ 588.60

Ayes—Supervisors Canepa, Colman, Hayden, McGovern, McSheehy, Miles, Rossi, Shannon, Spaulding, Stanton, Suhr, Toner—12.

Absent—Supervisors Andriano, Gallagher, Havenner, Peyser, Power, Roncovieri—6.

Appropriation, Expense of Supervisor Suhr as San Francisco's Official Representative on Good Will Pacific Cruise of San Francisco Chamber of Commerce.

Also, Resolution No. 31917 (New Series), as follows:

Resolved, That the sum of $5,000 be and the same is hereby set aside and appropriated out of Publicity and Advertising, Appropriation 54, and authorized in payment to Fred Suhr, Supervisor, for his expense as official representative of the City and County of San Francisco in accompanying the San Francisco Chamber of Commerce on its good will Pacific cruise on the steamship "Mololo," as authorized by Resolution No. 31369, New Series. (Claim dated December 30, 1929.)

Ayes—Supervisors Canepa, Colman, Hayden, McGovern, McSheehy, Miles, Rossi, Shannon, Spaulding, Stanton, Suhr, Toner—12.

Absent—Supervisors Andriano, Gallagher, Havenner, Peyser, Power, Roncovieri—6.

Appropriation, $7,500, Additional Emergency Supplies, Board of Health.

Also, Resolution No. 31918 (New Series), as follows:

Resolved, That the sum of $7,500 be and the same is hereby set aside, appropriated and authorized to be expended out of "Urgent Necessity," Budget Item No. 24, Fiscal Year 1929-1930, for additional and emergency supplies by the Board of Health under the direction of the Superintendent of the Relief Home.

Ayes—Supervisors Canepa, Colman, Hayden, McGovern, McSheehy, Miles, Rossi, Shannon, Spaulding, Stanton, Suhr, Toner—12.

Absent—Supervisors Andriano, Gallagher, Havenner, Peyser, Power, Roncovieri—6.

Oil Tank Permits.

On recommendation of Fire Committee.

Resolution No. 31919 (New Series), as follows:

Resolved, That the following revocable permits be and the same are hereby granted:

Eugene Conway, 153 Eighth avenue, 1,500 gallons capacity.

Gray and Danielson, southeast corner of Nineteenth and Bryant streets, 1,500 gallons capacity.

Haley Bros., northeast corner of Turk and Polk streets, 1,500 gallons capacity.

Albert E. Hawley, northeast corner of Jackson and Walnut streets, 1,500 gallons capacity.

Ben Liebman, southwest corner of Fillmore street and Retiro Way, 1,500 gallons capacity.

Marian Realty Company, southwest corner of Pacific and Laguna streets, 1,500 gallons capacity.

C. N. Miller, south side of Marina boulevard, 150 feet east of Avila way, 1,500 gallons capacity.

National Sanitary Rag Company, 148 Townsend street, 1,500 gallons capacity.

New Eureka Laundry, 329 Noe street, 1,500 gallons capacity.

W. W. Nutter, 71 San Felipe avenue, 1,500 gallons capacity.

Sutter Theatre, west side of Steiner street, 120 feet south of Sutter street, 1,500 gallons capacity.

W. R. Voorhies, south side of Washington street, 165 feet west of Locust street, 1,500 gallons capacity.

The rights granted under this resolution shall be exercised within six months, otherwise said permits shall become null and void.

Ayes—Supervisors Canepa, Colman, Hayden, McGovern, McSheehy, Miles, Rossi, Shannon, Spaulding, Stanton, Suhr, Toner—12.

Absent—Supervisors Andriano, Gallagher, Havenner, Peyser, Power, Roncovieri—6.

Reimbursements to Board of Works for Work Done on Public Buildings.

On recommendation of Public Buildings and Lands Committee.

Resolution No. 31920 (New Series), as follows:

Resolved, That the following amounts be and the same are hereby set aside and appropriated out of the hereinafter mentioned Budget Items, General Fund, 1929-1930, to the credit of Bureau of Building Repair, Board of Public Works, Budget Item No. 442; being reimbursements for labor and materials furnished for account of work performed on public buildings, to-wit:

From "City Hall Repairs and Painting," Budget Item No. 54, for the gilding of ornamental iron work, City Hall.......$ 2,782.65

From "Repairs to Public Buildings, other than School Buildings," Budget Item No. 53, for construction of pits at Fire Department Corporation Yard 4,362.92

For flooring, etc., detective room, Hall of Justice........... 388.41

For miscellaneous carpentry, metal grills, etc., Juvenile Detention Home 1,367.90

For plumbing, etc., Chemical Engine No. 7................. 675.28

For repairs, plumbing, etc., Engine No. 21................. 725.68

For electrical work, Coroner's office 226.36

For construction of kitchen, Engine No. 6................. 1,106.40

For handball court, Engine House No. 10.................... 287.85

For new counter, etc., office of Chief of Police............. 780.00

Total $12,703.45

Ayes—Supervisors Canepa, Colman, Hayden, McGovern, McSheehy, Miles, Rossi, Shannon, Spaulding, Stanton, Suhr, Toner—12.

Absent—Supervisors Andriano, Gallagher, Havenner, Peyser, Power, Roncovieri—6.

Blasting Permit, Mount Vernon Avenue.

On recommendation of Streets Committee.

Resolution No. 31921 (New Series), as follows:

Resolved, That H. V. Tucker Company, Inc., be and is hereby granted permission, revocable at will of the Board of Supervisors, to explode blasts while grading on Mt. Vernon avenue, between Howth and Getz streets, and on Williar street between Mt. Vernon and Niagara streets, provided said permittee shall execute and file a good and sufficient bond in the sum of $5,000 as fixed by the Board of Public Works and approved by his Honor, the Mayor, in accordance with Ordinance No. 1204 (New Series); provided, also, that said blasts shall be exploded only between the hours of 7 a. m. and 6 p. m. and that the work of blasting shall be performed to the satisfaction of the Board of Public Works, and that if any of the conditions of this resolution be violated by said H. V. Tucker Company, Inc., then the privileges and all the rights accruing thereunder shall immediately become null and void.

Ayes—Supervisors Canepa, Colman, Hayden, McGovern, McSheehy, Miles, Rossi, Shannon, Spaulding, Stanton, Suhr, Toner—12.

Absent—Supervisors Andriano, Gallagher, Havenner, Peyser, Power, Roncovieri—6.

(At this point in the proceedings Supervisor Gallagher was noted present.)

Changing Grades on Sanchez Street Between the Southerly Line of Twenty-first Street and the Northerly Curb Line of Hill Street.

Also, Bill No. 9154, Ordinance No. 8661 (New Series), as follows:

Changing and reestablishing the official grades on Sanchez street between the southerly curb line of Twenty-first street and the northerly curb line of Hill street.

Whereas, the Board of Supervisors, on the written recommendation of the Board of Public Works, did on the 18th day of October, 1929, by Resolution No. 31508 (New Series), declare its intention to change and reestablish the grades on Sanchez street between the southerly curb line of Twenty-first street and the northerly curb line of Hill street.

Whereas, said resolution was so published for ten days, and the Board of Public Works within ten days after the first publication of said resolution of intention caused notices of the passage of said resolution to be conspicuously posted along all streets specified in the resolution, in the manner and as provided by law; and

Whereas, more than forty days has elapsed since the first publication of said resolution of intention; therefore,

Be it ordained by the People of the City and County of San Francisco as follows:

Section 1. The grades on the following named streets at the points hereinafter named and at the elevations above City base as hereinafter stated are hereby changed and established as follows:

Sanchez Street.

Twenty-first street northerly line 355 feet. (The same being the present official grade.)

Fifteen feet northerly from Twenty-first street southerly line 358.83 feet. (The same being the present official grade.)

Westerly curb line of, 47.91 feet northerly from the end of the arc, 61.55 feet southerly from Twenty-first street 360.30 feet.

Easterly curb line of, at points of reverse curve at Twenty-first street 360.30 feet.

Westerly curb line of, 16.76 feet southerly from the end of the arc, 61.55 feet northerly from Hill street 353.29 feet.

Easterly curb line of, 20.32 feet southerly from the end of the arc, 61.55 feet northerly from Hill street 353.29 feet.

Westerly curb line of, 47.90 feet southerly from the end of the arc, 61.55 feet northerly from Hill street 347.63 feet.

Easterly curb line of, at the point of reverse curve at Hill street 347.63 feet.

Fifteen feet southerly from Hill street northerly line 346.05 feet. (The same being the present official grade.)

Hill street southerly line 343 feet. (The same being the present official grade.)

On Sanchez street between the southerly curb line of Twenty-first street and the northerly curb line of Hill street changed and established to conform to true gradients between the grade elevations above given therefor.

Section 2. This ordinance shall take effect immediately

Ayes—Supervisors Canepa, Colman, Gallagher, Hayden, McGovern, McSheehy, Miles, Rossi, Shannon, Spaulding, Stanton, Suhr, Toner—13.

Absent—Supervisors Andriano, Havenner, Peyser, Power, Roncovieri—5.

Changing Grades on Goettingen Street Between Woolsey and Dwight Streets.

Also, Bill No. 9155, Ordinance No. 8662 (New Series), as follows:

Changing and reestablishing the official grades on Goettingen street between Woolsey and Dwight streets.

Whereas, the Board of Supervisors, on the written recommendation of the Board of Public Works, did on the 2nd day of November, 1929, by Resolution No. 31596 (New Series), declare its intention to change and reestablish the grades on Goèttingen street between Woolsey and Dwight streets.

Whereas, said resolution was so published for ten days, and the Board of Public Works within ten days after the first publication of said resolution of intention caused notices of the passage of said resolution to be conspicuously posted along all streets specified in the resolution, in the manner and as provided by law; and

Whereas, more than forty days has elapsed since the first publication of said resolution of intention; therefore,

Be it ordained by the People of the City and County of San Francisco as follows:

Section 1. The grades on the following named streets at the points hereinafter named and at the elevations above City base as hereinafter stated, are hereby changed and established as follows:

Goettingen Street.

Woolsey street southerly line, 81 feet. (The same being the present official grade.)

100 feet southerly from Woolsey street, 94.14 feet.

175 feet southerly from Woolsey street, 106.28 feet.

250 feet southerly from Woolsey street, 123 feet.

(Vertical curve passing through the last three described points.)

Dwight street northerly line, 161 feet. (The same being the present official grade.)

On Goettingen street between Woolsey and Dwight streets changed and established to conform to true gradients between the grade elevations above given therefor.

Section 2. This ordinance shall take effect immediately.

Ayes—Supervisors Canepa, Colman, Gallagher, Hayden, McGovern, McSheehy, Miles, Rossi, Shannon, Spaulding, Stanton, Suhr, Toner—13.

Absent—Supervisors Andriano, Havenner, Peyser, Power, Roncovieri—5.

Changing Grades on Corbett Avenue.

Also, Bill No. 9156, Ordinance No. 8663 (New Series), as follows:

Changing and reestablishing grades on Corbett avenue from Clayton street to Portola drive, as hereinafter described.

Whereas, the Board of Supervisors, on the written recommendation of the Board of Public Works, did, on the 2d day of November, 1929, by Resolution No. 31594 (New Series), declare its intention to change and reestablish the grades on Corbett avenue from Clayton street to Portola drive, etc., as shown on that certain diagram entitled "Grade Map of Corbett avenue from Clayton street to Portola drive showing the proposed change and establishment of grades on Corbett avenue and adjoining streets."

Whereas, said resolution was so published for ten days, and the Board of Public Works within ten days after the first publication of said resolution of intention ·caused notices of the passage of said resolution to be conspicuously posted along all streets specified in the resolution, in the manner and as provided by law; and

Whereas, more than forty days has elapsed since the first publication of said resolution of intention; therefore,

Be it ordained by the People of the City and County of San Francisco as follows:

Section 1. The grades on the following named streets, at the points hereinafter named and at the elevations above city base as hereinafter stated, are hereby changed and established as follows:

On Corbett avenue from Clayton street to Portola drive, etc., as shown on that certain diagram entitled "Grade Map of Corbett avenue from Clayton street to Portola drive showing the proposed change and establishment of grades on Corbett avenue and adjoining streets."

Section 2. This ordinance shall take effect immediately.

Ayes—Supervisors Canepa, Colman, Gallagher, Hayden, McGovern, McSheehy, Miles, Rossi, Shannon, Spaulding, Stanton, Suhr, Toner—13.

Absent—Supervisors Andriano, Havenner, Peyser, Power, Roncovieri—5.

Amending Section 2, Ordinance No. 6512 (New Series), Spur Track on Twelfth Street.

Also, Bill No. 9157, Ordinance No. 8664 (New Series), as follows:

Amending Section 2 of Ordinance No. 6512 (New Series) granting permission, revocable at will of the Board of Supervisors, to the Southern Pacific Company to operate with steam locomotives and cars over the tracks belonging to the City and County of San Francisco, formerly the property of the Ocean Shore Railway Company, as hereinafter described.

Be it ordained by the People of the City and County of San Francisco as follows:

Section 1. Section 2 of Ordinance No. 6512 (New Series), the title of which is above recited, is hereby amended to read as follows:

Section 2. "Provided, that no locomotive, car or cars shall be taken over this spur track on Twelfth street from Harrison street to Howard street, except between the hours of 6 o'clock a. m. and 8 a. m. and 1 p. m. and 4 o'clock p. m., and that the crossings of Harrison street and Folsom street be flagged on the passing of locomotives, car or cars."

Section 2. This ordinance shall take effect immediately.

Ayes—Supervisors Canepa, Colman, Gallagher, Hayden, McGovern, McSheehy, Miles, Rossi, Shannon, Spaulding, Stanton, Suhr, Toner—13.

Absent—Supervisors Andriano, Havenner, Peyser, Power, Roncovieri—5.

Changing Grades on Olney Avenue.

Also, Bill No. 9158, Ordinance No. 8665 (New Series), as follows:

Changing and re-establishing the official grades on Olney avenue between Third street and San Bruno avenue.

Whereas, the Board of Supervisors, on the written recommendation of the Board of Public Works, did on the 2nd day of November, 1929, by Resolution No. 31597 (New Series), declare its intention to change and re-establish the grades on Olney avenue between Third street and San Bruno avenue; and

Whereas, said resolution was so published for ten days, and the Board of Public Works within ten days after the first publication of said resolution of intention caused notices of the passage of said resolution to be conspicuously posted along all streets specified in the resolution, in the manner and as provided by law; and

Whereas, more than forty days has elapsed since the first publication of said resolution of intention; therefore,

Be it ordained by the People of the City and County of San Francisco as follows:

Section 1. The grades on the following named streets at the points hereinafter named and at the elevations above city base as hereinafter stated, are hereby changed and established as follows:

Olney Avenue.

Northeasterly line of, at Third street, 141.00 feet. (The same being the present official grade.)

Southwesterly line of, at Third street, 145.00 feet. (The same being the present official grade.)

22.50 feet southwesterly from the northeasterly line of, 60 feet northwesterly from Third street, 143.85 feet.

22.50 feet southwesterly from the northeasterly line of, 100 feet northwesterly from Third street, 146.41 feet.

22.50 feet southwesterly from the northeasterly line of, 140 feet northwesterly from Third street, 151.81 feet.

Vertical curve passing through the last three described points.

22.50 feet southwesterly from the northeasterly line of, 150.45 feet northwesterly from Third street, 153.59 feet.

22.50 feet southwesterly from the northeasterly line of, 170.45 feet northwesterly from Third street, 156.04 feet.

22.50 feet southwesterly from the northeasterly line of, 190.45 feet northwesterly from Third street, 156.60 feet.

Vertical curve passing through the last three described points.

22.50 feet northeasterly from the southwesterly line of, 60 feet northwesterly from Third street, 144.55 feet.

22.50 feet northeasterly from the southwesterly line of, 100 feet northwesterly from Third street, 146.59 feet.

22.50 feet northeasterly from the southwesterly line of, 140 feet northwesterly from Third street, 151.81 feet.

Vertical curve passing through the last three described points.

22.50 feet northeasterly from the southwesterly line of, 170.45 feet northwesterly from Third street, 157.00 feet.

Northeasterly line of, at San Bruno avenue easterly line, 155.40 feet. (The same being the present official grade.)

Southwesterly line of, at San Bruno avenue easterly line, 158.00 feet. (The same being the present official grade.)

On Olney avenue between Third street and San Bruno avenue changed and established to conform to true gradients between the grade elevations above given therefor.

Ayes—Supervisors Canepa, Colman, Gallagher, Hayden, McGovern, McSheehy, Miles, Rossi, Shannon, Spaulding, Stanton, Suhr, Toner—13.

Absent—Supervisors Andriano, Havenner, Peyser, Power, Roncovieri—5.

Changing Grades on Margaret Avenue.

Also, Bill No. 9159, Ordinance No. 8666 (New Series), as follows:

Changing and reestablishing official grades on Margaret avenue between Lakeview avenue and Ridge lane; on Louisburg street between Ridge lane and a line parallel with Mount Vernon avenue and 200 feet southerly therefrom; on Majestic avenue between Ridge lane and a line parallel with Lakeview avenue and 544.02 feet northerly therefrom; on Tara street between Mount Vernon avenue and Ridge lane; and on Ridge lane between Caine avenue and Howth streets as hereinafter described.

Whereas, the Board of Supervisors, on the written recommendation of the Board of Public Works, did on the 28th day of October, 1929, by Resolution No. 31,595 declare its intention to change and reestablish the grades on Margaret avenue between Lakeview avenue and Ridge lane; on Louisburg street between Ridge lane and a line parallel with Mount Vernon avenue and 200 feet southerly therefrom; on Majestic avenue between Ridge lane and a line parallel with Lakeview avenue and 544.02 feet northerly therefrom; on Tara street between Mount Vernon avenue and Ridge lane; and on Ridge lane between Caine avenue and Howth street as shown on that certain diagram entitled "Grade Map showing the proposed change and establishment of grades on Margaret avenue between Lakeview avenue and Ridge lane; on Louisburg street between Ridge lane and a line parallel with Mount Vernon avenue and 200 feet southerly there-from; on Majestic avenue between Ridge lane and a line parallel with Lakeview avenue and 544.02 feet northerly therefrom; on Tara street between Mount Vernon avenue and Ridge lane; and on Ridge lane between Caine avenue and Howth street."

Whereas, said resolution was so published for ten days, and the Board of Public Works within ten days after the first publication of said resolution of intention caused notices of the passage of said resolution to be conspicuously posted along all streets specified in the resolution in the manner as provided by law; and

Whereas, more than forty days has elapsed since the first publication of said resolution of intention; therefore

Be it ordained by the People of the City and County of San Francisco as follows:

Section 1. The grades on the following named streets at the points hereinafter named and at the elevations above City base as hereinafter stated, are hereby changed and established as follows:

On Margaret avenue between Lakeview avenue and Ridge lane; on Louisburg street between Ridge lane and a line parallel with Mount Vernon avenue and 200 feet southerly therefrom; on Majestic avenue between Ridge lane and a line parallel with Lakeview avenue and 544.02 feet northerly therefrom; on Tara street between Mount Vernon avenue and Ridge lane; and on Ridge lane between Caine avenue and Howth street as shown on that certain diagram entitled "Grade Map showing the proposed change and establishment of grades on Margaret avenue between Lakeview avenue and Ridge lane; on Louisburg street between Ridge lane and a line parallel with Mount Vernon avenue and 200 feet southerly therefrom; on Majestic avenue between Ridge lane and a line parallel with Lakeview avenue and 544.02 feet northerly therefrom; on Tara street between Mount Vernon avenue and Ridge lane; and on Ridge lane between Caine avenue and Howth street."

Section 2. This ordinance shall take effect immediately.

Ayes—Supervisors Canepa, Colman, Gallagher, Hayden, McGovern, McSheehy, Miles, Rossi, Shannon, Spaulding, Stanton, Suhr, Toner—13.

Absent—Supervisors Andriano, Havenner, Peyser, Power, Roncovieri—5.

Width of Sidewalks on Campbell Avenue Between San Bruno Avenue and Goettingen Street.

Also, Bill No. 9160, Ordinance No. 8667 (New Series), as follows:

Amending Ordinance No. 1061 entitled "Regulating the Width of Sidewalks," approved December 18, 1903, by amending sections Four-hundred and ninety-two and Six hundred and fifty-two thereof.

Be it ordained by the People of the City and County of San Francisco as follows:

Section 1. Ordinance No. 1061 entitled "Regulating the Width of Sidewalks," approved December 18, 1903, be and is hereby amended in accordance with the communication of the Board of Public Works, filed in this office December 19, 1929, by amending sections Four hundred and ninety-two and Six hundred and fifty-two thereof, to read as follows:

Section 492. The width of sidewalks on Campbell avenue between San Bruno avenue and Goettingen street shall be ten (10) feet.

The width of sidewalks on Campbell avenue between Goettingen street and Alpha street shall be as shown on that certain map entitled "Map of Campbell avenue between Goettingen street and Alpha street," showing the location of street and curb lines and the width of sidewalks.

Section 652. The width of sidewalks on Campbell avenue, the northerly side of, between Alpha street and Rutland street shall be twenty (20) feet.

The width of sidewalks on Campbell, the southerly side of, between Alpha street and Rutland street shall be ten (10) feet.

The width of sidewalks on Campbell avenue between Rutland street and Hoyt street shall be twelve (12) feet.

Section 2. Any expense caused by the above change of walk widths shall be borne by the property owners.

Section 3. This ordinance shall take effect and be in force from and after its passage.

Ayes—Supervisors Canepa, Colman, Gallagher, Hayden, McGovern, McSheehy, Miles, Rossi, Shannon, Spaulding, Stanton, Suhr, Toner—13.

Absent—Supervisors Andriano, Havenner, Peyser, Power, Roncovieri—5.

Width of Sidewalks on Alpha Street Between Goettingen Street and Tucker Avenue, Etc.

Also, Bill No. 9161, Ordinance No. 8668 (New Series), as follows:

Amending Ordinance No. 1061 entitled "Regulating the Width of Sidewalks," approved December 18, 1903, by amending section Six hundred and fifty-seven thereof.

Be it ordained by the People of the City and County of San Francisco as follows:

Section 1. Ordinance No. 1061 entitled "Regulating the Width of Sidewalks," approved December 18, 1903, be and is hereby amended in accordance with the communication of the Board of Public Works, filed in this office December 19, 1929, by amending section Six hundred and fifty-seven thereof, to read as follows:

Section 657. The width of sidewalks on Alpha street between Goettingen street and Tucker avenue shall be seven (7) feet.

The width of sidewalks on Alpha street between Tucker avenue and Campbell avenue shall be ten (10) feet.

The width of sidewalks on Alpha street between Campbell avenue and Teddy avenue shall be as shown on that certain map entitled "Map of Alpha street between Campbell avenue and Teddy avenue," showing the location of street and curb lines and the width of sidewalks.

The width of sidewalks on Alpha street between Teddy avenue and Leland avenue shall be ten (10) feet.

Section 2. Any expense caused by the above change of walk widths shall be borne by the property owners.

Section 3. This ordinance shall take effect and be in force from and after its passage.

Ayes—Supervisors Canepa, Colman, Gallagher, Hayden, McGovern, McSheehy, Miles, Rossi, Shannon, Spaulding, Stanton, Suhr, Toner—13.

Absent—Supervisors Andriano. Havenner, Peyser, Power, Roncovieri—5.

Width of Sidewalks on Somerset Street.

Also, Bill No. 9162, Ordinance No. 8669 (New Series), as follows:

Amending Ordinance No. 1061, entitled "Regulating the Width of Sidewalks," approved December 18, 1903, by adding thereto a new section to be numbered Ten hundred and eighty-eight.

Be it ordained by the People of the City and County of San Francisco as follows:

Section 1. Ordinance No. 1061, entitled "Regulating the Width of Sidewalks," approved December 18, 1903, be and is hereby amended in accordance with the communication of the Board of Public Works, filed in this office December 18, 1929, by adding thereto a new section to be numbered Ten hundred and eighty-eight, to read as follows:

Section 1088. The width of sidewalks on Somerset street between Campbell avenue and a point 112 feet northerly from Campbell avenue are hereby dispensed with and abolished.

The width of sidewalks on Somerset street between Campbell avenue and Rodeo avenue shall be as shown on that certain map entitled "Map of Somerset street between Campbell avenue and Rodeo avenue," showing the location of street and curb lines and the width of sidewalks.

Section 2. Any expense caused by the above change of walk widths shall be borne by the property owners.

Section 3. This ordinance shall take effect and be in force from and after its passage.

Ayes—Supervisors Canepa, Colman, Gallagher, Hayden, McGovern, McSheehy, Miles, Rossi, Shannon, Spaulding, Stanton, Suhr, Toner—13.

Absent—Supervisors Andriano, Havenner, Peyser, Power, Roncovieri—5.

Ordering the Improvement of Castro Street Between Twenty-ninth and Thirtieth Streets and on Thirtieth Street Easterly to the Existing Pavement.

Also, Bill No. 9163, Ordinance No. 8670 (New Series), as follows:

Ordering the performance of certain street work to be done in the City and County of San Francisco, approving and adopting specifications therefor.

Be it ordained by the People of the City and County of San Francisco as follows:

Section 1. The Board of Public Works, in written communication filed in the office of the Clerk of the Board of Supervisors December 10, 1929, having recommended the ordering of the following street work, the same is hereby ordered to be done in the City and County of San Francisco in conformity with the provisions of the Street Improvement Ordinance of 1918 of said City and County of San Francisco, said work to be performed under the direction of the Board of Public Works, and to be done in accordance with the specifications prepared therefor by said Board of Public Works, and on file in its office, which said plans and specifications are hereby approved and adopted.

That said Board of Supervisors, pursuant to the provisions of Part II of the said Street Improvement Ordinance of 1918 of said City and County of San Francisco, does hereby determine and declare that the assessment to be imposed for the said contemplated improvements, respectively, may be paid in twenty installments; that the period of time after the time of the payment of the first installment when each of the succeeding installments must be paid is to be six months from the time of the payment of the preceding installment, and that the rate of interest to be charged on all deferred payments shall be seven per centum per annum.

The improvement of Castro street from the existing pavement at the south line of Twenty-ninth street to Thirtieth street, and of Thirtieth street easterly to the existing pavement on Thirtieth street, by grading to official line and grade; by the construction of reinforced concrete stairways with 2-pipe railing, reinforced concrete wall, curbs, fence, gutters and coping; by the construction of ironstone pipe sewers with accompanying manholes, Y branches and side sewers; by the construction of brick catchbasins with accompanying 10-inch ironstone pipe culverts; by the construction of gutter sump and storm water inlets with accompanying ironstone pipe connections; by performing the necessary conform work at Twenty-ninth, Day and Thirtieth streets; by the construction of red warning lights and reflectors to be furnished and installed on concrete fence; by the construction of an asphaltic concrete pavement, consisting of a 6-inch concrete foundation and a 1½-inch asphaltic concrete wearing surface; and of a concrete pavement; and artificial stone sidewalks, all to conform to Plans A-7491 and A-7492, on file in the office of the City Engineer.

Section 2. This ordinance shall take effect immediately.

Ayes—Supervisors Canepa, Colman, Gallagher, Hayden, McGovern, McSheehy, Miles, Rossi, Shannon, Spaulding, Stanton, Suhr, Toner—13.

Absent—Supervisors Andriano, Havenner, Peyser, Power, Roncovieri—5.

Plans for Fifteenth Street Sewer Authorized.

Also, Bill No. 9164, Ordinance No. 8671 (New Series), as follows:

Authorizing the preparation of plans and specifications for the construction of the Fifteenth street sewer, Section "A," Contract No. 3; ordering the construction of said sewer in accordance with said plans and specifications prepared therefor; authorizing and directing the Board of Public Works to enter into contract for the construction of said sewer, and permitting progressive payments to be made during the course of said work, the cost of said work to be borne out of Sewer Bonds, 1929.

Be it ordained by the People of the City and County of San Francisco as follows:

Section 1. The Board of Public Works is hereby authorized, instructed and empowered to prepare plans and specifications for the construction of Fifteenth street sewer, Section "A," Contract No. 3, and to enter into contract for the construction of said sewer, hereinbefore specified, which is hereby ordered, in accordance with said plans and specifications prepared therefor. The cost of said sewer to be borne out of funds of the Sewer Bonds, 1929.

Section 2. The Board of Public Works is hereby authorized and permitted to incorporate in the contract for the construction of said sewer conditions that progressive payments shall be made in the manner set forth in said specifications, on file in the office of the Board of Public Works, and as provided for by the Charter of the City and County of San Francisco.

Section 3. This ordinance shall take effect immediately.

Ayes—Supervisors Canepa, Colman, Gallagher, Hayden, McGovern, McSheehy, Miles, Rossi, Shannon, Spaulding, Stanton, Suhr, Toner—13.

Absent—Supervisors Andriano, Havenner, Peyser, Power, Roncovieri—5.

Appropriations for Boulevard Improvements.

Also, Resolution No. 31922 (New Series), as follows:

Resolved, That the following amounts be and the same are hereby set aside, appropriated and authorized to be expended out of Boulevard Bond Fund, Issue 1927, for the hereinafter mentioned boulevard improvements, to-wit:

(1) For improvement of Bay Shore boulevard, Section A, Potrero avenue to Silver avenue, Contract 6, to enable final payment $22,500.00

(2) For the improvement of the Sunset ·boulevard by grading 18,000.00

(3) For the improvement of the Great Highway, upper roadway, between Lincoln way and Sloat boulevard, by the placing of fill (Granfield, Farrar & Carlin contract)........ 37,875.50

Ayes—Supervisors Canepa, Colman, Gallagher, Hayden, McGovern, McSheehy, Miles, Rossi, Shannon, Spaulding, Stanton, Suhr, Toner—13.

Absent—Supervisors Andriano, Havenner, Peyser, Power, Roncovieri—5.

Appropriation, County Road Fund, Improvement of Evans Avenue.

Also, Resolution No. 31923 (New Series), as follows:

Resolved, That the sum of $3,425.10 be and the same is hereby set aside, appropriated and authorized to be expended out of County Road

Fund for the payment of the city's portion of the liability for the paving and sewering of Evans avenue from Marin to Army streets, and the paving of Evans avenue bridge and intersection at Selby street.

Ayes—Supervisors Canepa, Colman, Gallagher, Hayden, McGovern, McSheehy, Miles, Rossi, Shannon, Spaulding, Stanton, Suhr, Toner—13.

Absent—Supervisors Andriano, Havenner, Peyser, Power, Roncovieri—5.

Appropriation for Improvement of Miguel Street at Fairmount Park.

Also, Resolution No. 31924 (New Series), as follows:

Resolved, That the sum of $1,980 be and the same is hereby set aside, appropriated and authorized to be expended out of "Street Work in Front of City Property," Budget Item No. 34, for the improvement of Miguel street, fronting Fairmount Park, city property.

Ayes—Supervisors Canepa, Colman, Gallagher, Hayden, McGovern, McSheehy, Miles, Rossi, Shannon, Spaulding, Stanton, Suhr, Toner—13.

Absent—Supervisors Andriano, Havenner, Peyser, Power, Roncovieri—5.

Appropriation, County Road Fund, for Improvement of Waterville Street Between Silver Avenue and Augusta Street.

Also, Resolution No. 31925 (New Series), as follows:

Resolved, That the sum of $665 be and the same is hereby set aside, appropriated and authorized to be expended out of County Road Fund for the sewering and paving of Waterville street between Silver avenue and Augusta street and northerly portion of Silver avenue between Waterville street and Elmira street.

Ayes—Supervisors Canepa, Colman, Gallagher, Hayden, McGovern, McSheehy, Miles, Rossi, Shannon, Spaulding, Stanton, Suhr, Toner—13.

Absent—Supervisors Andriano, Havenner, Peyser, Power, Roncovieri—5.

Ordering the Improvement of Kirkham Street, Etc.

Also, Bill No. 9165, Ordinance No. 8672 (New Series), as follows:

Ordering the performance of certain street work to be done in the City and County of San Francisco, approving and adopting specifications therefor.

Be it ordained by the People of the City and County of San Francisco as follows:

Section 1. The Board of Public Works, in written communication filed in the office of the Clerk of the Board of Supervisors, May 7, 1929, having recommended the ordering of the following street work, the same is hereby ordered to be done in the City and County of San Francisco in conformity with the provisions of the Street Improvement Ordinance of 1918 of said City and County of San Francisco, said work to be performed under the direction of the Board of Public Works, and to be done in accordance with the specifications prepared therefor by said Board of Public Works, and on file in its office, which said plans and specifications are hereby approved and adopted.

That said Board of Supervisors, pursuant to the provisions of Part II of the said Street Improvement Ordinance of 1918 of said City and County of San Francisco, does hereby determine and declare that the assessment to be imposed for the said contemplated improvements, respectively, may be paid in ten installments; that the period of time after the time of the payment of the first installment when each of the succeeding installments must be paid is to be one year from the time of the payment of the preceding installment, and that the rate of interest to be charged on all deferred payments shall be seven per centum per annum.

The improvement of Kirkham street between the westerly line of Sixteenth avenue as produced southerly from the northwesterly corner of Sixteenth avenue and Kirkham street and the easterly line of Seventeenth avenue, by the construction of concrete curbs; by the construction of a 12-inch ironstone pipe sewer with accompanying Y branches and side sewers, and by the construction of an asphaltic concrete pavement, consisting of a 6-inch concrete foundation and a 1½-inch asphaltic concrete wearing surface, on the roadway thereof.

Section 2. This ordinance shall take effect immediately.

Ayes—Supervisors Canepa, Colman, Gallagher, Hayden, McGovern, McSheehy, Miles, Rossi, Shannon, Spaulding, Stanton, Suhr, Toner—13.

Absent—Supervisors Andriano, Havenner, Peyser, Power, Roncovieri—5.

PRESENTATION OF BILLS AND ACCOUNTS.

Your Finance Committee, having examined miscellaneous demands not required by law to be passed to print, and amounting to $82,888.81, recommends same be allowed and ordered paid.

Approved by the following vote:

Ayes—Supervisors Canepa, Colman, Gallagher, Hayden, McGovern, McSheehy, Miles, Rossi, Shannon, Spaulding, Stanton, Suhr, Toner—13.

Absent—Supervisors Andriano, Havenner, Peyser, Power, Roncovieri—5.

NEW BUSINESS.

Passed for Printing.

The following matters were *passed for printing*:

Authorizations.

On recommendation of Finance Committee.

Resolution No. ———— (New Series), as follows:

Resolved, That the following amounts be and the same are hereby authorized to be expended out of the hereinafter mentioned funds in payment to the following named claimants, to-wit:

Hetch Hetchy Construction Fund, Bond Issue 1928.

(1) Best Steel Casting Co., car wheels, Hetch Hetchy construction (claim dated Dec. 27, 1929)...................$ 716.25
(2) J. H. Creighton, truck hire (claim dated Dec. 27, 1929).. 626.29
(3) Del Monte Meat Co., meats (claim dated Dec. 27, 1929) 1,402.66
(4) Del Monte Meat Co., meats (claim dated Dec. 28, 1929).. 1,231.02
(5) Grier & Mead, steel concrete forms (claim dated Dec. 30, 1929) 1,750.00
(6) Delbert Hansen, truck hire (claim dated Dec. 30, 1929).. 1,262.42
(7) W. Haslam, hauling cement and sand (claim dated Dec. 27, 1929) 1,390.02
(8) Hammond Lumber Co., lumber (claim dated Dec. 27, 1929) 1,145.77
(9) John Johnson, truck hire (claim dated Dec. 28, 1929).... 586.50
(10) Montague Pipe & Steel Co., steel air pipe (claim dated Dec. 30, 1929) 2,014.03
(11) Owen-Oregon Lumber Co., lumber (claim dated Dec. 30, 1929) 1,247.63
(12) Alfred Pereira & Brothers, hauling cement, sand, etc. (claim dated Dec. 27, 1929)........................... 1,324.25
(13 Santa Cruz Portland Cement Co., cement (claim dated Dec. 30, 1929) 2,319.00
(14) St. Paul's Hospital, hospital service furnished Hetch Hetchy employees (claim dated Dec. 28, 1929)........... 833.55
(15) United States Rubber Co., rubber boots and coats (claim dated Dec. 30, 1929)................................. 1,777.40
(16) Virden Packing Co., meats (claim dated Dec. 30, 1929) 537.60

(17) Dodge, Sweeney Co., groceries (claim dated Jan. 2, 1930)   592.62

(18) General Electric Co., battery locomotive parts (claim dated Jan. 2, 1930).................................   514.42

(19) The Giant Powder Co. Con., explosives (claim dated Jan. 2, 1930) 4,500.00

(20) Ingersoll-Rand Co. of Calif., machinery parts (claim dated Jan. 2, 1930) 1,697.55

(21) Owen-Oregon Lumber Co., lumber (claim dated Jan. 2, 1930) 1,246.18

(22) Santa Fe Lumber Co., lumber (claim dated Jan. 2, 1930)   895.50

(23) Santa Cruz Portland Cement Co., cement (claim dated Jan. 2, 1930) 4,399.00

(24) Standard Oil Co. of Calif., gasoline and oils (claim dated Jan. 2, 1930) 757.90

(25) Western Iron Works, foot bridge truss span (claim dated Jan. 2, 1930) 509.75

(26) M. D. Jones, truck hire (claim dated Jan. 2, 1930)....   1,057.25

(27) Bald Eagle Meat Market, meat (claim dated Jan. 7, 1930)   551.54

(28) Pope & Talbot, lumber (claim dated Jan. 7, 1930)....   1,055.76

(29) Santa Cruz Portland Cement Co., cement (claim dated Jan 7, 1930) 896.50

Special School Tax.

(30) Jacks & Irvine, extra work, general construction of Roosevelt Junior High School (claim dated Jan. 4, 1930)..$ 7,597.56

(31) Anderson & Ringrose, extra work on general construction of Marina Elementary School (claim dated Dec. 30, 1929) 1,090.00

(32) D. A. Pancoast Co., for the furnishing of "Von Duprin" type panic bolts and dogging hooks for various schools (claim dated Dec. 30, 1929).........................   2,888.69

(33) Jacks & Irvine, seventh payment, general construction of Roosevelt Junior High School (claim dated Jan. 4, 1930)   8,477.59

(34) Larsen & Larsen, first payment, brick, tile and stone work for Roosevelt Junior High School (claim dated Jan. 7, 1930) 5,256.31

(35) Scott Co., fifth payment, mechanical equipment furnished Roosevelt Junior High School (claim dated Jan. 7, 1930) 2,746.20

(36) Scott Co., fifth payment, plumbing and gas-fitting for Roosevelt Junior High School (claim dated Jan. 7, 1930)   3,735.75

(37) Meyer Bros., second payment, general construction of additions to the Sunshine School (claim dated Jan. 4, 1930)   3,068.37

(38) Scott Co., first payment, mechanical equipment furnished for addition to Sunshine School (claim dated Jan. 7, 1930) 2,373.60

(39) Alta Electric Co., fifth payment, electrical work for Park-Presidio Junior High School (claim dated Jan. 7, 1930)   896.26

(40) Meyer Bros., fifth payment, general construction of Park-Presidio Junior High School (claim dated Jan. 4, 1930) ..   27,960.00

(41) Scott Co., fourth payment, plumbing and gas-fitting furnished Park-Presidio Junior High School (claim dated Jan. 7, 1930) 5,648.52

(42) Scott Co., fifth payment, mechanical equipment for Park-Presidio Junior High School (claim dated Jan. 7, 1930)....   2,529.75

(43) Alta Electric Co., third payment, electric work for Geary Street School (claim dated Jan. 7, 1930)................   1,147.50

(44) Meyer Bros., sixth payment, general construction of Geary Street School (claim dated Jan. 4, 1930)........   8,611.61

(45) Scott Co., third payment, mechanical equipment for Geary Street School (claim dated Jan. 7, 1930)............   1,660.50

(46) Scott Co., first payment, mechanical equipment for addi-

tion to Francisco Junior High School (claim dated Jan. 7, 1930) 1,946.25

(47) MacDonald & Kahn, second payment, general construction of viewing stand at the third unit of South Side (Balboa) High School (claim dated Jan. 4, 1930)............ 11,980.93

(48) The Electric Corporation of San Francisco, conduit furnished for schools (claim dated Jan. 6, 1930)............ 529.50

(49) J. H. McCallum, lumber furnished for schools (claim dated Jan. 6, 1930) 1,103.73

(50) Alta Electric Co., final payment, electrical work for Marina Elementary School (claim dated Jan. 7, 1930)...... 2,261.00

(51) Anderson & Ringrose, final payment, general construction of Marina Elementary School (claim dated Jan. 7, 1930) 43,135.23

Park Fund.

(52) Standard Fence Company, construction of fences for the Park, including labor and material (claim dated Jan. 10, 1930) ....$ 2,150.99

(53) Tay-Holbrook, Inc., pipe and plumbing supplies furnished the Park (claim dated Jan. 10, 1930)............... 2,837.20

Playground Fund.

(54) J. H. McCallum Lumber Company, lumber furnished for playgrounds (claim dated Jan. 8, 1930)...................$ 655.14

(55) State Compensation Insurance Fund, premium on insurance covering playground employments (claim dated Jan. 8, 1930) 973.86

(56) Tay-Holbrook, Inc., plumbing supplies furnished playgrounds (claim dated Jan. 8, 1930)..................... 749.66

Bernal Cut Construction Fund, Bond Issue 1927.

(57) MacDonald & Kahn, eleventh payment, improvement of Bernal Cut (claim dated Jan. 7, 1930)...................$17,700.00

Boulevard Construction Fund, Bond Issue 1927.

(58) Eaton & Smith, seventh payment, improvement of Junipero Serra boulevard (claim dated Jan. 7, 1930)........$13,500.00

(59) Federal Construction Company, seventh payment, improvement of Bay Shore boulevard, Section "E" (claim dated Jan. 7, 1930)..................................... 3,500.00

Spring Valley Water Bonds, Issue 1928.

(60) Thomson, Wood & Hoffman, for professional services, examining proceedings and opinion furnished (claim dated Jan. 6, 1930)...$ 3,750.00

Municipal Railway Fund.

(61) San Francisco City Employees' Retirement System, for pensions covering prior service of railway employees (claim dated Jan. 3, 1930)...................................$ 1,123.23

(62) Board of Public Works (Street Repair Department), reimbursement for paving work on replacement jobs for Municipal Railway during November, 1929 (claim dated Jan. 7, 1930)... 795.69

(63) Board of Public Works (Street Repair Department), reimbursement for asphalt repairs to Municipal Railway right of way during November, 1929) (claim dated Jan. 7, 1930).. 1,571.60

County Road Fund.

(64) Ajax Construction Company, first payment, for rearrangement of auxiliary water supply system pipe line in Rankin street between Islais Creek and Custer avenue (claim dated Dec. 30, 1929)...$ 1,000.00

(65) Eaton & Smith, City's portion of cost for improvement of Laidley street from Thirtieth to Noe streets (claim dated Jan. 7, 1930)... 11,061.52

(66) M. J. Lynch, City's portion of improvement of Twentieth street between Sanchez and Noe streets (claim dated Jan. 2, 1930) 24,571.58

Hetch Hetchy Power Operative Fund.

(67) The Diamond Match Company, material furnished for account of Hetch Hetchy Water Supply (claim dated Dec. 27, 1929) ....$ 991.02

(68) Hetch Hetchy Construction Fund, Bond Issue 1928, for material, supplies, equipment and services furnished and rendered the Hetch Hetchy Power Operative Fund during November, 1929 (claim dated Dec. 30, 1929)............... 9,351.82

(69) State Compensation Insurance Fund, premium covering insurance on Hetch Hetchy employments (claim dated Dec. 27, 1929) 764.50

(70) Standard Oil Company of California, gasoline and oils furnished (claim dated Dec. 27, 1929)..................... 1,343.13

Water Works Fund.

(71) H. O. Lindemann, refund of deposit, per Resolution No. 95613 (Second Series), Board of Public Works, for period July to December, 1929)...............................$ 1,110.20

Municipal Railway Fund.

(72) American Brake Shoe and Foundry Company of California, brake shoes furnished (claim dated Dec. 31, 1929)...$ 2,219.20

(73) Westinghouse Electric and Manufacturing Company, electric railway supplies (claim dated Dec. 31, 1929)........... 788.83

(74) Mack International Motor Truck Corporation, one 29-passenger bus, less allowance on used "White" bus (claim dated Dec. 27, 1929).. 7,797.00

(75) Pacific Gas and Electric Company, for the furnishing and installing of underground cable and overhead cable connecting Station "N" with Municipal Railway, Forest Hill Station, Twin Peaks Tunnel (claim dated Dec. 27, 1929)....... 1,536.78

(76) Payne's Bolt Works, tie rods for Municipal Railways (claim dated Dec. 27, 1929)............................. 503.28

(77) United States Steel Products Company, 200 rolled steel car wheels (claim dated Dec. 27, 1929)................... 7,200.00

Henri F. Windel Trust Fund.

(78) Duncan Matheson, Treasurer of City and County, for purchase of one Boulevard Bond, Issue 1927, No. 1352, maturing 1934, for the Henri F Windel Trust Fund; authorized by Resolution No. 31866 (New Series) (claim dated Jan. 3, 1930) 1,000.00

Municipal Airport Fund.

(79) California Construction Company, second payment, construction of San Francisco Airport pavement, Contract 13 (claim dated Dec. 30, 1929)...........................$ 7,000.00

General Fund, 1929-1930.

(80) John Kitchen, Jr., Co., Superior Court minute books furnished the County Clerk (claim dated Oct. 18, 1929)........$ 696.00

(81) Recorder Printing and Publishing Company, printing Supervisors' Calendar, Journal, etc. (claim dated Jan. 13, 1930) 927.97

(82) Recorder Printing and Publishing Company, printing Superior Court Calendars, etc. (claim dated Jan. 13, 1930).. 515.00

(83) William J. Quinn, contingent expense for Chief of Police,
month of January (claim dated Jan. 6, 1930).............. 750.00

(84) The Texas Company, gasoline furnished Police Department (claim dated Jan. 6, 1930)......:.............. 1,173.64

(85) Patrick & Co., license plates furnished the Auditor (claim
dated Jan. 13, 1930)..................................... 2,777.03

(86) Associated Charities, widows' pensions (claim dated Jan.
17, 1930) 7,450.00

(87) Eureka Benevolent Society, widows' pensions (claim
dated Jan. 17, 1930)..................................... 1,037.50

(88) Little Children's Aid, widows' pensions (claim dated Jan.
17, 1930) 5,999.59

(89) Dion R. Holm, legal services rendered in telephone rate
case, month of January (claim dated Jan. 7, 1930)......... 850.00

(90) N. Randall Ellis, engineering services rendered for month
of January in telephone rate case (claim dated Jan. 7, 1930). 750.00

(91) John J. Dailey, legal services rendered City Attorney for
month of January (claim dated Jan. 8, 1930).............. 850.00

(92) M. J. Lynch, first payment, furnishing, delivering and
erecting street signs (claim dated Jan. 7, 1930)............ 2,250.00

(93) Lindsay Construction Company, refund of amount expended for construction of auxiliary main sewer in London
street between France and Italy avenues (claim dated Jan. 7,
1930) 526.30

(94) County Road Fund (Ordinance No. 8462, New Series),
being reimbursement for account of expenditures in the covering of main sewers during November (claim dated Dec. 30,
1929) 1,354.50

(95) West Coast Iron and Wire Works, mesh wire, posts and
gates furnished San Francisco Health Farm (claim dated
Dec. 31, 1929)... 3,577.00

(96) O'Brien, Spotorno, Mitchell & Campagno, turkeys furnished Laguna Honda Home Dec. 21st (claim dated Dec. 31,
1929) 864.00

(97) Blue Ribbon Products Company, coffee furnished Laguna
Honda Home (claim dated Dec. 30, 1929).................. 613.00

(98) Dairydale San Francisco Dairy Company, milk furnished
Laguna Honda Home (claim dated Dec. 30, 1929).......... 2,341.20

(99) J. T. Freitas Co., eggs furnished Laguna Honda Home
(claim dated Dec. 31, 1930)............................. 2,006.25

(100) A. Levy and J. Zentner Co., produce furnished Laguna
Honda Home (claim dated Dec. 31, 1930).................. 878.60

(101) Spring Valley Water Company, water service thru Fire
Department hydrants during December (claim dated Dec. 31,
1929) 15,551.96

Adopted.

The following resolutions were *adopted*:

Appropriations, Sewer Construction and Auxiliary Water System.

On recommendation of Finance Committee.

Resolution No. 31926 (New Series), as follows:

Resolved, That the following amounts be and the same are hereby
set aside, appropriated and authorized to be expended out of the hereinafter mentioned funds for the following purposes, to-wit:

Extension and Reconstruction of Sewers, Budget Item No. 37.

(1) For cost of reconstructing existing sewer in De Long
street between San Diego avenue and Santa Cruz avenue..$ 490.00

General Fund, 1929-1930.

(2) For expense of rearrangement of water supply system pipe line in Rankin street between Islais street and Custer avenue, additional to enable final payment..............$ 120.15

Ayes—Supervisors Canepa, Colman, Gallagher, Hayden, McGovern, McSheehy, Miles, Rossi, Shannon, Spaulding, Stanton, Suhr, Toner—13.

Absent—Supervisors Andriano, Havenner, Peyser, Power, Roncovieri—5.

Cancellation of Sale of Property for Delinquent Taxes.

Also, Resolution No. 31927 (New Series), as follows:

Whereas, the following described property, now standing of record in the Veterans' Welfare Board of the State of California, was sold to the State June 27, 1929, for 1928 delinquent taxes. The same being State property the Auditor has recommended that said tax sales be cancelled and the City Attorney having consented thereto; therefore,

Resolved, That the Auditor be directed to cancel, as provided in Section 3804a of the Political Code, the following tax sales:

Vol. 11, Block 1578, Lot 20—Thos. J. and Rose C. Ryan; Sale No. 614.

Vol. 14, Block 1814, Lot 38—Henry Doelger; Sale No. 799.

Vol. 14, Block 1824, Lot 26-B—Joseph Estate Co.; Sale No. 805.

Vol. 14, Block 1825, Lot 21 and Imp.—Fredk. J. Luippold; Sale No. 807.

Vol. 15, Block 1918, Lot 14 and Imp.—Nels P. and Hedrig Johnson; Sale No. 859.

Vol. 15, Block 2026, Lot 5 and Imp.—Geo. H. and Mabel E. McCarthy; Sale. No. 901.

Vol. 16, Block 2116, Lot 1-B and Imp.—Oscar Swanson; Sale No. 980.

Vol. 16, Block 2201, Lot 1-P and Imp.—M. A. Calloghy; Sale No. 1064.

Vol. 16, Block 2201, Lot 4-G and Imp.—H. W. and E. F. Armbrust; Sale No. 1067.

Vol. 17, Block 2330, Lot 1-A and Imp.—Gensler-Lee Investment Corp.; Sale No. 1104.

Vol. 20, Block 2917, Lot 34 and Imp.—Peter Furnell; Sale No. 1424.

Vol. 22, Block 3158, Lot 15—John Leregen; Sale No. 1565.

Vol. 22, Block 3176, Lot 25 and Imp.—D. and E. M. McGilvery; Sale No. 1570.

Vol. 35, Block 5910, Lot 11 and Imp.—Peter Nelson; Sale No. 2391.

Vol. 35, Block 5910, Lot 18—Veterans' Welfare Board; Sale No. 2392.

Vol. 36, Block 6073, Lot 7 and Imp.—Emil Peterson; Sale No. 2479.

Vol. 36, Block 6074, Lot 8-B and Imp.—A. J. and H. A. Olsen; Sale No. 2480.

Vol. 38, Block 6402, Lot 3 and Imp.—Crocker Estate Co.; Sale No. 2671.

Vol. 42, Block 6992, Lot 3—Malessa H. Kaemmerling; Sale No. 3052.

Ayes—Supervisors Canepa, Colman, Gallagher, Hayden, McGovern, McSheehy, Miles, Rossi, Shannon, Spaulding, Stanton, Suhr, Toner—13.

Absent—Supervisors Andriano, Havenner, Peyser, Power, Roncovieri—5.

(At this point in the proceedings Supervisors Andriano and Roncovieri were noted present.)

Passed for Printing.

The following matters were *passed for printing*:

Amending Ordinance No. 5460 (New Series), Known as the "Ordinance of Additional Positions," in re County Clerk.

On recommendation of Finance Committee.

Bill No. 8166, Ordinance No. ———— (New Series), as follows:

Amending Section 14 of Ordinance No. 5460 (New Series), known as the "Ordinance of Additional Positions."

Be it ordained by the People of the City and County of San Francisco as follows:

Section 1. Section 4 of Ordinance No. 5460 (New Series), known as the "Ordinance of Additional Positions," is hereby amended to read as follows:

Subdivision (d) Fifty-four assistant register clerks, each at a salary of $2,400 a year. $129,600.

Subdivision (e) Twenty-two copyists, each at a salary of $2,400 a year, $52,800.

Section 2. This ordinance shall take effect from and after its passage.

Ordering the Construction of Film Vault, San Francisco Hospital, Plans and Specifications, Receipt of Bids, and Award of Contract.

Also, Bill No. 8167, Ordinance No. ———— (New Series), as follows:

Ordering the construction of film vault on the roof of the San Francisco Hospital in accordance with plans and specifications prepared for same which are hereby authorized to be prepared; authorizing and directing the Board of Public Works to enter into contract for said construction in accordance with plans and specifications prepared therefor.

Be it ordained by the People of the City and County of San Francisco as follows:

Section 1. The construction of a film vault on the roof of the San Francisco Hospital is hereby ordered, and the Board of Public Works is hereby authorized, instructed and empowered to prepare plans and specifications for the construction of said film valult, and to enter into contract for said construction in accordance with said plans and specifications prepared therefor.

Section 2. This ordinance shall take effect immediately.

Oil Tank and Boiler Permits.

On recommendation of Fire Committee.

Resolution No. ———— (New Series), as follows:

Resolved, That the following revocable permits be and are hereby granted:

Oil Tanks.

C. Heller, 1980 Jackson street, 1500 gallons capacity.

E. L. Shaffer, south side of Chestnut street, 261 feet west of Scott street, 300 gallons capacity.

Boiler.

National Sanitary Rag Company, 160 Townsend street, 50-horsepower.

The rights granted under this resolution shall be exercised within six months, otherwise said permit shall become null and void.

Granting Pacific Gas & Electric Company (San Francisco Division), Commercial Garage, Block Bounded by Shotwell, Folsom, Eighteenth and Nineteenth Streets.

Also, Resolution No. ———— (New Series), as follows:

Resolved, That Pacific Gas and Electric Company be and is hereby granted permission, revocable at will of the Board of Supervisors, to maintain and operate a commercial garage in block bounded by Shotwell, Folsom, Eighteenth and Nineteenth streets.

The rights granted under this resolution shall be exercised within six months, otherwise said permit shall become null and void.

Granting Automobile Parking Station Permit, W. J. Winthrop, North Side of Brannan Street, 80 Feet East of Third Street.

Also, Resolution No. ———— (New Series), as follows:

Resolved, That W. J. Winthrop be and is hereby granted permission, revocable at will of the Board of Supervisors, to maintain and operate an automobile parking station on the north side of Brannan street, 80 feet east of Third street.

The rights granted under this resolution shall be exercised within six months, otherwise said permit shall become null and void.

Granting Automobile Parking Station Transfer, Bert Brock, 210 Taylor Street.

Also, Resolution No. ———— (New Series), as follows:

Resolved, That Bert Brock be and is hereby granted permission, revocable at will of the Board of Supervisors, to have transferred automobile parking station permit heretofore granted J. N. Hughes by Resolution No. 25973 (New Series), for premises at 210 Taylor street.

The rights granted under this resolution shall be exercised within six months, otherwise said permit shall be come null and void.

Automobile Supply Station, F. W. Metzger, Scott and Waller Streets.

Also, Resolution No. ———— (New Series), as follows:

Resolved, That F. W. Metzger be and is hereby granted permission, revocable at will of the Board of Supervisors, to maintain and operate an automobile supply station on the northeast corner of Scott and Waller streets.

The rights granted under this resolution shall be exercised within six months, otherwise said permit shall become null and void.

(At this point in the proceedings Supervisor Power was noted present.)

Adopted.

The following resolutions were *adopted*:

Masquerade Ball Permit, San Francisco Schwaben Verein, Saturday, January 18, 1930, California Hall, Polk and Turk Streets.

On recommendation of Police Committee.

Resolution No. 31928 (New Series), as follows:

Resolved, That San Francisco Schwaben Verein be and it is hereby granted permission to hold a masquerade ball in California Hall, Polk and Turk streets, Saturday evening, January 18, 1930.

Ayes—Supervisors Andriano, Canepa, Colman, Gallagher, Havenner, Hayden, McGovern, McSheehy, Miles, Power, Roncovieri, Rossi, Shannon, Spaulding, Stanton, Suhr, Toner—17.

Absent—Supervisor Peyser—1.

Award of Contract, Velour Drapes and Valances, Mayor's Office.

On recommendation of Supplies Committee.

Resolution No. 31929 (New Series), as follows:

Resolved, That award of contract be hereby made to National Theatre Supply Company, on bid submitted December 23, 1929 (Proposal No. 546), for furnishing and installing velour drapes and valances in Mayor's suite of offices, City Hall, for the sum of $560.

Resolved, That a bond in the amount of $100 be required for faithful performance of contract.

Resolved, That all other bids submitted thereon be rejected.

Ayes—Supervisors Andriano, Canepa, Colman, Gallagher, Havenner, Hayden, McGovern, McSheehy, Miles, Power, Roncovieri, Rossi, Shannon, Spaulding, Stanton, Suhr, Toner—17.

Absent—Supervisor Peyser—1.

Loading Zones.

On recommendation of Traffic and Safety Committee.

Resolution No. 31930 (New Series), as follows:

Resolved, That the following list of loading zones, of the lengths specified, be established in front of or near the following addresses, in accordance with the provisions of Section No. 36 of Ordinance No. 7691 (New Series), as amended:

395-399—Ashton avenue, 18 feet—Richards' Drug Co.; U. S. Sub-Postoffice.

48 Beale street, 27 feet—Schroeder Dray Co., warehouse.

124 Buchanan street, 18 feet—State Teachers' College Library.

154 Buchanan street, 18 feet—State Teachers' College, main entrance.

372-380 Ellis street, 27 feet—Hetty Bros. Electric Co.; Olympic Flower Shop.

754-756 Folsom street, 18 feet—Associated Paint Mfg. Co.

243-247 Fremont street, 27 feet—O'Callaghan Drug Co., warehouse; 1 elevator.

135 Howard street, 27 feet—Payne's Bolt Works; 1 elevator; 5 entrances.

155 Howard street, 18 feet—Payne's Bolt Works; 2 freight entrances.

201 Main street, 45 feet—Payne's Bolt Works; 3 elevators; 3 entrances.

2664 Mission street, 27 feet—Metropolitan Chain Store Co.; 1 elevator.

1368 Ninth avenue, 18 feet—Vogue Furniture Co.

1600 Ocean avenue, 18 feet—Westwood Cleaners; Blair's Hdw. Co.

859 O'Farrell street, 27 feet—Blanco's Restaurant.

1695 O'Farrell street, 27 feet—Onorato Market, freight entrance.

115 Post street, 18 feet—L. C. Smith Co., 1 elevator; assists street car loading.

280 Post street, 18 feet—Maison Mendessolle Co.; assists street car loading.

621 Stockton street, 18 feet—Altair Apts., 1 oil intake.

242 Turk street, 27 feet—Von Dorn Hotel, 1 elevator, 1 oil intake.

Ayes—Supervisors Andriano, Canepa, Colman, Gallagher, Havenner, Hayden, McGovern, McSheehy, Miles, Power, Roncovieri, Rossi, Shannon, Spaulding, Stanton, Suhr, Toner—17.

Absent—Supervisor Peyser—1.

Establishing Loading Zones.

Also, Resolution No. 31931 (New Series), as follows:

Resolved, That the following list of loading zones, of the lengths specified, be established in front of or near the following addresses, in accordance with the provisions of Section No. 36 of Ordinance No. 7691 (New Series), as amended:

1155 California street, 27 feet; Worden Hotel Apartments.

110 Davis street, 27 feet; Sand and Warehouse Company.

115 Davis street, 18 feet; Wright Popcorn and Nut Specialty Factory.

423 Ellis street, 18 feet; Liberty Grocery; Manila Cleaners.

441 Ellis street, 36 feet; Lassen Hotel Apartments; Artistic Laundry; Marty Grocery; 1 oil intake.

810 Jones street, 18 feet; Queen Anne Apartments; 1 oil intake.

520-522 Mason street, 27 feet; Medico-Dental Building; freight entrance; 1 oil intake.

9-11 Main street, 27 feet; Bay Building; 5 stores.

628 Montgomery street, 36 feet; Montgomery Block; Postal Telegraph Company; 1 oil intake.

151 Powell street, 18 feet; Herbert's Grill; 2 shops; 1 elevator.

43-49 Spear street, 27 feet; Southern Pacific Building, Annex "A"; 1 elevator.

2041 Polk street, 18 feet; Anderbery-McCoron Tin Shop.

Ayes—Supervisors Andriano, Canepa, Colman, Gallagher, Havenner, Hayden, McGovern, McSheehy, Miles, Power, Roncovieri, Rossi, Shannon, Spaulding, Stanton, Suhr, Toner—17.

Absent—Supervisor Peyser—1.

Rescinding and Reestablishing Loading Zones.

Also, Resolution No. 31932 (New Series), as follows:

Resolved, That the following loading zones, of the lengths specified, be rescinded and reestablished as specified herein, in front of or near the following addresses, in accordance with the provisions of Section No. 36 of Ordinance No. 7691 (New Series), as amended:

151-159 Powell street, existing length 36 feet, abolished; Herbert's Grill and Hotel; 2 small shops; 1 elevator.

207-217 Powell street, existing length 27 feet, new length 36 feet; 8-story loft building; Edwin Clapp Shoe Company; Apparel Shoppe; 2 elevators; Pacific Hair Goods Company.

Ayes—Supervisors Andriano, Canepa, Colman, Gallagher, Havenner, Hayden, McGovern, McSheehy, Miles, Power, Roncovieri, Rossi, Shannon, Spaulding, Stanton, Suhr, Toner—17.

Absent—Supervisor Peyser—1.

Establishing Passenger Loading Zones.

Also, Resolution No. 31933 (New Series), as follows:

Resolved, That the following list of passenger loading zones, of the lengths specified, be established in front of or near the following addresses, in accordance with the provisions of Section No. 36 of Ordinance No. 7691 (New Series), as amended:

79 Leavenworth street, 27 feet; Wm. Taylor Hotel passenger entrance.

100 McAllister street, 27 feet; Wm. Taylor Hotel passenger entrance.

516 O'Farrell street, 27 feet; Shawmut Hotel.

159 Powell street, 18 feet; Herbert's Bachelor Hotel.

1100 Union street, 27 feet; La Mirada Community Apartments.

Ayes—Supervisors Andriano, Canepa, Colman, Gallagher, Havenner, Hayden, McGovern, McSheehy, Miles, Power, Roncovieri, Rossi, Shannon, Spaulding, Stanton, Suhr, Toner—17.

Absent—Supervisor Peyser—1.

ROLL CALL FOR THE INTRODUCTION OF RESOLUTIONS, BILLS AND COMMUNICATIONS NOT CONSIDERED OR REPORTED UPON BY A COMMITTEE.

Advertising Community Chest Drive on Street Cars.

Supervisor Colman presented:

Resolution No. 31934 (New Series), as follows:

Resolved, That the Market Street Railway Company be and it is hereby granted permission to display cloth banners advertising the Community Chest campaign on the outside of their cars during the dates of the intensive drive, February 24 to March 7, 1930.

Adopted by the following vote:

Ayes—Supervisors Andriano, Canepa, Colman, Gallagher, Havenner, Hayden, McGovern, McSheehy, Miles, Power, Roncovieri, Rossi, Shannon. Spaulding, Stanton, Suhr, Toner—17.

Absent—Supervisor Peyser—1.

Statement of Supervisor Rossi on Behalf of Finance Committee.

SUPERVISOR ROSSI: We have before us today demands running possibly $50,000 to $55,000. I have received today a bill for $3,000 which I am informed was not authorized by this Board of Supervisors. Now, the reason this plan is being adopted is that we feel that it will place your Finance Committee in a position to know just exactly how every fund in the City and County finances will be from day to day, and I am sure that no member of the Board wants to place your Finance Committee in the position of their not being in a position to meet the obligations of the City when presented.

Just how some of the bills will be met I do not know. Your Finance Committee is endeavoring to see whether it is possible—through the City Attorney and the Auditors—for transfer to be made legally whereby all of the obligations can be faced.

Whether or not these bills were all legally and properly incurred, so far as I am concerned, I believe that all of these merchants who furnished goods or merchandise, or those who rendered services in good faith should be paid for those goods and services, and that this Board of Supervisors is, morally at least, obligated to see that they are paid, but in the future I suggest that this Board, the various committees of this Board and the various City departments, adopt the plan that no bills be contracted for without there first being presented to the Finance Committee, and they, in turn, will make a report to the Board. This is not intended in any spirit of criticism to any one, and we want your cooperation. We have our particular duty and function to perform and we are going to do it as well as we know how, and in doing it, we ask the cooperation of every member of the Board.

One other thing I want to report, the Police Department was good enough to assign one of the cars of that department with one of the chauffeurs to the Board for their use, but inasmuch as we have two other cars at the disposal of the Board, which was deemed sufficient, a communication was sent to the Police Department returning the car and the chauffeur to them and thanking them. In reference to another car, the use of which was discontinued, that was assigned to the Auditorium Committee and Supervisor Hayden has decided it will not be necessary, and speaking for myself individually in the matter I will not require it.

That's all I have to say, and I hope for the cooperation of the members of the Board.

SUPERVISOR SHANNON: I would like to ask, Mr. Mayor, due to the fact arrangements have been made by the representatives of the Horse Show, based on an appropriation that we made of $7,500, or a guarantee of the payment of $7,500, and that they have gone ahead with their preliminary arrangements, and the show is to be held next month, telegrams, as the result of the publicity given this entire matter, are being received by them. I understand the Los Angeles papers are printing daily entire columns and exact reproductions of everything that appears in the San Francisco papers, with a lot added——

SUPERVISOR ROSSI (interrupting): Boosts?

SUPERVISOR SHANNON: No, a lot of added knocks from the Los Angeles papers. Telegrams have come to Doctor Creely asking if the show is to be cancelled, and wanting to know just exactly what the position is, and people as far away as Denver have been sending in communications. I want to know if there is any legal way for the transfer of money, or if there is any question of guarantees being given Doctor Creely or representatives of this Horse Show, so that they will be able to answer telegrams, even if only tentative, to show that San Francisco is endeavoring to cooperate with them in this annual exhibit.

SUPERVISOR ROSSI: In reply to Supervisor Shannon, I will repeat again that in so far as the Finance Committee is concerned, we are making an honest endeavor to pay all obligations committed by this Board and members of this Board which have been made in the past. However, even the horses are in this position, there is a matter in Judge Goodell's court in which the decision, I understand, is to be given tomorrow, that will place us in a position to know whether any transfers of funds can be made from other city funds to the Publicity and Advertising Fund. If no transfers can be made to the Publicity and Advertising Fund, the next step is this: The City Attorney and the Auditors are going over all expenditures charged to the Publicity and Advertising Fund, and if any of those items can be charged up to any other fund, legally, we shall try and have that done, and it may give us leeway to take care of some of these obligations. Just how many demands are in the hands of the Auditors at this time I do not know, but I think in the neighborhood of $15,000 or $20,000. We have this condition confronting us: We have practically a commitment of approximately $50,000 confronting us at this time. Referring to the newspaper comments only, the Redwood Empire Association claims a commitment of $4,000 Christmas decorations, there is a demand in the Auditor's office of $5,000; another, of the California Development Association exhibit, $2,800; the float in the Pasadena Rose Tournament, approximately $1,000; these are obligations which have to be paid. Then there are other items of lesser amounts, and I repeat, totaling altogether a deficit of about $50,000. Then I received a bill here today for $3,000 for electrical work along the Golden Gate Park Panhandle. That was only presented today. How many other bills there are I do not know. Now, you can figure out the problem we have in seeing how they can be met. I am not in a position—I don't know what the other members of the Finance Committee think—but personally I am not in a position of guaranteeing any amount for a few days until it is decided whether transfers can be made. In the meantime, the City Attorney and Auditors are devising ways and means whereby these obligations can be met.

Finance Committee Requested to Make an Appropriation for Audit of Mills Field Municipal Airport From Its Inception Up to Date.

Supervisor Spaulding presented:

Resolution No. ————— (New Series), as follows:

Resolved, That the Finance Committee be and it is hereby requested to make an appropriation for the purpose of making a complete audit of the financial transactions of Mills Field Municipal Airport from the date of its inception to date.

Referred to Finance Committee.

Invitation Accepted, Central Mission Improvement Association.

Communication from Central Mission Improvement Association inviting attendance at its installation of officers January 14, 1930.

Invitation *accepted* on motion of Supervisor Gallagher.

Reclassification of Property on Marina.

A protest of property owners against reclassification of certain property on the Marina was read and *referred to the Committee on Industries and City Planning, meeting in chambers January 15, 1930, at 2 p. m.*

Supervisor Stanton moved that the Board of Public Works be requested to hold up permits until these committees report.

Motion *carried.*

Location of Veteran Hospital in San Francisco.

Supervisor Spaulding presented:

Resolution No. 31935 (New Series), as follows:

Whereas, the Rogers Bill (H. R. 234), which has been enacted by Congress and signed by the President on December 24, 1929, appropriates funds for additional hospital, domicilary and out-patient dispensary facilities for persons entitled to hospitalization under the World War Veterans' Act of 1924 as amended, and for other purposes; and

Whereas, the report of the House Committee accompanying said bill when brought up for vote before the House approved the program of the United States Veterans' Bureau for the expenditure of said moneys and the location of said hospitals, which was pursuant to recommendations of the National Rehabilitation Committee of the American Legion; and

Whereas, the program so approved includes the expenditure of the sum of $1,000,000.00 for a "New Hospital with facilities for diagnostic center and regional office" to be located at San Francisco; and

Whereas, on account of the fact that the ·bill itself leaves the ultimate location of the hospitals therein provided for to the discretion of the Director of the United States Veterans' Bureau, subject to the approval of the President, other communities in California are taking steps to secure for their respective communities the construction of said hospital recommended for San Francisco; and

Whereas, the proposed hospital is primarily designed to be a diagnostic center, and San Francisco by reason of its medical schools is the recognized center on the Pacific Coast of the most eminent medical specialists and for that reason was recommended as the place of location of said hospital which would be to the best interests of the veterans to be served as well as the medical profession involved; now, therefore, be it

Resolved, That this Board of Supervisors take active steps to secure and assure the carrying out of said report locating said hospital at San Francisco and that it urge upon the Director of the Veterans' Bureau that selfish community interests be not permitted to interfere with the welfare of veterans entitled to medical aid, and that the hospital be located as recommended at San Francisco; be it

Further Resolved, That a copy of this resolution, duly attested, be transmitted to the President of the United States, General Frank T. Hines, Director of the United States Veterans' Bureau, our two United States Senators, all Congressmen and the Congresswoman from California, the public press, and the Chamber of Commerce of San Francisco; and that a special committee of this Board be appointed by the Mayor to take such other and further immediate steps to that end as they may be advised, and to report back to this Board.

Adopted by the following vote:

Ayes—Supervisors Andriano, Canepa, Colman, Gallagher, Havenner, Hayden, McGovern, McSheehy, Miles, Power, Roncovieri, Rossi, Shannon, Spaulding, Stanton, Suhr, Toner—17.

Absent—Supervisor Peyser—1.

Honolulu Thanks Board for Reception of Its Fire Chief.

Communication from Mayor Rolph, transmitting resolutions of the Board of Supervisors of the City of Honolulu thanking San Francisco for courtesies extended to its Fire Chief during his recent visit, and a copy of the communication in reply sent by Mayor Rolph.

Read by the Clerk, who was directed to acknowledge in behalf of the Board of Supervisors.

San Francisco Census.

The following was read by the Clerk:

Communication from Felton Taylor, Supervisor of Census, Sixth District of California, advising that the census enumeration of the population of San Francisco will be taken by the United States Bureau of Census from April 1 to 15, 1930, bespeaking cooperation in said work and offering to appear and address the Board on the subject any time after January 15, 1930. ˘

Referred to Finance and Industrial Development Committee and Clerk directed to extend invitation to Mr. Taylor to address the Board.

Dirigible Base at Sunnyvale.

The following was read by the Clerk:

Communication from Florence P. Kahn, member of Congress, assuring Board of her continued efforts in behalf of the selection of Sunnyvale as site for the proposed naval dirigible base; also, acknowledging resolution of Board of Supervisors on subject.

Ordered *filed*.

Sale of School Property.

A communication from the Mayor, transmitting resolution of Board of Education, recommending sale of unnecessary school property, formerly Boys' High School.

Referred to Public Buildings Committee.

Conference for Revision of State Road District Act.

The following was read by the Clerk:

Communication from Redwood Empire Association, calling attention to meeting of Supervisors of Northern California in Sacramento January 17, 1930, for the purpose of going fully into the matter of the proposed revision of the State Road District Act, and requesting that San Francisco send representatives.

Supervisors Suhr, Gallagher and Canepa were delegated to attend.

ADJOURNMENT.

There being no further business the Board at 6:15 p. m. adjourned.

J. S. DUNNIGAN, Clerk.

Approved by the Board of Supervisors February 3, 1930.

Pursuant to Resolution No. 3402 (New Series) of the Board of Supervisors of the City and County of San Francisco, I, John S. Dunnigan, hereby certify that the foregoing are true and correct copies of the Journal of Proceedings of said Board of the dates stated and approved as above recited.

JOHN S. DUNNIGAN,
Clerk of the Board of Supervisors,
City and County of San Francisco.

Vol. 25—New Series

No. 3

Monday, January 20, 1930

Journal of Proceedings
Board of Supervisors

City and County of San Francisco

The Recorder Printing and Publishing Company
337 Bush Street, S. F.

JOURNAL OF PROCEEDINGS
BOARD OF SUPERVISORS

MONDAY, JANUARY 20, 1930, 2 P. M.

In Board of Supervisors, San Francisco, Monday, January 20, 1930, 2 p. m.

, The Board of Supervisors met in regular session.

CALLING THE ROLL.

· The roll was called and the following Supervisors were noted present:

Supervisors Andriano, Canepa, Colman, Gallagher, Havenner, Hayden, McGovern, McSheehy, Miles, Roncovieri, Rossi, Shannon, Spaulding, Stanton, Suhr, Toner—16.

Absent—Supervisors Peyser, Power—2.

Quorum present.

His Honor Mayor Rolph presiding.

APPROVAL OF JOURNAL.

The Journal of Proceedings of the previous meeting was laid over for approval until next meeting.

ROLL CALL FOR PETITIONS AND COMMUNICATIONS.

Joint Highway District Laws Study.

The following was presented and read by the Clerk:

Communication, from Andrew J. Gallagher and Victor J. Canepa, delegates to the Joint Committee of the Senate and the Assembly to Study Joint Highway District Laws of the State of California, declaring that the said Joint Committee met in Sacramento on Friday, January 18, 1930, at 10 a. m., at which time they proceeded to discuss the present Joint Highway District Act. A quorum of the committee not being present, the meeting resolved itself into a discussion of the shortcomings of the Act and possible recommendations for its amendment. In view of the fact that the actions of the Joint Senate and Assembly Committee may result in the saving of millions of dollars to the people of San Francisco, we advise and suggest that this Board and the highway districts of which we are a part be hereafter represented at each of these meetings, and that we offer them every cooperation.

Ordered *filed.*

Relating to the Preservation of the Coast Line of the State of California.

The following was presented and read by the Clerk:

Communication, from George R. Bliss, secretary of the Joint Legislative Committee on Seacoast Conservation, inviting the Board of Supervisors to attend the coming session of the committee, to be held at 10 a. m. Monday, January 27, Room 803 Associated Realty Building, Los Angeles, at which time a map of a portion of Santa Barbara County, showing results of survey of waterfront of that county, will be exhibited and cooperation will be asked in getting a survey made of the entire coast line from Mexico to Oregon, with a view to the development of navigation, commerce, fisheries, mineral and oil production, as well as the development of sites for residential, recreational and scenic purposes.

Ordered *filed*.

James Allan & Sons' New Abattoir.

Supervisor Gallagher presented:

Communication, from James Allan & Sons, calling attention to the near completion of a new reinforced concrete building for slaughter-house and livestock purposes, and declaring that they have endeavored to make it a modern and model plant in every respect, representing a large investment in the Butchertown district, and requesting assistance in having the street on Evans avenue approaching said property brought to grade to enable the installation of sidewalks at proper levels and to give necessary drainage facilities for carrying on the business in a sanitary way.

Referred to Streets Committee.

Protest Against Operation of Amphibian Planes at the Marina.

Communication, from the Marina District Improvement Association, calling attention to their previous appeal for protection against the establishment and operation of a seaplane base at the Marina and stating that the Curtis-Wright Flying Service has been operating an amphibian plane transportation and ferry service north of Marina boulevard, between Laguna and Buchanan streets, and declaring that the operation of this base is affecting the health, happiness and welfare of many citizens on account of the excessive noise of the plane, low flying and attendant danger, and, therefore, again appealing to the Board of Supervisors for relief, believing that it is within the authority of the City, through its police powers and existing official ordinances governing transportation business, to bring action looking to the discontinuance of the alleged unnecessary amphibian plane and base operations at the Marina.

Referred to the Education, Parks and Playgrounds Committee.

Request That War Memorial Construction Be Expedited.

The following was presented and read by the Clerk:

Communication from North Beach Promotion Association transmitting copy of resolution unanimously adopted by said Organization, declaring that any further delay in the construction of the War Memorial would be disgraceful and inexcusable, and urging those in authority, in the interest of the unemployed, the veterans and the general public, bury their differences and proceed immediately with the project.

Ordered *filed*.

Embarcadero Bottle Neck.

The following was presented and read by the Clerk:

Communication from Board of State Harbor Commissioners, referring to property on the west line of The Embarcadero between Clay and Merchant streets which encroaches on The Embarcadero to such an extent as to cause a bottle neck through which narrow passage it is difficult for vehicles to pass and which especially interferes with the Fire Department equipment; declaring that said Board of Harbor Commissioners has set aside budget appropriation of $150,000 toward the acquisition of this property and requesting that the sum of $55,000 be provided by the City of San Francisco toward the purchase price of $205,000, with a view to correcting this condition.

Referred to Streets Committee.

Communication from Jesse C. Colman, Supervisor.

Calling attention to two blocks on Pacific avenue from Lyon street to Presidio avenue recently paved with brick, declaring that the grades are very steep and in wet weather there have been an unusually large number of accidents, and requesting that steps be taken to eliminate this hazardous condition.

Referred to Streets Committee.

Yacht Harbor Development.

Supervisor Gallagher presented;

Communication from the Associated Boat Industries, transmitting data on yacht harbors located in Southern California, which purports to give information as to the value of a large fleet of pleasure boats to San Francisco as a means of additional revenue, and with an idea of inducing San Francisco to exert itself in every way to bring about the expansion of facilities for mooring or parking boats, in order that the boat building industry might be stimulated.

Also, communication from the Associated Boat Industries, addressed to the Board of Supervisors, transmitting copy of resolution of its organization, adopted January 17, requesting the cooperation of San Francisco in the development of the Yacht Harbor on the Marina at the earliest possible date.

Referred to Joint Committee on Education, Parks and Playgrounds and Industrial Development.

Action Deferred.

The following matter was *laid over one week and made a Special Order of Business for 4 p. m., Monday, January 27, 1930:*

RULES OF PROCEEDINGS OF THE BOARD OF SUPERVISORS.

Resolved, That the rules hereinafter set forth be and the same are hereby adopted as the Rules of Proceedings of this Board of Supervisors, to-wit:

STANDING COMMITTEES.

1. The following shall constitute the standing committees of the Board (the first named member to be chairman thereof):

Airport and Aeronautics—Spaulding, Peyser, Miles.

Auditorium—Hayden, Canepa, Colman.

Civil Service—Havenner, McSheehy, Rossi.

Education, Parks and Playgrounds—McSheehy, Suhr, Andriano.

Finance—Rossi, Power, Hayden.

Fire—Canepa, Peyser, Toner.

Industrial Development and City Planning—Gallagher, Stanton, Hayden.

Judiciary—Suhr, Andriano, Roncovieri.

Lighting, Water and Telephone Service and Electricity—Stanton, McGovern, Shannon.

Municipal Concerts and Public Celebrations—Roncovieri, Colman, Toner.

Police and Licenses—Andriano, Shannon, McGovern.

Public Buildings and Lands—Shannon, Rossi, Suhr.

Public Health—Toner, McSheehy, Roncovieri.

Public Utilities—Colman, Spaulding, Havenner.

Public Welfare and Publicity—Peyser, Spaulding, Miles.

Streets and Tunnels—Power, Canepa, Gallagher.

Supplies—Miles, Stanton, Power.

Traffic—McGovern, Havenner, Gallagher.

Every Committee shall set a stated time of meeting, or the Committee may meet at a time to be set by the chairman, and every member will be expected to attend every meeting of his Committee, and to be present promptly on time. The clerk of each Committee shall keep a record of the attendance of the members, and he shall report such record to the Clerk of the Board, and the Clerk of the Board shall have the report of the attendance of members at committee meetings available at all times for the information of any or all members of the Board.

DUTIES OF COMMITTEES.

2. The respective duties of each of the foregoing Committees and the time of meetings are hereby defined as follows:

AIRPORT AND AERONAUTICS—To have control and management of the Municipal Airport; to report and recommend on applications for leasing of hangars and concessions in said Airport; to consider and report on all matters relating to said Airport.

AUDITORIUM—To have control and management of the Municipal Auditorium and entertainments held therein under the auspices of the City as provided in Ordinance No. 5320 (New Series); to lease said building and the several halls and apartments therein; to report and recommend on applications for leasing of said building for public assemblages and gatherings; to consider and report on all matters relating to the management, conduct and maintenance of said Auditorium.

CIVIL SERVICE AND RETIREMENT SYSTEM—To consider all matters relating to Civil Service in the several departments and to promote efficiency and economy in expenditures; to consider matters relating to the Retirement System, and all reports of the Board of Administration of the Retirement System shall be referred to it for investigation and report thereon.

COMMERCIAL AND INDUSTRIAL DEVELOPMENT AND CITY PLANNING—To assist in promoting the establishment of industries in San Francisco and to cooperate with commercial and industrial organizations in all efforts to establish new industries; to consider measures helpful in developing San Francisco as an industrial center and to encourage delegations to points where needed to bring new industries, and generally to consider manufacturing problems as related to the industrial needs of the community; to cooperate with the United States, State officials and civic organizations in support of national and state legislation designed to promote world trade and the United States Merchant Marine; to bring about the location of a foreign trade zone within the City and County of San Francisco; to inaugurate a movement to the end that the management, control and development of San Francisco's harbor be placed locally, and also to cooperate with the Federal and State authorities on all matters, especially legislation, that tend for the further development and utilization of San Francisco's harbor to meet the needs of the world's commerce; to promote friendly relations between the City and contiguous and neighboring communities, to consider all matters relating to the City's expansion, and to act in an advisory capacity between the City Planning Commission and the Board of Supervisors and to hear such matters concerning city planning as may be referred to it by the Board of Supervisors; to propose measures for developing and accelerating transcontinental railway and inter-urban railroad transportation on this peninsula; to confer with adjacent cities, towns and counties on inter-community problems and to suggest to the Board in what manner other committees may be of help in peninsula development.

EDUCATION, PARKS AND PLAYGROUNDS—To consider and report upon all matters relating to the Departments of Education, Parks and Playgrounds and recreation centers, including the Aquatic Park, and to cooperate with the Board of Education, Playground Commission and Park Commission regarding the development and increased usefulness of these departments.

FINANCE—To perform all duties required by the Charter; to audit all bills and report on all matters that may be referred to it by the Board of Supervisors; to act as a budget committee for the Board, hold hearings on budget estimates of and with all departments, receive recommendations from all other committees of the Board, and formulate a budget for submission to the Board on or before the second Monday of May. (Meets Fridays at 2:30 p. m.)

FIRE—To consider all matters relating to the Fire Department; to report on all applications for garage, boiler, laundry and other permits referred to it.

JUDICIARY—To consider and report upon Charter amendments and all matters referred to it by the Board.

LIGHTING, WATER SERVICE, TELEPHONE SERVICE AND ELECTRICITY—To attend to the proper lighting of streets, public parks and public buildings; to investigate and correct complaints of water service and extensions thereof, and telephone service; to recommend installation and removal of City telephones; to recommend from time to time extensions of underground wire system, and to have general charge of all matters pertaining to electricity other than public lighting and amendments to the building laws.

MUNICIPAL CONCERTS AND PUBLIC CELEBRATIONS—To have charge of the Municipal Band and conduct all concerts that are given under the auspices of the City and County of San Francisco (except those concerts under the management of the Park Commissioners and the Auditorium Committee of this Board); to assist in promotion of all semi-public celebrations, dedications, etc.

POLICE AND LICENSES—To consider legislation concerning the Police Department; to investigate the management and character of penal institutions; to consider all matters affecting public morals; to report upon applications for permits referred to it by the Board, including free licenses to those deserving them, and report on all licenses, including taxicabs and public conveyances for hire.

PUBLIC BUILDINGS AND LANDS—To consider the erection of all public buildings and the purchase of sites for all public buildings upon recommendation of the respective departments; to consider and report upon the repairs to public buildings, and to recommend as to the janitorial, elevator and other service required for the proper conduct of all buildings of the City and County; also to assign to the various offices and departments the various rooms and places in the City Hall and Hall of Justice; to investigate and report upon proposed purchases of lands; to formulate plans for leasing City lands not needed for public purposes; to consider transfer of lands from one department to another, and all other matters pertaining to the realty of the City other than school property and airport property.

PUBLIC HEALTH—To consider all matters relating to health and sanitation; to see that institutions under the control of the Board of Health are properly conducted; to establish and maintain a high standard of service in public hospitals and Relief Home; to consider and report upon all complaints of nuisances; to make recommendations upon applications for permits which may be referred to it by the Board; also removal and destruction of garbage.

PUBLIC UTILITIES—To consider and pass upon all matters relating to public utilities, their acquisition, construction, control and management, whether municipally or privately owned, including transbay bridges, transportation, lighting, power, water and steamheating.

PUBLIC WELFARE AND PUBLICITY—To consider matters relating to the social well-being of the community other than those heretofore provided for, and generally to act upon all matters of public advertising, and pass on all bills chargeable against the advertising fund; to consider all matters relating to the Bureau of Weights and Measures.

RULES—To consider amendments to the Rules and such other matters as may be referred to it by the Board. To have supervision of and give instructions to the chauffeurs of the Board of Supervisors.

STATE LAWS AND LEGISLATION—To be appointed by the Finance Committee when occasion requires. To consider all matters pending before the Legislature and proposed legislation which affects the City and County of San Francisco, directly or indirectly, and to make such recommendations to the Board as may be deemed advisable, and to appear before the State Legislature in advocacy of any measures or in opposition to measures as the Board may advise.

STREETS AND TUNNELS—To consider all matters relating to the construction, improvement and maintenance of streets and sewers, including highways outside the County, for which the City and County is authorized to appropriate money, the closing, opening and widening of streets and the cleaning of streets; to designate the streets for the improvement and repair of which appropriations may be made in the budget and to allocate the same. Also direct the expenditure of money received from the State for the construction of public highways; to consider and report upon applications for spur and industrial tracks; to consider and report upon all matters relating to tunnels.

SUPPLIES—To consider and have charge of the purchase of all supplies as provided by the Charter; to prepare schedules for general supplies and to recommend award of contracts; to inspect deliveries and quality and quantity of supplies; to pass on all requisitions for non-contract supplies; to supervise the purchase and distribution of all books, stationery, etc.

TRAFFIC AND SAFETY—To investigate and report on matters relative to traffic conditions in the City and propose Ordinances regulating traffic and the promotion of safety in connection therewith.

CONVENING OF BOARD.

3. The Board shall convene at 2 o'clock p. m. on each Monday, and the Clerk shall immediately, after the call to order, which shall be at 2 o'clock p. m., call the roll of the members of the Board and shall record those present and absent. The Clerk shall also record the time of arrival of those members of the Board who arrive after 2 o'clock p. m., and the name of such member and the time of his arrival shall be entered upon the journal.

It shall be the duty of each Committee charged with the duty of cooperating with any particular department to investigate the financial needs of such department to be provided for in the annual budget; to consider such department's budget estimates and to recommend to the Finance Committee such modifications or changes thereof as it may deem proper.

The designations and duties of the foregoing Committees are hereby made part of these rules.

RULES OF ORDER.

4. The Mayor shall be President of the Board of Supervisors. He shall call each regular, adjourned or special meeting to order at the hour appointed and shall proceed with the order of business. In the absence of the Mayor, the Clerk shall call the roll and the Board shall appoint a presiding officer pro tempore from its own members, who shall have the same right to vote as other members.

The presiding officer shall preserve order and decorum.

The Clerk shall, immediately after the call to order, call the roll of members of the Board, and the record of those present and absent shall be entered upon the Journal.

5. Whenever it shall be moved and carried by 12 members that the Board go into Committee of the Whole, the President shall leave the chair and the members shall appoint a chairman of the Committee of the Whole, who shall report the proceedings of said Committee.

6. The rules of the Board shall be observed in the Committee of the Whole.

7. A motion, in Committee of the Whole, to rise and report the question, shall be decided without debate.

8. The Clerk shall have clips, upon which shall be kept all Bills, Ordinances, Resolutions and Reports to be acted upon by the Board, except those not reported upon by a Committee.

9. No Bill, Ordinance or Resolution shall be considered by the Board unless it has been introduced by a member of the Board or by a Committee of the Board, and the Bill, Ordinance or Resolution must be read by the Clerk in open meeting before being referred to Committee. At the time of introduction the presiding officer shall first indicate to what Committee a Bill, Ordinance or Resolution ought to be referred, and it shall be so referred unless, upon majority vote without debate, the Board shall order it referred to some other committee.

Action by the Board shall not be taken upon any Bill, Ordinance or Resolution until it has been referred to and acted upon by a Committee of the Board.

10. The Order of Business, which shall not be departed from except by the consent of twelve members, shall be as follows:

    1. Roll Call.

    2. Approval of Journal.

    3. Calendar Business.

    4. Roll Call for the Introduction of Resolutions, Bills and Communications Not Considered or Reported on by a Committee.

11. If any question under debate contains several points, any member may have the points segregated and acted upon separately.

12. When a motion has been made and carried or lost, it shall be in order for any member voting with the prevailing side to move to "reconsider the vote" on that question.

A member may change his vote before the result is announced in order to move to "reconsider the vote" on that question. The vote upon such motion to reconsider shall not be taken before the next regular meeting of the Board. No question shall be reconsidered more than once. Motion to reconsider shall have precedence over every other motion. It shall require a majority vote to carry any motion to reconsider the vote by which any Bill, Ordinance or Resolution has been passed or defeated.

13. A motion to refer or lay on the table until decided shall preclude all amendments to the main question. A motion to lay on the table or to postpone indefinitely shall require a majority vote of the members present.

14. It shall be the duty of the Clerk to issue such certificates as may be required by Ordinances or Resolutions and transmit copies of said Ordinances or Resolutions to the various departments affected thereby. It shall also be the duty of the Clerk to cause the publication in the official newspaper of all Bills, Ordinances, proposals and awards as required by the Charter.

15. All accounts and bills shall be referred to the Finance Committee, provided that any Committee having jurisdiction over subject of expenditures may request that bills be first sent to that Committee before being acted upon by the Finance Committee and the Board.

16. The President shall preserve order and decorum, and prevent demonstrations of approval or disapproval on the part of persons in the Chambers of the Board, and shall decide questions of order, subject to an appeal to the Board.

17. When a Supervisor desires to address the Board he shall arise in his place, address the presiding officer, and when recognized he shall proceed to speak. No Supervisor shall be recognized when seated or when away from his seat.

18. No Supervisor shall speak more than twice in any one debate on the same subject, and at the same stage of the Bill, Ordinance, Resolution or Motion without the consent of a majority of the Board, and Supervisors who have once spoken shall not again be entitled to

the floor so long as any Supervisor who has not spoken desires to speak. No Supervisor shall be allowed to speak more than five minutes on any question except by permission of the Board, except that the author shall have five minutes to open and ten minutes to close.

19. No Supervisor shall be interrupted when speaking without his consent.

20. When two or more Supervisors arise at the same time to address the Board, the presiding officer shall designate the Supervisor who is entitled to the floor.

21. No motion shall be debated until the same *has been seconded* and distinctly announced by the presiding officer.

22. After a motion has been stated by the President, it shall be in the possession of the Board. It may be withdrawn by the mover thereof, with the consent of the second, before it is acted upon.

23. Upon a call of the Board the names of the members shall be called by the Clerk, and the absentees noted. Those for whom no excuse or insufficient excuses are made may, by order of those present, be sent for and be brought to the Chambers of the Board by the Sergeant-at-Arms or by special messengers appointed for the purpose.

24. When a question is under debate, no action shall be entertained except:

To adjourn.
Call of the Board.
To lay on the table.
The previous question.
To postpone.
To commit or amend.

which several motions shall have precedence in the order in which they are arranged; provided, however, that during a call of the Board it may consider and transact any matter or business that the Supervisors there present shall unanimously decide to consider.

25. A motion to adjourn is not debatable.

26. The previous question shall be put in the following form: "Shall the previous question be now put?" It shall only be admitted when demanded by three Supervisors, and its effect shall be to put an end to all debate except that the author of the Bill, Ordinance, Resolution or Motion or Amendments shall have the right to close, and the question under discussion shall thereupon be immediately put to a vote. On a motion for the previous question prior to a vote being taken by the Board a call of the Board shall be in order.

27. Every member present when a question is put shall vote for or against it, unless disqualified by the Charter. No member shall be permitted to vote upon a question unless present when his name is called or before the vote is announced. A roll call shall not be interrupted for debate or personal privilege, but a member may file, in writing, an explanation of his vote.

29. After the Board has acted, the names of those who voted for and those who voted against the question shall be entered upon the Journal, not only in cases required by law, but when any member may require it, and on all Bills, Ordinances and Resolutions on final passage the ayes and nays shall be recorded.

30. All appointments of officers and employees shall be made by a majority of the members of the Board. The Clerk shall assign the assistant clerks to their several duties, and shall immediately transmit to the Mayor all Resolutions and Ordinances which, under the law, require executive approval.

31. No member shall leave the Board during its session without permission from the Board.

32. All Committees shall be appointed by the Board unless otherwise ordered by the Board. Committees shall report on any subject referred to them by the Board and their recommendations thereon. *Unless otherwise ordered, a Committee shall report upon all subjects referred to it within thirty days thereafter.* It shall be the right of

any member of a Committee to move a roll call (in Committee), on any pending motion, and the Chairman or Acting Chairman of said Committee shall, with or without debate, order the roll call. In Committees of three members or less a motion by a member thereof shall not require a second.

33. The Clerk shall prepare and cause to be printed and placed on the desks of the members on days of meeting, at least 30 minutes before such a meeting, a calendar of matters to be presented to the Board at said meeting. Every petition or other written instrument intended to be presented to the Board must be delivered to the Clerk not later than 12 o'clock noon on Saturday, or on the day preceding the meeting; upon the request of the President or of any member its contents shall be read in full.

34. All petitions, protests and communications of a routine character shall be referred by the Clerk to the proper Committee.

35. Ten members shall constitute a quorum to transact business, and no Bill, Ordinance, Resolution or Amendment thereto shall pass without the concurrence of at least that number of members, but a smaller number may adjourn from day to day.

36. Except when otherwise provided by these rules, the Charter or law, a majority vote of the members present shall be necessary for the adoption of any motion.

37. The Clerk shall keep a record of all requests and instructions directed by the Board of Supervisors to any officer or board of the City and County and the action thereon of such officer or board. The record of such requests and instructions, until acted upon by such officer or board, shall be read by the Clerk at each regular meeting of the Board of Supervisors.

38. The privilege of the floor shall not be granted to others than members of the Board, except those entitled to the same under the Charter, or public officials of the City and County of San Francisco. This rule shall not be suspended, except by unanimous consent of all members present.

39. In debate a member must confine himself to the question before the Board.

40. On any questions or points of order not embraced in these rules the Board shall be governed by the rules contained in Robert's Rules of Order.

41. No member of the Board of Supervisors, chairman of a Committee, or Committee of said Board, shall employ or engage the services of any person, or authorize or incur any charge, debt or liability against the City and County unless authority therefor shall have been first given by the Board of Supervisors by Resolution or Ordinance, except as otherwise provided by law.

42. No standing rule or order of the Board shall be suspended or amended without the affirmative vote of twelve members, except that the rule as to the privilege of the floor shall require the unanimous consent of all members present.

43. No special order shall be placed on the Calendar except by order of the Board.

MEMORANDUM OF CHARTER PROVISIONS.

Page 4, Section 3, Chapter 1, Article II—Quorum consists of 10 members.

Page 5, Section 8, Chapter 1, Article II—No Bill shall become an Ordinance or Resolution be adopted unless it receives 10 votes.

Page 7, Section 16, Chapter 1, Article II—14 votes necessary to override Mayor's veto of Resolution or Ordinance.

Page 13, Chapter 2, Article II—Lease of City lands requires two-thirds vote of Board (12 votes).

Page 19, Section 6, Chapter 2, Article II—Street railway franchises require three-fourths vote (14 votes) of all the members of the Board, while five-sixths vote (15 votes) of all the members of the Board is necessary to pass these ordinances if MAYOR VETOES SAME.

Page 22, Section 9, Chapter 2, Article II—Sale of City lands requires 15 votes.

Page 30, Section 3, Chapter 1, Article III—Budget Ordinance requires 10 votes.

Page 30, Section 4, Chapter 1, Article III—15 votes are necessary to override Mayor's veto of Budget.

Page 31, Section 8, Chapter 1, Article III—15 votes necessary to appropriate from Urgent Necessity Fund.

Page 33, Section 13, Chapter 1, Article III—To suspend temporarily limit of taxation to meet emergency requires unanimous vote of 18 members of the Board and approval of the Mayor.

Page 76, Section 1, Chapter 1, Article VI—Contracts for street work require 14 votes.

Page 78, Section 2, Chapter 2, Article VI—When cost of sewer or drain is in excess of $5 per linear front foot of abutting property and work is disapproved by Board of Works, it requires 14 votes of the Board of Supervisors to pass ordinance ordering such work done.

If application for work is made, the expense of which is to be paid by City and County, and work is not recommended by the Board of Public Works, it requires 14 votes of the Board of Supervisors to order such work done.

Page 98, Section 33, Chapter 2, Article VI—Ordinance providing for street improvements in 10-year installments requires 15 votes.

Page 100, Section 1, Chapter 3, Article VI—Opening and improvement of streets, etc., requires 12 votes.

Page 120, Section 17, Chapter 6, Article VI—15 votes are required to modify or change procedure as provided in the Charter for changing street grades and the performance of work in connection therewith.

Page 121, Section 1, Chapter 8, Article VI—Ordinance providing for tunnel, subway and viaduct construction requires 12 votes.

Page 218, Section 19, Article XVI—Suspension of an elected officer by the Mayor requires approval of 14 votes of the Board of Supervisors to cause removal.

Page 223, Section 35, Article XVI—Appointments of additional deputies, clerks or employees require 14 votes.

Action Deferred.

The following matter was, on motion, *laid over sixty days*:

HEARING OF APPEAL.

Henry Cowell Lime and Cement Company.

Hearing of appeal of Henry Cowell Lime and Cement Company from the action and decision of the Board of Public Works in overruling the protest of Henry Cowell Lime and Cement Company against the improvement of the north half of Commercial street from the west line of The Embarcadero to a line at right angles with Commercial street and one hundred and twenty-five (125) feet six and three-eighths (6⅜) inches west of the west line of The Embarcadero, by the construction of full width artificial stone sidewalks, where sidewalks are not now to official grade, and the construction of a retaining wall to support this sidewalk, as set forth in Resolution of Intention No. 96689 (Second Series).

PRESENTATION OF PROPOSALS.

Two Motor Trucks With Dump Bodies, 2½-Ton.

Sealed proposals were received and opened between the hours of 2 and 3 p. m. this date for furnishing two motor trucks with dump bodies, 2½ tons, and *referred to the Supplies Committee.*

Dry Goods and Wearing Apparel.

Sealed proposals were received and opened between the hours of 2 and 3 p. m. this date for furnishing dry goods and wearing apparel and *referred to the Supplies Committee.*

Printing Auditor's Report.

Sealed proposals were received and opened between the hours of 2 and 3 p. m. this date for furnishing 800 copies of Auditor's Annual Report, 1928-29, and *referred to the Supplies Committee.*

UNFINISHED BUSINESS.

Final Passage.

The following matters, heretofore passed for printing, were taken up and *finally passed* by the following vote:

Authorizations.

On recommendation of Finance Committee.

Resolution No. 31936 (New Series), as follows:

Resolved, That the following amounts be and the same are hereby authorized to be expended out of the hereinafter mentioned funds in payment to the following named claimants, to-wit:

Hetch Hetchy Construction Fund, Bond Issue 1928.

(1) Best Steel Casting Co., car wheels, Hetch Hetchy construction (claim dated Dec. 27, 1929)....................$ 716.25

(2) J. H. Creighton, truck hire (claim dated Dec. 27, 1929)..   626.29

(3) Del Monte Meat Co., meats (claim dated Dec. 27, 1929) 1,402.66

(4) Del Monte Meat Co., meats (claim dated Dec. 28, 1929).. 1,231.02

(5) Grier & Mead, steel concrete forms (claim dated Dec. 30, 1929) 1,750.00

(6) Delbert Hansen, truck hire (claim dated Dec. 30, 1929).. 1,262.42

(7) W. Haslam, hauling cement and sand (claim dated Dec. 27, 1929) 1,390.02

(8) Hammond Lumber Co., lumber (claim dated Dec. 27, 1929) 1,145.77

(9) John Johnson, truck hire (claim dated Dec. 28, 1929)....   586.50

(10) Montague Pipe & Steel Co., steel air pipe (claim dated Dec. 30, 1929) 2,014.03

(11) Owen-Oregon Lumber Co., lumber (claim dated Dec. 30, 1929) 1,247.63

(12) Alfred Pereira & Brothers, hauling cement, sand, etc. (claim dated Dec. 27, 1929)............................. 1,324.25

(13 Santa Cruz Portland Cement Co., cement (claim dated Dec. 30, 1929) 2,319.00

(14) St. Paul's Hospital, hospital service furnished Hetch Hetchy employees (claim dated Dec. 28, 1929)...........   833.55

(15) United States Rubber Co., rubber boots and coats (claim dated Dec. 30, 1929)............................... 1,777.40

(16) Virden Packing Co., meats (claim dated Dec. 30, 1929)   537.60

(17) Dodge, Sweeney Co., groceries (claim dated Jan. 2, 1930)   592.62

(18) General Electric Co., battery locomotive parts (claim dated Jan. 2, 1930)...................................   514.42

(19) The Giant Powder Co. Con., explosives (claim dated Jan. 2, 1930) 4,500.00

(20) Ingersoll-Rand Co. of Calif., machinery parts (claim dated Jan. 2, 1930) 1,697.55

(21) Owen-Oregon Lumber Co., lumber (claim dated Jan. 2, 1930) 1,246.18

(22) Santa Fe Lumber Co., lumber (claim dated Jan. 2, 1930)   895.50

(23) Santa Cruz Portland Cement Co., cement (claim dated Jan. 2, 1930) 4,399.00

(24) Standard Oil Co. of Calif., gasoline and oils (claim dated Jan. 2, 1930) 757.90

(25) Western Iron Works, foot bridge truss span (claim dated Jan. 2, 1930) 509.75

(26) M. D. Jones, truck hire (claim dated Jan. 2, 1930).... 1,057.25

(27) Bald Eagle Meat Market, meat (claim dated Jan. 7, 1930)   551.54

(28) Pope & Talbot, lumber (claim dated Jan. 7, 1930)....   1,055.76
(29) Santa Cruz Portland Cement Co., cement (claim dated
Jan 7, 1930) 896.50

Special School Tax.

(30) Jacks & Irvine, extra work, general construction of
Roosevelt Junior High School (claim dated Jan. 4, 1930)..$ 7,597.56
(31) Anderson & Ringrose, extra work on general construction of Marina Elementary School (claim dated Dec. 30,
1929) 1,090.00
(32) D. A. Pancoast Co., for the furnishing of "Von Duprin"
type panic bolts and dogging hooks for various schools
(claim dated Dec. 30, 1929).........................   2,888.69
(33) Jacks & Irvine, seventh payment, general construction
of Roosevelt Junior High School (claim dated Jan. 4, 1930)   8,477.59
(34) Larsen & Larsen, first payment, brick, tile and stone
work for Roosevelt Junior High School (claim dated Jan.
7, 1930) 5,256.31
(35) Scott Co., fifth payment, mechanical equipment furnished Roosevelt Junior High School (claim dated Jan. 7,
1930) 2,746.20
(36) Scott Co., fifth payment, plumbing and gas-fitting for
Roosevelt Junior High School (claim dated Jan. 7, 1930)   3,735.75
(37) Meyer Bros., second payment, general construction of
additions to the Sunshine School (claim dated Jan. 4, 1930)   3,068.37
(38) Scott Co., first payment, mechanical equipment furnished for addition to Sunshine School (claim dated Jan.
7, 1930) 2,373.60
(39) Alta Electric Co., fifth payment, electrical work for
Park-Presidio Junior High School (claim dated Jan. 7, 1930)   896.26
(40) Meyer Bros., fifth payment, general construction of Park-
Presidio Junior High School (claim dated Jan. 4, 1930).. 27,960.00
(41) Scott Co., fourth payment, plumbing and gas-fitting furnished Park-Presidio Junior High School (claim dated Jan.
7, 1930) 5,648.52
(42) Scott Co., fifth payment, mechanical equipment for Park-
Presidio Junior High School (claim dated Jan. 7, 1930)....   2,529.75
(43) Alta Electric Co., third payment, electric work for Geary
Street School (claim dated Jan. 7, 1930)................   1,147.50
(44) Meyer Bros., sixth payment, general construction of
Geary Street School (claim dated Jan. 4, 1930)........   8,611.61
(45) Scott Co., third payment, mechanical equipment for
Geary Street School (claim dated Jan. 7, 1930)..........   1,660.50
(46) Scott Co., first payment, mechanical equipment for addition to Francisco Junior High School (claim dated Jan.
7, 1930) 1,946.25
(47) MacDonald & Kahn, second payment, general construction of viewing stand at the third unit of South Side (Balboa) High School (claim dated Jan. 4, 1930)............ 11,980.93
(48) The Electric Corporation of San Francisco, conduit furnished for schools (claim dated Jan. 6, 1930)............   529.50
(49) J. H. McCallum, lumber furnished for schools (claim
dated Jan. 6, 1930) 1,103.73
(50) Alta Electric Co., final payment, electrical work for
Marina Elementary School (claim dated Jan. 7, 1930)......   2,261.00
(51) Anderson & Ringrose, final payment, general construction of Marina Elementary School (claim dated Jan. 7,
1930) 43,135.23

Park Fund.

(52) Standard Fence Company, construction of fences for
the Park, including labor and material (claim dated Jan.
10, 1930) ....$ 2,150.99

(53) Tay-Holbrook, Inc., pipe and plumbing supplies furnished the Park (claim dated Jan. 10, 1930) 2,837.20

Playground Fund.

(54) J. H. McCallum Lumber Company, lumber furnished for playgrounds (claim dated Jan. 8, 1930) ....$ 655.14

(55) State Compensation Insurance Fund, premium on insurance covering playground employments (claim dated Jan. 8, 1930) 973.86

(56) Tay-Holbrook, Inc., plumbing supplies furnished playgrounds (claim dated Jan. 8, 1930) 749.66

Bernal Cut Construction Fund, Bond Issue 1927.

(57) MacDonald & Kahn, eleventh payment, improvement of Bernal Cut (claim dated Jan. 7, 1930) $17,700.00

Boulevard Construction Fund, Bond Issue 1927.

(58) Eaton & Smith, seventh payment, improvement of Junipero Serra boulevard (claim dated Jan. 7, 1930) $13,500.00

(59) Federal Construction Company, seventh payment, improvement of Bay Shore boulevard, Section "E" (claim dated Jan. 7, 1930) 3,500.00

Spring Valley Water Bonds, Issue 1928.

(60) Thomson, Wood & Hoffman, for professional services, examining proceedings and opinion furnished (claim dated Jan. 6, 1930) ....$ 3,750.00

Municipal Railway Fund.

(61) San Francisco City Employees' Retirement System, for pensions covering prior service of railway employees (claim dated Jan. 3, 1930) ....$ 1,123.23

(62) Board of Public Works (Street Repair Department), reimbursement for paving work on replacement jobs for Municipal Railway during November, 1929 (claim dated Jan. 7, 1930) 795.69

(63) Board of Public Works (Street Repair Department), reimbursement for asphalt repairs to Municipal Railway right of way during November, 1929) (claim dated Jan. 7, 1930) .. 1,571.60

County Road Fund.

(64) Ajax Construction Company, first payment, for rearrangement of auxiliary water supply system pipe line in Rankin street between Islais Creek and Custer avenue (claim dated Dec. 30, 1929) ....$ 1,000.00

(65) Eaton & Smith, City's portion of cost for improvement of Laidley street from Thirtieth to Noe streets (claim dated Jan. 7, 1930) 11,061.52

(66) M. J. Lynch, City's portion of improvement of Twentieth street between Sanchez and Noe streets (claim dated Jan. 2, 1930) 24,571.58

Hetch Hetchy Power Operative Fund.

(67) The Diamond Match Company, material furnished for account of Hetch Hetchy Water Supply (claim dated Dec. 27, 1929) ....$ 991.02

(68) Hetch Hetchy Construction Fund, Bond Issue 1928, for material, supplies, equipment and services furnished and rendered the Hetch Hetchy Power Operative Fund during November, 1929 (claim dated Dec. 30, 1929) 9,351.82

(69) State Compensation Insurance Fund, premium covering insurance on Hetch Hetchy employments (claim dated Dec. 27, 1929) 764.50

(70) Standard Oil Company of California, gasoline and oils furnished (claim dated Dec. 27, 1929) 1,343.13

Water Works Fund.

(71) H. O. Lindemann, refund of deposit, per Resolution No. 95613 (Second Series), Board of Public Works, for period July to December, 1929).............................$ 1,110.20

Municipal Railway Fund.

(72) American Brake Shoe and Foundry Company of California, brake shoes furnished (claim dated Dec. 31, 1929)...$ 2,219.20

·(73) Westinghouse Electric and Manufacturing Company, electric railway supplies (claim dated Dec. 31, 1929)........... 788.83

·(74) Mack International Motor Truck Corporation, one 29-passenger bus, less allowance on used "White" bus (claim dated Dec. 27, 1929)..................................... 7,797.00

(75) Pacific Gas and Electric Company, for the furnishing and installing of underground cable and overhead cable connecting Station "N" with Municipal Railway, Forest Hill Station, Twin Peaks Tunnel (claim dated Dec. 27, 1929)....... 1,536.78

(76) Payne's Bolt Works, tie rods for Municipal Railways (claim dated Dec. 27, 1929)............................. 503.28

(77) United States Steel Products Company, 200 rolled steel car wheels (claim dated Dec. 27, 1929)................... 7,200.00

Henri F. Windel Trust Fund.

(78) Duncan Matheson, Treasurer of City and County, for purchase of one Boulevard Bond, Issue 1927, No. 1352, maturing 1934, for the Henri F Windel Trust Fund; authorized by Resolution No. 31866 (New Series) (claim dated Jan. 3, 1930) 1,000.00

Municipal Airport Fund.

(79) California Construction Company, second payment, construction of San Francisco Airport pavement, Contract 13 (claim dated Dec. 30, 1929).............................$ 7,000.00

General Fund, 1929-1930.

(80) John Kitchen, Jr., Co., Superior Court minute books furnished the County Clerk (claim dated Oct. 18, 1929)........$ 696.00

(81) Recorder Printing and Publishing Company, printing Supervisors' Calendar, Journal, etc. (claim dated Jan. 13, 1930) 927.97

(82) Recorder Printing and Publishing Company, printing Superior Court Calendars, etc. (claim dated Jan. 13, 1930).. 515.00

(83) William J. Quinn, contingent expense for Chief of Police, month of January (claim dated Jan. 6, 1930).............. 750.00

(84) The Texas Company, gasoline furnished Police Department (claim dated Jan. 6, 1930)......................... 1,173.64

(85) Patrick & Co., license plates furnished the Auditor (claim dated Jan. 13, 1930)..................................... 2,777.03

(86) Associated Charities, widows' pensions (claim dated Jan. 17, 1930) 7,450.00

(87) Eureka Benevolent Society, widows' pensions (claim dated Jan. 17, 1930)..................................... 1,037.50

(88) Little Children's Aid, widows' pensions (claim dated Jan. 17, 1930) 5,999.59

(89) Dion R. Holm, legal services rendered in telephone rate case, month of January (claim dated Jan. 7, 1930).......... 850.00

(90) N. Randall Ellis, engineering services rendered for month of January in telephone rate case (claim dated Jan. 7, 1930). 750.00

(91) John J. Dailey, legal services rendered City Attorney for month of January (claim dated Jan. 8, 1930).............. 850.00

(92) M. J. Lynch, first payment, furnishing, delivering and erecting street signs (claim dated Jan. 7, 1930)............ 2,250.00

(93) Lindsay Construction Company, refund of amount expended for construction of auxiliary main sewer in London

street between France and Italy avenues (claim dated Jan. 7, 1930) 526.30
(94) County Road Fund (Ordinance No. 8462, New Series), being reimbursement for account of expenditures in the covering of main sewers during November (claim dated Dec. 30, 1929) 1,354.50
(95) West Coast Iron and Wire Works, mesh wire, posts and gates furnished San Francisco Health Farm (claim dated Dec. 31, 1929)... 3,577.00
(96) O'Brien, Spotorno, Mitchell & Campagno, turkeys furnished Laguna Honda Home Dec. 21st (claim dated Dec. 31, 1929) 864.00
(97) Blue Ribbon Products Company, coffee furnished Laguna Honda Home (claim dated Dec. 30, 1929).................. 613.00
(98) Dairydale San Francisco Dairy Company, milk furnished Laguna Honda Home (claim dated Dec. 30, 1929).......... 2,341.20
(99) J. T. Freitas Co., eggs furnished Laguna Honda Home (claim dated Dec. 31, 1930)............................. 2,006.25
(100) A. Levy and J. Zentner Co., produce furnished Laguna Honda Home (claim dated Dec. 31, 1930)................... 878.60
(101) Spring Valley Water Company, water service thru Fire Department hydrants during December (claim dated Dec. 31, 1929) 15,551.96

Ayes—Supervisors Andriano, Canepa, Colman, Gallagher, Havenner, Hayden, McGovern, McSheehy, Miles, Roncovieri, Rossi, Shannon, Spaulding, Stanton, Suhr, Toner—16.
Absent—Supervisors Peyser, Power—2.

Amending Ordinance No. 5460 (New Series), Known as the "Ordinance of Additional Positions," in re County Clerk.

Also, Bill No. 8166, Ordinance No. 8673 (New Series), as follows:
Amending Section 14 of Ordinance No. 5460 (New Series), known as the "Ordinance of Additional Positions."
Be it ordained by the People of the City and County of San Francisco as follows:
Section 1. Section 4 of Ordinance No. 5460 (New Series), known as the "Ordinance of Additional Positions," is hereby amended to read as follows:
Subdivision (d) Fifty-four assistant register clerks, each at a salary of $2,400 a year. $129,600.
Subdivision (e) Twenty-two copyists, each at a salary of $2,400 a year, $52,800.
Section 2. This ordinance shall take effect from and after its passage.

Ayes—Supervisors Andriano, Canepa, Colman, Gallagher, Havenner, Hayden, McGovern, McSheehy, Miles, Roncovieri, Rossi, Shannon, Spaulding, Stanton, Suhr, Toner—16.
Absent—Supervisors Peyser, Power—2.

Ordering the Construction of Film Vault, San Francisco Hospital, Plans and Specifications, Receipt of Bids, and Award of Contract.

Also, Bill No. 8167, Ordinance No. 8674 (New Series), as follows:
Ordering the construction of film vault on the roof of the San Francisco Hospital in accordance with plans and specifications prepared for same which are hereby authorized to be prepared; authorizing and directing the Board of Public Works to enter into contract for said construction in accordance with plans and specifications prepared therefor.
Be it ordained by the People of the City and County of San Francisco as follows:
Section 1. The construction of a film vault on the roof of the San

Francisco Hospital is hereby ordered, and the Board of Public Works is hereby authorized, instructed and empowered to prepare plans and specifications for the construction of said film vault, and to enter into contract for said construction in accordance with said plans and specifications prepared therefor.

Section 2. This ordinance shall take effect immediately.

Ayes—Supervisors Andriano, Canepa, Colman, Gallagher, Havenner, Hayden, McGovern, McSheehy, Miles, Roncovieri, Rossi, Shannon, Spaulding, Stanton, Suhr, Toner—16.

Absent—Supervisors Peyser, Power—2.

Oil Tank and Boiler Permits.

On recommendation of Fire Committee.

Resolution No. 31937 (New Series), as follows:

Resolved, That the following revocable permits be and are hereby granted:

Oil Tanks.

C. Heller, 1980 Jackson street, 1500 gallons capacity.

E. L. Shaffer, south side of Chestnut street, 261 feet west of Scott street, 300 gallons capacity.

Boiler.

National Sanitary Rag Company, 160 Townsend street, 50-horsepower.

The rights granted under this resolution shall be exercised within six months, otherwise said permit shall become null and void.

Ayes—Supervisors Andriano, Canepa, Colman, Gallagher, Havenner, Hayden, McGovern, McSheehy, Miles, Roncovieri, Rossi, Shannon, Spaulding, Stanton, Suhr, Toner—16.

Absent—Supervisors Peyser, Power—2.

Granting Pacific Gas & Electric Company (San Francisco Division), Commercial Garage, Block Bounded by Shotwell, Folsom, Eighteenth and Nineteenth Streets.

Also, Resolution No. 31938 (New Series), as follows:

Resolved, That Pacific Gas and Electric Company be and is hereby granted permission, revocable at will of the Board of Supervisors, to maintain and operate a commercial garage in block bounded by Shotwell, Folsom, Eighteenth and Nineteenth streets.

The rights granted under this resolution shall be exercised within six months, otherwise said permit shall become null and void.

Ayes—Supervisors Andriano, Canepa, Colman, Gallagher, Havenner, Hayden, McGovern, McSheehy, Miles, Roncovieri, Rossi, Shannon, Spaulding, Stanton, Suhr, Toner—16.

Absent—Supervisors Peyser, Power—2.

Granting Automobile Parking Station Permit, W. J. Winthrop, North Side of Brannan Street, 80 Feet East of Third Street.

Also, Resolution No. 31939 (New Series), as follows:

Resolved, That W. J. Winthrop be and is hereby granted permission, revocable at will of the Board of Supervisors, to maintain and operate an automobile parking station on the north side of Brannan street, 80 feet east of Third street.

The rights granted under this resolution shall be exercised within six months, otherwise said permit shall become null and void.

Ayes—Supervisors Andriano, Canepa, Colman, Gallagher, Havenner, Hayden, McGovern, McSheehy, Miles, Roncovieri, Rossi, Shannon, Spaulding, Stanton, Suhr, Toner—16.

Absent—Supervisors Peyser, Power—2.

Granting Automobile Parking Station Transfer, Bert Brock, 210 Taylor Street.

Also, Resolution No. 31940 (New Series), as follows:

Resolved, That Bert Brock be and is hereby granted permission, revocable at will of the Board of Supervisors, to have transferred automobile parking station permit heretofore granted J. N. Hughes by Resolution No. 25973 (New Series), for premises at 210 Taylor street.

The rights granted under this resolution shall be exercised within six months, otherwise said permit shall be come null and void.

Ayes—Supervisors Andriano, Canepa, Colman, Gallagher, Havenner, Hayden, McGovern, McSheehy, Miles, Roncovieri, Rossi, Shannon, Spaulding, Stanton, Suhr, Toner—16.

Absent—Supervisors Peyser, Power—2.

Automobile Supply Station, F. W. Metzger, Scott and Waller Streets.

Also, Resolution No. 31941 (New Series), as follows:

Resolved, That F. W. Metzger be and is hereby granted permission, revocable at will of the Board of Supervisors, to maintain and operate an automobile supply station on the northeast corner of Scott and Waller streets.

The rights granted under this resolution shall be exercised within six months, otherwise said permit shall become null and void.

Ayes—Supervisors Andriano, Canepa, Colman, Gallagher, Havenner, Hayden, McGovern, McSheehy, Miles, Roncovieri, Rossi, Shannon, Spaulding, Stanton, Suhr, Toner—16.

Absent—Supervisors Peyser, Power—2.

Confirming Sale of City Land.

On recommendation of Public Buildings and Lands Committee.

Bill No. 8168, Ordinance No. 8675 (New Series), as follows:

Confirming the sale of land owned by the City and County of San Francisco and situate in the City and County of San Francisco, State of California.

Whereas, by Ordinance No. 8544 (New Series), approved October 1, 1929, the Board of Supervisors determined that public interest and necessity demanded the sale of the land hereinafter described and hereinbefore referred to, and by said ordinance directed the Mayor of the City and County to sell all of said land at public auction, to be held on the 4th day of November, 1929, and directed that notice of said sale be given for three weeks successively next before the sale as required by law; and

Whereas, the Clerk of the Board of Supervisors thereafter proceeded to publish notice of said sale in the official newspaper and one other daily newspaper published in the City and County for three weeks successively next before said sale was directed to be made, describing the land to be sold therein with common certainty and stating the date on or after which said sale would be made, as specified in Ordinance No. 8544 (New Series), and that all bids or offers would be received by the Mayor at the chambers of the Board of Supervisors in the City Hall, City and County of San Francisco, State of California, on or after said date; and

Whereas, the Mayor, the Assessor and the Chairman of the Finance Committee, being the Board of Appraisement constituted by the Charter of the City and County of San Francisco for such purpose, thereafter duly met and made an appraisement of said land and fixed the fair value thereof and reported said appraisement to the Board of Supervisors in writing; and

Whereas, thereafter, and on the 18th day of November, 1929, at public auction the Mayor sold said property to R. H. Hawkes for the sum of $17,000 and accepted from said R. H. Hawkes a deposit, being a certified check in the sum of $1,700, and being 10 per cent or more of the amount bid as aforesaid, and thereupon and on the 5th day of December, 1929, duly notified the Board of Supervisors in writing of the fact of such sale, stating the sum bid, the name of the bidder, and requesting that the Board confirm the sale; and

Whereas, the Clerk of the Board of Supervisors immediately thereupon proceeded to give notice by publication in the official newspaper and one other newspaper in the City and County of San Francisco, for a period of three weeks from and after the 7th day of December, 1929, that at a meeting of the Board of Supervisors to be held on the 30th day of December, 1929, the matter of said sale would come up for confirmation, stating also in said notice the fact of the sale, the amount for which the property had been sold as aforesaid, and the name of the purchaser, and also stating that if at such meeting on the 30th day of December, 1929, an offer of 10 per cent more in amount than that named in said notice should be made to the Supervisors in writing by a responsible person, the Supervisors would confirm such sale to such person, or order a new sale; and

Whereas, the date of confirmation specified in said notice has arrived and action in said matter was deferred for one week, and on the 6th day of January, 1930, the matter was again deferred for one week, and on this, the 13th day of January, 1930, consideration of the matter was had, and a higher bid has not been obtained, and it appearing to the Board of Supervisors that the sum of $17,000 bid as aforesaid by R. H. Hawkes is not disproportionate to the value of the property sold and that a greater sum cannot be obtained; therefore,

Be it ordained by the People of the City and County of San Francisco as follows:

Section 1. The said sale of the said land hereinafter described to R. H. Hawkes for the sum of $17,000 is hereby ratified, approved and confirmed, and the Mayor and the Clerk of the Board of Supervisors are hereby authorized to execute and deliver to said purchaser, upon payment of the balance of the purchase price, a good and sufficient conveyance in the name of the City and County of San Francisco, conveying to R. H. Hawkes all the right, title and interest of the City and County of San Francisco in and to the land sold as aforesaid, and more particularly described as follows, to-wit:

Commencing at a point on the easterly line of Nineteenth avenue, distant thereon 255 feet southerly from the present southerly line of Wawona street, running thence southerly along said easterly line of Nineteenth avenue 150 feet; thence at a right angle easterly 275.26 feet; thence at a right angle northerly 150 feet; thence at a right angle westerly 275.26 feet to the easterly line of Nineteenth avenue and point of commencement. Being a portion of Outside Land Block 1258. also known as Lot 2 in Block No. 2540 on Assessor's Map Book.

Section 2. The City Attorney is hereby directed to prepare the necessary conveyance and supervise the delivery of deed upon payment of purchase price as aforesaid.

Section 3. This ordinance shall take effect immediately.

Ayes—Supervisors Andriano, Canepa, Colman, Gallagher, Havenner, Hayden, McGovern, McSheehy, Miles, Roncovieri, Rossi, Shannon, Spaulding, Stanton, Suhr, Toner—16.

Absent—Supervisors Peyser, Power—2.

PRESENTATION OF BILLS AND ACCOUNTS.

Your Finance Committee, having examined miscellaneous demands not required by law to be passed to print, and amounting to $58,953.18, recommends same be allowed and ordered paid.

Ayes—Supervisors Andriano, Canepa, Colman, Gallagher, Havenner, Hayden, McGovern, McSheehy, Miles, Roncovieri, Rossi, Shannon, Spaulding, Stanton, Suhr, Toner—16.

Absent—Supervisors Peyser, Power—2.

Urgent Necessity.

Edna Nelson et al, compensation insurance···················$ 104.15
Spring Valley Water Co., water, horse troughs··············   25.04
California School for the Deaf, clothing for San Francisco
  inmates 51.80

Ayes—Supervisors Andriano, Canepa, Colman, Gallagher, Havenner, Hayden, McGovern, McSheehy, Miles, Roncovieri, Rossi, Shannon, Spaulding, Stanton, Suhr, Toner—16.

Absent—Supervisors Peyser, Power—2.

NEW BUSINESS.

Passed for Printing.

The following matters were *passed for printing*:

Authorizations.

On recommendation of Finance Committee.

Resolution No. ———— (New Series), as follows:

Resolved, That the following amounts be and the same are hereby authorized to be expended out of the hereinafter mentioned funds in payment to the following named claimants, to-wit:

Library Fund.

(1) American Building Maintenance Co., janitor service furnished public libraries (claim dated Dec. 31, 1929) $ 810.00
(2) Mullen Manufacturing Co., book cases and fixtures furnished public libraries (claim dated Dec. 31, 1929).......   1,586.36
(3) Gunn, Carle & Co., tile floor furnished public library (claim dated Dec. 31, 1929)...........................   1,077.00
(4) C. E. Gordon, painting public libraries (claim dated Dec. 31, 1929) 847.00
(5) Finnell System, Inc., scrubber and water vacuum for public library (claim dated Dec. 31, 1929)...............   660.00
(6) Foster & Futernick Co., binding library books (claim dated Dec. 31, 1929)...................................   2,584.00
(7) San Francisco News Co., library books (claim dated Dec. 31, 1929) 4,454.84
(8) G. E. Stechert & Co., library books (claim dated Dec. 31, 1929) 2,511.43
(9) Sather Gate Book Shop, library books (claim dated Dec. 31, 1929) 3,238.24
(10) San Francisco News Co., library books (claim dated Dec. 31, 1929) 1,139.60

Special School Tax.

(11) Park Commissioners, reimbursement for care of school grounds (claim dated Jan. 10, 1930) ....$ 1,300.00
(12) J. H. McCallum, lumber for schools (claim dated Jan. 13, 1930) 527.72
(13) D. A. Pancoast Co., "Van Duprin" type Panic Bolts for schools (claim dated Jan. 13, 1930)....................   3,549.02
(14) C. F. Ernst, final payment for plumbing, gas fitting and cooking equipment furnished second unit South Side (Balboa) High School (claim dated Jan. 15, 1930)...........   15,088.68
(15) J. A. Mohr & Sons, Inc., final payment, painting of second unit South Side High School (claim dated Jan. 15, 1930) 1,985.25
(16) Scott Co., final payment, mechanical equipment, second unit South Side (Balboa) High School (claim dated Jan. 15, 1930) 8,601.75

(17) Mission Concrete Co., final payment, general construction of second unit South Side (Balboa) High School (claim dated Jan. 15, 1930) 77,505.58

(18) A. Lettich, first payment, plumbing work on Viewing Stand at South Side (Balboa) High School (claim dated Jan. 15, 1930) 968.40

(19) San Francisco City Employees' Retirement System, to match contributions by employees, for month of December, 1929 (claim dated Jan. 15, 1930) 968.69

California Palace, Legion of Honor, Appropriation 59.

(20) P. W. French, payment on purchase of "Moses and Aaron" tapestries, for California Palace, Legion of Honor (claim dated Jan. 10, 1930) .... $ 5,000.00

County Road Fund.

(21) Calaveras Cement Co., cement for street reconstruction (claim dated Jan. 11, 1930) .... $ 871.20

(22) Eclipse Lime & Cement Co., cement for street reconstruction (claim dated Jan. 11, 1930) 879.12

(23) Shell Oil Co., oil furnished in connection with street reconstruction (claim dated Jan. 11, 1930) 526.40

(24) The Texas Co., gasoline furnished in connection with street reconstruction (claim dated Jan. 11, 1930) 748.15

(25) Street Repair Department, Board of Public Works, reimbursement for cost of redressing curbs used in street reconstruction (claim dated Jan. 8, 1930) 643.75

(26) Street Repair Department, Board of Public Works, reimbursement for cost of redressing curbs used in street reconstruction (claim dated Jan. 8, 1930) 852.50

(27) San Francisco City Employees' Retirement System, to match contributions from employees engaged on street reconstruction (claim dated Jan. 15, 1930) 1,282.39

(28) Fay Improvement Co., sixth payment, improvement of Portola drive, from Twenty-fourth street to Fowler avenue (claim dated Jan. 15, 1930) 9,600.00

Hetch Hetchy Construction Fund, Bond Issue 1928.

(29) Bodinson Manufacturing Co., Inc., one double duplex classifier, Hetch Hetchy construction (claim dated Jan. 10, 1930. . . .. $ 4,370.00

(30) Consolidated Mills Co., Inc., lumber (claim dated Jan. 10, 1930) 567.71

(31) Ingersoll-Rand Co. of California, machinery parts (claim dated Jan. 10, 1930) 689.30

(32) Owen-Oregon Lumber Co., lumber (claim dated Jan. 10, 1930) 1,871.27

(33) Santa Cruz Portland Cement Co., cement (claim dated Jan. 10, 1930) 2,606.00

(34) Sherry Bros., Inc., eggs (claim dated Jan. 10, 1930) 554.40

(35) Utah Fuel Co., coal (claim dated Jan. 10, 1930) 232.80

(36) Western Pipe & Steel Co., steel tunnel form, steel carriage, etc. (claim dated Jan. 10, 1930) 4,392.00

(37) W. H. Worden Co., Inc., wire rope (claim dated Jan. 10, 1930) 527.19

(38) Best Steel Casting Co., castings and car wheels (claim dated Jan. 9, 1930) 969.58

(39) J. H. Creighton, truck hire (claim dated Jan. 9, 1930).. 1,262.80

Boulevard Bonds, Issue 1927.

(40) Spring Valley Water Co., laying of 8 and 12-inch water mains in Bay Shore boulevard and adjacent street (claim dated Jan. 10, 1930) .... $ 7,572.56

(41) Louis J. Cohn, fourteenth payment, improvement of Bay
Shore bolevard, Sec. A, Contract 6, Potrero to Silver avenue (claim dated Jan. 15, 1930) 15,000.00

Municipal Railway Fund.

(42) Ohio Brass Co., clinch trolley ears, Municipal Railways
(claim dated Jan. 10, 1930)......................$ 504.08
(43) Pacific Gas & Electric Co., electric power furnished Municipal Railways (claim dated Jan. 10, 1930)............. 43,359.76
(44) San Francisco City Employees' Retirement System, to
match contributions from Municipal Railway employees,
month of December, 1929 (claim dated Jan. 8, 1929)..... 7,742.13
(45) The Texas Co., gasoline furnished Municipal Railways
during November, 1929 (claim dated Jan. 10, 1930)....... 1,823.51

De Young Museum—Appropriation 58.

(46) P. J. Enright, third payment, heating and ventilating
M. H. de Young Memorial Museum (claim dated Jan. 17,
1930) ....$ 766.10

Auditorium Fund.

(47) Musical Association of San Francisco, for services of
San Francisco Symphony Orchestra, concert of Jan. 14,
1930 (claim dated Jan. 20, 1930).......................$ 2,000.00
(48) Selby C. Oppenheimer, for services of Dusolina Giannini
at concert of Jan. 14, 1930 (claim dated Jan. 20, 1930)... 1,200.00

General Fund, 1929-1930.

(49) San Francisco Chronicle, official advertising (claim
dated Jan. 20, 1930) ....$ 1,881.63
(50) Mendocino State Hospital, maintenance of criminal insane (claim dated Jan. 20, 1930)........................   561.33
(51) Pacific Gas & Electric Co., street lighting, month of
December, 1929 (claim dated Jan. 20, 1930).............. 65,767.94
(52) Old Homestead Bakery, bread furnished County Jails
(claim dated Jan. 15, 1930) 729.88
(53) Barnard & Bunker, beans for County Jails (claim dated
Jan. 15, 1930) 1,556.00
(54) Frank J. Reilly, general construction of addition to M.
H. de Young Memorial Museum, eighth payment (claim
dated Jan. 17, 1930) 10,425.00
(55) P. J. Enright, heating and ventilating M. H. de Young
Memorial Museum, third payment (claim dated Jan. 17,
1930) 3,046.41
(56) Children's Agency, maintenance of minors (claim dated
Jan. 9, 1930) 30,905.38
(57) Little Children's Aid, maintenance of minors (claim
dated Jan. 9, 1930) 12,324.68
(58) Eureka Benevolent Society, maintenance of minors
(claim dated Jan. 9, 1930)............................ 2,890.00
(59) St. Vincent's School, maintenance of minors (claim
dated Jan. 9, 1930)................................... 1,227.23
(60) Roman Catholic Orphan Asylum, maintenance of minors
(claim dated Jan. 9, 1930) 1,931.56
(61) The Albertinum Orphanage, maintenance of minors
(claim dated Jan. 8, 1930)............................   758.42
(62) Lybrand, Ross Bros. & Montgomery, professional services rendered in connection with system installation at San
Francisco Juvenile Court (claim dated Jan. 7, 1930)...... 1,919.95
(63) The Texas Co., gasoline furnished for street cleaning
(claim dated Jan. 13, 1930). 735.15
(64) Spring Valley Water Co., water furnished public buildings, month of December (claim dated Jan. 13, 1930)..... 2,197.93

(65) Pacific Gas & Electric Co., gas and electric service, Fire Department (claim dated Dec. 31, 1929)............   2,332.47

(66) The Seagrave Corporation, apparatus parts, Fire Department (claim dated Dec. 31, 1929).....................   601.95

(67) Spring Valley Water Co., water furnished Fire Department buildings, and installation of hydrants (claim dated Dec. 31, 1929) ....:..   2,302.35

(68) Standard Oil Co. of California, fuel oil, etc., for Fire Department (claim dated Dec. 31, 1929).................   1,164.05

(69) The Texas Co., gasoline furnished Fire Department (claim dated Dec. 31, 1929) 1,638.61

(70) Tire Service Co., tires and tubes, Fire Department (claim dated Dec. 31, 1929) 851.53

(71) The Spring Valley Water Co., rental, June 30 to Dec. 30, 1929, for 60 acres Lake Merced property, occupied as Fleishhacker Park, in accordance with agreement dated Dec. 24, 1929 (claim dated Jan. 20, 1930) 6,029.11

(72) California Meat Co., meat for Laguna Honda Home (claim dated Dec. 31, 1929) 1,660.56

(73) Del Monte Meat Co., meat furnished Laguna Honda Home (claim dated Dec. 31, 1929).......................   3,384.04

(74) Richfield Oil Co., fuel oil furnished Laguna Honda Home (claim dated Dec. 31, 1929) 1,900.69

(75) Baumgarten Bros., meat furnished Laguna Honda Home (claim dated Dec. 31, 1929) 813.71

(76) Spring Valley Water Co., water service rendered hospitals (claim dated Dec. 31, 1929) 1,700.59

Appropriations, Special School Tax, School Purposes.

Also, Resolution No. ————— (New Series), as follows:

Resolved, That the following amounts be and the same are hereby set aside, appropriated and authorized to be expended out of Special School Tax for the following purposes, to-wit:

(1) For the cost of installing gridiron and stage equipment at the Galileo High School.....................$ 3,481.00

(2) For cost of electrical fixtures for the Marina Elementary School 734.00

(3) For architectural services in the preparation of plans and specifications for the James Lick Junior High School..   7,200.00

Appropriations, Various Funds, Various Purposes.

Also, Resolution No. ————— (New Series), as follows:

Resolved, That the following amounts be and the same are hereby set aside, appropriated and authorized to be expended out of the hereinafter mentioned funds for the following purposes, to-wit:

Health Bonds, Issue 1928.

(1) For engineering plans and preparations of plans for roof ward buildings at the San Francisco Hospital............$ 5,000.00

Boulevard Bonds, Issue 1927.

(2) For cost of installing safety island on the Bay Shore boulevard at the county line............................$ 720.00

County Road Fund.

(3) For repairs and fills on Noriega street, from Thirty-fourth to Thirty-ninth avenues..........................$ 672.50

Fire House (Parkside), Budget Item No. 61.

(4) For engineering services in connection with construction of new engine house to be erected on west side of Eighteenth avenue between Quintara and Rivera streets.......$ 1,000.00

Municipal Airport Fund.

(5) For cost of cable installation at San Francisco Municipal Airport, in connection with construction of runway and drainage system ....$ 613.20

Reimbursements to Board of Public Works for Account Building Repairs.

Also, Resolution No. ————— (New Series), as follows:

Resolved, That the following amounts be set aside to the credit of Bureau of Building Repair, Board of Public Works, Budget Item 442, from the following Budget items, General Fund, 1929-1930, being reimbursements for work performed for various departments, Public Buildings, to-wit:

From repairs to public buildings, Budget Item No. 53, for work performed, as follows:

Grill work, etc., Juvenile Detention Home....................$	450.00
Bathroom, shower, plumbing, etc., Engine House No. 9.....	570.00
Kitchen construction, etc., Engine House No. 7.............	1,040.00
Elevator doors, etc., Hall of Justice........................	560.00
Electric switchboard, wiring, etc., Hall of Justice...........	950.00
Room 103, Detective Bureau, Hall of Justice...............	850.00
Room 102, Detective Bureau, Hall of Justice...............	568.00
Office, Chief of Police, Hall of Justice.....................	780.00
Electric work, signals, etc., office of Chief of Police.........	250.00
Cleaning hardwood floors, etc., Memorial Home, Chief of Fire Department	310.00
Boiler, San Francisco Hospital............................	1,934.00
Electric wiring and lights, office of Registrar...............	300.00

From City Hall repairs and painting, Budget Item 54, for work performed, as follows:

Building room, removing counters, etc., office of Registrar...	945.00
Building cashier's cages, office of Tax Collector.............	2,795.00
Partitions, etc., office of City Engineer....................	575.00
Changes in office of Chief Building Inspector...............	1,635.00

From contractual services, Department of Elections, Budget Item No. 188, for work performed, as follows:

For alterations, Department of Elections................... 1,500.00

Payment of Tax Judgment.

Also, Resolution No. ————— (New Series), as follows:

Resolved, That the following amounts be and the same are hereby set aside and appropriated out of "Tax Judgments," Appropriation 57, and authorized in payment to the hereinafter named claimants; being payments of one-tenth the amount of final judgments and interest, as approved by the City Attorney, to-wit:

(1) To Tobin & Tobin, attorneys for judgment creditors, seventh installment, per schedule attached (claim dated Dec. 27, 1929) ....$ 7,928.39
(2) To Charles W. Slack and Edgar T. Zook, attorneys for judgment creditors, per schedule attached (claim dated Jan. 2, 1930) 4,241.05
(3) To Southern Pacific Company, judgment creditor (claim dated Jan. 31, 1930) 19,084.77
(4) To The Western Pacific Railroad, judgment creditor (claim dated Dec. 29, 1929) 687.66

Payment for Property Damage, Bernal Cut.

Also, Resolution No. ————— (New Series), as follows:

Resolved, That the sum of $1,808 be and the same is hereby set aside and appropriated out of Bernal Cut Bond Fund, Issue 1927, and authorized in payment to James Millar and Jeannetta F. Millar, and

Title Insurance & Guaranty Co.; being payment in full release of damages to Lot 20, Block 6662, as per the Assessor's Block Books; also known as 71 Randall street; damages caused by the construction of Bernal Cut. Approved by Resolution No. 31899 (New Series) (claim dated Dec. 23, 1929).

Payments for Properties Required for Boulevards.

Also, Resolution No. ————— (New Series), as follows:

Resolved, That the following amounts be and the same are hereby set aside and appropriated out of Boulevard Bond Fund, Issue 1927, and authorized in payment to the hereinafter named persons; being payments for properties required for boulevard purposes, to-wit:

(1) To Ed Logue and Catherine Logue, and California Pacific Title & Trust Company, for portions of Lots 3 and 4, Block 7140 (47x24 irregular), as per the Assessor's Block Books, required for the opening of Alemany boulevard, and approved by Resolution No. 31896 (New Series) (claim dated Dec. 24, 1929) ....$ 5,500.00

2) To Mrs. Ernest Scossa and Title Insurance & Guaranty Co., for all of Lots 5 and 6 and portions of Lots 7 and 9, Block 5819, as per the Assessor's Block Books, and required for the opening of Alemany boulevard; approved by Resolution No. 31895 (New Series) (claim dated Dec. 31, 1929)   1,155.00

(3) To Maud E. Welch and Title Insurance & Guaranty Co., for portion of Lot 4, Block 7157 (20x90), as per the Assessor's Block Books, and required for the widening of San Jose avenue as an approach to Alemany boulevard. Purchase approved by Resolution No. ————— (New Series) (claim dated Jan. 14, 1930)......................   1,861.00

Adopted.

The following resolutions were *adopted*:

Appropriation, $25, Improvement of Stairs, Mono Street.

On recommendation of Finance Committee.

Resolution No. 31942 (New Series), as follows:

Resolved, That the sum of $25 be and the same is hereby set aside, appropriated and authorized to be expended out of County Road Fund, for the cost of the improving of the stairs on Mono street between Market and Eagle streets, to conform with new pavement on Eagle street.

Ayes—Supervisors Andriano, Canepa, Colman, Gallagher, Havenner, Hayden, McGovern, McSheehy, Miles, Roncovieri, Rossi, Shannon, Spaulding, Stanton, Suhr, Toner—16.

Absent—Supervisors Peyser, Power—2.

Dion Holm, Assistant City Attorney, to Attend Washington Hearing on Telephone Rate Investigation.

Also, Resolution No. 31943 (New Series), as follows:

Whereas, there is pending before the Senate of the United States, Senate Resolution No. 80, introduced by Honorable James Couzens, United States Senator from the State of Michigan, which said resolution provides that the Committee on Interstate Commerce of the Senate of the United States shall investigate the relationship existing between the different kinds of communication service used in interstate and foreign commerce, including radio, telephone, telegraph, and all kinds of wireless and cable service, and to investigate the connection, relationship, ownership and control of corporations and persons engaged in carrying on interstate and foreign communication services and other trade practices and trade activities, including contracts and stock ownership, and to investigate any and all other connections, relationships and activities of persons or corporations engaged in interstate and foreign communications by either wire or wireless, as said committee may deem necessary.

And, whereas, it will be of great benefit to the people of the City and County of San Francisco that said rates and activities be so investigated, for the reason that all of said matters have a direct bearing on the charges made and tolls collected by the Pacific Telephone & Telegraph Company for its services to the people of the City and County of San Francisco. Now, therefore,

Be It Resolved, That Dion R. Holm, an assistant to the City Attorney of the City and County of San Francisco, be and he is hereby directed to proceed to the City of Washington and be present at the hearing or hearings on said resolution before the Interstate Commerce Committee of the United States Senate, to be held on or about the 27th day of January, 1930, and to then and there present for and on behalf of the City and County of San Francisco, all data collected, learned or ascertained by him in the recent hearings before the Railroad Commission of the State of California in the matter of the application of the Pacific Telephone & Telegraph Company, that said commission establish and fix just rates of compensation for its services rendered. And be it

Further Resolved, That the Finance Committee be and it is hereby requested to appropriate the necessary money to defray the expense of said Dion R. Holm to and from the City of Washington and while he remains thereat during said hearing.

Ayes—Supervisors Andriano, Canepa, Colman, Gallagher, Havenner, Hayden, McGovern, McSheehy, Miles, Roncovieri, Rossi, Shannon, Spaulding, Stanton, Suhr, Toner—16.

Absent—Supervisors Peyser, Power—2.

Passed for Printing.

The following resolution was *passed for printing*:

Appropriation, Expense of Assistant City Attorney Dion R. Holm, to Represent San Francisco at Washington, D. C., $750.

On recommendation of Finance Committee.

Resolution No. ———— (New Series), as follows:

Resolved, That the sum of $750 be and the same is hereby set aside and appropriated out of "Telephone Rate Investigation Expense," Budget Item No. 59, and authorized in payment to Dion R. Holm, Assistant City Attorney, for his expense to, from and at Washington, D. C., in representing San Francisco before the U. S. Senate Committee on Interstate Commerce in its investigation on interstate and foreign communication service, etc., as authorized by Resolution No. 31943 (New Series).

Adopted.

The following resolution was *adopted*:

Accepting Offer of Maud E. Welch to Sell Land Required for Widening San Jose Avenue.

On recommendation of Finance Committee.

Resolution No. 31944 (New Series), as follows:

Resolved, That the offer of sale made by the following named owner to sell to the City and County of San Francisco the following described land, required for the widening of San Jose avenue as an approach to Alemany boulevard, for the sum set forth opposite her name be accepted:

Maud E. Welch, $1,861.00—Portion of Lot 4, Block 7157, as per the Assessor's Blocks Books of the City and County of San Francisco. (As per detailed description and written offer on file.)

As a further consideration Maud E. Welch is to receive a deed from the City and County of San Francisco to the following described parcel of land which was acquired for street purposes and is no longer necessary for street purposes:

Portion of Lots 2 and 3, Block 7157, as per the Assessor's Block Books of the City and County of San Francisco. (As per detailed description and written offer on file.)

And the City Attorney is hereby authorized to examine the title to said property, and if the same is found satisfactory to accept, on behalf of the City, a deed conveying said property to the City, free and clear of all encumbrances, and to record said deed, together with a copy of this resolution, in the office of the Recorder of the City and County of San Francisco.

The Mayor and the Clerk of the Board of Supervisors are hereby authorized and directed to execute a deed from the City and County of San Francisco to said Maud E. Welch conveying said parcel of land hereinabove described.

Ayes—Supervisors Andriano, Canepa, Colman, Gallagher, Havenner, Hayden, McGovern, McSheehy, Miles, Roncovieri, Rossi, Shannon, Spaulding, Stanton, Suhr, Toner—16.

Absent—Supervisors Peyser, Power—2.

Cancellation of Sale of Property for Non-Payment of Taxes.

Also, Resolution No. 31945 (New Series), as follows:

Whereas, the Tax Collector and Auditor have reported that the taxes for the year 1928 on the following described property were paid, but, through error, were not stamped "paid" on the Assessment Roll, and that the property was sold to the State of California on the 27th day of June, 1929, under Sales Nos. 2196 and 2399; therefore,

Resolved, That the Auditor be directed to cancel Sales Nos. 2196 and 2399, in accordance with the provisions of Sections 3776 and 3805 of the Political Code, of the following property:

Lot No. 14, Block No. 5526, Vol. No. 33, page No. 96, assessed to Catherine Lynch et al.

Lot No. 22, Block 5932, Vol. No. 36, page No. 26, assessed to Jean and B. Gregoine.

Ayes—Supervisors Andriano, Canepa, Colman, Gallagher, Havenner, Hayden, McGovern, McSheehy, Miles, Roncovieri, Rossi, Shannon, Spaulding, Stanton, Suhr, Toner—16.

Absent—Supervisors Peyser, Power—2.

Passed for Printing.

The following matters were *passed for printing*:

Ordering Improvement, Clayton and Market Streets.

On recommendation of Finance Committee.

Bill No. 8169, Ordinance No. ———— (New Series), as follows:

Ordering the improvement of the intersection of Clayton and Market streets, authorizing the preparation of plans and specifications for the said improvement of the intersection of Clayton and Market streets, and directing the Board of Public Works to enter into contract for said improvement in accordance with plans and specifications prepared therefor, which plans and specifications are hereby approved. The cost of said improvement to be borne out of County Road Fund.

Be it ordained by the People of the City and County of San Francisco as follows:

Section 1. The improvement of the intersection of Clayton and Market streets is hereby ordered, and the Board of Public Works is hereby authorized, instructed and empowered to prepare plans and specifications for said improvement of the intersection of Clayton and Market streets, and to enter into contract for said improvement in accordance with the plans and specifications prepared therefor, which plans and specifications are hereby approved. The cost of said improvement to be borne out of County Road Fund.

Section 2. This ordinance shall take effect immediately.

Ordering the Construction of Fire Department Engine House, Eighteenth Avenue Between Quintara and Rivera Streets.

Also, Bill No. 8170, Ordinance No. ———— (New Series), as follows:

Ordering the construction of Fire Department engine house, to be erected on the west side of Eighteenth avenue between Quintara and Rivera streets, in accordance with plans and specifications, which plans and specifications are hereby authorized to be prepared; authorizing and directing the Board of Public Works to enter into contract for said construction in accordance with the plans and specifications prepared therefor; permitting progressive payments to be made during the progress of construction.

Be it ordained by the People of the City and County of San Francisco as follows:

Section 1. The construction of Fire Department engine house is hereby ordered, and the Board of Public Works is hereby authorized, instructed and empowered to prepare plans and specifications for the said construction of Fire Department engine house, to be erected on the west side of Eighteenth avenue between Quintara and Rivera streets, and to enter into contract for said construction in accordance with the plans and specifications prepared therefor, which plans and specifications are hereby approved.

Section 2. The said Board of Public Works is hereby authorized and permitted to incorporate in the contract for the said construction of Fire Department engine house conditions that progressive payments shall be made in the manner set forth in said specifications on file in the Board of Public Works, and as provided by Section 21, Chapter I, Article VI of the Charter.

Section 3. This ordinance shall take effect immediately.

Ordering Construction of James Lick Junior High School.

Also, Bill No. 8171, Ordinance No. ———— (New Series), as follows:

Ordering the construction of the James Lick Junior High School, to be erected in block bounded by Twenty-fifth and Clipper streets, Noe and Castro streets, in accordance with plans and specifications, which plans and specifications are hereby authorized to be prepared; authorizing and directing the Board of Public Works to enter into contract for the said construction in accordance with the plans and specifications prepared therefor and as approved by the Board of Education. Permitting progressive payments to be made during the progress of construction.

Be it ordained by the People of the City and County of San Francisco as follows:

Section 1. The construction of the James Lick Junior High School is hereby ordered, and the Board of Public Works is hereby authorized, instructed and empowered to prepare plans and specifications for said construction of the James Lick Junior High School, to be erected in the block bounded by Twenty-fifth and Clipper streets, Noe and Castro streets, and to enter into contract for said construction in accordance with the plans and specifications prepared therefor and as approved by the Board of Education.

Section 2. The Board of Public Works is hereby authorized and permitted to incorporate in the contract for the said construction of James Lick Junior High School conditions that progressive payments shall be made in the manner set forth in said specifications on file in the Board of Public Works, and as provided by Section 21, Chapter I, Article VI of the Charter.

Section 3. This ordinance shall take effect immediately.

Ordering Construction of Ward Building "F", Relief Home Tract.

Also, Bill No. 8172, Ordinance No. ————— (New Series), as follows:

Ordering the construction of Ward Building "F," Relief Home Tract; authorizing and directing the Board of Public Works to prepare plans and specifications for the construction of Ward Building "F," Relief Home Tract, and to enter into contract for said construction in accordance with the plans and specifications prepared therefor, which plans and specifications are hereby approved. The cost of said construction to be borne out of Health Bonds, Issue 1928.

Be it ordained by the People of the City and County of San Francisco as follows:

Section 1. The construction of Ward Building "F," Relief Home Tract, is hereby ordered, and the Board of Public Works is hereby authorized, instructed and empowered to prepare plans and specifications for the construction of said Ward Building "F," Relief Home Tract, and to enter into contract for said construction in accordance with the plans and specifications prepared therefor, which plans and specifications are hereby approved. The cost of said construction of Ward Building "F," Relief Home Tract, to be borne out of the Health Bond Fund, Issue 1928.

Section 2. This ordinance shall take effect immediately.

Adopted.

The following resolution was *adopted*:

Fixing Salary of Bond and Ordinance Clerk at $175 Per Month.

On recommendation of Finance Committee.

Resolution No. 31946 (New Series), as follows:

Resolved, That the salary of Frederick J. Moran, bond and ordinance clerk, per authorization by Resolution No. 31867 (New Series), is hereby fixed at $175 per month.

Ayes—Supervisors Andriano, Canepa, Colman, Gallagher, Havenner, Hayden, McGovern, McSheehy, Miles, Power, Roncovieri, Rossi, Shannon, Spaulding, Stanton, Suhr, Toner—17.

Absent—Supervisor Peyser—1.

Passed for Printing.

The following matters were *passed for printing*:

Appropriation to Enable Final Payment for Improvement of Junipero Serra Boulevard, Contract No. 13.

On recommendation of Finance Committee.

Resolution No. ————— (New Series), as follows:

Resolved, That the sum of $28,500.00 be and the same is hereby set aside, appropriated and authorized to be expended out of Boulevard Bond Issue, 1927, for the improvement of Junipero Serra boulevard, from Sloat boulevard to the county line, Contract No. 13, additional to enable final payment.

Oil and Boiler Permits.

On recommendation of Fire Committee.

Resolution No. ————— (New Series), as follows:

Resolved, That the following revocable permits be and are hereby granted:

Oil Tanks.

Rothschild Bros.—West side Steiner street, 82 feet south of Broadway, 750 gallons capacity.

Rothschild Bros.—West side Steiner street, 55 feet south of Broadway, 750 gallons capacity.

Frank Risso—Northwest corner of Tenth avenue and Anza street, 750 gallons capacity.

Grace Cathedral—South side of Sacramento street, 125 feet east of Jones street, 2000 gallons capacity.

T. A. Amitage—1561 Francisco street, 1500 gallons capacity.

Sommer & Kaufmann—South side Ellis street, 150 feet west of Stockton street, 1500 gallons capacity.

J. L. Snigewald—West side Capp street, 200 feet south of Twenty-third street, 1500 gallons capacity.

Boiler.

Gray & Danielson—Southwest corner of Nineteenth and Bryant streets, 40 horsepower.

The rights granted under this resolution shall be exercised within six months, otherwise said permit shall become null and void.

Transfer of Automobile Supply Station, W. J. Higgins, Polk Street, North of Fell Street.

Also, Resolution No. ———— (New Series), as follows:

Resolved, That John M. Hearn be and is hereby granted permission, revocable at will of the Board of Supervisors, to have transferred automobile supply station permit heretofore granted W. J. Higgins by Resolution No. 31191 (New Series) for premises on west side of Polk street, 35 feet north of Fell street.

The rights granted under this resolution shall be exercised within six months, otherwise said permit shall become null and void.

Transfer of Automobile Supply Station Permit, H. Heskins, Southwest Corner Cabrillo Street and Forty-seventh Avenue.

Also, Resolution No. ———— (New Series), as follows:

Resolved, That H. Heskins be and is hereby granted permission, revocable at will of the Board of Supervisors, to have transferred automobile supply station permit heretofore granted C. Leonard by Resolution No. 30736 (New Series) for premises on southwest corner of Cabrillo street and Forty-seventh avenue.

The rights granted under this resolution shall be exercised within six months, otherwise said permit shall become null and void.

Action Deferred.

The following bill was, on motion of Supervisor Gallagher, *laid over one week and made a Special Order for 2:30 p. m.*:

Prohibiting Return of Certain Class of Merchandise by Purchaser.

Bill No. ————. Ordinance No. ———— (New Series).

Prohibiting the return by purchaser of merchandise which by use may become a source of infection and a menace to the public health.

Be it Ordained by the People of the City and County of San Francisco as follows:

Section 1. It is unlawful for any person, firm or corporation engaged in the sale at retail of the following articles of merchandise, to-wit:

a. Mattresses, blankets, sheets, comforters, pillows and other bedding.

b. Heating pads and metal hot water bottles, stockings made of rubber, reducing rollers, water bags and other rubber goods.

c. Combs, hair brushes, tooth brushes, barettes, bath brushes, powder puffs, lipsticks, compacts, broken packages of powder, creams, rouges.

d. Corsets, brassiers, underwear, union suits, bloomers, bathing suits.

e. Articles made of hair and veils.

to accept from the purchaser of any of above articles, once delivery is effected, provided that this section shall not be construed to prohibit the return of articles misfitting or defective in their construction, which shall be disinfected before being offered for re-sale.

Section 2. Any person, firm or corporation violating any of the provisions of this ordinance shall be deemed guilty of a misdemeanor and upon conviction thereof, shall be punished by a fine of not more than one hundred dollars ($100) or by imprisonment in the County Jail for a period not exceeding thirty (30) days, or by both such fine and imprisonment.

Adopted.

The following resolutions were *adopted*:

City Attorney to Prepare Ordinance, Inspection of Gas Appliances.

On recommendation of Public Health Committee.

Resolution No. 31947 (New Series), as follows:

Whereas, during the present month there have been numerous deaths by asphyxiation caused by gas leaking from defective gas appliances and piping within residences and apartments in the City and County of San Francisco; and

Whereas, at the present time the City and County of San Francisco maintains no adequate inspection of the installation of gas appliances in residences and other places; now, therefore, be it

Resolved, That the City Attorney be and he is hereby directed to present to this Board an ordinance providing for the adequate inspection of all gas pipes, fixtures and appliances installed in residences and other places in the City and County of San Francisco, and for the licensing of those persons engaged in the installation of said pipes and fixtures.

Ayes—Supervisors Andriano, Canepa, Colman, Gallagher, Havenner, Hayden, McGovern, McSheehy, Miles, Power, Roncovieri, Rossi, Shannon, Spaulding, Stanton, Suhr, Toner—17.

Absent—Supervisor Peyser—1.

Masquerade Ball Permit, Independent Rifles, California Hall, Turk and Polk Streets, Saturday, January 11, 1930.

On recommendation of Police Committee.

Resolution No. 31948 (New Series), as follows:

Resolved, That the Independent Rifles be and they are hereby granted permission to conduct a masquerade ball at California Hall, Turk and Polk streets, Saturday, January 11, 1930.

Ayes—Supervisors Andriano, Canepa, Colman, Gallagher, Havenner, Hayden, McGovern, McSheehy, Miles, Power, Roncovieri, Rossi, Shannon, Spaulding, Stanton, Suhr, Toner—17.

Absent—Supervisor Peyser—1.

Masquerade Ball Permit, Bayern Bund, California Hall, Turk and Polk Streets, Saturday, January 25, 1930.

Also, Resolution No. 31949 (New Series), as follows:

Resolved, That the Bayern Bund of San Francisco be and it is hereby granted permission to conduct a masquerade ball Saturday, January 25, 1930, in California Hall, Turk and Polk streets.

Ayes—Supervisors Andriano, Canepa, Colman, Gallagher, Havenner, Hayden, McGovern, McSheehy, Miles, Power, Roncovieri, Rossi, Shannon, Spaulding, Stanton, Suhr, Toner—17.

Absent—Supervisor Peyser—1.

Masquerade Ball Permit, Germania Club, California Hall, Polk and Turk Streets, Saturday, February 8, 1930.

Also, Resolution No. 31950 (New Series), as follows:

Resolved, That the Germania Club be and it is hereby granted permission to conduct a masquerade ball at California Hall, Polk and Turk streets, Saturday, February 8, 1930.

Ayes—Supervisors Andriano, Canepa, Colman, Gallagher, Havenner, Hayden, McGovern, McSheehy, Miles, Power, Roncovieri, Rossi, Shannon, Spaulding, Stanton, Suhr, Toner—17.

Absent—Supervisor Peyser—1.

Passed for Printing.

The following bill was *passed for printing*:

Directing Sale of City Land Situate Sutter Street Near Gough Street, Heretofore Site of Lowell High School.

On recommendation of Public Buildings and Lands Committee.

Bill No. 8173, Ordinance No. ——————— (New Series), as follows:

Providing for the disposal at public auction of certain lands belonging to the City and County of San Francisco in accordance with provisions of Article II, Chapter II, Section 9 of the Charter.

Be it ordained by the People of the City and County of San Francisco as follows:

Section 1. That public interest and necessity demand the sale of the following described parcel or piece of land owned and held by the City and County of San Francisco. Said parcel of land is situated in the City and County of San Francisco, State of California, and more particularly described as follows, to-wit:

Commencing at a point on the northerly line of Sutter street, distant thereon 137 feet 6 inches westerly from the westerly line of Gough street, running thence northerly 137 feet 6 inches; thence at right angles westerly 68 feet 9 inches; thence at right angles northerly 137 feet 6 inches to the southerly line of Bush street; thence at right angles westerly along said southerly line of Bush street 68 feet 9 inches; thence at right angles southerly 275 feet to the northerly line of Sutter street; thence at right angles easterly 137 feet. 6 inches to the point of commencement; being a portion of Block 673 (W. A. 158).

Section 2. The said piece or parcel of land hereinabove described shall be sold for cash, in United States gold coin, at public auction to be held in accordance with the provisions of Article II, Chapter II, Section 9 of the Charter.

Section 3. The Clerk of the Board of Supervisors is hereby directed to publish in the official newspaper and in one other daily newspaper for three weeks successively next before the day on which the sale is to be made, a notice of such sale, describing the land to be sold with common certainty.

Section 4. The Mayor, Assessor and the Chairman of the Finance Committee of the Board of Supervisors are hereby directed to appraise said land within three weeks after the final passage of this ordinance as required by Article II, Chapter II, Section 9 of the Charter.

Section 5. Upon receipt and examination of bids or offers for said land as aforesaid, the Mayor shall accept the highest bid made, provided said bid be for at least 90 per cent of the value found by said appraisers, and shall immediately thereafter, at the next meeting of the Supervisors, report the fact of such sale to the Supervisors with a statement of the sum bid and the name of the highest bidder, with a request that the Board confirm such sale.

Adopted.

The following resolution was adopted

Exchange of Property, Aptos Avenue, Board of Education and Playground Commission.

On recommendation of Public Buildings and Lands Committee.

Resolution No. 31951 (New Series), as follows:

Resolved, That, in accordance with a communication from the Playground Commission, and in accordance with the request of the Board of Education set forth therein, the following described properties are hereby exchanged between the said Playground Commission and the Board of Education for their respective use and purposes, to wit:

Playground Commission to Board of Education:

Commencing at a point on the easterly line of Aptos avenue, distant southerly thereon an arc distance of 290.207 feet from the southerly termination of that curve of 10-foot radius at the intersection of said easterly line with the southerly line of Upland drive, as said curve is shown on that certain map entitled "Map of Blocks 8260 to 8269, inclusive, Balboa Terrace Addition," and recorded in Map Book "L," pages 29 to 33, inclusive, records of the City and County of San Francisco, and running thence southerly along said easterly line of Aptos avenue, being a curve to the right, radius 1618 feet, an arc distance of 42.828 feet; thence deflecting 102 deg. 07 min. 49 sec. to the left from the tangent to the preceding curve, and running easterly parallel with said southerly line of Upland drive 232.466 feet; thence deflecting 169 deg. 28 min. 10 sec. to the left and running westerly along the radial line extended through the point of commencement 227.994 feet to the easterly line of Aptos avenue and the point of commencement. Being a portion of Block 8266 of said Balboa Terrace Addition and a portion of San Aleso avenue, as said avenue existed prior to its closing and abandonment by Resolution No. 28866, dated April 24, 1928, of the Board of Supervisors of the City and County of San Francisco.

Board of Education to Playground Commission:

Commencing at a point on the easterly line of Block 8265, as said block is shown on that certain map entitled "Map of Blocks 8260 to 8269, inclusive, Balboa Terrace Addition," and recorded in Map Book "L," pages 29 to 33, inclusive, records of the City and County of San Francisco, distant southerly thereon an arc distance of 864.567 feet from the southerly line of Upland drive, and running thence northerly along said easterly line of said Block 8265, being a curve to the left, radius 1968 feet, an arc distance of 22.854 feet; thence deflecting 100 deg. 86 min. 50 sec. to the left from the tangent to the preceding curve, and running westerly parallel with said southerly line of Upland drive 124.068 feet; thence deflecting 169 deg. 28 min. 10 sec. to the left and running easterly along the radial line through the point of commencement 122.076 feet to the easterly line of said Block 8265 and the point of commencement. Being a portion of said Block 8265 and a portion of San Aleso avenue, as said avenue existed prior to its closing and abandonment by Resolution No. 28866, dated April 24, 1928, of the Board of Supervisors of the City and County of San Francisco.

Passed for Printing.

The following resolution was passed for printing:

Condemnation of Land for School Purposes in Holly Park Tract.

On recommendation of Public Buildings and Lands Committee.

Resolution No. ——————— (New Series), as follows:

Resolved, by the Board of Supervisors of the City and County of San Francisco, that public interest and necessity require the acquisition by the City and County of San Francisco, a municipal corporation, of the following properties situated in the City and County of San Francisco, State of California, more particularly described as follows, to-wit:

Being all of Block No. 2, Holly Park Tract, as per map recorded in the office of the City and County Recorder July 5, 1883, excepting Lot No. 22 and a portion of Lot No. 21 on said original map which said land excepted is now vested in the City and County of San Francisco. The said block is also known as Block No. 5714 on Assessor's Map Book, bounded by Appleton, Patton and Highland streets and Holly Park Circle; and be it

Further Resolved, That said properties are suitable, adaptable, necessary and required for the public use of said City and County of San Francisco for school purposes. It is necessary that a fee simple title be taken for such use.

The City Attorney is hereby ordered and directed to commence proceedings in eminent domain against the owners of said parcels of land and of any and all interests therein or claims thereto, for the condemnation thereof for the public use of the City and County of San Francisco, as aforesaid.

Referred.

The following resolution was, on motion of Supervisor Rossi, referred to the Finance Committee:

Recommending Bond Issue for Acquisition of Lands, Extension of Leavenworth Street Through From McAllister to Market Within the Civic Center.

Resolution No. ———— (New Series), as follows:

Whereas, there is urgent need that the City should acquire certain property in the Civic Center to enable it to extend Leavenworth street from its present termination at McAllister street to a junction with Market street and to complete the entrance of the Civic Center from Market street; and

Whereas, it appears that the amount necessary to acquire said property cannot be taken from the ordinary revenue of the City; now, therefore, be it

Resolved, That the Finance Committee of the Board of Supervisors be requested to recommend to this Board the necessary ordinances looking to the issuance of a bonded indebtedness in an amount sufficient to acquire said properties.

Passed for Printing.

The following matters were passed for printing:

Spur Track Permit, Southern Pacific Company, Across Second, King and Gale Streets.

On recommendation of Streets Committee.

Bill No. 8174, Ordinance No. ———— (New Series), as follows:

Granting permission, revocable at will of the Board of Supervisors, to Southern Pacific Company (a corporation) to construct, maintain and operate spur tracks across Second, King and Gale streets as hereinafter described.

Be it ordained by the People of the City and County of San Francisco as follows:

Section 1. Permission, revocable at will of the Board of Supervisors, is hereby granted to the Southern Pacific Company (a corporation) to construct, maintain and operate spur tracks as follows:

(a) Beginning at a point on the center line of an existing Southern Pacific Company track in King street, said point being approximately 25 feet southwesterly from the northeasterly line of Second street 22 feet, more or less, southeasterly from the northwesterly line of King street; thence in a northeasterly direction and crossing portion of

the intersection of King and Second streets to a point on the northwesterly line of King street; thence continuing into private property.

(b) Beginning at a point on the center line of an existing Southern Pacific Company track in King street, said point being distant
southeasterly 5 feet, more or less, from the northwesterly line of King
street and 8 feet, more or less, northeasterly from the northeasterly
line of Second street; thence in a northeasterly direction and crossing portion of King street to a point on the northwesterly line of
King street; thence continuing into private property.

(c) Beginning at a point on the southwesterly line of Gale street,
distant northwesterly thereon 40 feet, more or less, from the northwesterly line of King street; thence in a northeasterly direction crossing Gale street to a point on the northeasterly line thereof; thence
continuing into private property.

(d) Beginning at a point on the southwesterly line of Gale street,
distant northwesterly thereon 53 feet, more or less, from the northwesterly line of King street; thence in a northeasterly direction crossing Gale street to a point on the northeasterly line thereof; thence
continuing into private property.

(e) Beginning at a point on the southwesterly line of Gale street,
distant northwesterly thereon 67 feet, more or less, from the northwesterly line of King street; thence in a northeasterly direction crossing Gale street to a point on the northeasterly line thereof; thence
continuing into private property.

Said permission is granted subject to the provisions of Ordinance
No. 69 (New Series) of the Board of Supervisors, approved October
12, 1906, and the provisions and conditions of Section 8 thereof are
hereby specifically contained in the permit hereby granted and shall
be construed as a part hereof as completely as though the same were
written in this ordinance.

Provided, that said spur tracks shall be laid with girder rails under
the supervision and to the lines and grades as furnished by the City
Engineer's office, and that any and all expenses connected with the
installation of the tracks, restoration of the pavement and any additional requirements for the surface drainage to be paid for by the
Southern Pacific Company; provided, that Southern Pacific Company
shall erect and maintain all-night lighted arc lamps to be placed where
directed by the Lighting Committee of the Board of Supervisors.

Section 2. This ordinance shall take effect immediately.

Repealing Ordinances Numbered 8612 (New Series) and 8621 (New Series), Ordering the Removal of Sand and Construction of Bulkheads on Thirty-second Avenue and on Balboa Street.

Also, Bill No. 8175, Ordinance No. ——— (New Series), as follows:

Repealing Ordinance No. 8612 (New Series) and Ordinance No. 8621
(New Series), ordering the removal of sand and the construction of
bulkheads on Thirty-second avenue and on Balboa street as hereinafter described.

Be it ordained by the People of the City and County of San Francisco as follows:

Section 1. Ordinance No. 8612 (New Series), ordering the removal
of sand and the construction of bulkheads on the west one-half of
Thirty-second avenue from the south line of Geary street to a line
parallel with and 100 feet 0 inches south of the south line of Geary
street.

Ordinance No. 8621 (New Series), ordering the removal of sand and
the construction of bulkheads on the south one-half of Balboa street
from the west line of Twenty-fourth avenue to a line parallel with and
82 feet 0 inches west of the west line of Twenty-fourth avenue, by
the removal of sand from the roadway and sidewalk area and the con
struction of a bulkhead be and the same are hereby repealed.

Section 2. This ordinance shall take effect immediately.

Ordering Street Work, Flood Avenue and Other Streets.

Also, Bill No. 8176, Ordinance No. ——— (New Series), as follows:

Ordering the performance of certain street work to be done in the City and County of San Francisco, approving and adopting specifications therefor.

Be it ordained by the People of the City and County of San Francisco as follows:

Section 1. The Board of Public Works in written communication filed in the office of the Clerk of the Board of Supervisors January 7, 1930, having recommended the ordering of the following street work, the same is hereby ordered to be done in the City and County of San Francisco in conformity with the provisions of the Street Improvement Ordinance of 1918 of said City and County of San Francisco, said work to be performed under the direction of the Board of Public Works, and to be done in accordance with the specifications prepared therefor by said Board of Public Works, and on file in its office, which said plans and specifications are hereby approved and adopted.

That said Board of Supervisors, pursuant to the provisions of Part II of the said Street Improvement Ordinance of 1918 of said City and County of San Francisco, does hereby determine and declare that the assessment to be imposed for the said contemplated improvements, respectively, may be paid in three installments; that the period of time after the time of the payment of the first installment when each of the succeeding installments must be paid is to be one year from the time of the payment of the preceding installment, and that the rate of interest to be charged on all deferred payments shall be seven per centum per annum.

The improvement of the south one-half of Flood avenue from the east line of Genesee street to a line parallel with and 100 feet east of the east line of Genesee street and the west one-half of Twenty-seventh avenue from a line parallel with and 100 feet north of the north line of Taraval street to a line parallel with and 125 feet north of the north line of Taraval street and the west one-half of Twnty-third avenue from a line parallel with and 265 feet south of the south line of Judah street to a line parallel with and 290 feet south of the south line of Judah street; and the west one-half of Eleventh avenue from a line parallel with and 200 feet north of the north line of Lawton street to a line parallel with and 225 feet north of the north line of Lawton street; and the east one-half of Nineteenth avenue from a line parallel with and 225 feet south of the south line of Moraga street to a line parallel with and 375 feet south of the south line of Moraga street; and the north one-half of Balboa street from the west line of Forty-third avenue to a line parallel with and 100 feet west of the west line of Forty-third avenue; and the east one-half of Twenty-sixth avenue from a line parallel with and 250 feet south of the south line of California street to a line parallel with and 325 feet south of the south line of California street; by the construction of artificial stone sidewalks, six feet in width, where artificial stone or bituminous rock sidewalks, six feet or more in width, have not already been constructed to the official grade; and the improvement of the west one-half of Eighth avenue from a line parallel with and 125 feet south of the south line of Anza street to a line parallel with and 175 feet south of the south line of Anza street; and the south one-half of Anza street from a line parallel with and 53 feet 4 inches east of the east line of Ninth avenue to a line parallel with and 105 feet east of the east line of Ninth avenue; and the west one-half of Mission street from the north line of Twenty-second street to a line parallel with and 112 feet 9 inches north of the north line of Twenty-second street; and the east one-half of Mission street from the north line of Twenty-third street to a line parallel with and 85 feet north of the north line of Twenty-third street; and the west one-half of Larkin street from the north line of Pine street to a line parallel with and 137 feet 6 inches north of the north line of Pine street; and the east one-half of Seventeenth avenue from the south line of Lincoln way to a line parallel with and 100 feet south of the south line of Lincoln way; and the south one-half of Twenty-ninth street from a line parallel with and 30 feet west of the west line of Noe street to a line parallel with and 55 feet west of the west line of Noe street; and the south one-half of Twenty-ninth street from a line parallel with and 80 feet west of the west line of Noe street to a line parallel with and 105 feet west of the west line of Noe street, by the construction of artificial stone sidewalks of the full official width, where artificial stone or bituminous rock sidewalks of the full official width have not already been constructed to the official grade.

Section 2. This ordinance shall take effect immediately.

Ordering Street Work, Silliman Street and Other Streets.

Also, Bill No. 8177, Ordinance No. ———— (New Series), as follows:

Ordering the performance of certain street work to be done in the City and County of San Francisco, approving and adopting specifications therefor.

Be it ordained by the People of the City and County of San Francisco as follows:

Section 1. The Board of Public Works in written communication filed in the office of the Clerk of the Board of Supervisors January 7, 1930, having recommended the ordering of the following street work, the same is hereby ordered to be done in the City and County of San Francisco in conformity with the provisions of the Street Improvement Ordinance of 1918 of said City and County of San Francisco, said work to be performed under the direction of the Board of Public Works, and to be done in accordance with the specifications prepared therefor by said Board of Public Works, and on file in its office, which said plans and specifications are hereby approved and adopted.

That said Board of Supervisors, pursuant to the provisions of Part II of the said Street Improvement Ordinance of 1918 of said City and County of San Francisco, does hereby determine and declare that the assessment to be imposed for the said contemplated improvements, respectively, may be paid in three installments; that the period of time after the time of the payment of the first installment when each of the succeeding installments must be paid is to be one year from the time of the payment of the preceding installment, and that the rate of interest to be charged on all deferred payments shall be seven per centum per annum.

The improvement of the following streets: Silliman street between Dartmouth street and Hamilton street; Felton street between Somerset street and Hamilton street; Burrows street between San Bruno avenue and Girard street; Bacon street between Somerset street and Hamilton street; Wayland street between Brussels street and Hamilton street; north half Woolsey street between Somerset street and Goettingen street; Olmstead street between San Bruno avenue and Brussels street; Girard street between Dwight street and Mansell street; Goettingen street between Wayland street and Bacon street; Somerset street between Wayland street and Silliman street; Holyoke street between Wayland street and Felton street; Hamilton street between Felton street and Silver avenue; Bowdoin street between Felton street and Silver avenue, by the construction of artificial stone sidewalks, six feet in width, where artificial stone or bituminous rock sidewalks, six feet or more in width, have not already been constructed.

Section 2. This ordinance shall take effect immediately.

Ordering the Improvement of the West One-Half of Twenty-second Avenue.

Also, Bill No. 8178, Ordinance No. ————— (New Series), as follows:

Ordering the performance of certain street work to be done in the City and County of San Francisco, approving and adopting specifications therefor.

Be it ordained by the People of the City and County of San Francisco as follows:

Section 1. The Board of Public Works in written communication filed in the office of the Clerk of the Board of Supervisors January 7, 1930, having recommended the ordering of the following street work, the same is hereby ordered to be done in the City and County of San Francisco in conformity with the provisions of the Street Improvement Ordinance of 1918 of said City and County of San Francisco, said work to be performed under the direction of the Board of Public Works, and to be done in accordance with the specifications prepared therefor by said Board of Public Works, and on file in its office, which said plans and specifications are hereby approved and adopted.

That said Board of Supervisors, pursuant to the provisions of Part II of the said Street Improvement Ordinance of 1918 of said City and County of San Francisco, does hereby determine and declare that the assessment to be imposed for the said contemplated improvements, respectively, may be paid in three installments; that the period of time after the time of the payment of the first installment when each of the succeeding installments must be paid is to be one year from the time of the payment of the preceding installment, and that the rate of interest to be charged on all deferred payments shall be seven per centum per annum.

The improvement of the west one-half of Twenty-second avenue from a line parallel with and 225 feet north of the north line of Moraga street to a line parallel with and 300 feet north of the north line of Moraga street, by the removal of sand from the roadway and sidewalk area and the construction of a bulkhead.

Section 2. This ordinance shall take effect immediately.

Ordering the Improvement of the North One-Half of Nineteenth Street.

Also, Bill No. 8179, Ordinance No. ————— (New Series), as follows:

Ordering the performance of certain street work to be done in the City and County of San Francisco, approving and adopting specifications therefor.

Be it ordained by the People of the City and County of San Francisco as follows:

Section 1. The Board of Public Works in written communication filed in the office of the Clerk of the Board of Supervisors January 7, 1930, having recommended the ordering of the following street work, the same is hereby ordered to be done in the City and County of San Francisco in conformity with the provisions of the Street Improvement Ordinance of 1918 of said City and County of San Francisco, said work to be performed under the direction of the Board of Public Works, and to be done in accordance with the specifications prepared therefor by said Board of Public Works, and on file in its office, which said plans and specifications are hereby approved and adopted.

That said Board of Supervisors, pursuant to the provisions of Part II of the said Street Improvement Ordinance of 1918 of said City and County of San Francisco, does hereby determine and declare that the assessment to be imposed for the said contemplated improvements, respectively, may be paid in three installments; that the period of time after the time of the payment of the first installment when each of the succeeding installments must be paid is to be one year from the time of the payment of the preceding installment, and that the rate of interest to be charged on all deferred payments shall be seven per centum per annum.

The improvement of the north one-half of Nineteenth street from a line parallel with and 100 feet east of the east line of Sanchez street to a line parallel with and 150 feet east of the east line of Sanchez street, by the removal of sand from the roadway and sidewalk area and the construction of a bulkhead 3 feet in height.

Bidder is to name price per lineal foot of bulkhead for this work.

Section 2. This ordinance shall take effect immediately.

Adopted.

The following resolutions were *adopted*:

Approving Map Showing the Widening of Silver Avenue Between San Bruno and Quesada Avenues and Charter Oak Avenue Between Silver Avenue and Augusta Street.

On recommendation of Streets Committee.

Resolution No. 31952 (New Series), as follows:

Whereas, the Board of Public Works did, by Resolution No. 108947 (Second Series), approve a map showing the widening of Silver avenue between San Bruno and Quesada avenues; also Charter Oak avenue between Silver avenue and August street; now, therefore, be it

Resolved, That the map showing the widening of Silver avenue between San Bruno and Quesada avenues, also Charter Oak avenue between Silver avenue and Augusta street, be and the same is hereby approved.

Further Resolved, That the parcels shown hatched on said map, parcels 2 to 17a, inclusive, as Silver avenue, and parcels 18 to 23, inclusive, as Charter Oak avenue, are hereby dedicated to public use and are declared to be open public streets.

Ayes—Supervisors Andriano, Canepa, Colman, Gallagher, Havenner, Hayden, McGovern, McSheehy, Miles, Power, Roncovieri, Rossi, Shannon, Spaulding, Stanton, Suhr, Toner—17.

Absent—Supervisor Peyser—1.

Extension of Time to Complete Improvements of Kirkham and Moraga Streets and Forty-third Avenue Where Not Already Done.

Also, Resolution No. 31953 (New Series), as follows:

Resolved, That the Municipal Construction Company is hereby granted an extension of ninety days' time from and after December 27, 1929, within which to complete the improvement of Kirkham street between Thirty-second and Thirty-third avenues, Kirkham street between Forty-fourth and Forty-fifth avenues, Moraga street between Forty-third and Forty-fourth avenues, Moraga street between Forty-fourth and Forty-fifth avenues, and Forty-third avenue between Lawton and Moraga streets, where not already improved under public contract.

This recommendation is granted upon the recommendation of the Board of Public Works for the reason that the grading is well under way and the contractor has been delayed by inclement weather.

Ayes—Supervisors Andriano, Canepa, Colman, Gallagher, Havenner, Hayden, McGovern, McSheehy, Miles, Power, Roncovieri, Rossi, Shannon, Spaulding, Stanton, Suhr, Toner—17.

Absent—Supervisor Peyser—1.

Extension of Time, M. Bertolino, Improvement of Swiss Avenue Between Surrey and Sussex Streets.

Also, Resolution No. 31954 (New Series), as follows:

Resolved, That M. Bertolino is hereby granted an extension of forty-five days' time from and after December 26, 1929, within which to complete the improvement of Swiss avenue between Surrey and Sussex streets, under public contract.

This extension of time is granted upon the recommendation of the Board of Public Works for the reason that the delay has been caused by inclement weather.

Ayes—Supervisors Andriano, Canepa, Colman, Gallagher, Havenner, Hayden, McGovern, McSheehy, Miles, Power, Roncovieri, Rossi, Shannon, Spaulding, Stanton, Suhr, Toner—17.

Absent—Supervisor Peyser—1.

Extension of Time to Complete Improvement of Victoria Street.

Also, Resolution No. 31955 (New Series), as follows:

Resolved, That M. Bertolino be granted an extension of thirty days' time from and after January 7, 1930, within which to complete the improvement of Victoria street between Sargent and Randolph streets under a public contract.

This extension is granted upon the recommendation of the Board of Public Works for the reason that the work is about 50 per cent complete. This is the first extension of time.

Ayes—Supervisors Andriano, Canepa, Colman, Gallagher, Havenner, Hayden, McGovern, McSheehy, Miles, Power, Roncovieri, Rossi, Shannon, Spaulding, Stanton, Suhr, Toner—17.

Absent—Supervisor Peyser—1.

Extension of Time to Complete the Uncompleted Portions of Twenty-second Avenue Between Noriega and Ortega Streets.

Also, Resolution No. 31956 (New Series), as follows:

Resolved, That James McElroy is hereby granted an extension of ninety days' time from and after January 19, 1930, within which to complete the uncompleted portions of Twenty-second avenue between Noriega and Ortega streets under public contract.

This extension of time is granted upon the recommendation of the Board of Public Works for the reason that the contractor has been delayed by inclement weather.

Ayes—Supervisors Andriano, Canepa, Colman, Gallagher, Havenner, Hayden, McGovern, McSheehy, Miles, Power, Roncovieri, Rossi, Shannon, Spaulding, Stanton, Suhr, Toner—17.

Absent—Supervisor Peyser—1.

Extension of Time to Complete Improvement of Noriega Street Between Thirty-third and Thirty-fourth Avenues.

Also, Resolution No. 31957 (New Series), as follows:

Resolved, That Federal Construction Company is hereby granted an extension of forty-five days' time from and after January 19, 1930, within which to complete the contract for the improvement of Noriega street between Thirty-third and Thirty-fourth avenues, under a public contract.

This extension is granted upon the recommendation of the Board of Public Works for the reason that the work is practically completed and the contractor has been delayed by inclement weather.

Ayes—Supervisors Andriano, Canepa, Colman, Gallagher, Havenner, Hayden, McGovern, McSheehy, Miles, Power, Roncovieri, Rossi, Shannon, Spaulding, Stanton, Suhr, Toner—17.

Absent—Supervisor Peyser—1.

Intention to Close a Portion of Seneca Avenue Lying Southeasterly From Otsego Avenue.

Also, Resolution No. 31958 (New Series), as follows:

Resolved, That the public interest requires that the certain following described portion of Seneca avenue, lying southeasterly from Otsego avenue, be closed and abandoned; and be it

Further Resolved, That it is the inention of the Board of Supervisors to close and abandon all that portion of Seneca avenue, more particularly described as follows, to-wit:

Beginning at the point of intersection of the southeasterly line of Otsego avenue and the northeasterly line of Seneca avenue; thence southerly on a curve to the left, tangent to said line of Otsego avenue, radius 80.102 feet, central angle 48 deg. 30 min. 27. sec., a distance of 67.816 feet to the southwesterly line of Seneca avenue; thence deflecting 41 deg. 29 min. 33 sec. to the left from the tangent to the preceding curve, and running southeasterly along the southwesterly line of Seneca avenue 157.967 feet to the southeasterly termination of Seneca avenue; thence deflecting 77 deg. 46 min. 30 sec. to the left and running northeasterly along said southeasterly termination 61.392 feet to the northeasterly line of Seneca avenue; thence northwesterly along the northeasterly line of Seneca avenue 198 feet to said line of Otsego avenue and the point of beginning.

Said closing and abandonment of said portion of said avenue shall be done and made in the manner and in accordance with the provisions of Section 2, Chapter 3 of Article VI of the Charter of the City and County of San Francisco, as amended, and the sections of said chapter and article following Section 2; and be it

Further Resolved, That the damage, cost and expense of said closing and abandonment be paid out of the revenue of the City and County of San Francisco.

And the Clerk of this Board is hereby directed to transmit to the Board of Public Works a certified copy of this resolution, and the Board of Public Works is hereby directed to give notice of said contemplated closing and abandonment of said portion of said avenue in the manner provided by law, and to cause notice to be published in the official newspaper as required by law.

Ayes—Supervisors Andriano, Canepa, Colman, Gallagher, Havenner, Hayden, McGovern, McSheehy, Miles, Power, Roncovieri, Rossi, Shannon, Spaulding, Stanton, Suhr, Toner—17.

Absent—Supervisor Peyser—1.

Award of Contract, Bathing Suits for Park Commission.

On recommendation of Supplies Committee.

Resolution No. 31959 (New Series), as follows:

Resolved, That award of contract be hereby made to Gantner & Mattern Co. on bid submitted January 6, 1930 (Proposal No. 549), for furnishing the following, viz.:

Bathing Suits for Park Commissioners—60 dozen bathing suits, on sample of Lot No. 831, at $24.50 per dozen.

Resolved, That no bond be required, as same are for immediate delivery.

Ayes—Supervisors Andriano, Canepa, Colman, Gallagher, Havenner, Hayden, McGovern, McSheehy, Miles, Power, Roncovieri, Rossi, Shannon, Spaulding, Stanton, Suhr, Toner—17.

Absent—Supervisor Peyser—1.

Rereferred.

The following matters were *rereferred to the Committee on Traffic and Safety.*

Loading Zones.

Resolution No. ———— (New Series), as follows:

Resolved, That the following list of loading zones, of the lengths specified, be established in front of or near the following addresses, in accordance with the provisions of Section No. 36 of Ordinance No. 7691 (New Series), as amended:

5-21 Belvedere street, 27 feet; San Francisco Bank, money entrance.

537-543 Front street. 18 feet; A. Giorlani & Bro., wholesale grocery.

224 Hemlock street, 27 feet; Lincoln University, freight entrance; 1 oil intake.

1195 Page street, 18 feet; Dr. Hawkin, office and clinic.

Passenger Loading Zones.

Also, Resolution No. ————— (New Series), as follows:

Resolved, That the following list of passenger loading zones, of the lengths specified, be established in front of or near the following addresses, in accordance with the provisions of Section No. 36 of Ordinance No. 7691 (New Series), as amended:

555 Baker street, 18 feet; Native Daughters' Home and Club Building.

1122 California street, 36 feet; Grace Cathedral.

2335 Pacific avenue, 18 feet; St. Xavier Apartments.

ROLL CALL FOR THE INTRODUCTION OF RESOLUTIONS, BILLS AND COMMUNICATIONS NOT CONSIDERED OR REPORTED UPON BY A COMMITTEE.

Leave of Absence, Supervisor Angelo J. Rossi.

The following was presented and read by the Clerk:

San Francisco, Calif., January 20, 1930.

To the Honorable Board of Supervisors, City Hall, San Francisco, Calif.

Gentlemen: Application has been made to me by Honorable Angelo J. Rossi, member of the Board of Supervisors, for a leave of absence, with permission to absent himself from the State of California, for a period of thirty (30) days, commencing January 22, 1930.

Will you please concur with me in granting this leave of absence?

Very sincerely yours,

JAMES ROLPH, JR., Mayor.

Whereupon, the following resolution was presented and *adopted*:

Resolution No. 31960 (New Series), as follows:

Resolved, That, in accordance with the recommendation of his Honor the Mayor, Hon. Angelo J. Rossi, member of the Board of Supervisors, is hereby granted a leave of absence for a period of thirty days, commencing January 22, 1930, with permission to leave the State.

Ayes—Supervisors Andriano, Canepa, Colman, Gallagher, Havenner, Hayden, McGovern, McSheehy, Miles, Power, Roncovieri, Rossi, Shannon, Spaulding, Stanton, Suhr, Toner—17.

Absent—Supervisor Peyser—1.

Supervisor Hayden, Acting Chairman Finance Committee.

On motion of Supervisor Colman, Supervisor Hayden was appointed Acting Chairman of the Finance Committee during Supervisor Rossi's absence.

Opinion of City Attorney in re Consideration by Board of Supervisors of Appeals from Action of City Planning Commission.

January 20, 1930.

Dear Sirs: You have asked that I advise you as to the procedure to be adopted by the Board of Supervisors upon the consideration of an appeal taken from the action of the City Planning Commission in re-zoning property.

Opinion.

The right to appeal to the Board of Supervisors from the action of the City Planning Commission in re-zoning property is found in Section 4 of Article XVIII of the Charter, adopted by the people in November, 1928. This section regulates the manner in which the Commission itself shall re-classify or re-zone property, and also provides for appeals to the Board of Supervisors from the action taken by the Commission. The section provides that if an application for a re-zoning is approved, that the order of the Commission shall not become effective for thirty days thereafter, and that property owners affected by the ruling may, within the period mentioned, file their protests in writing with the Board of Supervisors, which protests must state the reasons for the protest, the location of the property owned by the protestant 'and his postoffice address. The protests having been filed with the Board of Supervisors, it becomes the duty of the Board to check the signatures to the protests, and if the protest or protests are signed by twenty per cent of the property owners designated on the map or plat which the section provides shall be filed with the Commission upon the application for re-zoning, to thereupon set a day for the hearing of the protests. The Charter language on the matter of hearing is as follows: "And if such protest is subscribed to by the owners of twenty per cent or more of the property delineated on said map, the Supervisors shall fix a time and place for hearing said objections not less than thirty days thereafter, and the Supervisors shall hear the objections urged at the time specified."

While on the first reading of the language quoted there was some doubt in my mind whether the hearing should be held within the period of thirty days or at the expiration thereof, a more careful consideration of the matter leads me to the conclusion that, irrespective of what the intention of the framers of the amendment was, the use of the expression "not less than thirty days thereafter," means that the hearing on the protests cannot be heard until the expiration of a period of thirty days after the protests have been checked and the Board has ascertained that twenty per cent of the affected property owners have joined in the protest. When the protests are heard the hearing must be before the Board itself and not before a committee thereof. It is the duty of the Clerk of the Board to notify all parties interested, both proponents and protestants, as to the time and place of the hearing. On the conclusion of the hearing, it lies within the power of the Board of Supervisors, by a two-thirds vote of all of its members, to disapprove the ruling of the Commission, or by a majority vote to approve it. The power of modification of the ruling of the Commission does not lie in the Board of Supervisors; it can only approve or disapprove.

I would suggest, therefore, that if the signatures to the protests have been checked, and it is ascertained that the requisite number of signatures to the protest have been obtained, that the Board fix a date for the hearing of said protest, which date must be more than thirty days from the date at which said hearing is fixed.

Very truly yours,

JNO. J. O'TOOLE, City Attorney.

Referred to Industrial Development Committee.

Fixing February 10, 1930, at 3 P. M., as Time for Hearing Appeal from Decision of City Planning Commission in re Zoning Property on Marina Boulevard as First Residential.

Resolution No. 31961 (New Series), as follows:

Whereas, the City Planning Commission, on its own motion, by its Resolution No. 175, adopted December 10, 1929, placed the property on both sides of Marina boulevard between Buchanan street and Webster street in the First Residential District, where not already so zoned, said property being more particularly described in said Resolution No. 175, as follows:

City Planning Commission Resolution No. 175:

Resolved, That Section 2 of the Use of Property Zone Maps, constituting a part of the Building Zone Ordinance, is hereby changed so as to place the property fronting on the southwesterly line of Marina boulevard between the westerly line of Buchanan street and the westerly line of Webster street, produced southerly, in the First Residential District, where not already so zoned, and also to place the following described property in the First Residential District instead of the Light Industrial District:

Beginning at the point of intersection of the westerly line of Buchanan street and the northeasterly line of Marina boulevard; thence northwesterly along said line of Marina boulevard 573.504 feet; thence continuing northwesterly along said line of said Marina boulevard, on a curve to the right, tangent to the preceding course, radius 103.528 feet, central angle 42 deg. 15 min., a distance of 76.342 feet to tangency with the easterly line of Webster street; thence northerly along said line of Webster street 1.167 feet to a point distant thereon 130 feet southerly from the northerly line of Marina boulevard, produced easterly; thence at right angles easterly 100 feet; thence at right angles southerly parallel with said line of Webster street 1.167 feet; thence southeasterly on a curve to the left, tangent to the preceding course and concentric with the above-mentioned curve, radius 3.528 feet, central angle 42 deg. 15 min., a distance of 2.602 feet; thence southeasterly along a line parallel with and distant 100 feet at right angles northeasterly from the northeasterly line of Marina boulevard 462.413 feet to the westerly line of Buchanan street; thence deflecting 42 deg. 15 min. to the right and running southerly along said line of Buchanan street 148.728 feet to the northeasterly line of Marina boulevard and the point of beginning.

Ayes—Commissioners Sullivan, Kendrick, Chapin and Mrs. Maddux.

December 10, 1929.

Whereas, there was filed with the Board of Supervisors on January 9, 1930, within the time fixed for filing appeals from the decision of the City Planning Commission, as set forth in Section 4, Article XVIII of the Charter, a protest from owners of property within the district to be affected by requested change of zone classification; and

Whereas, an examination of said protests shows signatures of the owners of more than twenty (20%) per cent of the property affected, as delineated on map filed with the City Planning Commission in connection with the original application, as required under the provisions of said Section 4, Article XVIII of the Charter; therefore, be it

Resolved, That Monday, February 10, 1930, at the hour of 3 p. m., in the chambers of the Board of Supervisors, is hereby fixed as the time and place for hearing the appeal of property owners from the decision of the City Planning Commission placing the property on both sides of Marina boulevard between Buchanan street and Webster street, as described in said Resolution No. 175, in the First Residential District, where not already so zoned.

Adopted by the following vote:

Ayes—Supervisors Andriano, Canepa, Colman, Gallagher, Havenner, Hayden, McGovern, McSheehy, Miles, Power, Roncovieri, Rossi, Shannon, Spaulding, Stanton, Suhr, Toner—17.

Absent—Supervisor Peyser—1.

Motions.

Supervisor Gallagher moved that the Clerk be directed to have a copy of the resolution and a map of the district sought to be rezoned sent to each member and also to the Mayor.

Supervisor Stanton requested that the City Attorney furnish an opinion as to whether these people (company operating amphibian planes on the Marina) are operating legally, and whether, this being a ferry terminal, and they in the ferry business, should not first apply for and receive a franchise from this Board.

Veterans' Old Age Welfare Pension Legislation Endorsed.

Supervisor Havenner presented:

Resolution No. 31962 (New Series), as follows:

Resolved, That the Board of Supervisors òf the City and County of San Francisco hereby expresses its approval of the purposes of the legislation now pending before the Congress of the United States, as represented in Senate Bill 4559, House Bill known as The Indian War Bill, House Bill 2829, Senate Bill 476, and House Bill 2562; and be it

Further Resolved, That the Board of Supervisors respectfully recommends to the Senators from the State of California and the Representatives of the districts comprised within the City and County of San Francisco in the House of Representatives, in so far as they can consistently do so, to give their support and their encouragement to the legislation herein set forth; and be it

Further Resolved, That copies of this resolution be sent to United States Senators Johnson and Shortridge and to Representatives Kahn and Welch.

Adopted by the following vote:

Ayes—Supervisors Canepa, Colman, Gallagher, Havenner, Hayden, McGovern, McSheehy, Miles, Power, Roncovieri, Rossi, Shannon, Spaulding, Stanton, Suhr, Toner—16.

No—Supervisor Andriano—1.

Absent—Supervisor Peyser—1.

Explanation of Vote.

Supervisor Andriano explained his vote by saying he knew nothing about it save what he heard in Supervisor Havenner's statement.

Salaries of Chauffeurs in Board of Public Works.

Supervisor Power moved that the Clerk send a letter to the President of the Board of Public Works, calling attention to the status of the fund for salaries of chauffeurs, resulting in the laying off of some employees, and asking the Board of Public Works to confine itself to the item as laid down in the Budget.

Sale of Highway and Sewer Bonds.

Supervisor Power declared that the Streets Committee had recommended to the Finance Committee the sale of $2,000,000 of highway bonds and $1,000,000 of sewer bonds, which recommendations would have been concurred in if it were not that there is a gentlemen's agreement with the Bank of Italy syndicate that took over $41,000,000 of Spring Valley bonds, not to offer any other bonds until the $41,000,000 are sold. He said that the Finance Committee intended to get a release of that agreement and put the bonds up for sale at the earliest possible date.

Nuisance at War Memorial Site.

Supervisor Shannon called attention of the Health Committee to the condition of the lots on the west side of Van Ness avenue, opposite the City Hall. He declared that the stagnant pools of water, covered with green scum, afforded a breeding place for mosquitoes, and constituted a serious menace to the health of the community as well as a danger to boys of the neighborhood, who may be seen wading in the water every day. "If the pools were on private property," he said, "the Board of Health would long ago have compelled the owner to abate the nuisance."

His Honor Mayor Rolph said, in part:

"I have received many letters urging me to resubmit my appointments to the Board of Trustees. Likewise many resolutions, including several from veterans' organizations. If the Board wishes I'll have the names here in five minutes."

Joseph Claridge, secretary of the County Council of the American Legion, he said, some time ago wrote a letter to W. H. Crocker, member of the old board of trustees of the War Memorial, "demanding an accounting of the $2,000,000 fund" subscribed by citizens. It was this letter Mayor Rolph denounced as an insult to a leading citizen.

On motion of Supervisor Hayden, Mr. Claridge was given the privilege of the floor to explain the matter. Mr. Claridge declared that he was sorry, but that letter had no mention of the Mayor or the Board of Supervisors. It was addressed to the old board of trustees, "so there is nothing to explain to this Board."

Raymond A. Burr, past commander Golden Gate Post, which has adopted a resolution urging ratification of the Mayor's nominations, told the Board that his post wanted action so that work could be given unemployed veterans.

Mayor Rolph said: "Construction would have started months ago if the nominations had not needed the approval of the Board of Supervisors."

In reply to an inquiry from Supervisor Hayden, his Honor the Mayor further announced that within two weeks he would submit a report and call a special meeting on the War Memorial, going back to April, 1918, and that in the meantime he would confer with the advisory committee of the veterans in an effort to settle the pending differences.

Communication from Northern Federation of Civic Organizations re Auditorium.

San Francisco, Calif., June 16, 1928.

To the Honorable the Board of Supervisors, City Hall, San Francisco.

Gentlemen: In view of the present deficit in the funds of the Exposition Auditorium, a resolution has been adopted by this federation, urging that your Honorable Board provide by ordinance the following:

(1) Make it a condition of renting that there shall be no free admissions;

(2) Increase the rents to the level of rents charged for other halls with similar accommodations;

(3) Allow no free use of the halls, except for charitable and humanitarian purposes, or for veteran organizations.

Very truly yours,

Northern Federation of Civic Organizations,

By Frank Fischer, Secretary.

Limitation of Height of Buildingss Ordinance Proposed.

Resolution No. ———— (New Series), as follows:

Resolved, That the City Planning Commission be requested to hear and consider a proposed ordinance limiting the height of buildings in the district bounded by Chestnut street, Fillmore street, Laguna street and Lewis street to 40 feet, and to transmit to this Board its recommendation in connection therewith.

Referred to Public Buildings Committee.

Dr. David Starr Jordan Congratulated on 79th Birthday.

Resolution No. 31963 (New Series), as follows:

Be it Resolved, That His Honor the Mayor and the Board of Supervisors, representing the City and County of San Francisco, send greetings to Dr. David Starr Jordan on this the 79th anniversary of his birth.

During the past year Dr. Jordan has been ill. He has slowly climbed back to health, for which we are truly happy.

The world owes much to Dr. Jordan as a scientist, a humanitarian, a teacher and an administrator. He has added much to the comfort and enlightenment of mankind. Although he was not born in California, we Californians claim him as our own and are proud of him.

He is aptly termed "The Sage of Stanford."

Under his sagacious guidance Stanford University ranks among the foremost educational institutions of the world. Under his tutelage Herbert Hoover received the training and inspirations that fitted him for his high position of President of the United States.

We extend to him our sincere congratulations and heartfelt wishes that he may spend many more birthdays in his Palo Alto home. Be it

Further Resolved, That this resolution be signed by the Mayor of

San Francisco and the Clerk of the Board of Supervisors; that a copy be spread upon our minutes and another be sent to Dr. David Starr Jordan.

SUPERVISOR TONER: I move you the suspension of the rules and the adoption of the resolution.

SUPERVISOR HAVENNER: Second the motion.

SUPERVISOR McSHEEHY: Second the motion.

SUPERVISOR TONER: We have with us an alumnus of Stanford University, a graduate of Stanford University, a man who has done credit to his Alma Mater, and an outstanding official of the Board of Supervisors of San Francisco. I know that Mr. Havenner loves David Starr Jordan, and I would ask him to say a word on this seventy-ninth anniversary of his birth.

SUPERVISOR HAVENNER: Mr. Mayor, I am very glad indeed to second the resolution presented by Doctor Toner, and I feel sure that all of my colleagues on the Board subscribe most heartily to the sentiments that he has set forth in that resolution. Doctor David Starr Jordan has been, for many years, the most notable figure in educational circles on the Pacific Coast. He was the active president of Stanford when I was a student there. He was the most beloved figure on the campus then, and I think that still, with all due deference to his successor in office, who is likewise beloved, and perhaps equally beloved, Doctor Jordan stands first in the hearts of all Stanford alumni because of the fact that he pioneered the way in establishing, under the endowment of the Stanford family, that outstanding university on the Pacific Coast. I am extremely glad to pay my tribute to him and join with the members of the Board in wishing that his life may be continued.

Tribute to the Memory of Cyril Williams.

Mayor James Rolph, Jr., acted as the presiding officer.

SUPERVISOR HAVENNER: Before adjournment, I desire to say that by unusual circumstances here in the affairs of the Board, no official tribute has been paid, at a meeting of this Board, to Mr. Cyril Williams, who passed away from us just before the beginning of the new year. I understand what was done. I understand that at an informal meeting of members of the Board, when there was not a quorum present, that instructions were issued to the Clerk to have suitable resolutions prepared and transmitted to the members of his family. But I do feel that in the case of Mr. Williams there ought to be in the record of some duly called meeting of this Board a proper recognition of his services to the City. Personally, I think that Mr. Williams was the most remarkable employee of the City and County of San Francisco of whom I have had any knowledge. His record is pretty well known, I think, to everybody who has ever been associated with official life in the City Hall. He was an employee of the City, I believe, for about half a century—forty-three years. His record of faithful attention to his duties during all of that time, up until the beginning of his last illness, I think, is probably without parallel in the records of municipal service anywhere. As I recall, it was stated to me that Mr. Williams had never missed a day at his desk until his final illness began. He was the most remarkably accurate man whom I have ever had any knowledge of in matters of municipal accounting. He was the standard authority in the City Hall on all the intricate details that entered into the calculations of our annual tax rate, and I say it with almost awe, with amazement that a human being could be capable of the kind of service that he rendered, that I never knew him to be in error concerning any statement of financial detail he was called upon by the Finance Committee to submit. He was a most lovable man, an extraordinary man in all of his accomplishments and in his fidelity to duty, and I deem it my duty, as well as my privilege and honor, to make this statement for the record at this time.

SUPERVISOR TONER: I would suggest that Supervisor Havenner's remarks be put in print and sent Mrs. Williams.

THE MAYOR: So ordered.

Tribute to the Memory of Mrs. Thomas Cleary.

SUPERVISOR HAYDEN: Mr. Mayor, at this time, and during these moments of eulogium to our recently departed financial expert, Mr. Cyril Williams, so beautifully done by my associate, Supervisor Havenner, I want to call to the attention of the Mayor and the members of the Board the passing of the wife of Thomas Cleary. Thomas Cleary, as you know, Mr. Mayor, has been in intimate contact with your office and with the Board of Supervisors, as a Clerk of this Board, for a period of seventeen years. In fact, he came in with you at the beginning of your administration. We know what a great sorrow has come into his life, an irreparable loss, and, by a strange coincidence, I attended the funeral this morning of the late Mrs. Cleary, and Tom tells me that today would be the forty-fourth anniversary of their married life. I know that a word of sympathy from this Board, carrying with it the sympathy of the Chief Clerk and his staff to Mr. Cleary at this time, would find a place in his heart and a consolation that would be deeply appreciated.

We admire the ability of Mr. Cleary, we admire the wonderful family that he has raised, a good Christian family, all grown up and taking their places in society. I met them this morning, and I have met them on other occasions. And Tom Cleary can indeed be proud of the family that he raised in San Francisco. And it is with a great deal of sorrow, Mr. Mayor, that I have occasion to refer to the passing of Mrs. Cleary. As I say, it is a loss to Tom Cleary and to his dear family, and I would move that, when we adjourn, we adjourn out of respect to the memory of the late Mrs. Thomas Cleary.

SUPERVISOR STANTON: Second the motion.

THE MAYOR: I would like to just add a word to that. I could not go to the funeral this morning, but I sent former Chief of Police Walsh to represent me. Tom Cleary is a fine man. He had a fine wife and a fine family. He is the encyclopedia of this City Hall, and he knows how many rivets, how many shims, how many columns, how many glass windows, how many stairs to the top of the dome; he knows every detail of every part of this building, and when you want to know something about this building in particular all you have to do is to ask Tom Cleary. And he is one of the most efficient, able clerks we have here.

SUPERVISOR HAYDEN: In addition to my motion I would like to add that a letter of sympathy to Mr. Cleary be prepared by the Clerk.

So ordered.

Action Deferred.

The following resolution was presented by Supervisor Toner and made a *Special Order for* 2:30 *p. m. next Monday:*

Removal of Hog Ranches.

Resolution No. ———— (New Series), as follows:

Whereas, the Department of Public Health of the City and County of San Francisco has reported its inability to secure through agreement the removal of the following so-called hog ranches:

300 Lane street, corner Davidson—Mildred Goodsell, owner; Henry Suhling, lessee.

301 Lane street, corner Davidson—Henry Suhling, owner; Sacramento Hog Co. (P. Grech), lessee.

Mendell street, near Custer avenue—Chas. and Louis Nonnemann et al., owners; Attilio Del Grandi, lessee.

Northwest corner Custer avenue and Mendell street—C. and L. Nonnemann et al., owners; Castentini Bros., lessees.

Davidson avenue, in rear of 1520 Evans avenue—C. & C. of San Francisco, owners; American Hog Co. (Jos. and Roger Isolo and Jos. DiSantoro), lessee.

1288 Davidson avenue—George Wagner et al., owners; Henry Suhling, lessee.

1202-6 Evans avenue, corner Keith—Arcadio and Marianna Martinelli et al., owners; Martinelli Bros., lessees.

1290 Evans avenue—Mildred Goodsell, owner; R. Dolbeziero, lessee.

Mendell street between Custer avenue and Jennings—Barsotti and P. Fouchet, owners.

And whereas, the existence of said hog ranches within the City and County of San Francisco is in violation of Ordinance No. 1410 of our City and County, and constitutes a menace to the health and well being of our residents; now, therefore, be it

Resolved, That the City Attorney be and he is hereby authorized and requested to institute such legal action or actions as may be necessary to secure the abatement and removal of said hog ranches.

San Francisco Wins First Prize, Pasadena's Rose Festival.

The following was read by the Clerk:

Communication, from his Honor Mayor Rolph, transmitting telegram from H. L. Carnahan, stating that he had the honor of accepting, on behalf of San Francisco, a beautiful silver cup awarded to this City as first prize for class A civic body, and that the trophy is being forwarded to him; also that Chairman Hal Reynolds expressed deep appreciation of the good will manifested by San Francisco in her graceful and outstanding contribution to the success of Pasadena's New Year's Rose Tournament. Also Mayor's reply to above telegram.

Clerk directed to express thanks and appreciation of Board of Supervisors.

In re Board of Equalization Appraisal Bureau and Dismissal of John J. Barry.

Supervisor McSheehy, referring to a newspaper article of recent date, read in part as follows: "Appraiser dropped. No new bureau to be named by Supervisors. Dismissal of John J. Barry, a holdover from the staff which made the Stafford appraisal here several years ago, at a cost of more than $200,000, was announced by Supervisor Angelo J. Rossi, chairman of the Finance Committee."

Now, Mr. Chairman, through you, may I ask the chairman of the Finance Committee how this matter came before his committee last Friday?

SUPERVISOR ROSSI: Mr. Mayor and members of this Board: My attention was called to the fact that there was a gentleman, I did not know his name, who was employed, and being paid at the rate of $300 a month, on this appraisal. I called Mr. Joe Phillips, who has charge, or the right of way agent, who I understand has charge of that work, and he informed us that Mr. Barry, as I learned since, had no particular duties other than to give information to the public, so your Finance Committee, in its wisdom, recommended that the services of Mr. Barry be dispensed with as of January 31st.

SUPERVISOR McSHEEHY: Then you received the information from Mr. Phillips, the right of way engineer?

SUPERVISOR ROSSI: That has no bearing on the case, where we received the information. There was no further need of Mr. Barry's services and your Finance Committee deemed it advisable to dispense with his services.

Statement of Supervisor McSheehy.

Whereupon, Supervisor McSheehy read a statement purporting to show discrepancies and inequalities in property assessments made by the Assessor's office in various parts of the city in comparison with the true value of such property as found in the Stafford appraisal.

Supervisor Havenner also addressed the Board at length in justification of the establishment of the appraisal bureau and the need of its continuance.

Mr. John J. Barry, employee, was heard, and, in response to questions put by Supervisor Shannon, explained what information is afforded by the appraisal bureau and the class of citizens and organizations that come to the office for such service.

Supervisor Colman also discussed the matter, contending "that it was his thought that the original expenditure for the appraisal bureau would result, unwittingly, no doubt, and not by original intention, in the creation of a few jobs. It is obvious to me now that the records Mr. Barry refers to cannot serve the purpose claimed for them, as they are not up to date.

Mr. Boyd, representing the Assessor's office, declared, in part, that the Assessor's office was reluctant in the extreme to take any part in this discussion as to the continuance of the Stafford appraisal. It is something that the Assessor's office would prefer not to speak on. The purpose of the appraisal, he said, as generally given out to the public, was to provide an aid to the Board of Supervisors sitting as a Board of Equalization. If the Assessor were to object to its continuance, he said, he would be in the position of a man who resents a certified public accountant checking his books, and I want to say that Assessor Wolden welcomes any kind of an investigation of the assessed valuations of San Francisco.

Action Deferred.

Whereupon, the subject-matter was, on motion of Supervisor McSheehy, continued three weeks and a copy of Supervisor McSheehy's statement sent to the Assessor.

ADJOURNMENT.

There being no further business, the Board at 6:30 p. m. adjourned.

J. S. DUNNIGAN, Clerk.

Approved by the Board of Supervisors February 10, 1930.

Pursuant to Resolution No. 3402 (New Series) of the Board of Supervisors of the City and County of San Francisco, I, John S. Dunnigan, hereby certify that the foregoing is true and correct copy of the Journal of Proceedings of said Board of the date stated and approved as above recited.

JOHN S. DUNNIGAN,
Clerk of the Board of Supervisors,
City and County of San Francisco.

Vol. 25—New Series   No. 4

Monday, January 27, 1930

Journal of Proceedings
Board of Supervisors

City and County of San Francisco

The Recorder Printing and Publishing Company
337 Bush Street, S. F.

JOURNAL OF PROCEEDINGS
BOARD OF SUPERVISORS

MONDAY, JANUARY 27, 1930, 2 P. M.

In Board of Supervisors, San Francisco, Monday, January 27, 1930, 2 p. m.

CALLING THE ROLL.

The roll was called and the following Supervisors were noted present:

Supervisors Andriano, Canepa, Colman, Gallagher, Hayden, Miles, Power, Roncovieri, Spaulding, Suhr, Toner—11.

Absent—Supervisors Havenner, McGovern, McSheehy, Peyser, Rossi, Shannon, Stanton—7.

Supervisor Peyser reported ill.

Supervisor Rossi on leave of absence.

Quorum present.

His Honor Mayor Rolph presiding.

APPROVAL OF JOURNAL.

The Journal of Proceedings of January 6, 1930, was considered read and approved.

Action Deferred.

Removal of Hog Ranches.

The matter of the removal of hog ranches in San Francisco was, on motion, *laid over one week and made a Special Order of Business for 2:30 p. m. next Monday.*

Fixing Rate of Interest for City Funds Deposited in Bank.

The following was presented and read by the Clerk:

San Francisco, Cal., January 27, 1930.

Honorable Board of Supervisors, City Hall, San Francisco, California.

Gentlemen: This is to certify that, in compliance with the Charter, Article 4, Chapter 3, Section 2, the rate of interest for the current calendar year is hereby fixed at 3 per cent per annum on all moneys deposited in banks pursuant to law.

Very truly yours,
JAMES ROLPH, JR.,
Mayor City and County of San Francisco.
DUNCAN MATHESON,
Treasurer City and County of San Francisco.
THOS. F. BOYLE,
Auditor City and County of San Francisco.

Filed and ordered spread in Journal.

Standardization of Salaries.

The following was presented and read by the Clerk:

Communications, from Labor Council and Office Employees' Association, re standardization of salaries.

Motion.

Supervisor Havenner moved that the Clerk be instructed to send copy to Civil Service Commission, with the request that the Commission advise this Board at its earliest convenience as to when its report on standardization will be received.

So ordered.

Preservation of Wild Life on Spring Valley Water Company Reservation.

Supervisor Thomas Hickey of San Mateo County was granted the privilege of the floor. He called attention to the fact that it has been the policy of the Spring Valley Water Company to maintain their vast properties as a refuge and reservation of wild life, prohibiting hunting or fishing there. As a result of this policy the water properties are teeming with wild life—deer, quail, doves, etc.—which is fast passing away in other parts of California. He asked that the City continue this policy of protection and seek the aid of the State in making this reserve a permanent feature of the peninsula.

His Honor Mayor Rolph responded, enthusiastically favoring the idea, saying that he intended to do all in his power to carry on. He commended Supervisor Hickey for his very able and timely presentation of the subject.

Leave of Absence, Wm. F. Benedict, Member of Board of Education.

The following was presented and read by the Clerk:

San Francisco, Cal., January 21st, 1930.

Honorable Board of Supervisors, City Hall, San Francisco, California.

Gentlemen: Application has been made to me by Mr. William F. Benedict, member of the Board of Education of this City and County, for leave of absence, with permission to leave the State of California, for a period of ten days, beginning January 24, 1930.

Will you please concur with me in granting said leave of absence?

Respectfully submitted,

JAMES ROLPH, JR., Mayor.

Whereupon, the following resolution was presented and *adopted*:

Resolution No. 31994 (New Series), as follows:

Resolved, That in accordance with the recommendation of his Honor the Mayor, Mr. William F. Benedict, member of the Board of Education, is hereby granted a leave of absence for a period of ten days, commencing January 24, 1930, with permission to leave the State.

Ayes—Supervisors Andriano, Canepa, Colman, Gallagher, Havenner, Hayden, McSheehy, Miles, Power, Roncovieri, Spaulding, Stanton, Suhr, Toner—14.

Absent—Supervisors McGovern, Peyser, Rossi, Shannon—4.

SPECIAL ORDER—2:30 P. M.

Passed for Printing.

The following matter was *passed for printing*:

Prohibiting Return of Certain Class of Merchandise by Purchaser.

On recommendation of Public Health Committee.

Bill No. 8180, Ordinance No. ————— (New Series), as follows:

Prohibiting the return by purchaser of merchandise which by use may become a source of infection and a menace to the public health.

Be it Ordained by the People of the City and County of San Francisco as follows:

Section 1. It is unlawful for any person, firm or corporation engaged in the sale at retail of the following articles of merchandise, to-wit:

a. Mattresses, blankets, sheets, comforters, pillows and other bedding.

b. Heating pads and metal hot water bottles, stockings made of rubber, reducing rollers, water bags and other rubber goods.

c. Combs, hair brushes, tooth brushes, barettes, bath brushes, powder puffs, lipsticks, compacts, broken packages of powder, creams, rouges.

d. Corsets, brassiers, underwear, union suits, bloomers, bathing suits.

e. Articles made of hair and veils.

to accept from the purchaser of any of above articles, once delivery is effected, provided that this section shall not be construed to prohibit the return of articles misfitting or defective in their construction, which shall be disinfected before being offered for re-sale.

Section 2. Any person, firm or corporation violating any of the provisions of this ordinance shall be deemed guilty of a misdemeanor and upon conviction thereof, shall be punished by a fine of not more than one hundred dollars ($100) or by imprisonment in the County Jail for a period not exceeding thirty (30) days, or by both such fine and imprisonment.

SPECIAL ORDER—4 P. M.

The following matter was taken up:

RULES OF PROCEEDINGS OF THE BOARD OF SUPERVISORS.

Resolved, that the rules hereinafter set forth be and the same are hereby adopted as the Rules of Proceedings of this Board of Supervisors, to wit:

STANDING COMMITTEES.

1. The following shall constitute the standing committees of the Board (the first named member to be chairman thereof):

Airport and Aeronautics—Spaulding, Peyser, Miles.
Auditorium—Hayden, Canepa, Colman.
Civil Service—Havenner, McSheehy, Rossi.
Education, Parks and Playgrounds—McSheehy, Suhr, Andriano.
Finance—Rossi, Power, Hayden.
Fire—Canepa, Peyser, Toner.
Industrial Development and City Planning—Gallagher, Stanton, Hayden.
Judiciary—Suhr, Andriano, Roncovieri.
Lighting, Water and Telephone Service and Electricity—Stanton, McGovern, Shannon.
Municipal Concerts and Public Celebrations—Roncovieri, Colman, Toner.
Police and Licenses—Andriano, Shannon, McGovern.
Public Buildings and Lands—Shannon, Rossi, Suhr.
Public Health—Toner, McSheehy, Roncovieri.
Public Utilities—Colman, Spaulding, Havenner.
Public Welfare and Publicity—Peyser, Spaulding, Miles.
Streets and Tunnels—Power, Canepa, Gallagher.
Supplies—Miles, Stanton, Power.
Traffic—McGovern, Havenner, Gallagher.

Every Committee shall set a stated time of meeting, or the Committee may meet at a time to be set by the chairman, and every member will be expected to attend every meeting of his Committee, and to be present promptly on time. The clerk of each Committee shall keep a record of the attendance of the members, and he shall report such record to the Clerk of the Board, and the Clerk of the Board shall have the report of the attendance of members at committee meetings available at all times for the information of any or all members of the Board.

DUTIES OF COMMITTEES.

2. The respective duties of each of the foregoing Committees and the time of meetings are hereby defined as follows:

AIRPORT AND AERONAUTICS—To have control and management of the Municipal Airport; to report and recommend on applications for leasing of hangars and concessions in said Airport; to consider and report on all matters relating to said Airport.

AUDITORIUM—To have control and management of the Municipal Auditorium and entertainments held therein under the auspices of the city as provided in Ordinance No. 5320 (New Series); to lease said building and the several halls and apartments therein; to report and recommend on applications for leasing of said building for public assemblages and gatherings; to consider and report on all matters relating to the management, conduct and maintenance of said Auditorium.

CIVIL SERVICE AND RETIREMENT SYSTEM—To consider all matters relating to Civil Service in the several departments and to promote efficiency and economy in expenditures; to consider matters relating to the Retirement System, and all reports of the Board of Administration of the Retirement System shall be referred to it for investigation and report thereon.

COMMERCIAL AND INDUSTRIAL DEVELOPMENT AND CITY PLANNING—To assist in promoting the establishment of industries in San Francisco and to cooperate with commercial and industrial organizations in all efforts to establish new industries; to consider measures helpful in developing San Francisco as an industrial center and to encourage delegations to points where needed to bring new industries, and generally to consider manufacturing problems as related to the industrial needs of the community; to cooperate with the United States, State officials and civic organizations in support of national and state legislation designed to promote world trade and the United States Merchant Marine; to bring about the location of a foreign trade zone within the City and County of San Francisco; to inaugurate a movement to the end that the management, control and development of San Francisco's harbor be placed locally, and also to cooperate with the Federal and State authorities on all matters, especially legislation, that tend for the further development and utilization of San Francisco's harbor to meet the needs of the world's commerce; to promote friendly relations between the City and contiguous and neighboring communities, to consider all matters relating to the City's expansion, and to act in an advisory capacity between the City Planning Commission and the Board of Supervisors and to hear such matters concerning city planning as may be referred to it by the Board of Supervisors; to propose measures for developing and accelerating transcontinental railway and inter-urban railroad transportation on this peninsula; to confer with adjacent cities, towns and counties on inter-community problems and to suggest to the Board in what manner other committees may be of help in peninsula development.

EDUCATION, PARKS AND PLAYGROUNDS—To consider and report upon all matters relating to the Departments of Education, Parks and Playgrounds and recreation centers, including the Aquatic Park, and to cooperate with the Board of Education, Playground Commission and Park Commission regarding the development and increased usefulness of these departments.

FINANCE—To perform all duties required by the Charter; to audit all bills and report on all matters that may be referred to it by the Board of Supervisors; to act as a budget committee for the Board, hold hearings on budget estimates of and with all departments, receive recommendations from all other committees of the Board, and formulate a budget for submission to the Board on or before the second Monday of May. (Meets Fridays at 2 p. m.)

FIRE—To consider all matters relating to the Fire Department; to report on all applications for garage, boiler, laundry and other permits referred to it.

JUDICIARY—To consider and report upon Charter amendments and all matters referred to it by the Board.

LIGHTING, WATER SERVICE, TELEPHONE SERVICE AND ELECTRICITY—To attend to the proper lighting of streets, public parks and public buildings; to investigate and correct complaints of water service and extensions thereof, and telephone service; to recommend installation and removal of City telephones; to recommend from time to time extensions of underground wire system, and to have general charge of all matters pertaining to electricity other than public lighting and amendments to the building laws.

MUNICIPAL CONCERTS AND PUBLIC CELEBRATIONS—To have charge of the Municipal Band and conduct all concerts that are given under the auspices of the City and County of San Francisco (except those concerts under the management of the Park Commissioners and the Auditorium Committee of this Board); to assist in promotion of all semi-public celebrations, dedications, etc.

POLICE AND LICENSES—To consider legislation concerning the Police Department; to investigate the management and character of penal institutions; to consider all matters affecting public morals; to report upon applications for permits referred to it by the Board, including free licenses to those deserving them, and report on all licenses, including taxicabs and public conveyances for hire.

PUBLIC BUILDINGS AND LANDS—To consider the erection of all public buildings and the purchase of sites for all public buildings upon recommendation of the respective departments; to consider and report upon the repairs to public buildings, and to recommend as to the janitorial, elevator and other service required for the proper conduct of all buildings of the City and County; also to assign to the various offices and departments the various rooms and places in the City Hall and Hall of Justice; to investigate and report upon proposed purchases of lands except lands needed for streets, roads, boulevards and tunnel purposes; to formulate plans for leasing City lands not needed for public purposes; to consider transfer of lands from one department to another, and all other matters pertaining to the realty of the City other than school property and airport property.

PUBLIC HEALTH—To consider all matters relating to health and sanitation; to see that institutions under the control of the Board of Health are properly conducted; to establish and maintain a high standard of service in public hospitals and Relief Home; to consider and report upon all complaints of nuisances; to make recommendations upon applications for permits which may be referred to it by the Board; also removal and destruction of garbage.

PUBLIC UTILITIES—To consider and pass upon all matters relating to public utilities, their acquisition, construction, control and management, whether municipally or privately owned, including transbay bridges, transportation, lighting, power, water and steam heating.

PUBLIC WELFARE AND PUBLICITY—To consider matters relating to the social well-being of the community other than those heretofore provided for, and generally to act upon all matters of public advertising, and pass on all bills chargeable against the advertising fund; to consider all matters relating to the Bureau of Weights and Measures.

RULES—To consider amendments to the Rules and such other matters as may be referred to it by the Board. To have supervision of and give instructions to the chauffeurs of the Board of Supervisors.

STATE LAWS AND LEGISLATION—To be appointed by the Finance Committe when occasion requires. To consider all matters pending before the Legislature and proposed legislation which affects the City and County of San Francisco, directly or indirectly, and to make such recommendations to the Board as may be deemed advisable, and to appear before the State Legislature in advocacy of any measures or in opposition to measures as the Board may advise.

STREETS AND TUNNELS—To consider all matters relating to the construction, improvement and maintenance of streets and sewers, including highways outside the County, for which the City and County is authorized to appropriate money, the closing, opening and widening of streets and the cleaning of streets; to designate the streets for the improvement and repair of which appropriations may be made in the budget and to allocate the same. Also direct the expenditure of money received from the State for the construction of public highways; to consider and report upon applications for spur and industrial tracks; to consider and report upon all matters relating to tunnels.

SUPPLIES—To consider and have charge of the purchase of all supplies as provided by the Charter; to prepare schedules for general supplies and to recommend award of contracts; to inspect deliveries and quality and quantity of supplies; to pass on all requisitions for non-contract supplies; to supervise the purchase and distribution of all books, stationery, etc.

TRAFFIC AND SAFETY—To investigate and report on matters relative to traffic conditions in the City and propose Ordinances regulating traffic and the promotion of safety in connection therewith.

CONVENING OF BOARD.

3. The Board shall convene at 2 o'clock p. m. on each Monday, and the Clerk shall immediately, after the call to order, which shall be at 2 o'clock p. m., call the roll of the members of the Board and shall record those present and absent. The Clerk shall also record the time of arrival of those members of the Board who arrive after 2 o'clock p. m., and the name of such member and the time of his arrival shall be entered upon the journal.

It shall be the duty of each Committee charged with the duty of cooperating with any particular department to investigate the financial needs of such department to be provided for in the annual budget; to consider such department's budget estimates and to recommend to the Finance Committee such modifications or changes thereof as it may deem proper.

The designations and duties of the foregoing Committees are hereby made part of these rules.

RULES OF ORDER.

4. The Mayor shall be President of the Board of Supervisors. He shall call each regular, adjourned or special meeting to order at the hour appointed and shall proceed with the order of business. In the absence of the Mayor, the Clerk shall call the roll and the Board shall appoint a presiding officer pro tempore from its own members, who shall have the same right to vote as other members.

The presiding officer shall preserve order and decorum.

The Clerk shall, immediately after the call to order, call the roll of members of the Board, and the record of those present and absent shall be entered upon the Journal.

5. Whenever it shall be moved and carried by 12 members that the

Board go into Committee of the Whole, the President shall leave the chair and the members shall appoint a chairman of the Committee of the Whole, who shall report the proceedings of said Committee.

6. The rules of the Board shall be observed in the Committee of the Whole.

7. A motion, in Committee of the Whole, to rise and report the question, shall be decided without debate.

8. The Clerk shall have clips, upon which shall be kept all Bills, Ordinances, Resolutions and Reports to be acted upon by the Board, except those not reported upon by a Committee.

9. No Bill, Ordinance or Resolution shall be considered by the Board unless it has been introduced by a member of the Board or by a Committee of the Board, and the Bill, Ordinance or Resolution must be read by the Clerk in open meeting before being referred to Committee. At the time of introduction the presiding officer shall first indicate to what Committee a Bill, Ordinance or Resolution ought to be referred, and it shall be so referred unless, upon majority vote without debate, the Board shall order it referred to some other committee.

Action by the Board shall not be taken upon any Bill, Ordinance or Resolution until it has been referred to and acted upon by a Committee of the Board.

10. The Order of Business, which shall not be departed from except by the consent of twelve members, shall be as follows:

    1. Roll Call.
    2. Approval of Journal.
    3. Calendar Business.
    4. Roll Call for the Introduction of Resolutions, Bills and Communications Not Considered or Reported on by a Committee.
    5. Communications and Reports from City and County Officers.

11. If any question under debate contains several points, any member may have the points segregated and acted upon separately.

12. When a motion has been made and carried or lost, it shall be in order for any member voting with the prevailing side to move to "reconsider the vote" on that question.

A member may change his vote before the result is announced in order to move to "reconsider the vote" on that question. The vote upon such motion to reconsider shall not be taken before the next regular meeting of the Board. No question shall be reconsidered more than once. Motion to reconsider shall have precedence over every other motion. It shall require a majority vote to carry any motion to reconsider the vote by which any Bill, Ordinance or Resolution has been passed or defeated.

13. A motion to refer or lay on the table until decided shall preclude all amendments to the main question. A motion to lay on the table or to postpone indefinitely shall require a majority vote of the members present.

14. It shall be the duty of the Clerk to issue such certificates as may be required by Ordinances or Resolutions and transmit copies of said Ordinances or Resolutions to the various departments affected thereby. It shall also be the duty of the Clerk to cause the publication in the official newspaper of all Bills, Ordinances, proposals and awards as required by the Charter.

15. All accounts and bills shall be referred to the Finance Committee, provided that any Committee having jurisdiction over subject of expenditures may request that bills he first sent to that Committee before being acted upon by the Finance Committee and the Board.

16. The President shall preserve order and decorum, and prevent demonstrations of approval or disapproval on the part of persons in the Chambers of the Board, and shall decide questions of order, subject to an appeal to the Board.

17. When a Supervisor desires to address the Board he shall arise in his place, address the presiding officer, and when recognized he shall proceed to speak. No Supervisor shall be recognized when seated or when away from his seat.

18. No Supervisor shall speak more than twice in any one debate on the same subject, and at the same stage of the Bill, Ordinance, Resolution or Motion without the consent of a majority of the Board, and Supervisors who have once spoken shall not again be entitled to the floor so long as any Supervisor who has not spoken desires to speak. No Supervisor shall be allowed to speak more than five minutes on any question except by permission of the Board, except that the author shall have five minutes to open and ten minutes to close.

19. No Supervisor shall be interrupted, when speaking, without his consent.

20. When two or more Supervisors arise at the same time to address the Board, the presiding officer shall designate the Supervisor who is entitled to the floor.

21. No motion shall be debated until the same *has been seconded* and distinctly announced by the presiding officer.

22. After a motion has been stated by the President, it shall be in the possession of the Board. It may be withdrawn by the mover thereof, with the consent of the second, before it is acted upon.

23. Upon a call of the Board the names of the members shall be called by the Clerk, and the absentees noted. Those for whom no excuse or insufficient excuses are made may, by order of those present, be sent for and be brought to the Chambers of the Board by the Sergeant-at-Arms or by special messengers appointed for the purpose.

24. When a question is under debate, no action shall be entertained except:

To adjourn.
Call of the Board.
To lay on the table.
The previous question.
To postpone.
To commit or amend.

Which several motions shall have precedence in the order in which they are arranged; provided, however, that during a call of the Board it may consider and transact any matter of business that the Supervisors there present shall unanimously decide to consider.

25. A motion to adjourn is not debatable.

26. The previous question shall be put in the following form: "Shall the previous question be now put?" It shall only be admitted when demanded by three Supervisors, and its effect shall be to put an end to all debate except that the author of the Bill, Ordinance, Resolution or Motion or Amendments shall have the right to close, and the question under discussion shall thereupon be immediately put to a vote. On a motion for the previous question prior to a vote being taken by the Board a call of the Board shall be in order.

27. Every member present when a question is put shall vote for or against it, unless disqualified by the Charter. No member shall be permitted to vote upon a question unless present when his name is called or before the vote is announced. A roll call shall not be interrupted for debate or personal privilege, but a member may file, in writing, an explanation of his vote.

29. After the Board has acted, the names of those who voted for and those who voted against the question shall be entered upon the Journal, not only in cases required by law, but when any member may require it, and on all Bills, Ordinances and Resolutions on final passage the ayes and nays shall be recorded.

30. All appointments of officers and employees shall be made by a majority of the members of the Board. The Clerk shall assign the

assistant clerks to their several duties, and shall immediately transmit to the Mayor all Resolutions and Ordinances which, under the law, require executive approval.

31. No member shall leave the Board during its session without permission from the Board.

32. All Committees shall be appointed by the Board unless other-wise ordered by the Board. Committees shall report 'on any subject referred to them by the Board and their recommendations thereon. *Unless otherwise ordered, a Committee shall report upon all subjects referred to it within thirty days thereafter.* It shall be the right of any member of a Committee to move a roll call (in Committee), on any pending motion, and the Chairman or Acting Chairman of said Committee shall, with or without debate, order the roll call. In Committees of three members or less a motion by a member thereof shall not require a second.

33. The Clerk shall prepare and cause to be printed and placed on the desks of the members on days of meeting, at least 30 minutes before such a meeting, a calendar of matters to be presented to the Board at said meeting. Every petition or other written instrument intended to be presented to the Board must be delivered to the Clerk not later than 12 o'clock noon on Saturday, or on the day preceding the meeting; upon the request of the President or of any member its contents shall be read in full.

34. All petitions, protests and communications of a routine character shall be referred by the Clerk to the proper Committee.

35. Ten members shall constitute a quorum to transact business, and no Bill, Ordinance, Resolution or Amendment thereto shall pass without the concurrence of at least that number of members, but a smaller number may adjourn from day to day.

36. Except when otherwise provided by these rules, the Charter or law, a majority vote of the members present shall be necessary for the adoption of any motion.

37. The Clerk shall keep a record of all requests and instructions directed by the Board of Supervisors to any officer or board of the City and County and the action thereon of such officer or board. The record of such requests and instructions, until acted upon by such officer or board, shall be read by the Clerk at each regular meeting of the Board of Supervisors.

38. The privilege of the floor shall not be granted to others than members of the Board, except those entitled to the same under the Charter, or public officials of the City and County of San Francisco. This rule shall not be suspended, except by unanimous consent of all members present.

39. In debate a member must confine himself to the question before the Board.

40. On any questions or points of order not embraced in these rules the Board shall be governed by the rules contained in Roberts' Rules of Order.

41. No member of the Board of Supervisors, chairman of a Committee, or Committee of said Board, shall employ or engage the services of any person, or authorize or incur any charge, debt or liability against the City and County unless authority therefor shall have been first given by the Board of Supervisors by Resolution or Ordinance, except as otherwise provided by law.

42. No standing rule or order of the Board shall be suspended or amended without the affirmative vote of twelve members, except that the rule as to the privilege of the floor shall require the unanimous consent of all members present.

43. No special order shall be placed on the Calendar except by order of the Board.

MEMORANDUM OF CHARTER PROVISIONS.

Page 4, Section 3, Chapter 1, Article II—Quorum consists of 10 members.

Page 5, Section 8, Chapter 1, Article II—No Bill shall become an Ordinance or Resolution be adopted unless it receives 10 votes.

Page 7, Section 16, Chapter 1, Article II—14 votes necessary to override Mayor's veto of Resolution or Ordinance.

Page 13, Chapter 2, Article II—Lease of City lands requires two-thirds vote of Board (12 votes).

Page 19, Section 6, Chapter 2, Article II—Street railway franchises require three-fourths vote (14 votes) of all the members of the Board, while five-sixths vote (15 votes) of all the members of the Board is necessary to pass these ordinances if MAYOR VETOES SAME.

Page 22, Section 9, Chapter 2, Article II—Sale of City lands requires 15 votes.

Page 30, Section 3, Chapter 1, Article III—Budget Ordinance requires 10 votes.

Page 30, Section 4, Chapter 1, Article III—15 votes are necessary to override Mayor's veto of Budget.

Page 31, Section 8, Chapter 1, Article III—15 votes necessary to appropriate from Urgent Necessity Fund.

Page 33, Section 13, Chapter 1, Article III—To suspend temporarily limit of taxation to meet emergency requires unanimous vote of 18 members of the Board and approval of the Mayor.

Page 76, Section 1, Chapter 1, Article VI—Contracts for street work require 14 votes.

Page 78, Section 2, Chapter 2, Article VI—When cost of sewer or drain is in excess of $5 per linear front foot of abutting property and work is disapproved by Board of Works, it requires 14 votes of the Board of Supervisors to pass ordinance ordering such work done.

If application for work is made, the expense of which is to be paid by City and County, and work is not recommended by the Board of Public Works, it requires 14 votes of the Board of Supervisors to order such work done.

Page 98, Section 33, Chapter 2, Article VI—Ordinance providing for street improvements in 10-year installments requires 15 votes.

Page 100, Section 1, Chapter 3, Article VI—Opening and Improvement of streets, etc., requires 12 votes.

Page 120, Section 17, Chapter 6, Article VI—15 votes are required to modify or change procedure as provided in the Charter for changing street grades and the performance of work in connection therewith.

Page 121, Section 1, Chapter 8, Article VI—Ordinance providing for tunnel, subway and viaduct construction requires 12 votes.

Page 218, Section 19, Article XVI—Suspension of an elected officer by the Mayor requires approval of 14 votes of the Board of Supervisors to cause removal.

Page 223, Section 35, Article XVI—Appointments of additional deputies, clerks or employees require 14 votes.

Amendments.
Duties of Committees.

On motion of Supervisor Andriano, under "Duties of Committees," the hour of meeting of the Finance Committee was amended to read 2 p. m. instead of 2:30 p. m.

Public Buildings and Lands Committee.

On motion of Supervisor Power, after the word "lands," ninth line thereof, the following words were added: "except lands needed for streets, roads, boulevards and tunnel purposes."

Supervisor Gallagher moved that the following be added to the last line: "investigate and report on all applications for certificates of public necessity and convenience in the matter of the operation of cabs and other vehicles under the law and to be empowered to make such other investigations as it deems proper as to the sufficiency of the securities thereof."

The following was accepted as a substitute for the foregoing:

To be empowered to and, "as far as their authority permits, to carry out the provisions of Ordinance No. 8637 (New Series)."

Streets and Tunnels.

Add to end of paragraph "and to make all necessary purchases of lands for roads, streets and boulevard purposes."

Standing Committees and Duties of Committees Approved.

Whereupon, on motion of Supervisor Gallagher, the foregoing standing committees and duties of committees as amended, and including paragraph 3, "Convening of Board," was approved without objection.

Rules of Order.

On motion of Supervisor Andriano, Rule 6 was amended by adding the words "except Rule 18, limiting the time of speaking, and Rule 38, relating to the privilege of the floor.

On motion of Supervisor Andriano, the old "Order of Business" was accepted in lieu of that recommended by the committee, to-wit:

1. Roll call.
2. Approval of Journal.
3. Calendar matters (uncontested).
4. Roll call for the introduction of resolutions, bills and communications not considered or reported on by a committee.
5. Completion of calendar business.
6. Communications and reports from City and County officers.
7. Reports of committees.
8. Roll call for the introduction of resolutions, bills and communications not considered or reported on by a committee.

Reconsideration Rule.

Rule 12, line 9, after the word "vote," insert the words "of the Board."

Referred to Rules Committee.

Supervisor Hayden, seconded by Supervisor Stanton, moved to amend Rule 12, line 8, after the word "once," by adding the words: "A notice of reconsideration shall apply only to the main question."

Motion *carried.*

Supervisor Roncovieri, seconded by Supervisor Power, moved to insert at the end of Rule 12 the following words: "It shall require fourteen votes to carry any motion for reconsideration."

Referred.

Supervisor Havenner moved rereference of the matter to the Rules Committee.

So ordered.

Rule 38 was, on motion of Supervisor Gallagher, laid over until Supervisor Peyser can be present.

On motion of Supervisor Power, Rule 41 was laid over temporarily.

Rule 42 was laid over until Rule 38 is agreed upon.

Supervisor Gallagher moved to add a new rule, to-wit:

Special Orders.

"44. When a time has been especially set for the consideration of a pending question, bill or resolution, the Clerk shall, when the hour arrives, call attention to said special order, and such especially set matter shall, unless otherwise decided by majority vote of the members present, suspend and supersede any pending question."

The purpose of this rule is to guarantee to the public that consideration of any question shall be given a hearing at the time set.

Referred to Rules Committee.

Rules as Amended Adopted.

Whereupon, on motion of Supervisor Andriano, the rules as amended, except such as were referred for further consideration, were *adopted.*

UNFINISHED BUSINESS.

Final Passage.

The following matters, heretofore passed for printing, were taken up and *finally passed by the following vote*:

Authorizations.

On recommendation of Finance Committee.

Resolution No. 31964 (New Series), as follows:

Resolved, That the following amounts be and the same are hereby authorized to be expended out of the hereinafter mentioned funds in payment to the following named claimants, to-wit:

Library Fund.

(1) American Building Maintenance Co., janitor service furnished public libraries (claim dated Dec. 31, 1929) $ 810.00

(2) Mullen Manufacturing Co., book cases and fixtures furnished public libraries (claim dated Dec. 31, 1929)....... 1,586.36

(3) Gunn, Carle & Co., tile floor furnished public library (claim dated Dec. 31, 1929)............................. 1,077.00

(4) C. E. Gordon, painting public libraries (claim dated Dec. 31, 1929) 847.00

(5) Finnell System, Inc., scrubber and water vacuum for public library (claim dated Dec. 31, 1929)................ 660.00

(6) Foster & Futernick Co., binding library books (claim dated Dec. 31, 1929)..................................... 2,584.00

(7) San Francisco News Co., library books (claim dated Dec. 31, 1929) 4,454.84

(8) G. E. Stechert & Co., library books (claim dated Dec. 31, 1929) 2,511.43

(9) Sather Gate Book Shop, library books (claim dated Dec. 31, 1929) 3,238.24

(10) San Francisco News Co., library books (claim dated Dec. 31, 1929) 1,139.60

Special School Tax.

(11) Park Commissioners, reimbursement for care of school grounds (claim dated Jan. 10, 1930) ....$ 1,300.00

(12) J. H. McCallum, lumber for schools (claim dated Jan. 13, 1930) 527.72

(13) D. A. Pancoast Co., "Van Duprin" type Panic Bolts for schools (claim dated Jan. 13, 1930)...................... 3,549.02

(14) C. F. Ernst, final payment for plumbing, gas fitting and cooking equipment furnished second unit South Side (Balboa) High School (claim dated Jan. 15, 1930)............ 15,088.68

(15) J. A. Mohr & Sons, Inc., final payment, painting of second unit South Side High School (claim dated Jan. 15, 1930) 1,985.25

(16) Scott Co., final payment, mechanical equipment, second unit South Side (Balboa) High School (claim dated Jan. 15, 1930) 8,601.75

(17) Mission Concrete Co., final payment, general construction of second unit South Side (Balboa) High School (claim dated Jan. 15, 1930) 77,505.58

(18) A. Lettich, first payment, plumbing work on Viewing Stand at South Side (Balboa) High School (claim dated Jan. 15, 1930) 968.40

(19) San Francisco City Employees' Retirement System, to match contributions by employees, for month of December, 1929 (claim dated Jan. 15, 1930) 968.69

California Palace, Legion of Honor, Appropriation 59.

(20) P. W. French, payment on purchase of "Moses and Aaron" tapestries, for California Palace, Legion of Honor (claim dated Jan. 10, 1930) ....$ 5,000.00

County Road Fund.

(21) Calaveras Cement Co., cement for street reconstruction (claim dated Jan. 11, 1930) ....$ 871.20

(22) Eclipse Lime & Cement Co., cement for street reconstruction (claim dated Jan. 11, 1930).................. 879.12

(23) Shell Oil Co., oil furnished in connection with street reconstruction (claim dated Jan. 11, 1930).............. 526.40

(24) The Texas Co., gasoline furnished in connection with street reconstruction (claim dated Jan. 11, 1930).......... 748.15

(25) Street Repair Department, Board of Public Works, reimbursement for cost of redressing curbs used in street reconstruction (claim dated Jan. 8, 1930)............... 643.75

(26) Street Repair Department, Board of Public Works, reimbursement for cost of redressing curbs used in street reconstruction (claim dated Jan. 8, 1930)............... 852.50

(27) San Francisco City Employees' Retirement System, to match contributions from employees engaged on street reconstruction (claim dated Jan. 15, 1930)................ 1,282.39

(28) Fay Improvement Co., sixth payment, improvement of Portola drive, from Twenty-fourth street to Fowler avenue (claim dated Jan. 15, 1930) 9,600.00

Hetch Hetchy Construction Fund, Bond Issue 1928.

(29) Bodinson Manufacturing Co., Inc., one double duplex classifier, Hetch Hetchy construction (claim dated Jan. 10, 1930. ....$ 4,370.00

(30) Consolidated Mills Co., Inc., lumber (claim dated Jan. 10, 1930) 567.71

(31) Ingersoll-Rand Co. of California, machinery parts (claim dated Jan. 10, 1930) 689.30

(32) Owen-Oregon Lumber Co., lumber (claim dated Jan. 10, 1930) 1,871.27

(33) Santa Cruz Portland Cement Co., cement (claim dated Jan. 10, 1930) 2,606.00

(34) Sherry Bros., Inc., eggs (claim dated Jan. 10, 1930).... 554.40

(35) Utah Fuel Co., coal (claim dated Jan. 10, 1930)...... 232.80

(36) Western Pipe & Steel Co., steel tunnel form, steel carriage, etc. (claim dated Jan. 10, 1930)................. 4,392.00

(37) W. H. Worden Co., Inc., wire rope (claim dated Jan. 10, 1930) 527.19

(38) Best Steel Casting Co., castings and car wheels (claim dated Jan. 9, 1930) 969.58

(39) J. H. Creighton, truck hire (claim dated Jan. 9, 1930).. 1,262.80

Boulevard Bonds, Issue 1927.

(40) Spring Valley Water Co., laying of 8 and 12-inch water mains in Bay Shore boulevard and adjacent street (claim dated Jan. 10, 1930) ....$ 7,572.56

(41) Louis J. Cohn, fourteenth payment, improvement of Bay
Shore bolevard, Sec. A, Contract 6, Potrero to Silver avenue (claim dated Jan. 15, 1930) 15,000.00

Municipal Railway Fund.

(42) Ohio Brass Co., clinch trolley ears, Municipal Railways
(claim dated Jan. 10, 1930)..............................$ 504.08
(43) Pacific Gas & Electric Co., electric power furnished Municipal Railways (claim dated Jan. 10, 1930)............. 43,359.76
(44) San Francisco City Employees' Retirement System, to
match contributions from Municipal Railway employees,
month of December, 1929 (claim dated Jan. 8, 1929)..... 7,742.13
(45) The Texas Co., gasoline furnished Municipal Railways
during November, 1929 (claim dated Jan. 10, 1930)....... 1,823.51

De Young Museum—Appropriation 58.

(46) P. J. Enright, third payment, heating and ventilating
M. H. de Young Memorial Museum (claim dated Jan. 17,
1930) . . . .$ 766.10

Auditorium Fund.

(47) Musical Association of San Francisco, for services of
San Francisco Symphony Orchestra, concert of Jan. 14,
1930 (claim dated Jan. 20, 1930)......................$ 2,000.00
(48) Selby C. Oppenheimer, for services of Dusolina Giannini
at concert of Jan. 14, 1930 (claim dated Jan. 20, 1930)... 1,200.00

General Fund, 1929-1930.

(49) San Francisco Chronicle, official advertising (claim
dated Jan. 20, 1930) ....$ 1,881.63
(50) Mendocino State Hospital, maintenance of criminal insane (claim dated Jan. 20, 1930)...................... 561.33
(51) Pacific Gas & Electric Co., street lighting, month of
December, 1929 (claim dated Jan. 20, 1930)............... 65,767.94
(52) Old Homestead Bakery, bread furnished County Jails
(claim dated Jan. 15, 1930) 729.88
(53) Barnard & Bunker, beans for County Jails (claim dated
Jan. 15, 1930) 1,556.00
(54) Frank J. Reilly, general construction of addition to M.
H. de Young Memorial Museum, eighth payment (claim
dated Jan. 17, 1930) 10,425.00
(55) P. J. Enright, heating and ventilating M. H. de Young
Memorial Museum, third payment (claim dated Jan. 17,
1930) 3,046.41
(56) Children's Agency, maintenance of minors (claim dated
Jan. 9, 1930) 30,905.38
(57) Little Children's Aid, maintenance of minors (claim
dated Jan. 9, 1930) 12,324.68
(58) Eureka Benevolent Society, maintenance of minors
(claim dated Jan. 9, 1930)............................ 2,890.00
(59) St. Vincent's School, maintenance of minors (claim
dated Jan. 9, 1930)................................... 1,227.23
(60) Roman Catholic Orphan Asylum, maintenance of minors
(claim dated Jan. 9, 1930) 1,931.56
(61) The Albertinum Orphanage, maintenance of minors
(claim dated Jan. 8, 1930)............................   758.42
(62) Lybrand, Ross Bros. & Montgomery, professional services rendered in connection with system installation at San
Francisco Juvenile Court (claim dated Jan. 7, 1930)...... 1,919.95
(63) The Texas Co., gasoline furnished for street cleaning
(claim dated Jan. 13, 1930) 735.15
(64) Spring Valley Water Co., water furnished public buildings, month of December (claim dated Jan. 13, 1930)..... 2,197.93

(65) Pacific Gas & Electric Co., gas and electric service, Fire Department (claim dated Dec. 31, 1929)............ 2,332.47

(66) The Seagrave Corporation, apparatus parts, Fire Department (claim dated Dec. 31, 1929).................... 601.95

(67) Spring Valley Water Co., water furnished Fire Department buildings, and installation of hydrants (claim dated Dec. 31, 1929) 2,302.35

(68) Standard Oil Co. of California, fuel oil, etc., for Fire Department (claim dated Dec. 31, 1929).................. 1,164.05

(69) The Texas Co., gasoline furnished Fire Department (claim dated Dec. 31, 1929) 1,638.61

(70) Tire Service Co., tires and tubes, Fire Department (claim dated Dec. 31, 1929) 851.53

(71) The Spring Valley Water Co., rental, June 30 to Dec. 30, 1929, for 60 acres Lake Merced property, occupied as Fleishhacker Park, in accordance with agreement dated Dec. 24, 1929 (claim dated Jan. 20, 1930) 6,029.11

(72) California Meat Co., meat for Laguna Honda Home (claim dated Dec. 31, 1929) 1,660.56

(73) Del Monte Meat Co., meat furnished Laguna Honda Home (claim dated Dec. 31, 1929)...................... 3,384.04

(74) Richfield Oil Co., fuel oil furnished Laguna Honda Home (claim dated Dec. 31, 1929) 1,900.69

(75) Baumgarten Bros., meat furnished Laguna Honda Home (claim dated Dec. 31, 1929) 813.71

(76) Spring Valley Water Co., water service rendered hospitals (claim dated Dec. 31, 1929) 1,700.59

Ayes—Supervisors Andriano, Canepa, Colman, Gallagher, Hayden, Miles, Power, Roncovieri, Spaulding, Suhr, Toner—11.

Absent—Supervisors Havenner, McGovern, McSheehy, Peyser, Rossi, Shannon, Stanton—7.

Appropriations, Special School Tax, School Purposes.

Also, Resoltuion No. 31965 (New Series), as follows:

Resolved, That the following amounts be and the same are hereby set aside, appropriated and authorized to be expended out of Special School Tax for the following purposes, to-wit:

(1) For the cost of installing gridiron and stage equipment at the Galileo High School....:.........................$ 3,481.00

(2) For cost of electrical fixtures for the Marina Elementary School 734.00

(3) For architectural services in the preparation of plans and specifications for the James Lick Junior High School.. 7,200.00

Ayes—Supervisors Andriano, Canepa, Colman, Gallagher, Hayden, Miles, Power, Roncovieri, Spaulding, Suhr, Toner—11.

Absent—Supervisors Havenner, McGovern, McSheehy, Peyser, Rossi, Shannon, Stanton—7.

Appropriations, Various Funds, Various Purposes.

Also, Resolution No. 31966 (New Series), as follows:

Resolved, That the following amounts be and the same are hereby set aside, appropriated and authorized to be expended out of the hereinafter mentioned funds for the following purposes, to-wit:

Health Bonds, Issue 1928.

(1) For engineering plans and preparations of plans for roof ward buildings at the San Francisco Hospital............$ 5,000.00

Boulevard Bonds, Issue 1927.

(2) For cost of installing safety island on the Bay Shore boulevard at the county line..............................$ 720.00

County Road Fund.

(3) For repairs and fills on Noriega street, from Thirty-fourth to Thirty-ninth avenues..........................$ 672.50

Fire House (Parkside), Budget Item No. 61.

(4) For engineering services in connection with construction of new engine house to be erected on west side of Eighteenth avenue between Quintara and Rivera streets.......$ 1,000.00

Municipal Airport Fund.

(5) For cost of cable installation at San Francisco Municipal Airport, in connection with construction of runway and drainage system ....$ 613.20

Ayes—Supervisors Andriano, Canepa, Colman, Gallagher, Hayden, Miles, Power, Roncovieri, Spaulding, Suhr, Toner—11.

Absent—Supervisors Havenner, McGovern, McSheehy, Peyser, Rossi, Shannon, Stanton—7.

Reimbursements to Board of Public Works for Account Building Repairs.

Also, Resolution No. 31967 (New Series), as follows:

Resolved, That the following amounts be set aside to the credit of Bureau of Building Repair, Board of Public Works, Budget Item 442, from the following Budget items, General Fund, 1929-1930, being reimbursements for work performed for various departments, Public Buildings, to-wit:

From repairs to public buildings, Budget Item No. 53, for work performed, as follows:

Grill work, etc., Juvenile Detention Home..................$	450.00
Bathroom, shower, plumbing, etc., Engine House No. 9.....	570.00
Kitchen construction, etc., Engine House No. 7.............	1,040.00
Elevator doors, etc., Hall of Justice.......................	560.00
Electric switchboard, wiring, etc., Hall of Justice..........	950.00
Room 103, Detective Bureau, Hall of Justice................	850.00
Room 102, Detective Bureau, Hall of Justice................	568.00
Office, Chief of Police, Hall of Justice.....................	780.00
Electric work, signals, etc., office of Chief of Police........	250.00
Cleaning hardwood floors, etc., Memorial Home, Chief of Fire Department	310.00
Boiler, San Francisco Hospital............................	1,934.00
Electric wiring and lights, office of Registrar..............	300.00

From City Hall repairs and painting, Budget Item 54, for work performed, as follows:

Building room, removing counters, etc., office of Registrar...	945.00
Building cashier's cages, office of Tax Collector.............	2,795.00
Partitions, etc., office of City Engineer....................	575.00
Changes in office of Chief Building Inspector..............	1,635.00

From contractual services, Department of Elections, Budget Item No. 188, for work performed, as follows:

For alterations, Department of Elections.................. 1,500.00

Ayes—Supervisors Andriano, Canepa, Colman, Gallagher, Hayden, Miles, Power, Roncovieri, Spaulding, Suhr, Toner—11.

Absent—Supervisors Havenner, McGovern, McSheehy, Peyser, Rossi, Shannon, Stanton—7.

Payment of Tax Judgment.

Also, Resolution No. 31968 (New Series), as follows:

Resolved, That the following amounts be and the same are hereby set aside and appropriated out of "Tax Judgments," Appropriation 57, and authorized in payment to the hereinafter named claimants; being payments of one-tenth the amount of final judgments and interest, as approved by the City Attorney, to-wit:

(1) To Tobin & Tobin, attorneys for judgment creditors, seventh installment, per schedule attached (claim dated Dec. 27, 1929) ....$ 7,928.39

(2) To Charles W. Slack and Edgar T. Zook, attorneys for judgment creditors, per schedule attached (claim dated Jan. 2, 1930) 4,241.05

(3) To Southern Pacific Company, judgment creditor (claim dated Jan. 31, 1930) 19,084.77

(4) To The Western Pacific Railroad, judgment creditor (claim dated Dec. 29, 1929) 687.66

Ayes—Supervisors Andriano, Canepa, Colman, Gallagher, Hayden, Miles, Power, Roncovieri, Spaulding, Suhr, Toner—11.

Absent—Supervisors Havenner, McGovern, McSheehy, Peyser, Rossi, Shannon, Stanton—7.

Payment for Property Damage, Bernal Cut.

Also, Resolution No. 31969 (New Series), as follows:

Resolved, That the sum of $1,808 be and the same is hereby set aside and appropriated out of Bernal Cut Bond Fund, Issue 1927, and authorized in payment to James Millar and Jeannetta F. Millar, and Title Insurance & Guaranty Co.; being payment in full release of damages to Lot 20, Block 6662, as per the Assessor's Block Books; also known as 71 Randall street; damages caused by the construction of Bernal Cut. Approved by Resolution No. 31899 (New Series) (claim dated Dec. 23, 1929).

Ayes—Supervisors Andriano, Canepa, Colman, Gallagher, Hayden, Miles, Power, Roncovieri, Spaulding, Suhr, Toner—11.

Absent—Supervisors Havenner, McGovern, McSheehy, Peyser, Rossi, Shannon, Stanton—7.

Payments for Properties Required for Boulevards.

Also, Resolution No. 31970 (New Series), as follows:

Resolved, That the following amounts be and the same are hereby set aside and appropriated out of Boulevard Bond Fund, Issue 1927, and authorized in payment to the hereinafter named persons; being payments for properties required for boulevard purposes, to-wit:

(1) To Ed Logue and Catherine Logue, and California Pacific Title & Trust Company, for portions of Lots 3 and 4, Block 7140 (47x24 irregular), as per the Assessor's Block Books, required for the opening of Alemany boulevard, and approved by Resolution No. 31896 (New Series) (claim dated Dec. 24, 1929) ....$ 5,500.00

(2) To Mrs. Ernest Scossa and Title Insurance & Guaranty Co., for all of Lots 5 and 6 and portions of Lots 7 and 9, Block 5819, as per the Assessor's Block Books, and required for the opening of Alemany boulevard; approved by Resolution No. 31895 (New Series) (claim dated Dec. 31, 1929) 1,155.00

(3) To Maud E. Welch and Title Insurance & Guaranty Co., for portion of Lot 4, Block 7157 (20x90), as per the Assessor's Block Books, and required for the widening of San Jose avenue as an approach to Alemany boulevard. Purchase approved by Resolution No. ———— (New Series) (claim dated Jan. 14, 1930)..................... 1,861.00

Ayes—Supervisors Andriano, Canepa, Colman, Gallagher, Hayden, Miles, Power, Roncovieri, Spaulding, Suhr, Toner—11.

Absent—Supervisors Havenner, McGovern, McSheehy, Peyser, Rossi, Shannon, Stanton—7.

Appropriation, Expense of Assistant City Attorney Dion R. Holm, to Represent San Francisco at Washington, D. C., $750.

Also, Resolution No. 31971 (New Series), as follows:

Resolved, That the sum of $750 be and the same is hereby set aside and appropriated out of "Telephone Rate Investigation Expense," Budget Item No. 59, and authorized in payment to Dion R. Holm, Assistant City Attorney, for his expense to, from and at Washington, D. C., in representing San Francisco before the U. S. Senate Committee on Interstate Commerce in its investigation on interstate and foreign communication service, etc., as authorized by Resolution No. 31943 (New Series).

Ayes—Supervisors Andriano, Canepa, Colman, Gallagher, Hayden, Miles, Power, Roncovieri, Spaulding, Suhr, Toner—11.

Absent—Supervisors Havenner, McGovern, McSheehy, Peyser, Rossi, Shannon, Stanton—7.

Ordering Improvement, Clayton and Market Streets.

Also, Bill No. 8169, Ordinance No. 8676 (New Series), as follows:

Ordering the improvement of the intersection of Clayton and Market streets, authorizing the preparation of plans and specifications for the said improvement of the intersection of Clayton and Market streets, and directing the Board of Public Works to enter into contract for said improvement in accordance with plans and specifications prepared therefor, which plans and specifications are hereby approved. The cost of said improvement to be borne out of County Road Fund.

Be it ordained by the People of the City and County of San Francisco as follows:

Section 1. The improvement of the intersection of Clayton and Market streets is hereby ordered, and the Board of Public Works is hereby authorized, instructed and empowered to prepare plans and specifications for said improvement of the intersection of Clayton and Market streets, and to enter into contract for said improvement in accordance with the plans and specifications prepared therefor, which plans and specifications are hereby approved. The cost of said improvement to be borne out of County Road Fund.

Section 2. This ordinance shall take effect immediately.

Ayes—Supervisors Andriano, Canepa, Colman, Gallagher, Hayden, Miles, Power, Roncovieri, Spaulding, Suhr, Toner—11.

Absent—Supervisors Havenner, McGovern, McSheehy, Peyser, Rossi, Shannon, Stanton—7.

Ordering the Construction of Fire Department Engine House, Eighteenth Avenue Between Quintara and Rivera Streets.

Also, Bill No. 8170, Ordinance No. 8677 (New Series), as follows:

Ordering the construction of Fire Department engine house, to be erected on the west side of Eighteenth avenue between Quintara and Rivera streets, in accordance with plans and specifications, which plans and specifications are hereby authorized to be prepared; authorizing and directing the Board of Public Works to enter into contract for said construction in accordance with the plans and specifications prepared therefor; permitting progressive payments to be made during the progress of construction.

Be it ordained by the People of the City and County of San Francisco as follows:

Section 1. The construction of Fire Department engine house is hereby ordered, and the Board of Public Works is hereby authorized, instructed and empowered to prepare plans and specifications for the said construction of Fire Department engine house, to be erected on the west side of Eighteenth avenue between Quintara and Rivera streets, and to enter into contract for said construction in accordance with the plans and specifications prepared therefor, which plans and specifications are hereby approved.

Section 2. The said Board of Public Works is hereby authorized and permitted to incorporate in the contract for the said construction of Fire Department engine house conditions that progressive payments shall be made in the manner set forth in said specifications on file in the Board of Public Works, and as provided by Section 21, Chapter I, Article VI of the Charter.

Section 3. This ordinance shall take effect immediately.

Ayes—Supervisors Andriano, Canepa, Colman, Gallagher, Hayden, Miles, Power, Roncovieri, Spaulding, Suhr, Toner—11.

Absent—Supervisors Havenner, McGovern, McSheehy, Peyser, Rossi, Shannon, Stanton—7.

Ordering Construction of James Lick Junior High School.

Also, Bill No. 8171, Ordinance No. 8678 (New Series), as follows:

Ordering the construction of the James Lick Junior High School, to be erected in block bounded by Twenty-fifth and Clipper streets, Noe and Castro streets, in accordance with plans and specifications, which plans and specifications are hereby authorized to be prepared; authorizing and directing the Board of Public Works to enter into contract for the said construction in accordance with the plans and specifications prepared therefor and as approved by the Board of Education. Permitting progressive payments to be made during the progress of construction.

Be it ordained by the People of the City and County of San Francisco as follows:

Section 1. The construction of the James Lick Junior High School is hereby ordered, and the Board of Public Works is hereby authorized, instructed and empowered to prepare plans and specifications for said construction of the James Lick Junior High School, to be erected in the block bounded by Twenty-fifth and Clipper streets, Noe and Castro streets, and to enter into contract for said construction in accordance with the plans and specifications prepared therefor and as approved by the Board of Education.

Section 2. The Board of Public Works is hereby authorized and permitted to incorporate in the contract for the said construction of James Lick Junior High School conditions that progressive payments shall be made in the manner set forth in said specifications on file in the Board of Public Works, and as provided by Section 21, Chapter I, Article VI of the Charter.

Section 3. This ordinance shall take effect immediately.

Ayes—Supervisors Andriano, Canepa, Colman, Gallagher, Hayden, Miles, Power, Roncovieri, Spaulding, Suhr, Toner—11.

Absent—Supervisors Havenner, McGovern, McSheehy, Peyser, Rossi, Shannon, Stanton—7.

Ordering Construction of Ward Building "F", Relief Home Tract.

Also, Bill No. 8172, Ordinance No. 8679 (New Series), as follows:

Ordering the construction of Ward Building "F," Relief Home Tract; authorizing and directing the Board of Public Works to prepare plans and specifications for the construction of Ward Building "F," Relief Home Tract, and to enter into contract for said construction in accordance with the plans and specifications prepared therefor, which plans and specifications are hereby approved. The cost of said construction to be borne out of Health Bonds, Issue 1928.

Be it ordained by the People of the City and County of San Francisco as follows:

Section 1. The construction of Ward Building "F," Relief Home Tract, is hereby ordered, and the Board of Public Works is hereby authorized, instructed and empowered to prepare plans and specifications for the construction of said Ward Building "F," Relief Home Tract, and to enter into contract for said construction in accordance with the plans and specifications prepared therefor, which plans and specifications are hereby approved. The cost of said construction of Ward Building "F," Relief Home Tract, to be borne out of the Health Bond Fund, Issue 1928.

Section 2. This ordinance shall take effect immediately.

Ayes—Supervisors Andriano, Canepa, Colman, Gallagher, Hayden, Miles, Power, Roncovieri, Spaulding, Suhr, Toner—11.

Absent—Supervisors Havenner, McGovern, McSheehy, Peyser, Rossi, Shannon, Stanton—7.

Appropriation to Enable Final Payment for Improvement of Junipero Serra Boulevard, Contract No. 13.

Also, Resolution No. 31972 (New Series), as follows:

Resolved, That the sum of $28,500.00 be and the same is hereby set aside, appropriated and authorized to be expended out of Boulevard Bond Issue, 1927, for the improvement of Junipero Serra boulevard, from Sloat boulevard to the county line, Contract No. 13, additional to enable final payment.

Ayes—Supervisors Andriano, Canepa, Colman, Gallagher, Hayden, Miles, Power, Roncovieri, Spaulding, Suhr, Toner—11.

Absent—Supervisors Havenner, McGovern, McSheehy, Peyser, Rossi, Shannon, Stanton—7.

Appropriations Out of Bond Funds for Advertising and Expense in Connection With Holding Bond Elections.

Also, Resoltuion No. 31973 (New Series), as follows:

Resolved, That the following amounts be and the same are hereby set aside and appropriated out of the hereinafter mentioned Bond Funds, and placed to the credit of the General Fund, fiscal year 1927-1928, as reimbursement of said General Fund for amounts advanced for advertising and incidental expense in connection with the holding of Bond Elections, to-wit:

From Spring Valley Water Bond Fund......................$ 7,255.18
From Hetch Hetchy Bond Fund........................... 7,056.77
Boulevard Bond Fund 7,850.94
Bernal Cut Bond Fund.................................. 30,003.65
War Memorial Bond Fund............................... 29,009.65

Ayes—Supervisors Andriano, Canepa, Colman, Gallagher, Hayden, Miles, Power, Roncovieri, Spaulding, Suhr, Toner—11.

Absent—Supervisors Havenner, McGovern, McSheehy, Peyser, Rossi, Shannon, Stanton—7.

Oil and Boiler Permits.

On recommendation of Fire Committee.

Resolution No. 31974 (New Series), as follows:

Resolved, That the following revocable permits be and are hereby granted:

Oil Tanks.

Rothschild Bros.—West side Steiner street, 82 feet south of Broadway, 750 gallons capacity.

Rothschild Bros.—West side Steiner street, 55 feet south of Broadway, 750 gallons capacity.

Frank Risso—Northwest corner of Tenth avenue and Anza street, 750 gallons capacity.

Grace Cathedral—South side of Sacramento street, 125 feet east of Jones street, 2000 gallons capacity.

T. A. Amitage—1561 Francisco street, 1500 gallons capacity.

Sommer & Kaufmann—South side Ellis street, 150 feet west of Stockton street, 1500 gallons capacity.

J. L. Snigewald—West side Capp street, 200 feet south of Twenty-third street, 1500 gallons capacity.

Boiler.

Gray & Danielson—Southwest corner of Nineteenth and Bryant streets, 40 horsepower.

The rights granted under this resolution shall be exercised within six months, otherwise said permit shall become null and void.

Ayes—Supervisors Andriano, Canepa, Colman, Gallagher, Hayden, Miles, Power, Roncovieri, Spaulding, Suhr, Toner—11.

Absent—Supervisors Havenner, McGovern, McSheehy, Peyser, Rossi, Shannon, Stanton—7.

Transfer of Automobile Supply Station, W. J. Higgins, Polk Street, North of Fell Street.

Also, Resolution No. 31975 (New Series), as follows:

Resolved, That John M. Hearn be and is hereby granted permission, revocable at will of the Board of Supervisors, to have transferred automobile supply station permit heretofore granted W. J. Higgins by Resolution No. 31191 (New Series) for premises on west side of Polk street, 35 feet north of Fell street.

The rights granted under this resolution shall be exercised within six months, otherwise said permit shall become null and void.

Ayes—Supervisors Andriano, Canepa, Colman, Gallagher, Hayden, Miles, Power, Roncovieri, Spaulding, Suhr, Toner—11.

Absent—Supervisors Havenner, McGovern, McSheehy, Peyser, Rossi, Shannon, Stanton—7.

Transfer of Automobile Supply Station Permit, H. Heskins, Southwest Corner Cabrillo Street and Forty-seventh Avenue.

Also, Resolution No. 31976 (New Series), as follows:

Resolved, That H. Heskins be and is hereby granted permission, revocable at will of the Board of Supervisors, to have transferred automobile supply station permit heretofore granted C. Leonard by Resolution No. 30736 (New Series) for premises on southwest corner of Cabrillo street and Forty-seventh avenue.

The rights granted under this resolution shall be exercised within six months, otherwise said permit shall become null and void.

Ayes—Supervisors Andriano, Canepa, Colman, Gallagher, Hayden, Miles, Power, Roncovieri, Spaulding, Suhr, Toner—11.

Absent—Supervisors Havenner, McGovern, McSheehy, Peyser, Rossi, Shannon, Stanton—7.

Directing Sale of City Land Situate Sutter Street Near Gough Street, Heretofore Site of Lowell High School.

On recommendation of Public Buildings and Lands Committee.

Bill No. 8173, Ordinance No. 8680 (New Series), as follows:

Providing for the disposal at public auction of certain lands belonging to the City and County of San Francisco in accordance with provisions of Article II, Chapter II, Section 9 of the Charter.

Be it ordained by the People of the City and County of San Francisco as follows:

Section 1. That public interest and necessity demand the sale of the following described parcel or piece of land owned and held by the City and County of San Francisco. Said parcel of land is situated in the City and County of San Francisco, State of California, and more particularly described as follows, to-wit:

Commencing at a point on the northerly line of Sutter street, distant thereon 137 feet 6 inches westerly from the westerly line of Gough street, running thence northerly 137 feet 6 inches; thence at right angles westerly 68 feet 9 inches; thence at right angles northerly 137 feet 6 inches to the southerly line of Bush street; thence at right angles westerly along said southerly line of Bush street 68 feet 9 inches; thence at right angles southerly 275 feet to the northerly line of Sutter street; thence at right angles easterly 137 feet 6 inches to the point of commencement; being a portion of Block 673 (W. A. 158).

Section 2. The said piece or parcel of land hereinabove described shall be sold for cash, in United States gold coin, at public auction to be held in accordance with the provisions of Article II, Chapter II, Section 9 of the Charter.

Section 3. The Clerk of the Board of Supervisors is hereby directed to publish in the official newspaper and in one other daily newspaper for three weeks successively next before the day on which the sale is to be made, a notice of such sale, describing the land to be sold with common certainty.

Section 4. The Mayor, Assessor and the Chairman of the Finance Committee of the Board of Supervisors are hereby directed to appraise said land within three weeks after the final passage of this ordinance as required by Article II, Chapter II, Section 9 of the Charter.

Section 5. Upon receipt and examination of bids or offers for said land as aforesaid, the Mayor shall accept the highest bid made, provided said bid be for at least 90 per cent of the value found by said appraisers, and shall immediately thereafter, at the next meeting of the Supervisors, report the fact of such sale to the Supervisors with a statement of the sum bid and the name of the highest bidder, with a request that the Board confirm such sale.

Ayes—Supervisors Andriano, Canepa, Colman, Gallagher, Hayden, Miles, Power, Roncovieri, Spaulding, Suhr, Toner—11.

Absent—Supervisors Havenner, McGovern, McSheehy, Peyser, Rossi, Shannon, Stanton—7.

Condemnation of Land for School Purposes in Holly Park Tract.

Also, Resolution No. 31977 (New Series), as follows:

Resolved, by the Board of Supervisors of the City and County of San Francisco, that public interest and necessity require the acquisition by the City and County of San Francisco, a municipal corporation, of the following properties situated in the City and County of San Francisco, State of California, more particularly described as follows, to-wit:

Being all of Block No. 2, Holly Park Tract, as per map recorded in the office of the City and County Recorder July 5, 1883, excepting Lot No. 22 and a portion of Lot No. 21 on said original map which said land excepted is now vested in the City and County of San Francisco. The said block is also known as Block No. 5714 on Assessor's Map Book, bounded by Appleton, Patton and Highland streets and Holly Park Circle; and be it

Further Resolved, That said properties are suitable, adaptable, necessary and required for the public use of said City and County of San Francisco for school purposes. It is necessary that a fee simple title be taken for such use.

The City Attorney is hereby ordered and directed to commence proceedings in eminent domain against the owners of said parcels of land and of any and all interests therein or claims thereto, for the condemnation thereof for the public use of the City and County of San Francisco, as aforesaid.

Ayes—Supervisors Andriano, Canepa, Colman, Gallagher, Hayden, Miles, Power, Roncovieri, Spaulding, Suhr, Toner—11.

Absent—Supervisors Havenner, McGovern, McSheehy, Peyser, Rossi, Shannon, Stanton—7.

Spur Track Permit, Southern Pacific Company, Across Second, King and Gale Streets.

On recommendation of Streets Committee.

Bill No. 8174, Ordinance No. 8681 (New Series), as follows:

Granting permission, revocable at will of the Board of Supervisors, to Southern Pacific Company (a corporation) to construct, maintain and operate spur tracks across Second, King and Gale streets as hereinafter described.

Be it ordained by the People of the City and County of San Francisco as follows:

Section 1. Permission, revocable at will of the Board of Supervisors, is hereby granted to the Southern Pacific Company (a corporation) to construct, maintain and operate spur tracks as follows:

(a) Beginning at a point on the center line of an existing Southern Pacific Company track in King street, said point being approximately 25 feet southwesterly from the northeasterly line of Second street 22 feet, more or less, southeasterly from the northwesterly line of King street; thence in a northeasterly direction and crossing portion of the intersection of King and Second streets to a point on the northwesterly line of King street; thence continuing into private property.

(b) Beginning at a point on the center line of an existing Southern Pacific Company track in King street, said point being distant southeasterly 5 feet, more or less, from the northwesterly line of King street and 8 feet, more or less, northeasterly from the northeasterly line of Second street; thence in a northeasterly direction and crossing portion of King street to a point on the northwesterly line of King street; thence continuing into private property.

(c) Beginning at a point on the southwesterly line of Gale street, distant northwesterly thereon 40 feet, more or less, from the northwesterly line of King street; thence in a northeasterly direction crossing Gale street to a point on the northeasterly line thereof; thence continuing into private property.

(d) Beginning at a point on the southwesterly line of Gale street, distant northwesterly thereon 53 feet, more or less, from the northwesterly line of King street; thence in a northeasterly direction crossing Gale street to a point on the northeasterly line thereof; thence continuing into private property.

(e) Beginning at a point on the southwesterly line of Gale street, distant northwesterly thereon 67 feet, more or less, from the northwesterly line of King street; thence in a northeasterly direction crossing Gale street to a point on the northeasterly line thereof; thence continuing into private property.

Said permission is granted subject to the provisions of Ordinance No. 69 (New Series) of the Board of Supervisors, approved October 12, 1906, and the provisions and conditions of Section 8 thereof are hereby specifically contained in the permit hereby granted and shall be construed as a part hereof as completely as though the same were written in this ordinance.

Provided, that said spur tracks shall be laid with girder rails under the supervision and to the lines and grades as furnished by the City Engineer's office, and that any and all expenses connected with the installation of the tracks, restoration of the pavement and any additional requirements for the surface drainage to be paid for by the Southern Pacific Company; provided, that Southern Pacific Company shall erect and maintain all-night lighted arc lamps to be placed where directed by the Lighting Committee of the Board of Supervisors.

Section 2. This ordinance shall take effect immediately.

Ayes—Supervisors Andriano, Canepa, Colman, Gallagher, Hayden, Miles, Power, Roncovieri, Spaulding, Suhr, Toner—11.

Absent—Supervisors Havenner, McGovern, McSheehy, Peyser, Ross, Shannon, Stanton—7.

Repealing Ordinances Numbered 8612 (New Series) and 8621 (New Series), Ordering the Removal of Sand and Construction of Bulkheads on Thirty-second Avenue and on Balboa Street.

Also, Bill No. 8175, Ordinance No. 8682 (New Series), as follows:

Repealing Ordinance No. 8612 (New Series) and Ordinance No. 8621 (New Series), ordering the removal of sand and the construction of bulkheads on Thirty-second avenue and on Balboa street as hereinafter described.

Be it ordained by the People of the City and County of San Francisco as follows:

Section 1. Ordinance No. 8612 (New Series), ordering the removal of sand and the construction of bulkheads on the west one-half of Thirty-second avenue from the south line of Geary street to a line parallel with and 100 feet 0 inches south of the south line of Geary street.

Ordinance No. 8621 (New Series), ordering the removal of sand and the construction of bulkheads on the south one-half of Balboa street from the west line of Twenty-fourth avenue to a line parallel with and 82 feet 0 inches west of the west line of Twenty-fourth avenue, by the removal of sand from the roadway and sidewalk area and the construction of a bulkhead be and the same are hereby repealed.

Section 2. This ordinance shall take effect immediately.

Ayes—Supervisors Andriano, Canepa, Colman, Gallagher, Hayden, Miles, Power, Roncovieri, Spaulding, Suhr, Toner—11.

Absent—Supervisors Havenner, McGovern, McSheehy, Peyser, Rossi, Shannon, Stanton—7.

Ordering Street Work, Flood Avenue and Other Streets.

Also, Bill No. 8176, Ordinance No. 8683 (New Series), as follows:

Ordering the performance of certain street work to be done in the City and County of San Francisco, approving and adopting specifications therefor.

Be it ordained by the People of the City and County of San Francisco as follows:

Section 1. The Board of Public Works in written communication filed in the office of the Clerk of the Board of Supervisors January 7, 1930, having recommended the ordering of the following street work, the same is hereby ordered to be done in the City and County of San Francisco in conformity with the provisions of the Street Improvement Ordinance of 1918 of said City and County of San Francisco, said work to be performed under the direction of the Board of Public Works, and to be done in accordance with the specifications prepared therefor by said Board of Public Works, and on file in its office, which said plans and specifications are hereby approved and adopted.

That said Board of Supervisors, pursuant to the provisions of Part II of the said Street Improvement Ordinance of 1918 of said City and County of San Francisco, does hereby determine and declare that the assessment to be imposed for the said contemplated improvements, respectively, may be paid in three installments; that the period of time after the time of the payment of the first installment when each of the succeeding installments must be paid is to be one year from the time of the payment of the preceding installment, and that the rate of interest to be charged on all deferred payments shall be seven per centum per annum.

The improvement of the south one-half of Flood avenue from the east line of Genesee street to a line parallel with and 100 feet east of the east line of Genesee street and the west one-half of Twenty-seventh avenue from a line parallel with and 100 feet north of the north line of Taraval street to a line parallel with and 125 feet north of the north line of Taraval street and the west one-half of Twenty-third avenue from a line parallel with and 265 feet south of the south line of Judah street to a line parallel with and 290 feet south of the south line of Judah street; and the west one-half of Eleventh avenue from a line parallel with and 200 feet north of the north line of Lawton street to a line parallel with and 225 feet north of the north line of Lawton street; and the east one-half of Nineteenth avenue from a line parallel with and 225 feet south of the south line of Moraga street to a line parallel with and 375 feet south of the south line of Moraga street; and the north one-half of Balboa street from the west line of Forty-third avenue to a line parallel with and 100 feet west of the west line of Forty-third avenue; and the east one-half of Twenty-sixth avenue from a line parallel with and 250 feet south of the south line of California street to a line parallel with and 325 feet south of the south line of California street; by the construction of artificial stone sidewalks, six feet in width, where artificial stone or bituminous rock sidewalks, six feet or more in width, have not already been constructed to the official grade; and the improvement of the west one-half of Eighth avenue from a line parallel with and 125 feet south of the south line of Anza street to a line parallel with and 175 feet south of the south line of Anza street; and the south one-half of Anza street from a line parallel with and 53 feet 4 inches east of the east line of Ninth avenue to a line parallel with and 105 feet east of the east line of Ninth avenue; and the west one-half of Mission street from the north line of Twenty-second street to a line parallel with and 112 feet 9 inches north of the north line of Twenty-second street; and the east one-half of Mission street from the north line of Twenty-third street to a line parallel with and 85 feet north of the north line of Twenty-third street; and the west one-half of Larkin street from the north line of Pine street to a line parallel with and 137 feet 6 inches north of the north line of Pine street; and the east one-half of Seventeenth avenue from the south line of Lincoln way to a line parallel with and 100 feet south of the south line of Lincoln way; and the south one-half of Twenty-ninth street from a line parallel with and 30 feet west of the west line of Noe street to a line parallel with and 55 feet west of the west line of Noe street; and the south one-half of Twenty-ninth street from a line parallel with and 80 feet west of the west line of Noe street to a line parallel with and 105 feet west of the west line of Noe street, by the construction of artificial stone sidewalks of the full official width, where artificial stone or bituminous rock sidewalks of the full official width have not already been constructed to the official grade.

Section 2. This ordinance shall take effect immediately.

Ayes—Supervisors Andriano, Canepa, Colman, Gallagher, Hayden, Miles, Power, Roncovieri, Spaulding, Suhr, Toner—11.

Absent—Supervisors Havenner, McGovern, McSheehy, Peyser, Rossi, Shannon, Stanton—7.

Ordering Street Work, Silliman Street and Other Streets.

Also, Bill No. 8177, Ordinance No. 8684 (New Series), as follows:

Ordering the performance of certain street work to be done in the City and County of San Francisco, approving and adopting specifications therefor.

Be it ordained by the People of the City and County of San Francisco as follows:

Section 1. The Board of Public Works in written communication filed in the office of the Clerk of the Board of Supervisors January 7, 1930, having recommended the ordering of the following street work, the same is hereby ordered to be done in the City and County of San Francisco in conformity with the provisions of the Street Improvement Ordinance of 1918 of said City and County of San Francisco, said work to be performed under the direction of the Board of Public Works, and to be done in accordance with the specifications prepared therefor by said Board of Public Works, and on file in its office, which said plans and specifications are hereby approved and adopted.

That said Board of Supervisors, pursuant to the provisions of Part II of the said Street Improvement Ordinance of 1918 of said City and County of San Francisco, does hereby determine and declare that the assessment to be imposed for the said contemplated improvements, respectively, may be paid in three installments; that the period of time after the time of the payment of the first installment when each of the succeeding installments must be paid is to be one year from the time of the payment of the preceding installment, and that the rate of interest to be charged on all deferred payments shall be seven per centum per annum.

The improvement of the following streets: Silliman street between Dartmouth street and Hamilton street; Felton street between Somerset street and Hamilton street; Burrows street between San Bruno avenue and Girard street; Bacon street between Somerset street and Hamilton street; Wayland street between Brussels street and Hamilton street; north half Woolsey street between Somerset street and Goettingen street; Olmstead street between San Bruno avenue and Brussels street; Girard street between Dwight street and Mansell street; Goettingen street between Wayland street and Bacon street; Somerset street between Wayland street and Silliman street; Holyoke street between Wayland street and Felton street; Hamilton street between Felton street and Silver avenue; Bowdoin street between Felton street and Silver avenue, by the construction of artificial stone sidewalks, six feet in width, where artificial stone or bituminous rock sidewalks, six feet or more in width, have not already been constructed.

Section 2. This ordinance shall take effect immediately.

Ayes—Supervisors Andriano, Canepa, Colman, Gallagher, Hayden, Miles, Power, Roncovieri, Spaulding, Suhr, Toner—11.

Absent—Supervisors Havenner, McGovern, McSheehy, Peyser, Rossi, Shannon, Stanton—7.

Ordering the Improvement of the West One-Half of Twenty-second Avenue.

Also, Bill No. 8178, Ordinance No. 8685 (New Series), as follows:

Ordering the performance of certain street work to be done in the City and County of San Francisco, approving and adopting specifications therefor.

Be it ordained by the People of the City and County of San Francisco as follows:

Section 1. The Board of Public Works in written communication filed in the office of the Clerk of the Board of Supervisors January 7, 1930, having recommended the ordering of the following street work, the same is hereby ordered to be done in the City and County of San Francisco in conformity with the provisions of the Street Improvement Ordinance of 1918 of said City and County of San Francisco, said work to be performed under the direction of the Board of Public Works, and to be done in accordance with the specifications prepared therefor by said Board of Public Works, and on file in its office, which said plans and specifications are hereby approved and adopted.

That said Board of Supervisors, pursuant to the provisions of Part II of the said Street Improvement Ordinance of 1918 of said City and County of San Francisco, does hereby determine and declare that the assessment to be imposed for the said contemplated improvements, respectively, may be paid in three installments; that the period of time after the time of the payment of the first installment when each of the succeeding installments must be paid is to be one year from the time of the payment of the preceding installment, and that the rate of interest to be charged on all deferred payments shall be seven per centum per annum.

The improvement of the west one-half of Twenty-second avenue from a line parallel with and 225 feet north of the north line of Moraga street to a line parallel with and 300 feet north of the north line of Moraga street, by the removal of sand from the roadway and sidewalk area and the construction of a bulkhead.

Section 2. This ordinance shall take effect immediately.

Ayes—Supervisors Andriano, Canepa, Colman, Gallagher, Hayden, Miles, Power, Roncovieri, Spaulding, Suhr, Toner—11.

Absent—Supervisors Havenner, McGovern, McSheehy, Peyser, Rossi, Shannon, Stanton—7.

Ordering the Improvement of the North One-Half of Nineteenth Street.

Also, Bill No. 8179, Ordinance No. 8686 (New Series), as follows:

. Ordering the performance of certain street work to be done in the City and County of San Francisco, approving and adopting specifications therefor.

Be it ordained by the People of the City and County of San Francisco as follows:

Section 1. The Board of Public Works in written communication filed in the office of the Clerk of the Board of Supervisors January 7, 1930, having recommended the ordering of the following street work, the same is hereby ordered to be done in the City and County of San Francisco in conformity with the provisions of the Street Improvement Ordinance of 1918 of said City and County of San Francisco, said work to be performed under the direction of the Board of Public Works, and to be done in accordance with the specifications prepared therefor by said Board of Public Works, and on file in its office, which said plans and specifications are hereby approved and adopted.

That said Board of Supervisors, pursuant to the provisions of Part II of the said Street Improvement Ordinance of 1918 of said City and County of San Francisco, does hereby determine and declare that the assessment to be imposed for the said contemplated improvements, respectively, may be paid in three installments; that the period of time after the time of the payment of the first installment when each of the succeeding installments must be paid is to be one year from the time of the payment of the preceding installment, and that the rate of interest to be charged on all deferred payments shall be seven per centum per annum.

The improvement of the north one-half of Nineteenth street from a line parallel with and 100 feet east of the east line of Sanchez street to a line parallel with and 150 feet east of the east line of Sanchez street, by the removal of sand from the roadway and sidewalk area and the construction of a bulkhead 3 feet in height.

Bidder is to name price per lineal foot of bulkhead for this work.

Section 2. This ordinance shall take effect immediately.

Ayes—Supervisors Andriano, Canepa, Colman, Gallagher, Hayden, Miles, Power, Roncovieri, Spaulding, Suhr, Toner—11.

Absent—Supervisors Havenner, McGovern, McSheehy, Peyser, Rossi, Shannon, Stanton—7.

PRESENTATION OF BILLS AND ACCOUNTS.

Your Finance Committee, having examined miscellaneous demands not required by law to be passed to print, and amounting to $72,032.87, recommends same be allowed and ordered paid.

Approved by the following vote:

Ayes—Supervisors Andriano, Canepa, Colman, Gallagher, Hayden, Miles, Power, Roncovieri, Spaulding, Suhr, Toner—11.

Absent—Supervisors Havenner, McGovern, McSheehy, Peyser, Rossi, Shannon, Stanton—7.

NEW BUSINESS.

Passed for Printing.

The following matters were *passed for printing*:

Authorizations.

On recommendation of Finance Committee.

Resolution No. ———— (New Series), as follows:

Resolved, That the following amounts be and the same are hereby authorized to be expended out of the hereinafter mentioned funds in payment to the following named claimants, to-wit:

Hetch Hetchy Construction Fund, Bond Issue 1928.

(1) Ingersoll-Rand Co. of Calif., machinery parts (claim dated Jan. 15, 1930) ....$ 2,235.48

(2) Myers-Whaley Co., Inc., conveyor belts, etc. (claim dated Jan. 15, 1930) 1,371.60

(3) Pioneer Rubber Mills, digger belts and air hose (claim dated Jan. 15, 1930) 1,165.35

(4) Santa Cruz Portland Cement Co., cement (claim dated Jan. 15, 1930) 1,510.00

(5) Santa Fe Lumber Co, lumber (claim dated Jan. 15, 1930) 608.48

(6) San Francisco City Employees Retirement System, to match contributions of Hetch Hetchy employees (claim dated Jan. 15, 1930) 630.99

(7) State Compensation Insurance Fund, premium covering Hetch Hetchy employments (claim dated Jan. 15, 1930) . 6,654.15

(8) M. D. Jones, truck rental (claim dated Jan. 16, 1930).. 1,134.40

(9) Best Steel Casting Co., castings (claim dated Jan. 20, 1930) 529.65

(10) Boiler Tank & Pipe Co., remodeling of tunnel forms (claim dated Jan. 20, 1930)............................ 810.00

(11) Consolidated Mills Co., lumber (claim dated Jan. 20, 1930) 2,241.86

(12) Del Monte Meat Co., meat (claim dated Jan. 20, 1930) 1,963.01

(13) W. Haslam, truck rental and hauling (claim dated Jan. 20, 1930) 1,780.91

(14) Hammond Lumber Co., lumber (claim dated Jan. 20, 1930) 586.22

(15) Mally's Grill & Coffee Shop, Livermore, Cal., fish, turkeys and eggs furnished (claim dated Jan. 20, 1930)... 763.07

(16) J. H. McCallum, lumber (claim dated Jan. 20, 1930)... 517.03

(17) Montague Pipe & Steel Co., steel pipe (claim dated Jan. 20, 1930)... 1,928.76

(18) Owen-Oregon Lumber Co., lumber (claim dated Jan. 20, 1930).. 3,641.69

(19) Santa Cruz Portland Cement Co., cement (claim dated Jan. 20, 1930) 502.00

(20) St. Paul's Hospital, Livermore, hospital service rendered Hetch Hetchy employees (claim dated Jan. 20, 1930) 984.85

Park Fund.

(21) William Good, fertilizer furnished Harding Park (claim dated Jan. 24, 1930) ....$ 502.50

(22) Granfield, Farrar & Carlin, tractor hire for Fleishhacker Playfield (claim dated Jan. 24, 1930)............ 569.62

(23) Haskins & Sells, audit of Park accounts (claim dated Jan. 24, 1930) 1,264.45

(24) Standard Fence Co., wire fencing, cage, etc., for parks (claim dated Jan. 24, 1930) 677.37

(25) State Compensation Insurance Fund, premium covering insurance of park employments (claim dated Jan. 24, 1930) 574.56

(26) Berringer & Russell, hay, etc., for parks (claim dated Jan. 24, 1930) 788.20

(27) Meyer Rosenberg, loam for parks (claim dated Jan. 24, 1930) 1,876.25

Playground Fund.

(28) Playground Commission, for reimbursement of Mather Revolving Fund, account of expenditures as per vouchers attached (claim dated Jan. 22, 1930).................$ 708.00

Hetch Hetchy Power Operative Fund.

(29) Hetch Hetchy Construction Fund, Bond Issue 1928, for material, supplies and services furnished Hetch Hetchy Power Operative during December, 1929 (claim dated Jan. 21, 1930) ....$ 8,981.19

(30) Depreciation Fund, Hetch Hetchy Power Operative, as reserve for depreciation, for January, per Charter requirement (claim dated Jan. 21, 1930)...................... 14,583.00

(31) Reynier Lumber Co., redwood ties (claim dated Jan. 21, 1930) 548.00

(32) State Compensation Insurance Fund, premium covering insurance of Hetch Hetchy employments (claim dated Jan. 21, 1930) 966.29

Boulevard Construction Fund, Bond Issue 1927.

(33) Wm. Bateman, furnishing of survey stakes (claim dated Jan. 15, 1930)..$ 757.25

(34) Granfield, Farrar & Carlin, improvement of Great Highway (upper roadway) by placing of fill (claim dated Jan. 15, 1930) 37,875.00

(35) Granfield, Farrar & Carlin, improvement of Sunset boulevard, by grading (claim dated Jan. 15, 1930)....... 18,000.00

(36) Eaton & Smith, ninth payment, improvement of Nineteenth avenue from Sloat boulevard to Worcester avenue (claim dated Jan. 22, 1930) 67,000.00

County Road Fund.

(37) E. J. & M. J. Treacy, for improvement of Twentieth street between San Bruno avenue and Vermont street, and crossing (claim dated Jan. 15, 1930) ....$ 2,943.05

(38) James T. Tobin, for grading of 12-foot roadway on Kirkwood street from Mendell street to point 200 feet easterly (claim dated Jan. 15, 1930)................... 1,000.00

(39) Municipal Construction Co., City's portion for improvement of Evans avenue, Marin to Army streets, and intersection of Evans avenue and Selby street (claim dated Jan. 21, 1930) 2,883.40

(40) Property Owners Grading Co., for removal of sand from Twenty-fourth, Twenty-fifth, Twenty-seventh, Twenty-eighth, Twenty-ninth and Thirtieth avenues between Rivera and Santiago streets (claim dated Jan. 21, 1930)... 650.00

(41) James A. and Gesina Jenkins, reimbursement for damage to property at 3433 Market street; being in full satisfaction and settlement of claim (claim dated Jan. 21, 1930) 632.00

Special School Tax.

(42) Western Asbestos Magnesia Co., Acousti Celotex for Polytechnic High School (claim dated Jan. 20, 1930)....$ 4,125.00

(43) Pacific Coast Aggregates, Inc., concrete mix for Sunset Primary School (claim dated Jan. 20, 1930)............. 941.00

(44) W. H. Crim, seventh payment, architectural services for Park-Presidio Junior High School (claim dated Jan. 21, 1930) 888.83

(45) D. A. Pancoast Co., "Von Duprin" type panic bolts for schools (claim dated Jan. 22, 1930) 2,529.00

Tax Judgments—Appropriation 57.

(46) Percy E. Towne, attorney for judgment creditors, sixth installment, one-tenth of final judgment and interest, per schedule attached; approved by City Attorney (claim dated Jan. 8, 1930) ....$ 2,039.31

General Fund—1929-1930.

(47) Burroughs Adding Machine Co., one Burroughs adding-subtracting machine, for use of Auditor (claim dated Jan. 27, 1930) ....$ 750.50

(48) Board of Park Commissioners, reimbursement for Civic Center beautification (claim dated Jan. 24, 1930)...   656.43

(49) A. P. Jacobs, rental of No. 333 Kearny street, Jan. 3 to Feb. 3, 1930 (claim dated Jan. 27, 1930) 1,120.75

(50) San Francisco Chronicle, official advertising (claim dated Jan. 27, 1930) 688.88

(51) Stephenson Construction Co., fifth payment, repairs to Palace of Fine Arts (claim dated Jan. 24, 1930) 3,405.00

(52) Preston School of Industry, maintenance of minors (claim dated Jan. 23, 1930) 800.00

(53) Lybrand, Ross Bros. & Montgomery, professional services, installation of accounting system at Juvenile Court (claim dated Jan. 21, 1930) 1,401.90

(54) Municipal Construction Co., improvement of Rodeo avenue between Teddy and San Bruno avenues (claim dated Jan. 15, 1930) 1,690.00

(55) Pacific Gas & Electric Co., lighting public buildings during month of December (claim dated Jan. 14, 1930)   5,271.42

(56) Special School Tax, reimbursement for stock withdrawals, used by Board of Public Works during October, November and December, 1929 (claim dated Jan. 14, 1930)..   897.51

(57) Special School Tax, reimbursement for stock withdrawals by Board of Public Works during October, November and December, 1929 (claim dated Jan. 14, 1930)........   917.39

(58) Special School Tax, reimbursement for stock withdrawals by Board of Public Works during Octomber, November and December, 1929 (claim dated Jan. 14, 1930)........   901.44

(59) E. J. Treacy, construction of 8-inch ironstone pipe sewer, etc., in Chestnut street between Kearny and Montgomery streets (claim dated Jan. 22, 1930)..............   1,600.00

(60) Joseph Hagan & Sons, burial of indigent dead (claim dated Jan. 23, 1930) 860.00

(61) Pacific Gas & Electric Co., electricity furnished San Francisco Hospital (claim dated Jan. 23, 1930)..........   582.10

(62) Walton N. Moore Dry Goods Co., pajamas furnished San Francisco Hospital (claim dated Dec. 31, 1929) 577.28

(63) Herbert F. Dugan, chemical and surgical supplies for San Francisco Hospital (claim dated Dec. 31, 1929) 884.62

(64) Sussman Wormser & Co., coffee and oil, San Francisco Hospital (claim dated Dec. 31, 1929) 532.00

(65) San Francisco International Fish Co., fish, etc., for San Francisco Hospital (claim dated Dec. 31, 1929)......   615.00

(66) Ralphs-Pugh Co., Inc., sheeting for San Francisco Hospital (claim dated Dec. 31, 1929) 700.00

(67) Old Homestead Bakery, bread for San Francisco Hospital (claim dated Dec. 31, 1929) 2,123.12

(68) Wilsey, Bennett Co., eggs for San Francisco Hospital claim dated Dec. 31, 1929)...............................   2,394.04

(69) Fred L. Hilmer Co., butter, etc., San Francisco Hospital (claim dated Dec. 31, 1929) 2,142.20
(70) San Francisco Dairy Co., milk furnished hospitals (claim dated Dec. 31, 1929) 4,315.58
(71) Scatena-Galli Fruit Co., fruit and produce, San Francisco Hospital (claim dated Dec. 31, 1929)............. 956.10
(72) A. Lagomarsino & Co., produce, San Francisco Hospital (claim dated Dec. 31, 1929)............................... 1,362.83
(73) Richfield Oil Co., fuel oil, San Francisco Hospital (claim dated Dec. 31, 1929) 2,274.77
(74) California Meat Co., meat for San Francisco Hospital (claim dated Dec. 31, 1929) 1,518.77
(75) Del Monte Meat Co., meat for San Francisco Hospital (claim dated Dec. 31, 1929) 1,356.85
(76) Ames, Harris, Neville Co., curtains and awnings, San Francisco Hospital (claim dated Dec. 31, 1929)........... 869.00

Appropriations, Plumbing, Etc., Bay View Police Station, and Street Signs.

Also, Resolution No. ———— (New Series), as follows:

Resolved, That the following amounts be and the same are hereby set aside, appropriated and authorized to be expended out of the hereinafter accounts, General Fund, 1929-1930, for the following purposes, to-wit:

Repairs to Public Buildings, Budget Item No. 53.

(1) For general overhauling of plumbing in Bay View Police Station, and furnishing and installing of urinal and two high closet tanks on first floor and one toilet and shower on second floor .. ..$ 450.00

Traffic Signals, Budget Item 57.

(2) To the credit of "Street Signs," Budget Item 63, to reimburse for installation of 17 rubber slow signs at various locations during January, 1930 .. ..$ 52.00

Adopted.

The following resolutions were *adopted*:

Monthly Salaries, Employees of Traffic Bureau, Department of Engineering, Month of January, 1930.

On recommendation of Finance Committee.

Resolution No. 31978 (New Series), as follows:

Resolved, That the following amounts be and the same are hereby set aside, appropriated and authorized to be expended out of "Traffic Signals," Budget Item No. 57, for the payment of salaries of employees attached to the Traffic Bureau, being for the month of January, 1930, to-wit:

    Traffic Engineer .. ..:............$300
    Assistant Traffic Engineer 225
    Clerk and stenographer 175
                                                        ————
        Total $700

Ayes—Supervisors Andriano, Canepa, Colman, Gallagher, Hayden, Miles, Power, Roncovieri, Spaulding, Suhr, Toner—11.

Absent—Supervisors Havenner, McGovern, McSheehy, Peyser, Rossi, Shannon, Stanton—7.

Board of Health Reimbursing Board of Works for Work Performed and Materials Furnished.

Also, Resolution No. 31979 (New Series), as follows:

Resolved, That the following amounts be and the same are hereby

set aside to the credit of Budget Item No. 442, Board of Public Works, from the following Budget Items, Department of Public Health; being reimbursements for material and services furnished and performed by the Board of Public Works for the Department of Public Health, to-wit:

From Budget Item 784, Central Office.......................$ 32.92
From Budget Item 836, Laguna Honda Home...............   447.50
From Budget ·Item 992, San Francisco Hospital............. 5,947.58
From Budget Item 1010, Emergency Hospitals 46.28
From Budget Item 51, Preventorium, San Mateo County.....   303.94

Being for period October 1 to December 31, 1929. (Board of Health recommendation dated January 21. 1930.)

Ayes—Supervisors Andriano, Canepa, Colman, Gallagher, Hayden, Miles, Power, Roncovieri, Spaulding, Suhr, Toner—11.

Absent—Supervisors Havenner, McGovern, McSheehy, Peyser, Rossi, Shannon, Stanton—7.

Board of Health Transfer of Amounts for Reimbursement of Interdepartmental Accounts.

Also, Resolution No. 31980 (New Series), as follows:

Resolved, That the following amounts be and the same are set aside to the credit of Budget Item 838, Department of Public Health, from the following Budget Items, Department of Public Health; being reimbursements for commodities furnished or services rendered, to-wit:

From Budget Item 994, San Francisco Hospital.............$ 427.00
From Budget Item 1010, Emergency Hospitals..............   834.53
From Budget Item 51, Preventorium, San Mateo County.... 1,945.76
And from Budget Item 1010, Emergency Hospitals, to the
    credit of Budget Item 992, San Francisco Hospital........   224.72

(Recommendation of Department of Public Health, dated January 21, 1930.)

Ayes—Supervisors Andriano, Canepa, Colman, Gallagher, Hayden, Miles, Power, Roncovieri, Spaulding, Suhr, Toner—11.

Absent—Supervisors Havenner, McGovern, McSheehy, Peyser, Rossi, Shannon, Stanton—7.

Accepting Percentage of Passenger Receipts, Market Street Railway Company.

Also, Resolution No. 31981 (New Series), as follows:

Resolved, That the statements heretofore filed by the Market Street Railway Company, showing gross receipts from passenger fares for the months of November and December, 1929, upon which percentages in the following amounts are due the City and County, be and the same are hereby accepted, to-wit:

November—
    Twentieth avenue, Taraval street, etc. $541.99
    Gough street 39.96
    Parnassus avenue, etc.......................   257.07
December—
    Twentieth avenue, Taraval street, etc.........$545.05
    Gough street 39.35
    Parnassus avenue, etc. 247.07

Further Resolved, That the Market Street Railway Company is here·by directed to deposit with the Treasurer of the City and County the hereinabove mentioned sums, the same to be placed to the credit of the General Fund.

Ayes—Supervisors Andriano, Canepa, Colman, Gallagher, Hayden, Miles, Power, Roncovieri, Spaulding, Suhr, Toner—11.

Absent—Supervisors Havenner, McGovern, McSheehy, Peyser, Rossi, Shannon, Stanton—7.

Payment of City and County Aid to Aged Needy Persons, Statute 1929, Chapter 530.

Also, Resolution No. 31982 (New Series), as follows:

Whereas, the Director of the County Welfare Department, City and County of San Francisco, has reported to the Board of Supervisors that 39 aged needy persons are entitled to City and County aid under Statute 1929, Chapter 530, have been approved by the Finance Committee and recommended to the Board of Supervisors for its approval; therefore, be it

Resolved, That the amounts, none of which individually exceed $30, recommended to these several persons be and the same are hereby approved, allowed and ordered to be paid out of money raised by taxation under the aforesaid statute, for payment of January, 1930, allowances to the persons named in said report as submitted by said Welfare Board and filed with the Board of Supervisors and the Auditor. Being demand No. 1, for the needy aged.

Ayes—Supervisors Andriano, Canepa, Colman, Gallagher, Hayden, Miles, Power, Roncovieri, Spaulding, Suhr, Toner—11.

Absent—Supervisors Havenner, McGovern, McSheehy, Peyser, Rossi, Shannon, Stanton—7.

Passed for Printing.

The following matters were *passed for printing*:

Automobile Supply Station Permit, J. H. Frietzsche, Northeast Corner of Third Street and Revere Avenue.

On recommendation of Fire Committee.

Resolution No. ————— (New Series), as follows:

Resolved, That Philip Parodi be and is hereby granted permission, revocable at will of the Board of Supervisors, to have transferred to him automobile supply station permit heretofore granted to J. H. Frietzsche by Resolution No. 29199 (New Series) for premises on northeast corner of Third street and Revere avenue.

The rights granted under this resolution shall be exercised within six months, otherwise said permit shall become null and void.

Transfer of Automobile Supply Station Permit, F. J. Harlis, Northeast Corner of Fell and Baker Streets.

Also, Resolution No. ————— (New Series), as follows:

Resolved, That Edward B. Rowan be and is hereby granted permission, revocable at will of the Board of Supervisors, to have transferred to him automobile supply station permit heretofore granted F. J. Harlis by Resolution No. 31256 (New Series) for premises at northeast corner of Fell and Baker streets.

The rights granted under this resolution shall be exercised within six months, otherwise said permit shall become null and void.

Transfer of Garage Permit, Thos. J. Lowe, 1250 McAllister Street.

Also, Resolution No. ————— (New Series), as follows:

Resolved, That Thos. J. Lowe be and is hereby granted permission, revocable at will of the Board of Supervisors, to have transferred to him public garage permit heretofore granted F. J. Gahren by Resolution No. 30413 (New Series) for premises at 1250 McAllister street.

The rights granted under this resolution shall be exercised within six months, otherwise said permit shall become null and void.

Transfer of Garage Permit, O. J. Gilli, 2035 Divisadero Street.

Also, Resolution No. ————— (New Series), as follows:

Resolved, That O. J. Gilli be and is hereby granted permission, revocable at will of the Board of Supervisors, to have transferred to

him public garage permit heretofore granted Alfred Whittle by Reso- .
lution No. 30738 (New Series) for premises at 2035 Divisadero street.

The rights granted under this resolution shall be exercised within
six months, otherwise said permit shall become null and void.

Automobile Parking Station Permit, E. A. Hicks, Hoff Avenue, South of Sixteenth Street.

Also, Resolution No. ————— (New Series), as follows:

Resolved, That E. A. Hicks be and is hereby granted permission,
revocable at will of the Board of Supervisors, to maintain and operate
an automobile parking station on the easterly line of Hoff avenue, 211
feet 10½ inches southerly from the southerly line of Sixteenth street.

The rights granted under this resolution shall be exercised within
six months, otherwise said permit shall become null and void.

Laundry Permits.

Also, Resolution No. ————— (New Series), as follows:

Resolved, That the following revocable permits be and are hereby
granted:

Laundries.

Eloise Aiso, 1089 Pine street.
John Batsere, 976 Pine street.
Anna Biscay, 992 Sutter street.
Ruth Clausen, 94 Seventh street.
Mrs. V. J. Laurent, 447 Ellis street.
J. Nongue, 707 O'Farrell street.
Mme. P. Pomme, 1147 McAllister street.
Marie Sabacca, 808 Post street.
Mme. J. Saffores, 841 Powell street.
Mrs. A. Termello, 41 Franklin street.
Louise Vannucci and Gloria Cheader, 405 O'Farrell street. .

The rights granted under this resolution shall be exercised within
six months, otherwise said permits shall become null and void.

Blanket protest filed by Mr. Alford, Board of Trade, Laundry Industry.

Oil Tank Permits.

Also, Resolution No. ————— (New Series), as follows:

Resolved, That the following revocable permits be and are hereby
granted:

Oil Tanks.

Jules H. Bernheim, southwest corner San Fernando way and St.
Francis boulevard, 750 gallons capacity.

Mrs. C. Van Straaton, 1622 Washington street, 1500 gallons capacity.

N. George Weinholz, north side of Washington street, 62 feet east of
Laurel street, 1500 gallons capacity.

O. E. Carlson, south side Duboce avenue, 60 feet east of Guerrero
street, 1500 gallons capacity.

B. A. Ilg, 610 El Camino Del Mar, 1500 gallons capacity.

Jos. C. Linale, 1915 Baker street, 1500 gallons capacity.

The rights granted under this permit shall be exercised within six
months, otherwise said permits shall become null and void. .

Regulating Keeping and Feeding Dogs, Cats, Etc.

On recommendation of Public Health Committee.

Bill No. ————, Ordinance No. ————— (New Series), as follows:

Regulating the keeping and feeding of dogs, cats, hares, rabbits,
guinea pigs, chickens, turkeys, geese, ducks, doves, pigeons, parrots or
other fowl; providing penalties for the violation thereof, and repealing
Ordinance No. 384 (New Series) and all ordinances or parts of ordinances in conflict therewith.

Be it ordained by the People of the City and County of San Francisco as follows:

Section 1. It shall be unlawful for any person, firm or corporation, without first obtaining a permit from the Board of Health, to keep or feed, or cause to be kept or fed, or permit to be kept or fed on premises over which any such person, firm or corporation may have control, the following: Hares, rabbits, guinea pigs, chickens, turkeys, geese, ducks, doves, pigeons, parrots of any species, game birds of any species, dogs and cats within the First and Second Residential Districts as at present defined by Ordinance No. 5464 (New Series), or as may hereafter be defined by the City Planning Commission of the City and County of San Francisco; provided, however, that dogs and cats to the limit of two may be kept upon any premises within the First and Second Residential Districts, provided the same are kept and maintained in a manner that does not violate the State Housing Law or be in themselves a nuisance to any person or persons in the neighborhood.

Provided, however, that when a permit has been issued for the maintenance of any of the above the same shall be kept and fed in coops or inclosures complying with the following requirements, to-wit:

(a) The floor of said coop or enclosure shall be of concrete not less than two (2) inches thick and covered either with a layer of cement not less than one-half (½) inch thick or asphalt not less than one (1) inch thick.

(b) The said coop or enclosure shall be entirely surrounded by a brick or concrete wall at least five (5) inches in thickness and one (1) foot high.

(c) The said coop or enclosure shall be entirely surrounded by a galvanized iron wire mesh fence, wall or sides extending at least six (6) feet above the ground, which mesh shall not be greater than one-half (½) inch in size.

Provided, however, that said dogs, cats, hares, rabbits, guinea pigs, chickens, turkeys, geese, ducks, doves, pigeons, parrots, game birds or other fowl shall be permitted between the hours of sunrise and sunset to run at large within the limits of the premises in which said coops or inclosures shall be kept closed during the time that said dogs, cats, hares, rabbits, guinea pigs, chickens, turkeys, geese, ducks, doves, pigeons, parrots, game birds or other fowl are so running at large and that said premises be safely fenced so that said animals and fowls cannot escape therefrom.

Section 2. It shall be unlawful for any person, firm or corporation to keep or feed, or cause to be kept or fed, or permit to be kept or fed, dogs, cats, hares, rabbits, guinea pigs, chickens, turkeys, geese, ducks, doves, pigeons, game birds, parrots of any species, or other fowl, in moveable or portable coops in premises which are not ratproof unless the said coops are constructed with a metal bottom and metal sides to a height of at least one (1) foot, surmounted by a metal cage of one-half (½) inch wire mesh.

Section 3. It shall be unlawful for any person, firm or corporation to engage in the business of keeping, feeding or breeding any hares, rabbits, guinea pigs, chickens, turkeys, geese, ducks, doves, pigeons, parrots of any species, game birds of any species, dogs or cats or any other animals for commercial purposes within the First and Second Residential Districts, as defined by the Zoning Ordinance.

Section 4. All ordinances or parts or portions of any and all ordinances in conflict with the provisions of this ordinance and Ordinance No. 384 (New Series) are hereby repealed.

Section 5. Any person, firm or corporation violating the provisions of this ordinance shall be guilty of a misdemeanor and, upon conviction thereof, shall be punished by a fine of not more than five hundred ($500) dollars, or by imprisonment in the County Jail for not more than six (6) months, or by both fine and imprisonment.

Section 6. This ordinance shall take effect immediately upon its passage.

Motion.

Supervisor Andriano moved rereference to the Health Committee. Motion *lost* by the following vote:

Ayes—Supervisors Andriano, Canepa, Havenner, Stanton, Suhr—5.

Noes—Supervisors Colman, Gallagher, Hayden, McSheehy, Miles, Power, Roncovieri, Spaulding, Toner—9.

Absent—Supervisors McGovern, Peyser, Rossi, Shannon—4.

Amendment.

Supervisor Toner moved as an amendment to the foregoing bill that everything relating to dogs and cats be eliminated.

Amendment *carried* by the following vote:

Ayes—Supervisors Andriano, Canepa, Hayden, McSheehy, Miles, Power, Stanton, Suhr, Toner—9.

Noes—Supervisors Colman, Gallagher, Havenner, Roncovieri, Spaulding—5.

Absent—Supervisors McGovern, Peyser, Rossi, Shannon—4.

Passed for Printing.

Whereupon, the foregoing bill, amended as follows, was *passed for printing*:

Bill No. 8181, Ordinance No. ———— (New Series), as follows:

Regulating the keeping and feeding of hares, rabbits, guinea pigs, chickens, turkeys, geese, ducks, doves, pigeons, parrots or other fowl; providing penalties for the violation thereof, and repealing Ordinance No. 384 (New Series) and all ordinances or parts of ordinances in conflict therewith.

Be it ordained by the People of the City and County of San Francisco as follows:

Section 1. It shall be unlawful for any person, firm or corporation, without first obtaining a permit from the Board of Health, to keep or feed, or cause to be kept or fed, or permit to be kept or fed on premises over which any such person, firm or corporation may have control, the following: Hares, rabbits, guinea pigs, chickens, turkeys, geese, ducks, doves, pigeons, parrots of any species, game birds of any species, within the First and Second Residential Districts as at present defined by Ordinance No. 5464 (New Series), or as may hereafter be defined by the City Planning Commission of the City and County of San Francisco.

Provided, however, that when a permit has been issued for the maintenance of any of the above the same shall be kept and fed in coops or inclosures complying with the following requirements, to-wit:

(a) The floor of said coop or enclosure shall be of concrete not less than two (2) inches thick and covered either with a layer of cement not less than one-half (½) inch thick or asphalt not less than one (1) inch thick.

(b) The said coop or enclosure shall be entirely surrounded by a brick or concrete wall at least five (5) inches in thickness and one (1) foot high.

(c) The said coop or enclosure shall be entirely surrounded by a galvanized iron wire mesh fence, wall or sides extending at least six (6) feet above the ground, which mesh shall not be greater than one-half (½) inch in size.

Provided, however, that said hares, rabbits, guinea pigs, chickens, turkeys, geese, ducks, doves, pigeons, parrots, game birds or other fowl shall be permitted between the hours of sunrise and sunset to run at large within the limits of the premises in which said coops or inclosures shall be kept closed during the time that said hares, rabbits, guinea pigs, chickens, turkeys, geese, ducks, doves, pigeons, parrots, game birds or other fowl are so running at large and that said premises be safely fenced so that said animals and fowls cannot escape therefrom.

Section 2. It shall be unlawful for any person, firm or corporation to keep or feed, or cause to be kept or fed, or permit to be kept or fed, hares, rabbits, guinea pigs, chickens, turkeys, geese, ducks, doves, pigeons, game birds, parrots of any species, or other fowl, in moveable or portable coops in premises which are not ratproof unless the said coops are constructed with a metal bottom and metal sides to a height of at least one (1) foot, surrounted by a metal cage of one-half (½) inch wire mesh.

Section 3. It shall be unlawful for any person, firm or corporation to engage in the business of keeping, feeding or breeding any hares, rabbits, guinea pigs, chickens, turkeys, geese, ducks, pigeons, parrots of any species, game birds of any species, for commercial purposes within the First and Second Residential Districts, as defined by the Zoning Ordinance.

Section 4. All ordinances or parts or portions of any and all ordinances in conflict with the provisions of this ordinance and Ordinance No. 384 (New Series) are hereby repealed.

Section 5. Any person, firm or corporation violating the provisions of this ordinance shall be guilty of a misdemeanor and, upon conviction thereof, shall be punished by a fine of not more than one hundred ($100) dollars, or by imprisonment in the County Jail for not more than thirty (30) days, or by both fine and imprisonment.

Section 6. This ordinance shall take effect immediately upon its passage.

Ayes—Supervisors Andriano, Canepa, Colman, Gallagher, Havenner, Hayden, McSheehy, Miles, Power, Roncovieri, Spaulding, Stanton, Suhr, Toner—14.

Absent—Supervisors McGovern, Peyser, Rossi, Shannon—4.

Passed for Printing.

The following resolution was *passed for printing*:

Stable Permit, Nunzio Caruso, 149 Brewster Street.

On recommendation of Health Committee.

Resolution No. ———— (New Series), as follows:

Resolved, That Nunzio Caruso be and is hereby granted permission, revocable at will of the Board of Supervisors, to maintain and operate stable for one (1) horse only on premises at 149 Brewster street.

The rights granted under this resolution shall be exercised within six months, otherwise said permit shall become null and void.

Adopted.

The following resolution was *adopted*:

Street Lights.

On recommendation of Lighting Committee.

Resolution No. 31983 (New Series), as follows:

Resolved, That the Pacific Gas & Electric Company be and it is hereby authorized and requested to remove and install street lights as follows:

Remove 250 M. R.

Lake street, Arguello boulevard to Fourteenth avenue (1).
Valley street between Castro and Diamond streets.
Joost avenue between Baden and Arcadia.
Twenty-sixth avenue between Geary and Clement streets.
Banks street and Eugenia avenue.
Banks street and Cortland avenue.
Twenty-third avenue between Fulton and Cabrillo streets.
Twenty-third avenue between Cabrillo and Balboa streets.
Twenty-first avenue and Santiago street.

Twenty-first avenue between Taraval and Santiago streets.
Stevenson street between Duboce avenue and McCoppin streets.
Thirty-fifth avenue between Fulton and Cabrillo streets.

Remove 400 M. R.

Lake street, Arguello boulevard to Fourteenth avenue (29).
Twenty-third avenue and Cabrillo street.
Fifth avenue between Irving and Judah streets.
Thirty-seventh avenue between Irving and Judah streets.
Pierce street between Post and Sutter streets.
Carl street between Clayton and Cole streets.
Clayton street opposite Carl street.
Northeast corner Twenty-ninth avenue and Santiago street.
Twenty-ninth avenue between Santiago and Rivera streets.
North and south sides Waller street between Laguna and Buchanan streets.
Waller street between Scott and Divisadero streets.
Thirty-fifth avenue and Cabrillo streets.
Sacramento street between Taylor and Kearny streets (8)
Southwest corner Lake street and Arguello boulevard.
Lake street from Arguello boulevard to Fifteenth avenue, each corner.
Lake street between Third and Fourth avenues, Fourteenth and Fifteenth avenues.

Install 250 O. B. R.

East and west sides Stevenson street between Duboce avenue and McCoppin streets.
Opposite Nos. 36 and 130 Crown Terrace.
Brosnon street between Valencia and Guerrero streets.
Banks street and Eugenia avenue.
Banks street and Cortland avenue.
East and west sides Twenty-third avenue between Fulton and Cabrillo streets and Cabrillo and Balboa streets.
Install 250 O. B. R., Ingleside District, and remove electric meter service.

Remove 600 M. R.

Sacramento street between Taylor and Kearny streets (5).

Install 400 O. B. R.

Northeast and southwest corners Lake street from Arguello boulevard to Fourteenth avenue.
Lake street between Arguello boulevard and Fourteenth avenue (one in each block).
Northeast and southwest corners Lake street and Second avenue to Fifteenth avenue.
Lake street between Arguello boulevard and Fifteenth avenue (one each block).

Install 400 C. P. O. B. R.

Leland avenue and Sawyer street.
Visitacion avenue and Sawyer street.
North and south sides Carl street between Clayton and Cole streets.
Clayton street opposite Carl street.
Sussex street between Swiss avenue and Conrad street.
Bay and Broderick streets.
South side Bay street between Divisadero and Broderick streets.
Broderick street between Chestnut and Francisco streets.
Gloria court, east of Geneva avenue.
Eighteenth street between Valencia street and Lexington avenue.
Day street between Castro and Diamond streets (front of 526).
Ulloa street and Laguna Honda boulevard (two in front of church).
Northeast corner Ulloa street and Laguna Honda boulevard.
Valley street between Castro and Diamond streets.
Pierce street between Post and Sutter streets.
East and west sides Pierce street between Post and Sutter streets.

Cayuga avenue and Oneida street.

East and west sides Thirty-seventh avenue between Irving and Judah streets.

End of Carmelita street.

Detroit street between Hearst avenue and Monterey boulevard (bottom of stairway).

North and south sides Joost avenue between Baden and Arcadia streets.

East and west sides Fifth avenue between Irving and Judah streets.

Northeast and southwest corners Divisadero and Waller streets.

North and south sides Waller street between Scott and Divisadero streets.

Northwest and southeast corners Sixth and Mission streets.

Ingleside lane opposite Police Station.

Ingleside lane between Police Station and present light.

Guttenberg street between Morse and Brunswick streets.

Joost avenue between Arcadia and Baden streets.

East and west sides Twenty-ninth avenue between Rivera and Santiago streets.

Northeast corner Santiago street and Twenty-ninth avenue.

Northeast corner Nineteenth avenue and Judah street (front of church).

Wawona street and Twenty-fourth avenue.

Twenty-fourth avenue between Wawona and Vicente streets.

Forty-seventh avenue between Rivera and Santiago streets.

Shields and Ralston streets.

Monticello street between Shields and Sargent streets.

Southwest corner Worcester and Chester avenues.

Oakwood street, near Nineteenth street.

Thirtieth avenue between Kirkham and Lawton streets.

Crown Terrace and Twin Peaks boulevard.

Otsego avenue between Onondaga and Oneida avenues.

East and west sides Twenty-sixth avenue between Geary and Clement streets.

York street between Army and Twenty-sixth streets.

Banks street and Eugenia avenue and Bank street and Cortland avenue.

East and west sides Twenty-third avenue between Fulton and Cabrillo streets.

East and west sides Twenty-third avenue between Cabrillo and Balboa streets.

Northeast corner Twenty-third avenue and Cabrillo street.

East and west sides Twenty-first avenue between Taraval and Santiago streets.

Northeast corner Twenty-first avenue and Santiago street.

Opposite 261 Hickory avenue.

East and west sides Thirty-fifth avenue between Fulton and Cabrillo streets.

Thirty-fifth avenue and Cabrillo street.

East and west sides Congo street between Mangels avenue and Stellings street.

Kirkwood avenue between Phelps and Quint streets.

Install Type "C" 400 C. P.

Sea Cliff, as per map filed, and remove double inverted gas.

North and south sides Sacramento street between Kearny street and Grant avenue.

North and south sides Sacramento street between Grant avenue and Stockton street.

North and south sides Sacramento street between Stockton and Powell streets.

North and south sides Sacramento street between Powell and Mason streets.

North and south sides Sacramento street between Mason and Taylor streets.

Northwest corner Sacramento and Yerba Buena streets.

Northeast and southwest corners Sacramento and Mason streets.

Northeast and southwest corners Sacramento and Powell streets. ·

Northeast and southwest corners Sacramento and Stockton streets.

Ayes—Supervisors Andriano, Canepa, Colman, Gallagher, Havenner, Hayden, McSheehy, Miles, Power, Roncovieri, Spaulding, Stanton, Suhr—13.

Absent—Supervisors McGovern, Peyser, Rossi, Shannon, Toner—5.

Passed for Printing.

The following bill was *passed for printing*:

Establishing an Underground District, Sutter Street, from East Line of Steiner Street to West Line of Divisadero Street; Sutter Street From West Line of Octavia Street to West Line of Fillmore Street.

Bill No. 8182, Ordinance No. ———— (New Series), as follows:

Amending Order No. 214 (Second Series), entitled "Providing for placing wires and conduits underground in the City and County of San Francisco", by adding a new section to be known as Section 1 kk.

Be it ordained by the People of the City and County of San Francisco as follows:

Section 1 kk. An additional district to those heretofore described within which it shall be unlawful to maintain poles and overhead wires after July 1, 1930, is hereby designated, to-wit:

Underground District No. 45. Sutter street from east line of Steiner street to west line of Divisadero street, approximately 1520 feet; and

Sutter street from west line of Octavia street to the west line of Fillmore street, approximately 1925 feet.

Action Deferred.

The following matter, presented without recommendation from the joint Committee on Police, Public Welfare and Civil Service, was, on motion, *laid over one week and made a Special Order for 3 p. m.*

Police Commission Requested to Reconsider Action, Examinations for Promotion of Corporals.

Resolution No. ———— (New Series), as follows:

Whereas, a condition exists in the Police Department of the City and County of San Francisco which seems to have created a serious and unjust handicap on the men in the rank of patrolman in that department; and

Whereas, a majority of the men of said rank of patrolman are honorably discharged war veterans; and

Whereas, the men of the said rank of patrolman have not had an opportunity to engage in a competitive Civil Service examination for promotion in said Police Department since August 9, 1923, due to the fact that when the Civil Service Commissioners of the City and County of San Francisco announced their readiness to hold an examination from the rank of patrolman to the rank of corporal during the early part of the year 1927, they, the said Civil Service Commissioners, were requested by the Board of Police Commissioners not to hold the said examination as they, the Police Commissioners, then felt that the rank of corporal was sufficiently manned for some time to come; and

Whereas, records show that additional appointments were made by the Board of Police Commissioners to the rank of corporal on the following dates:

December 31, 1925—21 additional corporals;
September 1, 1926—18 additional corporals;
December 27, 1926—27 additional corporals; and

records further show that the date following appointment of the last 27 corporals as herein shown the said Police Department had a total strength of 136 men in the said rank of corporal; and

Whereas, the Budgets prepared for the fiscal years by this Board of Supervisors, as hereinafter shown, did make provisions for salaries for numerical strength in the said rank of corporal in said Police Department:

Fiscal year 1927-1928—129 corporals;
Fiscal year 1928-1929—119 corporals;
Fiscal year 1929-1930—119 corporals; and

Whereas, the strength of the said rank of corporal of police at the present time is 103 men, there is created, under budget provisions, 16 vacancies in the said rank; and

Whereas, the number of men in the said rank of corporal in the Police Department has been reduced by 33 men since December 28, 1926; and

Whereas, The strength of the rank of patrolmen on December 28, 1926, was 842 men as against a strength of 950 patrolmen authorized by the budget of the present fiscal year; and

Whereas, a proposed Charter amendment was submitted to the electorate of this City and County at the general election, held November, 1928, which proposed Charter amendment intended the abolition of the rank of corporal in the said Police Department; the said proposed Charter amendment was, however, decidedly defeated by an overwhelming majority, thereby conclusively showing the wishes of the people of this municipality to retain the said rank of corporal in their Police Department; and

Whereas, any condition which stifles ambition and obstructs legitimate aspirations of members of the Police Department in the rank of patrolman, who desire to seek advancement and promotion, based upon Civil Service competitive examination, is detrimental to police efficiency and to the morale of said Police Department; be it therefore

Resolved, That it is the sense of this Board of Supervisors that we call upon the Board of Police Commissioners to reconsider their action of 1927, when they called on the Civil Service Commission not to hold an examination for promotion to the rank of corporal at that time, and that the said Board of Police Commissioners be requested to communicate with said Civil Service Commission, asking that an examination be held and that an eligible list be adopted from which present and future vacancies in the rank of corporal may be filled and that said examination be held within a reasonable time; and be it

Further Resolved, That it is the sense of this Board of Supervisors that the same rules be followed in holding examinations for promotion to the rank of corporal of police as appertains to the other promotional ranks in the Police and Fire Departments, that is, that eligible lists be adopted and abolished at definite periods as prescribed by Civil Service regulations.

Adopted.

The following resolutions were *adopted*:

Approval of Taxicab Stand Permits.

On recommendation of Police Committee.

Resolution No. 31984 (New Series), as follows:

Resolved, That the following taxicab stand permits be and they are hereby approved:

Red Top Cab Company, 3343 Mission street, one cab.

Blue Bird Taxicab Co., 1600 Hyde street, one cab.

Thomas J. Oliver, 3399 Fulton street, one cab.

Yellow Cab Company, 80 Sixth street, one cab (transfer from 19 Sixth street).

Ayes—Supervisors Andriano, Canepa, Colman, Gallagher, Havenner, Hayden, McSheehy, Miles, Power, Roncovieri, Spaulding, Stanton, Suhr—13.

Absent—Supervisors McGovern, Peyser, Rossi, Shannon, Toner—5.

Cancellation of Taxicab Stand Permits.

Also, Resolution No. 31985 (New Series), as follows:

Resolved, That the following taxicab stand permits be and they are hereby cancelled:

Little Black Cab Company—677 Ellis street, 681 Ellis street, 1725 O'Farrell street.

Mrs. Ardelle C. Lewys—Thirty-third avenue and Clement street.

Lo Fare Cab Company—606 Kearny street.

Yellow Cab Company—2399 Ocean avenue, 3749 Geary street, 1470 Leavenworth street, 1319 Mason street, 2387 California street, 3132 California street, 2002 Divisadero street, 1505 Eddy street, 1701 Laguna street, 1101 Leavenworth street, 592 O'Farrell street, 2995 Sixteenth street.

Ayes—Supervisors Andriano, Canepa, Colman, Gallagher, Havenner, Hayden, McSheehy, Miles, Power, Roncovieri, Spaulding, Stanton, Suhr—13.

Absent—Supervisors McGovern, Peyser, Rossi, Shannon, Toner—5.

Masquerade Ball Permit, Garibaldi Guards, Garibaldi Hall, 441 Broadway, Saturday, March 8, 1930.

Also, Resolution No. 31986 (New Series), as follows:

Resolved, That the Garibaldi Guards be and they are hereby granted permission to conduct a masquerade ball at Garibaldi Hall, 441 Broadway, Saturday, March 8, 1930.

Ayes—Supervisors Andriano, Canepa, Colman, Gallagher, Havenner, Hayden, McSheehy, Miles, Power, Roncovieri, Spaulding, Stanton, Suhr—13.

Absent—Supervisors McGovern, Peyser, Rossi, Shannon, Toner—5.

Masquerade Ball Permit, Hermann Sons, Civic Auditorium, Saturday, February 15, 1930.

Also, Resolution No. 31987 (New Series), as follows:

Resolved, That Hermann Sons be and they are hereby granted permission to conduct a masquerade ball at Civic Auditorium, Saturday, February 15, 1930, with permission to run until 2 a. m.

Ayes—Supervisors Andriano, Canepa, Colman, Gallagher, Havenner, Hayden, McSheehy, Miles, Power, Roncovieri, Spaulding, Stanton, Suhr—13.

Absent—Supervisors McGovern, Peyser, Rossi, Shannon, Toner—5.

Masquerade Ball Permit, Dania Branch Nos. 2 and 3, California Hall, Polk and Turk Streets, Saturday, February 15, 1930.

Also, Resolution No. 31988 (New Series), as follows:

Resolved, That Dania Branch Nos. 2 and 3 be and they are hereby granted permission to conduct a masquerade ball at California Hall, Polk and Turk streets, Saturday, February 15, 1930.

Ayes—Supervisors Andriano, Canepa, Colman, Gallagher, Havenner, Hayden, McSheehy, Miles, Power, Roncovieri, Spaulding, Stanton, Suhr—13.

Absent—Supervisors McGovern, Peyser, Rossi, Shannon, Toner—5.

Masquerade Ball Permit, San Francisco Gymnastic Club, 2450 Sutter Street, Friday, February 21, 1930.

Also, Resolution No. 31989 (New Series), as follows:

Resolved, That San Francisco Gymnastic Club be and it is hereby granted permission to conduct a masquerade ball at 2450 Sutter street, Friday, February 21, 1930.

Ayes—Supervisors Andriano, Canepa, Colman, Gallagher, Havenner, Hayden, McSheehy, Miles, Power, Roncovieri, Spaulding, Stanton, Suhr—13.

Absent—Supervisors McGovern, Peyser, Rossi, Shannon, Toner—5.

Action Deferred.

The following matter was *laid over one week*:

Award of Contract, Laundry Machinery.

Resolution No. ———— (New Series), as follows:

Resolved, That award of contract be hereby made to American Laundry Machinery Co on bid submitted December 30, 1929 (Proposal No. 548), for furnishing the following, viz.: Laundry machinery for City Prison, to conform to circulars enclosed with bid giving detailed description:

One washer, 28 by 48 inches; single-geared Sterling Monel metal washer, for $1,480.00.

One extractor, 24 inches; American under-driven solid curb extractor, laundry type, vertical motor driven, for $828.00.

Above machines f. o. b. laundry room, City Prison, set in place ready for other contractors to make the necessary steam, water and electrical connections.

Resolved, That no bond be required, as said awards are for immediate delivery.

Resolved, That all other bids submitted thereon be rejected.

Adopted.

The following resolutions were *adopted*:

Award of Contract, Hospital Equipment.

On recommendation of Supplies Committee.

Resolution No. 31990 (New Series), as follows:

Resolved, That award of contract be hereby made on bids submitted November 18, 1929 (Proposal No. 536), for furnishing the following, viz.:

Hospital Equipment for San Francisco Hospital.

Item No. 1—24 beds, with Mount Sinai bottom; head and foot 1-inch National seamless tubing, 14 gauge; card holder for 3x5 card to be welded on fracture bar; painting three coats nitro cellulose, base lacquer first coat baked, color white; equipped with Colson #L-367 3-in. casters; height, head 49½ in. or 50 in., foot 36 in. or 37 in.; fabric 27 inches, including casters; cross rods ⅝ in., five filler rods ⅝ in; cross rods and filler rods 15 in. gauge; inside fracture bar 1 in. x 1¼ in., length of 78 in. inside, 36 in. wide inside; fabric to be National rust proof; on sample made by Simmons Co., $40.15 each; W. & J. Sloane.

Item No. 2 (a)—24 cribs, both sides sliding; size 2 ft. 6 in. x 5 O. D., equipped with Colson casters L-367 3 in.; pillars 1 in. 14 gauge National seamless bedstead tubing; cross rods ½ in., 16 gauge upright fillers ⅜ in.; top and bottom rods insides ⅝ in.; fillers not over 3½ inches apart; Colson white, three coats nitro cellulose base lacquer, first coat baked; to have card holder for 3 in. x. 5 in. card welded on fracture bar ends, also metal insert for card; in other respects as Hall Cat. page 49, Model 1109, $30.37 each; Colson Co. of the Pacific.

Item No. 2 (b)—12 cribs; specifications same as above, excepting length to be six feet; on sample made by Simmons Co., $35.75 each; W. & J. Sloane.

Item No. 3—100 sets casters, Eames casters; on sample, $5.20 set; Eames Co.

Item No. 4—6 basket trucks; Eames trucks; on sample, $32.00 each; Eames Co.

Item No. 5—1 truck; Colson Cat., p. 4, No. 2531; equipped with 4-in. P. C. I. wheels and 3-in. B. C. I. swivel, $32.88 each; Colson Co. of the Pacific.

Item No. 6—6 wheel chairs; Colson Cat., page 37, Model C-39B; selected oak seat and slatted back; to be equipped with 26-in. ball-bearing wheels and two 10-in. ball-bearing disc wheels; head rims attached to rims, $48.69 each; Colson Co. of the Pacific.

Resolved, That no bonds be required, as said awards are for immediate delivery.

Note—All above awards are made to the lowest bidder, except when award is made in consideration of deliveries or on account of the quality as determined by such tests as required or recommended by the Purchaser of Supplies.

Resolved, That all other bids submitted thereon be rejected.

Ayes—Supervisors Andriano, Canepa, Colman, Gallagher, Havenner, Hayden, McSheehy, Miles, Power, Roncovieri, Spaulding, Stanton, Suhr—13.

Absent—Supervisors McGovern, Peyser, Rossi, Shannon, Toner—5.

Loading Zones.

On recommendation of Traffic and Safety Committee.

Resolution No. 31991 (New Series), as follows:

Resolved, That the following list of loading zones, of the lengths specified, be established in front of or near the following addresses, in accordance with the provisions of Section No. 36 of Ordinance No. 7691 (New Series), as amended:

5-21 Belvedere street, 27 feet; San Francisco Bank, money entrance.

537-543 Front street, 18 feet; A. Giorlani & Bro., wholesale grocery.

224 Hemlock street, 27 feet; Lincoln University, freight entrance; 1 oil intake.

1195 Page street, 18 feet; Dr. Hawkin, office and clinic.

Ayes—Supervisors Andriano, Canepa, Colman, Gallagher, Havenner, Hayden, McSheehy, Miles, Power, Roncovieri, Spaulding, Stanton, Suhr—13.

Absent—Supervisors McGovern, Peyser, Rossi, Shannon, Toner—5.

Passenger Loading Zones.

Also, Resolution No. 31992 (New Series), as follows:

Resolved, That the following list of passenger loading zones, of the lengths specified, be established in front of or near the following addresses, in accordance with the provisions of Section No. 36 of Ordinance No. 7691 (New Series), as amended:

555 Baker street, 18 feet; Native Daughters' Home and Club Building.

1122 California street, 36 feet; Grace Cathedral.

2335 Pacific avenue, 18 feet; St. Xavier Apartments.

Ayes—Supervisors Andriano, Canepa, Colman, Gallagher, Havenner, Hayden, McSheehy, Miles, Power, Roncovieri, Spaulding, Stanton, Suhr—13.

Absent—Supervisors McGovern, Peyser, Rossi, Shannon, Toner—5.

ROLL CALL FOR THE INTRODUCTION OF RESOLUTIONS, BILLS AND COMMUNICATIONS NOT CONSIDERED OR REPORTED UPON BY A COMMITTEE.

Creation of an Athletic Commission.

Supervisor Gallagher presented:

Resolution No. ———— (New Series), as follows:

Whereas, the various forms of athletic activity have become a part of the life of the people of San Francisco; and

Whereas, the major forms, such as football and golf and baseball, have grown to such a degree as to call into action the numerous departments of the City government, as well as officials of different organizations, for the proper handling of said contests; be it, therefore,

Resolved, That the City Attorney is respectfully requested to prepare and submit to this Board of Supervisors the proper ordinance or the proper form of legislation for the initiation of an Athletic Commission of the City and County of San Francisco, to have charge of all public athletic contests.

Referred to Public Welfare and Finance Committees jointly.

Celebration of Washington's and Lincoln's Birthdays.

Supervisors Canepa and Colman presented:

Resolution No. 31993 (New Series), as follows:

Whereas, for many consecutive years the City of San Francisco has observed the anniversaries of the births of the "Father of our Country," George Washington, and of the "Savior of our Country," Abraham Lincoln; and

Whereas, the patriotic and civic organizations of the City of San Francisco and the citizens at large are deeply interested in the perpetuation of this splendid testimonial by the municipal government to the distinguished service rendered by these two immortal Americans; and

Whereas, the birthdays of George Washington and Abraham Lincoln occur during the month of February and thus it becomes possible and desirable to hold an impressive joint commemoration; therefore, be it

Resolved, That his Honor the Mayor be requested to appoint a Citizens' Committee, in cooperation with the Auditorium Committee, to make suitable arrangements for this civic event; that the use of the Civic Auditorium on the morning of February 12, 1930, be granted.

Adopted by the following vote:

Ayes—Supervisors Andriano, Canepa, Colman, Gallagher, Havenner, Hayden, McSheehy, Miles, Power, Roncovieri, Spaulding, Stanton, Suhr, Toner—14.

Absent—Supervisors McGovern, Peyser, Rossi, Shannon—4.

Discrimination Against San Francisco Merchants by Alameda County Chambers of Commerce.

Supervisor Gallagher presented:

Communication, from the four Chambers of Commerce of Alameda County, attempting to prevail upon the people of that community to make no purchases of goods, let no contracts, and patronize no concern outside Alameda County.

Referred.

Supervisor Gallagher called attention to the necessity of San Francisco meeting the situation by similar action as regards persons employed by the City and living outside the City and County. He moved that the matter be referred to the Commercial Development and City Planning Committee, and, moreover, that a copy of this letter be made and, through the Mayor's office, be presented, with any comment the Mayor wished to make, to the heads of every department in the City government.

So ordered.

Lighting Standards.

Supervisor Colman moved that the matter of boulevard lighting standards be made a Special Order of Business for next Monday at 3:30 p. m.

So ordered.

Adopted.

The following resolution was *adopted*:

Appropriations, Plumbing, Bay View Police Station, and Street Signs.

Resolution No. 31995 (New Series), as follows:

Resolved, That the following amounts be and the same are hereby set aside, appropriated and authorized to be expended out of the hereinafter accounts, General Fund, 1929-1930, for the following purposes, to-wit:

Repairs to Public Buildings, Budget Item No. 53.

(1) For general overhauling of plumbing in Bay View Police Station, and furnishing and installing of urinal and two high closet tanks on first floor and one toilet and shower on second floor, $450.

Traffic Signals, Budget Item No. 57.

(2) To the credit of "Street Signs," Budget Item No. 63, to reimburse for installation of 17 rubber slow signs at various locations during January, 1930, $52.

Adopted by the following vote:

Ayes—Supervisors Andriano, Canepa, Colman, Gallagher, Hayden, Miles, Power, Roncovieri, Spaulding, Suhr, Toner—11.

Absent—Supervisors Havenner, McGovern, McSheehy, Peyser, Rossi, Shannon, Stanton—7.

ADJOURNMENT.

There being no further business, the Board at the hour of 6:15 p. m. adjourned.

J. S. DUNNIGAN, Clerk.

Approved by the Board of Supervisors March 3, 1930.

Pursuant to Resolution No. 3402 (New Series) of the Board of Supervisors of the City and County of San Francisco, I, John S. Dunnigan, hereby certify that the foregoing is true and correct copy of the Journal of Proceedings of said Board of the date stated and approved as above recited.

JOHN S. DUNNIGAN,
Clerk of the Board of Supervisors,
City and County of San Francisco.

Vol. 25—New Series   No. 5

Monday, February 3, 1930

Journal of Proceedings
Board of Supervisors

City and County of San Francisco

The Recorder Printing and Publishing Company
337 Bush Street, S. F.

JOURNAL OF PROCEEDINGS
BOARD OF SUPERVISORS

MONDAY, FEBRUARY 3, 1930, 2 P. M.

In Board of Supervisors, San Francisco, Monday, February 3, 1930, 2 p. m.

The Board of Supervisors met in regular session.

CALLING THE ROLL.

The roll was called and the following Supervisors were noted present:

Supervisors Andriano, Canepa, Colman, Havenner, Hayden, McGovern, McSheehy, Miles, Peyser, Power, Roncovieri, Rossi, Spaulding, Toner—14.

The following Supervisors were noted present subsequent to the roll call:

Supervisor Gallagher, 2:18 p. m.; Supervisor Shannon, 2:10 p. m.; Supervisor Stanton, 2:18 p. m.; Supervisor Suhr, 2:15 p. m.

Quorum present.

His Honor Mayor Rolph presiding.

APPROVAL OF JOURNAL.

The Journal of Proceedings of January 13, 1930, was considered read and approved:

ROLL CALL FOR PETITIONS AND COMMUNICATIONS.

Additional Golf Course at Sharpe's Park.

The following was presented by Supervisor McSheehy and read by the Clerk:

Communication, from the San Francisco Municipal Golfers' Association, transmitting copy of resolution adopted at meeting of its board of directors, requesting an appropriation in next year's budget for the construction of an additional municipal golf course at Sharpe's Park, and that said construction commence without delay.

Referred to Education, Parks and Playgrounds Committee.

Boys' Aid Society Property Investigation.

Supervisor Havenner presented:

Communication, from Hon. C. J. Goodell, Presiding Judge, Superior Court, stating that Judges Dunne, Murasky, Roche and himself were named a committee to look into the conditions affecting the Boys' Aid Society property, and are ready to meet with the representatives of the School Department and Juvenile Probation Board at any time, to go into the matter.

Referred to Finance and Education, Parks and Playgrounds Committees.

Approval of Leave of Absence, George Bistany, Zoological Expert, Golden Gate Park.

The following was presented and read by the Clerk:

Communication, from the Park Commissioners, requesting approval of leave of absence for George Bistany, zoological expert, for three months, beginning February 1, 1930, to permit him to visit Northern Africa and procure a shipment of animals, birds and reptiles already donated by citizens of San Francisco for the new zoo in the Fleishhacker Playfield.

Referred to Education, Parks and Playgrounds Committee.

[235]

Leave of Absence, Joseph Marr Gwinn, Superintendent of Schools.

The following was presented and read by the Clerk:

San Francisco, Cal., February 3, 1930.

Honorable Board of Supervisors, City Hall, San Francisco.

Gentlemen: Application has been made to me by Mr. Joseph Marr Gwinn, Superintendent of Schools, for leave of absence, with permission to leave the State of California, for a period February 15 to March 5, 1930, inclusive.

I hereby request that you concur with me in granting said leave of absence.

Yours very truly,

JAMES ROLPH, JR., Mayor.

Whereupon, the following resolution was presented and *adopted*:

Resolution No. 32029 (New Series), as follows:

Resolved, That, in accordance with the recommendation of his Honor the Mayor, Mr. Joseph Marr Gwinn, Superintendent of Schools, is hereby granted a leave of absence from February 15 to March 5, 1930, inclusive, with permission to leave the State.

Ayes—Supervisors Andriano, Canepa, Colman, Gallagher, Havenner, Hayden, McGovern, McSheehy, Miles, Peyser, Power, Roncovieri, Rossi, Shannon, Spaulding, Stanton, Suhr, Toner—18.

SPECIAL ORDER—2:30 P. M.

On recommendation of Public Health Committee.

Removal of Hog Ranches.

Resolution No. ———— (New Series), as follows:

Whereas, the Department of Public Health of the City and County of San Francisco has reported its inability to secure through agreement the removal of the following so-called hog ranches:

300 Lane street, corner Davidson—Mildred Goodsell, owner; Henry Suhling, lessee.

301 Lane street, corner Davidson—Henry Suhling, owner; Sacramento Hog Co. (P. Grech), lessee.

Mendell street, near Custer avenue—Chas. and Louis Nonnemann et al., owners; Attilio Del Grandi, lessee.

Northwest corner Custer avenue and Mendell street—C. and L. Nonnemann et al., owners; Castentini Bros., lessees.

Davidson avenue, in rear of 1520 Evans avenue—C. & C. of San Francisco, owners; American Hog Co. (Jos. and Roger Isolo and Jos. DiSantoro), lessee.

1288 Davidson avenue—George Wagner et al., owners; Henry Suhling, lessee.

1202-6 Evans avenue, corner Keith—Arcadio and Marianna Martinelli et al., owners; Martinelli Bros., lessees.

1290 Evans avenue—Mildred Goodsell, owner; R. Dolbeziero, lessee.

Mendell street between Custer avenue and Jennings—Barsotti and P. Fouchet, owners.

And whereas, the existence of said hog ranches within the City and County of San Francisco is in violation of Ordinance No. 1410 of our City and County, and constitutes a menace to the health and well being of our residents; now, therefore, be it

Resolved, That the City Attorney be and he is hereby authorized and requested to institute such legal action or actions as may be necessary to secure the abatement and removal of said hog ranches.

Privilege of the Floor.

Mrs. Holmes, representing the City and County Federation of Improvement Clubs; Harry E. Koch, George McLaughlin, and Mrs. Hamilton of the Housewives' League, were heard favoring the passage of the resolution.

Chauncey Tramutolo, attorney, representing the hog men, and Mr. Martinelli, representing himself in the hog industry, were heard in opposition.

Adopted.

Whereupon, the roll was called and the resolution *adopted* by the following vote:

Ayes—Supervisors Andriano, Canepa, Colman, Gallagher, Havenner, Hayden, McGovern, McSheehy, Miles, Peyser, Power, Roncovieri, Rossi, Shannon, Spaulding, Stanton, Suhr, Toner—18.

Explanation of Vote.

Supervisor Power voted *aye*, and gives the following explanation of his vote:

I am voting aye because these hog ranches apparently exist in violation of law, but it is regrettable that no official action has been taken to enact an ordinance stipulating certain regulatory clauses under which they may exist. I deem it advisable to have such an ordinance enacted before the City Attorney presses the condemnation action. If there is any way whereby these hog ranches can exist under proper law I would favor it rather than be a party to putting them out of business.

SPECIAL ORDER—3 P. M.

The following matter was taken up:

Police Commission Requested to Reconsider Action, Examinations for Promotion of Corporals.

Resolution No. ———— (New Series), as follows:

Whereas, a condition exists in the Police Department of the City and County of San Francisco which seems to have created a serious and unjust handicap on the men in the rank of patrolman in that department; and

Whereas, a majority of the men of said rank of patrolman are honorably discharged war veterans; and

Whereas, the men of the said rank of patrolman have not had an opportunity to engage in a competitive Civil Service examination for promotion in said Police Department since August 9, 1923, due to the fact that when the Civil Service Commissioners of the City and County of San Francisco announced their readiness to hold an examination from the rank of patrolman to the rank of corporal during the early part of the year 1927, they, the said Civil Service Commissioners, were requested by the Board of Police Commissioners not to hold the said examination as they, the Police Commissioners, then felt that the rank of corporal was sufficiently manned for some time to come; and

Whereas, records show that additional appointments were made by the Board of Police Commissioners to the rank of corporal on the following dates:

December 31, 1925—21 additional corporals;
September 1, 1926—18 additional corporals;
December 27, 1926—27 additional corporals; and

records further show that the date following appointment of the last 27 corporals as herein shown the said Police Department had a total strength of 136 men in the said rank of corporal; and

Whereas, the Budgets prepared for the fiscal years by this Board of Supervisors, as hereinafter shown, did make provisions for salaries for numerical strength in the said rank of corporal in said Police Department:

Fiscal year 1927-1928—129 corporals;
Fiscal year 1928-1929—119 corporals;
Fiscal year 1929-1930—119 corporals; and

Whereas, the strength of the said rank of corporal of police at the present time is 103 men, there is created, under budget provisions, 16 vacancies in the said rank; and

Whereas, the number of men in the said rank of corporal in the Police Department has been reduced by 33 men since December 28, 1926; and

Whereas, The strength of the rank of patrolmen on December 28, 1926, was 842 men as against a strength of 950 patrolmen authorized by the budget of the present fiscal year; and

Whereas, a proposed Charter amendment was submitted to the electorate of this City and County at the general election, held November, 1928, which proposed Charter amendment intended the abolition of the rank of corporal in the said Police Department; the said proposed Charter amendment was, however, decidedly defeated by an overwhelming majority, thereby conclusively showing the wishes of the people of this municipality to retain the said rank of corporal in their Police Department; and

Whereas, any condition which stifles ambition and obstructs legitimate aspirations of members of the Police Department in the rank of patrolman, who desire to seek advancement and promotion, based upon Civil Service competitive examination, is detrimental to police efficiency and to the morale of said Police Department; be it therefore

Resolved, That it is the sense of this Board of Supervisors that we call upon the Board of Police Commissioners to reconsider their action of 1927, when they called on the Civil Service Commission not to hold an examination for promotion to the rank of corporal at that time, and that the said Board of Police Commissioners be requested to communicate with said Civil Service Commission, asking that an examination be held and that an eligible list be adopted from which present and future vacancies in the rank of corporal may be filled and that said examination be held within a reasonable time; and be it

Further Resolved, That it is the sense of this Board of Supervisors that the same rules be followed in holding examinations for promotion to the rank of corporal of police as appertains to the other promotional ranks in the Police and Fire Departments, that is, that eligible lists be adopted and abolished at definite periods as prescribed by Civil Service regulations.

Privilege of the Floor.

Charles Skelly, secretary of the Board of Police Commissioners, was heard at length in explanation of the policy of the Police Department in abolishing the rank of corporal, and declared that the Police Commission had not officially heard of the complaint of the men.

Action Deferred.

Whereupon, Supervisor Havenner moved that the Clerk of this Board be directed to notify the Police Commission that this Board has postponed this subject-matter and permitted it to lie on the calendar, and that the commission be asked to provide a hearing for the men involved and notify this Board of its decision in the matter.

Motion *carried*.

Action Deferred.

The following matter was, on motion of Supervisor Colman, *laid over until February* 19, 1930, *Special Order*, 2:30 *p. m.*

SPECIAL ORDER—3:30 P. M.

Boulevard Lighting Standards.

On motion of Supervisor Colman consideration of the matter of selection of boulevard lighting standards was made a Special Order of Business for 3:30 p. m. this day.

Hyde Street Lighting.

Under the 30-day rule Supervisor Gallagher called up the matter of Hyde street lighting by assessment district for next Monday, Special Order at 5 p. m.

PRESENTATION OF PROPOSALS.

Sugar.

Sealed proposals were received and opened between the hours of 2 and 3 p. m. this date, for furnishing sugar, and *referred to Supplies Committee.*

Manufactured Furniture.

Sealed proposals were received and opened between the hours of 2 and 3 p. m. this date, for furnishing manufactured furniture for School Department, and *referred to Supplies Committee.*

Foodstuffs.

Sealed proposals were received and opened between the hours of 2 and 3 p. m. this date, for furnishing foodstuffs, and *referred to Supplies Committee.*

UNFINISHED BUSINESS.

Final Passage.

The following matters, heretofore passed for printing, were taken up and *finally passed* by the following vote:

Authorizations.

On recommendation of Finance Committee.

Resolution No. 31995 (New Series), as follows:

Resolved, That the following amounts be and the same are hereby authorized to be expended out of the hereinafter mentioned funds in payment to the following named claimants, to-wit:

Hetch Hetchy Construction Fund, Bond Issue 1928.

(1) Ingersoll-Rand Co. of California, machinery parts (claim dated Jan. 15, 1930) ....$ 2,235.48

(2) Myers-Whaley Co., Inc., conveyor belts, etc. (claim dated Jan. 15, 1930) 1,371.60

(3) Pioneer Rubber Mills, digger belts and air hose (claim dated Jan. 15, 1930) 1,165.35

(4) Santa Cruz Portland Cement Co., cement (claim dated Jan. 15, 1930) 1,510.00

(5) Santa Fe Lumber Co, lumber (claim dated Jan. 15, 1930) 608.48

(6) San Francisco City Employees Retirement System, to match contributions of Hetch Hetchy employees (claim dated Jan. 15, 1930) 630.99

(7) State Compensation Insurance Fund, premium covering Hetch Hetchy employments (claim dated Jan. 15, 1930). 6,654.15

(8) M. D. Jones, truck rental (claim dated Jan. 16, 1930).. 1,134.40

(9) Best Steel Casting Co., castings (claim dated Jan. 20, 1930) 529.65

(10) Boiler Tank & Pipe Co., remodeling of tunnel forms (claim dated Jan. 20, 1930)......................... 810.00

(11) Consolidated Mills Co., lumber (claim dated Jan. 20, 1930) 2,241.86

(12) Del Monte Meat Co., meat (claim dated Jan. 20, 1930) 1,963.01

(13) W. Haslam, truck rental and hauling (claim dated Jan. 20, 1930) 1,780.91

(14) Hammond Lumber Co., lumber (claim dated Jan. 20, 1930) 586.22

(15) Mally's Grill & Coffee Shop, Livermore, Cal., fish, turkeys and eggs furnished (claim dated Jan. 20, 1930)... 763.07

(16) J. H. McCallum, lumber (claim dated Jan. 20, 1930)... 517.03

(17) Montague Pipe & Steel Co., steel pipe (claim dated Jan. 20, 1930)... 1,928.76

(18) Owen-Oregon Lumber Co., lumber (claim dated Jan. Jan. 20, 1930)... 3,641.69

(19) Santa Cruz Portland Cement Co., cement (claim dated
Jan. 20, 1930) 502.00
(20) St. Paul's Hospital, Livermore, hospital service rendered Hetch Hetchy employees (claim dated Jan. 20, 1930) 984.85

Park Fund.

(21) William Good, fertilizer furnished Harding Park
(claim dated Jan. 24, 1930) ....$ 502.50
(22) Granfield, Farrar & Carlin, tractor hire for Fleishhacker Playfield (claim dated Jan. 24, 1930)............ 569.62
(23) Haskins & Sells, audit of Park accounts (claim dated
Jan. 24, 1930) 1,264.45
(24) Standard Fence Co., wire fencing, cage, etc., for parks
(claim dated Jan. 24, 1930) 677.37
(25) State Compensation Insurance Fund, premium covering
insurance of park employments (claim dated Jan. 24, 1930) 574.56
(26) Berringer & Russell, hay, etc., for parks (claim dated
Jan. 24, 1930) 788.20
(27) Meyer Rosenberg, loam for parks (claim dated Jan.
24, 1930) 1,876.25

Playground Fund.

(28) Playground Commission, for reimbursement of Mather
Revolving Fund, account of expenditures as per vouchers
attached (claim dated Jan. 22, 1930)...................$ 708.00

Hetch Hetchy Power Operative Fund.

(29) Hetch Hetchy Construction Fund, Bond Issue 1928, for
material, supplies and services furnished Hetch Hetchy
Power Operative during December, 1929 (claim dated Jan.
21, 1930) ....$ 8,981.19
(30) Depreciation Fund, Hetch Hetchy Power Operative, as
reserve for depreciation, for January, per Charter requirement (claim dated Jan. 21, 1930)...................... 14,583.00
(31) Reynier Lumber Co., redwood ties (claim dated Jan.
21, 1930) 548.00
(32) State Compensation Insurance Fund, premium covering
insurance of Hetch Hetchy employments (claim dated Jan.
21, 1930) 966.29

Boulevard Construction Fund, Bond Issue 1927.

(33) Wm. Bateman, furnishing of survey stakes (claim dated
Jan. 15, 1930)..$ 757.25
(34) Granfield, Farrar & Carlin, improvement of Great
Highway (upper roadway) by placing of fill (claim dated
Jan. 15, 1930) 37,875.00
(35) Granfield, Farrar & Carlin, improvement of Sunset
boulevard, by grading (claim dated Jan. 15, 1930)....... 18,000.00
(36) Eaton & Smith, ninth payment, improvement of Nineteenth avenue from Sloat boulevard to Worcester avenue
(claim dated Jan. 22, 1930) 67,000.00

County Road Fund.

(37) E. J. & M. J. Treacy, for improvement of Twentieth
street between San Bruno avenue and Vermont street,
and crossing (claim dated Jan. 15, 1930) ....$ 2,943.05
(38) James T. Tobin, for grading of 12-foot roadway on
Kirkwood street from Mendell street to point 200 feet
easterly (claim dated Jan. 15, 1930)................... 1,000.00
(39) Municipal Construction Co., City's portion for improvement of Evans avenue, Marin to Army streets, and intersection of Evans avenue and Selby street (claim dated
Jan. 21, 1930) 2,883.40

(40) Property Owners Grading Co., for removal of sand from Twenty-fourth, Twenty-fifth, Twenty-seventh, Twenty-eighth, Twenty-ninth and Thirtieth avenues between Rivera and Santiago streets (claim dated Jan. 21, 1930)...   650.00

(41) James A. and Gesina Jenkins, reimbursement for damage to property at 3433 Market street; being in full satisfaction and settlement of claim (claim dated Jan. 21, 1930) 632.00

Special School Tax.

(42) Western Asbestos Magnesia Co., Acousti Celotex for Polytechnic High School (claim dated Jan. 20, 1930)....$ 4,125.00

(43) Pacific Coast Aggregates, Inc., concrete mix for Sunset Primary School (claim dated Jan. 20, 1930).............   941.00

(44) W. H. Crim, seventh payment, architectural services for Park-Presidio Junior High School (claim dated Jan. 21, 1930) 888.83

(45) D. A. Pancoast Co., "Von Duprin" type panic bolts for schools (claim dated Jan. 22, 1930).................... 2,529.00

Tax Judgments—Appropriation 57.

(46) Percy E. Towne, attorney for judgment creditors, sixth installment, one-tenth of final judgment and interest, per schedule attached; approved by City Attorney (claim dated Jan. 8, 1930) ....$ 2,039.31

General Fund—1929-1930.

(47) Burroughs Adding Machine Co., one Burroughs adding-subtracting machine, for use of Auditor (claim dated Jan. 27, 1930) ....$ 750.50

(48) Board of Park Commissioners, reimbursement for Civic Center beautification (claim dated Jan. 24, 1930)...   656.43

(49) A. P. Jacobs, rental of No. 333 Kearny street, Jan. 3 to Feb. 3, 1930 (claim dated Jan. 27, 1930).............. 1,120.75

(50) San Francisco Chronicle, official advertising (claim dated Jan. 27, 1930) 688.88

(51) Stephenson Construction Co., fifth payment, repairs to Palace of Fine Arts (claim dated Jan. 24, 1930)...... 3,405.00

(52) Preston School of Industry, maintenance of minors (claim dated Jan. 23, 1930) 800.00

(53) Lybrand, Ross Bros. & Montgomery, professional services, installation of accounting system at Juvenile Court (claim dated Jan. 21, 1930) 1,401.90

(54) Municipal Construction Co., improvement of Rodeo avenue between Teddy and San Bruno avenues (claim dated Jan. 15, 1930) 1,690.00

(55) Pacific Gas & Electric Co., lighting public buildings during month of December (claim dated Jan. 14, 1930) 5,271.42

(56) Special School Tax, reimbursement for stock withdrawals, used by Board of Public Works during October, November and December, 1929 (claim dated Jan. 14, 1930)..   897.51

(57) Special School Tax, reimbursement for stock withdrawals by Board of Public Works during October, November and December, 1929 (claim dated Jan. 14, 1930)........   917.39

(58) Special School Tax, reimbursement for stock withdrawals by Board of Public Works during October, November and December, 1929 (claim dated Jan. 14, 1930)........   901.44

(59) E. J. Treacy, construction of 8-inch ironstone pipe sewer, etc., in Chestnut street between Kearny and Montgomery streets (claim dated Jan. 22, 1930)............. 1,600.00

(60) Joseph Hagan & Sons, burial of indigent dead (claim dated Jan. 23, 1930) 860.00

(61) Pacific Gas & Electric Co., electricity furnished San
Francisco Hospital (claim dated Jan. 23, 1930).......... 582.10
(62) Walton N. Moore Dry Goods Co., pajamas furnished
San Francisco Hospital (claim dated Dec. 31, 1929)...... 577.28
(63) Herbert F. Dugan, chemical and surgical supplies for
San Francisco Hospital (claim dated Dec. 31, 1929)...... 884.62
(64) Sussman Wormser & Co., coffee and oil, San Francisco
Hospital (claim dated Dec. 31, 1929) 532.00
(65) San Francisco International Fish Co., fish, etc., for
San Francisco Hospital (claim dated Dec. 31, 1929)...... 615.00
(66) Ralphs-Pugh Co., Inc., sheeting for San Francisco
Hospital (claim dated Dec. 31, 1929) 700.00
(67) Old Homestead Bakery, bread for San Francisco Hospital (claim dated Dec. 31, 1929) 2,123.12
(68) Wilsey, Bennett Co., eggs for San Francisco Hospital
claim dated Dec. 31, 1929)............................... 2,394.04
(69) Fred L. Hilmer Co., butter, etc., San Francisco Hospital (claim dated Dec. 31, 1929) 2,142.20
(70) San Francisco Dairy Co., milk furnished hospitals
(claim dated Dec. 31, 1929) 4,315.58
(71) Scatena-Galli Fruit Co., fruit and produce, San Francisco Hospital (claim dated Dec. 31, 1929).............. 956.10
(72) A. Lagomarsino & Co., produce, San Francisco Hospital
(claim dated Dec. 31, 1929)............................. 1,362.83
(73) Richfield Oil Co., fuel oil, San Francisco Hospital
(claim dated Dec. 31. 1929) 2,274.77
(74) California Meat Co., meat for San Francisco Hospital
(claim dated Dec. 31, 1929) 1,518.77
(75) Del Monte Meat Co., meat for San Francisco Hospital
(claim dated Dec. 31, 1929) 1,356.85
(76) Ames, Harris, Neville Co., curtains and awnings, San
Francisco Hospital (claim dated Dec. 31, 1929).......... 869.00

Ayes—Supervisors Andriano, Canepa, Colman, Havenner, Hayden, Mc-
Govern, McSheehy, Miles, Peyser, Power, Roncovieri, Rossi, Spaulding,
Toner—14.

Absent—Supervisors Gallagher, Shannon, Stanton, Suhr—4.

Automobile Supply Station Permit, J. H. Frietzsche, Northeast Corner of Third Street and Revere Avenue.

On recommendation of Fire Committee.

Resolution No. 31996·(New Series), as follows:

Resolved, That Philip Parodi be and is hereby granted permission,
revocable at will of the Board of Supervisors, to have transferred to
him automobile supply station permit heretofore granted to J. H.
Frietzsche by Resolution No. 29199 (New Series) for premises on
northeast corner of Third street and Revere avenue.

The rights granted under this resolution shall be exercised within
six months, otherwise said permit shall become null and void.

Ayes—Supervisors Andriano, Canepa, Colman, Havenner, Hayden, Mc-
Govern, McSheehy, Miles, Peyser, Power, Roncovieri, Rossi, Spaulding,
Toner—14.

Absent—Supervisors Gallagher, Shannon, Stanton, Suhr—4.

Transfer of Automobile Supply Station Permit, F. J. Harlis, Northeast Corner of Fell and Baker Streets.

Also, Resolution No. 31997 (New Series), as follows:

Resolved, That Edward B. Rowan be and is hereby granted permission, revocable at will of the Board of Supervisors, to have transferred to him automobile supply station permit heretofore granted
F. J. Harlis by Resolution No. 31256 (New Series) for premises at
northeast corner of Fell and Baker streets.

The rights granted under this resolution shall be exercised within six months, otherwise said permit shall become null and void.

Ayes—Supervisors Andriano, Canepa, Colman, Havenner, Hayden, McGovern, McSheehy, Miles, Peyser, Power, Roncovieri, Rossi, Spaulding, Toner—14.

Absent—Supervisors Gallagher, Shannon, Stanton, Suhr—4.

Transfer of Garage Permit, Thos. J. Lowe, 1250 McAllister Street.

Also, Resolution No. 31998 (New'Series), as follows:

Resolved, That Thos. J. Lowe be and is hereby granted permission, revocable at will of the Board of Supervisors, to have transferred to him public garage permit heretofore granted F. J. Gahren by Resolution No. 30413 (New Series) for premises at 1250 McAllister street.

The rights granted under this resolution shall be exercised within six months, otherwise said permit shall become null and void.

Ayes—Supervisors Andriano, Canepa, Colman, Havenner, Hayden, McGovern, McSheehy, Miles, Peyser, Power, Roncovieri, Rossi, Spaulding, Toner—14.

Absent—Supervisors Gallagher, Shannon, Stanton, Suhr—4.

Transfer of Garage Permit, O. J. Gilli, 2035 Divisadero Street.

Also, Resolution No. 31999 (New Series), as follows:

Resolved, That O. J. Gilli be and is hereby granted permission, revocable at will of the Board of Supervisors, to have transferred to him public garage permit heretofore granted Alfred Whittle by Resolution No. 30738 (New Series) for premises at 2035 Divisadero street.

The rights granted under this resolution shall be exercised within six months, otherwise said permit shall become null and void.

Ayes—Supervisors Andriano, Canepa, Colman, Havenner, Hayden, McGovern, McSheehy, Miles, Peyser, Power, Roncovieri, Rossi, Spaulding, Toner—14.

Absent—Supervisors Gallagher, Shannon, Stanton, Suhr—4.

Automobile Parking Station Permit, E. A. Hicks, Hoff Avenue, South of Sixteenth Street.

Also, Resolution No. 32000 (New Series), as follows:

Resolved, That E. A. Hicks be and is hereby granted permission, revocable at will of the Board of Supervisors, to maintain and operate an automobile parking station on the easterly line of Hoff avenue, 211 feet 10½ inches southerly from the southerly line of Sixteenth street.

The rights granted under this resolution shall be exercised within six months, otherwise said permit shall become null and void.

Ayes—Supervisors Andriano, Canepa, Colman, Havenner, Hayden, McGovern, McSheehy, Miles, Peyser, Power, Roncovieri, Rossi, Spaulding, Toner—14.

Absent—Supervisors Gallagher, Shannon, Stanton, Suhr—4.

Action Deferred.

The following resolution was, on motion of Supervisor McGovern, *laid over one week*:

Laundry Permits.

Also, Resolution No. ——— (New Series), as follows:

Resolved, That the following revocable permits be and are hereby granted:

Laundries.

Eloise Aiso, 1089 Pine street.
John Batsere, 976 Pine street.
Anna Biscay, 992 Sutter street.
Ruth Clausen, 94 Seventh street.
Mrs. V. J. Laurent, 447 Ellis street.

J. Nougue, 707 O'Farrell street.
Mme. P. Pomme, 1147 McAllister street.
Marie Sabacca, 808 Post street.
Mme. J. Saffores, 841 Powell street.
Mrs. A. Termello, 41 Franklin street.
Louise Vannucci and Gloria Cheader, 405 O'Farrell street.
The rights granted under this resolution shall be exercised within six months, otherwise said permits shall become null and void.

Blanket protest filed by Mr. Alford, Board of Trade, Laundry Industry.

Final Passage.

The following resolution, heretofore passed for printing, was taken up and *finally passed* by the following vote:

Oil Tank Permits.

On recommendation of Fire Committee.

Resolution No. 32001 (New Series), as follows:

Resolved, That the following revocable permits be and are hereby granted:

Oil Tanks.

Jules H. Bernheim, southwest corner San Fernando way and St. Francis boulevard, 750 gallons capacity.

Mrs. C. Van Straaton, 1622 Washington street, 1500 gallons capacity.

N. George Weinholz, north side of Washington street, 62 feet east of Laurel street, 1500 gallons capacity.

O. E. Carlson, south side Duboce avenue, 60 feet east of Guerrero street, 1500 gallons capacity.

B. A. Ilg, 610 El Camino Del Mar, 1500 gallons capacity.

Jos. C. Linale, 1915 Baker street, 1500 gallons capacity.

The rights granted under this permit shall be exercised within six months, otherwise said permits shall become null and void.

Ayes—Supervisors Andriano, Canepa, Colman, Havenner, Hayden, McGovern, McSheehy, Miles, Peyser, Power, Roncovieri, Rossi, Spaulding, Toner—14.

Absent—Supervisors Gallagher, Shannon, Stanton, Suhr—4.

Rereferred.

The following matter, heretofore passed for printing, was taken up and *laid over one week*:

Regulating Keeping and Feeding Hares, Rabbits, Birds and Fowl.

Bill No. 8181, Ordinance No. ———— (New Series), as follows:

Regulating the keeping and feeding of hares, rabbits, guinea pigs, chickens, turkeys, geese, ducks, doves, pigeons, parrots or other fowl; providing penalties for the violation thereof, and repealing Ordinance No. 384 (New Series) and all ordinances or parts of ordinances in conflict therewith.

Be it ordained by the People of the City and County of San Francisco as follows:

Section 1. It shall be unlawful for any person, firm or corporation, without first obtaining a permit from the Board of Health, to keep or feed, or cause to be kept or fed, or permit to be kept or fed on premises over which any such person, firm or corporation may have control, the following: Hares, rabbits, guinea pigs, chickens, turkeys, geese, ducks, doves, pigeons, parrots of any species, game birds of any species, within the First and Second Residential Districts as at present defined by Ordinance No. 5464 (New Series), or as may hereafter be defined by the City Planning Commission of the City and County of San Francisco.

Provided, however, that when a permit has been issued for the maintenance of any of the above the same shall be kept and fed in coops or inclosures complying with the following requirements, to-wit:

(a) The floor of said coop or enclosure shall be of concrete not less than two (2) inches thick and covered either with a layer of cement not less than one-half (½) inch thick or asphalt not less than one (1) inch thick.

(b) The said coop or enclosure shall be entirely surrounded by a brick or concrete wall at least five (5) inches in thickness and one (1) foot high.

(c) The said coop or enclosure shall be entirely surrounded by a galvanized iron wire mesh fence, wall or sides extending at least six (6) feet above the ground, which mesh shall not be greater than one-half (½) inch in size.

Provided, however, that said hares, rabbits, guinea pigs, chickens, turkeys, geese, ducks, doves, pigeons, parrots, game birds or other fowl shall be permitted between the hours of sunrise and sunset to run at large within the limits of the premises in which said coops or inclosures shall be kept closed during the time that said hares, rabbits, guinea pigs, chickens, turkeys, geese, ducks, doves, pigeons, parrots, game birds or other fowl are so running at large and that said premises be safely fenced so that said animals and fowls cannot escape therefrom.

Section 2. It shall be unlawful for any person, firm or corporation to keep or feed, or cause to be kept or fed, or permit to be kept or fed, hares, rabbits, guinea pigs, chickens, turkeys, geese, ducks, doves, pigeons, game birds, parrots of any species, or other fowl, in moveable or portable coops in premises which are not ratproof unless the said coops are constructed with a metal bottom and metal sides to a height of at least one (1) foot, surrounted by a metal cage of one-half (½) inch wire mesh.

Section 3. It shall be unlawful for any person, firm or corporation to engage in the business of keeping, feeding or breeding any hares, rabbits, guinea pigs, chickens, turkeys, geese, ducks, doves, pigeons, parrots of any species, game birds of any species, for commercial purposes within the First and Second Residential Districts, as defined by the Zoning Ordinance.

Section 4. All ordinances or parts or portions of any and all ordinances in conflict with the provisions of this ordinance and Ordinance No. 384 (New Series) are hereby repealed.

Section 5. Any person, firm or corporation violating the provisions of this ordinance shall be guilty of a misdemeanor and, upon conviction thereof, shall be punished by a fine of not more than one hundred ($100) dollars, or by imprisonment in the County Jail for not more than thirty (30) days, or by both fine and imprisonment.

Section 6. This ordinance shall take effect immediately upon its passage.

Final Passage.

The following matters, heretofore passed for printing, were taken up and *finally passed* by the following vote:

Prohibiting Return of Certain Class of Merchandise by Purchaser.

On recommendation of Public Health Committee.

Bill No. 8180, Ordinance No. 8687 (New Series), as follows:

Prohibiting the return by purchaser of merchandise which by use may become a source of infection and a menace to the public health.

Be it Ordained by the People of the City and County of San Francisco as follows:

Section 1. It is unlawful for any person, firm or corporation engaged in the sale at retail of the following articles of merchandise, to-wit:

a. Mattresses, blankets, sheets, comforters, pillows and other bedding.

b. Heating pads and metal hot water bottles, stockings made of rubber, reducing rollers, water bags and other rubber goods.

c. Combs, hair brushes, tooth brushes, barettes, bath brushes, powder puffs, lipsticks, compacts, broken packages of powder, creams, rouges.

d. Corsets, brassiers, underwear, union suits, bloomers, bathing suits.

e. Articles made of hair and veils.

to accept from the purchaser of any of above articles, once delivery is effected, provided that this section shall not be construed to prohibit the return of articles misfitting or defective in their construction, which shall be disinfected before being offered for re-sale.

Section 2. Any person, firm or corporation violating any of the provisions of this ordinance shall be deemed guilty of a misdemeanor and upon conviction thereof, shall be punished by a fine of not more than one hundred dollars ($100) or by imprisonment in the County Jail for a period not exceeding thirty (30) days, or by both such fine and imprisonment.

Ayes—Supervisors Andriano, Canepa, Colman, Havenner, Hayden, McGovern, McSheehy, Miles, Peyser, Power, Roncovieri, Rossi, Shannon, Spaulding, Toner—15.

Absent—Supervisors Gallagher, Stanton, Suhr—3.

Stable Permit, Nunzio Caruso, 149 Brewster Street.

Also, Resolution No. 32002 (New Series), as follows:

Resolved, That Nunzio Caruso be and is hereby granted permission, revocable at will of the Board of Supervisors, to maintain and operate stable for one (1) horse only on premises at 149 Brewster street.

The rights granted under this resolution shall be exercised within six months, otherwise said permit shall become null and void.

Ayes—Supervisors Andriano, Canepa, Colman, Havenner, Hayden, McGovern, McSheehy, Miles, Peyser, Power, Roncovieri, Rossi, Shannon, Spaulding, Toner—15.

Absent—Supervisors Gallagher, Stanton, Suhr—3.

Establishing an Underground District, Sutter Street, from East Line of Steiner Street to West Line of Divisadero Street; Sutter Street From West Line of Octavia Street to West Line of Fillmore Street.

On recommendation of Lighting Committee.

Bill No. 8182, Ordinance No. 8688 (New Series), as follows:

Amending Order No. 214 (Second Series), entitled "Providing for placing wires and conduits underground in the City and County of San Francisco", by adding a new section to be known as Section 1 kk.

Be it ordained by the People of the City and County of San Francisco as follows:

Section 1 kk. An additional district to those heretofore described within which it shall be unlawful to maintain poles and overhead wires after July 1, 1930, is hereby designated, to-wit:

Underground District No. 45. Sutter street from east line of Steiner street to west line of Divisadero street, approximately 1520 feet; and

Sutter street from west line of Octavia street to the west line of Fillmore street, approximately 1925 feet.

Ayes—Supervisors Andriano, Canepa, Colman, Havenner, Hayden, McGovern, McSheehy, Miles, Peyser, Power, Roncovieri, Rossi, Shannon, Spaulding, Toner—15.

Absent—Supervisors Gallagher, Stanton, Suhr—3.

PRESENTATION OF BILLS AND ACCOUNTS.

Your Finance Committee, having examined miscellaneous demands not required by law to be passed to print, and amounting to $66,457.81, recommends same be allowed and ordered paid.

Approved by the following vote:

Ayes—Supervisors Andriano, Canepa, Colman, Havenner, Hayden, Mc. Govern, McSheehy, Miles, Peyser, Power, Roncovieri, Rossi, Shannon, Spaulding, Toner—15.

Absent—Supervisors Gallagher, Stanton, Suhr—3.

NEW BUSINESS.

Passed for Printing.

The following matters were *passed for printing*:

Authorizations.

On recommendation of Finance Committee.

Resolution No. ———— (New Series), as follows:

Resolved, That the following amounts be and the same are hereby authorized to be expended out of the hereinafter mentioned funds in payment to the following named claimants, to-wit:

Hetch Hetchy Construction Fund, Bond Issue 1928.

(1) Ingersoll-Rand Company of California, three jack hammers (claim dated Jan. 21, 1930)........................$ 585.00

(2) Santa Fe Lumber Company, lumber (claim dated Jan. 21, 1930) 1,704.10

(3) Coos Bay Lumber Company, lumber (claim dated Jan. 21, 1930) 1,529.34

(4) Del Monte Meat Company, meat (claim dated Jan. 22, 1930) 614.29

(5) Dr. Paul E. Dolan, medical services rendered Hetch Hetchy employees (claim dated Jan. 22, 1930).............   853.25

(6) Edison Storage Battery Supply Company, Edison battery cells (claim dated Jan. 22, 1930)........................   2,134.87

(7) Hercules Powder Company, explosives and wire (claim dated Jan. 22, 1930)....................................   2,648.15

(8) Higgins & Sons, Inc., payment for land required for San Miguel Reservoir of the Hetch Hetchy Water Supply (claim dated Jan. 22, 1930). Purchase approved by Resolution No. 31884 (New Series)................................   1,000.00

(9) Ingersoll-Rand Company of California, jack hammers and machinery parts (claim dated Jan. 22, 1930).............   1,341.86

(10) The Charles Nelson Company, wood wedges (claim dated Jan. 22, 1930)......................................   663.30

(11) Santa Cruz Portland Cement Company, cement (claim dated Jan. 22, 1930)...................................   2,474.50

(12) Sherry Bros., Inc., eggs (claim dated Jan. 22, 1930)....   882.00

(13) Utah Fuel Company, coal (claim dated Jan. 22, 1930)..   760.42

(14) Wilsey-Bennett Co., butter and cheese (claim dated Jan. 22, 1930) 541.40

(15) Best Steel Casting Company, castings (claim dated Jan. 28, 1930) 967.40

(16) J. H. Creighton, truck hire (claim dated Jan. 28, 1930)   1,360.92

(17) Pacific Coast Aggregates, Inc., concrete sand (claim dated Jan. 28, 1930)......................................   560.65

(18) Alfred Pereira & Brothers, hauling during December (claim dated Jan. 28, 1930)...........................   1,124.79

(19) Shell Oil Company, gasoline, oils, etc. (claim dated Jan. 28, 1930) 607.70

County Road Fund.

(20) Equitable Asphalt Maintenance Company, resurfacing
of asphalt, street reconstruction (claim dated Jan. 23, 1930.$ 716.44
(21) Graham Fuel & Drayage Company, coal used in reconstruction of streets (claim dated Jan. 23, 1930)...........   570.64
(22) Santa Cruz Portland Cement Company, cement for street
reconstruction (claim dated Jan. 23, 1930)..............   879.12

Auditorium Fund.

(23) Thomas F. Boyle, as Auditor of the City and County,
for payment of claims for account of the expense of municipal Christmas Eve celebration held at Auditorium December 24, 1929 (claim dated Feb. 3, 1930)..................$ 1,980.25

Municipal Railway Fund.

(24) Lilian Murphy Prevonak, in. full settlement and payment for account of any damage due to injuries sustained
by reason of being struck by a Municipal Railway street
car at Kearny and Market streets August 31, 1923 (claim
dated Jan. 27, 1930).....................................$ 1,129.75
(25) The Texas Company, gasoline furnished Municipal Railways December, 1929 (claim dated Jan. 27, 1930).........   1,948.70
(26) United States Steel Products Company, track material
furnished (claim dated Jan. 24, 1930)...................   9,613.40
(27) United States Steel Products Company, track material
furnished (claim dated Jan. 23, 1930)................... 38,975.21

School Bond Fund, Issue 1923.

(28) Fred Medart Manufacturing Company, gymnasium
equipment for Polytechnic High School (claim dated Jan.
28, 1930) ....$ 613.20

Special School Tax.

(29) J. H. McCallum, lumber for school repairs (claim dated
Jan. 23, 1930)..$ 667.94
(30) Larsen & Larsen, second payment, brick work, etc., for
Roosevelt Junior High School (claim dated Jan. 27, 1930). 9,670.79
(31) D. A. Pancoast Company, for "Von Duprin" type panic
bolts, for various schools (claim dated Jan. 28, 1930)...... 2,748.00

Boulevard Bond Fund, Issue 1927.

(32) California State Automobile Association, eight battery
type arterial stop signs for Bay Shore boulevard, Section
"C" (claim dated Jan. 23, 1930)........................$ 560.00

Park Fund.

(33) Pacific Gas and Electric Company, gas and electric service for parks (claim dated Jan. 31, 1930)...............$ 1,541.28
(34) Spring Valley Water Company, water service for parks
(claim dated Jan. 31, 1930)............................   1,269.80
(35) Berringer & Russell, hay, etc., for parks (claim dated
Jan. 31, 1930)..   1,016.18
(36) Standard Fence Company, posts, wire, etc., for parks
(claim dated Jan. 31, 1930)............................   1,224.84

General Fund, 1929-1930.

(37) Stockton State Hospital, maintenance of criminal insane
(claim dated Feb. 3, 1930)............................$ 521.00
(38) San Francisco Society for the Prevention of Cruelty to
Animals, impounding, feeding, etc., of animals (claim dated
dated Feb. 3, 1930)...................................   1,500.00
(39) The Electric Corporation, cable, batteries, etc., for Department of Electricity (claim dated Dec. 31, 1929).......   1,192.26

(40) The Texas Company, gasoline furnished Police Department (claim dated Jan. 27, 1930)........................ 1,320.15

(41) James F. Waters, one De Soto phaeton for Police Department (claim dated Jan. 27, 1930)................... 977.70

(42) Spring Valley Water Company, water service furnished fire hydrants (claim dated Jan. 31, 1930)................. 15,587.10

(43) Richfield Oil 'Company of California, fuel oil furnished Civic Center power house (claim dated Jan. 23, 1930)..... 1,231.76

(44) Arata & Peters, potatoes, Laguna Honda Home (claim dated Dec. 31, 1929)...................................... 750.00

(45) Spring Valley Water Company, water service furnished Laguna Honda Home (claim dated Dec. 31, 1929).......... 1,023.07

(46) L. M. Wilbor, M. D., Superintendent of San Francisco Hospital, room rent allowance for employees of San Francisco Hospital (claim dated Dec. 31, 1929)................ 3,500.00

(47) O'Brien, Spotorno & Mitchell, turkeys furnished San Francisco Hospital (claim dated Jan. 31, 1930)........... 605.44

(48) Arata & Peters, Inc., potatoes furnished San Francisco Hospital (claim dated Jan. 31, 1930)..................... 900.00

(49) Building Supplies Company, supplies for San Francisco Hospital (claim dated Dec. 31, 1929)..................... 805.88

Maintenance of Aquarium, Appropriation 56.

(50) California Academy of Sciences, for expense of maintaining the Steinhart Aquarium during month of January, 1930 (claim dated Feb. 3, 1930)........................$ 3,506.26

Appropriation, $1,690.90, Purchase of Land for Widening of Portola Drive.

Also, Resolution No. ————— (New Series), as follows:

Resolved, That the sum of $1,690.90 be and the same is hereby set aside and appropriated out of County Road Fund and authorized in payment to Wells Fargo & Company, a corporation; being payment for portion of Lot 3, Block 2871 (56x105); portion of Lot 3, Block 2871 (290x 40); portion of Lot 1 and all of Lot 2 in Block 2868 (174x134), all irregular, and as per Assessor's Block Books of the City and County of San Francisco, purchase approved by Resolution No. ——— (New Series), and required for Portola drive (claim dated January 8, 1930.)

Appropriations, Payment Out of "Publicity and Advertising" for Services and Materials, Construction of San Francisco Float, Pasadena Tournament of Roses.

Also, Resolution No. ————— (New Series), as follows:

Resolved, That the following amounts be and the same are hereby set aside and appropriated out of "Publicity & Advertising," Appropriation 54, fiscal year 1929-1930, and authorized in payment to the hereinafter named claimants; being payments for account of services rendered and materials furnished and used in the construction of San Francisco's float exhibited at the Tournament of Roses, Pasadena, California, January 1, 1930, to-wit:

(1) To Rudolph G. Theurkauf, for services rendered and materials furnished (claim dated Feb. 3, 1930)..............$ 1,018.07

(2) To Mission Florist, flowers, ferns, etc., and express charges furnished and paid (claim dated Feb. 3, 1930).... 991.50

Appropriations, Various Funds, for Various Purposes.

Also, Resolution No. ————— (New Series), as follows:

Resolved, That the following amounts be and the same are hereby set aside, appropriated and authorized to be expended out of the hereinafter mentioned accounts, General Fund, 1929-1930, for the following purposes, to-wit:

Street Work in Front of City Porperty—Budget Item 34.

(1) To defray cost of constructing artificial stone sidewalks
at City playground, Lenox way between Ulloa and Taraval
streets .. ..$ 700.00
(2) To defray cost of constructing sidewalks at City playground, east side of Hampshire street from Army to Twenty-sixth streets 670.00

Repairs to Public Building, Etc.—Budget Item No. 53.

(3) For cost of furnishing and installing an additional feed
water heater in the engine room of the Hall of Justice....$ 975.00

Appropriations for Street Improvement, County Road Fund.

Also, Resolution No. ————— (New Series), as follows:

Resolved, That the following amounts be and the same are hereby
set aside, appropriated and authorized to be expended out of County
Road Fund for the following purposes, to-wit

(1) For the reconstruction of Grant avenue between Chestnut
and Bay streets ....$ 5,500.00
(2) For the reconstruction of Sherman street between Folsom
and Harrison streets 7,125.00
(3) For the improving of Second street between Berry and
Townsend streets, by straightening existing curbs and resurfacing with asphaltic concrete wearing surface........   4,000.00
(4) For reconstruction of Washington street between Polk
and Larkin streets, by construction of new curb and resurfacing existing pavement 2,277.00
(5) To defray cost of constructing necessary parapet wall,
warning lights, reflector signs and coping at the east side
of the intersection of Vicksburg and Twenty-second streets   825.00

Appropriations for Street Reconstruction, County Road Fund.

Also, Resolution No. ————— (New Series), as follows:

Resolved, That the following amounts be and the same are hereby
set aside, appropriated and authorized to be expended out of County
Road Fund for the reconstruction of the following streets, to-wit:

(1) Hyde street, from Lombard to Chestnut street..........$ 3,200.00
(2) Leavenworth street, from Lombard to Chestnut street..   2,100.00
(3) Jones street, from Chestnut to Bay street.............   2,300.00
(4) Bay street, from Columbus avenue to Jones street......   1,500.00
(5) Broderick street, from Sacramento to Jackson street....   3,600.00
(6) Baker street, from Jackson street to Pacific avenue......   4,100.00
(7) Baker street, from Jackson to Washington street......   1,500.00
(8) Seventeenth avenue, from Fulton to Cabrillo street......   3,400.00
(9) Masonic avenue, from Java street to Upper Terrace....   2,240.00

Total $23,940.00

Adopted.

The following resolutions were *adopted*:

Appropriations, Various Purposes.

On recommendation of Finance Committee.

Resolution No. 32003 (New Series), as follows:

Resolved, That the following amounts be and the same are hereby
set aside, appropriated and authorized to be expended out of the hereinafter mentioned funds, for the following purposes, to-wit:

County Road Fund.

(1) For cost of reconstructing barrier at termination of
Twenty-first avenue with Presidio Reservation...........$ 95.00
(2) For construction of a bulkhead and removal of sand from

the street and sidewalk area, west side of Eighteenth ave-
' nue from 225 feet to 375 feet south of Ortega street........   450.00
(3) For removal of sand from Thirty-eighth avenue between
Taraval and Santiago streets 499.00
(4) For removal of sand from the crossing of Seventeenth
avenue and Moraga street..............................   250.00
(5) For payment to Mrs. Johanna Franziska Schomacker as
reimbursement for account of fill which encroached on her
property in connection with the improvement of Yukon
street ....: 499.00

Street Work in Front of City Property—Budget Item No. 34.

(6) For cost of improving entrances to Golden Gate Park, on
Fulton street at Arguello boulevard, Park-Presidio drive,
and at Twenty-fourth avenue, by reconstructing curbs and
sidewalks, and for replacing of curb, where necessary, between Twelfth and Twenty-fourth avenues.............$ 195.00
(7) For cost of constructing sidewalks at City property, on
Stillman street between Second and Third streets.........   135.00

Ayes—Supervisors Andriano, Canepa, Colman, Havenner, Hayden,
McGovern, McSheehy, Miles, Peyser, Power, Roncovieri, Rossi, Shannon, Spaulding, Suhr, Toner—16.

Absent—Supervisors Gallagher, Stanton—2.

Appropriation, Publicity and Advertising.

Also, Resolution No. 32004 (New Series), as follows:

Resolved, That the sum of $465 be and the same is hereby set aside,
appropriated and authorized to be expended out of Publicity and Advertising, Appropriation 54, for San Francisco's share in the expense
of the holding of the 19th Annual Convention of the National Association of Builders Exchanges, to be held in San Francisco February 10
to 13, 1930, and being for the publicity and advertising of San Francisco.

Ayes—Supervisors Andriano, Canepa, Colman, Havenner, Hayden,
McGovern, McSheehy, Miles, Peyser, Power, Roncovieri, Rossi, Shannon, Spaulding, Suhr, Toner—16.

Absent—Supervisors Gallagher, Stanton—2.

Accepting Offers to Sell Land Required for Bernal Cut.

Also, Resolution No. 32005 (New Series), as follows:

Resolved, That the offers of sale made by the following named persons to sell to the City and County of San Francisco the following
described land, required for the opening of Bernal Cut, for the sums
set forth opposite their respectives names, be accepted:

Joseph Francis Callaghan, $1—Portion of Lot 2, Block 6723, as per
the Assessor's Block Books of the City and County of San Francisco.
(As per detailed description and written offer on file.)

Frank O. Carlson and Annie Carlson, $1—Portion of Lot 26, Block
6723, as per the Assessor's Block Books of the City and County of
San Francisco. (As per detailed description and written offer on file.)

And the City Attorney is hereby authorized to examine the title to
said property, and if the same is found satisfactory, to accept, on behalf of the City, deeds conveying said property to the City, free and
clear of all encumbrances, and to record the said deeds, together with
copy of this resolution, in the office of the Recorder of the City and
County of San Francisco.

Ayes—Supervisors Andriano, Canepa, Colman, Havenner, Hayden,
McGovern, McSheehy, Miles, Peyser, Power, Roncovieri, Rossi, Shannon, Spaulding, Suhr, Toner—16.

Absent—Supervisors Gallagher, Stanton—2.

Accepting Offers to Sell Property Required for the Widening of Chenery Street.

Also, Resolution No. 32006 (New Series), as follows:

Resolved, That the offers of sale made by the following named persons to sell to the City and County of San Francisco the following described land, required for the widening of Chenery street, for the sums set forth opposite their respective names, be accepted:

John W. Martin and Aura E. Martin, $10—Portion of Lot 17, Block 6727, as per the Assessor's Block Books of the City and County of San Francisco. (As per detailed description and written offer on file.)

Patrick Reilly and Mary Reilly, $437.20—Portion of Lot 19, Block 6727, as per the Assessor's Block Books of the City and County of San Francisco. (As per detailed description and written offer on file.)

Mathias Bohnert and Louise Bohnert, $10—Portion of Lot 4, Block 6685, as per the Assessor's Block Books of the City and County of San Francisco. (As per detailed description and written offer on file.)

And the City Attorney is hereby authorized to examine the title to said property, and if the same is found satisfactory, to accept, on behalf of the City, deeds conveying said property to the City, free and clear of all encumbrances, and to record said deeds, together with copy of this resolution, in the office of the Recorder of the City and County of San Francisco.

Ayes—Supervisors Andriano, Canepa, Colman, Havenner, Hayden, McGovern, McSheehy, Miles, Peyser, Power, Roncovieri, Rossi, Shannon, Spaulding, Suhr, Toner—16.

Absent—Supervisors Gallagher, Stanton—2.

Accepting Offer of A. Tiscornia in Sum of $75 to Release City From All Claim of Damages Caused by Construction of Alemany Boulevard.

Also, Resolution No. 32007 (New Series), as follows:

Whereas, the following owner of property adjacent to the proposed Alemany boulevard has offered to release the City and County of San Francisco, its contractors or agents, from all claim or claims of damages to his property or the improvements thereon caused by the establishment of grades on the proposed Alemany boulevard and adjacent streets and the grading and construction of the proposed Alemany boulevard to the proposed official grade and the grading and construction of adjacent streets to said proposed Alemany boulevard; and

Whereas, the City Attorney has recommended the acceptance of the said offer as per the following terms, namely:

Antonio Tiscornia, $75—All that certain piece or parcel of land situated in the City and County of San Francisco, State of California, and known as Lot 2, in Block 6959, as per the Assessor's Block Books of the City and County of San Francisco.

Resolved, That the said offer be accepted and the City Attorney be authorized to close negotiations and superintend the payment of money to the above mentioned person upon the receipt of the proper releases.

Ayes—Supervisors Andriano, Canepa, Colman, Havenner, Hayden, McGovern, McSheehy, Miles, Peyser, Power, Roncovieri, Rossi, Shannon, Spaulding, Suhr, Toner—16.

Absent—Supervisors Gallagher, Stanton—2.

Reimbursing Board of Works Accounts, Interdepartmental.

Also, Resolution No. 32008 (New Series), as follows:

Resolved, That the following amounts be and the same are hereby set aside out of the hereinafter Budget items, Board of Public Works, to the credit of Budget Item 461, Board of Public Works; being reimbursements for repairs to equipment of various bureaus, to-wit:

From Budget Item 552 (Street Cleaning) $402.12

From Budget Item 565 (Sewer Repair) 240.75

From Budget Item 577 (Auto Maintenance) 70.25
From Budget Item 469 (Stores and Yards)........... 4.50
From Budget Item 504 (Bureau of Engineering)...... 36.00
(Request of Board of Works, dated Jan. 25, 1930.)

Ayes—Supervisors Andriano, Canepa, Colman, Havenner, Hayden, McGovern, McSheehy, Miles, Peyser, Power, Roncovieri, Rossi, Shannon, Spaulding, Suhr, Toner—16.

Absent—Supervisors Gallagher, Stanton—2.

Approving Payments Out of Islais Creek Reclamation District Funds.

Also, Resolution No. 32009 (New Series), as follows:

Resolved, That the following warrants of Islais Creek Reclamation District—No. 1, to Stuart F. Smith, for $45; No. 2, to California Pacific Title & Trust Company, for $50; No. 3, to Foster, Mingins & Sekins, for $33; No. 4, to A. Carlisle & Co., for $135, and No. 5, to State Banking Department, for $924.50—payable out of the funds of said district, be and the same are hereby approved, and that the Mayor of the City and County of San Francisco, as chairman of the Board of Supervisors thereof, and the Clerk of said Board be and they are hereby authorized and directed to sign and certify to the foregoing approval of said warrants on each of said warrants.

Ayes—Supervisors Andriano, Canepa, Colman, Havenner, Hayden, McGovern, McSheehy, Miles, Peyser, Power, Roncovieri, Rossi, Shannon, Spaulding, Suhr, Toner—16.

Absent—Supervisors Gallagher, Stanton—2.

Accepting Offer of Allan St. John Bowie to Sell Land Required for San Miguel Reservoir.

Also, Resolution No. 32010 (New Series), as follows:

Resolved, That the offer of sale made by the following named person to sell to the City and County of San Francisco the following described lands, required for the San Miguel Reservoir of the Hetch Hetchy Water Supply Project, for the sum set forth opposite his name, be accepted:

Allan S. John Bowie, $2,000—Lots 17 to 34, inclusive, Block 2899, as per the Assessor's Block Books of the City and County of San Francisco. (As per detailed description and written offer on file.)

The City Attorney is hereby authorized to examine the title to said property, and, if the same is found satisfactory, to accept, on behalf of the City, a deed conveying said property to the City, free and clear of all encumbrances, and to record said deed, together with copy of this resolution, in the office of the Recorder of the City and County of San Francisco.

Ayes—Supervisors Andriano, Canepa, Colman, Havenner, Hayden, McGovern, McSheehy, Miles, Peyser, Power, Roncovieri, Rossi, Shannon, Spaulding, Suhr, Toner—16.

Absent—Supervisors Gallagher, Stanton—2.

Accepting Offer of Wells Fargo & Co. to Sell Lands for the Widening of Portola Drive for the Sum of $1,690.90.

Also, Resolution No. 32011 (New Series), as follows:

Resolved, That the offer of sale made by the following named corporation to sell to the City and County of San Francisco the following described lands, required for the widening of Portola drive, for the sum set forth opposite its name, be accepted:

Wells Fargo & Company, a corporation, $1,690.90—

Parcel 1: Portion of Lot 3, Block 2871, as per the Assessor's Block Books of the City and County of San Francisco. (Northeasterly portion.)

Parcel 2:   Portion of Lot 3, Block 2871, as per the Assessor's Block Books of the City and County of San Francisco. (Southwesterly portion.)

Parcel 3:   Portion of Lot 1 and all of Lot 2, Block 2868, as per the Assessor's Block Books of the City and County of San Francisco. (All as per detailed description and written offer on file.)

As a further consideration it is understood that said Wells Fargo & Company is to receive a deed to a portion of Lot 7, Block 2871, as per the Assessor's Block Books of the City and County of San Francisco, which said property is being held in trust for said City and County of San Francisco by California Pacific Title and Trust Company; said parcel of land is described as Parcel "A" in that certain written offer on file.

As a further consideration said hereinabove named grantor is to receive a deed to that certain piece or parcel of land, now a portion of Portola drive, which said portion is to be closed and abandoned in accordance with the provisions of the Act of May 1, 1911. Said parcel of land is described as Parcel "B" in that certain written offer on file, and is described as follows, to-wit:

Commencing at a point on the westerly line of La Place avenue (formerly Twin Peaks avenue), distant northerly thereon 87.162 feet from the northerly line of Army street; thence deflecting 74 degrees 47 minutes 43 seconds to the left from said westerly line of La Place avenue and running northwesterly 68.490 feet to the true point of beginning of this description, said true point of beginning being on the northeasterly line of Portola drive, 66.092 feet at right angles westerly from said westerly line of La Place avenue and 105.125 feet at right angles northerly from said northerly line of Army street; thence deflecting 24 degrees 52 minutes 51 seconds to the right and running northwesterly along said northeasterly line of Portola drive 101.631 feet; thence continuing northwesterly along said northeasterly line, on a curve to the left, tangent to the preceding course, radius 135 feet, central angle 7 degrees 01 minutes 10 seconds, a distance of 16.54 feet to the easterly line of the property now or formerly belonging to J. L. La Place and P. J. Drioton; thence deflecting 107 degrees 08 minutes 58 seconds to the left from the tangent to the preceding curve and running, southerly 3.57 feet; thence deflecting 2 degrees 09 minutes 57 seconds to the left and continuing southerly 45.428 feet; thence southeasterly on a curve to the right, tangent to a line deflected 89 degrees 47 minutes 38 seconds to the left from the preceding course, radius 300 feet, central angle 1 degree 14 minutes 52 seconds, a distance of 6.532 feet; thence continuing southeasterly tangent to the preceding curve 99.957 feet to the northeasterly line of Portola drive and the true point of beginning.

And the City Attorney is hereby authorized to examine the title to said property, and, if the same is found satisfactory, to accept, on behalf of the City and County of San Francisco, deed conveying said property to said City and County, free and clear of all encumbrances, and to record said deed, together with copy of this resolution, in the office of the Recorder of the City and County of San Francisco.

And immediately after the closing and abandonment of said portion of Portola drive, hereinabove described as Parcel "B", the Mayor and the Clerk of the Board of Supervisors, in the name of the City and County of San Francisco, are hereby authorized and directed to execute a deed conveying said Parcel "B" to said Wells Fargo & Company.

Ayes—Supervisors Andriano, Canepa, Colman, Havenner, Hayden, McGovern, McSheehy, Miles, Peyser, Power, Roncovieri, Rossi, Shannon, Spaulding, Suhr, Toner—16.

Absent—Supervisors Gallagher, Stanton—2.

Cancellation of Erroneous Assessments.

Also, Resolution No. 32012 (New Series), as follows:

Resolved, That, in accordance with the recommendation of the Assessor, in a communication dated January 23, 1930, the following duplicate assessment of personal property for the year 1929 having been erroneously assessed, be cancelled in accordance with Section 3805 of the Political Code:

Vol. 15, page 30, line 21, unsecured personal property assessed to W. K. Glasby in the sum of $290.

Ayes—Supervisors Andriano, Canepa, Colman, Havenner, Hayden, McGovern, McSheehy, Miles, Peyser, Power, Roncovieri, Rossi, Shannon, Spaulding, Suhr, Toner—16.

Absent—Supervisors Gallagher, Stanton—2.

Passed for Printing.

The following matters were *passed for printing*:

Oil and Boiler Permits.

On recommendation of Fire Committee.

Resolution No. ————— (New Series), as follows:

Resolved, That the following revocable permits be and are hereby granted:

Oil Tanks.

D. Rudee, 3876 California street, 1500 gallons capacity.

A. Sutro, Sutro Forest (top Twin Peaks), 1500 gallons capacity.

S. A. Born, southeast corner Larkin and Pine streets, 1500 gallons capacity.

A. Wendell, 774 Howard street, 1500 gallons capacity.

James Allan & Sons, south side Evans avenue, approximately 200 feet east of Third street, 1500 gallons capacity.

O. Bussie, southeast corner of Grove street and Masonic avenue, 1500 gallons capacity.

Ferroni Bros., 3110 Laguna street, 1500 gallons capacity.

E. A. Hammer, 2615 Divisadero street, 1500 gallons capacity.

Henry Ahlers, 3876 Clay street, 1500 gallons capacity.

W. H. Jackson, 400 Yerba Buena avenue, 1500 gallons capacity.

J. Harris, 2041 Hyde street, 1500 gallons capacity.

Boiler.

A. Depaol, west side Dartmouth street, 100 feet north of Woolsey street, 50 horsepower.

The rights granted under this resolution shall be exercised within six months, otherwise said permit shall become null and void.

Transfer of Auto Supply Station Permit, Cresta Bros., Nantucket and San Jose Avenues.

Also, Resolution No. ————— (New Series), as follows:

Resolved, That Cresta Bros. be and are hereby granted permission, revocable at will of the Board of Supervisors, to have transferred to them automobile supply station permit heretofore granted Phillips & Filsinger by Resolution No. 27208 (New Series), for premises at northwest corner of Nantucket and San Jose avenues.

The rights granted under this resolution shall be exercised within six months, otherwise said permit shall become null and void.

Transfer of Garage Permit, L. J. Espel, 3130 California Street.

Also, Resolution No. ————— (New Series), as follows:

Resolved, That L. J. Espel be and is hereby granted permission, revocable at will of the Board of Supervisors, to have transferred to him public garage permit heretofore granted D. A. McKean by Resolution No. 18414 (New Series) for premises at 3130 California street.

The rights granted under this resolution shall be exercised within six months, otherwise said permit shall become null and void.

Transfer of Auto Supply Station Permit, Ernest and Leo Moretton, Mission and Tingley Streets.

Also, Resolution No. ————— (New Series), as follows:

Resolved, That Ernest and Leo Moretton be and are hereby granted permission, revocable at will of the Board of Supervisors, to have transferred to them automobile supply station permit heretofore granted Bernard R. Kerns by Resolution No. 30161 (New Series) for premises at southwest corner of Mission and Tingley streets.

The rights granted under this resolution shall be exercised within six months, otherwise said permit shall become null and void.

Adopted.

The following resolutions were *adopted*:

Extension of Time to Complete Improvement of Twentieth Street Between Iowa Street and Pennsylvania Avenue.

On recommendation of Streets Committee.

Resolution No. 32013 (New Series), as follows:

Resolved, That E. J. Treacy is hereby granted an extension of ninety days' time from and after January 26, 1930, within which to complete the improvement of Twentieth street between Iowa street and Pennsylvania avenue under a public contract.

This extension of time is granted upon the recommendation of the Board of Public Works for the reason that the contractor has been delayed owing to inclement weather. The work is under way and this second extension is recommended on account of the unsettled condition of the weather.

Ayes—Supervisors Andriano, Canepa, Colman, Havenner, Hayden, McGovern, McSheehy, Miles, Peyser, Power, Roncovieri, Rossi, Shannon, Spaulding, Suhr, Toner—16.

Absent—Supervisors Gallagher, Stanton—2.

Extension of Time to Complete Improvement of Evans Avenue Between Rankin and Marin Streets.

Also, Resolution No. 32014 (New Series), as follows:

Resolved, That Municipal Construction Company is hereby granted an extension of thirty days' time from and after January 20, 1930, within which to complete the improvement of Evans avenue between Rankin and Marin streets where not already improved, under public contract.

This extension of time is granted upon the recommendation of the Board of Public Works for the reason that the contractor was delayed because of the rain. The work is well under way, the curbs, side sewers and concrete base having been constructed.

Ayes—Supervisors Andriano, Canepa, Colman, Havenner, Hayden, McGovern, McSheehy, Miles, Peyser, Power, Roncovieri, Rossi. Shannon, Spaulding, Suhr, Toner—16.

Absent—Supervisors Gallagher, Stanton—2

Extension of Time to Complete Improvement of Nineteenth Street Between Mission and Bryant Streets.

Also, Resolution No. 32015 (New Series), as follows:

Resolved, That M. Bertolino is hereby granted an extension of ninety days' time from and after November 26, 1929, within which to complete the improvement of Nineteenth street between Mission and Bryant streets, by the construction of sidewalks.

This extension of time is granted upon the recommendation of the

Board of Public Works for the reason that the work is practically completed and this first extension is granted pending the issuance of the assessment.

Ayes—Supervisors Andriano, Canepa, Colman, Havenner, Hayden, McGovern, McSheehy, Miles, Peyser, Power, Roncovieri, Rossi, Shannon, Spaulding, Suhr, Toner—16.

Absent—Supervisors Gallagher, Stanton—2·

Extension of Time to Complete the Improvement of Portola Drive.

Also, Resolution No. 32016 (New Series), as follows:

Resolved, That the Fay Improvement Company is hereby granted an extension of sixty days' time from and after January 7, 1930, to complete the improvement of Portola drive between Twenty-fourth street and Fowler avenue.

This extension of time is granted upon the recommendation of the Board of Public Works for the reason that the work is practically completed, with the exception of a small amount of sidewalk construction now held up by weather conditions.

Ayes—Supervisors Andriano, Canepa, Colman, Havenner, Hayden, McGovern, McSheehy, Miles, Peyser, Power, Roncovieri, Rossi, Shannon, Spaulding, Suhr, Toner—16.

Absent—Supervisors Gallagher, Stanton—2·

Extension of Time to Complete Improvement of Nineteenth Avenue From Sloat Boulevard to Worcester Avenue.

Also, Resolution No. 32017 (New Series), as follows:

Resolved, That Eaton & Smith is hereby granted an extension of sixty days' time from and after January 16, 1930, to complete the improvement of Nineteenth avenue from Sloat boulevard to Worcester avenue.

This extension of time is granted upon the recommendation of the Board of Public Works for the reason that the work is practically completed, with the exception of a small amount of paving which could not be done until fills had settled sufficiently, completion of which is now held up by weather conditions.

Ayes—Supervisors Andriano, Canepa, Colman, Havenner, Hayden, McGovern, McSheehy, Miles, Peyser, Power, Roncovieri, Rossi, Shannon, Spaulding, Suhr, Toner—16.

Absent—Supervisors Gallagher, Stanton—2·

Intention to Change Grades on De Long Street, Etc.

Also, Resolution No. 32018 (New Series), as follows:

Resolved, That it is the intention of the Board of Supervisors to change and establish grades on the following named streets at the points hereinafter specified and at the elevations above city base as hereinafter stated, in accordance with Resolution No. 109121 (Second Series) of the Board of Public Works, adopted January 13, 1930, and written recommendation of said Board, filed January 14, 1930, to-wit:

On De Long street between Head street and a line at right angles to the southwesterly line of, 88.16 feet southeasterly from San Diego avenue, and on Santa Cruz avenue between De Long street and a line radial to the curve, 315.84 feet (measured along the center line) northerly from the County line.

The Board of Supervisors hereby declares that no assessment district is necessary as no damage will result from said change of grades, inasmuch as the streets are ungraded and there are no existing street improvements.

The Board of Public Works is hereby directed to cause to be conspicuously posted along the street or streets upon which such change or modification of grade or grades is contemplated, notice of the passage of this resolution of intention.

Ayes—Supervisors Andriano, Canepa, Colman, Havenner, Hayden, McGovern, McSheehy, Miles, Peyser, Power, Roncovieri, Rossi, Shannon, Spaulding, Suhr, Toner—16.

Absent—Supervisors Gallagher, Stanton—2.

Approving Map Showing the Widening of Elk Street at Sussex Street.

Also, Resolution No. 32019 (New Series), as follows:

Whereas, the Board of Public Works did, by Resolution No. 109189 (Second Series), approve a map showing the widening of Elk street at Sussex street; now, therefore, be it

Resolved, That the map showing the widening of Elk street at Sussex street be and the same is hereby approved.

Further Resolved, That the parcel shown hatched on said map is hereby declared an open, public street.

Ayes—Supervisors Andriano, Canepa, Colman, Havenner, Hayden, McGovern, McSheehy, Miles, Peyser, Power, Roncovieri, Rossi, Shannon, Spaulding, Suhr, Toner—16.

Absent—Supervisors Gallagher, Stanton—2.

Approval of Map Showing Proposed Establishment of Grades on Campbell Avenue, Etc.

Also, Resolution No. 32020 (New Series), as follows:

Whereas, the Board of Public Works did, by Resolution No. 108624 (Second Series), approve a map showing the proposed establishment of grades on Campbell avenue between Goettingen and Alpha streets; on Somerset street between Rodeo and Campbell avenues, and on Alpha street between Teddy and Campbell avenues; now, therefore, be it

Resolved, That the map showing the proposed establishment of grades on Campbell avenue between Goettingen and Alpha streets; on Somerset street between Rodeo and Campbell avenues, and on Alpha street between Teddy and Campell avenues be and the same is hereby approved.

Ayes—Supervisors Andriano, Canepa, Colman, Havenner, Hayden, McGovern, McSheehy, Miles, Peyser, Power, Roncovieri, Rossi, Shannon, Spaulding, Suhr, Toner—16.

Absent—Supervisors Gallagher, Stanton—2.

Approval of Map Showing Proposed Change and Establishment of Grades on Margaret Avenue Between Lakeview Avenue and Ridge Lane and on Other Streets.

Also, Resolution No. 32021 (New Series), as follows:

Whereas, the Board of Public Works did, by Resolution No. 108132 (Second Series), approve a map showing the proposed change and establishment of grades on Margaret avenue between Lakeview avenue and Ridge lane and on other streets; now, therefore, be it

Resolved, That the map showing the proposed change and establishment of grades on Margaret avenue between Lakeview avenue and Ridge lane and on other streets be and the same is hereby approved.

Ayes—Supervisors Andriano. Canepa, Colman, Havenner, Hayden, McGovern, McSheehy, Miles, Peyser, Power, Roncovieri, Rossi, Shannon, Spaulding, Suhr, Toner—16.

Absent—Supervisors Gallagher, Stanton—2.

Approval of Map of Corbett Avenue From Clayton Street to Portola Drive Showing the Proposed Change and Establishment of Grade on Corbett Avenue and Adjoining Streets.

Also, Resolution No. 32022 (New Series), as follows:

Whereas, the Board of Public Works did, by Resolution No. 108112 (Second Series), approved a map entitled "Grade map of Corbett avenue from Clayton street to Portola drive," showing the proposed change and establishment of grades on Corbett avenue and adjoining streets; now, therefore, be it

Resolved, That the grade map of Corbett avenue from Clayton street to Portola drive, showing the proposed change and establishment of grades on Corbett avenue and adjoining streets, be and the same is hereby approved.

Ayes—Supervisors Andriano, Canepa, Colman, Havenner, Hayden, McGovern, McSheehy, Miles, Peyser, Power, Roncovieri, Rossi, Shannon, Spaulding, Suhr, Toner—16.

Absent—Supervisors Gallagher, Stanton—2.

Approval of Map Showing Alley in Block 3005C, Known as "Globe Alley."

Also, Resolution No. 32023 (New Series), as follows:

Whereas, the Board of Public Works did, by Resolution No. 109275 (Second Series), approve a map showing the closing of an alley between Blocks 3005C and 3005D and opening of an alley in Block 3005C, Westwood Highlands, between Cresta Vista drive and Hazelwood avenue, known as Globe alley; now, therefore, be it

Resolved, That the map showing the closing of an alley between Blocks 3005C and 3005D, and the opening of an alley in Block 3005C, Westwood Highlands, between Cresta Vista drive and Hazelwood avenue, known as Globe alley, is hereby approved.

Further Resolved, That the parcel shown hatched on said map is declared to be an open public alley, to be known as Globe alley.

Ayes—Supervisors Andriano, Canepa, Colman, Havenner, Hayden, McGovern, McSheehy, Miles, Peyser, Power, Roncovieri, Rossi, Shannon, Spaulding, Suhr, Toner—16.

Absent—Supervisors Gallagher, Stanton—2.

Deed to Land for the Opening of an Alley Known as "Globe Alley."

Also, Resolution No. 32024 (New Series), as follows:

Resolved, That the deed executed on the 13th day of April, 1928, between Henry Stoneson and Hazel Stoneson, his wife, and the City and County of San Francisco, a municipal corporation, to lands for opening of an alley, as shown on map showing the closing of an alley between Blocks 3005C and 3005D, and opening of an alley in Block 3005C, Westwood Highlands, between Cresta Vista drive and Hazelwood avenue, known as Globe Alley, be and the same is hereby accepted.

Ayes—Supervisors Andriano, Canepa, Colman, Havenner, Hayden, McGovern, McSheehy, Miles, Peyser, Power, Roncovieri, Rossi, Shannon, Spaulding, Suhr, Toner—16.

Absent—Supervisors Gallagher, Stanton—2.

Passed for Printing.

The following matters were *passed for printing*:

Regulating the Width of Sidewalks on Quint Street Between Oakdale and Palou Avenues.

On recommendation of Streets Committee.

Bill No. 8183, Ordinance No. ———— (New Series), as follows:

Amending Ordinance No. 1061, entitled "Regulating the Width of Sidewalks," approved December 18, 1903, by adding thereto a new section to be numbered ten hundred and eighty-nine.

Be it ordained by the People of the City and County of San Francisco as follows:

Section 1. Ordinance No. 1061, entitled "Regulating the Width of Sidewalks," approved December 18, 1903, be and is hereby amended in accordance with the communication of the Board of Public Works, filed in this office January 21, 1930, by adding thereto a new section to be numbered ten hundred and eighty-nine, to read as follows:

Section 1089. The width of sidewalks on Quint street between Oakdale avenue and Palou avenue shall be ten (10) feet.

Section 2. Any expense caused by the above change of walk widths shall be borne by the property owners.

Section 3. This ordinance shall take effect and be in force from and after its passage.

Repealing Ordinance No. 8654 (New Series), Ordering the Improvement of Forty-first Avenue Between Kirkham and Lawton Streets Where Not Already Done.

Also, Bill No. 8184, Ordinance No. ———— (New Series), as follows:

Repealing Ordinance No. 8654 (New Series) ordering the improvement of Forty-first avenue between Kirkham and Lawton streets, where not already so improved.

Be it ordained by the People of the City and County of San Francisco as follows:

Section 1. Ordinance No. 8654 (New Series) ordering the improvement of Forty-first avenue between Kirkham and Lawton streets, where not already so improved, be and the same is hereby repealed.

Section 2. This ordinance shall take effect immediately.

Prohibiting Operation of Out of Doors Loud Speakers, Etc., Without Permit.

On recommendation of Police Committee.

Bill No. 8185, Ordinance No. ———— (New Series), as follows:

Prohibiting the maintenance or operation of loud speakers or amplifiers so that said instruments cause the sound therefrom to be projected outside of any building or out of doors without a permit; declaring maintenance or operation between certain hours and at certain times unlawful, and providing a penalty therefor.

Be it ordained by the People of the City and County of San Francisco as follows:

Section 1. It shall be unlawful for any person, firm, association or corporation to maintain, operate, connect, or suffer or permit to be maintained, operated or connected, any loud speaker or sound amplifier in such manner as to cause any sound to be projected outside of any building or out of doors in any part of the City and County of San Francisco between the hours of 10 o'clock a. m. and 10 o'clock p. m., except during public events and affairs of interest to the general public.

Section 2. It shall be unlawful for any person, firm, association or corporation to maintain, operate, connect, or suffer or permit to be maintained, operated or connected, any loud speaker or sound amplifier in such a manner as to cause any sound to be projected outside of any building, or out of doors, in any part of the City and County of San Francisco between the hours of 10 o'clock a. m. and 10 o'clock p. m., or after 10 o'clock p. m. during public events and affairs of interest to the general public, without a permit from the Board of Police Commissioners, which said permit shall be granted upon application therefor, but which said permit shall be revocable by said Board of Police Commissioners whenever any such loud speaker or sound amplifier shall be objectionable to or disturb the public peace, and in the event of the revocation of any such permit the same shall not be renewed without satisfactory proof to said Board of Police Commissioners that the public peace will no longer be disturbed.

Section 3. Any person, firm, association or corporation who shall violate the provisions of Sections 1 or 2 hereof shall be guilty of a misdemeanor and upon conviction thereof shall be punished by a fine not to exceed five hundred ($500) dollars, or by imprisonment in the

County Jail for not more than six (6) months, or by both such fine and imprisonment.

Section 4. This ordinance is hereby declared to be an emergency ordinance to take effect at once and which is rendered necessary for the preservation of the public peace.

Adopted.

The following resolutions were *adopted*:

Masquerade Ball Permit, United Slovenian Societies of San Francisco, Eagle's Auditorium, 375 Golden Gate Avenue, Sunday Evening, February 16, 1930.

On recommendation of Police Committee.

Resolution No. 32025 (New Series), as follows:

Resolved, That United Slovenian Societies of San Francisco be and they are hereby granted permission to conduct a masquerade ball in Eagle's Auditorium, 375 Golden Gate avenue, Sunday, February 16, 1930.

Ayes—Supervisors Andriano, Canepa, Colman, Havenner, Hayden, McGovern, McSheehy, Miles, Peyser, Power, Roncovieri, Rossi, Shannon, Spaulding, Suhr, Toner—16.

Absent—Supervisors Gallagher, Stanton—2.

Award of Contract, Laundry Machinery.

On recommendation of Supplies Committee.

Resolution No. 32026 (New Series), as follows:

Resolved, That award of contract be hereby made to American Laundry Machinery Co on bid submitted December 30, 1929 (Proposal No. 548), for furnishing the following, viz.: Laundry machinery for City Prison, to conform to circulars enclosed with bid giving detailed description:

One washer, 28 by 48 inches; single-geared Sterling Monel metal washer, for $1,480.00.

One extractor, 24 inches; American under-driven solid curb extractor, laundry type, vertical motor driven, for $828.00.

Above machines f. o. b. laundry room, City Prison, set in place ready for other contractors to make the necessary steam, water and electrical connections.

Resolved, That no bond be required, as said awards are for immediate delivery.

Resolved, That all other bids submitted thereon be rejected.

Ayes—Supervisors Andriano, Canepa, Colman, Havenner, Hayden, McGovern, McSheehy, Miles, Peyser, Power, Roncovieri, Rossi, Shannon, Spaulding, Suhr, Toner—16.

Absent—Supervisors Gallagher, Stanton—2.

Award of Contract, Printing Auditor's Report.

Also, Resolution No. 32027 (New Series), as follows:

Resolved, That award of contract be hereby made to Eureka District Publishing Company, on bid submitted January 20, 1930 (Proposal No. 551), for furnishing the following, viz.:

Printing Auditor's Report, 1928-1929.

800 copies Auditor's Annual Finance Report for the fiscal year ended June 30, 1929.

Size, 11 x 8¼ inches.

Style of composition, as per City sample.

Quality of paper, Substance No. 60 Clipper M. F. book or equal; light gray color.

Binding to be side wire stitched, 3 stitches; cover scored; one insert

13 x 15½, two inserts 11 x 16, printed one side on Substance No. 16, English Bond, or equal, to be folded and tipped in.

Galley and page proofs to be submitted to Auditor.

"Copy" may be seen in the Statistical Department, Auditor's office, City Hall.

To be delivered within 30 full working days from receipt of order, for the sum of $798.

Resolved, That a bond in the amount of $200 be required for faithful performance of contract.

Resolved, That all other bids submitted thereon be rejected.

Ayes—Supervisors Andriano, Canepa, Colman, Havenner, Hayden. McGovern, McSheehy, Miles, Peyser. Power, Roncovieri, Rossi, Shannon, Spaulding, Suhr, Toner—16.

Absent—Supervisors Gallagher, Stanton—2.

Fixing State Primary Election Day August 26, 1930, as Date for Bond Election to Acquire Properties of Pacific Gas and Electric Company and Great Western Power Company, and Directing City Attorney to Secure Stipulation From Companies That Deferring Election to This Date Will Not Be Considered a Lack of Diligence.

The following, on recommendation of Joint Committee on Public Utilities and Finance, was taken up:

Resolution No. ———— (New Series), as follows:

Whereas, the Board of Supervisors have heretofore initiated proceedings for the purpose of submitting to the people the matter of the acquisition of the properties of the Pacific Gas and Electric Company and of the Great Western Power Company, at the valuation fixed by the State Railroad Commission, and additions thereto caused by additions and betterments made to the properties of the respective companies since the evaluation proceedings were commenced; and

Whereas, it is the desire of the Board of Supervisors to submit the matter of the acquisition of said properties, and the voting of a bonded indebtedness for the purpose of acquiring the same, to the electors of the City and County of San Francisco at such time as will best afford said electors the opportunity of expressing themselves in the matter of the acquisition of said utilities; now, therefore, be it

Resolved, That it is the sense of the Board of Supervisors that when the date for the holding of said election for the purpose of voting a bonded indebtedness to acquire the said properties of the Pacific Gas and Electric Company and Great Western Power Company is fixed by ordinance calling for said election, that the same should be fixed for the date on which the State primary election is held, to-wit: the last Tuesday in August, 1930, provided that said Pacific Gas and Electric Company and Great Western Power Company will stipulate with the City that the deferring of said election until said date shall not be considered a lack of due diligence in calling and holding said election; and be it

Further Resolved, That the City Attorney be and he is hereby directed to obtain, if possible, from each of said companies a stipulation with the City to the effect that the deferring of said election until the date hereinabove set forth shall not be considered a lack of due diligence in calling and holding said election.

Action Deferred.

Supervisor Rossi, seconded by Supervisor Hayden, moved to lay over one week.

Motion *carried* by the following vote:

Ayes—Supervisors Andriano, Canepa, Colman, Hayden, McSheehy, Miles, Peyser, Power, Rossi, Shannon, Stanton, Suhr, Toner—13.

Noes—Supervisors Gallagher, Havenner, McGovern, Roncovieri—4.

Absent—Supervisor Spaulding—1.

ROLL CALL FOR THE INTRODUCTION OF RESOLUTIONS, BILLS AND COMMUNICATIONS NOT CONSIDERED OR REPORTED UPON BY A COMMITTEE.

Survey for Commercial Sites South of San Francisco.

Introduced by Supervisor Power:

Resolution No. ———— (New Series), as follows:

Whereas, it is advisable and necessary for the Board of Supervisors to give all possible encouragement to the fostering and bringing of industries and manufacturing institutions to San Francisco; and

Whereas, the Committee on Industrial and Commercial Development of the Board of Supervisors was created for that purpose; now, therefore, be it

Resolved, That said Committee be and is hereby requested to make the necessary plans for a complete survey of San Francisco and the territory bordering on San Francisco to the south as to available sites, water, light and electric energy, available market for output and such other data as may be necessary to intelligently present to prospective investors the reasons they should locate in San Francisco; and be it

Further Resolved, That the Industrial and Commercial Development Committee of the Board of Supervisors cooperate in every way with every agency or organization that is working to bring industries to San Francisco and the territory tributary thereto; and be it

Further Resolved, That there be and is hereby appropriated out of the General Fund $5,000 to be expended by the Committee on Industrial and Commercial Development of this Board for the purposes heretofore referred to.

Referred to Finance Committee.

Application for Rerouting Peninsula Bus Service Over Bay Shore Boulevard.

Supervisor Spaulding presented.

Resolution No. ———— (New Series), as follows:

Whereas, the Peninsula Rapid Transit Company and the Pacific Auto Stages, Inc., now operating motor coach lines from San Francisco to San Jose, have applied for permission to re-route a portion of their service via the Bay Shore Highway; and

Whereas, these companies have pioneered the motor transportation industry on the Peninsula and have rendered adequate service; and

Whereas, there is at present no motor coach service for the people and communities situated on the Bay Shore Highway; and

Whereas, such service would be a great advantage to the people and communities of the Bay Shore Highway in general, and to the San Francisco Municipal Airport (Mills Field) in particular; therefore, be it

Resolved, That the Board of Supervisors of the City and County of San Francisco does hereby endorse the applications of the Peninsula Rapid Transit Company and the Pacific Auto Stages, Inc., and urges the Honorable Railroad Commission of the State of California to grant the same; and be it

Further Resolved, That the City Attorney, as the official representative of the Board of Supervisors, be instructed to be present in the courtroom of the California Railroad Commission in San Francisco on February 18, 1930, and to appear as a witness in behalf of said applications.

Referred to Public Utilities Committee.

Death of Sarah Jones, School Principal.

Supervisor Power presented:

Resolution No. 32031 (New Series), as follows:

Whereas, death has removed an estimable and beloved character in the civic life of San Francisco in the person of Sarah Jones, pioneer teacher, principal and member of the Board of Education in the public schools of this city.

Resolved, That in the death of Sarah Jones there has been called from our midst a woman of outstanding character, the termination of whose distinguished career is a distinct and irreparable loss to the children of San Francisco, to whose culture and education she was ever devoted.

Adopted by the following vote:

Ayes—Supervisors Andriano, Canepa, Colman, Gallagher, Havenner, Hayden, McGovern, McSheehy, Miles, Peyser, Power, Roncovieri, Rossi, Shannon, Spaulding, Stanton, Suhr, Toner—18.

ADJOURNMENT.

There being no further business the Board at the hour of 6:15 p. m. adjourned.

J. S. DUNNIGAN, Clerk.

Approved by the Board of Supervisors March 10, 1930.

Pursuant to Resolution No. 3402 (New Series) of the Board of Supervisors of the City and County of San Francisco, I, John S. Dunnigan, hereby certify that the foregoing is true and correct copy of the Journal of Proceedings of said Board of the date stated and approved as above recited.

JOHN S. DUNNIGAN,

Clerk of the Board of Supervisors,
City and County of San Francisco.

Vol. 25—New Series   No. 6

Monday, February 10, 1930

Journal of Proceedings
Board of Supervisors

City and County of San Francisco

The Recorder Printing and Publishing Company
337 Bush Street, S. F.

JOURNAL OF PROCEEDINGS
BOARD OF SUPERVISORS

MONDAY, FEBRUARY 10, 1930, 2 P. M.

In Board of Supervisors, San Francisco, Monday, February 10, 1930, 2 p. m.

CALLING THE ROLL.

The roll was called and the following Supervisors were noted present:

Supervisors Andriano, Canepa, Colman, Havenner, Hayden, McGovern, Miles, Peyser, Power, Roncovieri, Rossi, Spaulding, Stanton, Suhr—14.

Supervisor Gallagher noted present at 2:30 p. m.
Supervisor McSheehy noted present at 2:10 p. m.
Supervisor Toner noted present at 3:40 p. m.
Absent—Supervisor Shannon—1.
Quorum present.
His Honor Mayor Rolph presiding.

APPROVAL OF JOURNAL.

The Journal of Proceedings of January 20, 1930, was considered read and approved.

PRESENTATION OF PROPOSALS.

Underground Cable.

Sealed proposals were received and opened between the hours of 2 and 3 p. m. this date, for furnishing 15,000 feet of underground cable for the Department of Electricity, and *referred to Supplies Committee.*

Nurses' Uniforms.

Sealed proposals were received and opened between the hours of 2 and 3 p. m. this date, for furnishing nurses' uniforms for San Francisco Hospital, and *referred to Supplies Committee.*

Sheet Music for School Department.

Sealed proposals were received and opened between the hours of 2 and 3 p. m. this date, for furnishing sheet music for School Department, and *referred to Supplies Committee.*

HEARING OF APPEAL—3 P. M.

Rezoning Marina Boulevard.

Hearing of appeal of property owners from the decision of the City Planning Commission placing property on both sides of Marina boulevard between Buchanan street and Webster street, as described in Resolution No. 175 of the City Planning Commission, in the First Residential District, where not already so zoned.

Protest of Pacific Gas and Electric Company.

Communication, from Pacific Gas and Electric Company, protesting against ruling of City Planning Commission approving the rezoning or reclassification of the property fronting on the north side of Marina boulevard, between Buchanan and Webster streets, for a depth of one hundred feet, from Light Industrial to First Residential, and also the rezoning or reclassification of the property fronting on the south side of Marina boulevard, between Buchanan and Webster streets, for a depth of one hundred feet, from Commercial to First Residential.

Also, communication from Sierra and San Francisco Power Company making same protest.

Action Deferred.

Whereupon, on motion of Supervisor Gallagher, the hearing on appeal was *continued until March* 10, 1930, *and made a Special Order of Business for 3 p. m.*

Action Deferred.

The following matter was *laid over one week*:

Appraisal Bureau.

Consideration of the matter of the discontinuance of the Appraisal Bureau of the Board of Equalization.

Rules of Proceedings.

Consideration of the matter of the adoption of Rules of Proceedings of the Board of Supervisors was, on motion of Supervisor Peyser, *laid over one week and made a Special Order of Business for 3 p. m.*

UNFINISHED BUSINESS.

Final Passage.

The following matters, heretofore passed for printing, were taken up and *finally passed* by the following vote:

Authorizations.

On recommendation of Finance Committee.

Resolution No. 32054 (New Series), as follows:

Resolved, That the following amounts be and the same are hereby authorized to be expended out of the hereinafter mentioned funds in payment to the following named claimants, to-wit:

Hetch Hetchy Construction Fund, Bond Issue 1928.

(1) Ingersoll-Rand Company of California, three jack hammers (claim dated Jan. 21, 1930).......................$ 585.00

(2) Santa Fe Lumber Company, lumber (claim dated Jan. 21, 1930) 1,704.10

(3) Coos Bay Lumber Company, lumber (claim dated Jan. 21, 1930) 1,529.34

(4) Del Monte Meat Company, meat (claim dated Jan. 22, 1930) 614.29

(5) Dr. Paul E. Dolan, medical services rendered Hetch Hetchy employees (claim dated Jan. 22, 1930) 853.25

(6) Edison Storage Battery Supply Company, Edison battery cells (claim dated Jan. 22, 1930)........................ 2,134.87

(7) Hercules Powder Company, explosives and wire (claim dated Jan. 22, 1930)...................................... 2,648.15

(8) Higgins & Sons, Inc., payment for land required for San Miguel Reservoir of the Hetch Hetchy Water Supply (claim dated Jan. 22, 1930). Purchase approved by Resolution No. 31884 (New Series)................................. 1,000.00

(9) Ingersoll-Rand Company of California, jack hammers and machinery parts (claim dated Jan. 22, 1930)............. 1,341.86

(10) The Charles Nelson Company, wood wedges (claim dated Jan. 22, 1930)....................................... 663.30

(11) Santa Cruz Portland Cement Company, cement (claim dated Jan. 22, 1930)................................... 2,474.50

(12) Sherry Bros., Inc., eggs (claim dated Jan. 22, 1930).... 882.00

(13) Utah Fuel Company, coal (claim dated Jan. 22, 1930).. 760.42
(14) Wilsey-Bennett Co., butter and cheese (claim dated Jan. 22, 1930) 541.40
(15) Best Steel Casting Company, castings (claim dated Jan. 28, 1930) 967.40
(16) J. H. Creighton, truck hire (claim dated Jan. 28, 1930) 1,360.92
(17) Pacific Coast Aggregates, Inc., concrete sand (claim dated Jan. 28, 1930)...................................... 560.65
(18) Alfred Pereira & Brothers, hauling during December (claim dated Jan. 28, 1930)............................. 1,124.79
(19) Shell Oil Company, gasoline, oils, etc. (claim dated Jan. 28, 1930) 607.70

County Road Fund.

(20) Equitable Asphalt Maintenance Company, resurfacing of asphalt, street reconstruction (claim dated Jan. 23, 1930.$ 716.44
(21) Graham Fuel & Drayage Company, coal used in reconstruction of streets (claim dated Jan. 23, 1930)............ 570.64
(22) Santa Cruz Portland Cement Company, cement for street reconstruction (claim dated Jan. 23, 1930)................ 879.12

Auditorium Fund.

(23) Thomas F. Boyle, as Auditor of the City and County, for payment of claims for account of the expense of municipal Christmas Eve celebration held at Auditorium December 24, 1929 (claim dated Feb. 3, 1930)....................$ 1,980.25

Municipal Railway Fund.

(24) Lilian Murphy Prevonak, in full settlement and payment for account of any damage due to injuries sustained by reason of being struck by a Municipal Railway street car at Kearny and Market streets August 31, 1923 (claim dated Jan. 27, 1930)......................................$ 1,129.75
(25) The Texas Company, gasoline furnished Municipal Railways December, 1929 (claim dated Jan. 27, 1930)......... 1,948.70
(26) United States Steel Products Company, track material furnished (claim dated Jan. 24, 1930).................... 9,613.40
(27) United States Steel Products Company, track material furnished (claim dated Jan. 23, 1930).................... 38,975.21

School Bond Fund, Issue 1923.

(28) Fred Medart Manufacturing Company, gymnasium equipment for Polytechnic High School (claim dated Jan. 28, 1930) ....$ 613.20

Special School Tax.

(29) J. H. McCallum, lumber for school repairs (claim dated Jan. 23, 1930)..$ 667.94
(30) Larsen & Larsen, second payment, brick work, etc., for Roosevelt Junior High School (claim dated Jan. 27, 1930). 9,670.79
(31) D. A. Pancoast Company, for "Von Duprin" type panic bolts, for various schools (claim dated Jan. 28, 1930)...... 2,748.00

Boulevard Bond Fund, Issue 1927.

(32) California State Automobile Association, eight battery type arterial stop signs for Bay Shore boulevard, Section "C" (claim dated Jan. 23, 1930)........................$ 560.00

Park Fund.

(33) Pacific Gas and Electric Company, gas and electric service for parks (claim dated Jan. 31, 1930)................$ 1,541.28
(34) Spring Valley Water Company, water service for parks (claim dated Jan. 31, 1930)............................ 1,269.80
(35) Berringer & Russell, hay, etc., for parks (claim dated Jan. 31, 1930)....................................... 1,016.18

(36) Standard Fence Company, posts, wire, etc., for parks (claim dated Jan. 31, 1930)............................ 1,224.84

General Fund, 1929-1930.

(37) Stockton State Hospital, maintenance of criminal insane (claim dated Feb. 3, 1930)............................$ 521.00

(38) San Francisco Society for the Prevention of Cruelty to Animals, impounding, feeding, etc., of animals (claim dated Feb. 3, 1930).................................... 1,500.00

(39) The Electric Corporation, cable, batteries, etc., for Department of Electricity (claim dated Dec. 31, 1929)....... 1,192.26

(40) The Texas Company, gasoline furnished Police Department (claim dated Jan. 27, 1930)...................... 1,320.15

(41) James F. Waters, one De Soto phaeton for Police Department (claim dated Jan. 27, 1930)................... 977.70

(42) Spring Valley Water Company, water service furnished fire hydrants (claim dated Jan. 31, 1930)................. 15,587.10

(43) Richfield Oil Company of California, fuel oil furnished Civic Center power house (claim dated Jan. 23, 1930)..... 1,231.76

(44) Arata & Peters, potatoes, Laguna Honda Home (claim dated Dec. 31, 1929)...................................... 750.00

(45) Spring Valley Water Company, water service furnished Laguna Honda Home (claim dated Dec. 31, 1929).......... 1,023.07

(46) L. M. Wilbor, M. D., Superintendent of San Francisco Hospital, room rent allowance for employees of San Francisco Hospital (claim dated Dec. 31, 1929)............... 3,500.00

(47) O'Brien, Spotorno & Mitchell, turkeys furnished San Francisco Hospital (claim dated Jan. 31, 1930)........... 605.44

(48) Arata & Peters, Inc., potatoes furnished San Francisco Hospital (claim dated Jan. 31, 1930).................... 900.00

(49) Building Supplies Company, supplies for San Francisco Hospital (claim dated Dec. 31, 1929).................... 805.88

Maintenance of Aquarium, Appropriation 56.

(50) California Academy of Sciences, for expense of maintaining the Steinhart Aquarium during month of January, 1930 (claim dated Feb. 3, 1930)..........................$ 3,506.26

Ayes—Supervisors Andriano, Canepa, Colman, Havenner, Hayden, McGovern, Miles, Peyser, Power, Roncovieri, Rossi, Spaulding, Stanton, Suhr—14.

Absent—Supervisors Gallagher, McSheehy, Shannon, Toner—4.

Appropriation, $1,690.90, Purchase of Land for Widening of Portola Drive.

Also, Resolution No. 32032 (New Series), as follows:

Resolved, That the sum of $1,690.90 be and the same is hereby set aside and appropriated out of County Road Fund and authorized in payment to Wells Fargo & Company, a corporation; being payment for portion of Lot 3, Block 2871 (56x105); portion of Lot 3, Block 2871 (290x 40); portion of Lot 1 and all of Lot 2 in Block 2868 (174x134), all irregular, and as per Assessor's Block Books of the City and County of San Francisco, purchase approved by Resolution No. ——— (New Series), and required for Portola drive (claim dated January 8, 1930.)

Ayes—Supervisors Andriano, Canepa, Colman, Havenner, Hayden, McGovern, Miles, Peyser, Power, Roncovieri, Rossi, Spaulding, Stanton, Suhr—14.

Absent—Supervisors Gallagher, McSheehy, Shannon, Toner—4.

Appropriations, Payment Out of "Publicity and Advertising" for Services and Materials, Construction of San Francisco Float, Pasadena Tournament of Roses.

Also, Resolution No. 32033 (New Series), as follows:

Resolved, That the following amounts be and the same are hereby set aside and appropriated out of "Publicity & Advertising," Appropriation 54, fiscal year 1929-1930, and authorized in payment to the hereinafter named claimants; being payments for account of services rendered and materials furnished and used in the construction of San Francisco's float exhibited at the Tournament of Roses, Pasadena, California, January 1, 1930, to-wit:

(1) To Rudolph G. Theurkauf, for services rendered and materials furnished (claim dated Feb. 3, 1930) ....$ 1,018.07

(2) To Mission Florist, flowers, ferns, etc., and express charges furnished and paid (claim dated Feb. 3, 1930).... 991.50

Ayes—Supervisors Andriano, Canepa, Colman, Havenner, Hayden, McGovern, Miles, Peyser, Power, Roncovieri, Rossi, Spaulding, Stanton, Suhr—14.

Absent—Supervisors Gallagher, McSheehy, Shannon, Toner—4.

Appropriations, Various Funds, for Various Purposes.

Also, Resolution No. 32034 (New Series), as follows:

Resolved, That the following amounts be and the same are hereby set aside, appropriated and authorized to be expended out of the hereinafter mentioned accounts, General Fund, 1929-1930, for the following purposes, to-wit:

Street Work in Front of City Porperty—Budget Item 34.

(1) To defray cost of constructing artificial stone sidewalks at City playground, Lenox way between Ulloa and Taraval streets .. ..$ 700.00

(2) To defray cost of constructing sidewalks at City playground, east side of Hampshire street from Army to Twenty-sixth streets 670.00

Repairs to Public Building, Etc.—Budget Item No. 53.

(3) For cost of furnishing and installing an additional feed water heater in the engine room of the Hall of Justice....$ 975.00

Ayes—Supervisors Andriano, Canepa, Colman, Havenner, Hayden, McGovern, Miles, Peyser, Power, Roncovieri, Rossi, Spaulding, Stanton, Suhr—14.

Absent—Supervisors Gallagher, McSheehy, Shannon, Toner—4.

Appropriations for Street Improvement, County Road Fund.

Also, Resolution No. 32035 (New Series), as follows:

Resolved, That the following amounts be and the same are hereby set aside, appropriated and authorized to be expended out of County Road Fund for the following purposes, to-wit

(1) For the reconstruction of Grant avenue between Chestnut and Bay streets ....$ 5,500.00

(2) For the reconstruction of Sherman street between Folsom and Harrison streets 7,125.00

(3) For the improving of Second street between Berry and Townsend streets, by straightening existing curbs and resurfacing with asphaltic concrete wearing surface........   4,000.00

(4) For reconstruction of Washington street between Polk and Larkin streets, by construction of new curb and resurfacing existing pavement 2,277.00

(5) To defray cost of constructing necessary parapet wall, warning lights, reflector signs and coping at the east side of the intersection of Vicksburg and Twenty-second streets   825.00

Ayes—Supervisors Andriano, Canepa, Colman, Havenner, Hayden, McGovern, Miles, Peyser, Power, Roncovieri, Rossi, Spaulding, Stanton, Suhr—14.

Absent—Supervisors Gallagher, McSheehy, Shannon, Toner—4.

Appropriations for Street Reconstruction, County Road Fund.

Also, Resolution No. 32036 (New Series), as follows:

Resolved, That the following amounts be and the same are hereby set aside, appropriated and authorized to be expended out of County Road Fund for the reconstruction of the following streets, to-wit:

(1) Hyde street, from Lombard to Chestnut street.........$ 3,200.00
(2) Leavenworth street, from Lombard to Chestnut street.. 2,100.00
(3) Jones street, from Chestnut to Bay street............. 2,300.00
(4) Francisco street, from Columbus avenue to Jones street.. 1,500.00
(5) Broderick street, from Sacramento to Jackson street.... 3,600.00
(6) Baker street, from Jackson street to Pacific avenue...... 4,100.00
(7) Baker street, from Jackson to Washington street...... 1,500.00
(8) Seventeenth avenue, from Fulton to Cabrillo street...... 3,400.00
(9) Masonic avenue, from Java street to Upper Terrace.... 2,240.00

Total $23,940.00

Ayes—Supervisors Andriano, Canepa, Colman, Havenner, Hayden, McGovern, Miles, Peyser, Power, Roncovieri, Rossi, Spaulding, Stanton, Suhr—14.

Absent—Supervisors Gallagher, McSheehy, ·Shannon, Toner—4.

Oil and Boiler Permits.

On recommendation of Fire Committee.

Resolution No. 32037 (New Series), as follows:

Resolved, That the following revocable permits be and are hereby granted:

Oil Tanks.

D. Rudee, 3876 California street, 1500 gallons capacity.

A. Sutro, Sutro Forest (top Twin Peaks), 1500 gallons capacity.

S. A. Born, southeast corner Larkin and Pine streets, 1500 gallons capacity.

A. Wendell, 774 Howard street, 1500 gallons capacity.

James Allan & Sons, south side Evans avenue, approximately 200 feet east of Third street, 1500 gallons capacity.

O. Bussie, southeast corner of Grove street and Masonic avenue, 1500 gallons capacity.

Ferroni Bros., 3110 Laguna street, 1500 gallons capacity.

E. A. Hammer, 2615 Divisadero street, 1500 gallons capacity.

Henry Ahlers, 3876 Clay street, 1500 gallons capacity.

W. H. Jackson, 400 Yerba Buena avenue, 1500 gallons capacity.

J. Harris, 2041 Hyde street, 1500 gallons capacity.

Boiler.

A. Depaol, west side Dartmouth street, 100 feet north of Woolsey street, 50 horsepower.

The rights granted under this resolution shall be exercised within six months, otherwise said permit shall become null and void.

Ayes—Supervisors Andriano, Canepa, Colman, Havenner, Hayden, McGovern, Miles, Peyser, Power, Roncovieri, Rossi, Spaulding, Stanton, Suhr—14.

Absent—Supervisors Gallagher, McSheehy, Shannon, Toner—4.

Transfer of Auto Supply Station Permit, Cresta Bros., Nantucket and San Jose Avenues.

Also, Resolution No. 32038 (New Series), as follows:

Resolved, That Cresta Bros. be and are hereby granted permission, revocable at will of the Board of Supervisors, to have transferred to them automobile supply station permit heretofore granted Phillips & Hilsinger by Resolution No. 27208 (New Series), for premises at northwest corner of Nantucket and San Jose avenues.

The rights granted under this resolution shall be exercised within six months, otherwise said permit shall become null and void.

Ayes—Supervisors Andriano, Canepa, Colman, Havenner, Hayden, McGovern, Miles, Peyser, Power, Roncovieri, Rossi, Spaulding, Stanton, Suhr—14.

Absent—Supervisors Gallagher, McSheehy, Shannon, Toner—4.

Transfer of Garage Permit, L. J. Espel, 3130 California Street.

Also, Resolution No. 32039 (New Series), as follows:

Resolved, That L. J. Espel be and is hereby granted permission, revocable at will of the Board of Supervisors, to have transferred to him public garage permit heretofore granted D. A. McKean by Resolution No. 18414 (New Series) for premises at 3130 California street.

The rights granted under this resolution shall be exercised within six months, otherwise said permit shall become null and void.

Ayes—Supervisors Andriano, Canepa, Colman, Havenner, Hayden, McGovern, Miles, Peyser, Power, Roncovieri, Rossi, Spaulding, Stanton, Suhr—14.

Absent—Supervisors Gallagher, McSheehy, Shannon, Toner—4.

Transfer of Auto Supply Station Permit, Ernest and Leo Moretton, Mission and Tingley Streets.

Also, Resolution No. 32040 (New Series), as follows:

Resolved, That Ernest and Leo Moretton be and are hereby granted permission, revocable at will of the Board of Supervisors, to have transferred to them automobile supply station permit heretofore granted Bernard R. Kerns by Resolution No. 30161 (New Series) for premises at southwest corner of Mission and Tingley streets.

The rights granted under this resolution shall be exercised within six months, otherwise said permit shall become null and void.

Ayes—Supervisors Andriano, Canepa, Colman, Havenner, Hayden, McGovern, Miles, Peyser, Power, Roncovieri, Rossi, Spaulding, Stanton, Suhr—14.

Absent—Supervisors Gallagher, McSheehy, Shannon, Toner—4.

Action Deferred.

The following resolution was, on motion, *laid over one week*:

Laundry Permits.

Also, Resolution No. ———— (New Series), as follows:

Resolved, That the following revocable permits be and are hereby granted:

Laundries.

Eloise Aiso, 1089 Pine street.
John Batsere, 976 Pine street.
Anna Biscay, 992 Sutter street.
Ruth Clausen, 94 Seventh street.
Mrs. V. J. Laurent, 447 Ellis street.
J. Nougue, 707 O'Farrell street.
Mme. P. Pomme, 1147 McAllister street.
Marie Sabacca, 808 Post street.
Mme. J. Saffores, 841 Powell street.
Mrs. A. Termello, 41 Franklin street.
Louise Vannucci and Gloria Cheader, 405 O'Farrell street.

The rights granted under this resolution shall be exercised within six months, otherwise said permits shall become null and void.

Blanket protest filed by Mr. Alford, Board of Trade, Laundry Industry.

Final Passage.

The following bill, heretofore passed for printing, was taken up and *finally passed* by the following vote:

Prohibiting Operation of Out of Doors Loud Speakers, Etc., Without Permit.

On recommendation of Police Committee.

Bill No. 8185, Ordinance No. 8689 (New Series), as follows:

Prohibiting the maintenance or operation of loud speakers or amplifiers so that said instruments cause the sound therefrom to be projected outside of any building or out of doors without a permit; declaring maintenance or operation between certain hours and at certain times unlawful, and providing a penalty therefor.

Be it ordained by the People of the City and County of San Francisco as follows:

Section 1. It shall be unlawful for any person, firm, association or corporation to maintain, operate, connect, or suffer or permit to be maintained, operated or connected, any loud speaker or sound amplifier in such manner as to cause any sound to be projected outside of any building or out of doors in any part of the City and County of San Francisco between the hours of 10 o'clock a. m. and 10 o'clock p. m., except during public events and affairs of interest to the general public.

Section 2. It shall be unlawful for any person, firm, association or corporation to maintain, operate, connect, or suffer or permit to be maintained, operated or connected, any loud speaker or sound amplifier in such a manner as to cause any sound to be projected outside of any building, or out of doors, in any part of the City and County of San Francisco between the hours of 10 o'clock a. m. and 10 o'clock p. m., or after 10 o'clock p. m. during public events and affairs of interest to the general public, without a permit from the Board of Police Commissioners, which said permit shall be granted upon application therefor, but which said permit shall be revocable by said Board of Police Commissioners whenever any such loud speaker or sound amplifier shall be objectionable to or disturb the public peace, and in the event of the revocation of any such permit the same shall not be renewed without satisfactory proof to said Board of Police Commissioners that the public peace will no longer be disturbed.

Section 3. Any person, firm, association or corporation who shall violate the provisions of Sections 1 or 2 hereof shall be guilty of a misdemeanor and upon conviction thereof shall be punished by a fine not to exceed five hundred ($500) dollars, or by imprisonment in the County Jail for not more than six (6) months, or by both such fine and imprisonment.

Section 4. This ordinance is hereby declared to be an emergency ordinance to take effect at once and which is rendered necessary for the preservation of the public peace.

Ayes—Supervisors Andriano, Canepa, Colman, Havenner, Hayden, McGovern, Miles, Peyser, Power, Roncovieri, Rossi, Spaulding, Stanton, Suhr—14.

Absent—Supervisors Gallagher, McSheehy, Shannon, Toner—4.

Rereferred.

The following recommendation of Streets Committee was, on motion, *rereferred to the Streets Committee*:

Regulating the Width of Sidewalks on Quint Street Between Oakdale and Palou Avenues.

Bill No. 8183, Ordinance No. ———— (New Series), as follows:

Amending Ordinance No. 1061, entitled "Regulating the Width of Sidewalks," approved December 18, 1903, by adding thereto a new section to be numbered ten hundred and eighty-nine.

Be it ordained by the People of the City and County of San Francisco as follows:

Section 1. Ordinance No. 1061, entitled "Regulating the Width of Sidewalks," approved December 18, 1903, be and is hereby amended in accordance with the communication of the Board of Public Works, filed in this office January 21, 1930, by adding thereto a new section to be numbered ten hundred and eighty-nine, to read as follows:

Section 1089. The width of sidewalks on Quint street between Oakdale avenue and Palou avenue shall be ten (10) feet.

Section 2. Any expense caused by the above change of walk widths shall be borne by the property owners.

Section 3. This ordinance shall take effect and be in force from and after its passage.

Final Passage.

The following bill, heretofore passed for printing, was taken up and *finally passed* by the following vote:

Repealing Ordinance No. 8654 (New Series), Ordering the Improvement of Forty-first Avenue Between Kirkham and Lawton Streets Where Not Already Done.

On recommendation of Streets Committee.

Bill No. 8184, Ordinance No. 8690 (New Series), as follows:

Repealing Ordinance No. 8654 (New Series) ordering the improvement of Forty-first avenue between Kirkham and Lawton streets, where not already so improved.

Be it ordained by the People of the City and County of San Francisco as follows:

Section 1. Ordinance No. 8654 (New Series) ordering the improvement of Forty-first avenue between Kirkham and Lawton streets, where not already so improved, be and the same is hereby repealed.

Section 2. This ordinance shall take effect immediately.

Ayes—Supervisors Andriano, Canepa, Colman, Havenner, Hayden, McGovern, Miles. Peyser, Power, Roncovieri, Rossi, Spaulding, Stanton, Suhr—14.

Absent—Supervisors Gallagher, McSheehy, Shannon, Toner—4.

PRESENTATION OF BILLS AND ACCOUNTS.

Your Finance Committee, having examined miscellaneous demands not required by law to be passed to print, and amounting to $43,615.26, recommends same be allowed and ordered paid.

Approved by the following vote:

Ayes—Supervisors Andriano, Canepa, Colman, Havenner, Hayden, McGovern, Miles, Peyser, Power, Roncovieri, Rossi, Spaulding, Stanton, Suhr—14.

Absent—Supervisors Gallagher, McSheehy, Shannon, Toner—4.

Urgent Necessity.

Spring Valley Water Company, water for horse troughs, $20.65.

Edna Nelson et al., compensation insurance, $104.95.

Approved by the following vote:

Ayes—Supervisors Andriano, Canepa, Colman, Havenner, Hayden, McGovern, Miles, Peyser, Power, Roncovieri, Rossi, Spaulding, Stanton, Suhr—14.

Absent—Supervisors Gallagher, McSheehy, Shannon, Toner—4.

NEW BUSINESS.

Passed for Printing.

The following matters were *passed for printing*:

Authorizations.

On recommendation of Finance Committee.

Resolution No. ———— (New Series), as follows:

Resolved, That the following amounts be and the same are hereby authorized to be expended out of the hereinafter mentioned funds in payment to the following named claimants, to-wit:

Hetch Hetchy Water Construction Fund, Bond Issue 1928.

(1) Bryan Provision Company, ham and bacon (claim dated Jan. 30, 1930)..$ 526.62

(2) Challenge Cream and Butter Association, canned milk (claim dated Jan. 30, 1930)............................... 525.00

(3) Coos Bay Lumber Company, lumber (claim dated Jan. 30, 1930)... 4,663.45

(4) Crucible Steel Company of America, steel (claim dated Jan. 30, 1930)... 4,357.95

(5) Del Monte Meat Company, meat (claim dated Jan. 30, 1930) 1,456.29

(6) Haas Brothers, groceries (claim dated Jan. 30, 1930).... 518.70

(7) Ingersoll Rand Company of California, machinery parts (claim dated Jan. 29, 1930)............................. 1,805.70

(8) Rees Blow Pipe Manufacturing Company, blower piping systems (claim dated Jan. 29, 1930)..................... 2,131.00

(9) Santa Cruz Portland Cement Company, cement (claim dated Jan. 30, 1930)................................... 3,084.00

(10) Sherry Bros., Inc., eggs (claim dated Jan. 30, 1930).... 524.40

(11) Soule Steel Company, steel (claim dated Jan. 30, 1930). 573.53

(12) United States Rubber Company, rubber boots, coats, etc. (claim dated Jan. 30, 1930)............................. 3,339.20

(13) Utah Fuel Company, coal (claim dated Jan. 30, 1930)... 597.49

(14) Coos Bay Lumber Company, lumber (claim dated Feb. 3, 1930) 502.32

(15) Ingersoll Rand Company of California, machinery parts (claim dated Feb. 3, 1930)............................. 1,409.65

(16) Santa Cruz Portland Cement Company, cement (claim dated Feb. 3, 1930)................................... 526.00

(17) Sherry Bros., Inc., eggs (claim dated Feb. 3, 1930)..... 529.20

Auditorium Fund.

(18) Musical Association of San Francisco, services of San Francisco Symphony Orchestra for concert of Feb. 18, 1930) ....$ 2,000.00

(19) Serge Prokoleff, services as soloist, concert of Feb. 18, 1930 (claim dated Feb. 7, 1930)........................ 675.00

Tax Judgments, Appropriation 57.

(20) Goldman, Nye & Spicer, attorneys for judgment creditors, seventh installment, one-tenth of final judgment as per schedule attached (claim dated Feb. 15, 1930).........$ 1,355.07

(21) William F. Humphrey, attorney for judgment creditors, fifth installment, one-tenth of final judgment per schedule attached (claim dated Feb. 6, 1930)..................... 2,769.31

Special School Tax.

(22) Alta Electric Company, sixth payment, electrical work, Park-Presidio Junior High School (claim dated Feb. 3, 1930) 4,055.62

(23) Meyer Bros., sixth payment, general construction, Park-Presidio Junior High School (claim dated Feb. 3, 1930)... 43,575.58

(24) Scott Company, sixth payment, mechanical equipment, Park-Presidio Junior High School (claim dated Feb. 3, 1930) 4,839.75

(25) Scott Company, fifth payment, plumbing and gas-fitting, Park-Presidio Junior High School (claim dated Feb. 3, 1930) 1,778.95

(26) Oscar Aaron, fourth payment, plumbing for Geary Street School (claim dated Feb. 3, 1930)................. 1,669.43

(27) Scott Company, second payment, mechanical equipment for addition to Francisco Junior High School (claim dated Feb. 3, 1930)... 562.50

(28) MacDonald & Kahn, third payment, general construction of viewing stand, South Side (Balboa) High School (claim dated Feb. 3, 1930)............................. 6,805.44

(29) A. Lettich, second payment, plumbing for viewing stand at South Side (Balboa) High School (claim dated Feb. 3, 1930) 959.93

(30) Oscar Aaron, final payment, plumbing system, Marina Elementary School (claim dated Feb. 4, 1930) 2,438.94

(31) Lee Dixon, final payment, painting for Marina Elementary School (claim dated Feb. 3, 1930) 1,317.12

(32) A. Lettich, final payment, mechanical equipment for Marina Elementary School (claim dated Feb. 4, 1930) 4,266.80

(33) Jacks & Irvine, eighth payment, general construction of Roosevelt Junior High School (claim dated Feb. 3, 1930).. 6,479.60

(34) Scott Company, sixth payment, mechanical equipment for Roosevelt Junior High School (claim dated Feb. 3, 1930) 4,075.39

(35) Scott Company, sixth payment, plumbing and gas-fitting for Roosevelt Junior High School (claim dated Feb. 3, 1930) 1,197.30

Bernal Cut Construction Fund, Bond Issue 1927.

(36) MacDonald & Kahn, Inc., twelfth payment, improvement of Bernal Cut, Contract No. 1 (claim dated Feb. 5, 1930)...$ 8,100.00

Boulevard Bond Construction Fund, Issue 1927.

(37) Louis J. Cohn, fifteenth payment, improvement of Bay Shore boulevard, Section A, Contract No. 6, Potrero avenue to Silver avenue (claim dated Feb. 5, 1930) ....$ 4,000.00

(38) Eaton & Smith, eighth payment, improvement of Junipero Serra boulevard, Contract No. 13, Sloat boulevard to county line (claim dated Feb. 5, 1930) 12,300.00

Sewer Bond Construction Fund, Issue 1929.

(39) Eaton & Smith, first payment, construction of Alemany boulevard storm drain, Section B (claim dated Feb. 4, 1930) ....$ 4,500.00

County Road Fund.

(40) Pacific Coast Aggregates, Inc., sand and gravel for street reconstruction (claim dated Jan. 28, 1930)........$ 3,078.10

(41) Standard Oil Company of California, asphalt for street reconstruction (claim dated Jan. 28, 1930) 3,867.15

(42) Standard Building Material Company, cement for street reconstruction (claim dated Jan. 28, 1930) 871.20

(43) Board of Public Works (Stores and Yards, Appropriation 30-A), reimbursement for repairs to equipment used in street reconstruction (claim dated Jan. 25, 1930) 1,624.00

(44) J. J. Calish, for removal of sand, etc., on Twenty-seventh avenue between Kirkham and Lawton streets (claim dated Feb. 3, 1930).. 2,250.00

(45) Chas. L. Harney, repairs, fills and bulkheads on Noriega street (claim dated Feb. 3, 1930) 672.50

(46) Pacific Coast Aggregates, Inc., gravel for street reconstruction (claim dated Feb. 3, 1930) 557.73

(47) Pacific Coast Aggregates, Inc., gravel for street reconstruction (claim dated Feb. 3, 1930) 678.69

(48) The Texas Company, gasoline furnished for account of street reconstruction (claim dated Feb. 3, 1930) 692.51

(49) The Fay Improvement Company, seventh payment, improvement of Portola drive from Twenty-fourth street to Fowler avenue (claim dated Feb. 4, 1930) 20,000.00

(50) Granfield, Farrar & Carlin, final payment for surfacing and drainage of Laidley street slide between Mateo and Roanoke streets (claim dated Feb. 5, 1930) 604.45

Municipal Airport.

(51) Meyer Rosenberg, replacing main lighting cable lead at Mills Field, San Francisco Airport (claim dated Feb. 4, 1930) ....$ 613.20

General Fund, 1929-1930.

(52) William J. Quinn, police contingent expense (claim dated Feb. 1, 1930).. $750.00

(53) W. C. Uhte, overhauling and painting Patrol Wagon No. 5 (claim dated Feb. 1, 1930).......................... 800.00

(54) Auto Registration Service, 109,754 registration cards for use of Assessor (claim dated Feb. 3, 1930)........... 625.60

(55) Phillips & Van Orden Co., printing statements for use of the Assessor (claim dated Feb. 3, 1930)............... 1,904.40

(56) Associated Charities, widows' pensions (claim dated Feb. 7, 1930) 7,802.70

(57) Eureka Benevolent Society, widows' pensions (claim dated Feb. 7, 1930)...................................... 946.01

(58) Little Children's Aid, widows' pensions (claim dated 7, 1930) 6,432.49

(59) San Francisco Chronicle, official advertising (claim dated Feb. 10, 1930) 1,404.84

(60) The Recorder Printing & Publishing Company, printing of Supervisors' Calendar, etc. (claim dated Feb. 10, 1930).. 673.63

(61) The Recorder Printing & Publishing Company, printing of Superior Court Calendars, etc. (claim dated Feb. 10, 1930) 515.00

(62) A. P. Jacobs, rent of premises No. 333 Kearny street, February 3 to March 3, 1930 .... 1,120.75

(63) Healy & Donaldson, tobacco furnished Laguna Honda Home (claim dated Jan. 23, 1930)....................... 899.04

(64) Monarch Flour Co, flour for Laguna Honda Home (claim dated Jan. 23, 1930).................................. 1,322.25

(65) C. Nauman & Co., seed potatoes for Laguna Honda Home (claim dated Jan. 23, 1930).......................... 945.33

(66) H. E. Teller Co., coffee for Laguna Honda Home (claim dated Jan. 23, 1930)..................................... 620.00

(67) Dion R. Holm, legal services rendered in connection with telephone litigation, month of February (claim dated Feb. 4, 1930).. 850.00

(68) N. Randall Ellis, engineering services rendered in connection with telephone litigation, month of February (claim dated Feb. 4, 1930)..................................... 750.00

(69) Southern Pacific Company, reimbursement of taxes paid, first installment, 1929-1930, as rental for Lot 4A, Block 3810, occupied by the City and County as Municipal Pipe Yard (claim dated Feb. 10, 1930)........................ 3,665.18

Appropriation for Traffic Engineering.

Also, Resolution No. ———— (New Series), as follows:

Resolved, That the sum of $1,635 be and the same is hereby set aside, appropriated and authorized to be expended out of "Traffic Signals," Budget Item 57, to defray the cost of traffic engineering for the month of February, 1930.

Adopted.

The following resolution was *adopted*:

Auditor to Cancel Duplicate Assessments of Unsecured Personal Property.

On recommendation of Finance Committee.

Resolution No. 32041 (New Series), as follows:

Whereas, the Tax Collector has reported that the following assessments are duplicate assessments for the year 1929 and should be cancelled; therefore,

Resolved, That the Auditor be directed to cancel, in compliance with Section 3805 of the Political Code, the following assessments:

Vol. 15, page 154, line 10, Unsecured Personal Property, assessed to B. H. McCown in the sum of $560. For duplicate see Vol. 11, page 178, line 24, Unsecured Personal Property.

Vol. 15, page 11, line 5, Unsecured Personal Property, assessed to Robert Bush in the sum of $90. For duplicate see Vol. 11, page 84, line 8, Unsecured Personal Property.

Ayes—Supervisors Andriano, Canepa, Colman, Havenner, Hayden, McGovern, McSheehy, Miles, Peyser, Power, Roncovieri, Rossi, Spaulding, Stanton, Suhr—15.

Absent—Supervisors Gallagher, Shannon, Toner—3.

Fixing State Primary Election Day August 26, 1930, as Date for Bond Election to Acquire Properties of Pacific Gas and Electric Company and Great Western Power Company, and Directing City Attorney to Secure Stipulation From Companies That Deferring Election to This Date Will Not Be Considered a Lack of Diligence.

The following recommendation of Joint Committee on Public Utilities and Finance was taken up:

Resolution No. ———— (New Series), as follows:

Whereas, the Board of Supervisors have heretofore initiated proceedings for the purpose of submitting to the people the matter of the acquisition of the properties of the Pacific Gas and Electric Company and of the Great Western Power Company, at the valuation fixed by the State Railroad Commission, and additions thereto caused by additions and betterments made to the properties of the respective companies since the evaluation proceedings were commenced; and

Whereas, it is the desire of the Board of Supervisors to submit the matter of the acquisition of said properties, and the voting of a bonded indebtedness for the purpose of acquiring the same, to the electors of the City and County of San Francisco at such time as will best afford said electors the opportunity of expressing themselves in the matter of the acquisition of said utilities; now, therefore, be it

Resolved, That it is the sense of the Board of Supervisors that when the date for the holding of said election for the purpose of voting a bonded indebtedness to acquire the said properties of the Pacific Gas and Electric Company and Great Western Power Company is fixed by ordinance calling for said election, that the same should be fixed for the date on which the State primary election is held, to-wit: the last Tuesday in August, 1930, provided that said Pacific Gas and Electric Company and Great Western Power Company will stipulate with the City that the deferring of said election until said date shall not be considered a lack of due diligence in calling and holding said election; and be it

Further Resolved, That the City Attorney be and he is hereby directed to obtain, if possible, from each of said companies a stipulation with the City to the effect that the deferring of said election until the date hereinabove set forth shall not be considered a lack of due diligence in calling and holding said election.

Motion.

Supervisor Havenner moved as a substitute for the whole that June 10, 1930, be fixed as the date for the bond election.

Motion *lost* by the following vote:

Ayes—Supervisors Andriano, Gallagher, Havenner, McGovern, McSheehy, Roncovieri, Suhr—7.

Noes—Supervisors Canepa, Colman, Hayden, Miles, Peyser, Power, Rossi, Spaulding, Stanton, Toner—10.

Absent—Supervisor Shannon—1.

Notice of Reconsideration.

Before the result of the foregoing vote was announced Supervisor Havenner changed his vote from *aye* to *no* and gave notice that he would move for reconsideration at next meeting.

Rereferred.

The following bill was presented and, on motion, *rereferred to the Joint Committee on Public Utilities and Finance*:

Prescribing the Procedure Under Which the Board of Public Works Shall Have Charge, Superintendence and Control of the Municipally Owned Water System, and Providing for the Creation of a Water Department, Etc.

Bill No. 8187, Ordinance No. ———— (New Series), as follows:

Setting forth and prescribing the procedure and limitations under which the Board of Public Works shall have charge, superintendence and control of the supplying of water for domestic purposes from the municipally owned and operated water system; providing for the creation of a water department; providing for the organization of the same; prescribing its powers and duties and the manner in which these shall be carried out.

Be it ordained by the People of the City and County of San Francisco as follows:

Section 1. *Direction to Board of Public Works.* The Board of Public Works, in exercising the powers granted to it under Paragraph 8 of Section 9 of Chapter I of Article VI of the Charter, relative to the superintendence and control of the construction, maintenance and operation of the public water supply of San Francisco, shall do so subject to the provisions of this ordinance.

Section 2. *San Francisco Water Department and Purposes and Powers.* The Board of Public Works shall create a Department of Water Supply, for the purpose of supplying water to the inhabitants of the City and County of San Francisco, and to such other persons and places as may hereafter be supplied with water by the City and County of San Francisco, which said department shall be designated as "San Francisco Water Department."

The maintenance and operation of the Spring Valley Water Company system, whenever the same shall come into possession of the City, and also the water system owned by the City and County of San Francisco, commonly known as the County Line Water Works, shall be vested in said San Francisco Water Department under the jurisdiction of the Board of Public Works, until a Charter amendment is adopted and approved providing for the creation of a Public Utilities Commission.

All construction work done in or about the properties of said system, whether for extensions thereto or for additions and betterments thereto, shall be done under the direction and supervision of the City Engineer, and said City Engineer shall from time to time recommend to the Board of Public Works such work as he deems necessary to be performed, or materials or equipment to be furnished, in and about the construction, operation or maintenance of said Water Department. And no extensions, additions or major improvements or replacements to the system shall be made except on the recommendation of the head of the department or the City Engineer.

The Board of Public Works shall establish all necessary rules and regulations for the conduct of the business of the department, and shall have full power and authority to collect any and all amounts due from any consumer for water furnished by said San Francisco Water Department, including all amounts due from any consumer for water furnished by the Spring Valley Water Company and remaining unpaid when the properties of the Spring Valley Water Company are taken

over by the City and County of San Francisco, and the said Board
of Public Works, or the head of the department, shall have full power
and authority to discontinue the service of any consumer who is delinquent to the Spring Valley Water Company or to the Water Department in the payment of amounts due for water furnished to or used
by said consumer, and may by civil action in the name of the City and
County enforce the collection of any and all amounts due for said
water. And said Board may also provide, by rule or by order, for
the requiring of security in such form and in such amount as may
be recommended by the head of the department, for the supplying of
water or rendering service to any person, and the furnishing of said
security may be made a prerequisite to the furnishing of said water
or service.

The Board of Public Works may, by resolution, authorize such banks
in the City and County of San Francisco as it may elect to receive
payment of water bills due or to be collected by the Water Department, and to issue receipts for the same in the name of the department, payment for such service to be at a rate not to exceed five cents
per account per month, and provided that all amounts paid to any
bank or banks selected for the purpose of receiving payment of said
water bills shall be by said banks daily transmitted to the Water Department and by said Water Department paid daily into the Treasury
of the City and County of San Francisco.

The Water Department shall observe all ordinances of the City and
County of San Francisco and rules and regulations of the Department
of Public Works relative to street openings, barricades, excavations,
replacing of pavement, and similar matters, and relative to such matters shall apply for and receive permits and pay the necessary fees for
said permits, and be subject to inspection and regulation, in the same
manner and at the same rates as a private person or corporation would
be if doing or performing any of said work or things.

All rules and regulations adopted or established by the Board of
Public Works for the conduct of said San Francisco Water Department shall, within thirty days after the date of the adoption thereof,
be printed, and shall be available for distribution to the public upon
application therefor.

Section 3. *Organization, Employees.* The Board of Public Works
shall appoint as head of the department, with appropriate title, a chief
executive, who shall possess the necessary executive, administrative
and technical qualifications to administer the affairs of the department, and who shall have sole executive control of said department,
subject to rules and regulations prescribed by the Board.

Employees of the Spring Valley Water Company in the operating
service thereof at the time the properties of said company are taken
over by the City, and who have been continuously employed in said
operating service for not less than one year immediately prior to the
taking over of said properties, shall be continued in their positions
and shall be considered to have been appointed to such positions under
the provisions of Article XIII of the Charter, and shall be entitled to
all civil service rights therein provided, and shall thereafter be considered employees of San Francisco Water Department. That if any
of said employees in said operating department of said Spring Valley
Water Company do not, at the time the properties of said company are
taken over by the City, possess the residential qualifications required
by Section 2 of Article XVI of the Charter, they shall be allowed a
period of one year within which to acquire the same, and any employee
not acquiring said residential qualifications within said period shall
be dismissed from his or her employment. All positions in the Water
Department shall be classified and graded by the Civil Service Commission as provided by the Charter, and vacancies in any of said
positions shall be filled, and promotions in said department shall be
made, as provided by Article XIII of the Charter and in accordance
with the rules and regulations of the Civil Service Commission.

The Board shall employ such engineers, superintendents, accountants, inspectors and other assistants and employees as the department head may certify to be necessary. All of said appointments shall be made in accordance with the provisions of Article XIII of the Charter and the rules and regulations of the Civil Service Commission, provided that temporary appointments made under the provisions of Section 10 of said article shall, pursuant to the provisions of said article, remain in force for a period not exceeding sixty (60) days and only until regular appointments can be made under the provisions of said article, and said appointments shall be limited to a period of sixty (60) days and shall not be subject to renewal.

Section 4. *Salaries of Present Employees of Spring Valley Water Company.* The salaries, wages and compensation of all employees of the Spring Valley Water Company, whose employment shall continue in force with the San Francisco Water Department, as hereinbefore set forth, shall be subject to standardization as provided in Section 14, Chapter II, Article II, of the Charter. That, pending the standardization of said wages, salaries and compensation, there shall be paid to said employees at least the minimum entrance salary, wage or compensation paid for similar service in any other utility at present being operated by the Board of Public Works, and if there are any positions or places of employment in said Water Department which are not common with those in said other utilities, then the compensation to be paid to said employees occupying said last-mentioned positions shall be at least the minimum entrance wage or compensation paid for similar service in other departments of the city government, provided that such minimum entrance rate in the clerical service shall not be less than $150 per month. Provided, however, that the salary, wage or compensation of any employee whose employment is continued in the Water Department shall not be reduced below the salary, wage or compensation which said employee received from the Spring Valley Water Company, as evidenced by its January, 1930, payroll, unless the duties of said employee have been diminished on his coming into the employment of the Water Department, or said salary, wage or compensation exceeds the maximum amount paid by the city for like service.

Section 5. *Accounts, Reports and Adjustments.* The accounts of the Water Department shall be maintained in accordance with the forms and requirements of the State Railroad Commission for water companies of similar character, in so far as said forms and requirements shall be applicable to a municipally-owned water system, and said accounts shall also show all matters and things provided to be shown or set up by Subdivision 3, Section 16, Article XII, of the Charter.

A complete operating statement, showing all the operations, receipts and disbursements of the Water Department for the previous month, shall be filed each month by the head of the department with the Board of Public Works, and with the Mayor, and with the Board of Supervisors, and the same shall be open for inspection by the public in the office of said Board of Public Works. In addition to the matters hereinbefore set forth, said statements shall show the increase or decrease in the number of employees of the Department since the end of the preceding month.

Commencing July 1, 1930, all amounts due to the Water Department for water used by or furnished to the other departments of the city, as well as all charges or rental for hydrant service, shall be carried on the books of the Water Department at the current rates provided for said water or for said service; and before the end of each fiscal year the Water Department shall determine the amount of taxes which would have been payable at the rate for the current year to the City and County upon the properties of the Water Department, if said properties were privately owned, and said amount of taxes shall offset any amounts which said accounts may show to be due for water or service from said municipal departments, in so far as the amount of said taxes and the amount due for water equal one another; and if the amount shown to be due for said water or for said service shall exceed the amount which would have been due for taxes if said property of said department was privately owned, the overplus shall be paid from the General or other funds of the City and County to the said Water Department, and charged against the various departments in accordance with the water and service furnished to each.

In making its annual budget each year, pursuant to the provisions of the Charter, the Board of Supervisors shall estimate the amount which shall become due from the other departments of the city government to the Water Department in the succeeding fiscal year, by reason of any difference between the amounts due for water and the amount of taxes which would be collected if the property of said Water Depart. ment was privately owned, and shall in said budget make provision for such difference.

During the remainder of the fiscal year 1929-1930, water shall be furnished without charge to those departments of the municipality to which appropriations have been made to defray the cost of water or hydrant service furnished to any of said departments, and water or service furnished to any other department shall be paid for at the current rates.

Commencing with the fiscal year 1930-1931, there shall be payable from the Water Department the sum of $250,000 per year as rental for the transbay Hetch Hetchy aqueduct, which said sum shall be payable into the 1910 Hetch Hetchy Bond Interest Fund, and for the remainder of the fiscal year the Water Department shall pay into said fund such portion of said sum of $250,000 as shall not have been paid as rental for said aqueduct for said year.

Section 6. *Budgets.* Not later than April 1, in the year 1930, and during the month of February in each succeeding year, the head of the Water Department shall transmit to the Board of Public Works a proposed budget for the next fiscal year, which said budget shall show in detail the estimated amounts of revenue from all sources to the department for said year, as well as an estimate of all amounts to be paid out by said department for all purposes, including payments to and from the various reserve and sinking funds maintained by said department. Such estimate, both of receipts and disbursements, shall be segregated and itemized so as to show the exact purpose of each item therein, and the amounts for salaries and wages shall be itemized so as to show the compensation paid to each class of employees, and the number of said employees in each class. Provided, however, that in estimating the cost of construction work, in the performance of which the employees will not be of a permanent character, the estimated number of said employees to be employed thereon need not be set forth. Said budget shall be prepared and transmitted to the Board of Public Works in quadruplicate.

The Board of Public Works shall consider said proposed budget, and upon approval of the same, shall transmit a copy thereof, with such changes, if any, indicated thereon, to the Mayor, and another to the Board of Supervisors, and another to the Auditor, which said copies shall be so transmitted not later than the first Monday in April of each year.

The Finance Committee of the Board of Supervisors shall submit said budget with its annual budget report to the Board, together with such recommendations as it deems proper. and said Board of Supervisors may reduce the estimate of expenditures or any item thereof. except proposed expenditures or appropriations as may be by law or by their nature fixed; and, subject, to such changes or reductions. said Board shall approve and adopt said budget at the same time at which the annual budget provided by Charter must be adopted, and shall thereupon transmit the same to the Auditor.

The adoption of said budget by the Board of Supervisors shall be considered an appropriation of the various amounts therein contained for the purposes therein set forth, and thereafter said sums so appropriated may be expended by the Board of Public Works, in the manner provided by law, for the purposes for which they are appropriated, without further order of the Board of Supervisors.

Expenditures or commitments in excess of amounts set up in the budget adopted as hereinbefore provided, or for purposes not therein specified, may be made only by the filing and adopting at any time in the manner as specified hereinbefore for each annual budget and within the estimated revenues of the department, of a supplemental budget for such additional expenditures; provided, however, that in case of an emergency involving the protection of life or property, emergency expenditures may be ordered and authorized by the head of the department, in which case full report to the Board of Public Works, with copy thereof to the Board of Supervisors and the Auditor, shall be made at the earliest possible time, together with an estimate of the additional cost, if any, of further expenditures occasioned by the emergency.

Temporary Budget. As soon after March 1st, 1930, as is possible, the head of the Department shall file with the Board of Public Works a budget of the estimated revenues and proposed expenditures of the Water Department for the period from March 3rd to June 30th, 1930, and the Board of Public Works shall act upon the same without delay and transmit one copy thereof as approved to the Mayor, and two copies thereof to the Board of Supervisors. Said budget, in so far as possible, shall be prepared in accordance with the provisions hereinbefore set forth relating to annual budgets in so far as said provisions may be applicable, provided that said budget shall show the number, title and rate of compensation of the employees of the Spring Valley Water Company immediately prior to the date on which the properties of said Company were taken over by the City, as well as the number, civil service title and proposed rates of compensation of said employees while in the employ of the Water Department. Upon receipt of said budget the Board of Supervisors shall act upon the same within ten days after receipt of same, and when the said budget is approved by said Board of Supervisors one copy of the same shall be transmitted to the Auditor with the approval of the Board attached thereto, and when so received by said Auditor the same shall be his authority for auditing any demands against the Water Department as set forth or included in said budget; and if said budget should not be received by said Auditor in due time to enable him to audit the demands of the employees of said Water Department as the same become due, the said Auditor may audit and the Treasurer pay the demands of said employees when they are approved by the head of the Water Department, the Board of Public Works, and the Civil Service Commission, as being in conformity with the provisions of Section 4 of this ordinance, and appropriation in an amount sufficient to pay said demands as so approved is hereby made from the revenues of said Water Department as the said revenues accrue.

Section 7. *Operating Expenses and Reserves.* The receipts from operation of the San Francisco Water Department shall be paid daily into the City Treasury and maintained in a special fund set aside therefor, which shall be designated "The Water Revenue Fund," and appropriations may from time to time be made by the Board of Supervisors from said receipts for the purposes in this section set forth and in accordance with budgets to be made as hereinbefore provided and as otherwise provided in this ordinance.

1. For the payment of the operating expenses of the water supply system, including expenditures or appropriations to reserves, pension charges, compensation insurance, injuries, damages, Hetch Hetchy aqueduct rental and taxes that may be assessed against property outside of San Francisco belonging to the City and under the control of the Water Department.

2. For repairs and reconstruction, and in order to provide properly for repairs and reconstruction due to depreciation, there shall be

created and established a depreciation reserve which shall be credited monthly with an amount equal to one-twelfth the annual depreciation requirements determined as elsewhere herein provided.

3. For the payment of interest and sinking fund on the bonds issued for the acquisition of the Spring Valley Water system, and for this purpose there shall be set aside monthly and transferred to the Spring Valley bond interest and redemption funds sums sufficient in the aggregate to meet, at the proper time, all interest and redemption charges against said utility as the same fall due.

4. For extensions, improvements and replacements, and in order to properly finance the necessary extensions, improvements and replacements out of earnings, there shall be established a Water Extension Reserve Fund, into which shall be paid monthly the sums necessary to provide for such extensions, improvements and replacements as may have been determined upon in a program adopted as elsewhere herein provided.

5. For the Charter Reserve Fund.

The Depreciation Reserve Fund shall be used only to cover costs of replacements due to a realized depreciation. The Board of Public Works shall cause an appraisal to be made by the City Engineer of the several classes of property involved in the Water System as to life and the amount of accrued depreciation, and determine the amount of the reasonable annual depreciation requirements necessary in order to provide properly for repairs or reconstruction due to realized physical and functional depreciation; provided, however, that at least every five years the Board shall cause a reappraisal to be made of the depreciation reserves, replacement expenditures therefrom, and probable useful life of each of the several kinds of property, and on the basis of such reappraisal shall redetermine the amount of the reasonable annual depreciation requirements. Provided, that the amount to be set aside each year into said depreciation fund shall be subject to budget by the Board of Supervisors. Until such time as the Board of Public Works has determined the reasonable annual depreciation requirements necessary by appraisal as above provided for, there shall be transferred to the Depreciation Reserve Fund from the receipts from operation of the Water Department at the end of each month, the sum of $5,000.

The Water Extension Reserve Fund shall be used only to cover costs of the construction of extensions, additions and betterments to the water system. The Board of Public Works upon the recommendation of the head of the Water Department shall from time to time establish a program of the necessary extensions, additions and betterments required in a period not extending over five years, and upon the approval of said program or any amendments thereto by the Board of Supervisors in any annual or supplemental budget, there shall be deposited monthly to the credit of the Extension Reserve one-twelfth of the annual contribution determined as necessary to complete the several elements of the program within the time required, provided, that for the first five years of operation the amount to be appropriated to the depreciation fund and the Water Extension Reserve Fund, considered together, shall be not less than $564,000 per year.

There shall be paid into the Charter Reserve Fund provided for in Subdivision 5, Section 7 of this ordinance all moneys not otherwise appropriated or used in conformity with the provisions of this ordinance, and the Board of Supervisors may from time to time make appropriations from said fund for any of the purposes provided for in this ordinance when respective funds herein provided for any of the specific purposes herein set forth are exhausted or insufficient to meet the demands upon them. Whenever the said Charter Reserve Fund shall exceed one-half of the payment for operating expenses in the preceding year, the Board of Supervisors may appropriate such excess to the General Fund of the City.

At any time that there is a surplus on deposit in the city treasury in any of the several funds herein provided for in an amount greater than is necessary for the immediate needs of the Water Department, the said department, through the Board of Public Works, shall notify the Treasurer, who shall make arrangements as provided by law for the proper investment or deposit of such funds, the interest accruing therefrom to be credited to the benefit of and to be applied to the fund from which invested.

Section 8. *Water Rates.* No water shall be furnished to any con-sumer, except as hereinbefore set forth, except at the current rates therefor fixed as in this section provided. The water rates in effect under the Spring Valley Water Company's management at the time of the City's acquisition of the system shall remain in effect for a period of at least one year. Thereafter, changes in the water rates shall only be made by the Board of Public Works upon the written recommendation of the head of the department and the approval of the Board of Supervisors.

No rates shall be established which in the aggregate will produce a revenue less than that necessary to safely cover all operating expenses and other expenses provided for in Section 6 hereof, and provide for and maintain the several reserves herein provided for and also to maintain the Charter reserve at a sum equal to one-half of the operat-ing expenses for the preceding year.

When any change in rates is contemplated, the head of the depart-ment shall submit to the Board of Public Works a financial report, in support of the proposed change, and the Board of Public Works shall fix a date for hearing the matter of said change in rates and cause to be published in the official newspaper of the City and County notice of said hearing at least ten days prior to the date thereof, specifying in said notice the time and place of said hearing. At said hearing any person, on behalf of himself or others interested, may be heard, or present in writing his views, after which the Board shall fix the rates and submit them to the Board of Supervisors, who shall within thirty days, by ordinance, approve or disapprove the same. Failure of the Board of Supervisors to act within the thirty days shall be con-strued as approval of the recommended rates. In fixing rates for water service, the same may be fixed at varying scales for different classes of service or consumers.

Section 9. *Service by Other Departments.* Services rendered by any other department of the City and County to the Water Depart-ment, upon request of the Water Department, shall be paid for by the Water Department at cost out of its revenues.

Section 10. *City Attorney.* The City Attorney shall be the legal ad-viser of the Department and shall render such legal services as the Board of Public Works or the head of the Department may deem nec-essary, and shall prosecute and defend all actions or proceedings af-fecting or involving the Water Department or any of its properties. He shall when necessary, upon the request of the Board of Public Works, appoint and detail one or more attorneys to perform the duties herein specified, and the compensation of said attorneys so detailed shall be approved by the Board of Public Works and fixed by the Board of Su-pervisors, and shall be paid from the revenues of the Water Depart-ment as an operating expense thereof.

Section 11. *Bonds of Employees.* The Board of Public Works may require a bond of indemnity from any of the employees of the Water Department, conditioned for the faithful performance of the duties of said employee or employees, and for the purpose of obtaining said bonds the said Board of Public Works may contract with any surety company authorized to write said bonds, to furnish the same, either for individual employees of groups thereof, and the cost of the same shall be charged as an operating expense of said Water Department.

Section 12. *Payment of Salaries and Wages.* Payrolls for all employees of the Water Department shall be segregated and made up according to the assembly or distribution points for the various employments, as determined by the head of the department, and each of said payrolls shall be approved as required by law and transmitted to the Auditor. Upon the approval of the items on said payroll or payrolls the Auditor shall issue his separate demand upon the Treasurer for each of the items thereon in the form provided for the payment of salaries in other departments of the city, and the same, with the respective payrolls for which said demands are issued, shall be delivered to such person as the head of the department shall, in writing filed with the Auditor, authorize to receive the same, and upon the delivery of the same said person shall receipt to said Auditor for said payrolls and said demands. The head of the department shall thereupon cause said demands to be delivered to the respective payees named therein at, or as near as possible to, the places of employment of said employees.

Section 13. *Revolving Fund.* For the purpose of paying petty expenses of the Water Department, and for making such other payments as cannot be conveniently paid by demands drawn upon the Treasurer and approved by the Auditor, the Water Department shall maintain in such bank or banks as may be designated by the Board of Public Works, a fund of $20,000, from which fund said petty expenses and other payments that cannot be conveniently paid by demands drawn upon the Treasurer shall be paid by check drawn by the head of the department or by such other persons in the employ of said department as the head of said department may authorize. The head of the department shall, from time to time, and at least once in each month, transmit to the Auditor a demand in favor of said fund for all amounts disbursed from it, to which demand shall be attached receipts for all payments so made, which said receipts shall show the name of the person receiving any payment from said fund, as well as the purpose for which said payment was made, and shall be signed by the party receiving said payment. When said demand is approved by the Auditor and paid by the Treasurer, it shall be delivered to the head of the Water Department and deposited to the credit of said fund. The Board of Supervisors shall appropriate the said sum of $20,000 for such fund, and may, from time to time, make such additional appropriations thereto from the revenues of said department as said Board shall deem proper.

Section 14. *Purchase of Materials, Supplies and Equipment.* Purchases of materials, supplies and equipment required by Water Department operations shall be made in accordance with the provisions of Chapter IV, Article II, and Section 6, Chapter I, Article III, of the Charter, and of Ordinance 5880 (New Series); provided, however, that specifications may be prepared under the direction of the head of the Water Department for all equipment required by the department, or for materials or supplies peculiar to said department operations and not in common use in other departments of the City and County, and the head of the department may designate the particular brand, kind or make of any equipment which may be necessary in the conduct of said department.

Section 15. *Constitutionality.* If any section, subsection, subdivision or provision of this ordinance is for any reason held to be unconstitutional, such decision shall not affect the validity of the remaining portions of this ordinance, the Board of Supervisors hereby declaring that it would have passed this ordinance and each section, subsection, subdivision, provision, sentence, clause and phrase thereof irrespective of the fact that any one or more sections, subsections, subdivisions, provisions, sentences, clauses or phrases hereof are declared unconstitutional.

Section 16. This ordinance shall become effective immediately upon its passage.

Adopted.

The following resolution was *adopted*:

City Attorney Requested to Submit Legislation for Creation of Athletic Commission.

On recommendation of Public Welfare and Finance Committees jointly.

Resolution No. 32042 (New Series), as follows:

Whereas, the various forms of athletic activity have become a part of the life of the people of San Francisco; and

Whereas, the major forms, such as football and golf and baseball, have grown to such a degree as to call into action the numerous departments of the City government as well as officials of different organizations, for the proper handling of said contests; be it, therefore,

Resolved, That the City Attorney is respectfully requested to prepare and submit to this Board of Supervisors the proper ordinance or the proper form of legislation for the initiation of an athletic commission of the City and County of San Francisco, to have charge of all public athletic contests.

Ayes—Supervisors Andriano, Canepa, Colman, Havenner, Hayden, McGovern, McSheehy, Miles, Peyser, Power, Roncovieri, Rossi, Spaulding, Stanton, Suhr—15.

Absent—Supervisors Gallagher, Shannon, Toner—3.

Passed for Printing.

The following resolutions were *passed for printing*:

Oil and Boiler Permits.

On recommendation of Fire Committee.

Resolution No. ———— (New Series), as follows:

Resolved, That the following revocable permits be and are hereby granted:

Oil Tanks.

A. L. Matthew, 434 Leavenworth street, 1500 gallons capacity.

G. Molinari, 1516 Larkin street, 1500 gallons capacity.

A. Depaoli, west side of Dartmouth street, 100 feet north of Woolsey streets, 1500 gallons capacity.

L. Kroner, 158 Jordan avenue, 1500 gallons capacity.

Boiler.

James Allan & Sons, south side Evans avenue, 200 feet east of Third street, 50 horsepower.

The rights granted under this resolution shall be exercised within six months, otherwise said permit shall become null and void.

Auto Supply Station Permit, Edw. J. O'Neill, Lombard and Lyon Streets.

Also, Resolution No. ———— (New Series), as follows:

Resolved, That Edw. J. O'Neill be and is hereby granted permission, revocable at will of the Board of Supervisors, to have transferred to him automobile supply station permit heretofore granted Sidney Franklin by Resolution No. 27269 (New Series) for premises at southeast corner of Lombard and Lyon streets.

The rights granted under this resolution shall be exercised within six months, otherwise said permit shall become null and void.

Auto Supply Station Permit, Luis Whiteman, San Jose Avenue and Dolores Street.

Also, Resolution No. ———— (New Series), as follows:

Resolved, That Luis Whiteman be and is hereby granted permission, revocable at will of the Board of Supervisors, to have transferred to him automobile supply station permit heretofore granted Luigi Bacigalupi by Resolution No. 31318 (New Series) for premises on gore of San Jose avenue and Dolores street.

The rights granted under this resolution shall be exercised within six months, otherwise said permit shall become null and void.

Auto Supply Station Permit, W. H. Woodfield, Jr., Bartlett and Twenty-second Streets.

Also, Resolution No. ———— (New Series), as follows:

Resolved, That Wm. H. Woodfield, Jr., be and is hereby granted permission, revocable at will of the Board of Supervisors, to maintain and operate an automobile supply station on the northwest corner of Bartlett and Twenty-second streets.

The rights granted under this resolution shall be exercised within six months, otherwise said permit shall become null and void.

Auto Supply Station Permit, Twin Peaks Parlor No. 214, Twenty-fourth and Diamond Streets.

Also, Resolution No. ———— (New Series), as follows:

Resolved, That Twin Peaks Parlor 214, Native Sons of the Golden West, be and is hereby granted permission, revocable at will of the Board of Supervisors, to maintain and operate an automobile supply station on the southeast corner of Twenty-fourth and Diamond streets.

The rights granted under this resolution shall be exercised within six months, otherwise said permit shall become null and void.

Adopted.

The following resolutions were *adopted*:

Masquerade Ball Permit, San Francisco Maennerchor, California Hall, Polk and Turk Streets, Saturday, February 22, 1930.

On recommendation of Police Committee.

Resolution No. 32043 (New Series), as follows:

Resolved, That San Francisco Maennerchor be and it is hereby granted permission to conduct masquerade ball at California Hall, Polk and Turk streets, Saturday, February 22, 1930.

Ayes—Supervisors Andriano, Canepa, Colman, Havenner, Hayden, McGovern, McSheehy, Miles, Peyser, Power, Roncovieri, Rossi, Spaulding, Stanton, Suhr—15.

Absent—Supervisors Gallagher, Shannon, Toner—3.

Masquerade Ball Permit, Green Valley Grove No. 145, U. A. O. D., Corinthian Hall, 4793 Mission Street, Sunday, March 9, 1930.

Also, Resolution No. 32044 (New Series), as follows:

Resolved, That Green Valley Grove No. 145, "Druids," be and it is hereby granted permission to conduct masquerade ball at Corinthian Hall, 4793 Mission street, Sunday, March 9, 1930.

Ayes—Supervisors Andriano, Canepa, Colman, Havenner, Hayden, McGovern, McSheehy, Miles, Peyser, Power, Roncovieri, Rossi, Spaulding, Stanton, Suhr—15.

Absent—Supervisors Gallagher, Shannon, Toner—3.

Passed for Printing.

The following resolution was *passed for printing*:

Condemnation for the Acquisition of Lands for School Purposes, Located at Morse Street, Southwest from Lowell Street, for Longfellow School.

On recommendation of Public Buildings and Lands Committee.

Resolution No. ———— (New Series), as follows:

Resolved, By the Board of Supervisors of the City and County of San Francisco, that public interest and necessity require the acquisition by the City and County of San Francisco, a municipal corporation, of the following property, situated in the City and County of San Francisco, State of California, more particularly described as follows, to-wit:

Commencing at a point on the southeasterly line of Morse street, distant thereon 267 feet southwesterly from the southwesterly line of Lowell street, running thence southwesterly along the said southeasterly line of Morse street 168 feet; thence at a right angle southeasterly 213 feet; thence at a right angle northeasterly 178 feet; thence at a right angle northwesterly 213 feet to the southeasterly line of Morse street and point of commencement. Being a portion of Blocks 51, 52, 58 and 96, West End Homestead Association, also known as Lots Nos. 26, 27, 28, 29 and 30, in Block 6474, on Assessor's Map Book. Be it

Further Resolved, That said property is suitable, adaptable, necessary and required for the public use of said City and County of San Francisco, to-wit: For school purposes. It is necessary that a fee simple title be taken for such use.

The City Attorney is hereby ordered and directed to commence proceedings in eminent domain against the owners of said parcel of land and of any and all interest therein, or claims thereto, for the condemnation thereof for the public use of the City and County of San Francisco, as aforesaid.

Rereferred.

The following resolution was, on motion, *rereferred to the Public Utilities Committee*:

Endorsing the Applications of the Peninsula Rapid Transit Company and the Pacific Auto Stages, Inc., for Permission to Reroute a Portion of Their Motor Coach Lines via the Bayshore Highway and Instructing the City Attorney to Appear Before the Railroad Commission in Behalf of Said Applications.

Resolution No. ———— (New Series), as follows:

Whereas, the Peninsula Rapid Transit Company and the Pacific Auto Stages, Inc., now operating motor coach lines from San Francisco to San Jose, have applied for permission to reroute a portion of their service via the Bay Shore Highway; and

Whereas, these companies have pioneered the motor transportation industry on the peninsula and have rendered adequate service; and

Whereas, there is at present no motor coach service for the people and communities situated on the Bay Shore Highway; and

Whereas, such service would be a great advantage to the people and communities of the Bay Shore Highway in general and to the San Francisco Municipal Airport (Mills Field) in particular; therefore, be it

Resolved, That the Board of Supervisors of the City and County of San Francisco does hereby endorse the applications of the Peninsula Rapid Transit Company and the Pacific Auto Stages, Inc., and urges the Honorable Railroad Commission of the State of California to grant the same; and be it

Further Resolved, That the City Attorney, as the official representative of the Board of Supervisors, be instructed to be present in the courtroom of the California Railroad Commission in San Francisco on February 18, 1930, and to appear as a witness in behalf of said applications.

Adopted.

The following resolution was *adopted*:

Acceptance of Resignation of Bartlett Stephens, Acting and Assistant Superintendent of Mills Field Municipal Airport.

On recommendation of Airport Committee.

Resolution No. 32045 (New Series), as follows:

Resolved, That the resignation of Bartlett Stephens as Acting and Assistant Superintendent of Mills Field Municipal Airport be and the same is hereby accepted, effective January 22, 1930.

Ayes—Supervisors Andriano, Canepa, Colman, Gallagher, Havenner, Hayden, McGovern, McSheehy, Miles, Peyser, Power, Roncovieri, Rossi, Spaulding, Stanton, Suhr—16.

Absent—Supervisors Shannon, Toner—2.

Captain Roy N. Francis Appointed Superintendent of Mills Field Municipal Airport.

Whereupon, Supervisor Spaulding moved the adoption of the following resolution:

Resolution No. ————— (New Series), as follows:

Resolved, That Captain Roy N. Francis be and he is hereby appointed Superintendent of Mills Field Municipal Airport, effective February 1, 1930.

Action Deferred.

Supervisor Gallagher, seconded by Supervisor McSheehy, moved as an amendment that the resolution lay over one week.

Amendment *carried* by the following vote:

Ayes—Supervisors Andriano, Canepa, Colman, Gallagher, Havenner, McGovern, McSheehy, Rossi, Suhr—9.

Noes—Supervisors Hayden, Miles, Peyser, Power, Roncovieri, Spaulding—6.

Absent—Supervisors Shannon, Stanton, Toner—3.

Rereferred.

The following resolution was *rereferred to the Finance Committee:*

Fixing Salary of Superintendent of Airport.

Resolution No. ————— (New Series), as follows:

Resolved, That the salary of Captain Roy N. Francis, Superintendent of the Mills Field Municipal Airport, be and is hereby fixed at $500 per month, effective February 1, 1930.

Action Deferred.

On motion of Supervisor Andriano the following resolution was *laid over one week*:

Airport Committee to Appoint Advisory Committee.

Resolution No. ————— (New Series), as follows:

Resolved, That the Airport and Aeronautics Committee be and is hereby authorized to select and appoint an Advisory Committee, to consist of citizens whose cooperation, advice and counsel, by reason of their training, experience and knowledge of aviation, would be of value and assistance to the Committee in the operation and management of Mills Field Municipal Airport; and be it

Further Resolved, That Resolution No. 30712 (New Series) be and the same is hereby repealed.

Adopted.

The following resolutions were *adopted*:

Award of Contract, Sugar.

On recommendation of Supplies Committee.

Resolution No. 32046 (New Series), as follows:

Resolved, That award of contract be hereby made to Sussman, Wormser & Co. on bid submitted February 3, 1930 (Proposal No. 554), for furnishing the following, viz.:

Sugar. Definite quantities for immediate delivery f. o. b. vendor's establishment. Sugar, beet, dry granulated, white, in 100-pound sacks.

Department	No. of Sacks
Laguna Honda Home	500
San Francisco Hospital	450
Emergency Hospitals	6
S. F. Health Farm	20
County Jail No. 1	25
County Jail No. 2	45
City Prison	12
Juvenile Detention Home	6
Total	1064

Price per 100 pounds, $4.997.

Resolved, That this contract not being a term award, no bond is required.

Resolved, That all other bids submitted thereon be rejected.

Ayes—Supervisors Andriano, Canepa, Colman, Gallagher, Havenner, Hayden, McGovern, McSheehy, Miles, Peyser, Power, Roncovieri, Rossi, Spaulding, Stanton, Suhr, Toner—17.

Absent—Supervisor Shannon—1.

Award of Contract, Padlocks.

Also, Resolution No. 32047 (New Series), as follows:

Resolved, That award of contract be hereby made to Dunham, Carrigan & Hayden Co. on bid submitted December 2, 1929 (Proposal No. 540), for furnishing the following, viz.: Padlocks for School Department.

5200 padlocks, keyless, Eagle No. 04942, with rivets depressed and face like sample No. T1 at $0.54 each.

Construction: Solid brass. Baked enamel dial in black with impressed white enamel markings.

Size: Diameter of case 1¾ inches; diameter of staple ¼ inch, length of staple 1 inch.

Resolved, That said contractor shall be required to sign a contract to be drawn by the City Attorney and said contractor shall file a bond in the amount of $2,000 for faithful performance of contract.

Resolved, That all other bids submitted thereon be rejected.

Ayes—Supervisors Andriano, Canepa, Colman, Gallagher, Havenner, Hayden, McGovern, McSheehy, Miles, Peyser, Power, Roncovieri, Rossi, Spaulding, Stanton, Suhr, Toner—17.

Absent—Supervisor Shannon—1.

Referred.

The following recommendation of Traffic and Safety Committee was, on motion of Supervisor Rossi, *referred to the Finance Committee*:

Approval of Traffic Control Budget.

Resolution No. ———— (New Series), as follows:

Whereas, the Board of Public Works has submitted a budget of expenditures for Traffic Control. for the five remaining months of the fiscal year, which budget has the approval of the Traffic Committee, the Police Department, the Traffic Law Enforcement Board and the California State Automobile Association; now, therefore, be it

Resolved, That the budget as submitted be approved, with the understanding that the several amounts specified are not to be construed as appropriations, and with the further understanding that the Board of Public Works will request appropriations in accordance with this budget setup, as the occasion may arise.

1. Painting (curb and pavement markings).................$ 7,000
2. Traffic signs (no parking, school zones, slow, warning, non-illuminated arterial and other traffic direction markings) 5,000

3. Turning buttons: Installing 1000 buttons and moving 500
   buttons 1,000
4. New Safety Zones:
   Installing 350 plain buttons ....$ 210
   Purchase 200 reflector type buttons............. 1,000
   Install 100 reflector type buttons.............   70

   _____

        Total   1,380
5. Maintenance of Safety Zones:
   (a) Replacing reflector type safety zone buttons
   with buttons containing new reflectors. Hauling buttons with broken reflectors to the yard,
   and installing new reflectors, 200 at 85 cents..$ 170
   (b) Installing new type reflector buttons on
   heavy traffic streets, 100 at 70 cents..........   70

   _____

        Total   240
6. Installing approximately 53,000 pedestrian lane markers
   at 7½ cents   4,000
7. Maintenance of illuminated stop signs, beacons and reflectors other than safety zone reflectors and reflectors
   maintained by C. S. A. A. (material only)..............   900
8.. Division of Street Traffic Engineering   8,508

   _____

        Subtotal $28,028
9. Illumination of concrete safety zones—Immediate importance (portion of cost from Traffic Fund):
   1. Laguna and Market streets.........................
   2. Haight, Gough and Market streets...................
   3. Van Ness avenue and Geary street..................
   4. South side Valencia street at Mission (including concrete work for new raised safety zone)...............$ 1,000
10. Curb cut-backs at (first importance; portion of cost from
    Traffic Fund):
    1. Examiner Building and at de Young Building........
    2. Southeast corner New Montgomery and Market streets
    3. Southeast corner Main and Market streets..........
    4. Northeast corner Taylor and Market streets.........
    5. Northeast corner Stockton and Market streets........
    6. Pedestrian safety island at Grant avenue and Market
    street   1,000
11. Installation, maintenance and electric current standard
    arterial stop signs   14,248

   _____

        Grand total $44,276

Adopted.

The following resolutions were *adopted*:

Passenger Loading Zones.

On recommendation of Traffic and Safety Committee:

Resolution No. 32048 (New Series), as follows:

Resolved, That the following list of passenger loading zones, of the lengths specified, be established in front of or near the following addresses, in accordance with the provisions of Section No. 36 of Ordinance No. 7691 (New Series), as amended:

160 Eddy street, 18 feet—Hotel William Penn.
1355 Franklin street, 27 feet—Century Club.
142-146 Kearny street, 18 feet—Sutter Hotel.
34 Turk street, 18 feet—Dalt Hotel.

Ayes—Supervisors Andriano, Canepa, Colman, Gallagher, Havenner,

Hayden, McGovern, McSheehy, Miles, Peyser, Power, Roncovieri, Rossi, Spaulding, Stanton, Suhr, Toner—17.

Absent—Supervisor Shannon—1.

Rescinding and Reestablishing Loading Zones.

Also, Resolution No. 32049 (New Series), as follows:

Resolved, That the following loading zones, of the lengths specified, be rescinded and reestablished as specified herein, in front of or near the following addresses, in accordance with the provisions of Section No. 36 of Ordinance No. 7691 (New Series), as amended:

142-146 Kearny street, 27 feet (rescinded)—Sutter Hotel.

1034 Market street, 27 feet, new length 36 feet—Six small stores; San Christina Building.

1008 Mission street, 27 feet, new length 36 feet—T. Rickey Wholesale Tobacco Co.; Nu-On Products Co.

1012 Mission street, 27 feet (rescinded)—Puresh Nursery Co.

18-24 Turk street, 18 feet, new length 27 feet—Leighton Dairy Lunch; one elevator.

42-48 Turk street, 36 feet, new length 27 feet—Wm. F. Heinz, tailor; Deckelman Bros.; one elevator.

512-514 Washington street, 36 feet (rescinded)—Sevin-Vincent Seed Company.

Ayes—Supervisors Andriano, Canepa, Colman, Gallagher, Havenner, Hayden, McGovern, McSheehy, Miles, Peyser, Power, Roncovieri, Rossi, Spaulding, Stanton, Suhr, Toner—17.

Absent—Supervisor Shannon—1.

Loading Zones.

Also, Resolution No. 32050 (New Series), as follows:

Resolved, That the following list of loading zones, of the lengths specified, be established in front of or near the following addresses, in accordance with the provisions of Section 36 of Ordinance No. 7691 (New Series), as amended:

501 Folsom street, 27 feet—Gimbal Candy Factory; one elevator; one oil intake.

141 Fourth street, 18 feet—Fourth Street Lunch; Bridgeway Garage; two oil intakes.

132-140 Kearny street, 18 feet—Eagleson's Co.; Royal Shoe Co.; tailor; two stores.

220-228 McAllister street, 36 feet—Presbyterian Book Co.; Woodbridge Bldg.; California Law Book Co.

315 Pine street, 36 feet—S. F. Stock Exchange.

155 Sansome street, 36 feet—S. F. Stock Exchange; two elevators.

645 Stockton street, 18 feet—Town House Apts.

1403 Sutter street, 18 feet—Century Club, tradesmen's entrance.

101-103 Turk street, 27 feet—Wakelee's drug warehouse; one elevator.

508-510 Washington street, 27 feet—A. L. Hettreck Shell Imp. Co.; one elevator.

310 Sansome street, 27 feet—Alaska Commercial Bldg.

Ayes—Supervisors Andriano, Canepa, Colman, Gallagher, Havenner, Hayden, McGovern, McSheehy, Miles, Peyser, Power, Roncovieri, Rossi, Spaulding, Stanton, Suhr, Toner—17.

Absent—Supervisor Shannon—1.

ROLL CALL FOR THE INTRODUCTION OF RESOLUTIONS, BILLS AND COMMUNICATIONS NOT CONSIDERED OR REPORTED UPON BY A COMMITTEE.

Commendation of Drs. Coffey and Humber on Cancer Treatment Discovery.

Supervisor McSheehy presented:

Resolution No. ———— (New Series), as follows:

Whereas, the medical world of scientific research has been aroused by the startling announcement of a treatment for cancer; and

Whereas, to Doctors Walter B. Coffey and John B. Humber of San Francisco is due the honor and glory of the extraordinary discovery; and

Whereas, the validity of the claim has been substantiated by numerous cures, so as to place it beyond the realm of theory; be it therefore

Resolved, That the Board of Supervisors of the City and County of San Francisco hereby offers Doctors Walter B. Coffey and John B. Humber its sincere homage and commendation for their marvelous research work, and expresses heartfelt gratitude for' their discovery of a treatment which will relieve the awful sufferings of thousands of humanity; and be it

Further Resolved, That a copy of this resolution be sent to Doctors Walter B. Coffey and John B. Humber.

Referred to Public Health Committee.

Plans for Construction of a Canopy and Installation of Electrical Equipment at Civic Auditorium.

Supervisor Hayden presented:

Bill No. ————, Ordinance No. ———— (New Series), as follows:

Ordering the preparation of plans and specifications for the construction of a gridiron, canopy and the installation of electrical equipment for the stage of the Civic Auditorium; authorizing and directing the Board of Public Works to enter into contract for said construction; and permitting progressive payments to be made during the progress of said work.

Be it ordained by the People of the City and County of San Francisco as follows:

Section 1. The Board of Public Works is hereby authorized, instructed and empowered to prepare plans and specifications for the gridiron, canopy and the installation of electrical equipment for the stage of the Civic Auditorium, and to enter into contract for the construction of said gridiron, canopy and the installation of electrical equipment for the stage of the Civic Auditorium in accordance with the plans and specifications so prepared.

Section 2. The said Board of Public Works is hereby authorized and permitted to incorporate in the contract for the construction of said gridiron, canopy and the installation of electrical equipment for the stage of the Civic Center Auditorium, conditions that progressive payments shall be made in the manner set forth in said specifications and as provided by Section 21, Chapter I, Article VI of the Charter.

Section 3. This ordinance shall take effect immediately.

Referred to Finance Committee.

Appointment of Committee to Represent Board of Supervisors at Meeting of Joint Senate and Assembly Committees on Highways at Los Angeles.

Resolution No. 32051 (New Series), as follows:

Resolved, That a member or not more than three members of the Streets and Finance Committees be and they are hereby appointed to represent the Board of Supervisors at the meeting of the Joint Senate and Assembly Committees on Highways, to be held at Los

Angeles February 14 and 15, 1930, said appointments to be made by his Honor, the Mayor.

Adopted by the following vote:

Ayes—Supervisors Andriano, Canepa, Colman, Gallagher, Havenner, Hayden, McGovern, McSheehy, Miles, Peyser, Power, Roncovieri, Rossi, Spaulding, Suhr—15.

Absent—Supervisors Shannon, Stanton, Toner—3.

Appointment of Supervisorial Committee to Attend Joint Senate and Assembly Committees on Highways, Los Angeles, February 14-15, 1930.

The following was read and ordered *spread in Journal*:

San Francisco, Cal., February 13, 1930.

Honorable Board of Supervisors, City Hall, San Francisco, California.

Gentlemen: Pursuant to the terms of Resolution No. 32051, I hereby appoint the Honorable James E. Power, Honorable Victor J. Canepa, and the Honorable Andrew J. Gallagher to represent the Board of Supervisors at the meeting of the joint Senate and Assembly Committees on Highways, to be held in Los Angeles, February 14 and 15, 1930.

Respectfully submitted,

JAMES ROLPH, JR., Mayor.

Appropriation, $300, Expenses of Delegates to Joint Senate and Assembly Committee Meeting at Los Angeles.

Resolution No. 32052 (New Series), as follows:

Resolved, That the sum of $300 be and is hereby appropriated out of Budget Item No. 22 to pay the expenses of representatives in attendance at the Joint Senate and Assembly Committee on Highways at Los Angeles, February 14 and 15, 1930.

Adopted by the following vote:

Ayes—Supervisors Andriano, Canepa, Colman, Gallagher, Havenner, Hayden, McGovern, McSheehy, Miles, Peyser, Power, Roncovieri, Rossi, Spaulding, Suhr—15.

Absent—Supervisors Shannon, Stanton, Toner—3.

Appropriations, Publicity and Advertising.

Resolution No. 32053 (New Series), as follows:

Resolved, That the following amounts be and the same are hereby set aside, appropriated and authorized to be expended out of Publicity and Advertising, Appropriation 54, for the following purposes, to-wit:

(1) For expense by the Junior Chamber of Commerce in connection with the advertising of San Francisco "Products Week," for the publicity and advertising of San Francisco..$475.00

(2) For expense of decorating Market street, in connection with the San Francisco Community Chest drive, for the publicity and advertising of San Francisco...................... 465.00

Adopted by the following vote:

Ayes—Supervisors Andriano, Canepa, Colman, Gallagher, Havenner, Hayden, McGovern, McSheehy, Miles, Peyser, Power, Roncovieri, Rossi, Spaulding, Suhr—15.

Absent—Supervisors Shannon, Stanton, Toner—3.

Relative to War Memorial Report and Meeting.

His Honor Mayor Rolph announced that on Friday night he had a conference in his chambers with a committee of War Memorial veterans, at which meeting a number of veterans were present. "I had with me," he said, "and I have completed a full report of the War Memorial project from the time it commenced, in 1918, ready to submit to you, but I really think that it ought to be printed as a matter of record, including a financial statement of the entire fund."

Motion.

Supervisor Miles, seconded by Supervisor Peyser, moved that the report be printed, so that all members may have a copy and have an opportunity to study the report.

Motion *carried.*

Relative to Leave of Absence, George Bistany, Zoological Expert, Golden Gate Park.

Supervisor McSheehy stated that he had been informed informally by the City Attorney, in re requested leave of absence for George Bistany, zoological expert, that under the Charter only officers of the City and County are required to secure a leave of absence from the Board of Supervisors upon the recommendation of his Honor the Mayor. Mr. Bistany, being an employee of the Park Commission, and not an officer, is under the sole jurisdiction of the Park Commission, and it is not necessary for the Board of Supervisors to approve his leave of absence.

Special Meeting of Board to Be Held February 18, 1930.

Supervisor Hayden moved that a special meeting be called for a week from tomorrow (February 18, 1930), at 2:30 p. m.

Motion *carried.*

Report on Operation of Amphibian Planes at Marina.

Supervisor McSheehy announced that on February 17, 1930, he would present a report on the matter of the operation of amphibian planes at the Marina. He requested that the matter be considered as a Special Order at 4 p. m.

Reapportionment of Congressional Districts.

Supervisor Havenner, referring to the Federal census, declared that there were several new congressional districts in California, and requested that the City Attorney pass upon legal procedure in matter of reapportionment of congressional districts in California.

ADJOURNMENT.

There being no further business, the Board at 7 p. m. adjourned.

J. S. DUNNIGAN, Clerk.

Approved by the Board of Supervisors March 24, 1930.

Pursuant to Resolution No. 3402 (New Series) of the Board of Supervisors of the City and County of San Francisco, I, John S. Dunnigan, hereby certify that the foregoing is true and correct copy of the Journal of Proceedings of said Board of the date stated and approved as above recited.

JOHN S. DUNNIGAN,

Clerk of the Board of Supervisors,
City and County of San Francisco.

Vol. 25—New Series   No. 7

Monday, February 17, 1930

Journal of Proceedings
Board of Supervisors

City and County of San Francisco

The Recorder Printing and Publishing Company
337 Bush Street, S. F.

JOURNAL OF PROCEEDINGS
BOARD OF SUPERVISORS

MONDAY, FEBRUARY 17, 1930, 2 P. M.

In Board of Supervisors, San Francisco, Monday, February 17, 1930, 2 p. m.

The Board of Supervisors met in regular session.

CALLING THE ROLL.

The roll was called and the following Supervisors were noted present:

Supervisors Andriano, Canepa, Colman, Havenner, Hayden, McGovern, McSheehy, Miles, Peyser, Power, Roncovieri, Rossi, Spaulding, Suhr, Toner—15.

Absent—Supervisors Gallagher, Shannon, Stanton—3.

Quorum present.

His Honor Mayor Rolph presiding.

APPROVAL OF JOURNAL.

The Journal of Proceedings of the previous meeting was laid over for approval until next meeting.

ROLL CALL FOR PETITIONS AND COMMUNICATIONS.

Suggested Amendment of Spring Valley Operating Ordinance.

The following was presented and read by the Clerk:

Communication, from Adolph Uhl, requesting that the Spring Valley Operating Ordinance, under consideration, be so drafted that the earnings from distribution of water will be credited to a "Hetch Hetchy Water Operating Fund," as it is his judgment that the parent water utility is Hetch Hetchy, and any water or power properties or distributing systems subsequently acquired become a unit of the parent utility. Therefore, the Spring Valley would become a unit of the parent utility and its receipts should be credited as suggested.

Referred to Finance and Public Utilities Committees.

Report of Dion R. Holm Regarding Appearance Before the Interstate Commerce Committee of the Senate Anent Telephone Rate Situation.

The following was presented and read by the Clerk:

Communication, from City Attorney, transmitting a report from Dion R. Holm concerning his appearance before the Interstate Commerce Committee of the Senate, Washington, D. C., relative to telephone rate investigation.

Referred to Public Utilities Committee.

Official Representation Requested by Down Town Association, Good-Will Tour of Old Mexico.

The following was presented and read by the Clerk:

Communication, from Down Town Association, announcing the association's excursion and good-will tour of Mexico, commencing on March 14th next, returning Wednesday, April 2, and requesting that San Francisco be officially represented on said trip.

Referred to Public Welfare Committee.

Distribution of Joint Highway District No. 1.

The following was presented and read by the Clerk:

Communication, from C. H. Purcell, State Highway Engineer, enclosing notice of hearing to be had before the State Department of Public Works on February 20, 1930, for the purpose of distributing the highway constructed by the Joint Highway District No. 1, and for decreeing the distribution thereto to the State of California. The hearing is to be held in technical compliance with the provisions of the Joint Highway District Act, and it is felt that unless you so desire it will not be necessary for any of the directors or others interested to appear at hearing.

Referred to Streets Committee.

Death of David J. Tobin.

The following resolution was *adopted unanimously by rising vote*: Resolution No. 32055 (New Series), as follows:

Whereas, David J. Tobin, a citizen of San Francisco, died February 15, 1930; and

Whereas, the said David J. Tobin was an energetic worker in public affairs; and

Whereas, to him, the district south of the Park owes much of its development and in recognition thereof had felicitously named him the Mayor of Parkside; and

Whereas, David J. Tobin was an excellent citizen, a genial companion with a host of friends, and lost none of them by his earnest endeavor in civic affairs; therefore, be it

Resolved, That the Board of Supervisors of the City and County of San Francisco hereby expresses tender sympathy and condolence to the widow of the late deceased; and be it further

Resolved, That a copy of this resolution be sent to Mrs. David J. Tobin and that this Board adjourn out of respect to the memory of the late David J. Tobin.

Fixing Monday, March 3, 1930, for Hearing Objections of Property Owners Against Closing Rhode Island Street.

Resolution No. 32080 (New Series), as follows:

Resolved, That Monday, March 3, 1930, is hereby fixed as the time for hearing the objections of property owners against the closing of Rhode Island street, as provided in Resolution of Intention No. 31892 (New Series).

Adopted by the following vote:

Ayes—Supervisors Andriano, Canepa, Colman, Gallagher, Havenner, Hayden, McGovern, McSheehy, Miles, Peyser, Power, Roncovieri, Rossi, Spaulding, Stanton, Suhr, Toner—17.

Absent—Supervisor Shannon—1.

In Memory of Robert S. Moore.

His Honor Mayor Rolph called attention to the passing of Robert S. Moore, distinguished citizen of San Francisco and president of the Moore Shipbuilding Company. He highly eulogized the character of the deceased and declared that his death meant a distinct loss to the civic life of San Francisco.

Whereupon, Supervisor McSheehy moved that a committe of three be appointed to draw suitable resolutions of condolence, and that when the Board adjourns that it does so out of respect to the memory of Robert S. Moore.

Adopted unanimously by rising vote:

Report of Delegates to Joint Committee of Legislature on Necessity of Revision of State Act Governing State Highway District Road Projects.

The following was presented and read by the Clerk:

February 17, 1930.

To the Honorable Board of Supervisors, City Hall, San Francisco, California.

Gentlemen: We, your delegates to session of the Joint Committee of the Legislature (Senate and Assembly) on the subject of study of the necessity of revision of the State act governing the conduct of the State Highway District road projects, beg leave to report as follows:

The session was held in the rooms of the California State Railroad Commission, Los Angeles, California, Friday, February 14th, and was attended by official representatives of about twenty cities or counties, especially the southern portion of the State.

Your representatives were given much time to state our views, i. e., that the language of the act was loose and ambiguous. In addition, we stressed the fact that our county (San Francisco) was now engaged in the expenditure of approximately eight million dollars (in conjunction with San Mateo and Santa Cruz counties) in the building of inter-county highways. We further appealed for a larger allotment by the State for these inter-county highways. Attorneys Donald Young and Mary Schwab appeared for Highway Districts Nos. 9 and 10 and discussed at length the legal defects of the act.

Mr. Thomas Hurley, Supervisor of San Diego County, speaking for the thirteen southern counties, stated that if the money for secondary roads was not diminished that the southern cities and counties were agreeable to some form of legislation providing a new tax to be used to assist these projects.

Further sessions of the Joint Committee will be held at different State points. We again recommend that your Board be represented.

Respectfully submitted,

JAMES E. POWER,
VICTOR J. CANEPA,
ANDREW J. GALLAGHER,
Delegates.

P. S. Vouchers covering expenditures will be filed with the Auditor.

PRESENTATION OF PROPOSALS.

Bread.

Sealed proposals were received and opened between the hours of 2 and 3 p. m. this date for furnishing bread from March 1 to June 30, 1930, and *referred to Supplies Committee.*

X-Ray Films for San Francisco Hospital.

Sealed proposals were received and opened between the hours of 2 and 3 p. m. this date for furnishing X-ray films for San Francisco Hospital, and *referred to Supplies Committee.*

Hospital Supplies.

Sealed proposals were received and opened between the hours of 2 and 3 p. m. this date for furnishing hospital supplies, roller bandages, absorbent cotton, gauze, lint, oiled muslin, adhesive plasters, and *referred to Supplies Committee.*

UNFINISHED BUSINESS.

Action Deferred.

The following matter, heretofore passed for printing, was *laid over one week:*

Laundry Permits.

Resolution No. ————— (New Series), as follows:

Resolved, That the following revocable permits be and are hereby granted:

Laundries.

Eloise Aiso, 1089 Pine street.
John Batsere, 976 Pine street.
Anna Biscay, 992 Sutter street.
Ruth Clausen, 94 Seventh street.
Mrs. V. J. Laurent, 447 Ellis street.
J. Nougue, 707 O'Farrell street.
Mme. P. Pomme, 1147 McAllister street.
Marie Sabacca, 808 Post street.
Mme. J. Saffores, 841 Powell street.
Mrs. A. Termello, 41 Franklin street.
Louise Vannucci and Gloria Cheader, 405 O'Farrell street.

The rights granted under this resolution shall be exercised within six months, otherwise said permits shall become null and void.

Indefinite Postponement.

The following was, on recommendation of Streets Committee, *indefinitely postponed.*

Regulating the Width of Sidewalks on Quint Street Between Oakdale and Palou Avenues.

Bill No. 8183, Ordinance No. ————— (New Series), as follows:

Amending Ordinance No. 1061, entitled "Regulating the Width of Sidewalks," approved December 18, 1903, by adding thereto a new section, to be numbered ten hundred and eighty-nine.

Be it ordained by the People of the City and County of San Francisco as follows:

Section 1. Ordinance No. 1061, entitled "Regulating the Width of Sidewalks," approved December 18, 1903, be and is hereby amended in accordance with the communication of the Board of Public Works, filed in this office January 21, 1930, by adding thereto a new section, to be numbered ten hundred and eighty-nine, to read as follows:

Section 1089. The width of sidewalks on Quint street between Oakdale avenue and Palou avenue shall be ten (10) feet.

Section 2. Any expense caused by the above change of walk widths shall be borne by the property owners.

Section 3. This ordinance shall take effect and be in force from and after its passage.

PRESENTATION OF BILLS AND ACCOUNTS.

Your Finance Committee, having examined miscellaneous demands not required by law to be passed to print, and amounting to $59,361.81, recommends same be allowed and ordered paid.

Approved by the following vote:

Ayes—Supervisors Andriano, Canepa, Colman, Havenner, Hayden, McGovern, McSheehy, Miles, Peyser, Power, Roncovieri, Rossi, Spaulding, Suhr, Toner—15.

Absent—Supervisors Gallagher, Shannon, Stanton—3.

NEW BUSINESS.

Passed for Printing.

The following matters were *passed for printing:*

Authorizations.

On recommendation of Finance Committee.

Resolution No. ————— (New Series), as follows:

Resolved, That the following amounts be and the same are hereby

authorized to be expended out of the hereinafter mentioned funds in payment to the following named claimants, to-wit:

Library Fund.

(1) American Building Maintenance Co., janitor service for public libraries (claim dated Jan. 31, 1930) ....$ 828.00

(2) Maundrell & Bowen, painting for public libraries (claim dated Jan. 31, 1930) 960.26

(3) Maundrell & Bowen, painting of public library (claim dated Jan. 31, 1930) 560.25

(4) J. H. Keefe Co., painting main public library (claim dated Jan. 31, 1930) 740.00

(5) C. E. Gordon, painting of public library (claim dated Jan. 21, 1930) 730.00

6) Foster & Futernick Co., rebinding library books (claim dated Jan. 31, 1930) 2,718.00

.7) G. E. Stechert & Co., library books (claim dated Jan. 31, 1930) 1,451.91

(8) Sather Book Shop, library books (claim dated Jan. 21, 1930) 614.96

(9) San Francisco News Co., library books (claim dated Jan. 21, 1930) 1,690.02

M. H. de Young Memorial Museum—Appropriation 58.

(10) P. H. Enright, fourth payment, heating and ventilating the M. H. de Young Memorial Museum (claim dated Feb. 14, 1930) ....$ 1,290.90

Park Fund.

(11) C. J. Holzmueller, furnishing and installing 4500 lamps and sockets for Christmas trees, Panhandle of Golden Gate Park (claim dated Feb. 14, 1930) ....$ 3,000.00

(12) Joel W. Kaufman, chairman Finance Committee, Christmas Fete Committee, decorations of Christmas tree, public park decorations, etc., Christmas celebration (claim dated Feb. 14, 1930) 5,000.00

(13) The Turner Company, labor and material, installing heating system in Park Lodge (claim dated Feb. 14, 1930) 586.50

(14) Berringer & Russell, alfalfa, etc., for parks (claim dated Feb. 14, 1930) 724.28

Hetch Hetchy Construction Fund, Bond Issue 1928.

(15) Coos Bay Lumber Co., lumber (claim dated Feb. 4, 1930) ....$ 1,012.95

(16) Del Monte Meat Co., meat (claim dated Feb. 4, 1930). 1,175.24

(17) Ingersoll-Rand Co. of California, machinery parts (claim dated Feb. 4, 1930) 555.15

(18) Department Public Health (San Francisco Hospital), hospital service rendered Hetch Hetchy employees, July 1 to Dec. 21, 1929 (claim dated Feb. 4, 1930) 882.50

(19) Santa Fe Lumber Co., lumber (claim dated Feb. 4, 1930) 1,091.82

(20) Coos Bay Lumber Co., lumber (claim dated Feb. 6, 1930) 2,159.52

(21) Ingersoll-Rand Co. of California, machinery parts (claim dated Feb. 6, 1930) 2,271.50

(22) Montague Pipe & Steel Co., pipe (claim dated Feb. 6, 1930) 1,882.25

(23) Santa Fe Lumber Co., lumber (claim dated Feb. 6, 1930) 601.49

(24) Santa Cruz Portland Cement Co., cement (claim dated Feb. 6, 1930) 2,908.90

Municipal Railway Fund.

(25) American Brake Shoe & Foundry Co. of California, brake shoes (claim dated Feb. 5, 1930) ....$ 819.19

(26)   Department of Public Works (Bureau of Street Repair), asphalt repairs to Municipal Railway right of way (claim dated Feb. 5, 1930)................................   859.80
(27)   Dunham, Carrigan & Hayden Co., bolts and spikes (claim dated Feb. 7, 1930) 1,223.00
.28)   San Francisco City Employees' Retirement System, for employees pensions, etc. (claim dated Feb. 3, 1930).......   752.85

General Fund, 1929-1930.

(29)   Pacific Gas & Electric Co., street lighting during January (claim dated Feb. 17, 1930)..........................$66,662.67
(30)   County Road Fund, reimbursement of expenditures in connection with the covering of main sewers during December (claim dated Feb. 3, 1930).................... 1,133.10
(31)   Board of Park Commissioners, reimbursement for account of beautification of Civic Center (claim dated Feb. 14, 1930) 4,640.56
(32)   Clinton-Stephenson Construction Co., Ltd., sixth payment, repairs to Palace of Fine Arts building (claim dated Feb. 14, 1930)..   857.25
(33)   Eureka Benevolent Society, maintenance of minors (claim dated Feb. 7, 1930) 2,975.92
(34)   Little Children's Aid, maintenance of minors (claim dated Feb. 7, 1930) 11,675.50
(35)   Children's Agency, maintenance of minors (claim dated Feb. 7, 1930) 30,931.87
(36)   St. Vincent's School, maintenance of minors (claim dated Feb. 7, 1930) 1,171.56
(37)   Albertinum Orphanage, maintenance of minors (claim dated Feb. 7, 1930) 713.81
(38)   Roman Catholic Orphanage, maintenance of minors (claim dated Feb. 7, 1930) 2,015.90
(39)   Neal, Stratford & Kerr, printing for Police Department (claim dated Feb. 10, 1930) 646.50
(40)   American LaFrance & Foamite Co., Fire Department apparatus parts (claim dated Jan. 31, 1930).............. 1,122.20
(41)   Enterprise Foundry Co., grate and section bars, Fire Department (claim dated Jan. 31, 1930).................   516.60
(42)   Graham Fuel & Drayage Co., coal, etc., Fire Department (claim dated Jan. 31, 1930) 1,072.48
(43)   Pacific Gas & Electric Co., gas and electricity, Fire Department (claim dated Jan. 31, 1930) 2,601.23
(44)   Spring Valley Water Co., water furnished Fire Department, and installation of hydrants (claim dated Jan. 31, 1930) 2,053.29
(45)   The Texas Co., gasoline and oil, Fire Department (claim dated Jan. 31, 1930) 1,221.63
(46)   Union Oil Co. of California, fuel oil, Fire Department (claim dated Jan. 31, 1930) 712.64
(47)   Joseph Hagan & Sons, burial of indigent dead (claim dated Feb. 13, 1930)......................................   869.00
(48)   H. F. Dugan Company, surgical supplies for San Francisco Hospital (claim dated Jan. 31, 1930)...............   789.11
(49)   Kahn & Co., X-ray films for San Francisco Hospital (claim dated Jan. 31, 1930) 1,019.52
(50)   Sussman, Wormser & Co., groceries, San Francisco Hospital (claim dated Jan. 31, 1930) 1,527.00
(51)   Scatena-Galli Fruit Co., groceries and produce, San Francisco Hospital (claim dated Jan. 31, 1930)....... 1,194.87
(52)   Spring Valley Water Co., water service, San Francisco Hospital (claim dated Jan. 31, 1930).................... 1,761.43
(53)   Mangrum-Holbrook Co., dishes for San Francisco Hospital (claim dated Jan. 31, 1930) 2,062.00

(54) Sherry Bros. Inc., butter for Laguna Honda Home
    (claim dated Jan. 31, 1930)............................. 2,036.21
(55) Baumgarten Bros., meat for Laguna Honda Home
    (claim dated Jan. 31, 1930) 1,018.48
(56) California Meat Co., meat, Laguna Honda Home (claim
    dated Jan. 31, 1930) 2,651.70
(57) Dairy Dale, San Francisco Dairy Co., milk for Laguna
    Honda Home (claim dated Jan. 31, 1930)................. 2,324.60
(58) Del Monte Meat Co., meat for Laguna Honda Home
    (claim dated Jan. 31, 1930) 3,242.66
(59) J. T. Freitas Co., eggs for Laguna Honda Home (claim
    dated Jan. 31, 1930) 1,575.00
(60) Healy & Donaldson, tobacco for Laguna Honda Home
    (claim dated Jan. 31, 1930) 987.60
(61) Richfield Oil Co., fuel oil for Laguna Honda Home
    (claim dated Jan. 31, 1930) 1,882.72
(62) Schweitzer & Co., meat for Laguna Honda Home (claim
    dated Jan. 31, 1930) 1,051.49
(63) Sherry Bros. Inc., butter for Laguna Honda Home
    (claim dated Jan. 31, 1930) 1,547.10
(64) Spring Valley Water Co., water furnished Laguna
    Honda Home (claim dated Jan. 31, 1930) 1,153.32
(65) John J. Dailey, legal services rendered the City Attor-
    ney, month of February, 1930 ....   850.00

Appropriation From Urgent Necessity, Additional Emergency Supplies by the Board of Health.

Also, Resolution No. ———— (New Series), as follows:

Resolved, That the sum of $7,000 be and the same is hereby set aside, appropriated and authorized to be expended out of Urgent Necessity, Budget Item No. 24, Fiscal Year 1929-1930, for additional and emergency supplies by the Board of Health under the direction of the Superintendent of the Relief Home.

Appropriations for Construction of Ward Building "F," Relief Home Tract.

Also, Resolution No. ———— (New Series), as follows:

Resolved, That the following amounts be and the same are hereby set aside, appropriated and authorized to be expended out of Hospital Bond Construction Fund, Issue 1929, for the construction of Ward Building "F," Relief Home Tract, to-wit:
(1) General construction (Spivock & Spivock contract).... $95,900.00
(2) Electrical work (Knut Smith contract)............... 2,137.00
(3) Plumbing and gasfitting work (Scott Co. contract)..... 11,537.00
(4) Mechanical equipment (Scott Co. contract)........... 8,160.00
(5) Architectural fees 4,274.42
(6) Extras, incidentals and inspection................... 10,000.00

    Total $132,008.42

Appropriations Out of County Road Fund, Various Improvements.

Also, Resolution No. ———— (New Series), as follows:

Resolved, That the following amounts be and the same are hereby set aside, appropriated and authorized to be expended out of County Road Fund for the following purposes, to-wit:
(1) For the improving of Chestnut street from a line 220 feet easterly from Grant avenue to the easterly line of Kearny street, and Kearny street from Chestnut street to to a line 79½ feet southerly from Chestnut street, at City property . . . .:.............. $3,400.00
(2) For the improvement of the intersection of Burnside

avenue and Bosworth street, City's liability, and the construction of walls and stairs.............................. 1,850.00

(3) For the improvement of Division street between Bryant and Florida streets, Treat avenue between Florida and Alameda streets, and Alameda street between Harrison street and Treat avenue; assessment against City property used as Corporation Yard 3,379.26

(4) For the reconstruction of Tehama street westerly from Second street 3,000.00

(5) For the reconstruction of Clementina street easterly from Third street...................................... 700.00

(6) For the resurfacing of Castro street between Seventeenth and Nineteenth streets......................... 2,305.00

Appropriations Out of County Road Fund for Street Improvements.

Also, Resolution No. ———— (New Series), as follows:

Resolved, That the following amounts be and the same are hereby set aside, appropriated and authorized to be expended out of the County Road Fund for the improvement of the following streets, to-wit:

Grand View avenue conform.............................. $1,984.13
Havelock street, Edna to Circular........................ 1,557.50
Josiah and Ridge lane.................................... 962.05

Appropriations, Work in Front of City Property.

Also, Resolution No. ———— (New Series), as follows:

Resolved, That the following amounts be and the same are hereby set aside, appropriated and authorized to be expended out of "Work in Front of City Property," Budget Item 34, for the following street work at City property, to-wit:

(1) Thirty-first avenue, Kirkham to Lawton streets and crossing $3,397.00

(2) Short street, Market to Yukon streets.................. 773.11

(3) For the improvement of Twenty-sixth street between York and Hampshire streets, City's portion of cost.............. 1,930.00

Appropriation for Construction Due to Boulevard Construction.

Also, Resolution No. ———— (New Series), as follows:

Resolved, That the sum of $1,045 be and the same is hereby set aside, appropriated and authorized to be expended out of Boulevard Bond Issue Construction Fund for the improvement of Le Conte avenue at crossing of Lane street ($857), and reconstruction of Lane street and San Bruno avenue ($188), necessitated by the construction of the Bay Shore boulevard.

Appropriations for Building Repairs and Painting Traffic Signs, Etc.

Also, Resolution No. ———— (New Series), as follows:

Resolved, That the following amounts be and the same are hereby set aside, appropriated and authorized to be expended out of the hereinafter mentioned funds for the following purposes, to-wit:

Repairs to Public Buildings, Budget Item No. 53.

(1) For the replacing of nineteen flanged control valves on fresh water supply piping from tanks on roof of Hall of Justice $678.00

Traffic Signals, Etc., Budget Item No. 57.

(2) For the painting of traffic signs, lines and curbs during month of February, 1930............................... 700.00

Reimbursement of Board of Public Works for the Painting of Traffic Signs, Etc.

Also, Resolution No. ———— (New Series), as follows:

Resolved, That the sum of $941.20 be and the same is hereby set aside and appropriated out of "Traffic Signals," Budget Item No. 57, to the credit of "Reimbursements," Budget Item No. 442, Board of Public Works, being reimbursement for labor and materials furnished and used in the painting of traffic signs, lines and curbing during the month of December, 1929.

Appropriations for Repairs to County Jail No. 1.

Also, Resolution No. ———— (New Series), as follows:

Resolved, That the following amounts be and the same are hereby set aside and appropriated out of "Maintenance, Subsistence and Equipment," office of the Sheriff, Budget Item No. 269, to the credit of Budget Item No. 442, Board of Public Works, and authorized to be expended for the following purposes, to-wit:

(1) For the painting of the south wing at County Jail No. 1.$ 1,960.00
(2) For changing eighteen windows in County Jail No. 1 to pivot type windows.....................................   695.00

Adopted.

The following resolutions were *adopted*:

Appropriations, Work in Front of City Property.

On recommendation of Finance Committee.

Resolution No. 32057 (New Series), as follows:

Resolved, That the following amounts be and the same are hereby set aside, appropriated and authorized to be expended out of "Work in Front of City Property," B. I. 34, for the following street work at City property, to-wit:

(1) Truett place, Mason street west......................$	68.75
(2) Beach street, opposite Polk...........................	499.38
(3) Ortega street and Forty-fourth avenue................	14.54
(4) Ortega street and Twenty-fifth avenue...............	138.75
(5) Twenty-fifth avenue, Ortega street to Pacheco street....	452.00
(6) Forty-third avenue, Kirkham street to Lawton street...	180.00
(7) Twenty-seventh and Twenty-eighth avenues, Fulton street to Cabrillo street.............................	288.00
(8) Jackson and Montgomery streets.....................	25.00
(9) Circular and Havelock streets........................	153.20
(10) Thirty-first avenue and Moraga street................	123.75
(11) Harrison street between Fifteenth and Sixteenth streets	422.76
(12) Fourteenth avenue, Ulloa street to Vicente street......	120.00
(13) Eighteenth avenue, Kirkham street to Lawton street...	120.00

Ayes—Supervisors Andriano, Canepa, Colman, Havenner, Hayden, McGovern, McSheehy, Miles, Peyser, Power, Roncovieri, Rossi, Spaulding, Suhr, Toner—15.

Absent—Supervisors Gallagher, Shannon, Stanton—3.

Appropriations Out of County Road Fund for Street Improvements.

Also, Resolution No. 32058 (New Series), as follows:

Resolved, That the following amounts be and the same are hereby set aside, appropriated and authorized to be expended out of the County Road Fund for the improvement of the following streets, to-wit:

De Long and Chrystal streets.............................$	49.45
Isabel and Wolfe streets..................................	87.10
Market street to Danvers street..........................	312.00

Niagara avenue and Ridge lane	50.00
Valley street, Castro street to Diamond street	250.00
Reset hydrant, Noe and Twentieth streets	22.50
Manhole, Forty-fifth avenue and Moraga street	110.00
Peralta avenue and Hampshire street	150.00
Sidewalk, Third and Thornton streets	15.00
Falmouth and Shipley streets	30.00
Thirtieth and Wisconsin streets	49.15
Catchbasins, Thirtieth avenue and Noriega street	160.00

Ayes—Supervisors Andriano, Canepa, Colman, Havenner, Hayden, McGovern, McSheehy, Miles, Peyser, Power, Roncovieri, Rossi, Spaulding, Suhr, Toner—15.

Absent—Supervisors Gallagher, Shannon, Stanton—3.

Appropriations, Various Purposes.

Also, Resolution No. 32059 (New Series), as follows:

Resolved, That the following amounts be and the same are hereby set aside, appropriated and authorized to be expended out of the hereinafter mentioned funds for the following purposes, to-wit:

County Road Fund.

(1) For the construction of temporary pavement over unfinished portion of Roanoke street between Chenery and Laidley streets ....$ 500.00

(2) For the construction of 120 feet of guard rail fence, painted white, on south side of Roosevelt way at the intersection of Sixteenth street........................... 125.00

Street Work in Front of City Property, Budget Item No. 34.

(3) For construction of sewer, with branches and manholes, in Yale street between Silver avenue and Silliman street, at City property ....$ 495.00

(4) For the improvement of Santiago street at the crossings of Forty-second and Forty-third avenues; City's liability.. 225.00

Traffic Signals, Budget Item No. 57.

(5) For the installation of 150 lenses in safety zone buttons and 10 rubber "Slow" signs, by Board of Public Works....$ 40.75

Boulevard Bond Construction Fund.

(6) For the cost of paving a portion of Blanken street between Tunnel avenue and Bay Shore boulevard, necessitated due to construction of Bay Shore boulevard.........$ 97.92

Ayes—Supervisors Andriano, Canepa, Colman, Havenner, Hayden, McGovern, McSheehy, Miles, Peyser, Power, Roncovieri, Rossi, Spaulding, Suhr, Toner—15.

Absent—Supervisors Gallagher, Shannon, Stanton—3.

Passed for Printing.

The following resolution was *passed for printing*:

Condemnation of Land Required for Opening Ord Court.

On recommendation of Finance Committee.

Resolution No. ———— (New Series), as follows:

Resolved, By the Board of Supervisors of the City and County of San Francisco, that public interest and necessity require the acquisition by the City and County of San Francisco, a municipal corporation, of the following properties, situated in the City and County of San Francisco, State of California, more particularly described as follows, to-wit:

Parcel 1: Beginning at the southwesterly corner of Lot 37 of Lyon

& Hoag's Subdivision No 2 of Ashbury Terrace, as per map thereof recorded in Map Book "G," pages 89 and 90, records of the City and County of San Francisco; thence northwesterly along the southwesterly line of Lot 36 of above mentioned map 19.028 feet; thence northeasterly on a curve to the right whose tangent deflects 89 deg. 14 min. 19 sec. from the preceding course, radius 23 feet, central angle 46 deg. 38 min. 48 sec., a distance of 18.725 feet to the westerly line of said Lot 37; thence southwesterly along the westerly line of said Lot 37 20.684 feet to the southwesterly corner of said Lot 37 and the point of beginning.

Being a portion of Lot 36 of above mentioned map.

Parcel 2: Beginning at the southeasterly corner of Lot 39 of Lyon & Hoag's Subdivision No 2 of Ashbury Terrace, as per map thereof recorded in Map Book "G," pages 89 and 90, records of the City and County of San Francisco; thence northwesterly along the southwesterly line of Lots 39 and 38 of above mentioned map, 60 feet to the southeasterly corner of Lot 37 of above mentioned map; thence at right angles northeasterly along the northeasterly line of said Lot 37 17.50 feet; thence at right angles southeasterly along a line parallel with and distant 17.50 feet at right angles northeasterly from the southwesterly line of said Lots 38 and 39 60 feet to the southeasterly line of Lot 12 of Block 13, Flint Tract Homestead Association, as per map thereof recorded in Map Book 1, page 148, records of the City and County of San Francisco; thence at right angles southwesterly along said line of said Lot 12 and along the southeasterly line of said Lot 39 17.50 feet to the southeasterly corner of said Lot 39 and the point of beginning.

Being portions of Lots 38 and 39 of the aforesaid Ashbury Terrace and a portion of Lot 12, Block 13, Flint Tract, as mentioned above.

Parcel 3: Beginning at the southeasterly corner of Lot B of Lyon & Hoag's Subdivision No. 2 of Ashbury Terrace, as per map thereof recorded in Map Book "G," pages 89 and 90, records of the City and County of San Francisco; thence northwesterly along the southwesterly line of Lots B and A of above mentioned map 50 feet to the southeasterly line of Lot 39 of aforenamed map; thence at right angles northeasterly along said line of Lot 39 and along the southeasterly line of Lot 12, Block 13, Flint Tract Homestead Association, as per map thereof recorded in Map Book 1, page 148, records of the City and County of San Francisco, 17.50 feet; thence at right angles southeasterly along a line parallel with and distant 17.50 feet at right angles northeasterly from the southwesterly line of said Lots A and B 50 feet to the southeasterly line of Lot 14 of the above mentioned Flint Tract; thence at right angles southwesterly along said line of said Lot 14 and along the southeasterly line of above mentioned Lot B 17.50 feet to the southeasterly corner of said Lot B and the point of beginning.

Being all of Lots A and B of the aforesaid Ashbury Terrace and portions of Lots 13 and 14, Block 13, of the Flint Tract, as mentioned above.

Parcel 4: Beginning at the southeasterly corner of Lot F of Lyon & Hoag's Subdivision No 2 of Ashbury Terrace, as per map thereof recorded in Map Book "G," pages 89 and 90, records of the City and County of San Francisco; thence northwesterly along the southwesterly line of said Lot F 25 feet to the southeasterly line of Lot E of the above mentioned map; thence at right angles northeasterly along the southeasterly line of said Lot E and along the southeasterly line of Lot 17, Block 13, Flint Tract Homestead Association, as per map thereof recorded in Map Book 1, page 148, records of the City and County of San Francisco, 17.50 feet; thence at right angles southeasterly along a line parallel with and distant 17.50 feet at right angles northeasterly from the southwesterly line of said Lot F 25 feet to the southeasterly line of Lot 18, Block 13, of the above mentioned Flint Tract; thence at right angles southwesterly along said line of Lot 18 and along the southeasterly line of the aforesaid Lot F 17.50 feet to the southeasterly corner of Lot F and the point of beginning.

Being all of Lot F of the aforesaid Ashbury Terrace and a portion of Lot 18, Block 13, Flint Tract, as above mentioned.

Parcel 5: Beginning at the southeasterly corner of Lot J of Lyon & Hoag's Subdivision No. 2 of Ashbury Terrace, as per map thereof recorded in Map Book "G," pages 89 and 90, records of the City and County of San Francisco; thence northwesterly along the southwesterly line of said Lot J 25 feet to the southeasterly line of Lot I of aforesaid map; thence at right angles northeasterly along said line of said Lot I and along the southeasterly line of Lot 21, Block 13, Flint Tract Homestead Association, as per map thereof recorded in Map Book 1, page 148, records of the City and County of San Francisco, 17.50 feet; thence at right angles southeasterly along a line parallel with and distant 17.50 feet northeasterly from the southwesterly line of aforesaid Lot J 10.883 feet; thence easterly on a curve to the left, tangent to the preceding course, radius 136.868 feet, central angle 5 deg. 55 min. 12 sec., a distance of 14.142 feet to the southeasterly line of Lot 22, Block 13, of said aforesaid Flint Tract; thence southwesterly along said line of said Lot 22 and along the southeasterly line of aforementioned Lot J 18.23 feet to the southeasterly corner of aforesaid Lot J and the point of beginning.

Being all of Lot J of aforesaid Ashbury Terrace and a portion of Lot 22, Block 13, Flint Tract, as above mentioned. Be it

Further Resolved, That said properties are suitable, adaptable, necessary and required for the public use of said City and County of San Francisco, to-wit: For the opening, widening, construction and maintenance of Ord court. It is necessary that a fee simple title be taken for such use.

The City Attorney is hereby ordered and directed to commence proceedings in eminent domain against the owners of said parcels of land, and of any and all interests therein or claims thereto, for the condemnation thereof for the public use of the City and County of San Francisco, as aforesaid.

Adopted.

The following resolutions were *adopted*:

Accepting Offer to Sell Land for the Widening of Ord Court.

On recommendation of Finance Committee.

Resolution No. 32060 (New Series), as follows:

Resolved, That the offer of sale made by the following named corporation to sell to the City and County of San Francisco the following described land required for the opening, extension and widening of Ord Court, for the sum set forth opposite its name, be accepted:

Pope-Talbot Land Company, $1—Beginning at the southeasterly corner of Lot J of Lyon & Hoag's Subdivision No. 2 of Ashbury Terrace, as per map thereof recorded in Map Book "G," pages 89 and 90, Records of the City and County of San Francisco; thence southeasterly along the northeasterly line of Lot 34 of the above named map 42.54 feet to the southwesterly boundary line of the above mentioned subdivision; thence southeasterly along last named southwesterly boundary line 59.17 feet to the southwesterly line of the property belonging to the City and County of San Francisco; thence deflecting 166 deg. 46 min. to the left and running northwesterly along said line of the property of said City and County 86.53 feet to a point distant 10 feet at right angles northeasterly from the first named course of this description; thence deflecting 6 deg. 51 min. 20 sec. to the right and running northwesterly along a line parallel with and distant 10 feet at right angles northeasterly from the first course of this description 12 feet to the southeasterly line of aforesaid Lot J; thence at right angles southwesterly along said line of Lot J 10 feet to the southeasterly corner of said Lot J and the point of beginning.

And the City Attorney is hereby authorized to examine the title to said property, and if the same is found satisfactory, to accept on behalf of the City, deed conveying said property to the City, free and clear of all encumbrances, and to record said deed, together with a copy of this resolution, in the office of the Recorder of the City and County of San Francisco, State of California.

Ayes—Supervisors Andriano, Canepa, Colman, Havenner, Hayden, McGovern, McSheehy, Miles, Peyser, Power, Roncovieri, Rossi, Spaulding, Suhr, Toner—15.

Absent—Supervisors Gallagher, Shannon, Stanton—3.

Accepting Offer to Sell Land for Widening of Chenery Street.

Also, Resolution No. 32061 (New Series), as follows:

Resolved, That the offer of sale made by the following named person to sell to the City and County of San Francisco the following described land, required for the widening of Chenery street, for the sum set forth opposite his name, be accepted:

J. P. Loustaunau, $17.50—Portion of Lot 20, Block 6727, as per the Assessor's Block Books of the City and County of San Francisco. (As per detailed description and written offer on file.)

And the City Attorney is hereby authorized to examine the title to said property, and if the same is found satisfactory, to accept on behalf of the City, deed conveying said property to the City, free and clear of all encumbrances, and to record said deed, together with a copy of this resolution, in the office of the Recorder of the City and County of San Francisco.

Ayes—Supervisors Andriano, Canepa, Colman, Havenner, Hayden, McGovern, McSheehy, Miles, Peyser, Power, Roncovieri, Rossi, Spaulding, Suhr, Toner—15.

Absent—Supervisors Gallagher, Shannon, Stanton—3.

Accepting Offer of Elizabeth Christian and Elizabeth Kelly to Sell Land for Widening of Chenery Street.

Also, Resolution No. 32062 (New Series), as follows:

Resolved, That the offers of sale made by the following named persons to sell to the City and County of San Francisco the following described land, required for the widening of Chenery street, for the sums set forth opposite their respective names, be accepted:

Elizabeth Christian, $435—Portion of Lot 18, Block 6727, as per the Assessor's Block Books of the City and County of San Francisco. (As per detailed description and written offer on file.)

Elizabeth Kelly, $162.75—Portion of Lots 4 and 5, Block 6685, as per the Assessor's Block Books of the City and County of San Francisco. (As per detailed description and written offer on file.)

And the City Attorney is hereby authorized to examine the title to said property, and if the same is found satisfactory, to accept on behalf of the City, deeds conveying said property to the City, free and clear of all encumbrances, and to record said deeds, together with copy of this resolution, in the office of the Recorder of the City and County of San Francisco.

Ayes—Supervisors Andriano, Canepa, Colman, Havenner, Hayden, McGovern, McSheehy, Miles, Peyser, Power, Roncovieri, Rossi, Spaulding, Suhr, Toner—15.

Absent—Supervisors Gallagher, Shannon, Stanton—3.

Accepting Offer to Sell Land for the Widening of Corbett Avenue.

Also, Resolution No. 32063 (New Series), as follows:

Resolved, That the offer of sale made by the following named owners to sell to the City and County of San Francisco the following described land, required for the widening of Corbett avenue, for the sum set forth opposite their names, be accepted:

W. O. and Irma B. Smith, $5,125—Portions of Lots 7 and 8, Block 2712, as per the Assessor's Blocks Books of the City and County of San Francisco. (As per detailed description and written offer on file.)

And the City Attorney is hereby authorized to examine the title to said property, and if the same is found satisfactory to accept, on behalf of the City, a deed conveying said property to the City, free and clear of all encumbrances, and to record said deed, together with a copy of this resolution, in the office of the Recorder of the City and County of San Francisco.

Ayes—Supervisors Andriano, Canepa, Colman, Havenner, Hayden, McGovern, McSheehy, Miles, Peyser, Power, Roncovieri, Rossi, Spaulding, Suhr, Toner—15.

Absent—Supervisors Gallagher, Shannon, Stanton—3.

Accepting Offer of Charles Monestier to Sell Land for Market Street Extension.

Also, Resolution No. 32064 (New Series), as follows:

Resolved, That the offer of sale made by the following named owner to sell to the City and County of San Francisco the following described land, required for the extension of Market street, for the sum set forth opposite his name, be accepted:

Charles Monestier, $725—Lot 14, Block 2659, as per the Assessor's Block Books of the City and County of Francisco. (As per detailed description and written offer on file.)

And the City Attorney is hereby authorized to examine the title to said property, and if the same is found satisfactory to accept, on behalf of the City, a deed conveying said property to the City, free and clear of all encumbrances, and to record said deed, together with a copy of this resolution, in the office of the Recorder of the City and County of San Francisco.

Ayes—Supervisors Andriano, Canepa, Colman, Havenner, Hayden, McGovern, McSheehy, Miles, Peyser, Power, Roncovieri, Rossi, Spaulding, Suhr, Toner—15.

Absent—Supervisors Gallagher, Shannon, Stanton—3.

Accepting Offer to Sell Land for Opening and Widening of Cayuga Avenue at Its Intersection With Greece Street.

Also, Resolution No. 32065 (New Series), as follows:

Resolved, That the offer of sale made by the following named owner to sell to the City and County of San Francisco the following described land, required for the opening and widening of Cayuga avenue at its intersection with Greece street, for the sum set forth opposite its name, be accepted:

Andrea Sbarboro & Sons, $185—Portion of Lots 4 and 5, Block 6959B, as per the Assessor's Block Books of the City and County of San Francisco. (As per detailed description and written offer on file.)

And the City Attorney is hereby authorized to examine the title to said property, and, if the same is found satisfactory, to accept, on behalf of the City, a deed conveying said property to the City, free and clear of all encumbrances, and to record said deed, together with a copy of this resolution, in the office of the Recorder of the City nad County of San Francisco.

Ayes—Supervisors Andriano, Canepa, Colman, Havenner, Hayden, McGovern, McSheehy, Miles, Peyser, Power, Roncovieri, Rossi, Spaulding, Suhr, Toner—15.

Absent—Supervisors Gallagher, Shannon, Stanton—3.

Passed for Printing.

The following matters were *passed for printing*:

Board of Public Works to Prepare Plans, Etc., Receive Bids and Award of Contract for 60,000 Lane Markers.

On recommendation of Finance Committee.

Bill No. 8186, Ordinance No. ———— (New Series), as follows:

Authorizing and directing the Board of Public Works to prepare plans and specifications, receive bids and award contract for installing approximately 60,000 pedestrian lane markers, 1000 traffic turning buttons, removing and installing 500 traffic turning buttons, installing 1000 plain safety zone buttons, installing 200 reflector type safety zone buttons, replacing approximately 400 reflector type safety zone buttons with buttons containing whole reflectors, hauling buttons to Corporation Yard and replacing broken reflectors with new ones.

Be it ordained by the People of the City and County of San Francisco as follows:

Section 1. The Board of Public Works is hereby authorized and directed to prepare plans and specifications, receive bids and award contract for installing approximately 60,000 pedestrian lane markers, 1000 traffic turning buttons, removing and installing 500 traffic turning buttons, installing 1000 plain safety zone buttons, installing 200 reflector type safety zone buttons, replacing approximately 400 reflector type safety zone buttons with buttons containing whole reflectors, hauling buttons to Corporation Yard and replacing broken reflectors with new ones.

Section 2. This ordinance shall take effect immediately.

Boiler Permits.

On recommendation of Fire Committee.

Resolution No. ———— (New Series), as follows:

Resolved, That the following revocable permits be and are hereby granted:

Boilers.

Lesters. Limited, 609 Mission street, 15-horsepower.

Gilt Edge Creamery, 2498 Fillmore street, 10-horsepower.

The rights granted under this resolution shall be exercised within six months, otherwise said permit shall become null and void.

Captain Roy N. Francis Appointed Superintendent of Mills Field Municipal Airport.

The following matter was taken up:

Resolution No. ———— (New Series), as follows:

Resolved, That Captain Roy N. Francis be and he is hereby appointed Superintendent of Mills Feld Municipal Airport, effective February 1, 1930.

Statement of Supervisor McSheehy.

Supervisor McSheehy, referring to conversation he had with Mr. Edw. E. Moulton, declared that Mr. Moulton had asked him to take up the matter of Captain Francis' qualification for Superintendent of the Municipal Airport, alleging that the Advisory Committee had not unanimously endorsed the appointment of Captain Francis; that Captain Francis did not have a pilot's license, and that the last action that he was in favor of, with other members of the Advisory Committee, was the retention of Bartlett Stephens as acting superintendent.

Motion.

Supervisor Havenner moved, in light of the statement of Supervisor McSheehy, the resolution be laid over one week and made a Special Order for 4 p. m., and that the Advisory Committee be invited to attend, especially Mr. Moulton and Captain Brant.

Motion *carried* by the following vote:

Ayes—Supervisors Andriano, Colman, Gallagher, Havenner, McGovern, McSheehy, Roncovieri, Suhr, Toner—9.

Noes—Supervisors Canepa, Hayden, Miles, Peyser, Power, Rossi, Spaulding, Stanton—8.

Absent—Supervisor Shannon—1.

Action Deferred.

The following matter was *laid over one week*:

Airport Committee to Appoint Advisory Committee.

Resolution No. ————— (New Series), as follows:

Resolved, That the Airport and Aeronautics Committee be and is hereby authorized to select and appoint an Advisory Committee, to consist of citizens whose cooperation, advice and counsel, by reason of their training, experience and knowledge of aviation, would be of value and assistance to the Committee in the operation and management of Mills Field Municipal Airport; and be it

Further Resolved, That Resolution No. 30712 (New Series) be and the same is hereby repealed.

Adopted.

The following resolutions were *adopted*:

Exchange of Properties Between Board of Education and Playground Commission, Aptos Avenue, and Repeal of Resolution No. 31951 (New Series).

On recommendation of Public Buildings and Lands Committee.

Resolution No. 32066 (New Series), as follows:

Resolved, That, in accordance with a communication from the Playground Commission, and in accordance with the request of the Board of Education set forth therein, the following described properties are hereby exchanged between the said Playground Commission and the Board of Education for their respective use and purposes, to-wit:

Playground Commission to Board of Education:

Commencing at a point on the easterly line of Aptos avenue, distant southerly thereon an arc distance of 290.207 feet from the southerly termination of that curve of 10 feet radius at the intersection of said easterly line with the southerly line of Upland drive, as said curve is shown on that certain map entitled "Map of Blocks 3260 to 3269, inclusive, Balboa Terrace Addition," and recorded in Map Book "L," pages 29 to 33, inclusive, records of the City and County of San Francisco, and running thence southerly along said line of Aptos avenue, on the arc of a curve to the right, radius 1618 feet, central angle 1 deg. 31 min. 44 sec., a distance of 43.174 feet to a point in a line parallel to and distant 340 feet at right angles southerly from the southerly line of Upland drive; thence deflecting 103 deg. 02 min. 15 sec. to the left from the tangent to the preceding curve and running easterly along said parallel line 216.370 feet to a point distant westerly 141.193 feet measured along said parallel line from its point of intersection with the northwesterly line of Mt. Davidson Manor, as per map thereof recorded in Map Book "K," pages 55 to 62, inclusive, records of the City and County of San Francisco; thence deflecting 168 deg. 29 min. 29 sec. to the left and running northwesterly along the radial line of said curve of 1618 feet radius hereinbefore mentioned extended easterly through the point of commencement of this description 211.444 feet to the easterly line of Aptos avenue and the point of commencement.

Being a portion of Block 3266 of said Balboa Terrace Addition and a portion of San Aleso avenue, as said avenue existed prior to its closing and abandonment by Resolution No. 28866 (New Series), dated

April 24, 1928, of the Board of Supervisors of the City and County of San Francisco. Containing 4560 square feet.

Board of Education to Playground Commission:

Commencing at a point on the easterly line of Block 3265 as said block is shown on that certain map entitled "Map of Balboa Terrace Addition," and recorded in Map Book "L," pages 29 to 33, inclusive, records of the City and County of San Francisco, distant southerly thereon an arc distance of 370.296 feet from the southerly line of Upland drive and running thence northerly along said easterly line of Block 3265 on a curve to the left, radius 1968 feet, an arc distance of 28.171 feet to its intersection with a line parallel to and distant 340 feet at right angles southerly from said southerly line of Upland drive; thence deflecting 100 deg. 41 min. 18 sec. to the left from the tangent to the preceding curve and running westerly along said parallel line 141.193 feet to a point distant easterly 216.370 feet, measured along said parallel line, from the easterly line of Aptos avenue; thence deflecting 168 deg. 29 min. 29 sec. to the left and running southeasterly along the radial line of said curve of 1968 feet radius, hereinbefore mentioned, 138.556 feet to the easterly line of said Block 3265 and the point of commencement.

Being a portion of said Block 3265 and a portion of San Aleso avenue as said avenue existed prior to its closing and abandonment by Resolution No. 28866 (New Series), dated April 24, 1928, of the Board of Supervisors of the City and County of San Francisco. Containing 1953 square feet.

Resolution No. 31951 (New Series) is hereby repealed.

Ayes—Supervisors Andriano, Canepa, Colman, Havenner, Hayden, McGovern, McSheehy, Miles, Peyser, Power, Roncovieri, Rossi, Spaulding, Suhr, Toner—15.

Absent—Supervisors Gallagher, Shannon, Stanton—3.

Mayor Authorized and Requested to Sell at Public Auction Frame Building Adjoining Polytechnic High School.

Also, Resolution No. 32067 (New Series), as follows:

Resolved, That, in accordance with a communication from the Board of Education, filed January 24, 1930, his Honor the Mayor be and he is hereby authorized and requested to sell, at public auction, in accordance with provisions of the Charter, the certain frame building belonging to the City and County and situate as follows:

On the south line of Frederick street, immediately adjoining the Polytechnic High School on the easterly side, consisting of three flats and known as Nos. 643-645-647 Frederick street.

Ayes—Supervisors Andriano, Canepa, Colman, Havenner, Hayden, McGovern, McSheehy, Miles, Peyser, Power, Roncovieri, Rossi, Spaulding, Suhr, Toner—15.

Absent—Supervisors Gallagher, Shannon, Stanton—3.

Favoring the Establishment of Motor Bus Service From San Francisco to San Jose Via the Bay Shore Highway, and Requesting City Attorney to Appear Before California Railroad Commission in Behalf of Such Service.

On recommendation of Public Utilities Committee.

Resolution No. 32068 (New Series), as follows:

Whereas, there are pending before the California Railroad Commission applications for permits to operate motor coach lines from San Francisco to San Jose via the Bay Shore highway; and

Whereas, there is at present no motor coach service for the people in the communities situated on the Bay Shore highway; and

Whereas, such service would be a great advantage to the people and communities of the Bay Shore highway in general, and to the San

Francisco Municipal Airport (Mills Field) in particular; now, therefore, be it

Resolved, That the Board of Supervisors of the City and County of San Francisco does hereby favor the establishment of this motor bus service as a public necessity and convenience to the public; and be it

Further Resolved, That the City Attorney, as the official representative of the Board of Supervisors, be requested to be present in the courtroom of the California Railroad Commission in San Francisco on February 18, 1930, when these applications are to be heard, not in behalf of any particular application, but to urge upon the said California Railroad Commission the necessity, benefit and advantage of the establishment of motor bus transportation between San Francisco and San Jose via the Bay Shore highway.

Ayes—Supervisors Andriano, Canepa, Colman, Havenner, Hayden, McGovern, McSheehy, Miles, Peyser, Power, Roncovieri, Rossi, Spaulding, Suhr, Toner—15.

Absent—Supervisors Gallagher, Shannon, Stanton—3.

Passed for Printing.

The following matters were *passed for printing*:

Prescribing the Procedure Under Which the Board of Public Works Shall Have Charge, Superintendence and Control of the Municipally Owned Water System, and Providing for the Creation of a Water Department, Etc.

On recommendation of Public Utilities and Finance Committees.

Bill No. 8187, Ordinance No. ———— (New Series), as follows:

Setting forth and prescribing the procedure and limitations under which the Board of Public Works shall have charge, superintendence and control of the supplying of water for domestic purposes from the municipally owned and operated water system; providing for the creation of a water department; providing for the organization of the same; prescribing its powers and duties and the manner in which these shall be carried out.

Be it ordained by the People of the City and County of San Francisco as follows:

Section 1. *Direction to Board of Public Works.* The Board of Public Works, in exercising the powers granted to it under Paragraph 8 of Section 9 of Chapter I of Article VI of the Charter, relative to the superintendence and control of the construction, maintenance and operation of the public water supply of San Francisco, shall do so subject to the provisions of this ordinance.

Section 2. *San Francisco Water Department and Purposes and Powers.* The Board of Public Works shall create a Department of Water Supply, for the purpose of supplying water to the inhabitants of the City and County of San Francisco, and to such other persons and places as may hereafter be supplied with water by the City and County of San Francisco, which said department shall be designated as "San Francisco Water Department."

The maintenance and operation of the Spring Valley Water Company system, whenever the same shall come into possession of the City, and also the water system owned by the City and County of San Francisco, commonly known as the County Line Water Works, shall be vested in said San Francisco Water Department under the jurisdiction of the Board of Public Works, until a Charter amendment is adopted and approved providing for the creation of a Public Utilities Commission.

All construction work done in or about the properties of said system, whether for extensions thereto or for additions and betterments thereto, shall be done under the direction and supervision of the City Engineer, and said City Engineer shall from time to time recommend to the Board of Public Works such work as he deems necessary to be performed, or materials or equipment to be furnished, in and about the construction, operation or maintenance of said Water Department. And no extensions, additions or major improvements or replacements to the system shall be made except on the recommendation of the head of the department or the City Engineer.

The Board of Public Works shall establish all necessary rules and regulations for the conduct of the business of the department, and shall have full power and authority to collect any and all amounts due from any consumer for water furnished by said San Francisco Water Department, including all amounts due from any consumer for water furnished by the Spring Valley Water Company and remaining unpaid when the properties of the Spring Valley Water Company are taken over by the City and County of San Francisco, and the said Board of Public Works, or the head of the department, shall have full power and authority to discontinue the service of any consumer who is delinquent to the Spring Valley Water Company or to the Water Department in the payment of amounts due for water furnished to or used by said consumer, and may by civil action in the name of the City and County enforce the collection of any and all amounts due for said water. And said Board may also provide, by rule or by order, for the requiring of security in such form and in such amount as may be recommended by the head of the department, for the supplying of water or rendering service to any person, and the furnishing of said security may be made a prerequisite to the furnishing of said water or service.

The Board of Public Works may, by resolution, authorize such banks in the City and County of San Francisco as it may elect to receive payment of water bills due or to be collected by the Water Department, and to issue receipts for the same in the name of the department, payment for such service to be at a rate not to exceed five cents per account per month, and provided that all amounts paid to any bank or banks selected for the purpose of receiving payment of said water bills shall be by said banks daily transmitted to the Water Department and by said Water Department paid daily into the Treasury of the City and County of San Francisco.

The Water Department shall observe all ordinances of the City and County of San Francisco and rules and regulations of the Department of Public Works relative to street openings, barricades, excavations, replacing of pavement, and similar matters, and relative to such matters shall apply for and receive permits and pay the necessary fees for said permits, and be subject to inspection and regulation, in the same manner and at the same rates as a private person or corporation would be if doing or performing any of said work or things.

All rules and regulations adopted or established by the Board of Public Works for the conduct of said San Francisco Water Department shall, within thirty days after the date of the adoption thereof, be printed, and shall be available for distribution to the public upon application therefor.

Section 3. *Organization, Employees.* The Board of Public Works shall appoint as head of the department, with appropriate title, a chief executive, who shall possess the necessary executive, administrative and technical qualifications to administer the affairs of the department, and who shall have sole executive control of said department, subject to rules and regulations prescribed by the Board.

Employees of the Spring Valley Water Company in the operating service thereof at the time the properties of said company are taken over by the City, and who have been continuously employed in said operating service for not less than one year immediately prior to the taking over of said properties, shall be continued in their positions and shall be considered to have been appointed to such positions under the provisions of Article XIII of the Charter, and shall be entitled to all civil service rights therein provided, and shall thereafter be considered employees of San Francisco Water Department. That if any of said employees in said operating department of said Spring Valley Water Company do not, at the time the properties of said company are taken over by the City, possess the residential qualifications required by Section 2 of Article XVI of the Charter, they shall be allowed a period of one year within which to acquire the same, and any employee not acquiring said residential qualifications within said period shall be dismissed from his or her employment. All positions in the Water Department shall be classified and graded by the Civil Service Commission as provided by the Charter, and vacancies in any of said positions shall be filled, and promotions in said department shall be made, as provided by Article XIII of the Charter and in accordance with the rules and regulations of the Civil Service Commission.

The Board shall employ such engineers, superintendents, accountants, inspectors and other assistants and employees as the department head may certify to be necessary. All of said appointments shall be made in accordance with the provisions of Article XIII of the Charter and the rules and regulations of the Civil Service Commission, provided that temporary appointments made under the provisions of Section 10 of said article shall, pursuant to the provisions of said article, remain in force for a period not exceeding sixty (60) days and only until regular appointments can be made under the provisions of said article, and said appointments shall be limited to a period of sixty (60) days and shall not be subject to renewal.

Section 4. *Salaries of Present Employees of Spring Valley Water Company.* The salaries, wages and compensation of all employees of the Spring Valley Water Company, whose employment shall continue in force with the San Francisco Water Department, as hereinbefore set forth, shall be subject to standardization as provided in Section 14, Chapter II, Article II, of the Charter. That, pending the standardization of said wages, salaries and compensation, there shall be paid to said employees at least the minimum entrance salary, wage or compensation paid for similar service in any other utility at present being operated by the Board of Public Works, and if there are any positions or places of employment in said Water Department which are not common with those in said other utilities, then the compensation to be paid to said employees occupying said last-mentioned positions shall be at least the minimum entrance wage or compensation paid for similar service in other departments of the city government, provided that such minimum entrance rate in the clerical service shall not be less than $150 per month. Provided, however, that the salary, wage or compensation of any employee whose employment is continued in the Water Department shall not be reduced below the salary, wage or compensation which said employee received from the Spring Valley Water Company, as evidenced by its January, 1930, payroll, unless the duties of said employee have been diminished on his coming into the employment of the Water Department, or said salary, wage or compensation exceeds the maximum amount paid by the city for like service.

Section 5. *Accounts, Reports and Adjustments.* The accounts of the Water Department shall be maintained in accordance with the forms and requirements of the State Railroad Commission for water companies of similar character, in so far as said forms and requirements shall be applicable to a municipally-owned water system, and said accounts shall also show all matters and things provided to be shown or set up by Subdivision 3, Section 16, Article XII, of the Charter.

A complete operating statement, showing all the operations, receipts and disbursements of the Water Department for the previous month, shall be filed each month by the head of the department with the Board of Public Works, and with the Mayor, and with the Board of Supervisors, and the same shall be open for inspection by the public in the office of said Board of Public Works. In addition to the matters hereinbefore set forth, said statements shall show the increase or de-

crease in the number of employees of the Department since the end
of the preceding month.

Commencing July 1, 1930, all amounts due to the Water Department for water used by or furnished to the other departments of the
city, as well as all charges or rental for hydrant service, shall be
carried on the books of the Water Department at the current rates
provided for said water or for said service; and before the end of each
fiscal year the Water Department shall determine the amount of taxes
which would have been payable at the rate for the current year to the
City and County upon the properties of the Water Department, if said
properties were privately owned, and said amount of taxes shall offset
any amounts which said accounts may show to be due for water or
service from said municipal departments, in so far as the amount of
said taxes and the amount due for water equal one another; and if
the amount shown to be due for said water or for said service shall
exceed the amount which would have been due for taxes if said
property of said department was privately owned, the overplus shall
be paid from the General or other funds of the City and County to the
said Water Department, and charged against the various departments
in accordance with the water and service furnished to each.

In making its annual budget each year, pursuant to the provisions of
the Charter, the Board of Supervisors shall estimate the amount which
shall become due from the other departments of the city government
to the Water Department in the succeeding fiscal year, by reason of any
difference between the amounts due for water and the amount of
taxes which would be collected if the property of said Water Department was privately owned, and shall in said budget make provision for
such difference.

During the remainder of the fiscal year 1929-1930, water shall be
furnished without charge to those departments of the municipality to
which appropriations have been made to defray the cost of water or
hydrant service furnished to any of said departments, and water or
service furnished to any other department shall be paid for at the
current rates.

Commencing with the fiscal year 1930-1931, there shall be payable
from the Water Department the sum of $250,000 per year as rental
for the transbay Hetch Hetchy aqueduct, which said sum shall be payable into the 1910 Hetch Hetchy Bond Interest Fund, and for the
remainder of the fiscal year the Water Department shall pay into said
fund such portion of said sum of $250,000 as shall not have been paid
as rental for said aqueduct for said year.

Section 6. *Budgets.* Not later than April 1, in the year 1930, and
during the month of February in each succeeding year, the head of the
Water Department shall transmit to the Board of Public Works a
proposed budget for the next fiscal year, which said budget shall show
in detail the estimated amounts of revenue from all sources to the
department for said year, as well as an estimate of all amounts to be
paid out by said department for all purposes, including payments to
and from the various reserve and sinking funds maintained by said
department. Such estimate, both of receipts and disbursements. shall
be segregated and itemized so as to show the exact purpose of each
item therein, and the amounts for salaries and wages shall be itemized
so as to show the compensation paid to each class of employees, and
the number of said employees in each class. Provided. however. that
in estimating the cost of construction work, in the performance of
which the employees will not be of a permanent character. the estimated number of said employees to be employed thereon need not be
set forth. Said budget shall be prepared and transmitted to the Board
of Public Works in quadruplicate.

The Board of Public Works shall consider said proposed budget, and
upon approval of the same. shall transmit a copy thereof. with such
changes. if any. indicated thereon, to the Mayor, and another to the
Board of Supervisors, and another to the Auditor, which said copies

shall be so transmitted not later than the first Monday in April of each year.

The Finance Committee of the Board of Supervisors shall submit said budget with its annual budget report to the Board, together with such recommendations as it deems proper, and said Board of Supervisors may reduce the estimate of expenditures or any item thereof, except proposed expenditures or appropriations as may be by law or by their nature fixed; and, subject, to such changes or reductions, said Board shall approve and adopt said budget at the same time at which the annual budget provided by Charter must be adopted, and shall thereupon transmit the same to the Auditor.

The adoption of said budget by the Board of Supervisors shall be considered an appropriation of the various amounts therein contained for the purposes therein set forth, and thereafter said sums so appropriated may be expended by the Board of Public Works, in the manner provided by law, for the purposes for which they are appropriated, without further order of the Board of Supervisors.

Expenditures or commitments in excess of amounts set up in the budget adopted as hereinbefore provided, or for purposes not therein specified, may be made only by the filing and adopting at any time in the manner as specified hereinbefore for each annual budget and within the estimated revenues of the department, of a supplemental budget for such additional expenditures; provided, however, that in case of an emergency involving the protection of life or property, emergency expenditures may be ordered and authorized by the head of the department, in which case full report to the Board of Public Works, with copy thereof to the Board of Supervisors and the Auditor, shall be made at the earliest possible time, together with an estimate of the additional cost, if any, of further expenditures occasioned by the emergency.

Temporary Budget. As soon after March 1st, 1930, as is possible, the head of the Department shall file with the Board of Public Works a budget of the estimated revenues and proposed expenditures of the Water Department for the period from March 3rd to June 30th, 1930, and the Board of Public Works shall act upon the same without delay and transmit one copy thereof as approved to the Mayor, and two copies thereof to the Board of Supervisors. Said budget, in so far as possible, shall be prepared in accordance with the provisions hereinbefore set forth relating to annual budgets in so far as said provisions may be applicable, provided that said budget shall show the number, title and rate of compensation of the employees of the Spring Valley Water Company immediately prior to the date on which the properties of said Company were taken over by the City, as well as the number, civil service title and proposed rates of compensation of said employees while in the employ of the Water Department. Upon receipt of said budget the Board of Supervisors shall act upon the same within ten days after receipt of same, and when the said budget is approved by said Board of Supervisors one copy of the same shall be transmitted to the Auditor with the approval of the Board attached thereto, and when so received by said Auditor the same shall be his authority for auditing any demands against the Water Department as set forth or included in said budget; and if said budget should not be received by said Auditor in due time to enable him to audit the demands of the employees of said Water Department as the same become due, the said Auditor may audit and the Treasurer pay the demands of said employees when they are approved by the head of the Water Department, the Board of Public Works, and the Civil Service Commission, as being in conformity with the provisions of Section 4 of this ordinance, and appropriation in an amount sufficient to pay said demands as so approved is hereby made from the revenues of said Water Department as the said revenues accrue.

Section 7. *Operating Expenses and Reserves.* The receipts from operation of the San Francisco Water Department shall be paid daily into the City Treasury and maintained in a special fund set aside therefor, which shall be designated "The Water Revenue Fund," and appropriations may from time to time be made by the Board of Supervisors from said receipts for the purposes in this section set forth and in accordance with budgets to be made as hereinbefore provided and as otherwise provided in this ordinance.

1. For the payment of the operating expenses of the water supply system, including expenditures or appropriations to reserves, pension charges, compensation insurance, injuries, damages, Hetch Hetchy aqueduct rental and taxes that may be assessed against property outside of San Francisco belonging to the City and under the control of the Water Department.

2. For repairs and reconstruction, and in order to provide properly for repairs and reconstruction due to depreciation, there shall be created and established a depreciation reserve which shall be credited monthly with an amount equal to one-twelfth the annual depreciation requirements determined as elsewhere herein provided.

3. For the payment of interest and sinking fund on the bonds issued for the acquisition of the Spring Valley Water system, and for this purpose there shall be set aside monthly and transferred to the Spring Valley bond interest and redemption funds sums sufficient in the aggregate to meet, at the proper time, all interest and redemption charges against said utility as the same fall due.

4. For extensions, improvements and replacements, and in order to properly finance the necessary extensions, improvements and replacements out of earnings, there shall be established a Water Extension Reserve Fund, into which shall be paid monthly the sums necessary to provide for such extensions, improvements and replacements as may have been determined upon in a program adopted as elsewhere herein provided.

5. For the Charter Reserve Fund.

The Depreciation Reserve Fund shall be used only to cover costs of replacements due to a realized depreciation. The Board of Public Works shall cause an appraisal to be made by the City Engineer of the several classes of property involved in the Water System as to life and the amount of accrued depreciation, and determine the amount of the reasonable annual depreciation requirements necessary in order to provide properly for repairs or reconstruction due to realized physical and functional depreciation; provided, however, that at least every five years the Board shall cause a reappraisal to be made of the depreciation reserves, replacement expenditures therefrom, and probable useful life of each of the several kinds of property, and on the basis of such reappraisal shall redetermine the amount of the reasonable annual depreciation requirements. Provided, that the amount to be set aside each year into said depreciation fund shall be subject to budget by the Board of Supervisors. Until such time as the Board of Public Works has determined the reasonable annual depreciation requirements necessary by appraisal as above provided for, there shall be transferred to the Depreciation Reserve Fund from the receipts from operation of the Water Department at the end of each month, the sum of $5,000.

The Water Extension Reserve Fund shall be used only to cover costs of the construction of extensions, additions and betterments to the water system. The Board of Public Works upon the recommendation of the head of the Water Department shall from time to time establish a program of the necessary extensions, additions and betterments required in a period not extending over five years, and upon the approval of said program or any amendments thereto by the Board of Supervisors in any annual or supplemental budget, there shall be deposited monthly to the credit of the Extension Reserve one-twelfth of the annual contribution determined as necessary to complete the several elements of the program within the time required, provided, that for the first five years of operation the amount to be appropriated to the depreciation fund and the Water Extension Reserve Fund, considered together, shall be not less than $564,000 per year.

There shall be paid into the Charter Reserve Fund provided for in Subdivision 5, Section 7 of this ordinance all moneys not otherwise appropriated or used in conformity with the provisions of this ordinance, and the Board of Supervisors may from time to time make appropriations from said fund for any of the purposes provided for in this ordinance when respective funds herein provided for any of the specific purposes herein set forth are exhausted or insufficient to meet the demands upon them. Whenever the said Charter Reserve Fund shall exceed one-half of the payment for operating expenses in the preceding year, the Board of Supervisors may appropriate such excess to the General Fund of the City.

At any time that there is a surplus on deposit in the city treasury in any of the several funds herein provided for in an amount greater than is necessary for the immediate needs of the Water Department, the said department, through the Board of Public Works, shall notify the Treasurer, who shall make arrangements as provided by law for the proper investment or deposit of such funds, the interest accruing therefrom to be credited to the benefit of and to be applied to the fund from which invested.

Section 8. *Water Rates.* No water shall be furnished to any consumer, except as hereinbefore set forth, except at the current rates therefor fixed as in this section provided. The water rates in effect under the Spring Valley Water Company's management at the time of the City's acquisition of the system shall remain in effect for a period of at least one year. Thereafter, changes in the water rates shall only be made by the Board of Public Works upon the written recommendation of the head of the department and the approval of the Board of Supervisors.

No rates shall be established which in the aggregate will produce a revenue less than that necessary to safely cover all operating expenses and other expenses provided for in Section 6 hereof, and provide for and maintain the several reserves herein provided for and also to maintain the Charter reserve at a sum equal to one-half of the operating expenses for the preceding year.

When any change in rates is contemplated, the head of the department shall submit to the Board of Public Works a financial report, in support of the proposed change, and the Board of Public Works shall fix a date for hearing the matter of said change in rates and cause to be published in the official newspaper of the City and County notice of said hearing at least ten days prior to the date thereof, specifying in said notice the time and place of said hearing. At said hearing any person, on behalf of himself or others interested, may be heard, or present in writing his views, after which the Board shall fix the rates and submit them to the Board of Supervisors, who shall within thirty days, by ordinance, approve or disapprove the same. Failure of the Board of Supervisors to act within the thirty days shall be construed as approval of the recommended rates. In fixing rates for water service, the same may be fixed at varying scales for different classes of service or consumers.

Section 9. *Service by Other Departments.* Services rendered by any other department of the City and County to the Water Department, upon request of the Water Department, shall be paid for by the Water Department at cost out of its revenues.

.Section 10. *City Attorney.* The City Attorney shall be the legal adviser of the Department and shall render such legal services as the Board of Public Works or the head of the Department may deem necessary, and shall prosecute and defend all actions or proceedings affecting or involving the Water Department or any of its properties. He shall when necessary, upon the request of the Board of Public Works, appoint and detail one or more attorneys to perform the duties herein specified, and the compensation of said attorneys so detailed shall be approved by the Board of Public Works and fixed by the Board of Supervisors, and shall be paid from the revenues of the Water Department as an operating expense thereof.

Section 11. *Bonds of Employees.* The Board of Public Works may require a bond of indemnity from any of the employees of the Water Department, conditioned for the faithful performance of the duties of said employee or employees, and for the purpose of obtaining said bonds the said Board of Public Works may contract with any surety company authorized to write said bonds, to furnish the same, either for individual employees of groups thereof, and the cost of the same shall be charged as an operating expense of said Water Department.

Section 12. *Payment of Salaries and Wages.* Payrolls for all employees of the Water Department shall be segregated and made up according to the assembly or distribution points for the various employments, as determined by the head of the department, and each of said payrolls shall be approved as required by law and transmitted to the Auditor. Upon the approval of the items on said payroll or payrolls the Auditor shall issue his separate demand upon the Treasurer for each of the items thereon in the form provided for the payment of salaries in other departments of the city, and the same, with the respective payrolls for which said demands are issued, shall be delivered to such person as the head of the department shall, in writing filed with the Auditor, authorize to receive the same, and upon the delivery of the same said person shall receipt to said Auditor for said payrolls and said demands. The head of the department shall thereupon cause said demands to be delivered to the respective payees named therein at. or as near as possible to, the places of employment of said employees.

Section 13. *Revolving Fund.* For the purpose of paying petty expenses of the Water Department, and for making such other payments as cannot be conveniently paid by demands drawn upon the Treasurer and approved by the Auditor, the Water Department shall maintain in such bank or banks as may be designated by the Board of Public Works, a fund of $20,000, from which fund said petty expenses and other payments that cannot be conveniently paid by demands drawn upon the Treasurer shall be paid by check drawn by the head of the department or by such other persons in the employ of said department as the head of said department may authorize. The head of the department shall, from time to time, and at least once in each month, transmit to the Auditor a demand in favor of said fund for all amounts disbursed from it, to which demand shall be attached receipts for all payments so made, which said receipts shall show the name of the person receiving any payment from said fund, as well as the purpose for which said payment was made, and shall be signed by the party receiving said payment. When said demand is approved by the Auditor and paid by the Treasurer, it shall be delivered to the head of the Water Department and deposited to the credit of said fund. The Board of Supervisors shall appropriate the said sum of $20,000 for such fund, and may, from time to time, make such additional appropriations thereto from the revenues of said department as said Board shall deem proper.

Section 14. *Purchase of Materials, Supplies and Equipment.* Purchases of materials, supplies and equipment required by Water Department operations shall be made in accordance with the provisions of Chapter IV, Article II, and Section 6, Chapter I, Article III. of the Charter, and of Ordinance 5880 (New Series); provided. however. that specifications may be prepared under the direction of the head of the Water Department for all equipment required by the department, or for materials or supplies peculiar to said department operations and not in common use in other departments of the City and County, and the head of the department may designate the particular brand, kind or make of any equipment which may be necessary in the conduct of said department.

Section 15.. *Constitutionality.* If any section, subsection, subdivision or provision of this ordinance is for any reason held to be unconstitutional, such decision shall not affect the validity of the remaining portions of this ordinance, the Board of Supervisors hereby declaring that it would have passed this ordinance and each section, subsection, subdivision, provision, sentence, clause and phrase thereof irrespective of the fact that any one or more sections, subsections, subdivisions, provisions, sentences, clauses or phrases hereof are declared unconstitutional.

Section 16. This ordinance shall become effective immediately upon its passage.

Privilege of the Floor.

Adolph Uhl was granted the privilege of the floor and requested that section 3 be so amended that the earnings from the distribution of water will be credited to a "Hetch Hetchy Water Operating Fund," as it is his judgment that the parent water utility is Hetch Hetchy, and any water or power properties or distributing systems subsequently acquired become a unit of the parent utility and its receipts should be credited as suggested.

Opinion of City Attorney in re Spring Valley Operating Ordinances.

January 20, 1930.

To the Public Utilities Committee, Board of Supervisors.

Dear Sirs: On the 16th instant you submitted two drafts of an ordinance relative to the operation of the Spring Valley Water System when the same is taken over by the City. I understand that one of said ordinances was submitted to you by the Department of Engineering and the other by the Board of Public Works. The drafts are similar in effect with the exception that the one submitted by the Engineering Department commits control of the system to the Department of Engineering and makes the recommendation of the City Engineer a prerequisite to the appointment of its employees, while the one submitted by the Board of Public Works lodges complete control in that body.

You have asked me to report specifically upon the legality of the following provisions of the drafts:

(1) Is it legal to make the Water Department a bureau in the Department of Engineering?

(b) Is it legal to place the Hetch Hetchy project under the jurisdiction of the Water Department or to consolidate the Water Department with the Hetch Hetchy project?

(c) Can the appointment of the head and other employees of the Water Department be made conditional upon the approval of the City Engineer?

(d) Can the Board of Public Works, on the recommendation of the City Engineer, be authorized to employ an attorney to attend to such legal matters as may arise in the Water Department?

(e) In addition, you have asked that I comment upon the legality of the other provisions of both ordinances.

Opinion.

Question a. Is it legal to make the Water Department a bureau in the Department of Engineering?

There is no provision in the Charter for a Department of Engineering in the Department of Public Works, and if such a department exists it is by virtue of the power of the Board to make rules and regulations for its government and for the performance of its duties. (Sec. 4; Chap. I, Art. VI, Charter.) It is needless to state that such rules cannot contravene any Charter provision. Subdivision 8 of Section 9 of the same chapter lodges in the Board of Public Works, subject to ordinances of the Board of Supervisors, the charge, superintendence and control of the construction, maintenance and operation of any and all public utilities owned, operated or controlled by the City. Section 11 of the same chapter provides for the appointment of a City Engineer, and prescribes his duties, which duties may be summed up in the language contained in the opening sentence of the second paragraph, to-wit: "He shall perform all civil engineering and surveying required in the prosecution of the public works and improvements done under the direction and supervision of said Board, and shall certify to the progress and completion of the same." In my opinion this section commits the construction work of any utility to the City Engineer, as an official of the Board of Public Works, but I can find no Charter language which in any way vests him with its management. True, Subdivision 8 of Section 9, above mentioned, provides that the Board of Public Works may, when authorized by ordinance, "contract for work to be performed, or materials or equipment to be furnished, or for expert or technical or professional services to be rendered, wherever the same are certified by the City Engineer to be necessary, etc." At most, this language authorizes the City Engineer to recommend to the Board of Public Works what he may deem necessary to the utility, but it is not sufficiently broad to vest him with control, which is, by more definite language, lodged in the Board itself.

I am, therefore, of the opinion that there is no provision in the Charter which compels the management of a public utility to be vested in the City Engineer. This being the case, it follows that it is not within the power of the Board of Supervisors to compel the Board of Public Works to commit the management of the Water Department to the Department of Engineering, for the reason that Section 13 of Chapter I, above mentioned, provides that "The Board (of Public Works) shall appoint the necessary heads of departments under its charge." Should the Board of Supervisors, by ordinance, place the Water Department under the jurisdiction of the Department of Engineering it would be practically appointing the head of the Water Department, which would be a usurpation of power which is, by the above-mentioned section, vested in the Board of Public Works. Understand, however, that if the Board of Public Works itself desires to make the City Engineer manager of the Water Department, it may do so.

Question b. Is it legal to place the Hetch Hetchy project under the jurisdiction of the Water Department, or to consolidate the Water Department with the Hetch Hetchy project?

With the exception of the production of hydro-electric power at Moccasin Creek, the Hetch Hetchy project is as yet in the progress of construction, and as a water proposition is not a producing utility, and, being in the progress of construction, is, by the Charter, committed to the City Engineer, under the jurisdiction of the Board of Public Works. I have already stated that the management of the Water Department cannot, by ordinance of the Board of Supervisors, be committed to the Department of Engineering. Therefore, to commit the construction project to the Water Department might be taking the former from the City Engineer, where it properly belongs. However, I see even a more serious objection to a consolidation of the two departments. As both projects have to do with water for San Francisco, I am fearful that committing the construction, maintenance and operation of both projects to the San Francisco Water Department would be practically merging them both into one utility, i. e., the water utility of San Francisco. The Supreme Court, in Uhl vs. Badaracco, 199 Cal. 270, decided that the earnings of a municipally owned utility could be applied only in the order set forth in Section 16, Article XII of the Charter, and that said earnings could not be applied to extensions and improvements before full provision had been made for bond interest and redemption. Applying the principle decided to the instant case it might be that, if the utilities were consolidated, the earnings of the Spring Valley would be liable for the bond issue for the Hetch Hetchy project, and that until suitable provision was made from said earnings for interest and redemption on the obligations of both projects we could not use any portion of the earnings for the extensions or improvement of Spring Valley. I note that an attempt has been made in the ordinances submitted (Sec. 4, p. 3) to compel the segregation of the earnings of each utility. If the courts should determine that the ordinance merged them, such a provision would be ineffective, for the Charter must prevail over the ordinance. Therefore, aside from the right of the City Engineer to continue in charge of the Hetch Hetchy project, I deem it unwise, if not unlawful, to attempt a consolidation of the projects at this time. Understand, however, that the foregoing is not to be understood that the City Engineer could not be placed at the head of both projects, even if they are separated, should the Board of Public Works desire to do so.

Question c. Can the appointment of the head and other employees of the Water Department be made conditional upon the approval of the City Engineer?

This question is answered upon the assumption that the Water Department cannot by ordinance of the Board of Supervisors be made a part of the Department of Engineering, and that the Board of Public Works does not make the City Engineer its head. Section 3, Chapter I, Article VI, of the Charter, gives to the Board of Public Works the right to employ all necessary clerks, superintendents, etc. Section 13 of the same chapter provides that "The Board shall appoint the necessary heads of departments under its charge." The right to appoint is absolute under the Charter, and it cannot be qualified except by other Charter provisions, such as civil service regulations, by making the right to appoint dependent on the recommendation of another person, unless the appointing power has authority by rule to make it so. This principle was determined in Crowley vs. Freud, 132 Cal. 440, wherein it was determined by our Supreme Court that where the Constitution failed to give the Charter framers the right to require civil service qualifications for the deputies of the county officers, that the Charter had no right to make the appointment of such deputies dependent upon the certification of the Civil Service Commission that they possessed such qualifications. The only language in the Charter which could give rise to any other conclusion is that contained in Subdivision 8, Section 9, Chapter I, Article VI, above referred to, which gives to the Board of Public Works, under authority of proper ordinances, the right to "contract for work to be performed, or materials or equipment to be furnished, or for expert, technical or professional services to be rendered wherever such work, services, materials or equipment are certified by the City Engineer to be necessary, etc." I am, however, of the opinion, that, in view of the positive language vesting the power of the appointment of subordinates in the Board of Public Works, that the above provision runs entirely to the character of the service to be rendered rather than to the personnel of those who render it. However, should the Board of Public Works desire to lodge in the head of the Water Department the power of recommending employees for appointment, it may do so, as Section 4 of Chapter I, Article VI, gives to the Board the right to make rules for its government and for the performance of its duties, and Section 13 of the same chapter provides that the head of each department shall have sole executive control in its own department, subject to the rules and regulations prescribed by the Board. This, however, is a matter of discretion vested in the Board of Public Works, coming to that body by direct provision of the Charter, and not by ordinance of the Board of Supervisors.

Question d. Can the Board of Public Works, on the recommendation

of the City Engineer, employ an attorney to attend to such legal matters as arise in the Water Department?

Section 2, Chapter II, Article V, of the Charter, defines the duties
of the City Attorney and in no uncertain terms charges him with the
obligation of representing the City and all of its officials and departments in all litigation in which any of them may be interested, and
also to give to such officers, boards or departments, legal advice on
all matters committed to them when requested to do so. That the
Charter language is sufficiently broad to prevent officers, boards or
departments from retaining counsel independent of the City Attorney
has more than once been determined by our Supreme Court. (See
Denman vs. Webster, 139 Cal. 452.)

Referring to the right of the Board of Education of San Francisco
to employ an attorney, the Court said:

"The obvious purpose of the Charter in providing for the election
of a City Attorney, and prescribing his duties and compensation, was
to take from the various city officials and boards the power to employ
other counsel, and to burden the City and County or the School District with the payment of fees fixed, or to be fixed, by the officers or
boards employing them, thus nullifying the Charter provision."

Also, Rafael vs. Boyle, 31 Cal. App. 623, where the District Court of
Appeal determined that the Civil Service Commission had not the
right to employ an attorney, using the following language, after quoting the Charter provision relative to the duties of the City Attorney:

"This express provision clearly indicates an intention that the City
Attorney should handle all the legal work of the various departments
of the city government, except where special provision is made for
additional counsel. The manifest intention of the framers of the
Charter in the adoption of this provision was to systematize the conduct of the city's legal business, and to limit the power of the authorities to incur expenditures for this character of service; and the mere
power given the commission to institute and prosecute legal proceedings does not imply that this above-quoted provision of the Charter
should be inoperative with regard to the Civil Service Commission
so as to empower it to employ another attorney to perform the duties
belonging to the law officer of the municipality. The Charter having
provided a City Attorney upon whom the Board can call when a defense to any suit is necessary, it, by implication, makes it incumbent
upon the Board to avail itself of his services, and it cannot ignore
this provision and employ some other attorney to render those services
which it is the duty of the City Attorney to perform. (Denman vs.
Webster, 139 Cal. 452, 73 Pac. 139; Merrian vs. Barnum, 116 Cal. 619,
48 Pac. 727.)"

Also, McQuillan on Municipal Corporations, 2d Ed., par. 521:

"Whether attorneys may be employed in behalf of the municipal
corporation will depend upon the proper construction of the law under
which such employment is sought to be sustained, the nature of the
services to be performed by the attorney, or, in the absence of legal
provisions pertaining thereto, the character of the litigation or legal
controversy involved and the interest which the public corporation
has therein. It has been held that a city or town as an incident to
its very corporate existence has power to employ an attorney, notwithstanding the Charter or applicable legislative act is silent on the
subject. This arises from power to sue and be sued, to contract and
to be contracted with. 'The power is indispensable to the proper exercise of the ordinary general powers of municipal bodies.' However,
courts are usually reluctant to imply power to employ attorneys, due,
no doubt, to the opportunity of abuse, and common experience and
knowledge of such abuse. But unless forbidden by law when a necessity arises therefor, and the interests of the municipal corporation
requires it, the employment of legal services will usually, and clearly
should be, sanctioned."

There are, however, times when the legislative body of a munic-. ipality has the power to employ an attorney in addition to the regu. larly elected official, but these occasions are usually where the em. ployment is for some special litigation, and not where one employed is likely to become a permanent employee of the City. This determina. tion was made by my predecessor, Mr. George Lull, when he advised the Board of Supervisors that they might authorize the Board of Public Works to enter into a contract with Mr. Robert Searls to render certain legal services of a temporary character in regard to legal matters arising on the Hetch Hetchy construction. Without passing on the correctness of Mr. Lull's opinion, it appears in the instant case that the services of an attorney in the Water Department are to be permanently required; that they, therefore, come within those services which the City Attorney and his assistants must render to all the departments when called upon to do so. You are, therefore, advised that the Board of Supervisors cannot authorize the Board of Public Works to employ an attorney to render services to the Water Department.

Question e. There are other provisions in the proposed ordinances the legality of which, as at present written, is questionable. And other provisions which involve matters of policy.

The short period of time which I have had to investigate this im- portant matter does not permit me to advert to them herein, and I will be pleased to discuss them with your committee, and thereafter make such recommendations as are necessary.

In view of the foregoing you are advised:

a. That the Charter commits the construction, operation and maintenance of a municipally owned utility to the Board of Public Works, and not to any particular bureau, department or division thereof, and that while the Board of Public Works has a perfect right to place the City Engineer at the head of the Water Department, the Board of Supervisors cannot by ordinance making that department a bureau in the Engineering Department, do indirectly what they are prevented from doing directly.

b. Even if the Board of Public Works should commit the manage- ment of the Water Department to the City Engineer, the consolidation of the Spring Valley project with the Hetch Hetchy project may lead to serious difficulties in regard to the use of the revenues of the first- mentioned project.

c. If the Board of Public Works should appoint the City Engineer head of the Water Department it may by rule clothe him, or whomso- ever shall be appointed, with the power of recommending the appoint- ment of employees of the department. It is not, however, within the power of the Board of Supervisors by ordinance to compel such pro- cedure.

d. The necessary legal work of the Water Department must be performed by the City Attorney or his deputies. It is, however, within the power of the Board of Supervisors to provide that such assistant of the City Attorney as may be engaged in serving the Water Depart- ment may be compensated from the revenues of that Department.

JNO. J. O'TOOLE, City Attorney.

Resolutions of the Board of Public Works.

Resolution No. 109132 (Second Series):

Resolved, That this Board approves the attached draft of ordinance prescribing the procedure and limitations under which the Board of Public Works shall have charge, superintendence and control of the supplying of water for domestic purposes from the municipally owned and operated water system; providing for the creation of a water de- partment; providing for the organization of the same; prescribing its powers and duties and the manner in which these shall be carried out, and transmits four copies of said proposed ordinance to the Board of Supervisors with the recommendation that said ordinance be enacted.

(Signed copy of resolution Board of Supervisors. Files of Secretary.)

Passed January 15, 1930, by the following vote:

Ayes—Commissioners Meyer, Stanton and Reardon. DRS.

Resolution No. 109165 (Second Series):

Resolved, That this Board amends Resolution No. 109132 (Second Series), passed January 15, 1930, by striking out that portion of the attached ordinance to said resolution contained on page 2, paragraph three (3), reading:

"The Board, upon the request of the department head, when such employment is necessary, as provided in Subsection 8 of Section 9, Chapter I of Article VI of the Charter, may employ an attorney to serve as special counsel for the Water Department, and fix his compensation; provided, however, that before any such special counsel is employed the City Attorney shall first approve the selection of the person to be employed."

(Signed copy of resolution to Board of Supervisors. Files of Secretary. City Attorney.)

Passed January 17, 1930, by the following vote:

Ayes—Commissioners Meyer, Stanton and Reardon. DRS.

Passed for Printing.

Whereupon, the foregoing bill was *passed for printing* by the following vote:

Ayes—Supervisors Andriano, Canepa, Colman, Gallagher, Havenner, Hayden, McGovern, McSheehy, Miles, Peyser, Power, Roncovieri, Rossi, Stanton, Suhr, Toner—16.

Absent—Supervisors Shannon, Spaulding—2.

Adopted.

The following resolutions were *adopted*:

Directing the Clerk to Advertise for Bids for Publishing Official Advertising for the Year Commencing April 1, 1930.

On recommendation of Public Welfare and Publicity Committee.

Resolution No. 32069 (New Series), as follows:

Resolved, That the Clerk be directed to advertise that sealed proposals will be received on Monday, the 10th day of March, 1930, at 3 o'clock p. m. for publishing the official advertising for the year commencing April 1, 1930.

Ayes—Supervisors Andriano, Canepa, Colman, Gallagher, Havenner, Hayden, McGovern, McSheehy, Miles, Peyser, Power, Roncovieri, Rossi, Stanton, Suhr, Toner—16.

Absent—Supervisors Shannon, Spaulding—2.

Directing the Clerk to Advertise for Bids for Publishing Delinquent Tax List, Fiscal Year 1929-1930.

Also, Resolution No. 32070 (New Series), as follows:

Resolved, That the Clerk of the Board is hereby directed to advertise that sealed proposals for printing, publishing and distributing the delinquent tax list, index to delinquent real estate taxpayers and printing the sales list and other matters incidental thereto for the fiscal year 1929-1930 will be received on Monday, March 10, 1930, at 3 o'clock p. m.

Ayes—Supervisors Andriano, Canepa, Colman, Gallagher, Havenner, Hayden, McGovern, McSheehy, Miles, Peyser, Power, Roncovieri, Rossi, Stanton, Suhr, Toner—16.

Absent—Supervisors Shannon, Spaulding—2.

Closing and Abandoning Portions of Grand View Avenue Between Market and Twenty-third Streets.

On recommendation of Streets Committee.

Resolution No. 32071 (New Series), as follows:

Closing and abandoning certain portions of Grand View avenue lying between Market street and Twenty-third street as described in Resolution of Intention No. 31853 (New Series).

Whereas, this Board has, by Resolution No. 31853 (New Series), declared its intention to close and abandon certain portions of Grand View avenue in the City and County of San Francisco; and

Whereas, proper notice of said proposed closing and abandonment of certain portions of Grand View avenue lying between Market street and Twenty-third street as described in Resolution of Intention No. 31853 (New Series) was duly given by the Board of Public Works of said City and County of San Francisco; and

Whereas, more than ten days have elapsed after the expiration of the time of publication of said notice; and

Whereas, no objection or objections to the closing and abandonment of said certain portions of Grand View avenue as described in Resolution of Intention No. 31853 (New Series) was or were made or delivered to the Clerk of the Board of Supervisors within said period of ten days or at all; and

Whereas, it is the opinion of this Board that the public interest and convenience will be conserved by the closing and abandonment of said certain portions of Grand View avenue; and

Whereas, in and by said Resolution of Intention No. 31853 (New Series) this Board did declare that the damages, costs and expenses of closing said certain portions of Grand View avenue are nominal and no assessment district is necessary to be formed for the purpose of paying the damages, costs and expenses thereof, the Board of Supervisors hereby declares and determines that the whole damage, cost and expense of closing said certain portions of Grand View avenue shall be paid out of the revenues of the City and County of San Francisco; and

Whereas, the said work is for the closing and abandonment of certain portions of Grand View avenue as described in Resolution of Intention No. 31853 (New Series) and it appears to this Board that no assessment is necessary; now, therefore, be it

Resolved, That the said closing and abandonment of certain portions of Grand View avenue, lying between Market street and Twenty-third street as described in Resolution of Intention No. 31853 (New Series) be and the same is hereby ordered and that said certain portions of Grand View avenue lying between Market street and Twenty-third street be and the same are hereby closed and abandoned as public streets; and

Further Resolved, That the Clerk of this Board transmit a certified copy of this resolution to the Board of Public Works and that the Board of Public Works be instructed to proceed thereafter as required by law and the Charter of the City and County of San Francisco, and the Clerk of this Board is hereby directed to advertise this resolution in the official newspaper as required by law.

Ayes—Supervisors Andriano, Canepa, Colman, Gallagher, Havenner, Hayden, McGovern, McSheehy, Miles, Peyser, Power, Roncovieri, Rossi, Stanton, Suhr, Toner—16.

Absent—Supervisors Shannon, Spaulding—2.

Intention to Change Grades on Third Street From Le Conte Avenue to Meade Avenue.

Also, Resolution No. 32072 (New Series), as follows:

Resolved, That it is the intention of the Board of Supervisors to change and establish grades on the following named streets, at the points hereinafter specified and at the elevations above city base, as hereinafter stated, in accordance with Resolution No. 109351 (Second Series) of the Board of Public Works, adopted February 3, 1930, and written recommendation of said Board filed February 3, 1930, to-wit:

Third Street.

Southeasterly line of, at Le Conte avenue southwesterly line, 104.30 feet. (The same being the present official grade.)

At a point 15 feet northwesterly at right angles to the southeasterly line of, at Le Conte avenue southwesterly line, 104.30 feet. (The same being the present official grade.)

Southeasterly line of, at Meade avenue northeasterly line produced, 119 feet. (The same being the present official grade.)

At a point 15 feet northwesterly at right angles to the southeasterly line of, at Meade avenue northeasterly line produced, 119 feet. (The same being the present official grade.)

On Third street between the southeasterly line of and a line parallel with and 15 feet northwesterly therefrom extending from Le Conte avenue to Meade avenue be changed and established to conform to true gradients between the grade elevations above given therefor.

The Board of Supervisors hereby declares that no assessment district is necessary as no damage will result from said change of grades, inasmuch as the streets are ungraded and there are no existing street improvements.

The Board of Public Works is hereby directed to cause to be conspicuously posted along the street or streets upon which such change or modification of grade or grades is contemplated, notice of the passage of this resolution of intention.

Ayes—Supervisors Andriano, Canepa, Colman, Gallagher, Havenner, Hayden, McGovern, McSheehy, Miles, Peyser, Power, Roncovieri, Rossi, Stanton, Suhr, Toner—16.

Absent—Supervisors Shannon, Spaulding—2.

Passed for Printing.

The following matters were *passed for printing*:

Changing Grades on Mt. Vernon Avenue Between Alemany Boulevard and Cayuga Avenue.

On recommendation of Streets Committee.

Bill No. 8188, Ordinance No. ———— (New Series), as follows:

Changing and reestablishing the official grades on Mt. Vernon avenue between the easterly line of Alemany boulevard produced and the westerly line of Cayuga avenue.   ⌐⌐eet

Changing Grades on Nineteenth Street Between San Potrero Avenues and on Utah Street Betv. Twentieth Streets.

Also, Bill No. 8189, Ordinance No. ———— (New Series),

Changing and reestablishing the official grades on Nineteenth between San Bruno and Potrero avenues and on Utah street between the northerly line of Eighteenth street and Twentieth street.

Changing Grades on Alta Street, 150 and 303 Feet Easterly From Montgomery Street.

Also, Bill No. 8190, Ordinance No. ———— (New Series), as follows:

Changing and reestablishing the official grades on Alta street between lines respectively 150 feet and 303 feet easterly from Montgomery street.

Whereas, the Board of Supervisors, on the written recommendation of the Board of Public Works, did, on the 6th day of December, 1929, by Resolution No. 31716 (New Series), declare its intention to change

and reestablish the grades on Alta street between lines respectively 150
feet and 303 feet easterly from Montgomery street.

Whereas, said resolution was so published for ten days, and the Board
of Public Works, within ten days after the first publication of said
resolution of intention, caused notices of the passage of said resolution
to be conspicuously posted along all streets specified in the resolution,
in the manner and as provided by law; and

Whereas, more than forty days has elapsed since the first publication
of said resolution of intention; therefore,

Be it ordained by the People of the City and County of San Francisco as follows:

Section 1. The grades on the following named streets at the points
hereinafter named, and at the elevations above city base as hereinafter
stated, are hereby changed and established as follows:

Alta Street.

6 feet southerly from the northerly line of, 150 feet easterly from
Montgomery street, 175.83 feet. (The same being the present official
grade.)

6 feet northerly from the southerly line of, 150 feet easterly from
Montgomery street, 175.83 feet. (The same being the present official
grade.)

175 feet easterly from Montgomery street, 174.15 feet.

200 feet easterly from Montgomery street, 171.99 feet.

225 feet easterly from Montgomery street, 168.86 feet.

(Vertical curve passing through the last three described points.)

303 feet easterly from Montgomery street, 156.80 feet.

On Alta street between lines respectively 150 feet and 303 feet easterly from Montgomery street, changed and established to conform to
true gradients between the grade elevations above given therefor.

Section 2. This ordinance shall take effect immediately.

Changing Grades on Oakdale Avenue Between Earl and Keith Streets and on Fitch, Griffith, Hawes, Ingalls and Jennings Streets Between Newcomb and Palou Avenues.

Also, Bill No. 8191, Ordinance No. ——— (New Series), as follows:

Changing and reestablishing the official grades on Oakdale avenue
between Earl and Keith streets, and on Fitch, Griffith, Hawes, Ingalls
and Jennings streets between Newcomb and Palou avenues.

Width of Sidewalks on Quint Street Between Oakdale and Palou Avenues.

Also, Bill No. 8192, Ordinance No. ——— (New Series), as follows:

of Amending Ordinance No. 1061, entitled "Regulating the Width of
street be an approved December 18, 1903, by adding thereto a new
streets; and umbered ten hundred and eighty-nine.

Further Resol'd by the People of the City and County of San Fran-
copy of this res.

Board of Pu··ordinance No. 1061, entitled "Regulating the Width of
Siueva···," approved December 18, 1903, be and is hereby amended
in accordance with the communication of the Board of Public Works,
filed in this office January 21, 1930, by adding thereto a new section
to be numbered ten hundred and eighty-nine, to read as follows:

Section 1089. The width of sidewalks on Quint street between Oakdale avenue and Palou avenue shall be ten (10) feet.

Establishing Grades on Ledyard Street.

Also, Bill No. 8193, Ordinance No. ——— (New Series), as follows:

Establishing grades on Ledyard street between Silver avenue and
a line parallel with and 707.50 feet southerly therefrom.

Be it ordained by the People of the City and County of San Francisco as follows:

Section 1. The grades on Ledyard street between Silver avenue and a line parallel with and 707.50 feet southerly therefrom are hereby established at points hereinafter named, and at heights above city base as hereinafter stated, in accordance with recommendation of the Board of Public Works, filed February 3, 1930:

Ledyard Street.

Westerly line of, at Silver avenue, 83.50 feet. (The same being the present official grade.)

Easterly line of, at Silver avenue, 85.00 feet.

183.50 feet southerly from Silver avenue, 88.50 feet.

707.50 feet southerly from Silver avenue, 78.00 feet.

On Ledyard street between Silver avenue and a line parallel with and 707.50 feet southerly therefrom be established to conform to true gradients between the grade elevations above given therefor.

Section 2. This ordinance shall take effect immediately.

Establishing Grades on Niagara Avenue Between Alemany Boulevard and Cayuga Avenue.

Also, Bill No. 8194, Ordinance No. ———— (New Series), as follows:

Establishing grades on Niagara avenue between Alemany boulevard and Cayuga avenue.

Be it ordained by the People of the City and County of San Francisco as follows:

Section 1. The grades on Niagara avenue between Alemany boulevard and Cayuga avenue are hereby established in accordance with recommendation of the Board of Public Works, filed February 3, 1930.

Adopted.

The following resolutions were *adopted*:

Approval of Map Showing Widening of Utah Street.

On recommendation of Streets Committee.

Resolution No. 32073 (New Series), as follows:

Whereas, the Board of Public Works did, by Resolution No. 109315 (Second Series), approve a map showing the widening of Utah street at Nineteenth street; now, therefore, be it

Resolved, That the map showing the widening of Utah street at Nineteenth street is hereby approved.

Ayes—Supervisors Andriano, Canepa, Colman, Gallagher, Havenner, Hayden, McGovern, McSheehy, Miles, Peyser, Power, Roncovieri, Rossi, Stanton, Suhr, Toner—16.

Absent—Supervisors Shannon, Spaulding—2.

Extension of Time to Complete Improvement of Garfield Street Between Vernon and Beverly Streets.

Also, Resolution No. 32074 (New Series), as follows:

Resolved, That Municipal Construction Company is hereby granted an extension of ninety days' time from and after January 20, 1930, within which to complete the improvement of Garfield street between Vernon and Beverly streets, under public contract.

This extension of time is granted upon the recommendation of the Board of Public Works for the reason that the contractor has been delayed by inclement weather.

Ayes—Supervisors Andriano, Canepa, Colman, Gallagher, Havenner, Hayden, McGovern, McSheehy, Miles, Peyser, Power, Roncovieri, Rossi, Stanton, Suhr, Toner—16.

Absent—Supervisors Shannon, Spaulding—2.

Extension of Time to Complete Improvement of Holladay Avenue.

Also, Resolution No. 32075 (New Series), as follows:

Resolved, That E. J. Treacy is hereby granted an extension of sixty days from February 6, 1930, within which to complete the improvement of Holladay avenue between Peralta avenue and a line 126 feet southerly from York street.

This extension of time is granted upon the recommendation of the Board of Public Works for the reason that the work has been delayed on account of weather conditions. The curbs and subgrading have been completed.

Ayes—Supervisors Andriano, Canepa, Colman, Gallagher, Havenner, Hayden, McGovern, McSheehy, Miles, Peyser, Power, Roncovieri, Rossi, Stanton, Suhr, Toner—16.

Absent—Supervisors Shannon, Spaulding—2.

Extension of Time to Complete Improvement of Ortega Street Between Forty-fifth and Forty-sixth Avenues.

Also, Resolution No. 32076 (New Series), as follows:

Resolved, That J. F. Dowling is hereby granted an extension of sixty days from February 7, 1930, to complete the improvement of Ortega street between Forty-fifth and Forty-sixth avenues.

This extension of time is granted upon the recommendation of the Board of Public Works for the reason the work has been completed with the exception of the asphaltic wearing surface.

Ayes—Supervisors Andriano, Canepa, Colman, Gallagher, Havenner, Hayden, McGovern, McSheehy, Miles, Peyser, Power, Roncovieri, Rossi, Stanton, Suhr, Toner—16.

Absent—Supervisors Shannon, Spaulding—2.

Extension of Time to Complete Improvement of Mt. Vernon Avenue Between Howth and Goetz Streets.

Also, Resolution No. 32077 (New Series), as follows:

Resolved, That Clarence B. Eaton is hereby granted an extension of ninety days' time from and after February 8, 1930, within which to complete the improvement of Mt. Vernon avenue between Howth and Goetz streets, under public contract.

This extension of time is granted upon the recommendation of the Board of Public Works for the reason that the contractor has been delayed by inclement weather.

Ayes—Supervisors Andriano, Canepa, Colman, Gallagher, Havenner, Hayden, McGovern, McSheehy, Miles, Peyser, Power, Roncovieri, Rossi, Stanton, Suhr, Toner—16.

Absent—Supervisors Shannon, Spaulding—2.

Extension of Time to Complete Improvement of Montcalm Street Between Peralta Avenue and York Street.

Also, Resolution No. 32078 (New Series), as follows:

Resolved, That T. M. Gallagher is hereby granted an extension of sixty days' time from and after February 4, 1930, within which to complete the improvement of Montcalm street between Peralta avenue and York street, under public contract.

This extension of time is granted upon the recommendation of the Board of Public Works for the reason that the contractor has been delayed by inclement weather.

Ayes—Supervisors Andriano, Canepa, Colman, Gallagher, Havenner, Hayden, McGovern, McSheehy, Miles, Peyser, Power, Roncovieri, Rossi, Stanton, Suhr, Toner—16.

Absent—Supervisors Shannon, Spaulding—2.

Award of Contract, Underground Cable.

On recommendation of Supplies Committee.

Resolution No. 32079 (New Series), as follows:

Resolved, That award of contract be hereby made to Standard Underground Cable Company on bid submitted February 10, 1930 (Proposal

No. 558) for furnishing the following, viz.: Underground cable for Department of Electricity—15,000 feet 6 pr. Cable No. 18 A. W. G. solid 0.22 M. F. average regular electric capacity, 3-wrap saturated paper, core tape 1/16 lead, 3 per cent tin, all in conformity with city specifications, at $0.143 per lineal foot.

Resolved, That a bond in the amount of $500 be required for faithful performance of contract.

Resolved, That all other bids submitted thereon be rejected.

Ayes—Supervisors Andriano, Canepa, Colman, Gallagher, Havenner, Hayden, McGovern, McSheehy, Miles, Peyser, Power, Roncovieri, Rossi, Stanton, Suhr, Toner—16.

Absent—Supervisors Shannon, Spaulding—2.

NOTICE OF RECONSIDERATION.

Bond Issue Election for Acquisition of Electrical Distribution System of Pacific Gas and Electric and Great Western Power Companies.

Supervisor Havenner, at the last meeting of the Board of Supervisors, gave notice that at this meeting he would move for a reconsideration of the vote whereby the following resolution, offered as a substitute for the one succeeding, was defeated:

Resolution No. ———— (New Series), as follows:

Resolved, That the Board of Public Works, through the City Engineer, be requested to file with this Board, without further delay, the plans and estimates of the cost of original construction of the properties of the Pacific Gas and Electric Company and the Great Western Power Company, which said plans and estimates have been called for by ordinance heretofore enacted by this Board. And be it

Further Resolved, That the City Attorney be and he is hereby directed, immediately upon the filing of said plans and estimates by the Board of Public Works, to prepare and present to this Board the ordinances and resolutions necessary to submit to the electors of the City and County of San Francisco, on the 10th day of June, 1930, the question of voting bonds in an amount sufficient to acquire the properties of both said companies.

February 10, 1930—*Refused passage* by the following vote:

Ayes—Supervisors Andriano, Gallagher, Havenner, McGovern, McSheehy, Roncovieri, Suhr—7.

Noes—Supervisors Canepa, Colman, Hayden, Miles, Peyser, Power, Rossi, Spaulding, Stanton, Toner—10.

Absent—Supervisor Shannon—1.

Before the result of the foregoing vote was announced Supervisor Havenner changed his vote from *aye* to *no* and gave notice of reconsideration.

Motion.

Supervisor Havenner moved reconsideration of the vote whereby foregoing resolution was defeated.

Privilege of the Floor.

MRS. WILLIAM KENT: Mr. Mayor and Members of the Board of Supervisors: I appreciate very deeply this recognition of the important part taken by William Kent in shaping and helping to pass this bill of Hetch Hetchy. I shared his enthusiasm for this bill and his great joy when it passed Congress. We were both more interested in the power clause of that bill even than we were in the water supply, necessary as that is, because the question of water power, publicly-owned water power, is one of the great world questions, and San Francisco has this marvelous opportunity of making a great demonstration to the world of its ability to so conduct this affair as to bring great benefit to every single person in San Francisco, because the question of water and the question of power affects every individual in our midst. I am not a voter in San Francisco, but I feel, from my connection with the intent in this bill and as a citizen of California, a very tremendous concern in this matter. And I know that William Kent felt that that clause in the bill was of great importance, which said that San Francisco might forfeit its right to the Hetch Hetchy benefactions if, at any time, it should not remain in public hands and be administered for the good of the people. So when Mrs. Gerberding told me that this was coming up before your honorable body this afternoon, we came here quite simply. I had not the least idea of being asked or allowed to say anything to you. But we have discussed it. Mrs. Gerberding, as you know, knows a great deal of this City's work, and we decided, as citizens, that, if such an important question was to be voted upon by us, that we would infinitely prefer that it came at a special election when the question would be alone submitted to us. If this thing can be brought to the people in an election by itself you are going to have a far more intelligent expression of opinion from the citizens of San Francisco, who are so vitally concerned in this matter, than if you put it into a general election at another date. So we feel that we are speaking for ourselves, as we regard such an important question, and that we, therefore, are representative of thousands of others who want such important questions decided on their own, not put in with a great many other things to discuss, but made the main issue so that a truly intelligent vote may be cast. And so I feel that I am not out of place, although I live in Marin County, to come and present to you my feeling that, if possible, this election on this bond issue, which means so much to every individual in this City, should come at a special election by itself rather than to be placed in a general election. I thank you very much.

MRS. ELIZABETH GERBERDING: Mr. Mayor, Members of the Board and Citizens: It seems to me a large portion of my life has been taken up in fighting for Hetch Hetchy, and it gives me great pleasure every time to be able to do a very little bit toward helping it along. This wealth that has been running down the mountains into the sea, that belongs to every citizen of this City, is a very important thing. We have lost a large portion of it. Now, San Francisco has her chance to get what belongs to her, the most vital thing in the world, more vital than gold and more vital than oil. Mr. Colman inadvertently omitted to state when he stated that he wished to see a large representation of voters, that it does not make the least particle of difference, the vote will be counted on two-thirds of the people who vote on that question, and not on the whole election, not for the Governor, not for the Lieutenant-Governor, not for all the other things that may be crowded onto the ballot, but for that one thing, and it does not make any difference how few people go there. I assume that every citizen of this City would not refuse the gift of this fortune, for it is a fortune, and unless, of course, there was some ulterior motive that influenced his opinion. If there is such a citizen, man or woman, I would like to meet him or her, and I beg of you not to have this thing blanketed under a lot of other things. We know that a tired man or woman going to the polls says, "When in doubt, vote no." Now, we do not want that to happen with our valuable power, we want to win, and we want to win for every citizen, man or woman, in this City. I thank you.

Reconsideration Defeated.

Whereupon, the roll was called on reconsideration of the vote taken at last meeting changing the date of election from August 26, 1930, to June 10, 1930, and the same was *defeated* by the following vote:

Ayes—Supervisors Andriano, Gallagher, Havenner, McGovern, Mc-Sheehy, Roncovieri, Suhr—7.

Noes—Supervisors Canepa, Colman, Hayden, Miles, Peyser, Power, Rossi, Spaulding, Stanton, Toner—10.

Absent—Supervisor Shannon—1.

Adopted.

Whereupon, the roll was called and the following resolution was *adopted* by the following vote:

Fixing State Primary Election Day August 26, 1930, as Date for Bond Election to Acquire Properties of Pacific Gas and Electric Company and Great Western Power Company, and Directing City Attorney to Secure Stipulation From Companies That Deferring Election to This Date Will Not Be Considered a Lack of Diligence.

Resolution No. 32081 (New Series), as follows:

Whereas, the Board of Supervisors have heretofore initiated proceedings for the purpose of submitting to the people the matter of the acquisition of the properties of the Pacific Gas and Electric Company and of the Great Western Power Company, at the valuation fixed by the State Railroad Commission, and additions thereto caused by additions and betterments made to the properties of the respective companies since the evaluation proceedings were commenced; and

Whereas, it is the desire of the Board of Supervisors to submit the matter of the acquisition of said properties, and the voting of a bonded indebtedness for the purpose of acquiring the same, to the electors of the City and County of San Francisco at such time as will best afford said electors the opportunity of expressing themselves in the matter of the acquisition of said utilities; now, therefore, be it

Resolved, That it is the sense of the Board of Supervisors that when the date for the holding of said election for the purpose of voting a bonded indebtedness to acquire the said properties of the Pacific Gas and Electric Company and Great Western Power Company is fixed by ordinance calling for said election, that the same should be fixed for the date on which the State primary election is held, to-wit: the last Tuesday in August, 1930, provided that said Pacific Gas and Electric Company and Great Western Power Company will stipulate with the City that the deferring of said election until said date shall not be considered a lack of due diligence in calling and holding said election; and be it

Further Resolved, That the City Attorney be and he is hereby directed to obtain, if possible, from each of said companies a stipulation with the City to the effect that the deferring of said election until the date hereinabove set forth shall not be considered a lack of due diligence in calling and holding said election.

Ayes—Supervisors Andriano, Canepa, Colman, Hayden, Miles, Peyser, Power, Rossi, Spaulding, Stanton, Toner—11.

Noes—Supervisors Gallagher, Havenner, McGovern, McSheehy, Roncovieri, Suhr—6.

Absent—Supervisor Shannon—1.

Explanation of Vote.

The hereinafter mentioned Supervisors explained their votes as follows:

SUPERVISOR HAVENNER: Mr. Mayor, I desire to make a statement of my vote for the record: I am whole-heartedly in favor of the adoption of the bond issues to be submitted at the August election. I intend to work, to the extent of my ability, for the success of those issues when they are submitted. I voted "no" merely as a protest against the selection of the date for the submission of this election.

I will be on the firing line, for what little I am worth, Mr. Mayor, devoting all of my time, if necessary, to attempt to bring about the adoption of these bond issues, and I know that my colleagues who voted with me today will also be found on that firing line, working night and day to persuade the people of the importance of this election.

SUPERVISOR ANDRIANO: After listening to the statement of Supervisor Havenner, I think that I ought to make an explanation of my vote. I consider that the vote in favor of the June election was a protest against the August election, but having failed to carry the June election date, and being in favor of submitting it to the people, I think it is consistent that I should vote "yes" for the August election.

SUPERVISOR GALLAGHER: Mr. Chairman, this record should follow the last vote: Convinced, as I am, that it is not a friendly act, however unconscious those may be who voted for it, that this submission of this great issue at the time proposed is to its detriment and not in its favor, I continued my vote, which was a vote for submission at a special election and against submission at a so-called "general election." I believe that unconsciously the vote to submit this at a general election was bringing the great question into danger. I am hopeful that my views may be found mistaken, and that the issue, on the date set, may be successful. And, of course, like every one else who believes in the fulfillment of the things to which the Charter dedicates us, I subscribe my whole effort to its adoption. I do, however, desire that the record shall immediately be appended to the vote just taken, and will show that the vote against the August submission was not as to submission of the issue, but against the date set.

SUPERVISOR COLMAN: Mr. Mayor, as the chairman of the Joint Public Utilities Committee and Finance Committee, I want to state that I cast my vote for the August election with a great deal of pride, and with the satisfaction and knowledge that I have done my duty. By this vote the Board of Supervisors has placed a very vital matter before the people for consideration, and they have placed it at a time when the people will be there to express their views. In so doing we have carried out, to the best of our ability, the principle of democracy, the principle upon which this country is founded, the right of suffrage. The people do not vote at special elections in the same numbers that they do vote at gubernatorial elections. There will be a tremendous outpouring of voters, and I have no fear whatsoever of the result, simply because of the fact that the largest possible number of our people will be there to express their will.

SUPERVISOR McSHEEHY: Mr. Mayor, as I said, as a rule I do not have to apologize for my vote on this Board. I try to investigate every matter that comes before this Board and vote according to the dictates of my conscience, but I believe, Mr. Mayor, that a mistake was made today. I think you yourself sounded the keynote, and a keynote that ought to have brought a change of date. You told us how certain officials might come here from Washington, could be brought here from Washington, and could tell the people of San Francisco the great necessity of voting this bond issue at this particular time, and I think that note of warning ought to have been warning enough to the members of this Board to follow the suggestion that you have made. As I stated, I have no apologies, but I want the record to show that I favor the bond issue and I will do everything that I can to advocate its passage. Whoever the committee might be, a committee of this Board or a committee of citizens, they can count on me going throughout this City advocating the passage of this bond issue.

SUPERVISOR McGOVERN: I believe, as long as there is an atmosphere of giving explanations, that I will state that, from what experience I have had in my political life, it has been well known that that is one of the policies which I have followed, municipal ownership. I will do in August what I thought I could do more successfully in

June, try to convince, as some of us have found, and we are speaking from practical experience, those that probably are interested in some special candidate, to interest themselves in this special bond election. That has been my experience in the past. I found that, though there are a great number of voters that go to the polls at a gubernatorial election, it is harder to get them interested in any one special thing that you might be interested in. But that shall be my duty and I will so try.

Mayor to Appoint Citizens' Committee for Bond Campaign, Acquisition of Electrical Distributing System.

The following resolution was presented by Supervisor Havenner and *adopted:*

Resolution No. 32083 (New Series), as follows:

Resolved, That His Honor the Mayor be and he is hereby authorized and requested to appoint a Citizens Campaign Committee for the purpose of properly presenting to the electors argument for the authorization of bonds for the acquisition of the properties of the Pacific Gas & Electric Company and Great Western Power Company at the valuation fixed by the State Railroad Commission at the election to be held August 26, 1930.

Ayes—Supervisors Andriano, Canepa, Havenner, Hayden, McSheehy, Miles, Peyser, Power, Rossi, Spaulding, Stanton—11.

Absent—Supervisors Colman, Gallagher, McGovern, Roncovieri, Shannon, Suhr, Toner—7.

SPECIAL ORDER—2:30 P. M.

Amendment of Food Terminal Ordinance.

Supervisor Stanton called up out of the Education, Parks and Playgrounds Committee the following entitled bill and moved its passage to print:

Bill No. ————, Ordinance No. ———— (New Series), entitled: Amending Ordinance No. 8140 (New Series), providing that wholesale food terminals, warehouses, freight yards and ferry terminals shall not be constructed or established, erected or constructed within a certain district of the City and County of San Francisco, and establishing the boundaries of said district, and providing for penalties for the violation of the provisions hereof, by including in said prohibited structures and callings airplane landings and hydroplane landings and the landing of passengers from airplanes and hydroplanes.

Privilege of the Floor.

Daniel A. Ryan, attorney representing James McNear, was heard in favor of the operation of amphibian planes at the Marina.

Captain Andersen, representing Sea Scouts; Mrs. Jones, representing the Parent-Teachers' Association; Mrs. Gerberding, Mrs. Holmes, Mrs. Boggs, Mrs. Leon and Mr. Olsen were heard in opposition.

Mr. Fred Widdling, representing the Associated Boat Industries, was also heard in opposition.

Motion.

Supervisor Power moved that the City Attorney's opinion be obtained as to the legality of passing or amending the ordinance proposed.

Motion *carried.*

Action Deferred.

Whereupon, on motion of Supervisor Andriano, the foregoing matter was *laid over one week* and made a special order for 2:30 p. m.

Motion *carried.*

Action Deferred.

The following matters were *laid over one week*:

SPECIAL ORDER—3:30 P. M.

Boulevard Lighting Standards.

On motion of Supervisor Colman, consideration of the matter of the selection of boulevard lighting standards was made a Special Order of Business for 3:30 p. m. this day.

Hyde Street Lighting.

Supervisor Gallagher, at a previous meeting, gave notice that he would, under the thirty-day rule, call out of the Lighting Committee the Hyde street lighting matter for consideration as a Special Order at 5 p. m.

Ventilation of Chambers.

Supervisor Power presented:

Resolution No. 32084 (New Series), as follows:

Resolved, That the Public Buildings and Lands Committee be and it is hereby requested to consider ways and means and provide for adequate ventilation of the Chambers of the Board of Supervisors.

Adopted by the following vote:

Ayes—Supervisors Andriano, Canepa, Havenner, Hayden, McSheehy, Miles, Peyser, Power, Rossi, Spaulding, Stanton—11.

Absent—Supervisors Colman, Gallagher, McGovern, Roncovieri, Shannon, Suhr, Toner—7.

Communication from City Attorney on Taking Over Properties of Spring Valley Water Company.

The following were read and *ordered spread in the Journal*:

February 17, 1930.

Honorable Board of Supervisors, City Hall, San Francisco, California.

Dear Sirs: I am herewith transmitting to you the following documents:

1. Resolution providing for the acquisition of operative properties of Spring Valley Water Company, including authority to the Mayor and to the Board of Supervisors to enter into the necessary agreements relative to the taking over of said properties on the 3rd day of March, 1930, and appropriating the necessary money therefor.

2. Resolution authorizing recording of deed from Spring Valley Water Company to the City, in the City and County of San Francisco and in the counties of San Mateo, Santa Clara and Alameda.

3. Two demands, one in favor of Spring Valley Water Company for $39,962,606.51, which is the amount to be paid to said company on March 3, 1930, and the other for $75,000, to be deposited with the Wells Fargo Bank and Union Trust Company, to meet such additional amounts as may be due to the company upon the final adjustment of all matters between the City and the company.

4. A letter, signed by the City Engineer and myself, setting forth the general terms and conditions as to the acquisition of the properties and the estimated amount to be paid therefor.

Resolution No. 1, above mentioned, should be passed to print on this date, provided that its terms are satisfactory to you, and should be finally adopted prior to March 1st, 1930.

Resolution No. 2 should be adopted so that the same may be attached to each of the deeds to be recorded.

The two demands should be approved and passed to print and finally adopted prior to March 1, 1930, so that the respective amounts mentioned will be available to close the Spring Valley transaction before noon on March 3.

It is the intention that the properties of the Spring Valley Water Company shall be taken over by the City prior to noon on Monday, March 3, 1930, and that the deeds for the properties shall be executed in quadruplicate, to the end that one copy may be recorded in each of the counties where the company's properties are situated prior to noon on March 3, to the end that the respective properties may be assessed to the City for the next fiscal year.

I have cooperated with the City Engineer and with his assistants in the determination of the correct amount to be paid for the properties of the company, under our option agreement and the company's offer of March 2, 1928, and the amounts mentioned in the accompanying letter of the City Engineer and myself are correct.

The title to all properties which the City is acquiring have been checked, and, where available, abstracts of these titles have been examined. Where abstracts have not been available, I have caused title companies in the counties where the properties are situate to examine the county records from the date of the Spring Valley bond mortgage to the present time, and have checked all properties as to the payment of taxes and adverse possession by the company for more than five years last past. The bond mortgage upon the properties will be released before the payment of the purchase price, and in so far as my investigation has extended I have found the titles to the property to be good.

The reason for not making a more extended examination of the titles to the various properties is that the cost of abstracts or title insurance would be almost prohibitive, and as the company has been in possession of its properties for many years, and has paid taxes upon the same, there is little likelihood of there being any serious defects in its titles. Furthermore, we are entitled to receive from the company only such title to its properties as the company itself possesses. However, the investigation which has been made regarding titles has been as complete as can be without causing an abstract to be made of each particular parcel of property, which, in my opinion, is not necessary.

Several properties are taken over subject to charges and agreements wherein the company is bound to furnish water to the former owners of said properties or to adjacent properties. The deed from the company to the City contains a complete statement of all such obligations, and the City is not assuming any obligation which is not now a charge upon the properties.

The amount of the total purchase price has been arrived at upon the report made by William Dolge Company, expert accountants for the City, and a re-check thereof made by representatives of the City Engineer's and City Attorney's office.

Sincerely,

JNO. J. O'TOOLE, City Attorney.

P. S. It will be necessary for your Board to hold a special or adjourned meeting on some date between the 25th and 28th of the present month for the purpose of finally acting on the above-mentioned resolution and the appropriation made to consummate the purchase of the properties of the water company.

February 14, 1930.

To the Honorable Board of Supervisors of the City and County of San Francisco.

Gentlemen: Under Resolution No. 28948 (New Series) the City Engineer's office was directed, in cooperation with the City Attorney, to examine, inquire into and report as to a correct list, statement and inventory of all properties which the City and County is entitled to acquire by virtue of the option held on the Spring Valley properties, and to report the correct amount to be paid therefor.

The final report as to certain inventories on hand, etc., and the exact purchase price, cannot be definitely fixed until after the company has closed its books on March 3, 1930. The purchase price will be affected by the expenditures of the company on new construction between De-

cember 31, 1929, and March 3, 1930, as well as by the operating revenues and expenditures, which affect the contributions to the amortization fund, and by certain other minor elements at present indeterminate.

This office has checked the list, statement and inventory of all of the
properties and the descriptions of the same as set forth in the deed of
conveyance prepared by the City Attorney, and the same are correct.
The City Attorney has caused examination of the title of all lands,
properties, easements and rights of way which the City is to receive,
and his findings are the subject of a separate report.

At this time, while the final price cannot be definitely determined,
it has been estimated to be $40,021,540.25, more or less. Of this sum
$39,962.606.51 is absolutely determinable, and under the terms of a
collateral agreement prepared by the representatives of the Spring
Valley Company and the City this amount is recommended as a direct
payment to be made to the company simultaneously with the conveyance of the deed.

To provide for the additional amount of the final purchase price,
which may be more or less than $58,933.74 (the difference between
the initial determined payment and the estimated purchase price), depending upon the construction expenditures and the credits to the
amortization fund and other minor details, the collateral agreement
provides for the deposit of the sum of $75,000 in escrow with the Wells
Fargo Bank and Union Trust Company, from which will be paid to
the company the additional amount of the purchase price as it may
be finally determined, and the balance will be returned to the City.
Under this arrangement the interests of the City are fully protected.

Respectfully,
M. M. O'SHAUGHNESSY, City Engineer.

Passed for Printing.

The following resolution was *passed for printing:*

**Accepting Offer of Spring Valley Water Company to Sell Its
Properties, Appropriating Moneys for the Payment Therefor and
Empowering the Mayor and Clerk of the Board of Supervisors
to Execute and Deliver Collateral and Supplemental Agreements
Incident Thereto.**

Resolution No. ———— (New Series), as follows:

Whereas, the electors of the City and County of San Francisco did
heretofore vote and authorize a bonded indebtedness of $41,000,000 for
the purpose of acquiring the operative properties, rights, equipment
and distribution system of the Spring Valley Water Company, which
are hereafter in this resolution referred to as the "properties" of said
Water Company, and which said properties are more particularly described in a certain offer under date of March 2, 1928, made by said
Water Company to the Board of Supervisors of the City and County
of San Francisco, to sell the same to said City and County;

And Whereas, it is now the intention of said City and County to
purchase said properties pursuant to the terms and upon the conditions set forth in said offer;

And Whereas, it is impossible to determine the exact amount of
money to be paid for said properties according to the terms of said
offer until a full accounting is had between the City and County and
the Water Company, as of the date on which said properties are actually
taken over by said City and County, and the total cost of additions
and betterments made to said properties subsequent to December 31,
1929, and credits to the amortization fund of said properties, have all
been computed;

And Whereas, it is the intention of the City and County to take over
said properties as of the 3d day of March, 1930, and prior to noon on
said day, and it is admitted that there will be due to said Water Company on said day for said properties the sum of $39,962,606.51, together

with such additional amounts as may be shown by said accounting, which said additional amounts are to be paid as hereinafter set
forth; now, therefore, be it

Resolved, That the City and County accept the offer of March 2, 1928,
of said Water Company to sell to said City and County the said properties described therein, and does hereby agree to purchase and take
over the same on the 3d day of March, 1930, and before noon of said
day, and to pay therefor the amount which will be due for said properties as of said date and time based on the terms and conditions of
said offer, and to pay for said properties as follows: $39,962,606.51 on
said last mentioned date upon the delivery of a good and sufficient deed
made, executed and delivered by the Water Company to the City and
County, conveying said properties to said City and County, and the
balance of said purchase price as soon thereafter as the exact amount
thereof can be determined after a full accounting of all reciprocal
demands and amounts can be had between the City and the Water
Company; and be it

Further Resolved, That for the purpose of meeting and paying such
additional amount as may hereafter be found due to the Water Company for said properties, that the City shall deposit, not later than
noon on the 3d day of March, 1930, with Wells Fargo Bank and Union
Trust Company, the sum of $75,000, which said sum shall be disbursed
in accordance with the terms and conditions of a certain collateral or
supplemental agreement between the City and County and the Water
Company, which said agreement shall bear date of March 3, 1930, and
embody and contain all the terms and conditions relative to the payment of the total purchase price for said properties, and all of the
terms and conditions which shall govern the final accounting between
the City and County and the Water Company, and the manner in which
said total purchase price shall be determined, and which said collateral
and supplemental agreement shall further provide for the settlement,
adjustment and agreement as to all matters and things which may
be properly, necessarily or incidentally settled and adjusted between
the City and County and the Water Company relative to the taking
over of said properties, and the continuation of the business of the
Company without interruption; and be it

Further Resolved, That the Mayor of the City and County and the
Clerk of the Board of Supervisors be and they are hereby authorized
and empowered to execute and deliver, for and on behalf of the City
and County, the aforesaid collateral or supplemental agreement, in,
or substantially in, the form submitted to this Board by the City
Attorney, and to agree, on behalf of the City and County, with the
Water Company upon all of its terms and conditions; and be it

Further Resolved, That said collateral agreement above mentioned,
and any and all amounts of money to be paid thereunder and any and
all checks, drafts, warrants or demands payable to Spring Valley Water
Company for said properties may be deposited with Union Securities
Corporation in escrow for the purpose of consummating the purchase
of said properties from said Water Company, and that the City Attorney and the City Engineer be, and they are hereby, given full power
and authority to agree upon all of the terms and conditions of said
escrow, for and on behalf of the City and County, and to execute said
escrow and all agreements relative thereto for and on behalf of said
City and County; and be it

Further Resolved, That the Mayor and the Clerk of the Board of
Supervisors be and they are hereby given full power and authority to
enter into and execute, for and on behalf of the City and County, such
additional or supplemental agreements, escrows and documents. and
to do such other and further things as may be necessary to fully consummate the purchase of said properties pursuant to the said offer of
March 2, 1928, of said Water Company: and be it

Further Resolved, That there be and there is hereby appropriated
from the moneys realized from the proceeds of the sale of the bonds

of the City and County, known as "Spring Valley Bonds," the sum of $40,037,606.51, for the purpose of consummating the purchase of said above-mentioned properties from said Water Company, of which said sum $39,962,606.51 shall be payable to the Spring Valley Water Company upon the delivery of its deed for said properties to the City, and the remainder of said sum, to-wit, the sum of $75,000, shall be payable to Wells Fargo Bank and Union Trust Company for the purpose of meeting and paying such additional amounts as may be due to said Water Company in accordance with adjustments to be made as of March 3, 1930, as may be provided for in said collateral agreement hereinbefore mentioned. And the Board of Supervisors does hereby authorize the payment of said sum of $39,962,606.51 to the Spring Valley Water Company, and the payment of said sum of $75,000 to Wells Fargo Bank and Union Trust Company for the respective purposes hereinbefore set forth.

Ayes—Supervisors Andriano, Canepa, Colman, Gallagher, Havenner, Hayden, McGovern, McSheehy, Miles Peyser, Power, Roncovieri, Rossi, Spaulding, Stanton, Suhr, Toner—17.

Absent—Supervisor Shannon—1.

City Attorney to Receive and Record Deed, Spring Valley Water Company.

Resolution No. 32086 (New Series), as follows:

Whereas, this Board, by Resolution No. 32085 (New Series), did accept the offer dated March 2, 1928, made to the Board of Supervisors of the City and County of San Francisco, by the Spring Valley Water Company, to sell to the City and County of San Francisco its water system and operative properties more particularly described and referred to in said offer, for a sum or price to be determined in the manner set out in said offer; and

Whereas, a deed of conveyance, to be executed as of Monday, the 3rd day of March, 1930, which by its terms conveys all of the said water system properties to the said City and County, has been prepared under the direction of the City Attorney and approved by him; therefore, be it

Resolved, That the City Attorney is hereby authorized to accept said deed of conveyance on behalf of the City and County of San Francisco and is hereby directed to immediately thereafter cause said deed, with a copy of this resolution attached thereto, to be recorded in the offices of the County Recorder of the City and County of San Francisco and the County Recorders of the counties of San Mateo, Alameda and Santa Clara, State of California.

Adopted by the following vote:

Ayes—Supervisors Andriano, Canepa, Colman, Gallagher, Havenner, Hayden, McGovern, McSheehy, Miles, Peyser, Power, Roncovieri, Rossi, Spaulding, Stanton, Suhr, Toner—17.

Absent—Supervisor Shannon—1.

Committee on Reception to Ex-President Calvin Coolidge.

Supervisor Peyser presented:

Resolution No. 32082 (New Series), as follows:

Whereas, it has come to the attention of the Board of Supervisors that Calvin Coolidge, former President of the United States of America, is due to arrive in San Francisco this week; and

Whereas, it is fitting, becoming and patriotic that a public reception be given said dignitary; and

Whereas, a necessary expenditure will be required to correctly receive the former President of the United States of America; be it, therefore,

Resolved, That the Finance and Public Welfare Committees of the Board of Supervisors of the City and County of San Francisco, be, and are hereby authorized, to make suitable preparations for the proper reception of former President Calvin Coolidge, and are authorized to incur such indebtedness as will enable the Committees to receive the ex-President in the manner becoming the City and County of San Francisco.

Adopted by the following vote:

Ayes—Supervisors Andriano, Canepa, Havenner, Hayden, McSheehy, Miles, Peyser, Power, Rossi, Spaulding, Stanton—11.

Absent—Supervisors Colman, Gallagher, McGovern, Roncovieri, Shannon, Suhr, Toner—7.

Motion.

Supervisor Colman thereupon moved that the Board meet again in special session Wednesday, February 26, 1930, at 2:30 p. m., for the purpose of giving final passage to Spring Valley purchase matters heretofore passed for printing.

Motion *carried*.

ADJOURNMENT.

There being no further business, the Board at 7:15 p. m. adjourned.

J. S. DUNNIGAN, Clerk.

Approved by the Board of Supervisors April 7, 1930.

Pursuant to Resolution No. 3402 (New Series) of the Board of Supervisors of the City and County of San Francisco, I, John S. Dunnigan, hereby certify that the foregoing is a true and correct copy of the Journal of Proceedings of said Board of the date stated and approved as above recited.

JOHN S. DUNNIGAN,

Clerk of the Board of Supervisors,
City and County of San Francisco.

Tuesday, February 18, 1930, 2:30 p. m.
Tuesday-Wednesday, February 18-19, 1930, 11 p. m.
Wednesday, February 19, 1930, 3 a. m.

Journal of Proceedings
Board of Supervisors

City and County of San Francisco

The Recorder Printing and Publishing Company
337 Bush Street, S. F.

JOURNAL OF PROCEEDINGS
BOARD OF SUPERVISORS

(Note—The following Proceedings of February 18 and 19 cover the original transactions of the meetings and the Mayor's report on the War Memorial. The Proceedings appear in a narrower measure to differentiate them from the War Memorial Report proper.)

TUESDAY, FEBRUARY 18, 1930, 2:30 P. M.

In Board of Supervisors, San Francisco, Tuesday, February 18, 1930, 2:30 p. m.

The Board of Supervisors met in regular session.

CALLING THE ROLL.

The roll was called and the following Supervisors were noted present:

Supervisors Canepa, Gallagher, Havenner, Hayden, McSheehy, Miles, Peyser, Power, Roncovieri, Rossi, Spaulding, Stanton, Suhr—13.

Absent—Supervisors Andriano, Colman, McGovern, Shannon, Toner—5.

Quorum present.

His Honor Mayor Rolph presiding.

THE CLERK: Supervisor Toner excused himself yesterday, he had professional matters to attend to. If the Board please, I would like to be excused to attend to some duties for the Finance Committee.

SUPERVISOR HAYDEN: I move the Clerk be excused.

THE MAYOR: If there are no objections, it is so ordered.

SUPERVISOR HAYDEN: And that Mr. Rogers take his place.

THE MAYOR: Gentlemen of the Board, Men and Women of the Army and Navy Services of our Nation and my Fellow Citizens: This time of this day was set apart to hear a message from the Mayor, giving a review of the facts in connection with the efforts made to build a War Memorial in San Francisco. And I have prepared a special message, addressed to the Honorable Board of Supervisors of the City and County of San Francisco.

San Francisco, February 15, 1930.

To the Honorable Board of Supervisors, City and County of San Francisco:

Gentlemen: I beg to submit to you, and through you to the people of San Francisco, a chronological review of facts relating to the highly patriotic desire of the people of San Francisco to erect, for the living and in loving memory of the dead who served our country in stress of strife, a War Memorial, and for the purpose of giving this message to your Honorable Board a designation I shall title it "History of the San Francisco War Memorial."

In April, 1918, a group of citizens interested in the musical development of San Francisco determined to erect a Symphony Hall. Later this plan was expanded to include an Opera House and Art Museum. Leaders of this group were W. H. Crocker, Templeton Crocker, John Drum, Milton Esberg, Herbert Fleishhacker, E. S. Heller, Walter Martin and John D. McKee. John Drum was made chairman.

During 1918 and 1919 these men worked actively securing subscriptions to carry out this magnificent project, and from a comparatively small group of subscribers obtained pledge tou $1,635,000.

On September 1, 1919, an option was taken on the former St. Ignatius lot bounded by Hayes, Franklin and Grove streets and Van Ness avenue.

On February 28, 1920, the St. Ignatius lot held under option was purchased for $300,000.

Early in 1920 members of the American Legion suggested to John Drum that his group dedicate their great project as San Francisco's War Memorial. This idea was enthusiastically accepted, and it was determined to hold a city-wide drive for funds to bring the entire public into the project.

A War Memorial Committee of the American Legion was appointed to handle the Legion's participation in the project. This committee consisted of forty-six members and was a pro-rata representation of the membership of each San Francisco Post. The committee was as follows:

Charles H. Kendrick, Chairman Conference Committee.

Frank F. Kilsby, Secretary Conference Committee.

San Francisco Post—Edward Crowley, Post Chairman; Humphrey Sullivan, Jesse Colman, Wm. S. Williams, Charles Elliott, Norman Livermore, Rev. F. W. Clampett, Louis T. Grant, Charles H. Kendrick, Rev. Jos. McQuaide, Henry G. Mathewson, Sydney Van Wyck, A. E. Graupner, Bertram Cadwalader, Dr. Morton R. Gibbons, Allen Wright, Gen. Hunter L. Liggett, Bruce Cornwall, Mark L. Gerstle, Wm. L. Laurence, Paul Bancroft, W. W. Crocker.

Golden Gate Post—J. W. Jackson, Post Chairman; M. D. Sapiro, C. Willard Evans, F. F. Bebergall, David J. McCoy, W. I. Garren, Kimball C. Kaufman, Col. James M. Kennedy, Richard M. Budd, John Channing, Dr. Julian L. Waller, J. Paulding Edwards, Frederick W. Kant, Geo. E. Kammerer, Rollo Bishop Watt, Frank F. Kilsby, E. M. Dunnivant.

Zane Post—Arthur P. Crist, Post Chairman; Admiral Jayne, Col. Hugh Matthews.

George Washington Post—Donald Henderson, Post Chairman; Israel Weinstein.

Irwin Post—C. J. Kelly, Frank J. Sullivan.

On May 19, 1920, a great mass meeting was held in the Civic Auditorium to open the drive. At this meeting the fund of $1,635,000 already subscribed was first made known to the public.

In November, 1920, the city-wide drive closed with a total subscription of about $2,012,000. This sum was payable in installments over a period of years. The Regents of the University of California were designated as Trustees for the subscribers.

On August 19, 1921, a formal trust agreement was entered into with the Regents of the University of California and the following persons were designated as Trustees of the War Memorial: Wm. H. Crocker, Herbert Fleishhacker, John Drum, Milton Esberg, Charles Kendrick, Frank Kilsby, Walter Martin, Templeton Crocker, John D. McKee, E. S. Heller.

In the preparation of this trust agreement the attorneys for the Regents determined that the pledges signed by the subscribers were legally insufficient, and as a condition of the acceptance of the trust by the Regents the Trustees were obliged to secure new signatures from the subscribers on pledge forms satisfactory to the Regents. This was a huge task as there were several thousand subscribers and many persons losing their first enthusiasm took advantage of the situation and refused to sign on the new forms. About two years was required to accomplish this work.

The War Memorial Trustees were further specifically obligated by the Regents not to enter into any expenditures or contracts for the War Memorial until at least $1,800,000 in subscriptions had been signed up on the new form designated by them.

On October 11, 1922, an Architectural Advisory Committee was appointed by th........ This advisory committee consisted of eight leading San Francisco architects, as follows: Bernard Maybeck, chairman; Willis Polk, John Galen Howard, Ernest Coxhead, G. Albert Lansburg, John Reid, Jr., Fred Meyer, Arthur Brown.

On November 3, 1922, the Architectural Advisory Committee reported unanimously that the St. Ignatius lot was too small to carry out the War Memorial project as conceived.

On November 3, 1922, the War Memorial Trustees appointed a committee, consisting of Messrs. Drum, Heller and Kendrick, to present to the Board of Supervisors a proposition to purchase the two blocks of land immediately west of the City Hall for War Memorial purposes, these two blocks being a part of the original Civic Center area.

On December 5, 1922, the committee from the War Memorial Trustees met with City Attorney Lull and Supervisor McLaren to discuss plans for condemnation of the two blocks immediately west of the City Hall. The Board of Supervisors had shortly before this date filed an injunction against certain persons who had started the erection of a storage house on the southwest corner of Van Ness and McAllister.

On December 28, 1922, the War Memorial Trustees, on request of the Board of Supervisors, advanced $89,000 to purchase the southwest corner of Van Ness and McAllister. This action was made necessary as the only means of preventing the erection of the warehouse already started on this site. The City and County repaid the loan of $89,000, without interest, on June 30, 1924.

On January 27, 1923, the following was presented, read and ordered spread in the Journal:

"To his Honor the Mayor and the Honorable Board of Supervisors of the City and County of San Francisco, City Hall, San Francisco, California:

The Trustees of the San Francisco War Memorial, mindful of the plans for the Civic Center to the west of the City Hall and comprising the area between McAllister, Franklin and Grove streets and Van Ness avenue, as prepared by the Civic Center Architectural Commission, are desirous of cooperating with the City and County in the achievement and completion of these plans so as to afford the city the public places and grounds it desires. The Trustees of the San Francisco War Memorial will erect the following buildings, viz.: Opera House, American Legion Building, Art Museum, and they will be made to harmonize with this Civic Center plan.

The public of San Francisco has subscribed to the funds of which we are Trustees and it is our desire to complete the buildings as soon as possible. To that end we will agree to use part of the area bounded by Van Ness avenue, McAllister, Grove and Franklin streets, approximately equal to the area of the St. Ignatius lot, for the erection thereon of the contemplated group of buildings. To complete this general project cooperation between the City and County of San Francisco and the Trustees is necessary.

Therefore, if the City and County will purchase, through condemnation proceedings or otherwise, the remainder of the two blocks above referred to, the Trustees of the San Francisco War Memorial will join in said purchase, sharing the cost fifty-fifty with the City and County. To expedite such purchase the Trustees will advance necessary money, from time to time, with the understanding and agreement entered into with the City and County that one-half of the total purchase price shall be refunded to the Trustees of the San Francisco War Memorial in five annual installments, necessary resolutions to make this agreement legally effective to be approved by the City Attorney and the attorney for the said Trustees.

Upon acquisition of the aforesaid property the Trustees will proceed forthwith to erect thereon the group of buildings, which, upon completion, will be held by the University of California under the terms of our trust.

It goes without saying that the exerior design of the buildings to be erected are to meet with your approval.

The interest of the Trustees and the City and County in the lot recently purchased at the southwest corner of Van Ness avenue and McAllister street will naturally be taken into consideration in the carrying out of the plan.

Yours very truly,

(Signed)   JOHN S. DRUM,

Chairman of the Trustees of the San Francisco War Memorial.

WM. H. CROCKER,

TEMPLETON CROCKER,

CHAS. H. KENDRICK,

MILTON ESBERG,

FRANK F. KILSBY.

HERBERT FLEISHHACKER,

Trustees."

ACCEPTING OFFER.

Whereupon, the following resolution was presented to the Board of Supervisors and adopted by the following vote:

Resolution No. 20725 (New Series), as follows:

"Whereas, the San Francisco War Memorial Committee, in a communication dated January 27, 1923, has offered to use a part of the area bounded by Van Ness avenue, McAllister, Grove and Franklin streets for the construction of an Opera House, American Legion Building and Art Museum, approximately equal to the St. Ignatius lot now owned by said committee, provided that the City and County of San Francisco purchase the privately owned property in said area; and

Whereas, the said War Memorial Committee offers to pay one-half of the purchase cost of said property, provided the City pays the other one-half; and

Whereas, said offer is advantageous to the City; now, therefore, be it

Resolved, That said offer be accepted and that the City Attorney confer with the attorneys for said committee and report back a proposed contract to this Board embodying the offer of the War Memorial Committee for the approval of the Board.

Ayes—Supervisors Bath, Colman, Deasy, Hayden, McGregor, McLaren, McSheehy, Morgan, Mulvihill, Robb, Rossi, Scott, Shannon, Welch, Wetmore—15.

Excused—Supervisor Hynes—1.

Absent—Supervisors Powers, Schmitz—2."

CONDEMNATION OF CIVIC CENTER LANDS.

Resolution No. 20726 (New Series), as follows:

"Resolved, That public interest and necessity require the acquisition by the City and County of San Francisco of the following described lands, and any and all rights and claims thereto, for the continuation and expansion of the Civic Center, to-wit: All the lots, pieces or parcels of land included in the following descriptions, to-wit:

1. Being all of that lot, block or parcel of land bounded on the north by Fulton street, on the east by Van Ness avenue, on the south by Grove street and on the west by Franklin street.

2. Beginning at the point of intersection of the southerly line of McAllister street with the easterly line of Franklin street, running thence southerly and along the easterly line of Franklin street 275 feet to its point of intersection with the northerly line of Fulton street; thence at a right angle easterly and along said northerly line of Fulton street 384 feet 9 inches to its point of intersection with the westerly line of Van Ness avenue; thence at a right angle northerly

and along said westerly line of Van Ness avenue 155 feet to its point of intersection with the northerly line of Ash street; thence at a right angle and along the northerly line of Ash street 219 feet 6 inches; thence at a right angle northerly 120 feet to the southerly line of Mc-Allister street; thence at a right angle westerly and along said southerly line of McAllister street 165 feet to the point of commencement.

That all the lands, rights and claims above described are hereby declared to be suitable, adaptable and necessary for a public use by the City and County of San Francisco.

The City Attorney is hereby instructed to commence proceedings against the owner or owners of said lots, pieces or parcels of land inclosed within said hereinabove description, and any and all rights and claims thereto and interest therein for the condemnation thereof for the use of the City and County of San Francisco, as aforesaid, and to prosecute such proceedings to a speedy termination.

Ayes—Supervisors Bath, Colman, Deasy, Hayden, McGregor, Mc-Leran, McSheehy, Morgan, Mulvihill, Robb, Rossi, Scott, Shannon, Welch, Wetmore—15.

Absent—Supervisors Powers, Schmitz—2."

On March 16th, 1923, the City Attorney filed condemnation proceedings on all the property ownerships contained in the two blocks immediately west of the City Hall.

During 1923, 1924 and 1925 the City, in conjunction with the War Memorial Trustees, purchased, by negotiation and suit, the twenty-eight parcels of land comprising the two blocks bounded by Van Ness avenue, McAllister, Grove and Franklin streets.

On April 25th, 1924, the War Memorial Trustees, on the advice of the Architectural Advisory Committee, contracted with Willis Polk, Arthur Brown, Jr., and G. Albert Lansburg to undertake the plans for the War Memorial.

On October 4th, 1924, the War Memorial Trustees sold St. Ignatius lot to the Board of Education for $350,000, which sum practically reimbursed the War Memorial fund for all expenses in the purchase of that property.

Late in 1924 the Trustees authorized Messrs. Polk, Brown and Lansburg to establish drafting rooms and employ the necessary personnel to carry on the architectural work.

Early in 1926, when estimates were taken on the general studies and plans for the Memorial project, it was determined that the funds subscribed were entirely inadequate to construct a Memorial in keeping with the dignity and grandeur which the people of San Francisco were entitled to expect of such an undertaking. During the following year the Trustees considered several plans to raise additional funds, but no proposed solution of the problem seemed feasible.

In the latter part of 1926 Mr Otts, chairman of the United Veterans' Council War Memorial Committee, met several times with Messrs. Kilsby and Kendrick, Trustees, and discussed fully the provisions being made for veteran occupancy in the Memorial. It should be noted that the United Veterans' Council is the central veteran body, representing all veterans of the Civil War, Spanish War and World War. Mr. Otts later, as well as Mr. Harold Hotchner, of the American Legion War Memorial Committee, visited the drafting rooms and examined the Memorial plans. Many other veteran representatives called to examine the plans, among whom were Mr. Gerlack, Mr. French, Mr. Schary and Mr. Wiedenfeld.

On February 18th, 1927, the publishers of the five San Francisco newspapers were called into conference with the Trustees. It was their unanimous opinion that the plans for the Memorial as prepared by the Trustees should not be curtailed, and that the public be asked to vote a bond issue sufficient to carry out the project in full. The publishers also agreed to give this bond issue the full support of their newspapers.

· *On February* 24th, 1927, a meeting was held between the Finance Committee and the other members of the Board of Supervisors and the publishers and the Trustees, at which meeting the Supervisors present agreed to submit a bond issue of $4,000,000 to the public.

In March, 1927, members of the War Memorial Trustees were advised by City Attorney John O'Toole that he had eliminated from the resolution for the $4,000;000 bond issue all direct mention of an Art Museum and Opera House in order to make sure that the bond issue conform to the California statutes. However, the Board of Supervisors were fully aware that the bond issue was to provide for the then accepted Memorial plan of two buildings—one a Music Auditorium, or so-called Opera House, and the other a Veterans' and Arts Building. This was also stressed in all the newspapers during the bond campaign.

On May 2nd, 1927, an ordinance, numbered 7516 (New Series), was passed by the Board of Supervisors of this City and County, submitting to the voters a proposition for a bond issue for the War Memorial, as follows:

"Bill No. 8003, Ordinance No. 7516 (New Series). Calling and providing for a special election to be held in the City and County of San Francisco on Tuesday, the 14th day of June, 1927, for the purpose of submitting to the said voters of the City and County of San Francisco a proposition to incur a bonded debt of the City and County of San Francisco to the amount of four million ($4,000,000) dollars for the acquisition, construction and completion of a permanent improvement, to-wit: the construction, completion and equipment of permanent buildings in or adjacent to the Civic Center, in the City and County of San Francisco, to be used as a Memorial Hall for War Veterans and for educational, recreational, entertainment and other municipal purposes, and the purchase of all equipment and furnishings necessary for said buildings.

Be it ordained by the People of the City and County of San Francisco as follows:

Section 1. A special election is hereby called and ordered to be held in the City and County of San Francisco on Tuesday, the 14th day of June, 1927, for the purpose of submitting to the electors of said City and County the folowing proposition, to-wit: To incur a bonded debt of the City and County of San Francisco to the amount of four million ($4,000,00) dollars, for the purpose of the acquisition, construction and completion of a permanent improvement, to-wit: The construction, completion and equipment of permanent buildings in or adjacent to the Civic Center, in the City and County of San Francisco, to be used as a Memorial Hall for War Veterans and for educational, recreational, entertainment and other municipal purposes, and the purchase of all equipment and furnishings necessary for said buildings.

Section 2. The estimated cost of the acquisition, construction and completion of the permanent improvement described herein was by plans and estimates of the Board of Public Works procured through the City Engineer and filed with the Board of Supervisors on the 11th day of April, 1927, and was and is fixed by Bill No. 7997, Ordinance No. 7501 (New Series), in the sum of four million ($4,000,000) dollars.

Section 3. By Bill No. 7997, Ordinance No. 7501 (New Series), it was declared that no part of the said sum of four million ($4,000,000) dollars could be paid out of the annual revenue of the City and County in addition to the other necessary expenses thereof or other funds derived from taxes levied for that purpose, and will require the incurring of a bonded debt to the amount of four million ($4,000,000) dollars for the purposes herein recited. The method and manner of payment of the estimated cost of said described permanent improvement are by the issuance of bonds of the City and County of San Francisco to the amount required therefor and the application of the proceeds arising from the sale thereof to defray the cost of the acquisition, construction and completion of said permanent improvement herein described.

Section 4. The special election hereby called and ordered to be held shall be held and conducted, and the votes thereat received and canvassed, and the returns thereof made, and the result thereof ascertained, determined and declared as herein provided and according to the laws of the State of California providing for and governing elections in the City and County of San Francisco, and the polls for such election shall be and remain open during the time required by said laws.

Section 5. The ballots to be used at said special election shall be such as may be required by law to be used thereat, and, in addition to any other matter to be required by law to be printed thereon shall appear thereon the following:

Memorial Halls. To incur a bonded indebtedness in the sum of four million ($4,000,000) dollars for the acquisition, construction and completion of a permanent improvement, consisting of public buildings in or adjacent to the Civic Center of the City and County of San Francisco, to be used as memorial halls for war veterans and for educational, recreational, entertainment and other municipal purposes, and the purchase of all equipment and furnishings necessary for said buildings.

To vote for the proposition, and thereby authorize the incurring of a bonded indebtedness to the amount of and for the purpose stated herein, stamp a cross (X) in the blank space to the right of the word 'YES.' To vote against the proposition, and thereby refuse to authorize the incurring of a bonded indebtedness to the amount of and for the purpose stated herein, stamp a cross (X) in the blank space to the right of the word 'NO.'

YES	
NO	

Bonds issued for the acquisition, construction and completion of the permanent improvement herein described shall bear interest at the rate of 4½ per centum per annum, payable semi-annually.

Section 6. Where voting machines are used at said special election, and said voting machines shall be so arranged that any qualified elector may vote for the proposition by pulling down a lever over the word 'YES' under or near a statement of the proposed proposition appearing on cardboard, paper or other material placed on the front of the machine, and said act shall constitute a vote for the proposition, and by pulling down a lever over the word 'NO' under or near a statement of the proposed proposition appearing on cardboard, paper or other material placed on the front of the machine, shall constitute a vote against the proposition. Said voting machines and the preparation of the same are to be used in accordance with the provisions of Chapter 96 of the Statutes of 1923.

Each cross (X) stamped in the square to the right of the word 'YES' appearing on the printed ballot, where printed ballots are used, shall constitute a vote in favor of and to authorize the incurring of a bonded indebtedness for the purpose set forth in the proposition, and each cross (X) stamped in the square to the right of the word 'NO' shall be counted as a vote not in favor of, and a refusal to authorize the incurring of a bonded indebtedness for the purpose set forth in the proposition.

Section 7. The election precincts and the numbers, names and boundaries thereof for said special election, and the places of voting, and the officers to conduct such election, and all other necessary proceedings in that behalf shall be respectively defined, designated, selected, appointed and had by the Board of Election Commissioners of the City and County of San Francisco, and said board is hereby authorized and directed to procure and provide all supplies that may be necessary to properly and lawfully conduct such special election.

When the polls are closed the officers of election shall count the ballots cast at such election and canvass the votes cast respectively for and against the proposition herein stated and make return thereof in time, form and manner required for the counting, canvassing and returning of votes cast at other municipal elections held in the City and County of San Francisco. The Board of Election Commissioners shall, as soon as the said returns and ballots have been received by said board, canvass said returns and declare the result thereof in the manner provided by law for canvassing returns and declaring results in other elections, and shall also certify said results to the Board of Supervisors.

Section 8. If, at such special election, it shall appear that two-thirds of all the votes cast thereat were in favor of and authorized the incurring of a bonded debt for the purpose set forth in said proposition, then such proposition shall be deemed to have been accepted by the electors and bonds will be issued to defray the cost of the permanent improvements described therein. Such bonds shall be of the form and character known as 'serials.' All of said bonds shall be dated July 1, 1927, shall bear interest at the rate of 4½ per centum per annum, payable semi-annually, shall be of the denomination of one thousand dollars each, and the principal and interest thereof shall be payable in gold coin of the United States. Said bonds shall be called 'Memorial Halls Bonds.'

Bonds issued for the purpose stated shall be numbered from 1 to 4000, both inclusive, and shall be payable two hundred thousand ($200,000) dollars thereof five years from the date of said bonds, beginning with the lowest numbers, and two hundred thousand ($200,-000) dollars thereof of the next higher numbers on the same day in each succeeding year until all of said bonds shall be paid.

THE MAYOR: It is the purpose to read to you everything that has transpired in connection with this War Memorial, giving you facts from the very inception in 1918. I feel at the present moment that the balance of the bond election printed matter, which went before the people, which is customary in all cases, from now on, with your permission, and yielding in no way whatsoever to reading verbatim the whole history of the record, I will, for your convenience, if you accept it in such manner, just leave to the printing of the record the full ballot as it appeared, as I have it here.

SUPERVISOR HAYDEN: How many pages is that, Mr. Mayor?

THE MAYOR: These were $1,000 bonds of the United States of America, State of California, City and County of San Francisco, and known as "Memorial Halls Bonds," $1,000 each, bearing interest at the rate of 4½ per cent, and payable at the fiscal agency of the City and County of San Francisco, in the City and State of New York, and all matters relating to law are included in this bond issue, which was approved by City

Attorney O'Toole, I think. And it takes the four signatures of the Mayor, the Treasurer, the Auditor and the Clerk of the Board, and it gives the form of the coupon and the form of the registration. It sets forth the purpose and intent of the tax provision and says: "This ordinance shall take effect immediately," and it was finally passed by the Board of Supervisors, San Francisco, May 2, 1927.

Section 9. Said bonds and coupons shall be in substantially the following form:

THE UNITED STATES OF AMERICA.

State of California.

City and County of San Francisco.

MEMORIAL HALLS BOND

No........ $1,000.00

For value received the City and County of San Francisco, a municipal corporation organized and existing under the laws of the State of California, hereby acknowledges itself indebted and promises to pay to the bearer, on the first day of ...., 19..., one thousand dollars, with interest thereon at the rate of 4½ per centum per annum, payable semi-annually January 1 and July 1, on presentation and surrender of the coupons hereto attached as they respectively become due, both principal and interest being payable in gold coin of the United States at the office of the Treasurer of said City and County, or, at the option of the holder, at the fiscal agency of said City and County of San Francisco in the City and State of New York.

This bond is issued under and pursuant to the Constitution and statutes of the State of California and the Charter of said City and County of San Francisco and amendments thereto and under and pursuant to ordinances and proceedings of said City and County duly adopted and taken, and a vote and assent of more than two-thirds of all the qualified electors of said City and County voting at a special election duly and legally called and held for that purpose.

It is hereby certified, recited and declared that all acts, conditions and things required by law to exist, happen and be performed precedent to and in the issuance of this bond have existed, happened and been performed in due time, form and manner as required by law, and that the amount of this bond, together with all other indebtedness of said City and County, does not exceed any limit prescribed by the Constitution or statutes of said State or Charter of said City and County, and that provision has been made, as required by the Constitution and statutes of said State and the Charter of said City and County, for the collection of an annual tax sufficient to pay the interest on this bond as it falls due, and also provision to constitute a sinking fund for the payment of the principal of this bond on or before maturity. The full faith and credit of said City and County are hereby pledged for the punctual payment of the principal and interest of this bond.

This bond may be converted into a registered bond upon presentation to the Treasurer of the City and County of San Francisco, in which event such Treasurer shall cut off and cancel the coupons of this bond, and shall sign a statement stamped, printed or written upon the back or face of the bond to the effect that this bond is registered in the name of the owner and that thereafter the interest and principal of this bond are payable to the registered owner. Thereafter, and from time to time, this bond may be transferred by such registered owner in person, or by attorney duly authorized, on presentation of this bond to the Treasurer, and the bond be again registered as before, a similar statement being stamped, printed or written thereon.

This bond is exempt from all taxation within the State of California.

In witness whereof, said City and County of San Francisco has caused this bond to be executed under its corporate seal, signed by its

Mayor and Treasurer, and countersigned by its Auditor, and has caused the interest coupons hereto attached to be signed with the engraved or lithographed signature of its Treasurer, and this bond to be dated the first day of July, 1927.

....
                                                          Mayor.

....
                                                          Treasurer.
Countersigned:

....
                                                          Auditor.

FORM OF COUPON.

No. .... $ ....
   On .... 1, 19.., the City and County of San Francisco, California, will pay to bearer, at the office of the Treasurer of said City and County, or, at the option of the holder, at the fiscal agceny of the City and County of San Francisco, in the City and State of New York, ... dollars ($........) in gold coin of the United States, being six months' interest then due on its bond dated July 1, 1927, No. ......

....
                                                          Treasurer.

FORM OF REGISTRATION.

San Francisco, ..., 19...
   This bond is registered pursuant to Charter of the City and County of San Francisco, State of California, in the name of ...., and the interest and principal thereof are hereafter payable to such owner.

....
                                                          Treasurer.

Section 10. The amount of tax levy to be made for the payment of said four million dollars' bonds issued under said proposition shall be in the sum of one hundred eighty thousand dollars for the first five years from date of said bonds to pay the annual interest on said bonds, and, in season to pay such interest as it becomes due, and for the sixth year after the date of said bonds in the sum of one hundred seventy-one thousand dollars to pay and in season to pay the interest on such of said bonds as remain outstanding after the two hundred thousand dollars thereof due five years from their date have been paid, and for the seventh year after the date of said bonds the sum of one hundred sixty-two thousand dollars to pay and in season to pay the interest on such of said bonds as remain outstanding after the two hundred thousand dollars thereof due six years from their date have been paid, and so on, a sum each year for seventeen succeeding years until said bonds are all paid, sufficient for interest and in season to pay interest on all of said bonds outstanding, which sum for interest will diminish each year by the amount of nine thousand dollars by reason of the payment each year, beginning five years from date of said bonds, of two hundred thousand dollars of said bonds, and the sum of two hundred thousand dollars each year, beginning four years from the date of said bonds, to pay and in season to pay the principal of such bonds as they respectively become due, and continuing each succeeding year for nineteen years until the principal of all of said bonds has been paid.

The purpose and intent of the foregoing tax provisions are, and it is hereby expressly provided, that at the time of levying the municipal tax, and in the manner provided for such tax levy, the Supervisors shall levy and collect annually a tax sufficient to pay the annual interest on such bonds, and also such part of the bonded indebtedness as will fall due within the succeeding fiscal year. Such taxes shall be in addition to all other taxes levied for municipal purposes, and shall be collected at the same time and in the same manner as other municipal taxes are collected.

Section 11. This ordinance shall be published for at least ten days in the official newspaper, and at the expiration of said ten days notice of such special election shall be given and published as required by law.

Section 12. This ordinance is the third of a series of ordinances which will be adopted by the Board of Supervisors relating to and designed to secure the acquisition, construction and completion of the permanent improvement named.

Section 13. This ordinance shall take effect immediately.

Finally passed—Board of Supervisors, San Francisco, May 2, 1927.

Ayes—Supervisors Byington, Colman, Deasy, Gallagher, Harrelson, Havenner, Hayden, Kent, McSheehy, Marks, Powers, Schmidt, Shannon, Stanton, Todd.

Absent—Supervisors Badaracco, Bath, Roncovieri.

J. S. DUNNIGAN, Clerk.

Approved, San Francisco, May 2, 1927, 10:40 a. m.

JAMES ROLPH, JR., Mayor."

THE MAYOR (reading): The argument accompanying the ordinance last quoted is as follows:

"THE WAR MEMORIAL.

The land for the War Memorial is bought, and $1,200,000 cash is waiting in the bank. Thus the people of this city, by issuing $4,000,000 in bonds, will gain a beautiful public project costing almost $7,000,000. The rest is already donated privately or given by the city.

This group of buildings, occupying two entire blocks on one side of Vàn Ness avenue, with the City Hall opposite, will greatly beautify our city. The location is ideal. The purpose—to commemorate our heroes of the World War—is idealistic and patriotic.

The utilitarian value of these buildings alone merits their construction. One of them will be the Veterans' Building, housing all the veterans' organizations in San Francisco. It was to give these splendid organizations a permanent headquarters in the name of the public which honors their deeds that the War Memorial fund orginally was launched.

The other building will contain San Francisco's long-needed Symphony Hall and Opera Auditorium. Originally this was planned for a less advantageous location at the eastern end of the Civic Center. We have one of the finest Symphony Orchestras in the United States, and it should have a fitting place in which to perform. The San Francisco Opera Chorus, with the Municipal Chorus, foreshadows the day when the musical productions here will take rank with those produced in Chicago and New York; and a home for all the future will here be provided, second to none in beauty. Art gallery and museum features also are included in the plans. *The War Memorial* deserves unanimous support. Vote 'YES.'

CIVIC LEAGUE OF IMPROVEMENT CLUBS AND
ASSOCIATIONS OF SAN FRANCISCO.
W. W. WATSON, President.
GEORGE W. GERHARD, Secretary."

"Resolution No. 27286 (New Series).

The following resolution was adopted by the Board of Supervisors of the City and County of San Francisco at its meeting on Monday, May 16, 1927, and approved by Mayor James Rolph, Jr.:

Whereas, the Civic League of Improvement Clubs and Associations has recommended to the voters of the City and County of San Francisco in favor of the acquisition of the Spring Valley Water System, the extensions of the Municipal Railways, the construction of the Bernal Cut and the War Memorial project; therefore, be it

Resolved, That the Registrar is hereby authorized and directed to include, on behalf of the Board of Supervisors, the arguments of the Civic League of Improvement Clubs and Associations in favor of those projects, with the sample ballots mailed to the voters, as provided in

Section 10, Article XI, Chaper 3, of the Charter of the City and County of San Francisco.

> JOHN B. BADARACCO,
> LEWIS F. BYINGTON,
> JESSE C. COLMAN,
> ANDREW J. GALLAGHER,
> W. H. HARRELSON,
> FRANCK R. HAVENNER,
> J. EMMET HAYDEN,
> MILO F. KENT,
> JAMES B. McSHEEHY,
> MILTON MARKS,
> CHARLES J. POWERS,
> ALFRED RONCOVIERI,
> WALTER J. SCHMIDT,
> WARREN SHANNON,
> WILLIAM P. STANTON,
> CHARLES F. TODD,
>   Supervisors.

Approved: JAMES ROLPH, JR., Mayor.

June 6, 1927, the Board of Supervisors adopted the following resolution:

"Resolution No. 27631 (New Series), as follows:

Resolved, That, in the event of the approval by the people of the War Memorial bonds, to be voted upon on June 14, 1927, this Board of Supervisors pledges itself to the policy of not appropriating the money to be derived from the sale of said bonds for the construction of the War Memorial Building until the official plans for such building shall have received the formal approval of a majority of duly constituted representatives of all the war veteran organizations now existing in San Francisco.

Adopted by the Board of Supervisors June 6, 1927.

Ayes—Supervisors Badaracco, Gallagher, Havenner, Hayden, Mc-Sheehy, Powers, Roncovieri, Schmidt, Shannon, Stanton, Todd—11.

Absent—Supervisors Bath, Byington, Colman, Deasy, Harrelson, Kent, Marks—7.

                                   J. S. DUNNIGAN, Clerk.

Approved June 13, 1927.

                              JAMES ROLPH, JR., Mayor."

On June 14, 1927, the election for the $4,000,000 bond issue was held and the bonds carried by a large majority.

On July 14, 1927, a vacancy occurring on the Board of Trustees of the War Memorial, the Chairman of the Finance Committee of the Board of Supervisors, Mr. James B. McSheehy, was unanimously elected to fill the vacancy. Later Supervisors Franck R. Havenner and Jesse C. Colman were added to the Board.

On July 25, 1927, at 7:30 p. m., a meeting of various veteran representatives was held in the drafting rooms of the War Memorial architects and the plans were considered in detail. The suggestions for additions or alterations made by the veterans were carefully noted and wherever practicable were afterwards incorporated in the plans.

September 1, 1927, at the request of the veterans the auditorium on the first floor of the Veterans' Building was radically changed to permit the addition of a club room on the third floor for dancing and smokers.

March 16, 1928, at the request of veteran representatives, the auditorium on the first floor was replaced by a club room similar to the one on the third floor.

March 19, 1928, the official War Memorial Committee of the American Legion finally approved the plans for the Veterans' Building and it was hoped by the Trustees that work could now be started on the Memorial. These plans bear the signatures of the following committee members:

Duncan, A. Don—Galileo Post.
Cabaniss, Geo. H., Jr.—Blackstone Post.
Hotchner, Harold—Golden Gate Post.
Angel, Dr. Peter R.—Hellenic Post.
Harris, Earle H.—Advance Post
French, Leon—Daylight Post.
Cerkel, Ivy Perkins—Eliz. Lee Post.
Kendrick, Chas. H.—California Post.
Burns, James B.—Zane Irwin Post.
Schofield, A. E.—West Twin Peaks Post.
Schary, Edward—George Washington Post.
Foley, Thos. M.—Disabled American War Veterans.
Flynn, Wm. D.—San Francisco Post.
Ainsworth, F. F.—Thomas Post.

Attest: I hereby certify that the foregoing are signatures of duly authorized and accredited members of the American Legion War Memorial Committee.

J. S. CLARIDGE, Secretary.

After the signing of the plans by the Legion representatives the Trustees immediately prepared specifications for excavation for foundations.

June 7th, 1928, the Trustees decided to cut down the width of both Memorial buildings by ten feet. This was made necessary by acoustic requirements. This change reduced the net space allocated to the veterans from 105,760 square feet to 102,647 square feet, a difference of 3113 square feet. However, upon rechecking the plans, the architects, by changing widths of corridors, were able to give the veterans an area even larger than that provided in the plans approved by the veterans. The amount of space provided for veterans does not include provisions made for corridors, toilets, exits, retiring rooms, etc.

June 7th, 1928, the War Memorial Committee of the American Legion voted to disapprove the Memorial plans as above modified, giving as the reason, so I was informed by Mr. H. W. Glensor at a meeting held in my office on November 15th, 1929, with representatives of various Legion Posts, that when the new plans were prepared and presented to the veteran bodies they were approved and later disapproved because said plans had been changed to conform to another set of plans which had theretofore been disapproved by the veterans on account of space allotted inside, and which objection didn't go entirely to the exterior of the building.

June 22nd, 1928, the War Memorial Committee of the American Legion voted to disapprove the Memorial plans as above modified for the reason given.

June 29th, 1928, at the request of City Attorney O'Toole, the Trustees submitted to him a form of Charter amendment providing means for the consolidation of the funds held by the Trustees with the funds voted in the bond issue. This form of Charter amendment, as originally submitted by the Trustees, was radically changed before being submitted to the Board of Supervisors, and further changes were made by the Supervisors themselves before its adoption.

August 24th, 1928, in a last effort to get together with the veterans, the Trustees held a meeting in the architect's drafting rooms, at which were present the Legion representatives as well as the chairman and other members of th United Veterans' Council. However, this meeting failed in securing harmony. Those present were:

Veterans—Boyd, Story, Scofield, Hotchner, Ainsworth, Gerlack, Wiedenfeld, Burns, French, Cabaniss, Caulfield, Schary, Flynn, Harris, Claridge.

Trustees—Drum, Kendrick, Kilsby, Martin, Crocker, Esberg, McKee, McSheehy, Colman.

Staff—Brown, Wagstaff, Widenham, architects.

November 6, 1928, Charter amendment No. 32, providing for appoint. ment of War Memorial Trustees by the City, was adopted by the people, notwithstanding that it was vigorously opposed by a number of veteran organizations. The Charter amendment is in the words and figures as follows, to-wit:

"WAR MEMORIAL—CHARTER AMENDMENT NO. 32

Creating of Board of Trustees of the War Memorial, providing for the manner of their appointment, defining their powers and duties.

Describing and setting forth a proposal to the qualified electors of the City and County of San Francisco, State of California, to amend the Charter of the City and County by adding a new article thereto, to be designated as Article XIV-D, relating to the War Memorial of San Francisco, and providing for the appointment of a Board of Trustees to have the management, superintendence, control and operation of said War Memorial, and prescribing the duties and powers of said Board.

The Board of Supervisors of the City and County of San Francisco hereby submits to the qualified electors of said City and County at the general election to be held on the sixth day of November, 1928, a proposal to amend the Charter as follows:

By adding a new article thereto, to be designated as Article XIV-D, reading as follows:

Section 1. There shall be a Board of Trustees of the San Francisco War Memorial to be erected and maintained in the Civic Center in the City and County of San Francisco, which said Board shall be known as the Board of Trustees of the War Memorial.

Section 2. The Trustees of the War Memorial shall, under such ordinances as the Board of Supervisors may from time to time adopt, have charge of the construction, administration, management, superintendence and operation of the War Memorial to be constructed in the Civic Center, and of the grounds set aside therefor, and of all of its affairs.

Section 3. The Trustees of said War Memorial shall consist of eleven members, who shall be appointed by the Mayor, subject to confirmation by the Board of Supervisors. The terms of said eleven members shall be for six years each; provided, that those first appointed shall so classify themselves by lot that the term of four of said Trustees shall expire on the 2nd day of January, 1931; four on the 2nd day of January, 1933, and three on the 2nd day of January, 1935. Thereafter appointments to said Board shall be for the full term of six years. Vacancies on said Board shall be filled by the Mayor, subject to confirmation by the Board of Supervisors, for the unexpired term becoming vacant. In making appointments to said Board, the Mayor shall give due consideration to veterans of all wars engaged in by the United States, and to such other classes of persons who may have a special interest in the purpose for which said War Memorial is to be constructed and maintained. All persons appointed to said Board shall be residents of the City and County. The members of said Board shall serve without compensation.

Section 4. The said Board of Trustees shall have power:

(a) To receive, on behalf of the City and County, gifts, devises and bequests for any purpose connected with said War Memorial or incident thereto.

(b) To administer, execute and perform the terms and conditions and trusts of any gift, devise or bequest which may be accepted by the Board of Supervisors of San Francisco for the benefit of said War Memorial, or incident thereto, and to act as trustee under any such trust when so authorized to do by said Board of Supervisors.

(c) To appoint a secretary to said Board and a managing director of said War Memorial, and such other employees as may be necessary for the conduct of its affairs and property, and to define their powers and prescribe their duties. The salaries of all of said officers and employees of said Board shall be fixed and standardized as provided by Section 14 of Chapter II of Article II of the Charter.

(d) To make rules and regulations not inconsistent with the provisions of the Charter and the ordinances of the Board of Supervisors for the government of all its officers and employees, and for the administration, government and protection of said War Memorial and its affairs, and the property belonging thereto or under the control of said Board, and to enforce the same.

Section 5. All employees of said Board, with the exception of the secretary and managing director, shall be subject to the provisions and entitled to the benefits of Article XIII of the Charter, and shall be appointed in conformity with the provisions of said article.

Section 6. The said Board shall appoint one of its members president thereof, who shall hold his office during the pleasure of the Board, Said Board shall meet at least once in each month, and at such other times as the president or any three members thereof shall request. A majority of said Board shall constitute a quorum.

Section 7. All moneys received by said Board from every source whatsoever shall immediately upon receipt of the same be deposited in the treasury of the City and County in a special fund to be designated by the Board of Supervisors, and the Board of Supervisors shall annually appropriate to said Board an amount sufficient to defray the cost of maintaining, operating and caring for said War Memorial, which said amount so appropriated shall not be within the limitation set forth in Sections 11 and 13 of Chapter I of Article III of the Charter, and said Board shall have control of the expenditure of said appropriation, subject to the limitations herein contained.

Section 8. The title of all property now owned or hereafter acquired for the said War Memorial, when not inconsistent with the terms of its acquisiiton, shall vest in the City and County, and in the name of the City and County may be sued for or defended by an action of law or otherwise.

Section 9. The powers herein expressly conferred on said Board of Trustees by this article shall not be construed as a limitation upon the powers which may be exercised by said Board, and said Board may exercise such other and further powers as may from time to time be conferred upon it by ordinance of the Board of Supervisors.

Ordered Submitted—Board of Supervisors, San Francisco, September 19, 1928.

Ayes—Supervisors Colman, Gallagher, Havenner, Hayden, Kent, Marks, McSheehy, Powers, Schmidt, Suhr, Todd, Toner—12.

Absent—Supervisors Andriano, Deasy, McGovern, Roncovieri, Shannon, Stanton—6.

J. S. DUNNIGAN, Clerk."

December 6th, 1928, at 8 p. m. a large public meeting was held at the City Hall at the request of and in the chambers of the Board of Supervisors for the purpose of having a full hearing on all War Memorial matters. Mr. John S. Drum, Chairman of the Board of Trustees of the San Francisco War Memorial, reviewed the entire history of the project at this meeting, all of which was taken down in shorthand by the official reporter of the Board of Supervisors and is as follows:

THE MAYOR: I tell you this is a full report, because I am going to explode a lot of charges and claims that have been

made, which are all answered here in this report, and I have
a full report. Now, whoever wants to listen to the report is
here to listen to it, if not——

SUPERVISOR POWER (interrupting): Have there been
any copies printed, Mr. Mayor?

THE MAYOR: Not yet, Colonel, no.

SUPERVISOR SPAULDING: Mr. Mayor, I think in courtesy to you that we should give you a ten-minute recess to
give you time to recuperate.

THE MAYOR: I thank you for that compliment, I think
it is due the Mayor. I have given over a year of my time to
this matter, and to this problem. I have tried to come to a
harmonious settlement of it. I am going to read all of the
testimony that has been taken down here of all these meetings
so that the new members of the Board will be familiar with it.
There are six of them. There is another exhibit, No. 7, which
is a financial statement of the moneys received by the Trustees
and the expenditure of every dollar thereof, and in reading
you a history of this entire matter, I am giving you a background of the whole history, all the ordinances and the votes
and everything connected with it. I am glad to have ten
minutes. I have been working very late. The reason it is not
printed is that I did not finish it until 3 o'clock this morning.
The Board will take a recess for ten minutes.

(Recess.)

Upon reconvening, the following proceedings were had:

SUPERVISOR HAYDEN: How many more pages have you,
Mr. Mayor?

THE MAYOR: Well, I have the record of the public meeting of the War Memorial Trustees, and I have other records
of meetings which have been held and resolutions of the Board
of Supervisors.

SUPERVISOR SUHR: Mr. Mayor, I suggest that we proceed.

SUPERVISOR POWER: Mr. Mayor, I am going to offer a
motion, that those proceedings of the meetings be considered
read. I understand there are a number of pages of it. I think
if we get down to the financial picture of the situation, why
that is what interests especially the new members. I offer a
motion that they be considered read.

SUPERVISOR SPAULDING: I second the motion.

THE MAYOR: Now, I want to tell you, I want to be relieved of all responsibility of the nonperformance of the building of the War Memorial. I think it is only fair to the Mayor.
This is not my work, this is the Board of Supervisors' work.
I have been asked to prepare a full and complete report of
all of the proceedings in connection with the building of the
War Memorial; members of the War Memorial Trustees that
conceived this idea in 1918, their activities, the activities of
the Board, the votes of the people down to a mass meeting
which took place here on December 6, 1928, have so far been
reviewed. Then you appointed three of your own members,
the veterans appointed three of their members, the War Memorial Trustees appointed three of their members, and you very
courteously paid a compliment to the Mayor by adding him to
the committee, and that made a committee of ten. From this
time on the activities of the committee of ten are entitled to
be heard by the Board. There should be no responsibility——

SUPERVISOR POWER (interrupting): If you will pardon
an interruption, if you believe that it should be read, I have
no objection. All I wanted to do was to save your time and
hours.

THE MAYOR: Well, I will tell you, Mr. Power, the responsibility rests somewhere.

SUPERVISOR POWER: Then I will withdraw the motion.

'THE MAYOR: If it is impossible for the Board of Supervisors to listen to a report, the Mayor has named, according to law, eleven worthy trustees, the Mayor is again prepared today to name eleven worthy trustees. If the Board of Supervisors are unwilling to confirm the eleven trustees, or any part of them, why, this matter will have to go to the people of San Francisco because it has come to an impasse where the Board of Supervisors is not free to act. Now, I have no desire to cause you inconvenience——

SUPERVISOR HAYDEN (interrupting): Mr. Mayor, I move you proceed with the reading of the report, up to six o'clock, at which time we will ask for an adjournment.

SUPERVISOR HAVENNER: I move to amend that to five, I will have to be excused at five.

SUPERVISOR ANDRIANO: Second the amendment.

SUPERVISOR HAYDEN: That is a matter for the Board.

SUPERVISOR SUHR: I would suggest we proceed.

THE MAYOR: I will give a reason for this, because, following the reading of this report of this meeting which took place here, the Board of Supervisors passed a resolution appointing a committee, which was known as an ironing-out committee, and you should be advised of what caused the necessity of the appointment of the ironing-out committee, on the motion made by Mr. Gallagher, and since they were appointed in December, 1928, a little over a year ago, you should know what they have been doing to try and iron this thing out. Now, that is only fair.

SUPERVISOR HAYDEN: I move the Mayor proceed.

SUPERVISOR POWER: Let us proceed.

THE MAYOR: What is the motion?

SUPERVISOR HAYDEN: I move the Mayor proceed.

SUPERVISOR ANDRIANO: Until five o'clock.

THE MAYOR (reading):

EXHIBIT NO. 1.
PUBLIC MEETING OF THE WAR MEMORIAL TRUSTEES.
Thursday, December 6, 1928, 8 O'clock p. m.

There were present the following War Memorial Trustees: John S. Drum, Chairman, and Trustees Crocker, Bentley, McKee, Martin, Colman, Havenner and Kilsby. There were also present James Rolph, Jr., Mayor, and Supervisors Shannon, Roncovieri, Schmidt, Stanton, Marks, Gallagher and Todd, members of the American Legion, the United War Veterans and interested citizens. Thereupon the following proceedings were had:

SUPERVISOR McSHEEHY: Your Honor, the Mayor, ladies and gentlemen: This meeting has been called by the Trustees of the War Memorial. I occupy a dual position, that of Supervisor and also as one of the Trustees of the War Memorial. At this time I deem it a privilege and a pleasure to introduce to you the Chairman of the evening, Mr. John S. Drum, Chairman of the Board of War Memorial Trustees. (Applause)

MR. DRUM (Chairman): Mr. Mayor, Mr. McSheehy, and friends: This meeting is called for a business purpose so we might just as well get down to business at once. The purpose of the meeting is to find out whether or not the misunderstandings that seem to have occurred over the past few months, regarding the progress work of the War Memorial can be taken care of and brushed aside tonight,

so that this great civic enterprise can go on. That is the purpose of
the meeting. We invited the Mayor of the city, the Board of Supervisors, the representatives of the various activities who were going
to occupy part of the space in these two big buildings, and we felt,
by having the city representatives with their powers, by having all
of those who were interested in seeing this work proceed, that we
could have a fair and a frank discussion of the entire work, what it
means, what its purpose is, what is going to be the benefit, not only
of those who are going to enjoy some part of the occupancy of the
building, but what really is the greater purpose. And that is so that
the people of this great city can enjoy, finally, this work that has
been promised so long and has been delayed through so many years.
I think it will serve a useful purpose if I merely outline a little bit
of the history of the development of the War Memorial, so that everybody here knows how·it began and knows exactly what it is that we
are trying to accomplish. It goes back to 1918. In 1918 the Musical
Association of San Francisco, a body that had been organized in 1909,
the body that is responsible for the symphony music in San Francisco,
concluded that it was both strong enough, and it had enough music-
loving people back of its efforts, so that they could build a symphony
hall. Their members talked it over, they concluded it was a proper
plan, they even went so far as to invite architects to make up some
plans for that theater. I think that was in April or May, 1918. In
the fall of 1918, and before the Armistice, it was with the thought
that it would strengthen the activity of the Musical Association if they
could have conjoined not only a symphony hall but an opera house
as well. San Francisco since the fire of 1906 had not had any opera
house. It had no place where the operas which had been given in the
years passed could then be given. And the Musical Association, join-
ing with those who were interested in seeing that this city had once
more the opera, the amusement that formerly existed here for all the
people, San Francisco being a music-loving city, we having, not only
a great many of our native population but a very large foreign population that enjoyed music, as part of their daily life, it was thought
that, by getting together those who wished to see an opera house
restored, and a symphony hall, that they could obtain enough in the
way of subscriptions from those interested in music to erect an opera
house that would serve a double purpose. They could give opera, they
could likewise have their symphony orchestra. And they joined forces,
as I say, towards the end of 1918. After the Armistice, it seemed to
those music-lovers that that served as a very fitting time to go back
to those conditions of peace following the Great War, and give to this
city, after the years of war, something that would upbuild the city,
contribute to its cultural life, make the city a more interesting place
to live in, and a better place to live in. So they discussed having not
only the activities of music, but likewise to have an art museum in
the center of the city. San Francisco likewise had lost its art museum
in the fire of 1906. It had been on Nob Hill in the old Hopkins building.
It had been burned down at the time of the fire and there was no art
museum in the city at that time. So they felt, those who were interested in music, felt that if they could line up those who were interested
in art that they could, by the construction of one building, and by
stating that that building was a war memorial, that it was a memorial
to peace, celebrating the termination of the war, that it would be a
matter of universal appeal to the city that, out of the war, would come
a better city, and a city where the conditions of peace were such as to
make the city a more enjoyable place to live. So they called the buildings which they desired to erect a "War Memorial." They likewise
stated that, so as to give it the absolute aspect of a war memorial, that
they should have a memorial court. Other cities over the country were
talking of erecting war memorial fountains, war memorial columns,
other war memorial objects in commemoration of the war, and it was

believed that if, joined to the purpose for which this building was
to be erected, they could likewise have a court that would serve as
the ideal memorial, such as other communities discussed, that they
could properly regard it as a war memorial. So they provided for a
memorial court. That was in 1918. They had no building site, but
they started in to get subscriptions and through 1919 they got a
certain number of people who said that they would subscribe a given
amount of money for the purposes named. In the summer of 1919 they
looked about for a site and they found this St. Ignatius College site
diagonally opposite the City Hall, and twenty-five men first guaranteed that they would sign an option to buy that property. Finally
fifty men signed for $5000 apiece to buy the property, in August or
September, 1919. They had no plans for the building, they had not
a subscription list whereby they could obtain the moneys to go ahead
with the building but, nevertheless, they concluded to buy the site
first and then get the subscriptions afterwards. So they bought the
site and paid for it in January or February, 1920.

After buying the property and during the year 1919, a certain committee was obtaining subscriptions for the purpose I have outlined.
In the spring of 1920, the amount of money that they had thus secured,
for the purpose which I have named, was about $1,400,000 or $1,-
500,000. At that time this committee was waited upon by a committee from The American Legion. They stated that it was splendid
to have a war memorial for the peace purposes outlined, it was a fine
thing to have a war memorial square or a war memorial court, but
they wondered whether it would not be a more practical purpose if,
instead of only contributing to the welfare and the happiness of the
people generally, that there were likewise some quarters provided
where The American Legion, which had lately been formed, could
find adequate housing. That appealed to the committee and they
discussed with that Legion committee how much space they wanted
and·what quarters they desired to occupy. The matter was discussed
generally, and it was finally concluded by the committee representing
the Legion, not the committee of the trustees because they were
not acquainted with the needs of the Legion, they discussed a matter
of 40,000 square feet in the new building. That was the suggestion
of the Legion which was approved by the committee. The committee
enlarged its personnel, which then had two representatives representing opera, two representatives representing symphony, two representing the Legion, and they put on—I mean two representatives representing the museum, and the two representatives representing the Legion.
And that committee practically from that day to this has been the
War Memorial Committee or Board of Trustees that has prosecuted
this work. After that committee was enlarged, there was a public
drive in San Francisco to get additional funds. All the various activities of the city combined to make the drive a success. The Mayor,
the Board of Supervisors, all of the members of the Legion. The drive
went forward. There were a great many small private subscriptions,
but as far as the total amount secured in addition to the fourteen
hundred thousand dollars or fifteen hundred thousand dollars that
was already secured before the Legion had become one of the activi-
tivities of the War Memorial, there was possibly four or five hundred
thousand dollars additionally subscribed. All of that sum was subscribed for the specific purpose of the activities named, with the exception of small subscriptions from 35,000 school children and small
subscriptions from the city generally I think to the number of 30.-
000 subscriptions, making 65,000 in all. The numbers in those subscriptions amounted in dollars to something under $50,000. The
amount that was subscribed by the activities which I have named,
amounted to the rest of the fund which finally came to a sum around
$2,000,000. After the moneys had been subscribed it was thought at
that time it would take about two and a half million dollars to com-

plete the buildings on the St. Ignatius lot. The plans went forward
through 1920, 1921, and 1922. At the end of 1922 Supervisor Ralph
McLeran appeared before the Board of Trustees and he stated that
the property at the corner of Van Ness and McAllister Street had
been purchased by some company that intended to erect a warehouse, that it would be an unsightly Civic Center, that it had always been the hope of the Board of Supervisors and the City authorities that they could add two squares opposite the City Hall to the
Civic Center so as to have a beautiful Civic Center on the west .s
well as on the east. He wanted to know whether or not the War
Memorial group could exchange its St. Ignatius Lot, which was diagonally opposite on Grove Street, to one of the two blocks, if the City
would purchase the second block, making the two blocks directly
opposite the City Hall instead of the St. Ignatius block which was
diagonally opposite. The matter was taken up, not only with the
Trustees but likewise with the City Authorities. We appeared before the Mayor and the Finance Committee. They agreed that they
would authorize the City to buy one of the two blocks and pay for
it. They said they had no funds at that time and they asked us if we
would buy out or advance the sum necessary to buy from this warehouse company, that had already had its excavation made, its steel
ordered, the steel delivered on the lot, whether or not we would buy
out that company, pay what they were in for the lot, and, as far
as they had gone on the building, and that then out of the next tax
levy they would pay us back. They did, out of that tax levy, and
the succeeding tax levy and the City has bought and paid for the
corner of McAllister and Van Ness Avenue a lot somewhere in the
neighborhood of 80 feet front by 180 or 190 feet in depth, and that
is the only property up to date. I am stating this as a statement of
fact, that its is the only property that the City so far has bought and
paid for on the two blocks opposite. After we had changed from the
St. Ignatius lot to these two lots we had to sell the St. Ignatius. lot.
We succeeded in selling it to the Board of Education. We had to
condemn sixty or seventy separate pieces of property in these two
blocks which took a given length of time. We had to likewise scrap
the architectural plans, we had for the St. Ignatius lot and start the
preparation of new plans on the two blocks opposite. We likewise
had to make those necessary changes that would give us what was
a working plan for the erection of the two buildings. That took us
through 1923, 1924, 1925, and the end of 1926 we had pretty nearly
all of the difficulties straightened out except the question of money.
We had no more money except the accumulation of interest, than we
had at the end of 1920, after the drive of May 1920. We figured out
how much it would cost for the two buildings after we had paid for
one block and the City had paid for the other block and our estimates of cost were so high that it was very evident that we could do
only one of three things: we could either ask those who had already
privately subscribed to this fund to contribute a further sum of money,
we could abandon the enterprise entirely, or we could see whether or
not private subscriptions, having collected the sum of $2,000,000
whether there was justification to go on with this work as a big civic
enterprise and get the balance of the money. And we thought that
there was no one so familiar with public opinion and public necessity
in this City as the daily press. We therefore, in February of 1927,
last year, invited the publishers of the press, the owners of the newspapers here who have always taken such an active part and such
a decided stand in the advancement of civic enterprise, to say what
they believed should or should not be done, and what, in their judgment, was or was not the public opinion of this City and in these
communities relative to the War Memorial. We met with these gentlemen on two or three different occasions. We did not suggest to
them what should be done. They gave us the benefit of their judg-

ment, and they stated, very definitely, that it was unthinkable for this enterprise to be abandoned, that it was an enterprise of some consequence to the welfare of this City, from so many different angles, that the proper thing to do was to proceed. They likewise felt that private subscription having collected the sum of $2,000,000, it was nothing more than right to ask the taxpayers of this City whether, by bonding themselves, they would not contribute double the amount of private subscriptions coming from probably three or four or five hundred people in the community and would not thereby furnish the adequate funds to go on with this enterprise. After we received that opinion from the publishers, we met and they met with us, the Mayor and the Finance Committee and later the Board of Supervisors of this City. We explained to them what I have just explained to you. The opinion of the Mayor and the Board of Supervisors was exactly the same as the publishers. It was that the thing to do was to go ahead, the thing to do was to bond the community, that the sum that the community was bonding itself for was relatively a small one considering the amount of the private subscriptions, and that it was their judgment that the community would accept the proposition and vote the bonds. Their judgment was correct. In June 14th of last year the bond issue for $4,000,000 was not only passed but was passed by an overwhelming vote. We began immediately with the pursuit of the plans, getting ready to invite bids to erect the two buildings. Up to that time we had never had any matter of dispute whatsoever with any of the activities that were going to enjoy the benefits of these buildings, those activities applying, not only to various organizations, but likewise practically applying to the entire City and County of San Francisco, the neighborhoods about the bay and those transient people who visited San Francisco from time to time. The idea of regarding this enterprise, in any of its pursuits, as a matter that refers only to a given group of the community, that nobody can enjoy the benefits of this enterprise except a relatively few who enjoy music, or a relatively few who enjoy museums, and that the great and overwhelming numbers are those who belong to the various veteran organizations, later on I think I will show this is not true in point of fact. As far as the plans were concerned, the plans which we placed before the publishers, the plans which we placed before the Board of Supervisors, were plans that contemplated two buildings. The first building for opera house purposes was of a given area. That building was to cost a given sum of money. There was no less sum of money or no less area except in regard to seating capacity, which was later changed whereby an opera house and symphony hall could be erected. In other words, the very purpose of the opera house and symphony hall required a building of a given type, covering a certain area and costing a certain sum of money. The plans which were filed with the Board of Public Works in April of last year upon which the Supervisors authorized the bond election are substantially the same plans that exist today, as far as the opera house is concerned, except that it is costing a little less money than was figured at that time, and a considerable additional less sum of money by reason of cutting down the capacity of the house, we appearing before the Board of Supervisors several months ago to get their consent to cut down that capacity.

As far as the Legion building is concerned, the situation is entirely different. When we presented to the publishers, when we presented to the Board of Supervisors, we presented at that time what we thought, and what we were led to believe was the amount of space which the veteran organizations needed for their purpose. The cost of the building, as presented to the Board of Public Works and confirmed by the Supervisors, confirmed by the publishers, was for a building housing, not only the Legion, but housing the art museum as well. The amount of square footage which the art museum was

to have, under that building as presented, was 55,000 square feet. The
amount which the Legion was to have had grown from the original
1920 estimate of 40,000 feet to an amount of 65,000 square feet. That
65,000 square feet, costing $1,685,000 was the amount of space which
was supposed to cover all of the Legion activities and likewise all
of the veteran activities. If there had been any question at that time
that there was not sufficient space, that there was the need for more
space costing more money, the obvious and the intelligent thing to
have done was to have gone to the people of this city and county
and asked for a sum of money that could properly pay for the activities which were to be housed in these two buildings. The question
even—I have forgotten whether it was before the publishers or before
the Supervisors—was raised at that time, was $4,000,000 an adequate
bond issue? And they were answered in the affirmative. The matter
was asked whether it would not be safer to have $5,000,000, and it
was felt that the amount of money being asked for, in addition to
the amount of money on hand, would appear like an extravagant
amount. Therefore, the bond issue was passed for the two buildings,
as I have said. For the time being we can abandon consideration both
of the size of the opera house and of the cost of the opera house
because it really has no place in the facts or circumstances that have
arisen since bond election of 1927.

Before the election, about a week before the election—I may have
my facts a little wrong, it is hearsay—but I understood certain veteran organizations appeared before the Supervisors and stated that
they were not satisfied with the promises theretofore made as to the
occupancy of this building, that unless there was something of a more
detailed character they would feel, in their interest, that they would
have to oppose the bonds. How the matter came up I do not know,
but it finally reached the Supervisors, and on June 7, eight days before
the election of June 14, the Supervisors passed a resolution to the
effect that none of the $4,000,000 should be spent in these buildings
unless the veteran organizations were entirely satisfied as to the plans
for their housing, prior to the expenditure of the moneys. After that
resolution, after the bonds were passed, it was then, for the first time,
that we knew the number of organizations which felt that they qualified under the resolution of the Board of Supervisors. We delayed
our plans until we could get all the facts. I might say that, although
original private subscription activity contemplated simply housing of
the Legion, between the time of that original conception and the time
when the trust deed was made with the University of California, the
trust deed was made broad enough to include, not only the Legion
Posts, but likewise other veteran Posts. But the position taken by
our Trustees was that we were not acquainted with the number of
these Posts, that the Legion was more acquainted with the veteran
organization, that the Legion was the primary activity that was to
occupy these quarters, and that the other veteran organizations should
adjust with the Legion the question of the occupancy and the use of
the space. That was a position that was not satisfactory to the other
veteran organizations. It was probably the reason why they appeared
before the Board of Supervisors. However, we recognized the resolution of the Board of Supervisors, we recognized the wishes of the
Board of Supervisors and the wishes of the public, as far as veteran
activities were concerned, and we sought to increase this space, originally starting with 40,000 square feet, the bond election based upon
an occupancy of 65,000 square feet, and we recast the plans and increased the amount of the Legion's space from 65,000 square feet to
80,000 square feet, cut down the museum space from 55,000 square
feet to 42,000 square feet. The plans were finally submitted to the
Legion representatives, they meanwhile having organized their Posts
so they had a central clearing committee authorized to act in all

matters pertaining to war memorial. The suggested space, the space planned, was not satisfactory to the Legion committee and they so notified us in February of this year. Following that notification, our representatives, or the representatives of the Legion on our committee, and those representatives likewise being on this clearing committee of the Legion, had many meetings with the Legion committee, likewise visited the drafting rooms of the Trustees, analyzed the space, analyzed their needs, and stated that, instead of the 80,000 square feet, they needed an amount of square footage which afterwards totalled 105,000 square feet. When that space was made up on five drawings which I have here in this room, this Legion committee went over this space, analyzed it, checked it, and finally, by a vote of all of the committee, I think seventeen members of the Legion committee, all of them unanimously approved the plans, so endorsed on the plans, with the exception of two of their members who did not vote. They accompanied the approval of the plans, however, by a letter to the effect that, while they approved the plans, they made two reservations: One was that they wanted to know how that space was to be specifically divided, and they wanted to feel that their subsequent approval was necessary on the specific division of the space. The second was that they wanted certain structural columns omitted. With those two exceptions they made no conditions, but they did annex to the letter a statement to the effect that it was to be regretted that the building of the Legion was to be in an unfinished condition. With that approval before us we went forward with the final drawings. After we were in the midst of those drawings, some acoustical experts for the opera house took the position that the number of seats in the opera house, the size of the opera house, was too large for good hearing, and they recommended cutting it down. We appeared before the Supervisors and got their permission. We explained at that time what the cutting down meant. It meant taking ten feet off the length of the opera house building, reducing the opera house building by I think three or four or five hundred feet, reducing the cost of the opera house and, of course, as both of the buildings must match in the frontage on Van Ness Avenue, it meant likewise cutting down the Legion building by 10 feet. That made both buildings 10 feet less in frontage than they were before. It resulted in a saving on the opera house building of about $120,000 and the Legion building of about $57,000. After that cutting down took place, we got a letter from the Legion committee to the effect that they were not satisfied with the space, and, finally, they passed a resolution repudiating entirely their approval of the previous March, that is, March of this year. As a result of their position, we met with the Legion committee last August. We sat for an entire afternoon threshing out the entire matter. We gave them most of the facts that I am giving you now. We likewise explained to them that, while in a technical sense we did not regard their approval of the previous March as something which, in a sense legal or moral bound them, but we did believe that we were justified in going ahead with this work on a basis where we could get this building under construction, the cry having naturally been made for years, was even made in the campaign documents of the Legion, that there had been an undue delay, and they had been kept out of the occupancy of this building. We were hurrying in every way possible to complete those plans. In the discussion that we had with the Legion at that time these are the facts that developed, as near as I understood them then, as I understand them now, as I understand has been the sole complaint of the Legion and the veterans, both at that meeting of last August, in their statements during the campaign, in the statements before the Board of Supervisors and their present position. It was this: That they regarded the private subscription of money as being something which the pri-

vate subscribers had the right to subscribe. As far as the bond issue
was concerned, that the primary purpose of that bond issue was to
furnish, through the resolution of the Board of Supervisors, housing
to their satisfaction, and a building and an amount of space to their
satisfaction, otherwise this enterprise should not go forward. They
took the position that it was an unfinished building because, on the
McAllister Street side for a length of 200 feet and a width of 50 feet
there was one jog in the building which did not give the building
a completed four sides, with the four sides finished in the outer
covering, whether terra cotta or granite. They took the position that
the City Library is an unfinished building. They took the position
that they were entitled to a building that was finished just as much
as the opera building was finished and that, as far as they were concerned, they would protest against the building going forward unless
that space was filled up, and it was a building having four sides with
completed building materials on the four sides. We explained to them
that by reason of the additional space which we gave them under
the resolution, or which had been provided for them under the
resolution of the Board of Supervisors, increasing the size of the
building from 65,000 square feet to 105,000 and at the present time we
have added 3,000 square feet more, 108,000 square feet, the cost estimated in April to the publishers of the papers, and to the Supervisors,
which would have provided sufficient funds to put up these two buildings, for the square footage that was then estimated had been changed
by adding nearly 40,000 square feet, over 40,000 square feet to their
needs, with the result that, instead of having sufficient moneys remaining from the private subscription fund, after buying the property, and
from the $4,000,000 of bonds, that the entire cost of the construction
of these two buildings would be short somewhere in the neighborhood
of three or four hundred thousand dollars. We believed, however,
with proper economy, and likewise with the bids coming in for final
approval, that we could make up the three or four hundred thousand
dollars. They mention: "You saved $120,000 on the opera house; you
saved $57,000 on the width of our building; there is $177,000; why
don't you put that in this building of the Legion?" We explained that
the amount that we were then short was somewhere in the neighborhood of $350,000 or $400,000, that $177,000 was only one portion of
that, and that the estimate of the amount of the additional 50 by 200
and some odd feet to add that final piece on the McAllister street side
would cost, under the estimates of the contractors, $540,000, and that
therefore, instead of having adequate funds, as the enterprise was already short by reason of the additional square feet, we would have an
additional shortage, not only of the difference between $400,000 less
$177,000, but plus $540,000 on top of that. In that discussion they
brought out—some of the members of this committee stated, very definitely, "It is not because we need additional square footage for our
purposes. We feel, with the square footage that now exists for our
occupancy, that we could take care of all of our activities. We do not
want to use the space if the space was there, because we have got adequate space, but we do not want to go into a building that is not completed, and we think we are entitled to a completed building just the
same as the opera house." The matter was left in that shape. The
Legion, I understand, had a meeting subsequent to our meeting with
them. There were one or two resolutions; one was to disapprove entirely, which was lost; the other was to approve, which was lost; and
the matter, as I understand it, has been in status quo since last August, when we had the meeting, as far as we are concerned. We have
never seen any of this clearing house committee of the Legion. They
have never asked anything in the way of modification or change since
that time.

And we now come to the charter amendment No. 32, which was
passed on November 6. Our attorneys and the City Attorney got to-

gether to know how legally the City could spend this $4,000,000 and this Board of Trustees could spend its million or a million and a quarter dollars, so that, legally, the money could go into the erection of those buildings. Both the City Attorney and our attorneys drew up the very charter amendment which was presented to the Supervisors. It was no fault of ours that the argument before the Supervisors, with all the amendments which they were proposing, lasted through the evening and lasted into the morning. There was no star chamber proceeding; it was simply a question of satisfying the Supervisors that they were willing to stand behind an amendment the purpose of which was obvious. It was nothing more than to clothe somebody, under public sanction, with the power to go forward with this long-delayed improvement, and see to the erection of those two buildings. You are familiar with the progress of the election. The newspapers unanimously approved the amendment, both editorially and in their recommendations as to the charter amendments which it passed. There was absolutely nothing to the amendment but merely the incidental clothing authority in somebody to proceed with this work. The veteran organizations opposed it. You are familiar with their arguments as they went over the radio every night during the campaign. The arguments are substantially the arguments which were made at our meeting last August. It was not a completed building; it was the case of devoting moneys which should go to veteran purposes for other activities: opera house, museum and the rest; that the Board of Trustees was dominated by men who had no sympathy with the Legion, that they were simply thinking of art museum, and they were thinking of opera, and that they were privately seeking to control, for their purposes, the expenditure of this money, so that they would have their purposes served and the Legion would be left to take what remained over.

Now, what are the facts? I have reviewed this whole thing as far as the facts are concerned. But what is the real status of this great big public enterprise? First of all, there is no question that this City is a city which, prior to the fire, always had probably in all parts of the country a status, both as to contentment, as to happiness and as to the enjoyment of the proper things of life, whether opera, or whether art, or anything else, ahead of any city in the country. It stood out pre-eminent. The papers never ceased to remark on what a wonderful community it was, in a music-loving sense, in a cultural sense, that there is here a music-loving population that does not apply to the tens or hundreds, but applies literally to the hundreds of thousands. What has made this community where not only its own people have had this enjoyment, but where it has been attractive to people coming from a distance? It has been those things that you find in the larger capitals of the world. It is a nice thing to read about what this English editor said the other day as to what a beautiful place San Francisco is. It is a beautiful place. But since the fire we have not had, in the way of those things that San Francisco has stood for, a place to adequately house them. And the form of entertainment which you can get in San Francisco in the way of amusement, where you have no opera house, where you have no museum, is the same character of entertainment, through the development of the growth of the moving picture theater, that you can get in any town of 500 in population or up. What is it which brings people from afar to San Francisco? I happen to be in a business that knows something about transient movement. I have lived here all of my life; I know something about the growth and development of this place. I know at the present time there are fewer transient people coming to San Francisco to stay here for the purposes of enjoyment than has ever existed in the history of the community. There are not those things despite the activity of our people; despite the love that our people have for the finer things. This is a cosmopolitan community; it is one of the few cosmopolitan communities of the world. But unless this community puts in those things, for not only its own people, but likewise for those people coming here that can put this city back in the ranks of a cosmopolitan community in the sense of having a plant, you can have all the love you want for these things, but unless you have a plant where they can be enjoyed, you may have cosmopolitan aspirations, but you have not that plant; you have not that opportunity to give the thousands and the tens of thousands and the hundreds of thousands of our own people an opportunity to enjoy those things that make this the greatest city on earth.

Now, this is a public purpose. The moneys that were subscribed originally were not for any opera house, or not for any museum, or not for any veteran activities, but for all those purposes combined. There is no more reason why there should be any dominance on the part of one activity than the other. It was supposed to be a combination where our soldiers, our veterans, could have something in the way of housing such as does not exist in the United States. But at the same time it was never intended that the housing of those veterans should contract that which had been the purpose and the object, from the very beginning, and which had been confirmed, not only by the publishers of the newspapers of San Francisco, not only by the Mayor and the Board of Supervisors, but likewise by the people themselves when they passed that bond issue of June 14, 1927. They did not vote only for housing. They voted for all those activities with which they were familiar and for which they had been waiting for years. There is no chance for any argument that there has been any shift or change, or any chance for the injection of the type of argument that it is a question of the enjoyment of the few against the occupancy of the many.

Now, let us come to the question of this housing. I wonder if all of us would realize what 108,000 square feet is? The biggest area of a block in San Francisco where most of our business houses are constructed is what is called the "50-vara lot," that is, 137 feet 6 inches in each direction. Those blocks are supposed to be the largest blocks in San Francisco. The largest buildings, outside of one or two, do not occupy a greater area than 137 feet 6 inches square. The amount of space that is devoted in this civic enterprise, for the purpose of these veteran organizations, amount to the area that would go into a building covering an entire 50-vara lot, 137 feet 6 inches square and a height of ten stories. And what goes into that area? There is everything that every lodge, that every club, social, political, religious or otherwise, has, either in their clubhouses or has in their lodgerooms. There are bowling alleys and there are handball courts and there are steam rooms and there are dining rooms and there are two halls seating seven or eight hundred people, with full equipment, maple floors for dancing, full equipment for banqueting. There are sixteen or seventeen lodgerooms. There are sixteen or seventeen anterooms. There is every activity that you can think of in those rooms. We have in the membership of our Masons, of our Knights of Columbus, of our Odd Fellows, we have buildings in this town that are not one fraction of the size of this building which is devoted to these veteran purposes. We have two clubs; our largest clubs are the Olympic and the Elks. Neither of those clubs contain anything in the nature of area that is here. We have likewise a question as to the membership which is to occupy this area. When this first arrangement in 1920 for giving the Legion and the other veterans' organizations was passed, the Legion asked for 40,000 square feet. They stated, three different Legion bodies —we got our facts from them—three different Legion bodies said that their membership at that time, the minimum, was 14,000 members, then another figured 15,000 and another figured 17,000. At a minimum 14,000, at a maximum 17,000, out of a potential 30,000 to occupy 40,-000 square feet. What is it today, eight or nine years later? I am not able to verify my facts, but, as far as I can gather—I have talked to

Legion people—I have figured the number of posts, and they have somewhere, without their women's auxiliaries, of 3100 to 3300 instead of 14,000 to 17,000. As far as their meeting places are concerned, I have tried to analyze every place that every veterans' organization in this town meets. We had when we began what we thought was sixteen; I think there were then twelve or thirteen posts and some veterans' organizations. We have taken and given adequate space to every veteran organization that we know of that has made a request. You can see the names of all the veterans' organizations in the protest against the charter amendment. Those veterans' organizations today meet in different halls. As I understand it, there is no one hall that houses more than 200 or 250 or 300 people, and that is only for one or several of the larger organizations of the veterans. These veteran organizations, I have figured how often they meet. There are twenty-eight of them that only meet once a week, there are fifteen that only meet twice a week and there are thirteen of them that meet once a week. These organizations, with the exception of the Legion, have gone on ever since the Civil War and probably before that. I am not familiar with the membership of all the organizations. Mr. Boyd, I believe, claims 3000 for his Spanish-American Veterans. But these organizations have gone on since the wars of the past and they have gotten along with their meetings once or twice a month, meeting in halls, or meeting at lunch time or meeting at dinners, with an amount of space that goes into a relative fractional sum of this amount. I feel that by this analysis, the City and County of San Francisco, in a most generous way and proper way—I am not opposing the Legion in any way or the veteran organizations, but I am saying, as far as the enjoyment of the activities that are going to be conducted in those two buildings across the street, I want to know what number of this community enjoy those quarters. We have, on the one hand, 108,000 square feet given to organizations which, in their total personnel numerically, may be up to 6000 or may be up to 7000, but they are the activities for those members to enjoy club life and lodge life and the rest in an amount of space that is overwhelming. We have on the contrary—and likewise half of that building, not the opera house building, half of that building or about one-third of that building, is given over to an art museum. We have a beautiful art museum at the Spreckels Museum. We have one or two other buildings in Golden Gate Park of a magnificent character. But there is no place in the modern sense where people can have the benefits, the school children can have the benefits, the university students can have the benefits, our people generally can have the benefits, of a central location where they can come to see the better art things of life displayed and where they can have lectures and where they can have explanations, and where they can enrich their lives as they are entitled to in this city. Some years ago in the old Fine Arts Building on the Marina we had two loaned collections brought here from a distance. The number of people in this community that cleared through to see those things and to hear those lectures amounted to two or three hundred thousand people. That is the art museum.

Take your opera house, so called. You cannot place on an opera house only the giving of opera; you cannot say because at the present time we have a building that is used for opera for two or three weeks, that for the other forty-eight or forty-nine weeks the people of this city, in symphony concerts, in spectacles, in other concerts will not get the benefit of that. And it cannot be said that a building which seats 3,400 people, and which allows for 600 standing room, an audience of 4,000 people, is a building that is devoted to a few people down town who are putting up their money for their own enjoyment. That building is not only for this community; it is for all the communities around this Bay. It is for all the transients that come to town, to make this community what it really is, one of the outstand-

ing communities of the country, and it is to build up and to enrich
once more, since the fire, the type of metropolitan life that this city
has always enjoyed. Now, what have we as a practical problem? I
can talk as much as I please about what I think or what the Trustees
think, or even what a good number of the community thinks as to
the type and the character of this civic enterprise which we want
to put up over here. We have had, I think, the opinion of the people
of this community twice: Once on a bond issue where, for their
enjoyment and for their use, the people of this community voted
themselves into $4,000,000 of bonds, so that all these purposes could
be served. Then, in this last election, where, despite an opposition
of a very potent character—any one reading that opposition, which
was put out by the Legion, and if they were not very well informed
about what it is, would naturally conclude that there was something
in what the Legion was objecting to. But, despite that, the people
of this community once more put their approval—it is true, it was a
vote of six or seven hundred, but likewise it was an unusual opposition—put their seal of approval on going ahead with all of these
enterprises. Now, as I say, I can talk, or anybody representing the
trustees or representing this community can talk about what are relative merits or demerits. If those soldiers, if those veterans for whom
we have the admiration and likewise for whom we have the sense of
obligation for what they did to preserve and allow to be developed
these purposes of peace, if those Legion men and those veterans are
dissatisfied, this enterprise should not go forward. If an enterprise
of this character, an enterprise that is outstanding in the country—
there is no civic center in this country comparable to San Francisco's
civic center, there is no enterprise in the way of a civic center, with
art purposes for people generally, and with housing purposes for
Legion and veteran organizations, that touches it. The Legion's largest housing is in Indianapolis, the headquarters. Here is housing for
their State organization, here is housing for every veteran organization, here is something in the way of housing that is unique in this
country. If, after this housing is provided, there is still room for
the arguments that the building is not finished, still room for the
arguments that certain men down town have selfish reasons in civic
enterprise of this character, I say, and I say very definitely, this
enterprise should not go on. If this big city cannot, in this great big
civic improvement, have back of it not only the support but likewise
the enthusiasm, not only of the Legion but of the city representatives,
the Board of Supervisors and the Mayor, I say, let us pause. We
have not that support. The Legion, or rather some members of the
Supervisors, put forward here last week a resolution that there should
be a majority of the Legion war veterans to constitute this new body.
The arguments made at that time repeated practically the arguments
existing on the part of the Legion in opposition to this going forward.
In addition to that, some of the Supervisors were concerned lest, in
some way, the Legion would be trapped and the Supervisors trapped,
despite their resolution, in moneys being spent before the Supervisors
and before the veterans had approved fully the plans. The fear was
expressed that, in some way or another, because, under the stress of
time, because we were summoned out here twice within the last year
before the Board of Supervisors and asked why we were not hastening
these plans, why weren't we going forward with this building, because
we have tried in every way we know how to advance this work, and
get it completed and have everybody enjoy it, the fear was expressed
that we were possibly unduly hastening the letting of the bids for
the foundations, and letting the bids for the steel work, so that, in
that indirect way, the Legion and the veterans would be bound by a
plan that afterward could not be set aside. There is no ground for
any such fear. This situation is one where either this plan should
go forward with the uanimous support, not only of the veteran bodies

but of the Supervisors, and if it cannot go forward on that basis, it should not go forward at all. There is a question here which has to be settled and settled right, and that is, is this enterprise going forward for the people of this community, as the moneys were subscribed, as the funds were voted for all of these purposes for the benefit of this community, or is it not? If for any reason an agreement cannot be reached whereby these Legion and veteran bodies are satisfied, then there is only one thing to do: Face the situation that this present Board of Trustees has under its control the ownership of this property across the street, with the exception of one lot; it has under its control money from private subscriptions, over a million dollars; it has, in land and money, over $2,000,000, with which, as trustees, it is specifically charged to see that it carries out the purpose of the trust. Anybody sitting on this Board of Trustees would, under the circumstances, of opposition or the circumstances of a definite cleavage here, as to whether these funds should be used as originally intended, or whether they should be turned over to this new Board, they would do as a duty just exactly what it is certain that this Board will do—that is, they will hold onto this money, they will hold onto this land, they will either turn back this money to the private subscribers, and do what they can to liquidate this land, or they will do that which they desire to do, and that is, see that a sensible, intelligent, enthusiastic and harmonious adjustment is made whereby, as people loving this city and desiring to see the people intelligently enjoy this greatest improvement, they would find the necessary ways and means of going forward, in an enthusiastic and expeditious way, without carping criticism or suspicions cast one on the other, with an intention and a determination to give to this city what is the greatest thing that has ever been given for the purposes served, to any city in the United States, up to the present time.

Now, how can that be done? I have outlined to you what the positions of the Trustees are. If they are not satisfied that they are going to be allowed, both by the veterans' organizations, by the Mayor and the Board of Supervisors, to decide what conscientiously they believe to be the duties of their trust.

But now I turn to the other side, and I make a like argument of strength as to having this matter settled where it meets the approval of the Legion and the approval of the Board of Supervisors. The Board of Supervisors are entirely correct that they have no right to see these moneys spent unless they likewise feel that the purposes of the original conception, the purposes of their resolution of June 7, are fully carried out. It would be futile and absurd for the Mayor, no matter what the personnel of the committee is, to appoint a committee that would not meet with the approval of the majority of the Board of Supervisors, and would not meet with the approval of the Legion and veteran bodies. We would be equally stultifying ourselves to have the representatives of the people, the Board of Supervisors, not satisfied, to have the soldiers, who have fought for us, who have the desire to have these quarters for the upbuilding of the citizenship of their numbers and the citizenship generally, not satisfied that they were getting everything that would enable them to pursue their activities. It would be futile, I say, to attempt to go forward merely by the selection of a committee which would not meet with the approval of the Supervisors or the Legion, and which would continue once more this status of suspicion and this status of failing to pull together in this great civic work.

I have a definite solution for that. My solution is that the Mayor, for the time being, postpone the selection of any committee. Let the committee which now represents the private subscriptions, let the veteran bodies, either by whole committee or subcommittee, or in any other way, sit down and thresh out and determine what is and what is not the intelligent thing to do, in the light of the purposes for which these moneys were subscribed. They are all public moneys. It does not make a particle of difference whether one came from a private source and the other came from a public source—they are all public moneys, because they were subscribed to serve a public purpose. I say, let the different parties in interest feel that they are discharging their duties as good citizens to the people of this community generally by putting an end to this argument and this criticism, and see that there is some adjusted and some harmonious and some united effort to go forward, and go forward immediately, in this work. I repeat again, there will not be a contract let, there will not be an extra dollar spent on that lot or an extra piece of work done, when this grading contract is finished, until this matter is settled. It happens that this is an opportune time to discuss this matter, and settle it once and for all, because nobody has gone so far that they cannot retrace their steps. This thing could be retraced on either side. Nothing has been done so far that will compel either the city taxpayers to spend their money or these private subscribers to spend this money for public purposes, unless we go forward with the united front, first of all having the confidence of this city administration back of us. If we have not that confidence, there is no reason to go ahead whatsoever. And, secondly, that we have this Legion body where they feel, not in terms of active or passive criticism, but in terms of enthusiastic support, that this is going to give them what has always been their dream and what they feel has been so long delayed in accomplishment. I feel, Mr. Mayor, that you are the principal officer of the city. You represent all the people. I have put this matter entirely as a matter in which the people are concerned first and foremost. Our activities, it is true, are of a special kind. Each of these activities has a given amount of selfishness in it, but all of these activities are supposed to be public activities, in the sense that the people of the entire community get the benefit of them; and I would like, if you are so minded, before this discussion becomes general, to have your support in that principle that we must—while I have put the alternative of what can be done, I am likewise adding, very definitely, that there is no alternative here, that there is just one thing that can be done, and that is to go forward with this work, in the shortest possible time, and with the most unanimous and overwhelming enthusiasm. And I call on you, first of all, before the discussion is general, for the support on that principle. (Applause.)

THE MAYOR: Mr. Drum, gentlemen representing the War Memorial Trustees, my colleagues of the Board of Supervisors, veterans of all wars, and my fellow citizens: I have never listened to a more brilliant presentation of a case than has just been presented to us tonight by Mr. John S. Drum, president of the War Memorial Trustees. I have endeavored, from the very inception of the idea advanced of an opera house, a musical hall combined with a war memorial that would give unto San Francisco the most outstanding war memorial in all the world. The opera house question dates back many years. Mr. William H. Crocker, Mr. Joseph D. Redding, Mrs. Phoebe Hearst, Mr. A. B. McCreery and many of our public-spirited citizens offered to build, upon the block of land owned by the city here in the Civic Center, an opera house. We were all enthusiastic about it; we wanted the opera house built. I was in favor of that, but the case was taken to the Supreme Court of the State and the Supreme Court of the State decided that private interests could not have any interest on public property. I vetoed the measure, and the measure was supported unanimously by the Board of Supervisors. Efforts have been made since that time to erect here an opera house, and nearly a million and a half dollars has been subscribed for that opera house. All that Mr. Drum has reviewed here tonight is true. The St. Ignatius lot was purchased. A big building was going up here, the Warehouse and Van Company of Oakland; the Standard Oil were ordered off with their oil station, and Mr. McLeran, as Chairman of the Finance Committee, with the approval of the Board, acquired that property. These gentlemen have all contributed to the tune of a million and a half; in fact, when I had some money I contributed $10,000 myself, so you can see I was interested. Now we are confronted with my good friends over there, the American Legion. And they know my support of their great order, and I do not have any other proof to offer than that I am honorary president of the mighty 363rd Division and the honorary president of the mighty 91st Division that plowed their way through the Argonne Forest. And it is too bad, my brothers, that there should be a difference of opinion in this great project here. Here we have the finest building in all the world, with a gold medal from the Government of France, and it certifies that it is the finest building in all the world. As I have told you before, its dome is forty-seven feet higher than the Capitol at Washington. (Laughter.) Now, look at the delay. Unemployment, men walking the streets, and $4,000,000, outside of the land, ready to go ahead. Now, if there are only 6,000 veterans, with all the organizations, from the Grand Army of the Republic, the Indian War Veterans, the Spanish American War Veterans, the World War Veterans, and all the veterans that there are, and the Women's Auxiliaries, only 6,000, and they have increased the space from 45,000 square feet to a building ten stories high on a 50-vara lot, how are you going to occupy all that space of ground? Now I am for you as far as I can go, but I do believe that these men who have guided the way, who have put their hands down in their pockets and have produced $1,500,000 toward this enterprise, and, because that private money was given, the people, out of admiration for what the American Legion did, and all the war veterans did, joined hand in hand with them, and produced the other money to complete the project. I must concur in what Mr. Drum has said. I think we all feel cheap tonight to think that an attack could be made on public-spirited men, seated here tonight at this table, who have put their hands down in their pockets for years to help the advancement of San Francisco. Mrs. Huntington came to me one day and said: "Mr. Mayor, will you accept Huntington Park for the people of San Francisco?" I said: "Mrs. Huntington, yes." Mr. Ignatz Steinhart came to me and said: "Mayor, would you like an aquarium in Golden Gate Park?" I said: "Yes, Mr. Steinhart." Mr. and Mrs. A. B. Spreckels came to me and said: "Would you like a beautiful Legion of Honor Building in Lincoln Park?" and I said, "Yes." All of which was confirmed by the Board of Supervisors. And General M. H. deYoung put millions of dollars into the M. H. deYoung Memorial in Golden Gate Park. I am trying to get things from these men all the time for the advancement of San Francisco. I have the money in the will of one of our distinguished citizens to build that zoo that I have advocated during the last campaign. I am trying to get these gentlemen to put money in their wills for the advancement of this city, to build playgrounds, to build parks, to build schools, and give unto the people of San Francisco something out of what they have earned for the good of the city that has done so well with them. But I cannot accomplish those things for the city of San Francisco if they are charged with selfish motives, if they are charged with doing something for themselves. We cannot expect gifts for our city if some one says: "He is benefiting by it or she is benefiting by it." Look at the wonderful Honora Sharpe Park you have down in the southern part of the City in San Mateo County. Look at the other gifts that are in Golden Gate Park! Look at the Sutro Heights that were given to Golden Gate Park by Mrs Sutro! Look at the land that they sold us around Lands End, where the railroad is running, the city's railroad is running. If we charge them at all times with making these gifts to San Francisco for selfish motives—I want to say here tonight I am sorry for that. You have done these things for this city, and you are conscientiously doing these things for this city. Look at Mr. Crocker, building a great cathedral on top of Nob Hill.

MR. CROCKER (interrupting): Wait a minute. That is not correct, Mr. Mayor.

THE MAYOR: Well, I stand corrected.

MR. CROCKER: Thank you.

THE MAYOR: Was not the old Crocker home given to Grace Cathedral?

MR. CROCKER: Mr. William H. Crocker did not do that.

THE MAYOR: Well, the Crocker family. Now, I really think, members of the Legion, that after that statement tonight of Mr. Drum's, and I think, gentlemen of the Board of Supervisors, we ought to sit down with Mr. Drum and his committee and iron this thing out. They want to do everything they can for you. As I see it, if I appoint a majority committee of the Legion as trustees of the War Memorial, who is going to guarantee $500,000 to bring the opera here? Who is going to pay the bill? Because the guaranty has to come from somebody? Who is going to bring the opera here? Can the Legion guarantee $500,000? And these are the gentlemen that guarantee, with others that are not here, $500,000 to bring the Metropolitan Opera Company here. And there is far more involved in the project than there is in any other project that we have undertaken. And I hope you will accept the suggestion of Mr. John Drum tonight, and sit down with him, with a special committee, and let us let that great work go ahead to the glory of San Francisco. Mr. Drum, I pledge you tonight my best efforts and my support for a continuance of the splendid work that you have done; I commend you in the name of the city, and I am going to do all I can to encourage the American Legion to join with you and your wonderful Board of Trustees, so that this work will go ahead and they will get all they want. (Applause.)

THE CHAIRMAN: The meeting is now an open one for any one to address the meeting for the purpose for which it was organized.

SUPERVISOR ANDRIANO: Mr. Mayor, I am sure we all appreciate very much the great work that you have performed in preparing this report. We appreciate also the generosity with which you are giving this report to us, neither sparing your voice nor your strength, and I think that we ought to be a little more considerate of your strength and of your energies than you seem to be yourself, Mr. Mayor. You have already spoken for two hours this afternoon, and I do not think that we should tax your energies any further. Therefore, at this time, I am going to make a motion that we stand adjourned to meet again at the call of the Mayor.

SUPERVISOR HAVENNER: Second the motion.

SUPERVISOR HAYDEN: When do you want to adjourn to?

SUPERVISOR ANDRIANO: I leave that matter in the hands of the Mayor, as far as the fixing of the date.

THE MAYOR: The motion is before the Board.

SUPERVISOR GALLAGHER: It is not subject to debate, however; that is the trouble.

THE MAYOR: Well, now, gentlemen of the Board——

SUPERVISOR ANDRIANO (interrupting): I am going to move to recess, if that will make it any——

SUPERVISOR GALLAGHER (interrupting): I would like to——

SUPERVISOR ANDRIANO (interrupting): I will change the motion from adjourning to recessing, so that the Supervisor may express his views on the subject.

SUPERVISOR GALLAGHER: Is that accepted?

THE MAYOR: Yes.

SUPERVISOR GALLAGHER: I would like to say a word before you speak, if your Honor will permit an interruption.

THE MAYOR: Certainly.

SUPERVISOR GALLAGHER: I appreciate and support the statements made by Supervisor Andriano and I share with him the sympathy for the task the Mayor has undertaken for himself, which I think he has done willingly and properly. However, we have reached a point now, Mr. Mayor, in the matter of this War Memorial that looks like a point of decision and I am anxious to get at it. His Honor is the best judge of his own strength in the matter, and we are subject to his desires as to the length to which he desires to go. I would like to see this, if he is so disposed, and desires to read more, or appoint somebody to read for him, that we go on to six o'clock, and I would like to see a time set, convenient, of course, if possible, to everybody's wishes, for this matter, so that probably by the end of the week by the very latest, if not within the next forty-eight hours, we should have reached some decision which would have some finality, so far as the attitude of the Board is concerned on the final question which I presume you will present, which will be whether or not the Board will hold to its action already taken, or rescind it and approve your appointees. And I am very anxious to get at that, and if you are willing to sacrifice some more of your strength to go on, I think you should go on to six o'clock. I do not want to talk as long as I am doing, but I do say, if we go to a recess, if it is the intention of the Board to do so, that the next meeting be an early one, be a night one, or be set early, so that, as I say, a vote could be taken, and you will know the position of the Board in the premises.

SUPERVISOR PEYSER: Mr. Mayor, I realize, also, the arduous task that you are performing now. I, as a new member of the Board, greatly appreciate it, and I presume that you are doing it largely for us who are new members of the Board and not fully acquainted with the subject. However, I feel that we want to get to the meat of the situation and decide the matter, and if your Honor feels that you have not the strength at this time to proceed, why, I suggest that the financial statement be printed and given to us to digest, and at the next meeting we could immediately proceed to the meat of the situation, have your appointees presented, or whatever procedure your Honor desires, and we could then proceed to the hearing, which would eliminate your arduous duty there of reading the report to us.

THE MAYOR: Thank you. Now, gentlemen, I know you realize that I am only doing this as a matter of public duty, and a desire to try and bring harmony out of this unfortunate situation we are in. And the Board of Supervisors are equally responsible with myself. My appointees must be confirmed by you likewise; we are the appointing power. I want to give the new members a thorough statement of facts. I have said nothing except facts that have transpired in this whole matter. I want to gain the friendship of the veterans over fair to them. They know I am fair to them. They have proven it by their honoring me on so many occasions. But a great responsibility rests upon us. There is nothing wrong with this financial statement, it is the receipts and the expenditures of moneys. I am afraid to let this get loose where a wrong impression might be gained, where parts of this report might be used and the whole report not be before you, and I think the whole report ought to be printed as a whole and given to you. You will want some time to study it over, if it is printed

between now and the time I call you into session the next
time, but I want to try and arrive, if I can, at the going
ahead of that proposition. And I want to impress upon you
the seriousness of this situation. I am telling you that suits
will be filed; I am telling you that litigation will be instituted; I am telling you that private funds already given will
not be given; I am telling you that the Regents of the University—and there is no power on earth to compel them to
turn this over to the Board of Supervisors—I am telling you
that the whole situation is as serious as anything can be,
and that mandamus proceedings will be filed upon the four
million dollars' worth of bonds if something is not done pretty
soon to get this straightened out. And the responsibility
rests with you and rests with me, and it is serious and we
do not want to go into litigation here. And if you will listen
to my report, and if the war veterans will listen to my report
and go through with it—it has only got down to the question
of two men, there is nothing else, there is nothing to argue
about. There never was a problem that could not be solved.
And it is a War Memorial that is so far greater than any War
Memorial there is in the country, there is not anything like
it. It was only yesterday that a national committeeman from
Kansas was in my office to see me, and I asked him what
memorial they had in Kansas City. Well, he said, they had
a war memorial in Kansas City, a shaft, with an elevator to
take people up to look around, and there are a few memorial
halls in it, and they are four or five hundred thousand dollars shy on it. It was all privately subscribed, about two
million dollars, and it needs four or five hundred thousand
dollars to finish it, and the subscribers' organization, a voluntary corporation, elected trustees for life, and they are
struggling along with it the best way they can. Here is Los
Angeles with its war memorial, and I was down there the
other night—$750,000, including furnishings, fixtures and
everything else, $738,000 for the buildings and the furnish-
ings and fixtures brings it up to $750,000, and the city gave
a block of land they owned to put it up on, $250,000 more, a
total of one million dollars. And then there was another
million dollars voted by the people down there for the Coliseum and that is for Los Angeles' war memorial. I have not
tried to find out what all the war memorials are in the
United States. The thing ought to be put in the hands of
the War Memorial Trustees to thrash this matter out. The
Charter provides that eleven trustees shall handle this proposition, and why are we struggling with it, except for the good
of the city? The opera house has to be built. I am only talking facts. I have not got into an argument yet and I do not
want to. I am only doing my duty, as the Mayor of the City,
to see that the funds are properly placed in the hands of a
board of trustees, representing all the interests involved in
this proposition, and to meet the requirements of the University Regents, who have to be satisfied before they will turn
over the deed to that piece of property over there, and turn
over the cash on hand, seven hundred seventy-eight thousand
and some odd dollars, drawing interest in four different banks
of San Francisco. It has got to be turned over. As you will
read in all the proceedings of the Board, I advised that the
Board of Supervisors themselves must have a contact. And
all the actions of the Board of Trustees, their actions must
be approved by the Board of Supervisors, and all the money
that you have to put into the budget, to take care of any
deficit over there, certainly the Board should be represented
on the Trustees. Now, there is an objection to having any

member of the Board on it. But how is the Board going
to keep its contact with the expenditure of the budget money
which you must put up every year, according to the Charter,
to maintain that War Memorial? Now, I am only giving
you facts, and I am doing it more sincerely than I have
done anything in my life, and I have never had a harder task
to perform. And this fine secretary of mine, Judge Smith,
and myself, we have been working indefatigably for a long,
long time on this matter, together with the signing of those
forty-one million dollars' worth of bonds for the Spring Valley. And I am pretty near tired out with night work until
3 o'clock in the morning. There is never a night that I do
not work. I want to get down to a point where it is in your
hands to approve or disapprove. You ought to approve, but
if you disapprove of any member of that committee of eleven,
there is no reason why you should not approve General Hunter Liggett; there is no reason why you should not vote for
him. There is not any reason why you should not vote for
George Cameron and George Hearst. The press all agreed
to this and put this over. And you take the position that
you will vote for eleven or none. Now, what kind of a position——

SUPERVISOR POWER (interrupting): Are the names of
the trustees before the Board at this time?

THE MAYOR: No, but they all will be when I finish,
Colonel.

SUPERVISOR POWER: I say, if you want to get action,
why not put them in and let us vote.

THE MAYOR: I know enough, while I am not a judge, I
know when the judge is told, they have heard enough, it is
about time to put the names before you. Let us have them
right now.

SUPERVISOR POWER: As one member of the Board, I
am going to ask the privilege, when they are submitted, of
voting on them individually, and I would like to ask whether
or not you have investigated, before making the appointment
of them, as to what their attitude was previous to the World
War, or when we entered it. Have you investigated that fact,
of all of them?

THE MAYOR: How do you mean their attitude, Supervisor?

SUPERVISOR POWER: Well, some of them may not
have been very much in accord—I do not know it for a fact—
but that question was raised by a party that I know, as to
what the attitude of certain members of the trustees was
towards the World War.

THE MAYOR: Towards America's cause in the war?

SUPERVISOR POWER: Yes.

THE MAYOR: Of any one of the eleven I have named?

SUPERVISOR POWER: Yes, I am just saying, have you
looked into that phase of it?

THE MAYOR: I will read you the names I submitted. If
there is any doubt about any of them—you have the eleven
that I named in my letter of transmission of August 26, 1929.
I will not read the whole letter, I will just read the names:
I appoint, as the trustees of the War Memorial, subject to
your confirmation, General Hunter Liggett, United States
Army, retired, and a Veteran of All Wars; Frank N. Belgrano, former State Commander American Legion; James I.
Herz, 363d Infantry (San Francisco's Own), 91st Division,
who stood by when the orders were given to fire; Major
Charles H. Kendrick, World War Veteran; Herbert Fleish-
hacker, president Anglo and London Paris National Bank;

Kenneth R. Kingsbury, president Standard Oil Company of California; Robert I. Bentley, president California Packing Corporation; George Cameron, publisher San Francisco Chronicle; George Hearst, publisher San Francisco Examiner; as an outstanding representative of labor I appoint, subject to your confirmation, James W. Mullen, publisher of the Labor Clarion, and as I was unable to appoint Colonel George L. Filmer because he could not accept, I appoint Supervisor Jesse C. Colman, World War Veteran. There are the eleven and the eleven all accepted and all were willing to serve, which I think they are as a whole, and the eleven were acceptable to the Regents of the University of California. And, with one exception, all were approved by the Board of Supervisors, informally.

SUPERVISOR GALLAGHER: What is that statement again?

THE MAYOR: I say, all was discussed in my office, my letter says on two or three occasions, and all approved, or the names approved as submitted.

SUPERVISOR GALLAGHER: By whom?

THE MAYOR: By the members of the Board that came into my office when I discussed it. I do not know where our boys that fought over there could get a better selection. I do not know how they are going to get the money. There are so many serious obstacles to this thing. I think you ought to accept the eleven, take your troubles to the eleven and work with them harmoniously, get the thing going, release the Supervisors of any pledges that you may have had them make to you. Let us forget and forgive and let us get this project going ahead. It is hard for me to turn anybody down after appointing them. It is a serious proposition. You represent the people and you have got a very big responsibility, and you have to share it with me, and I have to share it with you. Now, I have lots more here. I have only just begun because I am trying to make a full and complete report, and the more I go on the more convincing I will make it to you.

SUPERVISOR HAVENNER: Mr. Mayor, I think, of course, the Board should hear from the representatives of the Veteran organization, whose vital interest in this whole problem has been a controlling influence in the actions of the Board in the past, and I think the report should be printed so that we, as well as they, can have a chance to study it before we are asked to vote, and I want to second the motion made by Supervisor Andriano, that we now recess, and add to that, if I may, the motion that your report be printed and that your Honor call us into session at any convenient time.

SUPERVISOR SUHR: Mr. Mayor, could there be any objection on your part if we voted on those names seriatim, as suggested by Supervisor Power?

THE MAYOR: I do not believe the time has come for that. I think that might not look well with the public. I think you had better wait until I nominate them. The Supervisor was asking whom I nominated before to the Board and I gave the names because he questioned the Americanism of some of them.

SUPERVISOR POWER: I was judging from your statement and I thought the names had been submitted while I was out.

THE MAYOR: No, I have not submitted the names; that was my letter of August 26, 1929. The only time that your committee of the Board of Supervisors and myself took was from December until August when they were named.

SUPERVISOR PEYSER: Mr. Mayor, if Supervisor Havenner and Supervisor Andriano will consent, I would suggest, and if they consent, move, that the names, that your nominations be now presented to the Board, and that then a recess be declared, and that in the interim that a printed report be furnished us for study so that the matter can come up for debate and vote at the next session to be called by your Honor, so that there will be no further delay in that respect, and we can all study it and your nominations will be before the Board and we can vote.

SUPERVISOR ANDRIANO: As the mover of the motion to recess, I do not feel justified in accepting the suggestion of Supervisor Havenner, that the report be printed in the interim. I believe that your Honor, having gone to such trouble to prepare this voluminous report, is entitled to present it to the Board in the manner that your Honor deems best, and as far as the printing of the report is concerned, I think that it should rest with you, consequently I do not accept the suggested amendment, and insist upon a vote on my motion to recess, subject to the call of the Mayor.

SUPERVISOR HAVENNER: Well, Mr. Mayor, as I understand it, your Honor expressed a willingness yesterday to have the report printed. I have not advanced this suggestion with any idea that it would be repugnant to the Mayor. I know that his statement yesterday was that he intended to submit it to the printer.

SUPERVISOR ANDRIANO: He said today that he desired to present it to the Board before printing it, and I do not feel justified in interfering with his plans in that regard.

SUPERVISOR HAVENNER: I do not insist that it be printed before the Mayor finishes the presentation, but I do request that it be presented to us before we vote.

SUPERVISOR ANDRIANO: That is all right.

SUPERVISOR POWER: As a matter of fact, Mr. Mayor, the records of the Board will show that you submitted a report to the Board a week ago yesterday; it was received and a motion made that the matter be printed and copies furnished to each member of the Board. Yesterday you explained that that was not done, that you wished to read it. Even if printed, there is no reason why you should not still read the report; that is your privilege and your right, but I think, as has been suggested by Supervisor Peyser, that the veterans would have a far better opportunity to study the situation and be familiar with it if it was printed than they would to try and grasp the situation as you go along and read it.

THE MAYOR: I think if you will accept my suggestion in good faith in this matter, and let me be the judge of the situation, I think that it will be far better that I proceed to read the report to you in full. You can have it printed. I think it will serve your purpose the best of all, I think it will help the veterans because I know they have a lot of arguments today that I am answering, as I know what their statements are, and I am answering their statements, many of which will be withdrawn tonight in the renewal of their statements, which they have made, because I have answered some of them already. And I think by the time I answer all and make my report clear, that the statements which the Veterans' Committee are going to make will already have been answered by the report I submit to you, and I think they may withdraw some of the questions which they already have today, which they would take up now. I think, for your own satisfaction, I think for your own good, and I think for the public—and the responsibility is in your hands—you had better hear the Mayor in full and have it printed. That is what I think, and I think the veterans will be better pleased, too.

SUPERVISOR PEYSER: Mr. Mayor, I have no objection whatsoever to the report being read. As a matter of fact, it is a very good idea. But, nevertheless, a week ago Monday, if your Honor will recall, at your Honor's suggestion, by motion of the Board, it was moved that the report be printed and given to us for perusal. I for one would like, in addition to your reading it, I would like to study it, and I have no objection to your reading it and presenting it in any manner that you desire, but I would like to have it printed in accordance with the resolution, if there is no objection.

SUPERVISOR HAVENNER: If I may then, prior to the consideration of a motion for recess, I would like to move that the report be printed forthwith.

SUPERVISOR PEYSER: It was moved and passed a week ago.   .

SUPERVISOR HAVENNER: Has it been given to the Clerk?

THE CLERK: I have not got it; the Mayor has it; it has never been given to the Clerk.

THE MAYOR: I only finished it at 3 o'clock this morning. I have a little more to put in that the reporter cannot find.

SUPERVISOR HAVENNER: Is there a copy of the report available to be submitted to the printer?

THE MAYOR: The only copy I have is what I have here.

SUPERVISOR GALLAGHER: Have you an original and a stenographic copy?

THE MAYOR: No, I have only the original.

SUPERVISOR GALLAGHER: It seems that you absolutely intend to read it whether we like it or not, so we had better let you have your way.

THE MAYOR: No, it is not that; I want to be dead sure that it is all before you.

SUPERVISOR GALLAGHER: I am prepared to listen, I am prepared to meet tonight, I want to get this thing behind me. The Board is being accused of being dilatory. I think that you can read from now until doomsday and that the decision will be much the same, except for the new members of the Board, I mean by that, that nearly everybody has made up their mind. I suggest you go on reading until 6 o'clock.

SUPERVISOR SPAULDING: Mr. Mayor, I move then—I second the motion of Mr. Andriano that we recess and that we go into session again at 7:30 tonight and get it behind us.

SUPERVISOR HAVENNER: I cannot be present tonight.

SUPERVISOR ROSSI: I won't be able to be present either.

SUPERVISOR HAYDEN: Some of us have appointments for tonight and I will have to object to that.

THE MAYOR: Leave it to the original motion, that I call you after the recess.

SUPERVISOR ANDRIANO: Question.

SUPERVISOR McSHEEHY: Mr. Mayor, you have read a portion of the report, and part of that report, I remember well, was a verbatim report of a meeting we had here almost a year ago, in which Mr. Drum spoke for an hour and ten minutes. Now, I understand you have a number of statements or reports of various meetings; they are verbatim statements of meetings we have had that will take several hours, and you are going to read them to the Board here. I feel this way: if some of the members have important engagements for tonight, very well, excuse those members, but the people of San Francisco mean more to this Board, and this matter means more to them than any individual member of this Board. I personally have no objection whatsoever to excusing certain members. I would like to come back here tonight and sit here until midnight to hear your report. It will be taken down by our stenographer, and anyone that wishes the report can have it. But in that manner we will end this controversy, and that is what we are all anxious to do. I would like to hear from the veterans; I would like to get this matter behind us. They are here day in and day out. Any members that wish to be excused, very well, I personally will vote to excuse them, but stay with it until we end the matter. We have these two lots over here. I am perhaps as well posted on this matter as any member of this Board. We have these two lots over here. We have four million dollars of the people's money that can be brought into cash any day. I do not know, but there is practically a million dollars in money that we could start as a nucleus on these buildings. Now why not stay with it?

SUPERVISOR POWER: Has Supervisor McSheehy offered a motion?

THE MAYOR: Now let me say just another word.

SUPERVISOR HAYDEN: Sit down, Supervisor.

SUPERVISOR McSHEEHY: I will not sit down, Supervisor. Now, I wish you would stop that little heckling of yours. We are here to act.

SUPERVISOR HAYDEN: I rise to a point of order. We are getting nowhere with the Supervisor's statement, and I want to get somewhere.

SUPERVISOR McSHEEHY: I have not yielded the floor. If the Supervisor wishes to rise to a point of order—Supervisor Power really knows parliamentary law as well as any member on this Board, that is his privilege and you, as the presiding officer, will decide that point of order.

THE MAYOR: You have the floor.

SUPERVISOR HAVENNER: I am going to rise to a point of order. My point of order is that this Board has already, by a formal motion, ordered the printing of this report, and I make the point of order that the report be printed before this proceeding is concluded.

THE MAYOR: Well, of course, that matter is optional at the present time with the Mayor. The Board of Supervisors cannot order the Mayor to give up his report in order to print it before he has delivered it. Now, I want to tell you I am making a report. I am not making any comments. I have stated nothing but facts. I have made nothing but a statement of facts, nor discussed the subject in any way, and there is no need of anybody getting alarmed or anybody feeling that they are not going to have a chance to talk, because they will have a chance to talk as long as they want to, and at any time they want, after the Mayor has had the opportunity—and he is the responsible party—of making the report. And it is up to the Mayor to make his report before it is given out and everybody picks it to pieces, fly to the press and go after it before the Mayor has finished his report. There is no fairness in that. When the Mayor makes his report, and has submitted it to the Board of Supervisors, it is then public property and until that time it is the Mayor's private report. Is not that true?

SUPERVISOR POWER: That is true, Mr. Mayor, but you did submit it last Monday and you made half an hour's speech after you submitted it.

THE MAYOR: No, I have that speech, that is, only just about that much.

SUPERVISOR POWER: Well, it was submitted to the Board and it is in the hands of the Board.

THE MAYOR: I withdraw it now for reasons of my own. There has been a change of atmosphere come over the whole situation, as to what the Mayor's report was and all about it, and I want you to get the whole report as a whole, as a statement of fact, because I will have something to say myself in the discussion. Now I think, in fairness to me, you should let the Mayor submit his report to you, then order it printed, or do whatever you please with it.

SUPERVISOR HAYDEN: I would like to rise to a question of personal privilege.

THE MAYOR: I do not want to make this trouble any worse than it is at the present time, and just what is going to happen to the Mayor's statement of facts if they get out——

SUPERVISOR HAYDEN: What is the parliamentary situation?

THE MAYOR: The parliamentary situation is that Mr. Andriano, seconded by Mr. McSheehy, moved that the meeting take a recess, to be called together at some time this week convenient to the Mayor and the members of the Board of Supervisors.

SUPERVISOR McSHEEHY: I never seconded that because I am not in favor of it.

THE CLERK: Supervisor Andriano made the motion.

SUPERVISOR HAYDEN: I seconded it.

THE MAYOR: I appeal to the members of the Board, for their own good and for the good of the Mayor, that all members of the Board be present, as you are today, rather than have any criticism cast upon you, because this is a big question. It is the biggest thing there is before the people right now, next to the bond issue for the Hetch Hetchy power, that you carry this motion and we will get together, either day or night, and give due and proper notice so that all the veterans can be here when the report is finished and then we will proceed on parliamentary lines.

SUPERVISOR McSHEEHY: Supervisor Spaulding made a motion to amend the motion of Supervisor Andriano, that we recess and reconvene here tonight at 7:30 to hear your report. Your report is only half read or one-third read, perhaps. I favor Supervisor Spaulding's motion for the reason that we reconvene here tonight, and then we will hear your report and then we will have it; if it takes until midnight, all right. You are the Mayor of this City and County of San Francisco and we are duty bound to hear your report, therefore I favor Supervisor Spaulding's motion, which is seconded by Supervisor Gallagher, and I hope when we do recess that we reconvene here say at 8 o'clock tonight for that purpose.

SUPERVISOR GALLAGHER: I desire to address myself to the question which I consider before the house, the amendment to the motion to recess to a time set, namely 7:30. Now, I admit that this may cause some inconvenience to members of the Board, and I am very loath to do it. I know it causes me great inconvenience, greater than I would care to make known at the moment. The same with some of the others, but I submit that there may be enough members of the Board, particularly new members, who will respond to a call for 7:30. They will come if they care to, and we can promise that there will be no vote taken on the subject of appointments, and there can be none until your report is concluded. And many of the gentlemen here, including myself, are thoroughly familiar, except for the financial statement, with the entire situation. But it is not fair that new men be called upon to vote until they have had it clarified to their satisfaction. I submit to the members of the Board, unless their engagements are so pressing that it is impossible to come, in view of the public criticism reiterated and reiterated, that some of us are to blame for the delay——

SUPERVISOR McGOVERN (interrupting): We are not.

SUPERVISOR GALLAGHER: In view of the fact that the veterans' organizations are here represented and are pleading with us to go on and clear the situation as soon as possible, I submit that if there is a majority of this Board, particularly the new members, who can inconvenience themselves to come, and you can continue your report tonight, much will be accomplished, and a decision probably reached on this matter as to vote before the end of the week.

SUPERVISOR HAYDEN: I would like to ask the Mayor if the Mayor is free to appear tonight?

THE MAYOR: It would mean my canceling a dinner engagement which I made four weeks ago, and it would inconvenience a group of people that I had accepted the invitation from.

SUPERVISOR HAYDEN: Tomorrow morning at 10 o'clock.

THE MAYOR: Tomorrow night I have a dinner engagement at my sister's home with some relatives.

SUPERVISOR HAYDEN: How about 10 o'clock tomorrow morning?

THE MAYOR: Yes, at any time.

SUPERVISOR HAYDEN: Will you accept 10 o'clock tomorrow morning?

SUPERVISOR ANDRIANO: That is agreeable to me.

MR. GLENSOR: If you are going on and finish reading the report without printing the financial statement, we will be here any time. We are at your disposal.

SUPERVISOR HAYDEN: I would like to move that we take a recess until 10 o'clock tomorrow morning and the Mayor continue reading his report.

SUPERVISOR HAVENNER: May I ask whether you would have any objection to allowing the financial report, which I understand is a part of your report to the Board, to be printed? That is the thing which we have not had yet, and which we have not had time to study, and I cannot see that anybody would be injured if that be printed, in accordance with the motion adopted by the Board already. I understand that that is in the nature of a report of certified public accountants. There must be copies of it. It could go to the printer now, and that is the thing that I would like to see.

SUPERVISOR ANDRIANO: I rise to a point of order, that is not germane to the question before the Board now.

SUPERVISOR HAVENNER: I make the point of order that it is germane to the action already taken by this Board prior to this meeting today.

SUPERVISOR ANDRIANO: It is not material to the question before the Board now. Whether the Mayor desires to print the financial statement is, in my opinion, up to the Mayor. It is his report and he desires to present it in the manner that suits him best and I do not think that the question of printing or non-printing is before us now. I call for a vote upon my motion, as amended by Supervisor Hayden, that we recess to meet tomorrow at 10 o'clock.

SUPERVISOR HAYDEN: I second that motion.

THE MAYOR: Mr. Havenner, as long as we are going to meet tomorrow morning at 10 o'clock, I tell you that I put the financial report at the close of the full report to you here. Here it is, to show you that I have it. But if I give this out, I know there is just one thing going to happen to my whole report—and this report is nothing but the facts about the War Memorial, that is all—and I think the report ought to go on in chronological order. Curiosity killed the cat many a time.

SUPERVISOR HAVENNER: Mr. Mayor, I certainly do not desire to press any point that is going to be in any way discourteous to you, but I cannot, for the life of me, see why we should not save time in having this thing printed. There is no question about my constitutional right to stand on the point of order that the thing has to be printed. That has been done prior to this meeting and nobody, except this Board by rescinding its action, can prevent me from having this thing printed. Now, why should it be delayed until the very end?

THE MAYOR: The only thing that could prevent you from having it printed is, if the Mayor tells you it is not ready to be submitted.

SUPERVISOR HAVENNER: If the Mayor keeps it, that is true, and I do not want to be discourteous.

SUPERVISOR PEYSER: I rise to a question of personal privilege. Mr. Mayor, I just want to explain my vote, that I cannot possibly be here tomorrow morning at 10 o'clock.

THE MAYOR: Well, I want you here. When can you be here?

SUPERVISOR PEYSER: I can be here tomorrow afternoon. I have to appear in court tomorrow morning.

THE MAYOR: At half past one tomorrow?

SUPERVISOR ANDRIANO: No objection, that is agreeable.

SUPERVISOR STANTON: I will not be able to be here tomorrow. I am fairly familiar with everything but the financial part of your report. I have a meeting in the morning and in the afternoon which I must attend.

SUPERVISOR ROSSI: I will not be able to be here tomorrow either.

THE MAYOR: Well, then, we will make it Thursday.

SUPERVISOR CANEPA: We have a very important committee, the fire committee, and there are numerous applications pending for laundry permits, and if this Board meets Thursday it will seriously interfere with the committee meeting.

SUPERVISOR PEYSER: Make it tomorrow night.

SUPERVISOR SPAULDING: How much longer will it take for you to complete your report?

THE MAYOR: How long was I at it this afternoon?

MR. GLENSOR: You read about one-fifth of the transcript of that night meeting, Mr. Mayor, by actual count of the pages.

SUPERVISOR PEYSER: I believe that you, along with this Board, are trying to reach a solution of the War Memorial situation. I assume so, from the earnestness with which you have prepared your report, and from your own statements given to this Board. I am a war veteran and I am vitally interested and I am also vitally interested as a representative of the people of San Francisco. Now I cannot see, if it is going to be a matter of saving time, why we should not have the opportunity of digesting this at our leisure, at nights, and then your Honor could read the rest of it, if you wish, and we will be prepared to go to a vote. The way it is proceeding now, we will be reading here for another two days and then the matter will be printed anyway, and the veterans here, most of them who have to work, cannot come to these meetings continually, and I think, for the purpose of efficiency and expediency, that your Honor should be willing—and I make this merely in the form of a suggestion — to have this printed and have the war veterans heard on their problems, present your nominations, and then we can have the matter before the Board.

THE MAYOR: Well, leave it with me and I will do the best I can think of doing for the harmony——

SUPERVISOR POWER (interrupting): Question on the motion to meet tonight.

SUPERVISOR McSHEEHY: We do not seem to reach any conclusions with reference to any time we are going to meet. We have all come to the conclusion that we must continue, and you have stated positively that you will read this report to the Board before it is printed, and it is in such a form that I dare say you have to read it to the Board. Now, your Honor, I might ask you this question: Is there any way, if I am not asking too much, in behalf of the City of San Francisco I ask it, is there any way that you can ask to be relieved from the appointment that you have tonight, so that we can continue this meeting here tonight? Now, your Honor, especially if a few members cannot be here tonight, of course there will be no vote taken here tonight, and they will want to receive the report, but you must read the report yourself, so therefore I feel that, for the sake of time, and for the sake of our city, and if there is any way that you can be released from your appointment tonight, I feel that you should be released, if you feel that way.

SUPERVISOR PEYSER: Mr. Mayor, would it be in order to ask the privilege of the floor at this time for Mr. Glensor? He has something to say, representing the veterans.

SUPERVISOR RONCOVIERI: Mr. Mayor, I understand it is your desire to read the financial statement before you print it. Am I correct?

THE MAYOR: Yes, I do.

SUPERVISOR RONCOVIERI: I think that there are no Einsteins here, and I am no mathematician, able to grasp a thousand numbers and figures that you are going to read, and I doubt if there is an Einstein here. It would take one to understand a financial statement made by experts. And so you ought, it seems to me, to print the financial statement. I am willing, as one member of the Board, to accept your financial statement when printed, and I will not give a line to anyone else, and if the other members will agree—and I am saying that because now Supervisor Andriano is laughing, I would like him to follow it—the Mayor has stated that he does not want his printed report to be analyzed and chopped to pieces by others than this Board. And so I say, for one, I am willing not to give it to these men until he is ready. Then, of course, I will give them my copy, of course they will have it.

THE MAYOR: Everybody will have it.

SUPERVISOR RONCOVIERI: Of course, the better way would be to print it at once and let us study it in the next two or three days. It will take time to apprehend it. I say, there is not a single Einstein in here; nobody can understand that.

THE MAYOR: There have been so many insulting remarks made about the report and gross misstatements that are not true, a letter written to Mr. Crocker, which I have in my report, analyzing hearsay figures, I want all of you to hear the statements that have been made and the remarks made to Mr. Crocker, and for his personal attention, to which no reply has yet been made, and I want them to wind up with the final financial statement, and I want one of the certified public accountants here present to explain every item in the statement, so there will nothing go wrong and no haphazard charges made against Mr. Crocker and his institution, and the institution of these honorable men who have had the handling of their own money and of the subscribers who entrusted them with it. I do not want any misconception to go out about a report to the public until it is thoroughly analyzed and thoroughly analyzed and thoroughly understood, and, in my judgment, there is nothing wrong with it, and it is a fine, clean public document.

SUPERVISOR RONCOVIERI: Then, Mr. Mayor, what objection have you to publishing it, if it is clean, as you say it is, what objection have you to publishing it?

THE MAYOR: I have not any objection to publishing it, but I want to read the letter written to Mr. Crocker first, and give you the report afterwards.

SUPERVISOR ANDRIANO: I think that we have been discussing this question long enough, and as the author of the original motion, I think that we ought to take a vote on the motion pending and the amendment to the motion. May I before calling for a vote make the suggestion, which probably will meet with the approval of every one concerned, including your Honor: It has been stated here, by the representatives of the veterans, that only about one-fifth of the report has as yet been read.

MR. GLENSOR: Only about one-fifth of one transcript.

SUPERVISOR ANDRIANO: Your Honor has also stated that you are desirous of presenting the facts, and might it not be possible if we recess to say Thursday for your Honor to condense the report, as far as the arguments that took place in this Board are concerned, and just give us the facts, so that the new members may be apprised of them, and in that way we would all save a great deal of time and your Honor would be spared a great deal of unnecessary effort, and, nevertheless, your plan of procedure would be followed, of presenting the facts first, and then giving us the financial report, and then having the report printed, including the financial statement, so that we may study it and come back at a later date and vote upon your nominations? I think that, in my humble judgment, is the logical way to proceed and at the same time economize the time of all concerned.

SUPERVISOR POWER: Mr. Mayor, I would like to ask either through you or the Clerk whether or not a transcript of the proceedings referred to here has been made by the stenographer?

THE MAYOR: Yes, they are all the stenographic reports of meetings. These come from my own records. A copy has been sent to me every time they have taken place here.

SUPERVISOR POWER: I want to know if they were printed in the Journal.

THE MAYOR: They came over to me after every hearing. I have thousands of pages.

SUPERVISOR POWER: They have not been printed?

THE MAYOR: They have not been printed.

SUPERVISOR ANDRIANO: Question.

SUPERVISOR POWER: Question.

SUPERVISOR GALLAGHER: I rise to a point of order, this howl for "question" when a member of the body is on the floor. He is insisting that he has an amendment which is duly and properly made, and upon which I as a seconder demand a vote. I am prepared to go ahead tonight regardless of social couse-quences.

SUPERVISOR SPAULDING: It has been suggested by Super-visor Andriano that you wanted to get down to the facts in your report, and I am sure it is agreeable to me, and I am quite sure that it is agreeable to the Board. You pick out the facts that you want to present before us, and I know we will be glad to listen to them, and then you come to your financial statement and the report is complete. I do not think that you want to, or I do not think that we want to be bored by a lot of unnecessary transcripts that probably would be of no value to us. But if you yourself touch upon the facts, and if we come back here at 7:30 tonight, I am sure that you can clean that up tonight. It will be serious to me because I am indis-posed tonight myself, but if this continues on for two or three days—I have been here at a meeting every day since I have been a Supervisor, and as most of you know, I have to work for a living, and to come here for the next four or five days, it seems to me like it will be impossible for me to do it. I know it will be for Carl Miles and Peyser. So I suggest that we vote upon that amendment, go on at 7:30 and clean it up and get it behind us.

SUPERVISOR HAYDEN: By way of explanation, I have made an engagement with my wife back three or four weeks, for a particular social engagement this evening. I must keep that appointment. My wife is prepared to join me tonight and I shall have to vote "no" for the meeting tonight. I am free otherwise, any night or any day after tonight, but, under those circumstances, I have to vote "no" against 7:30.

SUPERVISOR POWER: I wish to make an explanation: I am going to keep the same engagement, but I will be back here just as soon as I get a bite to eat, whether it is 7:30 or 8.

THE MAYOR: Speaking to the remarks made by Supervisor Spaulding, I presume he will grant to the Mayor the courtesy of making his own report.

SUPERVISOR SPAULDING: I will be glad to do that, Mayor.

THE MAYOR: It is now 6 o'clock, and I have a dinner en-gagement myself, and I have not time, between now and a dinner engagement at 7, to get excused from the engagement which I have accepted. The Mayor's duties consist of many duties. Among those are functions and affairs that he has to attend. Now, inasmuch as I cannot get excused between now and 7 o'clock, it will be more convenient for me for you to set a time when you can meet in the same numbers as you have today, and at a time convenient to you all.

SUPERVISOR GALLAGHER: Could you be here at 8 o'clock?

THE MAYOR: I do not think so.

SUPERVISOR RONCOVIERI: Nine o'clock?

THE MAYOR: I will meet you here at 11 o'clock tonight.

SUPERVISOR McSHEEHY: I will be here.

SUPERVISOR GALLAGHER: That ought to suit everybody.

THE MAYOR: Is that acceptable to everybody?

SUPERVISOR HAYDEN: What hour did you set?

THE MAYOR: Eleven o'clock. Is that satisfactory to every-body? We will take a recess to meet at 11 o'clock. (Bringing down the gavel.)

TUESDAY-WEDNESDAY, FEBRUARY 18-19, 1930, 11 P. M.

(Mayor James Rolph, Jr., acted as Chairman of the meeting.)

THE MAYOR: Call the roll, Mr. Clerk.

(Roll call.)

THE CLERK: Not a quorum.

THE MAYOR: We will proceed with the continuation of the public meeting of the War Memorial Trustees on Thursday, December 6, 1928, at 8 o'clock P. M., from where I left off this afternoon, the Chairman announcing that, "The meeting is now an open one for anyone to address the meeting for the purpose for which it was organized."

MR. HUTCHINS: I want to endorse the Mayor's remarks, not as a member of any military organization, but as an honorably discharged soldier from the Spanish-American war and the late war. In my discussion with members of the American Legion I imagine that I understand their attitude.   It has been my experience to be present at the meetings, when I had the glorious opportunity of listening to our public benefactors when they subscribed so magnificently to this memorial, in the incipiency of its thoughts.   At that time there was nothing but a war memorial in mind.   There was no opera house, no nothing at all.   I was watching so closely that wonderful contribution, $50,000 by several of them.   What a noble gift to the soldiers! Later on we got assistance from the voters in issuing those bonds. There is no doubt, I do not think, in the minds of any person who hears this, that 75 per cent of those funds were intended for the benefit of the soldiers.   Now let us see where the money came from. Look at the enormous amount· that was subscribed that evening, not by soldiers at the front but by soldiers at the rear, and any one who is a student of history knows that a soldier at home is as important, and sometimes more so, than a soldier at the front.   Who would feed that soldier, who would take care of his many wants if it was not for the man behind the gun at home?   Those men did not only subscribe at that meeting, but they are on the tax roll for hundreds and hundreds of thousands of dollars.   They pay twice.   I do not pay anything—I am on the tax roll, but forget it, it is so small.   I did my little part in the war.   I ate three meals a day and wore the uniform. I can say that I did that much.   My discharge would indicate that. Now let it go at that.   The hour has come, gentlemen, when you must get together.   Now, remember that our military organizations are gradually dying—I mean now a physical death.   The Grand Army is soon off the map entirely.   The Indian War Veterans will soon be among the missing.   We are gradually going out.   But the musical end of life and the music lovers are growing every day.   I have not gone far enough in music to appreciate the symphony.   I like to hear something in music where I can follow the tune.   I cannot with the symphony; I am not musically educated, but there are hundreds of thousands that are.   And then we owe them a degree of courtesy, and they pay the bill.   Now let us get together.   It seems to me that the Legion are just a little bit displeased here because they do not feel as though they have been allowed enough.   Why don't you get in touch with these gentlemen that are the representatives of the subscribers, the people that have put up 90 per cent of this money, and see if you cannot immediately agree?   Let harmony prevail.   You heard what the Mayor said.

THE CHAIRMAN: Thank you, Mr. Hutchins, but the hour is very late, and I wonder whether you would not yield your time to some of the veteran organizations who have taken the position.   Thank you very much.   (Applause.)

THE CHAIRMAN: I think, gentlemen of the veteran organizations, or the Legion, if any of the members desire to speak, I think it would serve the purpose for which this meeting is called if we could hear from you.

SUPERVISOR MARKS: May I ask a couple of questions, Mr. Chairman?

THE CHAIRMAN: Surely.

SUPERVISOR MARKS: I would like to ask, Mr. Chairman, what the total amount is that has been made available for war memorial purposes, both by subscription and bond issue?

THE CHAIRMAN: Four million dollars bond issue, approximately $2,000,000 by private subscriptions, of which, for the time being, because the city has not yet paid for one of the two lots, the amount of money on hand, plus the amount of land purchased, is about a million to a million and a quarter.

SUPERVISOR MARKS: I would like to ask, in addition, the total cost of the land for both war memorial and the opera house?

THE MAYOR: I wish to say, for all present tonight, that Mr. John Drum was Chairman of the meeting.

THE CHAIRMAN: I cannot give it exactly. I think on one block it is somewhere in the neighborhood of $650,000, and the other block, due to the Locomobile Building, which had an added value, it is somewhere in the neighborhood of $800,000.

SUPERVISOR MARKS: That would be available for buildings approximately how much, for all of the buildings?

THE CHAIRMAN: The amount available for buildings, for building itself, that will be in the neighborhood of $5,000,000, without going into all the accounting back and forth.

SUPERVISOR MARKS: Now, of that $5,000,000, according to the present plans of the trustees, how much is allotted to the opera house and how much is allotted to the veterans' building?

THE CHAIRMAN: With the buildings cut down, for the opera house approximately $3,000,000 and for the veterans' building $1,870,000.

SUPERVISOR MARKS: Just one further question, Mr. Drum. You referred several times to a ten-story building upon a 50-vara lot. My computation makes that 187,000 square feet, which shows a discrepancy in your figures of about 82,000 square feet.

THE CHAIRMAN: That is correct according to the square footage, but I took the matter up with a contracting firm, and, making allowance for light wells and counting out all stairways and all hall-ways, toilets and closets, which we have done in figuring 108,000 square feet, they figured that the amount of available space in a building that tall would be about 108,000 square feet. Mr. Wagstaff, will you give me that book for a moment?

The committee representing the Legion is as follows: James B. Burns, Chairman; A. Don Duncan, George H. Cabaniss, Jr., Harold Hotchner, Dr. T. T. Angel, Earl J. Harris, Leon French, Ivy P. Cerkel, Charles H. Kendrick, Allison E. Schofield, Edward L. Schary, Thomas Foley, William D. Flinn, F. H. Ainsworth, Sr., Alvin Gerlach and Harold Weidenfeld. Mr. Burns, would you care to address the audience?

MR. JAMES B. BURNS: I will state, Mr. Chairman, that, with the exception of one name, that your statement of the Legion Committee is correct; that Mr. Kendrick has presented his resignation as a member of that committee, and he has been replaced as a representative on that committee. We are very glad that, after seven years, we have been notified, as the Mayor suggested, that there was going to be a meeting between the War Memorial Trustees and those interested. We are very much interested, of course, in learning what this meeting is for and in finding out just why it is called. I personally asked, and the Adjutant received a notice of this meeting, and it stated that it was to be a general meeting on the War Memorial. And that was all the information which we received with relation to the purposes for which this meeting was called. And we are very glad to sit here and listen so that we may be enlightened, and we will be very glad to listen to the discussions, and there may be questions which we may ask later, and there may be questions that we can answer later.

THE CHAIRMAN: Mr. Burns, I wonder whether—you are the Chairman of that committee; you gave us a letter in which you outlined the broad powers which your committee possessed. You likewise, in the last campaign, conducted a campaign in what you regarded as proper opposition to Amendment 32. We have made a very definite personal appeal for the co-operation of your committee, you and the personnel of your committee, and I wonder if you would not be willing, considering the public meeting is called, where you and your committee are very definite in your view, that you would not give us the benefit of what your point of view is, and whether or not, in your judgment, there is not some way in which, for the welfare of this enterprise, we can get together?

MR. BURNS: I will state, Mr. Drum, that during all of your able discourse, that you referred entirely and at all times to the Legion, and once or twice incidentally you mentioned other veteran organizations and other veterans. I want it thoroughly understood that there are many other veteran organizations who are here tonight. I do not know whether they were invited or not, but, nevertheless, on account of knowing as many veterans in the city as I do, I notice that many organizations are represented. We believe that there are a number of reasons, and we think they are valid reasons, why the San Francisco County Council of the American Legion, through its War Memorial Committee, opposed Amendment No. 32. At this moment I repeat that we feel that we would like to hear just a little more of the purposes of this meeting and, further, that we would like to be enlightened upon one other subject. As I understand it, under the amendment, as carried, this Board of Trustees, with relations to any other amounts than the $2,000,000 privately subscribed fund, goes out of existence as soon as the Legislature ratifies the charter amendment, and as soon as the Mayor makes his appointment. And at this time we are just a little doubtful as to the jurisdiction of this Board of Trustees, as it were, to ask the Legion to state a position, without taking into consideration all of the veterans' organizations in whose name the bond issue was presented to the people and ultimately carried. Now, as I stated before, I feel that we would like to have the meeting progress just a little further, so that we would know further the purposes thereof, and then we certainly do not desire to let the public believe that we do not care to present to the proper tribunal or the proper authorities our reasons for the position which we have taken.

THE CHAIRMAN: Why not regard this as a public meeting, Mr. Burns? There are several hundred citizens here—and present what you have to say.

MR. MILTON D. SAPIRO: Mr. Drum, I will state this on behalf of the American Legion——

THE CHAIRMAN (interrupting): Are you on this committee, Mr. Sapiro?

MR. SAPIRO: I have been asked to act with the committee. I am an ex-service man and a member of the American Legion and a citizen of San Francisco, and I participated in the original drive whereby you secured subscriptions for this War Memorial, and am familiar with the facts which you covered generally in a fairly correct way, and in some substantial matters a little in error. It is too bad that the Mayor did not stay. .

THE CHAIRMAN: He is just in the other room. He told me he would come right back.

MR. SAPIRO: He was very interesting in his outline of the gifts that were made by citizens to this community, and as a citizen of San Francisco I certainly appreciate the generosity that prompted those men to give so much of what they had. But if we are going to consider this on the basis of the merits of the men who gave gifts, I could just turn around and point out men in this room who did not give money to this city, but offered that which was far more than money, their lives; and many men who probably bear marks that they will carry through the rest of their days because of what they offered to the city. You asked what the attitude of the Legion is in this situation. The Legion, of course, as Mr. Burns has stated, is not the only one concerned. The other veteran organizations have a right to be heard and have a right to participate in this War Memorial, because the money that was secured from the citizens of San Francisco by the bond issue, which is the bulk of the money, was secured on the primary issue that it was to provide a housing place for veterans; and if you will take your campaign literature of that date, you will find that that is the fact. You stated in your talk that the principle which should govern this War Memorial is this: That there should be no more reason for dominance of one activity than the other, and we accept that principle; and it is on that principle that we stand. (Applause.) And it is because of the failure of your Board of Trustees to carry out that principle that you have had to call this meeting tonight to meet any objection on the part of the veteran body. And it is because of the failure of your Board of Trustees to carry out that principle that the veteran body had to carry their case before the Board of Supervisors representing the City and County of San Francisco. We have never failed to co-operate with you or your Board of Trustees. You have failed to co-operate with us. There has never been a time when this project was originally formed that it lacked enthusiasm. You were in error in your statement of the origin of the War Memorial in so far as the Legion was concerned. The American Legion in 1920 contemplated going before the Board of Supervisors of the City and County of San Francisco for the purpose of asking them to erect a veterans' building as a war memorial, just as was being done in a great many other cities throughout the country.

THE CHAIRMAN: Which cities, Mr. Sapiro, please?

MR. SAPIRO: Oakland, Los Angeles has had a building up for years, and we could have had if your committee had acted with efficiency and expedition instead of coming here eight years later to say why it was not built. But the fact is that eight years ago, in 1920, our Legion groups were meeting for the purpose of considering what form of War Memorial the City of San Francisco should erect in honor of those men who had given service to their country. This city was ready and willing to recognize the service that had been given by men who had gone to the World War and to previous wars. The memory of their deeds was fresh in their minds, and there would have been no difficulty whatsoever in coming before the Board of Supervisors that then sat in this chamber to secure a proper appropriation of the necessary sum to erect a building for our purposes, and we were ready to do that. However, we were approached—we did not see it—we were approached by a representative of the group that had been trying to erect an opera house in San Francisco. And they told us of their desires, and they told us of their wishes, which you have so well outlined this evening, to keep San Francisco the cultural center of the Pacific Coast, and to let music ring in the hearts of our people in the proper surroundings. We accorded with that wish. After all, the love of music does not reside in any particular group, and those of us who are service men are just as apt to have as fine an appreciation of music as any other group, and we recognize the value of an opera house to this city. And when the proposition came before us, and it was pictured that we should have a group of buildings on one lot, which would give us sufficient space for the meeting place of veterans,

and which would also provide space for the activities of the musical
groups and the art-loving groups of San Francisco, we acceded to that.
The group that came to us told us of the subscriptions that they had.
As a matter of fact, they had not been able to complete the full amount
of their subscriptions, and their pledges were as yet ineffective, and
they did not know just how long those pledges might be allowed to
continue to exist. And therefore we, desiring to accomplish your
object and our own, entered into an agreement with you whereby we
were going to take up and carry on the campaign for the type of
building which had been outlined to us. The campaign was carried
on. True it is that there was only four or five hundred thousand dollars of the $2,000,000 raised at that time, but it was much harder work
to raise that four or five hundred thousand dollars than it was to
raise the million dollars, because, as Mr. Drum has pointed out, we
got that money in pennies and nickels from those to whom it meant
probably a great deal more in financial sacrifice to furnish the funds
to build up that number of subscriptions. And you cannot compare
the rate of the subscription, because it is true that if we went out
alone for a private War Memorial Building that would have provided
a housing place for veterans, we would have had a building, and we
would have secured subscriptions from the same groups that had provided the other million and a half dollars for your musical purposes,
because we have no question but what they are just as patriotic—that
patriotic motives and the development of patriotic motives are just as
dear to them as they are to us. Now, that campaign was carried on,
and I want to say to you, Mr. Drum, and you will probably have to
admit that you never met a more enthusiastic group than the group
of ex-service men who had just come back fresh from the war fields
and wanted to put up something that would be peaceful in its nature,
to remind them, not of our deeds, but of the men and the spirit that
had gone before. And we went into that thing enthusiastically, threw
ourselves into it, with an effort to get the money and to provide the
funds to erect these buildings. What happened? We waited year
after year. The money was raised in 1920. In 1920 it was finally
decided, at the solicitation of Supervisor McLeran, to exchange lots.
It then took 1922, 1923, 1924, 1925 and 1926, almost, to draw up the
plans for the new structures and to decide that the money which you
then had on hand was insufficient. Do you wonder that the ardor
and the spirit of the war veterans grew cold? You talk of the places
that they are now meeting. True, they have meeting places that would
shame any organization. And it was to get away from that type of
meeting place, it was to put the veterans' organizations into the type
of home that they properly belong in, so that they might stimulate
the patriotic motives of this community, that they wanted this
memorial hall. And we waited for seven years. And then our enthusiasm became very low, I will admit. And we became very discour-
aged. All of this time there was money on hand; you had more than
a million dollars; you could have put up a building to house us,
and then gone out and put up the other building, or you could have
started something that would have indicated that there was going to
be progress in the work. But nothing was done. And do not think
that we were not trying to get information. We tried through our
committee, through everything possible, to get information from your
Board of War Memorial Trustees. The information was not forthcoming. As a matter of fact, we came here tonight thinking that we
were going to get an accounting of your stewardship, of everything
that had been entrusted to you, and we did get a history of the thing,
but not an accounting of what had been accomplished. And we have
always attempted to find out, from the Board of War Memorial Trustees, as to when that project was going to be put forward. Why,
when the time came for the $4,000,000 bond issue, we could have come
before this Board of Supervisors and said to them, "Gentlemen, we
are tired of this situation; we have waited in vain for a building

that would properly house our activities," and you know, as Mayor Rolph said, that the Supreme Court held that an opera house could not be built privately on city land; but the Supreme Court held that the city can build a War Memorial Building, and the late Judge Lennon said. in his decision, that it serves the most patriotic motives of the community, because what is more necessary in a community than the building up of a spirit of loyalty and patriotism to this country? And that has always been entrusted to the organizations composed of those men who served this country in time of war. It is those men who are called upon, despite their war service, to keep on with that service and build up that spirit in a community. And we are called upon to do that, but we wanted to do it in proper surroundings; and if, in May of 1927, we had come to this Board and stated, "Gentlemen, we are loath to any longer support the War Memorial, as it consists of an opera house with facilities for other musical organizations, we merely want a war memorial that will cost not more than a million and a half or two million dollars, that will be a housing place for veteran organizations," I feel quite sure, in my own heart, Mr. Drum, that this Board of Supervisors would have assented to that proposition, and there would have been no $4,000,000 bond issue placed on the ballot. But we did not want to take that attitude. We wanted the whole project completed. And we went forward and supported your measure. We did want to protect ourselves, however, because we had not been able to get proper information from your Board of Trustees. You talked 40,000 feet, and then in expanding measure. You said that that was the amount that the American Legion agreed to. True it was, but it was not the amount presented by the American Legion. We wanted more space, but it was pointed out to us in the origin that the money then on hand would have only permitted us to have this space, and that, if we had to get more, it would have been at the sacrifice of the other organizations. That amount of 40,000 square feet was not an original proposal from the American Legion; it was the result of barter and bargaining between the representatives of our Board and the representatives of the American Legion. We finally acceded to that in the same spirit of sacrifice and willingness to co-operate with all of the other units that we have shown the past eight years.

And so I say, when this bond issue came up we wanted to protect ourselves, and all the veteran organizations, too. And they came before the Board, and the Board passed a measure pledging themselves to protect the veteran organizations in their allotment of space. Now I am not going into the history of Amendment No. 32, except to answer one statement that you made when you stated that there was ample opportunity given for a presentation of that measure before the Board of Supervisors, so that anybody who was interested in it could have come up probably and opposed it. You did not say that, but that was the inference in your suggestion.

THE CHAIRMAN: I did not say that.

MR. SAPIRO: Did you know, Mr. Drum, that the Judiciary Committee of this Board of Supervisors sat for several months before that time, receiving charter amendments, holding space open for Charter Amendment No. 32, relating to the War Memorial, but it was not brought before them. It was not brought before a committee of this Board of Supervisors, where it could have been considered properly, in the right spirit, and with everybody having an opportunity to know about it. But it was first brought to the attention of this Board at 11 o'clock that night, on the next to the last day on which charter amendments could be submitted, and none of the war veteran organizations knew anything about it until after it had been placed on the ballot; and I doubt whether it would have been so placed if certain assurances, which we believe were distinctly incorrect, were not given this Board of Supervisors at that time.

THE CHAIRMAN: I was not in the State.

MR. SAPIRO: I do not say that you gave the assurance. I do not want any one to misunderstand me. I want to make that absolutely clear, Mr. Drum, so that you will not misunderstand me. I do not say that the statements came from you, but the persons who presented them—and I do not know that they were authorized by you.

THE CHAIRMAN: The only one who presented the matter was Mr. Hall, representing in a legal sense this Board, and Mr. O'Toole, the City Attorney, they regarding it merely as an amendment to legalize the prosecuting of this work—nothing else.

MR. SAPIRO: Of course, we could not see, even from a legal sense, why the city could not accept the money and the lands without the necessity of creating a Board of Trustees.

THE CHAIRMAN: Mr Martin tells me—I was not here—that the Legion was notified and did not appear.

MR. SAPIRO: That is incorrect; that statement is incorrect; the Legion was not notified, nor were any of the other veteran organizations that were interested in this project. Now, the fact is, Mr. Drum, you cannot take the result of that campaign as an issue with the people because, although you had the unanimous support of the newspapers, which was given on the theory that the failure to carry that thing through would have stopped the progress of this work for two years, as a matter of fact that was a very unfortunate argument. It convinced the newspapers and got their support. But unfortunately it is not a true argument, because you propose this evening, if I understand the gist of your remarks, that the Mayor forbear the appointment of the Board of Trustees under the new charter amendment, and that we go ahead with this project with the same old setup that we have had before.

THE CHAIRMAN: Oh, I did not make myself clear, Mr. Sapiro. My point was that the Mayor postpone; but it is not an indefinite postponement, but simply a postponement for a sufficient length of time for your Legion committee and all of the veteran bodies to state their reasons, in conjunction with the Board of Trustees, and see whether or not they cannot come to such an adjustment and agreement whereby the work can immediately go forward; that was the point.

MR. SAPIRO: Of course, you understand that the Mayor cannot appoint immediately anyway. The matter has to go before the Legislature for ratification.

THE CHAIRMAN: That is even a better reason why we should get together.

MR. SAPIRO: Which would probably take some time. I may state also it is rather difficult for us to understand why, since the money on the $4,000,000 bond issue has been available since May, 1927, and since at that time a representative of the Board of Trustees of the War Memorial came before the American Legion and asked us to approve the plans for the War Memorial building, or for the whole project, which was then completed by the architects, and stated, as a reason for asking us, that it was necessary, in order to alleviate the unemployment situation. We wanted to help in that. We had always shown a willingness to co-operate, and although the plans were not entirely satisfactory, we gave our approval of those plans. After our approval was given, subject to the two contingencies which you mentioned, you changed the plans. You stated that we repudiated—and you used that very harsh word—our former approval. I have here a copy of the letter that was sent to you, Mr. Drum, or to your Board. And I want to say that the Legion has never at any time repudiated any action that it has taken. The Legion just told you this——

THE CHAIRMAN (interrupting): I did not mean to infer that, Mr. Sapiro.

MR. SAPIRO: That word was used, and I just want—we are not going to be placed wrong in the eyes of anybody.

THE CHAIRMAN: I will withdraw the word; it was only a quick expression in an extemporaneous speech; all I meant to infer was: the Legion wanted to have the plans reviewed.

MR. SAPIRO: We disapproved the new plans; that was the correct situation. Now, we have never at any time taken the attitude that we will not sit down with the Board of Trustees, or with any other body or group that has to do with this Memorial, and work out the proper solution of the same. We have had, in our own behalf, one or two things put over on us. But even then that has not taken away from us the desire to forward the progress of this city, and if you meant, and your board meant what you said in your speech, and you desire to co-operate, and that no one activity should have dominance over the other, we can very well get together. Of course, you do not expect us here, at a meeting on a night like this, at a meeting where nobody was told in advance what it was to consist of, to sit down with you and say, "We want this reviewed or that reviewed." And if you want to know the spirit of the Legion, that is the spirit, and we are perfectly willing to co-operate with your group, or any other group, in order to see this War Memorial erected, and erected at the earliest possible date. (Applause.)

THE CHAIRMAN: I think that is fine, Mr. Sapiro, your last statement of not only a willingness, but a desire to co-operate. I think that will serve the entire purpose of this meeting, naturally at a date when we can sit down and review things thoroughly. As you very properly said, while I have always in most of my remarks spoken of the Legion, I necessarily included all the veterans' organizations. Mr. Boyd, I believe, in the United Veterans' organization, is the spokesman for the major part of the personnel or numbers at least of the other veteran organizations, and I think, Mr. Boyd, that the meeting would like to hear from you.

MR. BOYD: I want to say at the outset, Mr. Drum, that the United Veterans' Council is taking this position insofar as your Trustees are concerned, and we are taking this position wholly without any desire to appear disrespectful, but we maintain that, in view of the fact that the American Legion is the only veteran organization that is mentioned as a beneficiary in the trust agreement, that, insofar as your board is concerned, no other veteran organization is a beneficiary and has any rights, and having no rights, no other veteran organization can be damaged in any way or suffer any wrong at your hands. That is our position. It may be our position is not well taken; nevertheless it is our position and we will maintain it. We take the further position that, if our comrades of the American Legion have no confidence in the Board of Trustees that they have been in close association with for seven years, then it would be hardly right to expect that the other veteran organizations in San Francisco would place ourselves in your hands. And that, again, is said in all friendliness.

THE CHAIRMAN: Good fellowship.

MR. BOYD: The United Veterans' Council and the rest of the veteran organizations of San Francisco feel that our court of appeal is the Board of Supervisors. We feel that they are our representatives, they are the direct representatives of the people of San Francisco, and we feel that, inasmuch as the armed forces of the United States have always come direct from the people, that it is thoroughly proper for us to go to the direct representatives of the people. That is our position. Therefore, I must take up your remarks, Mr. Drum, from the time when you appealed to the people. When your group found they were unable to raise sufficient money to carry out their plans, you said that they had three courses open to them: One was to abandon, the other was to secure more money from private subscribers, and the third was to appeal to the taxpayers. The United Veterans'

Council asks that, regardless of who completes the War Memorial, if it be your present group or a group which the Mayor is to appoint under Charter Amendment 32, or it is the Board of Supervisors, we' ask that the pledge made to the people of San Francisco when you appealed to them for funds that you could not get elsewhere, that that pledge be kept. The pledge is of record.

THE CHAIRMAN: The pledge was based upon the facts then given to the Supervisors and presented to the Board of Public Works; that was the segregation of the bond money under the bond issue.

MR. BOYD: Let us see what the facts are, Mr. Drum. This is the argument in favor of the progress bonds, mailed to every voter in San Francisco for the bond election of June 14, 1927.

SUPERVISOR MARKS: Signed by whom?

MR. BOYD: I will come to that presently. Under the heading "War Memorial" it says, "The land for the War Memorial is bought and $1,200,000 cash is waiting in the bank. Thus the people of this city, by issuing $4,000,000 in bonds, will gain a beautiful public project costing almost $7,000,000. The rest is already donated privately or given by the city. The group of buildings occupying two entire blocks on one side of Van Ness avenue, with the City Hall opposite, would greatly beautify our city. The purpose, to commemorate our heroes of the war, is idealistic and patriotic. The utilitarian value of these buildings alone merits their construction. One of them will be the veterans' building, housing all the veterans' organiations in San Francisco." Now, I want to mark very carefully the next sentence. "It was to give these splendid organizations a permanent headquarters, in the name of the public which honors their deeds, that the War Memorial fund originally was launched." And the argument continues, "The other building will contain San Francisco's long-needed symphony hall and opera auditorium; art gallery and museum features also are included in the plant." And that says the other building. Well, Supervisor Marks has asked me whose names are signed to that. I will read them. "Hesse C. Colman, Andrew J. Gallagher, Frank R. Havenner, Emmet Hayden, Milo Kent, James B. McSheehy, Milton Marks, Charles J. Powers, Alfred Roncovieri, Walter J. Schmidt, Warren Shannon, William B. Stanton, Charles F. Todd, Supervisors. Approved, James Rolph Jr., Mayor." And further, "The foregoing arguments are approved and adopted by the Citizens' Campaign Committee of San Francisco for the San Francisco progress bonds." Signed, "Charles H. Kendrick, Chairman." Some other names follow; I will call just a couple of them: "Milton Esberg, Frank Kilsby, James D. Phelan, Matt I Sullivan." That was the argument put forward to the people of San Francisco when the $4,000,000 bond issue was asked. Not to repeat, but simply for the purpose of record, two of the present War Memorial Trustees, two members of this committee, approved that argument when it went to the people. You went to the people direct for money when you could not get it elsewhere. We come direct to the representatives of the people when, after seven years, the veterans of San Francisco, the American Legion as well as all the other veterans' organizations, are impatient at the delay. You told us tonight, Mr. Drum, that there never was an intention to give a preference to a given group. We will discard this argument. That clearly shows that there was an intention to give a preference to a given group. And we will go to Bill No. 8003, Ordinance No. 7516, which is the ordinance that authorizes the bonds, and it says: "The construction, completion and equipment of permanent buildings in or adjacent to the Civic Center of the City and County of San Francisco, to be used as a memorial hall for war veterans"; a given group is given preference under the ordinance which the people approved.

SUPERVISOR MARKS: Is that the title that you are reading?

MR. BOYD: No; the title is very long, but the title also includes that "to be used as a memorial hall for war veterans."

SUPERVISOR MARKS: Does it refer to an opera house?

MR. BOYD: It makes no mention of an opera house. It says, "For educational, recreational, entertainment and other municipal purposes." Possibly the Police Department could use the basement as a shooting gallery; that is certainly a municipal purpose. It is there in the ordinance. (Laughter and applause.)

Now, Mr. Drum,.I am representing fourteen organizations, and they are not strong numerically. And yet I believe that they are as strong numerically as the Art Association; I believe that they are as strong numerically as the San Francisco Opera Association. The Mayor very pertinently asks if we could guarantee $500,000 to bring the Metropolitan Opera Company, or any other opera company, to San Francisco, and I regret very much to say that we are not in a position to make such a guaranty. I make that statement for the purpose of the record. However——

THE CHAIRMAN (interrupting): How strong are you with your fourteen organizations, Mr. Boyd?

MR. BOYD: That would be rather difficult to say offhand, because I am speaking now for organizations of which I am not a member in any way. I am a member of only one organization, the Veterans of Foreign Wars, and I am a veteran of the World War; would have been of the Spanish-American War, only I was 8 years old the day it was declared. And I think it is worthy of comment, too, that there is no intention on the part of my friends of the American Legion, and there is no intention on my part to wave the flag. We have been soldiers, sailors, marines, because we happened to be born at the right time. If we had been born a little earlier, we would have been too old to go to war, and if we had been born a little later we would have been too young to go to war. Our age was an accident that gave us a chance to earn a title, the title of "veteran," which never can be taken away from us. (Applause.) We do not have to go to the people for a vote; it is always ours. The Supervisors, they become ex-Supervisors; possibly members of your Board of War Memorial Trustees become ex-trustees, but we remain veterans. (Applause.)

You said one thing tonight, Mr. Drum, and I realize that you were speaking extemporaneously, just as I am, and that possibly in an extemporaneous argument one makes a statement that, when you read it over in the transcript it looks differently than you meant it to sound. But, as I understand your statement tonight, you said that your Board of Trustees could do only that which they believed to be their duty as Trustees, and if I understood you correctly, you intimated that if the veteran organizations of San Francisco did not see their duty to be the same as your duty, that your Board of Trustees could only do one thing: you could retain your title to that property over there, and that you could give back the money to the people that subscribed it, and that this entire project would fall to the ground. You are placing the burden upon the veteran organizations. If we make a selection of our own rather than following your dictates, then that will be your attitude. And I do not think you meant that, Mr. Drum.

THE CHAIRMAN: I did not say it, Mr. Boyd. What I did say was this: that the private subscription fund for the public purpose contemplated given purposes to cost given sums of money; that the bond issue was predicated upon such additional sum of money and such a segregation of the expenditure of that money that will accomplish all of those purposes, and that I did not put any burden on the veterans. I did say that if any fact or circumstance should arise whereby the Trustees, responsible for $2,000,000 of money or property, found the enterprise in a position where those purposes cannot go forward, as confirmed by the Board of Supervisors, with the documents on file with the Board of Public Works before the election of June 11, then our Trustees would be in the position where they could not go forward with the amount of money which was subscribed for a general

purpose, for all of these purposes. I was not trying to put any burden on the veterans; I was only showing that the public purposes of all
of these activities, under the plans by which the money was raised,
would have to go on that way or it could not be accomplished according
to our trust.

MR. BOYD: That puts a different aspect on it, I think, Mr. Drum.
I was going to ask the reporter to read it, but it is not necessary.
There is only one thing I would like to say in conclusion, and it is
this: the Mayor has spoken of the love we all have for San Francisco.
My comrade, Milton Sapiro, has pointed out that certain members of
our organization have shown their affection for their city in a very
substantial way. And that is true. That takes care of the group at
this table and it takes care of the group at the other table. But there
is another group and they are not at any table. When you talk about
memorials, you do not build them for the living; you do not build memorials so that music and culture and the elegancies of life can be indulged in. Memorials are built, as I understand the word, to dead
men. (Applause.) You do not need any applause on that one because
of the men that are dead; they did not die amid cultural surroundings or refinements or elegancies of any kind. (Applause.)

THE CHAIRMAN: Just a word in reply to that, Mr. Boyd: Wouldn't
you agree with me that if those dead men could come back, and by
reason of their death they could find those things done in this community that would make better living men and women, that they
would feel their death was worth while and they had not been sacrificed?

MR. BOYD: Provided they did not think that the veterans' cause
had been cashed in to get $4,000,000 from the taxpayers when the
money could not be raised elsewhere. (Applause.)

THE CHAIRMAN: I have no reply to make to that, but I was going
to ask, Mr. Boyd, what is your suggestion, as Mr. Sapiro has made the
suggestion, of a co-operation whereby we can see that this great public enterprise goes forward? Have you any suggestion?

MR. BOYD: Yes, that there be no delay in making operative Charter Amendment 32, which was proposed, not by our group, but by
yours, that the Legislature ratify Charter Amendment 32, and that his
Honor, the Mayor, appoint members to that commission in accordance
with the dictates of Charter Amendment 32, and that this Board of
Supervisors, if I may make a suggestion to them, stand firmly behind
the vote that they took on Monday of this week, and see that six ex-
service men are named on that commission. That is my suggestion.

THE CHAIRMAN: Are there any other gentlemen present who wish
to speak?

SUPERVISOR HAVENNER: I happen to be the author of the resolution adopted last year, which pledged this Board of Supervisors, by
unanimous vote, adopted by unanimous vote—I am not trying to make
a speech, ladies and gentlemen; I merely want to restate a few facts—
I happen to be the author of the resolution adopted by the Board of
Supervisors by unanimous vote last year, which pledges this Board
not to expend any of the moneys voted by the people of San Francisco
for the War Memorial until such time as the official plans for the
project have been approved by the majority of the duly constituted
representatives of the war veterans' organizations of San Francisco.
I introduced that resolution, having in mind the argument which has
just been read to you by Mr. Boyd, which was advanced as a paramount argument at the time these bonds were submitted to the people
of San Francisco. There is no question that these bonds were sold
to you, the people of San Francisco, for the purpose of building a war
memorial. (Applause.) There was a deliberate subordination of reference, during that bond campaign, to the opera house. Now, I approve of
the opera house. I happen to be a good deal of a music lover. I think
it is a fine thing that we are going to have an opera house, but the

political tactics that were used at that time were unethical if there
was, in the minds of anybody at that time, an intention to use a majority of that money for the opera house as against the completion of
a war memorial building. Now, there is not any doubt about it; every
member of this Board of Supervisors knows that that is the fact. The
thing was discussed in campaign meetings and it was a deliberate
adoption of policy that we would not stress the opera house and that
this was to be for the War Memorial. Otherwise, in my humble opinion, these bonds might not have succeeded at all. They certainly would
not have succeeded by the majority which they received.

As an ex-officio prerequisite of my office here on the Board of Supervisors, I was appointed here by somebody or other this last year
as a member of this Board of Trustees of the War Memorial. I did not
attend the meetings, and I do not say this with any disparagement to
the gentlemen who conducted those meetings; they were busy; it had
been their custom to hold these meetings down town. My position,
however, so far as my personal action was concerned, was that this
had now been removed from the realm of private control into the
realm of public control; that the principal element of money to be
used is money entrusted by the people of San Francisco to the Board
of Supervisors for expenditure and that these meetings should be held
publicly in the public meeting place of the city government, which is
the City Hall. That view has recently been acceded to. But during all
of that time arrangements apparently went ahead to complete plans
for these two buildings, to be paid for by private subscription, which
I think was a very fine thing, and the public subscription amounting
to just about double the amount of the private subscription. This
Board of Supervisors has never had any progressive definite information as to what the details of these plans were. I say that, and I challenge any contradiction from my colleagues; they know that to be true.
There have been occasional reports to us, but we have been as much
in the dark, and perhaps more in the dark than the veterans have been
concerning these plans. And I say, with all respect to these gentlemen
who have done a very fine thing in raising this private subscription,
that their methods have been wrong, and that in my judgment that
mistake in procedure is very largely responsible for the regrettable
conflict of opinion that confronts us today. Now, I introduced two
weeks ago, after the passage of Charter Amendment No. 32, the resolution to which Mr. Drum referred here tonight. It provides merely
that we, the Board of Supervisors, who are invested by the mandate
of the people in adopting Charter Amendment No. 32, with the responsibility of confirming the nominations which his Honor the Mayor
may make to this new official Board of War Memorial Trustees; it
merely respectfully requests and recommends that the Mayor appoint
on this Board of War Memorial Trustees a majority which have seen
service in some branch of the armed forces of the nation. It does not
specify that they be members of any veteran organization. It has no
reference to the American Legion or the Veterans of Foreign Wars or
any other veteran organization. I went further and I explained my
attitude in so doing again by the argument that was made to the voters,
officially, by this Board of Supervisors and by his Honor the Mayor
and by the various other organizations which were signatories thereto.
I suggested in this resolution that his Honor the Mayor get the advice. I did not ask that he be bound by it, but that he seek the counsel of the veterans' organizations, because they are the only organized
bodies which represent this great group of men and women who served
in the wars. I do not know where else he could go or we could go to
get advice of that kind. I think it is eminently proper that this great
group should be consulted concerning their representatives, and I think
they are entitled, by every element of good faith, in view of our argument to the people, to have a majority representation on this Board
of War Memorial Trustees. Now, I want to say that my position—I

might as well say it here, because I understand this meeting was called for a full discussion of this whole situation—my position as a member of the Board of Trustees will be to adhere strictly to the declaration of policy unanimously adopted last year: that none of this public money will be expended, regardless of who may go ahead privately to draw plans; none of this public money will be expended, with my vote, until such time as these organized groups have been consulted. (Applause.) And through them, the only medium which we can consult, we may obtain an idea as to the attitude of the veterans themselves, the great group of veterans, as to the recognition which they think they should receive in this Memorial that was voted by the people for them. Now, that will be done, gentlemen, I think, by a majority of this Board. I think their past actions have clearly indicated it. And I think one of the things that ought to be decided in the immediate future is to bring these things out in the realm even of semi-private control—and I say that without any disrespect, but I submit it to you as a practical proposition; this conflict and this disagreement is going to continue so long as private plans are carried out to completion before they are submitted to the elected representatives of the people here. And that is not said with any jealousy of my prerogatives as a Supervisor; it is not because I want to have a say, but because I insist that this thing be done in a public fashion, in accordance with the intention of the charter of this City and the intention of the voters when they voted that money. I therefore disagree flatly with the recommendation made by Mr. Drum tonight that the Mayor should defer action on Charter Amendment No. 32. I respectfully suggest to your Honor that you have no right—I say that in no personal sense—that you nor no other Mayor would have a right to defer action on a mandate from the people that a Board of Trustees be appointed, particularly when the reason advanced or suggested is that we should settle these problems in private conference. Now, I want the advice and counsel of the veterans' organizations; but I want them given to the duly constituted Board which is going to take charge of this project, so far as both funds are concerned, in the immediate future. And I suggest to you, respectfully, that it would be a very serious mistake in the eyes of all the people of San Francisco, so soon as they shall become familiar with these facts, to defer action on Charter Amendment No. 32, your Honor. I would like to say just this additional thing to you, Mr. Mayor: in your statement commending Mr. Drum's speech here tonight, and pointing out to the war veterans the recognition that you think is due to this fine group of citizens for their generous contributions to this very worthy project, you asked them how they could possibly further the production of opera in the War Memorial building if they were on the Board of Trustees. Well, they would not have a thing to do with that, your Honor. The Opera Association is a private association which has to bear its own financial guarantees, and there is nothing in Charter Amendment No. 32, or in any other power of this city and county government at this time, by which we are committed to any support of opera. We are going ahead with this opera building, we are going to put up a building there, but there has never been any provision made for any municipal support of opera up to this time, and it does not make any difference whether they are war veterans or these gentlemen or any of this group of citizens out here. They would not underwrite any opera that comes in there. So I merely point that out to you respectfully, because it will have no bearing whatever on the whole situation. The opera will be either carried out as at present by the Opera Association, a private organization, or with the remote possibility that some time in the future the City itself might see fit to subsidize opera. (Applause.)

THE CHAIRMAN: I express the same respect for the views of Supervisor Havenner that he has expressed for mine, but I think for the sake of the record it is only fair to point out two things to the Supervisor: one is, he says that at the moment that a bond issue is passed where public moneys are to be spent that there should be a public hearing. Not a dollar of public money has been spent or has been attempted to be spent. It is perfectly usual to meet in that place which is of convenience, and for years we have met down town, simply because all the members of the committee, or most of them, are down town. We are not a public committee, we are not spending the public's money, we have not attempted to go forward on any private enterprise where anybody is committed to a set of plans prepared by a private corporation to be forced upon the public expenditure of money. But we have been asked before this Board of Supervisors twice to explain what we have been doing since June of 1927. We have had representatives of the veterans' organizations here, urging us to proceed in the preparation of those plans. The plans that we have prepared—they are about 80· per cent complete—are plans that have been prepared without a dollar of money spent by any bond issue voted by the people. If there is any one that has any objection to the expenditure of money thus far, it is those who have subscribed privately to the amount of money other than the bond issue. It would seem to me, under those circumstances, that it is hardly a fair comment to put, either upon that expenditure or the place of meeting the aspect on the part of this committee of the endeavor to discharge a public function in a private place.

SUPERVISOR HAVENNER: May I not ask whether the committee has not gone ahead to prepare complete plans for the entire project?

THE CHAIRMAN: It has.

SUPERVISOR HAVENNER: Those plans have not been prepared, as would be necessary under the terms of this charter, I think, by the duly constituted agents of the city government, the City Engineer's office, or his architects.

THE CHAIRMAN: We thought we had the Legion organizations and the other veteran organizations, or rather the Legion organization, pass and approve those plans last March; that was our thought at that time.

SUPERVISOR HAVENNER: I do not want to do any injustice to anybody, Mr. Drum; I want to be frank, however. I attended the meeting that your Trustees held out here in the City Hall shortly after Charter Amendment No. 32 was adopted. At that time I was advised that plans were under way for the letting of a contract for the foundation of these buildings.

THE CHAIRMAN: That is correct.

SUPERVISOR HAVENNER: I am a layman, but I cannot understand how it would be possible for your board, before this new official Board of Trustees goes into existence, and before this Board of Supervisors commences to spend public moneys, how it would be possible for your board to let a contract for the foundations of both of these buildings, out of the money under your control, without committing us almost irrevocably to the necessity of building the rest of the buildings to fit your foundation plans, and if that does not commit us to a procedure, I do not understand the whole thing. I have consulted engineers and the building department of this City and they tell me, "Yes, we would be committed if that were ever done."

THE CHAIRMAN: I agree with you in every statement made. It would be impossible to do that without committing you, but the invitation to bid was not the letting of bids, and with these statements made as to haste and to get forward at that meeting which you attended, I merely stated that we desired to invite bids for that work. We have not, by the invitation to these bids we have not authorized that work, and when this matter assumed the shape that it has, as between the requests of the veteran organizations and the Board of Supervisors, we purposely postponed for two weeks, until December 20, the opening of bids. If this situation continues, we won't open any bids, and we won't authorize a dollar of work. The matter is entirely in our hands in the sense of neither committing the public nor committing those who subscribed privately to that money. But we did gain a matter of two or three weeks; we expected this excavation work would be finished some time between the 10th and 20th of December, under their contract, so that if, with time of the essence, that we would at least be in shape to avoid the delay of thirty to forty days in the invitation for bids. We agree perfectly, but no one is committed and no one intended to commit any one. The next point, I think, for the sake of the record, Supervisor, that it would only be fair for me to state, and that is you said that you challenged any one to produce any evidence of having explained fully what the plans and costs of these buildings were. We appeared, after the meeting with the publishers and before the bond issue, before an informal meeting in the Mayor's office, at which the entire Board of Supervisors was invited—I do not know whether you were there or not. We then held two subsequent meetings with the Finance Committee, and I think you were there at that time. I happened to be the spokesman, and I outlined in every detail the cost of both buildings, taking the area of both buildings, taking the purposes of both buildings, and I was asked by the city authorities to see that it would be put in proper shape and filed with the Board of Public Works, where it is on file now, with such specific detail that the Supervisors would thereby be putting a confirmation on the purposes of the bond issue, both as to how the money would be spent and on what purposes. Those papers are on file today. I only want to make both of those points, because I believe the record should state the facts.

SUPERVISOR GALLAGHER: Mr. Drum, could I ask you this question: I think we all share the idea that we would like to see the work go forward and, after all, I think we have heard a good deal of the history tonight that we did not know. Without going into the question of criticism, do you think now there has been presented enough evidence to your Board of Trustees to indicate that perhaps there is a feeling, a suspicion, whether justified or not, that the plans and the preparation of the plans has been all too unconsciously private for the good of the project?

THE CHAIRMAN: I would say, Supervisor Gallagher, in answer to that, the following: that no criticism or no suggestion by any member of any of the veteran organizations, acting under the resolution of the Board of Supervisors of June 7, 1927, that they should approve, that nothing of a disapproving character has occurred regarding the amount of square footage that they have had; the only thing is the nature of criticism they did not have a completed building, even though, if that additional wing was put up, they could not occupy the space. At the meeting last August, called for the express purpose, at which all the veteran organizations were present, there was not a single claim made—it was then 105,000 square feet—that 105,000 square feet would not serve every possible housing problem that all the veterans' organizations in San Francisco had. The only point that was made as a point of criticism was, "You finished the opera house as a building and you have not finished the veterans' building; we want as good a building as the opera house."

SUPERVISOR GALLAGHER: Is that the fact? I am trying to grip this, and perhaps I may be dull; is it a fact that, as things stand, as the plans are drawn, and as money is available, taking both moneys, that the opera house will be a completed building and the veterans' building, so called, will not be?

THE CHAIRMAN: It is according to the definition of what is complete and incomplete. You can tour this country and you can find monumental buildings, completed only to the extent of one-third of what the veterans' building is, and regarded as completed buildings. The whole idea on a monumental building is, do not add any more square footage to the cost of the building until you can use the contents. This is a pretty rich city, and we have had a library that, if this building is not completed, with a little strip fifty feet by two hundred on McAllister Street and Franklin unfinished, then the library across the street is very far from being completed. It is according to the definition of what is completed. I would say that the building is eminently completed. Of course, one thing that has been overlooked in this discussion, and that is that the memorial court from the St. Ignatius lot, of 8,000 square feet, has been made into a memorial court opposite the City Hall of 150 by 350 feet, about 52,000 square feet.

SUPERVISOR GALLAGHER: Could you say to me again, in money, what the so-called or presumed incompleted portion of the building would cost?

THE CHAIRMAN: Five hundred and forty thousand dollars.

SUPERVISOR GALLAGHER: Would that reconcile the difference as to space?

THE CHAIRMAN: Pardon me?

SUPERVISOR GALLAGHER: Would that reconcile the difference as to space?

THE CHAIRMAN: As I have understood the argument, it would reconcile their ideas of a completed building, but they would not need the space after it was completed, and so stated.

SUPERVISOR GALLAGHER: Is that last statement correct?

MR. BURNS: That statement was never made.

SUPERVISOR GALLAGHER: Is the statement made by Mr. Drum, that $500,000 would complete the building to your satisfaction and as to space, is that correct?

MR. BOYD: As to the amount of money, Mr. Gallagher? The principal thing, if it was a completed building, would the veterans be satisfied?

SUPERVISOR GALLAGHER: With the space situation now?

MR. SAPIRO: No, it is not a question of more space; it is a question of proper plans. We approved a set of plans; we stand by that approval. The Board of Trustees changed those plans after the approval was given; we disapproved the subsequent plans.

SUPERVISOR MARKS: What were the changes made after your approval generally?

MR. BOYD: May I make this point——

THE CHAIRMAN (interrupting): Pardon me, could I hear the answer to that question?

SUPERVISOR MARKS: One set of plans was approved at one time, I understood you to say, in August. .

THE CHAIRMAN: In March of this year, 1928.

MR. BURNS: Mr. Hotchner is the Chairman of the Plans Subcommittee.

MR. HOTCHNER: I would like to explain that Mr. Drum is slightly in error in the statement that we were eminently satisfied with 105,000 square feet. It just happened to figure that that is the square footage that was there. It never was set by us. There are forty-odd organizations to be housed in that building. On our attempt to get, or rather to obtain the footage that would be required for all of these organizations, we were informed by a member of the Trustees that this information should not be obtained at that time, due to the fact that dissension might occur that we, the Legion, were the only beneficiaries under the trust agreement, and we were the only ones that they were looking to at that time. Answering your direct question as to whether or not we would be satisfied if this building was finished, the statement has been made to us that, if that section was finished it would not be available for veterans; that it would go to the other occupants of the building. Now, this building was cut down— I will answer Mr. Marks' question—this building was cut down after we approved the plans; ten feet was removed from the building.

Then, to offset this footage, a mezzanine, absolutely impracticable for useful purposes, was inserted. The .plans now show practically, I believe, 1,000 square feet more than what we approved. That, in a way, would seem to be more footage than we originally approved, but that is offset by a mezzanine that was inserted in the section of the building that is supposed to be the State headquarters for all of the organizations, making not only that square footage unusable, but the square footage below it unusable.

MR. BOYD: May I make this point, please, simply for the purpose of the record and the information of the Board: All of the discussion as to the plans being approved or disapproved, all of the discussion as to the space being acceptable or not acceptable, thus far has been entirely by the American Legion. The other fourteen veteran organizations have never seen a set of plans, have never had a statement as to the space available, and have no opinion of record with your Committee, or with anyone else, as to whether or not they are satisfied; and those other fourteen organizations are most certainly included in Supervisor Havenner's resolution of June 6, 1927.

THE CHAIRMAN: Mr. Boyd, the only answer I can make to that is——

MR. BOYD (interrupting):   It was not a question; it was a statement of fact.

THE CHAIRMAN: The only answer I can make in reply to that statement of fact is that, after the bond issue was passed, the amount of space figured was then 65,000 square feet. It was then increased to 107,000 or 108,000 square feet. I do not know what the contract was, but I know those representatives of the Legion on our committee were in contact with a number of veteran organizations; they were bringing us in every week a number of organizations. I assumed that they had some contact whereby they knew the number, because the number increased from sixteen veteran posts—I mean Legion posts—to sixty-one separate organizations, with the statements made as to the space they had to occupy and the number of lodge rooms that there should be.

MR. BOYD: That is quite true; but the fact remains that none of those organizations have ever seen a set of plans, nor have they ever been told, by anyone speaking with authority, as to the space that would be available for them in that building.

SUPERVISOR GALLAGHER: Mr. Boyd, could I ask a question? Is it not a fact that the American Legion is the only beneficiary mentioned in the trust agreement? Is there now being and ready to act a comprehensive and authoritative committee, or set of gentlemen, representing, besides the American Legion, all of the groups of which you speak, and, I presume, who are signed to this letter?

MR. BOYD: There is now, and there has been continuously such a group for the past ten years, Supervisor.

SUPERVISOR GALLAGHER: In other words, if a way were found to open some doors here that some people think are closed and others think are open; if somebody was asked to call groups together to settle, if we can, this thing, to the end that the work will go forward, there is now in being a constituted representative body authorized to speak for all of the veterans—that is, I mean, it is joined with the Legion?

MR. BOYD: Exactly. We are co-operating with the Legion, and we are in daily contact with our own duly constituted groups. We are a committee of five, and ready to proceed at any time to contact the other groups, show them what there is, and secure their approval or their disapproval; and I have made that proposition to one of the members of the War Memorial Trustees already, Mr. Gallagher. I made it, in fact, as far back as last March.

SUPERVISOR GALLAGHER: I am not clear yet. Every war veteran organization entitled to consideration in respect to this War

Memorial is, as I understand it, represented in one group, duly and regularly appointed.

MR. BOYD: Exactly. Let me make this analogy, and I know it will be clear to you: The American Legion, we will say, for the sake of this example, the American Legion's council can be compared to the Building Trades Council, and the United Veterans' Council can be compared to the Labor Council. Now, if you had a matter that concerned labor, you would call in the leaders from the Building Trades Council, the duly elected officers, and the Labor Council. And if there is ever a proposition to be made with regard to this War Memorial, it is a fact that has been known to the War Memorial Trustees for a long time they·could call in the War Memorial Committee of the County Council of the American Legion on the one hand, and the War Memorial Committee of the United Veteran Council on the other hand——

SUPERVISOR McSHEEHY: I am going to ask for a recess for ten minutes.

SUPERVISOR GALLAGHER: Get the page.

SUPERVISOR RONCOVIERI: If the Mayor can stand it, we ought to stand it.

THE MAYOR: Page 48, let me finish this. ——"and the War Memorial Committee of the United Veteran Council on the other hand, and the groups are not large; it is not a huge mob of men, and they can sit down together. But that has never been done."

SUPERVISOR GALLAGHER: Do you consider, then—and I am going to ask Mr. Drum a question in a moment—do you consider, or does anybody consider that represents these groups, that you have reached an impasse on this question of War Memorial plans?

MR. BOYD: Why, not at all.

SUPERVISOR GALLAGHER: Now, Mr. Drum, what is the intention of your War Memorial Trustees looking to, and being temporarily in charge of the situation, looking to bringing together these representative groups that will have a decisive say in this matter?

THE CHAIRMAN: A desire to have whatever is the representative of the sixty-five or sixty-six veteran organizations sit down and show where they can use any more square footage than 108,000 square feet, and likewise have them take the position that they have got a finished building when they have got the amount of building which takes care of 108,000 square feet.

SUPERVISOR GALLAGHER: Are you in an unyielding position in that regard?

THE CHAIRMAN: I am in no position at all.

SUPERVISOR GALLAGHER: I mean your Board?

THE CHAIRMAN: No. If the Supervisors desire, in the tax levy, or by an additional bond issue, to raise from half a million to three-quarters of a million, we will not only be glad to have the building completed, and $540,000 more paid, but give. all these Legion bodies the number of square feet, up to the discretion and judgment of the Board of Supervisors, if they will provide the money.

SUPERVISOR GALLAGHER: If the money is not provided, then do I get you clear—let us not misinterpret you—do I understand the attitude of the War Memorial Trustee Board you represent to be·that, unless more money is forthcoming, or unless they can be brought to an agreement with your mind, as you express it, that this is the end of the trail so far as you and your colleagues go?

THE CHAIRMAN: I will put it a little differently. We do not see how we are driven other than into the inevitable position that, if no more money is forthcoming, if the activities that have been approved by the people of this community in the other building are properly carried out, that there is no possible place where more square footage or more building cost can be added, other than by taking from the other building, which is to an irreducible minimum; and that we, not by reason of the Legion or Board of Supervisors or anybody else, but we, in the discharge of our duty as trustees, with all these various activities, have no means of carrying out to the people of this community a satisfactory accomplishment of all of these various purposes. It is simply a ground-hog case.

SUPERVISOR McSHEEHY: I move we recess for ten minutes. You have read for one hour and a quarter.

THE MAYOR: It does not seem like ten minutes.

SUPERVISOR RONCOVIERI: I object to a recess, and I do not want any ten minutes either, it will be twenty. As long as the Mayor can stand it we can stand it.

SUPERVISOR POWER: Let us go ahead.

THE MAYOR: I think the more I read——

SUPERVISOR RONCOVIERI (interrupting): The stronger you get.

THE MAYOR: The more I read the stronger this position is getting, that is a certainty in my own mind, and I want to tell you this: the best thing that has happened for this War Memorial is that I brought you the record. Will you announce when you want a recess and we will take it?

SUPERVISOR RONCOVIERI: I won't take one; I announce that now.

SUPERVISOR McSHEEHY: I am perfectly satisfied.

THE MAYOR: "Supervisor Havenner: May I ask you who has decided that the plans for the opera house have been brought down to an irreducible minimum?

"THE CHAIRMAN: The Board of Supervisors, the Mayor, the publishers of this city, acting in concert with us, and on their judgment and advice, in going forward with this bond issue."

Mind you, I appreciate your patience. It is your duty as Supervisors to listen, the responsibility is in your hands and I want to get through this record, which is just that little bit more, and then I get down to your resolution, passed by the Board of Supervisors, creating the committee of nine, you remember. Then you can stop and we go on from then when we put it in the hands of the committee of three and three and three and you added, as a compliment to me, you added me thereto and here I am tonight.

SUPERVISOR POWER: I move we have a call of the Board, Mr. Chairman.

SUPERVISOR GALLAGHER: I second that motion—while the report is read?

SUPERVISOR POWER: Yes.

SUPERVISOR GALLAGHER: And the Sergeant-at-Arms be instructed to call the members of the Board.

SUPERVISOR POWER: Go and get them wherever they are; get their home addresses.

THE MAYOR: Don't you think this is getting interesting as we go on? Don't you see the situation?

SUPERVISOR GALLAGHER: You are getting warm.

THE MAYOR: Anybody can see the situation now.

SUPERVISOR POWER: I want to say it is very interesting . to the new members. I presume the others have heard it, but I am very much concerned myself.

THE MAYOR: This is three years ago, and the committee that you put me on, we got action. We got down to an impasse, and I want to clear it up now and get those buildings going. If we stay here and listen to this, and get the report, you will vote quickly and I think the war veterans will say "Yes, put it in the hands of the Trustees and go ahead."

MR. GLENSOR: No.

THE MAYOR: All right, the Mayor is going to make the appointments anyway.

SUPERVISOR GALLAGHER: You have not hypnotized them yet.

SUPERVISOR HAVENNER: May I ask you who has decided that the plans for the opera house have been brought down to an irreducible minimum?

THE CHAIRMAN:

THE MAYOR: I would like to get down to the point where we began. I know I am detaining you, but I think I should finish. I am at page 100 and this report runs to 130, and then I get down to a resolution introduced by you on December 20th and from then on——

SUPERVISOR GALLAGHER (interrupting): Three, three and three.

THE MAYOR: Yes, three, three and three.

SUPERVISOR GALLAGHER: I think you ought to go to the three, three and three and then go on.

THE MAYOR: And then recess?

SUPERVISOR GALLAGHER: Yes.

THE MAYOR (reading):

THE CHAIRMAN: The Board of Supervisors, the Mayor, the publishers of this city, acting in concert with us, and on their judgment and advice, in going forward with this bond issue.

SUPERVISOR MARKS: On what occasion and by what act did the Board of Supervisors make that decision?

THE CHAIRMAN: They made it by having all of the facts presented to them as to what the size of the bond issue should be, what the money should be spent for, and how these things could be accomplished. And if it had not been by the action of the Board of Supervisors' confirmation of what was the expenditure of the irreducible minimum, being merely expressed in terms of building costs, we, as far as our activities are concerned, would not have asked for any bond issue, any more than we were stumped when we had $2,000,000 and no way of completing the enterprise.

SUPERVISOR MARKS: Was the Board of Supervisors advised at that time that, with the bond issue of $4,000,000, there would still be a disparity of about half a million dollars, as far as the Legion building was concerned?

THE CHAIRMAN: The Board of Supervisors were definitely informed that the $4,000,000 issue would take care of all of the activities that were then discussed and approved up to 65,000 square feet, devoted to veteran purposes. That was in April, when the Board of Supervisors authorized the bond issue. But eight days before the election, on June 7, Supervisor Havenner introduced a resolution, passed by the Board of Supervisors, which put upon the moneys subscribed privately in the bond issue a burden of an additional three or four hundred thousand dollars, and there was not thereby, by reason of that act, the same moneys which had been confirmed by the Board of Supervisors in April.

MR. SAPIRO: You have made a great deal of play about this additional area that has been given to the ex-service men over the 65,000 square feet that you registered down before the Board of Public Works. Isn't it a fact that practically that entire addition, or 33,000 square feet of it, comes about from the fact that you were making this excavation, and is basement space?

THE CHAIRMAN: No; 33,000 square feet is in the basement, and the other 75,000 is in the upper structure.

MR. SAPIRO: But the 33,000 is extra area that is merely basement excavation?

THE CHAIRMAN: There was always——

MR. HAVENNER: The bond election of June, 1927, was primarily proposed by this Board for the purpose of submitting to the people the Spring Valley purchase. The War Memorial bonds were brought in at that time and placed on the ballot as an added submission before the people by the group of which, I think, you were a member (referring to Mr. Drum), and, as is very customary in bond issues brought before us hastily, the plans and specifications were never explained in detail to this Board; and I challenge any contradiction of that statement, that the plans and specifications were ever brought in and explained in detail before this Board. It ought to be a fixed policy of this Board of Supervisors, and I have so declared before this Board since that time, since that experience, that this Board should never submit to the people any bond issue until every detail of that bond issue has been explained in full before the Board. In explanation, I might say that we had the right to believe this argument prepared and read here this evening was an argument in good faith, and we went ahead with the idea that this was primarily for the purpose of a War Memorial; and if we had not, I for one would not have done as I did. I may as well admit here and now, publicly, that this matter did not have the attention at that time it should have; but we are not bound, Mr. Drum, by any errors we may have committed, if any errors at that time. We have the opinion of the City Attorney; our City Attorney advises us we are not strictly bound by the terms of that act.

MR. BURNS: May we have an answer to the question of Mr. Sapiro? I would ask that the reporter, Mr. W. H. Girvin, read that question of Mr. Sapiro.

(Thereupon the question was read by the reporter.)

MR. SAPIRO: That was not exactly the question. You have made a great deal of play about this additional area that has been given to the ex-service men over the 60,000 square feet that you registered down before the Board of Public Works. Is it not a fact that practically that entire addition of 33,000 square feet additional has come about by reason of the fact that you are making this additional excavation?

MR. WAGSTAFF: Not entirely. There is a strip of 15,000 square feet in addition on Franklin Street; that was additional to the extra basement space.

MR. BURNS: How much does that amount to in the aggregate—that additional space outside of the basement?

MR. WAGSTAFF: And there is an additional fifty by fifty, due to the excavation in the basement.

MR. BURNS: As I understand it, there were some pillars in that basement originally. Is that correct?

MR. WAGSTAFF: There are.

MR. BURNS: Was it not contemplated, in connection with the War Memorial, to make a rearrangement of those pillars in order to make that basement space usable?

MR. WAGSTAFF: To make the space usable? It is usable, as approved by the plans.

MR. BURNS: When you say "approved by the plans," you are referring to the plans as approved on April 16?

MR. WAGSTAFF: Yes, those plans were approved by the Legion on the 16th of April.

MR. BURNS: Now, were any changes made in these plans with relation to the location of those pillars after the Legion had approved the plans?

MR. WAGSTAFF: No vital change.

MR. BURNS: Ah, no vital change?

MR. WAGSTAFF: No, no vital change. The building was made less than ten feet narrower, there was a ten-foot strip taken off, and it caused some rearrangement in the size of the rooms. For example, a room thirty by fifty might be changed to twenty-five by sixty. Changes of that nature—changes of shape, and not of capacity.

SUPERVISOR MARKS: Were those changes approved by the veterans?

MR. BURNS: Did you submit, or were those plans——

MR. WAGSTAFF (interrupting): No. '

MR. BURNS (continuing): —you say that they were not approved by the Legion?

MR. WAGSTAFF: Not officially.

MR. BURNS: Not officially? Were they approved by anyone representing himself to be a representative of the Legion?

MR. WAGSTAFF: Members of the Legion saw the plans at different places.

MR. BURNS: Who was that? Anyone representing the Legion?

MR. WAGSTAFF: Various members, who said they were from the Legion.

MR. BURNS: I see; various members who said they were members of some veterans' organization; simply came in and looked at the plans; but no one stated that he was approving the plans on behalf of the American Legion, did he?

MR. WAGSTAFF: Oh, no.

MR. BURNS: Were those plans ever submitted to the Legion thereafter for approval?

MR. WAGSTAFF: Not as finally approved.

MR. BURNS: In other words, the Legion never had them presented to them for approval?

MR. KILSBY: Mr. Wagstaff, following the approval of the plans by the Committee, and following the narrowing of the building by approximately ten feet, as you say, your office submitted two sets of plans; and did not those plans, were they not submitted, one copy to Mr. Burns and one copy to Mr. Hotchner?

THE CHAIRMAN: Does Mr. Wagstaff know he submitted them to Mr. Burns and Mr. Hotchner?

MR. KILSBY: No.

MR. BURNS: Would the reporter kindly read the question of Mr. Kilsby to Mr. Wagstaff?

(Question read.)

SUPERVISOR MARKS: What are the facts with reference to the submission by Mr. Kilsby of these plans to the Legion?

MR. WAGSTAFF: They probably were.

MR. BURNS: You do not know that they were, definitely?

MR. WAGSTAFF: No.

THE CHAIRMAN: If Mr. Kilsby knows, why not ask him? Mr. Burns, I would suggest to you that this is an informal public meeting; no one is supposed to be under cross-examination; it is just an informal meeting. You are taking the form of cross-examination.

MR. BURNS: I suppose I am inclined to revert to my early training, I admit I was trained along those lines just as you were trained in finance.

THE CHAIRMAN: Thank you for not including the law.

MR. BURNS: I want to ask this question, then, of the Board of Trustees: Were those plans which were not approved by the Legion submitted in the call for bids? In other words, when invitations were sent out to the contractors for bids for the concrete foundation work and the steel structural work, were those plans which had not been approved by the Legion used as the basis?

THE CHAIRMAN: No steel structural work—

MR. BURNS (interrupting): The concrete foundation work, then.

THE CHAIRMAN: There is no steel structural work in view yet; the foundation, yes.

MR. BURNS: In other words, plans which were not approved by the Legion?

THE CHAIRMAN: Yes. .

MR. BURNS: And if this condition which you have outlined had not arisen you would have gone on and received bids on those plans which had not been approved by the Legion?

THE CHAIRMAN: No, we should not; we had been put on ample notice after our meetings with the Legion's representatives, and we would not have taken the responsibility of carrying this enterprise to a position where it could not be stopped until we knew we had the absolute approval of every veterans' organization which was interested.

SUPERVISOR MARKS: Two or three weeks ago you called in bids, or took steps looking towards the issuing of bids for the foundation work, based upon plans not approved by the war veterans; is that correct?

THE CHAIRMAN: That is correct.

SUPERVISOR MARKS: But you say you would not have gone forward with the calling of bids under those plans unless they were approved?

THE CHAIRMAN: That is right.

SUPERVISOR MARKS: What was it that stopped the Trustees from continuing in securing those bids?

THE CHAIRMAN: Until the matter of the satisfaction of the veterans, and the co-operation of the veterans' organizations in the plan, we were going to go right to the point of having everything ready to go forward with this work without having any further delay than what was necessary. It was our intention to go no further than having the excavation work done, and the foundation work done, with the idea that completion of the foundation would not prevent the erecting of any type of building desired upon that foundation.

SUPERVISOR MARKS: In other words, if the veterans' organizations had not expressed dissent, the Trustees would have proceeded with the letting of bids and the completion of the foundation work?

THE CHAIRMAN: Oh, no; not after Mr. Havenner's resolution of June, 1927.

SUPERVISOR MARKS: But Supervisor Havenner's resolution was passed in June, 1927, and after that you had submitted plans, new plans which were not approved by the Legion, by the veterans' organizations.

THE CHAIRMAN: The plans were modified, yes; they were the plans approved by the Veterans' Commission.

SUPERVISOR MARKS: And now, two or three years ago, a year and a half after Mr. Havenner's resolution, you took bids looking to the letting of the work of excavating and constructing the foundation, and you were going ahead without the approval of the veterans? Now, what was it that stopped you, the dissatisfaction of the veterans?

THE CHAIRMAN: No, no; it was done by reason of Mr. Havenner's resolution.

SUPERVISOR MARKS: I don't quite get that.

THE CHAIRMAN: It was very definite that unless the veterans' organizations approved of our plans, the Board of Supervisors would not approve of the expenditure of a dollar.

SUPERVISOR MARKS: Supervisor Havenner's resolution calls for the approval of the plans before any money was called for. That resolution states that in the event of the approval by the people of the War Memorial bonds to be voted on the ballot, this Board—the Board of Supervisors—pledges itself to the policy of not appropriating any money whatsoever for the construction of the War Memorial building until the official plans for such building shall have received the formal approval of a majority of the duly constituted representatives of all the war veterans' organizations.

THE CHAIRMAN: That is correct.

SUPERVISOR MARKS: In other words, you planned to call for bids and have bids received?

THE CHAIRMAN: Absolutely.

SUPERVISOR MARKS: And subsequently have the plans approved by the veterans' organizations?

THE CHAIRMAN: No, the plans were up for approval; the matter of the change of plans. It would not incur any change whatever in the foundation plan; the foundation plans had nothing to do with the superstructure. We were under the impression that the only point upon which we had been led to believe the veterans were dissatisfied were three: First, that the space had been cut down by ten feet, which was not a structural change; second, was that they should know what the interior of the rooms at the time the were finished would be, which had nothing whatever to do with a structural change; third, which was a structural point that was whether the columns should or should not be in the basement. Outside of that there was nothing in the plans except for the foundation, except the possible addition to the foundation contract of that space 50 by 130 feet.

SUPERVISOR MARKS: Could you proceed to get bids' on the foundation without knowing whether additional pillars were to be in the building or not, in the basement?

THE CHAIRMAN: Absolutely; we were only wanting to get as far along as we could.

MR. SAPIRO: Is it not a fact that the set of plans which the Legion did approve were accompanied by a proviso that those pillars in the basement were to be removed?

THE CHAIRMAN: I said that.

MR. SAPIRO: Is it not a fact that the bids called for now show those pillars in the basement, and making, in our opinion, that space in the basement unsuable?

THE CHAIRMAN: That is correct, except we do not agree it is unusable.

MR. HOTCHNER: There are other objections, one of which is that the furnishing of this building—to begin with the trust agreement states that the building shall be adequately and completely furnished. From the architect's figures $45,000 is allocated to the furnishing of this building. I did receive the set of plans Mr. Wagstaff said was handed to me, and an investigation was immediately set on foot by the Plans Committee of our organization to find out if $45,000 was sufficient to adequately and completely furnish this building, and in our opinion, after this investigation, it is not. Up to the time that Charter Amendment No. 32 was passed we found out that it was totally inadequate. We found out from reliable bidders that the floor coverings alone, the linoleum and tarpaulin, would come to about $28,000, and the furnishings in the building outside of the tarpaulin and linoleum would run over $80,000. In other words, if we should cut our bid in half we would still be twice as much as the sum allocated by the Trustees. It must be kept in mind that the trust agreement specifically provides that the building shall be adequately and completely furnished.

THE CHAIRMAN: I think that is correct, Mr. Hotchner, but I think you will find that that will all work out. We find that on some of our estimates previously made, estimates before the inviting of bids, that on some of the estimates they are too low and on some of the estimates they are too high, but most of those estimates adjust themselves.

Supervisor Havenner, may I ask you, you were the author, as you say, of that resolution before the Board and it is your expectation to see that the policy of that resolution goes through and is carried out.

I want to ask you at this time whether you do not think it would
be in the expedition of this work and the creation of a harmonious
feeling between all concerned to have a sub-committee of your Board,
a sub-committee of our committee, and a committee representing all
of the Legion and veteran organizations, sit down together and see
whether we cannot thresh this thing out prior to the appointment of
the Board of Trustees by the Mayor?

SUPERVISOR HAVENNER: I cannot see any objection to that.

THE CHAIRMAN: Then, that would mean the postponement of
your resolution, the postponement of your pressing your resolution
before the Board until that could be done. Would you be willing to
do that?

SUPERVISOR HAVENNER: I don't think so. I feel that my resolution has nothing to do with this meeting, and that I shall press it
in the regular course.

THE CHAIRMAN: I am asking that for this reason: Without more
money and with a board of veterans feeling that they want more space,
and with the sum of money limited, that while such a Board of Trustees appointed by the Mayor would have complete control of the matter of the expenditure of the four millions voted by the public, they
would have absolutely no control over the two millions furnished by
private subscription, and over the ownership of the land. Don't you
feel under those circumstances that it would be better to thresh the
matter out and adjust all of the various points of difference before
the appointment of such a Board of Trustees representing the public's
money, so that the Board of Trustees when finally appointed representing the public's money that it will be equally divided between all
organizations interested in this matter?

SUPERVISOR HAVENNER: I don't see any logic in the adjustment at all. In the first place, Charter Amendment No. 32 was suggested by your representatives and brought into this Board of Supervisors by your committee and I can't see that at all. My resolution
does not commit the Mayor to the appointment of a Board; it has
nothing to do with this controversy. I believe that the fact that we
sold these War Memorial bonds to the people on this argument justifies us in asking the Mayor to see that the affairs of this institution
be administered by a group of men a majority of whom are representative of the veterans of our wars, because that is the plain language
of the argument, all of the selling argument, we made to the people of
San Francisco in selling these bonds.

THE CHAIRMAN: May I reply to that, Supervisor Havenner?

SUPERVISOR HAVENNER: Certainly.

THE CHAIRMAN: Don't you think that it would have this final
effect, along these lines? If the Mayor should select as this Board all
those who are veterans of the late war from among those who are
not members of these majority groups, that it would result that an
appeal would be made of the same character as is now made to the
Board of Trustees, of either increasing their space or completing their
building with an expenditure of at least an additional half a million
dollars where there is not the money on hand to do so? Then, if this
majority should refuse the veterans' application, wouldn't we find the
Legion equally dissatisfied with that Board as they are with us? Now,
we take the other angle, if, on the contrary, the majority of that Board
sympathizes with the veterans' organizations and with the Legion,
according to Mr. Havenner's resolution, that Board must follow
through to the point of satisfying the veterans no matter what sum
of money is expended. Then wouldn't we find the case to be where all
of the purposes of this War Memorial could not be carried forward,
and you could not possibly have the private trustees, the trustees
of the private funds subscribed, cooperating to go forward where they
could not feel that one or two or five of the purposes of this Memorial
would not be carried out properly. Wouldn't we be driven into that

position? Wouldn't it be better if before the Mayor can appoint this Board of Trustees, wouldn't it be wise to postpone anything in the nature of the resolution to proceed, together with the Supervisors and the representatives of the various veterans' organizations, and try and iron out these differences? We have got three or four weeks, and I, personally, don't see any possible objection to that.

SUPERVISOR HAVENNER: Of course, my resolution is not before this committee. It was brought into discussion and I have explained it, but it is not properly before this committee at this time.

I don't see any possible reason to apprehend any such situation as you picture. However, If it did arise we are going to reach an impasse some time in this matter anyway, if the conditions are going to be as you say, and if that is the case this impasse might as well be met now and gotten over with.

I can not understand how anyone who believes in a democratic form of government can possibly argue that in order to arrive at an harmonious agreement in this matter, that we must first reach an harmonious private agreement. I do not feel that we should ask his Honor the Mayor to delay the appointment of that Board until any private agreement can be reached in the matter.

MR. SAPIRO: May I ask a question? Do I understand from your statement that it would be the attitude of your Committee that if the Mayor appointed a Board of Trustees a majority of whom are from the various veterans' groups, your present Board of Trustees would not have confidence in that Board, and your Board of Trustees would refuse to transfer to the City and County of San Francisco, or to the people of San Francisco, or to that Board, that you would not transfer the money and land in your possession?

THE CHAIRMAN: Let me answer it this way: If the Mayor should appoint a committee which, under the advice of that committee should increase the building of the so-called Legion or Museum Building to the point where there would not be funds enough to complete both buildings, according to the plans and purposes laid before the Board of Supervisors and confirmed by them, then it would not be a case of the refusing or non-refusing to transfer by our Committee. It would then be our duty to hold on to the money and land we have, for the reason that we could not properly fulfill our responsibility and carry out the trust we have, according to its terms.

MR. SAPIRO: Then I am going to ask you this question: Then your Board of Trustees would refuse to transfer the money and property, which you have in trust, to the Board of Trustees appointed by the Mayor. To the Board properly constituted by this city under charter amendment. That you would not transfer this money and property unless they approved plans for the War Memorial satisfactory to your Committee. Is that your statement?

THE CHAIRMAN: No, sir.

MR. SAPIRO: I think it is. I can't see any difference.

THE CHAIRMAN: There is a difference.

MR. SAPIRO: What is the difference?

THE CHAIRMAN: I will tell you what it is. It is this: There is no Board of Supervisors, no Board, or no other body, that can compel me, as far as my private acts are concerned, or which can make me, regardless of any charter amendment or anything else, do something which is specifically against the purposes of the trust which I hold. I admit that may not be a strictly legal answer.

MR. SAPIRO: Of course you know that it is not a legal answer; you know that it is not an answer that any court in the land would sustain for a minute. You know that statement is not correct, and, as far as the legal feature of the thing is concerned, that all your Board of Trustees would have to do, that your Board of Trustees is empowered to pass a resolution authorizing the Board of Regents to transfer those lands and funds to the Board which the Mayor may appoint.

You know that you could do that immediately after that Board was appointed by the Mayor.

If your Board had in mind to do as you have said this evening, why aren't you honest enough to go before the people at the election and say so, instead of doing as you did so, and saying that you wanted to transfer these funds and property? Why didn't you honestly state to the people of San Francisco, "We want you to create a Board appointed by the Mayor, and then if we are satisfied with the plans of that Board, then we would transfer the lands and funds to them." Because you know very well that if you had ever said that to the people of San Francisco before the election they would have defeated that amendment so badly there would have been nothing to it. As a matter of fact, I told that to the Legion in meeting, that's what the present Board of Trustees intends to do is to dictate what the plans shall be; they are not going to transfer a thing unless the plans and specifications as approved by them are adopted, and not by the Board appointed by the Mayor. Now, I would like to know why you weren't honest enough to the people to go before the people before the election and tell them that you were not going to transfer this money and property to the Board appointed by the Mayor unless that Board would approve the plans of your committee, you having determined that beforehand?

THE CHAIRMAN: The only trouble, Mr. Sapiro, with your question is that you are going on the assumption that this Board of Trustees, before this election, or before the passage of this amendment, sat down and determined definitely what you have embodied in your question, which, if I said "Yes," I would then be admitting your statement is correct.

MR. SAPIRO: I don't know whether you determined it before or after the election, but you have determined it. If that isn't your determination, what is it?

THE CHAIRMAN: I will say that this matter has never been before the Board for review; that it has never been discussed, to my knowledge. I have never discussed it with any member of the Board of Trustees. I have stated the only thing I can say, not what the committee will or will not do, but I have stated that the purpose of our trust cannot be carried out unless the conditions for their proper carrying out are fulfilled. It is a question of whether or not your various bodies insist upon more money being spent, and then whether or not the Board of Supervisors believe that more money should be spent. If they believe that, and if you people believe you need more space, then it should be increased by bond issue or in some other way. My point is this: if we have a situation requiring more money, and if the Board of Supervisors want to pass more money, either out of tax levy or by bond issue, and then we have sufficient money in amount, money which they at your instance want to invest, I say we will turn everything we hold over to any board appointed by the Mayor.

MR. SAPIRO: Is that your personal opinion, or the opinion of the Committee?

THE CHAIRMAN: Yes, that is my personal opinion.

MR. SAPIRO: Then I understand that is not the opinion of your Committee?

THE CHAIRMAN: We have never discussed it—that is my personal opinion.

MR. SAPIRO: Didn't you understand by the passage of that charter amendment, and by the arguments used in favor of the amendment, that the funds and lands were to be turned over to a Board to be appointed by the Mayor? I presume that your attorneys, the attorneys for your Committee, advised you that your Board of Trustees could, by going into court and getting an order stating that the Board of Trustees of the City had now been created, which is going on with this project, could just turn this money and land over to them without further ado? Leaving the matter of carrying out the purposes of the project in the hands of the Board appointed by the Mayor. You knew that could be done, didn't you?

THE CHAIRMAN: I have expressed my personal opinion. Your question was, didn't I know when that amendment was proposed and when those arguments were made? My answer is that I did not. I was out of the city when the amendment was proposed. I had nothing whatever to do with the form it should take. I wasn't here.

MR. SAPIRO: Didn't you know that to be a fact?

THE CHAIRMAN: I wasn't even here.

MR. SAPIRO: Without pressing any personal responsibility upon you as to the amendment, don't you know as a matter of fact that it is a fact that what the Board of Trustees can do, they can turn the moneys and lands over today, or, rather, as soon as the Mayor has legally appointed the Board of Trustees under that amendment?

THE CHAIRMAN: I don't think they can unless they know how the money is to be spent, and whether there is going to be money enough to complete the plans and purposes for which that money was given.

MR. SAPIRO: There is nothing in the charter amendment to that effect, is there?

THE CHAIRMAN: No, but there is an awful lot in our trust agreement, in our responsibility for the private subscriptions. The purpose of the charter amendment was to enable the City, under the charter amendment, to enable the city to spend its four million dollars voted under the bonds, and to enable our Committee to return the private funds and the lands held under our trust.

MR. SAPIRO: Who is to prepare the plans, you or the Board of Trustees appointed by the Mayor?

THE CHAIRMAN: The Board appointed by the Mayor, but we have to know where the money is coming from.

MR. SAPIRO: Why do you say then that you have to approve the plans?

THE CHAIRMAN: I don't say that we have to approve the plans, but we do have to know where all the money is to come from which will pay for the carrying out of those plans when approved.

MR. SAPIRO: Is there anything in the law that makes this official body appointed by the City and County of San Francisco, by the Mayor of the City and County of San Francisco responsible to this informal body of yours?

THE CHAIRMAN: No, but neither is there anything which, by the adoption of the charter amendment, can compel our Board of Trustees to disregard their trust.

MR. SAPIRO: Are you going to assume then, in advance, that the men whom the Mayor is going to appoint are not going to perform their trust just as well as you gentlemen will perform your trust?

THE CHAIRMAN: They are in an entirely different trustees' position from what we are. If the new Board should have a majority from Mr. Boyd's organization, and Mr. Boyd's interpretation of how the four million-dollar bond issue should be spent is different and it is his desire to have more space and more money spent for their purposes, and then the new Board of Trustees should disregard the allocation of the money as between the two buildings, and the organizations represented by Mr. Burns and by Mr. Boyd should get what they desire for their building, cost what it may, and if thereafter with that conception of their trusteeship that should result, we have not fulfilled our trust. If we have previously turned over the money and property, we have not lived up to the purposes for which that money and property was put in our charge. We have nothing to do with trying to have our judgment control, the whole point of the desire to have a majority on the Board, is to do what you gentlemen

originally did indicate. We have to know where the money is going
to come from and how it is to be spent.

MR. BOYD: It is a War Memorial, and primarily was to be devoted to War Memorial purposes, and the veterans should control.
Now, nobody I know of, outside of your Board, your particular committee, has ever examined your plans or has ever had an opportunity
to see whether the money in your hands has been properly spent or
not. When we came here tonight we expected to get a stewardship,
an accounting of all of your funds; we don't know whether some of
the money has been expended or not, we do not know whether you
have expended or handled your funds with as much judgment as
another group might have. We don't expect to commit anybody in
advance on what plans they would approve. We realize that any
Board of Trustees—as a matter of fact, we particularly didn't favor
this charter amendment, mostly because of the way that it came
through the Board of Supervisors—but we also had in mind that
under this charter amendment the funds and lands held by your committee would be turned over to the new Board of Trustees, and not
be retained by the Board of Trustees who now hold it. To use a
common expression, your committee is in the position of "trying to
eat their pie and still have it." You say that unless your Board of
Trustees has their plans approved they will not transfer the funds
and property. In other words, the men the Mayor appoints will have
to say, "I will accept appointment and approve such and such
plans," otherwise under your statement you are not going to turn over
the money the public subscribed. You place yourselves in the position
that you feel that only you, that your group alone, your particular
Board alone will be able to define the particular kind of plans that
should be used. If your statement means anything else I would like
to know what it is.

SUPERVISOR MARKS: I understand that under the present plans
of the Trustees some three million dollars plus is going to be spent on
the opera house, some three and one-half million dollars on the opera
house, and about one million six hundred thousand, or thereabouts, on
the Veterans' building.

THE CHAIRMAN: $3,300,000 on the opera house, and $1,870,000 on
the Veterans' building.

SUPERVISOR MARKS: All right. Will the opera house be completed by the expenditure of that money?

THE CHAIRMAN: Yes.

SUPERVISOR MARKS: But the Veterans' building will not be completed?

THE CHAIRMAN: For the $1,870,000, yes, under these plans, but it
is not completed according to the interpretation they place upon it.

SUPERVISOR MARKS: May I ask if there is anything in your trust
agreement, to which you have referred, and wherein you state that
you must do certain things in order to properly discharge your trust,
which obligates the Trustees to build the opera house first and to defer
completion of the Veterans' building, or which gives in your trust any
priority of one building over another?

THE CHAIRMAN: No.

SUPERVISOR MARKS: Then how can you say that in order to properly carry out your responsibility under the terms of the trust you
must defer the possible completion of the Veterans' building and say
that unless you do that you have not discharged your trust?

THE CHAIRMAN: I say that if the trustee body appointed by the
Mayor, if that Board of Trustees is appointed by the Mayor, and that
body proceeds to revise the plans, and if, under that revision of the
plan, it requires more money than that now allocated under the bond
issue to the Veterans' building, we know that by reason of our trusts,
the contact which we have had with the costs it is going to be impos-

sible for us to discharge our trust, and will compel us to withhold the money.

SUPERVISOR MARKS: That is all predicated, is it not, upon your predetermination that the three million odd dollars is going to be expended for the completion of the opera house——

THE CHAIRMAN (interrupting): We have no predetermination in the matter whatever——

SUPERVISOR MARKS (interrupting): Well, you have determined that that $3,300,000 is going into the opera house, and that the opera house is going to be completed, and that of the total funds alloted you are going to spend the full amount for the opera house regardless?

THE CHAIRMAN: No, it does not mean that at all. Our whole conception of the trust is not to consider one building before the other, and not to proceed with the project unless both buildings can be completed in accordance with our private trust.

SUPERVISOR MARKS: Is there any description or allocation of funds, as to what proportion is to be spent for the opera house and what proportion is to be spent for the Veterans' building?

THE CHAIRMAN: None.

SUPERVISOR MARKS: It is discretionary with the Trustees, is it not?

THE CHAIRMAN: Yes.

SUPERVISOR MARKS: Will you indicate to us, of the $2,000,000 given to you from private subscriptions, what limitation is there on the Trustees as to how that money should be spent?

THE CHAIRMAN: There is no limitation, but of the amount subscribed there was $1,940,000 given by those subscribers who at the time stated that it was a subscription for one or the other purposes, of that amount $1,425,000 was subscribed by private persons for particular purposes.

SUPERVISOR MARKS: How about the $500,000 which was mentioned?

THE CHAIRMAN: He spoke of the $500,000 as though that had all been raised by the veterans, of that amount there was $40,000 raised by the drive of the veterans, and the rest of the $450,000 was raised by the same type of private subscriptions as the $1,425,000 already subscribed.

SUPERVISOR MARKS: Do you see any objection, any logical objection, to a composition of this Board of Trustees of the War Memorial wherein the veterans will constitute a majority of that Board, and if so, what is the objection?

THE CHAIRMAN: The basis of the objection is, as I have stated several times—this whole situation should be one of cooperation, of agreement, and of approval of plans, before there is any board of a character where one activity other than another activity has the majority on that Board.

SUPERVISOR MARKS: I am speaking of the Board of Trustees to be appointed pursuant to Charter Amendment No. 32, providing for such a Board. What is the objection against the composition of a Board of Trustees of that sort wherein the veterans shall be in the majority?

THE CHAIRMAN: For the reason that, as I have stated before, if the veterans are in the majority, as they have already indicated, it is their desire to see that there is a more equitable division of the money than as at present allocated. I am speaking now in terms of money, for the money has got to come from some place. If a majority of the Board is selected from among the veterans, and that Board proceeds to carry out the wishes of the veterans, and it then becomes impossible for us to carry out the original terms of our trust agreement, wherein we are entrusted with the responsibility of completing two buildings for four separate purposes, there would not be the money on hand to complete both buildings.

SUPERVISOR MARKS: You believe then, that if the Board was organized as you desire and your plans approved, your present allocation of funds would be more nearly adhered to than if they were a majority from the veterans?

THE CHAIRMAN: Oh, no, that is why I am asking if we cannot have a meeting on the matter, with a view to threshing out the differences on the basis of what every organization needs, have it fully and impartially investigated and an agreement reached as to the carrying out of these purposes before the appointment of the trustees. The point of difference is only very small, in my opinion. I don't see why it cannot be worked out in advance. I want to ask the group which is representing the Legion members—I want to ask, and I believe that practically all members representing the Legion and the various veterans' organizations are there in that box. What is it that you want particularly in addition to the plans as previously approved?

MR. BOYD: Don't include my group in the approval. We did not have anything to do with that approval.

THE CHAIRMAN: What is it you want, specifically?

MR. SAPIRO: You have approved a new set of plans. We have never seen these plans or had an opportunity to examine them. We don't want to approve them until we have seen them. We don't want to be brought in here at twelve o'clock midnight, have them presented to us at twelve o'clock midnight for approval. If those plans are presented to us properly we will go over them and point out just what objections we have to the set of plans.

SUPERVISOR GALLAGHER: What do you think of a suggestion of three, three and three? Three representing your group; three representing your group, the committee; and three of a subcommittee of the Supervisors? Take that group of nine and take up between you what Mr. Drum says on the one hand is entirely possible of adjustment, and what some of the others say is not, but being a human thing—I like that suggestion, Mr. Drum, I like your suggestion as to his resolution being held up to see if this cannot be ironed out. I like the suggestion you make, a group of three, three and three, and I think the Mayor ought to sit in——

THE MAYOR: That is where I came in.

SUPERVISOR GALLAGHER: ——and I think the Mayor ought to sit in, with the idea of seeing if, after all, you are as far apart as you think. They can take the plans and take a jab at them—it seems to me the differences can be compromised in some way.

MR. BOYD: We wish some such suggestion had been made a year and a half ago.

SUPERVISOR GALLAGHER: But that is water that has gone over the wheel, isn't it?

MR. BOYD: Yes, but it would appear now that this is being forced from the War Veterans, that we are being forced to do this. But we are perfectly willing to sit in with anyone at any time.

THE CHAIRMAN: I want to ask Mr. Burns—he is the chairman of this committee of the Legion, with all due respect to Mr. Sapiro—I don't think what he said from an attorney's point of view was responsive. Surely you are able to give us, in this public meeting——

MR. BURNS (interrupting): I am pretty sure I know what your question is going to be. I will state that the answer which Mr. Sapiro gave was my answer.

THE CHAIRMAN: May I not ask this: You went into certain plans in March, you approved the plans, and we cut down both buildings by ten feet, and only changed the shape of certain rooms, and that was over six months ago. Can't you give us at least some of the high spots of your objection? First, are you gentlemen willing to accept that building if that building is given to you with that strip off McAllister street of fifty by two hundred and thirty? What is the answer?

SUPERVISOR SCHMIDT: There is another group here. You are merely confining your question to the American Legion——

THE CHAIRMAN (interrupting): Mr. Supervisor, Mr. Boyd has said that he represents all of the other veterans' organizations except the Legion, and that he is cooperating with them.

SUPERVISOR SCHMIDT: Very well.

MR. BURNS: We cannot say that we would definitely approve those plans. We have pointed out here quite clearly that there are several considerations which enter into the approval of those plans. The previous approval of the plans was not an unanimous approval at that time, due to the unemployment situation existing, and due to the fact that we did not want to be placed in a position at that time of slowing up public work and not assisting in the alleviation of the unemployment situation which existed. Further, we claim these changes were made in the plans subsequent to our approval and that they are material changes which effect the useability of the building for the purposes for which it is to be used, leaving our any architectural and esthetic considerations, and only considering the use.

THE CHAIRMAN: Saving the point as to the interior of that building, so that you are not committed to anything in any way,—the reason I ask specifically is because, with all of the veterans' organizations present with your committee when you came in contact with us last August, you gentlemen stated very positively you would not be satisfied with that building, that you would regard it as an incomplete building, unless that strip was put up on McAllister street.

MR. BURNS: With other objections.

THE CHAIRMAN: Are you of the same mind still?

MR. BURNS: Certainly.

THE CHAIRMAN: Where is the $540,000 to come from for this work?

MR. BURNS: We would like an answer to the question first as to where the money in your trust is.

MR. BOYD: You are asking us where the five hundred thousand dollars is going to come from to complete our building. I am asking you where the practically two million dollars is going to come from to fulfill your function as trustee? All you have is about a quarter of a million, and you are obligated to complete this building.

THE CHAIRMAN: It is coming from the bond issue, plus that money.

MR. BOYD: The four million-dollar bond issue, and you have got, roughly, one and a quarter million dollars, and you have to complete those two buildings.

THE CHAIRMAN: Certainly.

MR. BOYD: Exactly. You, as trustee, are authorized to put up a building as an opera house costing three millions of dollars, and as trustee you are obligated to put up the Veterans' building costing about $1,800,000.

THE CHAIRMAN: Yes, about $4,180,000.

MR. BOYD: And, as trustee, it is your sacred obligation under this trust agreement to do that, but all you have to do that with is one and a quarter million dollars?

THE CHAIRMAN: Certainly.

MR. BOYD: And that is your position, and in order to hold that position you are attempting to dynamite this meeting tonight. That is what you are trying to do when you want us to approve your plan. You say it will cost another five hundred thousand dollars. I am speaking for fourteen organizations, and it is not all right with us, not at twelve o'clock midnight.

THE CHAIRMAN: Supervisor Havenner, would it be possible for you to postpone your resolution in the light of what Mr. Burns has stated? That is, that he has stated in conjunction with the other agencies or organizations, that they insist on this building which will mean an additional cost of five hundred thousand dollars?

MR. BURNS: We did not come to that latter conclusion.

SUPERVISOR HAVENNER: I don't think my resolution is involved at all. My resolution would have followed as a logical sequence of the previous resolution I introduced. I see no possible reason for delay.

SUPERVISOR GALLAGHER: Between now and Monday, Mr. Drum, it might be entirely possible for a situation to arise—The Supervisor in his present frame of mind is expressing his own thought. He says, "Not now." He might change between now and Monday. I don't think it is an element—I think the main thing to be done is to let the Board of Supervisors attend to that question.

SUPERVISOR HAVENNER: It is my right to press the resolution.

SUPERVISOR GALLAGHER: But it isn't possible for this gathering to agree tonight that at least—never mind these other features—at least we shall attempt to see if these differences cannot be reconciled so that the work will go forward.

SUPERVISOR SCHMIDT: I suggest a committee be appointed, that next Monday a committee representing the Board, and a committee representing your committee, and a committee representing the veterans, and the Mayor, and let them try to reconcile these differences.

SUPERVISOR COLMAN: I want to make this thought—if it has been expressed here tonight I have not heard it—that this whole project is a War Memorial. All of these buildings, the opera house, and the court, and the Veterans' building, together constitute it. An opera house is every bit as much a War Memorial as any other part, and that same applies to the court. War Memorials assume different shapes in different places according to the artistic or utilitarian view of the different people who build them. In various cities and various places we find War Memorials in various forms. I consider here that we have practiced no deceit on the veterans in connection with this opera house. San Francisco can spend money for an opera house and have it just as much a War Memorial as if the entire building were for the housing of veterans' organizations. As a matter of fact, in a certain light, the opera house is more essentially a War Memorial than the home of the veterans, inasmuch as it is to be used by a great deal more people.

THE CHAIRMAN: Gentlemen, this is an opening meeting, and I would like to ask that all speakers be afforded the courtesy of speaking without interruption.

SUPERVISOR COLMAN: I will repeat my statement that I consider each and every part of that project essentially a War Memorial. I want to state that I went out on the rostrum at the time the bonds were put before the voters, and at the bond election, and I spoke particularly on the War Memorial bonds probably twenty or thirty times all over San Francisco, and those bonds were sold to the people with the understanding that the south lot was to be an opera house and the north lot was to be a home for the veterans, and that all veteran activities were to be housed decently and cleanly, with ample room and ample comfort. If we fulfill that we are fulfilling our agreement in that respect.

I want to say with regard to Charter Amendment No. 32, that amendment was presented here to me by Mr. Hall, and I presented it to the Board of Supervisors. I knew nothing about it, neither did my colleague, Mr. McSheehy. It provided that a certain number of trustees would be veterans, three, I believe, and in our desire to do everything possible for the veterans, we placed it in the hands of the committee consisting of Supervisor Marks, the City Attorney, and Attorney Hall, who drew up the amendment and that amendment was passed. That amendment, as originally read here in the Board of Supervisors, provided that the Mayor could have appointed eleven instead of three or five or six.

To illustrate how even supervisors can disagree, I object to the resolution of Supervisor Havenner. I can see here tonight that it carries with it a lack of cooperation which may result disadvantageously to the project. I took the ground, it seems to me it is not properly presented. It suggests to his honor, the Mayor, that he make certain appointments from a certain group. The amendment specifically provides that the Mayor will make the appointments from certain groups. I don't think that should be done. I don't think it should be suggested to the Mayor where he should go for advice in naming his appointees. In the Mayor's seventeen years as Mayor he has had many appointments, and so far as I know he has been able to do it without asking any advice or suggestion from anyone. To me, it is out of order; to me, it is almost an insult to the intelligence of the Mayor to ask him to make appointments from any certain group.

SUPERVISOR HAVENNER: I submit that my resolution has no proper place here, and ask you to defer any discussion of it until the next meeting of the Board of Supervisors.

THE CHAIRMAN: Not being a member of the Board of Supervisors, I feel powerless to act.

SUPERVISOR COLMAN: I simply wanted some of the ladies and gentlemen to hear, first, that there was a small group, it is a small group, it is true, who do oppose this resolution, and I thought it was only fair that you ladies and gentlemen should know I was one of the group who did oppose it.

The statement of Mr. Sapiro earlier this evening was to me very hopeful, but possibly his later remarks may have dissipated that to some extent, but I believe this thing can be straightened out.

Mr. Marks brought out this point, that to build an opera house requires a certain specific amount of money, else it is not an opera house. It requires a certain number of chairs, stage space, orchestra space, and so forth. You can cut that to the irreducible minimum, but once you get below that you do not have an opera house. I do believe that the people of San Francisco want that, but to say that they want it as much as they want the veterans properly housed, I wouldn't state. I do know that there is very considerable and very keen interest in having the whole project go ahead, and we all want to bring that about. I do believe that if Mr. Drum's people and the Supervisors' Committee, with the Mayor, and the veterans' organizations, have proper cooperation—let's all try to get together and work this thing out. If we press this other resolution we will possibly be delaying matters more. It is my opinion, from the knowledge which I have of the Mayor, he will take the notice of it he thinks proper. The reason I think well of the Mayor's appointments, he appointed me. But I do feel that the veterans, of whom I am very proud to be one, and with whom I worked very hard when active in the Legion, I hope they will make this attempt to see this great project go on because I believe it can be done and I believe you will find a receptive group here on the Board.

THE CHAIRMAN: Supervisor Havenner, provided you cannot see your way clear to postponing the urging of your own motion on Monday, how do you feel about Mr. Gallagher's suggestions as to appointing that committee and having that committee get together on the matter? I would also suggest subcommittees not only from the Legion body but all activities represented by private subscriptions, such as the Musical Association of San Francisco, the opera house group, and others, and go all over the whole matter.

SUPERVISOR HAVENNER: I think the committee suggested by Supervisor Gallagher, of three members representing your Board, three members representing the veterans, and three from the Board, is all right.

MR. BURNS: It is absolutely satisfactory to the Legion.

MR. SAPIRO: We recognize it has no connection with Mr. Havenner's resolution.

SUPERVISOR GALLAGHER: I will expect Supervisor McSheehy

or Mr. Havenner, or Mr. Colman, as our representative on the Board to present that matter on Monday. We are sitting here unofficially, and if they don't I will.

THE CHAIRMAN: I think we have already kept you here very late, and we want to tender to all of you our thanks for the cooperation displayed. I feel that with the appointment of such a committee we will be able to go forward.

MAYOR ROLPH: I have listened very intently tonight to everything that has been said. I am not committed in any way, shape or form, to the appointment of anyone. I am just as free as when that charter amendment went through, but I can see brewing here a situation that arose the same as when Andrew Carnegie made a gift of $500,000 to the people of this city to build a public library here, and the people of San Francisco voted $25,000 and $50,000 branches throughout the city. The hue and cry arose that Andrew Carnegie's tainted money would not be accepted, and the matter brewed, and the matter brewed, until it became in such a condition it had to be submitted to the people of this city as to whether they would accept Andrew Carnegie's $500,000. Do you know that when the matter of that $500,000 gift was put before the people it was accepted by a vote of about forty to one? Do you know that the great mass of people here in this city are interested in public gifts to the city?

I hope that the three groups suggested here tonight will meet and discuss this matter and try to bring order out of chaos, which should be a matter easily accomplished, but while the project is in the position it is now I will make no appointments. We have had two members on your committee, and we have had two members of the veterans, Major Kendricks and Major Kilsby, and I am surprised to find that two members of this Board and two members of the veterans' organizations on your committee, it is not entirely familiar with all of these plans. I sat here in this chair when you and Supervisor McSheehy had all of the plans here in these chambers, when it was all discussed, and the Board agreed to curtail some three hundred seats in the opera house because of the acoustics.

It would seem to me that with two members of the Board on the committee, and two members of the veterans' organizations, these things should have been straightened out. If we don't find our selves getting this thing straightened out, I promise you it is going to the people by referendum.

THE CHAIRMAN: The meeting will stand adjourned.

THE MAYOR: Now, we are down to the introducing of the resolution on Monday by Supervisor Gallagher. I think it will be wise, as the hour is getting late, to take a recess until tomorrow morning at 8:00 o'clock.

SUPERVISOR GALLAGHER: I was going to suggest a recess of 15 minutes.

SUPERVISOR PEYSER: A recess of ten minutes.

SUPERVISOR GALLAGHER: I move we recess for 15 minutes.

SUPERVISOR STANTON: Second the motion.

THE MAYOR: It is moved and seconded that a recess be taken for 15 minutes. So ordered.

SUPERVISOR McSHEEHY: May I at this time ask the Sergeant-at-Arms that he provide the Board, and especially your Honor, with coffee and sandwiches. I do not think that there will be any objection on the part of the Finance Committee—one member is here.

SUPERVISOR GALLAGHER: The Finance Committee has already approved it.

(Thereupon a recess was taken. Upon reconvening the following proceedings were had:)

THE MAYOR (reading):

APPOINTMENT OF IRONING-OUT COMMITTEE.

On December 10th, 1928, following a general discussion Supervisor Frank R. Havenner suggested that an ironing out committee of three Supervisors, three Trustees, and three veterans be appointed to work out the problem.

The Board of Supervisors passed the following resolution:

Resolution No. 30102 (New Series), as follows:

Whereas, by resolution unanimously adopted on June 6, 1927, the Board of Supervisors is committed to the policy of withholding appropriations from funds resulting from sale of War Memorial Bonds until the official plans for the War Memorial have been approved by a majority of the duly constituted representatives of war veteran organizations; and

Whereas, by virtue of that resolution the Board of Supervisors have justly recognized as paramount the rights of the ex-service men and women of San Francisco, it being the deeds of such men, living as well as dead, that the War Memorial is intended to commemorate; and

Whereas, Charter Amendment No. 32, as approved by the people, provides for the appointment of a Board of Trustees to administer all matters pertaining to that War Memorial, and states, "The Mayor in making appointments shall give due consideration to the veterans of all wars in which the United States has engaged"; and

Whereas, Charter Amendment No. 32 invests in the Board of Supervisors the duty of confirming the appointments of all members of the Board of Trustees selected by the Mayor; now, therefore, be it

Resolved, That the Board of Supervisors respectfully urge and recommend that his Honor the Mayor appoint a majority of the members of the Board of War Memorial Trustees from that portion of the citizenry of San Francisco who have been in service with the Army, Navy or Marine Corps in time of war; and be it

Further Resolved, That the advice and counsel of the war veteran organizations, through the medium of the properly constituted representatives, be sought before said appointments are made, it being the opinion of the Board of Supervisors that every class or group of the people of San Francisco, with a confidence inspired by service in time of war, may look to such men for purposeful loyalty and unselfish devotion to San Francisco in time of peace

Adopted by the Board of Supervisors December 3, 1928.

Ayes—Supervisors Gallagher, Havenner, Kent, McGovern, Marks Powers, Roncovieri, Schmidt, Stanton, Suhr, Todd—11.

Noes—Supervisors Andriano, Colman, Hayden, McSheehy, Shannon, Toner—6.

> SUPERVISOR GALLAGHER: What page of the record?
> THE MAYOR: It is not in the record, it is in my report.
> SUPERVISOR GALLAGHER: That is my resolution.
> THE MAYOR: Your resolution? I thought it was Mr. Havenner's resolution.
> SUPERVISOR GALLAGHER: Is your record correct?
> THE MAYOR: I think so.
> SUPERVISOR GALLAGHER: Well, I just interpose that, I remember making a motion for three, three and three, but the resolution on the subject of a majority of directors of the War Memorial, I thought emanated from Mr. Havenner. I do this in your interest as to the record.
> THE MAYOR: Either of you would know.
> SUPERVISOR GALLAGHER: So that the Mayor may have his record correct. This does not say who presented it. A little later I may interrupt you, for corrections.

THE MAYOR: Because we dug this up from the records and from the information we got over here.
(Reading:)

Absent—Supervisor Deasy—1.

J. S. DUNNIGAN, Clerk.

San Francisco, December 21, 1928.

The foregoing resolution, heretofore on December 10, 1928, adopted by the Board of Supervisors, presented to his Honor the Mayor for his approval on December 11, 1928, and not returned by him with his signature within the time prescribed by Section 16, Chapter I, Article II of the Charter, has taken effect in accordance with the aforesaid provisions of the charter.

J. S. DUNNIGAN, Clerk.

THE MAYOR: I think Mr. Havenner's was the other one, and this yours.
SUPERVISOR HAVENNER: I think you are correct, Mr. Mayor.
THE MAYOR: I think this next one is yours. (Reading):

December 10, 1928, pursuant to the meeting on December 6, 1928 and as a result of suggestions made by Supervisor Andrew J Gallagher the Board of Supervisors passed the following resolution:
Resolution No. 30103 (New Series), as follows:
Whereas, at a public meeting of the War Memorial Trustees, held in the Board of Supervisors' chambers December 6, 1928, after a complete discussion by the trustees and others of the proposed plans, etc., it appeared that there was dissatisfaction among the veterans of all wars as to these plans; and
Whereas, it is advisable that this work proceed at the earliest possible date, and to that end these differences be harmonized, if possible; therefore, be it
Resolved, That a committee of three members of this board be appointed by the chair to serve with a joint committee consisting of his Honor the Mayor, three representatives of the present Board of War Memorial Trustees and three representatives of the veterans' organizations of San Francisco to study th differences that have arisen over the plans for the War Memorial project, and report to this board any suggestions as to a solution of the problems involved; and be it
Further Resolved, That this committee be authorized, in so far as this board can do so, to call meetings and conferences as in its judgment are advisable to bring about an agreement among all parties affected to permit the actual construction to proceed.
Adopted by the Board of Supervisors December 10, 1928.
Ayes—Supervisors Colman, Havenner, Hayden, Kent, McGovern, McSheehy, Marks, Powers, Roncovieri, Schmidt, Shannon, Stanton, Todd, Toner—14.
No—Supervisor Adriano—1.
Absent—Supervisors Deasy, Gallagher, Suhr—3.

J. S. DUNNIGAN, Clerk.

San Francisco, December 21, 1928.

The foregoing resolution, heretofore on December 10, 1928, adopted by the Board of Supervisors, presented to his Honor the Mayor for his approval on December 11, 1928, and not returned by him with his signature within the time prescribed by Section 16, Chapter I, Article II of the Charter, has taken effect in accordance with the aforesaid provisions of the Charter.

J. S. DUNNIGAN, Clerk.

SUPERVISOR GALLAGHER: For your record, the record of the Board's proceedings of Monday, December 3d—I do this for your record, and for my Memorial, if I may use the expression, the Public Welfare Committee, the report of the Public Welfare Committee on Supervisor Havenner's resolution providing for a majority representation of War Veterans on the Board of Trustees for the War Memorial. The following was read by the Clerk—this is on Monday, December 3, 1928, and the following was read by the Clerk: "San Francisco, December 3, 1928, Board of Supervisors, City and County of San Francisco. Gentlemen: A majority of the members of the Public Welfare and Auditorium Committee, to whom was referred Supervisor Havenner's resolution relating to appointment by the Mayor of the Trustees for the War Memorial, recommends the adoption of said resolution by the Board," and thereupon the following resolution was read and adopted, which, according to the record, is Resolution No. 30102, New Series, which I think is the one you read.

THE MAYOR: But that meeting took place on December 10th.

SUPERVISOR GALLAGHER: May I see the record? The resolution then follows.

THE MAYOR: I just read Resolution No. 30102, but that meeting took place on December 10th.

SUPERVISOR GALLAGHER: 30102 resolves—so that we won't take up too much time—resolves that the advice and counsel of the War Veterans organizations, through the medium of the properly constituted representatives, be sought before such appointments are made, it being the opinion of the Board of Supervisors that every class or group of the people of San Francisco, with the confidence inspired by service in time of war, may look to such men for purposeful loyalty, and so on. Supervisor McSheehy moved that the foregoing resolution be laid over one week. Motion lost by the following vote, the ayes were seven and the noes were ten. Adopted. And whereupon the roll call was called on the foregoing resolution and the same was adopted by the following vote: . A vote of 11 to 6.

THE MAYOR: Yes, I have that.

SUPERVISOR GALLAGHER: And before the result was announced Supervisor McSheehy changed his vote to give notice of reconsideration at the next meeting. Supervisor Gallagher moved the suspension of the rules for immediate consideration, and that was lost by a vote of ten to seven. So it went over to the next meeting. Your record is correct.

THE MAYOR: But that is December 10th.

SUPERVISOR GALLAGHER: The date is correct, but the name is wrong.

THE MAYOR: Yes, I have the resolution. All right. Now, we are down to December 19, 1928.

SUPERVISOR POWER: Did I understand, in the last resolution you read, Supervisor Gallagher's resolution, did you notice the absentees?

THE MAYOR: He was absent.

SUPERVISOR POWER: How did he introduce the resolution?

THE MAYOR: He introduced the other resolution, but he was absent on that resolution, as this report just shows.

SUPERVISOR GALLAGHER. I think you are in error there.

THE MAYOR: You were probably outside.

SUPERVISOR GALLAGHER: That is of no material moment.

THE MAYOR: The resolution was introduced, but all those resolutions took place, those which you have just read, and when the final vote came you just did not happen to be in the room, that was all.

SUPERVISOR POWER: He must have made a motion for the adoption of it.

SUPERVISOR GALLAGHER: I think you desire that your record shall be correct.

THE MAYOR: Yes.

SUPERVISOR GALLAGHER: And my recollection was that I thought it was at the meeting of the night you speak of, and I am sure that your stenographers followed it closely, it was on the night meeting that you spoke of.

THE MAYOR: December 6th, yes.

SUPERVISOR GALLAGHER: That I made the motion for the three, three and three because that meeting shows that Supervisor Havenner objected to the consideration of his resolution, which was for a majority of the Board veterans, and it is obvious I think that I could not have been absent when the motion—it was not a resolution, it was a motion— when the motion creating the three, three and three was adopted.

THE MAYOR: No, you voted yes on that.   Both resolutions were the same day, December 10th.

SUPERVISOR GALLAGHER: For your sake, if the record is straight, I am satisfied.

THE MAYOR: I have both resolutions and both votes, but you voted—it may have been this resolution, maybe Supervisor Havenner—I had you right on the resolution on which you voted.

SUPERVISOR GALLAGHER: Well, I voted 'Yes" on Supervisor Havenner's resolution.

THE MAYOR: You were not in the room then.   You voted "Yes" on his resolution, but you were not in the room on your own.

SUPERVISOR GALLAGHER: May I submit to his Honor, not for my own sake but for the sake of the record, that he permit of this motion: That the record be clarified, to the extent that the Mayor's report be examined as to its correctness, and be, with his permission, on proof submitted, corrected.

THE MAYOR: Absolutely, and, Mr. Girvin, when this report gets to you, you will have to insert what has transpired here tonight in going over this with Judge Smith, and you put it in.   There has been very little talking about anything tonight, but some few remarks like this have crept in, which will be put in to make it correct.   But you were not present, according to this report, on your own resolution.

SUPERVISOR GALLAGHER: Go right on, Mr. Mayor, and I may interrupt you later, with your permission.

THE MAYOR (reading):

December 19, 1928, the first meeting of the special ironing out committee——

Now, you remember you passed the resolution on the 10th, and the special ironing-out committee met on December 19, 1928——

(Reading:)

in formal session, under the resolution of the Board of Supervisors last quoted, was held in the mayor's office. There were present, the Mayor, representing the City and County of San Francisco; representing the veterans Messrs. Glensor, Boyd and Burns; representing the Supervisors Messrs. Kent, Marks and Hayden; representing the trustees Messrs. Drum, Kilsby and McSheehy. Others present at this meeting were Mr Claridge, Secretary Legion committee, Mr. McKee of the trustees, Architects Brown and Lansberg and from the drafting rooms Messrs. Wagstaff and Collupy.

March 21, 1929, meeting in the Mayor's office of the committee of nine. The advisory board of the Veterans' War Memorial committees submitted a report, dated March 20, 1929, in which the needs of the various veteran organizations were discussed and suggestions made regarding the growth of the organizations. This report is as follows:

REPORT OF ADVISORY BOARD OF
VETERANS WAR MEMORIAL COMMITTEES

San Francisco, Calif, March 20, 1929.

To the Veteran Organizations of San Francisco:

Comrades: At the meeting of this board with the Mayor and representatives of the War Memorial Trustees and the Supervisors, on December 18, 1928, it developed that, although plans for the War Memorial had been drawn and work started, no definite information had been collected regarding the needs of veteran and patriotic organizations requiring housing in the War Memorial. It was thereupon agreed that the Veterans' Advisory Board would make a survey of the needs of veteran and patriotic organizations, make a study of the plans and be prepared to submit the result of these studies to the above mentioned groups at the next meeting thereof.

Immediately steps were taken to carry this into effect. From the best available data, we find and submit the following facts and recommendations as our report to you:

Organizations in San Francisco Submitting Reports and Data to Us

Veterans of Foreign Wars .... 7 Units
American Legion .... 20 Units
United Spanish War Veterans .... 4 Units
Indian War Veterans .... 1 Unit
Auxiliaries, Patriotic Societies, Disabled American Veterans, etc. .... 33 Units
Organization State Headquarters .... 5 Units
Bands .... 5 Units
Drill Teams .... 3 Units
Drum Corps .... 2 Units
Scout Troops sponsored by Posts .... 11 Units

Times per month refreshments are served 43
Number members in reporting organizations 10,498
   (11 organizations reported auxiliaries without giving membership thereof)
Organizations reporting membership in 1925 31
Members reported for 1925 5,491

Increase in American Legion membership over 1925, 57 per cent.

Increase in Spanish War Veterans membership over 1925, 92 per cent plus.

Table of Meetings of Reporting Organizations

	First	Second	Third	Fourth
Monday	8	7	6	4
Tuesday	3	7	4	7
Wednesday	6	7	4	5
Thursday	5	6	7	5
Friday	6	5	8	2
Saturday	1	1		1
Sunday	1			

(2 organizations did not report their meeting nights, 2 organizations do not have night meetings—luncheon, 1 organization holds irregular meetings.)

Estimates of Future Growth

It is somewhat difficult to get any accurate figures on which to base estimates of future growth of veteran organizations. Based upon the history of the G. A. R., and the U. S. W. V., the following facts seem to be well established:

1.   Veterans' organizations reach the peak of their membership approximately 30 years after the war in which they participated.

2.   At the high point in their membership approximately 40 per cent of the eligibles belong to their respective organizations.

If the American Legion develops upon these premises there would be in 1925-1950 approximately 16,000 to 20,000 Legionnaires in San Francisco. This would probably mean 125 to 150 separate units.

3.   By 1940, perhaps 1935, there will be no more G. A. R. organizations; by 1945 the membership of the U. S. W. V. will begin to decline. By 1965 it will be about where the G. A. R. is today. By 1970 it will doubtless cease to exist as an organization. The membership of the World War Veterans' organizations should show no decline before 1965.

4.   The ratio of eligibles of World War Veterans to U. S. W. V. is about 16 to 1.

5.   At one time two Legion posts had an aggregate of 13,000 members in San Francisco.

6.   These estimates of future growth are made upon the supposition that we will have no more wars. Our history, however, has been a war for about every 30 years of our national existence.

Estimated Needs for Veteran and Patriotic Organizations

A building to house the veteran and patriotic organizations of San Francisco, and plans for same which we could recommend for approval, should contain the following:

1.   An auditorium with balcony, with combined seating capacity of 1500, to be arranged for on first floor of building.

This auditorium to be complete with fully equipped stage, dressing rooms, space for chair storage, check rooms, retiring rooms, toilets, stairways to basement, serving pantries, etc. The auditorium may, on occasion, be used as a banquet hall.

2.   Two meeting halls with a maximum seating capacity of 500.

3.   Eighteen meeting halls with maximum seating capacity ranging from 75 to 250.

4.   Kitchenette to be installed adjacent to each meeting hall. These kitchenettes in size should be consistent with the seating capacity of the meeting halls which they adjoin.

5.   A fully equipped kitchen, complete in every detail, with pantries, ranges, steam tables, dish-washing equipment, refrigerator, supply-rooms, dining room, toilets and lockers, rooms for help, elevators, stairways, serving pantries, etc., to be installed in the basement in a location so that same will be accessible to the auditorium and connect with the auditorium by means of electric dumbwaiters and stairways.

6.   One clubroom for men—minimum 2500 square feet.

7.   One clubroom for women—minimum 2000 square feet.

8.   Library, having as its adjunct, two reading rooms—1800 feet.

9.   Two band practice rooms, with instrument rooms and lockers adjoining same—3500 square feet. These band practice rooms are to be located in the basement and are to be sound proof.

10.   Flag lockers and lockers for the uniformed bodies of the organizations.

11.   Lockers for post records and paraphernalia; locker rooms on floors adjacent to meeting halls; five large lockers to be allotted to each meeting hall.

12.   One large meeting hall for subsidiary organizations such as the "40 and 8," Snakes, Cooties, etc.—4000 square feet. (Basement.)

13.   Souvenir and war relic room—2000 square feet.

14. Office space for American Legion State headquarters—7500 square feet.

15. Office space for "40 and 8" State headquarters—800 square feet.

16. Office space for U. S. W. V.—800 square feet.

17. Office space for American Legion County Council—800 square feet.

18. Office space for American Legion Auxiliary State headquarters —1800 square feet.

19. Office space for V. F. W. State headquarters and County Council —1000 square feet.

20. Office space for D. A. V.—1500 square feet.

21. Office space for desk room for individual units of the various organizations—5000 square feet.

22. Office space for Veterans' Employment Bureau—3000 square feet.

23. Minimum of 25 lockers for employees in various headquarters.

24. Storage space for old records—1000 square feet.

25. Vault with individual compartments for various headquarters.

Listen to this, this is an important matter, and I want you to listen to this, that all buildings under the plan of the architeets should conform to the Civic Center. (Reading):

26. The facade as set forth in existing plans for the War Memorial——

SUPERVISOR McSHEEHY (interrupting): Your Honor, I hate to interrupt you, but the coffee will be ready in about five minutes.

THE MAYOR: I am certainly glad to hear that.

SUPERVISOR McSHEEHY: It is really so, your Honor, and now I would suggest that we recess until 3:00 o'clock.

THE MAYOR (continuing reading):

26. The facade as set forth in existing plans for the War Memorial is, in our opinion, poorly designed. It contains neither dignity or detail and is inferior to a degree to the various public buildings now standing in the Civic Center. This building should be redesigned along more monumental lines, following out the design, to a certain extent, of the City Hall, Library, Auditorium, or any other monumental building, many of which grace less important sites throughout the State and Nation.

Particular criticism is directed to the lowest story, particularly the entrances, which are very weak and unattractive and give one the impression of entering a basement rather than a building dedicated to the purposes for which this structure is intended.

27. The plans for the Veterans' Building show an indentation on the McAllister street facade of some 50 feet, with a length of 236 feet. This indentation is consistent neither with good planning or good design, and should be eliminated, making a rectangular structure, even though some of our frontage on Van Ness avenue be sacrificed in so doing, and it is believed that if the program as herein presented be followed that it will be imperative that this objection be removed.

28. The mezzanine offices as shown on existing plans are not at all practical, inasmuch as same are neither light, nor do they contain any visible means of ventilation.

29. Recreational space, i. e., steam rooms, bowling alleys, etc. This recreational space provided for by the existing plans is desirable and would, if provided, doubtless be used by a substantial number of veterans. However, in San Francisco, all such advantages

may be secured elsewhere. In view of the fact that space and funds for furnishings, etc., is an object, the advisory board recommends that in the event that new plans are submitted that provide for the elimination of such facilities, the veterans approve such plans if by so doing a completed building may be provided suitable for the veterans' needs as herein outlined.

30. It is noted in the estimates submitted by the War Memorial executives that in the matter of a reduction in the Veterans' Building of 10 feet in width, that an allowance of 57,000 was set forth. In computing the cost per square foot it is ascertained that this allowance was made on the basis of approximately $3.30 per square foot of floor area.

It is further noted that a price of $540,000 is submitted in this estimate for finishing the McAllister street wing or indentation. This cost figures approximately $9.00 per square foot, which is wholly inconsistent, when but $3.30 per square foot is allowed for the elimination of identical floor area for which $9.00 per square foot is charged.

In view of the above it is recommended that the existing plans for the Veterans' Building be discarded in their entirety as they do not at all meet the requirements of the veteran and patriotic organizations, and obviously could not be revised to meet such needs.

Whenever plans, which substantially conform to the requirements as set forth above are submitted to this advisory board we are prepared to recommend their immediate approval by the veteran organizations.

THE MAYOR: Now, listen to this, I don't think you are getting all this. Listen, gentlemen, this is dated March 20th (reading):

It is our opinion that the solution of this entire problem is for the Mayor to immediately appoint the Board of War Memorial Trustees provided for by the Charter of the City and County of San Francisco. The War Memorial is a public project. Its destinies should be entrusted to the authorities constituted under the Charter.

Respectfully submitted,
ADVISORY BOARD TO VETERANS' WAR MEMORIAL
COMMITTEES

(Signed) H..J. BOYD,
(Signed) JAMES B. BURNS,
(Signed) H. W. GLENSOR.

THE MAYOR: This is from the Advisory Board to the Veterans' War Memorial Committees and is signed by H. J. Boyd, James B. Burns and H. W. Glensor.

I am not commenting or saying a thing. I am just reading facts.

SUPERVISOR POWER: What year is that?

THE MAYOR: This report is the report of the Advisory Board to the Veterans' War Memorial Committee dated March 20, 1929, after we were at work. You passed this resolution of December 10th and we were getting to work on the first meeting on December 19th, and then this was put over—I apologize, I did not want to argue with you.

SUPERVISOR McSHEEHY (interrupting): Pardon me, your Honor, the coffee is hot.

THE MAYOR: If there is no objection by any member, we will recess for a short time for refreshments.

(Thereupon the meeting took a recess from 2:55 a. m. to 3:00 a. m., after which the meeting proceeded.)

WEDNESDAY, FEBRUARY 19, 1930, 3:00 A. M.

THE MAYOR: The committee of nine met again on April 11, 1929, and the meeting of the committee of nine was held in the Mayor's office. (Continuing reading:)

April 11, 1929. Meeting of the committee of nine was held in the Mayor's office. A report, dated March 20, 1929, and the so-called Plan "C" were thoroughly discussed.

April 30, 1929. The Veterans' Advisory Committee, after consultation with all veteran groups, in a statement dated April 30, 1929, have advised that in the event of a deficit in carrying out Plan "C" they would submit to a reduction in the Veteran-Museum Building of ten feet on either the north or south sides, five feet on both the north and south sides, or ten feet in the center of the building. They suggested, in this respect, that if the reduction of the Veteran-Museum Building as heretofore stated, unbalances or destroys the symmetry of the project as a whole, that such objection may be overcome by a corresponding reduction of the Opera House. This is suggested by them as a method of taking care of the deficit of the whole project. The veterans are not willing to concede that their requests for space are such as to make any deficit necessary.

The statement above referred to is as follows:

REPORT OF ADVISORY BOARD TO VETERANS' WAR MEMORIAL COMMITTEES
April 30, 1929.

To the Mayor and the Committee of Nine:

Consistent with the policy of the veterans to submit all statements in writing regarding the matter now being considered by this committee, so that such statements may remain a matter of record for future reference, the Veterans' Advisory Board makes the following statement with respect to the matters submitted for their consideration at the meeting held on April 11th, 1929.

After careful consideration of the three plans submitted on that date, consultation with the heads of all the major veteran groups in San Francisco, and obtaining such expert opinion and advice as, in their circumstances, the veterans could obtain, the conclusion has been reached that plan "C" is the only one of the three plans that can be approved by the veterans. This is subject, however, to the following important qualification:

If it is finally determined to construct the Opera House and Art Center upon such a scale that there is certain to be a deficit (which point is hereafter discussed in more detail) the veterans will, if desired, receive from this Board a recommendation to approve plan "C" with the elimination of 10 feet on either the North or South sides of the Veteran-Museum Building, five feet on both the North and South sides or 10 feet in the center of the building.

In view of the suggestion submitted in the attached criticism of these plans that the auditorium planned in the Veteran-Museum Building is too wide for its depth, perhaps if the suggested modification is adopted it will be found advisable to put it into effect in accordance with the latter suggestion. If such reduction of the Veteran-Museum Building unbalaces or destroys the symmetry of the project as a whole, such objection may be overcome by a corresponding reduction in the size of the Opera House, and in such reduction we may find a happy solution to three problems:

1.   The contemplated deficit.

2.   The extended and spirited criticism of American and European technicians that the Opera House as presently planned is too large for proper acoustical effects in the production of opera.

3. The impending problem of handling traffic on McAllister and Grove streets, west of Van Ness avenue due to the width of these two streets. At present no provision has been made for the widening of these two streets and if constructed as planned, the War Memorial group will be so situated that it will practically make it impossible to ever widen these streets west of Van Ness avenue.   .

In connection with the selection of plan "C," the veterans are well aware of the fact that, according to the statement of the Trustees made to this Committee at the meeting of April 11th, this plan will create the larger deficit. The veterans, however, are far from convinced that it is necessary that there be any deficit at all, and are very firmly convinced that if there is any deficit it is not caused by the requirements of the veterans, nor is it chargeable to the veterans' portion of the building alone. Indeed it should not be considered in connection with the veterans' portion of the building at all. To make this clearly understood it is necessary to review the history of this project at some length. If such review exceeds a desirable brevity, it must be remembered that we are in reality dealing with not one, but two separate and distinct methods of financing one project, which methods must be reconciled and amalgamated, and under which plans have been in the making and/or operation over a period of eight years.

The entire project, so far as the veterans are concerned, started with the drive of 1920 for public subscriptions. If it is a fact, as stated at the last meeting, that prior thereto one and one-half million dollars had been subscribed or pledged to build an Art Building, Opera House, or either or both, the veterans regard it as of no moment because such sum has now been shown to be wholly inadequate for such purpose and unless supplemented by the other subscriptions would have been of no use whatever. The additional funds were sought by public subscription in 1920, at which time receipts for such subscriptions were given the subscribers in the following form:

No. 1040

SAN FRANCISCO WAR MEMORIAL

John S. Drum, Chairman,
300 Crocker Building

San Francisco,..............1920.

The undersigned hereby subscribes and agrees to donate and pay to the University of California the sum of $........in the manner indicated below:

$.........., cash (or check) received by solicitor, (If cash is paid the signature of solicitor will be a receipt)

$.........payable five dollars each month until the whole amount ($10 to $95) subscribed is paid in full

$.........payable in..........equal installments, the first installment to be paid upon its demand, and the remaining installments to be paid annually thereafter until the total amount of this donation is paid. The money so subscribed and donated is to be used for the purpose of purchasing a lot of land in the City and County of San Francisco, State of California, and for the purpose of erecting thereon a building or buildings devoted to music, fine arts, and a home for the American Legion, both the land and the building or buildings to be the property of the University of California.

The purpose is to honor in memory the soldiers, marines, sailors and war workers, men and women, who brought imperishable glory to California by their splendid contribution to the winning of the World War.

This receipt entitles the holder to place a memento in the cornerstone of the War Memorial Building.

A souvenir certificate will be mailed to each subscriber.

Solicitor ....   Name ....
Address ....   Address ....

As a result of this drive a fund was raised, (or the fund increased as the case may be) to $2,000,679.00 payable to the regents of the University of California, a corporation. A trust indenture was thereupon entered into between said Regents and a Board of War Memorial Trustees, three of whom are now members of this committee of nine, wherein there was named as beneficiaries|of the trust:

1. The San Francisco Art Association,
2. Musical Association of San Francisco and San Francisco Symphony Orchestra,
3. The San Francisco Posts of the American Legion.

This trust agreement provided with respect to the San Francisco Posts of the American Legion, among other things, as follows:

"REQUIREMENTS OF TRUST IN FAVOR OF SAN FRANCISCO POSTS OF THE AMERICAN LEGION

(1) The building to be occupied by the San Francisco Posts of the American Legion shall be occupied and used by the various duly organized and authorized San Francisco Posts of the American Legion without rent charge. The San Francisco Posts of the American Legion, or a majority of them, shall under such rules and conditions as they may prescribe, provide headquarters for Veterans of the Mexican War, Grand Army of the Republic, Spanish-American War Veterans, and such other patriotic organizations as said San Francisco Posts of the American Legion may from time to time desire to install. Should the San Francisco Posts of the American Legion be consolidated with or merged into some other national organization, then the organizations duly authorized by such other national organization shall have the same rights of occupancy as the San Francisco Posts of the American Legion, and the rights and obligations of the successor organization shall be the same as the rights and obligations of the San Francisco Posts of the American Legion as set-forth herein.

(2) The said building to be occupied by the San Francisco Posts of the American Legion shall be used by them as club and meeting rooms and for executive offices and auditorium purposes."

At all times since this trust agreement came into existence, the American Legion has considered the clause therein that "The San Francisco Posts of the American Legion or a majority of them, shall under such rules and conditions as they may prescribe provide headquarters . . ." for the veteran organizations other than the Legion, as a mandate and that they were thereby obligated to see that the Grand Army of the Republic, United Spanish War Veterans, Indian War Veterans, Veterans of Foreign Wars and other veteran and patriotic organizations were provided for. Therefore the statement made at the last meeting of this committee that until the passage of the four million dollar bond issue in 1927, the veterans as a whole, that is, other than the American Legion had no "fixed status" in relation to the War Memorial is wholly unfounded. The veterans of San Francisco have at all times been in a fixed and definite status so far as this project is concerned.

Following the drive for public subscriptions and donations for funds to erect the War Memorial apparently nothing real definite was done to carry the project through until early in 1927 when it was decided that the funds were insufficient to carry out what was planned. Accordingly steps were taken to provide a bond issue by the people of San Francisco sufficient to complete the project. As has been explained in detail on several occasions by the trustees, the publishers of the San Francisco papers, the Mayor and members of the Board of Supervisors were called into conference early in 1927 and agreed that the time was right to put this bond issue before the people. Steps were then taken to determine the amount of money necessary to complete the project.

Under date of March 21st, 1927, the Board of Supervisors passed ordinance No. 7450 directing the Board of Public Works to secure, through the City Engineer, plans and estimates of cost of the original construction, completion and equipment of permanent buildings in or adjacent to the Civic Center as described in said ordinance.

Persuant to instructions in this ordinance, the City Engineer, under date of April 9th, 1927, transmitted by letter to the Board of Public Works certain plans and estimates of cost above referred to. Under date of April 11th, 1927, the Board of Public Works by resolution (Their No. 96801, second series) approved and transmitted to the Board of Supervisors these plans and estimates of cost. (Copy of plan attached hereto).

Using as a basis the plans and estimates of cost prepared by the City Engineer and approved by the Board of Public Works it was determined that a sum of $4,000,000, in addition to the sum on hand in the publicly subscribed fund, would be necessary to complete, construct and equip the buildings shown by plans and referred to in ordinance No. 7450. Accordingly the Board of Supervisors passed on April 22d, 1927, ordinance No. 7501 authorizing a bond issue in the sum of $4,-000,000 for the above purpose. Thus the problem of the War Memorial was apparently solved.

It has, of course, long been a matter of public knowledge that such was not the case. A study of the plans submitted with the estimates of cost to the Board of Public Works by the City Engineer, then approved by the Board of Public Works and transmitted to the Board of Supervisors, clearly indicates, even to the layman, that it was the intention at that time to construct two buildings, rectangular in shape and identical in size. If such was not the real intent, then it is clear that this plan was an effort to at least convey that impression to those whose attention was directed to the plan. It is also of interest to point out at this time that neither this plan, or any other, was brought to the attention of the veterans; in fact none of the veteran organizations in San Francisco had any knowledge of what was intended in regard to the bond issue, or how the money was to be used.

Ordinance No. 7501, which provided for the four million dollar bond issue made reference only to buildings to be used for a "Memorial Hall for War Veterans—and for educational, recreational, entertainment and other municipal purposes."

An Art Museum is not mentioned.

An Opera House is not mentioned.

While the language of the ordinance might possibly be interpreted to include either or both of these purposes, it is too plain for argument that the main purpose for which the money was voted was for a building for veteran uses and purposes, and the educational, recreational, entertainment and other municipal purposes were incidental thereto.

Therefore, in addition to the privately subscribed trust fund, donated in part for the veterans' needs, there was provided by vote of the people $4,000,000 for building specifically designed to be used as a Memorial Hall for War Veterans, and incidentally for other purposes. Under the present plans only about two-thirds of the building which has commonly been referred to as the Veterans' Building is allocated to the veterans, the balance being dedicated to art purposes, yet an attempt is patently being made to create the impression that the entire deficit, if there be one, is due to the inordinate demands of the veterans.

The plans and estimates of cost prepared by the City Engineer were approved by the Board of Public Works on April 11th, 1927. The bond issue was approved by the people on June 14th, 1927. Not until November 1927 were any definite plans submitted to the veterans, and then only to the American Legion. These plans, dated November 1st, 1927, did not conform to the plans approved by the Board of Public Works in so far as the Veteran-Museum Building was concerned. Instead of a rectangular building, conforming in shape and size to the Opera House the veterans were offered for approval a plan that had been reduced by about one-third from the original plan on which the bond issue was based. This plan was of course not approved by the veterans.

In December, 1927, another set of plans for the Veteran-Museum Building were submitted to the American Legion showing some addition to the building, but not yet a completely finished rectangular structure. In January, 1928, still another set of plans was submitted to the American Legion, showing further changes, but still an uncompleted building. In February 1928, March 1928, May 1928, and December 1928, new plans were submitted to the American Legion, none of which gave to the veterans—in joint occupancy with the Art Association—a completely finished rectangular building as called for in the original plan on which the bond issue was based. Neither were any of these plans found acceptable to the American Legion, either in space or arrangement, although the representatives of a majority of the Legion Posts in San Francisco did approve one set of plans but only under great pressure from the trustees who definitely advised the American Legion that there was not sufficient money to warrant building a completely rectangular structure as desired by the American Legion and other veteran organizations. The further plea was made by the trustees that the Legion should hasten approval of the plans in order to get construction under way, an act which would be of inestimable benefit in relieving the unemployment situation in San Francisco at that time. Naturally, the dominant desire of the representatives of the American Legion was to get the War Memorial under way, regardless of employment conditions, and with that factor in addition to be considered the Legion representatives were doubly anxious to do anything reasonable to get work started on this project.

However, after one set of plans had received the approval of the American Legion, but not the approval of any other veteran bodies, and when work was about to get started, in fact after bids had been called for on foundations, it was discovered that the plans approved by the American Legion had been departed from and a building was to be erected not entirely in accordance with those approved plans. Of course, the American Legion complained of such action and work was held up.

The statement made at the last meeting of this committee that the present situation is due to changing requests and requirements of the veterans is utterly unfounded. The veterans have always wanted a completed building, conforming in shape and size to the Opera House, with an allotment of space sufficient for their actual needs. But, while the trustees had used great care to inform themselves as to the needs of the Art Association and the Musical Association, they had evidently made little effort to ascertain what the veterans actually needed. It was not until the survey made by this Advisory Board following the meeting of this committee on December 18th, 1928, that anything approaching a sound and reasonable estimate of veterans' needs was made available. With this in mind, the statement that the needs of the Opera House and the Art Association have never changed but have remained static, while the veterans' plans have been constantly changed, is more easily understood. The needs of the art and music interests were ascertained and fully provided for from the beginning. and what was left over was allotted to the veterans. There has been no change made in the requirements of the art and music interests, but the entire effort concentrated upon an attempt to square this remainder with the veterans' needs. In other words, to get the veterans to accept what was left over and be satisfied regardless of whether it was sufficient for their needs or not.

Now as to the matter of available funds. In the estimats of costs prepared by the City Engineer and approved by the Board of Public Works and transmitted to the Board of Supervisors we find the following:

```
Opera  House...............................................$4,127,000
Legion-Museum  .........................................  1,500,000
                                                          ───────────
                                                           5,627,000
Public  subscription  on  hand...........................  1,627,000
Balance  to  be  raised  by  bond  issue......................$4,000,000
```

Thus we find that the entire project was to cost the sum of $5,627,000 for the building, equipment and furnishings, and with a bond issue of $4,000,000 added to the sum in the hands of the trustees of the publicly subscribed fund, sufficient money would be available.

After the bond issue was passed, however, there were certain changes in the cost of the two buildings which reduced the cost of the Opera House some $700,000 below the original estimate and raised the cost of the Legion-Museum Building some $400,000 over the original estimate. There was also added an additional sum to construction costs for the Memorial Court of $76,000. This changed the Dinwiddie estimate, the basis for all figures being quoted by the trustees, to the following:

```
Memorial  Court  .........................................$   76,000
Opera  House  .........................................  3,429,679
Legion-Museum  .........................................  1,921,485
                                                         ───────────
                                                          $5,427,164
```

or $199,836 under the original estimate.

It was later found advisable to reduce the size of the Opera House which occasioned a corresponding reduction in the size of the Legion-Museum Building. Sixty thousand dollars more was also added to the cost of the Memorial Court. These changes brought the costs, according to the Dinwiddie estimate to the following:

```
Opera  House.............................................$3,309,679
Legion  Museum  .........................................  1,864,485
Memorial  Court  .........................................   136,000
                                                         ───────────
                                                          $5,310,164
```

or $316,836 below the original estimate.

A comparison of the figures set forth above clearly indicates that in April, 1927, with a project comprising two complete buildings of the exact size and shape, costing $5,627,000, there was, with the four million dollar bond issue, sufficient funds to complete the project. However, two years later, with no increase in building costs, and with one of the originally planned buildings having shrunk considerably in size, together with other reductions that have decreased the estimated costs more than three hundred thousand dollars, instead of there being sufficient money to complete the project, with a surplus, we are now informed that there is a deficit of $327,000. This information comes from the trustees of the publicly subscribed fund who have controlled the affairs of this project this far and who undoubtedly furnished the figures of the amount in their hands when the original estimate was made. With a reduction in estimated costs of more than three hundred thousand dollars and a declared deficit of more than three hundred thousand dollars then it would appear that the private fund has shrunk more than six hundred thousand dollars during the past two years.

This should emphasize the need, heretofore suggested, for a full detailed accounting by the trustees. The fund has been in existence for eight to nine years. Expenses have been incurred. Income has been received, but despite repeated requests, no accounting, other than a balance sheet as of September, 1928, has been made available.

It is not the desire of the veterans to be critical, but in face of the assertion of the trustees that the alleged deficit is due to the ever changing demands of the veterans, the veterans cannot remain silent. We therefore call attention to the following facts:

Prior to September 1st, 1926, the two parcels of land involved in this project were occupied by income producing properties. The tenants of these structures were summarily evicted prior to September, 1926, and the fact is that the land remained untouched for a period of two years following their eviction. During that period not a single dollar of revenue accrued, with the exception of the Locomobile building and the small corner leased to one of the oil companies for a service station. In other words, here were two square blocks of land occupied by various lines of business activity, each one contributing to the commercial well being of the neighborhood, and we find that—for no apparent reason—all of this commercial activity was forced to suspend, and that following that suspension the land lay idle, and now remains idle. We suggest that this is not in keeping with sound business practice.

We find, further, that despite the fact that the Trust Agreement very definitely provides that the title to this land shall vest in the Regents of the University of California, and, under such conditions, would be tax-exempt; the title to the properties not owned by the City has remained over a period of years in the hands of private corporation with a consequent drain on the trust fund by reason of tax payments.

We cannot quarrel with the principle that the City is entitled to the revenue, but we seriously question the wisdom of a policy that gives taxes to the City for a period of years, thereby bringing about a situation that may compel the people at a later date to furnish further fund for this project.

The block bounded by Fulton, Grove, Van Ness and Franklin streets was acquired during the calendar years 1924 and 1925, and the title thereto remained, exclusive of six parcels owned by the City, in the Mercantile Trust Company until March 4th, 1929. This is the block scheduled as the Opera House site.

The block bounded by Fulton, McAllister, Van Ness and Franklin streets, exclusive of lots 1 and 2, was acquired by the Mercantile Trust Company during the calendar year 1925 and the title to that land still remains in the Mercantile Trust Company.

It would seem that it is wholly in order to inquire why, when the transfer of Block 791 was made to the Regents, that a transfer was not made of Block 786, with a resultant saving in taxes for the fiscal year 1929-1930.

Upon all these facts, therefore, the veterans do not concede any necessity for a deficit. If there be a deficit, responsibility therefor must be placed where it belongs, upon the Opera House and Art Museum, and not upon the Veterans' Building, rather upon the fraction of the Veterans-Museum Building devoted to veterans' uses as distinguished from art purposes.

If it is finally determined to construct an Opera House and Art Museum upon a scale that will, if the bare necessities of the veterans are provided for, inevitably leave a deficit, the veterans do not deem it their privilege to criticize such a policy. Neither do they deem it their duty to find or suggest a solution as to the method of or for further financing.

However, the veterans deem it proper at this time to say that, if any appeal is made for further funds in connection with this project and it is charged that such further funds are necessary to complete the veterans' part of the Memorial, or that the appeal is caused by veterans' demands, the veterans will not support such an appeal. On the contrary, on our opinion, they will oppose it. We do not mean to say, however, that in our opinion the veterans will not do anything reasonable and proper to facilitate the erection of the War Memorial. As a matter of course they will do so, but the day when a building for the veterans can be used as a bait to induce the voting of money for an Opera House or an Art Museum, with supine acquiescence on the part of the veterans of San Francisco, is past.

This Advisory Board stands ready to recommend to the veterans of San Francisco the approval of plan "C," with the technical modifications as submitted in the attached criticism of that plan, and either with or without the elimination of 10 feet in width of the building as suggested earlier in this statement; but such approval will only be recommended when the duly constituted Board of War Memorial Trustees has been regularly appointed agreeable to the provisions of the Charter of the City and County of San Francisco.

Respectfully submitted,

ADVISORY BOARD TO VETERANS WAR MEMORIAL COMMITTEES,

(Signed)   H. J. BOYD,
JAMES B. BURNS,
H. W. GLENSOR

J. C. CLARIDGE, Secretary.

Cost estimates by City Engineer, approved by Board of Public Works, April 11th, 1927, and transmitted to Board of Supervisors with plans shown below to establish sum needed by bond issue:

Opera House...$4,127,000.00
Legion-Museum 1,500,000.00

$5,627,000.00
Public subscription on hand........................... 1,627,000.00

To be raised by bond issue...........................$4,000,000.00

THE MAYOR: These you haven't heard, because these came from the committee of nine.

THE MAYOR (reading):

RESULTS OF STUDY OF PLAN "C," AS COMPARED WITH THE STATEMENT OF ESTIMATED NEEDS OF VETERAN ORGANIZATIONS CONTAINED IN THE REPORT OF THIS BOARD UNDER DATE OF MARCH 20TH, 1929.

(Criticisms in this report are numbered same as items listed in above report of March 20th, 1929).

1.   The seating capacity of the auditorium is 150-odd seats less than tabulated on plans, and the shape of the auditorium is quite out of proportion, inasmuch as same represents a square arrangement rather than a rectangular one. Chair storage is shown on the second floor, which is a serious mistake, inasmuch as this storage should be taken care of on the first floor directly adjacent to the auditorium.

2.   The area of meeting halls mentioned is about 30 per cent shy of the required area.

4.   The kitchenettes as shown on plans are inadequate in size to care for the number of people who are to be served from same.

5.   The arrangement as shown will not function properly, on account of its inaccessibility to the auditorium.

8.   The library is short about 250 feet of space and no reading rooms have been shown.

9.   Band practice rooms are provided in basement in addition to band practice rooms on fourth floor.   These latter rooms can be utilized for another purpose.

10.   These lockers have been overlooked in plans, but space for same is available.

11.   These rooms and lockers have been overlooked in plans but space for same is available.

14-22 inc. Office space for various Veterans headquarters, as set forth in program, contains about 6000 feet less than required.

June 10, 1929. The following is an extract of the meeting of the Board of Supervisors, Monday, June 10, 1929:

THE MAYOR: This next is an extract of the meeting of the Board of Supervisors of June 10, 1929, a copy of the transcript (reading):

EXHIBIT NO. 2.

IN RE WAR MEMORIAL TRUSTEES.
Extract From Meeting of Board of Supervisors, Monday,
June 10, 1929, 10:00 A. M.

SUPERVISOR TODD: Mr. Chairman, I would like to make an inquiry. I have been away for the past fourteen weeks. I would like to make some inquiry as to what is being done across the street toward the War Memorial. There was a party out to see me, while I was out in the hospital, and told me that the steel had been ordered for this building, and it was being fabricated in the East. Now, I believe we are equipped to manufacture that steel in San Francisco, and I do not believe any contracts should be entered into by the War Memorial Trustees, or by any one else for a public building, to be fabricated in the East, when we have a great many men in San Francisco who are out of employment. I would like to know from some one the work that is ordered on this building, and just what has been done and just where we stand on it. It has been 1926 since those buildings were torn down across the street. Rents have been lost and there has been nothing done. I would like to know, as one member of the Board, just where we stand on this War Memorial and the Opera House.

THE CHAIRMAN: Supervisor McSheehy and Supervisor Colman are representatives of the Board on the committee.

SUPERVISOR COLMAN: I am very glad to give what information I have on the matter. You will recall a public meeting held here at which the Supervisors passed a resolution, I believe, authorizing, advising or recommending—suggesting to the Mayor that he appoint the trustees and telling the Mayor about the composition of this Board of Trustees. That the Mayor has not seen fit to do, for the reason that some funds are in the control of the present trustees and nothing can be done about appointing new trustees without full power to act. Now, the matter is in disagreement. The architects have a suggestion, the trustees are ready, but there is a difference of opinion between them and the veterans as to the way the building to the north should be built, the trustees claiming that there is ample room and accommodation for the veterans provided, but the veterans want a reallocation of the money, some taken from the Opera House and added to the corner building. The committee was appointed by the Mayor, three Supervisors, three veterans and three trustees to iron the matter out. I have not heard of the result of the last meeting. That is the present status.

SUPERVISOR RONCOVIERI: I would like to inquire if the Supervisor knows why—you may not know the answer—why are these trustees not appointed, is my question. Perhaps that question should be put to the Mayor himself—who has the authority—but if you know, I would like to hear it.

SUPERVISOR TODD: I understand that there were three members of the veterans and three members of this Board and three members of the Musical Association, as I remember it now, a committee of nine, who were to work out these plans and I would like to know who the members of the Board are and if they have had these meetings and what they have done. Who are the members of this Board that are members of this committee?

THE CHAIRMAN: Supervisor McSheehy.

SUPERVISOR HAYDEN: No, Supervisor Hayden, Kent and Marks. There is no report to make, Mr. Chairman and members of the Board.

This committee has met the Committee of Nine, has met with the Trustees of the War Memorial and the Advisory Committee of the veterans, and we do not seem to get anywhere. The veterans are making certain demands for more space and the Trustees of the War Memorial have offered three different plans giving certain additional space and with it additional cost. Now, that matter has been referred back to the veterans for them to select a certain plan that will meet their requirements. The Mayor is to call a meeting and the veterans are to report back at that meeting. That is all the progress I can report at this time.

SUPERVISOR TODD: When are you going to have another meeting?

SUPERVISOR HAYDEN: That is in the hands of the Mayor, the Mayor calls the meeting.

SUPERVISOR TODD: I think somebody is being very derelict in their duty in this War Memorial matter. I do not want to censure anyone, the members of the Board or anyone else. We tore those buildings down more than two years ago. The citizens of San Francisco voted $4,000,000 to complete those buildings. By private subscriptions we raised nearly $2,000,000 to purchase this land and construct these buildings and, up to date, there has been practically nothing done except wrecking the buildings and losing the rent, and now we have two holes, and that is all we have to show for it. It is high time we should take some action. Either the members of the Board who are on that committee should take the lead or the veterans, and get some where with it. This money has been voted by the people, and they want to see these buildings erected, and I would like to see some action taken by some one. I think the chair should call the members of this Board who are members of the committee into conference with the veterans and see if we cannot get something started. Every day four or five men come to my home looking for some kind of employment, and we have the money available.

THE CHAIRMAN: It is the Supervisor's privilege to make a motion calling for a report from the committee.

SUPERVISOR TODD: I will make such a motion, that a report from this committee of nine be submitted to this Board at next Monday's meeting, if I can get a second to it.

SUPERVISOR RONCOVIERI: Second the motion.

SUPERVISOR HAYDEN: I think it would be well to add to that that this matter be first submitted to the Mayor.

SUPERVISR TODD: I have no objection to that.

SUPERVISOR HAYDEN: The committee of nine is in no position to report. We are subject to the call of the Mayor and he is the presiding member of this committee of nine and we are helpless, under the circumstances.

SUPERVISOR TODD: I will amend my motion, that a request be made of the Mayor.

SUPERVISOR ANDRIANO: In my opinion, the serious mistake that was made by this Board was to appoint three members of this Board to act as arbitrators. It was evident at the time that there was an irreconcilable conflict between the veterans and between the Trustees, and it was bad judgment to appoint members of this Board as arbitrators because it was evident that all the members of this Board were leaning one way or the other. they were not impartial. they were not indifferent, they were not disinterested, and that is why nothing has been accomplished. If instead of three Supervisors, this Board had appointed or sought the appointment of three disinterested and impartial and eminent men of this City, who are not involved with one group or with the other, I believe we would have succeeded in adjusting the differences between the veterans and the trustees. But when you appoint arbitrators who are not thoroughly impartial and disinterested, it is impossible to reach a solution of a delicate and intricate problem such as confronts us at this time. And I do not think that as long as you have that committee composed of men, all of whom are in some way committed, we will ever succeed in straightening out the difficulty. The proper thing, in my opinion, after this report comes in, and no solution is reached, is to rescind our action of appointing three members of this Board as arbitrators, and to select three disinterested and impartial citizens of the City who have the best interests of the City at heart, and who are desirous of seeking a final solution of the controversy. And I trust that will be done when the proper time comes.

SUPERVISOR COLMAN: Mr. Chairman, I want to call attention to the maker of this motion that, whereas it is very timely, the subject that he brings up, and is one that should be discussed at all times, in my opinion, we trace back to the cause of this deadlock——

SUPERVISOR TODD (interrupting): Will you speak to the motion?

SUPERVISOR COLMAN: Yes, I want to give you additional information on it and favoring it.

SUPERVISOR TODD: I would suggest that the chair put the motion.

THE CHAIRMAN: Supervisor Colman has the floor.

SUPERVISOR TODD: Are you speaking to the motion?

THE CHAIRMAN: Supervisor Colman has the floor.

SUPERVISOR TODD: I rise to a point of order. You have not put the motion yet, Mr. Chairman.

THE CHAIRMAN: The motion, if you wish——

THE CLERK (interrupting): The motion is by Supervisor Todd, seconded by Supervisor Roncovieri, that his Honor be requested to make a report in time for the meeting of the Board next Monday relative to the status of the War Memorial project.

SUPERVISOR TODD: That is correct.

SUPERVISOR COLMAN: I desire to speak on that matter and throw some additional light on the subject. I am opposed to it. The deadlock can be traced, in my opinion, directly to this Board of Supervisors when they passed the resolution, stating that no plans would be approved for the construction of the War Memorial that were not agreeable to the veterans. That places this Board of Supervisors in a very biased situation in the matter because it places the control of the plans, before their approval, in the hands of the veterans. I merely call that to the Board's attention because that has a great deal of weight in the present discussion, and the Board is not impartial, and I think the Board, in its action on the other matter regarding the appointment of the trustees, has not been entirely impartial but has shown, without, in my opinion,—well, as clear an understanding of the matter as we members of the trustees have, a desire to side with the veterans in the matter. Now, the thought in Mr. Todd's mind to have the War Memorial built is a worthy one, and I am certainly for it with heart and soul. But we are faced here between two interests, and, in my opinion, the public are getting sick and tired of this difference of opinion, and they want a settlement, absolutely. They do not want the authority left on one side or the other, but they want the thing settled, they want to see the War Memorial built. That is my size-up of the situation regarding it. Supervisor Roncovieri asked about why not appoint the trustees? The answer is that there is $2,000,000 there available that the present trustees have as a trust, and they have assumed responsibility for this money, under certain clauses and certain conditions set by the Regents of the University of California, and they will not release this money to the new board of trustees until they feel assured that the conditions of trust under which they received the $2,000,000 will be faithfully carried out. Now, as a matter of fact at the present time, there is no cash available except this $2,000,000. The bonds have not been sold and possibly, for the immediate future, will not be offered until at least our bonding finances are in better shape than they are now. Now, that is why the Mayor has not appointed the trustees. And I agree with him and so stated at a meeting held in his office when he asked the opinion of the Supervisors who were present, whether we approved of his action under the circumstances in deferring the announcement of his appointees on this board of trustees. Now, that is the situation we are facing in the making of this resolution. Still the effort to bring about the solution is a worthy one, and I am happy to vote for it.

SUPERVISOR RONCOVIERI: I would like to ask the Supervisor, through you, a question. Do I understand that the Mayor hesitates or will not appoint the trustees until certain trustees who are holding money subscribed to the project, who may not be the trustees that the Mayor will appoint, act upon the plan, or the plan is satisfactory to them? In other words, are financiers, men who may not be appointed by the Mayor, or they may be, I do not know, going to hold this project up and say, "We won't turn over this $2,000,000 until we approve the plans," and that holds the money up? And that prevents the Mayor from appointing a group of nine trustees which the law empowers him to do?

SUPERVISOR COLMAN: Not the plan, they do not care about the plan, but they want to be assured that the terms of the trust under which they hold the money will be carried out by the new board, and unless they are sure they are assured that they can do, they will not release this money, because they received it under certain conditions.

SUPERVISOR RONCOVIERI: What assurance do they want? The law says that the Mayor shall appoint nine trustees.

SUPERVISOR COLMAN: Eleven.

SUPERVISOR RONCOVIERI: Eleven. These men hold this money and you say they want to be assured that everything that they want will be carried out by the eleven new trustees, of which they may not be members. Then they can hold that $2,000,000 out for ever. They may——

SUPERVISOR COLMAN (interrupting): If the conditions of their trust are fulfilled by the new trustees, they have nothing further to do.

SUPERVISOR RONCOVIERI: I ask again, what guarantee can be given to this nonofficial board that the official board will carry out its wishes?

THE CHAIRMAN: I would like to ask, how these private trustees are going to know whether their wishes are going to be carried out by the new committees before that committee is appointed? How can they possibly get any assurances? I do not think the Supervisor's explanation is logical, if I may be pardoned for making the statement.

SUPERVISOR COLMAN: I am telling you just what occurred.

SUPERVISOR RONCOVIERI: I would like to know—I have an indistinct recollection, and it seems to me that we passed some sort of a resolution, requesting the Mayor to appoint a certain number of war veterans on the board. I do not recall positively that we did that.

THE CHAIRMAN: That is correct.

SUPERVISOR RONCOVIERI: It seems now that we should release the Mayor and not hold him to anything. Let him appoint whoever he sees fit. The time has come to do something. Let the Mayor be free to appoint whomever he sees fit and go on with the job.

THE CHAIRMAN: After a very lengthy hearing, this Board adopted a resolution, merely recommending to the Mayor that a majority of the new trustees be representatives of the Veterans of the World War.

SUPERVISOR RONCOVIERI: It was merely a recommendation, we did not tie his hands?

THE CHAIRMAN: No, we did——

SUPERVISOR McSHEEHY (interrupting): Yes we did.

SUPERVISOR TODD: Yes. to be ratified by this Board.

SUPERVISOR COLMAN: We tied his hands because his appointments must be ratified by this Board.

SUPERVISOR RONCOVIERI: I think we should free the Mayor from that embarrassment. If we have practically said to the Mayor, we recommend that you appoint this number of war veterans and that means that, later on, when the appointments are submitted to us for ratification, we won't ratify them, I do not think it is fair to the

Mayor, I do not think it is fair to the people who are waiting for that job to be completed or to be commenced.

SUPERVISOR McSHEEHY: Mr. Mayor and members of the Board: Supervisor Todd was sick for several months, and of course is not very conversant with this matter. I am more than pleased that he has brought this matter up today, and I want to say to the members of the Board that, if any member of this Board can offer any motion that will solve this problem so that we can start that work over there, that he will find this Board, I think, in a receptive mood to follow that recommendation. San Francisco wants to see the work started and wants to see it started badly, but we are in a peculiar position here today, members of the Board, and our position is simply this, and Supervisor Colman has made it as clear as anyone can make it, and that is that the trustees appointed by the Regents of the University of California have in their custody in round sums or have had $2,000,000. They have spent, I think, somewhere in the neighborhood of $700,000 for the purchase of the land and other incidental expenses. Now, by reason of their trusteeship they have a duty to perform just as we have as members of the Board of Supervisors. And the trustees are men of standing. Three members of this Board are trustees, and the other trustees are some of our outstanding citizens here in our City, who have subscribed large sums of money to the fund. Now, they want to go on, they want to finish the work. And the veterans have their views in the matter and they are entitled to their views and they are asking for so many feet of floor space. That footage was granted to them, and they have revised their figure and requested a number of thousand more feet, and that number of thousand feet has been granted, and today a staff of architects have been employed for some months drawing up the plans, and I have personally seen the plans, and I can tell you that they are plans that we will be proud of, and they are entirely under the supervision of the architects who designed this building, Mr. Brown and entirely under the supervision of Mr. Lansburgh, who is one of our leading theater designers. The plans are about completed. It is simply an impasse that has been created, through some misunderstanding. Now if we can all get together and agree to give and take we can start that work, but we must be in that frame of mind. We cannot stand up and say, "You must do so and so, you must do so and so." You have got to go in there with a free hand to give and take because we both have rights in the matter

SUPERVISOR SHANNON: We, you say "we," who do you mean?

SUPERVISOR McSHEEHY: I mean we, the Board of Supervisors, we, representing the people of San Francisco. Friday night a meeting is to be held, which you have all seen a notice of in the newspapers, by the veterans, to which all of the various interests of San Francisco have been invited. I do not know that this Board has been invited individually, but any member that desires to attend can do so. It will be held in the Memorial Hall of the Auditorium, under the auspices of the Veterans of Foreign Wars. Now, members of the Board, the entire matter is in such shape today that it will take but little to complete an agreement between the Board of Trustees, the Veterans of Foreign Wars and this Board of Supervisors, representing the City and County of San Francisco, and the Mayor will not appoint the trustees or the Board of Trustees that the people voted for until we have ironed out our differences, so that they will go in with a free hand to function. And you cannot blame the Mayor in taking that stand. You would not want to go in as one of the directors, picking up something that others differed on. You would get no place. So that I say that your motion is a timely one and I hope the Board will pass it, and I feel that within the next week or two, these differences will be ironed out because I feel every one is in a receptive mood today and they want to start the work. Now, I am speaking as a Supervisor and also as a member of the present Board of Trustees. I have attended myself every meeting of the Board of Trustees from the day I was appointed some two years ago.

SUPERVISOR TODD: Do you know anything about any steel being ordered by this present Board of Trustees from some eastern factory?

SUPERVISOR McSHEEHY: There have been no contracts of any kind let by the present Board of Trustees. They have advertised for certain concrete and grating contracts but they have never been let, and they won't be let until this Board of Supervisors approves the plans and there will be no steel contract let until this Board approves the plans.

SUPERVISOR TODD: You know that is the story on the street, that a contract for steel has been let.

SUPERVISOR McSHEEHY: Well, I would say, as a member of the Board of Trustees, that is an erroneous story, and I am talking from positive knowledge, and I will say that to you, as a member of the Board of Trustees.

SUPERVISOR TODD: I move the previous question.

SUPERVISOR McSHEEHY: The plans are being drawn under the supervision of Mr. Brown and Mr. Lansburgh, on Montgomery and Sacramento Streets, on the northwest corner. There is a young man in charge of the office and I know he will be delighted to show the plans to any member of this Board that calls there.

THE CHAIRMAN: Supervisor Todd's motion, on adoption. Is there any objection?

(Bringing down the gavel.)

June 17, 1929. Motion in Board of Supervisors by Supervisor Todd: In accordance with motion of Supervisor Todd, made at last meeting of the Board, his Honor Mayor Rolph reported relative to the appointment on December 21, 1928, of a committee of nine to act with the Mayor regarding the prosecution of the work of constructing the War Memorial and Opera House. He declared that he had a complete record of all the meetings of the committee held in his office and reports made, but hoped to be able to give a complete report after conference with Mr. Fleishhacker. In the absence of Mr. Drum, who is in New York, Mr. Fleishhacker was requested to take, his place temporarily, and he has asked for ten days' time to get figures on the financial status of the project.

The Mayor requested that a special time be set for hearing report when figures are in.

Supervisor Todd moved to make a Special Order of Business for next Monday at 3 p. m.

Supervisor Hayden moved as an amendment that the matter be left in the hands of the Mayor to call a meeting at the earliest time suitable for a full attendance of the Board. Amendment carried.

On Wednesday, July 17, 1929, a special meeting of the Board of Supervisors was held at which were present members of the Board of Supervisors, War Memorial Trustees, representatives of veteran organizations and interested citizens. A full discussion of the War Memorial took place and a report of the War Memorial Committee, printed above, under date of July 17, 1929, was submitted to the Board of Supervisors and ordered printed. I refer hereto and make a part hereof the Reporter's Transcript of the meeting, dated July 17, 1929, because it contains very definite, important and interesting facts relating to the whole War Memorial question.

EXHIBIT NO. 3.

IN RE WAR MEMORIAL.

Special Meeting of the Board of Supervisors,
Wednesday, July 17, 1929.

A special meeting of the Board of Supervisors was held on the 17th day of July, 1929, beginning at the hour of 3:30 p. m. of said day, in the chambers of the Board of Supervisors, City Hall, San Francisco, California.

Mayor James Rolph Jr. presided.

(Andriano, here; Colman, absent; Deasy, here; Gallagher, ill; Havenner, out of town; Hayden, here; Kent, out of town; Marks, here; McGovern, absent; McSheehy, here; Powers, here; Roncovieri, here; Schmidt, absent; Shannon, out of town; Stanton, here; Suhr, here; Todd, out of town; Toner, absent.)

There were present beside the Supervisors, War Memorial Trustees, representatives of Veteran organizations, and interested citizens.

THE MAYOR: Have you any means of knowing, Mr. Clerk, whether or not we will have a quorum today?

THE CLERK. I do not know. Notices were sent yesterday and telephone messages were sent this morning to all the members.

THE MAYOR: Gentlemen of the Board: Pursuant to a resolution adopted by your honorable body, the Mayor was directed to communicate with the War Memorial Trustees and to expedite, as far as possible, the submitting to you of a report of their labors in connection with the building of the War Memorial across the street. You passed a resolution, directing that a committee of nine—complimenting the Mayor by adding him to that committee of nine—be appointed, to discuss the differences that then existed between the War Memorial Trustees and the committee appointed by the Veteran organizations. We held many meetings in the Mayor's office, and the Mayor's office has a full and complete record of all that transpired at those conferences. The reports submitted to the committee of nine are on file in the Mayor's office, in fact, they are here today, but they are so voluminous that it will take a very long period of time to review what the committee of nine, with the Mayor, has discussed during the period since last December when you appointed the committee of nine with the Mayor. Now, in response to the resolution last passed by your honorable body, the War Memorial Trustees are here today, the members of the committee of nine are here today and the San Francisco War Memorial Trustees have submitted to the Mayor for your consideration, and in response to your resolution, a completed report of all of the points involved in the building, the changes and the matters that have been before the committee of nine. And so that no further time may be lost I would respectfully suggest that the Clerk of the Board read to the Board the report of the War Memorial Trustees.

(The Clerk reads the report and a telegram from Mr. John S. Drum.)

THE MAYOR: That adds John S. Drum's name to the list.

(The Clerk reads a letter from Lansburgh & Brown, Architects, and also reads estimates and summaries.)

THE CLERK: That is the end of the report except the field notes.

THE MAYOR: Those figures—I have just perused them—are the detailed working figures of Dinwiddie & Company, known as leading constructors of buildings and being a part of this full report from the War Memorial Trustees. As we have not a quorum today, and as no action can be taken today without a quorum, I would respectfully suggest that these figures be thoroughly digested and thoroughly gone over, and each Supervisor familiarize himself with the figures, and the Board decide whether or not the Trustees shall be appointed, as provided for by the Charter, and the names submitted to the Board, and that this report be transferred to the new Trustees, as provided for by the charter amendment, and these reports turned over by the Board of Supervisors, discharging the committee of nine and the Mayor, and transferred to the new committee of eleven, confirmed by you, and that they have full charge of the construction. These are matters which, of course, require your consideration and your attention. I do not think that you can grasp those figures. You know, there is $4,000,000 on hand, you know that, to put a granite front on that building will cost some $700,000 or $800,000 more than if a terra cotta is put on. You are advised that it will take several hundred thousand dollars more to carry out this plan, you are advised that you will have to devise ways and means for raising that money, or you will have to submit to a reduction and curtailment of plans recommended by the representatives of the veteran organizations, and which the War Trustees have confirmed, and this report is based on *Plan C*, as set forth in the last report to the Committee on April 20th, of this year. Now, these are matters which will require your attention, and as I say, we cannot act without a quorum, the Board cannot direct the appointment of the Trustees without a quorum, because the committees of the Board have all agreed that until the plans are thoroughly thrashed out, why, the committee had better not be appointed. The War Memorial Trustees come forward now in making this final report and suggest that the Mayor make the appointments and have them confirmed by the Board. I was prepared to make the appointments today, but it is fruitless because you cannot confirm them, but to indicate the type of appointees the Mayor is going to appoint, the Mayor has appointed and has the acceptance of Major General Hunter Liggett as a member of the committee, second in command of the American Expeditionary Force at the Front.

Now, without a quorum nothing can be done. Has any Supervisor any suggestion to offer, or has any member of the War Trustees any suggestion to offer?

SUPERVISOR McSHEEHY: Mr. Mayor, members of the Board and members of the Board of Trustees and members of the veterans organizations: I hope that we will do something here today. We might not officially be able to do anything without a quorum, I realize that. There are nine members present, I am sorry there are not ten, for this reason: I think that we are all in accord that something should be started, I think that we all realize that we have these two lots over here, that you might say are an eyesore to the people of San Francisco. Practically around $700,000 has been invested in the property. In round sums there is about $900,000 in moneys in custody of the present trustees of the War Memorial. The people of San Francisco have stamped their approval by voting $4,000,000 worth of bonds. We are all anxious to do something, I think that we are all anxious to get together. So I hope this meeting will not adjourn without some expression of opinion from those present as to how we can come together and try and iron out our differences. I think you will find the present Board of Trustees in a receptive mood, ready to co-operate, ready to do anything to advance this construction work which will mean the advancement of San Francisco. We all realize the condition that exists here today. I happen to be engaged in the building industry, and I know the conditions that that industry is in today. Men are walking our streets. And men need work here in the erection of buildings. We have the money, and it is simply a difference of opinion. Now, I feel, as true San Franciscans, as true Americans, that we can come together and iron out our differences, and I hope some effort will be made here today. I realize that we cannot take any official recognition of the report as rendered without a quorum, but there are nine members present, and you, the Mayor of San Francisco, are also present, and I hope an expression will be rendered by all interested, to see if we cannot agree on something here today, so that the next time, your Honor, that you will call us together there will be a quorum present. I assure you that I am deeply sorry that a quorum is not present here today.

SUPERVISOR RONCOVIERI: I would like to ask Supervisor McSheehy, what are the differences that exist today?

SUPERVISOR McSHEEHY: The differences are many.

SUPERVISOR MARKS: Before you answer that, Mr. McSheehy, isn't it possible to obtain the presence of one more Supervisor?

THE MAYOR: I have spoken to the Clerk about it, and I have

spoken to the Sergeant-at-Arms to see if there was not one that we could possibly get hold of.

SUPERVISOR HAYDEN: I think we might get Supervisor Colman.

SUPERVISOR ANDRIANO: Supervisor Colman is out of town.

SUPERVISOR MARKS: I suggest, respectfully, while we are discussing the matter, the Sergeant-at-Arms make another effort to reach the members.

SUPERVISOR McSHEEHY: I think that suggestion is a worthy one. I cannot answer directly, only indirectly, and of course it might open up the debate and we are anxious to settle our differences. What was the question again?

SUPERVISOR RONCOVIERI: You were alluding to some differences in your talk and I wonder what those differences are today. I thought they had been ironed out.

SUPERVISOR McSHEEHY: I do not believe they have been ironed out, Supervisor. The differences, as I get them, are these: We have here two lots here across the street that have been purchased. We have, in round figures—let me use round figures entirely, not to get into too many details—we have in round figures practically $5,000,000 for the purpose of erecting two buildings. We have figures from our architects showing certain construction runs $8,000,000. We have other figures from our architects showing certain constructions that will cost $6,500,000. I am using round terms entirely. We have but $5,000,000. Now, the question is, can we erect two buildings that will meet with the approval of the interested parties for $5,000,000? Personally I am in the building business—and you know it for yourself— I feel that we can erect those two buildings. $5,000,000 is a huge sum of money. Construction work does not cost today what it cost one year ago or two years ago. Now, it is a matter of ironing out our differences so we can erect the buildings that will cost that amount of money. And, personally, I do not want to, at this time, enter into any debate with any one, but I would like to hear from some that are interested so that we could all have something to work on, so that we can iron out these differences.

SUPERVISOR RONCOVIERI: I would like to know what does the present committee recommend? I understand there is Plan A, I understand there is Plan B, and I understand there is Plan C. I would like to know what Plan A would cost, in round figures. Perhaps the architect could tell us, Mr. Lansburgh.

THE MAYOR: Mr. Lansburgh.

MR. LANSBURGH: You call it Plan A. I have not it down there under those categories. $8,200,000.

SUPERVISOR RONCOVIERI: And Plan B, the second plan?

MR. LANSBURGH: That is with the granite, the same plan, but with one the exterior is in granite and terra cotta with the other.

SUPERVISOR RONCOVIERI: It would be the same plan but the material would be terra cotta?

MR. LANSBURGH: Yes.

SUPERVISOR RONCOVIERI: And that would cost——

MR. LANSBURGH: $7,500,000. Then there is a reduced plan where the specifications have been changed and somethings have been changed.

SUPERVISOR RONCOVIERI: The plan itself has been reduced?

MR. LANSBURGH: No, not the plan itself, the specifications, something has been left out in heating and lighting and things of that sort.

SUPERVISOR RONCOVIERI: Did you reduce the size of the auditorium?

MR. LANSBURGH: No.

SUPERVISOR RONCOVIERI: You first proposed 4400.

MR. LANSBURGH: That has been reduced to 3300.

SUPERVISOR RONCOVIERI: Did not that make some economies?

MR. LANSBURGH: Yes.

SUPERVISOR RONCOVIERI: What is the lowest possible figure that it can be built for?

MR. LANSBURGH: $6,600,000.

SUPERVISOR RONCOVIERI: We have only $5,000,000.

MR. LANSBURGH: I think there is a little more, or $5,100,000. There is a deficit of $1,500,000.

SUPERVISOR RONCOVIERI: I do not know whether we have any authority, Mr. Mayor, but I would suggest that a bond issue be submitted this November for the difference between the money on hand and the money it will cost, $6,600,000, and I believe the people of San Francisco will vote this overwhelmingly. They know the men that are behind this movement, they have confidence in them and I believe they will vote for this. Everybody wants this finished, the Press is unanimous, that would be my suggestion. I do not know whether we have any authority in the matter, or whether this new committee you are about to appoint will have that authority, but I think that is the way out of it, to give them the money they need and do it as it has been done in the past, in the big way that this Civic Center and all that it contains has been done.

THE MAYOR: Do not forget the dome, either.

SUPERVISOR RONCOVIERI: Or the dome, either.

THE MAYOR: Mr. Fleishhacker, would you mind enlightening the Board upon the standpoint of the Trustees?

Mr. HERBERT FLEISHHACKER: Mr. Mayor and members of the Board: I think the letter sent by the Trustees covers very very fully everything that the Trustees have in mind at this time. To just listen to them and not know the real contents is quite misleading. Supervisor Roncovieri wanted to know what the difference was in Plan A and B and C. As I understand, A refers to the Opera House, B possibly to the Legion Building and so on, and to go into the details would take hours. The Board of Trustees have spent nearly five years in the perfecting of these plans, and I want to say at this time I regret exceedingly that our Chairman, Mr. John Drum, is not here. Mr. Drum was the one active man on the Board, he was Chairman of the Building Committee, and I know I express the thought of all my associates on the Board when I say John Drum was wrapped up, heart and soul, in the thought and the wish of developing for San Francisco the finest Opera House in the world and the finest home for the Legionnaires to be found anywhere in the world. Unfortunately, the plans were so very very fine that, before we got through listening to the wishes and desires of both sides, that the cost amounted very very much. We have reached a point somewhere between seven and eight million dollars, with a little less than $5,000,000 available. I cannot share with Supervisor Roncovieri his wish and desire to sell more bonds, because I think San Francisco is in a very terrible dilemma at this time. San Francisco has voted $4,000,000 worth of bonds for the completion of this project, and many millions of dollars for the acquisition of the water system. We cannot sell the bonds at this time. So I do not think you are losing any very valuable time in putting over this very important matter a few days. It will probably be two or three months before you will find any customer for these particular bonds, or any other bonds. The financial situation throughout the world is that investors are not looking for 4½ percent bonds at this time. The day will come when those bonds again will sell at a premium, and I dare say it will before the end of the year. So I do not believe that you have anything to worry about at this moment. I do not think, further, that we will ever accomplish very much until you have appointed your new Board of Trustees. It is a matter that will have to be thrashed over very very carefully. The architects, Messrs. Brown & Bakewell have given the very best that they have to design the very very best building that any architect could design. And I believe we have two of the foremost architects in the United States working on this wonderful plan.

THE MAYOR: Do not forget Albert Lansburgh.

MR. FLEISHHACKER: If the program continues he can smile because he will get a fee. I put a question to Mr. Brown and Mr. Lansburgh this morning before coming here. I asked them if they could build two buildings within the $5,000,000 limit, buildings that they thought would do credit to this marvelous Civic Center and this wonderful dome of yours, and they both answered in the affirmative that it could be done, but in order to do it, they would have to cut down materially the size of the Opera House building and also the Legion Building. I think those matters will have to be taken up by your new Board. If you attempt to have 50 or 500 men settle the building problem you will never get anywhere. A small committee who have the confidence of the Mayor and the Board and the people of San Francisco I think will very readily solve this important project, and, as Mr. McSheehy said, thrash out the small differences because, after all, the differences are very, very small, it is a question of cutting out some of the refinements and cutting down the size of these buildings. And the only thing I regret is that it will take time to redraft new plans. You could not start in immediately if the committee decide to build within the $5,000,000 available. I also asked that question of the architects, and they tell me it will take between four and five months to bring that about. So I do not think that you are going to make much speed by rushing this matter. It will require some little time, and if you attempt to put too much speed on, you will get nowhere at all.

SUPERVISOR MARKS: Mr. Mayor, may I ask as to some of the figures, with your permission? Do I understand the total cash available now is $4,890,000 approximately?

MR. KENDRICK: Yes.

MR. FLEISHHACKER: That includes a sum of almost $200,000 that has been expended. I believe that something like $70,000 has been expended in excavating. And it covers the full expense of the drafting of all plans.

MR. KENDRICK: It excludes it.

MR. FLEISHHACKER: There will be about $5,100,000, altogether.

SUPERVISOR MARKS: $5,100,000 available. And is there anything left to be paid on the land purchase?

MR. KENDRICK: Mr. Marks, I can tell you that there is $4,000,000 worth of bonds that are available and about $800,000 in Trustee's money. The land is all paid for but the Trustees have also plans that are worth about $300,000, including excavations, and that will add to the $800,000, making about $5,100,000 really being available, considering we had to buy new plans and have the excavation made.

SUPERVISOR MARKS: In other words, the money that is now on hand would be entirely available for building purposes, no part of that need be spent for excavation or for land?

MR. KENDRICK: No.

MR. FLEISHHACKER: Possibly for new plans if you decide to change the size.

SUPERVISOR MARKS: Some mention was made of three distinct kinds of plans which have been referred to as A, B and C.

MR. KENDRICK: Those are not three distinct sets of plans, it is the same plan for two of those, say A and B, one is with granite and the other with terra cotta. And then the third idea is taking the same plan, so far as the cubic contents are concerned, but cutting down the embellishments.

SUPERVISOR MARKS: What I meant when I used the word "plan"—I did not mean "Plan" in the architectural sense, I meant that scheme or design for building a building.

MR. KENDRICK: The same building in all three plans, the same exteriors.

SUPERVISOR MARKS: The same architectural plans but different combinations of specifications and so on?

MR. KENDRICK: Yes, and cutting down of some of the interior decorations or accessories.

SUPERVISOR MARKS: As I understand, Mr. Mayor, with one set, for granite construction, would be $8,200,000, but with terra cotta, with the same arrangement, would be $7,500,000, with another arrangement $7,250,000 for granite and $6,600,000 for terra cotta.

MR. KENDRICK: No, that is wrong. $8,200,000 for granite, $7,500,000 for terra cotta and about $6,500,000 by eliminating a great many of the interior arrangements.

THE MAYOR: Mr. Landsburgh, can you add to that?

MR. LANDSBURGH: There are two setups, Mr. Marks: One, the plans as they exist, with all the details shown, and the specifications as written, $8,200,000 and $7,000,000 and something.   Then those same plans, with the modification of specifications in detail but not structurally changed in any way, are, the reduced figures, $7,000,000 something and $6,500,000, $6,600,000.   So there is a deficit of the lowest possible figure of $1,500,000, approximately.

SUPERVISOR MARKS: There are not three different setups?

MR. LANSBURGH: No, the A, B and C that was referred to by the Mayor refers entirely to the Legion Building.   That was the scheme we discussed, as to which it showed three different dispositions for the arrangement of the Legion Building.   It has nothing whatsoever to do with this set of figures.

SUPERVISOR RONCOVIERI: Mr. Chairman, Mr. Fleishhacker stated that he believed that the buildings could be built within the amount now on hand, but if there is a $1,500,000 difference between the amount we have on hand and the amount necessary to build this $6,600,000 building, how can you obtain the same building?   There must be a loss somewhere.

MR. LANSBURGH: The size of the building would have to be cut down, you would have to have a building of a smaller seating capacity. The present plan calls for 3,500 seats, and it is possible that we will have to cut down to a 2,700 or 2,800 opera house.   But those are matters that the architects will have to ponder over, for weeks before they can answer.   But we cannot go on with the present plans with the amount of money available, that is definite, that we know.   If you want to complete the present idea, it will mean getting more money.

SUPERVISOR RONCOVIERI: Will the appearance of these buildings be such, that is of the $5,000,000 buildings, that it will not be at all what is in your minds, what you would like to have for the $6,600,000? Can you give us some idea of the difference in appearance of these buildings?   And also their interior?

MR. BROWN: It has not to do with the character of the exterior or the interior.

SUPERVISOR RONCOVIERI: The exterior will be the same in every case?

MR. BROWN: It will be of similar character but smaller, as 5 is to 8, it would go on those proportions as to cubic contents.   I think the 5 would be a very imposing building, yes.

SUPERVISOR RONCOVIERI: Would the smaller building satisfy the veterans, would that be satisfactory to them?

MR. BROWN: That I could not say, we would have to get together in detail.

SUPERVISOR RONCOVIERI: Have not they been consulted?

MR. BROWN: We have just about got what the veterans want now, we have not got any surplus, but I imagine that the veterans would perhaps shade their requirements to the amount of money that is available, I do not know.

SUPERVISOR RONCOVIERI: What would the seating capacity be on a $5,000,000 investment?

MR. BROWN: That is all pretty hard to answer, off-hand. Perhaps we could bring the seating capacity down to 3000, I imagine we could.

THE MAYOR: I do not like to excuse Mr. Fleishhacker. If there is any one desirous of asking him any questions—he has been elected to take the place of Mr. John Drum on the War Memorial Trustee's Committee. Now, as Chairman, and in substitution for Mr. Drum, who is now in New York and who, I am sorry, is not here today after years of service in this matter, if you wish to ask Mr. Fleishhacker any questions before he leaves, now is the time to do it. I know he has an important engagement because he mentioned it before I made the report to you, that we meet this afternoon, and we have not a quorum.

SUPERVISOR POWERS: I would like to ask Mr. Fleishhacker and the rest of the directors: The Board of Supervisors here passed a resolution that, when the plans are completed, they will have to be satisfactory to the War Veterans. You realize that, Mr. Fleishhacker?

MR. FLEISHHACKER: Mr. Mayor, I am very much gratified by your alluding to me as the "Chairman," but I want to say at this time that it will be impossible for me to accept the chairmanship of the committee. I am very much tied down with business, I am serving now as chairman of three committees, and I think I am doing my full share, and you will have to pass that on to somebody who is not so active as I am. I am just acting today as chairman. As a matter of fact, Mr. Walter Martin has been on the Building Committee—I have not—and so has Mr. Charles Kendrick, and I think both of these men are better qualified to answer questions in detail, than I am. I am just getting into this hoping we can solve the problem and go ahead with an Opera House and Legion Building plan at the earliest possible moment. We have wasted now, five years time, and I do not want another year or two wasted before real accomplishments.

THE MAYOR: Mr. Boyd, has your committee anything to say today?

SUPERVISOR RONCOVIERI: I understand Mr. Fleishhacker is going to go, and he does not agree with my idea of submitting to the people a bond issue for $1,500,000. Of course, if it is not necessary, neither do I want to submit a bond issue for $1,500,000, or any other amount. But I simply thought your architects and your committee had made a very fine study, an intensive study of your needs, and when you said $6,600,000 you had cut it to the bone. And it was upon that, that I thought we should get the $1,500,000 from the people. Now, is your objection directed to the eonomic conditions that exist, the cost of money, and all that sort of thing, financially, or do you think that you can get along with $5,000,000? Would you rather go ahead with $5.000.000?

MR. FLEISHHACKER: Both for financial reasons, and at the same time to save time. Were we to put another bond issue on the ballot, it would mean probably a year's delay. I want to say this, in justice to the architects present: They were not asked at any time by the Building Committee to get up a set of plans to have an Opera House and Legion Building within the $5,000,000 limit, and they are not to blame. And I think that should be understood because otherwise there is a possibility of them being criticized for running $1,500,000 in excess of the amount available. They were asked to get up a very beautiful building, one that would serve the purpose and that would answer the requirements of the Legionnaires. They have done that but now we will have to go back at them again with a definite lot of instructions, telling them to develop it, as best they can, for the $5.000,000. I believe they can do it and will have a building that will do credit to San Francisco.

SUPERVISOR RONCOVIERI: Will that be the type of building that San Francisco ought to have, the one that the City ought to have.

MR. FLEISHHACKER: These men have both answered it in the affirmative.

SUPERVISOR RONCOVIERI: Because I think that $1,500,000 is, over the years to come, a mere bagatelle. Posterity will go into that building, that building will be there, and $1,500,000 more invested in it, if that will make it the perfect 100 per cent building, I would rather see it now, than to tinker along now and try to cut out some of the embellishments that the architects have in mind in the interior of that building. It ought to be as beautiful as I know the exterior will be. And I would rather see the money obtained.

THE MAYOR: Let me put these thoughts before the Board: When the Exposition Directors presented to the City a million dollars for an Auditorium, the plans provided for a terra cotta front and terra cotta sides and back which still stands. The people would not stand for a terra cotta front, and therefore $234,000 was taken out of the Civic Center Fund to put a granite front on the Auditorium. Now, we have got to have a bond issue of $1,000,000 as soon as possible to cut Leavenworth Street through and Fulton Street, or we do not get the $5,000,000 Federal Building from the United States Government, because they cannot put up the building with Leavenworth Street as it is on the turn. If you are going to build a seven or eight million dollar building, I think the people would rather have it satisfy everybody and to erect a notable monument for the ages yet to come. As long as this other bond issue has to go up, the committee which I will appoint, having full charge of this matter, will discuss whether a bond issue, or whether taxation, or the providing of funds will be set forth in some way or other. So we have that proposition or we do not get the $5,000,000 Federal Building. The Government is waiting on us, and these things have all got to be discussed. As there is no quorum today, and as Mr. Fleishhacker has to go, and you want to think this over, there is no use in me making the appointments this afternoon. I will do so when a quorum is present, because the appointments need your confirmation, but again, if France can honor its Marshal Joffre and its Marshal Foch, surely the City of San Francisco can honor its Marshal, General Hunter Liggett, as a representative of the American Expeditionary Forces, and I give you exhibit number one of the appointments I am going to make.

SUPERVISOR McSHEEHY: May I say this to you, Mr. Mayor: I would suggest at this time that the Clerk be instructed to have one hundred copies of this report, as presented to this Board by the Trustees, made, one copy sent to every member of this Board and the other copies for anyone that would require the same, in other words, the Trustees want to spread out to the people of San Francisco, and to all interested parties, their report. I happen to be one and I know that is their attitude and I would ask at this time that the Clerk be so instructed.

THE MAYOR: And a copy sent to each member of the committee of nine and to the veterans' organizations.

SUPERVISOR McSHEEHY: Exactly, your Honor.

THE MAYOR: All right, all in favor of that motion——

SUPERVISOR McSHEEHY (interrupting): And the press, also.

THE MAYOR: And the press, also, and everybody get a copy.

THE CLERK: Do you want these sheets in there?

SUPERVISOR McSHEEHY: I would include everything that the Trustees have sent you, Mr. Clerk, so that everybody will have an entire copy of everything that the Trustees have done in this matter.

MR. FLEISHHACKER: Before you adjourn, I would like to suggest that you call upon Mr. Hall, representing the Regents of the University of California. You know they are very much interested in this project, they are trustees and I think we should listen to them.

MR. HALL: Mr. Mayor, and members of the Board of Supervisors and members of the veterans' organizations: I merely want to point out that, as far as the Regents are concerned, who are the trustees of the funds of the War Memorial, that it will be impossible for them to turn over this money and the property that stands in their name to the new board until they are satisfied that the new plan will be in conformity with the trust agreement which was made between the

War Memorial Trustees and the subscribers to the War Memorial, back in 1921. So that the situation will be that the new Board of Trustees will have to evolve a plan which will fit in with that agreement before these funds can be released, and, of course, these gentlemen, as trustees of the whole project, are just as much interested in seeing that that is done as the Regents are because the Regents were appointed by the War Memorial Trustees.

THE MAYOR: Thank you.

SUPERVISOR ANDRIANO: May we have a word from one of the representatives of the veterans' organizations, Mr. Boyd?

THE MAYOR: I would like to have Mr. Boyd speak.

MR. BOYD: Your Honor and gentlemen and members of the Trustees: The veterans are deeply gratified to find that the War Memorial Trustees are today recommending to your Honor the appointment of the permanent board be made. The members who sat in at the meetings of the committee of nine, and I think the members of the board as well—all the members of the board—know that from the beginning, from our first meeting in December, the veterans have urged that the one way, the only way, to get down to real business in this matter was for his Honor to make the appointment provided for in the charter. Mr. Drum asked that his Honor postpone that appointment. And I want to say, Mr. Fleishhacker, that the veterans are deeply grateful to you for your recommendation today that the board be appointed because, gentlemen of the board, there is no other way that this matter can be ever settled until, as Mr. Fleishhacker has told you, a group clothed with the proper authority can sit down and adjust these differences, if any differences there are. The veterans' organizations take the stand that there is no difference in fact. There may be some differences in opinion. But with the proper board appointed, the varying opinions can surely be adjusted and the work can start.

There is one matter I would like to speak to the board about, and that is a matter that was just touched upon by Mr. Hall in regard to the trust agreement. Mr. Hall has said that, unless the Regents of the University of California could be assured that the terms and provisions of the trust agreement would be carried out, that the regents could not release the board that the Mayor is to appoint, the funds that are available, and for the information of the board, and for the information of Mr. Hall, I will point out that the trust agreement specifically says: "It is expressly agreed and understood that this agreement may be in any way modified and amended at any time by subsequent agreement, in writing between the parties hereto, or their respective successors in interest."

SUPERVISOR PEYSER: May I interrupt for a moment, if your Honor please. You have been standing for quite some time and proven yourself quite a soldier, and I move that the Mayor be permitted to sit while reading the rest of the report.

SUPERVISOR GALLAGHER: Second the motion.

THE MAYOR: It is my duty, as Mayor, that I remain standing while addressing the Board of Supervisors.

SUPERVISOR PEYSER: I then move the suspension of the rules in that respect.

SUPERVISOR GALLAGHER: Second the motion.

THE MAYOR: It is just fine standing, and the light is very good, and I am now getting down to the meat of the cocoanut.

SUPERVISOR SPAULDING: I move that we take a ten-minute recess to wake up the Supervisors.

THE MAYOR (continuing reading):

So that if there is anything in this private trust agreement that would prevent this work from starting, whatever it is that might exist that would prevent the work from starting can be changed, and the trust agreement itself provides that that change can be made.

SUPERVISOR MARKS: Who are the parties to that agreement?

MR. BOYD: The Regents of the University of California and Walter S. Martin, Charles Templeton Crocker, John deGuigne, E. S.———— Charles H. Kendrick, Frank F. Kilsby, Milton H. Esberg, Herbert Fleishhacker, William H. Crocker and John S. Drum. So that, if there is any difference, a change can be made.

MR. HALL: Mr. Mayor, I might state that that agreement calls for a certain plan, an Opera House, a Court and the Veterans' Building. As far as amending the agreement is concerned, there is no question it can be done, so far as a matter of form is concerned, but if it is going to be amended so as to change the very gist of the trust, I doubt whether the regents would do it without getting authority from the subscribers themselves, because they were given authority to carry out a specific trust, and if it has to be modified in a very simple way, it would be done without referring it back to the subscribers, but they certainly would not change the whole plan.

MR. GLENSOR: Mr. Mayor, I do not think we need borrow any trouble about modifying the trust agreement at this time. The plan that has been approved by the veterans is one that I think any one examining the present trust agreement can see falls plainly into conformity with its terms because the veterans bodies of San Francisco are specifically named as beneficiaries under that private trust agreement, and they have asked nothing and want nothing that a beneficiary under a trust agreement cannot properly ask for. There is just one other thing that has been brought up here today I would like to briefly mention: It has been mentioned, over and over, by men prominently identified with this project, that there is to be a Legion Building. May I invite your attention, gentlemen, to the proposition that there is not going to be a Legion Building, there is going to be a Veterans' Building. The Legion is only one organization, of which I am a member, but it is only one organization of veterans, it is not the entire veteran bodies of San Francisco. The building just contemplated as the Veterans' Building for the American Legion, the G. A. R., the Spanish War Veterans, the Indian War Veterans, the Veterans of Foreign Wars and other affiliated and auxiliary and subsidiary bodies, and the Gold Star Mothers and all such identified bodies as that. And if it is possible for us to make a request that will be complied with, may we request that you cease thinking and speaking of this building as the Legion Building because it is not the Legion Building at all. That is not very important but it does amount to something. It is not a Legion Building, it is a Veterans' Building. Now, a plan was presented to the veterans, which we approved, and we thought and understood that all that was desired of the veterans was to say what their minimum requirements were, which we have submitted in writing, and would a plan that gave us those as minimum requirements and necessities meet with our aproval? We have done so, and we do not see that the veterans at this time can say anything further except that anything that will move this project along and carry those plans into execution will meet with the whole-hearted support and endorsement and the unanimous support and endorsement of all the veterans of San Francisco.

SUPERVISOR POWERS: Which plan did the veterans adopt? The $8,200,000 plan?

MR. GLENSOR: It was submitted to us and referred to as Plan C. The cost of that plan was only estimated, and just exactly what it is now, figured out in detail cost, we do not know unless it has been announced here this afternoon. Whichever plan it was that we approved the architects can tell you what it will cost better than I can.

MR. LANSBURGH: The one that they approved was the most expensive of the three schemes.

SUPERVISOR POWERS: $8,200,000?

MR. LANSBURGH: That is included in the figures we gave you today, I think there is a difference of about $450,000. That is all included in those figures, there is no additional added.

SUPERVISOR RONCOVIERI: $6,600,000?

MR. LANSBURGH: It is included in every one of them.

SUPERVISOR RONCOVIERI: How can that be reduced when you get down to the $5,000,000?

MR. LANSBURGH: It would have to be reduced in volume and capacity. It would be reduced proportionately to the Opera House, both buildings.

SUPERVISOR RONCOVIERI: Mr. Hall has brought up a doubt as to whether the University Trustees would turn over that money. What are the provisions of that contract that led you to say that? You say, if so and so, we will hold the money back, we will not release it. Now, what do you mean by that? I would like you to make that very clear.

MR. HALL: Mr. Supervisor, the money was turned over to the Regents of the University of California, in trust for the purpose of carrying out a very definite plan, as set forth in the trust agreement. That plan calls for the erection of an Opera House, a Memorial Court and a Veterans' Building. There were certain trust provisions in favor of the Opera Association, the Art Association and of the American Legion and other veteran bodies. They had certain rights. For instance, the veterans are to get their building rent free. The Opera and Musical Associations have certain rights regarding the use o the Opera House and auditorium and so on. The regents take the attitude that, if there is going to be a change in the plan which would call for the erection, say, of only one building, or a building which would not provide for these various groups mentioned in the trust, there would be such a change from the original plan that they would have to get the consent of the people who subscribed the $2,000,000 before they could turn that money over to the city. The agreement permits the regents to resign at any time and turn the property over to the City of San Francisco, or any other acceptable body, on the terms of that particular trust. So that, when they resign and turn it over, it has to be along the lines set forth in that agreement. Now, it does speak about modifications and amendments, and the regents have taken the attitude that the matter of changing that agreement in some minor details, they can do it without going back to the subscribers, but if the whole has to be changed, they certainly would not take a chance of doing it without knowing that the people who put up the $2,000,000 were satisfied. That is what I meant when I said they would want to be sure that the plan was acceptable to the people who put up the money.

SUPERVISOR RONCOVIERI: Are the regents familiar with Plan C?

MR. HALL: Oh, yes.

SUPERVISOR RONCOVIERI: Does that meet the views of the regents and the provisions of this contract?

MR. HALL: All of these plans carry out all the terms of the trust agreement. Of course, after the building was erected, there are other parts of that agreement that immediately come into effect. For instance, use of the Opera House and the use of the Veterans' Building, and those trusts will be attached to the property after it has been erected. But any one of these plans completely comes within the terms of the trust agreement.

SUPERVISOR RONCOVIERI: And you will turn over the money as soon as the trustees are appointed, if these plans are accepted?

MR. HALL: If those plans are accepted, or if there is any set of plans prepared which will encompass those particular features.

SUPERVISOR POWERS: Did I understand you right that the Regents would have jurisdiction on the buildings after they were completed?

MR. HALL: No, I merely said, Mr. Powers, when they turned that money over, the money and the real estate. You see, the real estate stands in their name, the south block entirely, that it would be immediately affected by the trust as included in that agreement, which would be that the buildings, when erected, would have to be used for the purposes set forth in that agreement, that the veterans would have to have their building rent free, and that the Art Association would have certain rights regarding the Museum and that the Opera Association and Musical Association would have certain rights regarding the opera house. As soon as it is turned over the Regents are out of the picture entirely.

SUPERVISOR RONCOVIERI: I would like to ask the Trustees, if those things are possible. After the buildings are built—the buildings to be used for certain purposes—now, will those purposes be possible, according to the plans?

MR. MARTIN: These modified plans?

SUPERVISOR RONCOVIERI: Yes.

MR. MARTIN: I do not see why not. It is only a question of the size, auditorium space and the opera house.

MR. HALL: There is no size included in that agreement, of course. There was nothing said about the size of the opera house or the size of the auditorium, or anything else. As long as there are two buildings, one an opera house and one a Veterans' building, each of which is complete enough to carry out the various terms, we would release the money and then it would be up to the new Board of Trustees to see that those buildings were used for the purposes of that trust, and the charter amendment automatically gives the new Board of Trustees the right to accept any trust in connection with that property.

SUPERVISOR RONCOVIERI: I assume, when the people subscribed their dollars and ten-cent pieces to make up that $2,000,000 they did not go into all this when they turned the money over to you. I presume they will take care of themselves.

MR. HALL: In 1921 they all signed this agreement.

SUPERVISOR RONCOVIERI: Not those that subscribed ten-cent pieces.

MR. HALL: Maybe not the ten-sent pieces, but there are thousands and thousands of them.

SUPERVISOR RONCOVIERI: There were thousands of children and teachers that did.

MR. HALL: That is probably so, whose names——

SUPERVISOR RONCOVIERI (interrupting): They simply put their names on for so much money, one dollar or fifty cents, or whatever it is. I think Mr. Widenham knows about the number it was.

MR. WIDENHAM: The gross amount of those subscriptions totaled approximately $10,000, so it is not an appreciable amount of the total sum, at all. These subscriptions, the small items like the school children, we did not go to the trouble of trying to get those signed up because it would have been an expensive proposition. The others were all signed under the general agreement.

SUPERVISOR ANDRIANO: Mr. Chairman, I am going to move that we stand adjourned, since we have not a quorum, and everything that we said here today will very likely have to be said over again when the Board, sitting as a Board of Supervisors, will take it up for action, so I see no reason why the discussion should be prolonged, and after the lady has made her remarks, I suggest that we stand adjourned.

SUPERVISOR STANTON: I was going to ask a question of the Mayor, if you have no objection, Mr. Mayor. I was going to ask you, when you are ready to announce the names, that you give us a few days in which to look them over.

THE MAYOR: Oh, certainly.

SUPERVISOR STANTON: What I had in mind is that we would want to have the matter laid over after you announce the names for another week. Or maybe, if you gave them to us in advance, then at the following meeting we could act on the names.

MRS. LEAH DAVIS: As the representative of the Gold Star Mothers of San Francisco, we are keenly interested in this project. As I understand it, memorials are erected for somebody who has given their life in the public cause, consequently we believe that it is San Francisco's tribute to the six hundred and fourteen hero dead of the World War that has brought about the desire to erect this proposed Memorial building. I want to pay honor to your judgment in placing General Hunter Liggett at the head of this proposed Board of Trustees, the man who saw service with our sons in the American Expeditionary Forces. Now that the architects are present, the members of the Board of Trustees, the veterans interested, and the public interested, I think it is appropriate, at this time particularly, as Mr. Glensor said, this is not a Legion building, but dedicated to veteran organizations, but when the plans are adopted and accepted, the exclusive headquarters to the mothers of these six hundred and fourteen hero dead of San Francisco be set aside, exclusively for our use, the headquarters for the Gold Star Mothers of San Francisco, to speak for the purpose for which this building is to be erected. We ask that, and I have been asking that of this committee for years. And I have never heard anything adopted in particular to this. I have been told that it will be laid over to the allocating committee. But we are particularly anxious at this time to be assured that, when plans are adopted and accepted, that the Gold Star Mothers will not be overlooked, that appropriate headquarters exclusively for our use will stand out in this building, honoring the memory of our sons.

MR. BOYD: May I say to his honor the Mayor and to the members of the Board that Mrs. Davis has the pledge of the ex-service men of San Francisco that her request will not be forgotten as far as we are concerned?

MRS. DAVIS: Thank you, Mr. Boyd.

THE MAYOR: The Board, I assume, accepts the report of the Mayor in transmitting the report of the War Memorial Trustees. It is now in the hands of the Board. There being no quorum, action on it, of course, cannot be taken today. It has been moved and seconded that the Board adjourn, and later make such disposition as they desire of the report of the Mayor and Trustees, as set forth in the stenographer's report of today's proceedings. The meeting stands adjourned.

THE MAYOR: Not this meeting, though.

SUPERVISOR GALLAGHER: Does the Mayor desire to rest?

SUPERVISOR RONCOVIERI: No, he don't.

THE MAYOR (continuing reading):

REPORT OF WAR MEMORIAL COMMITTEE.

July 17, 1920, the following report was submitted by the War Memorial Committee to the Board of Supervisors:

THE MAYOR: I have already read to you the contents of that report.

SUPERVISOR MILES: May I interrupt your Honor. Since a number of the boys have gone to sleep, may I suggest we have the bugler sound reveille?

SUPERVISOR POWER: It might be better to sound a warning that we go over the top at 5:00 a. m.

THE MAYOR (continuing reading):

July 17, 1929.

Hon. James Rolph, Jr., Mayor of San Francisco, San Francisco.

Dear Mr. Mayor: The architects have completed and submitted a scheme for the War Memorial buildings. That scheme is acceptable to the Trustees and to the veterans' organizations.

It provides for an adequate opera house, for the completion of the Veterans' building as demanded by the veterans' organizations and for the construction of the Memorial Court.

It provides for structures of distinctive dignity and beauty befitting their purpose and environs, conforming to the architectural treatment of the Civic Center and creditable to the City of San Francisco.

The architects submit round figure estimates of cost as follows:

1. Terra cotta exterior.....................................$7,500,000
2. Granite exterior. 8,200,000

cr, with certain modifications in specifications but adhering to the same general scheme:

1. Terra cotta exterior $6,600,000
2. Granite exterior. 7,250,000

Summary and detail of estimates are enclosed.

While the architects believe these estimates may be relied upon, they point out that vigilance will be required to maintain them because they are figured on narrow margins and include no contingency allowances.

The funds available or to be available for the realization of the War Memorial scheme, as disclosed by the accompanying financial statement, are:

Cash . . ..$ 890,664
Bonds 4,000,000

Total $4,890,664

The cash item represents the remainder of the private subscriptions collected or to be collected after capital expenditures of $301,346.74 for plans, excavations, etc., land purchase (south block) $330,965.80, and $328,287.44 land purchase (north block).

If the present plans are carried out, the capital expenditures of $301,346.75 which are included in the estimates of cost, would be added to the funds available or to be available, to make a total of $5,192,010.75.

The total of funds available is, in round figures, $1,400,000 less than the lowest estimate of cost.

When the issuance of $4,000,000 of War Memorial bonds was submitted to the people and ratified, the estimates of cost were based on plans which contemplated the present completion of the Opera House · and the War Memorial scheme, excepting only the McAllister and Franklin Streets facades of the Veterans' Building, which were not regarded as immediately essential and which could be completed later as needed. The veterans' organizations have demanded that these facades be included in the original construction. This inclusion accounts in part for the increase in costs.

From the foregoing it is obvious that further progress is contingent upon either the provision of additional funds or a radical revisions of plans.

Respectfully submitted,

FRANK F. KILSBY,
JESSE C. COLMAN,
CHARLES H. KENDRICK,
JAMES B. McSHEEHY,
WALTER S. MARTIN,
MILTON H. ESBERG,
R. I. BENTLEY,
JOHN D. McKEE,
HERBERT FLEISHHACKER,
WILLIAM H. CROCKER.

THE MAYOR: I have here a notation to the report which I read to you, which report is signed by the members of the War Memorial Committee (continuing reading):

(Note) Various parts of the report were discussed and a printed transcript was prepared of the remarks made at the meeting of the Board, which can be obtained from the Board's Reporter upon application of the Clerk of the Board of Supervisors. The balance of the above mentioned report dated July 17, 1929, is as follows:

THE MAYOR: Then follows copy of a telegram from New York to Mr. Herbert Fleishhacker by John S. Drum (continuing reading):

TELEGRAM.

New York, N. Y., July 12, 1929.

Herbert Fleishhacker, care Anglo & London Paris National Bank, San Francisco, Calif.

Many thanks for your telegram. Believe the Trustees have acted wisely and have adopted a very sound course. Kindest regards.

JOHN S. DRUM.

THE MAYOR: Then follows all of the detailed information which I have epitomized tonight. I have the record here of the full detail of every cost of every part of the building, way to the sidewalk lines, and stuccos, the painting, and every item which I am making a part of my report. (Continuing reading:)

San Francisco, June 25, 1929.

Mr. Herbert Fleishhacker, Member Board of Trustees, San Francisco War Memorial, San Francisco, California.

Dear Sir:

In answer to your inquiry, the careful estimates made recently at the War Memorial drafting rooms and verified by Mr. Dinwiddie indicate that the War Memorial buildings as at present delineated and specified would cost, in round figures:

    1. With Terra Cotta Exterior.................$7,500,000
    2. With Granite Exterior...................... 8,200,000

With certain modifications in specification as shown on the estimate sheets, but keeping the same approved scheme, another estimate was made showing possible modifications of the totals as follows:

    1. Terra Cotta Exterior......................$6,600,000
    2. Granite Exterior 7,250,000

The above figures include the completion of the Veterans' building as demanded by the Veteran organizations (involving $511,212 more than contemplated on the drawings) and also the construction of the Memorial Court ($250,000 to $300,000).

These figures we believe to be reliable, but it will require vigilance to maintain them as they are figured on narrow margins and include no contingency allowance.

In the case these figures are too high, in view of the available funds, the alternative would seem to be to redraw the plans with a modified program as to requirements both of the Veterans and Opera and with the accommodations strictly limited to the funds allowed.

ARTHUR BROWN, JR.,
G. L. LANSBURGH.

MEMORANDUM

Estimate Summary Discussed at War Memorial Trustees Meeting.
June 21, 1929.

Estimate A1 (with contingencies item deducted)
Opera House $3,934,783
Veterans' Building (including Memorial Court).......... 3,042,643

Total $6,977,426
Additional McAllister-Franklin wing demanded by
Veterans 511,212
Total $7,488,638

Estimate A2 (with contingencies item deducted and all cuts
made)
Opera House $3,326,896
Veterans' Building (including Memorial Court)........... 2,641,754

Total $5,968,650
Stage apparatus (bridges, etc.) put back................ 155,700

Total $6,124,350
Additional McAllister-Franklin wing demanded by
Veterans 439,959

Total $6,564,309
(This estimate is for terra cotta above base line.)   Extra
for granite (both buildings).........................$ 680,586

Bonds voted $4,000,000.00
Cash on hand September 30,
1928 (Auditor's report).. 1,215,475.00
Estimated accrued interest as
of July 1, 1929.......... 30,000.00
Subscriptions collected since
September 30, 1928....... 82,510.00

$5,327,985.00
Unpaid subscriptions collect-
able 135,500.00

$5,463,485.00
Expended since September 30,
1928 ....$ 230,791.31
Attorney's fee 13,742.25   244,533.56 $5,218,951.44
Deduct Participating Loan for purchase of portion of North
Block for City Account............................ 328,287.44

Total available cash July 1, 1929..................$4,890,664.00

It should be taken into consideration that the available cash should
be considered as the item shown (last item) plus following capital expenditures, which would naturally be included in the estimates of cost,
and which have already been expended.

Available cash July 1, 1929...........................$4,890,664.00
Drafting Room Expenditures $159,930.07
Architects 34,890.28
Excavation and Wrecking.................. 75,850.00
Special Engineering Services............. 30,676.40

$301,346.75
Capital Expenditures 301,346.75

Total $5,192,010.75

(A1 is estimate of May, 1929, revised)
(B is Dinwiddie estimate, 1927)

June 21, 1929.

Item	Description	Opera House Est. A1	Opera House Est. B	Veterans' Building and Memorial Court Est. A1	Veterans' Building and Memorial Court Est. B	Total Est. A1	Total Est. B
1-9	Foundations	$205,415	$372,654	$323,322	$245,965	$528,737	$618,619
10-11	Steel	486,200	506,970	280,682	320,844	766,882	827,814
12	Plumbing	83,636	87,200	46,364	48,730	130,000	135,930
13	Heating	114,770	76,000	179,927	60,500	294,697	136,500
14	Electrical	294,545	271,190	54,545	25,940	349,090	297,130
15	Concrete	345,909	230,100	290,454	130,272	636,363	360,372
16	Granite R.	109,818	93,870	225,909	74,390	335,727	168,260
16A	Granite (above B)	*(785,000)	(887,605)	(581,000)	(445,610)	(1,366,000)	(1,133,215)
17-18A	Terra Cotta	394,982	395,000	247,904	212,500	642,886	607,500
18	Masonry	130,473	78,618	115,732	51,367	246,205	129,985
19	Elevators	150,000	197,380	59,182	66,000	209,182	263,380
20	Roofing	127,057	59,044	48,955	39,085	176,012	98,129
21	Miscellaneous Steel	106,227	67,230	102,182	29,320	208,409	96,550
22	Vaults	1,091	......	182	......	1,273	......
23	Carpentry	90,909	77,895	90,909	54,741	181,818	132,636
24	Marble and Floors	276,711	125,588	183,923	69,323	460,634	194,911
25	Plastering	200,000	126,568	181,818	86,343	381,818	262,911
26	Tile Work	20,636	9,555	14,909	14,449	35,546	24,014
27	Painting	36,364	54,000	31,818	38,400	68,182	92,400
28	Glazing	26,361	12,700	31,818	10,018	68,182	22,718
29	Hardware	19,091	10,000	14,091	10,000	33,182	20,000
30	Furnishings	127,456	140,202	121,673	56,782	249,129	196,984
31	Fixtures	113,921	30,000	72,332	6,000	186,253	35,000
32	Stage Equipment	45,455	50,000	......	......	45,455	50,000
33	Buffet Equipment	28,182	......	14,000	......	42,182	......
34	Other Equipment	......	108,644	......	69,276	......	177,920
35	Sq. Lights	82	......	1,100	......	1,182	......
	Sub totls	$3,535,294	$3,230,408	$2,733,731	$1,719,245	$6,269,025	$4,949,653
	Contingencies (10%)	176,765		136,687		313,452	
	Contingencies (5%)		323,041		171,925		494,966
	Totals	$3,712,059	$3,553,449	$2,870,418	$1,891,170	$6,582,477	$5,444,619

*Not in first totals.

Item	Description	Opera House Est. A1	Opera House Est. B	Veterans' Building and Memorial Court Est. A1	Veterans' Building and Memorial Court Est. B	Total Est. A1	Total Est. B
	Brought Forward	$3,712,059	$3,553,449	$2,870,418	$1,891,170	$6,582,477	$5,444,619
	Direct (10/6/27)	.....	−317,900	.....	−189,000	.....	−506,900
	Subtotals	$3,712,059	$3,235,549	$2,870,418		$6,582,477	
A	Arct and general (6%)	222,724	194,130	172,225		394,949	296,256
	Totals	$	$3,429,679	$	$1,804,296	$5,233,975	
	Add (12/27/27)	.....		.....			
	Totals	$	$	$	$1,921,485	$5,351,164	
	The 10 feet	.....	−120,000	.....	−57,000		−177,000
	Subtotals	$	$3,309,679	$	$1,864,485	$5,174,164	
	Court	.....		.....			136,000
	Totals (terra cotta)	$3,934,783	$3,309,679	$3,042,643	$2,000,485	$6,977,426	$5,310,164
	Add granite	334,587	292,605	294,292	233,100	628,879	525,715
	Add 6% granite	20,075	17,556	17,658	13,987	37,733	31,543
	Totals (granite)	$4,289,445	$3,619,840	$3,354,593	$2,247,582	$7,644,038	$ 867,422

REDUCTION OF ESTIMATE A1 TO BASIS OF A2

	Opera House	Veterans' Building	Total
Totals as quoted	$3,888,823	$3,007,104	$6,895,927
10/11 ditto	3,535,294	2,733,731	6,269,025
Contingencies (5%)	176,765	136,687	313,452
Subtotals	$3,712,059	$2,870,418	$6,582,477
Architect and general (6%)	222,724	172,225	394,949
Totals (terra cotta)	$3,934,783	$3,042,643	$6,977,426
Add granite	334,587	294,292	8,879
Add 6% granite	20,075	17,658	37,733

(A2 is estimate of June, 1929)
(B is Dinwiddie estimate, 1927)

June 20, 1929.

Item	Description	Opera House		Masons' Building and …al Court		Total	
		Est. A2	Est. B	Est. A2	Est. B	Est. A2	Est. B
1-9	Foundations	$ 192,896	$ 372,654	$ 286,119	$ 245,965	$ 479,015	$ 618,619
10-11	Steel	461,434	506,970	279,546	320,844	740,980	827,814
12	Plumbing	76,665	87,200	40,975	48,730	117,630	135,930
13	Heating	105,224	76,000	155,382	60,500	260,606	136,500
14	Electrical	216,364	271,190	54,545	25,940	270,909	297,130
15	Concrete	364,177	230,100	236,351	130,272	600,528	360,372
16	Granite B	109,818	93,870	197,909	74,390	307,727	168,260
16A	Granite (for B)	*(712,696)	*(687,605)	(529,080)	(445,610)	(1,241,770)	(1,133,251)
17-18A	Granite	338,619	395,000	226,540	212,500	565,159	607,500
18	Masonry	79,366	78,618	91,696	51,367	171,062	129,985
19	Bars	78,546	197,380	59,180	66,000	137,726	263,380
20	Roofing	86,966	59,044	34,409	39,085	121,375	98,129
21	Miscellaneous Steel	102,863	67,230	99,182	29,320	202,045	96,550
22	Vaults	636	.....	182	.....	818	.....
23	Carpentry	59,174	77,895	90,935	54,741	150,109	132,636
24	…te and Floors	237,195	125,588	130,074	69,323	367,269	194,911
25	Plastering	163,636	176,568	152,727	86,343	316,363	262,911
26	Tile Work	19,182	9,555	13,545	14,449	32,727	24,004
27	Painting	29,571	54,000	23,884	38,400	53,455	92,400
28	Glazing	20,000	12,700	20,455	10,018	40,455	22,718
29	Hardware	15,273	10,000	11,273	10,000	26,546	20,000
30	Furnishings	127,456	140,202	108,423	56,782	235,879	196,984
31	Fixtures	52,173	30,000	45,112	5,000	97,285	35,000
32	Stage Equipment	45,455	50,000	.....	.....	45,455	50,000
33	Buffet Equipment	6,364	.....	14,000	.....	20,364	.....
34	…ther Equipment	.....	108,644	.....	69,276	.....	177,920
35	Sq. Lights	82	.....	1,100	.....	1,182	.....
	Subtotals	$2,989,125	$3,230,408	$2,373,544	$1,719,245	$5,362,669	$4,949,653

*Not in first totals.

Item	Description	Opera House		Veterans' Building and Official Court		Total	
		Est. A2	Est. B	Est. A2	Est. B	Est. A2	Est. B
	Brought Forward	$2,989,125	$3,230,408	$2,373,544	$1,719,245	$5,362,669	$4,949,653
	Contingencies (10%)	149,456	323,041	8677	171,925	268,133	494,966
	Contingencies (5%)	.....	.....	.....	.....	.....	.....
	Totals	$3,138,581	$3,553,449	$2,492,221	$1,891,170	$5,630,802	$5,444,619
	Deduct (10/6/27)	.....	–317,900	.....	–189,000	.....	–506,900
	Totals	$3,138,581	$3,235,549	$2,492,221	$1,702,170	$5,630,802	$4,937,719
	Met and general (6%)	188,315	194,130	149,533	102,126	337,848	296,256
	Totals	$	$3,429,679	$	$1,804,296	$	$5,233,975
	Add (12/27/27)	.....	.....	.....	117,189	.....	7,189
	Subtotals	$	$	$	$1,921,485	$	$5,351,164
	Reduce 10 feet	.....	–120,000	.....	–57,000	.....	–177,000
	Subtotals	$	$3,309,679	$	$1,864,485	$	$5,174,164
	Court	.....	.....	.....	136,000	.....	136,000
	Totals (terra cotta)	$3,326,896	$3,309,679	$2,641,754	$2,000,485	$5,968,650	$5,310,164
	Add granite	324,750	292,605	267,164	233,100	591,914	525,715
	Add 6% granite	19,485	17,556	16,030	13,987	35,515	31,543
	Totals (granite)	$3,671,131	$3,619,840	$2,924,948	$2,247,582	$6,596,079	$5,867,422

SAN FRANCISCO WAR MEMORIAL
COST ESTIMATES AND APPORTIONMENT

Dated June 21, 1929.

Item	Description	Opera House Est. A1	Opera House Est. A2	Veterans' Building and Memorial Court Est. A1	Veterans' Building and Memorial Court Est. A2	Total Est. A1	Total Est. A2
1-7.	Rough excavation and other completed items	$ 25,956	$ 25,956	$ 51,771	$ 51,771	$ 77,727	$ 77,727
8.	Well	......	......	3,883	3,883	3,883	3,883
9.	Finished excavation, basement concrete and waterproofing. Estimate A1 by Clinton. Estimate A2 by Evans. No deductions.	200,000	186,230	300,000	259,076	500,000	445,306
10-11.	Steel. Difference between A1 and A2 is due to closer pricing in A2. No deductions.	534,820	507,577	308,750	307,500	843,570	815,077
12.	Plumbing. Deductions—Opera House: 2 sinks, 30 toilets, 18 lavatories, 21 urinals—$7,679. Deductions—Veterans' Building: 21 toilets, 26 lavatories, 12 urinals—$5,928.	92,000	84,321	51,000	45,072	143,000	129,393
13.	Heating and mechanical equipment.	126,247	115,747	197,920	170,920	324,167	286,667
14.	Electrical work	324,000	238,000	60,000	60,000	384,000	298,000

Deductions—Opera House:

Galvanized iron udts	$ 5,500
Ice bar system	3,300
Temperature control on direct radiators	1,700
	$10,500

Deductions—Veterans' Building:

Carrier system $27,500

Deductions—Opera House: Side spots, color change spots, D. C. arc spots, bars 6-7-8-9-10, eg fots, projection room (gpt, motor lines for stage drops, revamp of stage switchboard ard other arrangement—$86,000.

No deductions in Veterans' Building.

Item	Description	Opera House Est. A1	Opera House Est. A2	Veterans' Building and Memorial Court Est. A1	Veterans' Building and Memorial Court Est. A2	Total Est. A1	Total Est. A2
15.	Superstructure .... note .... Estimate A1 by Hân. Estimate A2 by Evans. No l dtis.	$ 380,500	$ 400,595	$ 319,500	$ 259,986	$ 700,000	$ 660,581
16.	Granite base, curbs, steps and court.... No l dtis for Opera House. Deductions—Veterans' Building and court: Granite paving, 4 mns, and wlls of runways—$30,800.	120,800	120,800	248,500	217,700	369,300	338,500
16a.	Granite work above base....... Attic story behind bal tile —$72,304. Deductions—Opera House: Attic story behind bal title mn, $51,920. Deductions—Veterans' Building: Same	*(785,000)	(712,696)	(581,000)	(529,080)	(1,306,000)	(1,241,776)
17.	Furnishing terra cotta............ tis in price and tge. Deductions are due to tis in price and tge. Deductions—Opera House: Tonnage t rad from 2700 to 2400 ons by substituting tad note in atic story and top of sge block—$56,000. Deductions—Veterans' Building: Tonnage reduced from 1700 to 1600 tons. Similar omissions—$21,500.	356,000	300,000	222,000	200,500	578,000	500,500
18.	Setting terra cotta .... tis in tonnage. Deductions are due to tis in tonnage. Deductions—Opera House: 300 tons—$6,000. Deductions—Veterans' Buil xti 100 tons—$2,000.	78,480	72,480	50,695	48,695	129,175	121,175
18.	Masonry work .... tite: Subst tite metal lath for tile Deductions—Opera tite: Subst tite metal lath for tile · tl18. Deductions — Veterans' Building: Same omissions —$26,440.	143,520	87,302	127,305	100,865	270,825	188,167
19.	El .... eurs .... Deductions—Opera House:	165,000	86,400	65,100	65,100	230,100	151,000

1 fly estor	$17,500
4 orchestra elators	23,700
4 stage bridges	37,400
	$78,600

No deductions in Veterans' Building.

Item	Description	Opera House		and Memorial Court			
		Est. A1	Est. A2	Est. A1	Est. A2	Est. A1	Est. A2
20.	Roofing and sheet metal work..............	$ 139,763	$ 95,663	$ 53,850	$ 37,850	$ 193,613	$ 133,513
21.	Miscellaneous steel ornamental metal, and steel windows..	116,850	113,150	112,400	109,100	229,250	222,250
22.		1,200	700	200	200	1,400	900
23.		100,000	65,091	100,000	100,029	200,000	165,120
24.	Marble work and floors..........	304,382	260,915	202,315	143,081	506,697	403,996
25.	Plastering	220,000	180,000	200,000	168,000	420,000	348,000

20. Deductions—Opera House:
Substitute galvanized iron for lead-coated copper roofs $32,000
Omit wardrobes except in dressing rooms...... 8,600
Omit 1 fly elevator...... 3,500
$44,100

Deductions—Veterans' Building:
Roof as ... ave............ $16,000
...ing of galvanized iron roof was added to item 27.

21. ... House: $3,700.

22. Deductions—Veterans' Building: $3,300.
...ts ... re due to revised quotations on windows.

23. ... ns: 1 safe in Opera House—$500.
... and ...illwork.
Estimate A1 ...
Estimate A2 by ...
No ...

24. Deductions—Opera House: ... "..." for marble 20,000 square feet, and ... ns on marble —$43,467.
Deductions—Veterans' Building: Substitute 5200 square feet of "..." for ...able, and ... quotations on ...,234.

25. ... and deductions—Opera House: Substitute furred ... for ... atic and stage ... and exterior ... and $3,000 ...ter ... fixture. ... work in ...er of Paris ... Wall ... stone, ... and ... sand—$40,000.
Similar changes in Veterans' Building—$32,000.

Item	Description	Opera House Est. A1	Opera House Est. A2	Veterans' Building and Memorial Court Est. A1	Veterans' Building and Memorial Court Est. A2	Total Est. A1	Total Est. A2
26.	Tile work	$ 22,700	$ 21,100	$ 16,400	$ 14,900	$ 39,100	$ 36,000
27.	Painting	40,000	32,528	35,000	26,273	75,000	58,801
28.	Glazing	29,000	22,000	35,000	22,500	64,000	44,500
29.	Revised quotations.	21,000	16,800	15,500	12,400	36,500	29,200
30.	Revised quotations. …ings …and quotations for Veterans' Building.	140,202	140,202	133,840	119,265	270,042	259,467
31.	…les Revised …	125,313	57,391	79,565	49,622	204,878	107,013
32.	Stage equi… No …	50,000	50,000			50,000	50,000
33.	…buffet … in Opera House, except roughing and plumbing—$24,000. No … ors h Veterans' Building.	31,000	7,000	15,400	15,400	46,400	22,400
34.	…er equipment—None.						
35.	Sidewalk lights No deductions.	90	90	1,210	1,210	1,300	1,300
	Subtotals	$3,888,823	$3,288,038	$3,007,104	$2,610,898	$6,895,927	$5,898,936
	10-11 do	3,535,294	…25	2,733,731	2,373,544	6,269,025	5,362,669
	Contingencies, 5 per cent.	176,765	149,456	136,687	118,677	313,452	268,133
	Subtotals	$3,712,059	$3,138,581	$2,870,418	$2,492,221	$6,582,477	$5,630,802
	Architect and general, 6 per cent.	222,724	188,315	172,225	149,533	394,949	337,848
	Total (terra cotta)	$3,934,783	$3,326,896	$3,042,643	$2,641,754	$6,977,426	$5,968,650
	Add granite	334,587	324,750	294,292	267,164	628,879	591,914
	6 per cent granite.	20,075	19,485	17,658	16,030	37,733	35,515
	Total (granite)	$4,289,445	$3,671,131	$3,354,593	$2,924,948	$7,644,038	$6,596,079

APPOINTMENT OF TRUSTEES

August 26, 1929. Letter from Mayor to Board of Supervisors submitting names of Trustees of War Memorial:

"August 26, 1929.

"Honorable Board of Supervisors,
City and County of San Francisco.

Gentlemen:

There were submitted to the electors of the City and County of San
Francisco by your honorable board at an election held in this City and
County on November 6, 1928, a number of charter amendments, one of
which was entitled "War Memorial Charter Amendment No. 32." This
charter amendment was adopted by a majority of the electors at said
election. It provides for the appointment of a board of trustees to have
the management, superintendence, control and operation of said War
Memorial and prescribes the duties and powers of said board. Section
3 provides: "The trustees of said War Memorial shall consist of eleven
members, who shall be appointed by the Mayor, subject to confirmation
by the Board of Supervisors. The terms of said eleven members shall
be for six years each; provided, that those first appointed shall so
classify themselves by lot that the term of four of said trustees shall
expire on the 2nd day of January, 1931; four on the 2nd day of January, 1933, and three on the 2nd day of January, 1935. Thereafter appointments to said board shall be for the full term of six years.
Vacancies on said board shall be filled by the Mayor, subject to confirmation by the Board of Supervisors, for the unexpired term becoming vacant. In making appointments to said board, the Mayor
shall give due consideration to veterans of all wars engaged in by the
United States, and to such other classes of persons who may have a
special interest in the purpose for which said War Memorial is to be
constructed and maintained. All persons appointed to said board shall
be residents of the City and County. The members of said board
shall serve without compensation."

It is, therefore' incumbent upon me to appoint the said eleven trustees of said War Memorial, subject to confirmation by your Honorable
Board. I have given very thoughtful consideration to this important
authority resting upon your Honorable Board and the Mayor jointly;
I have conferred with your Honorable Board and the Mayor's office
in the discussion of appointments; I have discussed the appointments
with the Advisory Board to the Veterans' War Memorial Committee
of San Francisco:

H. W. Glensor, H. J. Boyd, James B. Burns.

I have received many applications from very worthy gentlemen for
appointment, with many splendid endorsements of their fitness for the
position; I have borne in mind at all times the provisions of the charter amendment relating to appointments; I have received a declination
which I regret, because its acceptance would have given general delight and commendation, to which I shall refer hereafter; I have been
compelled to listen to protest on applicants for appointment and I have
had many fine names submitted to me which I would like to have
presented to your Honorable Board which the complexion of the trus
tees at this time would not deem advisable, but later on vacancies will
occur and I shall have these names in my file for submission to your
Honorable Board by whomsoever the pleasant duty falls for making
such appointments.

I appoint as Trustees of the War Memorial, subject to your confirmation:

General Hunter Liggett, United States Army, retired.

Frank N. Belgrano, State Commander American Legion.

James I. Herz, 363rd Infantry (San Francisco's Own) 91st Division.

Charles H. Kendrick, World War Veteran.

Herbert Fleishhacker, President Anglo and London Paris National
Bank.

Kenneth R. Kingsbury, President Standard Oil Company of California.

Robert I. Bentley, President California Fruit Packers' Association.

George Cameron, Publisher San Francisco Chronicle.

George Hearst, Publisher San Francisco Examiner.

As an outstanding representative of Labor, I appoint, subject to your confirmation

James W. Mullen, Publisher of the Labor Clarion.

These appointments total ten and are equally divided between veterans of all wars engaged in by the United States and such other classes of persons who have a special interest in the purpose for which said War Memorial is to be constructed and maintained.

It has been a very keen disappointment to me and I know it will be to your Honorable Board and the citizens in general, that Colonel George L. Filmer, Captain of the First California Spanish War Veterans is unable, owing to many public committees which he is serving upon and a desired trip abroad the coming spring, to accept the appointment as a trustee.

I have had many requests made of me by veterans of all wars, and citizens generally, that I appoint Supervisor Colonel Jesse C. Colman as a trustee of the War Memorial. As a veteran, an honored citizen of this community, who has been a trustee of the War Memorial prior to the adoption of Charter Amendment No. 32 and as Section No. 2 of said charter amendment provides, "The trustees of the War Memorial shall, under such ordinances as the Board of Supervisors may from time to time adopt, etc," I am confident that his appointment, confirmed by your Honorable Board, will meet with general approval and give your Honorable Board a representative on said Board of War Memorial Trustees. I therefore, not unmindful, however, of a motion adopted by the members of your Honorable Board who attended the conferences in my chambers, that no member of the board would be expected to be appointed on said board of trustees, do hereby appoint Supervisor Colonel Jesse C. Colman, subject to the confirmation of your Honorable Board.

Respectfully submitted,
(Signed) JAMES ROLPH, JR.,
Mayor."

September 7, 1929. The Advisory Board to the Veterans' War Memorial Committees submitted the following report, dated September 7, 1929:

REPORT OF ADVISORY BOARD TO
VETERANS WAR MEMORIAL COMMITTEES.

September 7, 1929.

To the Board of Supervisors,
  City and County of San Francisco,
San Francisco, California.

SUPERVISOR GALLAGHER (interrupting): What page of what record is that?

THE MAYOR: This is a letter to the Board of Supervisors dated September 7, 1929, and signed by the Advisory Board of the Veterans' War Memorial Committee, H. J. Boyd, H. W. Glensor and James B. Burns.

THE MAYOR (continuing reading):

Gentlemen: The Veterans' Advisory Board has been instructed by the 20 posts of the American Legion in San Francisco, 5 posts of the Veterans of Foreign Wars, 4 camps of the United Spanish War Veterans, the Disabled American Veterans of the World War, and the United Veterans Council, the latter organization representing the other veteran organizations in San Francisco, to convey to your Honorable Board the information that the veteran organizations of San Francisco emphatically protest the confirmation of the Board of War Memorial Trustees now submitted to your board for confirmation. Therefore, the advisory board speaks to you for all active veteran organizations in San Francisco.

The advisory board has further been instructed to submit a written statement fully setting forth the veterans' objections and the reasons therefor.

The veterans first object to the appointment and confirmation of this board upon the ground that a majority of the members are not veterans.

By Ordinance No. 7516 New Series, a special election was called and held in this City on the 14th day of June, 1927, for the purpose of submitting to the voters a proposition to incur a bonded indebtedness in the sum of four million dollars for the acquisition of land and the construction of the War Memorial. The project was specifically described in the ordinance as:

"The construction, completion and equipment of permanent buildings in or adjacent to the Civic Center of the City and County of San Francisco to be used as a memorial hall for war veterans and for educational, recreational, entertainment and other municipal purposes."

By a resolution of your board, adopted at its meeting on Monday, May 16, 1927, signed by 16 members of the board and approved by the Mayor, an argument was ordered mailed by the Registrar to the voters on behalf of your board in support of the bond issue, in which argument the following statement was made, speaking of the contemplated building:

"The utilitarian value of these buildings, alone, merit their construction. One of them shall be the Veterans' Building, housing all the veteran organizations in San Francisco. It was to give these splendid organizations a permanent headquarters in the name of the public which honors their deeds that the War Memorial Fund originally was launched."

This argument is entirely consistent with the ordinance, because in such ordinance there is but one specific purpose named for the bond issue. That purpose is for the construction and equipment of buildings to be used as a Memorial Hall for war veterans. *Any other purpose is incidental thereto.* Such being the purpose as expressed by your board and by the people of San Francisco in the overwhelming vote by which the bonds were passed, the veterans of San Francisco are unable to see any valid reason why the erection, supervision, maintenance and administration of this building, designed and intended primarily as a place to house their organizations, should not be committed to a board, at least a majority of which are veterans who have served this country in some one of its wars.

The veterans of San Francisco recognize that the people of San Francisco could have created a War Memorial in any form that they wished, a monument, a bridge, an arch or a statue. They have in fact, however, adopted the practical rather than the idealistic form of memorial and provided for the erection of a building that will be of some real benefit to the living veterans as well as stand in commemoration of those who passed on in heroic sacrifice that the people of San Francisco might have peace and prosperity, and enjoyment of the arts and sciences which is now theirs.

The veterans of San Francisco do not now claim and never have claimed the entire use of these Memorial Buildings. All they have ever asked and all they are now asking is a sufficient space so arranged as to be a practical response to their minimum needs. They have waited almost ten years to secure this, and the wishes of the people of San Francisco have been thwarted by an evident attempt to defeat the needs of the veterans.

The veterans refused to stand idly by and have the monies subscribed and voted by the citizens of San Francisco used for a purpose that would defeat the pledges made to the citizens and the veterans of San Francisco. This resulted in controversy which finally led to the exposure of the inefficiency and extravagant wastefulness of the present private Board of Trustees that has spent several hundred thousand dollars for architects' fees and expenses and yet have not a plan for a War Memorial within the total sum subscribed and voted for use.

The veterans of San Francisco, for whose deeds and in whose name this War Memorial project was launched, demand that the purposes for which the War Memorial Fund was created be carried out. The main purpose was to erect a building to house the veterans' organizations of San Francisco. Other uses and purposes were incidental. This cannot be denied. The ordinance so provides in plain terms. In view of the determined effort that has been made to defeat this' purpose and divert the buildings to other uses, the veterans unhesitatingly assert that they can only be assured of the lawful purpose of the War Memorial being accomplished if a majority of war veterans are placed upon the board of trustees, which board is charged by law with the duties of erecting, equipping, maintaining and administering the same.

There is a sufficient group of men living in San Francisco today who have served this country in its armed forces in time of war from whose number a majority of qualified trustees can well be chosen. In all other cities of California, and we believe throughout the United States, when administrative bodies to administer the functions of War Memorials have been selected, their membership has consisted not of a majority of veterans but entirely of veterans. Only in San Francisco has there been an apparent and perhaps a deliberate neglect of the recognition to which war veterans are entitled. The War Memorial is a tribute to their services and why should not they be permitted to administer it during their lifetime as they are fully qualified to do?

THE MAYOR: This letter to the Board was presented to the Board before the action of the Board took place as to the nominations, but I will refer to that as we progress, we are doing pretty well so far. (Continuing reading:)

We are further directed to say that the veterans of San Francisco are opposed to the appointment and confirmation of any member of the Board of Supervisors as a member of such War Memorial Trustees. The objection of the veterans in this regard is not personal or political, but practical. There is also a precedent established by your board against making such appointment. Under the terms of the City Charter, the Board of War Memorial Trustees, in the erection and administration of the War Memorial are subordinate in many respects to the Board of Supervisors. Each and every member of the Board of Supervisors should be prepared to exercise calm, unbiased and impartial judgment with respect to all matters submitted to it by the Board of War Memorial Trustees. A member of the Board of Supervisors also serving upon the Board of War Memorial Trustees could not bring to the solution of problems submitted to him as supervisor, the calm, unbiased and impartial judgment in matters of administration or appropriation for the administration of such buildings, if he is also a member of the Board of Trustees and as such officially interested in the decisions. Such a situation is wrong in principle. The veterans respectfully urge upon your board that it is fundamentally unsound that a member of the legislative body, who must decide upon policies and pass ordinances governing the administrative body, should also be a member of such administrative body.

The members of the advisory board personally regret that under their instructions they are obliged to file specific objections to confirmation of any board of which one of their own number, namely, Charles H. Kendrick, is a member. In fairness to Col. Kendrick, it must be said that this is not any personal objection to him, but arises primarily by reason of certain differences of opinion which we concede to be honest with respect to the position of the veterans in connection with this project. In further explanation it should be said that nine years ago Col. Kendrick was a unanimous and very satisfactory choice of the American Legion to represent it on the board of trustees appointed to administer the privately subscribed trust fund. With the passage of time, there came differences of opinion to the end that the American Legion and other veterans concluded that Col. Kendrick did not represent the American Legion on such board of trustees. Finally, on November 1, 1928, the War Memorial Committee of the American Legion of San Francisco, composed of representatives of all posts of the American Legion in San Francisco, passed a motion that Col. Kendrick be immediately requested to resign as a member of the Board of Trustees for the reason that he had not represented the best interests of the American Legion, the body specifically selecting him for service on that board, and had taken action in a manner directly opposed to the expressed desires of the organization he represented. Thereafter and on November 14, 1928, Col. Kendrick appeared before the County Council of the American Legion and there stated that none of the present trustees would be anxious to continue serving in this capacity and would be glad of the opportunity to turn the whole matter over to the City and sever their connection with the War Memorial. In answer to a question by a member of the council as to why he did not resign in view of an admission he had made that he did not represent the American Legion, Col. Kendrick replied that he would resign when the project was turned over to the City. The foregoing statements are based upon excerpts from the minutes of the County Council and War Memorial Committee of the American Legion.

Under these circumstances, the veterans must emphatically protest against the confirmation of Col. Kendrick as a member of this or any other board of permanent trustees of the San Francisco War Memorial. Why one of the few veterans who have opposed the position and stand of the United Veteran Organizations of San Francisco and whose appointment was duly protested by these organizations, should be designated as one of the war veteran members of the new Board of Trustees, is beyond comprehension.

The veterans further object to the confirmation of this board upon the ground that the charter has amended by Charter Amendment No. 32 provides:

" * * * the Mayor in making appointments shall give due consideration to the veterans of all wars in which the United States has engaged * * "

and charge that in making these nominations the Mayor has not given due consideration to the veterans of all wars. In this connection you are advised that in March, 1929, the veterans of San Francisco, after careful and earnest consideration, submitted to the Mayor a list of names of fifteen veterans selected from the ranks of the United Spanish War Veterans, Veterans of Foreign Wars, Disabled Veterans, American Legion, Indian War Veterans, and other nationally known and accredited organizations.

These men were not selected for political expediency, but for their standing in the community, their business experience and ability to supervise the erection and administration of this six million dollar building project. Consideration had also been given to their intimate knowledge of the needs of the various veteran organizations in San Francisco, their activities and prospects of future growth. The veterans at that time stated that any of these men would be satisafactory to the veterans of San Francisco for appointment to the Board of War Memorial Trustees.

Not one of these men has been nominated to your board for confirmation. In this connection it is proper to say that two of the men whose names have been submitted to your board for confirmation were not selected by the veterans of San Francisco for the reason that at the time the veterans' list was submitted it was understood that these two men would be unable to serve. They are General Hunter Liggett and Frank N. Belgrano, Jr. The veterans are entirely satisfied with these two nominees and would be pleased to see them confirmed as members of the new Board of Trustees.

THE MAYOR: I would like to insert here these two names, General Hunter Liggett and Frank N. Belgrano, Jr.—I understand you concur in these nominations. (Continuing reading:)

The veterans further object to the confirmation of these nominees upon the ground that by resolution of this Board of Supervisors, adopted on December 10, 1928, this board urged and recommended that his Honor, the Mayor, appoint a majority of the members of the War Memorial Trustees from that portion of the citizenry of San Francisco that had seen service with Army, Navy or Marine Corps, and further resolved

"that the advice and counsel of the veterans' organizations through the medium of their properly constituted representatives be sought before said appointments are made, it being the opinion of the Board of Supervisors that every class or group of the people of San Francisco, with a confidence inspired by service in time of war, may look to such men for purposeful loyalty and unselfish devotion to San Francisco in time of peace."

The advice and counsel of the veteran organizations was not sought before the nomination of the proposed board, now before you, was made. In this connection it is fair to say that this advisory board met with the Mayor, at which time he presented a list of names, nine of which names are now before you. The veterans were then asked if they had any objection to the appointment of those men. With respect to one name submitted it was then emphatically stated that the veterans did object. There are now two names before you that were never submitted to the veterans at all. The board as now proposed has never been discussed with nor submitted to the veterans at all.

Obviously it is a useless matter to submit the names of individuals and ask the veterans if they have any objections to such individuals. Probably hundreds of names could be selected in San Francisco and the veterans could truthfully state that they had no objection to the appointment of any one of such men. It is, however, the constitution of the board as a whole to which consideration must be given and this board as a whole has never been submitted to the veterans, although at the time of the interview last referred to, it was stated by the Mayor that before a submission was made to the Board of Supervisors, the veterans would again be consulted.

In conclusion, the veterans of San Francisco, speaking with one voice, say to you that it is painful to thus be compelled to discuss frankly and publicly a board composed of men who individually are highly esteemed fellow citizens, and in some instances close personal friends. We feel, however, that we have been forced into this position by the effort that has been made over eight years, notwithstanding the express provisions of the agreement under which the people subscribed and paid nearly two million dollars; notwithstanding the plain terms of the ordinance above mentioned, to convert this project from a War Memorial, primarily of service to war veteran organizations, into some other type of project. If it is your intention to disregard the law and build art museums and/or other buildings, leaving to the veterans such scraps of space as may be available and which some of their bodies can use, the best and most conclusive way for your board to manifest such intention is to confirm these appointments.

If, on the other hand, you intend to follow the terms of the ordinance, pay due and proper tribute to the service our comrades have given, and build a building in accordance with Ordinance No. 7516—

"to be used as a Memorial Hall for war veterans"

we respectfully request that the erection and administration of such buildings be placed where it belongs, in the hands of the veteran bodies of San Francisco, and that this Board of Trustees as now constituted be not confirmed.

Respectfully submitted,
ADVISORY BOARD TO VETERANS WAR MEMORIAL
COMMITTEES.

H. J. BOYD,
H. W. GLENSOR,
JAMES B. BURNS.

J. C. CLARIDGE, Secretary.

September 16, 1929. The Board of Supervisors of the City and County of San Francisco refused to confirm the following named persons submitted by the Mayor as Trustees of the War Memorial. The names submitted are as follows:

General Hunter Liggett.
Frank N. Belgrano.
James I. Herz.
Charles H. Kendrick.
Herbert Fleishhacker.
Kenneth R. Kingsbury.
Robert I. Bentley.
George Cameron.
George Hearst.
James W. Mullen.
Supervisor Jesse C. Colman.

The Reporter's Transcript of the proceedings on confirmation is as follows:

EXHIBIT NO. 4.
IN RE PROCEEDINGS AS TO CONFIRMATION OR REJECTION OF THE APPOINTEES OF THE MAYOR ON THE BOARD OF WAR MEMORIAL TRUSTEES.
Monday, September 16, 1929, 10:00 A. M.

The regular meeting of the Board of Supervisors of the City and County of San Francisco was held on Monday, September 16, 1929, beginning at the hour of 10:00 o'clock A. M. of said day, in the chambers of the Board, City Hall, San Francisco, California.

Acting Mayor Havenner presided.

After the transaction of other business, the following proceedings were had in relation to the vote on the confirmation or rejection of the nominees of the Mayor for trustees of the Board of War Memorial Trustees.

SUPERVISOR SCHMIDT: Mr. Chairman and members of the Board: I move the privilege of the floor to Comrade Harry Glensor, who desires to address the Board with reference to the trustees.

THE CHAIRMAN: Is there any objection? (Bringing down the gavel).

SUPERVISOR SCHMIDT: I move that all of the absent members be sent for.

SUPERVISOR SHANNON: The Mayor requested to be present when this matter was taken up, and I am going to move at this time that the matter be continued until such time as the Mayor is in the City to hear the discussion.

THE CHAIRMAN: Is there a second to that motion? The motion
fails for lack of a second.

SUPERVISOR SCHMIDT: At the last meeting I desired to bring
this matter before the Board so the Mayor could hear the discussion.
But in view of the fact that the Mayor has charged a delay in the
appointment of the War Memorial Trustees, I feel that I do not want
to take any more responsibility of delay. I move, and I think that it
would be courtesy, that we send and find out if the Mayor is still in
town, to assure ourselves whether he is present or not. I so move,
that the Sergeant at Arms be instructed to wait upon the Mayor's
office and find out if the Mayor has left the City, and, if so, we can
deal with the situation as we see fit.

SUPERVISOR McSHEEHY: The papers have recorded the Mayor
as leaving here last night and the present Chairman is Acting Mayor.
He could tell you directly, by asking him the direct question, if Mayor
Rolph is in town?

THE CHAIRMAN: I have not been advised that the Mayor has
changed his plans. I just asked that the Mayor's office be requested
to advise us whether he left, according to his schedule, for the East.

SUPERVISOR McSHEEHY: Mr. Chairman, and members of the
Board: While the inquiry is being made, I feel this way about this
matter—and I happen to be one of the present trustees of the War
Memorial: A great deal has been said about our dilatory tactics in
appointing the trustees to succeed the present trustees, and I want to
say, as a member of the present trustees, that I do not, individually,
like to be charged with being dilatory in doing anything. I do not
do it in my private work, and I have never done it in public work
and I never will if I can help it. Now, I feel that this matter should
be heard here today, and that a stenographic report of all of the statements made by all should be sent to his Honor the Mayor, in whatever part of the East that he is in. I read in the newspapers where
the Mayor went east. I am sure that he has gone east according to
those statements, and I feel that we should carry this hearing on and
that everything pertaining to the statements made here should be
transcribed and sent to his Honor the Mayor.

SUPERVISOR GALLAGHER: I would like to know the parliamentary status.

THE CHAIRMAN: The privilege of the floor has been extended to
Mr. Glensor.

SUPERVISOR SCHMIDT: We are waiting to see if the Mayor can
be present or not.

THE CHAIRMAN: I am advised that the Mayor left for the East
last night. The privilege of the floor at this time——

SUPERVISOR RONCOVIERI (interrupting): I wish to know what
the parliamentary situation is.

THE CHAIRMAN: The privilege of the floor has been extended to
Mr. Glensor.

SUPERVISOR McSHEEHY: Mr. Chairman, as Chairman of the
Rules Committee, it is my duty to move an adjournment at 12:00
o'clock. I feel today that we have kept these gentlemen waiting and
I am going to move that we recess at 12:30.

H. W. GLENSOR: Members of the Board:

THE MAYOR: This original is the same report read by
Mr. Glensor——

SUPERVISOR GALLAGHER (interrupting): I was going
to observe that was repetition.

THE MAYOR: Yes, that is repetition, and with your permission, I will not read it again.

I ask leave to file that with your Board, as an official communication for the veteran bodies of San Francisco, and I also ask permission,
if you please, to step out of my character for a moment as a member
of the Advisory Board of the veterans, and to state to you, personally,

my views on this important question. Eight or nine years ago this project was launched, as you gentlemen said in the argument that was sent to the people of San Francisco to induce them to vote these bonds, primarily as a project to give a home to the veteran organizations of San Francisco. That was the whole motive, that was the whole tone of the big mass meeting that was held in the Civic Auditorium in the fall of 1920. You remember how the stage was dressed with all the flags of the soldiers, sailors, marines, war workers and so on. And that was all that was discussed, the whole undertone of the meeting was, "Let us give these veteran organizations a place to meet." The citizens of San Francisco subscribed over $2,000,000, and nearly $2,000,000 of that has been paid into the trust fund. That next made its appearance as a trust fund, under a declaration of trust, that was drawn with a board of seven trustees appointed. The beneficiaries of that trust fund were the American Legion, the San Francisco Opera Association and the San Francisco Art Association—maybe I have not got the names exactly right, but that is the sense of it. Under the terms of that trust agreement the American Legion was made a sort of subsidiary trustee for the benefit of all the other veteran organizations of San Francisco, to see that they had proper housing accommodations in this War Memorial building if and when it was built.

In 1927 the veterans were asked, and they did support, and very properly so, this bond issue, which was to complete the project. And the only specific designation you will find in that ordinance is a specific designation to build Memorial halls for veteran organizations, and all other purposes are incidental thereto. What happened? From the beginning of the original privately subscribed trust fund to this day no plans have ever been submitted to the veteran organizations of San Francisco, with one exception, that even approximately met their needs for housing purposes. When we come to examine it, we find that the principal project is something else entirely, and that the veterans' needs are subsidiary and subordinate. The tail is wagging the dog, if I may use such a homely illustration.

A set of plans were, at one time, submitted to the veterans which they did approve, and when we find construction work started we find it started upon an entirely different set of plans, upon an entirely different plan departing, radically and materially, from the plans which the veteran organizations had approved. Naturally, they objected, and we objected, and we are going to continue to object until the law is complied with and a Memorial Hall for veteran organizations is provided in accordance with law or the entire project is rescinded and comes before the people in honest guise, saying that they want to build an opera house and an art museum and use the money for that purpose. And if the people so will, we will be quiet and accept the will of the people.

And then buildings were removed from these lots across here, buildings that were bringing in revenue, tenants were evicted and excavations were dug, to carry on plans which were not in accordance with the law, which did not meet the needs of the veterans, and when the veterans objected the people who were trying to put this project across, according to their private views, rushed to the press with a statement that the veterans were impeding the progress of San Francisco, and that a few malcontents were holding up this great constructive project for the City of San Francisco. Gentlemen, the veterans would be derelict in the duty they owe to the people of San Francisco on the present state of the record if they did not object to this practical misappropriation of the funds which were provided by the people to build one type of project and have it converted into another type, and if that constitutes a malcontent, we are going to continue to be malcontents. But as to representing only a few of the veteran organizations of San Francisco, I want to assure you that I will be followed, briefly, by two or three of the leaders of the major veteran organizations of San

Francisco, and you will find that the veterans of San Francisco are
of one mind and speak with one voice on this project. We are going
to oppose the construction of a War Memorial in San Francisco until
and unless the plan, as laid down, is followed out according to the
law which has created the funds for the erection of that building. I
thank you for your attention.

SUPERVISOR HAYDEN: Mr. Chairman, might I ask Mr. Glensor
how many buildings does he anticipate in the plan of the War Memorial?

MR. GLENSOR: Two, I guess.

SUPERVISOR HAYDEN: One for the veterans and one for the
opera house?

MR. GLENSOR: Well, if that were so, it would be all right, I guess,
but there is one that is commonly and erroneously referred to as The
American Legion Building, which really should be referred to as the
Veterans' Building, in which approximately one-third of the space
will be allotted to the veterans, if I remember correctly, and about two-
thirds will be built into a Memorial Court and an art museum, if the
present plans were carried out.

SUPERVISOR HAYDEN: You have no objection to an opera house
as a part of the War Memorial?

MR. GLENSOR: Heavens no, we wish them all the luck in the
world, but what we want is a building, built in accordance with the
original plan that was submitted to the Board of Supervisors by the
City Engineer before this bond ordinance was ever submitted to the
people, and in which the veterans will be provided with sufficient
space, so arranged that it will be a practical response to their needs,
and that is all we want. We hope that there will be enough money
left over to build the finest opera house west of New York City.

SUPERVISOR HAYDEN: Will you say then that the four million-
dollar bond issue which was voted by the people ought to be devoted
exclusively to a building for the use of the war veterans?

MR. GLENSOR: That is the only project that is mentioned in the
ordinance.

SUPERVISOR HAYDEN: Then you claim that that money should
go exclusively to a building for the veterans?

MR. GLENSOR: No, not exclusively.

SUPERVISOR HAYDEN: You are willing then that it should be
evenly prorated between the opera house and the veterans and the
other purposes?

MR. GLENSOR: We are even willing that it should be unevenly
prorated so long as sufficient halls and an auditorium, locker rooms
and so forth are provided to meet the veterans' needs. We do not
care what is done with the rest of the money.

SUPERVISOR GALLAGHER: I would like to ask Mr. Glensor this
question: It has been stated somewhere, either by the chief executive
or by newspaper editorials, I am not sure, that these opinions expressed
by you, and heretofore expressed by others, on behalf of the County
Council, which I know is a representative body, do not represent, in
the main, the views of the rank and file of the veterans, the majority.
What is your statement as to that?

MR. GLENSOR: Well, the only reaction that we have obtained from
the rank and file is that, if we have been condemned at all, it has
been condemnation for the restraint we have imposed upon our expression of these views. We have made every effort to couch the views
in proper parliamentary language and still meet the reaction of the
rank and file, Mr. Gallagher.

SUPERVISOR GALLAGHER: The Board can be assured that not
only have the rank and file been consulted, but these views, despite
statements to the contrary, represent unquestionably their sentiments?

MR. GLENSOR: Mr. Gallagher, we have only heard one dissenting
voice from a gentleman who was formerly, some years ago, quite active

in the County Council of the American Legion, and in the American Legion in San Francisco, who has been out of touch for some time, and who is a business partner, I am informed, of one of the nominees. We have not heard a dissenting voice anywhere. If any criticism has been directed toward us, it has been for not pressing our claims more strenuously.

SUPERVISOR GALLAGHER: There are, I understand, something like 40,000 veterans of foreign wars in San Francisco; is that not true?

MR. GLENSOR: I think that is fair and sixty organizations now.

SUPERVISOR GALLAGHER: And your group here represents, in an organized sense, how many?

MR. GLENSOR: I should think about 30,000 men and women, counting auxiliaries and all that.

SUPERVISOR GALLAGHER: All organized as a part of 40,000 veterans and workers?

MR. GLENSOR: Yes, I think there are 40,000 men who are actually veterans. I think that we represent here the voice of approximately 30,000 people which include auxiliary organizations and state units.

SUPERVISOR GALLAGHER: You are organized and through organization you give expression——

MR. GLENSOR (interrupting): Yes. The personnel of this Advisory Board arises in the following manner: The American Legion has an Advisory Committee, consisting of representatives from each post. The Spanish War veterans act through their County Council—I happen to be a member also of the Spanish War Veterans—obviously, the entire 40,000 people cannot come up here and express their views. In order to get an avenue of communication on this thing, so that we would be coordinated and we would all talk about the same thing, they appointed an Advisory Board, comprising J. B. Burns, County and Area Commander, which is the same as the vice-president of the American Legion, and also a past commander of the County Council, Mr. Boyd, representing the Veterans of Foreign Wars, one of the major veteran organizations in San Francisco, and myself, primarily representing the views of the Spanish War Veterans, although I happen to be a member of both organizations, and that is the Advisory Board. The Advisory Board, gentlemen, does not purport to make or name any policy in connection with this War Memorial. We are merely the mouthpiece for expressing to you and to others, the organized views of the veterans of San Francisco.

SUPERVISOR SCHMIDT: May I say a word while on this question: In all discussions with the War Memorial Trustees there has never been one individual that appeared before this Board of Supervisors that denied the statement, made just a moment ago by Comrade Glensor, that the united body of veterans were standing behind the movement outline by the Advisory Board.

SUPERVISOR GALLAGHER: I wanted Mr. Glensor to bring out, for the press and the public, a statement which would be an answer to the statement frequently made, and authoritatively as I thought, or by somebody who thought it was authoritative, that the views expressed by the gentleman whom he represents, and for whom he speaks so well this morning, were not the views of a majority of the veterans involved. You have answered my question.

MR. GLENSOR: We have certified copies of resolutions from practically every one of these subordinate organizations, not instructing us in detail, but in principle as to what to say here, and the report which I have just read to you has been submitted to and approved by the commanders of all the major organizations in San Francisco, and, specifically, by the committees of the American Legion on the War Memorial and the Spanish War Veterans and the Veterans of Foreign Wars, the Disabled American Veterans and so forth. I will ask you gentlemen to be kind enough to hear from Mr. Sapiro briefly.

SUPERVISOR TODD: You made the statement that there was a

list of veterans sent to the Mayor, any of whom would be acceptable to your organization.

MR. GLENSOR: Yes.

SUPERVISOR TODD: How many names were in that list?

MR. GLENSOR: Fifteen.

SUPERVISOR TODD: Would you furnish this Board with a list of those names?

MR. GLENSOR: I would not feel at liberty to for this reason: We would have no objection to the Mayor furnishing the Board——

> THE MAYOR: Is Mr. Glensor here? Did you make that statement, you would have no objection to submitting that list of 15 names to the Board?
>
> MR. GLENSOR: I said I had no objection to your doing so. You will see there, I stated that I had no objection to your doing it, and I have none now.
>
> THE MAYOR (continuing reading):

SUPERVISOR TODD (interrupting): The Mayor has left the city for a month.

MR. GLENSOR: It was agreed at that time that list would be confidential as between the Advisory Committee and the Mayor, and I would not feel at liberty to break that confidence without his permission, but I am sure we would gladly consent to his furnishing them.

SUPERVISOR TODD: I would not want to ask you to if that was the arrangement.

SUPERVISOR SCHMIDT: I move the privilege of the floor to Comrade Sapiro.

MILTON D. SAPIRO: Mr. Chairman, members of the Board of Supervisors: I appear here this morning to add my voice to the report that was rendered by the Advisory Board, just for one purpose, and that is to refute the insinuation that some one has endeavored to spread among this Board, and probably to all the citizens of San Francisco, that the Advisory Board does not express the voice of the organized veterans of San Francisco. I want to say, Mr. Supervisor Gallagher, that you will perhaps remember that the Advisory Board, one of the members of which just addressed you, was created at your suggestion. You asked that the veteran groups of San Francisco get together and appoint a board of three men to whom this supervisorial body could look for accurate information representing the opinion and sentiment of the veterans of San Francisco. This Advisory Board was created by all of the veteran bodies. It does not take any independent action, however. It is the voice of the veteran bodies. And the letter just read by Mr. Glensor accurately represents the voice of every post in the American Legion in San Francisco, and accurately represents the voice of probably more than 90 per cent of the members of the organized bodies of the American Legion in San Francisco. I preside over the council that represents all of the posts in San Francisco and I know that that is their sentiment. And I happen to attend a great many meetings of the American Legion posts in San Francisco and I know that it is the sentiment of practically all the members of the American Legion in San Francisco. They want this Memorial, but they want a Memorial built under a Board of Trustees in whom they can have confidence, to carry out the vote of the people and the subscription of the people of San Francisco. They feel that it cannot be accomplished unless the resolution which you gentlemen adopted is carried out in spirit and in fact, that is, that there be a majority of that Board who are war veterans, and war veterans who are satisfactory to the veteran groups of San Francisco.

> THE MAYOR: I would like to make a statement there, but I am not making any statement. (Continuing reading:)

Now, I have seen the statements in the public press that perhaps this group of organized veterans does not represent all of the veterans of San Francisco. But if you gentlemen have had any experience with the organized veteran groups in San Francisco and California, such as is represented before you here today, you know that the man who has become a member of an organized veteran group is the man who has recognized that his service to his country did not cease when the war terminated, but that service to country meant doing something in time of peace to carry out the true purposes of citizenship, and that a man could only be an effective citizen through organization. And so the organized veteran is the man who has maintained his interest in the welfare of his country. The organized veteran in San Francisco is the man who has the interest of San Francisco at heart, and who is willing, not merely to sit back and read it in the newspapers, but to take an active part in creating public sentiment and in creating a policy that will make for the good of San Francisco. And his voice is the voice that is entitled to be heard because the unorganized man sits back and lets other people do the things for him. And when we come to you saying that we represent the voice of the organized veterans we represent those veterans who are the only ones to be entitled to be heard before the Board here, where other men are willing to sit back and not express themselves one way or another. We are not afraid to put ourselves on record on this thing; we are not afraid of the false cries that have been raised with reference to this thing. They say that the people of San Francisco want a War Memorial. Who wants a Memorial to the deeds of men who fought and bled and fell on the field of battle more than those of us who stood by their sides when they fell, who saw those men go to the last home that is given to man? Do you think that we do not want the War Memorial in San Francisco? But we want a War Memorial. There is nothing in anything that has been submitted to the people of San Francisco that says, "Do you want an opera house as a War Memorial?" We want to be fair to the people of San Francisco. We are perfectly willing that, along with these other garbage questions that you are going to submit to the people of San Francisco that you can submit this one: "Do you want the majority of the funds voted for War Memorial purposes to be used for building an opera house?" And if the people answer "Yes," we will accept their decision. But we know what their answer will be. And we know, and we are confident of the fact, that the people will support you in demanding that a War Memorial Board of Trustees be composed of a majority of veterans. Why, it is a shame in a city of this size, where there are thousands of veterans, as you say, Mr. Supervisor, that you appoint, not a majority of veterans, but that you do not appoint an entire board of war veterans to administer a War Memorial. Who says that all the intelligence and all the brains of San Francisco reside in a certain group? I understand that when the group was presented to your body that something was mentioned as to the wealth of the men that were appointed and the expectation of gifts from them. Is San Francisco too small to build its own War Memorial that it has to depend on wealth? Was wealth ever made the test of service to the nation? When we went out on the field of battle did they say, "How much money do you have; how much did you contribute to the army?" No. They looked at your heart and your soul and your willingness to serve. We want a War Memorial, but we do not want you to erect a building out there, or a set of buildings that we will point out to our children and say, "Yes, there is a beautiful structure, but empty in spirit and not representative of the heart of San Francisco." We do not want any hypocrisy associated with our War Memorial. We of the American Legion expect this Board of Supervisors to keep faith with us. When the ordinance was passed—and it was passed, of course, under very peculiar circumstances—you saw fit to insert in that ordinance a provision that the appointees would be subject to your confirmation, and then you went further. You said that you believed that it was proper to have a majority of appointees who are war veterans. Now, we want you to stay by the belief which we believe you sincerely held when you passed that resolution. We do not think that the ordinance was intended to make you a rubber stamp of the Mayor. You have the right to an independent judgment on those appointees, and in the name of the American Legion of San Francisco, I ask this Board to keep faith with its war veterans and insist that a majority of that Board be war veterans and war veterans who are acceptable to the group of ex-service men here.

SUPERVISOR SCHMIDT: Mr. Chairman——

SUPERVISOR SUHR: I am going to ask, if we are not going to adjourn, that Colonel Tobin be heard for just a moment.

SUPERVISOR SCHMIDT: I have been given the list of speakers that the veterans desire to have speak before this Board.

SUPERVISOR SUHR (interrupting): It will just take a moment.

SUPERVISOR SCHMIDT: I have no objection.

SUPERVISOR McSHEEHY: I gave notice that I would move to adjourn at 12:30. I am going to make that as a motion. You can vote it down if you wish. I could not present it under the conditions.

COLONEL TOBIN: Mr. Chairman and members of the honorable Board of Supervisors: Two weeks ago yesterday I came here in behalf of men of my regiment, who represented the City of San Francisco and were on the other side, and asked for a postponement in their behalf for one week. The Mayor granted it, and last week you were so busy, you worked until 7:00 o'clock, that you postponed it until today. I wish to thank you for that, and my one reason is that my men wanted to bring before your body, the fathers of this city, the true state of affairs, as I understand them. It is my duty to you. I do not belong to the Legion or to any organization. I believe that those men who live here, your sons and husbands and brothers represent those who are entitled to be heard. I am only a regular. But it is my duty to uphold my men when they call on me to do so.

SUPERVISOR SCHMIDT: I move the privilege of the floor to Comrade Harold Boyd.

SUPERVISOR McSHEEHY: Supervisor Schmidt just told me that there is only one more speaker and that is Mr. Boyd.

SUPERVISOR SCHMIDT: I believe that is all.

SUPERVISOR McSHEEHY: So I won't press my motion until he gets through.

MR. HAROLD J. BOYD: Mr. Chairman and Gentlemen of the Board: As Commander of the County Council of the Veterans of Foreign Wars, and as Chairman of the War Memorial Committee of the United Veterans Council, I am here to confirm the statement made by Mr. Glensor, and also the statement made by Mr. Sapiro, representing the American Legion. On behalf of the organization that I represent, I also want to express our sincere appreciation to this Board of Supervisors for the attitude that you have always assumed in the past in regard to the War Memorial. I think that the speakers that have preceded me have given you all of the facts. But I want you to know, and I want to take this opportunity to acquaint you with some of the questions that the rank and file of the veterans of San Francisco are asking us, because the three of us are their representatives. They are asking us why it is that there has been so much opposition to the veterans' views in this matter, no opposition from this Board but opposition from other quarters. The people we represent point out to us that, in June, 1927, this Board, by a unanimous resolution, decided that no money resulting from the sale of the $4,000,000 worth of bonds would ever be appropriated until and unless the plans for the War Memorial were approved by veteran organizations. They point out to us that two years went by without any plans being submitted to us for approval. The men that we represent point out to us, also, that at the last minute of the last hour of the last day upon which charter amendments could be submitted a charter amendment was submitted to this Board last year. Every member of the Board knows the text of that charter amendment. It was submitted to you. As originally submitted to you that Board of War Memorial Trustees would have been all powerful in connection with that project. This Board of Supervisors, in protection of veteran interests, if you please, saw fit to limit the power of that Board, and this Board of Supervisors saw fit to alter the amendment, as submitted, to the extent that this Board would have a voice in the final approval of the Board of War Memorial Trustees that his Honor the Mayor was to appoint. The men that we represent point out to us, also, that in December of last year a resolution was introduced in this Board, recommending to his Honor the Mayor that six of eleven trustees be chosen from the ranks of ex-service men. That resolution you are all familiar with. That resolution was fought here for three weeks and, finally, by a majority action, the Board adopted the resolution.

Gentlemen of the Board, I want to tell you that in January of this year we appealed to his Honor the Mayor to appoint the Board of Trustees, in January, and in February, and again in March, and his Honor took no action, and, finally, after eight months of study, he submitted a Board to you that his Honor the Mayor knew would be objected to by the veteran organizations. We want to say to you that we appreciate the problem that confronts you today.

SUPERVISOR McSHEEHY: Your Honor, it is six o'clock——

THE MAYOR: Yes, the sun is just coming up.

SUPERVISOR PEYSER: I was going to suggest——

SUPERVISOR GALLAGHER (interrupting): I move a call of the Board.

THE MAYOR: I intend to finish this report, if you will stay here.

SUPERVISOR HAVENNER: I would like to make a statement for the record.

THE MAYOR (continuing): That is the reason the record is here. I would like to continue now. (Continuing reading:)

We realize that you are serving simply as representatives of the people, and we know what a problem it is to serve as representatives of the people. For that reason we have given you our views in writing so that every member of the Board could have our reasons for objecting to the Board of Trustees as at present constituted. We realize the problem that you have to contend with, but we hope that you will continue to keep faith with the veteran organizations just as you have in the past on three specific occasions that I have mentioned. We realize that you are representatives, we realize that a representative sometimes has a hard, hard problem to handle. The veterans in San Francisco were at one time representatives. We represented not only San Francisco and California, but we represented all of the United States of America, in 1898, and in 1917-1918, and all we ask of you is that you do as well by us as we tried to do by you in those days. Thank you.

SUPERVISOR McSHEEHY: I move we recess until 2:30.

SUPERVISOR HAYDEN: Second that motion.

(Thereupon a recess was had until 2:30.)

————

AFTERNOON SESSION, 2:30 P. M.

THE CHAIRMAN: The Board will be in order.

THE CHAIRMAN: The matter before the Board is still the appointment of the War Memorial Trustees.

SUPERVISOR SCHMIDT: I move that the matter of the War Memorial Trustees be taken in the hands of the Board.

MR. GLENSOR: I would like to make about a five-minute statement
SUPERVISOR SCHMIDT: I withdraw that motion temporarily and move that the privilege of the floor be extended to Mr. Harry Glensor.
THE CHAIRMAN: No objection? Such will be the order.
MR. GLENSOR: Gentlemen of the Board: You may have gathered this morning that the members of the veterans who are here feel rather intensely on this matter, and due, perhaps, to the very intenseness of that feeling, we overlooked a matter that should be considered, and which is not covered by the typewritten letter which was submitted to you, for the reason that it has only come up since that report was prepared. I refer to the intimations that have been going around in the press—one of them is editorially noted in one of today's papers —that, unless action satisfactory to the people who subscribed to this private trust fund is taken, that the subscribers to the private trust fund might see fit to withdraw their subscriptions. Now, gentlemen, the answer of the veterans to that suggestion is that it simply cannot be done. The subscriptions to the private trust fund have been paid in, all or nearly all paid in, and there are some uncollected. Whether the uncollected can be collected or not is a question. But so far as any subscriber to the private trust fund withdrawing the money that has been paid into the private trust fund, it simply cannot be done, it is just foolish to talk about it. If such an attempt was made, the veterans might welcome it because it might result in our securing a full and complete accounting of that private trust fund, which we have been trying for eight years unsuccessfully to get. Now, what may happen is this: It may happen, no matter what action this Board takes, or what form the War Memorial project may take, the board of private trustees may, in their wisdom, refuse to turn over the privately subscribed trust fund to the public trustees who are eventually appointed by the Mayor and confirmed by this Board. That may happen no matter what this Board does or what form the War Memorial project may take. We cannot look into the future and say what those trustees are going to do. It is doubtful if they, even at this time, know themselves. But if such a contingency should occur, the answer to it is very simple, very simple: If the Board of War Memorial Trustees, as finally constituted, and this Board of Supervisors will sell the $4,000,000 bonds provided by the people and proceed to erect a structure in accordance with the mandates of the Ordinance which the people passed to house the veteran organizations of San Francisco, and for such other educational, recreational and other municipal purposes as may be incidental thereto——

SUPERVISOR HAYDEN (interrupting): What do you mean—right at that point and stage—by "other educational or recreational purposes that might be incidental thereto," in addition to the War Memorial Building?

MR. GLENSOR: I do not propose to interpret the Ordinance.
SUPERVISOR HAYDEN: How do you interpret that?
MR. GLENSOR: Why, I suppose that if there was room in the basement for a fire house or a police station, or some other incidental municipal purpose, and it was not being utilized for any other purpose, it could be used for any other city purpose. That is my personal idea. I suppose that the language of the Ordinance might furnish material for long and serious cogitation on the part of a Supreme Court sometime, I do not know.

SUPERVISOR HAYDEN: Do you assume that the people, in voting the $4,000,000, or do you agree that, when they voted that bond issue for $4,000,000 for a War Memorial, that the public had in mind also a building and an Opera House with the $2,000,000 that was already available?

MR. GLENSOR: I do not know what the public had in mind, Mr. Hayden, other than the language of the Ordinance itself, and perhaps it may be explained by the argument that this Board sent out to the people to induce them to vote it, and that was the language that was quoted there—maybe I did not quote it correctly from memory. It is quoted in the written memorandum which we submitted to you this morning, and the argument of the Board of Supervisors sent out in support thereof was that its primary purpose was to house the veteran organizations of San Francisco, that was the primary purpose for which the War Memorial project was launched. Well, now——

SUPERVISOR SHANNON (interrupting): Mr. Glensor, don't you think that in voting those bonds that was the main thought in the minds of the public?

MR. GLENSOR: Why, there can be no doubt of it, this Board has gone on record and so stated.

SUPERVISOR SHANNON: The thought just expressed by Mr. Glensor that it was for the veterans.

MR. GLENSOR: There can be no doubt of it, it has always been the underlying motive back of this War Memorial project, from the day of the first mass meeting in the Civic Center. Now, if in the highly inconceivable even that the private trustees should, in their wisdom, refuse to turn over this million or so dollars that may remain, the answer is very clear, it will only be necessary to comply with the law, and if you comply with the law, the Board of Trustees—and I presume they will—and this Board of Supervisors complies with the ordinance and the Charter of the City and County of San Francisco, there will be no trouble about that private fund of $1,000,000 or so because without it no progress can be made upon an Opera House, to any marked degree. And if the Board of Trustees and this Board takes the $4,000,000 and complies with the Ordinance in the construction of that building, the private trustees and the people that they represent, who are the proponents, principally, of an Opera House and an Art Museum, will be sitting on the front steps of the City Hall to turn over the private money to you so they can go on with the Opera House.

SUPERVISOR KENT: That has opened up a line of thought here to me. It was stated awhile back, I think by yourself, that at one time there was a different set of plans submitted by the City Engineer. Is that your statement?

MR. GLENSOR: Well, yes, that is qualifiedly true.

SUPERVISOR KENT: There was a different set of plans submitted by the City Engineer's office. When was that?

MR. GLENSOR: At the time the Ordinance was submitted to this Board, or prepared by this Board to be submitted to the people, it was accompanied by a draft of floor plans. I have them right here, a print taken from those plans, that were submitted by the City Engineer, showing two buildings, rectangular in shape, which constituted the War Memorial project. The plans, as drawn and submitted, the first plans that were drawn and submitted to the Legion—to the veterans, rather, for their approval—did not conform to this at all. One of the buildings was not rectangular in shape, and there were some other changes. Tentative plans were thereafter submitted but never have been definitely submitted.

SUPERVISOR KENT: There was a set of plans that was agreeable to veteran organizations?

MR. GLENSOR: Yes.

SUPERVISOR KENT: That is what I mean.

MR. GLENSOR: Yes, there was at one time.

SUPERVISOR KENT: Was that submitted by City Engineer O'Shaughnessy?

MR. GLENSOR: No, submitted by the private trustees.

SUPERVISOR KENT: By the private trustees?

MR. GLENSOR: Yes, sir, and then when construction started we discovered that they were being built according to other plans.

SUPERVISOR KENT: What was the ultimate cost to be of those suggested buildings? I want to find out what was the ultimate cost.

MR. GLENSOR: I have it all here, it may take a moment to find it. That was under the $4,000,000.

SUPERVISOR KENT: My question is that, in this particular set of plans that was submitted, and apparently met the approval of the veteran organizations, I asked, what was the cost figure on those plans?

MR. GLENSOR: The plans that we approved, I am not certain we ever had any cost figure on those, we have never had any definite cost figures—of the Veterans' Building was $1,806,000 and the total cost was $5,310,364, well within the amount of money available.

SUPERVISOR TODD: When was that set of plans approved?

MR. GLENSOR: Approved by the veterans? Just a minute, I will tell you; December, 1928.

SUPERVISOR TODD: What has become of those plans now?

MR. GLENSOR: I do not know what has become of the plans, but when they started work on the building it was plain to be seen that the building was to be built in accordance with other plans.

SUPERVISOR TODD: Who rejected this plan that has been approved by the veterans? Did the present Trustees of the War Memorial reject this plan?

MR. GLENSOR: Apparently so, because they started to build the building in accordance with other plans.

SUPERVISOR TODD: They have not started to do any building any more than excavating.

MR. GLENSOR: It is plain to be seen that is what is going to happen, and they drew up other plans.

SUPERVISOR TODD: I do not think they will get away with that.

SUPERVISOR KENT: At the time that these plans were submitted to you that you approved——

MR. GLENSOR: December, 1928.

SUPERVISOR KENT: Did they carry with it the Opera House feature also?

MR. GLENSOR: Yes.

SUPERVISOR KENT: And it was voluntarily submitted to you?

MR. GLENSOR: Yes. Well, voluntarily—we requested them.

SUPERVISOR KENT: I mean, it was their own architectural design.

MR. GLENSOR: Yes.

SUPERVISOR KENT: You do not think that there is a commitment in the adoption of any particular set of plans up to this time, is there? There is no commitment anywhere?

MR. GLENSOR: Well, so far as we know, the only commitment that has been made has been made to another set of plans, different than the ones we approved.

SUPERVISOR SCHMIDT: If that completes the various speakers that desired to discuss this matter, I move now that the matter be taken in the hands of the Board.

SUPERVISOR KENT: Second that motion.

THE CHAIRMAN: No objection? Such will be the order.

SUPERVISOR RONCOVIERI: Mr. Chairman, I believe that the parliamentary situation is this: When the Mayor presented the names to this Board. I believe that Supervisor Hayden moved that the group be ratified. That was seconded by some member of the Board, I have forgotten.

THE CLERK: Supervisor Shannon.

SUPERVISOR RONCOVIERI: I take it that that is the situation before us now.

SUPERVISOR SHANNON: No, there was another motion after that.

SUPERVISOR RONCOVIERI: What was it?

SUPERVISOR SHANNON: The Clerk will notify you.

THE CLERK: It went over a week.

SUPERVISOR SHANNON: Mr. Chairman, I know that after the motion was made by Mr. Hayden and seconded by myself, then the subject matter was discussed and it was brought out that there were only five veterans on the list, and I was about to withdraw my second when another motion was made, I do not recall just what it was, that I seconded. If the record is found——

THE CLERK (interrupting): I will read the record to you. On August 26th the communication from the Mayor was read, the consideration was continued a week, after some discussion. On September 3rd, one week later, it came up again, went over one week and was made a special order for 2:00 p. m.

SUPERVISOR SHANNON (interrupting): No, I am speaking about the first time that it was presented to the Board, I think, if Mr. Barry will look up the record he will find that there was another motion made after the original motion that was made by Mr. Hayden and seconded by myself.

THE CLERK: Moved to lay over one week. So ordered.

SUPERVISOR SHANNON: So as to bring the matter before the Board, I will allow my second to the motion to remain, with the understanding that it does not commit me to vote for the list.

SUPERVISOR RONCOVIERI: Call the roll.

SUPERVISOR SCHMIDT: Mr. Chairman and members of the Board, I merely desire to state my position upon this matter with reference to ratifying the trustees appointed by the Mayor. I have no differences with the appointments made by the Mayor, but I have a word that I gave by resolution that I would cast my vote in favor of the majority of the trustees being appointed from a veteran group, with no reflection to the Mayor and his appointments, those whom he has selected to serve as trustees. Nevertheless, I feel it my duty to cast a vote in opposition to ratification on account of the stand that I took when this resolution was passed by the Board of Supervisors.

THE CHAIRMAN: I would like to make a statement for the record, if I may be permitted to do so: I regret that I cannot vote to confirm the nominations of the Mayor, but I feel that an affirmative vote on my part at this time would be a stultification of the position which I have publicly taken in this Board on a number of occasions in connection with the War Memorial project. I was the author of the resolution unanimously adopted by this Board nearly two years ago, to the effect that this Board would not approve any appropriations from the bond issue voted for the War Memorial project until such time as the plans and specifications for that project had been approved by the representatives of a majority of the duly constituted war veterans organizations of San Francisco. I was also the author of the resolution requesting his Honor the Mayor to appoint a majority of the new Board of War Memorial trustees from the ranks of the veterans of the wars in which this Republic has been engaged. I regret that his Honor, the Mayor, did not see fit to meet the request of the Board, because I feel that the Charter amendment which provides for the creation of this new Board definitely places that joint responsibility for the appointment and confirmation of these trustees as between the Mayor and the Board, and I think that the request of the Board was entirely a proper one. I have no criticism whatever to make of any of the individuals who have been nominated by the Mayor for these trusteeships. I desire to say, publicly, that in my opinion every man, as a citizen, is worthy, in every respect, to fulfill the obligations of this trusteeship and to function as the citizens of San Francisco would have him function. But the question has become controversial, very bitterly controversial, in the community, and I personally agree with the viewpoint expressed by the representatives of the organized veterans who have appeared here. I know—and there can be no contradiction of the record—that in the appeal to the voters to ratify the bond issue proposed for the War Memorial project, the paramount argument was that this money would be used, first, to construct a building as a home for the San Francisco veterans of the Wars. There was little mention during that campaign of the proposal to build an Opera House. It was generally understood that an Opera House would probably be part of the

War Memorial project, but the voters were told that the money was to be used, primarily, for the other purpose first and that the residue of the money should be used then for such other purposes as the trustees might recommend. I desire at this time to express my conviction that the responsibility for the long delay in the carrying forward of this War Memorial project rests, squarely and exclusively, upon the shoulders of the men who have been acting as the private board of trustees for the War Memorial project. I have stated previously that, in my opinion, the responsibility rested mainly upon one or two individuals in that Board who had the fixed opinion that an Opera House of a certain size must be constructed, and that every other feature of that project must be subordinated to their opinion. If this matter had been in the hands of this Board of Supervisors, or of any other public body, public condemnation would have rested upon us, and justly, in severest fashion, but the responsibility here cannot be placed upon public officials. It rests in one place, and one place only, and that is where I have placed it in my statement to you. I think that this situation could be adjusted very simply, meeting the opinions of the War Veterans by just one or two changes. I would not presume to suggest what those changes should be, but it is obvious to all of us that, however fine the selections made by his Honor may be, there are in the citizenship of San Francisco other selections that could be made to give the War Veterans their proper representation, which would be equally satisfactory. And the change that need be made would be only very small. I feel it my duty, in view of my previously expressed public attitude on this question, to vote against confirmation.

I desire to make one additional statement: We have already been forewarned that the criticism will probably be made that the responsibility for a further delay rests upon this Board of Supervisors, if it does not today confirm the nominations made by his Honor the Mayor. I desire to point out to you that no such criticism at this time can logically be made because it will be a financial impossibility to sell any of those bonds on the present market until such time as the people of San Francisco have seen fit—I will modify that to this extent: Until such time as the conditions in the bond market shall improve, if they do, or until such time as the citizens of San Francisco shall see fit to authorize a change in the interest rate on our bonds.

SUPERVISOR STANTON: Mr. Chairman, I too feel that I should explain my vote, having been one of those who voted for a resolution, asking that a majority of the Committee be War Veterans. I do not know how I, or any member who at the time the resolution was introduced voted for it, could vote differently. I think the members of the Board have been exceedingly fair. We ask the Mayor and had a sitting with him, and I think explained our position very thoroughly, so that the matter could not be put up to us at this particular time as being the obstacle. We tried to nave people—not my choice or the choice of the Board of Supervisors, I do not think any member of the Board had any individual in sight—we were seeking to have a Committee appointed who would be satisfactory to the War Veterans, for, after all, we are building a War Memorial, dedicated to those who took part in the War and to those who lost their lives, and it seems to me no more than fair that we should go along with them and try to satisfy any reasonable request that they might make, and it seems to me that their requests have been reasonable. Therefore, I must vote against the motion.

SUPERVISOR ANDRIANO: Mr. Chairman, I would like to have a week's time to consider the arguments made by the veterans' organizations. It is the first time that I have heard these arguments. Some of them I was familiar with, others are entirely new, and I wish to examine this communication and wish to weigh the arguments that have been presented here orally. I feel that I am not in a position at the present time to pass intelligently upon their arguments. And for those reasons I make a motion, Mr. Chairman, that the matter of the confirmation of the Mayor's list of trustees be postponed for one week.

THE CHAIRMAN: Is there a second to that motion? The motion fails for lack of a second?

SUPERVISOR RONCOVIERI: Now, Mr. Chairman, I desire to make a brief statement of my vote. I hold the resolution that was passed December 3rd, 1928, in which the Board of Supervisors respectfully urge and recommend that his Honor the Mayor appoint a majority of the members of the Board of War Memorial Trustees from that portion of the citizenry of San Francisco who have been in service in the Army, Navy or Marine Corps in time of War. This resolution was adopted by eleven votes, six against and one absent. I am one of those who voted in favor. I assure you my fingers were not crossed when I said "Yes", I meant it. And I think it would have been a very easy matter for the Mayor to have selected, from that portion of our citizenry that has served our country, a group of men, at least a majority, but inasmuch as the Mayor has not seen fit to do it, I am going to vote, with the understanding that this will be sent back to him and that he will understand that he must appoint a majority at least, and that as long as I am on this Board I shall vote against any recommendations he may make, if they do not contain a majority of our citizenry who have served the country.

SUPERVISOR KENT: Mr. Chairman, on a point of information: What is to prevent the construction and equipment of a $4,000,000 project only on that site? Is the private money that has been subscribed, in the possession of those Trustees with any strings on it that could not be rectified at this time? I wonder if the subscribers to the private fund would be willing to donate to the City and County these two blocks of land which are held by private ownership today, pending the settlement of this controversy. If that was turned over to the city as a gift, as is, and whatever funds are to their credit, to the credit of the account, prorated and sent back to the subscribers, I think that that would be a good solution, and we could proceed, after the gift of the land, with the expenditure of this $4,000,000 in a War Memorial building that would take care of all the subsidiary considerations. It seems to me that when you analyze the declarations that were made at the time that the bond issue was put forth, there was no reference to any private fund. It was wholly and solely standing on its own two legs, a War Memorial. And for the project to be a secondary consideration, as far as the War Memorial Hall is concerned, in my opinion, would never survive. As a veteran I have the one feeling that, as the generations come and go, that monument must be paramount, that it was erected to the War Veterans of all of the Wars in the defense of their country. And I am sure that, if this Board would think wisely of that suggestion that perhaps we may pour oil over the troubled waters of today and ask that it be reconsidered from that standpoint: Would the private interests of today be willing to give to the city the present of the two block site that they have there for us to improve with public money that is available by a particular vote of last November?

SUPERVISOR McSHEEHY: Mr Chairman and members of the Board and Veterans of all foreign wars and citizens: I occupy perhaps a rather unique position on this Board today as a member of the present Board of Trustees. I am not alone, there are three members, members of the Board of Supervisors, members of that Board. In the latter part of 1926, October, I think it was, September or October, I was elected a member of the present Board of War Memorial Trustees, as Chairman of the Finance Committee at that time. I attended religiously every meeting of that Board. In May, 1927, it was suggested that a bond issue must take place to provide sufficient funds to erect the two buildings, and in June, 1927, I introduced that bond issue in this Board. I was the author of it. It was passed unanimously by all members present and the people of San Francisco, by a two-thirds vote, acquiesced in it. Now, may I say this to the veterans that are present: There was a disposition, on the part of the veterans, to vote against that bond issue, for the reasons that the plans—that they had not access to the plans, and they really did not know what it was all about. I waited on several organizations, and the outcome of it was that a committee was appointed and personally I took that committee to the architect's office on Bush street, and we went over the plans, and the outcome of that meeting was that the opposition was withdrawn and the veterans endorsed the plans and voted for them. And if they had not, I doubt if the bond issue would have carried. Now, the bond issue did carry and the private trustees, as we are called now, went ahead, and we submitted plans to the veterans. There was a difference of opinion, not once but several times. Now, the submission of the plans to the veterans, or anything in that line was entirely made by two members of the Board of Trustees who represented the veterans and who are veterans of foreign wars, one of their names was mentioned here today. And they reported back to the Trustees that everything was O. K. and that the plans were accepted. Now, here today your principal speaker made the statement that at that time—and I believe the statement is borne out by certain records here—that at that time—these are round figures, I just took them off roughly—that at that time the Veterans' Building would cost $1,850,000, round figures, and that there was approximately in the fund, in dollars and cents, $5,300,000, which woulld make the Opera House cost approximately $3,450,000. Now, the Trustees, at no time, ever contemplated spending over that amount of money for the Opera House, and about that amount of money for the Veterans' Building or the Memorial Building. Plans were drawn. I happen to be in the building business, I have been in it all my life, I am not an architect, but I do some drawing, and I know a plan from A to Z. I went over those plans, not once but a number of times, and those plans have cost approximately $150,000. The supervising architect is no less a person than Mr Brown, the man who supervised this very building, and I am not going to tell you about the dome. Now, those plans, in my opinion, are an architectural gem. They are perfect—as perfect as plans can be made. Specifications have been carried out, the estimates have been made, the last word in construction has been carried out. I do know—and I am not going into minute details—but I do know that the details are carried out to the very last word. Now, in asking for estimates we found that certain construction would run as high as $7,000,000, certain construction would run as high as $6,000,000 and certain construction was brought down to about $5,600,000. But I want to say that an agreement never could be reached. Now, a statement was made here by Supervisor Kent, only a minute ago, and that was if the present trustees could tender to the Supervisors, or to the public authorities of this city, the monies that are now in their custody. Why, that has been the object of the present trustees right along, and you passed a resolution in the form of an amendment last election which allows us to place that money in your hands, and we have had to change part of our charter to carry out that particular trust. But the trustees are in this position: They are responsible for that money. And they can, if they wish to take that position, and I do not think that they are going to take it, and I know I, as one member will not take it, speaking for myself, if they wish to take that position they can take the position that they are custodians of that money, and they have a right to know just where that money is being spent. Now, today you have approximately $1,-100,000. The plans have been paid for, the excavation has been paid for. Something has been said that they are building on a different set of plans. The land is paid for. Now, in reference to building on a different set of plans, there has been no attempt to build in any shape, manner or form. An excavation has been made. No harm at all has come out of making that excavation. The money has been spent on it. Now, the question up to this Board is simply this, and it is up to the citizens of San Francisco, and it is up to all of us, is to get together and erect two buildings, and erect them for approximately $5,000,000. That is a huge sum of money, and those two buildings can be erected for that sum of money. I am very sorry that his Honor the Mayor did not see fit to at least acquiesce in some of the—I won't say the demands, but the requests made by the veterans. If he had, I think the work would be on its way today. Personally, I would have liked to have served as one of the trustees, and this Board of Supervisors met in the Mayor's office, and a motion was made there and unanimously carried by the whole Board that the Mayor should not appoint any member of this Board, for the reason that that member would have to act in a dual position. And I made the statement, previous to the passing, or, at least right after that motion was made, that I would have liked to have served, but in the face of a suggestion of that kind and in the face of a motion of that kind, I gladly would acquiesce in the majority will of this Board. And that motion was carried, and I feel today—I do not feel hurt in any manner or form that I am personally not named on that Board. I consider that project greater than any man or any set of men. I consider that we need a War Memorial Building, I consider we need an Opera House. And I happen to be Chairman of the Auditorium Committee and I realize what the people of San Francisco want, for I have seen them in thousands attending the various concerts over there in the Auditorium. So I say to you here today that I hope we will be able to adjust our differences, and that the Mayor will acquiesce in your demands for the sake of harmony, for the sake of all of us, and that when the committee is appointed, that you will take those plans and by a small modification you can use them, you can save over $100,000 and you can erect two buildings on that site that will be a monument to the City of San Francisco. Now, I hope we will do something here today, something that is constructive. I cannot, in the face of the position that I now occupy as a trustee, I cannot in the face of the mandate made by the Mayor, do anything else but acquiesce in the appointment of the committee that he has named. I personally hope, in a way, that perhaps his demand will not be met by this Board, but I cannot do anything else but vote for the list, as recommended by the Mayor. I hope and trust that a way will be found out so that we can go along with this work, and that some sort of a compromise must be made. We must make a compromise, we must give and take in this matter and get this work on its way. I happen to be engaged in the building business and I know of thousands of men that are walking our streets, and they need work and we need the buildings.

SUPERVISOR RONCOVIERI: Mr Chairman, I desire, in order to set straight a few remarks made by Supervisor McSheehy, to read you what the two architects to whom he has referred, Arthur Brown, Jr. and G. L. Lansburgh, had to say regarding the plans. "To Mr. Herbert Fleishhacker, a member of the Board of Trustees: Dear Sir: In answer to your inquiry the careful estimates made recently at the War Memorial drafting rooms, and verified by Mr Dinwiddie—Mr Dinwiddie is one of our largest builders and contractors—indicate that the War Memorial buildings, as at present delineated and specified, would cost, in round figures, with terra cotta exterior, $7,500,000, with granite exterior, $8,200,000. With certain modifications in specifications as shown on the estimate sheet, but keeping the same approved scheme, another estimate was made showing the possible modifications in the total as follows: Terra cotta exterior, $6,600,000, granite exterior, $7,250,000. In case these figures are too high, in view of the available funds, the alternative would seem to be to redraw the plans with a modified program as to requirements both of the veterans and the opera, and with the accomodations strictly limited to the funds allotted." Now, those last two or three words "strictly limited to the funds allotted"—why, in the first place——

SUPERVISOR MARKS: What is the lowest figure?

SUPERVISOR RONCOVIERI: The lowest figure is, a terra cotta exterior, $6,600,000, or $1,600,000 more than they have got. And with terra cotta. And, surely, we expected granite the same as this building. The buildings should be in harmony at least to this one. But what I want to say is this: They knew that they had $5,100,000, there was not another dollar to be had, they knew that, but they made plans running up to $8,200,000. And would you call such trustees competent? Why, if I had $10,000 to build a little house, and I said I wanted six flats with the $10,000, the architect would say to me, "you cannot get it with that amount of money," and he would not even draw the plans, but if he did attempt it, he would drawn lead pencil sketches, he would not make complete working designs, as has been done in this case, that run up to $150,000 and I have been told, $200,000. And the other day, in the presence of Supervisor Suhr, one of these architects said to me that the changes will require another $100,000. You talk of incompetency! $300,000 wasted of the people's money for one set of plans! These are your so-called "big men." And I stated to the Mayor the other day, in the presence of many of you, that, had I my way, I would not have appointed one of those men upon this Board of Trustees, as they have proven themselves incompetent to the 'nth degree. They could not draw plans or run a little business for me of any kind. Now, gentlemen, that is what we are up against, and there is no use temporizing with this matter. The Mayor must appoint at least a majority—as long as they are satisfied with it, I am—but if I had my way, there are enough fine upstanding citizens in San Francisco who have served their country in time of need from whom, from that large group, the Mayor could select 11 gentlemen to run this thing properly. It is for them during their lifetime. Their lives are limited. The youngest is probably 30 years of age at present and the older men will not last many, many years. Why not give them the satisfaction of controlling this as they want to? And they have been extremely generous today. I was surprised to see such generosity. "We are willing to prorate a large part of this $5,000,000 that is left to the Opera House, so long as we have a decent place to point to as our War Memorial for us who are living and for those who have made the supreme sacrifice." I think that there is nothing before us, I cannot imagine any one voting in favor of the recommendations of the Mayor, He has made a mistake, an honest one if you wish, I am willing to call it that. He has had this resolution before him, and he knew how we stood, at least 11 of us stood, since last December. No rush. Still now we are told that if there is any further delay, it will be up to the Board of Supervisors. Well, I refuse—I resent that—I refuse to accept any such responsibility.

SUPERVISOR KENT: Mr. Chairman, if I may substantiate my thought with the figures that Mr. Roncovieri has read into the record. If everything was harmonious, on the face of it apparently we would court the creating of a deficit, there would be an unfinished product. As one member of the board, I have always been consistent in not running into any financial deficits in the last four years, and I think that is quite substantiated by the attitude of the entire membership of this board. So it would appear to me that the $1,100,000 that is still in the hands of private trustees can be returned back to the subscribers, the land as is can be given to the city, and we can proceed to build a War Memorial Hall, as it was designated in the bond issue, to cost $4,000,000, and certainly that will be a monument.

SUPERVISOR GALLAGHER (interrupting): I move that we recess until 8:00 o'clock tonight; do I get a second?

SUPERVISOR RONCOVIERI: I was going to ask if you

would be kind enough to read on page 55 the remarks that
I read.

THE MAYOR (reading):

"SUPERVISOR RONCOVIERI: The lowest figure is, a
terra cotta exterior, $6,600,000, or $1,600,000 more than they
have got"—I read all this.

SUPERVISOR RONCOVIERI: Yes, your Honor.

THE MAYOR (continuing reading):

SUPERVISOR SHANNON: Mr. Chairman, the question that we are
discussing today is the matter of the trustees, and I feel that we
should satisfy at least one group, and that is a very large group, and
that is the veterans. In the call for the bonds this was designated
as a Memorial Hall for War Veterans. And I think the thought expressed by Mr. Sapiro this morning is one that might be given very
serious consideration by the Mayor when this list of names is returned
to him, which I sincerely hope it will be, and that is, that he appoint
11 war veterans. They are competent, they are capable, they were
sufficiently competent and capable to go overseas and represent us, and
they did a good job, and they would do just as good a job in the
handling of the structure across the street as any group of 11 citizens
that could be named by any man in San Francisco. And I hope that
this list will be sent back to the Mayor because it was written into the
law and requested of the Mayor that he appoint war veterans, and
we requested a majority of war veterans. And I think that the Mayor
might have acceded to our request, and I daresay, if given another
opportunity, he will. There was another thing that was requested of
the Mayor by this Board of Supervisors, and that was that he appoint
no member of this Board of Supervisors on that Board of Trustees.
Now, Mr. Chairman, no chain is stronger than its weakest link. And
I think it would be a very fine thing if Mr. Colman stood up here
today and said he will request the Mayor to withdraw his name from
that list. We cannot allow any one's own personal desires, ambitions or
vanity, however worthy it may be—and this is not said disparagingly
—to interfere in a project that is very far greater than anybody's personal status in the matter. And that is the situation that Supervisor
Colman is facing today. I call on him to request that his name be withdrawn from that list, and I call upon the members of the board to
return the list to the Mayor without our ratification.

SUPERVISOR COLMAN: Mr. Chairman: I want to say, in the first
place, that if I were to present my resignation at this time, I would
not have to do it in writing, but were I to do it verbally, it would be
binding upon me. But I will say this, as a matter of just a brief history:
It is quite true what Supervisor McSheehy said. I also stated the other
day, in the presence of my colleagues, in the Mayor's chambers, that
"I was disappointed, but I felt competent, and in view of that situation
and the opinion of my colleagues, I will withdraw." I will state,
further, that had Captain George Filmer of the Spanish War Veterans
seen fit, in his judgment, to accept the offer of the Mayor, my name
would not have been considered in any way. The Mayor, however, did,
entirely voluntarily, come to me and tell me he would be glad to have
me serve as a trustee of the War Memorial. I reserved my answer to
him until I would take the matter up with some of my colleagues, those
who had expressed themselves perhaps the most at the meeting in the
Mayor's office. This I did and those of my colleagues assured me that
they had no objection, and rather gave me the opinion that it would
be proper, and felt that I was competent to serve. I then took the
matter up with the City Attorney, who also looked into the thing very
thoroughly, and assured me that my appointment was perfectly legal,
that I could sit legally, that it was not incompatible, in any way, with
my duty as a Supervisor, that in his opinion there was no ground for

ineligibility, and I was quite eligible to serve on the Board of Trustees.

I note here in the report, that the veterans object to a Supervisor, the statement being made, the objection of the veterans in this regard is not personal or political but practical. I want to thank the veterans for the statement that the objection to myself is not personal. That it is not political is of no moment to me, but I deeply appreciate the statement that it is not personal. Mr. Chairman. I think the members of the Board know me, at least I have been here—I am in my eighth year. My colleagues have served with me for from two, four, six to eight years, and I think know me probably as well as anybody knows me, if not better. Whatever action they may take in the matter is entirely up to them. I will not resign nor withdraw my name, as I deeply appreciate the honor paid me by the Mayor, and I feel thoroughly competent and capable of giving a square deal to the veterans in this matter, and of giving a square deal to the people of San Francisco. If I might express my views on the matter as it is now, it is this: A great deal has happened, a great many events have transpired. I do not dispute the facts, as stated by the various members of the Board, but I do simply make this statement: That they have taken place. It is water under the bridge. We can go back and bring up those matters that have occurred, and we can place the blame here and criticize there. To me this is not a constructive way of handling this problem. Whatever has taken place is no fault of any member of this Board. It has, however, taken place and we have reached the present day in the situation, and we consider the matter from the situation as it does exist today, and it seems to me that bringing up the past and fastening blame and criticism and all is certainly not going to build the War Memorial. It is not my purpose to take the floor today to speak well of the members that the Mayor has seen fit to appoint. I feel, too, that I would be a little disloyal to a distinguished citizen, whom I admire very much, and whom I am a personal friend of, if I did not say a word in his behalf, also because he has been mentioned in this report. And I want to say a word about Major Charles H. Kendrick, a distinguished San Franciscan and a friend of mine. Major Kendrick enlisted in the Army, he was, like myself, beyond the draft age. He volunteered his services, he was commissioned, he served his country across the water, came back and was quite active in the Legion for a period of years. Major Kendrick is past commander of his post, California Post Number 234, the post to which both General Liggett, Major Kent and myself, the three of us have the honor to belong. Major Kendrick was National Committeeman from this district, Major Kendrick was National Vice-Commander of the American Legion. I believe, though I am not quite sure about it, I believe that he has achieved the highest rank in the Legion of any San Franciscan. We have had a National Commander from California, Comrade John R. Quinn, living in Delano. As far as I know, Major Kendrick has reached, as I say, the highest rank here. Major Kendrick has taken a prominent part in the life of San Francisco. One year he was the director general of the Community Chest drive. Another year he directed the drive of the Salvation Army. Major Kendrick today is the president of the Schlage Lock Company, a San Francisco concern, with its factory on the Bay Shore Boulevard, employing some two to three hundred working men, with a payroll of approximately $50,000 monthly, making a splendid product that is being marketed all over the country. I want to call to your attention, too, the fact that Major Kendrick was the director of the bond drive, I believe the unsuccessful Spring Valley drive prior to the last one, and also was the Chairman of the drive against Amendment 24, an amendment which this Board was very desirous of having beaten, and it was not an easy problem at that time to secure a Chairman for the Citizens' Committee, a man of influence and ability, who would satisfactorily handle that particular fight. Major Kendrick fearlessly assumed this burden, worked very, very hard, giving a great deal of his time and no doubt some, I do not know how much, but some of his money toward this work, with the result that, to some degree—some great degree—that his campaign was successful, and that amendment was defeated. Therefore, I cannot help but feel that this Board of Supervisors is under a peculiar obligation to this citizen. I might mention, for many years he served on the City Planning Commission, a thankless job, a difficult job, served without remuneration. Apparently Major Kendrick is desirous of serving on this Board because he has resigned his position from the City Planning Commission in order to accept the nomination of the Mayor. So I hope, regardless of what action is taken, I hope the Board will remember the services by Mr. Kendrick, and that I feel he is entitled to some consideration from us, and I further feel that he, like myself, if chosen by this Board to serve on the Board of Trustees, will give the veterans a very square deal, and treat them the way they would be treated. I do not know, nor am I interested, in the criticism. I never made the statement that this Board would be criticized for a lack of action in the matter. And I do not mean to imply that for one instant. I simply mean that, looking at the project in a big, constructive way, that we are in no way helping the building of the War Memorial by indulging today in criticisms, and bringing up unpleasant past events, or at the same time I might say, we should hear at least from the other side because there are always two sides to every question. And every man, before being condemned, is entitled to a hearing, particularly by this Board, and I do not think it is just right, in a sense, that these gentlemen, whom I admire and I think are big men still, even though my colleague may sincerely believe they are not, I believe they are big men, and I believe, before they are condemned, they are entitled to a hearing and should be possibly here today before the Board would accept judgment from one side of the case. I feel this way, however: That today, if the Board thinks that it is proper, I am going to ask to be excused from voting as one of the names is mine. I have just one more thought: The project today has the $5,000,000 spoken of. I believe, without the question of a doubt, that this $5,000,000, can be spent, and in its spending will meet the just demands of every interested party in the building of the War Memorial.

SUPERVISOR SHANNON: I move that the request of Mr Colman that he be excused from voting be granted.

SUPERVISOR MARKS: (Second the motion.

THE CHAIRMAN: (Bringing down the gavel).

SUPERVISOR ANDRIANO: My colleagues on the Board, having refused me the privilege of considering this matter for a period of one week, I am obliged to express the thoughts that occur to me on the spur of the moment, without that consideration and deliberation which I would have liked to have given to the arguments presented by the veterans here today. As the situation presents itself to me, Mr. Chairman, it is greatly to be regretted that this discussion, this wrangling and squabbling, should take place here today. I deplore deeply that the trustees heretofore appointed, I mean the old trustees, did not see fit to deal more magnanimously with the veterans. I believe that they should have gone to all limits, not to please the veterans, but to express the gratitude and the appreciation of every citizen to the veterans, and that it should have been made impossible for the veterans to express a complaint. On the other hand, Mr. Chairman, I deplore just as deeply the fact that the veterans have to come here and exact something of this Board. It is truly a sorry spectacle that this wonderful thing, the War Memorial, the symbol of the glory, the nobility and the sacrifice of our citizens during the war, should be made a sort of a football to be kicked about. I would have a great deal more regard for the veterans, and I am satisfied that I am speaking the deep sentiments of the public of San Francisco, had they, in view of the fact that the trustees did not see fit to be more magnanimous, more generous and more liberal towards them, if they had simply said, "We will take what you give us. The sacrifice that we have made cannot be valued." You cannot put a price, Mr. Chairman, upon patriotism, upon heroism, upon sacrifice. And it seems to me, with all due deference to my good friends of the veteran organizations, that they are robbing their deeds of some of their luster. And then, too, I am satisfied that they will not have any cause to complain in the future, if this list of the Mayor is confirmed by this Board. They did declare here, in the presence of all of us, that the nine names submitted to them by the Mayor were satisfactory to them. Now, that only leaves two, Mr. Colman's name and Mr. Kendrick's name.

SUPERVISOR GALLAGHER (interrupting): I pause to move that Mr. Dunnigan be sent for immediately.

THE MAYOR: Mr. Dunnigan, the Clerk, will be sent for.

SUPERVISOR MILES: May I suggest that we have a five or ten minute recess at this time?

SUPERVISOR GALLAGHER: Is that all?

SUPERVISOR McSHEEHY: It is five minutes to seven——

SUPERVISOR SPAULDING (interrupting): I second the motion.

THE MAYOR: I don't think it is fair to the boys who have been waiting here all evening to take a recess without giving them the financial statement of this whole matter which they have been waiting for. I am pretty near down to it, I am going to read you certain letters and I was going to submit eleven nominees to you tonight; I am going to finish the job tonight, if you will stay with it.

SUPERVISOR MILES: I will withdraw the motion, Mr. Mayor.

SUPERVISOR McSHEEHY: May I ask your Honor, have you some more transcripts to read? It is about 7:00 o'clock——

THE MAYOR (interrupting): I wasn't noticing the time.

SUPERVISOR McSHEEHY: I say that in all kindness——

SUPERVISOR PEYSER (interrupting): I move we proceed.

THE MAYOR: If you will accept as a part of my report the balance of this transcript which I am now reading, and the transcript of the remarks of the Mayor dated October 7, 1929, and the transcript of the meeting of Monday, October 14, 1929, when I returned, and if you will accept the meeting of the Board of Supervisors of January 20, 1930, in regard to the appointment of the War Memorial Trustees, it will save my reading these records at this time.

SUPERVISOR McSHEEHY: I move that be accepted, and that they be considered read.

SUPERVISOR GALLAGHER: What were those last two?

THE MAYOR: My report dated October 14, 1929, after I got home from the East.

SUPERVISOR GALLAGHER: And what was the other one?

THE MAYOR: The report of the meeting of January 20, 1930.

SUPERVISOR McSHEEHY: I move it be accepted and considered read.

SUPERVISOR RONCOVIERI: Second the motion.

THE MAYOR: No objection, so ordered. (Bringing down the gavel.)

SUPERVISOR PEYSER: I propose, after your Honor has submitted the names and called for a vote, I propose to ask— if I move for a call of the Board, I would ask whether your Honor would be willing to proceed pending the arrival of the other members. As I understand, your Honor has the privilege of discontinuing until they are present, but I move now to ask for a call of the Board and that your Honor continue pending their arrival.

THE MAYOR: When this report is in your hands fully read by me, it will be then up to you to decide what you want to do with it.

SUPERVISOR PEYSER: I realize that, your Honor, but I desired to ask at this time whether if I now moved for a call of the Board your Honor would continue reading pending their arrival.

THE MAYOR: I haven't any objection to what you do.

SUPERVISOR PEYSER: I move for a call of the Board.

SUPERVISOR HAVENNER: If that call is with the idea that we vote without first studying the report, I am going to object to it. If we are going to sit here and have a call of the Board, for what is this call of the Board? I for one don't intend to vote without consideration.

SUPERVISOR PEYSER: The situation is this, to enlighten the Supervisor——

SUPERVISOR HAVENNER (interrupting): I will make the point of order now, that there isn't a quorum here.

SUPERVISOR McSHEEHY: You just stated a minute ago, your Honor, and members of the Board, a few minutes ago you stated that if we had no objection to not reading the transcripts of the two days, one in October and one in January, and the members as a whole, if that is carried through, then it would be right up to you to read the financial report and report of the nominees, and that will finish it, more or less. Now, members of the Board, just a minute. I don't know whether you heard that or not; his Honor, he asked us to kindly consider those two transcripts as read to save time.

THE MAYOR: No, you asked me if I was going to read any more transcripts.

SUPERVISOR McSHEEHY: Yes, sir, your Honor.

THE MAYOR: I told you I had two more of these dates, one after my return and the other coming up in January, a month ago, and then my report is in complete form as it will be.

SUPERVISOR McSHEEHY: Then will that be followed by the financial report?

THE MAYOR: It will be pretty close up to the financial report.

SUPERVISOR McSHEEHY: Members of the Board, you have heard the remarks just made, that that will be followed by the financial report and then by the report of the nominees, nominations of trustees, and I would say to keep right at it.

SUPERVISOR GALLAGHER: I demand a vote on the motion for a call of the Board.

SUPERVISOR HAVENNER: I am opposed to that; I think it might simply complicate things without accomplishing anything.

SUPERVISOR GALLAGHER: I would just as soon see the gentlemen come and see the sunrise.

SUPERVISOR McSHEEHY: I move we proceed.

SUPERVISOR MILES: There is a motion up before the Board, I believe, that certain transcripts be included in his report, one on his return from Washington here; you have suggested that they be inserted in the record.

SUPERVISOR McSHEEHY: I make that as a motion that they be inserted in the record, the meeting on October 14, 1929, and the meeting of January 20, 1930.

THE MAYOR: If there is no objection, such is the order, that will save a lot of time.

THE MAYOR (reading):

Mr. Colman has stated that he consulted the City Attorney and that the City Attorney told him that there is no incompatibility between his office as Supervisor and his office as Trustee of the War Memorial. The veterans themselves have stated that they have no objection to Mr. Colman. We, knowing Mr. Colman as we do, all concede that it would be difficult to find a more capable, a more efficient, a more high minded and more public spirited citizen than Mr. Colman to act as a trustee on the War Memorial. So that brings the number up to ten. What then is the bone of contention? Mr. Kendrick. They also concede that Mr. Kendrick is not objectionable to them as far as his ability is concerned, that they have nothing against Mr. Kendrick, but, forsooth, he is persona non grata to the veterans because of certain difficulties, certain disagreements that they had in the ranks of their own organization. They may be justified. We do not dispute the fact. But I say, recognizing the fact that Mr. Kendrick is also a high minded public spirited and capable citizen, what objection can there be, as far as this Board is concerned, to Mr. Kendrick? It seems to me, in all sincerity, Mr. Chairman that, after all, the members of the veteran organizations are fighting for an empty victory, for an academic triumph. They say that they are satisfied with the nine men submitted to them by the Mayor. They say that they have no objection to Mr. Colman, and yet they say that they feel that their hopes will not be realized if this list is confirmed. I submit that the conclusion does not follow from the premise. Last November the people of this city expressed themselves with regard to the new Board of Trustees. The Charter Amendment did not state that a majority of the trustees had to be members of war veteran organizations, or that they had even to be war veterans. It merely stated, as set forth in the letter addressed to the Board by the veteran organizations, that due representation or due consideration ought to be given to the veterans of all wars. They have not contended, so far, that due representation was not given to the members of all wars, but they do contend that a majority of the veterans were not appointed. Now, that question of the majority is merely a matter that this Board has gone on record about. But the people of San Francisco as yet have not gone on record on that question. And this Board cannot, in a matter of that sort, supersede the expressed will of the people. The people just simply declared that all of the veteran organizations should be given representation. That was done. The veterans themselves do not deny that the charter amendment of last November was complied with, and it must not be forgotten that the veteran organizations last November fought, and fought very bitterly, the adoption of this charter amendment, and yet the people, in their wisdom, saw fit to override the express wishes of the veteran organizations. But let us come down to the practical question that confronts us. I will say that it is not that I do not love the members of the veteran organizations—I do. But I do feel that, as a member of the Board of Supervisors, the primary question, the one that demands my conscientious consideration, is the welfare of the people of San Francisco as a whole, is the erection of that War Memorial as soon as practicable. And now let me ask the members of the veteran organizations, in all sincerity, have they any justification for feeling that this list of names, as presented to us by the Mayor, or these individuals, rather, will not give to them all that their hearts desire? After all, let us take the list. We have representatives of labor, we have representatives of the press, we have, in fact, two of the owners of the leading or two of the leading newspapers in San Francisco. Now, those men must surely have their hands upon the pulse of the public, and if they realize that the public does want the veterans to be given more space to have every desire gratified, they will see that it is done. I do not see, at the present time, any justification for my refusing confirmation of that list of names, viewing the question upon its merits. I am satisfied that the veterans will be satisfied because of the high class, high type of men in that Mayor's list. And so what will we gain if we do accede to their request now?

In my estimation, nothing except the loss of time. In my estimation we will put off the erection of that War Memorial for another six months or probably a year. I really believe that the past Board of Trustees, having failed to be as liberal as they might have been towards the veterans, in view of the high class of men on this present Board, or proposed Board, against whom the war veterans themselves have no objections, except in the case of one individual, Mr. Kendrick, and those objections, they have stated, are personal, what is the best thing to be done? I say, let us confirm this proposed Board of Trustees, and let them go ahead, and I feel confident, as every man and woman in this room must feel confident, that the matter will be straightened out to the satisfaction of the veterans because, after all what difference does it make whether they have a majority of so-called "Veterans" who might not even be in sympathy with the aims of the veterans? If they have a number of high minded, irreproachable men on that Board, that is all that they can ask, and I feel confident that they will get everything that they expect, everything that they wish for. But I see no justification, at the present time, in refusing to confirm the proposed Board of Trustees submitted to us by the Mayor, and in doing so, I want the veterans to understand that I have absolutely nothing against them. The only thing that I deplore is the fact that they have to come here before us and ask us to do something for them. We should have done it without their asking.

SUPERVISOR RONCOVIERI: I understood Supervisor Andriano to make the point that the veterans and the Mayor should have gotten together, something of that kind. I would like to read a word or two, I will make it very brief, from the statement of the gentleman made this morning. (Reading from the report of veteran organizations.) Now, his Honor failed in that promise to these gentlemen in not calling them before him and submitting that list. They would, in his private office, have told him what they thought of it. Just as the Mayor failed in calling the members of this Board a second time before coming here publicly and giving out the names. If you were there the first time, you recall that the Mayor said that he would call us a second time. He did not do so, but, out of a clear sky, came here and announced the names which you now have before you. All this could have been avoided, but it was not. His Honor saw fit to work it his own way.

SUPERVISOR McSHEEHY: I want to state one or two small facts, that are these: Number one. Supervisor Roncovieri stated and criticized the present Board of Trustees for having plans drawn that ran $7,000,000——

SUPERVISOR GALLAGHER (interrupting): I rise to a point of order, and I admit that the Chair, in ruling on this point of order, has permitted members to wander. I submit to the Chair, in view of the fact that the simple issue here, is confirmation or non-confirmation, that structural figures, costs, and so on have no point and should be now dispensed with.

THE CHAIRMAN: I think that the point of order is well taken. The Chair has exercised a great deal of latitude in this discussion, but I think the Supervisor's point of order is sound and it will be sustained.

SUPERVISOR McSHEEHY: I will state, Mr. Chairman, I am sorry the point has been raised, for the reason I simply wanted to make a statement as a trustee. I do not want to rise to a question of personal privilege.

SUPERVISOR GALLAGHER: I will withdraw the objection if that is the case.

SUPERVISOR McSHEEHY: Well. I do. I feel that way. Mr. Chairman. The present trustees have been criticized. There are three members of the Board of Trustees on this Board. I am the oldest member of that Board by almost two years. Supervisor Havenner is a member of the Board of Trustees and has never exercised that function in any manner or form and Supervisor Colman has been a member of the Board of Trustees only a short time. I simply say this: That a motion—I feel especially that the veterans and the citizens present should have this information, I will be very short and brief—a motion was made at the Board of Trustees that the buildings should not cost over $5,000,000. Mr. Crocker of the First National Bank made that motion, and I seconded it, at the meeting of the trustees with about nine members present. Now, that was made two years ago or thereabouts. And I want to say, secondly, that this Board is on record of not letting one contract until the plans are accepted. Not one contract can be let until the plans are accepted. Therefore, the trustees that have been nominated by the Mayor, those plans that those men will accept will have to be confirmed by this Board. Thirdly, I want to state that a statement has been made that the bonds cannot be sold. There is $1,100,000 in actual cash in the bank today that can be used as preliminary money to start that work on its way. There is a nucleus worth trying for, and that means something to the citizens of San Francisco. Now, we are in a nice position to start this work, and I feel that we should, if possible, agree to come together in some manner or form. Remember, we have the passing of the plans, and if those plans are not acceptable to the veterans they will not be passed by this Board. I am positive of that. So therefore, I cannot see, for the life of me, why we cannot pass the list of names as submitted to us by the Mayor.

SUPERVISOR STANTON: Will you answer a question? If we do not keep our word in the first place, can the veterans expect us to keep it in the second? First of all, we requested that they have six members on the board, secondly, we said that the plans would have to be O.K.'d before we passed them. If we do not keep our word in the first place they have no right to feel that we will keep it in the second.

SUPERVISOR McSHEEHY: May I say this, Supervisor: No one deplores more than I do that the Mayor did not meet with the suggestion made, but he has not met with it, and he has told you, for you were present and I was present, that he will not alter, he will not change one name. I wish the Mayor was here this afternoon. I have only one desire and that is the desire of seeing that work started. Again may I say this, in closing, you have plans that cost $150,000, which took the better part of one entire year for a corps of about 25 architects, under one of the best designers in San Francisco, to draw those plans. If they are scrapped I tell you, as one who has some knowledge of building construction, that it wall take at least another year to redesign those buildings. If the present plans are used and modified and shrunk, which they can be, to meet with the demands and the money that we have, we can start that work going in four or five months. Now, it is up to us and us only, and I hope there will be something come out of this entire matter that we can compromise and do something to start the work on its way. And I give you these facts as I have them.

SUPERVISOR MARKS: At the time the architects were asked to draw these plans of the buildings, were they told by the trustees how much money was available?

SUPERVISOR McSHEEHY: I was present at the time, Mr. Supervisor. I seconded the motion when Mr. Crocker, of the Crocker First National Bank, made the motion, that the buildings should not cost over $5,000,000.

SUPERVISOR MARKS: Was that conveyed to the architects?

SUPERVISOR McSHEEHY: I am almost positive they were present.

SUPERVISOR MARKS: How soon after the plans came back from the architects was it known that the plans would cost over $8,000,000?

SUPERVISOR McSHEEHY: It must have been a year after that particular motion was made.

SUPERVISOR MARKS: How long ago was that from the present time?

SUPERVISOR McSHEEHY: In time—I will say this to you: That the bond issue was in June, 1927, that would be two years ago that the bond issue was voted, and it was shortly after that issue that this motion was made, it might have been perhaps in August, 1927, perhaps later, I could not say right offhand, but I remember the particular meeting. And perhaps over a year passed on before we received the estimates from the architects as to the cost.

SUPERVISOR MARKS: Did the Board of Trustees have presented to it, at any time, by the architects, a set of plans for structures that could be built within the money limit that the Trustees placed upon it?

SUPERVISOR McSHEEHY: I would say yes. Following some plans submitted here today of $5,300,000 odd dollars, that the veterans agreed —the report came in that the veterans agreed to I think—now, this is all from memory and I might be wrong—I think the veterans agreed to 105,000 square feet or thereabouts, of floor space, and those plans were to cost, or that portion of the building was to cost, as was stated, practically $1,850,000 and the balance of $3,450,000, in round sums, was for the Opera House.

SUPERVISOR TODD: I have never seen fit, in the four years on this board, to explain my vote or make any apologies for any vote, nor do I intend to make any apology today. When I returned from my recent illness, the first meeting I attended that the Mayor was here, I asked him when he was going to appoint these committeemen. He said he had been working on this list hard for many nights, trying to get eleven men who would take the job. He finally called us into his office about three or four weeks ago and he handed us a list of men—I think the whole eighteen members of the board were present— and I believe that the Mayor understood at that time that this list would not be confirmed by certain members of the Board of Supervisors, inasmuch as there were not six veterans on the board, which eleven members of the board gave their word that there would be or that it would not be confirmed. I have nothing against any of these men whom the Mayor has seen fit to name. They are all outstanding men. I am told, by the representatives of the veterans, that they went over their entire membership, and they culled it down to fifteen outstanding men who are members of the veterans' organizations, who would be acceptable to them and they think acceptable to the citizens. Of course, this is a secret list and we do not know who these fifteen men were. The veterans do not want to give it to us on account of their confidence with the Mayor. I think that this matter should be sent back to the Mayor and his attention called to this list of fifeen men and at least six veterans put on this committee. With all due respect to my friend, Supervisor Colman, he was one of the eighteen that attended this meeting in the Mayor's office when the board unanimously agreed that no member of the board should sit on this commission. I think that this should be sent back to the Mayor without being confirmed and that will be my vote.

SUPERVISOR DEASY: Mr. Chairman, I wish to state that this is the first discussion I heard about the Memorial Building, and when that resolution was passed last year I was unfortunate enough to be sick in St. Mary's Hospital, I was not here when they voted to select six men from the veterans on this committee. What I want to see is that building started over there, and I was first willing to abide by the Mayor's selection, but after hearing the veterans talk today, I will have to vote against the Mayor's recommendations.

SUPERVISOR MARKS: I feel, Mr. Chairman and members of the Board: That the buildings to be erected across the way, because of their nature, because of the spirit behind them, should not have written upon the cornerstone that those structures: "These buildings, erected by the Board of Trustees, selected after a wrangle which lasted longer than the war which the buildings are sought to commemorate". Nor should there be written on the cornerstone: "This building erected by a Board of Trustees, the first group of which died on the field of battle in the Board of Supervisors after a very long struggle". And I am serious about that, Mr. Chairman, because I think that, even though it won't be written there physically, if this Board of Supervisors at some time elects a Board of Trustees, it must eventually, and has, at one time, refused by official vote confirmation of any group, inevitably that taint is going to remain with the War Memorial I think for all time, and as a result of that there is going to be, I am satisfied, some diminution of the respect and affection which the people will have for those structures, and always a spirit of looking back over past history where people will point to those buildings and think of the long struggle and activity of this Board of Supervisors in connection with it. I want to call attention of the Board to just what the motion is that is pending: It is a motion to confirm a group of men. I have listened to the discussions here today. I listened to the expressions of individuals. I gather from it that there is a feeling of unwillingness on the part of this Board to confirm the list which is pending before us. I think that is pretty plain from the expressions here. And I hope, Mr. Chairman, that that feeling does not go to an official vote until every possible opportunity is, thought to arise at an agreement by the confirmation of a Board of Trustees, either this group or a group with modifications, shall be the unanimous act of this Board. In other words, I would hate to see, individually I would hate to see, the record, at any time in the history of the War Memorial structure, where there was an adverse vote on the selection of a group. I would hate to see future generations say that the records of the Board of Supervisors showed such an adverse vote. While I do not like to see the Board delay the projects, and I deplore those delays as others of you have, I think that it is the duty of this Board to use every effort, until it appears impossible, if it should so appear, to try to get an agreement on the part of the members of the Board, semi-officially if you will, with the veterans, either on this group or on some other group, so that, when the matter does receive a vote, it shall receive, for the first time that it is voted upon, the seal of approval of every member of the Board, rather than to have the record show a negative vote at any stage of the proceedings. Now, I want to say just a word about Supervisor Colman, if I may. This is not a recommendation for a position, this is not a certificate of good character to him. I sat in that conference in the Mayor's office and I felt, theoretically, that there might be some objection to a member of the Board being upon the Board of Trustees of the War Memorial. It is deplorable and unfortunate that, in a project such as we have in contemplation across the street, it should be necessary, or it should be inevitable, that there would be discussions of the individual character and standing of citizens of San Francisco. I am satisfied, as far as Mr. Colman is concerned, I am satisfied, his nomination being before the Board by the Mayor, that he will manifest in this activity, if confirmed by this Board, the same high character and the same fair-mindedness that shows and has shown in all of his public activities. But that is not the particular matter that is before the Board. I believe that if Supervisor Andriano's suggestion is adopted, if he wants to renew the motion, and if this Board were to have a few days in which to think over this matter dispassionately, we ought to exert every possible effort, I repeat, to come back to this Board so that the record shall be plain and clear, and that whenever an official vote is taken upon confirmation of a Board of Trustees, there shall not be a dissenting vote which will in any way place a stain, for all time and posterity, upon those splendid structures to be erected across the way.

SUPERVISOR SCHMIDT: The Mayor has stated definitely to the Committee when we went there he would not change one member on that Board of Trustees that he selected. Are we going to confirm the names or not? If we are going to delay it we are taking the responsibility for delay after the statement made by the Mayor. Because many times we tried to confer with the Mayor, to meet the veterans again and settle with them on the members of the Board, and that did not take place. If there is any one that is confronted with the entire Board of Trustee's matter it is the Board of Supervisors. The whole trend of the situation has been placed in our lap. If the matter was again submited to the Supervisors, and the veterans, who are willing to confer but never had the opportunity to confer again protested, why, what else are we going to do? The Mayor is out of town and probably will be for a month, and in the meantime, by laying this matter over for a week, it won't change the mind of the Mayor. It will merely work delay and I do not want to be charged with any delay.

SUPERVISOR MARKS: Certainly a refusal to confirm any group will have the same result as postponement of a matter, with the addition that it will have the bad effect of a refusal to confirm. Now, I do not think either you or I want to ever have it said that the group that we eventually select was selected after an official vote wherein we have rejected a whole group of men because that will be the inevitable result of our vote if the vote should be negative on the motion to confirm. I do not think we want it said, I do not believe those men, I am sure those men would not want it said of them, and we would not want it said, that in selecting any group we had taken an official vote, as the result of which we—possibly I am not entitled to say that we refused to confirm—but where it might be said that we had done so, and created a bad atmosphere in connection with the War Memorial project. I have seen it done before, Mr. Schmidt, and you have too. I have seen matters come into this Board where it seemed impossible to arrive at an adjustment, where it seemed impossible to arrive at some arrangement, whereby all interests were satisfied, and then, after we had debated the matter, and after we have conferred on these situations and given mature thought to it, we have come, sensibly and calmly and deliberately to a satisfactory conclusion. I do not despair of that being possible in the War Memorial matter. It may be, after the open discussion we have had here, that the veterans themselves may be brought to a situation where they would be satisfied with these nominations, or it may be that some of the nominees themselves, realizing the situation, or the Mayor himself, or this Board can bring about a situation whereby appointments or a list can be brought in which will receive immediate and unanimous support, and that is the spirit I think the War Memorial should be founded upon.

SUPERVISOR SCHMIDT: May I ask Mr. Marks this question: Would it be possible for us, without confirming or disapproving the Mayor's appointments, to refer the entire matter back to the Mayor again for further consideration, if you do not want to go on record as opposed to the eleven trustees presented by the Mayor? It is merely camouflaging the issue, and I do not know whether we will get very far with it.

SUPERVISOR GALLAGHER: Question.

SUPERVISOR ANDRIANO: Following the invitation of Supervisor Marks to renew my motion, I am going to. I move we continue the matter for one week.

SUPERVISOR MARKS: Second the motion.

SUPERVISOR STANTON: I cannot help but say a little word, possibly a little out of order, and it takes us back to a month or so ago, which I am sort of pleased and delighted to see the feeling and the thought that some of the members have of people's standing in the community, for their honor and not wanting to hurt them. But I very well remember a few months ago, after this Board unanimously elected me as a member of the Board of Directors, without a reason—without a reason whatever—at the following meeting, came back and voted, almost unanimously, to kick me off. Did anybody give me any thought? Did anybody think anything about my standing in the community around here? They tried to bury me for all time right there and then. I want to tell you that chickens do come home to roost.

SUPERVISOR GALLAGHER: Question.

THE CHAIRMAN: I am doubtful about the parliamentary situation. The identical motion was put before and defeated and I doubt whether the same motion can be repeatedly submitted to the Board.

SUPERVISOR MARKS: It was put without a second.

THE CHAIRMAN: Without a second, I beg your pardon. Call the roll.

SUPERVISOR SHANNON: I would like to 'ask a question of the maker of the motion: If it is the thought that possibly the new Mayor we have can change the list in the coming week? Now, Mr. Chairman, you do not need to answer that because I do not want to put you in that position. But I made the motion, Mr. Chairman, at the very outset of the meeting to postpone until the Mayor returned, which would have saved us a day had it carried. Now, if the motion is made by Mr. Andriano that we continue this matter until the Mayor returns, I will be willing to vote for it, but to postpone a week and leave it in your lap during that time, I would not care to vote for that because nothing will be accomplished. Now, if the thoughts enunciated by Mr. Marks carry weight with the body, the proper motion to make, and for which I would be willing to vote, would be a continuance for three weeks or a month, until the Mayor returned, because he asked for a thirty day leave, and if we do vote to reject today, the matter would necessarily have to wait his arrival for a new list. So if we would vote to reject it would, as Mr. Marks said, be taken by some people as a slap at these men who have been nominated by the Mayor, and no new list would be forthcoming in the meantime. So if the members feel that they want to vote on this today, I am willing to vote on it; if they want to vote on a motion that might be amended to call for a month's continuance, a thirty day continuance, I would be willing to vote for that.

SUPERVISOR GALLAGHER: Mr. Chairman, I have not risen to speak on this question, nor do I intend to make any extended remarks now. This last motion, once having been refused, is now renewed. What is the issue here? Is it the issue whether we are saving somebody's feelings? Is it the out and out, cold blooded, unmistakable, unequivocal issue that we demand as representatives of the people, a majority of the Board of Trustees shall be Veterans, regardless of whose feelings are hurt? That is the out and out issue. Now, you are moving, after hours of debate, you are proposing now, after hours of talk, which I do not criticize you for, you are proposing to do the very old thing, which you are so often accused of and sometimes rightfully and sometimes wrongfully——

SUPERVISOR SHANNON (interrupting): Make that "we" instead of "you," if you please.

SUPERVISOR GALLAGHER: I shall say "we" instead of "you." Make that "we." I think I said "we," if I did not I fully intended to. Now, I propose to do one of the most regrettable things that I have to do. I am asked first, to vote on the subject of the confirmation of Mr. Colman. Nothing would please me better than to be able to do that. I am asked to vote on the subject of the confirmation of Mr. Cameron, Mr. Kendrick, another gentleman of high repute. But I am willing to meet the issue because the issue is not—their reputation will not be in the slightest degree tarnished by either confirmation or rejection. The issue is clear cut that the Mayor has made and I propose to meet it. I do not wish to wave any flags, nor do I wish to indulge in war talk, but it does seem to me that we are somewhat forgetful. The people of the City and County of San Francisco have written into their organic law that in the matter of positions throughout the government those that fought for their country have the preference. It is not a very far cry then to justify yourselves and to say that if there is to be a memorial to the deeds they performed, to the work that they have done, the things for which they stood for when we needed them, the thing to do is to trust them with their own War Memorial.

SUPERVISOR ANDRIANO: With the consent of my second, I will amend my motion to the effect that the matter be postponed for thirty days.

THE CHAIRMAN: Is there a second? I would like to clarify the situation suggested by Supervisor Shannon, the possibility that, in my present position as Acting Mayor I might see it to amend the Mayor's nominations. Whenever, by reason of my present position, as result of a necessitated absence from the state of the Mayor, I am called upon to act as Mayor, it will be my policy not to make any appointments which are vested by the charter, or by law, in his Honor the Mayor during his absence, unless he specifically requests me to do so.

SUPERVISOR McSHEEHY: The question before us is postponement for one week, nothing more but postponement for one week and that is all. Now, members of the Board, suppose we today do not confirm the nominees of the Mayor? The thing will go on just as it is going on now. If we postpone for one week what might happen? This, I hope, will happen, that the Acting Mayor will call this Board together, which he can, we are all conversant with the question, and we will try to agree, and I hope that we will be able to send the Mayor a telegram that we unanimously agree on so and so and forward to him the stenographic report here today. I hope that we will be able to do that. We will then be accomplishing something. If we vote down the recommendations of the Mayor, the matter will remain just as it is. We will mark time and that is all that will come out of it. I tried to give you all the facts as a present member of the Board of Trustees. I deplore that the Mayor did not see fit to nominate one member at least of the 15 recommended by the Veterans. And I say to you here now that we can do something and I hope we will do something so we can start this project on its way. Vote postponement down if you will, vote the recommendations of the Mayor down, if you will. You remain just as you are today and so you will remain until the Mayor returns. Vote postponement for one week and I hope the Acting Mayor will call us together and that we will unanimously agree on some program.

THE CLERK: On Supervisor Andriano's amendment, seconded by Supervisor Marks, that consideration be continued for one week.

THE CHAIRMAN: Call Mr. Andriano in. Roll call.

SUPERVISOR ANDRIANO: Aye.
SUPERVISOR COLMAN: Excused from voting.
SUPERVISOR DEASY: No.
SUPERVISOR GALLAGHER: No.
SUPERVISOR HAVENNER: No.
SUPERVISOR HAYDEN: No.
SUPERVISOR KENT: No.
SUPERVISOR MARKS: Aye.
SUPERVISOR McGOVERN: No.
SUPERVISOR McSHEEHY: Aye.
SUPERVISOR POWERS: No.

SUPERVISOR RONCOVIERI: No.
SUPERVISOR SCHMIDT: No.
SUPERVISOR SHANNON: No.
SUPERVISOR STANTON: No.
SUPERVISOR SUHR: No.
SUPERVISOR TODD: No.
SUPERVISOR TONER: Aye.
THE CLERK: Four ayes, thirteen noes, one excused.
THE CHAIRMAN: The motion is lost.   The question is, shall the appointments recommended by his Honor the Mayor to the Board of War Memorial Trustees, be confirmed.   Roll call.
SUPERVISOR ANDRIANO: Aye.
SUPERVISOR COLMAN: Excused from voting.
SUPERVISOR DEASY: No.
SUPERVISOR GALLAGHER: No.
SUPERVISOR HAVENNER: No.
SUPERVISOR HAYDEN: Aye.
SUPERVISOR KENT: No.
SUPERVISOR MARKS: Aye.
SUPERVISOR McGOVERN: No.
SUPERVISOR McSHEEHY: Aye.
SUPERVISOR POWERS: No.
SUPERVISOR RONCOVIERI: No.
SUPERVISOR SCHMIDT: No.
SUPERVISOR SHANNON: No.
SUPERVISOR STANTON: No.
SUPERVISOR SUHR: No.
SUPERVISOR TODD: No.
SUPERVISOR TONER: Aye.
THE CLERK: Five ayes, twelve noes, 1 excused.
SUPERVISOR ANDRIANO: I desire to change my vote from aye to no and give notice of reconsideration.
THE CLERK: The vote then becomes four ayes and thirteen noes.
SUPERVISOR RONCOVIERI: Mr. Chairman, I move immediate reconsideration.
SUPERVISOR TODD: I second the motion.
THE CHAIRMAN: Call the roll, the question is——
SUPERVISOR ANDRIANO (interrupting):   Mr. Chairman, as I understand it, a notice to reconsider is to afford an opportunity to the members of the Board to do just that very thing, to reconsider, and a motion cannot be reconsidered immediately after a vote is taken, the time is not sufficient.   Now, that rule of common sense has been disregarded by the members of this Board heretofore, but it has been disregarded illegally, and I now rise to a point of order, that such a motion is not in order.
THE CHAIRMAN: Your point of order is not well taken.
SUPERVISOR ANDRIANO: May I be permitted, if you please, to read the Charter.
SUPERVISOR KENT: It seems to me that a vote was taken to postpone for one week, and this notice of reconsideration is for the same purpose, and I believe the thing has already been voted on in another way and therefore this is out of order.
SUPERVISOR ANDRIANO: Section 12, Article II, Chapter I: "When a bill is put upon its final passage in the Board and fails to pass, and a motion is made to reconsider, the vote upon such motion shall not be acted upon before the expiration of twenty-four hours after adjournment.   No bill for the grant of any franchise shall be put upon its final passage within ninety days after its introduction, and no franchise shall be renewed before one year prior to its expiration.   Every ordinance shall, after amendment, be laid over for one week before its final passage."

That last has no bearing upon the point of order that I raised, but I submit that the first portion of it is exactly in point, that we cannot vote finally upon this question until the expiration of 24 hours. We may be able to disregard the by-laws of this Board, but I do not think the members of the Board will want to ignore the Charter.

SUPERVISOR SHANNON: It is the reconsideration of franchises.

THE CHAIRMAN: The Chair will rule that the point of order is not well taken because this section quoted by the Supervisor refers to reconsideration of franchises.

SUPERVISOR SHANNON: To get the matter properly before the Board, I will move the suspension of the rules for the purpose of immediate reconsideration.

SUPERVISOR SCHMIDT: Second the motion.

THE CHAIRMAN: Call the roll.

THE CLERK: Roll Call:

SUPERVISOR ANDRIANO: No.

SUPERVISOR COLMAN: Excused from voting.

SUPERVISOR DEASY: Aye.
SUPERVISOR GALLAGHER: Aye.
SUPERVISOR HAVENNER: Aye.
SUPERVISOR HAYDEN: Aye.
SUPERVISOR KENT: Aye.
SUPERVISOR MARKS: Aye.
SUPERVISOR McGOVERN: Aye.
SUPERVISOR McSHEEHY: No.
SUPERVISOR POWERS: Aye.
SUPERVISOR RONCOVIERI: Aye.
SUPERVISOR SCHMIDT: Aye.
SUPERVISOR SHANNON: Aye.
SUPERVISOR STANTON: Aye.
SUPERVISOR SUHR: Aye.
SUPERVISOR TODD: Aye.
SUPERVISOR TONER: No.

THE CLERK: Fourteen ayes, three noes, one excused.

(The Chairman brings down the gavel).

THE CHAIRMAN: The question is, shall the vote whereby this Board of Supervisors refused confirmation to the nominations of his Honor the Mayor be reconsidered.

SUPERVISOR ANDRIANO: I would just like to call your attention to the fact that that sentence that I have read does not refer exclusively to franchises. It says, "When a bill is put upon its final passage in the Board and fails to pass, and a motion is made to reconsider, the vote upon such motion shall not be acted upon before the expiration of twenty-four hours after adjournment."

That is a complete statement in itself. There is no reference in that sentence to franchises. And I submit that you cannot draw the conclusion that, because the following sentence refers to franchises, that therefore the sentence that I have read refers to franchises.

THE CHAIRMAN: The Chair would rule that the provisions of the Charter read does, however, in specific language refer to the final passage of a bill, and that the question before us is not the final passage of the bill.

SUPERVISOR ANDRIANO: I desire to appeal from the ruling of the Chair with regard to that point of order and I so move.

THE CHAIRMAN: The motion fails for lack of a second.

SUPERVISOR GALLAGHER: The gentleman desires to exercise his right to appeal 'from the decision of the Chair.

THE CHAIRMAN: I have no objection to putting the question.

SUPERVISOR GALLAGHER: I may be in error, but I know of no rule which provides that he must have a second.

SUPERVISOR SHANNON: Well, you are in error, Mr. Gallagher.

SUPERVISOR McSHEEHY: I will second the appeal.

THE CHAIRMAN: Call the roll. The question is, Shall the ruling of the Chair be upheld.

THE CLERK: Roll call.

SUPERVISOR ANDRIANO: No.

SUPERVISOR COLMAN: Excused from voting.

SUPERVISOR DEASY: Aye.

SUPERVISOR GALLAGHER: Aye.

SUPERVISOR HAVENNER: Excused from voting.

SUPERVISOR HAYDEN: Aye.

SUPERVISOR KENT: Aye.

SUPERVISOR MARKS: Aye.

SUPERVISOR McGOVERN: Aye.

SUPERVISOR McSHEEHY: Aye.

SUPERVISOR POWERS: Aye.

SUPERVISOR RONCOVIERI: Aye.

SUPERVISOR SCHMIDT: Aye.

SUPERVISOR SHANNON: Aye.

SUPERVISOR McSHEEHY: I want to change, I wish to vote no, I seconded Supervisor Andriano's motion, I wish to vote no.

SUPERVISOR STANTON: Aye.

SUPERVISOR SUHR: Aye.

SUPERVISOR TODD: Aye.

SUPERVISOR TONER: Aye.

THE CLERK: Fourteen ayes, two noes and two excused.

SUPERVISOR SHANNON: Mr. Chairman, so that Mr. Gallagher will know that I do not give any offhand decisions, I want to read Section 14: "A question of order takes precedence of the question giving rise to it, and must be decided by the officer without debate. If a member objects to the decision he says, 'I appeal from the decision of the chair.' If the appeal is seconded the Chairman immediately states the question as follows"——

SUPERVISOR GALLAGHER: Very much obliged, Mr. Robert.

THE CHAIRMAN: The question is, Shall the Board reconsider the vote whereby it refused to confirm the nominations of his Honor the Mayor.

THE CLERK: Roll call.

SUPERVISOR ANDRIANO: Aye.

SUPERVISOR COLMAN: Excused from voting.

SUPERVISOR DEASY: No.

SUPERVISOR GALLAGHER: No.

SUPERVISOR HAVENNER: No.

SUPERVISOR HAYDEN: No.

SUPERVISOR KENT: No.

SUPERVISOR MARKS: Aye.

SUPERVISOR McGOVERN: No.

SUPERVISOR McSHEEHY: Aye.

SUPERVISOR POWERS: No.

SUPERVISOR RONCOVIERI: No.

SUPERVISOR SCHMIDT: No.

SUPERVISOR SHANNON: No.

SUPERVISOR STANTON: No.

SUPERVISOR SUHR: No.

SUPERVISOR TODD: No.

SUPERVISOR TONER: Aye.

THE CLERK: Four ayes, thirteen noes, one excused.
THE CHAIRMAN: Reconsideration is denied.

————

October 7, 1929. Remarks of Mayor James Rolph, Jr., made before the Board of Supervisors upon his return from Washington in regard to War Memorial Trustees:

THE MAYOR: It is too late today for me to take up with the Board the question of the War Memorial Trustees. I would like to call the Board together or have the Board take a recess until Thursday afternoon, say at two o'clock, after the Mayor of Berlin leaves, when we can sit down here and discuss the appointment for that project.

SUPERVISOR McSHEEHY: May I ask, Mr. Mayor, we just agreed that a copy of your report in reference to the bridge matter be tendered to Mr. Harlan, I believe that is the name of the attorney. May I ask that a copy also be tendered to our Clerk as a record, so that, if any of us wish at any time to refer to it, we will have it here?

THE MAYOR: So ordered.

SUPERVISOR HAVENNER: Do I understand that you want to have a special meeting of the Board to discuss the War Memorial Trustees? May I call your attention to the parliamentary situation? There is nothing before the Board in regard to that.

THE MAYOR: Then I will call the Board in special session for two o'clock on Thursday afternoon to discuss appointments for the War Memorial, because I am going to present each name singly and have the Board vote on each name, so that we will find out whom you are for and whom you are against, that is all.

SUPERVISOR HAVENNER: I will have to raise a point of order at this time, and I will be obliged to raise that point of order. The Board is not, under the Charter amendment—and I consulted the City Attorney at the time—the Board is not required to vote seriatim, and I do not feel that that would be fair. The Charter specifically provides that the Board has the right of confirmation of denominations, not individually. The Board made itself very clear on that subject at the time that it took its vote. We do not object to any individual. Solely on the basis of the action previously taken by the Board, I will have to raise a point of order against any proposition to ask us to vote seriatim.

THE MAYOR: The point of order is not well taken, because voting on any matter seriatim is provided for in the Charter, for the budget, and everything else. The Mayor is going to take full advantage of passing every single name up, because there is no hope of getting unanimous consent on every name presented by the vote. We are going to have a seriatim vote on each name.

SUPERVISOR HAVENNER: I will ask that the City Attorney be requested to be here and advise us, as he did before.

THE MAYOR: We will have a vote on every name.

SUPERVISOR HAVENNER: I do not think we will.

SUPERVISOR GALLAGHER: The Streets Committee meets Thursday; cannot we meet some other day than Thursday?

THE MAYOR: I mean, convenient to the Board. I cannot have it before Thursday, because the Mayor of Berlin arrives tomorrow morning and will be here until Thursday morning, I understand.

SUPERVISOR GALLAGHER: If the Finance Committee does not object the Streets Committee could meet Friday. We have the Bay Shore and Redwood Empire matters before us. Wednesday we have a district highway meeting. We could meet then. But Thursday, I would ask for you not to call it on Thursday.

SUPERVISOR HAVENNER: At this time, in view of your announcement that you desire to call the Board in session to vote upon your nominations, I desire to call public attention to the fact that I think the Board was not treated entirely fairly by your Honor, perhaps not intentionally, in connection with the nominations for the War Memorial. You called tne entire Board into your office two months ago, I believe it was, and submitted to us a partial list of the names, which we discussed privately. It was at your invitation, you stated at that time that you did not desire, and that you did not believe that the Board desired, to bring this question to a public discussion and to have the issue of personalities raised in connection with the nominations. You presented to us a partial list of proposed nominations at that time, to which, individually, I think there was no objection raised. You told us that before you submitted the nominations, you desired to confer with us again. I desire to call the attention of the Board now publicly to the fact that we never had the opportunity to discuss this matter with you again, and that we have had no explanation of why we did not have that opportunity. The Board entered into this matter in good faith, hoping that the issue of personalities could be avoided, through the conference which you yourself, your Honor, suggested.

THE MAYOR: Yes.

SUPERVISOR HAVENNER: And we were not given the privilege, which you voluntarily proffered us, to discuss the entire list again before it was brought before the Board. Therefore, I want to submit to you that I think your proposition now, that we publicly discuss the issue of personalities, which we have officially disclaimed as any part of the reason for our refusing to confirm your list of nominations, is not in keeping with the suggestion that you made to us yourself.

THE MAYOR: But, Mr. Havenner, the last time I called the Board in—I know it was twice, I am not sure whether it was three times or not, but twice, anyway,—nearly every name on the list that I submitted was acceptable to all the members of the Board present in my office.

SUPERVISOR HAVENNER: That is true, but you did not submit to us a complete list. We had the right to expect at that time, and the thing that we insisted upon at the meeting in your office, Mr. Mayor, with all due respect, we merely insisted that, in view of the joint authority that the Charter placed upon us with yourself, that the official request that we had made, that a majority of the men who were to be nominated should be veterans of some department of the military service of the United States, should be complied with.

THE MAYOR: Well, all right, Mr. Havenner, there is nothing incumbent upon me to follow that resolution. I did not sign it, I let it go.

SUPERVISOR HAVENNER: I merely call your attention to it— I say it may have been an unintentional breach of good faith with the Board—but I think that, having publicly assured us—and every member of the Board was present—that we would be consulted again before you subjected this list to a public discussion, that it is not now fair to thrust upon us the issue of personalities.

THE MAYOR: Well, I refuse to go through any more executive conferences in my chambers and be turned down on some of the names that were agreed upon by every member of the Board present in my chambers. And I am not going to go into executive session in my chambers and get nowhere. The names that were agreed upon have been turned down and the Board has permitted, as near as I can find out while I have been away, slurs to be cast upon the names of some of those that I have nominated.

SUPERVISOR HAVENNER: That is absolutely untrue. I must deny it, it is not true. This Board, officially, went on record as saying that our sole objection was that you placed this Board in the position of repudiating its public pledge to the veterans of San Francisco, that we requested that a majority of those names be veterans. And it is inconceivable to me, Mr. Mayor—I regard every one of your nominations as worthy individually—and I will not be placed in the position of voting for one and voting against another. I serve notice now that I will not be placed in that position. But, Mr. Mayor, it is inconceivable to me that there are not others as worthy among this great army of men who offered their lives in the World War and the wars which have preceded it. And we merely requested——

THE MAYOR (interrupting): There are.

SUPERVISOR HAVENNER: (continuing): —that a majority of the nominations be men who have rendered that service to the United States.

THE MAYOR: If I had the appointment of all the men who served the country, I would appoint every one of them, but you drew the resolution limiting me to eleven.

SUPERVISOR ANDRIANO: I think that there is nothing before the Board at this time on this particular question, and I am going to make a motion that, if your Honor desires to present this matter before the Board, or if there is going to be any discussion at all, that it should be made a special order of business for some other day. I make a motion that three o'clock next Monday be set aside for that purpose.

SUPERVISOR HAVENNER: There is nothing before the Board.

SUPERVISOR ANDRIANO: There is nothing before the Board now.

THE MAYOR: I have had notice served on me this morning that many of those whom I have appointed are going to resign, that is all, and I cannot get anywhere with the Board in my chambers discussing names because you cannot agree on eleven names, all of you put together, you could not agree on eleven names, and I say that with all kindliness, I cannot do anything.

SUPERVISOR HAVENNER: I rise to a question of personal privilege with regard to that statement. We did not solicit the invitation to come to your office. We were invited by you, and it was your suggestion, and yours alone, that we come to your office——

THE MAYOR (interrupting): Yes.

SUPERVISOR HAVENNER: (continuing): —that we come to the office, for the purpose of discussing with you in private, before this matter was submitted to public discussion, the various names that you had in mind. And you submitted to us a partial list. To none of the individuals did we raise any objection.

THE MAYOR: I submitted all but one.

SUPERVISOR HAVENNER: There was no agreement at that time, and it was at your specific request, Mr. Mayor——

THE MAYOR (interrupting): It was.

SUPERVISOR HAVENNER (continuing): ——that we should meet with you again.

THE MAYOR: Yes.

SUPERVISOR HAVENNER: Now, it is not fair, Mr. Mayor, to get up here now before this audience and say that you won't consider a further private consultation in your office. We did not suggest that, you suggested it, sir.

THE MAYOR: I won't extend the invitation again. I think I was paying the Board a distinct compliment, but if you do not want the invitation, I won't extend it, we will have it here.

SUPERVISOR HAVENNER: For one, I would like to have the privilege of discussing again it with you.

THE MAYOR: I have no objection to having it here.

SUPERVISOR GALLAGHER: I would like to say a word, Mr. Mayor.

SUPERVISOR ANDRIANO: I rise to a point of order, Mr. President, there is nothing before the Board.

SUPERVISOR GALLAGHER: The Mayor has made a statement.

SUPERVISOR ANDRIANO: I rise to a point of order as to the Mayor's statement. There is nothing before the Board. If the Mayor desires to call a special meeting, it is his privilege, but there is nothing before us now, and I do not think it is the proper time to enter into any discussion on the War Memorial. Let us have it out at a special session for that purpose. If you desire to make a statement you can make it at that time. I rise to a point of order.

THE MAYOR: Would you object, Mr. Gallagher, to a special meeting?

SUPERVISOR GALLAGHER: I would not object to a special meeting, but I suggest that, in view of the fact that discussion has been permitted and I do not intend to go into it very deeply, I merely intend to make a suggestion that might be helpful. I have to wait, however, until you rule me out of order, on your own invitation.

THE MAYOR: I do not object to him talking, Mr. Andriano, if you do not.

SUPERVISOR GALLAGHER: I would like to say this in a helpful spirit: I wish to say that I was not at the meeting in your office, you know I was not in town, but you submitted a very fine list of names, there is no question about that, and it was so stated here by nearly everybody who spoke. The issue is, however, as to whether the Board and yourself can get together on this matter so that a majority—I do not care if anybody has a victory in this thing or not, it does not matter to me—so that a majority of these directors might be veterans of some war. Now, that is an issue, and you could help it out very nicely——

THE MAYOR (interrupting): Whom am I going to throw off?

SUPERVISOR GALLAGHER: I would not use that expression. Why not take Mr. Fleishhacker? I am very sure he would be quite willing if it would help the situation. He is on, I think, four or five different boards of the city now. You could say, "Would you object if I took your name off for some one of 40,000 veterans"—I do not care who it is. And I happen to know, Mr. Mayor, that some of the gentlemen that you named have themselves stated, personally, that if it would solve the situation—it is not a question of getting off—they would be tickled to death to get out of the work involved. And I really think that in view of the fact that you would calm this community in one sense, and, anyhow, that you would get something started in the other, and that if we won't let our own pride get too much in the way, you can solve this between now and the time we next meet. Now, here is the situation you will face when you come to the Board: You state that you are going to ask us to vote individually on every name. What a complexity and with what result? Now, if you force that issue, the answer is the same. If you could compel us—which you cannot, by the way, you will lose in that matter, I would like to predict to you now—but if you could compel us to vote on every single name, why, the answer is that to sustain the record we would vote down every single name. And I would ask you not to force that issue for this reason: It is the Board's dictum that when a matter is presented—and it makes its own rule on the subject and you and I cannot change it—that if it desires to vote on names or matters seriatim, it is within their decision. And what will you have here? You will have a war of the War Memorial, as we Irish say, a sort of a Donnybrook affair, and you will get nowhere. Now, I think you really want to get this Memorial started, and I would like to have you undertake the legal job of switching a couple of names. I think, if you will consult some of the men whom you have proposed, they would tell you that it is their personal view, although they are very grateful for the honor you tendered them, and that it might be made consistent with every ideal you have and yet meet, on all fours, the position, not only of the Board, but of thousands of citizens. And I appeal to you, sir, with no disrespect for the names that you sent in, because they were wonderful people, all of them, and I want to assure you, as did Mr. Havenner, that not one unkind word, not even by those who were permitted to talk from outside the Board, not one unkind word was uttered against any nominee. I think that you will find that to be the record.

THE MAYOR: May I interrupt you and ask you a question: Was a statement made that only two of those whom I had suggested were satisfactory to those who were opposing them?

SUPERVISOR GALLAGHER: If it was made—I think it was only two were unsatisfactory, there was some such statement made and reasons recited, but remember, when that remark was given responsibility, it was the remark of a citizen permitted to address the Board, and, frankly, was put forward in colorful criticism, respectful, not derogatory, certainly not derogatory. You could take as your witness anybody who sat during that hearing, and it was a hearing in which everything that was said, including that that was said by individuals from the outside, was addressed in the most respectful manner and the names were treated in that form. And if you will examine the record, which was taken down in full, I would invite your particular attention to the fact that everything respectful was said and nothing that could, in any sense, so far as I heard it, and I heard it all, be considered as a slur against any man. And, take Major Kendrick, for instance. I would not sit here for one second— and Major Kendrick was one of the men mostly under fire, I will say—I would not sit here, or anywhere else, for one second and permit anybody to insult the name of Major Kendrick, although I had to vote against his name as a War Memorial trustee. And I would not listen to a man who would attack the men on that Board or slur them. But there was another issue here and they all went down in that manner, and I would like to appeal to you to see if the Board and yourself cannot get together, and then you will come back here with your nominations and they will be approved.

THE MAYOR: Was there a kick at Sergeant Major Jimmie Hertz?

SUPERVISOR TODD: No, not by anybody.

SUPERVISOR MARKS: His name was not mentioned.

THE MAYOR: I have asked the War Department to send me a record of the 363rd. One of the most brilliant pages of the War were made by the 363rd, our San Francisco regiment.

SUPERVISOR MARKS: Mr. Mayor, his name was not mentioned in any discussion.

SUPERVISOR STANTON: When we left your office, the only time that I was over there, when we left you had some names, not a full list but a tentative list, and you were going to look for some other people. I do not believe that there was a member of the Board —at least, not in conference was there a member of the Board— that I heard suggest anybody's name, and I do not know any member of the Board that has any name to suggest. I am satisfied, Mr. Mayor. if you and the veterans of the wars. or their committee, agreed on a set of names, I am satisfied that this Board of Supervisors, without any further conference, would accept them. But we did agree with the veterans, the Board of Supervisors, that there should be a majority of the Board of Trustees war veterans. We gave that promise to them and we explained that in your office, that we had made the promise, and we sort of must go along with it. And that is just what we are up against. Nobody has any particular kick. We have no fault to find with these War Memorial trustees. It is the Veterans, the people who served the country, who would like to have a Board of Trustees, a majority of them people who would be friendly and kindly with them. That is all. We have no further thought in it; we want the thing to go along as harmoniously as possible, and we are willing to work to that end. But after giving a promise to the people who were interested in it, we cannot fall down on that promise.

THE MAYOR: I am willing to yield an awful lot to try to get that work going. I thought I had given you eleven of the finest names we could get here. I will see you sometime during the week. *October* 14, 1929. Meeting of the Board of Supervisors regarding letter from the Veterans mentioned in the morning papers of this date, and which referred to alleged opposition of the Veterans to the $4,000,000 bond issue for the War Memorial. The press reports of this letter were read to the Board of Supervisors and the same were discussed. The letter treats mainly of the alleged "gross mis-statement of facts" by the Mayor relative to the activities of Veteran organizations against the War Memorial Boards. The letter was not received by the Mayor at the time it was published in the morning newspapers but was received later on in the day, and after it had been discussed before the Board of Supervisors.

The letter was dated October 12th, 1929, addressed to the Mayor, signed by Milton B. Sapiro, Commander San Francisco County Council, The American Legion; Mr. E. F. Peckham, President San Francisco County Council, United Spanish War Veterans; Harold J. Boyd, Commander San Francisco County Council, Veterans of Foreign Wars; Hillary H. Crawford, President United Veterans Council of San Francisco; Thomas M. Foley, representing Disabled Veterans of the World War; Harold J. Boyd, H. W. Glensor, and James B. Burns, the latter three constituting the Advisory Board of the Veterans' War Memorial, committees appointed to consult with a committee of nine on War Memorial matters. This letter points out that the Mayor is quoted as having issued a statement to the effect that the War Veterans opposed the bond issue providing for the War Memorial. The War Veterans are laboring under a misapprehension, because I never at any time made any such statement, and if I was so quoted, it is an erroneous quotation. I may have inadvertently referred to the War Memorial, but I, in fact, meant that certain War Veteran organizations of the City and County of San Francisco opposed Charter Amendment No. 32, creating the Board of Trustees of the War Memorial, which provided for the manner of their appointment, defined their powers and their duties. Said Board is to consist of eleven members, who are to be appointed by the Mayor, subject to confirmation by the Board of Supervisors. The Amendment provides that "in making appointments to said Board the Mayor shall give due consideration to Veterans of all wars engaged in by the United States for which said War Memorial is to be constructed and maintained."

My reference to the position of certain Veteran organizations on Charter Amendment No. 32, voted on and passed by the citizens of this City and County at the November, 1928, election is based upon a leaflet which was given wide circulation at and before the time the amendment above referred to was to be voted upon. The leaflet I refer to is quoted as follows:

"A WAR MEMORIAL WITH
NO
WAR VETERANS
Is
NO
WAR MEMORIAL
VOTE
NO
On Amendment
No.
32

CITIZENS OF SAN FRANCISCO:

1. War Veterans, speaking for themselves—through their nationally recognized organizations—remind you that your bond issue

of $4,000,000.00 asked in the name of War Veterans, was intended primarily to provide a real War Memorial as a tribute to deceased Veterans of all Wars, and as headquarters for San Francisco War Veterans.

2.   Amendment 32 means that War Veterans have no assurance of a voice in the construction, arrangement, management, or control of the War Memorial—that they have been promised since 1919—a memorial which was to provide a permanent headquarters for Veterans of all Wars.

3.   Amendment 32 means that War Veterans have no assurance that the employees in the 'Veterans Building' of the War Memorial will be honorably discharged War Veterans.

4.   Amendment 32 means that the entire War Memorial project, as well as the control and administration thereof, may be in the hands of a group interested primarily in an opera house and art museum, without regard to the wishes, desires, or needs of the War Veterans.

5.   Those who submitted Amendment 32 did not consult any of the major War Veteran Organizations; they did not permit a suggestion or recommendation from any major War Veteran Organization; they did not in fact even notify any major War Veteran Organization of their intention to submit this amendment.

6.   Amendment 32 was presented at the last possible moment—within an hour of midnight—too late for any public hearings to be held.

7.   The War Veterans' Name. and their cause, have been and now are being used in an attempt to control and dominate an alleged War Memorial for the primary purpose of securing an opera house and an art museum.

VOTE NO ON AMENDMENT No. 32

Respectfully submitted in the name of, and under the specific authority of

>The Grand Army of the Republic
>National Indian War Veterans
>Veterans of Foreign Wars of the U. S.
>Disabled American Veterans of the World War
>United Veterans of the Republic
>Disabled Emergency Officers Association
>1st. California U. S. Volunteers
>347th Field Artillery Association
>United Spanish War Veterans
>United States Veteran Navy
>Imperial Order of the Dragon
>Dewey Congressional Medal Men
>Military Order -of the World War
>Woman's Relief Corps, G. A. R.
>363rd Infantry Association
>>The United Veterans Council
>>and
>>The American Legion"

I have been informed that some of the Veteran Organizations, whose names were attached to the leaflet heretofore mentioned, were not in fact opposed to the passage of Amendment No. 32, creating the so-called Board of War Memorial Trustees, and advised that the 363rd Infantry Association did not authorize the use of their name.   The reporter's transcript of the proceedings, "In re remarks of Mayor James Rolph, Jr., on appointment of Trustees of the War Memorial" is as follows:

THE MAYOR: Then follows: "In Re Remarks of Mayor James Rolph, Jr. On Appointment Of Trustees Of The War

Memorial," and then follows the transcript of the meeting
of Monday, October 14, 1929, at 10:00 o'clock a. m., and then
the transcript of the meeting of October 14, 1929, continues,
and a transcript of November 15, 1929:

IN RE REMARKS OF MAYOR JAMES
ROLPH, JR., ON APPOINTMENT OF TRUSTEES
OF THE WAR MEMORIAL.

Monday, October 14, 1929, 10:00 A. M.

The regular meeting of the Board of Supervisors was held on
Monday, the 14th day of October, 1929, beginning at the hour of
10:00 o'clock A. M. of that day, in the chambers of the Board,
City Hall, San Francisco, California.

After the transaction of other business and during the morning
session of the Board, the following proceedings were had:

THE MAYOR: Gentlemen of the Board, from the morning papers,
if the statements are correct, the headlines indicate that the Supervisors are to act on War Memorial Trustees today, and I see in both
papers this morning a printed open letter to the Mayor, which I
would like to have printed in the records of these proceedings.

(The letter referred to is as follows:

"Dear Mayor Rolph:

"In the afternoon papers of Thursday, October 10, and in the
morning papers of Friday, October 11, there has been published a
statement quoting you in reference to the War Memorial.

"This statement, if you are correctly quoted, contains some gross
mis-statements of fact, and as representatives of the various Veteran Organizations in San Francisco, we are compelled to call these
mis-statements to your attention and to the attention of the public
whose opinion you are evidently attempting to sway in reference
to a proposed Board of Trustees selected by you.

"You are quoted as saying that the Veterans or the Veteran Organizations opposed the bond issue providing for the War Memorial buildings. This statement is incorrect. The Veterans did
not oppose the bonds, but supported them.

"It seems strange to us that such a statement should be made
by you, for you should have been acquainted with the facts as they
existed at the time this bond issue passed in 1927 and in addition
you were personally informed by our advisory committee not many
weeks ago that the Veterans approved and worked for the passage
of the four-million-dollar bond issue. It was only through the
efforts of our Veteran Organizations and the use of the name of
the Veterans that the four-million-dollar bond issue was voted by
the people of San Francisco for the construction of buildings to
be used as a memorial hall for War Veterans and other municipal
purposes.

"As you should have known, the bond issue was approved and
authorized one year before the private Board of Trustees conceived
Amendment No. 32, presented at the November, 1928, election,
providing for the creation of a Board of Trustees to administer the
War Memorial funds. This had nothing to do with bonds, and the
war veterans opposed it. The war veterans opposed Amendment
No. 32, knowing that a Board of Trustees was absolutely unnecessary and that the scheme for the same was drawn up by the private Board of Trustees that had been maladministering this whole
memorial proposition and had failed to build it for a period of
eight years.

"We recognize that this measure was not proposed in good faith by the private Board of Trustees, and therefore we opposed the enactment of the legislation. Our suppositions in reference to this were confirmed at a public meeting held after the approval of the amendment, which was adopted by just a few hundred votes, and only because the people of San Francisco were not given the opportunity to learn the truth of the matter. Then we forced from Mr. John Drum, Chairman of the private Board of Trustees, an admission that he would not permit the transfer of assets from the private Board of Trustees unless a public board was created of which he would approve, and necessarily which he would dominate.

"In order to insure such a controlled board, the private Board of Trustees after this measure had carried requested you to delay your appointments to the Board of Trustees and thereby further delay the construction of the War Memorial. You followed their wishes and delayed the project.

"This private Board of Trustees had this memorial project in hand for a period of ten years. They originally asserted that $2,500,000 would be sufficient to complete the War Memorial. They then increased the sum to $6,500,000, and now, having spent hundreds of thousands of dollars in waste efforts, they bring forth plans which could only be carried out by the expenditure of more than $8,000,000, or $3,000,000 more than has been voted or subscribed for such purpose.

"The private Board of Trustees must be charged with gross inefficiency, waste and mismanagement. And yet you have selected four members of that private board on a new Board of Trustees, when those four men permitted one man to dominate the private Board of Trustees, and did not have enough public interest to find out for themselves what was happening in the private Board of Trustees.

"We suggest to you, as Mayor of San Francisco, that you, representing the citizens of San Francisco, demand of the private Board of Trustees a full accounting of the funds placed in their hands. Then maybe you will find out why they borrowed money from and paid interest to a bank controlled by one of the trustees, when they had hundreds of thousands of dollars on deposit which could have been used without making a loan. You might also find out what banks benefited by the deposit over a period of years of the hundreds of thousands of dollars that had been subscribed by the people of San Francisco, and whether or not those banks are controlled by members of the private Board of Trustees.

"If the people are indignant, as you are quoted, then they must be indignant about the failure of the private Board of Trustees to carry out their trusts and make a proper return and accounting to the people of San Francisco for the money which was placed in their hands.

"If they are indignant, they must be indignant about the waste of funds that has characterized the administration of the War Memorial project.

"If they are indignant, they must be indignant about the attempt to thwart the will of the people of San Francisco by depriving the war veteran organizations of proper meeting places and attempting to give them as little as possible of the use of the funds voted or subscribed by our citizens.

"We who served this country in the war are just as desirous of seeing the War Memorial completed as you are, but we want a War Memorial that will be built by a group of men in whom every citizen of San Francisco may have the utmost confidence, and which will not leave in the minds of the ex-service men, whose deeds brought forth this War Memorial project, a feeling that their service has been used to foster a private project so that the true desire and wish of the people of San Francisco has been defeated.

"There has been delay in the matter of constructing the War

Memorial, but that delay is chargeable to the inefficient private Board of Trustees from whose ranks you have seen fit to select four of the members of your present proposed board, and to yourself in failing to propose a board prior to this time and in failing to propose a proper Board of Trustees. Do not try to place that blame other than where it should rest.

"You now persist in carrying on the delay by not proposing a changed Board of Trustees. We would like to remind you that when the President of the United States submits a name of a citizen, even for an office as exalted as that of a member of his Cabinet, for approval by the United States Senate, and that name is not confirmed, the President does not try political means of securing confirmation of the same name that was rejected, but he submits a new name. Do you believe that you should have any different attitude than the President of the United States?

"The Supervisors have acted within their rights as given to them by the citizens of San Francisco when they refused to confirm your first appointments. The ordinance enacted did not contemplate that they would necessarily accept your appointments without the exercise of independent judgment.

"Unless you submit to the Board of Supervisors another Board of Trustees, you are the only one who can be charged with delay, and that Board of Trustees must necessarily be different from the one that you previously submitted.

"We also call your attention to the fact that the demand of the veterans that a majority of that board be composed of veterans is a proper demand. In the first place, a decent respect for the deeds of the men who served this country would have prompted you to have appointed a board consisting entirely of veterans, and so pay honor to such men during the short lifetime that they might have.

"In the second place, the course of the War Memorial in the past several years has made it clear that the interest of the people of San Francisco in seeing that a War Memorial was built which would provide meeting places for veterans can only be carried out if a majority of the Board of Trustees are veterans.

"If a majority is not composed of veterans, then there will be the attempt, as there has been in the past, to subvert the purpose for which money was voted and subscribed, and to make the veterans' participation in the buildings a minor one and not sufficient for their purposes.

"In closing we must repeat that we are compelled to write this letter because you are quoted to have made the incorrect statement that the veterans opposed the $4,000,000 bond issue. The support of the veteran organizations carried the bonds, and their watchfulness has protected the citizens from an improper disposition of the funds.

"Inasmuch as you have made your statements, not to the veterans' organizations, but to the public through the newspapers, we are sending a copy of this communication to the newspapers of San Francisco so that the public may be truthfully and accurately informed in respect to conditions concerning the War Memorial."

THE MAYOR: The headlines state that "The War Veterans Accuse Memorial Board and Issue Reply to Mayor's Statement." And it goes on further to say: "Declaring recent declarations of Mayor Rolph concerning the proposed War Memorial contained 'gross misstatements of facts' and denying specifically as incorrect a statement attributed to the Mayor that veterans' organizations had opposed the bond issue for the War Memorial buildings, an open letter was addressed to the Mayor yesterday, signed by commanders, presidents and representatives of five veterans' organizations in San Francisco." I am sorry that the veterans did not do the Mayor the courtesy of at least sending him a copy. The letter points out that it was through the efforts of veteran organizations that the original $4,000,000 bond issue was voted in 1927, a year before the private Board of Trustees drew up Amendment 32, creating a Board of Trustees to administer the Memorial funds, explaining why the veterans opposed Amendment 32. The letter in effect goes on to charge the original private board with gross inefficiency, mismanagement and waste, adding "they borrowed money from and paid interest to a bank controlled by one of the trustees." The open letter then follows, which I have asked to be included in the proceedings of today.

The letter, which I presume in the Chronicle is a full text of the letter, also appears, in abbreviated form, in this morning's San Francisco Examiner, the headlines of which are "Rolph Wrong on Memorial Vets Charge. Check on Funds Demanded in Letter to Mayor. Showdown on the Board Looms for Today. On the eve of a showdown on the entire War Memorial controversy, war veterans of San Francisco in an open letter last night charged Mayor James Rolph, Jr., with bad faith in his appointment of a Board of Trustees. The Mayor's nominations for a board were turned down by Supervisors. Today Rolph declared that he will demand that the Supervisors reconsider their action and confirm the eleven men he has named. The members of the Board of Supervisors have stated positively that they will decline to confirm the Mayor's nominations. Gross misstatement. With the Mayor and Supervisors at loggerheads, here are the accusations leveled at Rolph in a communication addressed to him by the veterans: 1. That Rolph has made gross misstatements, evidently attempting to sway public opinion. Chief among these is the allegation that the veterans opposed the War Memorial bond issue, when in fact they merely opposed Charter Amendment 32 calling for creation of the Board of Trustees. 2. That the Mayor alone is responsible for present delay, having followed the wishes of the private trustees in refusing to appoint a public board that would contain a majority of veterans and win approval of the Supervisors. The communication was signed by Milton D. Sapiro, Commander of the San Francisco County Council of the American Legion; E. F. Peckham, President San Francisco County Council, United Spanish War Veterans; Harold J. Boyd, Commander San Francisco County Council, Veterans of Foreign Wars; Hilary H. Crawford, President the United Veterans Council of San Francisco; Thomas M. Foley, representing the Disabled American Veterans of the World War, and by H. J. Boyd, H. W. Glensor and James B. Burns, as members of the Advisory Board to Veterans' War Memorial Committee." The letter says, in part: "This private Board of Trustees had this memorial project in hand for a period of ten years. They originally asserted that $2,500,000 would be sufficient to complete the War Memorial. They then increased the sum to $6,500,000, and now, having spent hundreds of thousands of dollars in waste efforts, they bring forth plans which could only be carried out by the expenditure of more than $8,000,000, or $3,000,000 more than has been voted or subscribed for such purpose.

"The private Board of Trustees must be charged with gross inefficiency, waste and mismanagement. And yet you have selected four members of that private board on a new Board of Trustees, when those four men permitted one man to dominate the private Board of Trustees and did not have enough public interest to find out for themselves what was happening in the private Board of Trustees.

"We suggest to you, as Mayor of San Francisco, that you, representing the citizens of San Francisco, demand of the private Board of Trustees a full accounting of the funds placed in their hands. Then maybe you will find out why they borrowed money from and paid interest to a bank controlled by one of the trustees, when they had hundreds of thousands of dollars on deposit which could have been used without making a loan. You might also find out what banks benefited by the deposit over a period of years of the hundreds of thousands of dollars that had been subscribed by the people of San Francisco, and whether or not those banks are controlled by members of the private Board of Trustees."

Permit me to call your attention to the fact that on May 2, 1927, your Honorable Board, by a vote of fifteen members, three absent, passed Bill No. 8003, Ordinance No. 7516, New Series, calling and providing for a special election to be held in the City and County of San Francisco on Tuesday, the 14th day of June, 1927, for the purpose of submitting to the said voters of the City and County of San Francisco a proposition to incur a bonded indebtedness of the City and County of San Francisco to the amount of $4,000,000 for the acquisition, construction and completion of a permanent improvement, to-wit: The construction, completion and equipment of permanent buildings in or adjacent to the Civic Center in the City and County of San Francisco, to be used as a Memorial Hall for War Veterans and for educational, recreational, entertainment and other municipal purposes, and the purchase of all equipment and furnishings necessary for said buildings. All of the terms are set forth in that bill and ordinance, the form of the bond and so forth. After being approved by the Mayor at 10:40 A. M., immediately after you passed it on May 2, 1927, it was submitted to the people and was carried by the necessary two-thirds vote of the people on the 14th day of May, the date of the election. The only literature that was sent out for the purpose of asking the people of this City and County to approve this bond issue is here submitted and sent out by the Registrar of Voters: "The land for a War Memorial is bought and $1,200,000 cash is waiting in the bank. Thus the people of this city, by issuing $4,000,000 in bonds, will gain a beautiful public project costing almost $7,000,000. The rest is already donated privately or given by the city. This group of buildings, occupying two entire blocks on one side of Van Ness Avenue, with the City Hall opposite, will greatly beautify our city. The location is ideal, the purpose to commemorate our heroes of the World War is idealistic and patriotic. The utilitarian value of these buildings alone merits their construction. One of them will be the Veterans' Building, housing all the veterans' organizations in San Francisco. It was to give these splendid organizations a permanent headquarters in the name of the public which honors their deeds that the War Memorial fund originally was begun. The other building will contain San Francisco's long-needed Symphony Hall and Opera Auditorium. Originally this was planned for a less advantageous location at the eastern end of the Civic Center. We have one of the finest symphony orchestras in the United States, and it should have a fitting place in which to perform. The San Francisco Opera Chorus, with the Municipal Chorus, foreshadows the day when the musical productions here will take rank with those produced in Chicago and New York, and a home for all the future will here be provided, second to none in beauty. Art gallery and museum features also are included in the plans. The War Memorial deserves unanimous support. Vote Yes. Civic League of Improvement Clubs and Associations of San Francisco, W. W. Watson, President; George W. Gerhard, Secretary." With that bond issue carried and the Board of Supervisors providing in that resolution, section 12, "This Ordinance is the third of a series of Ordinances which will be adopted by the Board of Supervisors relating to and designed to secure the acquisition, construction and completion of the permanent improvements named," later on——

SUPERVISOR HAVENNER (interrupting): Mr. Mayor, may I interrupt you just a moment? Do I understand you to say that that is the only argument you find there?

Mr, Mayor, that is not the official argument of the Board of Supervisors, but it is the argument of the Civic League of Improvement Clubs.

THE MAYOR: Mr. Havenner, I want to be as fair as I can. I sent to the Registrar's office this morning. This, of course, has come upon me out of a clear sky, I have had no letter, I have had no communication, I find it in the morning papers. And I sent to the Registrar's office this morning, for the purpose of finding out what messages were sent to the voters when this bond issue was before them, and this, the Registrar says, is the only one that went out from the Board. Now, I will finish, please.

SUPERVISOR HAVENNER: I think you will find that he is in error in that. I am quite sure that an official argument was sent out by the Citizens' Committee in charge of the bonds in the campaign.

THE MAYOR: Now, as I proceed, permit me to say, and I will state, with your permission, other facts which I have here, simply as a preliminary presentation to you of all of the facts relating to the original subscriptions and what they were for, the last ten years which has been referred to in this open letter to the Mayor, where the money came from, who has the money, what was done with it, and what all the plans were in connection with it, because I have never been at a meeting, never invited to attend a meeting. The Board has had three members on the Committee of Trustees representing the Board, and I have listened to the progress which I presumed was going on, toward the completion of this $6,000,000 project. I am going to ask you now, so that, as I proceed, you will know that I am seeking other information, I am not making a full and a complete report this morning, I am answering the charges, briefly, that have been referred to in this open letter to the Mayor, I am answering that as a preliminary report, but positive facts I will present in a full report to the Board in due time. I have not the office staff nor the help in my office to dig up all the data necessary in the compilation of this report. I would respectfully request this morning that you detail to me, to work with my assistant secretary, Judge Smith, one of the young attorneys from the City Attorney's office and some clerical help from your office, that I might dig up and that I might answer and I might prepare a full and complete reply to the open letter which has been addressed to the Mayor this morning and is in the public mind for discussion. If you will give me that help, I will bring here, in due time, a full and complete, unbiased statement of the facts, because I yield to no man in my desire, and my advocacy, and my voice and my efforts to pass that bond issue, to build a War Memorial in honor of those who served their country and who sacrificed their lives for our country, and I yield to no man in his efforts, during the entire period of the war, giving up my time, doing the best I could in the interests of those that were called, in the interests of the war and in the interest of keeping the home fires burning here in San Francisco. These are gross libelous charges against honest men in this community, charges of dishonesty, inefficiency and waste of money, men who gave their own money. Practically charges of graft, charged that, because the property across the street stands in the name of the Mercantile Trust Company, that John Drum was going to get away with it. Charges which I want, now that I am in it—I have never been in it since this Board of Supervisors passed the resolution last December appointing three of your own number, three war veterans, three Trustees, and you included the Mayor. And I took hold of that, and I struggled, as that committee of ten did, to try and arrive at a solution of this problem and try and bring amity out of what appears to be years of bitterness, over a great public project. I went to get these facts together The statement that I issued was to the effect that I did not wish to put you in a jam on the eve of an election. And there is nothing in my statement that I was going to have a show-down with you today, or

anything to that effect, except a kindly statement that we would let
the matter lay over until after election, so it would not be dragged
in, which, I think, had the approval of the members of the Board.
Now, these charges cannot go unanswered. And they will not go un-
answered, so far as I am concerned, with the highest respect, the
loftiest dignity and honor to the veteran organizations, and my
tribute at all times to them. But when charges are made like this
against honest citizens of this city, and spread broadcast throughout
the Nation, it is about time that an honest statement was made of the
situation. And if I may have that help, we will proceed immediately
to dig up the information, Mr. Havenner, which you have just suggested, that there is other data which is not in my possession.

SUPERVISOR HAVENNER: Mr. Mayor, I am going to ask that
your request be approved, and in so moving, there is just one issue
that has been raised here, which, I think, is unfair to this Board, and
which ought to be clarified in the public mind. The statement has
been made from various sources, and published in the press, that if
there were not immediate action on the confirmation of a Board of
Trustees, which I heartily desire, the construction of the War Memorial would be delayed by that very failure at this moment. Well,
those of us who are on the Board and who are familiar with the fiscal
affairs of the city, Mr. Mayor, know that that is not the fact. At this
moment we all know that we could not sell our bonds, not even if we
had a Board in operation which recommended their sale tomorrow.
And there is not in the War Memorial fund sufficient money to carry
out the recommendations of the present private Board of War Memorial Trustees, and permit those bonds to be taken by the contractor.
So we are up against a financial problem which faces the entire country, and in which San Francisco is not in a unique position. We are
facing a national situation in the bond market. So that even if the
appointment of the War Memorial Trustees should be delayed a few
weeks, which I trust it will not be, we will not be contributing to any
delay in the construction of the project. I move that the Mayor's request be approved.

SUPERVISOR POWERS: I second that motion.

SUPERVISOR SCHMIDT: I desire to second the motion made by
Supervisor Havenner, that the necessary help be given to you to obtain all information pertaining to the War Memorial.

SUPERVISOR POWERS: I am in favor of that motion, but I
would like to have one remark which is being spread throughout San
Francisco clarified, and that is that. this Board of Supervisors is
responsible for digging the two holes across the street. which you and
every member of this Board of Supervisors realizes that this
Board of Supervisors had nothing to do with digging the two holes
across the street. which we are now being charged with. and I think
that should be straightened out in the public's mind throughout San
Francisco.

THE MAYOR: All in favor of giving the Mayor the necessary help,
an attorney from the City Attorney's office to cooperate with Judge
Smith and what clerical help I need to compile a full and complete
statement of this matter, will please say aye.

(Ayes). Contrary minded, no. (No response.) The ayes have it, and
it is unanimously adopted.

SUPERVISOR ANDRIANO: I desire to inquire whether a copy of
that communication which appeared in the public press was sent to
this Board by the veterans?

THE MAYOR: I do not know, I have not been honored with a
copy, so I do not know whether any of you have it or not.

SUPERVISOR HAVENNER: Mr. Mayor, I have inquired of the
Clerk and I understand that it has not been, I want it to be understood, of course, that this statement is not of an official nature, and
that the members of the Board were not aware of its preparation
and knew nothing about it until it appeared in the press.

THE MAYOR: The slightest courtesy would prompt sending a copy of those communications to the Board of Supervisors and to the Mayor. I am reading from the press.

SUPERVISOR TONER: Mr. Mayor, might I ask you the date of the communication which was read by you and which appears in the morning papers, if there is a date on it? The Chronicle has the full text of the letter, Mr. Mayor.

THE MAYOR: It has no date, appearing in the Chronicle, nor the abbreviated text of it in the Examiner. And now permit me to proceed. There are so many matters in this full text requiring a reply, of bad faith being charged, Mr. John Drum's name being mentioned, charges of extravagnce and waste and practically dishonesty and mismanagement, four men reappointed. The only member of the original Board that is on this list that I have named and presented to you for confirmation is Herbert Fleishhacker. Mr. Crocker and McKee and Mr. Walter Martin and others who live down the peninsula were ineligible by reason of the fact that the act provides that they must be residents of the City and County of San Francisco. And the only one of the original trustees in securing the first $2,000,000 was Herbert Fleishhacker. Mr. Kingsbury never was on it as a trustee. Mr. James——

SUPERVISOR RONCOVIERI (interrupting): Mr. Mayor, Mr. Drum was.

THE MAYOR: Mr. Drum's name has not been submitted to this Board. Mr. Drum's name is not amongst the 11 submitted.

SUPERVISOR RONCOVIERI: That is true.

THE MAYOR: Mr. Bentley was head of the Musicial Association, never met or a member of the Board that raised the first $2,000,000. And yet the headlines say that four men were reappointed. And then reference is made to the President sending nominations to Congress. Why, the President never yet has sent nominations to Congress of a group, such as the Farm Board, an agricultural group, but what they have discussed the names of the men singly, and if there is one upon the group that is not satisfactory, the whole Board is not turned down. And it is these points brought out in this open letter that I want now, for your benefit, and my benefit, and for the citizens of San Francisco knowledge of what the facts are, I want to present it in a proper form.

Now, as a matter of fact, one thing that you want to keep in mind is that the County Council of the American Legion had a committee of 16 members functioning for two years on the plans, going over them carefully, and this committee, or 14 of them, or this committee of 16, had full power to act, and they approved the plans now in the hands of the Board of Trustees; that is, 14 of them, and the plans have got their signatures, and their signatures are attached, and the plans are now in the hands of the Board of Trustees. I am trying to borrow those plans, if I can, with the 14 original signatures signed to those plans, in whose hands they were for over two years' time.

SUPERVISOR SCHMIDT: With reference to those plans, it was charged, before this Board, that the original plans that the veterans signed had been changed, and they were entirely different than the altered plans that are now in effect.

THE MAYOR: Now, Mr. Schmidt, I am giving you just a preliminary report, for your good as well as mine, to let the public know today that there are some points involved in this matter, so they won't get a wrong impression of what the actual facts are. The plans were changed ten feet, but it did not take a square foot away from the purposes of the War Memorial nor the activities of the veterans. The halls were narrowed slightly, but every inch is still there on those plans. And then a new committee was appointed because they could not agree, and you had three members of your honorable Board, Mr. McSheehy, Mr. Colman and Mr. Havenner, representing you at all of the meetings of the Board, when held.

SUPERVISOR SCHMIDT: Mr. Mayor, I was going to state that it would be well if we could get that transcript of the statements made by the various veterans for your information. It would be well for you to go over that, because there were a lot of statements made that would help you out in your investigations.

THE MAYOR: I now ask for that statement, which I have a memorandum of. Will the Board authorize the reporter to compile for you and for me a full statement of the transcript taken the day the hearing was held before you?

SUPERVISOR SCHMIDT: I so move, Mr. Mayor, that a transcript be made.

SUPERVISOR HAVENNER: I will second that motion.

THE MAYOR: It has been moved and seconded that the reporter compile a full statement of what transpired when the names of the Mayor's appointments were before the Board for consideration.

SUPERVISOR HAVENNER: And for your further guidance, Mr. Mayor, if you have no objection, I think it would be worth while to have transcribed for your benefit the proceedings before this Board, in committee, some time last year, when the entire Board of War Memorial Trustees appeared here and the representatives of the veterans, to discuss the plans that were then under consideration, if you have no objection. I think there was a fuller discussion on that particular evening than on any other occasion, Mr. Mayor.

SUPERVISOR SCHMIDT: I second the motion.

THE MAYOR: All in favor of the motions made that a full transcript be made of the hearings here when the nominations were before the Board, and also at the meeting referred to by Supervisor Havenner, all in favor will please say aye. (Ayes.) Contrary no. (No response.) The ayes have it and it is unanimously carried. I want to call your attention to the fact, so that the public may know it as a preliminary report, that in all three banks, not one bank, all told, there was not more than two hundred to three hundred thousand dollars out of the $2,000,000. They were in three banks, not one; they were in the Anglo, the Crocker and the American. And the reason that the money was put in those banks was to pay running expenses, architect's fees, appraisements, and one thing and another, as an operating fund.

And another matter that I want to call the people's attention to is that the people who gratuitously subscribed the two million dollars had four years to pay it in, and some of them are still paying. This money which was subscribed and collected was the property of the Regents of the University of California, and placed in their hands as Trustees. A portion of the money, approximately two hundred to three hundred thousand dollars, was held to pay current expenses, such as purchasing property, about 30 parcels, and Mr. Phillips and Mr. Dunnigan, the Clerk, did most of the negotiating, the appraisers were——

THE CLERK (interrupting): Mr. Phillips was not in it at all.

THE MAYOR: Well, Mr. Dunnigan has the honor.

THE CLERK: No, it is not a matter of honor, it is a matter of record. The Trustees and the California Title Company carried on the transactions and I sent for the owners, that is all I did.

＊　　＊　　＊　　＊　　＊　　＊　　＊　　＊　　＊　　＊

THE MAYOR: There were about 30 parcels purchased in this block across the street here, and Mr. Dunnigan did most of the negotiating. The appraisers were representatives of banks, insurance companies and real estate firms, all well qualified.

THE CLERK: The appraisers were the Real Estate Board.

THE MAYOR: The Real Estate Board, and done under the supervision of the Board of Supervisors. Now, I respectfully call your attention to the fact that when you desired to merge the $2,000.000 with the $4,000,000 you passed the necessary legislation here so that it could be merged, and the War Memorial, for which there was not sufficient money, and the Opera House, for which there was $2,000,000, could go hand in hand, and two blocks of land acquired. The block on the corner, you remember, was leased to a van and storage company, and that we had a lot of difficulty in getting them to go off the land, and the Standard Oil was on the corner, and the trustees of the private fund advanced to the City $500,000 in cash in order that that block could be purchased, and the two blocks then lie side by side, so that this beautiful War Memorial could be built as two buildings, on one side, with the closing of Fulton street.

Now, this circular was broadcasted by the thousands: "A War Memorial with no veterans is no War Memorial. Vote no on Charter Amendment Number 32. Citizens of San Francisco, war veterans speaking for themselves, through their nationally recognized organizations, remind you that your bond issue of $4,000,000, asked in the name of war veterans, was intended primarily to provide a real War Memorial as a tribute to deceased veterans of all wars, and as headquarters for San Francisco war veterans. Amendment 32 means that war veterans have no assurance of a voice in the construction, arrangement, management or control of the War Memorial, and they have been promised since 1919 a Memorial which was to provide a permanent headquarters for veterans of all wars. Amendment 32 means that war veterans have no assurance that the employees in the Veterans' Building or the War Memorial will be honorably discharged war veterans. Amendment 32 means that the entire War Memorial project, as well as the control and administration thereof, may be in the hands of a group of people interested, primarily, in an Opera House and Art Museum, without regard to the wishes, desires or needs of the war veterans. Those who submitted Amendment 32"—this is the Board of Supervisors—"those who submitted Amendment 32 did not consult any of the major war veterans' organizations. They did not permit a suggestion or recommendation from any major war veteran organization. They did not, in fact, even notify any major war veteran organization of their intention to submit this amendment. Amendment 32 was presented at the last possible moment, within an hour of midnight, too late for any public hearings to be held. The war veterans' name and their cause have been and now are being used in an attempt to control and dominate an alleged War Memorial for the primary purpose of securing an Opera House and an Art Museum. Vote no on Amendment 32."

Now, permit me to read to you an editorial which——

SUPERVISOR RONCOVIERI (interrupting):   What was Amendment 32, please? What was it, definitely?

THE MAYOR: It is what we are working on now.

SUPERVISOR RONCOVIERI: Creating the Trustees?

THE MAYOR: Yes, everything, and the people carried that by a very substantial majority.

In yesterday morning's Examiner, dated San Francisco, October 13, 1929, there appears an article, written by Redfern Mason, the title of which is: "Speedy Solution of the War Memorial Difficulty Needed."

"It seems a thousand pities that there should be so much delay about the building of the War Memorial. Opera and Symphony are homeless; we have not, in the whole of San Francisco, a hall which is worthy of the high ministry of music.

"One thing some of the disputants in this matter seem to lose sight of. The War Memorial is not and never will be the property of the Musical Association, the Opera Association, or the American Legion. It is the property of the people of San Francisco, and of them alone. Theirs is the interest to be considered before all others, and they it is who ought to have the dominating voice in its administration.

"Two million dollars were subscribed by private donation to make the Memorial, for which that money was given, an actuality. The

purpose, as set forth in the deed by which the University of California
was made recipient of the funds, was 'To honor the soldiers, sailors,
marines and war workers, men and women, who brought imperishable
glory by their splendid contribution to the World War.'

"But the two millions was insufficient, and the citizens of San Francisco voted $4,000,000 'to complete the War Memorial.' The total,
$6,000,000, is available, or will be available, when the actual work is
undertaken.

"Meanwhile the Opera waits and the Symphony hopes against hope;
but nothing is done.

"The official representatives of the American Legion, which in San
Francisco numbers about 4,000 out of a total of 40,000 war veterans,
demand a majority of six out of the eleven members of the Board of
Trustees. Mayor Rolph gave them five; but his recommendation has
been rejected by the Board of Supervisors.

"So things are at an impasse and meanwhile the people of San
Francisco suffer.

"Looking at the ideal which the Memorial is intended to serve
brings to light the fact that one element is entirely unrepresented
among the Trustees. That element is the war workers, the men and
women of the Red Cross, the two 'Y's,' the Knights of Columbus, the
Jewish Welfare Board and Salvation Army. If the Mayor would
nominate some representative citizen from among these bodies he
might very well act as a moderator and harmonizer to bring the
other elements of the board into organic unity. Such a man would
not be unacceptable to the Legion, for the war workers were
veritably brothers and sisters to them during the fighting. On the
other hand, they would not be swayed by allegiance to any body
which, by its nature, may become political.

"Some of the veterans think of the War Memorial in too narrow
terms. Its purpose is to honor the dead, indeed: but the best way
to do that is help the living. The memorial will last for centuries;
the Legion will march away within a few decades. But their children will remain, and their children's children. It is they whom
the Memorial is intended to benefit. Its purpose is, through the
gentle ministrations of art, to bring up a generation that shall have
outgrown the brutalities of war.

"As far as actual space is concerned, the Legionaires are well
taken care of. They have the use of 105,000 square feet, which is
equal to a building 100 feet long and as many broad, ten stories
high. True, the Legion building has a total content of 155,109
square feet, but 49,322 square feet are to be devoted to the art
museum. But the museum is for the veterans just as much as it
is for the civilian. The same is true of the opera house. But the
Legion has this advantage over the opera and the symphony that,
whereas the musical organizations will have to pay whenever they
use the Memorial, the Legion gets its quarters for nothing.

"Moreover, the $2,000,000 of the original donation is not the
only contribution of the private citizens. They pay their quota of
the bond issue, and, seeing that the richest people in the community
were among their number, it follows that their contribution is cor-
respondingly large.

"As for the crticisms passed on the building, it must not be forgotten that last year the plans received the formal approval of the
Legion. Here is a copy of that approval:

" 'This set of plans, consisting of five sheets, is hereby approved
by the San Francisco Posts of the American Legion. Signed, San
Francisco, California, March 19, 1928, American Legion War Memorial Committee, James B. Burns.' And the plans bear the names
of the representatives of fourteen of then existing posts.

"In fifty years San Francisco will probably have a population of
two million people. To place the War Memorial under the control

of any organization whatsoever would be unjust to the populace as a whole. The Memorial is a people's Memorial, not a Legion Memorial. When America went to war the whole people participated, though only the enlisted men fought on the field. To the whole people, therefore, the War Memorial belongs and the domination of their interest should be assured on the Board of Trustees."

Gentlemen, as a preliminary report on this matter I leave this preliminary statement of facts in the hands of the reporter, and in due time, with the help you have given me this morning, I will make you a full and completed report. I will not drag the matter into the issues of the campaign at this time; I will not embarrass any of you, or anybody else, over it, but I will take the responsibility of giving you a report, a fair report, an unbiased report, and in the report pay the highest possible tribute to the men and to the women and to all who served their country when their country needed them the most.

October 14, 1929 (Continued)--

Of course, the name of Mr. John S. Drum was not submitted to the Board of Supervisors, and the private Board of Trustees have at no time requested me to delay the appointment of the War Memorial Trustees authorized by the people of the City and County of San Francisco under Charter Amendment No. 32. The suggestion was made by some, whom I do not recall, that the veterans should get together and approve a workable plan for space necessary for their needs and that the new Board of Trustees to be appointed under Amendment No. 32 be given the whole matter with a definite plan to work on. To date this has not been done.

The veteran organizations have, from what I have been able to learn from the various meetings with their representatives and the present War Memorial Trustees, changed their demands from time to time so that when definite space was agreed upon and plans and specifications drawn they would be disapproved. While it is true the War Memorial is to be an opera house and a war veterans' building, the whole project belongs to the people of San Francisco. It is the people's money that will build it to honor the war veterans of all American wars.

The Mayor submitted a list of representative citizens of San Francisco to the Board of Supervisors. The veterans objected to them. The Board of Supervisors of this City and County, at the insistence of the veterans, refused to confirm the list because the veterans had indicated they would withdraw their support at the polls for any Supervisor who refused to vote against any list the Mayor may submit if it did not contain a majority of veterans. The answer is clear. The members of the veteran organizations desire to manage the construction of a project voted by the people for the honor and convenience of the veterans of all wars and to be under the full control of their own Board of War Memorial Trustees also authorized to represent the whole people.

The present plans exceeded the amount provided by the $4,000,-000 bond issue.

The veterans have charged the present War Memorial Board of Trustees with "Gross inefficiency, waste and mismanagement." Yet the financial report of their status, certified by public accountants, shows competence, efficiency and careful management. This certified account follows hereafter (on page 177).

I urgently appeal to you to confirm the War Memorial Trustees I have nominated and submited to you, and that a war memorial, memorial court and opera house be forthwith started, and if the veterans want something providing more space that they appear before the War Memorial Trustees and work out a financial plan whereby their additional requests may be promptly satisfied.

The Supervisors have passed a resolution at the request of the veterans which recommends that the Mayor appoint a majority of veterans as Trustees of the War Memorial. The act of the people creating the War Memorial did not so provide. The people of this City empowered the Mayor to appoint a Board of War Memorial Trustees, to be confirmed by the Board of Supervisors, and in the naming of said Board due consideration is to be given veterans of all American wars.

November 15, 1929. Representatives of various Legion Posts met in the Mayor's office, specifically urging that the Mayor eliminate the names of Major Charles H. Kendrick and Supervisor Jesse C. Colman from the list submitted to the Board of Supervisors.

Your Honorable Board is hereby requested to provide space for storage of the records of the Trustees of the War Memorial in a vacant room on the fourth floor of the City Hall and to permit them to use for convenience the Board chambers at such times as you may not require same.

December 3, 1929. The following letter was received by me from Senator James D. Phelan, and former Mayor of San Francisco:

"JAMES D. PHELAN
760 MARKET STREET
SAN FRANCISCO, CALIFORNIA.
                              "December 3, 1929.

"Honorable James Rolph, Jr., Mayor, San Francisco—

"My Dear Mr. Mayor:

"I have followed the newspaper reports concerning the embarrassment which you apparently have experienced, through the opposition of certain members of the American Legion to the personnel of the Memorial Trustees appointed by you, and whose names were presented to the Board of Supervisors for confirmation.

"I was glad to see that you would not yield to their unreasonable demands. I think that Major Charles H. Kendrick and Colonel Jesse C. Colman are men of such fine character, sound judgment, public spirit and proven capacity that it would be nothing less than a calamity for you to surrender your position. You were authorized by law to name the Trustees, and you have made an excellent selection.

"As you know, I am interested in art as represented by the theater, the museum and the gallery, which give pleasure to and gratify the higher aspirations of the people. In that spirit I contributed to the original citizens' fund for the Memorial Buildings. I now believe that if the Trustees of that fund surrender to the demand of an unauthorized body, not even pretending to promote the public benefit, but their own, it would be a betrayal, and it probably could be stopped by the courts. It is so purely selfish that the people resent it.

"As I understood the citizens' fund, it was to be used principally for an opera house and museum. It was never intended to make it a clubhouse for preferred individuals.

"As I have great regard and appreciation for veterans who have fought under the flag, I deplore the fact that some of them—who certainly cannot be called representative of all—seek to mar the generous purpose of our citizens in privately contributing to the fund and recently voting to increase it.

"I have known Major Kendrick many years. He entered the service as a volunteer; was wounded in action and decorated. Col. Colman, also a volunteer, has an honorable record, and both of these gentlemen have been in the public service and are intimately known to you. The people have learned to trust them. You should not withdraw such names as these and thus greatly impoverish your Board, which shall make very large expenditures and are charged with grave responsibilities. I am convinced that most of the veterans of our wars, if they had a voice, would disapprove of your surrendering your judgment.

"Very truly yours,
"(Signed) JAMES D. PHELAN."

January 20, 1930. At the regular meeting of the Board of Supervisors on the afternoon of Monday, January 20, 1930, there was discussed the War Memorial matter, entitled in the shorthand reporter's transcript "Appointment of War Memorial Trustees." At the close of the meeting the Mayor said that, after he has had a conference with the veterans, he will call a special meeting on this important matter, and said transcript is attached hereto and made a part hereof.

THE MAYOR: This is the one included in your motion——

SUPERVISOR PEYSER (interrupting): If you will pardon the interruption, your Honor, I again in view of the importance of this matter, and in view of the fact that you and some of the members of the Board have been here over 12 hours, and that a number of our citizens and members of the various Veteran organizations have been here and desire to see action taken in this matter, and, further, in view of the fact that they are willing to submit this matter to the Board now or at any time, I now move for a call of the Board and ask if you are willing to have that call of the Board made while you are continuing your reading of your report?

SUPERVISOR SPAULDING: Second that motion.

SUPERVISOR HAVENNER (interrupting): I must strenuously oppose that motion, he is not going to be here after 10:00 o'clock, and it is going to be physically impossible to finish out a call of the Board within two hours. I personally know of one member who is not within call at this time, and furthermore, I intend to discuss this question myself, and I know there are other members who intend to discuss it before it comes to a vote. Now, I have sat here all night, and I would say that out of courtesy to the Mayor, because he is entitled to the closing argument in the matter, we should not try to force this through now. I am not going to state my position is now where it was before, I am going to discuss it and I am going to object to anyone leaving here now while you make a call of the Board. You won't get anybody here within two hours. For what purpose do you want a call of the Board now? In order that we may have a continuous session? To what purpose? We can have an orderly session at another time——

THE MAYOR (interrupting): May I clarify the situation to a little extent? I am simply submitting to you facts of record. I haven't begun to discuss the matter at all as yet. You understand that. Nobody has had an opportunity to discuss it, the veterans will have an opportunity and the Board will have an opportunity. When I finish here, I would suggest that the Clerk be ordered to have it printed at once, and when it is ready and the Board reconvenes—or you can take a vote right now. I am willing to stay with it all day——

SUPERVISOR McSHEEHY (interrupting): If your Honor please, a minute ago I understood your Honor was almost closing, that there were only a few pages more, that you were close to the close. I know there is no attempt on the part of Supervisor Peyser to ask that this matter be taken into the hands of the Board for a vote——

SUPERVISOR HAVENNER (interrupting): That's what a call of the Board means. That's what you intended, wasn't it?

SUPERVISOR PEYSER: Yes, sir, I believe the matter

should be settled, it has been pending for eight or nine years and been thoroughly discussed, and the veterans have been sitting here all night, and they are willing to submit it to the Board without argument. As far as the Board itself is concerned, I have no desire to stifle the Board, but we are here now, let's finish it, and then we are through.

THE MAYOR: You do what you please, but when I get to arguing the charges that have been made against me and against my nominations which I have made, I will have something to say, no matter who it hurts or who it hits; I won't stand this responsibility for 12 years——

SUPERVISOR McSHEEHY (interrupting): Members of the Board, I sincerely hope this motion won't be pressed. I hope the Mayor will be allowed to continue; he has just stated he will finish in a half hour or so——

THE MAYOR: I will finish this, but I will promise you that when the argument comes, I will have the last word.

SUPERVISOR McSHEEHY: I would say this, members of the Board, and your Honor, why not continue and when you have finished your message, then you can take the matter up.

THE MAYOR: You are about through with the statement of facts, and you will come in just a few minutes to the financial statement.

SUPERVISOR PEYSER: Your Honor, I am not, as a matter of fact, my motion was made with the understanding that the Mayor would proceed while the motion was enforced. I have no desire whatsoever to prevent the Mayor from proceeding, and that in the meantime we might proceed with the call of the Board and thereafter come to a vote. However, if the members desire, I would be willing to withdraw my motion with the understanding that the meeting recess until tonight at 8 o'clock, or whatever time is convenient to all. I intend to put this thing through, not hurriedly, but we should get it behind us. If we have a meeting tonight at 8 o'clock, I am willing to withdraw my motion.

SUPERVISOR McSHEEHY: I would say this, members of the Board, I yield to no man in attempting to put this through, but allow the Mayor to proceed and finish, and when he has finished, then some motion will prevail that we will agree upon.

THE MAYOR: You will get the financial report from me in a half hour.

SUPERVISOR McSHEEHY: I would ask that the Mayor be permitted to proceed.

SUPERVISOR PEYSER: I withdraw my motion.

SUPERVISOR SPAULDING: I withdraw the second.

EXHIBIT No. 6

IN RE APPOINTMENT OF WAR MEMORIAL TRUSTEES.

Monday, January 20, 1930, 2 o'clock p. m.

The regular meeting of the Board of Supervisors of the City and County of San Francisco was held on Monday, the 20th day of January, 1930, beginning at the hour of 2 o'clock p. m. of that day in the chambers of the Board, City Hall, San Francisco, California.

Mayor James Rolph, Jr., presided.

After the transaction of other business the following proceedings were had in relation to the appointment of the War Memorial Trustees.

SUPERVISOR SHANNON: Mr. Mayor, I would like to call to the attention of the Health Committee the condition in the lots across the way from the City Hall. It is no laughing matter, Mr. Mayor; it is a very serious matter. Boys are wading in the pond over there, and there is a green scum on the water, and they have little floats that they are using in there, and yesterday a friend of mine told me, while standing viewing the boys playing in there, a mosquito lit on his head. Now, we all know that mosquitos are the carriers of disease, and if that property was owned by a private individual, the Health Committee would be after that individual at once to have him clean that up. And I would like to have the Health Committee take notice of this and call it to the attention of the Health Officer so that the proper steps be taken to fix those lots over there so that the water will not accumulate and cause this condition to exist.

SUPERVISOR TONER: We will do it right away.

SUPERVISOR HAYDEN: While on that subject, I would like to ask your Honor what is the status of the appointment of the War Memorial Trustees which is now pending in your office?

THE MAYOR: Well, I have promised the Trustees that I would submit to them and show them my completed report on the whole War Memorial matter from its beginning up to the present time, together with the Certified Public Accountant's report on the finances. But it is impossible to sell the $4,000,000 worth of bonds. I do not know the temper of the Board with regard to the appointees. I have submitted eleven names. I have some letters, very strong letters, urging me to resubmit to this Board those eleven fine outstanding men whom I named several months ago. It is a difficult thing for me to turn down any one of them. The Board has turned them down. Resolutions are being passed by organizations which are being formed, representing the Veterans, condemning the action of the committee of the Veterans in their opposition to the names submitted by the Mayor. Now, resolutions are being passed, they are coming to my office, some of the vets who are not on the committee demand that it be built, demand that I resubmit to you those eleven names, and it will be up to you and the burden will be upon you whether or not you accept those eleven names or say which ones you will not accept, and that the War Memorial work go on. Now, I have completed my work up to the minute. If the $4,000,000 worth of bonds were salable and the work could go on, I would bring the report in to you, after a meeting with the Veterans which I promised first, immediately. If you say you will confirm the eleven names I gave to you that you have turned down, I will submit them this afternoon. Now, pending that action and until I know the temper of this Board, because I do not want to slaughter good men's names, men in this community who have served their city, who are honored men and respected men, who have fought, who have honored and been decorated in the service of their country. There is no delay on the part of the Mayor. But it is a difficult thing for the Mayor to yield when there is a feeling against one or two men, and a demand made by this Board of Supervisors, pre-election promises, that you would not confirm the names unless there were six veterans on the board. Now, where am I going to get? You ask me the situation. Some man attempted to cover, in a coffin, a redwood box, a wax figure, thinking it was the burial of the War Memorial. Now, we know who did that, and the Board of Works took the redwood coffin, with the wax figure in it, and was going to send it to the door of the man who put it in there. But we did not want to do anything like that because we treat this matter seriously, and it is a serious proposition.

SUPERVISOR HAYDEN: Where did you find that?

THE MAYOR: Over here off the sidewalk Now, there is a lot I could tell you, and I do not want to break my promise because I never break a promise when it comes to a matter of that kind. And I want to have this meeting. But my office is now deluged with resolutions, unanimously adopted by Veterans of the World War, of the Spanish-American War, and other organizations, demanding that the Mayor resubmit the eleven names that he submitted, and that they be confirmed by the Board and the work go on. Now, if you will remember, I did not want to submit those eleven names, but a resolution was passed in here, and the Veterans demanded that I submit the names, and I said it was only going to bring trouble. And I said that the committee appointed by your honorable Board, the three from the Veterans and the three others and myself, a committee of ten, struggle with this problem until we agreed upon it before passing a resolution, demanding that I immediately bring in here eleven names just to be slaughtered. I have a letter from Senator Phelan that, when you hear it, it is a masterpiece and answers the question one hundred per cent, but I cannot read it to you now, and I have had it since early December, in order to keep my face with the three gentlemen, Mr. Claridge, Mr. Boyd and Mr. Glensor. There is where it rests at the present time and I work every night, from eight o'clock at night until two and three o'clock in the morning, signing those Spring Valley bonds, and I simply have not had time to call a meeting at night, nor to call a meeting in the daytime, but I will call it just as soon as I finish those bonds. And when the bond market reaches par and accrued interest, and the $4,000,000 worth of bonds can be sold, I will have a meeting the minute that point is reached and I will immediately report to you thereafter. That is the situation.

SUPERVISOR GALLAGHER: I am not going into the question of the integrity or standing of the men you appointed, nor am I going to rehash the question of the wisdom or unwisdom of your appointees. If you think, in view of the changed personnel of this Board, if it is legally possible that the resubmission of those names will facilitate the erection of the Memorial, I, for one, would have no objection to the resubmission. As I say, there is a legal procedure involved. Secondly, if, as I understand it, you promise a report to the Board on this subject matter, I do not know whether you set a date or not, I thought you did——

THE MAYOR (interrupting): No, I did not.

SUPERVISOR GALLAGHER: We should like to have it. Very well. The three, three, three committee has never made a report except one brief report here, verbally, since their appointment. They were not to report to his Honor the Mayor, they were to report to the Board, if you will recollect the terms of the motion by which they were appointed.

THE MAYOR: But they did report and were discharged by the Board in writing, too.

SUPERVISOR GALLAGHER: If they did I am ignorant of it. Is that the fact, Mr. Clerk?

THE CLERK: I do not recall all the details of that discussion.

SUPERVISOR COLMAN: I cannot remember, there are many committee reports.

SUPERVISOR GALLAGHER: It is quite likely you may be in error. It may be while we were away, some of us, but as my recollection serves me, Mr. Mayor, a report was made here, verbally one day, and that is all, and it was not a report, it was just an explanation. Now, there is something in what you say, that the bonds may not be immediately salable at this time, but the day is coming shortly, and very shortly, if we are to believe the financial prognosticators, when they will be salable. You ought to, in my judgment—and I say this in a kindly spirit—complete your chain of events involved in this matter, one of which was, as I understand it, that you thought you might adjust it, and, in any event, you were to hold a meeting with the Veterans' County Board in the meantime. I think that ought to be done and soon, and I will state the reason for it presently. If, as I say, you feel that you can legally resubmit the names that you had in prospect for appointment, and you believe there may be a change in the vote here, certainly I shall be the last one to offer an objection. I am moving to this point: it is conceivable that a number of the members of the Board will not change their positions. And you do not know, unless you care to canvass the Board privately——

THE MAYOR (interrupting): I have not done so.

SUPERVISOR GALLAGHER: It is your right, of course.

THE MAYOR: But I have not done it.

SUPERVISOR GALLAGHER: However, unless—and this is not said threateningly; it is said perhaps as the ultimate answer to the mixed position in which your office and our own find ourselves, and our inability to reach an agreement. If, however, in the near future—and I should say that that won't be long—some solution, looking to permitting whoever is appointed to go on their way and commence to do the things they are legalized to do under the ordinance, I am of the opinion that you will face a special election on the question at issue. The builders of San Francisco and the mechanics of San Francisco are not, I frankly state, much concerned about the differences existing between the names that are to be appointed, as between yourself and the Board. They are, however, vitally concerned over the fact that four odd million dollars and more can be turned loose in San Francisco to give work to hundreds of mechanics, with hundreds of thousands of dollars spent for materials, and, therefore, giving work, indirectly, to a great number of other people, and they are inclined, unless our differences can be settled—and I hope they can be—either through this Board, or if it can be obtained privately, or not privately, to prepare a petition which will compel a solution and a settlement of the question. I do not blame them myself. The logic of their position is unquestionable, they are not accountable for the fact that we disagree. We might have our own conscientous belief, you yours and we ours, but at the same time they think that, unless we can reconcile our differences and operations start, not actual buildings, it is true, but the legal operations looking to the sale of the bonds when the market is ready, which ought to be very shortly, and these are a kind of bond that will appeal, both to the heart and to the head—they are of the opinion that steps must be taken to get this money in circulation. Now, that is not a criticism of your appointments, nor of your Honor, nor of your policy, nor is it altogether one of the Board's. They realize that this is apparently a static condition, that the Board—the last Board, at least—and the Mayor, have reached apparently a deadlock on an issue that might seem simple, but which does not appear to be so. And so I would plead with you, sir, too, in view of the fact that the Board has remained silent on it up to this moment while you are making up your mind as to the future policy to be pursued and to be presented, I would appeal to you, sir, and I think, while I am not an official and while I am not a member in any sense, that I have a right to speak, but I think I would not be rebuked in my appeal to you to call such meetings, as in your judgment should be called, to announce to the Board the exact position in which you find yourself, to place, either of reaffirmation or of new affirmation or of rejection, before the Board, and then, perhaps, it may have to be taken out of your hands and the issue, the only issue apparently at present, withholding the legal steps looking to actual operations, may have to be taken on the outside. I would hate to see it done. You speak of men on that committee that you have appointed. I would like just this brief word; there is not a doubt about their splendid ability, their service to the community and their standing. The issue is not that. I am not going into it academically. You have one man appointed on there that his name presented singly to me for any position that I know of that he would care to take, I would most enthusiastically support him. I just give his name as an example—and the others are in like character—Charles Kendrick, for instance. I would not raise a finger to hurt either his reputation, his feelings or his standing. But he is presented with others on an issue entirely different. Now, I wish to close what I have to say by saying I plead with you, as one member of this Board, to, if you will, please, bring the matter forward at the earliest possible date, to the end that the issues either be resubmitted here in the Board, or between us, or an opportunity might be presented to decide by vote of the people.

THE MAYOR: Now, Mr. Gallagher, in replying to you, I thank

you for all you have said. I have a very difficult situation in hand,
a most difficult. It is very unfortunate the Board, for the first time
in the history of the Board of Supervisors of this City, put into that
charter amendment that the names submitted by the Mayor had to
be confirmed by the Board of Supervisors. Now, that was not necessary. You know I would not appoint, on a great trust like that, anybody but the best and outstanding men of the community to carry
that project through. Now, I am threatened with the resignation of
the whole eleven. I am threatened with every kind of disaster
to that enterprise. I am threatened with the refusal of the Board of
Regents of the University of California to turn over that money. That
money is in their hands and that property over there stands in
their hands, and to whoever it is turned over to the provisions provide that they must be satisfactory to the Regents of the University of California. Those eleven men were all acceptable to the
Regents of the University of California. Now, you cannot knock
and go about knocking, questioning the honor and integrity and the
honesty of those men. You cannot write letters calling them practically thieves and robbers. You cannot write a letter to Mr. William
H. Crocker, within the last three weeks, the most disrespectful, most
dishonorable, most outrageous, blasphemous letter that I ever read,
was sent to Mr. Crocker, trying to prove that Mr. Crocker got away
with money in the handling of the finances. You cannot attack men
like John Drum, and charge John Drum with owning the property
because it stood in the name of the Mercantile Trust Company of
California. You cannot do those things and have men like Kenneth
Kingsbury and General Hunter Liggett and Crocker—he cannot serve
because it provides that none but residents of San Francisco can
serve—you cannot attack Robert I. Bentley, and expect those men to
serve the City and go through what they have gone through in abuse
and charges of theft and dishonesty. And I sent for Mr. Claridge the
morning after a copy of that letter came to me, and I was mad about
it because I have had enough trouble of this thing, more than any
proposition I have had since I have been Mayor, and I asked him
what right he had to write such a letter as that to one of our representative citizens of San Francisco, who had put up the most money
of the private contributions for this War Memorial. I said, it is the
most outrageous letter that ever was written. I said, "What did you
write such a thing as that for when I am trying to solve this problem
with all the diplomacy that I have got?" Well, he said he did not
write it. "Well," I said, "who did write it?" "I cannot tell you who
wrote it because one of my superior officers wrote the letter." And
when you hear that letter you will be up in arms just as much as I
was when I got a copy of it the next day. You yourself would not
stand for a letter like that being written to Mr. Crocker, or to anybody else, you would not have it written to a street sweeper.

SUPERVISOR HAYDEN: It must be an anonymous letter.

THE MAYOR: No, it was signed by Mr. Claridge, the secretary of
the committee. Mr. Claridge is right here, he has been here all
afternoon. You do not know what I have been up against. Mr. Kingsbury says he does not want to serve, and I have word that none want
to serve, and if one goes, they will all resign. I have been threatened
that they will take back their private subscriptions. Some have said
that, "We gave our money as a War Memorial to build an opera house.
Give us our money back if you are not building any opera house."
I hear it on the street. The Post would not give Mr. Sapiro one day
longer to stay last week when his term of office expired. Not one day
longer and they passed resolutions and overruled him. Now, you ask
me some questions. I am telling you the troubles I have got over
that one.

SUPERVISOR HAYDEN: Can I ask Mr. Claridge if he was responsible for that letter?

THE MAYOR: Yes, you can ask him, but he said "No."

SUPERVISOR HAYDEN: Mr. Claridge, what is your position in connection with the veteran organization?

MR. CLARIDGE: I am secretary of the County Council of the American Legion.

SUPERVISOR HAYDEN: Did you hear the statement just made by his Honor the Mayor?

MR. CLARIDGE: I did.

SUPERVISOR HAYDEN: That an insulting letter was sent to Mr. Crocker over your signature?

MR. CLARIDGE: I heard the statement.

SUPERVISOR HAYDEN: Was it a typewritten signature?

MR. CLARIDGE: No.

SUPERVISOR HAYDEN: Was it in your own handwriting?

MR. CLARIDGE: It was in my own handwriting, I was responsible for the letter, I did not tell the Mayor that I did not write the letter, I told him that the expression of that letter was not mine, but I wrote it because I was instructed to, but nevertheless it contains my personal views, and I also told his Honor the Mayor that that letter had nothing to do with the appointment of the Board of Trustees. It is a matter between the American Legion, as the beneficiary of the trust fund, and a certain group of gentlemen downtown as the custodians of that fund. It is entirely aside from the appointment matter of the Public Board of Trustees. It is a matter that has been pending since October, 1928. The letter was directed to Mr. Crocker, does not concern his Honor the Mayor, does not concern this Board of Supervisors and does not concern anybody but the American Legion and the private Board of Trustees of the San Francisco War Memorial.

SUPERVISOR HAYDEN: A letter of that kind does not serve the purpose the Mayor is trying to bring about, to appoint a Board of Trustees that will be satisfactory to this Board of Supervisors, especially where——

MR. CLARIDGE (interrupting): I will call your Honor's attention to this fact that that letter does not accuse Mr. Crocker of being a thief, of being a robber, and of attempting to get away with funds. I have that letter in my office and my files.

THE MAYOR: I would suggest that you go over to your office and read it to the Board.

MR. CLARIDGE: I will be very glad to bring this letter before the Board at the proper time.

THE MAYOR: Well, do it now.

MR. CLARIDGE: It is not an issue in this Board.

SUPERVISOR HAYDEN: It has been used here; it is in our records.

MR. CLARIDGE: The letter is not a matter in your records.

SUPERVISOR HAYDEN: The Mayor's reference to it is a matter of record now.

MR. CLARIDGE: It is perfectly all right with me; the Mayor's reference is incorrect.

SUPERVISOR POWER: Is Mr. Crocker one of the men that you propose as a director?

THE MAYOR: No, I could not because he is a resident of San Mateo County.

SUPERVISOR POWER: I agree with Mr. Claridge that really the subject matter is not before us at this time. I think that, if you make a new recommendation, as has been suggested by Supervisor Gallagher, I will say, without making any commitment on these trustees, that I am as free as the air. I made no promise to anyone, the veterans' organizations or anyone else, previous to the campaign, and I think it will be well to sound out the sentiment of the six new members of the board.

THE MAYOR: Well, I purposely have not tried to bring this before the Board. I have tried to settle this matter. I will have my promised meeting of the veterans. There is no man thinks

more of the veterans than I do. I am the only civilian in the
United States that has been recognized by the veterans. I am the
Honorary President of the finest fighting division of the war; I
am the Honorary President of the 91st Division, and I am the Honorary President of the 363d, San Francisco's own, that lost 1,284
men out of their own regiment, your own San Francisco regiment,
the greatest number of casualties in the war, whose flags are honored as no other flags are honored in any public building, right
here in the City Hall. No other civilian in the United States has
been honored as I have been honored by them, and I am trying
my best to please the veterans, to show them every courtesy and
to give them the greatest honor. I take my hat off to them and
to their flags every time I pass them; I glory in them, and as long
as I live I will thank them, and tell my children following me to
thank them for the services they have rendered their country. But
they keep putting me in a position where the Mayor cannot put
in front of the Board of Supervisors, a body of eleven outstanding
men in this city. Some of them will naturally pass on; time may
bring six; I do not care in the future if the whole eleven are veterans of the World War or any of the wars of our country; possibly they will be; I will be glad to see it. I have been advised,
by members of this Board and by others, "Mayor, at least when you
start this matter off, put somebody on the eleven trustees that
knows something about the War Memorial from its beginning—
how it started, who has handled the funds, who has contributed
and given confidence to the Regents of the University of Cáli-
fornia." If I had my way, and I could pick out eleven, I would.
But I must appoint General Hunter Liggett; I must appoint Kenneth Kingsbury, one of the largest subscribers to the fund; I must
appoint Robert I Bentley, the head of the Musical Association of
San Francisco; I must appoint Herbert Fleischhacker. He does
not want to go on this board because he is a large contributor to
it. He is a great public-spirited citizen of this city. I know you
get a laugh at him at times, but he is giving his money—$50,000
a year to the Park. He is giving that Zoo out there for the benefit
of San Francisco. And I must appoint some of these other men.
And I appointed Charles H. Kendrick because he had been on the
Board of Trustees with Mr. McSheehy. You have had three members on this board for five or six years; Mr. McSheehy was on, Mr.
Havenner was on, Mr. Coleman was on, representing the Board of
Supervisors during all these years. And I am confronted with the
appointment of eleven men that require your approval. The War
Memorial, if I did not have to have that approval, would have been
on its way. This Board has had many meetings. This Board has
met to appoint committees. This Board has met on several organization meetings. It would be the easiest thing in the world for
this Board, without my offending the Board, to go into special session and see what you can do to help the Mayor out. That is what
you can do. Let me know what the temper of the Board is. I do
not want to go and buttonhole any member of this Board. I want
to come in here and give you all the facts and present everything
to you as I have it, including the financial report. And you ought
to go into executive session and tell me what you will do; whether
you will stand for those eleven. You have a board of eleven there
who will do that building for you, hold all the money, hold the
Regents of the University of California, sell your bonds, and employ
labor and get it going. The opera house has to be finished. The
committee does not want the opera house finished. How about
these people who have put in nearly $2,000,000 for an opera house?
And the only thing that there is in it is that possibly that wall
over on the farther corner of the veterans' building will have to
remain in brick for some period of time, like when the Panama-

Pacific International Exposition gave us a million dollars out of the World Exposition fund to build an Auditorium, they had nothing but sandstone or brick, the City itself put in $346,000 to put the stone front on it. We will put the money up to put that over. We will finish that. We will do the job well.

SUPERVISOR SUHR: Mr. Mayor, I believe I read in the paper a short while ago that one of the organizations was in favor of that Board of Trustees. Mr. Ray Burr is here representing them.

THE MAYOR: I am glad to hear from any of them.

SUPERVISOR HAYDEN: Let us have the privilege of the floor for Mr. Burr.

MR. RAYMOND BURR: Mr. Mayor, Golden Gate Post No. 40 of the American Legion on Tuesday last passed a motion asking our delegates to the County Council to take such steps as they might to provide for the immediate construction of the War Memorial project, and we urge the members of the Board of Supervisors to confirm the names submitted by Mayor Rolph as members of the Board of Trustees, or to be submitted. The matter was passed as a method suggested to try and reach a decision in the matter and to end the present deadlock. We hold, in our Post, that the question of securing employment of some thousands of veterans that are walking the streets here is paramount to any other issue involved, and the time has come when some one must give or take, and the decision we reached to that end, that the many thousands of men applying at our United States Veteran Bureau Employment Office for jobs, that some of them can be taken care of. That was the position of our Post.

SUPERVISOR MILES: Mr. Mayor, a few minutes ago you stated that you had promised the veterans that you were going to call them in on another meeting.

THE MAYOR: I am.

SUPERVISOR MILES: You further stated a little later that you always make good your promises.

THE MAYOR: I will.

SUPERVISOR MILES: Now, my suggestion would be this: That you call this meeting with the veterans, make good that promise, and then see what the result of that meeting is. Perhaps you can effect an agreement there whereby, when the War Memorial is started, that we won't have to stop it again with other litigation. And I feel, for the best interests of the City, that this meeting with the veterans should be called immediately and this matter brought before this Board for final settlement.

SUPERVISOR McSHEEHY: I happen to be one of the Trustees of the present War Memorial, and I have been a Trustee for the past three years. We had a meeting here about six weeks ago, and I want to say to the members of this Board that the Trustees, as constituted today, are unanimous in trying to solve this problem, and they are in a very receptive mood; they are willing to do anything almost to start this work on its way. Now, it is up to us, the members of this Board, as to whether we shall accept from the Mayor his nominees are not. Now, we are all looking for action, and the building industry of this City requires action, because hundreds of our citizens—yes, thousands—are walking our streets. Now, we have one million dollars in a round sum to start this work going immediately. We will sell bonds to the extent of $4,000,000 and we will erect two buildings over there that will cost approximately $5,000,000. We have spent approximately $150,000 for plans. These plans are there now. Of course those plans, as they stand today, overrun the estimate; they overrun the actual money that we have on hand; but the architects have been going over those plans for the last three months, and they are in a position today to report to this Board that the buildings can be erected for the amount of money—$5,000,000. Now, it is up to this Board to act, and I am going to suggest, or I am going to make a motion directly here that, when we adjourn here today, that we meet on next Thursday, at 2 o'clock, to receive from the Mayor his report as to the membership of the Trustees for the War Memorial. I make that as a motion.

SUPERVISOR HAYDEN: If the Mayor is ready.

THE MAYOR: Be a little considerate of me. As long as you cannot sell these $4,000,000 worth of bonds, if you will give me a few days longer time, I think I can finish those $12,000,000 this week by writing every night.

SUPERVISOR McSHEEHY: A week from Thursday?

THE MAYOR: That is all right, I will have it by then.

SUPERVISOR TONER: I second that motion.

SUPERVISOR POWER: I was going to suggest to the mover of the motion that, following the suggestion you made, that the Board go into executive session and take perhaps an expression from the members as to the nominees.

SUPERVISOR GALLAGHER: We cannot do that, that is against the Charter.

SUPERVISOR POWER: However, I have not looked at the Charter for some time—

SUPERVISOR GALLAGHER (interrupting): I would make an amendment to that motion.

SUPERVISOR POWER: However, the idea of it was to carry out the intention to get an expression from the members of the Board to see whether the sentiment is changed in view of the election of six new members.

SUPERVISOR GALLAGHER: I make an amendment to that motion, that the Chairman of the Finance Committee of the Board confer with his Honor as to a convenient date, that he be authorized to call us into conference at a convenient place to the members of the Board on the subject matter of discussing this situation and looking to relief.

SUPERVISOR POWER: Do you offer that as an amendment to my motion?

SUPERVISOR GALLAGHER: No, you did not make the motion.

SUPERVISOR POWER: I do not think that is quite the idea. The idea is to have our own meeting and exchange our ideas and find out. We may call in representatives of the Veterans and call in representatives of the Trustees and so forth and get the picture. Some of us know nothing of it. So that I will say that rather than the Mayor call a conference that the chairman of the Finance Committee call a conference, if that is the proper term.

SUPERVISOR GALLAGHER: I will withdraw my motion and substitute in favor of that, that the Mayor and the chairman of the Finance Committee, acting jointly, be authorized to, at a date convenient and within the next two weeks, call a special meeting of this Board, the purpose of which shall be two-fold. The purpose of it shall be to acquaint the new members of the Board with all of the information at hand on the subject of this Memorial, and to have, if possible now—and I used the word advisedly—an expression from members of the Board as to their attitude thereon.

SUPERVISOR ROSSI: If that motion is carried, so far as I am concerned, I would be perfectly willing to meet Thursday night of this week. We can discuss it among ourselves.

SUPERVISOR HAVENNER: There is no use discussing anything until we know what the Mayor is going to propose to us, and, so far as I am concerned, I am going to object to any executive session, conference or anything else on the subject. If his Honor the Mayor asks us to meet with him, and it be his request that this be a private conference, that is different. I object to any executive conference on the part of this Board.

THE MAYOR: I have faithfully kept my pledge to the Veterans,

I have not revealed or divulged a single thing in connection with this report, and I propose to keep it that way until I can call this meeting. I know they know I am busy signing bonds because I have had letters exchanged over it. As soon as I am down within two or three million dollars worth of bonds, I can rattle those off sometimes in a day and a half—Mr. Giannini and Mr. Ferrari have been after me all the time— they have been threatened with cancellation of the sale of their bonds to people who have bought them on account of non-delivery. As soon as I am ready, and after finishing with the Veterans, I will get in touch with the Board, but I will promise you that we will have it within two weeks, and I will promise you, Mr. Claridge, that we will get together some night within ten days' time.

SUPERVISOR McSHEEHY: Do I understand, then, that you will call a meeting of this Board to forward to this Board your report inside of two weeks?

THE MAYOR: My message is to the Board, certainly.

SUPERVISOR McSHEEHY: Inside of two weeks?

THE MAYOR: Yes.

SUPERVISOR McSHEEHY: If that is your wish, Mayor, I will withdraw my motion because the results will be obtained by your wish in the matter.

THE MAYOR: Why, it is a message dating back to April, 1918.

SUPERVISOR POWER: I did not so understand the Mayor's request, if I followed him correctly. He does not wish to recommend to this Board a set of Trustees unless he knows the sentiment of the Board. He is not going to meet with a rebuff, at least he does not wish it. I do not care whether it is a private conference or a public conference, or anything of the sort, I would like to have a conference so that I can have all the light necessary from the representatives of the Veterans and also the representatives of the original trustees, or the Trustees themselves, so that I can make up my mind intelligently what to do. I, as one member of this Board, do not wish to be accused of any delay in connection with the construction of the War Memorial.

SUPERVISOR McSHEEHY: I have only one object in view, and that is to start the work on its way. Action is what we are all looking for. We have been criticized for not acting in this matter. Now, the question is the time. If the Mayor states that he wishes this Board to meet in conference at his office at any time, I am ready to meet in conference, and receive from him whatever names he wishes to suggest.

THE MAYOR: I will tell you what we will do. After I have had the conference with the Veterans, I will call a special meeting of this Board.

SUPERVISOR McSHEEHY: That is satisfactory, I will withdraw my motion.

THE MAYOR (continuing reading):

"February 7, 1930. The Veterans' Advisory Committee, consisting of Messrs. Glensor, Boyd and Burns and Secretary Claridge, met with the Mayor this evening at 8:30 p. m."

THE MAYOR: I told you, if you remember, that I would have a meeting with the Veterans' Committee before submitting the names to you. All right.

SUPERVISOR McSHEEHY (interrupting): Not to interrupt, your Honor, but our Clerk, Mr. Dunnigan, is here and I am going to ask that Mr. Rogers be excused.

THE MAYOR: If there is no objection, it is so ordered (continuing reading):

February 7, 1930. The Veterans' Advisory Committee, consisting of Messrs. Glensor, Boyd and Burns and Secretary Claridge, met with the Mayor this evening at 8:30 p. m. There attended quite a number of interested ex-service men. The discussion lasted for about two and one-half hours, principally over the appointment of Trustees. The Veterans' Advisory Committee opposed the appointments of Messrs. Kendrick and Colman and demanded six Veterans on the Board. In order to come to a definite conclusion, I said that newspaper reports were that either or both Supervisors Stanton and Gallagher were considering resigning and if either did, I would offer the appointment to James W. Mullen as Supervisor and if he accepted, that would cause a vacancy on the War Memorial Trustees Board and I would fill it with an ex-service man. They immediately agreed to it, provided I would immediately not name James W. Mullen and by not waiting for a vacancy to occur on the Board of Supervisors. I told them I could not do such a thing, because I had tendered the appointment to the War Memorial Board to Mr. James W. Mullen, representing labor and someone said 85 per cent of the ex-service men. Here the meeting adjourned.

The buildings, other than the War Veterans' Building, to be erected in the group, the War Veterans Committee say, are incidental to the War Memorial. They have in the past, are now and always have been considered as a group. The additional recreational, entertainment and other municipal purposes naturally require a building and it was always definitely understood the Opera House was referred to for the purpose mentioned.

I now reprint a full financial report, dated November 5, 1929, of the disbursements of the private subscriptions prepared by Messrs. F. W. Lafrentz & Company, Bullock, Kellogg & Mitchell, certified public accountants.

SUPERVISOR POWER: Have you reached the financial statement?

THE MAYOR: Now, right now.

SUPERVISOR POWER: I respectfully suggest that you read it slowly in order that we may get the figures.

THE MAYOR: Yes, certainly (continuing reading):

EXHIBIT No. 7

REPORT OF AUDIT
FOR THE PERIOD FROM SEPT. 30, 1928, TO OCT. 31, 1929

F. W. LAFRENTZ & CO.
BULLOCK, KELLOGG & MITCHELL
Certified Public Accountants
1018-1021 Russ Building
San Francisco, Calif.

November 5, 1929.

The Board of Trustees, San Francisco War Memorial, San Francisco, California.

Dear Sirs: We have made an audit of the books and records of account of the San Francisco War Memorial for the period from September 30, 1928, to October 31, 1929. The statements annexed hereto set forth the condition of the fund on October 31, 1929, the receipts and disbursements for the period under review, and the receipts and disbursements from the inception to October 31, 1929.

STATEMENT OF CONDITION, OCTOBER 31, 1929.

The following comments are explanatory and refer to items appearing in this statement:

Cash—$772,652.57

Cash was verified by communication and reconciliation of balances. As at October 31, 1929, the custody of the cash rested as follows:

Cash with the Regent of University of California:

Banks:

Anglo California Trust Co. (Savings Account $306,481.38
Bank of America (Savings Account)······   721.08

$307,202.46

Certificates of Deposit:

Anglo California Trust Co., No. 5206······	56,424.68	
Anglo California Trust Co., No. 5207······	56,424.68	
Anglo California Trust Co., No. 5208······	112,849.38	
Anglo California Trust Co., No. 5209······	112,849.38	
Anglo California Trust Co., No. 5222······	29,589.10	
Crocker First National Bank No. 303······	29,444.49	397,581.71

Cash on Hand—Regents of U. C............   64,985.78

Total Monies in Hands of Regents of U. C..... $769,769.95
Revolving Fund American Trust Co..........   2,882.62

$772,652.57

Subscriptions Receivable—$231,442.41

The individual balances aggregating this figure are set forth in Schedule 1 of Exhibit "A." During the period under review uncollectible subscriptions totaling $26,500 were written off the books. We were advised that approximately $132,000 of the remaining $231,442.41 would be collected. The balance consists of items which will apparently have to be charged off.

Accrued Interest Receivable—$6,834.67

The interest accrued to October 31, 1929, on monies in the custody of the Regents of the University of California is represented here.

Real Estate—South Block—$325,514.50

This item represents the cost of the parcels in the block bounded by Van Ness Avenue, Franklin, Grove and Fulton streets. The only change in this account during the period under review was an item in amount $6.20. We were advised that title to these parcels is in the name of the Regents of the University of California.

Real Estate—North Block—$328,287.44

The purchase of portions of the block bounded by McAllister, Fulton, Van Ness and Franklin is represented here. We were advised that title to these parcels is vested in the Regents of the University of California.

Purchase Locomobile Company Lease—North Block—$21,000

This item is self-explanatory.

Real Estate Income—Net—$8,685.83

The above figure represents the net income on the South and North blocks to October 31, 1929, analyzed as hereunder:

North Block ....$ 14,723.83
South Block 6,038.00

$ 8,685.83

Architects, Drafting, Excavation, Engineering Services, etc.—$319,664.51

This figure represents the amount paid for construction and engineering services, and is analyzed as follows:

Draftsmen's Salaries	$127,272.86
Rent, Drafting Room	9,905.07
Blue Prints	3,006.68
Drafting Room Supplies and Expense	8,133.41
Advisory Architects	8,415.55
Architects' Fees	24,999.99
Engineering Fees—Consultants	6,155.00
Engineering Fees—Structural	21,174.94
Engineering Fees—Acoustics	2,346.46
Engineering Fees—Electrical	3,500.00
Ground Breaking	1,465.02
Excavation Expense	78,489.53
Auxiliary Fire Protection System and Sewers	24,800.00
	$319,664.51

Furniture and Fixtures—$2,250.40

Furniture and Fixtures acquired consisting for the most part of articles for the drafting room are represented here.

War Memorial Fund—$1,836,216.20 (Collected and Collectible)

The aggregate of subscriptions and donations less such adjustments as were necessary constitutes the above figure. The adjustments referred to are the writing off of uncollectible items, and the subscription of $100,000 by the City and County of San Francisco, as this was repaid to the city to clear title of the St. Ignatius property.

Accretions to Fund—$162,744.47

The net addition to the fund from sources apart from donations comprises the above figure. An analysis is given hereunder:

Additions:

Interest Received and Accrued	$394,350.50	
Miscellaneous	224.50	$394,575.00

Deductions:

Interest Expense (includes $42,814.11, Account of Purchase of Portions of No. Block for City and County of San Francisco)	$151,852.53	
Campaign Expense	25,243.71	
Progress Bond Campaign Expense	2,851.90	
Administrative Salaries Expense, 10 Years	31,524.76	
Loss on St. Ignatius Property	4,122.24	
P. P. I. E. Expense	1,055.68	
Commission on Securities	735.63	
Charter Amendment Campaign	617.50	
Legal Expense	13,826.58	231,830.53
		$162,744.47

Liabilities

This audit did not include an investigation of construction contracts and the liability thereon.

Annexed to this report are the following statements:

Exhibit "A"—Statement of Condition as at October 31, 1929.

Exhibit "A," Schedule 1—Subscription Balances as at October 31, 1929.

Exhibit "B"—Statement of Cash Receipts and Disbursements for the Period from Inception to October 31, 1929.

Respectfully submitted,

F. W. LAFRENTZ & CO.,

BULLOCK, KELLOGG & MITCHELL,

Certified Public Accountants.

By H. A. Kellogg.

(EXHIBIT "A.")

SAN FRANCISCO WAR MEMORIAL.
STATEMENT OF CONDITION AS AT OCTOBER 31, 1929.

ASSETS

Cash:
Cash—With Regents of the University of California $769,769.95
Revolving Fund.......................... 2,882.62 $772,652.57

Subscriptions Receivable—Schedule 1......... 231,442.41
Accrued Interest Receivable.................. 6,834.67
Real Estate:
Cost of South Block............$325,514.50
Cost of North Block...........:. 328,287.44
Purchase—Locomobile Lease
North Block................. 21,000.00

$674,801.94
Less: Real Estate Income—Net 8,685.83 666,116.11

Architects, Drafting, Excavation,
Engineering Services, etc..... 319,664.51 985,780.62
Furniture and Fixtures........ 2,250.40

Total Assets.............. $1,998,960.67

SURPLUS

War Memorial Fund from Subscriptions and
Donations $1,836,216.20
Accretions to Fund by Excess of Revenues
Over Expenses.......................... 162,744.47

$1,998,960.67

EXHIBIT "B."

SAN FRANCISCO WAR MEMORIAL.

STATEMENT OF CASH RECEIPTS AND DISBURSEMENTS FOR THE PERIOD FROM INCEPTION TO OCTOBER 31, 1929.

	Period October 1, 1928, to October 31, 1929			Period Inception to October 31, 1929		
Balance, Beginning of Period			$1,216,476.70			$1,216,476.70
Receipts:						
Subscriptions and Donations		$ 87,060.00			$391,551.10	
Interest Received	$ 63,254.63			$391,551.10		
Less: Interest Disbursed	36,768.20	16,486.43		151,852.55	239,698.55	
North Block—Rents, etc. Net		14,723.83			14,723.83	
Miscellaneous					224.50	
Total Receipts			$ 118,270.26			$1,856,420.67
Total Receipts and Balance			$1,333,746.96			$1,856,420.67
Disbursements:						
Purchase of St. Ignatius Property				$354,122.24		
Less: Amount Repaid on Sale				350,000.00	$ 4,122.24	
Purchase of South Block				$330,966.80		
Less: Received from Sale of Buildings				5,467.50	325,508.30	
Taxes—South Block	$ 5,072.74			$ 24,004.63		
Insurance—South Block	9.82			2,279.55		
Notary Fees—South Block	6.20			6.20		
Repairs—South Block		6,088.76		69.56		
Less: Rentals Received South Block				$ 26,359.94		
				20,316.74	6,044.20	
Purchase of Locomobile Lease North Block					21,000.00	
Purchase of North Block		328,287.44			328,287.44	

	Period October 1, 1928, to October 31, 1929	Period Inception to October 31, 1929
Engineering and Construction:		
Auxiliary Fire Protection System add Sewer $4800	$ 19,600.00	$ 19,600.00
Advisory Archi tcts		8,415.55
Drafting Salaries	63,725.67	127,272.86
Drafting Room Rent and Supplies Expense	5,386.25	20,364.59
Architect's Fees		24,999.99
Consulting Engineering Fees	1,000.00	6,155.00
Plumbing Engineering Fees		3,666.66
Structural Engineering	3,560.00	12,500.00
El etal Engineering	7,000.00	7,000.00
Acoustic Engineering		2,346.46
Ground Breaking		1,465.02
Excavating	67,489.53	85, 197.81
	167,701.45	318,983.94
Administration:		
Campaign Expense		$ 25,231.71
Salaries	1,520.00	18,929.80
Regents, University of California	421.36	6,853.15
Rents and Sundries	1,942.84	7,919.63
Progress Bond Campaign		2,851.90
Furniture and Fixtures	3,884.20	61,786.19
Panama Pacific Int. Exp. Expense	391.66	1,800.40
Commission and Tax on Liberty Bonds		1,055.68
After Amendment Campaign	617.50	735.63
Paid to American Trust Co.—Advances	41,295.80	617.50
Legal Expense (# Law Suits, Court Proceedings and Negotiations Incident to the Collection of Delinquent Acco uls)	13,826.58	13,826.58
Total Disbursements	561,093.39	1,083,768.10
	$ 772,652.57	772,652.57
Balance, October 31, 1929		$ 772,652.57

BLOCK 75

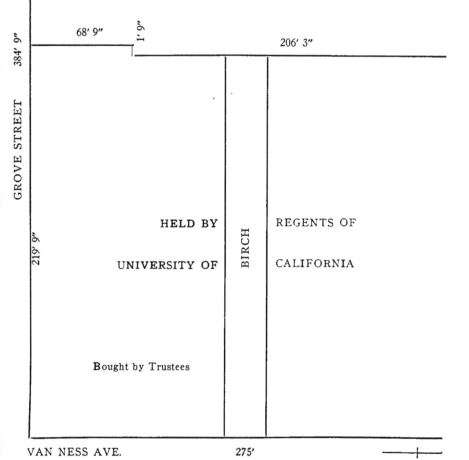

BLOCK 76
FRANKLIN STREET   275'

HELD BY | OF | REGENTS

UNIVERSITY | OF | CALIFORNIA

165' 0"

ASH

137' 6"

Bought by Trustees on behalf of City, but City put up no money. Trustees paid it all through Regents.
Advanced by: Crocker Bank ¼; Anglo Bank ¼; American Trust Co. ½. Approximately $330,000.

Street closed by Ordinance
110' 0"

137' 6"

219' 9"

HELD BY | CITY | AND COUNTY

OF

SAN | FRANCISCO

Warehouse to buy out $89,000. Trustees drew their check to Finance Company.
McLeran.

St. James Hotel

NESS AVE.   275'   ⟶ N

THE MAYOR: I offer this statement now to the Board of Supervisors as part of the record I am making here, and which will be included in the final summing up of my report.

SUPERVISOR POWER: Subscriptions Receivable, you say $213,442.41. They are considered still good?

THE MAYOR: Yes. Continuing my report:

I reprint an editorial appearing in the San Francisco Chronicle under date of January 25, 1930, which clearly states the exact status of the private subscription fund, and its use by authorized officials of the San Francisco War Memorial Trustees:

"CLEARING A MISCONCEPTION OF ORIGINAL WAR MEMORIAL FUND.

Discussion of the War Memorial question is complicated by a common misconception. This has to do with the status of the $2,000,000 fund subscribed by private citizens and now in the hands of their Trustees. Even some of those most active in the current discussions do not seem to understand this matter.

Two funds are concerned in the War Memorial. The first, amounting to $2,000,000, was subscribed by private individuals. Out of this fund has come all the expenditure so far made, including the purchase of land for the Memorial site.

The second fund is that voted by the people of San Francisco when it was seen that the original private fund would not be enough for the purpose. The City's bond issue was for $4,000,000. No cash has yet been realized from these bonds, which are still unsold and in the City Treasury.

The private fund is still in the hands of Trustees representing the subscribers. In the nature of things, these Trustees, while they hold the money, are accountable only to the subscribers who gave it. They have a very definite responsibility to the subscribers which it is not in their power to alter.

When the project is at last organized under the new public Board of Trustees provided for by vote of the people, the private Trustees are to turn over to it the fund now in their hands. Since the City's Board of Trustees has not yet been confirmed and organized, the private Trustees are compelled to keep the money for lack of anyone to take it over.

But when this transfer does take place, these two funds—private and municipal—will become partners in the War Memorial project. In this partnership the City will naturally assume the responsibility to the private subscribers now borne by the present private Trustees.

With the lapse of so much time since the project was started it is not remarkable that the people should have lost sight of the fundamental facts and relationships. The private fund has been confused with the public funds later voted by the people. As a result much has been said and much attempted to be done that is wholly irrelevant.

It is well to get back to the facts of the partnership and a clear view of the relations of the two funds involved in the War Memorial."

Here follows a copy of my remarks, made before the Board of Supervisors, Monday, February 10, 1930, and a copy of Supervisor Hayden's motion that this report be printed and sent to the Board of Supervisors:

THE MAYOR: Then follows a copy of my remarks concerning the appointment of the War Memorial Trustees, which I think is already in the record, and a copy of the letter from James D. Phelan, already read.

EXHIBIT NO. 8.

IN RE REMARKS OF MAYOR JAMES ROLPH, JR., CONCERNING APPOINTMENT OF WAR MEMORIAL TRUSTEES.

Monday, February 10, 1930, 2 p. m.

THE MAYOR: Gentlemen of the Board, I have finished the signing of the Spring Valley bonds and made full delivery today to the Bank of Italy of the entire $41,000,000 worth. On Friday night I had a conference, in my chambers, with the committee of the War Memorial veterans, at which meeting a number of other veterans were present. I had with me, and I have completed a full report of the war veterans' project, from the time it commenced in 1918, ready to submit to you, but I really think that it ought to be printed, as a matter of record. It dates back nearly 12 years. It comprises all the proceedings, all the motions, all the resolutions, all the reports of the War Veterans Committees, proceedings which have taken place at meetings which have been held, the appointment of your committee of ten, a financial statement of the entire fund. And it seems to me that it is of sufficient importance to have it set up in type rather than have me read it to you, taking a very long period of time. And it is a record of the City. Now, I told you that, after having a meeting with the war veterans last Friday night, I would call you into special session probably tomorrow, or this meeting could adjourn until tomorrow to take this matter up.

SUPERVISOR MILES: I so move you, that the record be printed so that we will all have a copy, and therefore we will have an opportunity to study the report before it is decided.

SUPERVISOR PEYSER: Second the motion.

THE MAYOR: It is moved and seconded that the report requested of the Mayor with regard to a record of the War Memorial proceedings be printed so that copies may be had by the Supervisors. And when you get a rough copy you can order as many copies as you want printed. Now, I have had a request that the meeting not be held tomorrow because it is the day before Lincoln's birthday, and a number who would like to be present cannot be present tomorrow. The question with you now is whether you want to wait until this report is printed and then study it and then have the meeting. To be candid with you, the whole point at issue now is, boiled down, who will comprise the Board of eleven Trustees? That is the whole problem which is before you. I tried to make several compromises. I used all my persuasive power on Friday night's meeting, but nothing was accomplished, and the matter is in the same status quo as it was when I submitted the names of eleven Trustees to you on the 26th of August last. I am going to be confronted with submitting to you the same eleven names in the final report which I make to you because there is no opportunity of coming to an adjustment of this matter. I am told, further today, that some want the whole eleven turned down, and I have been told that they would be satisfied if two were removed. And yet I made a proposition to them last Friday night which was satisfactory, provided it was done last Friday night. I have read, by the newspapers, that Supervisor Stanton and Supervisor Gallagher might retire from the Board. I have a labor man on the committee of eleven, Mr. James W. Mullen, a very fine capable labor man of this city, and I agreed to appoint in his place—I agreed to put him on the Board of Supervisors and put a veteran of the World War, or one of the wars, the Spanish-American War, in his place, if he came on this Board. They were perfectly satisfied with that if that happened Friday night. Now, I know nothing about any vacancy on the Board, but I am confronted with this letter particularly, of Senator Phelan, which is similar to many letters which I received, which, I think, will show you the position. Here is a letter to me from James D. Phelan, dated December 3:

"Honorable James Rolph, Jr., Mayor, San Francisco.

My Dear Mr. Mayor: I have followed the newspaper reports con-

cerning the embarrassment which you apparently have experienced
through the opposition of certain members of the American Legion to
the personnel of the War Memorial Trustees appointed by you and
whose names were presented to the Board of Supervisors for confirmation. I was glad to see that you would not yield to their unreasonable demands. I think that Major Charles H. Kendrick and
Colonel Jesse C. Colman are men of such fine character, sound judgment, public spirit and proven capacity that it would be nothing less
than a calamity for you to surrender your position. You were authorized by law to name the Trustees and you have made an excellent
selection. As you know, I am interested in art, as represented by the
theater, the museum and the galleries, which give plaesure to and
gratify the higher aspirations of the people. In that spirit I contributed to the original citizens' fund for the Memorial buildings.
I now believe that if the Trustees of that fund surrender to the demands of an unauthorized body, not even pretending to promote the
public benefit, but their own, it would be a betrayal, and it probably
could be stopped by the courts. It is so purely selfish that the people
resent it. As I understood the citizens' fund, it was to be used principally for an Opera House and a Museum, it was never intended to
make it a clubhouse for preferred individuals. As I have great regard
and appreciation for the veterans who have fought under the flag I
deplore the fact that some of them, who certainly cannot be called
representatives of all, seem to mar the generous purpose of our citizens in privately contributing to the fund, and recently voting to increase it. I have known Major Kendrick many years. He entered the
service as a volunteer, was wounded in action and decorated. Colonel
Colman, also a volunteer, has an honorable record. And both of these
gentlemen have been in the public service and are intimately known
to you. The people have learned to trust them. You should not withdraw such names as these and thus greatly impoverish your Board,
which shall make very large expenditures and are charged with grave
responsibilities. I am convinced that most of the veterans of our
wars, if they had a voice, would disapprove of your surrendering your
judgment.

Very truly yours,
JAMES D. PHELAN."

Now, I have just returned from Los Angeles, where I went down as
the guest of honor of the mighty 91st Division and of its southern sector. With 500 veterans present I was given honorary membership in that
organization. While there the meetings took place in their War
Memorial. Their War Memorial is a beautiful building, eight stories
high, on a piece of land a hundred feet wide and one hundred and
fifty feet long, cost $738,000, and the furnishings brought it up to
$750,000, and the land was owned by the city. The War Memorial was
erected away out on South Figueroa street, and the land, as estimated
today, is worth approximately $250,000, or a total investment of
$1,000,000. And everybody is satisfied, and it is handled by the mem-
bers of the veterans' organizations. In adidtion to that, the city and
county bonded itself for another million dollars, which they used for
the creation of a War Memorial in the shape of a Coliseum, where the
great football games are played and where the great parades, in fact,
all of the parades, take place. And those are the War Memorials of the
City of Los Angeles.

Last Friday night I was asked to turn over the $4,000,000 bond issue
voted by the people, turn it all over to a Board of War Memorial
Trustees, for the purpose of building a $4,000,000, plus the block of
land, a $4,000,000 War Memorial. That leaves a block of land and
$772.000 in the Treasury for the building of the Opera House. The
charter amendment provides that it shall not be used except for War
Memorial purposes and municipal purposes. You know as well as I
do that to build a $4,000,000 War Memorial for a building simply for
the veterans' uses alone, which, after thirty or forty or fifty years the

veterans, like all of us, pass away, and there will be standing on a block of land over there a building for War Memorial purposes and for veterans' purposes that cost more than the Olympic Club, the Elks' club and the William Taylor Hotel combined. Now, I am convinced that there will be no Opera House, which the people of this City intended there shall be, except one unfinished and a disgrace to the City unless it is completely finished. It seems too bad that, when the City of Los Angeles puts up a building, furnished, at a cost of $750,000, that it seems to be necessary to put up nearly a $4,000,000 building here in San Francisco, and I am sure that you will not be a party to a wreckage of an Opera House on the two blocks of land standing over there, one standing in the name of the City and County of San Francisco and the other one standing in the name of the Regets of the University of California. The eleven names that I have submitted to you are approved by the Regents of the University of California, to whom this money will be turned over. Several of them are men who have been, for almost 12 years, gathering the fund, administering the fund, and the architectural plans were all satisfactory and the names of all, including the veterans, signed to the plans.

Now, this is a problem which you, my colleagues of the Board of Supervisors, have got to help to solve with me. It has become a great public question. I submitted the names on the 26th of August, and I am powerless to go ahead and do anything unless you confirm the names which I submit to you. You have taken the position that there must be all or none. How can any human being foretell than he can submit eleven names to your body, the entire eleven being satisfactory to you? Now, this work ought to go on. The bond market is pretty near reaching the point where we can sell the bonds at 4½ per cent, and that $4,000,000, plus $772,000-odd in cash, in four banks in this City, together with a public certified accountant's report of where every dollar has gone, is ready for submission to you. I could not submit it to anybody else. My duty is to submit it to my colleagues first. And there was nobody disposed to listen to the long report, anyway. And it has resolved itself down to the point now, who are the Trustees going to be? Everybody is quite willing to turn over the management of the building to be used by the veterans to the veterans the moment it is finished. But the funds cannot be dissipated in building one building without finishing the building of the other building. And my observation is, with all due respect to the gentlemen who comprise the committee, that if the money is placed entirely in their hands, the most of it will be spent on a building on the one block far too great for the need of the veterans compared with what Los Angeles has. And there are as many veterans down there as there are here, because there were 20,000 out of California alone in the 91st Division, and 60,000 in the Western States, consisting of eight States and two Territories. And they are all thoroughly satisfied. But I cannot turn around and put into the hands of the veterans solely $6,000,000 to be used exclusively for a building, unless I know the opera house is going to be built. And the opera house is a memorial. The Coliseum is a memorial. Statues have been built as memorials. Other places have been built as memorials. This City voted a large amount of money and also private subscriptions for a memorial for President Harding, who died in this City, and they created a golf link and named it the Harding Golf Link. Now, I need your advice. I want to know whether you want that opera house built, which will be a great memorial and will last on, like the Grand Opera House in Paris, forever? The other building, in the course of time, fifty or sixty years from now, there will be no veterans left. What are you going to do with the building? The opera house can remain, the musical associations, the choruses, the operas, for places of amusement for generations to come, and there should be enough

money left and there should be enough money divided, with
$4,000,000 in cash, the plans ready, the property excavated, the
architects' fees paid for, and the tenants evicted for the purpose of
opening up the streets and making the excavations, expecting that
this would go right ahead. Now, it is your responsibility; it is up
to you to say who is going to handle this. It is up to you to decide,
because the burden is not upon my shoulders any longer. And I
do hope that, between the time that I have spoken to you this afternoon, frankly, giving you the situation, and the time you get a copy
of my report, you will talk it over amongst yourselves, because,
after all, the authority rests with you. If you decide to elect General Hunter Liggett, well, elect him. If you decide to elect Frank
Belgrano, elect him. If you decide to elect Jimmy Herz, elect him.
If you decide to elect R. I. Bentley, President of the San Francisco
Musical Association, elect him. If you decide to elect Colonel Coleman, elect him. If you decide to elect Major Kendrick here, elect
him. He has been honored from the very beginning; he knows;
he is one of the best posted veterans that you have got, and it is
some internal strife among the veterans against Major Kendrick.
And it is because Jesse Coleman is a member of the Board of
Supervisors.

Now, all the money that is going to go out has to be passed by
your Board. I would think they would be tickled to death to have
a veteran and a Supervisor on the Board of Trustees who could
come in here and explain to the members of the Board what you
needed the money for, and get it immediately. And the other one
is Herbert Fleishhacker, who is the only one of the three that is
left since the very beginning, twelve years ago. And he is quite
willing to get off. I tell you now, he is quite willing to get off;
but if he goes off, Kenneth R. Kingsbury, President of the Standard
Oil Company, goes off; R. I. Bentley goes off, and others go off, and
we do not get the money from the Regents of the University of
California. That is the law.

Now, I say, let us appoint eleven honorable men, thoroughly
capable of handling this $6,000,000 project, and go ahead with it;
and, as vacancies come, why, gradually appoint a veteran, because
we all love the veterans. I am singing their praises all the time.
I have told you how many honorary memberships I have. You
know I am the Honorary President of the 363d, you know I am the
Honorary President of the 91st, the northern sector, and no other
honorary member, as long as they exist, will ever be elected, because
it is part of the by-laws. And my heart is with them. But I am
entrusted with a $6,000,000 proposition over there for the City of
San Francisco, which wants to build a War Memorial. Now, that
is practically the way the matter stands at the present time. and
as long as you have ordered this printed, why, we will have it
printed, and you can read it over and you will see the whole status
of the situation, and I ask and I beg your co-operation with me
to get this thing going.

SUPERVISOR POWER: Mr. Mayor, I know you do not wish to
leave the impression that there is anything placed before the Board
at this time on this matter?

THE MAYOR: No, certainly not. So that there may be no misunderstanding, I am just explaining to you, my colleagues and my
fellow citizens, the exact status of this matter, because today was
the day that you were going to have a hearing—tomorrow is the
probable day that we were going to have a special meeting. Now,
the special meeting has been put off until the printer can print
this report, and then the Board will take it up, and nothing is
expected of the Board today, because I have not resubmitted the
names of the Trustees.

SUPERVISOR HAYDEN: On motion of Supervisor Miles, the

Clerk was instructed to have your report printed, and I would like to ask the Clerk just how long it will take to get that copy into the hands of the membership?

THE CLERK: I don't know how long it is—a day or two.

SUPERVISOR HAYDEN: I recommend to you that you call a special meeting a week from tomorrow, which would be the 18th, a special meeting of the Board of Supervisors.

THE MAYOR: That is, if the printer has it ready.

SUPERVISOR HAYDEN: Yes, at an hour to be satisfactory to the Board—Tuesday, the 18th, at 2:30 P. M.

SUPERVISOR McSHEEHY: Second the motion.

THE MAYOR: All in favor say aye. (Ayes. The ayes have it.)

SUPERVISOR HAYDEN: And, of course, the veteran organizations will be invited to attend that meeting?

THE MAYOR: Everybody—a public meeting.

* * * * * * *

THE MAYOR: May I ask the Board—I named most of those Trustees—that the Clerk be instructed to insert two others that I just remembered.   Mr. George Cameron of the Chronicle has accepted appointment on the Board of Trustees and Mr. George Hearst has accepted appointment on the Board of Trustees.   So I think I have now named the eleven.

The following is a copy of a letter dated February 11, 1930, written by the Advisory Board to Veterans War Memorial Committees to the members of the Board of Supervisors, transmitting a copy of their letter, dated September 7, 1929, to the Board of Supervisors, which appears hereinbefore in this report under that date:

"San Francisco, California, February 11, 1930.

"To the Members of the Honorable Board of Supervisors,
    City and County of San Francisco.

"Gentlemen: The Mayor has stated that he will resubmit to your Board for action, the same eleven names for the position of Trustees of the San Francisco War Memorial Board as submitted by him and on which confirmation was refused by the Board of Supervisors under date of September 16, 1929.

"This Advisory Board has been instructed by the Veteran organizations of San Francisco to voice to you the opposition of the Veteran organizations to confirmation of such nominees when submitted to your Board.

"In order to refresh your memories on this subject, we submit herewith a written statement which was filed with the Board of Supervisors in opposition to the Mayor's nominations on the occasion of them being first presented to you, which statement was in writing at that time and is a part of the record of proceedings of the Board of Supervisors.

"It is our understanding that a special meeting of your Board will be held on Tuesday, February 18, 1930, for the purpose of considering the War Memorial question, and of undoubtedly considering the Mayor's nominees for the office of Trustees.   In order that you may be fully informed as to all the facts pertinent to this issue it is requested that you permit this Advisory Board to appear before you at such meeting to present to you additional grounds for the Veterans' opposition to the Mayor's nominees, additional facts and figures not contained in the enclosed statement.

"Trusting that you will accord us the courtesy of a full and complete hearing, we are,

"Respectfully yours,

"ADVISORY BOARD TO VETERANS WAR MEMORIAL
         COMMITTEES.
                    "By J. C. CLARIDGE, Secretary."

For the purposes of this historical report, I include a letter, dated January 7, 1930, sent by the American Legion War Memorial Committee to Mr. William H. Crocker, chairman Board of Trustees, San Francisco War Memorial, and I question the authority of the American Legion War Memorial Committee to write such a letter over the heads of the legally authorized committee of Messrs. Glensor, Boyd and Burns.

(For the personal attention of Mr. William H. Crocker.)

January 7, 1930.

Mr. William H. Crocker, Chairman, Board of Trustees, San Francisco War Memorial, 244 Kearny Street, San Francisco, Cal.

Dear Sir: In response to the request of the Veterans transmitted to you as chairman of the Board of War Memorial Trustees having the administration of the privately subscribed trust fund, the Veterans of San Francisco have been favored with a reply from Mr. Widenham, signing himself as secretary of the Trustees, purporting to give his personal understanding of the provisions of the trust indenture of August 19, 1921.

In the first place, the Veterans of San Francisco are not at all interested in Mr. Widenham's "understanding" of the provisions of the trust indenture. In the second place, the "understanding" is obviously incorrect, a conclusion which anyone able to read the English language and who has taken the trouble to read the trust indenture in question cannot fail to reach.

The Veterans note from the incomplete and fragmentary financial statement, made as of June 21, 1929, and printed in the journal of procedings of the Board of Supervisors under date of July 12-15-17, 1929, that from September 30, 1928, to the date of the statement, June 21, 1929, the Trustees spent the sum of $13,742.25 for counsel fees. It seems peculiar, to say the least, that in securing $13,000 worth of advice and service from your counsel you have not asked them to pass upon the question as to who are the beneficiaries under the trust, but at this late date disposed of the matter upon the basis of your secretary's "understanding."

With respect to his statement that the San Francisco posts of the American Legion are not beneficiaries of the trust, but are only entitled to the beneficial use of the buildings that come into being through the use of the trust funds, not only is this erroneous, but the attempt to so distinguish in order to avoid the rendition of a financial report we regard as puerile, evasive, quibbling and equivocation, and unworthy of a group of men entrusted with public funds.

Furthermore, while it is entirely true that the Veterans want this accounting so they may have some knowledge of the manner in which the trust fund has been administered, it is wanted more particularly for a reason which is directly beneficial to the Trustees themselves.

The Veterans of San Francisco, and to a marked degree the public of San Francisco, have long been asking a reason for the cloud of secrecy that has been thrown around the administration of this trust fund. The question is daily propounded to our advisory board as to whether or not the secrecy surrounding the administration of the trust fund and the violent opposition to the appointment of a Board of Trustees by the Mayor on the part of certain interests and certain persons in San Francisco is not due to the fact that this private trust fund has been subjected to such maladministration, inefficient and unbusiness-like use, that a disclosure of what has occurred would create a great public scandal that would rock San Francisco to its foundations. They are asked why should the Trustees borrow $328,000 from banks and pay interest thereon when, according to their own statement, they had on hand somewhere between $600,000 and $1,200,000, the character of our information being so vague that the amount cannot be determined except between those limits. They are asked why were the tenants evicted and the buildings razed upon the property long before bonds had been voted by the people in an amount sufficient to complete the War Memorial, and at a time when it was not known whether such bonds would be voted or not. They are asked why the Trustees expended $159,000 for drafting room expenses, $34,000 for architects' fees, $30,000 for special engineering services, and have not yet produced a set of plans upon which it is possible to erect a War Memorial. There are many other questions they have been asked, and which the public is now asking, and to which our advisory board has been unable to supply an answer. Substantial numbers of the Veterans are in favor of instituting court proceedings for the purpose of securing this accounting. Our advisory board has been able to avoid this course by assuring them that when the accounting was prepared it would be furnished to the Veterans; that the caliber of the men upon the Board of War Memorial Trustees insured such a course being followed.

Many of the Veterans we represent subscribed to this trust fund, and as subscribers have requested us to demand for them an accounting of the funds placed in your hands.

For all these reasons, may we suggest that your Board of Trustees reconsider this matter and immediately furnish us with the accounting which we have so long requested. If you determine not to do so, will you at least do us the courtesy to definitely say so as a Board of Trustees and not favor us with any evasive statements of your secretary's "understanding" in the premises?

Finally, may we say we have noted the veiled threat embodied in your secretary's letter to the effect that unless the Board of Trustees to be appointed by the Mayor function, and agree to function in the manner which your Board thinks it proper, you will not turn over the privately subscribed trust fund. We are not interested in this phase of the matter at all. When the time comes to turn over the private trust fund, it will be turned over, and if not the War Memorial will be erected anyway.

Yours faithfully,
AMERICAN LEGION WAR MEMORIAL COMMITTEE,
By J. C. Claridge, Secretary.

THE MAYOR: That is the letter that I spoke to you about, one of the most defamatory, most incendiary and most contemptible letters that I ever heard written of anyone, and I asked who wrote the letter, I requested to know who wrote the letter, and Supervisor Hayden asked who wrote the letter, and Mr. Claridge said that he had written it, and when Mr. Hayden asked him he said he was directed to write the letter and originally signed it. If you think, gentlemen of the Board, that is conducive to bringing harmony about in connection with the $2,000,000 fund which was subscribed by private citizens to the Trustees who have that fund and who have expended it honestly and without gross inefficiency and mismanagement and dishonesty, I would say the time has come when there must be a break between the two factions, the one of the veterans and the one of the War Memorial Trustees who hold that fund.

February 11. This is after giving due consideration to all appointments involved in this matter, this is giving due consideration to the Veterans, to the names submitted to me; this is giving consideration to the demand that seven members of the Veteran Committee go on that Board. They opposed Supervisor Colman because he was in favor of the Opera House. Do you think I am going to make an appointment that is going to thwart the wishes of the people that an Opera House be built? Not much. When you dig into this thing, when you find out the reasons why Supervisor Colman and Major Kendrick are being threatened, if you will give some thought and attention, and if you have your ear to the ground as I have mine all throughout the city, you will find as expressed by former Senator Phelan, and you will wake up and appoint a Board of Trustees you can have confidence in to build this great memorial here in San Francisco, and there will be nothing like it in any part of the world. If you hear, as I do, of those fine eleven sterling, outstanding men, men who are foremost in the city of San Francisco, men whose names cannot be impeached, men who stand for the very highest things, men whose names can be written in unlimited amounts, men of intelligence, men of spirit and men of action, men whom the people can have confidence in. I make tonight, after all the study and all the consideration and all the thought and all the advice and all the requests that are made upon me by men of the ex-service organization, the appointment of these men and they are all men whom you cannot quarrel with. You need that right now, you cannot get anywhere with this proposition unless you appoint men as trustees as demanded by the Charter and men in whom the people have confidence and trust, and let us appoint and confirm these fine eleven men and go ahead about our business.

THE MAYOR (reading):

I appoint, under the law directing me to do so, as Trustees of the War Memorial, subject to your confirmation:

General Hunter Liggett, United States Army, retired Veteran of All Wars.

Frank N. Belgrano, former State Commander American Legion.

James I. Herz, 363d Infantry (San Francisco's Own), 91st Division.

Major Charles H. Kendrick, World War Veteran.

Herbert Fleishhacker, president Anglo and London Paris National Bank.

Kenneth R. Kingsbury, president Standard Oil Company of California.

Robert I. Bentley, president California Packing Corporation.

George Cameron, publisher San Francisco Chronicle.

George Hearst, publisher San Francisco Examiner.

James W. Mullen, publisher of the Labor Clarion.

Colonel Jesse C. Colman, Supervisor, World War Veteran.

And I earnestly appeal to your fairness to confirm them and then we can refer all matters relating to San Francisco War Memorial to these Trustees for action.

I have submitted to you facts, no arguments or personal opinions. You have the authority to decide now the building of the San Francisco War Memorial with this history of twelve years' effort in your hands.

Respectfully submitted,

JAMES ROLPH, JR., Mayor.

POSTSCRIPT TO THE REPORT OF MAYOR JAMES ROLPH, JR., ON THE WAR MEMORIAL.

Meeting of the Board of Supervisors of the City and County of San Francisco, Wednesday, February 19, 1930.

THE MAYOR: As a postscript, let me add, these eleven trustees are satisfactory to the Regents of the University of California. The money will be turned over to these eleven trustees named by the Mayor.

Nobody ever asked me about a man who is named on that Board of Trustees. I never conferred with them, I never asked who they wanted on the Board. The men of the Legion, several of them said to me, "Give us some men at least upon this Board of Trustees who have

been in this thing for the last twelve years so that we can start off
with some advice and some help, some one who is familiar with all
of these things to help us on the road so that we can build this
$6,000,000 project."

I have put on there the earlier members of the Board. I cannot permit one Veteran to abuse another. I cannot permit, in my fairness as
Mayor, I cannot permit a committee to knock Supervisor Jesse Colman, who wore the cloth of a Veteran just as much as any other
Veteran. And I cannot permit personal criticism against Major Kendrick. I cannot permit personal animosity against any of the Committee whom I have appointed to delay and defeat this. I have appointed as fine a body of men as you will find anywhere.

This list has been appointed from August 26th last, and the more
I hear of this measure around this City, and the more I hear of it from
the Veterans, the more I hear of the discussion, the more convinced I
am everybody is getting sick of it, and the more they want this thing
to go ahead. Nobody is holding it up, and nobody is doing anything
to defeat it except the Committee appointed by the Veterans, who want
to charge every man with every kind of dishonesty, dishonor, want
to malign every one connected with it except themselves. The time
has come when the interests of the City of San Francisco is paramount
to everything else. When it comes to the honor and dignity and character of the men and women who died and served for their country in
stress and strife, this Board meets the requirements and adds dignity
to the requirements. They will discuss, but not in fear, all of the
questions in connection with this matter, so I request that you put it
in the hands of the people who are opposed to this delay, and this will
put it in the hands where the law demands that it should go, and I
earnestly appeal to you to give consideration to all of these things
before you vote on the names which the Mayor again submits to you
as the nominees for the San Francisco War Memorial trustees.

THE MAYOR: What is the pleasure of the Board?

SUPERVISOR PEYSER: I move we recess until eight
o'clock tonight——

THE MAYOR: Mr. Peyser, I have two cousins arriving here
tonight——

SUPERVISOR PEYSER (interrupting): I didn't know you
had an engagement, your Honor.

THE MAYOR (continuing): ——arriving from Toronto,
Canada, today, and sailing on the Malolo Saturday, and I have
a dinner engagement to meet them at my sister's home tomorrow night, and I really must attend that family reunion.

SUPERVISOR PEYSER: I withdraw the motion.

SUPERVISOR McSHEEHY: Mr. Chairman and members of
the Board, I would imagine everyone is anxious to receive
the financial report, I imagine we all are more or less anxious
to receive——

THE MAYOR: What is the pleasure of the Board? The
whole report is going to be ready, what is the pleasure?

SUPERVISOR McSHEEHY: I will make a motion, your
Honor.

THE MAYOR: If you will move that I hand it to the
Finance Committee, and they in turn hand it to the reporter
to have copies made, that is perfectly legal and proper.

SUPERVISOR ROSSI: I so move, your Honor.

(Seconded by several voices.)

SUPERVISOR McSHEEHY: It is all agreed. I think, your
Honor, the financial report is all we are anxious for and I will
make that motion, if you wish.

THE MAYOR: It is all a part of my report.

SUPERVISOR McSHEEHY: I move that the Clerk be instructed to press the financial part of your report, print one

hundred copies and have it distributed to each member of the Board——

SUPERVISOR HAVENNER: I, for one, want to see the report.

SUPERVISOR POWER: I suggest Supervisor McSheehy hand them to the Board.

SUPERVISOR STANTON: When are you going to have them printed, right away?

THE CLERK: Right away, yes.

SUPERVISOR POWER: I presume we are going to hear from the representatives of the Veterans and of the Legion and I also realize that probably we are not going to come to a vote in view of the absentees at this time, but I want to ask a question. I noticed an article in the paper the other day that General Hunter Liggett was going to Honolulu, and as I recollect the article, he was going to remain there indefinitely as a resident on account of his health. I was wondering if that would make him unlikely to serve on this board.

THE MAYOR: He has not sent me any such word, and it would be a very great mistake not to recognize General Hunter Liggett when the citizens of San Francisco have presented him with a home, and he is a resident of San Francisco, and until he says he cannot serve I think we should appoint him, I think he ought at least to get the honor.

SUPERVISOR POWER: The fact he was presented with a home, and I, too, think he should have the honor, but this article said he was going to reside in Honolulu indefinitely, and I was wondering whether that would make any difference with him.

THE MAYOR: Until I receive word from him, I think he should have the honor of appointment.

SUPERVISOR POWER: I should like to ask you whether or not in the course of investigation, and I understood you to say that you had, you made a careful investigation of the qualifications of all of your nominees. I would like to ask if you would put yourself out to look up the records in 1917 and see whether or not James Mullen did not refuse at that time to act as a member of the War Draft Board or Examination Board.

THE MAYOR: I know lots who did.

SUPERVISOR POWER: If he did, when members of our families were going over and serving, I will say that notwithstanding any other considerations, if that is his attitude, I don't think he is qualified to serve as one of the members of your Board of Trustees. So I would like you to investigate it if you would.

THE MAYOR: All right. No quorum being present, nothing can be done further at this time, I presume.

SUPERVISOR POWER: The Veterans have got to be heard.

MR. GLENSOR: We want to see the financial report.

SUPERVISOR McSHEEHY: I make a motion we recess until Tuesday at two o'clock.

(Unreported discussion between members.)

SUPERVISOR HAVENNER: I move at this time that consideration of this matter be continued until Tuesday night at seven-thirty o'clock, Tuesday, the 25th, at seven-thirty p. m.

THE MAYOR: If I have to go to Los Angeles to meet President Coolidge to pay him the compliments of the City, you would let me off, I suppose, for that purpose.

SUPERVISOR McSHEEHY: Certainly, your Honor.

SUPERVISOR RONCOVIERI: I would like to ask a question, how long it will take to publish that report, Mr. Clerk?

THE CLERK: A few hours.

THE MAYOR: If there is no objection, the further consideration of this matter will be continued until seven-thirty o'clock on Tuesday, February 25, 1930.

SUPERVISOR GALLAGHER: I want to ask or make a motion, that all of the staff be excused who have been on duty here tonight.

THE MAYOR: If there is no objection, it is so ordered.

SUPERVISOR McSHEEHY: I move we adjourn.

SUPERVISOR RONCOVIERI: Second the motion.

THE MAYOR: If there is no objection, we stand adjourned. (Bringing down the gavel.)

Approved by the Board of Supervisors April 14, 1930.

Pursuant to Resolution No. 3402 (New Series) of the Board of Supervisors of the City and County of San Francisco, I, John S. Dunnigan, hereby certify that the foregoing are true and correct copies of the Journal of Proceedings of said Board of the dates stated and approved as above recited.

J. S. DUNNIGAN,
Clerk of the Board of Supervisors,
City and County of San Francisco.

Monday, February 24, 1930

urnal of Proceedings
Board of Supervisors

City and County of San Francisco

The Recorder Printing and Publishing Company
337 Bush Street, S. F.

JOURNAL OF PROCEEDINGS
BOARD OF SUPERVISORS

MONDAY, FEBRUARY 24, 1930, 2 P. M.

In Board of Supervisors, San Francisco, Monday, February 24, 1930, 2 p. m.

CALLING THE ROLL.

The roll was called and the following Supervisors were noted present:

Supervisors Andriano, Canepa, Gallagher, Hayden, Miles, Peyser, Power, Rossi, Shannon, Spaulding, Suhr, Toner—12.

Supervisor Colman noted present at 2:15 p. m.

Supervisor McGovern noted present at 2:10 p. m.

Supervisor McSheehy noted present at 2:07 p. m.

Supervisor Stanton noted present at 2:30 p. m.

Absent—Supervisors Havenner, Roncovieri—2.

Quorum present.

His Honor Mayor Rolph presiding.

APPROVAL OF JOURNAL.

The Journal of Proceedings of the previous meeting was laid over for approval until next meeting.

ROLL CALL FOR PETITIONS AND COMMUNICATIONS.

Citizens' Committee to Celebrate Taking Over Properties of Spring Valley Water Company.

The following was presented and read by the Clerk:

Communication from his Honor James Rolph, Jr., advising that he has appointed a Citizens Committee to celebrate the taking over of the properties of the Spring Valley Water Company on March 9, 1930. All members of the Board of Supervisors are requested to act on the committee and attend a meeting on February 27, 1930, at 2:30 p. m., in his office, to make preliminary arrangements.

Ordered *filed.*

Additional Head Clerk for Treasurer, to Handle Receipts and Disbursements of San Francisco Water Department.

The following was presented and read by the Clerk:

Communication from his Honor, James Rolph, Jr., recommending the appointment of an additional head clerk for the Treasurer's office, whose duty it shall be to handle receipts and disbursements of the San Francisco Water Department, recently created.

Referred to Finance Committee.

Ordinance Providing for Bureau of Fire Prevention and Public Safety.

The following was presented and read by the Clerk:

Communication from the San Francisco Junior Chamber of Commerce transmitting proposed ordinance providing for a Bureau of Fire Prevention and Public Safety to supersede the present ordinance; declaring that the Chamber has had the earnest and helpful cooperation of the Chief Engineer of the Fire Department, the Fire Marshal and other officials in its preparation, and expressing the belief that it will bring about material improvement in the hazardous conditions at present prevailing, and requesting careful study and final approval by Board.

Referred to Fire Committee.

Letter of Appreciation, Mrs. Mary Tobin.

The following was presented and read by the Clerk:

Communication from Mrs. Mary Tobin expressing her appreciation of the resolution adopted by the Board of Supervisors commemorating the death of her husband, David J. Tobin.

Ordered *filed.*

Memorial Grove, Golden Gate Park.

Communication from Edna A. Urmy, President Grove of Memory Association, Native Daughters of the Golden West and Native Sons of the Golden West, advising that the Native Sons of the Golden West have requested the Park Commissioners be instructed by the Board of Supervisors to expend the appropriation of $10,000 (Item 73 in the Budget, 1929-1930) for the development of the Memorial Grove in Golden Gate Park.

Referred to Education, Parks and Playground Committee.

Relative to Appointment of Superintendent of Airport.

The following matters were presented and read during the discussion of the subject indicated:

Telegram from Lieut.-Col. A. C. Brandt, declaring that he considered Captain Roy Francis best qualified applicant for the appointment of Superintendent of Mills Feld, asserting that his previous training and knowledge of aviation should render his services of great value to the City.

Ordered *filed.*

Also, communication from C. L. Smith, Adjutant, Floyd Bennett Aviation Post No. 333, American Legion, advising that the Floyd Bennett Aviation Post No. 333 of the American Legion, comprised of World War flyers, commends the action of the Airport Committee of the Board of Supervisors in the appointment of Captain Roy N. Francis as the Superintendent of Mills Field, declaring that his experience in aeronautical affairs dates back to the pre-war days, covers a record of outstanding achievements for the Government in the teaching of airport engineering and management, and that his executive ability and integrity are above question.

Ordered *filed.*

Leave of Absence, Jesse C. Colman, Supervisor.

The following was presented and read by the Clerk:

San Francisco, Cal., February 24, 1930.

Honorable Board of Supervisors, City and County of San Francisco, City Hall, San Francisco, California.

Gentlemen: The Honorable Jesse C. Colman, Supervisor, has made application to me for leave of absence, with permission to leave the State, commencing February 25, 1930, for a period of thirty (30) days.

Will you please concur with me in granting this leave?

Very sincerely yours,

(Signed) JAMES ROLPH, Jr., Mayor.

Whereupon, the following resolution was presented and *adopted:*

Resolution No. 32114 (New Series), as follows:

Resolved, That, in accordance with the recommendation of his Honor the Mayor, Honorable Jesse C. Colman, member of the Board of Supervisors, is hereby granted a leave of absence for a period of thirty days, commencing February 25, 1930, with permission to leave the State.

Ayes—Supervisors Andriano, Canepa, Colman, Gallagher, Havenner, McGovern, McSheehy, Miles, Peyser, Power, Roncovieri, Rossi, Shannon, Spaulding, Stanton, Suhr, Toner—17.

Absent—Supervisor Hayden—1.

SPECIAL ORDER—2:30 P. M.

The following matter was taken up:

Amendment to Food Terminal Ordinance.

Bill No. 8208, Ordinance No. ——— (New Series), as follows:

Amending Ordinance No. 8140 (New Series), providing that wholesale food terminals, warehouses, freight yards and ferry terminals shall not be constructed or established, erected or constructed within a certain district in the City and County of San Francisco, and establishing the boundaries of said district, and providing for penalties for the violation of the provisions hereof, by including in said prohibited structures and callings airplane landings and hydroplane landings, and the landing of passengers from airplanes or hydroplanes.

Be it ordained by the People of the City and County of San Francisco as follows:

That Ordinance No. 8140, the title of which is hereinbefore recited, is hereby amended to read as follows:

Section 1. No wholesale food terminal, warehouse, freight yard, or ferry terminal, or airplane landing or hydroplane landing, or any building or structure to be used as a wholesale food terminal, warehouse, freight yard, ferry terminal, airplane landing or hydroplane landing, shall be constructed, erected or established within the territory bounded on the north by the waters of San Francisco Bay, on the east by the westerly line of Van Ness avenue, on the south by Jackson street, and on the west by the westerly line of Lyon street, nor shall any structure for any of the purposes above mentioned be constructed or erected, projecting into the waters of the bay from the land included in the above described district.

Section 2. No building permit shall be issued or granted by the Board of Public Works for the erection, construction or alteration of any building, or structure, contrary to the provisions of this ordinance, and any permit so issued or granted shall be void.

Section 3. No certificate of occupancy shall be issued or granted by the Board of Health authorizing or permitting any person, firm or corporation to occupy or use any building or structure in place within the above bounded district for or as a wholesale food terminal, warehouse, freight yard or ferry terminal.

Section 4. Any person, firm or corporation violating any of the provisions of this ordinance shall be guilty of a misdemeanor, and upon the conviction thereof shall be punishable by a fine not to exceed $500.00 or by imprisonment in the County Jail not to exceed six months, or by both such fine and imprisonment. And any person, firm or corporation violating any of the provisions of this ordinance shall be deemed guilty of a separate offense for each and every day during any portion of which any violation of this ordinance is committed, permitted or continued by such person, firm or corporation.

Amendment and Reference.

The foregoing ordinance, amended on motion of Supervisor Stanton by the inclusion of the words "or airplane landing or hydroplane landing," was, on motion, *rereferred to the City Planning Commission* for approval.

Death of John J. Calish.

Supervisors Toner and Hayden presented:

Resolution No. 32109 (New Series), as follows:

Whereas, the Almighty, in His wisdom, has called from our midst John J. Calish, a late and respected resident of San Francisco. Mr. Calish was born in New York State, but resided in San Francisco for the past sixty years. His love for this, the city of his adoption, has been manifested by his activities in every forward movement that had for its object the betterment of San Francisco. He was especially active in the development of the Sunset District. His energies in that section have been so active that he was affectionately termed "The Mayor of the Sunset." He has frequently appeared before this Board with constructive policies for that district. In his passing San Francisco has lost a valuable citizen; the Sunset District has lost a valiant advocate and his friends have lost an associate of sterling character.

Resolved, That when this Board adjourns today it does so out of respect to his memory; be it

Further Resolved, That a copy of this resolution be spread upon the minutes and that a copy be sent to his bereaved family.

Adopted by the following vote:

Ayes—Supervisors Andriano, Canepa, Colman, Gallagher, Havenner, Hayden, McGovern, McSheehy, Miles, Peyser, Power, Roncovieri, Rossi, Shannon, Spaulding, Stanton, Suhr, Toner—18.

Remarks eulogizing the character, worth and civic activities of John J. Calish over a period of fifty years in San Francisco were made by his Honor Mayor Rolph, Supervisors Toner, Havenner, Hayden and others.

SPECIAL ORDER—4 P. M.

The following, on recommendation of the Airport Committee, were taken up:

Captain Roy N. Francis Appointed Superintendent of Mills Field Municipal Airport.

Resolution No. ————— (New Series), as follows:

Resolved, That Captain Roy N. Francis be and he is hereby appointed Superintendent of Mills Field Municipal Airport, effective February 1, 1930.

Airport Committee to Appoint Advisory Committee.

Resolution No. ————— (New Series), as follows:

Resolved, That the Airport and Aeronautics Committee be and is hereby authorized to select and appoint an Advisory Committee, to consist of citizens whose cooperation, advice and counsel, by reason of their training, experience and knowledge of aviation, would be of value and assistance to the Committee in the operation and management of Mills Field Municipal Airport; and be it

Further Resolved, That Resolution No. 30712 (New Series) be and the same is hereby repealed.

In re Appointment of Captain Roy N. Francis as Superintendent of Mills Field Municipal Airport.

The following was presented and read by the Clerk:

February 21, 1930.

To whom it may concern:

I have before me a transcript marked as "Meeting of the Board of Supervisors of the City and County of San Francisco, Monday, February 17, 1930, at 2 p. m." In re No. 25 on the calendar: Appointment of Captain Roy N. Francis as superintendent of Mills Field Municipal Airport.

I have never at any time since my resignation from the Citizens
Advisory Committee opposed, endorsed or have I anything derogatory
to say concerning any applicant for the superintendency of Mills Field,
as that is not a matter pertaining to this office.

All my recommendations are contained in the minutes of the meetings of the Citizens Advisory Committee attended by myself. The
last meeting I attended was on January 20, 1930.

(Sgd) EDISON E. MOUTON,
Supervising Inspector.

Oakland Airport, Oakland, Cal.

Supervisor Spaulding also read telegram from G. C. Brandt, Lieu-
tenant-Colonel Aviation Corps, United States Army, stating that he
considered Captain Roy Francis the best qualified applicant for appointment as Superintendent of airport.

Privilege of the Floor.

C. L. Smith, member of the American Legion, and representing Mr.
Mouton, was granted the privilege of the floor, on motion of Supervisor
Spaulding. He declared that he took up with Mr. Mouton the statement made by Mr. McSheehy "that he (Mouton) objected to the appointment of Captain Francis, and positively stated to me that at the
meeting that was held at Mr. Marvin's office, at 315 Montgomery street,
the committee did not endorse the appointment of Mr. Francis, and he
requested me (Supervisor McSheehy) to bring this matter to the attention of the Board today."

Mr. Mouton declared to me that he did not make that statement;
that he never at any time made a statement derogatory to the ability
or the character of Captain Roy Francis. He also denied the statement of Supervisor McSheehy to the effect that Captain Roy Francis
did not have a pilot's license.

Mr. Marvin, member of the Advisory Board, Municipal Airport, was
also heard at length as to the transaction at the last meeting of the
Advisory Board and the appointment of Captain Francis.

Captain Francis was also granted the privilege of the floor and was
interrogated by Supervisor McSheehy as to his qualifications.

Motion.

Supervisor Havenner moved that the Board issue a subpoena for Mr.
Mouton to appear at the next meeting.

Supervisor Shannon moved the previous question, seconded by Supervisor Canepa.

Motion Lost.

Whereupon, the roll was called on Supervisor Havenner's motion and
the same was *defeated* by the following vote:

Ayes—Supervisors Havenner, McSheehy, Power—3.

Noes—Supervisors Andriano, Canepa, Colman, Gallagher, Hayden,
McGovern, Miles, Peyser, Roncovieri, Rossi, Shannon, Spaulding, Stanton, Suhr, Toner—15.

Adopted.

Whereupon, the following resolutions were *adopted* by the following
vote:

Resolution No. 32099 (New Series), as follows:

Resolved, That Captain Roy N. Francis be and he is hereby appointed
Superintendent of the Mills Field Municipal Airport, effective February
1, 1930.

Ayes—Supervisors Andriano, Canepa, Colman, Gallagher, Havenner,
Hayden, McGovern, Miles, Peyser, Power, Roncovieri, Rossi, Shannon,
Spaulding, Stanton, Suhr, Toner—17.

No—Supervisor McSheehy—1.

Supervisor Hayden was excused by the meeting at 6:55 p. m. by the following vote:

Ayes—Supervisors Andriano, Canepa, Colman, Gallagher, Havenner, McGovern, Miles, Peyser, Power, Roncovieri, Rossi, Shannon, Spaulding, Stanton, Suhr, Toner—16.

No—Supervisor McSheehy—1.

Absent—Supervisor Hayden.

Resolution No. 32110 (New Series), as follows:

Resolved, That the salary of Captain Roy N. Francis, Superintendent of the Mills Field Municipal Airport, be and is hereby fixed at $500 per month, effective February 1, 1930.

Ayes—Supervisors Andriano, Canepa, Colman, Gallagher, Havenner, McGovern, Miles, Peyser, Power, Roncovieri, Rossi, Shannon, Spaulding, Stanton, Suhr, Toner—16.

No—Supervisor McSheehy—1.

Absent—Supervisor Hayden—1.

Rereferred.

Whereupon, on motion of Supervisor Shannon, the resolution providing for the appointment of an Advisory Board was ordered *rereferred to the Airport Committee.*

UNFINISHED BUSINESS.

Final Passage.

The following matters, heretofore passed for printing, were taken up and *finally passed* by the following vote:

Authorizations.

On recommendation of Finance Committee.

Resolution No. 32087 (New Series), as follows:

Resolved, That the following amounts be and the same are hereby authorized to be expended out of the hereinafter mentioned funds in payment to the following named claimants, to-wit:

Hetch Hetchy Water Construction Fund, Bond Issue 1928.

(1) Bryan Provision Company, ham and bacon (claim dated Jan. 30, 1930)...$ 526.62

(2) Challenge Cream and Butter Association, canned milk (claim dated Jan. 30, 1930)............................   525.00

(3) Coos Bay Lumber Company, lumber (claim dated Jan. 30, 1930)...   4,663.45

(4) Crucible Steel Company of America, steel (claim dated Jan. 30, 1930)..   4,357.95

(5) Del Monte Meat Company, meat (claim dated Jan. 30, 1930) 1,456.29

(6) Haas Brothers, groceries (claim dated Jan. 30, 1930)....   518.70

(7) Ingersoll Rand Company of California, machinery parts (claim dated Jan. 29, 1930)............................   1,805.70

(8) Rees Blow Pipe Manufacturing Company, blower piping systems (claim dated Jan. 29, 1930).....................   2,131.00

(9) Santa Cruz Portland Cement Company, cement (claim dated Jan. 30, 1930).....................................   3,084.00

(10) Sherry Bros., Inc., eggs (claim dated Jan. 30, 1930)....   524.40

(11) Soule Steel Company, steel (claim dated Jan. 30, 1930).   573.53

(12) United States Rubber Company, rubber boots, coats, etc. (claim dated Jan. 30, 1930)............................   3,339.20

(13) Utah Fuel Company, coal (claim dated Jan. 30, 1930)...   597.49

(14) Coos Bay Lumber Company, lumber (claim dated Feb. 3, 1930) 502.32

(15) Ingersoll Rand Company of California, machinery parts (claim dated Feb. 3, 1930)............................... 1,409.65

(16) Santa Cruz Portland Cement Company, cement (claim dated Feb. 3, 1930)... 526.00

(17) Sherry Bros., Inc., eggs (claim dated Feb. 3, 1930)..... 529.20

Auditorium Fund.

(18) Musical Association of San Francisco, services of San Francisco Symphony Orchestra for concert of Feb. 18, 1930) ....$ 2,000.00

(19) Serge Prokoleff, services as soloist, concert of Feb. 18, 1930 (claim dated Feb. 7, 1930)......................... 675.00

Tax Judgments, Appropriation 57.

(20) Goldman, Nye & Spicer, attorneys for judgment creditors, seventh installment, one-tenth of final judgment as per schedule attached (claim dated Feb. 15, 1930).........$ 1,355.07

(21) William F. Humphrey, attorney for judgment creditors, fifth installment, one-tenth of final judgment per schedule attached (claim dated Feb. 6, 1930)..................... 2,769.31

Special School Tax.

(22) Alta Electric Company, sixth payment, electrical work, Park-Presidio Junior High School (claim dated Feb. 3, 1930) 4,055.62

(23) Meyer Bros., sixth payment, general construction, Park-Presidio Junior High School (claim dated Feb. 3, 1930)... 43,575.58

(24) Scott Company, sixth payment, mechanical equipment, Park-Presidio Junior High School (claim dated Feb. 3, 1930) 4,839.75

(25) Scott Company, fifth payment, plumbing and gas-fitting, Park-Presidio Junior High School (claim dated Feb. 3, 1930) ....:............... 1,778.95

(26) Oscar Aaron, fourth payment, plumbing for Geary Street School (claim dated Feb. 3, 1930)................ 1,669.43

(27) Scott Company, second payment, mechanical equipment for addition to Francisco Junior High School (claim dated Feb. 3, 1930)... 562.50

(28) MacDonald & Kahn, third payment, general construction of viewing stand, South Side (Balboa) High School (claim dated Feb. 3, 1930)............................. 6,805.44

(29) A. Lettich, second payment, plumbing for viewing stand at South Side (Balboa) High School (claim dated Feb. 3, 1930) 959.93

(30) Oscar Aaron, final payment, plumbing system, Marina Elementary School (claim dated Feb. 4, 1930)............ 2,438.94

(31) Lee Dixon, final payment, painting for Marina Elementary School (claim dated Feb. 3, 1930).............. 1,317.12

(32) A. Lettich, final payment, mechanical equipment for Marina Elementary School (claim dated Feb. 4, 1930)..... 4,266.80

(33) Jacks & Irvine, eighth payment, general construction of Roosevelt Junior High School (claim dated Feb. 3, 1930).. 6,479.60

(34) Scott Company, sixth payment, mechanical equipment for Roosevelt Junior High School (claim dated Feb. 3, 1930) 4,075.39

(35) Scott Company, sixth payment, plumbing and gas-fitting for Roosevelt Junior High School (claim dated Feb. 3, 1930) 1,197.30

Bernal Cut Construction Fund, Bond Issue 1927.

(36) MacDonald & Kahn, Inc., twelfth payment, improvement of Bernal Cut, Contract No. 1 (claim dated Feb. 5, 1930)...$ 8,100.00

Boulevard Bond Construction Fund, Issue 1927.

(37) Louis J. Cohn, fifteenth payment, improvement of Bay
Shore boulevard, Section A, Contract No. 6, Potrero avenue
to Silver avenue (claim dated Feb. 5, 1930)..............$ 4,000.00
(38) Eaton & Smith, eighth payment, improvement of
Junipero Serra boulevard, Contract No. 13, Sloat boulevard
to county line (claim dated Feb. 5, 1930)................ 12,300.00

Sewer Bond Construction Fund, Issue 1929.

(39) Eaton & Smith, first payment, construction of Alemany
boulevard storm drain, Section B (claim dated Feb. 4,
1930) ....$ 4,500.00

County Road Fund.

(40) Pacific Coast Aggregates, Inc., sand and gravel for
street reconstruction (claim dated Jan. 28, 1930)........$ 3,078.10
(41) Standard Oil Company of California, asphalt for street
reconstruction (claim dated Jan. 28, 1930).............. 3,867.15
(42) Standard Building Material Company, cement for street
reconstruction (claim dated Jan. 28, 1930).............. 871.20
(43) Board of Public Works (Stores and Yards, Appropriation 30-A), reimbursement for repairs to equipment used
in street reconstruction (claim dated Jan. 25, 1930)....... 1,624.00
(44) J. J. Calish, for removal of sand, etc., on Twenty-seventh
avenue between Kirkham and Lawton streets (claim dated
Feb. 3, 1930)... 2,250.00
(45) Chas. L. Harney, repairs, fills and bulkheads on Noriega
street (claim dated Feb. 3, 1930)....................... 672.50
(46) Pacific Coast Aggregates, Inc., gravel for street reconstruction (claim dated Feb. 3, 1930).................... 557.73
(47) Pacific Coast Aggregates, Inc., gravel for street reconstruction (claim dated Feb. 3, 1930).................... 678.69
(48) The Texas Company, gasoline furnished for account of
street reconstruction (claim dated Feb. 3, 1930).......... 692.51
(49) The Fay Improvement Company, seventh payment, improvement of Portola drive from Twenty-fourth street to
Fowler avenue (claim dated Feb. 4, 1930)................ 20,000.00
(50) Granfield, Farrar & Carlin, final payment for surfacing
and drainage of Laidley street slide between Mateo and
Roanoke streets (claim dated Feb. 5, 1930).............. 604.45

Municipal Airport.

(51) Meyer Rosenberg, replacing main lighting cable lead at
Mills Field, San Francisco Airport (claim dated Feb. 4,
1930) ....$ 613.20

General Fund, 1929-1930.

(52) William J. Quinn, police contingent expense (claim dated
Feb. 1, 1930)... $750.00
(53) W. C. Uhte, overhauling and painting Patrol Wagon
No. 5 (claim dated Feb. 1, 1930)........................ 800.00
(54) Auto Registration Service, 109,754 registration cards
for use of Assessor (claim dated Feb. 3, 1930)........... 625.60
(55) Phillips & Van Orden Co., printing statements for use
of the Assessor (claim dated Feb. 3, 1930).............. 1,904.40
(56) Associated Charities, widows' pensions (claim dated
Feb. 7, 1930) 7,802.70
(57) Eureka Benevolent Society, widows' pensions (claim
dated Feb. 7, 1930)..................................... 946.01
(58) Little Children's Aid, widows' pensions (claim dated
7, 1930) 6,432.49
(59) San Francisco Chronicle, official advertising (claim
dated Feb. 10, 1930) 1,404.84

(60) The Recorder Printing & Publishing Company, printing
of Supervisors' Calendar, etc. (claim dated Feb. 10, 1930)..   673.63
(61) The Recorder Printing & Publishing Company, printing
of Superior Court Calendars, etc. (claim dated Feb. 10,
1930) 515.00
(62) A. P. Jacobs, rent of premises No. 333 Kearny street,
February 3 to March 3, 1930 ....   1,120.75
(63) Healy & Donaldson, tobacco furnished Laguna Honda
Home (claim dated Jan. 23, 1930)........................   899.04
(64) Monarch Flour Co, flour for Laguna Honda Home (claim
dated Jan. 23, 1930)....................................   1,322.25
(65) C. Nauman & Co., seed potatoes for Laguna Honda Home
(claim dated Jan. 23, 1930).............................   945.33
(66) H. E. Teller Co., coffee for Laguna Honda Home (claim
dated Jan. 23, 1930)....................................   620.00
(67) Dion R. Holm, legal services rendered in connection
with telephone litigation, month of February (claim dated
Feb. 4, 1930)...   850.00
(68) N. Randall Ellis, engineering services rendered in connection with telephone litigation, month of February (claim
dated Feb. 4, 1930).....................................   750.00
(69) Southern Pacific Company, reimbursement of taxes paid,
first installment, 1929-1930, as rental for Lot 4A, Block
3810, occupied by the City and County as Municipal Pipe
Yard (claim dated Feb. 10, 1930)........................   3,665.18

Ayes—Supervisors Andriano, Canepa, Gallagher, Hayden, Miles,
Peyser, Power, Roncovieri, Rossi, Shannon, Spaulding, Suhr, Toner—13.
Absent—Supervisors Colman, Havenner, McGovern, McSheehy, Stan-
ton—5.

Appropriation for Traffic Engineering.

Also, Resolution No. 32088 (New Series), as follows:

Resolved, That the sum of $1,635 be and the same is hereby set aside,
appropriated and authorized to be expended out of "Traffic Signals,"
Budget Item 57, to defray the cost of traffic engineering for the month
of February, 1930.

Ayes—Supervisors Andriano, Canepa, Gallagher, Hayden, Miles,
Peyser, Power, Roncovieri, Rossi, Shannon, Spaulding, Suhr, Toner—13.
Absent—Supervisors Colman, Havenner, McGovern, McSheehy, Stau-
ton—5.

Oil and Boiler Permits.

On recommendation of Fire Committee.

Resolution No. 32089 (New Series), as follows:

Resolved, That the following revocable permits be and are hereby
granted:

Oil Tanks.

A. L. Matthew, 434 Leavenworth street, 1500 gallons capacity.

G. Molinari, 1516 Larkin street, 1500 gallons capacity.

A. Depaoli, west side of Dartmouth street, 100 feet north of Woolsey
streets, 1500 gallons capacity.

L. Kroner, 158 Jordan avenue, 1500 gallons capacity.

Boiler.

James Allan & Sons, south side Evans avenue, 200 feet east of Third
street, 50 horsepower.

The rights granted under this resolution shall be exercised within
six months, otherwise said permit shall become null and void.

Ayes—Supervisors Andriano, Canepa, Gallagher, Hayden, Miles,
Peyser, Power, Roncovieri, Rossi, Shannon, Spaulding, Suhr, Toner—13.
Absent—Supervisors Colman, Havenner, McGovern, McSheehy, Stan-
ton—5.

Auto Supply Station Permit, Edw. J. O'Neill, Lombard and Lyon Streets.

Also, Resolution No. 32090 (New Series), as follows:

Resolved, That Edw. J. O'Neill be and is hereby granted permission, revocable at will of the Board of Supervisors, to have transferred to him automobile supply station permit heretofore granted Sidney Franklin by Resolution No. 27269 (New Series) for premises at southeast corner of Lombard and Lyon streets.

The rights granted under this resolution shall be exercised within six months, otherwise said permit shall become null and void.

Ayes—Supervisors Andriano, Canepa, Gallagher, Hayden, Miles, Peyser, Power, Roncovieri, Rossi, Shannon, Spaulding, Suhr, Toner—13.

Absent—Supervisors Colman, Havenner, McGovern, McSheehy, Stanton—5.

Auto Supply Station Permit, Luis Whiteman, San Jose Avenue and Dolores Street.

Also, Resolution No. 32091 (New Series), as follows:

Resolved, That Luis Whiteman be and is hereby granted permission, revocable at will of the Board of Supervisors, to have transferred to him automobile supply station permit heretofore granted Luigi Bacigalupi by Resolution No. 31318 (New Series) for premises on gore of San Jose avenue and Dolores street.

The rights granted under this resolution shall be exercised within six months, otherwise said permit shall become null and void.

Ayes—Supervisors Andriano, Canepa, Gallagher, Hayden, Miles, Peyser, Power, Roncovieri, Rossi, Shannon, Spaulding, Suhr, Toner—13.

Absent—Supervisors Colman, Havenner, McGovern, McSheehy, Stanton—5.

Auto Supply Station Permit, W. H. Woodfield, Jr., Bartlett and Twenty-second Streets.

Also, Resolution No. 32092 (New Series), as follows:

Resolved, That Wm. H. Woodfield, Jr., be and is hereby granted permission, revocable at will of the Board of Supervisors, to maintain and operate an automobile supply station on the northwest corner of Bartlett and Twenty-second streets.

The rights granted under this resolution shall be exercised within six months, otherwise said permit shall become null and void.

Ayes—Supervisors Andriano, Canepa, Gallagher, Hayden, Miles, Peyser, Power, Roncovieri, Rossi, Shannon, Spaulding, Suhr, Toner—13.

Absent—Supervisors Colman, Havenner, McGovern, McSheehy, Stanton—5.

Auto Supply Station Permit, Twin Peaks Parlor No. 214, Twenty-fourth and Diamond Streets.

Also, Resolution No. 32093 (New Series), as follows:

Resolved, That Twin Peaks Parlor 214, Native Sons of the Golden West, be and is hereby granted permission, revocable at will of the Board of Supervisors, to maintain and operate an automobile supply station on the southeast corner of Twenty-fourth and Diamond streets.

The rights granted under this resolution shall be exercised within six months, otherwise said null and void.

Ayes—Supervisors Andriano, Canepa, Gallagher, Hayden, McSheehy, Miles, Peyser, Power, Roncovieri, Rossi, Shannon, Spaulding, Suhr, Toner—14.

Absent—Supervisors Colman, Havenner, McGovern, Stanton—4.

Condemnation for the Acquisition of Lands for School Purposes, Located at Morse Street, Southwest from Lowell Street, for Longfellow School.

On recommendation of Public Buildings and Lands Committee.

Resolution No. 32094 (New Series), as follows:

Resolved, By the Board of Supervisors of the City and County of San Francisco, that public interest and necessity require the acquisition by the City and County of San Francisco, a municipal corporation, of the following property, situated in the City and County of San Francisco, State of California, more particularly described as follows, to-wit:

Commencing at a point on the southeasterly line of Morse street, distant thereon 267 feet southwesterly from the southwesterly line of Lowell street, running thence southwesterly along the said southeasterly line of Morse street 168 feet; thence at a right angle southeasterly 213 feet; thence at a right angle northeasterly 178 feet; thence at a right angle northwesterly 213 feet to the southeasterly line of Morse street and point of commencement. Being a portion of Blocks 51, 52, 58 and 96, West End Homestead Association, also known as Lots Nos. 26, 27, 28, 29 and 30, in Block 6474, on Assessor's Map Book. Be it

Further Resolved, That said property is suitable, adaptable, necessary and required for the public use of said City and County of San Francisco, to-wit: For school purposes. It is necessary that a fee simple title be taken for such use.

The City Attorney is hereby ordered and directed to commence proceedings in eminent domain against the owners of said parcel of land and of any and all interest therein, or claims thereto, for, the condemnation thereof for the public use of the City and County of San Francisco, as aforesaid.

Ayes—Supervisors Andriano, Canepa, Gallagher, Hayden, McSheehy, Miles, Peyser, Power, Roncovieri, Rossi, Shannon, Spaulding, Suhr, Toner—14.

Absent—Supervisors Colman, Havenner, McGovern, Stanton—4.

Action Deferred.

The following resolution was, on motion, *laid over one week*:

Laundry Permits.

Resolution No. ———— (New Seriese), as follows:

Resolved, That the following revocable permits be and are hereby granted:

Laundries.

Eloise Aiso, 1089 Pine street.
John Batsere, 976 Pine street.
Anna Biscay, 992 Sutter street.
Ruth Clausen, 94 Seventh street.
Mrs. V. J. Laurent, 447 Ellis street.
J. Nougue, 707 O'Farrell street.
Mme. P. Pomme, 1147 McAllister street.
Marie Sabacca, 808 Post street.
Mme. J. Saffores, 841 Powell street.
Mrs. A. Termello, 41 Franklin street.
Louise Vannucci and Gloria Cheader, 405 O'Farrell street.

The rights granted under this resolution shall be exercised within six months, otherwise said permits shall become null and void.

Blanket protest filed by Mr. Alford, Board of Trade, Laundry Industry.

PRESENTATION OF BILLS AND ACCOUNTS.

Your Finance Committee, having examined miscellaneous demands not required by law to be passed to print, and amounting to $83,722.30, recommends same be allowed and ordered paid.

Approved by the following vote:

Ayes—Supervisors Andriano, Canepa, Gallagher, Hayden, McSheehy,

Miles, Peyser, Power, Roncovieri, Rossi, Shannon, Spaulding, Suhr, Toner—14.

Absent—Supervisors Colman, Havenner, McGovern, Stanton—4.

NEW BUSINESS.

Passed for Printing.

The following matters were *passed for printing*:

Authorizations.

Resolution No. ———— (New Series) as follows:

On recommendation of Finance Committee.

Resolved, That the following amounts be and the same are hereby authorized to be expended out of the hereinafter mentioned funds in payment to the following named claimants, to-wit:

1928 *Hetch Hetchy Water Bonds.*

(1) Coos Bay Lumber Co., lumber (claim dated Feb. 7, 1930).$ 2,003.44
(2) Del Monte Meat Co., meat (claim dated Feb. 7, 1930).... 1,156.50
(3) Ingersoll-Rand Co. of California, nine Drifter complete and machinery parts (claim dated Feb. 7, 1930)........... 4,116.20
(4) Pacific Coast Steel Corporation, steel (claim dated Feb. 7, 1930) 1,239.44
(5) Santa Cruz Portland Cement Co., cement (claim dated Feb. 7, 1930) 526.00
(6) Sherry Bros. Inc., eggs (claim dated Feb. 7, 1930)....... 619.50
(7) United States Rubber Co., rubber coats and boots (claim dated Feb. 7, 1930) 770.40
(8) Worthington Machinery Corporation of California, Ltd., six pumps and parts (claim dated Feb. 6, 1930)........... 1,033.25
(9) Cement Gun Co., Inc., one cement gun equipped (claim dated Feb. 10, 1930) 1,640.21
(10) Consolidated Mills Co., Inc., lumber (claim dated Feb. 10, 1930) 552.41
(11) Coos Bay Lumber Co., lumber (claim dated Feb. 10, 1930) 1,499.58
(12) Haas Brothers, groceries (claim dated Feb. 10, 1930)... 559.72
(13) State Compensation Insurance Fund, premium on insurance covering Hetch Hetchy employments (claim dated Feb. 10, 1930) 6,924.35
(14) Santa Cruz Portland Cement Co., cement (claim dated Feb. 10, 1930) 1,578.00

Robinson Bequest Interest Fund.

(15) James Rolph Jr., Mayor, for relief of destitute women and children (claim dated Feb. 17, 1930).................$ 1,260.00

Playground Fund.

(16) C. F. Weber & Co., portable bleachers for playgrounds (claim dated Feb. 19, 1930) ....$ 526.10

Municipal Railway Fund.

(17) Pacific Gas and Electric Co., electricity furnished Municipal Railways, month of January, 1930 (claim dated Feb. 10, 1930) $43,899.00
(18) San Francisco City Employees' Retirement System, to match contributions from Municipal Railway employees, month of January, 1930 (claim dated Feb. 7, 1930)........ 7,967.18

Special School Tax.

(19) D. A. Pancoast, for "Von Duprin" type panic bolts furnished various schools (claim dated Feb. 8, 1930)........$ 4,210.22
(20) Park Commissioners, care of school grounds for month of January (claim dated Feb. 7, 1930)................... 1,383.33

(21) J. H. McCallum, lumber for schools (claim dated Feb. 11, 1930) 667.96

(22) Meyer Bros., final payment, general construction of addition to Sunshine School (claim dated Feb. 11, 1930) 4,272.23

(23) Samuel Lightner Hyman and A. Appleton, final payment for architectural services rendered for account of Second Unit of the South Side (Balboa) High School (claim dated Feb. 11, 1930) 3,446.20

(24) W. H. Crim, eighth payment, architectural services for Park-Presidio Junior High School (claim dated Feb. 19, 1930) 1,271.26

(25) Edward F. Dowd, first and final payment, electrical fixtures for Marina Elementary School (claim dated Feb. 19, 1930) 734.00

County Road Fund.

(26) Spring Valley Water Co., water for concrete work, reconstruction of streets (claim dated Feb. 8, 1930)..............$ 1,067.16

(27) Eclipse Lime & Cement Co., cement for street reconstruction (claim dated Feb. 13, 1930)......................... 881.76

(28) Board of Public Works, Budget Item 461, reimbursement for repairs to equipment used in street reconstruction (claim dated Feb. 17, 1930) 1,351.75

(29) Board of Public Works, Budget Item 524, reimbursement for redressing of curbs used in street reconstruction (claim dated Feb. 7, 1930) 505.00

(30) Board of Public Works, Budget Item 524, reimbursement for redressing of curbs used in street reconstruction (claim dated Feb. 7, 1930) 998.12

(31) Board of Public Works, Budget Item 524, reimbursement for redressing of curbs used in street reconstruction (claim dated Feb. 7, 1930) 826.25

(32) Board of Public Works, Budget Item 521, reimbursement for asphalt-labor used in street reconstruction work (claim dated Feb. 7, 1930) 1,480.80

General Fund, 1929-1930.

(33) Neal, Stratford & Kerr, field books for Assessor (claim dated Feb. 18, 1930) ....$ 544.00

(34) Berringer & Russell, hay, etc., Police Department (claim dated Feb. 17, 1930) 1,241.23

(35) Glaser Bros.-Judell Co., tobacco furnished County Jail (claim dated Feb. 14, 1930) 666.93

(36) Old Homestead Bakery, bread furnished County Jails (claim dated Feb. 14, 1930) 840.79

(37) H. F. Dugan Co., hospital supplies, San Francisco Hospital (claim dated Jan. 31, 1930)........................ 785.85

(38) Kahn & Co., X-ray films, San Francisco Hospital (claim dated Jan. 31, 1930) 1,324.80

(39) Old Homestead Bakery, bread for San Francisco Hospital (claim dated Jan. 31, 1930) 1,119.36

(40) San Francisco International Fish Co., fish for San Francisco Hospital (claim dated Jan. 31, 1930).............. 649.36

(41) J. T. Freitas Co., Inc., eggs, San Francisco Hospital (claim dated Jan. 31, 1930) 2,470.72

(42) San Francisco Dairy Co., milk, San Francisco Hospital (claim dated Jan. 31, 1930) 4,453.04

(43) Fred L. Hilmer Co., butter, San Francisco Hospital (claim dated January 31, 1930) 2,238.95

(44) Troy Laundry Machinery Co., laundry extractor, furnished and installed in San Francisco Hospital (claim dated Jan. 31, 1930) 1,288.50

(45) Richfield Oil Co., fuel oil furnished San Francisco Hospital (claim dated Jan. 31, 1930) 2,399.68

(46) Schweitzer & Co., meat, San Francisco Hospital (claim dated Jan. 31, 1930) 1,662.78

(47) Del Monte Meat Co., meat for San Francisco Hospital (claim dated Jan. 31, 1930) 811.70

(48) California Meat Co., meat for San Francisco Hospital (claim dated January 31, 1930) 2,657.86

(49) Western Meat Co., meat for San Francisco Hospital (claim dated Jan. 31, 1930) 765.71

(50) Mangrum-Holbrook Co., crockery for Laguna Honda Home (claim dated Jan. 31, 1930) 796.27

(51) Pacific Gas & Electric Co., electricity furnished Tubercular Preventorium (claim dated Feb. 20, 1930) 611.80

(52) Edw. Barry Co., real estate rolls furnished Assessor (claim dated Feb. 18, 1930) 1,136.25

(53) M. J. Lynch, second payment, furnishing and erecting street signs (claim dated Feb. 19, 1930) 3,590.00

(54) Pacific Gas & Electric Co., lighting public buildings (claim dated Feb. 17, 1930) 6,540.15

(55) County Road Fund, reimbursement of expenditures in connection with covering of main sewers (claim dated Feb. 13, 1930) 935.99

(56) Spring Valley Water Co., water furnished public buildings (claim dated Feb. 13, 1930) 2,058.08

(57) Gurley-Lord Tire Co., seven pairs Gruss Air Springs for street cleaning trucks (claim dated Feb. 13, 1930) 1,354.50

Special School Tax.

(56) Fred Medart Mfg. Co., gymnasium equipment for Balboa High School (claim dated Feb. 18, 1930) .... $ 877.50

(57) Meyer Bros., acceptance payment, general construction of Geary Street School (claim dated Feb. 21, 1930) 32,036.75

Payments for Property, County Road Fund.

Also, Resolution No. ———— (New Series), as follows:

Resolved, That the following amounts be and the same are hereby set aside and appropriated out of County Road Fund, and authorized in payment to the following named persons; being payments for properties required for the following purposes, to-wit:

(1) To W. O. Smith and Irma E. Smith and California Pacific Title and Trust Company, for portions of Lots 7 and 8 in Block 2712 (87 ft. x 60 ft. irregular), as per the Assessor's Block Books, and required for the widening of Corbett avenue, approved by Resolution No. 32063, New Series (claim dated Feb. 10, 1930)........................... $5,125.00

(2) To Charles Monestier and Title Insurance & Guaranty Co., for all of Lot 14 in Block 2659, as per the Assessor's Block Books, and required for the extension of Market street, approved by Resolution No. 32064, New Series (claim dated Jan. 29, 1930)................................... 725.00

Adopted.

The following resolution was *adopted*:

Payments for Properties, County Road and Boulevard Funds.

On recommendation of Finance Committee.

Resolution No. 32095 (New Series), as follows:

Resolved, That the following amounts be and the same are hereby set aside and appropriated out of the hereinafter mentioned funds, and authorized in payment to the following named claimants; being payments for properties required for purposes, to-wit:

County Road Fund.

(1) To Elizabeth Christian and Title Insurance & Guaranty Co., for portion of Lot 18 in Block 6727 (25 x 5, irregular), as per the Assessor's Block Books, and required for the widening of Chenery street; per acceptance of offer by Resolution No. 32062, New Series (claim dated Jan. 29, 1930). $435.40

(2) To Patrick Reilly and Mary Reilly and Title Insurance & Guaranty Co., for portion of Lot 19 in Block 6727 (6 x 25), as per the Assessor's Block Books, and required for the widening of Chenery street; per acceptance of offer by Resolution No. 32006, New Series (claim dated Jan. 21, 1930). 437.20

(3) To J. P. Loustaunau and Title Insurance & Guaranty Co, for portion of Lot 20 in Block 6727 (32 x 3), as per the Assessor's Block Books, and required for the widening of Chenery street; per acceptance of offer by Resolution No. 32061, New Series (claim dated Feb. 3, 1930)............ 17.50

(4) To John W. Martin and Aura E. Martin and Title Insurance & Guaranty Co:, for portion of Lot 17 in Block 6727 (1 x 27), as per the Assessor's Block Books, and required for the widening of Chenery street; per acceptance of offer by Resolution No. 32006, New Series (claim dated Jan. 21, 1930).. 10.00

(5) To Mathias Bohnert and Louis Bohnert and Title Insurance & Guaranty Co., for portion of Lot 4 in Block 6685 1 x 29), as per the Assessor's Block Books, and required for the widening of Chenery street; per acceptance of offer by Resolution No. 32006, New Series (claim dated Jan. 21, 1930). 10.00

(6) To Andrea Sbarboro & Sons and California Pacific Title & Trust Co., for portions of Lots 4 and 5 in Block 6959B (50 x 21), as per the Assessor's Block Books, and required for the opening and widening of Cayuga avenue; per acceptance of offer by Resolution No. 32065, New Series claim dated Feb. 3, 1930).............................. 185.00

Boulevard Bond Fund, Issue 1927.

(7) To Antonio Tiscornia, for release of damages to Lot 2, as per the Assessor's Block Books of the City and County, caused by construction operations of the opening of Alemany boulevard; as per Resolution No. 32007, New Series (claim dated Jan. 15, 1930)........................... 75.00

Ayes—Supervisors Andriano, Canepa, Colman, Gallagher, Havenner, Hayden, McSheehy, Miles, Peyser, Power, Roncovieri, Rossi, Shannon, Spaulding, Suhr, Toner—16.

Absent—Supervisors McGovern, Stanton—2.

Passed for Printing.

The following matters were *passed for printing*:

Appropriation for Cancer Treatment by Board of Health.

On recommendation of Finance Committee.

Resolution No. ———— (New Series), as follows:

Resolved, That the sum of $20,000 be and the same is hereby set aside, appropriated and authorized to be expended out of "Urgent Necessity," Budget Item No. 24, for expenses of cancer treatment by the Department of Public Health.

Appropriation for Employment of Bricklayer and Hodcarrier, Department of Public Works.

Also, Resolution No. ———— (New Series), as follows:

Resolved, That the sum of $2,500 be and the same is hereby set aside and appropriated out of County Road Fund to the credit of the Department of Public Works, for the employment of additional hod carrier and bricklayer in the Sewer Repair Division for the balance of the present fiscal year. (Request of Board of Public Works, Resolution No. 109358.)

(To credit of Budget Item 559, $1,375.)
(To credit of Budget Item 560, $1,125.)

Adopted.

The following resolutions were *adopted*:

Appropriation, $279, for Work at City Property.

On recommendation of Finance Committee.

Resolution No. 32096 (New Series), as follows:

Resolved, That the sum of $279 be and the same is hereby set aside, appropriated and authorized to be expended out of "Work in Front of City Property," Budget Item No. 34, for the construction of artificial stone sidewalks on the west side of Somerset street between Felton and Silliman streets, at City property.

Ayes—Supervisors Andriano, Canepa, Colman, Gallagher, Havenner, Hayden, McSheehy, Miles, Peyser, Power, Roncovieri, Rossi, Shannon, Spaulding, Suhr, Toner—16.

Absent—Supervisors McGovern, Stanton—2.

Board of Works Interdepartmental, Transfer of Funds.

Also, Resolution No. 32097 (New Series), as follows:

Resolved, That the following amounts be and the same are hereby set aside and appropriated out of the hereinafter mentioned accounts, Board of Public Works, to the Credit of Bureau of "Stores and Yards," Budget Item No. 461; being reimbursements for expenditures in connection with repairs to equipment for the various bureaus, to-wit:

(1) Street Cleaning, Budget Item 552	$362.68
(2) Sewer Repair, Budget Item 565	230.06
(3) Auto Maintenance, Budget Item 577	110.63
(4) Building Repair, Budget Item 446	21.63
(5) Bureau of Engineering, Budget Item 504	16.87
(6) Stores and Yards, Budget Item 469	33.75
Total	$775.62

Ayes—Supervisors Andriano, Canepa, Colman, Gallagher, Havenner, Hayden, McSheehy, Miles, Peyser, Power, Roncovieri, Rossi, Shannon, Spaulding, Suhr, Toner—16.

Absent—Supervisors McGovern, Stanton—2.

Passed for Printing.

The following resolution was *passed for printing*:

Appropriations for Repairs to County Jail No. 1.

On recommendation of Finance Committee.

Resolution No. ———— (New Series), as follows:

Resolved, That the sum of $3,770 be and the same is hereby set aside and appropriated out of "Maintenance, Subsistence and Equipment," Budget Item No. 269, Sheriff's Department, to the credit of Department of Public Works, Budget Item No. 442, for the reconstruction of the floors in Federal wing and felony wing, County Jail No. 1. (Request of Sheriff, dated February 12, 1930.)

Adopted.

The following resolution was *adopted*:

Transferring $5,000 From Fire Department Personal Service to Equipment.

On recommendation of Finance Committee.

Resolution No. 32098 (New Series), as follows:

Resolved, That the sum of $5,000 be and the same is hereby set aside out of Fire Department "Personal Services," Appropriation 41-A. to the credit of Fire Department, "Equipment," Appropriation 41-E.

Ayes—Supervisors Andriano, Canepa, Colman, Gallagher, Havenner, Hayden, McSheehy, Miles, Peyser, Power, Roncovieri, Rossi, Shannon, Spaulding, Suhr, Toner—16.

Absent—Supervisors McGovern, Stanton—2.

Passed for Printing.

The following matters were *passed for printing*:

Appropriation for Construction in Office of the Treasurer.

On recommendation of Finance Committee.

Resolution No. ——— (New Series), as follows:

Resolved, That the sum of $1,110 be and the same is hereby set aside. appropriated and authorized to be expended out of "City Hall Repairs and Painting," Budget Item No. 54, for construction of wood and glass partition and the removing and reinstalling, with necessary additions, one steel and glass booth, to new location, in office of the Treasurer. City Hall.

Appropriations.

Also, Resolution No. ——— (New Series), as follows:

Resolved, That the following amounts be and the same are hereby set aside, appropriated and authorized to be expended out of Boulevard Bond Fund, Issue 1927. for the following constructions, to-wit:

(1) For the improvement of the Great Highway, lower road, from Ulloa street to Lincoln way, including engineering, inspection and extras, per contract awarded Federal Construction Company $123,000

(2) For construction of public comfort stations at the Great Highway and Judah street. and at the Great Highway and Taraval street. including engineering, inspection and extras. per contract awarded Clinton-Stephenson Construction Company $60.000

Reimbursing Board of Public Works for Gilding Iron Work. City Hall.

Also. Resolution No. ——— (New Series). as follows:

Resolved, That the sum of $988.67 be and the same is hereby set aside and appropriated out of "City Hall Repairs and Painting." Budget Item No. 54. to the credit of Department of Public Works. Budget Item No. 442; being reimbursement for expenditure in the gilding of ornamental iron work of the City Hall.

Plans, Etc., Gridiron, Canopy, Electrical Equipment for Stage for Civic Auditorium.

Also. Bill No. 8195. Ordinance No. ——— (New Series), as follows:

Ordering the preparation of plans and specifications for the construction of a gridiron. canopy, and the installation of electrical equipment for the stage of the Civic Auditorium; authorizing and directing the Board of Public Works to enter into contract for said construction, and permitting progressive payments to be made during the progress of said work.

Be it ordained by the people of the City and County of San Francisco as follows:

Section 1. The Board of Public Works is hereby authorized, instructed and empowered to prepare plans and specifications for the gridiron, canopy, and the installation of electrical equipment for the stage of the Civic Auditorium, and to enter into contract for the construction of said gridiron, canopy, and the installation of electrical equipment for the stage of the Civic Auditorium, in accordance with the plans and specifications so prepared.

Section 2. The said Board of Public Works is hereby authorized and permitted to incorporate in the contract for the construction of said gridiron, canopy, and the installation of electrical equipment for the stage of the Civic Auditorium conditions that progressive payments shall be made in the manner set forth in said specifications and as provided by Section 21, Chapter I, Article VI, of the Charter.

Section 3. This ordinance shall take effect immediately.

Ayes—Supervisors Andriano. Canepa, Colman, Gallagher, Hayden, Miles, Peyser, Power, Roncovieri, Rossi, Shannon, Spaulding, Suhr, Toner—14.

Noes—Supervisors Havenner, McSheehy—2.

Absent—Supervisors McGovern, Stanton—2.

(Supervisors Havenner and McSheehy explained that they would vote *aye* next week, when the report of the Finance Committee was in "on the condition of the funds.")

Appropriation, $55,000, County Road Fund, for Property Between Clay and Merchant Streets, Adjoining The Embarcadero.

Also, Resolution No. ————— (New Series), as follows:

Resolved, That the sum of $55,000 be and the same is hereby set aside, appropriated and authorized to be expended out of County Road Fund for the purchase of property between Clay and Merchant streets, adjoining The Embarcadero.

Adopted.

The following resolution was *adopted*:

Creation of Positions of Eight Welfare Investigators to Be Assigned to County Welfare Board and Report on Old Age Pension Applications.

On recommendation of Finance Committee.

Resolution No. 32100 (New Series), as follows:

Resolved, That his Honor the Mayor is hereby requested to approve the creation of eight additional positions under the Board of Supervisors. Said positions to be designated eight Welfare Investigators at $150 per month each. The duties of these Welfare Investigators will be to investigate and report on applications for pensions for needy aged persons as provided by State law. Said Welfare Investigators to be assigned to the County Welfare Board.

Ayes—Supervisors Andriano, Canepa, Colman. Gallagher, Havenner, Hayden, McGovern, McSheehy, Miles, Peyser, Power, Roncovieri, Rossi, Shannon, Spaulding, Stanton, Suhr, Toner—18.

Passed for Printing.

The following resolutions were *passed for printing*:

Oil Tanks.

On recommendation of Fire Committee.

Resolution No. ————— (New Series), as follows:

Resolved, That the following revocable permits are hereby granted:

Oil Tanks.

Enterprise Foundry Co., southwest side Fremont street, 150 feet southeast of Folsom street, 1500 gallons capacity.

A. Germarro, 503 Cabrillo street, 1500 gallons capacity.

H. O. Lindeman, west side Nineteenth avenue, 225 feet north of California street, 1500 gallons capacity.

Mary Scheffer, 493 Eddy street, 1500 gallons capacity.

O. Mueller, 1535 Sacramento street, 1500 gallons capacity.

P. Bellegarde, 1627 Clay street, 1500 gallons capacity.

M. Solomon, southeast corner of La Playa and Balboa street, 1500 gallons capacity.

The rights granted under this resolution shall be exercised within six months, otherwise said permit shall become null and void. ·

Public Garage Transfer, D. C. Parker and John Boido, 1737 Jackson Street.

Also, Resolution No. ———— (New Series), as follows:

Resolved, That D. C. Parker and John Boido be and are hereby granted permission, revocable at will of the Board of Supervisors, to have transferred to them public garage permit heretofore granted E. S. Allen by Resolution 28325 (New Series) for premises at 1737 Jackson street.

The rights granted under this resolution shall be exercised within six months, otherwise said permit shall become null and void.

Public Garage Transfer, Foote & Sarin, 1301 Pierce Street.

Also, Resolution No. ———— (New Series), as follows:

Resolved, That Foote & Sarin be and are hereby granted permission, revocable at will of the Board of Supervisors, to have transferred to them public garage permit heretofore granted Geo. D. Guenley by Resolution No. 26214 (New Series) for premises at 1301 Pierce street.

The rights granted under this resolution shall be exercised within six months, otherwise said permit shall become null and void.

Automobile Supply Station Transfer. W. W. Stone and A. E. Walsh, Southwest Corner of Cabrillo Street and Forty-seventh Avenue.

Also, Resolution No. ———— (New Series), as follows:

Resolved, That W. W. Stone and A. E. Walsh be and are hereby granted permission, revocable at will of the Board of Supervisors, to have transferred to them automobile supply station permit heretofore granted H. Heskins by Resolution No. 31976 (New Series) for premises at southwest corner of Cabrillo street and Forty-seventh avenue. ·

The rights granted under this permit shall be exercised within six months, otherwise said permit shall become null and void.

Automobile Supply Station, George Bepler, Southeast Corner of Seventeenth and Connecticut Streets.

Also, Resolution No. ———— (New Series), as follows:

Resolved, That Geo. Bepler be and is hereby granted permission, revocable at will of the Board of Supervisors, to maintain and operate an autombile supply station on the southeast corner of Seventeenth and Connecticut streets.

The rights granted under this resolution shall be exercised within six months, otherwise said permit shall become null and void.

Automobile Supply Station, George Gaspar, Northwest Corner of Cortland and San Bruno Avenues.

Also, Resolution No. ———— (New Series), as follows:

Resolved, That George Gaspar be and is hereby granted permission, revocable at will of the Board of Supervisors, to maintain and operate an automobile supply station on premises at the northwest corner of Cortland avenue and San Bruno avenue.

The rights granted under this resolution shall be exercised within six months, otherwise said permit shall become null and void.

Protest filed.

Commercial Garage Permit, Gilmore Oil Company, Ltd., North Side of Eighteenth Street, 70 Feet East of Third Street.

Also, Resolution No. —————— (New Series), as follows:

Resolved, That the Gilmore Oil Company, Ltd., be and is hereby granted permission, revocable at will of the Board of Supervisors, to maintain and operate a commercial garage on the north side of Eighteenth street, 70 feet east of Third street.

The rights granted under this resolution shall be exercised within six months, otherwise said permit shall become null and void.

Automobile Supply Station, Gilmore Oil Company, Ltd., Northeast Corner of Eighteenth and Third Streets.

Also, Resolution No. —————— (New Series), as follows:

Resolved, That the Gilmore Oil Company, Ltd., be and is hereby granted permission, revocable at will of the Board of Supervisors, to maintain and operate an automobile supply station at premises on the northeast corner of Eighteenth and Third streets.

The rights granted under this resolution shall be exercised within six months, otherwise said permit shall become null and void.

Adopted.

The following resolutions were *adopted*:

Commending Doctors Walter B. Coffey and John B. Humber for Their Cancer Treatment.

On recommendation of Public Health Committee.

Resolution No. 32101 (New Series), as follows:

Whereas, the medical world of scientific research has been aroused by the startling announcement of a treatment for cancer; and

Whereas, to Doctors Walter B. Coffey and John B. Humber of San Francisco is due the honor and glory of the beneficent discovery; and

Whereas, the validity of the claim has been substantiated by numerous cures, so as to place it beyond the realm of theory; be it therefore

Resolved, That the Board of Supervisors of the City and County of San Francisco hereby offers Doctors Walter B. Coffey and John B. Humber its sincere homage and commendation for their marvelous research work, and expresses heartfelt gratitude for their discovery of a treatment which will relieve the awful sufferings of thousands of humanity; and be it

Further Resolved, That a copy of this resolution be sent to Doctors Walter B. Coffey and John B. Humber.

Ayes—Supervisors Andriano, Canepa, Colman, Gallagher, Havenner, Hayden, McGovern, McSheehy, Miles, Peyser, Power, Roncovieri, Rossi, Shannon, Spaulding, Stanton, Suhr, Toner—18.

Street Lights.

On recommendation of Street Lighting Committee.

Resolution No. 32102 (New Series), as follows:

Resolved, That the Pacific Gas and Electric Company be and it is hereby authorized and requested to remove and install street lights as follows:

Remove 400 M. R.

East side Twenty-ninth avenue between Taraval and Ulloa streets.

Eighteenth avenue between Irving and Judah streets.

Corner Ninth avenue and Ortega and Pacheco streets.
Ninth avenue between Ortega and Pacheco streets.
Corner Visitacion avenue and Desmond street.
Greenwich street from Broderick street to Lyon street (4).
Shotwell street between Twenty-fifth and Twenty-sixth streets.
Thirty-third avenue between Taraval and Ulloa streets.
Yosemite avenue, second pole west of Lane street.
Pine and Steiner and Pierce streets.
North and south sides Pine street from Fillmore street to Pierce
street.
Steiner and Waller streets.
Waller street between Fillmore and Steiner streets.
Twenty-fourth avenue between Lawton and Moraga streets.
Corner Forty-sixth avenue and Anza and Balboa streets.
East side Forty-sixth avenue, first south of Anza streets.
Turk street, Market street to Van Ness avenue (15).
Ashbury street between Frederick and Clayton streets (7).
Turk street between Van Ness avenue and Laguna street (6).
Turk street, Jones to Van Ness avenue (15).

Remove 250 M. R.

Paris street between Persia and Russia avenues.
East side Forty-sixth avenue, opposite Sutro Heights avenue.
Winfield avenue between Eugenia and Virginia streets.
State street (6).

Install 400 Type "C" C. P.

Laguna street, Bay street to Marina boulevard (13).

Remove 600 M. R.

West side Laguna street between Bay street and Marina boulevard (3).

Remove Gas.

Balboa Terrace.

Install 250 Type "C."

Balboa Terrace as per map.

Install 400 C. P. O. B.

Divisadero street between Jefferson and Beach streets.
Divisadero street between Jefferson and Marina streets.
East and west sides Paris street between Persia and Russia avenues.
Bon View street between Coso and Esmeralda.
Bocana street and Eugenia avenue.
Turk street, Jones street to Van Ness avenue, northeast and south-
west corners, east and west sides.
Ashbury street between Frederick and Clayton streets (10).
North and south sides Turk street from Van Ness avenue to Laguna
street.
Northeast and southwest corners Turk and Franklin, Gough, Octavia
and Laguna streets.
Hudson avenue between Keith and Lane streets.
Yosemite avenue, second and fourth poles west of Lane street.
East and west sides Ninth avenue between Ortega and Pacheco
streets.
Northwest and southeast corners Ortega and Pacheco streets.
East and west sides Eighteenth avenue between Irving and Judah
streets.
Peninsula avenue, south of Lathrop street.
Northeast corner Desmond street and Visitacion avenue.
South side Visitacion avenue between Bay Shore Highway and Des-
mond street.
Northeast and southwest corners Shotwell and Twenty-fifth street
and Twenty-sixth street.

East and west sides Shotwell street between Twenty-fifth and Twenty-sixth streets.

East and west sides Twenty-ninth avenue between Taraval and Ulloa streets.

East and west sides San Jose avenue between Thirtieth and Randall streets.

San Jose avenue between Twenty-ninth and Thirtieth streets.

North and south sides Greenwich street from Broderick street to Lyon street.

Northwest and southeast corners Greenwich and Baker streets and Lyon street.

Northwest corner Greenwich and Broderick streets.

Alabama street between Army street and Precita avenue.

East and west sides Thirty-third avenue between Taraval and Ulloa streets.

Capitol avenue between Ocean avenue and De Montford street.

Felton and Amhurst streets.

Divisadero street between Jefferson street and Marina boulevard.

Divisadero street between Beach and Jefferson streets.

Rhode Island street between Twenty-second and Twenty-third streets.

Lyon street between Chestnut and Lombard streets.

Mississippi street between Nineteenth and Twentieth streets.

Twentieth street and Pennsylvania avenue.

North and south sides Pine street, Fillmore street to Pierce street.

Northeast and southwest corners Pine street, Steiner and Pierce streets.

North and south sides Waller street between Fillmore and Steiner streets.

Northeast and southwest corners Waller and Steiner streets.

Jules avenue (front of 318.)

Sussex street, 25 feet north of No. 11.

Duncan and Douglass streets.

Bon View street between Coso and Esmeralda avenues.

Third street, Thomas avenue to intersection of San Bruno avenue (26).

East and west sides Twenty-fourth avenue between Lawton and Moraga streets.

East and west sides Twenty-fifth avenue between Lawton and Moraga streets.

Northeast corner Thirtieth avenue and Lawton street.

Northeast and southwest corners Forty-sixth avenue and Anza street and Balboa street.

Southwest corner Forty-sixth avenue and Sutro Heights avenue.

East side Forty-sixth avenue between Anza street and Sutro Heights avenue.

Seventeenth street between Ord and Saturn streets.

Winfield avenue between Eugenia and Virginia streets.

Guerrero and Hill streets.

Hale street between Merrill and Barneveld streets.

Milan street between Huron and Moneta avenues.

Southeast corner Alemany boulevard and Admiral street.

Alemany boulevard, third pole south of Admiral street.

Alemany boulevard, first pole north of Silver avenue.

Alemany boulevard, first pole south of Silver avenue.

State street (install 6).

Turk street, Jones to Van Ness avenue (6 to each block).

Remove 600 *C. P. O. B.*

East side Taylor street, first north of Ellis street.

Southwest corner Taylor and Ellis streets.

Turk street, Van Ness avenue to Laguna street (2).

Install 600 C. P. O. B.

Geary street and Presidio avenue.

Install 300-Watt Electrolier.

Northeast corner Fourth and Shipley streets.

Install 400 Type "C."

Amazon avenue and Naples street, front of church (2).

Install 250 O. B.

Berwick and Heron streets.

Girard street, Silver avenue to Mansell (1 in center of each block).

Ayes—Supervisors Andriano, Canepa, Colman, Gallagher, Havenner, Hayden, McGovern, McSheehy, Miles, Peyser, Power, Roncovieri, Rossi, Shannon, Spaulding, Stanton, Suhr, Toner—18.

Masquerade Ball Permit, Booker T. Washington Community Center, Friday, February 21, 1930, Scottish Rite Hall.

On recommendation of Police Committee.

Resolution No. 32103 (New Series), as follows:

Resolved, That Booker T. Washington Community Center be and it is hereby granted permission to conduct a masquerade ball Friday, February 21, 1930, in Scottish Rite Hall, Van Ness avenue and Sutter street.

Ayes—Supervisors Andriano, Canepa, Colman, Gallagher, Havenner, Hayden, McGovern, McSheehy, Miles, Peyser, Power, Roncovieri, Rossi, Shannon, Spaulding, Stanton, Suhr, Toner—18.

Award of Contract, Nurses' Uniforms.

On recommendation of Supplies Committee.

Resolution No. 32104 (New Series), as follows:

Resolved, That award of contract be hereby made to Doctors and Nurses Outfitting Co., Inc., on bid submitted February 10, 1930 (Proposal No. 555) for furnishing the following, viz., uniforms for nurses for San Francisco Hospital, individual fittings for each nurse, as same may be ordered from time to time during the calendar year 1930. Deliveries must conform to city samples.

Item No. 1—170 suits, gingham, blue and white striped; $3.95 each.

Item No. 2—282 aprons and bibs, pequot, bleached; $1.40 per set.

Item No. 3—288 caps, pequot, bleached; $0.30 each.

Item No. 4—552 cuffs, pequot, bleached; $0.30 per pair.

Item No. 5—282 collars, No. 1 special, bleached; $0.30 each.

Item No. 6—54 dresses, white; Burton's Irish poplin, removable buttons (for graduation); $5.95 each.

Item No. 7—45 capes, cadet blue cloth, turkey-red flannel lined; $13.25 each.

Resolved, That a bond in the amount of $500 be required for faithful performance of contract.

Resolved, That all other bids submitted thereon be rejected.

Ayes—Supervisors Andriano, Canepa, Colman, Gallagher, Havenner, Hayden, McGovern, McSheehy, Miles, Peyser, Power, Roncovieri, Rossi, Shannon, Spaulding, Stanton, Suhr, Toner—18.

Award of Contract, X-Ray Supplies.

Also, Resolution No. 32105 (New Series), as follows:

Resolved, That award of contract be hereby made on bids submitted February 17, 1930 (Proposal No. 561) for furnishing the following, viz.: X-Ray supplies for San Francisco Hospital.

Note—The quantities stated below are for immediate delivery.

Option—The right is reserved to the City to place additional orders on any or all of the given items for quantities not to exceed 20 per cent of the stated quantities, provided said option be exercised before June 30, 1930.

Eastman Safety X-Ray Films Company.

Item No. 1—288 doz. 8 x 10, $2.76⅓; General Electric X-Ray Corporation, contractor.

Item No. 2—216 doz. 11 x 14, $5.48½; General Electric X-Ray Corporation, contractor.

Item No. 3—288 doz., 14 x 17, $8.33; General Electric X-Ray Corporation, contractor.

Item No. 4—12 doz. cans developer powder, Eastman No. 4, $25.20; Eastman Kodak Stores, Inc., contractor.

Resolved, That all other bids submitted thereon be rejected.

Resolved, That no bonds be required.

Ayes—Supervisors Andriano, Canepa, Colman, Gallagher, Havenner, Hayden, McGovern, McSheehy, Miles, Peyser, Power, Roncovieri, Rossi, Shannon, Spaulding, Stanton, Suhr, Toner—18.

Award of Contract, Hospital Supplies.

Also, Resoltuion No. 32106 (New Series), as follows:

Resolved, That award of contract be hereby made on bids submitted February 17, 1930 (Proposal No. 562), for furnishing the following, viz.: Hospital supplies for Department of Public Health.

Item No. 1—1412 rolls bandages, roller gauze, 40x44 mesh, 1x10 yards, at 81 cents per roll—Reid Bros., Inc.

Item No. 2—1700 lbs. cotton, absorbent, plain, best grade, long fiber, absolutely free from seeds and other particles, in 1-lb. packages, at 27 cents per lb.—Seabury & Johnson.

Item No. 3—200 rolls gauze, plain, absorbent, 24x20 mesh, in 100-yard rolls, at $3.25 per roll—Reid Bros., Inc.

Item No. 4—912 rolls gauze, plain, 16x20 mesh, 36-inch flat roll, in 100-yard rolls, at $2.80 per roll—Reid Bros., Inc.

Item No. 5—160 lbs. lint, absorbent, 1-lb. carton, at 99 cents per lb.—Reid Bros., Inc.

Item No. 6—67 rolls muslin, oiled opal, in 5-yard rolls, at $3.70 per roll—Reid Bros., Inc.

Item No. 7—620 rolls plaster, adhesive, zinc oxide, in rolls 12-inch x 5 yards, at 82 cents per roll—Reid Bros., Inc.

Item No. 8—100 rolls gauze, 16x20 mesh, 100-yard rolls, 4-inch, 4-ply, at $2.80 per roll—Reid Bros., Inc.

Item No. 9—500 lbs. cotton, absorbent, cheap grade, in 1-lb. rolls, at 19 cents per lb.—Johnson & Johnson.

Item No. 10—100 rolls gauze, 16x20, 18-inch fold, in rolls of 100 yards, at $2.80 per roll—Reid Bros., Inc.

Delivery: One-half of the above stated "quantity required" upon each item must be delivered within 15 days of date of award of contract and the balance within 30 days of date of award of contract.

Note: All above awards are made to the lowest bidder, except when award is made in consideration of deliveries or on account of the quality as determined or recommended by the Purchaser of Supplies.

Resolved, That no bonds be required.

Resolved, That all other bids submitted hereon be rejected.

Ayes—Supervisors Andriano, Canepa, Colman, Gallagher, Havenner, Hayden, McGovern, McSheehy, Miles, Peyser, Power, Roncovieri, Rossi, Shannon, Spaulding, Stanton, Suhr, Toner—18.

Award of Contract, Sheet Music.

Also, Resolution No. 32107 (New Series), as follows:

Resolved, That award of contract be hereby made for furnishing sheet music for School Department on bids submitted February 10,

1930 (Proposal No. 559), and tabulation thereof on file in the Bureau of Supplies, which is by this reference made a part hereof; said matter having heretofore received full consideration in an open public meeting of the Supplies Committee of the Board of Supervisors and the awards herein approved by it, same are now made to the following, viz.:

Bid No. 1—Henry Grobe, contractor.
Bid No. 2—Sherman, Clay & Co., contractor.
Bid No. 3—John P. Broder, Inc., contractor.
Bid No. 4—Waters & Ross, contractor.
Resolved, That no bonds he required.
Resolved, That all other bids submitted thereon be rejected.

Ayes—Supervisors Andriano, Canepa, Colman, Gallagher, Havenner, Hayden, McGovern, McSheehy, Miles, Peyser, Power, Roncovieri, Rossi, Shannon, Spaulding, Stanton, Suhr, Toner—18.

Award of Contract, Bread.

Also, Resolution No. 32108 (New Series), as follows:

Resolved, That award of contract be hereby made on bids submitted February 17, 1930 (Proposal No. 557), for furnishing the following, viz.: Fresh bread for four months' period commencing March 1 and ending June 30, 1930:

Part I. Awarded to Peoples Baking Co.
Delivery to be made to the public institutions daily except Sundays.
Note: The Park Commissioners are excluded from bid on Part I.

Hearth, $0.0625 per lb.; Vienna, $0.0625 per lb.; round French, $0.0625 per lb.; whole wheat, $0.0625 per lb.; graham, $0.0625 per lb.; pan, $0.0625 per lb.; rye, $0.0625 per lb.; twist, $0.0625 per lb.; raisin, $0.0725 per lb.; bran, $0.0625 per lb.; gluten, $0.25 per lb.

Part II. For Park Commissioners, for playground and restaurant activities. It is understood that the City may order as it needs these goods in any quantities it sees fit and deliveries will be made promptly by the contractor at such times.

The City will endeavor to place orders daily before 8:30 a. m. and the contractor must make deliveries within 2 hours thereafter. Later in the day, if the occasion arises, additional orders may be placed and the contractor shall be obliged to make immediate delivery, this being necessary to take care of the public if there should be a rush of trade.

Quality—To be the same as served at first-class restaurants.
Pullman Loaves—2-lb., awarded to Peoples Baking Co., per lb., $0.071.
Pullman Loaves—4-lb., awarded to Peoples Baking Co., per lb., $0.071.

Buns (for Frankfurters)—Awarded to Langendorf United Bakeries, Inc., per doz., $0.15.
Resolved, That bonds for faithful performance of contract be required as follows, viz.:
Peoples Baking Co., in the amount of $500.
Langendorf United Bakeries, Inc., in the amount of $100.
Resolved, That all other bids submitted thereon be rejected.

Ayes—Supervisors Andriano, Canepa, Colman, Gallagher, Havenner, Hayden, McGovern, McSheehy, Miles, Peyser, Power, Roncovieri, Rossi, Shannon, Spaulding, Stanton, Suhr, Toner—18.

Mayor Retires.

At 4:25 p. m. his Honor the Mayor retired and Supervisor Rossi was elected to preside.

Stafford Appraisal.

Supervisor Rossi moved that next Monday, at 3 p. m., be fixed as Special Order to hear report of Finance Committee on the Stafford appraisal and the employment of John Barry.
So ordered.

Hyde Street Lighting Assessment District.

Supervisor Gallagher moved that the Hyde street lighting assessment matter be made a Special Order for 2:30 p. m. next Monday.

So ordered.

SPECIAL ORDER—3 P. M.

The following matters were taken up:

RULES OF PROCEEDINGS OF THE BOARD OF SUPERVISORS.

Resolved, that the rules hereinafter set forth be and the same are hereby adopted as the Rules of Proceedings of this Board of Supervisors, to wit:

STANDING COMMITTEES.

1. The following shall constitute the standing committees of the Board (the first named member to be chairman thereof):

Airport and Aeronautics—Spaulding, Peyser, Miles.

Auditorium—Hayden, Canepa, Colman.

Civil Service—Havenner, McSheehy, Rossi.

Education, Parks and Playgrounds—McSheehy, Suhr, Andriano.

Finance—Rossi, Power, Hayden.

Fire—Canepa, Peyser, Toner.

Industrial Development and City Planning—Gallagher, Stanton, Hayden.

Judiciary—Suhr, Andriano, Roncovieri.

Lighting, Water and Telephone Service and Electricity—Stanton, McGovern, Shannon.

Municipal Concerts and Public Celebrations—Roncovieri, Colman, Gallagher.

Police and Licenses—Andriano, Shannon, McGovern.

Public Buildings and Lands—Shannon, Rossi, Suhr.

Public Health—Toner, McSheehy, Roncovieri.

Public Utilities—Colman, Spaulding, Havenner.

Public Welfare and Publicity—Peyser, Spaulding, Miles.

Streets and Tunnels—Power, Canepa, Gallagher.

Supplies—Miles, Stanton, Power.

Traffic—McGovern, Havenner, Toner.

Every Committee shall set a stated time of meeting, or the Committee may meet at a time to be set by the chairman, and every member will be expected to attend every meeting of his Committee, and to be present promptly on time. The clerk of each Committee shall keep a record of the attendance of the members, and he shall report such record to the Clerk of the Board, and the Clerk of the Board shall have the report of the attendance of members at committee meetings available at all times for the information of any or all members of the Board.

DUTIES OF COMMITTEES.

2. The respective duties of each of the foregoing Committees and the time of meetings are hereby defined as follows:

AIRPORT AND AERONAUTICS—To have control and management of the Municipal Airport; to report and recommend on applications for leasing of hangars and concessions in said Airport; to consider and report on all matters relating to said Airport.

AUDITORIUM—To have control and management of the Municipal Auditorium and entertainments held therein under the auspices of the city as provided in Ordinance No. 5320 (New Series); to lease said building and the several halls and apartments therein; to report and recommend on applications for leasing of said building for public assemblages and gatherings; to consider and report on all matters relating to the management, conduct and maintenance of said Auditorium.

CIVIL SERVICE AND RETIREMENT SYSTEM—To consider all matters relating to Civil Service in the several departments and to promote efficiency and economy in expenditures; to consider matters relating to the Retirement System, and all reports of the Board of Administration of the Retirement System shall be referred to it for investigation and report thereon.

COMMERCIAL AND INDUSTRIAL DEVELOPMENT AND CITY PLANNING—To assist in promoting the establishment of industries in San Francisco and to cooperate with commercial and industrial organizations in all efforts to establish new industries; to consider measures helpful in developing San Francisco as an industrial center and to encourage delegations to points where needed to bring new industries, and generally to consider manufacturing problems as related to the industrial needs of the community; to cooperate with the United States, State officials and civic organizations in support of national and state legislation designed to promote world trade and the United States Merchant Marine; to bring about the location of a foreign trade zone within the City and County of San Francisco; to inaugurate a movement to the end that the management, control and development of San Francisco's harbor be placed locally, and also to cooperate with the Federal and State authorities on all matters, especially legislation, that tend for the further development and utilization of San Francisco's harbor to meet the needs of the world's commerce; to promote friendly relations between the City and contiguous and neighboring communities, to consider all matters relating to the City's expansion, and to act in an advisory capacity between the City Planning Commission and the Board of Supervisors and to hear such matters concerning city planning as may be referred to it by the Board of Supervisors; to propose measures for developing and accelerating transcontinental railway and interurban railroad transportation on this peninsula; to confer with adjacent cities, towns and counties on intercommunity problems and to suggest to the Board in what manner other committees may be of help in peninsula development.

EDUCATION, PARKS AND PLAYGROUNDS—To consider and report upon all matters relating to the Departments of Education, Parks and Playgrounds and recreation centers, including the Aquatic Park, and to cooperate with the Board of Education, Playground Commission and Park Commission regarding the development and increased usefulness of these departments.

FINANCE—To perform all duties required by the Charter; to audit all bills and report on all matters that may be referred to it by the Board of Supervisors; to act as a budget committee for the Board, hold hearings on budget estimates of and with all departments, receive recommendations from all other committees of the Board, and formulate a budget for submission to the Board on or before the second Monday of May. (Meets Fridays at 2 p. m.)

FIRE—To consider all matters relating to the Fire Department; to report on all applications for garage, boiler, laundry and other permits referred to it.

JUDICIARY—To consider and report upon Charter amendments and all matters referred to it by the Board.

LIGHTING, WATER SERVICE, TELEPHONE SERVICE AND ELECTRICITY—To attend to the proper lighting of streets, public parks and public buildings; to investigate and correct complaints of water service and extensions thereof, and telephone service; to recommend installation and removal of City telephones; to recommend from time to time extensions of underground wire system, and to have general charge of all matters pertaining to electricity other than public lighting and amendments to the building laws.

MUNICIPAL CONCERTS AND PUBLIC CELEBRATIONS—To have charge of the Municipal Band and conduct all concerts that are given under the auspices of the City and County of San Francisco (except those concerts under the management of the Park Commissioners and the Auditorium Committee of this Board); to assist in promotion of all semi-public celebrations, dedications, etc.

POLICE AND LICENSES—To consider legislation concerning the Police Department; to investigate the management and character of penal institutions; to consider all matters affecting public morals; to report upon applications for permits referred to it by the Board, including free licenses to those deserving them, and report on all licenses, including taxicabs and public conveyances for hire.

PUBLIC BUILDINGS AND LANDS—To consider the erection of all public buildings and the purchase of sites for all public purposes (except airport) upon recommendation of the respective departments; to consider and report upon the repairs to public buildings, and to recommend as to the janitorial, elevator and other service required for the proper conduct of all buildings of the City and County; also to assign to the various offices and departments the various rooms and places in the City Hall and Hall of Justice.

PUBLIC HEALTH—To consider all matters relating to health and sanitation; to see that institutions under the control of the Board of Health are properly conducted; to establish and maintain a high standard of service in public hospitals and Relief Home; to consider and report upon all complaints of nuisances; to make recommendations upon applications for permits which may be referred to it by the Board; also removal and destruction of garbage.

PUBLIC UTILITIES—To consider and pass upon all matters relating to public utilities, their acquisition, construction, control and management, whether municipally or privately owned, including transbay bridges, transportation, lighting, power, water and steam heating; to be empowered to, as far as their authority permits, carry out the provisions of Ordinance No. 8637 (New Series).

PUBLIC WELFARE AND PUBLICITY—To consider matters relating to the social well-being of the community other than those heretofore provided for, and generally to act upon all matters of public advertising, and pass on all bills chargeable against the advertising fund; to consider all matters relating to the Bureau of Weights and Measures.

RULES—To consider amendments to the Rules and such other matters as may be referred to it by the Board. To have supervision of and give instructions to the chauffeurs of the Board of Supervisors.

STATE LAWS AND LEGISLATION—To be appointed by the Finance Committe when occasion requires. To consider all matters pending before the Legislature and proposed legislation which affects the City and County of San Francisco, directly or indirectly, and to make such recommendations to the Board as may be deemed advisable, and to appear before the State Legislature in advocacy of any measures or. in opposition to measures as the Board may advise.

STREETS AND TUNNELS—To consider all matters relating to the construction, improvement and maintenance of streets and sewers, including highways outside the County, for which the City and County is authorized to appropriate money, the closing, opening and widening of streets and the cleaning of streets; to designate the streets for the Improvement and repair of which appropriations may be made in the budget and to allocate the same. Also direct the expenditure of money received from the State for the construction of public highways; to consider and report upon applications for spur and industrial tracks;

to consider and report upon all matters relating to tunnels, and to recommend all necessary purchases of lands for road, street and boulevard purposes.

SUPPLIES—To consider and have charge of the purchase of all supplies as provided by the Charter; to prepare schedules for general supplies and to recommend award of contracts; to inspect deliveries and quality and quantity of supplies; to pass on all requisitions for non-contract supplies; to supervise the purchase and distribution of all books, stationery, etc.

TRAFFIC AND SAFETY—To investigate and report on matters relative to traffic conditions in the City and propose Ordinances regulating traffic and the promotion of safety in connection therewith.

CONVENING OF BOARD.

3.   The Board shall convene at 2 o'clock p. m. on each Monday, and the Clerk shall immediately, after the call to order, which shall be at 2 o'clock p. m., call the roll of the members of the Board and shall record those present and absent. The Clerk shall also record the time of arrival of those members of the Board who arrive after 2 o'clock p. m., and the name of such member and the time of his arrival shall be entered upon the journal.

It shall be the duty of each Committee charged with the duty of cooperating with any particular department to investigate the financial needs of such department to be provided for in the annual budget; to consider such department's budget estimates and to recommend to the Finance Committee such modifications or changes thereof as it may deem proper.

The designations and duties of the foregoing Committees are hereby made part of these rules.

RULES OF ORDER.

4.   The Mayor shall be President of the Board of Supervisors. He shall call each regular, adjourned or special meeting to order at the hour appointed and shall proceed with the order of business.   In the absence of the Mayor, the Clerk shall call the roll and the Board shall appoint a presiding officer pro tempore from its own members, who shall have the same right to vote as other members.

The presiding officer shall preserve order and decorum.

The Clerk shall, immediately after the call to order, call the roll of members of the Board, and the record of those present and absent shall be entered upon the Journal.

5.   Whenever it shall be moved and carried by 12 members that the Board go into Committee of the Whole, the President shall leave the chair and the members shall appoint a chairman of the Committee of the Whole, who shall report the proceedings of said Committee.

6.   The rules of the Board shall be observed in the Committee of the Whole, except Rule 18, limiting the time of speaking, and Rule 38, relating to the privilege of the floor.

7.   A motion, in Committee of the Whole, to rise and report the question, shall be decided without debate.

8.   The Clerk shall have clips, upon which shall be kept all Bills, Ordinances, Resolutions and Reports to be acted upon by the Board, except those not reported upon by a Committee.

9.   No Bill, Ordinance or Resolution shall be considered by the Board unless it has been introduced by a member of the Board or by a Committee of the Board, and the Bill, Ordinance or Resolution must be read by the Clerk in open meeting before being referred to Committee.   At the time of introduction the presiding officer shall first indicate to what Committee a Bill, Ordinance or Resolution ought to be referred, and it shall be so referred unless, upon majority vote

without debate, the Board shall order it referred to some other committee.

Action by the Board shall not be taken upon any Bill, Ordinance
or Resolution until it has been referred to and acted upon by a Committee of the Board.

10.   The Order of Business, which shall not be departed from except
by the consent of 12 members, shall be as follows:

    1.   Roll Call.

    2.   Approval of Journal.

    3.   Calendar Matters (uncontested).

    4.   Roll Call for the Introduction of Resolutions, Bills and
Communications Not Considered or Reported on by a Committee.

    5.   Completion of Calendar Business.

    6.   Communications and Reports From City and County
Officers.

    7.   Reports of Committees.

    8.   Roll call for the Introduction of Resolutions, Bills and
Communications Not Considered or Reported On by a Committee.

11.   If any question under debate contains several points, any member may have the points segregated and acted upon separately.

12.   When a motion has been made and carried or lost, it shall be
in order for any member voting with the prevailing side to move to
"reconsider the vote" on that question.

A member may change his vote before the result is announced in
order to move to "reconsider the vote" on that question.   The vote
upon such motion to reconsider shall not be taken before the next
regular meeting of the Board.   No question shall be reconsidered more
than once, and motion to reconsider shall apply only to the main question.   Motion to reconsider shall have precedence over every other
motion.   It shall require 10 votes to carry any motion to reconsider the
vote by which any Bill, Ordinance or Resolution has been passed or
defeated.

13.   A motion to refer or lay on the table until decided shall pre-
elude all amendments to the main question.   A motion to lay on the
table or to postpone indefinitely shall require a majority vote of the
members present.

14.   It shall be the duty of the Clerk to issue such certificates as
may be required by Ordinances or Resolutions and transmit copies of
said Ordinances or Resolutions to the various departments affected
thereby.   It shall also be the duty of the Clerk to cause the publication
in the official newspaper of all Bills, Ordinances, proposals and awards
as required by the Charter.

15.   All accounts and bills shall be referred to the Finance Committee, provided that any Committee having jurisdiction over subject of
expenditures may request that bills he first sent to that Committee
before being acted upon by the Finance Committee and the Board.

16.   The President shall preserve order and decorum, and prevent
demonstrations of approval or disapproval on the part of persons in
the Chambers of the Board, and shall decide questions of order, subject
to an appeal to the Board.

17.   When a Supervisor desires to address the Board he shall arise
in his place, address the presiding officer, and when recognized he
shall proceed to speak.   No Supervisor shall be recognized when
seated or when away from his seat.

18.   No Supervisor shall speak more than twice in any one debate
on the same subject, and at the same stage of the Bill, Ordinance,
Resolution or Motion without the consent of a majority of the Board.
and Supervisors who have once spoken shall not again be entitled to
the floor so long as any Supervisor who has not spoken desires to
speak.   No Supervisor shall be allowed to speak more than five min-

utes on any question except by permission of the Board, except that the author shall have five minutes to open and ten minutes to close.

19. No Supervisor shall be interrupted, when speaking, without his consent.

20. When two or more Supervisors arise at the same time to address the Board, the presiding officer shall designate the Supervisor who is entitled to the floor.

21. No motion shall be debated until the same *has been seconded* and distinctly announced by the presiding officer.

22. After a motion has been stated by the President, it shall be in the possession of the Board. It may be withdrawn by the mover thereof, with the consent of the second, before it is acted upon.

23. Upon a call of the Board the names of the members shall be called by the Clerk, and the absentees noted. Those for whom no excuse or insufficient excuses are made may, by order of those present, be sent for and be brought to the Chambers of the Board by the Sergeant-at-Arms or by special messengers appointed for the purpose.

24. When a question is under debate, no action shall be entertained except:

To adjourn.
Call of the Board.
To lay on the table.
The previous question.
To postpone.
To commit or amend.

Which several motions shall have precedence in the order in which they are arranged; provided, however, that during a call of the Board it may consider and transact any matter or business that the Supervisors there present shall unanimously decide to consider.

25. A motion to adjourn is not debatable.

26. The previous question shall be put in the following form: "Shall the previous question be now put?" It shall only be admitted when demanded by three Supervisors, and its effect shall be to put an end to all debate except that the author of the Bill, Ordinance, Resolution or Motion or Amendments shall have the right to close, and the question under discussion shall thereupon be immediately put to a vote. On a motion for the previous question prior to a vote being taken by the Board a call of the Board shall be in order.

27. Every member present when a question is put shall vote for or against it, unless disqualified by the Charter. No member shall be permitted to vote upon a question unless present when his name is called or before the vote is announced. A roll call shall not be interrupted for debate or personal privilege, but a member may file, in writing, an explanation of his vote.

29. After the Board has acted, the names of those who voted for and those who voted against the question shall be entered upon the Journal, not only in cases required by law, but when any member may require it, and on all Bills, Ordinances and Resolutions on final passage the ayes and nays shall be recorded.

30. All appointments of officers and employees shall be made by a majority of the members of the Board. The Clerk shall assign the assistant clerks to their several duties, and shall immediately transmit to the Mayor all Resolutions and Ordinances which, under the law, require executive approval.

31. No member shall leave the Board during its session without permission from the Board.

32. All Committees shall be appointed by the Board unless otherwise ordered by the Board. Committees shall report on any subject referred to them by the Board and their recommendations thereon. *Unless otherwise ordered, a Committee shall report upon all subjects referred to it within thirty days thereafter.* It shall be the right of

any member of a Committee to move a roll call (in Committee), on any pending motion, and the Chairman or Acting Chairman of said Committee shall, with or without debate, order the roll call. In Committees of three members or less a motion by a member thereof shall not require a second.

33. The Clerk shall prepare and cause to be printed and placed on the desks of the members on days of meeting, at least 30 minutes before such a meeting, a calendar of matters to be presented to the Board at said meeting. Every petition or other written instrument intended to be presented to the Board must be delivered to the Clerk not later than 12 o'clock noon on Saturday, or on the day preceding the meeting; upon the request of the President or of any member its contents shall be read in full.

34. All petitions, protests and communications of a routine character shall be referred by the Clerk to the proper Committee.

35. Ten members shall constitute a quorum to transact business, and no Bill, Ordinance, Resolution or Amendment thereto shall pass without the concurrence of at least that number of members, but a smaller number may adjourn from day to day.

36. Except when otherwise provided by these rules, the Charter or law, a majority vote of the members present shall be necessary for the adoption of any motion.

37. The Clerk shall keep a record of all requests and instructions directed by the Board of Supervisors to any officer or board of the City and County and the action thereon of such officer or board. The record of such requests and instructions, until acted upon by such officer or board, shall be read by the Clerk at each regular meeting of the Board of Supervisors.

38. The privilege of the floor shall not be granted to others than members of the Board, except those entitled to the same under the Charter, or public officials of the City and County of San Francisco. This rule shall not be suspended, except by unanimous consent of all members present.

39. In debate a member must confine himself to the question before the Board.

40. On any questions or points of order not embraced in these rules the Board shall be governed by .the rules contained in Roberts' Rules of Order.

41. No member of the Board of Supervisors, chairman of a Committee, or Committee of said Board, shall employ or engage the services of any person, or authorize or incur any charge, debt or liability against the City and County unless authority therefor shall have been first given by the Board of Supervisors by Resolution or Ordinance, except as otherwise provided by law.

42. No standing rule or order of the Board shall be suspended or amended without the affirmative vote of twelve members, except that the rule as to the privilege of the floor shall require the unanimous consent of all members present.

43. No special order shall be placed on the Calendar except by order of the Board. When the time of special order arrives the presiding officer or a member of the Board may call up said order, and it shall not be set aside unless by order of the Board.

MEMORANDUM OF CHARTER PROVISIONS.

Page 4, Section 3, Chapter 1, Article II—Quorum consists of 10 members.

Page 5, Section 8, Chapter 1, Article II—No Bill shall become an Ordinance or Resolution be adopted unless it receives 10 votes.

Page 7, Section 16, Chapter 1, Article II—14 votes necessary to override Mayor's veto of Resolution or Ordinance.

Page 13, Chapter 2, Article II—Lease of City lands requires two-thirds vote of Board (12 votes).

Page 19, Section 6, Chapter 2, Article II—Street railway franchises require three-fourths vote (14 votes) of all the members of the Board, while five-sixths vote (15 votes) of all the members of the Board is necessary to pass these ordinances if MAYOR VETOES SAME.

Page 22, Section 9, Chapter 2, Article II—Sale of City lands requires 15 votes.

Page 30, Section 3, Chapter 1, Article III—Budget Ordinance requires 10 votes.

Page 30, Section 4, Chapter 1, Article III—15 votes are necessary to override Mayor's veto of Budget.

Page 31, Section 8, Chapter 1, Article III—15 votes necessary to appropriate from Urgent Necessity Fund.

Page 33, Section 13, Chapter 1, Article III—To suspend temporarily limit of taxation to meet emergency requires unanimous vote of 18 members of the Board and approval of the Mayor.

Page 76, Section 1, Chapter 1, Article VI—Contracts for street work require 14 votes.

Page 78, Section 2, Chapter 2, Article VI—When cost of sewer or drain is in excess of $5 per linear front foot of abutting property and work is disapproved by Board of Works, it requires 14 votes of the Board of Supervisors to pass ordinance ordering such work done.

If application for work is made, the expense of which is to be paid by City and County, and work is not recommended by the Board of Public Works, it requires 14 votes of the Board of Supervisors to order such work done.

Page 98, Section 33, Chapter 2, Article VI—Ordinance providing for street improvements in 10-year installments requires 15 votes.

Page 100, Section 1, Chapter 3, Article VI—Opening and Improvement of streets, etc., requires 12 votes.

Page 120, Section 17, Chapter 6, Article VI—15 votes are required to modify or change procedure as provided in the Charter for changing street grades and the performance of work in connection therewith.

Page 121, Section 1, Chapter 8, Article VI—Ordinance providing for tunnel, subway and viaduct construction requires 12 votes.

Page 218, Section 19, Article XVI—Suspension of an elected officer by the Mayor requires approval of 14 votes of the Board of Supervisors to cause removal.

Page 223, Section 35, Article XVI—Appointments of additional deputies, clerks or employees require 14 votes.

Amendments Proposed.

The following motions were made in approval of the rules and amendatory thereof, and action upon taken as indicated:

Supervisor Gallagher moved to amend "Duties of Committees," "Public Buildings and Land," by inserting the following words in the third line, after the words "except airport": "and lands for road, street and boulevard purposes."

Rereferred to Rules Committee on motion of Supervisor Spaulding.

"Streets and Tunnels Committee" duties also *rereferred to Rules Committee* on motion of Supervisor Spaulding.

On motion of Supervisor Hayden the Board authorized the exchange of transfer of committee assignments of Supervisors Gallagher and Toner in accord with their wishes.

Supervisor Peyser moved that Rule No. 12 as presented, relative to "reconsideration of votes," be adopted.

Motion *carried.*

On motion of Supervisors Shannon and Peyser, Rule No. 32 was amended to read as follows:

32. All committees of the Board shall be appointed by the Board unless otherwise ordered by the Board. Committees must report on any subject referred to them by the Board and must give their recom-

mendations thereon. *Unless otherwise ordered, a committee shall report upon all subjects referred to it within thirty days thereafter.* It shall be the right of any member of a committee to move a roll call (in committee) on any pending motion, and the chairman or acting chairman of said committee shall, with or without debate, order the roll call. In committees of three members or less a motion by a member thereof shall not require a second.

Privilege of the Floor Rule.

Supervisor Stanton moved that Rule No. 38 be amended to provide for a two-thirds vote instead of a unanimous vote for suspension of the rules.

Motion *lost* by the following vote:

Ayes—Supervisors Canepa, Gallagher, McGovern, Roncovieri, Stanton—5.

Noes—Supervisors Andriano, Colman, Havenner, Hayden, McSheehy, Miles, Peyser, Power, Rossi, Shannon, Spaulding, Suhr, Toner—13.

Supervisor Peyser moved that Rule No. 38 be amended to permit, besides members of the Board, representatives of the Labor Council and civic bodies such as Twenty-ninth and Castro Improvement Club, Park-Presidio and others, to address the Board on matters pending.

Ayes—Supervisors Andriano, Canepa, Colman, Hayden, McSheehy, Miles, Peyser, Power, Rossi, Shannon, Spaulding, Suhr, Toner—13.

Noes—Supervisors Gallagher, Havenner, McGovern, Roncovieri, Stanton—5.

Rule No. 42, on motion of Supervisor Peyser, was *approved.*
Rule No. 12, on motion of Supervisor Peyser, was *approved.*
Rule No. 43, on motion of Supervisor Gallagher, was *approved.*
Rule No. 33, on motion of Supervisor Gallagher, was *approved.*

Supervisor Gallagher presented:

Rule No. 44. It shall be the duty of the chairman of the Rules Committee (during the interim between meetings of the Board), upon the arrival or departure of distinguished persons or delegations, the demise of those whom the Board would note, or on any occasion or meeting calling for Board representation, to appoint committees or representatives to attend, and to provide conveyance and facilities therefor, and the Finance Committee is authorized to approve expense incurred hereunder.

Referred to Rules Committee.

Correction of Board of Works Resolution.

Supervisor Power moved that the Clerk call attention of the Board of Public Works to error in its Resolution No. 109503 and to ask correction, changing Bay street to Francisco street.

So ordered.

Notice of Meeting, Final Passage of Spring Valley Matters.

Supervisor Rossi moved that the Clerk send notices to members of meeting on Wednesday to finally pass Spring Valley Water Company acquisition matters.

So ordered.

Census Enumeration.

Supervisor Canepa presented:

Resolution No. 32111 (New Series), as follows:

Whereas, in accordance with the provisions of the Constitution of the United States Government, on April 2d the fifteenth decennial census will be taken; and

Whereas, it is the civic duty of all persons, organizations, societies, etc., to assist in this great undertaking; and

Whereas, the City and County of San Francisco has been sadly neglected in the past in securing a correct census of population; therefore, be it

Resolved, That the Board of Supervisors assembled do hereby pledge their moral and financial support to the Department of Commerce of the United States Government and to work and cooperate with the Supervisors of Census, Senator Thomas A. Maloney of the Seventh District, San Francisco, California, and Mr. Felton Taylor of the Sixth District, San Francisco, California, to the end that San Francisco will receive a correct enumeration of all of its inhabitants; be it

Further Resolved, That the Supervisors of Census mentioned be invited to address this Board of Supervisors on Monday, March 3d, at 3:30 p. m.

Adopted by the following vote:

Ayes—Supervisors Andriano, Canepa, Colman, Gallagher, Havenner, McGovern, McSheehy, Miles, Peyser, Power, Roncovieri, Rossi, Shannon, Spaulding, Stanton, Suhr, Toner—17.

Absent—Supervisor Hayden—1.

Reception to Ben Greet Players.

Supervisor Hayden presented:

Resolution No. 32112 (New Series), as follows:

Whereas, the City and County of San Francisco will be honored by the world-famous actor, Sir Philip Ben Greet, and his company of players, by an engagement at a local theatre on March 24, 1930; and

Whereas, the histrionic worth of the Ben Greet Players has always been of a most excellent nature, and quite in tune with the spirit and work of the Bard of Avon; and

Whereas, all true lovers of the legitimate stage will again be given the opportunity of witnessing the mystery play, "Everyman," with which Sir Philip Ben Greet first manifested his extraordinary stage versatility in San Francisco a quarter of a century ago; now, therefore, be it

Resolved, That the Board of Supervisors of the City and County of San Francisco heartily welcomes Sir Philip Ben Greet and his players; and be it

Further Resolved, That his Honor the Mayor be respectfully requested to appoint a committee of citizens to act officially as a committee of welcome to Sir Philip Ben Greet and his company of players.

Adopted by the following vote:

Ayes—Supervisors Andriano, Canepa, Colman, Gallagher, Havenner, McGovern, McSheehy, Miles, Peyser, Power, Roncovieri, Rossi, Shannon, Spaulding, Stanton, Suhr, Toner—17.

Absent—Supervisor Hayden—1.

Death of Mrs. Rosetta E. Hayden.

Supervisor Rossi presented:

Resolution No. 32113 (New Series), as follows:

Whereas, God in His eternal wisdom has called to her reward Rosetta E. Hayden, the step-mother of the Honorable J. Emmet Hayden, Supervisor of the City and County of San Francisco; and

Whereas, the late Rosetta E. Hayden by her noble life of good deeds done, according to the law and pattern set forth in the tradition of the ages, had endeared herself to her family, to her associates and to all with whom she came in contact; and

Whereas, the demise of a good woman is always a fact exuding sorrow and grief to immediate relatives and to the world at large; now, therefore, be it

Resolved, That the Board of Supervisors of the City and County of San Francisco expresses regret at the death of Rosetta E. Hayden, and offers sincere sympathy and condolences to those she has reared in this world, and particularly to the Honorable Supervisor J. Emmet Hayden; and be it

Further Resolved, That a copy of this resolution be spread upon the minutes of this Board, that a copy be presented to Supervisor J. Emmet Hayden, and that this Board adjourn, when it does adjourn today, out of respect to the memory of Rosetta E. Hayden.

Adopted by the following vote:

Ayes—Supervisors Andriano, Canepa, Colman, Gallagher, Havenner, McGovern, McSheehy, Miles, Peyser, Power, Roncovieri, Rossi, Shannon, Spaulding, Suhr, Toner—16.

Absent—Supervisors Hayden, Stanton—2.

Garbage Incineration.

The following was presented and *referred to the Health Committee*:

Whereas, the electors of the City and County of San Francisco did, at the general election held on the 5th day of November, 1929, express and declare as their policy that the garbage collected in the City and County of San Francisco should be disposed of by incineration; and

Whereas, in order to carry out said policy, as so declared and expressed, it is necessary that an incinerator be constructed in the City and County of San Francisco for the purpose of incinerating the garbage collected therein; and

Whereas, there is urgent necessity that said incinerator should be constructed without further delay; and

Whereas, the limit of taxation fixed by the Charter of the City and County of San Francisco will not permit the levying of a sufficient amount of tax to defray the cost of the construction of said incinerator; and

Whereas, it is the sense of the Board of Supervisors that in view of the large bond issue that must be submitted to the people during the year 1930 for the purpose of acquiring the properties of the Pacific Gas and Electric Company and Great Western Power Company, heretofore evaluated by the State Railroad Commission of California, that no additional bond issues should be submitted for approval until after said bond issues for the acquisition of the properties of said Pacific Gas and Electric Company and Great Western Power Company are disposed of; now, therefore, be it

Resolved, That the Board of Supervisors of the City and County of San Francisco does hereby declare that an incinerator should be constructed by private capital under the following conditions:

(a) That said incinerator should be constructed at or near the site of the present incinerator at Fifteenth and De Haro streets, either upon the property belonging to the City or upon privately owned property, and if constructed upon property now owned or hereafter acquired by the City, that a reasonable rental should be paid by the person, firm or corporation erecting and operating said incinerator.

(b) That said incinerator should have a capacity of incinerating at least seven hundred and fifty tons of garbage per day in the most up-to-date and economical manner, and without necessitating the segregation of the wet from the dry garbage by the householders of the City and County, and without any discharge of odor or undue amount of smoke, and with the least possible amount of unconsumed material remaining after said incineration.

(c) That the person, firm or corporation constructing and operating said incinerator shall agree with the City and County that said City and County may acquire and take over said incinerator and all of the equipment thereof and the land upon which the same is situated, if said land is not already owned by the City, at the cost thereof, less a reasonable amount for depreciation on said incinerator and equipment, figured as of the date on which the same may be taken over by the City, and that if said incinerator is not taken over by the City before the expiration of the term during which the constructor of

said incinerator has been given the privilege of incinerating the garbage collected in the City and County of San Francisco, that the City
shall, at the expiration of said term, have the right of acquiring said
incinerator and the property on which the same is situated at the
fair and reasonable value thereof, and that if the amount to be paid
for said incinerator and said property cannot be agreed upon between
the owner thereof and the City, the said amount shall be fixed by
arbitration, the owner of said incinerator and the City each to appoint
one arbiter, and the two so appointed to choose a third, and the price
fixed for said incinerator and said land shall be the price at which the
City may acquire the same.

(d) That the person, firm or corporation erecting said incinerator
shall be given the exclusive privilege, for a period of at least twenty-
five years, of incinerating all garbage collected in the City and County
of San Francisco, with the exception of that character of garbage
commonly known as "swill," which may be collected from hotels,
restaurants and other similar places, provided that said swill must
also be incinerated if circumstances require the disposition of the same
by incineration.

(e) That the person, firm or corporation given the privilege of
erecting said incinerator shall file with the Board of Supervisors a bond
in such sum as the Board of Supervisors shall direct for the completion
of said incinerator in accordance with the plans and specifications submitted therefor, as well as an additional bond that said incinerator
will properly incinerate all garbage under the provisions contained in
any agreement for the construction thereof, and that said person, firm
or corporation constructing said incinerator will, when given the exclusive privilege of incinerating the garbage collected in the City and
County of San Francisco, perform his contract with said City and
County for the full term thereof or until said incinerator is taken
over by said City and County; be it

Further Resolved, That any and all persons offering to construct
said incinerator shall present to the Board of Supervisors with any
offer to construct the same full and complete plans and specifications
showing the construction of the same in detail, and the character and
kind of material used in and about said construction, and shall, in
addition thereto, specify the price or charge which shall be made for
the incineration of said garbage; and, be it

Further Resolved, That, for the purpose of carrying out and making
effective the terms of this resolution, that the Board of Public Works,
through the City Engineer, be directed to forthwith report to this
Board the most feasible site at or near the site of the present incinerator, which may be found available for the construction and maintenance of said incinerator, and the approximate cost at which said site
may be obtained, if the same is not already owned by the City, and
that upon a site for said incinerator being agreed upon by this Board,
that the said Board of Public Works, through the City Engineer, be
directed to make suitable borings and investigations to ascertain if
said site is suitable for the purposes mentioned; and be it

Further Resolved, That, upon a suitable site being determined for
the construction of said incinerator, that this Board enact suitable
legislation calling for the receipt of proposals for the construction of
said incinerator and for the incineration of the garbage collected in
the City, and authorizing the entering into a contract with the person,
firm or corporation who will construct said incinerator according to
the plans and specifications deemed most beneficial to the City, and
who will agree to incinerate the garbage collected in said City at the
least possible cost and with the greatest return for the privilege of so
doing, said privilege to exist for a period not longer than twenty-five
years. That the least amount to be paid to the City for the privilege

of incinerating said garbage shall be three per cent of the annual net receipts of said incinerator.

Thirty-Second Annual Convention, F. O. E.

Supervisor Shannon presented:

Whereas, the thirty-second annual session of the Grand Aerie and the state convention of the Fraternal Order of Eagles will be held at San Francisco, August 11 to 16, inclusive, 1930; and

Whereas, said convention brings to San Francisco the national delegates of this great fraternal order and is the occasion of general public demonstration and welcome; and

Whereas, said Fraternal Order of Eagles successfully sponsored and promoted the humanitarian Old Age Pension Bill of California; now, therefore, be it

Resolved, That the Finance Committee of the Board of Supervisors be requested to appropriate $10,000 in the coming budget for the purpose of contributing toward the holding of the thirty-second annual session of the Grand Aerie and the state convention of the Fraternal Order of Eagles in San Francisco, to be held from August 11 to 16, inclusive, 1930, for the publicity and advertising of San Francisco.

Referred to Public Welfare and Publicity Committee.

ADJOURNMENT.

There being no further business the Board at the hour of 7:40 p. m. adjourned.

J. S. DUNNIGAN, Clerk.

Approved by the Board of Supervisors April 14, 1930.

Pursuant to Resolution No. 3402 (New Series) of the Board of Supervisors of the City and County of San Francisco, I, John S. Dunnigan, hereby certify that the foregoing is a true and correct copy of the Journal of Proceedings of said Board of the date thereon stated and approved as recited.

JOHN S. DUNNIGAN,
Clerk of the Board of Supervisors.
City and County of San Francisco.

Tuesday, February 25, 1930
Wednesday, February 26, 1930
Monday, March 3, 1930

Journal of Proceedings
Board of Supervisors

City and County of San Francisco

The Recorder Printing and Publishing Company
337 Bush Street, S. F.

JOURNAL OF PROCEEDINGS
BOARD OF SUPERVISORS

TUESDAY, FEBRUARY 25, 1930, 7:30 P. M.

In re Submission by the Mayor to the Board of Supervisors of Nominees for War Memorial Trustees.

A special meeting of the Board of Supervisors of the City and County of San Francisco was held on Tuesday, the 25th day of February, 1930, beginning at the hour of 7:30 p. m. of that day in the chambers of the Board of Supervisors, City Hall, San Francisco, Caifornia. Mayor James Rolph, Jr., acted as the presiding officer.

CALLING THE ROLL.

THE MAYOR: Call the roll, Mr. Clerk.

THE MAYOR: I would like to say I have a message from Mr. Gallagher in which he states that he is very sick, he is in bed with a very severe cold, the doctor has refused to permit him to leave his home tonight, and he expressed the deepest regret that he could not be here, because he wanted to be here at this particular meeting. Under the circumstances there was nothing else for me to do but to excuse him. Call the roll again, Mr. Clerk.

(Second roll call.)

THE MAYOR: Did not I see Dr. Toner here a little while ago? Supervisor Hayden today, at Mr. John J. Calish's funeral, told me that an engagement which he had would prevent his being present tonight, much as he wanted to be here, so he could not come. I therefore, under the circumstances, could do nothing else but excuse him. Will the Sergeant-at-Arms kindly notify the Supervisors that are outside to come in. With the exception of Supervisor Gallagher, who is excused, and Supervisor Hayden, who is excused, Mr. Sergeant-at-Arms, according to the rules of the Board, please telephone the homes of the other members of the Board to ascertain whether they will be present.

SUPERVISOR McSHEEHY: Supervisor Colman has been excused.

THE MAYOR: Supervisor Colman has been excused and left for the East tonight; he is therefore excused. I am trying, gentlemen of the Board, to see if we cannot expedite this matter just as much as possible, because the people are greatly agitated over it, and we have not had a more important matter before us for a long time, and we really should do something and get somewhere with this proposition, and if it should ccme to a vote tonight, why, there is just a bare quorum here, and it is neither fair to the project, nor is it fair to the people of San Francisco who have entrusted us with the settlement of this problem. The nominees are before the Board and it is up to the Board now, and I think we should get as many of the members of the Board present as possible. We will wait until we hear from the Sergeant-at-Arms. Call the roll, Mr. Clerk.

THE CLERK (calling the roll):

SUPERVISOR ANDRIANO: Here.

SUPERVISOR CANEPA: Here.

SUPERVISOR COLMAN: On leave.

SUPERVISOR GALLAGHER: Ill.

SUPERVISOR HAVENNER: Here.

SUPERVISOR HAYDEN: Absent.
SUPERVISOR McGOVERN: Here.
SUPERVISOR McSHEEHY: Here.
SUPERVISOR MILES: Here.
SUPERVISOR PEYSER: Here.
SUPERVISOR POWER: Here.
SUPERVISOR RONCOVIERI: Here.
SUPERVISOR ROSSI: Here.
SUPERVISOR SHANNON: Absent.
SUPERVISOR SPAULDING: Here——
THE MAYOR (interrupting): Sergeant-at-Arms, what became of Mr. Shannon?
THE SERGEANT-AT-ARMS: He is at a theater and may be down later on when he returns from the theater.
THE CLERK (continuing calling the roll):
SUPERVISOR SPAULDING: Here.
SUPERVISOR STANTON: Here.
SUPERVISOR SUHR: Here.
SUPERVISOR TONER: Here.
(Supervisor Hayden came into the meeting later on.)
THE MAYOR: What is the pleasure of the Board?
SUPERVISOR SUHR: Mr. Mayor, I want to explain my delay tonight.
THE MAYOR: You will have to do it in writing, Supervisor.
SUPERVISOR SUHR: It is not necessary to explain in writing. I told you today that I could not be here until 8 o'clock.
MR. JAMES W. MULLEN: Mr. Mayor, I rise to a point of personal privilege concerning a statement made at the close of the session last Tuesday night and Wednesday morning, a statement made by Supervisor Power. He said: "I would like to ask you whether or not in the course of your investigation——"
SUPERVISOR POWER (interrupting): Just a minute, Mr. Mullen. I move that the privilege of the floor be granted to Mr. Mullen.
SUPERVISOR McGOVERN: I second the motion.
THE MAYOR: Are there any objections? Go ahead.
MR. MULLEN: "I would like to ask you whether or not in the course of your investigation, and I understood you to say that you had, you made a careful investigation of the qualifications of all your nominees. I would like to ask you if you will put yourself out to look up the records in 1917 and see whether or not James Mullen did not refuse at that time to act as a member of the War Draft Board or Examining Board.

"If he did, when members of our families were going over and serving, I will say that notwithstanding any other considerations, if that is his attitude, I don't think he is qualified to serve as one of the members of your Board of Trustees. So I would like you to investigate it if you would.

"THE MAYOR: All right. No quorum being present, nothing can be done further at this time, I presume."

Now, I desire, of course, to repudiate the insinuation contained——
SUPERVISOR POWER (interrupting): Just a minute, Mr. Mullen; I would like to ask the Mayor what investigation he carried on, if any, and what his investigation found out?
THE MAYOR: Well, I found out, as I have always known, that Mr. Mullen was one of the outstanding representatives of labor; that in my meeting in my chambers with the members of this Board of Supervisors, called for the purpose of discussing names, Mr. Roncovieri suggested that labor should have a representative on the Board of eleven Trustees. And I thought the point was well taken, and I tried to find an outstanding representative of labor. I made many inquiries concerning Mr. Mullen. I spoke to labor leaders at the time. I spoke to the president of the Board of Public Works, Mr. Timothy A. Rear-

don. I think I spoke to the president of the Board of Civil Service Commissioners, Mr. McCabe, former president of the San Francisco Labor Council. I spoke to a great many men. I remembered that I personally had appointed him on the Draft Board in 1917 when the appointments were all made by the Mayor, and after making a thorough investigation, to the minutest detail, trying to find a labor representative that would be satisfactory to labor and to the Veterans and to the Board of Supervisors and to the people, I selected Mr. James W. Mullen, after that thorough and full investigation. Now, he has the privilege of the floor, and he is here, at his own request. I have not discussed the matter with him except he came here tonight and asked me if I had a copy of the statement that was made, and I said I had not. I tried to find it in the report of last Tuesday's meeting, but the Clerk said, at the request of Supervisor Power, a copy had been made for him, and the Clerk handed me a copy of what was said, and it was immediately handed to Mr. Mullen. I do not know what more minute details I could go into than to try and find a man who represented labor, and all the Board wanted a man representing labor, and the investigations I made about James W. Mullen——

SUPERVISOR POWER (interrupting): Mr. Mayor, I am only concerned in the statement that I made and the request I made of you. The information conveyed to me that Mr. Mullen declined to serve as a member, and you were asked to investigate that, and I took it upon myself to investigate and I thought perhaps you would do likewise.

THE MAYOR: Go ahead, Mr. Mullen; you have the floor.

MR. MULLEN: Well, Mr. Mayor, he says he has investigated. If he has anything further to add to this statement, I would like very much for him to present it in order that I may be able to respond to it this evening, in as brief a time as possible.

SUPERVISOR POWER: Proceed, Mr. Mullen, and make any statement you want, and when you have finished, I will be very glad to make a part of the records of this Board what are the records at Washington.

MR. MULLEN: Mr. Mayor, I have an abundance of evidence here with me. If you will remember, in May, 1917, you appointed me a member of the Draft Board.

THE MAYOR: I did.

MR. MULLEN: I accepted the appointment and served on the Draft Board for five months, though in December, 1916, the doctor had put me in a plaster cast, a cast that covered my body from my hips clear up over my shoulders, up around my neck and under my chin. I was unable to bend over. I worked for five or six days right after being appointed in copying down in the Registrar's office. I put in days and days bending over, and as soon as the doctor discovered that this bending over was hurting the fractured vertebrae in my neck, he began advising me to retire from the Board and refrain from bending over. Supervisor Gallagher—I am sorry he is not here this evening; he was a member of the board of directors of the Labor Clarion at the same time, and he tried to persuade me to quit this bending over stuff, and to take a leave of absence of several months, in order that my fractured vertebrae might be righted. In August, President Wilson went to President Gompers of the American Federation of Labor and asked that an organization of labor be perfected to offset the propaganda of an institution known as the Citizens' Council, a red bolshevik organization that had been circulating propaganda throughout the entire United States. President Gompers asked me to come from California and to bring another representative with me to a gathering in Minneapolis, to organize such an institution as President Wilson had suggested. I took with me James J. McTiernan, a teacher in the Polytechnic High School——

SUPERVISOR POWER (interrupting): Pardon me, Mr. Mayor, I do not wish to be discourteous to Mr. Mullen, but the question is, if he declined to serve as a member of the Draft Board; that is all I am interested in. I know all about his labor record and everything about it, and that is the statement that has been made, and he has since verified it, and I have verified it in the records in Washington. He resigned as a member of the Draft Board. There is no personal reflection made when the statement was made. I made the statement that I could not conscientiously vote for such a man as Trustee, and with all due respect to his illness, Mr. Mullen was in the same position as some fellow who went overseas and then tried to get out of it. That is the way I look at it. That might not have been his attitude at all, but that is the way I look at it in connection with my vote on this Board. So I say, there is no sense of going into all the details of what Mr. Mullen accomplished.

MR. MULLEN: Well, Mr. President, I have stated that I did not decline to serve on the Draft Board, and as documentary evidence to that effect, I have here, from the President of the United States of America, "All to whom these present come greeting," and it shows where I was appointed a member of the Draft Board; this is an official document from Washington, countersigned by General Crowder, and signed by other representatives of the department in Washington.

SUPERVISOR POWER: Nobody doubts that, either, and nobody doubts that you were appointed and served, but the statement is made that you declined to serve longer, and you verify that statement, don't you; you resigned, didn't you?

MR. MULLEN: I positively did not decline to serve.

SUPERVISOR POWER: Didn't you resign?

MR. MULLEN: I sent in my resignation to Mayor Rolph on the 21st day of September, 1917, and gave my reasons for it.

SUPERVISOR POWER: Did you resign or not?

MR. MULLEN: I did, yes.

SUPERVISOR POWER: Well——

SUPERVISOR ANDRIANO (interrupting): I move that Mr. Mullen be extended the privilege of the floor, to make any statement that he desires to make in connection with this mattr.

MR. MULLEN: I sent in my resignation to Mayor Rolph on the 21st day of September, 1917, on the advice of my doctor. I will first read you what my doctor has to say on that: "To all whom it may concern. This is to say that Mr. James Mullen at my advice was sent to St. Luke's Hospital, where a plaster cast was applied to his neck and shoulder for a previous fracture of the cervical vertebrae, and was in this cast from December, 1916, to September, 1917, and upon my repeated advice that the bending over work he was doing on the Draft Board was interfering with his recovery, he resigned from the said board." Signed "Avery B. McGill, M. D." That shows the reason I resigned. In my letter to the mayor—the reason I was touching on this Minneapolis business was to show that some busybody, I do not know who, while I was in attendance on this convention to organize the American Alliance for Labor and Democracy, in the month of September, somebody wrote a letter to General Boree at Sacramento, and in my letter to the Mayor I quoted from the letter I received from General Boree and then wound up with this statement to the Mayor— Boree said that some one told him that I had private business that I would not desert and that I had to attend to that private business and neglect the meetings of the Draft Board. I said to the Mayor: "Now, I do not know the source of his information, but he has been misinformed to some extent, as, of course, I have no private business to demand practically all of my time, and I have devoted a goodly share of my time to the duties of the Exemption Board. However, I cannot give all of my time to that work, and I have only recently had a plaster cast taken off of my neck, and my physician informs me that I am retarding my recovery through bending over and doing the work of a clerical character required on the Board. Under the circumstances I feel I ought to be relieved of the work, and I hereby tender to you my resignation, to take effect at the earliest possible time." Now, that is my letter to the Mayor.

I have plenty of other documents here. Assertions have been made, since the publication of Supervisor Power's statement in the Daily News, that I was pro-German before the war and during the war.

SUPERVISOR POWER: Just a minute, Mr. Mullen. I did not make any statement to the Daily News. I was courteous enough to tell you that over the telephone, and the statement that I made you have been furnished a copy of it, at my request. I told the stenographer to make copies of it, and just confine yourself to that statement and not anything in the Daily News. I am not responsible for what is published in the Daily News, or any other paper.

MR. MULLEN: I do not need to take the Daily News. I have an official copy of what you said.

SUPERVISOR POWER: Just confine yourself to that and I will be satisfied.

MR. MULLEN: And the least that can be said is, there is a rather slanderous insinuation in the statement you made as a public official at a public meeting in this chamber, and I resent it, and I propose, if an opportunity is given me, to prove that there is absolutely no foundation for it. I brought along with me the volume of the Labor Clarion from February 9, 1917, to February 1, 1918, including editorials that I wrote before Congress declared war, stating that the United States ought to go into the war and punish the German government, and they ought to go in and become associated with the Allies in prosecuting that war. I also have them here, if you want me to read them. I will read them to you; they are all here. I do not want to take up so much of your time, but I have all of these editorials here that were printed 13 years ago, expressing my sentiments. I have another document here that the Red Brigade circulated and distributed all through the Labor Council because I was supporting the war and supporting the President of the United States. They distributed this document, headed, "Labor Judas," distributed it all over town on me, and called mé everything, a traitor to labor and a Judas and everything else because I was supporting the war. Now, as I say, I have all of these editorials here, I have them marked, and I will read you a paragraph or two of the first one here to show you what I did on March 30, before Congress assembled at all, on the special call of President Wilson. "Not since the Civil War period has there been a Congress called together that meant so much to the American people as the one that will convene in Washington next Monday. President Wilson has not yet indicated just what action he will ask Congress to take, and from comments in the public prints and by members of Congress it is impossible to determine what the general disposition of the members may be. But one thing at the present time stands out clearly, and that is that the people have made up their minds that there shall be no submitting to the barbarous submarine policy of the German government. As to the manner of preventing the German ruthlessness, there are differences of opinion. Whether the United States should go into the war on the side of the Allies, with an agreement with them as to the conditions under which terms of peace might be signed, or whether we should go in alone, in a purely defensive way under conditions such as would enable us to point out when Germany indicated her disposition to yield to our contention as to the freedom of the seas, there are on the subject a variety of different opinions. It is our opinion that this country is in no condition to carry on a separate war, and in the event war is declared by the Congress, that some understanding should be had with the allied governments as to separate peace terms. While Germany is engaged with the allied governments she cannot, of course, do any great amount of damage to us either on land or sea. But if we should go in alone with the war with the German government, the German government could then make peace with the Allies, and devote all of her attention to the United States. Under such conditions we could doubtless mobilize a force to prevent Germany from successfully invading this country, while, on the other hand, an invasion of Germany by American troops with any chance of success would be out of the question. In such an event, command of the seas would be the determining factor. At pres. ent the German navy is more powerful than ours, and she would start with that advantage in her favor. With our practically unlimited re. sources we doubtless could build a navy that in time would give us control of the seas, but at a tremendous expenditure of both blood and treasure. If this reasoning is sound, then it would seem to be the part of wisdom for us, if we are to be involved at all, to set aside all other considerations and go into the war on the side of the Allies, throwing all the power at our command into the conflict, so as to bring the whole affair to a speedy end and re-establish peace and con. cord in the world. Under other conditions there are possibilities that the war with us involved might spread out over a long period of years, keeping the world in turmoil and confusion. There are those who believe we should confine ourselves strictly to protecting Amer. ican lives and American ships on the seas. But even a defensive cam. paign of this kind would mean war and expose us to the dangers cited above. So that it does not look a wise course to follow. Again, others believe that the greatest need of the Allies is money, and we could best protect ourselves by loaning it to them, or even by giving them money outright. Of this plan it cannot be said that it would not in any degree remove the danger of a costly and prolonged war be. tween Germany and the United States after the close of hostilities in Europe. If this be true, then would it not be wise to bring to an end the whole terrible conflict? We believe we should either do this or sit back and mutely endure such wrongs as Germany may heap upon us. In saying this we have not taken into account the cause of either the Allies or the Germans, so far as merit is concerned. We have had in mind only the idea of the best means of achieving the just pur. poses of our own government and properly safeguarding the interests of our own people. However, there is no person in the Usited States in an official position to be so well qualified to advise in these matters as President Wilson, and his past record assures us that he has the wisdom and the foresight and the patriotism to properly handle the entire situation. He .has also demonstrated beyond the shadow of a doubt that he is a lover of peace and is possessed of an almost un. limited supply of patience, so that we can with serene confidence be guided by his recommendations. The people of America will follow his lead."

That sounds like I was pro-German, writing that stuff?

Then, after war was declared, I introduced a resolution in the Labor Council, placing the Labor Council on record as supporting the Presi. dent and the country in war, without any qualifications whatever. I will read you what I said in the Labor Clarion the following week. I will read you first the resolution—no, here is the editorial first: "The hour for action is at hand and all differences of opinion must be set aside in the interest of the united, vigorous and effective service to our common country. Organized labor has been in favor of doing everything within the bounds of reason to maintain peace, and the country has been fortunate in having in the White House a man as devoted to peace as any loyal American could be, but an ambitious, tyrannical and overbearing European autocrat has forced war upon us, and we must so prosecute it as to bring to an end forever the possibility of a repetition of such a condition in future world affairs." Then I go on and quote what President Wilson said, and after quoting what he said, I said this: "Our country is not all we should like to have it. We have some grievances against it. Injustices have at times been done the workers. We have bad laws upon the statute books that ought to be wiped out. But with all her faults, the United States of America, from the standpoint of the wage worker, is the best government in the world, and if there is a nation anywhere on earth that deserves the support of its working people, that nation is ours. The fight of the United States in the war now upon us is not to be for gain or glory, but for right and freedom and humanity. Such a fight is the fight of the organized labor movement, and every man will do his duty. Now that the enemy is at our gates with his submarines, the time for hesitating and deliberating has passed, and with action swift and fearful we must drive them back."

Now, those were my sentiments expressed before war was actually declared. Then I introduced this resolution in the Labor Council: "Whereas, the government of the United States for more than two years has submitted, in the interest of peace, to the numerous wrongs heaped upon it by the imperial German government; and whereas, the President and Congress of the United States have declared that a point has been reached in our affairs where peace is no longer possible, owing to the fact that the German government is now waging war upon us, destroying our commerce and taking the lives of our citizens while engaged in the peaceful pursuit of their legitimate activities; therefore, be it resolved, that the San Francisco Labor Council, in regular session assembled this 6th day of April, 1917, pledges its loyal and united support to the Nation and the State in this hour of trial, and invites the constituted authorities to call upon it for any service that it may be possible for it to render to our common country, in the interests of justice and freedom and humanity; and be it further resolved, that we express our faith and confidence in the high purposes that have governed President Woodrow Wilson in his conduct of the government's affairs during the trying years of the great world conflict, and assure him of our readiness to follow his lead in the effort to maintain the rights of human kind; and be it further resolved; that copies of these resolutions be forwarded to the President, the members of the California delegation in Congress, and to the Governor and the Legislature of the State of California."

That is the end of the resolution. I say after that: "The organized workers seek but justice in peace or in war, and they insist that all other persons must be satisfied with just that and nothing more. If the captains of industry and commerce stand as loyally and unselfishly by the country as do the workers, there will be no cause for complaint, and a speedy and victorious end of the war will be the result."

Now, those were my sentiments, expressed in the beginning, and long before I was asked to serve on the Draft Board. I have all through this issue of 1917, printed 13 years ago, sentiments of that kind expressed by me, and I was told, no later than yesterday, that Supervisor Power said that I was not in favor of the war, and that I was not willing to support the government in the prosecution of the war. I do not know whether he said that or not, but I was told that he did.

SUPERVISOR POWER: Who made the statement?

MR. MULLEN: When you tell me who furnished you with such information as you have, I will tell you who made the statement. You refused over the telephone to tell me whom your informant was.

SUPERVISOR POWER: I would say, Mr. Mayor, that as a member of this Board, that if there are any statements made here for the record, that I will insist, if my name is used, or any language attributed to me, that it also be put in the record who made the statement so I will have the opportunity of replying.

MR. MULLEN: As soon as you tell me whom your informant was, I will make that statement. Now, there are a whole lot more here that I might read to support my position in connection with this. I want to——

SUPERVISOR POWER (interrupting): Just a minute, Mr. Mullen. Mr. Mayor, I would ask that the record show that Mr. Mullen declined to notify me or this Board who made that statement.

THE MAYOR: Well, I must also reply by saying that Mr. Power himself refused to comply with the request of Mr. Mullen.

SUPERVISOR POWER: Mr. Power did nothing of the sort, and has never been asked on this Board by you or any member.

THE MAYOR: I ask you now.

SUPERVISOR POWER: At the proper time I will give the information.

THE MAYOR: It is only fair to the man, it is only fair to the public and the citizens.

SUPERVISOR POWER: I have not attacked any man. This thing has gone far afield. And you confine yourself to the statement I made, and the question I asked you, which was a courteous one and a fair question, and I was trying to arrive at a decision here on my vote on these Trustees. I am as anxious to expedite the erection of this Memorial, and perhaps more so than you are, and I was trying to arrive at a fair and just decision, and I was trying to bring myself to that point when I asked that question, and that is the only reason I asked it. The party that told it to me, I told them I would investigate. A member of this Board told it to me first.

THE MAYOR: Surely, Mr. Power, you do not think that the American Federation of Labor of the United States of America is going to permit a remark like that, an insinuation, to go unchallenged? The whole American Federation of Labor of the United States is back of this man.

SUPERVISOR POWER: Just a minute; I insist that you confine yourself to the subject; never mind the American Federation of Labor, or anything else; just confine yourself to the question I put to you; that is, the subject before this Board.

THE MAYOR: What is the question you put to me?

SUPERVISOR POWER: You have the record there; read it.

THE MAYOR: Well, I am simply—I have answered your question; I have told you of all the investigation that I made. I tell you that Mr. James W. Mullen is the choice of the American Federation of Labor of the United States as a Trustee of this War Memorial, if labor is to be represented on the board as the Board of Supervisors asked me to do. But that is not the point. The point is that you asked the record to show that Mr. Mullen refused to answer a question of yours, and I say, in quotation marks from him, that you refused to answer a question which he propounded to you. That is fair.

MR. MULLEN: I will say again that I am perfectly willing to give my authority for the statement as soon as the Supervisor sees fit to inform me concerning who has furnished him with his alleged information. Now, I want to say this concerning this War Memorial situation: I have not spoken to a single member of this Board of Supervisors concerning the War Memorial trusteeship; not one. From the time the Mayor called me and asked me if I would permit my name to be submitted as a War Memorial Trustee, I have not even discussed it with the Mayor.

THE MAYOR: That is true.

MR. MULLEN: It was not my purpose to come anywhere near this Board of Supervisors in any manner whatever connected with the War Memorial trusteeship. I am here this evening solely because of the slanderous insinuations sent out a week ago against me by a toy soldier. I say this to the real soldiers who are present, a toy colonel——

SUPERVISOR POWER (interrupting): Now, Mr. Mayor, I rise as a member of this Board, and on a question of personal privilege, and I appeal to you as the presiding officer, that Mr. Mullen has no right to cast any such personal reflections. For your information, you probably know I was a member of the Board at the time, and for Mr. Mullen's information, if he wishes it, I volunteered my services to the United States, a matter of record at .Washington, and was offered a captaincy as a disbursing officer in the military aeronautics, and failed to pass the overseas examination. I declined to take a stay-at-home majorship in the Ordinance Department at Washington. And that is a matter of record at Washington. So I resent that you allow Mr. Mullen to make any personal attack, and this thing has gone very far afield because I asked a fair question, and now to allow Mr. Mullen— and I just say, if he persists in that kind of attack, I will have to take my own means of protecting myself. My brother served for 24 years in the United States navy, served 19 months on the destroyers overseas. And my brother-in-law served 30 years in the United States navy and was the first man to report for service after being retired. And I won't stand here and permit Mr. Mullen, or anyone else, to attack my sincerity or make any reflection upon my character. The regiment that he refers to, for his information, that I was the head of, furnished many boys in the late war, and I am not going to, as I say, permit such an attack from Mr. Mullen, and I trust that you will be fair enough not to, otherwise I will have to protect myself.

SUPERVISOR ANDRIANO: Mr. Mayor, a moment ago I rose to move that Mr. Mullen be granted the privilege of the floor, to make any statement he wished in his own defense. I now rise to move that the remarks of Mr. Mullen relative to a member of this Board be stricken from the record, and that he confine himself, if he desires to continue to speak, to his own defense, and not to any counter-attack on any member of this Board.

SUPERVISOR RONCOVIERI: I second that motion.

THE MAYOR: So ordered. (Bringing down the gavel.)

MR. MULLEN: Mr. Mayor, I am going to close in a few minutes. As I say, I had no intention of coming down here; it was made necessary for me to come here because of the remarks made by Supervisor Power last week. Otherwise, I would not have been here at all. I want to say, too, before I close, that if any additional evidence is needed to indicate where I stood during the war, or to indicate why I resigned from the Draft Board, I have abundance of it here with me. The only reason I am not going through all of it is because I do not want to take up your time. I want to say this, too, is closing, that, while I could not myself be in the war, in the army, my brother was in the army, and I was responsible, after the close of the war, for organizing Golden Gate Council of the American Legion. It was organized in the Labor Temple. I started the ball rolling and began the organization of that Golden Gate Post. I got Fred Bebergol, the first Adjutant of the California Legion, to handle that work; my brother helped me, Jim McTiernan's son helped me, and during the time the Liberty bonds campaigns were on I campaigned during every Liberty bond campaign. I have letters here from the head of the Federal Reserve Bank, thanking me for my services in that connection. I have a letter here from the chairman of the Committee of One Thousand handling the Liberty bond campaigns, thanking me again for my assistance in that connection. And I say that this is the first time in my lifetime that I have ever had my Americanism questioned, and I assure you that I could not allow my first instance to pass unnoticed, and that is the only reason I am here addressing you this evening. Otherwise, I would not have been here, and I hope that such a circumstance will never arise again to bring me here, or before any other public body, to defend myself as to my patriotism and my Americanism. Now, I want to thank the Mayor and the members of the Board of Supervisors for giving me this opportunity, and I am going to close my remarks, and I will have no more to say to you unless I again be attacked by some Supervisor. I sincerely thank you for the opportunity.

SUPERVISOR POWER: Mr. Mayor, I submit for the record the

question I put to you on last Wednesday morning and the records from the Adjutant General's office at Washington.

THE CLERK (reading):

"Excerpts from the proceedings of the special meeting of the Board of Supervisors, Tuesday-Wednesday, February 18-19, 1930:

"SUPERVISOR POWER: I would like to ask you whether or not in the course of your investigation, and I understood you to say that you had, you made a careful investigation of the qualifications of all your nominees. I would like to ask you if you will put yourself out to look up the records in 1917 and see whether or not James Mullen did not refuse at that time to act as a member of the War Draft Board or Examining Board.

"If he did, when members of our families were going over and serving, I will say that, notwithstanding any other considerations, if that is his attitude, I don't think he is qualified to serve as one of the members of your Board of Trustees. So I would like you to investigate it if you would.

"THE MAYOR: All right. No quorum being present, nothing can be done further at this time, I presume."

"Washington, D. C., February 25, 1930. Honorable James E. Power. Received following communication today from General C. H. Bridges, Adjutant General: 'The records on file in this office show that James Mullen was appointed June 23, 1917, as a member of the Local Board for Division Number 3, San Francisco, California, that he took the oath of office on July 3, 1917, and that he served until November 16, 1917. It appears from correspondence on file that he tendered his resignation as a member of the Draft Board and the records show that he served until his successor was appointed.' Richard M. Welch, M. C."

SUPERVISOR POWER: I move they both be made a part of the record.

THE MAYOR: I would respectfully suggest, and I am sure Supervisor Power will have no objection, to inserting in the records the copy of the telegram which he sent to Congressman Welch.

SUPERVISOR POWER: No, that is here, sent from this office.

THE MAYOR: Can we put that in the record?

SUPERVISOR POWER: Yes, surely; I merely followed out what I told Mr. Mullen I would do, and what I told you I would do, that I would investigate.

THE MAYOR: Will the Clerk find that telegram?

THE CLERK: I have not it.

THE MAYOR: Where is it, Mr. Power?

SUPERVISOR POWER: Mr. Ashe will get it.

MR. MULLEN: I withdraw the remark I made concerning the toy soldier, I think I ought to, and I do it.

SUPERVISOR POWER: It is a good thing you did, Mr. Mullen.

THE CLERK: "San Francisco, February 21, 1930. Honorable Richard J. Welch, House of Representatives, Washington, D. C. Please ascertain from the Adjutant General's office the time served by James Mullen on draft or exemption board in San Francisco, 1917, and the reason for his resigning therefrom. Please wire all particulars by Tuesday next. Kind regards. James E. Power, Supervisor."

SUPERVISOR POWER: I move that that be made a part of the record also.

THE MAYOR: Well, it having been read it is in the record, of course, naturally.

Now, gentlemen of the Board, and gentlemen of the veterans' organizations, and my fellow citizens: We are meeting for the purpose of building a War Memorial. We are meeting to see if we cannot amicably come to an understanding whereby a War Memorial and the other buildings for municipal purposes provided for by the act cannot be built in San Francisco. It seems too bad that so many personalities are indulged in, it seem too bad that men's Americanism is questioned, it seems too bad that one of the outstanding representatives of labor in America should have his Americanism questioned simply because he has been recommended to the Mayor as one of the outstanding representatives of labor that furnished 85 per cent of the men who put on the uniform, and it seems too bad that we have to go to Washington 13 years later to find out and question the Americanism of this labor leader. You requested me to put a labor leader on this Board of Trustees, and you agreed on a labor leader to go on the Board of Trustees, in my office. I chose, after making all the inquiries that I could make, I chose the man recommended by labor. He, in his personality, represents, as I said, 85 per cent of the men who donned the uniforms of our country, and in putting on that labor leader, which you requested me to do, I figured that five veterans with five of the oldest representatives of the 13 years that this War Memorial project and the Opera House has been going on, that it was a nice offset to the whole program, to accept your suggestion, and I appointed James W. Mullen. I come to his defense tonight because he did not resign as a slacker, he did not resign for any cowardice, he did not resign for any other reason than the proof, which is here tonight, that it was his health which compelled him to resign. I think——

SUPERVISOR POWER (interrupting): Mr. Mayor, I want to interrupt and I ask you, did anybody say that Mr. Mullen resigned because he was a slacker, or any other reason given for resigning?

THE MAYOR: I am confining myself, Mr. Power——

SUPERVISOR POWER (interrupting): I would like you to answer that question, you are getting into the record here a statement, and I am not going to permit it unless you confine yourself to the question I put to you.

THE MAYOR: Let me tell you, you cannot prevent me, nor have you the authority to prevent me to put anything that I want to in the record as Mayor of San Francisco.

SUPERVISOR POWER: Oh, yes, I can prevent you or anyone else from putting any false statements in this record, it is not your province because you are the presiding officer to make them any more than it is mine to make them as a member of this Board, and I am not going to stand here as a member and have you imply that I said certain things when I did not.

THE MAYOR: If we want a discussion, you have not any right to stand without the permission of the Chair, which you have not yet.

SUPERVISOR POWER: I will rise as a member of this Board and the Chair has to recognize me whenever I rise, that is my prerogative, and it is your prerogative, as the presiding officer, to recognize me.

THE MAYOR: I have had so many years of experience I think I know how to preside.

SUPERVISOR POWER: That is all right, but I think I know my rights as a member of this Board.

THE MAYOR: Nobody is denying you your right, any more than you can tell me that I cannot make an explanation in defense of an honorable American.

SUPERVISOR POWER: There is nobody denying you the privilege of making a defense, if you feel that he needs a defense. But I do insist, though, that you do not imply that, in any inquiry I put to you, which is a matter of record of this Board, that I cast any reflection on Mr. Mullen, as you say. No reference to a slacker, fartherest from my thoughts, and I am not going to stand here, as a member of this Board, and permit you or anyone else to get that in the record without denying it.

THE MAYOR: Any word that I have put in the record tonight will not be withdrawn.

SUPERVISOR POWER: It may not be withdrawn, but it will be corrected.

THE MAYOR: The telegram to Washington asking for Mr. Mullen's record was an indication that there was doubt somewhere, that he had been a slacker because he resigned. It may be the word does not suit the Supervisor, but, nevertheless, it is a word that is applicable under the charges which have been made against an honorable American and a representative of the great working class of our country.

SUPERVISOR POWER: I am going to ask again, Mr. Mayor, that you state what are the charges made against the man that you are defending, what are the charges?

THE MAYOR: I do not care to encumber the record any more than it is, I let the record stand as it is. I think anyone and every one in the room tonight, as the press will carry in the morning, and the papers of the United States will carry, and the American Federation of Labor will take it up, that charges of doubt have arisen over the appointment of Mr. James W. Mullen, whom I appointed at the request of the Board of Supervisors.

SUPERVISOR POWER: I again ask you, as a member of the Board, what are the charges?

SUPERVISOR ANDRIANO: Mr. Mayor, may I ask the Clerk to read the motion made by Supervisor Power at the last meeting of the Board?

SUPERVISOR POWER: It was not a motion, I sought information.

SUPERVISOR ANDRIANO: The request. I will ask it so that the matter may be clear in my own mind.

THE CLERK (reading): "Supervisor Power: I would like to ask you whether or not in the course of your investigation, and I understood you to say that you had, you made a careful investigation of the qualifications of all your nominees. I would like to ask you if you will put yourself out to look up the records in 1917 and see whether or not James Mullen did not refuse at that time to act as a member of the War Draft Board or Examining Board. If he did, when members of our families were going over and serving, I will say that notwithstanding any other considerations, if that is his attitude, I don't think he is qualified to serve as one of the members of your Board of Trustees. So I would like you to investigate it if you would."

"THE MAYOR: All right. No quorum being present, nothing can be done further at this time, I presume."

THE MAYOR: Mr. Andriano.

SUPERVISOR ANDRIANO: I desire to ask the Supervisor, in all candor, whether that statement does not cast some aspersion upon the honor and integrity and Americanism of the gentleman in question, the fact that he refused to serve on the Draft Board? Now I happened to be secretary of one of the local Draft Boards right at the beginning, and if some one said that I was requested to act as secretary and that I had refused, I would certainly consider it an aspersion upon my character.

SUPERVISOR POWER: I would say, for the benefit of the Supervisor, the same as I said earlier in the meeting, Mr. Mayor, that I was seeking information in order to arrive at a fair and just decision, in so far as my vote is concerned, on your Trustees, and when that information was given to me, I asked the question of you, and I asked it in all fairness, and I thought you would do the very thing that I had done and investigate. I sent a telegram to the Adjutant General of the State of California, asking for the draft records, and he replied that they were with the Adjutant General at Washington, and I wired Congressman Welch, our Representative, and asked him if he would go to the office and kindly secure the record. Now, I have the information I want, so far as judging my vote is concerned. If you people want to believe that is a reflection upon anybody, and there are charges made and so forth, go right ahead and bring them.

THE MAYOR: I think that the Board of Supervisors, in view of all that has transpired, ought to give an expression of confidence by vote tonight to Mr. James W. Mullen in order that the record might be thoroughly cleared up. I think he is entitled to it. I think all that has been said tonight has clearly proven that James W. Mullen did everything he could, humanly possible he could do, to show that his colors were the Stars and Stripes of America. I think he is entitled to that vote from the Board after what has taken place.

SUPERVISOR ANDRIANO: I make such a motion, Mr. Mayor.

SUPERVISOR SUHR: I second it.

THE MAYOR: All in favor will please say aye——

SUPERVISOR POWER (interrupting): I will decline to vote on that after the attack Mr. Mullen made on me.

SUPERVISOR McGOVERN: Mr. Mayor, I think this is leading into avenues far-fetched. I think that Supervisor Power simply asked for a record that was in Washington, he did not know the reason of Mr. Mullen's retirement from the Draft Board. That has been explained to you at the present time, hasn't it, Supervisor?

SUPERVISOR POWER: As far as I am concerned.

SUPERVISOR McGOVERN: Therefore, I think you would realize that he was justified in retiring under the physical condition that he was in, and I do not think that we ought to carry that too far, because, realize this, Mr. Mayor, that Mullen, the man, is the editor of a paper that represents a great group of people here in San Francisco. That paper is run by a group of trustees, not by Mullen, and any aspersions made on Mullen as to his Americanism would reflect, probably, on me and many more of us who subscribe to the paper, and I know Jim Power well enough to know that he does not mean that. So, for that reason, I think that Mullen has made enough of an explanation to justify any of us in realizing that he had to resign because of the physical condition he was in. Naturally, Supervisor Power did not know of that when he asked for the record from Washington. That has been given at the present time; let us forget it.

THE MAYOR: All in favor of the motion will please say aye. (Ayes.) Contrary, no.

SUPERVISOR POWER: No.

THE MAYOR: The ayes have it and it is so ordered. What is the pleasure of the Board. Mr. Mullen, I thank you for coming here tonight and making your statement in a very manly way.

MR. MULLEN: Mr. Mayor, I thank you and the Board of Supervisors.

SUPERVISOR McSHEEHY: When we adjourned a week ago tomorrow morning at about 8:30 o'clock, at that time, your Honor, I believe you stated that you had not entirely finished your report to this Board. And I am going to ask you—we are all here, we are here tonight to try and transact some business, and I hope we will transact some business—and I am going to ask you——

(At this point members of the American Legion, carrying the American flag and a regimental flag, enter the room.)

THE MAYOR: Will the color-bearers kindly bring the colors to the front, and not to the rear? Will the color-bearer of the American flag please sit at my right? Will the color-bearer of the regimental flag please sit at my left.

Mr. McSheehy.

SUPERVISOR McSHEEHY: Your Honor, when we adjourned here one week ago tomorrow, Wednesday, you stated at that time that you had not completed your report to this Board, and, as I just stated, we are here tonight to do business, and I hope we will transact some direct business. So I am going to ask you at this time if you wish, or if you intend, to complete your report to this Board, and I feel that you really have the floor, if such is the case, because you stated that you had not completed the report at that time, one week ago tomorrow.

THE MAYOR: Replying to Mr. McSheehy, there has been printed, and I think a thousand copies——

THE CLERK: 200.

THE MAYOR: 200 "History of the San Francisco War Memorial," ordered printed by resolution of the Board of Supervisors, because the Board themselves and the veterans and some few others interested wanted copies. Those copies have been distributed, and those copies contain a full, exact and accurate statement of the facts, and nothing else. I have not yet made any criticisms. I have not yet made any replies. I have prepared, after weeks of effort, and upon resolution of the Board of Supervisors, an exact history of the facts, and there is nothing in this history that is not a fact. Every word in this history is a fact. It took place, it gives discussions that took place, it gives both sides of everything that took place in the years that have transpired since we have been trying to build our War Memorial. So far as the history of the San Francisco War Memorial, Mr. McSheehy, to the present time, it is complete. Since its completion the Mayor has been subject to daily attacks, particularly one on February 21st in the San Francisco Examiner, the headlines of which are, "Vets Attack Rolph Report on Memorial." Now, I would like to know where any attack can be made on a statement of facts?

SUPERVISOR POWER: That was what I was trying to find out, Mayor.

THE MAYOR: It is the first time in anybody's knowledge where attacks can be made on statements of fact of record. Everything in that report is of record, and there is nothing in this report that is not of record here or record somewhere else. Now, the Veterans' Committee—the report goes on to say: "The Board of Trustees assailed in list of questions submitted with explanation demanded." I believe that the floor should be given to the chairman of the Veterans' Committee to ask the questions which have been asked through the columns of the press, so that they may, if possible, be answered tonight, and the Clerk be requested to continue the stenographic reports of this meeting, and that it will be made a part of the history of the War Memorial. Now, Mr. Glensor is chairman. I really think that we should now give you the floor, to ask the questions which you say are the only questions you want answered; to ask those questions so that we may have them in the record, and not from the newspapers.

MR. GLENSOR: I have not had the privilege of reading that article that you quote there; I do not know what is in it. There are a great many questions and some statements that the veterans are willing and ready to make to this Board, if they care to hear them, and I am willing to make them all now, but I do not care to be limited to any particular question. We will state our entire position and ask numerous questions, and I am prepared to do it if the Board and the Mayor are willing to hear it.

THE MAYOR: I am.

SUPERVISOR CANEPA: I move that Mr. Glensor be given the privilege to make his statement before this Board.

SUPERVISOR HAVENNER: Second the motion.

SUPERVISOR PEYSER: Second the motion.

THE MAYOR: Is that what you arose for, Mr. Havenner?

SUPERVISOR HAVENNER: I was going to move the privilege of the floor to Mr. Glensor and the other representatives.

THE MAYOR: All in favor say aye. (Ayes.) The ayes have it. Mr. Glensor.

MR. H. W. GLENSOR: Could I ask you to let me see that clipping? I do not know just exactly which one you refer to or what is in it. Oh, I see.

THE MAYOR: Here is the other one, Mr. Glensor.

MR. GLENSOR: Is there another one?

THE MAYOR: I will read it for you, from the San Francisco Bulletin: "Mayor scored as evader by Legion head; expenditure for plans of buildings condemned as sheer waste. 'The Mayor talked 12 hours

and put everybody to sleep, and still did not answer the questions
we have been asking these many months.' This was the statement
today of Harry Glensor, County Commander of the American Legion
and a member of the General Veterans' Committee on the War Memorial. 'There are three questions we would like answered,' Mr. Glensor continued. 'We would like to know why War Memorial property
was held in the name of a bank and taxes were paid on it when it
could have been held in the name of the University of California
Regents and no taxes need have been paid. Why borrow money? We
would like to know why it was necessary to borrow money from a
certain bank when the fund contained hundreds of thousands of
dollars. We would also like to know why $216,000 was spent on plans
and not one of the plans drawn can be carried out with the money
that is available.' The Mayor said that later in the day he will get
one of the trustees to make a detailed reply to the questions asked by
Mr. Glensor. Mr. Glensor said he will call a meeting of American
Legion Councils this week to consider the Mayor's report, and he announced also that, notwithstanding the Mayor's record for long-distance
oratory, the veterans still believed that a majority of the War Memorial Trustees should be ex-service men." Now, let me read the
other one that I just gave to you. The San Francisco Examiner,
February 21, 1930: "Vets attack Rolph report on Memorial Board of
Trustees and Memorial. Board of Trustees assailed in list of questions submitted, with explanation demanded. Members of the Board
of Supervisors, other City officials and war veterans who sat through
Mayor Rolph's record-breaking endurance talkfest on the War Memorial Tuesday night and Wednesday morning, began returning to
their jobs yesterday, and for the first time in the twenty-four hours
that elapsed since the Mayor made his long report those interested
were able to make some comment on the controversy. Although the
Mayor presented a chronological report of the War Memorial project
since its inception in 1918 as a statement of facts which could not
become the subject of controversy, many phases of his report drew
fire from the veterans of the War Memorial Advisory Board, which
the Mayor accused of being entirely responsible for the years of delay
in the construction of the Memorial Building. The veterans center
their attack on the accounting of the $2,000,000 fund privately sub-
scribed to the War Memorial. The veterans demanded an explanation
of the shrinkage of approximately $625,000 in this fund. Harold Boyd,
H. W. Glensor, James B. Burns, members of the Advisory Board and
J. C. Claridge, Secretary, met to consider the report of the Mayor.
They will demand an answer, they said, to these questions: 'Why did
the private Board of Trustees spend $216,000 for plans which are use-
less, in view of the amount of money available to be spent? Why did
the Board of Trustees pay out $155,000 in interest on a loan from a
San Francisco bank when the Board had at its disposal plenty of its
own money?' This is another question: 'Why has the Board of Trustees failed to collect $234,000 in subscriptions after they had gone to
the trouble of having all of the subscribers renew their pledges on a
form which was legal and binding upon them?' The questions asked by
the veterans were addressed to the Mayor, who made a reply at once.
Mayor Rolph said: 'The audit clearly shows that the charges of the
veterans of misappropriation of funds are untrue. The Board of Trustees never took a dime wrongfully. In regard to their questions the
administration of the funds was purely a matter of policy. I had
nothing to do with that, and my statement was merely one of facts.
These questions, I am sure, can be answered to the satisfaction of
every one, and in due time I will have such an answer.' "
    Mr. Glensor.
    MR. GLENSOR: Now, I want you to thoroughly understand my
position here at this time; what I think you gentlemen refer to as
"the parliamentary situation." These questions have been propounded,
and I am prepared to state the entire position of the veteran bodies

of San Francisco that my colleagues and myself represent here tonight, and during that time I will propound those and other questions. Now, is it you gentlemen's desire that if there is a member of the Board— or a representative of the Board—of private Memorial Trustees present, he be first permitted to answer those categorical questions which are propounded in the newspaper articles, after which I will make our presentation, in part, followed by my colleagues, if you will grant them an audience, or shall I go ahead now? I am at your disposal, gentlemen.

THE MAYOR: Well, speaking for the Board, we are at your disposal. If you wish those questions answered, and I take it those are questions in the form in which you desire them answered, I am prepared to answer all four of them, in writing.

MR. GLENSOR: Well, do you wish to do it before?

THE MAYOR: No, I do not wish to do anything that displeases you.

MR. GLENSOR: On the contrary, I do not wish to displease you. Inasmuch as you brought up those specific questions, and say that you are prepared to answer them, my colleagues and myself think that we would like to have them answered, and it may materially change the things that we have to say.

SUPERVISOR POWER: I would like to ask Mr. Glensor a question.

MR. GLENSOR: Yes.

SUPERVISOR POWER: The appointment of the Trustees, as recommended by the Mayor, is that displeasing to you?

MR. GLENSOR: We are instructed to oppose the Board.

SUPERVISOR POWER: The Mayor just propounded a question to you that he did not wish to do anything to displease you and I thought that your answer might be to kindly nominate the Trustees you wish and then we can all go home.

MR. GLENSOR: Well, that might be a happy solution.

THE MAYOR: Let the record show that the Mayor is earnest in his efforts to solve this big problem. Let the record show that the Mayor has approached this matter with malice towards none and charity to all, in the words of Abraham Lincoln. Let the record show that after 12 years the Board of Supervisors put the job up to the Mayor by resolution, and a committee of nine, three Veterans, three members of the former Board of Trustees and three Supervisors, and added the Mayor to the committee of ten, and the Mayor has never yet finished working on this job. Let the record show that I have no personal feeling against any one, and I have nothing but a sincere desire to build the War Memorial that others who had it in their hands for 11 years got nowhere with. And we are getting somewhere now, because we are meeting to try and solve the problem, and I never found a problem yet that could not be solved, and we are going to build the War Memorial. The first question Mr. Glensor asked me to answer, I will give the same credit to the Daily News——

SUPERVISOR TONER (interrupting): Mr. Mayor, prior to your answering the question, I understood Mr. Glensor to say, and I think that my understanding was substantiated from the fact that he did not know what was in those clippings, were those the questions that you want answered?

MR. GLENSOR: Yes, and others.

SUPERVISOR TONER: I would like to hear him propound those individually and specifically so that we will know that those are the questions that he wants propounded.

THE MAYOR: May I assist Mr. Glensor. Mr. Glensor, is this your first question: Why did the private Board of Trustees spend $216,000 for plans which are useless, in view of the amount of money available to be spent?

MR. GLENSOR: That is one question we would like answered, yes, very much.

THE MAYOR: All right. In answering that question I make this reply: First, on March 19, 1928, the special American Legion War

Memorial Committee approved plans for the Veterans' building submitted by the Trustees, photostatic copy of these plans and signatures on same are submitted herewth. Here are the plans and here are the photostatic copy of all representatives of the American Legion War Veterans' Committee attached to the plans and made a part hereof, and here are all the detailed plans, photostatic copies of all of the plans which were drawn and bear the signatures. "The within set of plans, consisting of five sheets, is hereby approved by the San Francisco Posts of the American Legion, San Francisco, California, March 19, 1928 American Legion War Memorial Committee; James B. Burns, chairman; A. Don Duncan, Geo. H. Cabaniss, Jr., Harold Hotchner, Dr. Peter R. Angel, Earle H. Harris, Leon French, Ivy Perkins Cerkel, Chas. H. Kendrick, James B. Burns, A. E. Schofield, Edward Schary, Thos. M. Foley, Wm. D. Flynn and F. F. Ainsworth. I hereby certify that the foregoing are signatures of duly authorized and accredited members of the American Legion War Memorial Committee. J. C. Claridge, Adjutant, S. F. County Council, American Legion, Secretary, War Memorial Committee." "Estimates based on the plans existing at the time of above approval indicated that these plans could be carried out for within a few hundred thousand dollars of the funds available. In order to reduce the cost of the project both buildings were made ten feet narrower, this ten feet being taken from hallways only and not reducing the net amount of usable space allotted to the Veterans, which space is approximately 105,700 square feet. This space is equivalent to a building 100 feet square and ten stories high, without including necessary hallways, elevator shafts and so forth. Working drawings for the construction of buildings in accordance with the above plan are now in the hands of the trustees and practically completed. Second, amount expended for plans is not excessive. It is also a fact that a great deal of highly technical information was necessary and was required because of the character of the structure contemplated." And here is a beautiful design from a water colored drawing by Francis McComas of the San Francisco War Memorial. That is where the $216,000 went, the plans were approved, and the plans bear the signatures of the trustees entrusted with the building of this building. Now, so far as the funds are concerned, I never was on the board, never was invited to attend a meeting, I was never appointed on any board whatsoever until December, 1928, when the impasse came, and I have been striving since that time with this matter, and I made my nominations eight months later, after my appointment to the committee of ten. This is the explanation I give from the Honcrable Board of War Memorial Trustees who spent their own money, of private subscriptions, and none of the City's money, and not a dollar of the City's money has yet been touched. Two hundred and sixteen thousand dollars of the private subscribers' money was used in drawing these plans, which met with the approval of the Veterans, and I give you the proof of the signatures.

SUPERVISOR HAYDEN: What was that date, Mr. Mayor?

THE MAYOR: March 19, 1928.

SUPERVISOR HAYDEN: Might I ask you, at the same time, what was the estimated cost of those two buildings at that time?

THE MAYOR: That is in the record; it is in the history of the War Memorial.

SUPERVISOR HAYDEN: I was not here the other night.

THE MAYOR: They are all in there.

SUPERVISOR PEYSER: May I ask, those plans which you have exhibited to this Board, are they the entire plans, those five pages?

THE MAYOR: Yes.

SUPERVISOR PEYSER: And it is those which cost the amount of money?

THE MAYOR: For the architects' fees, for the engineers' fees, for the working in of plans to protect it against earthquakes, making the structures earthquake proof, all the details included in that financial statement of how that $216,000 was expended, not including the gratuitous service of many architects that gave their services gratis.

SUPERVISOR PEYSER: And those are the plans?

THE MAYOR: Completed.

SUPERVISOR TONER: Mr. Mayor, is the amount that the excavations cost also in that?

THE MAYOR: Yes.

SUPERVISOR TONER: The excavations?

THE MAYOR: Yes, sir, and the high pressure system put in by the Fire Department; we used pipe that was not used after the earthquake and fire; we used pipe and the high pressure system is in there, all ready to connect up with the building.

SUPERVISOR McSHEEHY: I happen to be, I want all to know one of the trustees of the present War Memorial. I happened to be at a meeting yesterday when this matter was brought up. I want to say, particularly in answer to Supervisor Peyser, those do not represent the plans exactly, because we have working plans that are as large as that blackboard, perhaps—oh, I do not know—the 24 sheets that are known as working plans. Those plans are complete, those plans can be sent out for bids; they are in a complete state, with specifications.

SUPERVISOR RONCOVIERI: May I, through you, ask a question of Mr. McSheehy? The plans are complete, you have just stated. You can call for bids upon them; they are ready to shoot?

THE MAYOR: May I answer that? Yes, the detailed drawings are complete, and the Dinwiddie Construction Company are the ones—it was agreed by the three veterans, the three War Memorial Trustees, the three Supervisors and myself, agreed on in my office at one of the meetings we held, to call upon Dinwiddie Construction Company to give us an estimate of what those plans would cost if the building was put up upon them. We have the detailed drawings.

SUPERVISOR RONCOVIERI: And the estimate was $8,200,000, and your Trustees had $5,000,000. Now, if that is good common sense, I fail to see it. They may be big men in their own affairs, but they could not build two flats for me, if I told them that I had $10,000 and they brought me plans for $20,000. Now, no architect could build for me if he brought me in plans for nearly twice the amount of money that I had on hand. Now, they must have known that they had $5,000,000. They bring in a beautiful set of plans. I do not blame these men for having signed that beautiful set of plans, I would have signed it, not knowing what the cost would be, but assuming that the architects and that those big men knew their business and then would submit to me a plan for $8,200,000, why, I cannot imagine men doing such a thing—$8,200,000—and they knew they only had $5,000,000.

THE MAYOR: No, Mr. Roncovieri, they had $6,000,000. (Laughter.) Now, please, I ask everybody present——

SUPERVISOR SPAULDING (interrupting): I rise to a point of order at this time, because I am, at this time, going to ask you to show all courtesy to the Mayor, and to the men who represent the veteran bodies of San Francisco, and in so doing you show the caliber of men you are, not only to the Mayor, but to this Board and to the men that represent you. And I know that you are men that will do it. So kindly refrain from any demonstration in the future. (Applause.)

THE MAYOR: Mr. Roncovieri, if you will take those figures, you will find that to put a granite front all around all those buildings, the estimate of the increased cost which that involves, increased by the amount of square feet requested by the veterans from their original amount which they wanted, to 105,870 square feet, which means, as you heard said the other day, a building 137 feet 6 inches square and ten stories high, which increased these original plans, which all were agreeable to, mind you, and raised the price to $8,200,000, and if in terra cotta you will find the cost was $7,000,000.

SUPERVISOR RONCOVIERI: $7,500,000 and they had only $5,000,-000?

THE MAYOR: They had $6,000,000, Mr. Roncovieri, $2,000,000 from the private subscriptions invested in the blocks of land and in the cash on hand and in accounts receivable and the interest earned plus the two blocks they had, and cash on hand, and the $4,000,000 bond issue of the City and County of San Francisco, which has not yet been sold. So the very lowest, then, is $6,000,000, four and two.

SUPERVISOR RONCOVIERI: They had $6,000,000 before they bought the land, yes; after they bought the land they had $5,000,000 for the buildings; they had $5,100,000 for the buildings and still they went to work and made plans for $8,200,000, and if of terra cotta, $7,500,000. Then they made the second set of plans, and they went awry again; the granite exterior would have been $7,250,000 and the terra cotta exterior $6,600,000. And then they proceed to say, "It indicates that these figures are too high in view of the available funds, and the alternative would seem to be to redraw the plans with a modified program." Now, they are going to have a third set of plans. Well, what are they going to cost? How much is that going to add to the $216,000 for two sets of plans?

THE MAYOR: If I had any authority, Supervisor Roncovieri, or if you had any authority—the men whom this Board are expected by the people of San Francisco to confirm, these matters will be answered by that authorized body, authorized by the people of San Francisco to answer those questions, and take charge of the building of the War Memorial, according to the Charter amendment.. We have no authority here, nobody here. We are just here trying to get a Board of Trustees confirmed so that we can put the plans in the hands of the board and tell them to go ahead, and they will have all the meetings. They will hear the veterans, they will hear the Supervisors, they will hear everybody, but they are the only people that can act, and that is the reason the War Memorial is held up. The Board of Supervisors cannot do anything with it.

SUPERVISOR RONCOVIERI: The plans have cost in actual money $216,000 and the building was not started. What will it cost in addition for superintendency of that building by the architects—four, five or six per cent, or whatever they get in addition. The third set of plans will have to be made. I can see here some four or five hundred thousand dollars expended for architects' fees by the time that this job is finished, and it is that which particularly I criticise on the part of the Trustees who have held the money for twelve years, as you said. And you have renamed some of the very gentlemen who, to my mind, have erred financially. It is inescapable, in my mind, that these gentlemen did not know what was going on. They must have left this work to some particular individual, perhaps to the committee, or to the architects themselves, without telling them, in advance, "We have $5,100,000 after buying these lands and digging the holes. Now, be sure not to exceed that; try to keep your plans within that amount." Now, they did not do it. And I say, in justice to them, they are busy men, they probably did not know what was going on. But you have renamed them.

THE MAYOR: Say, Mr. Supervisor, this Board had three members of its own members upon this War Memorial Board.

SUPERVISOR RONCOVIERI: Only lately.

THE MAYOR: All the time.

SUPERVISOR RONCOVIERI: Not all the time.

THE MAYOR: Not within the first few years, but I mean, during the last—the greater number of years. Why, you have had Supervisor McSheehy, you have had Supervisor Colman. Supervisor Havenner was named, but he did not serve, but you had your own members there and they approved these plans.

SUPERVISOR RONCOVIERI: That does not change the situation one iota.

THE MAYOR: Well, I cannot change it.

SUPERVISOR RONCOVIERI: You could.

THE MAYOR: How?

SUPERVISOR RONCOVIERI: By not naming these men and naming a majority of veterans. You spoke of an outstanding labor leader. I was the one that suggested to you, in your office, before these members, that a labor leader, a prominent labor man, should be on this Board of Trustees.

THE MAYOR: So we did discuss it in my office, the names?

SUPERVISOR RONCOVIERI: We did, but I believe that labor has within its ranks outstanding men who are ex-service men and who have served their country. I feel that there are other men in other walks of life, bankers, if you wish, lawyers, if you wish, other citizens who have served their country. Why, you can make the whole eleven ex-service men if it is desired. That is all right. All we asked you, in a resolution introduced by Supervisor Havenner, was to name a majority, six out of eleven. That was easy to do, it seemed to me. Unfortunately, you have not done it, and here we have reached this impasse.

THE MAYOR: The only impasse is that the Board won't vote.

SUPERVISOR RONCOVIERI: I am willing to vote and vote "no."

THE MAYOR: Call the roll now.

SUPERVISOR RONCOVIERI: And I suggest a roll call right now and we will end this matter right at this meeting.

THE MAYOR: Call the roll, begin with the first name on the list.

SUPERVISOR HAVENNER: Oh, no, Mr. Mayor, I object, and I move that the roll be called on the entire list of nominees.

SUPERVISOR PEYSER: Second the motion.

SUPERVISOR POWER: As I understand, the privilege of the floor has been given Mr. Glensor.

SUPERVISOR RONCOVIERI: I withdraw that motion.

THE MAYOR: I am simply replying to Mr. Roncovieri, who has asked me some questions.

SUPERVISOR POWER: I want some light myself from the veterans' side, I have never heard of it, outside of what you read.

THE MAYOR: Of course, Mr. Glensor has asked me to answer the questions which he has propounded. I have just answered No. 1. Now, Mr. Glensor.

SUPERVISOR POWER: Regarding this set of plans, would .you mind saying what date were they approved?

THE MAYOR: March 19, 1928, almost two years ago.

SUPERVISOR POWER: That was after the $4,000.000 bond issue was adopted by the people?

THE MAYOR: Yes.

MR. GLENSOR: Yes, sir.

THE MAYOR: Now, Mr. Glensor.

MR. GLENSOR: In due course we will show that another set of plans was drawn under date of May 24, 1928. We have them here, and they are different, materially different. Also to answer, for the information of the Board, a question that has recently come up, I find in the record the following statement, that is, with regard to the members of this Board who are also on the Board of War Memorial Trustees: "July 14, 1927. A vacancy occurring on the Board of Trustees of the War Memorial, the Chairman of the Finance Committee of the Board of Supervisors, Mr. James B. McSheehy, was unanimously elected to fill the vacancy. Later, Supervisors Franck R. Havenner and Jesse C. Colman were added to the Board." It would appear from that, which is my only information on the subject, that no member of this Board was on the Board of private War Memorial Trustees until July 14, 1927. Now, gentlemen, as I understand the

question on which you are presently to vote is the question, whether
the Board of Trustees to administer the War Memorial, pursuant to
the Charter of the City, nominated by his Honor the Mayor of this
City, and coming to you for confirmation pursuant to the Charter
shall or shall not be confirmed. This same Board, composed of the
identical individuals, when submitted to this Board of Supervisors
for confirmation, under date of August 25, and pursuant to instructions from certain veteran organizations, we appeared and filed written
opposition to the confirmation, upon the grounds stated in writing at
that time, and in the wisdom of this Board it saw fit to vote to not confirm that Board of Trustees. From September 16, the date on which that
vote was taken, until February 7, 1930, there is no doubt in my mind,
knowing this situation as I do, that this entire controversy could have
been very easily and amicably settled by making a few changes in
those nominees. Conferences were held with his Honor the Mayor in
an endeavor to get him to make such changes and to submit to this
Board nominations of a Board of War Memorial Trustees that we,
as representatives of the veterans, could come before you and ask
you to confirm. And you must observe tonight that the result of those
conferences was unsuccessful because you are now confronted with
the same Board of individuals which, on September 16, 1929, this
Board refused to confirm. I mention the date of February 7 because
that was the date of the last conference in which we attempted to
reach an understanding and an amicable adjustment in this matter,
that the men we represent would authorize and instruct us to ask
you gentlemen of the Board to confirm. A proposal was made at
that time, and we took it back to a meeting of the organizations which
we represent the next day, at which meeting three members of your
Board were present, and the Mayor himself was invited to be present,
and we submitted that proposal or recommendation and asked for instructions, and we received those instructions, and we are here under
those instructions tonight to voice the opinion and the position of the
veteran organizations of San Francisco on this question, which is of
all importance to them. We have been instructed by the twenty posts
of the American Legion in San Francisco, five posts of the Veterans
of Foreign Wars, four camps of the United Spanish War Veterans,
the United Veterans' Council, the Disabled American Veterans of the
World War, the United Veterans of the Republic, and numerous
auxiliaries and affiliated organizations, to say to this Board that these
organizations oppose the Board of War Memorial Trustees now before
you for confirmation upon the following grounds: First, all of the
grounds stated in the written objections filed with the Board on
September 16, 1929, under date, however, of September 7, because the
meeting was continued to the time when this same Board of Trustees
was nominated and confirmation thereof was refused by this Board.
Secondly, upon the ground not made before, that the nominations now
before you include four men who have served upon the Board of
Trustees of the private trust fund; thirdly, upon the ground that in
all of the places in California, and elsewhere, of which we have been
able to obtain any record or any knowledge, having War Memorials,
which are in the form of housing facilities for the veteran organizations, the administration of those buildings has been placed in the
hands of the veteran organizations that occupy them. It is not my
intention to speak at any greater length upon this matter than is
necessary to carry out the instructions of the organizations which we
represent, and, of course, we recognize the fact that we are limited by
the graciousness with which you gentlemen give us your time. But
if you will permit me, I would like to briefly sketch most of the points
of these objections and the veterans' position thereon, and leave some
of them to be disposed of by my colleagues on the Advisory Board,
and by Mr. Sapiro, the past commander of the County Council of the
American Legion. And I promise you now that we will endeavor to

be just as brief in our presentation as may be consistent with clarity. When the Board was submitted before, our opposition may be summarized as follows: First, that a majority of the Board was not composed of veterans. San Francisco is the only City of which we have been able to obtain any record anywhere, in the State of California or elsewhere, that has a War Memorial, or contemplates a War Memorial, and which has denied the veteran organizations who will occupy it the right to administer their own War Memorial. In Berkeley, across the bay, there is a War Memorial building, built jointly by the city and county, housing the veteran organizations of that city. The commission governing the building is composed of the City Commissioner of Buildings and five other commissioners selected by the veterans' organizations themselves: The American Legion, Spanish War Veterans, Veterans of Foreign Wars, Disabled American Veterans of the World War and the Grand Army of the Republic. Oakland has a War Memorial housing the veteran organizations of that city, and the commission governing it is composed of six veterans, selected by the nationally recognized veteran organizations and authorized by the Board of Supervisors to govern the War Memorial. The same is true in Los Angeles. To go outside of the borders of our own State. The State of Ohio has a War Memorial law authorizing political subdivisions of that State to erect War Memorials and the State law provides that those War Memorials shall be administered by a Board composed of five members selected by the veterans themselves: The Grand Army of the Republic, the Spanish War Veterans and the American Legion. Before the Board of Supervisors, on October 7, 1929, the Mayor, addressing you, said: "If I had the appointment of all the men who served the country, I would appoint every one of them, but you drew the resolution"—apparently referring to the Charter amendment—"but you drew the resolution limiting me to eleven." But, gentlemen, of these eleven we are only asking for six. We are not asking for eleven, although I think the veterans would be justified, based upon the practice in regard to War Memorials in other communities, we would be justified in asking eleven, but we are only asking six. Heretofore, and up until February 7, the meeting which I referred to in my opening remarks, the veterans would have been contented, I think they would have been satisfied, if not contented, with six men who were veterans in fact, on this War Memorial Committee. Now, in all kindness, in all sincerity and without any desire to offend anyone, I state simply as a fact that when we reported the results of our conference of February 7, 1930, the veteran organizations which we represent concluded that they were being trifled with in this matter, and they thereupon very definitely instructed us that they and we were now to take the position that we wanted a majority, not of veterans in fact, but of veterans who were members, who were sympathetic of and who were familiar with the aims, objects and the work that was being carried on by these veteran organizations. Now, gentlemen, I want to invite your attention to the fact that that is not an unreasonable demand. War Memorials, when built in this form, as housing accommodations for veteran organizations, are occupied, not by individual veterans, but by organizations. Those organizations are units of the Grand Army of the Republic, Women's Relief Corps, camps of the Spanish War Veterans, posts of the Veterans of Foreign Wars, posts of the American Legion and auxiliaries. Those organizations are carrying on, and trying to carry on, in this country a definite work. I wont go into in detail, it is a long story and most of you are familiar with it, but I may summarize it by saying that it is an endeavor, within the limits of our humble beliefs, to make this country, this Nation, this State and the community in which we live a better place in which to live. We recognize the fact that our service to this country did not end when we were given our discharges, a red chevron, and permission from a grateful government to buy

TUESDAY, FEBRUARY 25, 1930. 623

tickets home at a reduced rate, on government-operated railroads, so long as we did not insist on the better class trains. We recognize the fact that that service continues to this day, and we are trying to do certain work in the way of Americanism, for the benefit of the community. To bring an example home to you, we are cooperating in the Community Chest drive in San Francisco right now, and we are doing it through organizations, and those organizations are the veteran organizations that will occupy the War Memorial, if and when built. And it is entirely reasonable that the men who should administer that War Memorial, as representatives of the Veterans, should be members of these organizations, should know what these organizations mean, should know what they are trying to do, and should understand their relationships one with the other.

In November, shortly after the Armistice celebration, his Honor very graciously invited the War Memorial Committee of the American Legion to visit him at his chambers for the purpose of discussing this matter, and my predecessor, as commander of the County Council of the American Legion, took us all up there, some 22 or 23 men, and there in the presence of all of those men, and in the presence of the press and some visitors, we all understood him to say that he would submit ultimately a Board upon which at least some changes would be made. Yet tonight we are confronted by the same Board. At the meeting of February 7 we again made certain proposals which we thought we could get approved by the organizations that we represented, and the only proposal that we could take back to them was this: That it had been rumored in the press that two members of this Board were going to resign; that, if they resigned—first, it was suggested that we withdraw all opposition to confirmation of this Board. Then if the two members resigned, Mr. Mullen would be taken from the Board of War Memorial Trustees and appointed upon this Board as a member of the Board of Supervisors. And then if Mr. Mullen resigned from the Board of War Memorial Trustees, which I take it is not necessary for him to do unless he wanted to, some outstanding veteran, whom we do not know, would be appointed in his place, and there would be six veterans in fact upon the administrative body, controlling the War Memorial. That was the proposal which we took back to the organizations which we represent, the next day, and that was the time when, as I told you a moment before, they concluded that they were being trifled with and instructed us not only to oppose the confirmation of this Board upon all the grounds stated on September 16, 1929, but upon the additional grounds that they object to any members of the old Board, for reasons which I will hereafter develop, being appointed on the new Board, and they also will not be satisfied—I am not saying they may not ultimately have to take them —but they will never be satisfied unless there are six veterans upon the Board of War Memorial Trustees who are satisfactory to the veteran organizations, who are going to use the War Memorial. In that connection I may say, and I take it that any discussion here tonight to be of any value must be frank, that the veterans regard this present Board of Trustees as containing but one man that is serviceable to them as a veteran who has knowledge of and is sympathetic with veteran organizations and the work they are doing. One veteran has reached advanced years and his health is poor, a man whom we revere and respect, and in whom we have the highest confidence, and for whom we have the greatest esteem; his health is failing; he has reached the highest office in military life that his country can give with one or two exceptions. He has devoted his whole life to the service of the country, and we think that it would be unfair to expect from him the understanding of the detailed work in the administration of this War Memorial which the veterans' needs require. And for the other three veterans, they are veterans in fact, but with respect to the veteran organizations that will occupy those buildings, they are either apathetic or avowedly hostile.

The veterans object to the confirmation of this Board upon the ground that this Board of Supervisors has gone on record interpreting the Charter Amendment, Charter Amendment 32, which says that, in making the appointments, due consideration shall be given to the veterans of all wars, that a majority of the Board should be veterans, and there is not a majority of the Board proposed veterans, either in fact or in deed. Now, on September 16, when the other Board was proposed, we filed objections to any Board of Trustees which contains a member of the Board of Supervisors. And that objection was not personal, gentlemen, and it was not political. It is a practical objection which we base on a matter of principle. We have stated it fully in the written argument which we filed on September 16, which has been printed and submitted to you, and I will make no further argument on that point. There is one other member of the Board to which we are instructed to specifically object, and I will leave that matter to be discussed by Mr. Burns, the matters having arisen while he was commander of the County Council of the American Legion, if you will accord him a hearing. We object to the confirmation of a Board containing any of the old Board of Trustees; that is. the Board that has administered this private trust fund for 12 long years. Those of you who sat here the other night and heard this long ,record read must have caught, from time to time, flashes of the fact that for 12 years, notwithstanding the fact that these Trustees had signed their names to a trust indenture naming the San Francisco Posts of the American Legion specifically as a beneficiary, that for 12 years there had been active opposition and covert hostility to the San Francisco posts of the American Legion. This record is replete with incidents which show that, during all this time, there has been no attempt to ascertain the needs and to comply with the wishes of the veteran organizations. On the contrary, this record throughout the long statement made by Mr. Drum, especially in the latter part of the statement that he made, and at the public meeting of December 6, 1928, when he was examined or when questions were propounded to him, it shows that it has been a game of chess with these Trustees, not to carry out and discharge the trusts which they accepted when they signed this trust indenture, but to defeat those rights of the veteran organizations of San Francisco.

THE MAYOR: Will you excuse me just a moment, Mr. Glensor? I see Mr. Marks, a former member of the Board and a member of the committee. Will you come forward, Mr. Marks, and have a seat somewhere? You might be interested in this. Mr. Marks was one of the committee of three appointed by the Board of Supervisors to act in ironing out this affair.

MR. GLENSOR: I will join his Honor in inviting my brother at the bar in. His Honor mentioned that committee of nine. In passing, I just want to call your attention to one most significant fact, gentlemen, about the records which are submitted to you in this book, as emanating from that committee of nine. Look through them and will you find one word, in writing, emanating from that committee of nine, that was not submitted by the veteran organizations of San Francisco? Not one. We put every statement that was filed with that committee of nine in writing, as an indisputable record to be referred to thereafter, as to what our position was at all times, and not one other word emanated from that committee of nine in writing, other than the records which we submitted to them. So much for that.

To return to our objections to the old Board of Trustees, we think that their refusal to account to the beneficiaries of this trust fund alone is a sufficient ground for their rejection as trustees of any other trust fund, public or private. Do you recall in that report of December 6, 1928, where the veterans said, when they came in, they said, "Well, you gentlemen are here; what do you want?" And they said, "Why, we came up here and we thought that we were going to get the accounting we were waiting for so long of this trust fund. What happened to it?" Again, in the long written document which is printed in here, filed under date of April 20, 1929, there is a passage, you will find a passage somewhere like this—I won't stop to find it and quote it, but I remember it quite well because I wrote it myself: We think, perhaps, that if you do so and so it will be a very happy solution, because that would carry with it the accounting which the veterans have so long desired. And now that the matter has been called to your attention we have no doubt but it will be immediately forthcoming. The fund had then been in existence for eight or nine years, expenses had been incurred, income had been received and definite and repeated requests had been made for a financial statement or accounting, and those requests had all been refused except a sketchy and fragmentary balance sheet which was filed as of September, 1928. Many other requests were made for an accounting, and finally, after there had been a change in the chairmanship of the Board of private Trustees we addressed a letter to his successor, Mr. William H. Crocker, in which we asked him very graciously for an accounting. In reply we received a letter from a gentleman signing himself the secretary to the Board of War Memorial Trustees, and it read substantially as follows: According to my understanding the veterans of San Francisco are not direct beneficiaries of the trust fund, but are only entitled to the beneficial use of the buildings when built. Now, one of the most significant documents in connection with this whole controversy is the trust indenture of August 19, 1921. And in it you will find this language— I do not know whether it is in here or not, it certainly was not read to you—"requirements of trust in favor of San Francisco Posts of the American Legion. The building to be occupied by the San Francisco Posts of the American Legion shall be occupied and used by the various duly organized and authorized San Francisco Posts of the American Legion without rent charge. The San Francisco Posts of the American Legion, or a majority of them, shall, under such rules and conditions as they may prescribe, provide headquarters for veterans of the Mexican War, Grand Army of the Republic, Spanish-American War veterans, and such other patriotic organizations as such San Francisco Posts of the American Legion may from time to time desire to install." Then follows a provision in case the American Legion should ever merge in any other organization, what would happen, and finally it says: "The said building to be occupied by the San Francisco Posts of the American Legion shall be used both as a club and meeting rooms of the executive offices and for auditorium purposes." That is the provision of the private trust fund.

SUPERVISOR HAVENNER: What is the date of that?

MR. GLENSOR: August 19, 1921. Now, that is the trust indenture under which the private Trustees took the money and administered it. I won't read it all, it is a nine-page closely typewritten legal-size document, but in it there are provisions that they should take this money, acquire land and build the buildings for certain purposes, and among them that is one of the purposes. Now, that very clearly makes the San Francisco Posts of the American Legion beneficiaries, and if there is anything that is settled, gentlemen, in the law of trusts, as your City Attorney or your colleagues on the Board who are members of the bar can tell you, it is that a beneficiary of a trust fund may have an accounting at all reasonable and proper times from his trustee. Well, we wrote and asked for such an accounting, and finally, from the latest chairman of this Board of War Memorial Trustees, in reply we received this letter, saying that, according to his secretary's understanding of the trust fund we were not beneficiaries. And in reply to that we replied in a letter, which has been read to this Board at least twice, once on January 20, 1930, and again at the long meeting a week ago tonight. And in that letter we said substantially this: Dear Mr. Crocker: We are not interested in your secretary's understanding of the trust indenture. What we want is an accounting. We want it for your benefit as well as our own. There are many rumors of mis-

management and waste, and we would like to have an answer for
those rumors, and we would like to answer our own members, and we
would like to answer the public that are saying that there has been
mismanagement and waste. Furthermore, we want to call your attention to the fact that your secretary's understanding is wrong. And
then we invited attention to the trust indenture which makes the
American Legion Posts beneficiaries. And finally we said: We note in
the financial statement that you filed with the Board of Supervisors
that you have spent, over a period of years, $13,000 for legal expenses,
and we ask you, is it possible that in buying $13,000 worth of legal
advice you have not taken occasion to ask your counsel who are the
beneficiaries of the trust fund, but now, twelve years after its inception, you are obliged to rely for that information upon your secretary's
understanding? And that is the letter, gentlemen, about which our
Mayor has expressed such violent indignation—not violent indignation
that Trustees of a great quasi-public trust should deny one of the
beneficiaries the accounting to which they are entitled, but indignation
that they should ask for it, an indignation in which I cannot share.
In this report his Honor saw fit to read you an editorial from one
of the great San Francisco dailies. Now, as all citizens do, living
under this government of the people, for the people and by the newspapers, I recognize the right of the general press to express themselves on every topic. And this editorial stated that the trustees of this
private fund are only accountable to the donors. Now, passing for a
moment the fact that practically all the veterans who are interested
in this matter are donors of this trust fund—of course, they did not
give as much as some, but they gave what they could—it happened
that in that particular instance this gentleman or this editorial writer
was wrong, just a little bit wrong, but, nevertheless, he was somewhat wrong. It is true they are responsible and accountable to the
donors of the trust fund, but they are also accountable and responsible
to the beneficiaries. And to match editorial with editorial, may I read
you an excerpt from an editorial which appeared in another great San
Francisco paper. "Is it proper," it is said in this editorial, "to appoint
men as trustees of a great public trust fund who, for nine years, have
been trustees of a two million dollar private fund and who refuse to
make an accounting of their trusteeship?"

Now, soon after his honor announced that he would make this complete investigation, which has culminated in this report which is before
you, an announcement that was received by the veterans with great
enthusiasm because we welcomed it, my predecessor as commander of
the County Council of the American Legion, Mr. Milton Sapiro, sent
a communication to the Mayor, in which the following was said, among
other things:

"Dear Mayor Rolph: In connection with the various statements that
have been made in reference to the War Memorial project, and to assist
in your preparation of a complete report on this subject, we refer you
to the following data:

"First, let it be noted that you probably will have access to more
data than has been made available to the veteran organizations as the
trustees under the present existing trust have failed and neglected to
furnish a detailed financial statement to the veteran organizations,
although they promised to furnish the same more than one year ago.

"If you will secure a copy of the financial statement submitted by
the auditors, Bullock, Kellog and Mitchell, to the Board of Trustees,
dated September 30, 1928, you will find that at that date this Board
of Trustees had deposited in banks and trust companies $306,211.54,
and in addition had $910,017.27 on certificates of deposit representing
money deposited with banks but for which the banks had issued such
certificates.

"We believe that your failure to take this fact into account resulted
in the statement which you made to the Board of Supervisors that

there never was more than two to three hundred thousand dollars deposited with banks. We know that you did not intend to give the erroneous impression that no other money was deposited with banks, and that you will recognize that the money represented by these certificates of deposit was just as much a deposit as money placed in a savings or commercial account.

"We have not been informed as to the interest rate on these certificates of deposit, but you will be able to ascertain that and whether the rate was the customary rate of two or four per cent."

Try and find it in this report.

"If you will refer to the same report, you will find that the trustees borrowed from the American Trust Company $328,287.44, upon which interest was paid. Interest on such a loan at the usual rate of 6% is $1641.43 per month. The reports and accounts of the Board of Trustees establish conclusively that this money was borrowed at a time when the trustees held these certificates of deposit, which could have been turned into cash and used, instead of borrowing money from a bank at a loss of $1641.00 a month. We think that you should get a very definite statement as to the amount of interest paid in both instances and determine whether there has been any discrepancy unfavorable to the trust fund."

I have made a very careful examination of this financial statement, and had an examination made by two certified public accountants. Although you appreciate, gentlemen, it is difficult for a lawyer to admit that there is anything that he cannot extricate from a written document, nevertheless I admit it, and had an analysis made by two certified public accountants and it cannot be determined from this report what interest was received on the money on deposit, on how much money it was received, over what period it was received, nor can it be determined what rate of interest was paid, on how much money it was paid, or over what period it was paid. There are just two entries: Received interest, so much; paid interest, so much; difference, so much. That does not mean anything. It might have been at one per cent, or one-half of one per cent by weight and volume, or it might have been at eight or ten per cent. Nobody can tell.

"In further considering the financial account, we ask that a report be made concerning the reasons why the two blocks on Van Ness Avenue were excavated before plans had been prepared and approved by all necessary parties so as to deprive the trust fund of the income from the Locomobile building standing on one of the blocks and the oil stations standing on the corner of one of the blocks. The amount of rental lost should appear in the trustees' records."

Find an answer to that in anything that has been submitted to you.

"We also suggest that you ascertain definitely the reason why title to the property involved was held in the Mercantile Trust Company for a period of more than four years, thus resulting in an expenditure of taxes from the trust fund, which expenditure would not have been necessary if the property had been transferred to the board of regents of the University of California as contemplated."

Another item that is not reported to you and not of record.

For twelve years we have been trying to get a statement. What we finally got is embodied in here, and what it is, gentlemen, is what a bookkeeper would colloquially, and perhaps slangily, refer to as "a balance sheet," or a statement pulled off the books. It shows what the books show, the books of the War Memorial Trustees, and nothing else. To begin with, it is uncertified, although made by certified public accountants, it is not certified. And whether a public accountant is certified or not, if he does not append his certificate, he is merely doing the work of a bookkeeper, and that implies no criticism of the accountants who made this report whatsoever because we have not the slightest doubt but what they did just what they were told. It shows cash on hand in the sum of $64,000. Now, $64,000 is important

money in any language, and it is difficult to understand why men who
are submitted to you to be trustees and administrators of $4,000,000
of the money of the people of the City and County of San Franisco,
should actually carry, not on interest but cash on hand, over an unde-
termined period, $64,000 odd. Subscriptions receivable, $231,442.41.
And the report says that individual balances representing that are
appended in the schedule, and that schedule is not, for some unknown
reason, printed in this report. We might find in there, if we were
favored with a knowledge of its contents, some of our most constructive critics who had not paid their subscription to the War Memorial
Fund. Interest receivable is shown as $6,834.67 and interest accrued.
$394,350.50, but it does not appear at what rate, on what amount, or
over what period, and there is no way of determining that except by
getting information which has not been made available to us. Interest charges, $151,852.52. And we have asked—we have asked no later
than here tonight, and would be very pleased to receive an answer
from anybody, why was it necessary, with all this money on hand—
there has apparently never been a time since the Trustees invested a
dollar in land that they have not had a very large sum of money on
hand—why, gentlemen, is it necessary to deplete this trust fund by
spending $151,000 for interest?

You will find another item in this financial statement of $21,000 for
the Locomobile lease. Now, $21,000 for that lease may have been a
most reasonable amount; it might have been a great buy at that
time; it might have represented a very sharp bargain on the part of
the Trustees, and, on the other hand, it might not. It might have only
had a month to run; we do not know, and we cannot determine, and
there is no explanation in this so-called "accounting".

Architects, drafting, and so forth, $319,664.51. Now, that includes
the $78,000 for excavating which you asked about a few moments ago,
but the figure that was before you at that moment does not; the figure
that was before you then was some two hundred-odd thousand dollars.

SUPERVISOR TONER: $216,000.

MR. GLENSOR: Right, and that does not include the excavation,
but this figure does. Now, that is carried as an asset. And, in part,
it is an asset; the excavation is properly an asset. I suppose the
place had to be excavated some time, and it is, in part, an asset; but
the $216,000 for plans are certainly not an asset, because it is con-
ceded by the Trustees themselves, as I am going to read to you in a
moment, that the plans must be redrawn. And the only answer that
we have had to that so far is that the veterans approved the plans;
that is, the American Legion approved the plans. That is true, they
approved those plans. I have no intention of denying it. I would be
foolish if I did. But, gentlemen, that is one of the most—I was going
to say "vicious"; I won't use that word—annoying kind of statement
to answer; it is half truth. The veterans did approve those plans,
and I am going to leave to my colleague, Mr. Burns, if you will listen
to him a few moments when I am finished, and I assure you I am
going to finish some time. I am going to leave to him to explain to
you under what circumstances they approved the plans. Then we will
show you another set of plans which were produced afterwards and
which have never been referred to here at all. We have them right
here. Now, I said a moment ago that it was conceded by the Board
of Trustees themselves that the plans must be redrawn. At a meeting
in this room on July 17, 1929, we have this statement from one of
the trustees, Mr. Herbert Fleishhacker, and I am reading from page
90 of this printed report: "Both for financial reasons and at the same
time to save time. Were we to put another bond issue on the ballot,
it would mean probably a year's delay. I want to say this, in justice
to the architects present: They were not asked at any time by the
building committee to get up a set of plans to have an opera house
and Legion building within the $5,000,000 limit, and they are not to

blame. And I think that should be understood because otherwise there is a possibility of them being criticised for running $1,500,000 in excess of the amount available. They were asked to get up a very beautiful building, one that would serve the purpose and that would answer the requirements of the Legionnaires. They have done that, but now we will have to go back at them again with a definite lot of instructions, telling them to develop it, as best they can, for the $5,000,000. I believe they can do it and will have a building that will do credit to San Francisco." In other words, go back at them and have them redraw the plans to conform to the money available. Now, this report does show that the Trustees have received over $2,000,000, to be exact, from the money received from all sources—without repeating the various figures it is $2,239,477. Now, if you deduct from that the land, the purchase price of the south block, the north block, the Locomobile lease, excavation, fire protection service, ground breaking—ground breaking is being carried as an asset, $1,465 for ground breaking expense is being carried as an asset in this report, furniture and fixtures, legal expense, commission on bonds, administration and salaries, what else is there, gentlemen? If you deduct all of those things, you have $1,381,303, and if you take out of that the amount of cash, admittedly now on hand, of $772,652.57, you have left $608,651.17 that has been administered away by this board of private War Memorial Trustees somewhere. I do not know where. I wish I did. We have been trying for years to find out, and we have not found out yet, but it has been administered away. Extricate it from that report if you can—certified public accountants cannot—but you get it out if you can. And you are asked now to confirm four of these men upon a Board of Public Trustees, to administer the San Francisco War Memorial. One of the San Francisco papers published this morning an editorial in which it tried to reconcile those figures. On the one hand it set down what it thought was all the money received, and on the other hand it set down what had been expended, and it then said: "These plans are certainly of some value." But the difference between those figures, gentlemen, was $450,445. Where is it?

In the argument which was sent out and induced people to vote the $4,000,000 bonds, the written statement was made: "The land is bought and the money, $2,000,000, is in the bank," and if this report shows anything, it shows that $2,000,000 was never in the bank.

Now, gentlemen, a few moments more and I will finish, and then, if you will be good enough to listen to my colleagues, we will all be through. There has been a tremendous amount of misrepresentation disseminated in connection with the veterans' position in this matter, and I feel that I must call attention to some of the things that have been said and point out that they are erroneous.

On January 20, 1930, in this Board his honor, the Mayor, on page 4, said: "My office is now deluged with resolutions, unanimously adopted by veterans of the World War, of the Spanish American War and other organizations," demanding that the Mayor resubmit the eleven names that he has now submitted. Gentlemen, I won't endeavor to speak for the veterans of the World War because there are many local and unit organizations, what we call "reunion organizations." And I suppose they could be called "veterans of the World War," but it so happens that I am a veteran of the last two wars. I do not say that boastfully, but merely cite it as a lack of common sense. And it so happens that I am vice-commander of the Spanish War Veterans' County Council. And I immediately went to every one of the camps of the Spanish War Veterans in San Francisco, and I asked them to give me a copy of any resolution or any document with which they had deluged the Mayor of the City of San Francisco, asking that he resubmit this Board, and I have been assured, in going over the list of these organizations, that not one of them has ever made such a suggestion, and if his Honor has any such resolutions, I would ask they be produced here

that they may be made a part of the record for our benefit because
if he is being deluged with resolutions from organizations that we
represent I think, in fairness to us, we ought to have the privilege of
going to them.

On February 10th, page 2, his honor made the statement that, at
the meeting of February 7th with the veterans' organizations, he had
tried to make several compromises—"I tried to make several compromises." Now, I am sure that in making such a statement his honor
was losing sight of what had occurred in the exigencies of parliamentary debate because I sat through that entire meeting on February
7th, right directly in front of him, with my colleagues at my side, and
the only proposal that was made, if it could be called such, was that if
a couple of the Supervisors resigned he would appoint Mr. Mullen,
and then if Mr. Mullen resigned he would appoint an outstanding
veteran in his place. Again, in this report on page 177 it is said that
we immediately accepted it. Again I must say his honor was mistaken
because I personally stated to him at least three times on that occasion
that we were acting under instructions; we were merely a mouthpiece
for the veteran organizations that we represented, and we had no
right and no authority to accept anything, and his honor said to me
that he understood that, and we told him that we would report whatever proposal he made to our organizations, and we invited him to
come up there and see if he could convince them that it was a fair
solution to this matter, and he declined to do so.

THE MAYOR: I apologize for that remark. I did not decline to do
so. I told you that it was midnight, and that I had a lot of things to
do, and I asked you to kindly excuse me and you said you would
under the circumstances. I never declined to go at any time, and I
ask several of the vets to rise in their seats and defend my position
that night when I was asked. They were present at the meeting.
(Two men stand up among the audience.)

MR. —————: Mr. Glensor, we did not suppose we were veterans.
We think we are.

MR. GLENSOR: Now that that is over, I will make it a little more
clear: The meeting to which we invited the Mayor was to occur the
next day, and there were three members of the Board of Supervisors
there, and I believe his honor said, in order to make it perfectly fair
and make it perfectly clear, that you had to go and see a relative off
on a boat that was sailing at noon. Isn't that right? That is correct,
isn't it?

THE MAYOR: I did. Was there any objection to that?

MR. GLENSOR: No, but I want to make it just as equally clear
that we did not accept any proposal that was made that night, and
I may say to you now that we have no authority, and have never
assumed any, and will not assume any, to accept any deal of any
nature whatsoever in regard to this matter. We are voicing the wishes
of certain people whom we represent and that is all we are doing.

On February 10th last, this appears on page 6 of the report of the
proceedings of that meeting, his honor said: "Last Friday night I
was asked to turn over the $4,000,000 bond issue voted by the people,
turn it all over to a Board of War Memorial Trustees for the purpose
of building a $4,000,000, plus the block of land, a $4,000,000 War Memorial. That leaves a block of land and $772,000 in the treasury for
the building of an opera house. The charter amendment provides
that it shall not be used except for War Memorial purposes and
municipal purposes. You know as well as I do that to build a $4,000,-
000 War Memorial for a building simply for the veterans' uses alone
which, after 30 or 40 or 50 years, the veterans, like all of us, pass
away, and there will be standing on a block of land over there a
building for War Memorial purposes and for veterans' purposes that
cost more than the Olympic Club, the Elks Club and the William
Taylor Hotel combined."

Now, I am very glad that he made that statement. I am very glad that his honor said that, because it gives me a chance to say to you gentlemen of the Board of Supervisors and to say to you gentlemen of the press, and to say to you people of the City of San Francisco something that I have wanted to say and something that the veterans have wanted to say to all of you for a long time. The veterans of San Francisco don't want any $4,000,000 building for their purposes, and if any enthusiastic or over-zealous person, either official or private, should come forward with the proposal to take $4,000,000 of the people's money and build with it a building exclusively for the veterans, the veterans of San Francisco would be the very first to call the gentleman to his senses. So far as we know, the most expensive building in the State of California which is devoted exclusively to veterans cost somewhere in the neighborhood of $1,000,000. Now, I want to say to you gentlemen that I am no builder and do not pretend to know anything about building costs, and I am not standing here and telling you that a building could be built in San Francisco for $1,000,000 for veterans' purposes. But I do know this, that it would not cost $4,000,000, and that with the consent of the veterans of San Francisco no building exclusively for the use of veterans will ever be erected at a cost of $4,000,000 in San Francisco. What we have said and what I am glad to repeat is this: That the bond ordinance provides $4,000,000 for a Memorial Hall for War Veterans and for educational, recreational, entertainment and other municipal purposes. It does not follow that you must use any part of that $4,000,000 bond issue to erect an opera house, an art museum, or a War Memorial Court. I don't want to believe—and I would like to settle for all time on behalf of the veterans of San Francisco whom we represent here—that we have never asked for and do not want a building for veteran purposes costing $4,000,000. That we should want a $4,000,000 building for our purposes is ridiculous and absurd, and we would never take such a position.

I want now, gentlemen, to anticipate a few arguments that I know are going to be made.

There has been read to this Board, at least twice, a letter from Senator Phelan in which he stated, to put it very baldly, that the veterans of San Francisco were wholly selfish and of malvision, and the statement is made in that letter that he understood when he made his donation that he was donating his money to be used principally for an opera house. I don't know what Senator Phelan understood, and I don't know and probably nobody else knows exactly what he understood, but here is what he signed when he gave it:

"The undersigned hereby subscribes and agrees to donate and pay to the University of California the sum of $ in the manner indicated below:

"$ Cash"—and stating the manner of payment, and then it reads: "The first installment to be paid upon its demand, and the remaining installments to be paid annually thereafter until the total amount of this donation is paid. The money so subscribed and donated is to be used for the purpose of purchasing a lot of land in the City and County of San Francisco, State of California, and for the purpose of erecting thereon a building or buildings devoted to music, fine arts, and a home for the American Legion, both the land and the building or buildings to be the property of the University of California."

That is what the gentleman signed.

SUPERVISOR McSHEEHY: What is the page of that?

MR. GLENSOR: That is the form of agreement, subscription agreement everyone signed.

SUPERVISOR McSHEEHY: What is the page?

MR. GLENSOR: That is the one which was circulated in 1920.

SUPERVISOR ANDRIANO: There was one subscription agreement signed originally when they subscribed in the first place which was found to be unsatisfactory by the regents of the University of California, and they prepared a new blank which was resubmitted to their donors for signature, and I would like to know whether this is the first or second subscription agreement.

MR. GLENSOR: This is the one payable to the University of California.

SUPERVISOR ANDRIANO: But is it the first or the second agreement?

MR. GLENSOR: I have only the one before me at the present time.

MR. BOYD: Supervisor Andriano has the record there from which he may read.

SUPERVISOR ANDRIANO: In 1921 the Regents of the University of California determined that the pledges signed, or the attorneys for the Regents of the University of California, determined that the pledges signed in the first instance were not entirely sufficient and that as a condition to the acceptance of the trust the trustees were pledged to secure new signatures on such form as then prescribed. This was a very huge task, and several thousand of the subscribers who had pledged their money took advantage of the situation and refused to sign on the new form, and what I wanted to know was whether this blank from which you were reading and which you have before you was the first or second form of subscription agreement?

MR. SAPIRO: The first.

THE MAYOR: For the benefit of the record, permit me to say that Senator Phelan signed the second or new agreement to take the place of the first, which he signed. He signed the first agreement and then signed the second agreement as well.

SUPERVISOR TONER: Are they identical as far as wording concerning the War Memorial and Fine Arts and so on is concerned?

MR. GLENSOR: Yes, they just simply signed twice; no difference in the terms used, I believe, in that respect.

Finally, gentlemen, before I close I would like to state that it will be urged upon you that everybody is heartily sick of this thing and wants to get action on it. Well, who wants action on it any more than the veterans themselves? There is a great deal more to it than action. If that were true, if that were sound argument, and all that is necessary is action, then we would never have this question settled upon a basis of right or wrong. All that we would have to do with any question of this kind would be to drag it along for 10 or 12 years and then say, "Let's do it, right or wrong." We have not been responsible for the delay and have always been in favor of expediting action and cannot be charged with this long lapse of time. Any basis —the only basis upon which this question can be settled to the advantage of the people of San Francisco and to the advantage of all of the people directly interested in the War Memorial—is upon the basis of right or wrong, and that is the only basis upon which we present it to you.

There has been in the public press of this City over the past few months resolutions purporting to emanate from the veteran bodies, two from Posts of the American Legion with respect to which, with respect to those two resolutions I would speak, and I am able to speak with authority, if there is any lingering doubt in the minds of anyone as to the position of the American Legion in this matter. One post of the American Legion passed a resolution, at a special meeting that was called for no other purpose, by a majority of one vote. This resolution was passed approving and asking the resubmission of this Board of War Memorial Trustees. When the matter was called to their attention and the effect which it would have upon this situation, and the facts laid before them, they very promptly put another story in the press to the effect this action had been withdrawn. Another post passed another similar resolution. That is, that is not true; it was a proposed resolution which was referred to a committee for debate and then withdrawn while in committee and never voted upon at all.

So much for the American Legion.

There has been a great deal of comment in the public press on a resolution or resolutions purporting to emanate from an organization, what is known as a reunion organization. May I explain, just briefly, what is meant by a reunion organization. To an ex-soldier, when you speak of the veteran organizations he means the nationally organized veteran organizations. Every one of the regiments, many of the ships, often battalions, and various other units, which participated in the World War, after returning home formed divisional, regimental, battalion organizations. I myself belong to one such organization, and the purpose of these organizations is to meet once a year for the purpose of having a reunion. One of these organizations, there was a story in the press to the effect that they had passed a resolution unanimously endorsing these trustees.

Now with respect to this particular resolution, and this particular reunion organization, and the manner in which this resolution was passed and under what circumstances, I, of my own knowledge, know nothing. All I do know is what I have been told by members of that organization, and they told me this: That this particular organization is designed to meet once a year; that it is run by an executive committee; that this particular resolution was passed by three members of the executive committee, and not in the meeting, and was sent to the press.

THE MAYOR: What is the name of the organization, Mr. Glensor?

MR. GLENSOR: The 363d organization. I want to make it clear to you gentlemen I know nothing about this——

(At this point Mr. Glensor was interrupted by two men and a woman standing up in the rear of the room.)

THE MAYOR: Now, just let's wait——

(Several voices: Sit down, sit down.)

A SPECTATOR: We have a few of our men here——

SUPERVISOR HAVENNER (interrupting): I wish to state that this is a duly called and regular meeting of this Board of Supervisors, and until such time as this gentleman has been granted the privilege of the floor, I shall have to ask him to sit down.

MR. GLENSOR: Gentlemen, I want to say, if you will permit me, I have nothing but the highest regard and respect for the regiment in question, and it was not my purpose, until directly interrogated, to mention their names.

THE MAYOR: We all knew it, anyway. We might as well have it in the record, and those boys will have something to say when the time comes.

MR. GLENSOR: I myself served in the division of which this regiment formed a part, and I know it is a very excellent organization. I am not discussing the merits of this organization at all, because, if you know soldiers, you know that they will all admit, if they are questioned closely, that the particular division which they happened to be a member of was the best division in the army, and that they will admit that the regiment in which they served was the best regiment in that division, and that the battalian in which they served was the best battalion in the regiment, and that their company was the best company in the battalian, and if you press them just a little bit more, they will probably admit that their squad was the best squad in the company. I am not criticizing at all. I am telling the stories which were brought to me by men whom I know were members during the war of this organization. Whether they are true or not I do not propose or pretend to say. Those are merely the stories which were brought to me by members of this organization. This organization has about 1100 members, as I understand, of whom about three or four hundred are in San Francisco, and the purpose of the organization

is to meet once a year for a reunion. By its by-laws and constitution
it has an executive committee having certain powers to act for the
organization, but under the by-laws and constitution this executive
committee is prohibited from taking action upon such a question.
Now, that may not all be true; I know nothing about it, I am simply
passing it on to you for what it is worth.

Finally, and in conclusion, I would like to ask why has this particular Board of Trustees been resubmitted? We have a city of some
750,000 people. Are these eleven men the only men in our entire City,
in our entire population, capable of administering properly this War
Memorial? There are probably 40,000 veterans in San Francisco, and
only five have been appointed, and only one of those is an active member of a veteran organization.

This board, after full consideration, on September 16, 1929, had
voted—has voted to not confirm this Board of War Memorial Trustees.
The veterans objected to them then, upon stated grounds, and object
to them now. It is difficult to seek a reason why they should be resubmitted to you some five or six months later.
The only reason that we have been able to discover comes from the
mouth of the Mayor in language which may be found at page 173 of
this report. Speaking before this board on January 20, 1930, speaking
about the Board of War Memorial Trustees, the Mayor said:
"I must appoint Kenneth Kingsbury, one of the largest subscribers
to the fund; I must appoint Robert I. Bentley, the head of the Musical
Association of San Francisco; I must appoint Herbert Fleishhacker.
He does not want to go on this board because he is a large contributor
to it. He is a great public spirited citizen of this city. I know you
get a laugh at him at times, but he is giving his money—$50,000 a
year—to the park. He is giving that zoo out there for the benefit of
San Francisco. And I must appoint some of these other men."

Gentlemen, in that remark we find embodied something that has
emanated from our Mayor this evening. These trustees were administering their own money. Gentlemen, I want to point out to you the
fallacy of that observation. As soon as that money was paid into the
trust fund it ceased to be their money; it was the beneficiaries' money.
It had emanated from many owners. A little of it—a small part, it is
true—was mine once, but it isn't any more. It belongs to the beneficiaries, not to me or to these men, any of these men. Is this the
main and final reason why the veterans cannot have the administration
of their own War Memorial? Is it because these men have made large
contributions to the fund and are contributing money to the City of
San Francisco? If that is the reason, and you gentlemen subscribe
to that doctrine, then the veterans must curl up and say, "Approve
of this board, because we cannot point to a single veteran that has
contributed $50,000 a year to the park; we cannot point to a single
veteran in San Francisco that has ever presented the City of San
Francisco with a zoo." If you are going to confirm this Board of War
Memorial Trustees upon the basis of money contributed, then this
board must be confirmed. I could point out, perhaps, veterans who
have made substantial contributions, of their own kind, to the City
of San Francisco, and not only to the City of San Francisco but to
the whole United States of America. Out at Letterman General Hospital, down at Palo Alto, and at all of the hospitals throughout the
country there are men who are still contributing to the welfare of
San Francisco and to the welfare of the whole United States. Over
in France, in Suresnes and Romagne-sous-Montfaucon, there are men
who have made the most substantial contribution to the welfare of this
country that it is possible for any man to make. They have given
their lives, and lie there, their graves marked by a little white cross.
We cannot compete on any such basis as that suggested by his honor,
and in asking for the appointment of this Board of War Memorial

Trustees upon that basis we can only say that none of them have given as much in money, but some have given arms, and some have given legs; they gave what they had. If that is the solution, if that is to be the final word in this matter, that it is to be determined upon a basis of money and not of sacrifice, then you will have to determine to appoint this board.

I have spoken the last word I probably shall speak to you upon this matter before you vote upon it. I thank you for the patience and courtesy with which you have listened to me. I have spoken much longer than I expected, and I think that I may safely say, in speaking for my colleagues, that none of them will tire you as long as I have. I thank you. (Prolonged applause.)

SUPERVISOR ANDRIANO: I wish to ask, through the Chair, if I may, I want to ask Mr. Glensor one question in order to clear up one point which is not clear in my own mind. I understood you to state that there was only one name on this list that is acceptable to the war veterans. I am not sure whether you said one of the five veterans named in the list or one of the whole list.

MR. GLENSOR: There is one of the five veterans—there are two that are acceptable, General Hunter Liggett and Major Frank N. Belgrano. There is only one, however, to whom we can look for active support upon this board.

SUPERVISOR ANDRIANO: I think you used the words "that was desired by the veterans."

MR. GLENSOR. I did not intend to. General Hunter Liggett belongs to my particular post, but I understand that at the present time he is quite an ill man and has gone away for a protracted stay for his health. I hope I am in error, but I understand he is a very ill man. His loyalty and his devotion to the veterans is not questioned by us. He is a man whom we respect and revere, but we did not feel that it was fair to him to ask him to take an appointment involving the duties and worries in such a complex problem as this at this time, and we therefore do not lean upon him, if you please to allow me to state it that way, in this War Memorial work.

SUPERVISOR ANDRIANO: I understood you to say that none of the old trustees were acceptable to the veterans.

MR. GLENSOR: That is correct.

SUPERVISOR ANDRIANO: How many, then, if I may ask the question, of the present names on the list are acceptable or suitable to the desires of the veterans?

MR. GLENSOR: General Hunter Liggett and Frank N. Belgrano.

SUPERVISOR ANDRIANO: Those are the only two the Legion will recommend?

MR. GLENSOR: Those are the only two members the veterans do not object to.

SUPERVISOR PEYSER: Mr. Chairman, I move that the privilege of the floor be granted to Mr. James B. Burns.

SUPERVISOR MILES: Second the motion.

(The meeting then at 11:25 o'clock p. m. took a five minute recess until 11:30 p. m.)

THE MAYOR: The Board will please come to order. Mr. Glensor has the floor, I believe.

SUPERVISOR PEYSER: The privilege of the floor was requested for Mr. Burns.

MR. GLENSOR: If your Honor please, I would like to ask if I could make one correction for the record——

SUPERVISOR HAYDEN (interrupting): Before you do that, just for the purpose of getting the sense of the Board, coming to an understanding with the membership of the Board, the other night the Board sat through the whole night, and some of the members have suffered since that time by reason of indisposition. Supervisor Gallagher is ill by reason of a cold contracted on that night through sitting at an all night session——

SUPERVISOR POWER (interrupting): How do you feel, Emmett?

SUPERVISOR HAYDEN: All right, for myself. I don't think that the Board wants to go into an all-night session up to 8:00 o'clock in the morning. Personally, in the morning tomorrow I have to cross the bay to go to a funeral, and I feel that I owe that to my family to be there. I would simply like to get the sentiment of the Board at this time, and I would like to move that we adjourn at half past twelve.

SUPERVISOR ANDRIANO: I second the motion.

SUPERVISOR HAYDEN: Or, at least, that a·vote be taken at that time.

MR. GLENSOR: That is agreeable to us; we will finish in 25 minutes. There are only Mr. Burns and Mr. Sapiro to follow me.

SUPERVISOR HAYDEN: I have spoken to Mr. Burns and he said that he felt he would be able to finish by that time.

MR. GLENSOR: We will be through by 12:00 o'clock.

SUPERVISOR SPAULDING: May I interrupt for a minute? It is true that I was one of those who sat here all night until 8:00 in the morning, and we then went away having heard only one side of the question. Now, regardless of the length of time it takes, rather than go into another session, I feel that we should hear the facts as they are presented by the veterans, and I am sure that the Mayor would like to answer. I don't think that time should be an issue. If it takes all night, I, for one, am willing to stay here and listen.

SUPERVISOR HAYDEN: That is for the Board to determine by vote.

SUPERVISOR SPAULDING: I understand that.

SUPERVISOR HAYDEN: I am merely trying to get an expression from the Board so that I will not have to sit here all night. I am perfectly willing, if the Board is not through by half past twelve and if the veterans need a longer time, to meet at any other time, any other night, or day and night. I think they should be granted all the hearing they consider necessary, if it takes a week to do it, but for this particular night I am going to move that a vote be taken to adjourn at 12:30. If I can get a second to that motion, I will make it.

SUPERVISOR ANDRIANO: I second the motion.

THE MAYOR: You don't mean to say a vote and then postpone this meeting for a week or two without hearing all the facts?

SUPERVISOR HAYDEN: Your Honor, if the members are ready to vote at that time——

THE MAYOR (interrupting): I shall certainly like to set a few matters clear. I want to show to you certain facts. My friends, you haven't any cause to quarrel with the Mayor. I am the Mayor of the City and County of San Francisco, and I am entitled to your respect. I have gained that and I have earned that. You have never found me doing a thing that was not fair in all of the years I have been Mayor, and you see tonight that the responsibility is in the hands of the Mayor and the Mayor is trying to solve this problem with malice towards none and charity towards all. Put yourselves in the Mayor's position tonight and see how you feel; how you would feel in trying to solve a problem which affects the whole City of San Francisco, and give him a chance to answer the questions propounded to him. I was permitted to answer one question only and Mr. Glensor decided to take the floor and continue his speech without interruption, and without letting me answer the questions which he asked me to answer, and which were propounded through the columns of the press.

Let me point out to you—I am not going to take your time now—let me point out to you before you make up your minds to say whether the Mayor has been fair or not; let me point out to you some other facts that affect the appointment of this Board of Trustees, and whether you are going to get this $2,000,000 or not. Let me point out to you where I am told that there may be enough lawsuits filed over this money that would equal the spots on a zebra's back. Let me point out to you something to contemplate in the quietude of your home, that this is a matter which affects all the people of the City and County of San Francisco. I am trying my very best to find the proper solution, with no malice on my part, but with charity to all, and I give you as a thought what was said by one veteran who sat in there through the meeting the other day, and after the meeting he sat there with a crippled leg and he said to me, "Mayor, I was against you, but now I am for you, because you are full of guts."

I want to tell you there is a responsibility here that you do not appreciate, nor have these responsibilities been brought to you. The Supervisors indicate that they are going to turn down eleven men without saying which ones they will stand for and which ones they will not stand for. Let's see whether the Supervisors stand up. We are going to have an opinion from the City Attorney, and the legal authorities of this City and County, as to whether or not this Board of Supervisors are going to turn down interminably 11 full names submitted by the Mayor of the City, and we are going to see whether the Supervisors are going to be men enough to stand up and say which ones they are going to turn down. Don't fool anybody about the situation before us. Every one of you Supervisors is going to vote "yes" or "no," whether they are for General Hunter Liggett or not. I mentioned that he was entitled to the honor of the votes because he was the second in command, and it was up to us to let him have that honor as long as he lived, or, at least, as long as he lived with us. When he leaves he will at least have died with the honor of having been given a home by the people of the city in which he lived, and that he was at least good enough during his lifetime to receive your vote of confidence in time of peace. Old age—why old age? It is provided that when there is a death among the Board of Trustees the vacancy shall be filled and the confirmation made by the Board of Supervisors. Would you turn down General Hunter Liggett, the man who gave you orders to proceed and to fire; who commanded you in war? I say you won't turn down General Hunter Liggett under any circumstances, and I am going to have an opinion here from the City Attorney and other legal authorities as to whether or not this Board of Supervisors can interminably keep this thing going. I am going to find out if I have to pick and pick and pick for eleven names, not knowing who they will accept, and it is the duty of this Board of Supervisors to vote for those they favor and those they do not favor. That is fair to the Mayor, that is fair to you, it is fair to everybody. And then it is the duty of the Mayor to make other nominations and it is your duty to vote on them. In fairness to the Mayor, I haven't done you any wrong, I have championed your cause, and when I get through reading the trustee agreement between the Regents of the University of California, which Mr. Glensor says that he has never seen, and which I have never seen, maybe you will see another light on this subject. Maybe after dispassionate discussions a solution of this great problem can be arrived at, with our hearts full of gratitude for the veterans. The veterans will, of course, manage and control the affairs of the War Memorial building when that building is completed, but let me tell you, the Opera House, too, has to be built, and the Art Museum has to be built, and the Memorial Court has to be built, and the War Memorial building has to be built. You don't think I am going to appoint a board pledged against the building of an Opera House or pledged against the building of an Art Museum, or pledged against the building of a Memorial Court, and put the whole of the matter in the hands of the veterans and no facts yet shown as to how much it is going to cost the City of San Francisco to maintain this $4,000,000 War Memorial building? I grant you now the veterans will be given an opportunity to manage the War Memorial building; it will be managed by veterans of the World War when it is built.

So we cannot come to a vote tonight. You can postpone and post-pone and postpone, but the Mayor will certainly in justice to all be permitted to answer all the remarks appearing in the continuation of the record. I have something to say of interest to all of you, and I ask you that when Mr. Glensor and Mr. Burns and Mr. Sapiro and Mr. Claridge, and when the boys of the 363d have finished, and a few others have been heard, that I be given an opportunity to answer all of these remarks.

If James I. Herz, 363d Infantry, San Francisco's own, who is hon-ored here in this very hall, is going to be turned down tonight, there is something more which is going to be said before we come to a vote. They exploited this thing tonight, but it is in the hands of the Mayor, who appears to have full responsibility in his hands and don't get all the support he might in a problem which affects the entire people of this mighty city of 750,000 people. I am trying to carry on to the best of my ability, according to law and according to the agreement made, and trying to get the money in hands of the Regents of the University of California, which will not come along the lines being discussed tonight.

SUPERVISOR HAYDEN: If your Honor please, then, as we interpret your statement you have asked an opinion from the City Attorney——

THE MAYOR (interrupting): I will; I haven't yet, but I will

SUPERVISOR HAYDEN: You have asked——

THE MAYOR (interrupting): If the Board is willing to vote seriatim as provided in the charter, so that the law will apply in this case, the law which states where items can be segregated, a seriatim vote can be asked for, and this is a case where they certainly can be segregated. It is immaterial to the Mayor if you vote; then I will know who you are turning down, but if the Mayor must continue to pick and pick without knowing——

SUPERVISOR HAYDEN (interrupting): Do I understand you, your honor, that you ask the Board to postpone a vote until you have an opinion from the City Attorney?

THE MAYOR: Not if the Board is willing to vote seriatim. If the Board is willing to proceed tonight and vote on each name you can go ahead and I will know where I stand. I will know who I haven't got and I must then submit other names.

SUPERVISOR POWER: I don't know of any reason why we cannot come to a vote tonight. If you will just wait until the gentlemen finish, then you undoubtedly will have all the opportunity you desire——

THE MAYOR (interrupting): Don't you understand, Supervisor Power, that I cannot permit a number of these remarks to go un-answered?

SUPERVISOR HAYDEN: I am merely seeking the sense of the Board. I understood——

SUPERVISOR POWER (interrupting): I realize Supervisor Hayden has an appointment in the morning.

SUPERVISOR HAYDEN: I want to get a voice or sentiment about sitting all night. At the proper time, after we have heard from the Veterans, we can take a recess and adjourn to another time, or if you are prepared to vote after getting through with that, I am ready to vote.

THE MAYOR: If I understood, the Board will take a recess at 12:00 midnight and then meet again and meet again until the Mayor has finished the hearing; all right, but don't let it be final according to this statement at 12:00 o'clock midnight tonight.

SUPERVISOR HAYDEN: Your Honor, we have a meeting here tomorrow afternoon at 2:30 o'clock on the final passage of the ordi-nance in connection with Spring Valley, and that matter will be over in a very few minutes, it is merely an automatic act, practically, on the part of the Board, and we could adjourn tonight until tomorrow afternoon and continue the hearing then. I was just trying to emphasize the fact, and I have talked to a number of the Supervisors and we are agreed that we are not going to sit here all night again tonight.

THE MAYOR: I am not keeping you.

SUPERVISOR POWER: I move that the Veterans continue with their statements; we have wasted twenty minutes arguing here now.

THE MAYOR: It is not wasted.

SUPERVISOR POWER: I understood Mr. Burns was to be given the privilege of the floor.

SUPERVISOR HAYDEN: I second the motion of Supervisor Power, Mr. Mayor.

SUPERVISOR POWER: Mr. Glensor would like to correct one statement, he informs me.

THE MAYOR: Mr. Glensor, you have the floor.

MR. GLENSOR: I would like to correct one thing. My attention has been called that in answer to a Supervisor's question I stated something in a way that has been misunderstood, not only by him, but by men who have heard the same statement before. That with respect to the members of this Board of War Memorial Trustees we do not object to, and originally, let me make this clear, originally asked you not to confirm this entire Board. We have said in this written statement (referring to a document in his hand) which you have all been furnished a copy of, and this states exactly what our position is. I have tried again here today to make it clear. We do not object to, and would be very glad to see you confirm, General Hunter Liggett and Frank Belgrano on any board that you do ultimately confirm. That is all we have said. You will find it in writing, stated very concisely, in this document which has been filed with you tonight.

THE MAYOR: Has that report been filed for entry in this record?

MR. GLENSOR: Yes, sir, your Honor, it is in this report.

SUPERVISOR McSHEEHY: Mr. Mayor, if I might, I would like to ask through the Chair, if I may ask Mr. Glensor one or two questions.

THE MAYOR: Mr. McSheehy has the floor.

SUPERVISOR McSHEEHY: Following your last remark, Mr. Glensor, you say you are not opposed to all of the names mentioned by the Mayor. Have you any objection—I say this to you, I don't mean personal objection—but do you think your organizations have any objections to us taking up the names seriatim? How are we going to separate them otherwise?

MR. GLENSOR: Gentlemen of the Board, I feel that that is a matter which must be committed to the Board of Supervisors. I don't see how the Veterans could take a position upon a matter of procedure for your own Board to determine. We have no directions in that regard. However, in this statement (referring to letter of Advisory Board to Veterans War Memorial Committee, dated September 7, 1929), if we are asked, and we have been asked, "Do you object to A? do you object to C?" we could probably go through a large portion of the citizenry of San Francisco on that basis and name people whom the Veterans do not object to, but you understand, it is the constitution of this board as a whole that is important to the Veterans of San Francisco, not as to whether one particular man is on it or another man is on it. If we had probably six or seven men of our own selection we should probably not be at all interested, except as you just heard me say, that we are instructed to object to any of the old Board of Trustees, and we have been specifically directed to object to Major Kendrick as a member of this Board.

SUPERVISOR PEYSER: Your Honor, may I ask Mr. Glensor a question, through the Chair?

SUPERVISOR PEYSER: Is it not a fact, Mr. Glensor, that one of the objections that the Veterans organizations have to the constituted board as submitted by his Honor is that the majority of that board are not Veterans?

MR. GLENSOR: That is right.

SUPERVISOR PEYSER: Your Honor, that being the case, I fail to see how a seriatim vote could determine in any way the paramount question which is at issue here, and that is, whether or not there shall be a majority of Veterans on this Board. You can proceed to vote seriatim, vote on each one and by a process of elimination you will be in exactly the same position as to the number of Veterans on that Board as you were before. I don't think that under that circumstance it would be a fair thing to submit to this Board a matter of that type to determine when the only real issue before us at this time is whether or not a majority of Veterans shall constitute that Board.

THE MAYOR: Do you not see that one of the outstanding Veterans of the World War, decorated with the decorations which came from valued services in the war, is declined nomination and confirmation tonight—James I. Herz, San Francisco's own? Will the same thing happen if the Mayor names six fine outstanding Veterans? Or must I take the six that are opposed to the opera house and that are opposed to Major Kendrick and opposed to Colonel Colman? They appointed Major Kendrick and appointed Supervisor Colman and now they are against them because they are for the building of the opera house. Now, you are turning down James I. Herz, one of the outstanding veterans of the World War——

SUPERVISOR POWER (interrupting): Is he going to be turned down by this Board? We don't know until we come to a vote.

THE MAYOR: I am asking the question.

SUPERVISOR PEYSER: I believe I had the floor, your Honor.

THE MAYOR: Supervisor Peyser, you have the floor.

SUPERVISOR PEYSER: The first issue then to submit to this Board is whether or not this Board of War Memorial Trustees should be constituted of six Veterans, in other words, a majority of Veterans. After that has been determined, your Honor, your Honor might be correct in submitting that matter to us, but that cannot be determined by voting seriatim on these eleven men whom you have nominated. If more than six Veterans are selected on this Board, then the Board could vote on whether they wish to adopt only five Veterans, but they have been given no opportunity to determine whether or not there shall be a majority of Veterans on the Board, which is the real issue here.

THE MAYOR: The statement has been made here tonight, forgetting for the moment——

SUPERVISOR PEYSER (interrupting): But, Mr. Mayor——

THE MAYOR (continuing): that Major Kendrick is opposed, that Robert I. Bentley is opposed, that Herbert Fleishhacker is opposed, that Mr. George Cameron of the Chronicle is opposed, that Mr. George Hearst of the Examiner is opposed. If you eliminate any of those men and the Mayor comes in with any new names you will ultimately get six Veterans——

SUPERVISOR PEYSER (interrupting): Well, Mr. Mayor——

THE MAYOR (continuing): Are you going to refuse to vote seriatim on those names? I don't know which ones are unsatisfactory to you. I don't know how you are going to ever solve this without voting seriatim. I tell you now that until eleven trustees satisfactory to the Regents of the University of California, under the terms of the trust agreement, are appointed, you will not get your money. Unless they are satisfied with the eleven trustees, you won't get the money. Now, I say to you, if the same is decided, and you vote seriatim and will let me know who are unsatisfactory to you, so that I may be able to eliminate them and nominate others——

SUPERVISOR PEYSER (interrupting): May I call your attention to this fact, your Honor? The objection to these men is not a personal objection, the objection is because the Board as now constituted —the very thing your Honor suggests is the very thing which would lead this Board into doing that which no Board and no member of this Board of Supervisors wants to do. I am sure none of the Supervisors want to vote to reject any of these fine outstanding citizens. By forcing us to vote seriatim on these names, you are forcing us to accept five names as Veterans only. If you take the names of Herbert Fleishhacker, Kenneth R. Kingsbury, Robert I. Bentley, George Cameron, George Hearst and James W. Mullen, and we accept those men as representative citizens, it leaves only five men to vote for as Veterans. That is the very thing which is at stake here, namely, whether or not this Board shall consist of a majority of Veterans or not. I don't think it is fair to put us in that position.

THE MAYOR: I am going to put you in that position just the same.

SUPERVISOR PEYSER: You are not going to put me in that position.

THE MAYOR: I will go to the courts to do it. I will get a vote from the Board of whom they are for and who they are against.

SUPERVISOR PEYSER: Your idea is, you are not going to give this Board an opportunity to express themselves on whether they want a majority of Veterans on this Board or not.

THE MAYOR: I am.

SUPERVISOR PEYSER: This Board is on record by resolution to that effect.

THE MAYOR: I didn't pass that resolution or approve of it.

SUPERVISOR PEYSER: The Board of Supervisors passed it.

THE MAYOR: The Board of Supervisors, in my opinion, hadn't any right to pass any such resolution, particularly when tied up with this agreement connected with this $2,000,000.

Now, I am going to find out, why should I let you off from saying who you are for and who you are against. These are fine men, eleven fine outstanding men of San Francisco——

SUPERVISOR PEYSER (interrupting): Put six Veterans on the Board, give us an opportunity to choose six Veterans and there will be no difficulty in choosing the other five, but your Honor is not doing that——

(Interrupted by applause.)

SUPERVISOR ANDRIANO: I cannot see how the Supervisor can make that statement in view of the repeated statement made by Mr. Glensor of who on this Board are unsatisfactory to them, and from the statement by Supervisor Roncovieri that all of the old trustees would be unsatisfactory, and some of the other Supervisors also.

SUPERVISOR PEYSER: I am replying to the Supervisor. The reason why we object to those men, because, as the Board is now constituted there isn't an opportunity in the world to give expression or to fix how many Veterans there shall be on the Board. We are forced into the position of rejecting a group of wonderfully fine outstanding citizens of this city in a trick measure to get us to accept five Veterans on this Board; that is why the Veterans oppose those men, it is not from any personal objection to the men themselves.

THE MAYOR: You vote, and if one of these fine outstanding gentlemen you say you won't stand for——

SUPERVISOR PEYSER (interrupting): Why should we vote on them?

THE MAYOR: I submit the names and——.

SUPERVISOR PEYSER (interrupting): Give us fifteen names to choose from and we will pick the eleven.

(Laughter and applause.)

THE MAYOR: The Board of Supervisors have got themselves in this position——

SUPERVISOR POWER (interrupting): Mr. Burns, I believe, has the privilege of the floor, and I request that he be permitted to make his statement.

SUPERVISOR TONER: If your Honor please, before going any further, I would ask that I be excused at 12:30. I have a big operation for tomorrow morning, and I do not feel that I can stay any later. I am perfectly willing to come here every day next week, or for the next two weeks, but I don't propose to stay here all night tonight.

SUPERVISOR POWER: Mr. Burns has the floor, I believe.

SUPERVISOR TONER: Your Honor, may I be excused at 12:30?

SUPERVISOR HAVENNER: I move that Supervisor Toner be excused.

THE MAYOR: If there is no objection, it is so ordered.

SUPERVISOR POWER: Mr. Burns has the floor.

THE MAYOR: Mr. Burns, you have the floor.

MR. BURNS: Mr. Mayor, members of the Board of Supervisors, first, I hope this half hour won't be charged against my time, Mr. Hayden.

SUPERVISOR HAYDEN: You will have all the time you want' Mr. Burns.

MR. BURNS: A great deal has been said, gentlemen, about the plans which the Veterans approved. The Mayor has them on his desk, and he shows you the plans and the signatures which appear thereon. I want to touch for a few brief moments, upon those plans.

First of all, those plans were submitted to the War Memorial Committee of the American Legion. No other organization, no other Veteran organization ever saw them. No other Veteran organization ever took any action upon them, nor did any other Veteran organization know anything about the existence of that particular set of plans. The American Legion, as you know, has 20 posts in San Francisco. By scrutinizing the plans you will find 14 signatures in addition to the Chairman and Secretary appearing thereon. In other words, 14 American Legion posts are signatory thereto. At the time those plans were presented to the American Legion they were brought to us by a member of the present board of private trustees and we were told at that time a story about the unemployment situation in San Francisco, and we were told also that if we did not approve those plans we would be charged with not desiring to ameliorate that unemployment situation.

There was a great deal of discussion over the plans. The plans were unsatisfactory, even to the War Memorial Committee of the American Legion, not considering all of the other Veteran organizations at all. Nevertheless, after a great deal of discussion, and after several members of the War Memorial Committee of the American Legion refused to sign their names to them, 14 members did sign their names for the purpose of trying to get this project under way, and acting upon the representation made to us at that time that that was all we could get, anyway, and that if we did not approve those plans we would be charged with not desiring to take care of this unemployment situation I referred to. All right. At the time we approved those plans, that approval was a conditional approval, and that does not appear in this pamphlet——

THE MAYOR (interrupting): Mr. Burns, please may I interrupt you; that is no pamphlet, that is a history of the War Memorial submitted by the Mayor, and I do not——

MR. BURNS (interrupting): I am simply making a statement, that they have this report before them. I did not make the statement in any way to reflect.

On March 15, 1928, this letter was written to the Board of War Memorial Trustees:

"March 15, 1928.

"Board of Trustees,
"San Francisco War Memorial,
"Phelan Building,
"San Francisco, California.

"Gentleman:

"Please be advised that at the meeting of the War Memorial Committee of the American Legion, held Wednesday, March 14, 1928, this Committee conditionally approved the last set of plans submitted to it. Final approval of these plans is contingent upon the carrying out of the following recommendations of the Committee:

"1· That the interior arrangement and allocation of space be decided upon at a future date.

"2. That the building be constructed to allow for the removal and rearrangements of pillars now shown in the basement, so as to allow for large halls that would be useable, and to allow a ceiling clearance in the basement of approximately 13 feet.

"Your attention is also directed to the following resolution passed by this Committee at the above mentioned meeting: This Committee expresses its regrets to the Trustees of the War Memorial and to the Board of Supervisors of San Francisco because it is contemplated to erect the Veterans building with an uncompleted area on the McAllister street side thereof, and it urges these bodies to make every effort to include such area in the completed plans for the erection of the Veterans building.

"Yours very truly,

"JAMES B. BURNS,
"Commander, San Francisco County Council
"Chairman, War Memorial Committee.

"Official: J. C. Claridge, Adjutant San Francisco County Council,
    Secretary War Memorial Committee."

Your attention is also directed to the following resolution passed by this Committee of the American Legion at the above-mentioned meeting:

"This Committee expresses its regrets to the Trustees of the War Memorial and to the Board of Supervisors of San Francisco because it is contemplated to erect the Veterans building with an uncompleted area on the McAllister street side thereof, and it urges these bodies to make every effort to include such area in the completed plans for the erection of the Veterans building."

That is signed by myself as Commander of the San Francisco County Council of the American Legion.

All right——

THE MAYOR (interrupting): But you signed these plans, didn't you, Mr. Burns?

MR. BURNS: Conditionally, your Honor, and I am proceeding along those lines.

It later came to our attention, speaking now of the American Legion only, because no other Veteran organization knew anything about these plans. All right. These plans bearing the signatures indicating approval of these different posts were changed, and on June 23, 1928, the following letter was dispatched to the Board of Trustees of the War Memorial, over my signature:

"June 23, 1928.

"Board of Trustees,
"San Francisco War Memorial,
"Phelan Building,
"San Francisco, California.

"Gentlemen:

"You are hereby advised that the American Legion War Memorial Committee, having already conditionally approved plans for the Veterans building of the War Memorial group, does not disapprove the proposed modifications of those plans as shown on set of plans dated May 24, 1928, and submitted to this Committee for its consideration.

"This action was taken at a meeting of the Committee held at the Bellevue Hotel, Friday, June 22, 1928.

"Very truly yours,

"JAMES B. BURNS,

"Commander, San Francisco County Council.

"Chairman, War Memorial Committee.

"Official: J. C. Claridge, Adjutant, San Francisco County Council, Secretary War Memorial Committee."

THE MAYOR: What was the date of that letter?

MR. BURNS: June 23, 1928.

THE MAYOR: Does that letter appear in my report?

MR. BURNS: And that letter also is not in your report.

THE MAYOR: What is the date of that letter? Did you read some letter dated previously to that?

MR. BURNS: I read a letter which was sent on March 15, 1928.

THE MAYOR: And what was that letter in relation to?

MR. BURNS: Stating that we had conditionally approved the plan, and then on June 23, 1928, the Board was advised that we disapproved these plans because of modifications made therein and which were made subsequently to our approval of the original plan. All of these facts were called to your attention under date of November 21, 1929, by Mr. Milton Sapiro, then Commander of the San Francisco County Council of the American Legion, and I will read just one portion of that letter:

"You have made the statement to the Board of Supervisors that the Veterans approved the plans, and as this is not a fair statement of the situation, you should know that the approval of the plans, which approval was by the American Legion only and not by other Veteran organizations, was conditional upon certain changes being made. The approval sent to the Board of Trustees on March 15, 1928, specifically set forth these conditions, and the Board of Trustees promised the Veteran organizations that the plans would be changed.

"Subsequently, and without notice to the American Legion, the plans were modified so that they could not meet the approval of the Veteran organizations, and as soon as this was ascertained the Veteran organizations advised the Board of Trustees by letter of June 23, 1928, that such plans were disapproved.

"There can be no justification for any bald statement that the Veteran organizations approved the plans."

Subsequent to that, and without notice to the American Legion, the plans were modified so that they could not meet with the approval of the Veteran organizations, and as soon as this fact was ascertained, the Veterans advised the Board by the letter of June 15, 1928. There can be no justification for any false statement that the Veterans' organizations approved the plans. That was in our letter to your Honor dated November 21, 1929.

I will refer briefly to pages 51 and 52 of the History of the San Francisco War Memorial. That portion of this history refers to the open meeting which was held in these chambers and at which meeting Mr. John S. Drum presided, on December 6th, I believe, 1928, and we were referring at that time to the manner in which the request of the Veterans for more space was complied with, and incidentally and simply in passing by reference to this you will note that there was considerable reference made to the large amount of space allocated to the Veterans in the basement of the Veterans building.

THE MAYOR: Well, I didn't make it, that's history.

MR. BURNS: On this date, and referring to the portion of the history which I mentioned I happened to ask this question: "Was it not contemplated, in connection with the War Memorial to make a rearrangement of those pillars in order to make that basement space usable?

"MR. WAGSTAFF: To make the space usable? It is usable, as approved by the plans.

"MR. BURNS: When you say 'approved by the plans,' you are referring to the plans as approved on April 16?

"MR. WAGSTAFF: Yes, those plans were approved by the Legion on the 16th of April.

"MR. BURNS: Now, were any changes made in these plans with relation to the location of those pillars after the Legion had approved the plans?

"MR. WAGSTAFF: No vital change.

"MR. BURNS: Ah, no vital change?

"MR. WAGSTAFF: No, no vital change. The building was made less than ten feet narrower, there was a ten-foot strip taken off, and it caused some rearrangement in the size of the rooms. For example, a room thirty by fifty might be changed to twenty-five by sixty. Changes of that nature—changes of shape, and not of capacity.

"SUPERVISOR MARKS: Were those changes approved by the Veterans?

"MR. BURNS: Did you submit, or were those plans——

"MR. WAGSTAFF (interrupting): No.

"MR. BURNS (continuing): —you say that they were not approved by the Legion?

"MR. WAGSTAFF: Not officially.

"MR. BURNS: Not officially? Were they approved by anyone representing himself to be a representative of the Legion?

"MR. WAGSTAFF: Members of the Legion saw the plans at different places.

"MR. BURNS: Who was that? Anyone representing the Legion?

"MR. WAGSTAFF: Various members, who said they were from the Legion.

"MR. BURNS: I see; various members who said they were members of some Veterans' organization; simply came in and looked at the plans; but no one stated that he was approving the plans on behalf of the American Legion, did he?

"MR. WAGSTAFF: Oh, no.

"MR. BURNS: Were those plans ever submitted to the Legion thereafter for approval?

"MR. WAGSTAFF: Not as finally approved."

In other words, gentlemen of the Board, all of this statement with reference to the Veterans having approved the plans is not a fair statement to make. The record here, the trustees themselves, admit that they made changes in the plans even after having had the purported approval of one of the groups of organized Veterans.

One other little matter, and it won't take but a moment, I want to refer to another portion of the record which refers to the plans which were the basis of the $4,000,000 bond issue. At that time it was decided that in order to construct an opera house and the Legion Museum building that it would be necessary in addition to the $1,625,-000 then stated to be on hand to have $4,000,000 additional, and that was the basis of the $4,000,000 bond issue requested at that time, and I have over here the original tracing—that is simply a copy of it— and I will show it to you. It provided for two buildings equal in size, extent, area and shape. That was the basis of ·the $4,000,000 bond issue that came before this Board and was approved by the Board at the time that issue went on the ballot.

I make no further reference to that other than to call it to your attention and state that that is in the record in the City Hall here.

THE MAYOR: Let's put that in the record tonight.

MR. BURNS: You have already read it into the record.

THE MAYOR: Put it in the record.

MR. BURNS: It is in your report.

THE MAYOR: I know it is, but not the picture or design. Does
it show the opera house there?

MR. BURNS: It shows two buildings, your Honor, one labeled
"Opera House" and one labeled "Veterans Building," and it is a plot
plan for the proposed San Francisco Memorial Hall. Here is the
dome of the City Hall, right here. (Laughter.)

THE MAYOR: Put this picture in the record, Mr. Stenographer.

MR. BURNS: Now, there is another matter, gentlemen, which I
desire to refer to, and that will be in conclusion, and I think I have
kept my promise with relation to the time limit.

SUPERVISOR HAYDEN: Thank you, Mr. Burns.

MR. BURNS: His Honor made the statement, and I am sure he
did not intend that statement to sound just as it did, when he said
we are against Major Kendrick because he wants to build an opera
house. Now, gentlemen, no statement could be more unfair than that.

THE MAYOR: It is in the record.

MR. BURNS: No, it is not in the record, your honor. No statement could be more unfair than that.

THE MAYOR: That's in the record.

MR. BURNS: I think, with all sincerity, your honor and members
of the Board, that is not in the record, and I question the language that
the veterans oppose Major Kendrick because he wants to build an
opera house.

When the matter of the confirmation of this Board of Trustees——

THE MAYOR: Mr. Burns, if you will permit an interruption, would
you mind, for the sake of the record, indicating your objections to
Major Kendrick here.

MR. BURNS: If you will pardon me, that is just what I am doing,
Mr. Mayor.

When this same Board of War Memorial Trustees was presented in
September to this Board of Supervisors for approval, this same group
of veterans appeared before you and voiced its objections to Major
Charles H. Kendrick. The record which the Mayor read the other
night states those objections which we stated then and we state now,
what those objections are, and it is a matter of great personal regret
to the members of this advisory group that we must take objection to
one of our own members, Charles H. Kendrick. We have put forward
these specific objections to him, but in fairness to him it must be said
that this is no personal objection to him. Major Kendrick eight or nine
years ago was the unanimous choice, almost, of the American Legion
to represent them on the War Memorial Committee. However, as the
years went by a great many differences of opinion arose and finally,
in 1928, the American Legion called upon Major Charles H. Kendrick
to resign from that private board of trustees, which Mr. Kendrick
refused to do. The veterans, the American Legion particularly, concluded that because of the activities of Major Kendrick in connection
with the War Memorial over a period of years, that he did no longer
represent the group which had placed him on the Board of Trustees,
and, in fact, that is borne out by Major Kendrick's own statement at
the meeting of the San Francisco County Council of the American
Legion on November 1st—no, November 14, 1928. At that time Major
Kendrick appeared before that body and he stated at that time that
he did not believe that he had, that he owed his first duty to the
American Legion, but believed that his duty was to the city and to
the citizens of San Francisco. He was asked, in view of that statement, why he did not resign if he admitted baldly he no longer represented the group he was supposed to represent, and he said that when
the committee was to turn over all of the monies to the Board of
Trustees which will finally build the project, not only himself, but all
other members of the old Board of Trustees would be very glad to
resign.

That is a matter of record in the minutes of the meetings of the

San Francisco County Council of the American Legion, and it is also a matter of record in the history of the San Francisco War Memorial, that when the project was turned over to the City that he would resign from the Board of Trustees.

Now, gentlemen, as I stated, we have no personal objections to Major Charles H. Kendrick. The objection is based upon the conditions which have arisen and grown out of the War Memorial activities of Major Kendrick during a long period of time, and we respectfully again refer to you the objections which are in this record which we gave you at the time you refused to confirm the Board last September.

I have taken twenty minutes, when I only intended to take about fifteen. I appreciate very much having had this opportunity to say a few words to you, and I would like to state to you, as did his honor the Mayor, that what has been said has been said in all sincerity, and simply as the legal mouthpiece of the veterans whom I have the honor to represent.

(Applause.)

SUPERVISOR MILES: I move the privilege, Mr. Chairman, of the floor to Mr. Milton Sapiro.

THE MAYOR: Mr. Sapiro, you have the floor.

MR. MILTON SAPIRO: Gentlemen, Mr. Mayor, I will try and briefly give you a few facts in connection with this War Memorial controversy.

To those of us who represent the veteran organizations this question that has now been brought before the Board of Supervisors probably involves the most important issue in the civic life of the City of San Francisco that you gentlemen of the Board of Supervisors will probably face during your four years in office. I doubt that any question that will arise has as its foundation the opposition, or the basis for the opposition which there is to the confirmation of each of these gentlemen to the Board of Trustees nominated by his honor the Mayor. I want to say that those of us who are serving in the veteran ranks, that we are giving our time to a public cause because we believe in it. Every veteran who has spoken to you tonight and who will speak to you has told you nothing but the truth, and I am going to speak frankly and straight from the shoulder, and what I have got to say I am going to say in just a plain, straight manner. I am not going to try and obscure the facts or cloud the issue with a mountain of words such as is contained in this history of the San Francisco War Memorial. I am going to use words to reveal facts.

What I have to say is not intended to be personal in nature in any way, and if we have to refer to the acts of any officials or individuals, either in the discharge of their duties as such officials, or in connection with any of their official acts in connection with this War Memorial, or the official acts of officials of this City, those remarks have no personal application, but we are not in a position to spare any one's feelings in reference to this important subject.

Let me state to you that there has been a great deal of evasion on this subject. I believe when you come to study and analyze this report or history of the San Francisco War Memorial you will find that it has been presented at such great length, not merely to give a history of the matter, but that it has been presented in that design to build up a case for the private trustees who have mishandled this thing for so many years. I want to say to you gentlemen who are sitting here tonight in this great room that if you gentlemen of the Board of Supervisors were sitting here as a jury in a case and this were a case before a jury in a court of law, and the Mayor of San Francisco had presented the case for the defense as he has presented the case here in this report, that if he had appeared here as representing the detense, and I represented the prosecution, at the conclusion of the preseutation of that report I would have said to you, "Gentlemen, we submit our case on the statement of the case and the evidence presented by the defense." No more complete a record of a failure to perform a public trust ever existed in any city or county of this great country of ours than is contained in this history of the San Francisco War Memorial. This great City of ours that accomplishes things is able to turn out a history. History is usually supposed to be a record, an accurate record of things accomplished, things done. We in San Francisco who know how, are able to turn out a history which it takes fifteen hours to read, 193 pages of fine print. A history of what? A history of the construction of two holes over there over a period of eleven years. (Applause and laughter.)

The Mayor, in submitting the report to you, dared to use language in this report as follows:

"The veterans have charged the present War Memorial Board of Trustees with 'gross inefficiency, waste and mismanagement.' Yet the financial report of their status, certified by public accountants, shows competence, efficiency and careful management."

Tonight, when he wasn't thinking of the report which he had prepared for the City and which was read to you, and talking impromptu to you, what he said was that matters had been in the hands of others who had had it in their hands for eleven years and gotten nowhere with it. Now, do you think that any board who has had this matter in their hands for eleven years and has accomplished nothing is "competent and efficient," and that it shows careful management? Of course, when you think of the report which Mr. Glensor has rendered on this financial report, and the analysis of it, showing the vast amounts of money which have been spent for interest, $150,000, when this Board of Trustees had money in the bank, $21,000 to cancel the lease of the building in which the Locomobile Company was located at a time when they were not prepared to go ahead with the work, and it shows that they spent hundreds of dollars and thousands of dollars in administration expenses, legal expenses and expenses for a secretary and other matters. We gentlemen are wondering whether or not that secretary spent any time in the War Memorial office, judging by the records kept by that Board of War Memorial Trustees. We are wondering whether the money of the War Memorial was not used to pay the salary as secretary of one of the musical organizations of San Francisco which he also represented. Inefficiency and mismanagement of the grossest sort are shown in this report rendered to you by the Mayor of the City of San Francisco, yet in the face of that, what happened? Four of the men who are given a public trust of that kind are nominated by the Mayor. Don't think of it as a private fund, if you please. I contributed to that fund, and a great many other men who served their country contributed to that fund. Of course, I didn't contribute any $50,000 and I cannot point to any veteran who did contribute $50,000, but I do not place my contribution on the basis of dollars and cents. I attended a meeting the other night when an old veteran, a representative of the Grand Army, got up and stated to us, when sums were mentioned in this connection, and the statement was made that we had to appreciate the sums of money which had been contributed by some of our citizens: "I contributed $2 to the sum, too." That $2 meant more to him than $50,000 contributed by some one to whom that did not mean a sacrifice. He sacrificed something— he deprived himself of some tobacco or the pleasure of going to a show, something to eat, or something of that sort, while a man who is in a position to contribute $50,000 to a fund of that kind, while we appreciate his interest and his generosity in giving it, he does not have to sacrifice to contribute $50,000. He isn't deprived of a bit of food, he isn't deprived even of any pleasure—he doesn't sacrifice a thing. And while, as I say, we appreciate it being given, what else could he do with the money? Let it pile up and pile up until maybe the pile will fall over on him? Gentlemen, that is no basis for the test. You cannot debate this on a basis of dollars and cents. We, as veterans, strongly resent there coming to this Board in report after report the statement that we must consider these men because of the financial contributions they have made either to the City or to this project. I say to you that when you see the truth of that charge of lack of interest and of negligence in the performance of a public trust which those men have been guilty of, and they have been guilty of that charge beyond the shadow of a doubt, and nothing can be said that will gainsay the truth of that statement.

As I said before, they had a public trust. The public contributed money to this project, and that money had to be held by somebody and it was held by those men through a trust agreement with the Regents of the University of California. The Mayor has stated to you this evening that although it has been a huge task and that it has kept him occupied from October to the present day in order to prepare this great report, or great history, that he himself did not read the trust agreement, one of the important documents, if not the most important document, in connection with the project. Then he says this history contains facts. What are the facts in this report? It is not an accurate report when it says that this War Memorial project was started in 1918. You can only take it from the beginning of 1920 when the American Legion first got together with a bunch who had a lot of stale subscriptions on their hands. They had subscriptions signed up which they had had signed up for some years, but they had not received a total sum sufficient to do anything, and the signers of the subscriptions were withdrawing them. The American Legion finally came forward saying, "We are the persons responsible for the War Memorial, and you can start another group. You don't have to be afraid this particular group is not going ahead." I want to say right now, and I want to pin this down fast, so that there can be no mistake about it. No veteran organization ever suggested that we abandon the building of the opera house, nor have we ever suggested to the Mayor that the names of any of the men indicated by him as members of this Board of Trustees be withdrawn because they were in favor of the building of the opera house. That statement has been made to the Board and we want to say that it is entirely unfounded, and has been repeatedly refuted. And I want to see the proof of it. And I tell you it cannot be furnished to you of any statement by anybody representing any of the veteran organizations that we opposed the building of an opera house. We have always said that we favored the building of the opera house but that we were not willing to sacrifice the Veterans' building to it—sacrifice the Veterans' building to put up the opera house. As John Drum said, if anything was to be left uncompleted it was to be the Veterans' building, and we are not going to stand by and see the wishes of the people of San Francisco treated in that manner. The people of this City voted for a War Memorial for the veterans.

You gentlemen of the Board of Supervisors here have at stake, in our belief, a principle which is greater than even the War Memorial itself, and that is the real principle of democracy. The War Memorial Trustees are to be appointed by the Mayor subject to the confirmation of the Board of Supervisors. That gave to this Board of Supervisors a very definite power, definite powers and rights. They have the right to confirm or not confirm those nominees, and when they pleased not to confirm the names submitted by the Mayor it was the Mayor's duty to submit to the Board of Supervisors a new list of names to be confirmed or rejected.

You know as well as I do the truth of what Washington said: "Eternal vigilance is the price of liberty." It is an eternal struggle between democracy and autocracy, a struggle between the interests of the people and the rule of the autocrat. In this City and County the Mayor of this City should be governed by the charter. The Mayor should not attempt to impose his will beyond question upon this Board of Supervisors when the Board is acting entirely within its right, and you were entirely within your rights in rejecting the Board of Trustees submitted by the Mayor.

We have a very apt example. You remember the case of Mr. Warren, who was named by President Coolidge for Attorney General. At the time the question of the confirmation of Mr. Warren came up for vote, Mr. Dawes, then Vice-President, was takin a nap in the Senate ante-chamber. As a result of the fact that he was taking a nap at that time the nominee of President Coolidge could not be appointed. It was shy one vote. Mr. Dawes returned to the Senate chamber and President Coolidge knew that through the vote he would receive by Mr. Dawes' presence there in the Senate, that if he returned the name of Warren, Warren would be nominated as Attorney General. What did President Coolidge do? He recognized the true principle of democracy. He recognized that our government depends upon the operation of a proper system of check and balances, and in order to preserve the true principles of democracy he submitted a new name for Attorney General and did not try to insist on forcing through his first nominee, although he knew he could have the nomination of the man he really wanted for the position by again submitting his name. That should be the situation in this City and County. There should not be an attempt to impose upon this Board of Supervisors some Board of Trustees which you once turned down. It was entirely within your rights to turn down that Board because you did not consider it constituted, in accordance with the ordinance and in accordance with your request to the Mayor. The report of the Mayor showed that you were subject to threats. I resent that, and I can very honestly and conscientiously say, and there isn't a Supervisor here who can say that I have ever uttered one word of threat to any Supervisor whatsoever or to any one in connection with this matter. All I have asked from them, from this Board of Supervisors in the name of the veterans of San Francisco, is just fair play. We come before you on that showing, and on that issue we are entitled to have this Board turned down as it was in the past.

Now, gentlemen, we wonder ourselves when we read this report of his Honor, why the Mayor does not appoint a Board consisting entirely of veterans. In one meeting the Mayor stated, on one page of the transcript at one meeting that, "If I had my way, and I could pick out eleven, I would." That is on page 173 of this report, and as late as January 20, 1930, when he said, "If I had my way, and I could pick out eleven, I would." What stopped him from doing it? That's what we want to know; that is what we would like to know. Certainly, there isn't an invisible government in the City government of San Francisco. I know, I have read the trust agreement under which the Regents of the University of California hold the trust fund. I happen to be an attorney and to have a little knowledge of law. I have no fear or question on that score. They would not retain the money if the Mayor was to appoint such a Board, and they would not turn the money back to the subscribers. Gentlemen, this so-called fear of what they are going to do held over our heads was held over our heads once by John Drum, on December 19, 1928. Mr. Drum, I am sorry, isn't here to answer for his accounting of the War Memorial funds, his handling of them. These other men left the matter entirely in his hands, and he used them in a way which he wanted. He did not accomplish anything in a way which will be a credit to that Board. He is no longer a member of San Francisco, and therefore cannot be appointed as a member of this Board. But should he be given an opportunity to sit as a member of this Board and should the Mayor be permitted to reject thousands of veterans of San Francisco and not consider them? Now, if he could be appointed, why couldn't all the members of that Board be veterans? After all, you know, the veteran groups of San Francisco—you cannot believe for one minute that there are not men in the veterans just as much interested in opera, and just as much interested in culture as in any other group. A great many of them don't, perhaps, know what a symphony or concerts are, but we do know that we are not all uneducated, and of no culture, and that there are no men among the veterans able to fill a position of that kind. A great many veterans are just as well qualified to rule a project of this kind, and to rule the whole project as any other group in San Francisco.

As a matter of fact, if this were a private group and not a public body, and you had secured $4,000,000 from various people on the same representations that were made to secure these monies, you would be obligated to appoint a Board entirely of veterans because, you will remember if your memory will serve you right, before the bond campaign in 1927 the rumor went around the City that the name of the veterans was being used to exploit an opera house. It is very interesting to note on page 7 of this history of the San Francisco War Memorial that City Attorney John J. O'Toole was very careful to take the words "art museum and opera house" out of the resolution for fear that it might ·invalidate the whole thing, because there was a rumor going around that the name of the veterans was being used to exploit some outside project. As a result the papers made a determined ·campaign to make it clear that the veterans would control the project. Your Board of Supervisors passed a resolution that the veterans would have the approval of the plans. Not the approval of the plans alone for the Veterans' building, but the approval of the plans for the entire project, both the Veterans' building and the opera house.

Both the San Francisco Examiner and the San Francisco Chronicle,' the San Francisco Examiner in the editorial column on June 8th referred to that rumor, that there was a rumor being circulated in the City to the effect that the name and reputation of the veterans was being exploited in connection with another purpose and that they would have no control over the type or uses of the War Memorial, and stating that these rumors, which are always more or less groundless, had been laid once and for all and that the veterans were to have the full control not only over the type, but also over the uses of the Veterans' building, first, foremost and all the time. That was the editorial which was published to the people of San Francisco. That said that we veterans would control not only the type but the uses of the project.

Now, gentlemen, as I said to you before, if you were a private corporation and had induced somebody, certain individuals, to subscribe $4,000,000 on the basis of people from a certain group having control of the use of that money and then you should try to avoid that obligation, you would be guilty of fraud and could be compelled to return the money. Now, your duty to the people of San Francisco is certainly not less than it would be if you were a private corporation. Under your obligation as representatives of the people and as public officials it is greater. You have a public trust, and a person endowed with a public trust must show greater faith with the people even than in a private capacity with the people with whom he deals. We think on that basis we have an absolute right to ask that the veterans control this project. I want to say to you members of the Board of Supervisors that if the Mayor had seen fit to appoint a Board consisting of eleven veterans, not one month ago, but one year ago, when he could have done so under the charter, you would probably have a War Memorial now.

We have been brought up in a school of accomplishment. We had to go through a school of service where we had to be active and had to accomplish if we wanted to be alive. The veteran groups exist and are existing today for service to their city and country, so that they cannot sit back and neglect trusts that have been placed in their hands. I want to tell you something about what we think of the responsibility, about the responsibility for this so-called delay in this project. The Mayor of this City, however, tells us that he did not have any responsibility in the matter until December, 1928, when this Board of Supervisors passed a resolution stating that there should be this three, three and three committee and having the Mayor as an ex-officio or additional member. But, gentlemen, do you realize that in June, 1927, the people of the City of San Francisco voted $4,000,000 for the construction of a War Memorial? What did that mean? That meant that the executive officials of this City had in their charge $4,000,000 and that money was voted on the promise from this private Board of Trustees that if the $4,000,000 issue was voted they would turn over the $2,000,000 which they had to the City. It was not the understanding at any time that the City would turn over the $4,000,000 voted by the City of San Francisco to the trustees of this private fund. Section 2, Chapter I, Article IV of the City Charter states: "The Mayor shall from time to time recommend to the proper officers of the different departments such measures as he may deem beneficial to public interest." Why didn't the Mayor of the City of San Francisco take hold of the project in June, 1927, and recommend the necessary legislation to build this project? This Amendment 32 is almost a carbuncle on the City Charter. It is an indication of trying to create a self-perpetuating board, except in this particular instance the board isn't quite self-perpetuating. This amendment wasn't necessary to start the the War Memorial. The City was well qualified as such to immediately start building that War Memorial. Don't you think it rather strange that this City, after voting a $4,000,000 bond issue, should yet wait for the private board of trustees with $2,000,000—it was $2,000,000 but has shrunk to about $770,000—to prepare the plan to spend the City's $4,000,000, and the City, represented by the officials whom we must hold responsible, does nothing in reference to the thing.

There has been delay and delay and delay, and that delay can be placed at specific doors, but when there is any attempt to place it at the doors of any of the veteran groups, we maintain that such a charge is grossly unfair and unjustified. We have fought for the thing to which we are entitled, and we will continue to fight for that thing until the will of the people is carried out. The people said that we are entitled to a War Memorial and that we are entitled to control not only the type but the uses of that project.

I want to call your attention to one other thing. A number of times the statement has been made to the veterans: "What do you gentlemen need a building for, or what do you care what you get? In forty or fifty years you will all be dead and there will be no veteran organizations then, and what then will become of the building?" Gentlemen, any person who makes that remark doesn't understand the purposes of the veteran organizations. Not perhaps the purposes merely as expressions set forth in their Constitutions and By-Laws, but the purposes as expressed in the organizations themselves. You all well know that patriotism can only be kept alive when you teach it to the people and particularly to the children. On Admission Day, Armistice Day, Washington's birthday, the stores are all practically open. The dollar does not observe patriotism, and you cannot keep patriotism alive by making people successful alone. You have got to teach them the traditions of this country; you have got to make them realize what is at the foundation of the institution of democracy. The veteran organizations are doing that today. When we pass on, and we know that we are not going to live a great many years, but when we pass on there must be other organization who will keep this patriotic work going and who will keep these patriotic halls occupied to carry on our work. I want to tell you, gentlemen of the Board of Supervisors, that if those War Memorial halls ever become vacant through failure in this great City to have an organization to carry on our work, and you can only operate in this great society of today through organization, if they are not organized so that they want to instill patriotic efforts and thought in the minds of the people and use those halls, then I can tell you that we will have no use for an opera house because if patriotism is dead and democracy ceases to exist, you will not have even an autocracy; you will probably have a country that is ruined. We don't look for that because we know that we shall instill in the hearts of our children a patriotism that will endure and will keep alive in the minds of our future citizens the principles of democracy, and we are entitled to a better use and a better building than any person is entitled to consider even for opera purposes. Today opera is more in jeopardy than are the veterans. Today, with inventions of all sorts of mechanical devices, nobody knows what the future of an opera house will be. As a matter of fact, look at the trouble theatre owners are having right now. One owner of an opera house proposes to tear down two theatres which he owns and put up a hotel. Gentlemen, we don't know what will happen in this mechanical age we are living in today. An opera house is more apt to become a lodestone on the back of the City than is a War Memorial.

Gentlemen, I can go into this report in detail. If I should seek so to do and point out where you would not be justified in approving the nomination of any of the men who have served this City so poorly on this so-called Board of Private Trustees. Any of you who have heard any of the reports when Mr. Glensor read the statements of Mr. Fleishhacker to you that the Board of Trustees had not told the architects that they only had $5,000,000 to spend on buildings. Gentlemen, what do you think of that? Do you think that showed business interest in the affairs of San Francisco such as is characteristic of the personal ability of Mr. Fleishhacker? We don't doubt the personal ability or integrity of these men, but we do know that for the purposes of this War Memorial they have failed and failed dismally. They have no right to permit their names to go before this Board of Supervisors, nor has any one the right to suggest their names before this Board as future members of the Board of Trustees of this War Memorial. A group that has failed in their trust as they have should not ask for any further honor in the War Memorial at the hands of this City. I don't see how any group of men who have failed in their trust as they have for eleven years, and haven't done anything but waste money, which should convince you of that. For that reason we oppose their nomination and we ask you to vote on this Board of Trustees as a body, and on that you are entitled to do your will. It is not as individuals that we are opposed to them. The Mayor says that we are opposing Mr. Herz, Mr. Cameron, Mr. Bentley and Mr. George Hearst and others because they are in favor of and working for an opera house. We oppose the confirmation of the Board of Trustees upon which there are any members of the old private Board of Trustees, and we ask this on the basis of the showing which they have made, and which is a complete showing and an unanswerable showing. We ask you to do your duty by the City of San Francisco. As far as the War Memorial is concerned, I always feel, personally, that the building itself isn't going to mean so much for those of us who served in the war, and particularly for those of us who were not able to come home. A marble stone is all they will ever need. If we accomplished anything in our service, given unselfishly and with devotion to our country, if our service cannot speak for us, no stone will ever speak for us, but a War Memorial is something for the people of San Francisco. Not for those of us who may have served, but it is a question of such civic integrity, of the ability of the people of this City to recognize service and sacrifice, and if you are going to recognize service and sacrifice, do it in the right way and recognize them in the proper manner. They served their country, and they served their country well—and they are just as well qualified to serve their city as any particular private group of trustees that exist. Personally, I believe you could send a boy out on the street and tell him to pick out the first eleven men he came to, and those first eleven men picked out would serve the City more competently and more efficiently than the City has been served by those men who were on the Board of Private Trustees.

Gentlemen, we are asking just for fairness when we ask for a majority of veterans on the Board. We are seeking but little, and we believe in seeking that, that we are entitled to it, and we ask your support on the record of negligence and inefficiency as characterized by the record of this Board of Private Trustees in the past eleven years.

I thank you. (Applause.)

SUPERVISOR HAYDEN: I now move that we take a recess until tomorrow afternoon at 2:30 o'clock for the purpose of continuing this hearing.

SUPERVISOR ANDRIANO: Second the motion.

SUPERVISOR HAYDEN: Roll call, please.

THE MAYOR: A discussion of that matter is not debatable, but may I just ask the Board to direct the stenographer to prepare, as rapidly as he can, a full transcript of the proceedings of tonight?

SUPERVISOR ROSSI: Your Honor, I will be pleased to make such a motion.

SUPERVISOR HAYDEN: Second the motion.

THE MAYOR: There being no objection, such is the order.

SUPERVISOR CANEPA: May I ask if a copy of these proceedings may be furnished the members also .

THE CLERK: It will be printed the same as this report has been.

THE MAYOR: In view of the fact that you have asked me to close the discussion when the time arrived, I would like to get my copy as soon as possible.

It has been regularly moved and seconded that the Board now recess until 2:30 tomorrow afternoon.

SUPERVISOR HAYDEN: A roll call has been asked for.

THE MAYOR: The Clerk will call the roll.

THE CLERK (reading):

SUPERVISOR ANDRIANO: Aye.

SUPERVISOR CANEPA: Aye.

SUPERVISOR COLMAN: Absent.

SUPERVISOR GALLAGHER: Absent.

SUPERVISOR HAVENNER: Aye.

SUPERVISOR HAYDEN: Aye.

SUPERVISOR McGOVERN: Aye.

SUPERVISOR McSHEEHY: No.

SUPERVISOR MILES: No.

SUPERVISOR PEYSER: No.

SUPERVISOR POWER: No.

SUPERVISOR RONCOVIERI: No.

SUPERVISOR ROSSI: Aye.

SUPERVISOR SHANNON: Absent.

SUPERVISOR SPAULDING: No.

SUPERVISOR STANTON: Aye.

SUPERVISOR SUHR: Aye.

SUPERVISOR TONER: Aye.

THE CLERK: Nine ayes and six noes.

THE MAYOR: The hearing will recess until tomorrow afternoon at 2:30 o'clock p. m.

The following information was presented by his Honor the Mayor:

Why the War Memorial Property Was Held in Name of a Bank.

Why was the War Memorial property held in the name of a bank and taxes paid thereon, when it could have been held in the name of the Regents of the University of California and no payment of taxes would have been necessary?

In accordance with agreement made with the City's representatives through Mr. Ralph McLaren, Chairman of the Finance Committee of the Board of Supervisors, the City was to purchase the north block of the Memorial site and the Trustees the south block.

When the time came for the City to purchase parcels of the north block as same were available, it was then found there were no funds provided for this purpose, and at the request of Mr. McLaren the necessary money was borrowed for the City by the Trustees, with the understanding that same would be later repaid by the City out of the next tax levy.

Although numerous promises were made to pay this money, it was never repaid by the City and the monies loaned by the banks were finally repaid by the Trustees. The money advanced by the banks was secured by the property purchased and when the Trustees repaid the banks it was then possible to transfer title to the property to the regents and avoid further taxes.

The Trustees had this money advanced by the banks instead of using its own funds which were then invested, because it was believed by this plan complications, which would have risen had the property come directly into the hands of the regents, could be avoided.

Why Money Was Borrowed From Bank.

Why did the War Memorial Trustees borrow money from a bank when the money could have been used from the War Memorial fund?

Only money borrowed by the Trustees in addition to that specified in answering question No. 1 was the following:

First. When the War Memorial project was initiated the Trustees decided to purchase the old St. Ignatius lot for the Memorial site. No money was available for this purpose at that time as Memorial subscriptions were only then being secured. No considerable amount of money from these subscriptions was available before about January 1, 1922.

St. Ignatius lot was optioned in September, 1919.

St. Ignatius lot was purchased February 28, 1920.

Second. From time to time it became necessary to borrow money from banks to take care of current expenses in advance of payment of these expenses from the Regents of the University of California who were custodians of the trust funds. Said funds were by them kept invested.

Why Money Was Spent on Plans.

Why were $216,000 spent on plans and no plans drawn that could be carried out?

First. On March 19, 1928, the Special American Legion War Memorial Committee approved plans for the Veterans building submitted to them by the Trustees. (Photostatic copy of these plans and signatures on same submitted herewith.)

Estimates based on the plans existing at the time of above approval indicated that these plans could be carried out for within a few hundred thousand dollars of the funds available.

In order to reduce the cost of the project both buildings were made ten feet narrower. This ten feet being taken from hallways only and not reducing the net amount of usable space alloted to the veterans, which space is approximately 105,700 square feet. This space is equivalent to a building 100 feet square and ten stories high without including necessary hallways, elevator shafts, etc.

Working drawings for the construction of buildings in accordance with the above plans are now in the hands of the Trustees practically completed.

Second. Amount expended for plans is not excessive. It is also a fact that a great deal of highly technical information was necessary and was acquired because of the character of the structures contemplated.

Details of Trust Agreement.

What are the details of the private trust agreement between Regents of the University of California and the private Trustees, and would the City be obligated to pay an expense of $200,000 a year for the proposed opera house under the terms of the same?

Copy of trust agreement herewith. Said agreement does not contain any obligation to pay $200,000 per year.

It is expected that reasonable rentals shall be secured from the use of the opera house.

For example, the Symphony Orchestra will require the use of the opera house for about seventy performances each year.

The Grand Opera season will require the use of the opera house for from fifteen to twenty performances each year.

Artists' recitals should amount to twenty-five or thirty performances each year.

In addition to this there should be a great number of dramatic presentations, lectures, meetings, etc.

Trust agreement follows:

War Memorial Agreement.

THIS AGREEMENT, made this 19th day of August, one thousand nine hundred and twenty-one, by and between the Regents of the University of California, a corporation of the State of California, party of the first part, hereinafter for convenience called "Regents," and Walter S. Martin, Charles Templeton Crocker, John D. McKee, E. S. Heller, Charles H. Kendrick, Frank F. Kilsby, Milton H. Esberg, Herbert Fleishhacker, William H. Crocker and John S. Drum, trustees, parties of the second part, hereinafter for convenience called "trustees",

WITNESSETH:

Whereas, it is intended by this agreement to honor the memory of the soldiers, sailors, marines and war workers—men and women—who brought imperishable glory to California by their splendid contribution to the winning of the World War; and,

Whereas, a committee of citizens of San Francisco, represented by the said trustees, has for such purposes conceived the plan of a War Memorial in the ownership of the University of California, and to that end has recommended the purchase of a block of land, consisting of six fifty vara lots in the City and County of San Francisco, State of California, described as follows:

Bounded by Van Ness avenue, Franklin street, Hayes street and Grove street; saving and excepting therefrom approximately sixty-four hundred (6400) square feet conveyed or to be conveyed to the City and County of San Francisco;—and the erection thereon of a War Memorial consisting of a Memorial Court enclosed or partially enclosed by a building or group of buildings, viz: a theatre or auditorium building, a building to be used by the San Francisco Art Association, also called the San Francisco Institute of Art (and sometimes known as The Mark Hopkins Institute of Art) and a building to be used by the San Francisco Posts of the American Legion, an organization composed of veterans of the late World War, all for the purpose of commemorating in perpetuity the victory achieved by the United States of America, and it is contemplated that said group of buildings, or a part thereof, will be used for educational purposes in connection with the University work and University extension work of the University of California; and,

Whereas, to accomplish the aforesaid objects, arrangements have already been made by the trustees to acquire said block of land with funds to be obtained from the subscriptions hereinafter mentioned; and,

Whereas, the said trustees have procured from numerous and divers persons, associations, partnerships and corporations, subscriptions payable in terms to the University of California to provide the funds towards carrying out the said objects; and,

Whereas, the aggregate amount of such subscriptions at the present time, including cash subscriptions, is the sum of two million six hundred and seventy-nine ($2,000,679) dollars, or thereabout; and,

Whereas, said trustees have already incurred various expenses for the purpose of carrying out said objects and purposes, which expenses should be deducted from said subscriptions, including cash subscriptions; and,

Whereas, the said trustees may hereafter obtain other subscriptions in the same form for the same purposes as aforesaid; and,

Whereas, it was made conditional in said subscription agreements that the same as to each subscriber would be of no effect unless at least a total of one million five hundred thousand (1,500,000) dollars were subscribed to carry out the said objects, and whereas more than said sum has now been subscribed; and,

Whereas, the regents have heretofore accepted subscriptions to said fund and will hereafter accept subscriptions thereto only upon condition that each subscriber consents to this agreement and to the appointment of the said trustees as his irrevocable and perpetual agents for the carrying out of said trust and the terms of this agreement and any amendment or amendments thereof;

NOW, THEREFORE, THIS AGREEMENT WITNESSETH:

(1)   The Trustees agree that they will take immediate steps to secure the consent in writing of all the subscribers to the execution of this agreement and to the expenditure of the subscriptions in accordance herewith. This agreement shall not become operative as to the regents until the consent of subscribers whose subscriptions aggregate at least one million eight hundred thousand (1,800,000) dollars have been secured thereto. In addition, immediately after the execution of this agreement, written notice thereof, and either a copy thereof or a reference to a place where such copy may be examined, shall be sent to each subscriber who has not already given his said written consent hereto. Such notice and copies shall be prepared by the Trustees and shall be sent by the secretary of the regents.

The Trustees hereby jointly and severally warrant their authority to execute this agreement in behalf of all the subscribers to the end that at all times the regents may deal with the said Trustees, their successors and assigns, in such trust, as the sole agents and representatives of all the subscribers for every purpose connected with this agreement.

The Trustees shall remain in existence as an organized committee as long as the regents continue to hold the War Memorial and shall constitute a self-perpetuating body. In case of the death, resignation, incapacity or removal from the State of any of said Trustees, the remaining Trustees or a majority of them shall appoint a successor from the particular organization from which the vacancy occurs, as in this paragraph designated. Said Trustees shall consist in the first instance of the following persons: Walter S. Martin and Charles Templeton Crocker, representing the San Francisco Art Association; John D. Mc-Kee and E. S. Heller, representing the Musical Association of San Francisco; Charles H. Kendrick and Frank F. Kilsby, representing the San Francisco posts of the American Legion . Milton H. Esberg, Herbert Fleishhacker, William H. Crocker and John S. Drum. If requested by the regents, but not otherwise, the Trustees shall cause a corporation to be organized under the laws of the State of California and shall advise the regents thereof in writing, and thereafter all the rights and powers of the Trustees hereunder shall be vested in and devolve upon such corporation, including the perpetual and irrevocable right to act for and on behalf of the subscribers in connection with the trusts herein recited or referred to. The term subscribers, as hereafter used herein, shall mean those who have contributed or may hereafter contribute funds for the War Memorial. The Trustees shall be reimbursed out of the moneys paid in by the subscribers for the various expenses thus far or hereafter incurred in carrying out the objects and purposes of the trust.

(2)   The acts of the Trustees, or a majority of them, shall be binding upon all the Trustees, and shall be evidenced by a writing signed by the Trustees, or a majority of them. The Trustees may delegate any of their powers to an executive committee, in which event the acts of the executive committee (to be composed in part of representatives of the organizations which are given rights in the buildings to be erected) shall be evidenced by a writing signed by them or a majority of them. The regents shall be bound by a resolution duly passed by them.

(3)   The Trustees shall take all steps necessary, convenient or requisite to secure the payment of said subscriptions to the regents. The moneys and funds obtained through the payment of said subscriptions shall immediately be deposited in a bank or banks selected by the regents to the credit of the regents in an account to be designated "War Memorial Building Account," and such funds shall be paid out and expended upon the check or order of the regents, but only when and if a written demand therefor is made upon the regents by the Trustees or a majority of them, or by their executive committee, or a majority of it.

(4)   The Trustees shall construct said building or buildings upon said lot of land in accordance with plans and specifications to be adopted by them. Before any contracts are let for the construction of such buildings or any of them, or any part thereof, the general plan for the War Memorial shall first receive the approval of the regents in writing. The Trustees shall employ the architect, superintendent of construction, contractor or contractors, and all other agents necessary or convenient for the construction of said building or buildings, and the erection and completion thereof shall be exclusively under their direction and control. The contracts therefor shall be made in the name of the regents. The regents shall not be called upon to execute any contract for the construction, equipment or furnishing of any of the buildings or any part thereof, or to incur any liability of any character in connection therewith, unless the necessary funds to meet the financial obligations imposed have been paid into said War Memorial building account and are not otherwise appropriated. Neither the regents nor the State of California shall be under any liability whatever in the construction of said buildings or any of them, or at all, beyond the amount of said moneys actually collected and deposited in banks and available for such purpose or purposes as herein prescribed. nor shall any payment be made therefrom except upon the written demand of the Trustees, or a majority of them, or their executive committee, or a majority of it, as aforesaid.

(5) Inasmuch as said building or buildings are to be erected to comply with certain representations made by the said Trustees in obtaining said subscriptions, it is understood and agreed that when said building or buildings are completed, the same shall by the said Trustees be turned over to the regents, subject, however, to the carrying out by the regents of the trusts herein set forth, and which trusts the regents agree, as herein provided, to carry out and perform; provided, however, that in no event shall the regents be responsible or liable hereunder for any moneys beyond the actual receipts from said group of buildings and the amounts of the subscriptions actually paid to them.

(6) After said building or buildings are completed and turned over to the regents, it is agreed that the regents (a) will keep the exterior and roof of the buildings devoted to the San Francisco posts of the American Legion and to the San Francisco Art Association in good order, repair and condition, except as to any part of the buildings or any windows, glass or skylights which become broken through any act of the respective occupants; (b) will keep the theatre or auditorium its exterior and interior, and every part thereof, and the approaches thereto, in good order, repair and condition; (c) will maintain the Memorial Court and approaches thereto in good order, repair and condition; but this covenant is not intended to exonerate the City and County of San Francisco from the maintenance of any part of the Memorial Court, which it has agreed or may hereafter agree to maintain.

(7) The Trustees shall make written demand upon the regents for the said funds actually collected and deposited only for the purchase of the real property above described and for the construction of the following:

(a) The theatre or auditorium and its equipment; (b) the building for the use and occupancy of San Francisco Art Association; (c) the building for the use and occupancy of the San Francisco posts of the American Legion and its equipment.

(8) Out of the funds collected as aforesaid, said Trustees shall completely furnish and equip in a modern manner the buildings to be occupied by the San Francisco posts of the American Legion as executive offices, club and meeting rooms, and auditorium, expending a reasonable amount of money for these purposes.

(9) The occupation of the respective buildings and parts thereof to be used by the San Francisco posts of the American Legion and the San Francisco Art Association, respectively, shall be under the following covenants and conditions:

(a) The respective occupants shall be under no obligation to pay rent.

(b) Any wilful and continued violation by the respective occupants of the covenants and conditions herein expressed, or of any of them, shall give the regents the right to terminate the occupancy. No failure to exercise this right at any time shall be deemed a waiver of a subsequent breach of this subdivision.

(c) Each respective occupant shall comply with all laws, rules, orders, ordinances and regulations, Federal, State, County and Municipal, or any of their departments, which shall impose any duty upon the occupants with respect to the premises, including health, police and fire regulations.

(d) Each respective occupant will keep the interior of the building cleanly and in good order and repair, and promptly make and pay for all necessary repairs, replacements and renovations.

(e) No alterations, additions or improvements of any kind may be made without the written consent of the regents.

(f) The regents or their agents may enter upon the premises or any part thereof at all reasonable hours for the purpose of examining the same, or making such repairs, additions or alterations as the

regents deem necessary or proper for the safety or preservation thereof; but the stipulations in this subdivision (f) carry no obligation of
any kind upon the regents.

(g) The regents shall not be liable to any occupant for any damage
occurring to person or property, whether occasioned by or resulting
from the flow, leakage, breakage, or obstruction of any pipes, including
oil, steam, water, gas, air, vacuum, electricity or soil pipes, or from
any roof conduits or drain-ducts, or other leakage or overflow from
water, oil, gas, air, electricity, or steam in and about said premises, or
from any carelessness, negligence or improper conduct on the part of
the respective occupants, or their agents or guests in or about said
premises; and the regents shall not be liable for any damage, loss or
injury to any persons or property occurring by reason of any present,
future, latent or other defects in the form, character or condition of
the buildings, or any part thereof.

(h) Should the buildings or any of them be injured or destroyed
by any cause, there shall be no obligation on the part of the regents
to restore or replace the same. But if insurance is carried thereon by
the regents, the insurance moneys received shall be used for the restoration or replacement of the building or buildings so injured or destroyed in so far as they are sufficient for that purpose. The regents,
however, shall not be under any obligation to carry insurance on any
of said buildings.

(i) The respective occupants shall not assign, transfer or set over
their respective rights without written consent of the regents. Neither
shall the respective occupants lease, sublet or underlet any part or
portion of said premises without the written consent of the regents.
Should the rights of the occupant be assigned by operation of law in
any manner, then the regents may at their option terminate the occupancy; provided that any auditorium in the American Legion building
and rooms necessary to be used in connection therewith may be sublet
by the San Francisco posts of the American Legion, but no leasing
or renting or subletting or hiring shall be had to any tenant or tenants
or to any one or for any purpose or purposes objectionable to the
regents. The regents are hereby expressly given the right to forbid
or determine or veto any contract or agreement of letting, subletting,
or renting or hiring, of any part of said buildings.

(j) The respective occupants shall not use the said premises nor
any part thereof for any purpose deemed extra-hazardous by the
regents on account of fire, or use the said premises for any immoral
or illegal purposes.

(k) The respective occupants shall pay all taxes, assessments and
municipal charges whatsoever upon any property belonging to them
within said premises.

(l) The respective occupants shall pay for all heat, light, gas,
electricity, water, steam or other public utility used in or about their
respective premises, and shall pay for all janitor and elevator service.
This enumeration shall not be deemed exclusive, and the said respective occupants shall pay in full for all services and material of every
character used in or about their respective premises, and the regents
shall be under no obligation to pay for any part thereof.

(m) The respective occupants will repair and restore all glass in
windows, doors and skylights, and all plumbing and wiring which
have become broken through the acts, omissions or carelessness of the
respective occupants.

(n) The respective occupants will not use, or permit to be used.
the said respective premises for the purpose of any business, trade or
manufacture, or for lodging or for a hotel or boarding house, but said
respective occupants may permit necessary watchmen to lodge upon
said premises.

(o) The respective occupants shall not carry on upon said premises, or permit to be carried thereon, any offensive noises or odors, or permit any nuisance of any kind.

(p) The respective occupants shall not permit any signs to be affixed to the exterior of said premises, or upon any windows or doors, unless the size, form and location thereof are approved by the regents in writing.

(q) The respective occupants shall not cover any window or door with awnings unless the size, color and design of such awnings are first approved in writing by the regents.

(r) Should the regents decide upon maintaining a garden in any court in or about said buildings, or in or about the sidewalk adjacent to the same, the said respective occupants shall not interfere with the maintenance of such garden by the regents.

(s) Should any injury, loss or destruction of the said premises occur through the carelessness or negligence of the respective occupants or of their guests, then the respective occupants will pay the regents for the damage caused thereby.

(t) The respective occupants agree that all signs upon or adjacent to doors in the interior of said buildings shall be at their own expense, but the form, character and location thereof shall be approved by the regents in writing before the installation thereof.

(10) The trusts to be carried out by the said regents are as follows:

A.

Requirements of Trust in Favor of San Francisco Art Association.

The building to be occupied by San Francisco Art Association shall be used by that corporation (or by a non-profit association organized under the laws of the State of California, under the name of "Trustees of San Francisco Museum of Art" and authorized under the constitution and by-laws of San Francisco Art Association to act in association and conjunction with San Francisco Art Association in the matter of and in connection with the possession, custody, care, display and exhibition of fine paintings, statuary and other objects of art) to maintain therein an Art Gallery and Museum of Fine Arts, and the public shall have access thereto at reasonable times, and under conditions to be fixed by said San Francisco Art Association with the approval of the regents. Such parts or portions of said building as shall for the time being not be necessary to be used for the Art Gallery and Museum of Fine Arts may be used by the regents for any purpose the regents may desire. Such use and occupation on the part of the San Francisco Art Association shall be independent from any of the provisions of the so-called "Edward F. Searles Trust." For the purpose of maintaining exhibits the San Francisco Art Association may receive from donors or trustors works of art or endowments for maintenance or endowments for the purchase of works of art independent of the provisions of said "Edward F. Searles Trust." No works of art shall be maintained or exhibited in said Art Gallery or Museum of Fine Arts which are objectionable to the regents.

B.

Requirements of Trust in Favor of Musical Association of San Francisco and San Francisco Symphony Orchestra.

The theatre or auditorium to be erected upon said property and sufficient space about the same for convenient access thereto may be used and occupied by the Musical Association of San Francisco (a California corporation), which maintains the "San Francisco Symphony Orchestra." upon the following conditions:

(1) The Musical Association of San Francisco shall pay such rent for each performance in said theatre or auditorium as may be fixed by the regents. In case any rent remains due and unpaid for a period of two months after the same accrues and becomes due, the regents

shall have and they are hereby given the right and option of refusing
to permit said theatre or auditorium to be used by the Musical Association of San Francisco or said San Francisco Symphony Orchestra
until such rent is paid in full. In case any rent remains due and
unpaid for a period of four months after the same has accrued pursuant to the provisions hereof, then and in that event the regents shall
have and they are hereby given the right and option of terminating
the occupancy of said theatre or auditorium by said Musical Association of San Francisco or said San Francisco Symphony Orchestra, and
thereafter neither said Musical Association nor said San Francisco
Symphony Orchestra shall have any preferential rights of any character in or to said theatre or auditorium or any part thereof, and the
regents shall, in their discretion, manage and operate the said theatre
or auditorium and permit same to be used by those persons or organizations whom, in their discretion, they deem proper.

(2) The theatre or auditorum shall be maintained and kept in good
order and repair by the regents at their own expense.

(3) The regents shall at each performance and rehearsal given
under the auspices of the Musical Association of San Francisco furnish
at their own expense sufficient and proper light, heat, steam, water,
electricity, gas and other public utility in all parts of said theatre or
auditorium and the street approaches thereto.

(4) The regents shall at each performance and rehearsal given
under the auspices of the Musical Association of San Francisco furnish
necessary, proper, full and adequate service on the stage and in front
of the stage, including footmen, box office service, ticket takers, ushers
and first-class stage service.

(5) The regents shall at each performance and rehearsal given
under the auspices of the Musical Association of San Francisco use
their best endeavors to maintain proper order and decorum in all parts
of said theatre or auditorium and the approaches thereto.

(6) The Musical Association of San Francisco shall have the following preferential rights and privileges.

(a) The first preferential right to use the theatre or auditorium
for its future annual regular series of symphony, popular or choral
concerts as well as all rehearsals therefor, such season not to exceed
seven (7) consecutive months of each year between September fifteenth
and the following April fifteenth, upon as favorable terms and arrangements as to lease, license or occupancy as are or may be made during
such time with any other lessee, licensee or occupant giving symphony,
popular or choral concerts in said theatre or auditorium, excepting
the University of California or any department thereof or activity
directly affiliated therewith.

(b) The first preferential right to use the theatre or auditorium
for a season of musical festival, including rehearsals therefor, to be
given under the auspices of said Musical Association of San Francisco
after the conclusion of the regular series of concerts above mentioned,
such season not to exceed two (2) consecutive months in any year
between April fifteenth and June fifteenth, upon as favorable terms
and arrangements as to lease, license or occupancy as are or may be
made during such time with any other lessee, licensee or occupant
giving musical performances of a similar character in said theatre
or auditorium.

(c) The concerts or musical performances above mentioned may
be given in the day or night or both, as may be determined by said
Musical Association.

(d) The preferential rights above mentioned shall mean a first
right and option to be exercised by said Musical Association of San
Francisco before any arrangements shall be made by the regents
directly or indirectly with any other orchestra or musical organization
or those in control thereof or any impressario or concert manager for
any concerts or musical performances during the season that the
Musical Association of San Francisco may desire to give the above

mentioned concerts or musical performances. The preferential rights herein given to said Musical Association of San Francisco shall not extend to or cover the period in any calendar year from June fifteenth to September fifteenth. Such preferential rights shall be exercised by written notice given to the regents on or before August first in any calendar year for any use desired before the succeeding June fifteenth, and upon such written notice being given, the Musical Association of San Francisco shall become obligated to pay the rental to the regents for such use of the theatre or auditorium unless otherwise agreed by the regents in writing.

(7) Said regents may, if so advised, appoint any member of the regents and/or any of the faculty of the University of California and/or any agent as a Board of Administration to manage said auditorium or theatre and to provide for the entertainments to be given therein, and may, if so advised, appoint a business manager who will have such supervision and control over said auditorium or theatre as said regents may decide to confer; but nothing herein contained shall be deemed to deprive said Musical Association of the right to control and manage such concerts or musical performances as it may give in said theatre or auditorium.

C.

Requirements of and Trust in Favor of San Francisco Posts of the American Legion.

(1) The building to be occupied by the San Francisco Posts of the American Legion shall be occupied and used by the various duly organized and authorized San Francisco Posts of the American Legion without rent charge. The San Francisco Posts of the American Legion, or a majority of them, shall under such rules and conditions as they may prescribe, provide headquarters for Veterans of the Mexican War, Grand Army of the Republic, Spanish-American War Veterans, and such other patriotic organizations as said San Francisco Posts of the American Legion may from time to time desire to install. Should the San Francisco Posts of the American Legion be consolidated with or merged into some other national organization, then the organizations duly authorized by such other national organization shall have the same rights of occupancy as the San Francisco Posts of the American Legion, and the rights and obligations of the successor organization shall be the same as the rights and obligations of the San Francisco Posts of the American Legion, as set forth herein.

(2) The said building to be occupied by the San Francisco Posts of the American Legion shall be used by them as club and meeting-rooms and for executive offices and auditorium purposes.

(3) Should said San Francisco Posts of the American Legion or their successor by consolidation or merger cease to exist, then said building may be used by said regents for any purpose the regents may determine.

General Provisions.

(1) The regents shall in no event be liable for the erection or completion of the group of buildings herein described or any of them. Their only obligation in this connection shall be to pay out the subscriptions actually collected in the manner herein provided.

(2) The regents shall in no event be under any financial liability or responsibility for the maintenance, repair, or upkeep of said group of buildings, or any of them, over and above the net financial returns which may be received from the operation of the theatre or auditorium.

(3) In case the San Francisco Posts of the American Legion should cease to exist and there be no similar patriotic organization of like membership in existence at that time, the building to be erected for use by the San Francisco Posts of the American Legion shall thereafter be under the exclusive direction and control of the regents.

(4) In case the Musical Association of San Francisco should cease

to exist as an active musical association, the building to be erected for use by the Musical Association of San Francisco shall thereafter be under the exclusive direction and control of the regents.

(5) After the erection of the group of buildings herein provided for is completed and possession thereof delivered to the regents, neither the Trustees nor any of them, nor their executive committee, shall have any further connection with the said real property or group of buildings, except as provided in paragraphs (6) and (8) following.

(6) The regents may withdraw and retire from the trust hereby created in relation to said War Memorial at any time and resign as trustee hereunder. In case the regents determine so to withdraw and retire, a resolution to that effect shall be passed by the regents and a copy thereof deposited in the United States mail at San Francisco, California, postage prepaid, addressed to each of the following at San Francisco, California: Each post of the American Legion in San Francisco or its successor organization, if any; the Musical Association of San Francisco; the San Francisco Symphony Orchestra; San Francisco Art Association, the trustees herein individually named; and the corporation formed by the Trustees hereunder, if any. Within sixty (60) days after the completion of such mailing, the Trustees or the corporation formed by them pursuant hereto shall designate in writing a person, corporation, city, county or other governmental agency or political subdivision of the State of California, to whom the regents shall convey the said trust property and moneys then in their hands pursuant hereto. In case no such person, corporation, city, county or other governmental agency or political subdivision of the State of California is designated in writing by the Trustees or said corporation to be formed pursuant hereto, if any, and written notice of such designation given to the regents by depositing the same in the United States mail with the postage thereon prepaid, addressed to The Regents of the University of California, Berkeley, California, within said sixty (60) day period, then the regents may in their discretion convey the trust property and any moneys then in their hands pursuant hereto to any city, county, municipal corporation or political subdivision or agency of the State of California, as trustee, and upon making such conveyance the regents shall thereafter be under no further obligation of any character on account of the execution of this agreement, or in connection with the said War Memorial or the property or funds thereof.

(7) In order to protect the regents against any loss or liability in connection with the carrying out of the trusts herein recited and referred to, it is agreed that there shall first be deducted from the total amount of the moneys received by the regents the sum of one hundred thousand ($100,000) dollars; and in addition all of the net profits of the operation of said War Memorial buildings or any part thereof shall be accumulated by the regents and added to said fund of one hundred thousand ($100,000) dollars. The said fund shall be invested in such interest-bearing securities as the regents shall in their discretion deem proper and the regents may, in their discretion, invest and reinvest the same or any part thereof. Said fund shall be designated as the "War Memorial Contingent Fund" and either the income or the principal thereof may be used by the regents at any time, in their discretion, to make up any deficit in the operation of said War Memorial or for the purpose of making any necessary, convenient or desirable renewals, replacements, repairs or betterments in connection with said buildings, or the furnishing or equipment thereof.

(8) The Trustees hereby jointly and severally agree in their individual capacities that they will indemnify and hold harmless the regents against any financial loss of any character in the construction of the said War Memorial, and they hereby jointly and severally promise and agree that they will pay to the regents, upon demand, any loss which may have been suffered at any time by the regents in

the construction of the said War Memorial. It is the intention hereof
that the regents shall never be called upon to make any payments
on account of the construction of the said War Memorial except from
moneys actually paid to them by the said subscribers.

(9) In case any differences or disagreements arise between the
regents and the Trustees or its successor corporation, if any, concerning the interpretation of this agreement or the purchase of said
real property or the construction or operation of said buildings
thereon or any other matter or thing concerning said War Memorial
or this agreement or any amendment thereof, the parties hereto
hereby agree to submit the same for decision to a board of arbitration
consisting of three persons, to wit, the Chief Justice of the Supreme
Court of California, the Presiding Justice of the United States Circuit
Court of Appeals for the Ninth Circuit, and the Presiding Justice of
the District Court of Appeal of the State of California for the First
Appellate District, First Division, and the parties hereto shall be
bound by the decision of said board, and no suit or action shall be
maintained hereunder unless the matter in controversy shall first
have been submitted to said board of arbitration. If for any reason
any one of said three members of such board of arbitration shall not
be able to serve, then the other two members thereof shall select a
third arbitrator.

(10) The Trustees shall be deemed to be the representatives of and
their acts shall bind the San Francisco Posts of the American Legion,
the San Francisco Art Association and the Musical Association of
San Francisco, in all transactions with the regents pertaining to the
War Memorial.

(11) This agreement is executed by the Trustees for their own
account and as their own act and as the act of each' of them and for
the account of the said subscribers and as their act and as the act of
each of them.

(12) It is expressly agreed and understood that this agreement
may be in any way modified and amended at any time by subsequent
agreement in writing between the parties hereto, or their respective
successors in interest.

In Witness Whereof, the regents has, by its officers thereunto duly
authorized, caused its corporate name to be hereto subscribed and its
corporate seal to be hereto affixed, and the Trustees have hereunto
subscribed their names, all on the day and year first above written.

THE REGENTS OF THE UNIVERSITY OF CALIFORNIA,

By WM. D. STEPHENS,
Governor of the State of California
and ex-officio President of The Regents of the University of California.

By R. G. SPROUL,
Secretary of The Regents of the University of California.

(Seal)

WALTER S. MARTIN,
CHARLES TEMPLETON CROCKER,
JOHN D. McKEE,
E. S. HELLER,
CHAS. H. KENDRICK,
FRANK F. KILSBY,
MILTON H. ESBERG,
HERBERT FLEISHHACKER,
W.M. H. CROCKER,
JOHN S. DRUM.

State of California, County of Sacramento—ss.

On this 6th day of July, A. D. 1922, before me, R. T. McKisick, a
Notary Public in and for the County of Sacramento, State of California, residing therein, duly commissioned and sworn, personally

appeared Wm. D. Stephens, known to me to be the Governor of California and ex-officio President of The Regents of the University of California, the corporation that executed the within and annexed instrument, and he acknowledged to me that such corporation executed the same.

(Seal) R. T. McKISICK.
Notary Public in and for the County of
Sacramento, State of California.

State of California, County of Alameda—ss.

On this 28th day of June, A. D. 1922, before me, Frank C. Stevens, a Notary Public in and for the County of Alameda, State of California, residing therein, duly commissioned and sworn, personally appeared R. G. Sproul, known to me to be the Secretary of The Regents of the University of California, the corporation that executed the within and annexed instrument, and he acknowledged to me that such corporation executed the same.

(Seal) FRANK C. STEVENS,
Notary Public in and for the County of
Alameda, State of California,

State of California, City and County of San Francisco—ss.

On this 19th day of August in the year one thousand nine hundred and twenty-one, before me, W. W. Healey, a Notary Public in and for the said City and County, residing therein, duly commissioned and sworn, personally appeared Walter S. Martin, John D. McKee, E. S. Heller, Charles H. Kendrick (also known as Chas. H. Kendrick), Frank F. Kilsby, Milton H. Esberg, Herbert Fleishhacker, William H. Crocker (also known as Wm. H. Crocker) and John S. Drum, Trustees, known to me to be the persons described in, whose names are subscribed to and who executed the within instrument, and they acknowledged to me that they executed the same as such Trustees.

In Witness Whereof, I have hereunto set my hand and affixed my official seal, at my office in said City and County of San Francisco, the day and year in this certificate first above written.

(Seal) W. W. HEALEY,
Notary Public, in and for the said City
and County of San Francisco, State
of California, 208 Crocker Building.
My commission expires August 28, 1921

United States of America,
State of New York, County of New York—ss.

On this 24th day of August, in the year one thousand nine hundred and twenty-one, before me, John Jos. Lord, in and for the said County and State of New York, residing therein, duly commissioned and sworn, personally appeared Charles Templeton Crocker, Trustee, known to me to be the person described in, those name is subscribed to and who executed the within instrument, and he acknowledged to me that he executed the same as such Trustee.

In Witness Whereof, I have hereunto set my hand and affixed my official seal, at my office in said County of New York, the day and year in this certificate first above written.

(Seal) JOHN JOS. LORD,
Notary Public, New York County;
New York County Clerk's No. 1;
New York County Register's No. 3009.
Commission expires: March 30th, 1923.

No. 62619 Series B

State of New York, County of New York—ss.

I, William F. Schneider, Clerk of the County of New York, and also Clerk of the Supreme Court for the said County, the same being a Court of Record, do hereby certify, That John Jos. Lord whose name is subscribed to the deposition or certificate of the proof or acknowledgment of the annexed instrument, and thereon written, was, at the time of taking such deposition, or proof and acknowledgment, a Notary Public in and for such County, duly commissioned and sworn, and authorized by the laws of said State, to take depositions and to administer oaths to be used in any Court of said State and for general purposes; and also to take acknowledgments and proofs of deeds, of conveyances for land, tenements or hereditaments in said State of New York. And further, that I am well acquainted with the handwriting of such Notary Public, and verily believe that the signature to said depositiou or certificate of proof or acknowledgment is genuine.

In Testimony Whereof, I have hereunto set my hand and affixed the seal of the said Court and County, the 24th day of August, 1921.

(Seal)   WM. F. SCHNEIDER.
                                                         Clerk.

APPROVAL OF AGREEMENT BY AND WITH REGENTS OF THE UNIVERSITY OF CALIFORNIA.

An agreement dated —————— July, 1921, being about to be executed between the Regents of the University of California on one part, and Walter S. Martin, Charles Templeton Crocker, John D. McKee, E. S. Heller, Charles H. Kendrick, Frank F. Kilsby, Milton H. Esberg, Herbert Fleishhacker, William H. Crocker and John S. Drum, as Trustees, on the other part, respecting the acquisition, construction and operation of the San Francisco War Memorial (a copy of which agreement is on file at the office of Mercantile Trust Company, San Francisco, Crocker National Bank, San Francisco, and Anglo-California Trust Company, San Francisco, and is hereby made part hereof), the undersigned subscribers to said San Francisco War Memorial severally hereby agree to the execution of said agreement and the expenditure of the several subscriptions of the undersigned in accordance therewith; and hereby severally authorize said Trustees to execute and carry out said agreement in behalf of the undersigned and as their act and hereby irrevocably appoint said Trustees, their successors and assigns, as the agents and representatives of the undersigned for every purpose connected therewith. This agreement shall be deemed to have been executed by all of the undersigned on and as of the —— day of July, 1921.

This agreement was signed by subscribers whose subscriptions totaled $1,630,500.

On July 18, 1922, the Regents of the University of California and the Trustees passed the first amendment to the agreement dated August 19, 1921, covering paragraph 1, page 3.

———

THIS AGREEMENT, made this 18th day of July, one thousand nine hundred and twenty-two, by and between the Regents of the University of California, a corporation of the State of California, party of the first part, hereinafter for convenience called "Regents," and Walter S. Martin, Charles Templeton Crocker, John D. McKee, E. S. Heller, Charles H. Kendrick, Frank F. Kilsby, Milton H. Esberg, Herbert Fleishhacker, William H. Crocker and John S. Drum, Trustees, parties of the second part, hereinafter for convenience called "Trustees,"

WITNESSETH:

Whereas, the parties hereto have executed a certain agreement dated August 19, 1921, which contemplates the acquisition by the regents of certain land in the City and County of San Francisco and the erection thereon of a group of buildings which are to constitute and be known as the War Memorial, in accordance with certain terms and conditions set forth in said agreement; and

Whereas, it is provided in said agreement in paragraph 2 thereof that—

"This agreement shall not become operative as to the regents until the consent of subscribers whose subscriptions aggregate at least one million eight hundred thousand (1,800,000) dollars have been secured thereto," and

Whereas, it appears that the consent to said agreement of subscribers whose subscriptions aggregate at least one million eight hundred thousand (1,800,000) dollars has not been obtained, and the regents are willing to waive said requirement, and the Trustees represent to the regents that the consent to the execution of said agreement has been secured from subscribers whose subscriptions aggregate one million six hundred thirty thousand five hundred (1,630,500) dollars; and

Whereas, it is provided in said agreement, in paragraph 4 on page 19 thereof, that "it is expressly agreed and understood that this agreement may be in any way modified and amended at any time by subsequent agreement in writing between the parties hereto, or their respective successors in interest."

Now, therefore, it is hereby mutually agreed by and between the parties hereto that the Regents do hereby waive the requirements that said agreement shall not become operative as to the Regents until the consent of subscribers whose subscriptions aggregate at least one million eight hundred thousand (1,800,000) dollars have been secured thereto, and the parties hereto do hereby consent and agree to the modification and amendment of said agreement as herein provided.

In Witness Whereof, the Regents has, by its officers, thereunto duly authorized, caused its corporate name to be hereto subscribed and its corporate seal to be hereto affixed, and the Trustees have hereunto subscribed their names, all on the day and year first above written.

THE REGENTS OF THE UNIVERSITY OF CALIFORNIA,

By ....
Governor of the State of California and ex-officio President of the Regents of the University of California.

(Seal)　　　　　By ....
Secretary of the Regents of the University of California.

WALTER S. MARTIN,
CHARLES TEMPLETON CROCKER,
JOHN D. McKEE,
E. S. HELLER,
CHAS. H. KENDRICK,
FRANK F. KILSBY,
MILTON H. ESBERG,
HERBERT FLEISHHACKER,
WM. H. CROCKER,
JOHN S. DRUM.

(Acknowledgment taken by W. W. Healey, Notary Public, the 30th day of August, 1922.)

THIS AGREEMENT, made this............day of June, 1928, by and between the Regents of the University of California, a California corporation, hereinafter called the "Regents", and Walter S. Martin, James B. McSheehy, John D. McKee, R. I. Bentley, Charles H. Kendrick, Frank F. Kilsby, Milton H. Esberg, Herbert Fleishhacker, William H. Crocker, and John S. Drum, trustees, hereinafter called "Trustees",

WITNESSETH:

Whereas, the parties hereto have executed a certain agreement, dated August 19, 1921, providing for the erection of a War Memorial, (a copy of which agreement is hereto attached); and

.Whereas, it is provided in said agreement, on page 19 thereof, that "It is expressly agreed and understood that this agreement may be in any way modified and amended at any time by subsequent agreement, in writing, between the parties hereto, or their respective successors in interest"; and

Whereas, it is provided in said agreement, on page 1, that "Whereas, a committee of citizens of San Francisco, represented by said trustee, has for such purposes conceived the plan of a War Memorial in the ownership of the University of California, and to that end has recommended the purchase of a block of land, consisting of six vara lots, in the City and County of San Francisco, State of California, described as follows: 'Bounded by Van Ness avenue, Franklin street, Hayes street and Grove street; saving and excepting therefrom approximately sixty-four hundred (6,400) square feet, conveyed to or to be conveyed to the City and County of San Francisco'; and

Whereas, said described block of land was so purchased by the trustees but was found unsuitable for the purposes of said War Memorial and was thereafter sold and conveyed; and

Whereas, the trustees have purchased the following described real property in the City and County of San Francisco, to be used in connection with said War Memorial: Bounded by Van Ness avenue, Franklin street, McAllister street and Grove street; excepting therefrom lots 23 and 29 in the block bounded by McAllister street, Fulton street, Van Ness avenue and Franklin street, and lots 11, 12, 13, 14, 15 and 16 in the block bounded by Fulton street, Grove street, Franklin street and Van Ness avenue, which said excepted lots were purchased by the City and County of San Francisco for said War Memorial.

Now, therefore, it is hereby agreed by and between the parties hereto that the sale and conveyance hereinbefore mentioned of the block of land described as follows: "Bounded by Van Ness avenue, Franklin street, Hayes street and Grove street, saving and excepting therefrom approximately sixty-four hundred (6400) square feet conveyed or to be conveyed to the City and County of San Francisco", and the purchase hereinbefore mentioned of the blocks of land described as follows: "Bounded by Van Ness avenue, Franklin street, McAllister street and Grove street", saving and excepting the lots hereinabove described as having been purchased by the City and County of San Francisco, be ratified and adopted, and the same are hereby ratified and adopted.

It is hereby further agreed by and between the parties hereto that the second Whereas on page 1 of said agreement, which now reads as follows:

"Whereas, a committee of citizens of San Francisco, represented by the said trustees, has for such purposes conceived the plan of a War Memorial in the ownership of the University of California, and to that end has recommended the purchase of a block of land, consisting of six vara lots, in the City and County of San Francisco, State of California, described as follows: 'Bounded by Van Ness avenue, Franklin street, Hayes street and Grove street, saving and excepting therefrom approximately sixty-four hundred (6400) square feet conveyed or to be conveyed to the City and County of San Francisco'; is hereby amended to read as follows:

"Whereas, a committee of citizens of San Francisco, represented by the said trustees, has for such purposes conceived the plan of a War Memorial, and to that end certain blocks of land have been purchased in the City and County of San Francisco, State of California, described as follows: 'Bounded by Van Ness avenue, Franklin street, McAllister street and Grove street, saving and excepting therefrom lots 23 and 29 in the block bounded by McAllister street, Fulton street, Van Ness avenue and Franklin street, and lots 11, 12, 13, 14, 15 and 16 in the block bounded by Fulton street, Grove street, Franklin street and

Van Ness avenue, which said excepted lots were purchased by the City and County of San Francisco for said War Memorial.'

And it is hereby further agreed that all reference throughout said agreement to the block of land whereon the War Memorial should be constructed, which, for convenience, has been referred to in said agreement as "said block of land", or "said lot of land", or "the real property above-described", or other phrases referring to the block of land whereon the War Memorial shall be built, shall be construed to refer to the blocks of land described as follows, to-wit: "Those two blocks of land bounded by Van Ness avenue, Franklin street, Grove street, and McAllister street, in the City and County of San Francisco, State of California"; and

Whereas, it is further provided in said agreement that in certain contingencies certain portions of said War Memorial "shall be under the exclusive direction and control of the Regents" and/or may be used "for any purpose the Regents may desire", and/or may be used "for any purpose the Regents may determine";

Now, therefore, said agreement is hereby amended so as to provide that in such contingencies the Regents may only use or control said portions of said War Memorial for such charitable or patriotic purposes as they may desire; and

Whereas, E. S. Heller, named in said agreement as a trustee, is now dead, and Charles Templeton Crocker, also named as a trustee, has resigned; and

Whereas, R. I. Bentley and James B. McSheehy were duly appointed, in pursuance of the terms of said agreement, to fill vacancies occasioned by the death and resignation of E. S. Heller and Charles Templeton Crocker, respectively; and

Whereas, in view of the interest of the City and County of San Francisco in said War Memorial, it has been found desirable to increase the Board of Trustees, and to add Jesse Colman and Franck Havenner as trustees; and

Whereas, it is provided in said agreement, on page 4: "That said trustees shall consist in the first instance of the following persons: Walter S. Martin and Charles Templeton Crocker, representing the San Francisco Art Association; John F. McKee and E. S. Heller, representing the Musical Association of San Francisco; Charles H. Kendrick and Frank F. Kilsby, representing the San Francisco posts of the American Legion; Milton H. Esberg, Herbert Fleishhacker, William H. Crocker and John S. Drum."

Now, Therefore, it is hereby agreed that said agreement be amended, and is hereby amended, to read as follows:

"That said trustees shall consist of the following persons: Walter S. Martin and James McSheehy, representing the San Francisco Art Association; John D. McKee and R. I. Bentley, representing the Musical Association of San Francisco; Charles H. Kendrick and Frank F. Kilsby, representing the San Francisco posts of the American Legion; Milton H. Esberg, Herbert Fleishhacker, William H. Crocker, John S. Drum, Jesse Colman and Franck Havenner."

In Witness Whereof, the Regents have caused this agreement to be subscribed by its proper officers, thereunto duly authorized, and its corporate seal to be hereunto affixed, and the trustees have hereunto set their hands, all on the day and year first above written.

THE REGENTS OF THE UNIVERSITY OF CALIFORNIA.

By.......................................

By.......................................

RECESS.

Whereupon the Board took a recess until tomorrow, February 26, 1930, at 2:30 p. m.

J. S. DUNNIGAN, Clerk.

WEDNESDAY, FEBRUARY 26, 1930, 2:30 P. M.

· In Board of Supervisors, San Francisco, Wednesday, February 26, 1930, 2:30 p. m.

CALLING THE ROLL.

The roll was called and the following Supervisors were noted present:

Ayes—Supervisors Andriano, Canepa, Gallagher, Havenner, Hayden, McGovern, McSheehy, Miles, Peyser, Roncovieri, Rossi, Shannon, Spaulding, Stanton, Suhr—15.

Absent—Supervisors Colman, Power, Toner—3.

Supervisor Colman on leave of absence.

Supervisor Toner noted present at 3:05 p. m.

Quorum present.

His Honor Mayor Rolph presiding.

APPROVAL OF JOURNAL.

The Journal of Proceedings of the previous meeting was laid over for approval to the next meeting.

Final Passage.

The following matters heretofore passed for printing were taken up and finally passed by the following vote:

Prescribing the Procedure Under Which the Board of Public Works Shall Have Charge, Superintendence and Control of the Municipally Owned Water System, and Providing for the Creation of a Water Department, Etc.

On recommendation of Public Utilities and Finance Committees.

Bill No. 8187, Ordinance No. 8691 (New Series), as follows:

Setting forth and prescribing the procedure and limitations under which the Board of Public Works shall have charge, superintendence and control of the supplying of water for domestic purposes from the municipally owned and operated water system; providing for the creation of a water department; providing for the organization of the same; prescribing its powers and duties and the manner in which these shall be carried out.

Be it ordained by the People of the City and County of San Francisco as follows:

Section 1. *Direction to Board of Public Works.* The Board of Public Works, in exercising the powers granted to it under Paragraph 8 of Section 9 of Chapter I of Article VI of the Charter, relative to the superintendence and control of the construction, maintenance and operation of the public water supply of San Francisco, shall do so subject to the provisions of this ordinance.

Section 2. *San Francisco Water Department and Purposes and Powers.* The Board of Public Works shall create a Department of Water Supply, for the purpose of supplying water to the inhabitants of the City and County of San Francisco, and to such other persons and places as may hereafter be supplied with water by the City and County of San Francisco, which said department shall be designated as "San Francisco Water Department."

The maintenance and operation of the Spring Valley Water Company system, whenever the same shall come into possession of the City, and also the water system owned by the City and County of San Francisco, commonly known as the County Line Water Works, shall be vested in said San Francisco Water Department under the jurisdiction of the Board of Public Works, until a Charter amendment is adopted and approved providing for the creation of a Public Utilities Commission.

All construction work done in or about the properties of said system, whether for extensions thereto or for additions and betterments thereto, shall be done under the direction and supervision of the City Engineer, and said City Engineer shall from time to time recommend to the Board of Public Works such work as he deems necessary to be performed, or materials or. equipment to be furnished, in and about the construction, operation or maintenance of said Water Department. And no extensions, additions or major improvements or replacements to the system shall be made except on the recommendation of the head of the department or the City Engineer.

The Board of Public Works shall establish all necessary rules and regulations for the conduct of the business of the department, and shall have full power and authority to collect any and all amounts due from any consumer for water furnished by said San Francisco Water Department, including all amounts due from any consumer for water furnished by the Spring Valley Water Company and remaining unpaid when the properties of the Spring Valley Water Company are taken over by the City and County of San Francisco, and the said Board of Public Works, or the head of the department, shall have full power and authority to discontinue the service of any consumer. who is delinquent to the Spring Valley Water Company or to the Water Department in the payment of amounts due for water furnished to or used by said consumer, and may by civil action in the name of the City and County enforce the collection of any and all amounts due for said water. And said Board may also provide, by rule or by order, for the requiring of security in such form and in such amount as may be recommended by the head of the department, for the supplying of water or rendering service to any person, and the furnishing of said security may be made a prerequisite to the furnishing of said water or service.

The Board of Public Works may, by resolution, authorize such banks in the City and County of San Francisco as it may elect to receive payment of water bills due or to be collected by the Water Department, and to issue receipts for the same in the name of the department, payment for such service to be at a rate not to exceed five cents per account per month, and provided that all amounts paid to any bank or banks selected for the purpose of receiving payment of said water bills shall be by said banks daily transmitted to the Water Department and by said Water Department paid daily into the Treasury of the City and County of San Francisco.

The Water Department shall observe all ordinances of the City and County of San Francisco and rules and regulations of the Department of Public Works relative to street openings, barricades, excavations, replacing of pavement, and similar matters, and relative to such matters shall apply for and receive permits and pay the necessary fees for said permits, and be subject to inspection and regulation, in the same manner and at the same rates as a private person or corporation would be if doing or performing any of said work or things.

All rules and regulations adopted or established by the Board of Public Works for the conduct of said San Francisco Water Department shall, within thirty days after the date of the adoption thereof, be printed, and shall be available for distribution to the public upon application therefor.

Section 3. *Organization, Employees.* The Board of Public Works shall appoint as head of the department, with appropriate title, a chief executive, who shall possess the necessary executive, administrative and technical qualifications to administer the affairs of the department, and who shall have sole executive control of said department, subject to rules and regulations prescribed by the Board.

Employees of the Spring Valley Water Company in the operating service thereof at the time the properties of said company are taken over by the City, and who have been continuously employed in said operating service for not less than one year immediately prior to the taking over of said properties, shall be continued in their positions and shall be considered to have been appointed to such positions under the provisions of Article XIII of the Charter, and shall be entitled to all civil service rights therein provided, and shall thereafter be considered employees of San Francisco Water Department. That if any of said employees in said operating department of said Spring Valley Water Company do not, at the time the properties of said company are taken over by the City, possess the residential qualifications required by Section 2 of Article XVI of the Charter, they shall be allowed a period of one year within which to acquire the same, and any employee not acquiring said residential qualifications within said period shall be dismissed from his or her employment. All positions in the Water Department shall be classified and graded by the Civil Service Commission as provided by the Charter, and vacancies in any of said positions shall be filled, and promotions in said department shall be made, as provided by Article XIII of the Charter and in accordance with the rules and regulations of the Civil Service Commission.

The Board shall employ such engineers, superintendents, accountants, inspectors and other assistants and employees as the department head may certify to be necessary. All of said appointments shall be made in accordance with the provisions of Article XIII of the Charter and the rules and regulations of the Civil Service Commission, provided that temporary appointments made under the provisions of Section 10 of said article shall, pursuant to the provisions of said article, remain in force for a period not exceeding sixty (60) days and only until regular appointments can be made under the provisions of said article, and said appointments shall be limited to a period of sixty (60) days and shall not be subject to renewal.

Section 4. *Salaries of Present Employees of Spring Valley Water Company.* The salaries, wages and compensation of all employees of the Spring Valley Water Company, whose employment shall continue in force with the San Francisco Water Department, as hereinbefore set forth, shall be subject to standardization as provided in Section 14, Chapter II, Article II, of the Charter. That, pending the standardization of said wages, salaries and compensation, there shall be paid to said employees at least the minimum entrance salary, wage or compensation paid for similar service in any other utility at present being operated by the Board of Public Works, and if there are any positions or places of employment in said Water Department which are not common with those in said other utilities, then the compensation to be paid to said employees occupying said last-mentioned positions shall be at least the minimum entrance wage or compensation paid for similar service in other departments of the city government, provided that such minimum entrance rate in the clerical service shall not be less than $150 per month. Provided, however, that the salary, wage or compensation of any employee whose employment is continued in the Water Department shall not be reduced below the salary, wage or compensation which said employee received from the Spring Valley Water Company, as evidenced by its January, 1930, payroll, unless the duties of said employee have been diminished on his coming into the employment of the Water Department, or said salary, wage or compensation exceeds the maximum amount paid by the city for like service.

Section 5. *Accounts, Reports and Adjustments.* The accounts of the Water Department shall be maintained in accordance with the forms and requirements of the State Railroad Commission for water companies of similar character, in so far as said forms and requirements shall be applicable to a municipally-owned water system, and said accounts shall also show all matters and things provided to be shown or set up by Subdivision 3, Section 16, Article XII, of the Charter.

A complete operating statement, showing all the operations, receipts and disbursements of the Water Department for the previous month, shall be filed each month by the head of the department with the Board of Public Works, and with the Mayor, and with the Board of Supervisors, and the same shall be open for inspection by the public in the office of said Board of Public Works. In addition to the matters hereinbefore set forth, said statements shall show the increase or de- crease in the number of employees of the Department since the end of the preceding month.

Commencing July 1, 1930, all amounts due to the Water Depart- ment for water used by or furnished to the other departments of the city, as well as all charges or rental for hydrant service, shall be carried on the books of the Water Department at the current rates provided for said water or for said service; and before the end of each fiscal year the Water Department shall determine the amount of taxes which would have been payable at the rate for the current year to the City and County upon the properties of the Water Department, if said properties were privately owned, and said amount of taxes shall offset any amounts which said accounts may show to be due for water or service from said municipal departments, in so far as the amount of said taxes and the amount due for water equal one another; and if the amount shown to be due for said water or for said service shall exceed the amount which would have been due for taxes if said property of said department was privately owned, the overplus shall be paid from the General or other funds of the City and County to the said Water Department, and charged against the various departments in accordance with the water and service furnished to each.

In making its annual budget each year, pursuant to the provisions of the Charter, the Board of Supervisors shall estimate the amount which shall become due from the other departments of the city government to the Water Department in the succeeding fiscal year, by reason of any difference between the amounts due for water and the amount of taxes which would be collected if the property of said Water Depart- ment was privately owned, and shall in said budget make provision for such difference.

During the remainder of the fiscal year 1929-1930, water shall be furnished without charge to those departments of the municipality to which appropriations have been made to defray the cost of water or hydrant service furnished to any of said departments, and water or service furnished to any other department shall be paid for at the current rates.

Commencing with the fiscal year 1930-1931, there shall be payable from the Water Department the sum of $250,000 per year as rental for the transbay Hetch Hetchy aqueduct, which said sum shall be pay- able into the 1910 Hetch Hetchy Bond Interest Fund, and for the remainder of the fiscal year the Water Department shall pay into said fund such portion of said sum of $250,000 as shall not have been paid as rental for said aqueduct for said year.

Section 6. *Budgets.* Not later than April 1, in the year 1930, and during the month of February in each succeeding year, the head of the Water Department shall transmit to the Board of Public Works a proposed budget for the next fiscal year, which said budget shall show in detail the estimated amounts of revenue from all sources to the department for said year, as well as an estimate of all amounts to be paid out by said department for all purposes, including payments to and from the various reserve and sinking funds maintained by said department. Such estimate, both of receipts and disbursements, shall be segregated and itemized so as to show the exact purpose of each item therein, and the amounts for salaries and wages shall be itemized so as to show the compensation paid to each class of employees, and the number of said employees in each class. Provided, however, that in estimating the cost of construction work, in the performance of which the employees will not be of a permanent character, the esti- mated number of said employees to be employed thereon need not be set forth. Said budget shall be prepared and transmitted to the Board of Public Works in quadruplicate.

The Board of Public Works shall consider said proposed budget, and upon approval of the same, shall transmit a copy thereof, with such changes, if any, indicated thereon, to the Mayor, and another to the Board of Supervisors, and another to the Auditor, which said copies shall be so transmitted not later than the first Monday in April of each year.

The Finance Committee of the Board of Supervisors shall submit said budget with its annual budget report to the Board, together with such recommendations as it deems proper, and said Board of Supervisors may reduce the estimate of expenditures or any item thereof, except proposed expenditures or appropriations as may be by law or by their nature fixed; and, subject to such changes or reductions, said Board shall approve and adopt said budget at the same time at which the annual budget provided by Charter must be adopted, and shall thereupon transmit the same to the Auditor.

The adoption of said budget by the Board of Supervisors shall be considered an appropriation of the various amounts therein contained for the purposes therein set forth, and thereafter said sums so appropriated may be expended by the Board of Public Works, in the manner provided by law, for the purposes for which they are appropriated, without further order of the Board of Supervisors.

Expenditures or commitments in excess of amounts set up in the budget adopted as hereinbefore provided, or for purposes not therein specified, may be made only by the filing and adopting at any time in the manner as specified hereinbefore for each annual budget and within the estimated revenues of the department, of a supplemental budget for such additional expenditures; provided, however, that in case of an emergency involving the protection of life or property, emergency expenditures may be ordered and authorized by the head of the department, in which case full report to the Board of Public Works, with copy thereof to the Board of Supervisors and the Auditor, shall be made at the earliest possible time, together with an estimate of the additional cost, if any, of further expenditures occasioned by the emergency.

Temporary Budget. As soon after March 1st, 1930, as is possible, the head of the Department shall file with the Board of Public Works a budget of the estimated revenues and proposed expenditures of the Water Department for the period from March 3rd to June 30th, 1930, and the Board of Public Works shall act upon the same without delay and transmit one copy thereof as approved to the Mayor, and two copies thereof to the Board of Supervisors. Said budget, in so far as possible, shall be prepared in accordance with the provisions hereinbefore set forth relating to annual budgets in so far as said provisions may be applicable, provided that said budget shall show the number, title and. rate of compensation of the employees of the Spring Valley Water Company immediately prior to the date on which the properties of said Company were taken over by the City, as well as the number, civil service title and proposed rates of compensation of said employees while in the employ of the Water Department. Upon receipt of said budget the Board of Supervisors shall act upon the same within ten days after receipt of same, and when the said budget is approved by said Board of Supervisors one copy of the same shall be transmitted to the Auditor with the approval of the Board attached thereto, and when so received by said Auditor the same shall be his authority for auditing any demands against the Water Department as set forth or included in said budget; and if said budget should not be received by said Auditor in due time to enable him to audit the demands of the employees of said Water Department as the same become due, the said Auditor may audit and the Treasurer pay the demands of said employees when they are approved by the head of the Water Department, the Board of Public Works, and the Civil

Service Commission, as being in conformity with the provisions of Section 4 of this ordinance, and appropriation in an amount sufficient to pay said demands as so approved is hereby made from the revenues of said Water Department as the said revenues accrue.

Section 7. *Operating Expenses and Reserves.* The receipts from operation of the San Francisco Water Department shall be paid daily into the City Treasury and maintained in a special fund set aside therefor, which shall be designated "The Water Revenue Fund," and appropriations may from time to time be made by the Board of Supervisors from said receipts for the purposes in this section set forth and in accordance with budgets to be made as hereinbefore provided and as otherwise provided in this ordinance.

1. For the payment of the operating expenses of the water supply system, including expenditures or appropriations to reserves, pension charges, compensation insurance, injuries, damages, Hetch Hetchy aqueduct rental and taxes that may be assessed against property outside of San Francisco belonging to the City and under the control of the Water Department.

2. For repairs and reconstruction, and in order to provide properly for repairs and reconstruction due to depreciation, there shall be created and established a depreciation reserve which shall be credited monthly with an amount equal to one-twelfth the annual depreciation requirements determined as elsewhere herein provided.

3. For the payment of interest and sinking fund on the bonds issued for the acquisition of the Spring Valley Water system, and for this purpose there shall be set aside monthly and transferred to the Spring Valley bond interest and redemption funds sums sufficient in the aggregate to meet, at the proper time, all interest and redemption charges against said utility as the same fall due.

4. For extensions, improvements and replacements, and in order to properly finance the necessary extensions, improvements and replacements out of earnings, there shall be established a Water Extension Reserve Fund, into which shall be paid monthly the sums necessary to provide for such extensions, improvements and replacements as may have been determined upon in a program adopted as elsewhere herein provided.

5. For the Charter Reserve Fund.

The Depreciation Reserve Fund shall be used only to cover costs of replacements due to a realized depreciation. The Board of Public Works shall cause an appraisal to be made by the City Engineer of the several classes of property involved in the Water System as to life and the amount of accrued depreciation, and determine the amount of the reasonable annual depreciation requirements necessary in order to provide properly for repairs or reconstruction due to realized physical and functional depreciation; provided, however, that at least every five years the Board shall cause a reappraisal to be made of the depreciation reserves, replacement expenditures therefrom, and probable useful life of each of the several kinds of property, and on the basis of such reappraisal shall redetermine the amount of the reasonable annual depreciation requirements. Provided, that the amount to be set aside each year into said depreciation fund shall be subject to budget by the Board of Supervisors. Until such time as the Board of Public Works has determined the reasonable annual depreciation requirements necessary by appraisal as above provided for, there shall be transferred to the Depreciation Reserve Fund from the receipts from operation of the Water Department at the end of each month, the sum of $5.000.

The Water Extension Reserve Fund shall be used only to cover costs of the construction of extensions, additions and betterments to the water system. The Board of Public Works upon the recommendation of the head of the Water Department shall from time to time establish a program of the necessary extensions, additions and betterments required in a period not extending over five years, and upon the approval of said program or any amendments thereto by the Board of Supervisors in any annual or supplemental budget, there shall be deposited monthly to the credit of the Extension Reserve one-twelfth of the annual contribution determined as necessary to complete the several elements of the program within the time required, provided, that for the first five years of operation the amount to be appropriated to the depreciation fund and the Water Extension Reserve Fund, considered together, shall be not less than $564,000 per year.

There shall be paid into the Charter Reserve Fund provided for in Subdivision 5, Section 7 of this ordinance all moneys not otherwise appropriated or used in conformity with the provisions of this ordinance, and the Board of Supervisors may from time to time make appropriations from said fund for any of the purposes provided for in this ordinance when respective funds herein provided for any of the specific purposes herein set forth are exhausted or insufficient to meet the demands upon them. Whenever the said Charter Reserve Fund shall exceed one-half of the payment for operating expenses in the preceding year, the Board of Supervisors may appropriate such excess to the General Fund of the City.

At any time that there is a surplus on deposit in the City Treasury in any of the several funds herein provided for in an amount greater than is necessary for the immediate needs of the Water Department, the said department, through the Board of Public Works, shall notify the Treasurer, who shall make arrangements as provided by law for the proper investment or deposit of such funds, the interest accruing therefrom to be credited to the benefit of and to be applied to the fund from which invested.

Section 8. *Water Rates.* No water shall be furnished to any consumer, except as hereinbefore set forth, except at the current rates therefor fixed as in this section provided. The water rates in effect under the Spring Valley Water Company's management at the time of the City's acquisition of the system shall remain in effect for a period of at least one year. Thereafter, changes in the water rates shall only be made by the Board of Public Works upon the written recommendation of the head of the department and the approval of the Board of Supervisors.

No rates shall be established which in the aggregate will produce a revenue less than necessary to safely cover all operating expenses and other expenses provided for in Section 6 hereof, and provide for and maintain the several reserves herein provided for and also to maintain the Charter reserve at a sum equal to one-half of the operating expenses for the preceding year.

When any change in rates is contemplated, the head of the department shall submit to the Board of Public Works a financial report, in support of the proposed change, and the Board of Public Works shall fix a date for hearing the matter of said change in rates and cause to be published in the official newspaper of the City and County notice of said hearing at least ten days prior to the date thereof, specifying in said notice the time and place of said hearing. At said hearing any person, on behalf of himself or others interested, may be heard, or present in writing his views, after which the Board shall fix the rates and submit them to the Board of Supervisors, who shall within thirty days, by ordinance, approve or disapprove the same. Failure of the Board of Supervisors to act within the thirty days shall be construed as approval of the recommended rates. In fixing rates for water service, the same may be fixed at varying scales for different classes of service or consumers.

Section 9. *Service by Other Departments.* Services rendered by any other department of the City and County to the Water Department, upon request of the Water Department, shall be paid for by the Water Department at cost out of its revenues.

Section 10. *City Attorney.* The City Attorney shall be the legal adviser of the Department and shall render such legal services as the Board of Public Works or the head of the Department may deem necessary, and shall prosecute and defend all actions or proceedings affecting or involving the Water Department or any of its properties. He shall when necessary, upon the request of the Board of Public Works, appoint and detail one or more attorneys to perform the duties herein specified, and the compensation of said attorneys so detailed shall be approved by the Board of Public Works and fixed by the Board of Supervisors, and shall be paid from the revenues of the Water Department as an operating expense thereof.

Section 11. *Bonds of Employees.* The Board of Public Works may require a bond of indemnity from any of the employees of the Water Department, conditioned for the faithful performance of the duties of said employee or employees, and for the purpose of obtaining said bonds the said Board of Public Works may contract with any surety company authorized to write said bonds, to furnish the same, either for individual employees or groups thereof, and the cost of the same shall be charged as an operating expense of said Water Department.

Section 12. *Payment of Salaries and Wages.* Payrolls for all employees of the Water Department shall be segregated and made up according to the assembly or distribution points for the various employments, as determined by the head of the department, and each of said payrolls shall be approved as required by law and transmitted to the Auditor. Upon the approval of the items on said payroll or payrolls the Auditor shall issue his separate demand upon the Treasurer for each of the items thereon in the form provided for the payment of salaries in other departments of the city, and the same, with the respective payrolls for which said demands are issued, shall be delivered to such person as the head of the department shall, in writing filed with the Auditor, authorize to receive the same, and upon the delivery of the same said person shall receipt to said Auditor for said payrolls and said demands. The head of the department shall thereupon cause said demands to be delivered to the respective payees named therein at, or as near as possible to, the places of employment of said employees.

Section 13. *Revolving Fund.* For the purpose of paying petty expenses of the Water Department, and for making such other payments as cannot be conveniently paid by demands drawn upon the Treasurer and approved by the Auditor, the Water Department shall maintain in such bank or banks as may be designated by the Board of Public Works, a fund of $20,000, from which fund said petty expenses and other payments that cannot be conveniently paid by demands drawn upon the Treasurer shall be paid by check drawn by the head of the department or by such other persons in the employ of said department as the head of said department may authorize. The head of the department shall, from time to time, and at least once in each month, transmit to the Auditor a demand in favor of said fund for all amounts disbursed from it, to which demand shall be attached receipts for all payments so made, which said receipts shall show the name of the person receiving any payment from said fund, as well as the purpose for which said payment was made, and shall be signed by the party receiving said payment. When said demand is approved by the Auditor and paid by the Treasurer, it shall be delivered to the head of the Water Department and deposited to the credit of said fund. The Board of Supervisors shall appropriate the said sum of $20,000 for such fund, and may, from time to time, make such additional appropriations thereto from the revenues of said department as said Board shall deem proper.

Section 14. *Purchase of Materials, Supplies and Equipment.* Purchases of materials, supplies and equipment required by Water Department operations shall be made in accordance with the provisions of Chapter IV, Article II, and Section 6, Chapter I, Article III, of the Charter, and of Ordinance 5880 (New Series); provided, however, that specifications may be prepared under the direction of the head of the Water Department for all equipment required by the department, or for materials or supplies peculiar to said department operations and not in common use in other departments of the City and County, and the head of the department may designate the particular brand, kind or make of any equipment which may be necessary in the conduct of said department.

Section 15. *Constitutionality.* If any section, subsection, subdivision or provision of this ordinance is for any reason held to be unconstitutional, such decision shall not affect the validity of the remaining portions of this ordinance, the Board of Supervisors hereby declaring that it would have passed this ordinance and each section, subsection, subdivision, provision, sentence, clause and phrase thereof irrespective of the fact that any one or more sections, subsections, subdivisions, provisions, sentences, clauses or phrases hereof are declared unconstitutional.

Section 16. This ordinance shall become effective immediately upon its passage.

Ayes—Supervisors Andriano, Canepa, Havenner, Hayden, McGovern, McSheehy, Miles, Peyser, Roncovieri, Rossi, Shannon, Spaulding, Stanton, Suhr—14.

Absent—Supervisors Colman, Gallagher, Power, Toner—4.

Accepting Offer of Spring Valley Water Company to Sell Its Properties, Appropriating Moneys for the Payment Therefor and Empowering the Mayor and Clerk of the Board of Supervisors to Execute and Deliver Collateral and Supplemental Agreements Incident Thereto.

Resolution No. ————— (New Series), as follows:

Whereas, the electors of the City and County of San Francisco did heretofore vote and authorize a bonded indebtedness of $41,000,000 for the purpose of acquiring the operative properties, rights, equipment and distribution system of the Spring Valley Water Company, which are hereafter in this resolution referred to as the "properties" of said Water Company, and which said properties are more particularly described in a certain offer under date of March 2, 1928, made by said Water Company to the Board of Supervisors of the City and County of San Francisco, to sell the same to said City and County;

And Whereas, it is now the intention of said City and County to purchase said properties pursuant to the terms and upon the conditions set forth in said offer;

And Whereas, it is impossible to determine the exact amount of money to be paid for said properties according to the terms of said offer until a full accounting is had between the City and County and the Water Company, as of the date on which said properties are actually taken over by said City and County, and the total cost of additions and betterments made to said properties subsequent to December 31, 1929, and credits to the amortization fund of said properties, have all been computed;

And Whereas, it is the intention of the City and County to take over said properties as of the 3d day of March, 1930, and prior to noon on said day, and it is admitted that there will be due to said Water Company on said day for said properties the sum of $39,962,606.51, together with such additional amounts as may be shown by said accounting, which said additional amounts are to be paid as hereinafter set forth; now, therefore, be it

Resolved, That the City and County accept the offer of March 2, 1928, of said Water Company to sell to said City and County the said properties described therein, and does hereby agree to purchase and take over the same on the 3d day of March, 1930, and before noon of said day, and to pay therefor the amount which will be due for said properties as of said date and time based on the terms and conditions of said offer, and to pay for said properties as follows: $39,962,606.51 on said last mentioned date upon the delivery of a good and sufficient deed made, executed and delivered by the Water Company to the City and County, conveying said properties to said City and County, and the balance of said purchase price as soon thereafter as the exact amount thereof can be determined after a full accounting of all reciprocal demands and amounts can be had between the City and County and the Water Company; and be it

Further Resolved, That for the purpose of meeting and paying such additional amount as may hereafter be found due to the Water Company for said properties, that the City shall deposit, not later than noon on the 3d day of March, 1930, with Wells Fargo Bank and Union Trust Company, the sum of $75,000, which said sum shall be disbursed in accordance with the terms and conditions of a certain collateral or supplemental agreement between the City and County and the Water Company, which said agreement shall bear date of March 3, 1930, and embody and contain all the terms and conditions relative to the payment of the total purchase price for said properties, and all of the terms and conditions which shall govern the final accounting between the City and County and the Water Company, and the manner in which said total purchase price shall be determined, and which said collateral or supplemental agreement shall further provide for the settlement, adjustment and agreement as to all matters and things which may be properly, necessarily or incidentally settled and adjusted between the City and County and the Water Company relative to the taking over of said properties, and the continuation of the business of the Company without interruption; and be it

Further Resolved, That the Mayor of the City and County and the Clerk of the Board of Supervisors be and they are hereby authorized and empowered to execute and deliver, for and on behalf of the City and County, the aforesaid collateral or supplemental agreement, in, or substantially in, the form submitted to this Board by the City Attorney, and to agree, on behalf of the City and County, with the Water Company upon all of its terms and conditions; and be it

Further Resolved, That said collateral agreement above mentioned, and any and all amounts of money to be paid thereunder and any and all checks, drafts, warrants or demands payable to Spring Valley Water Company for said properties may be deposited with Union Securities Corporation in escrow for the purpose of consummating the purchase of said properties from said Water Company, and that the City Attorney and the City Engineer be, and they are hereby, given full power and authority to agree upon all of the terms and conditions of said escrow, for and on behalf of the City and County, and to execute said escrow and all agreements relative thereto for and on behalf of said City and County; and be it

Further Resolved, That the Mayor and the Clerk of the Board of Supervisors be and they are hereby given full power and authority to enter into and execute, for and on behalf of the City and County, such additional or supplemental agreements, escrows and documents, and to do such other and further things as may be necessary to fully consummate the purchase of said properties pursuant to the said offer of March 2, 1928, of said Water Company; and be it

Further Resolved, That there be and there is hereby appropriated from the moneys realized from the proceeds of the sale of the bonds of the City and County, known as "Spring Valley Bonds," the sum of $40,037,606.51, for the purpose of consummating the purchase of said above-mentioned properties from said Water Company, of which said sum $39,962.606.51 shall be payable to the Spring Valley Water Company upon the delivery of its deed for said properties to the City, and the remainder of said sum, to-wit, the sum of $75,000, shall be payable to Wells Fargo Bank and Union Trust Company for the purpose of meeting and paying such additional amounts as may be due to said Water Company in accordance with adjustments to be made as of March 3, 1930, as may be provided for in said collateral agreement hereinbefore mentioned. And the Board of Supervisors does hereby authorize the payment of said sum of $39,962,606.51 to the Spring Valley Water Company, and the payment of said sum of $75,000 to Wells Fargo Bank and Union Trust Company for the respective purposes hereinbefore set forth.

Ayes—Supervisors Andriano, Canepa, Havenner, Hayden, McGovern, McSheehy, Miles, Peyser, Roncovieri, Rossi, Shannon, Spaulding, Stanton, Suhr—14.

Absent—Supervisors Colman, Gallagher, Power, Toner—4.

In re Adoption of Spring Valley Ordinance.

In connection with the passage of the foregoing matters the following discussion was had:

Mayor James Rolph, Jr., acted as Chairman of the meeting.

(Roll Call.)

THE MAYOR: We are about to call the roll on the final act which will acquire by title today the properties of the Spring Valley Water Company, and for that purpose we met at special session at half past two. If there are any members outside the Sergeant-at-Arms will kindly advise them that we are ready to proceed because I am sure every member of the Board would like to have his name recorded upon the final legislation which will be enacted. Is there any other member outside?

(The Clerk reads the ordinance.)

THE MAYOR: The question is on final passage.

THE CLERK: (Roll call.)

SUPERVISOR ANDRIANO: Aye.

SUPERVISOR CANEPA: Aye.

SUPERVISOR COLMAN: Absent.

SUPERVISOR GALLAGHER: Absent.

SUPERVISOR HAVENNER: Aye.

SUPERVISOR HAYDEN: Aye.

SUPERVISOR McGOVERN: Aye.

SUPERVISOR McSHEEHY: Aye.

SUPERVISOR MILES: Aye.

SUPERVISOR PEYSER: Absent.

SUPERVISOR POWER: Absent.

SUPERVISOR RONCOVIERI: Aye.

THE MAYOR: Mr. Peyser, we are in the midst of a roll call for the purpose of adopting an ordinance for the operation of those Spring Valley Water Company properties when we take them over.

SUPERVISOR PEYSER: Aye.

SUPERVISOR ROSSI: Aye.

SUPERVISOR SHANNON: Aye.

SUPERVISOR SPAULDING: Aye.

SUPERVISOR STANTON: Aye.

SUPERVISOR SUHR: Aye.

SUPERVISOR TONER: Absent.

THE CLERK: Fourteen ayes, four absent.

THE MAYOR: The ayes have it and it is adopted.

THE CLERK: Final passage of resolution accepting offer of Spring Valley Water Company to sell its properties and appropriating the moneys therefor.

THE CLERK: (Roll Call.)

SUPERVISOR ANDRIANO: Aye.

SUPERVISOR CANEPA: Aye.

SUPERVISOR COLMAN: Absent.

SUPERVISOR GALLAGHER: Absent.

SUPERVISOR HAVENNER: Aye.

SUPERVISOR HAYDEN: Aye.
SUPERVISOR McGOVERN: Aye.
SUPERVISOR McSHEEHY: Aye.
SUPERVISOR MILES: Aye.
SUPERVISOR PEYSER: Aye.
SUPERVISOR POWER: Absent.
SUPERVISOR RONCOVIERI: Aye.
SUPERVISOR ROSSI: Aye.
SUPERVISOR SHANNON: Aye.
SUPERVISOR SPAULDING: Aye.
SUPERVISOR STANTON: Aye.
SUPERVISOR SUHR: Aye.
SUPERVISOR TONER: Absent.
THE CLERK: Fourteen ayes, four absent.
THE MAYOR: The ayes have it and it is so ordered.
(Bringing down the gavel.)
SUPERVISOR HAYDEN: Mr. Chairman——
SUPERVISOR HAVENNER (interrupting): Will the Supervisor yield just before we dispose of the Spring Valley matter?
SUPERVISOR HAYDEN: That is what I am going to speak on.
SUPERVISOR HAVENNER: I wanted to ask the City Attorney a question through the Chair. Mr. O'Toole, are these all of the legislative acts that are essential today to the taking over of the Spring Valley Water Company properties by the City?
CITY ATTORNEY O'TOOLE: Yes, the resolution for recording the deed is not a "passed to print" resolution, and was finally passed in your meeting of a week ago Monday. These two will enable us to take over the properties, record the deed and pay the money and acquire the properties on Monday.
SUPERVISOR HAYDEN: Mr. Chairman.
THE MAYOR: Mr. Hayden.
SUPERVISOR HAYDEN: Mr. Mayor and members of the Board of Supervisors, I think at this time, now that this transaction is completed, the taking over of the Spring Valley Water Company properties, and the Board has appropriated over $40,000,000 for the purchase of the same, that a word of compliment should be extended to the various departments who cooperated with the Finance Committee and the Public Utilities Committee in making possible the preparation of this operative ordinance. We have to first consider, Mr. Mayor, that the legal advice that was necessary in this matter naturally came from the City Attorney's office, headed by Mr. John J. O'Toole, assisted by Mr. Dion Holm and Mr. John Dailey. The statistical information, the financial set-up, and all that data that was available by way of information to the Joint Committee was prepared by Mr. Randall Ellis. The Board of Works sat in and cooperated and gave their advice to a great extent. The Engineer's office, Mr. O'Shaughnessy and Mr. Eckart in particular, who sat through all the hearings that we went through during a period of nearly thirty days continuously. And through that advice, Mr. Mayor and members of the Board, this operative ordinance and this final action of the Board appropriating this money was made possible. I think, Mr. Mayor and members of the Board, that this operative ordinance is a masterpiece of legislation, and I want to add, before I say anything further, the Bureau of Governmental Research, with Mr. Nanry's cooperation, was also a very valuable aid in the preparation of this ordinance, and I feel that the City of San Francisco is making history taking over this great utility, the utility of water, so essential to the life of any community, and, in addition to that, as Supervisor Rossi suggests, we had the cooperation of the San Francisco Labor Council and the Building Trades Council, those gentlemen gave us advice that was very helpful in ironing out our difficulties in the way of wages and the duties of the employees of the Spring Valley Water Company. As I say, Mr. Mayor, this is an historical moment, the passing of this

resolution and the appropriation of this money, and the Joint Committee of Public Utilities and Finance, and while I am expressing my own individual sentiments, I know I have the cooperation of the other members, that we should not allow this opportunity to go by without writing into the records our appreciation of this most valuable assistance given to us by way of cooperation by the gentlemen that I have named in the various departments of engineering, the law and the other departments necessary to make this legislation possible. Indeed, Mr. Mayor, after a long experience on this Board of Supervisors, I am really very happy and very proud to be a party to this occasion, and you, Mr. Mayor, after your long experience, I think will feel as I do, that you at last have realized the acquisition of a wonderful utility, one of which the City of San Francisco will be justly proud, and one which will redound to the prosperity of the community, industrially, commercially and every other way. I just want to emphasize this, Mr. Mayor, because that is my sentiment and I know it is the sentiment of the Joint Committee and this Board of Supervisors and I want to make that part of the record.

SUPERVISOR HAVENNER: Mr. Mayor, on behalf of the Public Utilities Committee I am very glad indeed to second the statement made by Supervisor Hayden, and to express the appreciation of that committee for the extremely painstaking work that has been done by all of the officials mentioned, in particular by Mr. O'Toole and his assistants, Mr. Holm and Mr. Ellis and Mr. Dailey, and Mr. Eckart of the Engineer's office.

THE MAYOR: Gentlemen of the Board, I wish to report to you that I have just signed the ordinances, the authority to pay the money and the payment of the money of $40,037,606.51 for the acquiring by the City of the properties of the Spring Valley Water Company, and the deed from the Company of the properties to the City and County of San Francisco will be vested in the City on the 3rd instant. I feel that this is a very great moment in the life of a progressive city. Ever since the Spring Valley Water Company started its system in a little spring up here on a hill and its properties at Mountain Lake, the citizens of San Francisco have been attempting to acquire these properties and many efforts have been attempted and many efforts lost in the presentation of the cause to the people of this City. The price we have paid today is small compared to the price the properties will be worth in the future because, as every day passes, as every soul comes into San Francisco, the properties increase in value. The history of the City is replete with political efforts to use those properties as the football of politics. Supervisors have been elected in the past, in the old ward system days, where they were pledged to fix the water rates in favor of Spring Valley, and to fix the gas rates in favor of the Pacific Gas & Electric Company, or its predecessor, the San Francisco Gas Company. And now, today, by your action you have removed Spring Valley from private interests and private control into public interests and to public control. In my platform of 1911 you will find a strong plank therein that we should acquire the properties of the Spring Valley Water Company at the earliest possible date. Nineteen years later we have acquired the properties by constant and persistent effort exerted to acquire them. I join in the remarks made by Mr. Hayden and seconded by Mr. Havenner, in giving thanks to all who have contributed through all these years, to all those forward-looking citizens of San Francisco who voted "yes" to acquire those properties, and now, particularly, to the members of the Board and the committees of the Board who have been so diligent, the Public Utilities Committee and the Finance Committee, the Joint Committee, and the Public Welfare Committee and every committee of the Board, the Judiciary Committee, and I pay special thanks to the City Attorney's office, Mr. John J. O'Toole and his assistants, Mr. Dion Holm, and I also pay special thanks to Mr. Ellis, who has had the burden all these years of keeping account of expenditures and arriving at the figure that we paid today. I pay particular thanks to the Treasurer, Duncan Matheson, for the part he has played in making it possible and making it easy for us to pay out this money, lawfully and rightly, so that this great sum will be paid. And I take particular pleasure in saying that the Board of Public Works has recognized the recommendation which I made to them, that Nelson Eckart be appointed to take full charge as General Manager of the properties which we take hold of today. Nelson Eckart has been in the Engineer's office as First Assistant for the nineteen years I have been Mayor. He has grown up in the Department, he has been Chief Assistant in all the big projects which we have had, and there is no one more capable nor more able nor who will go forward with greater confidence that the Board of Supervisors and the Board of Public Works are behind him than does this man, Nelson Eckart, who takes charge today of the properties for which we are paying. You have entrusted, by law, the properties to the Board of Public Works. You need have no fear about the Board of Public Works carrying out the terms and conditions of the ordinance which we passed today. And on the whole, it is a day of rejoicing, it is a day of gratification. And whosoever I have omitted from my expression of thanks for the people of this City, I add that vote of thanks on behalf of the people of the City to the people who have contributed to this success. And I join in thanking the Press for their ever alertness to this project, for their faithfulness to it, and for the great help that it has been to the City of San Francisco in putting the project over without charging the City any publicity fees. On the whole, a day of rejoicing has come in the acquisition and ownership of the properties of the Spring Valley Water Company.

SUPERVISOR HAYDEN: Just to complete the Mayor's compliments, it would be well if you should add in your compliments the name of Mr. Naury, representing the San Francisco Bureau of Governmental Research.

THE MAYOR: I add Mr. Naury's name and I ask the stenographic reporter to include it in the remarks that I have made.

SUPERVISOR TONER: I would like to be recorded as voting "yes" on this resolution, please.

THE MAYOR: If the Board has no objection to changing its rules, I would suggest that Doctor Toner's name be permitted to be recorded "yes".

THE CLERK: I may suggest, respectfully, that we can put a minute in the Journal. I have finished the record and you have signed it and it has gone on. We can put a minute in the Journal that, if Doctor Toner had been present, he would have voted "aye".

SUPERVISOR TONER: That is sufficient. Thank you, Mr. Mayor.

SUPERVISOR ROSSI: Mr. Mayor, and members of the Board: I, too, want to join with the members who have preceded me in expressing my sincere thanks and appreciation to our City Attorney, Mr. John J. O'Toole, and his assistants. I won't mention all those who took part in the preparation of the ordinance which we adopted finally here today, but the work that was accomplished through the City Attorney's office, together with the other individuals mentioned, is something that San Francisco can well be proud of. This has been a great task, and as important a document as this is, it has passed the Board in the shortest time than any other matter of such importance, to my way of thinking, in many a day. It means much in the history of San Francisco in the taking over of the Spring Valley Water Company properties, and I want to assure you, Mr. Mayor, as Chairman of the Finance Committee, that it is with a great deal of pride today that I signed a demand, together with other members of the Finance Committee, which would authorize the Treasurer to make the final payment when this property is taken over. I am sure that with the care that this ordinance was prepared, looking after every detail, that that project will be conducted along business lines and will be the success which every member of this Board hopes for it to be. And at this time, too, I want to say that under the able management of Mr. Nelson Eckart I am sure that it will be a success and San Francisco is to be congratulated.

SUPERVISOR HAVENNER: Mr. Mayor, I think that this record would be in one essential incomplete if the Board did not at this time express its thanks and gratitude to the committee of citizens who managed the successful Spring Valley Water Company Bond Campaign. Those men and women who finally were participants in the successful campaign to secure the ratification by the people of San Francisco of the Spring Valley Water Company purchase did an exceptional piece of work. It has been my experience to go through many political campaigns. I want to say that that particular campaign was in my judgment the most vigorous, the most intelligent and the most ably managed that I have seen, and a large number of our citizens devoted their time, both in the headquarters and on the platform, in presenting the issue to the people, and had they not done so, so ably, so vigorously, and so sincerely, we would not today be celebrating the taking over of this property. I move that the vote of thanks of this Board be extended to the Citizens' Committee who managed that campaign. I think also at this time we should repay the tribute that has been paid to the Bank of Italy, and its distinguished head, Mr. Giannini, for the part that they played in the financial transaction that makes this ratification today possible. I had the honor to suggest to Mr. Giannini the plan which was originally suggested to the City Attorney and the previous Finance Committee by Mr. Nelson Eckart, the plan whereby it might be possible to market our bonds without violation of the Charter, at a time when the bond market was below par and the bonds could not command a ready sale in the market at their par value, as required by the Charter. This was merely a year ago now. Mr. Giannini immediately expressed a great deal of interest in the plan, and said that he was hopeful that the market might improve in the near future to a point where it would be possible to swing the deal on the terms proposed, in the financial markets, and that he would instruct his organization to keep a strict watch on the condition of the bond market and to do everything possible to put this deal over. He kept his word, sent for the members of the Finance Committee and members of the Engineering Department and the City Attorney's office about a month before last Christmas, and said that he believed that the deal could be then put over, and threw the whole cooperation of his great organization behind this plan. To him is due again the thanks of this Board for a public spirited cooperation that enabled us to take over the properties at a time when they could not have been sold in the open market.

SUPERVISOR HAYDEN: Mr. Chairman, might I ask the Supervisor the name of the Chairman of that Citizens' Committee on the Spring Valley Bond Campaign?

SUPERVISOR HAVENNER: It was Senator Phelan.

SUPERVISOR SHANNON: Mr. Mayor, when Mr. Havenner arose I had the same thought in mind, as I was the Chairman of the Public Utilities Committee that offered to the Board the ordinance for the bonds. The same thought was in my mind, that full credit should be given to this Committee that handled the campaign. And, as Mr. Havenner has so ably covered it, I will let the remarks that he has made about the work and assistance of the Committee pass. But I do want to pay particular tribute to the gentleman who has just taken his seat for the work he did during that campaign. While all of the members of this Board were active in their desire to see those bonds pass, no member of the Board devoted as much time or gave as much, during the campaign, of his energy and his ability as Mr. Havenner, at all times. And at all times he was in touch with his Citizens' Committee and I feel that as a result of the activity of Mr. Havenner during that campaign, special mention should be made in the record so that his name will be included with those that helped to make this day possible.

SUPERVISOR HAYDEN: Second that motion.

SUPERVISOR HAVENNER: Thank you.

THE MAYOR: I add my meed of praise to all those whose names have just been mentioned, particularly to Mr. Havenner, and particularly again, to Mr. A. P. Giannini. because the records are full of grateful appreciation of what he did. And I have appointed, by resolution of the Board, introduced by Supervisor Gallagher, who asked that while he was the mover of the resolution, that Supervisor Havenner be made the Chairman, the Celebration Committee that will hold the celebration at the taking over of these properties at some place on Sunday, March 9th. And if I have not already, or my office has not already added every name on that committee. because I know Mr. Havenner has been over to my office and my secretaries have been working with him—if there is a single name that is not included in the list that I have already appointed, I want you. Mr. Havenner, to see that they are included. On Friday night of this week we are all to be the guests of the officials of the Spring Valley Water Company at a farewell dinner or dance and card party or supper at 11:30, at the Native Sons' Hall. It is a farewell party, breaking up of the connections of all of the employees of the Spring Valley Water Company, and a farewell to them all. I would respectfully suggest to the Chairman of the Committee that I have appointed that on the night of March 9 we give a welcome party in the Auditorium. with our Municipal Band, with all of the 454 employees of the Spring Valley, and with the officials of Spring Valley, welcoming them into the fold of the City and County of San Francisco—on Sunday night, the night before. I mean on Sunday night, not Saturday—that we give a return party to welcome into our fold all of the employees of Spring Valley. Now, there are three letters which I have written, at the request of Mr. Eastman, and approved by Mr. Matt. Sullivan. who was in my office the day that Mr. Eastman called. one was assuring the employees of the Spring Valley Water Company that they would come into the employ of the City and would be welcomed and would be taken into the fold and received, and that I knew that their services would be as faithful to the City as they had been to the Spring Valley Water Company, and that I was sure they would give the same service to us as to the Spring Valley Water Company. I have also written a letter to Mrs. William Bourne, the wife of the president of the company. Mr. Bourne is a hopeless paralytic cripple, in a wheel-chair, on the second floor in his home in San Mateo county, and will probably never get downstairs again. Mr. and Mrs. Bourne have enjoyed a ride. once in a great while. over the properties of the Spring Valley Water Company, and, at the suggestion of Mr. Eastman. I wrote a letter to Mrs. Bourne telling her that the City would acquire the properties that they have loved all these years. and that, remembering the many happy times they had together, the City wishes to give to them the same privilege of enjoying a ride over the properties which have now passed into the hands of the City. Likewise a letter to Mr. W. B. Lawrence. former superintendent of those properties and his father before him—all with the approval of Mr. Eastman. Matt I. Sullivan and several others that I have spoken to in connection with the matter. I will give you those letters and they will be on file. if Mr. Smith has not already sent them over here. And I hope that they will meet with the approval of the Board. Probably they will never ride over the properties again, because Mrs. Bourne is very, very ill and probably Mr. Bourne will never get out. but it is a courtesy from the City which Mr. Eastman said they would appreciate at this time of the transfer of their properties to the City.

SUPERVISOR ANDRIANO: Is the matter of Spring Valley finished?

THE MAYOR: Except to show you a deed. which will be signed

by the officials of the Spring Valley Water Company, duly attested by the City Attorney and the attorney for the Spring Valley Water Company, and which will be signed within a day or two so that they will become the properties of the City on the 3rd.

SUPERVISOR ANDRIANO: Is the matter on the confirmation of the trustees appointed by you, Mr. Mayor, properly before us at this time?

THE MAYOR: We took a recess last night for that purpose.

SUPERVISOR POWER: Mr. Mayor, I would like to record my vote "aye" on the final passage of Spring Valley ordinance.

THE MAYOR: The same remarks which the Mayor made regarding Doctor Toner will be applicable to Mr. Power and the Clerk will make the notation that he is making in connection with Supervisor Toner.

SUPERVISOR POWER: It gave me extreme pleasure to join with my colleagues on the Finance Committee, Supervisors Rossi and Hayden, in signing the demand of $40,037,606.51.

In re Submission by the Mayor to the Board of Supervisors of Nominees for War Memorial Trustees.

THE MAYOR: Mr. Andriano has the floor.

SUPERVISOR ANDRIANO: Mr. Mayor, in order to bring this matter of the confirmation of the Trustees to the War Memorial to a head, I am going to read to the members of this Board the wording of the Charter amendment under which the Mayor has made these appointments. Thereafter I propose to invoke the rule of our Board, and proceed to the confirmation, or to make a motion for the confirmation of the Trustees. The Charter amendment reads as follows, and I would like to have the members pay attention to the language of this Charter amendment for, after all, we must always bear in mind, whether we are in sympathy of the views of the veterans, or whether we are in sympathy with the views of the Mayor, we must always bear in mind that we are Supervisors of the entire City and County of San Francisco, representing all of the people of San Francisco, and not any particular group. "The trustees"—I call your attention to the language—"The Trustees"—not the Board of Trustees, but "The trustees of said War Memorial, shall consist of eleven members who"—the trustees, not the Board, but the trustees—"who shall be appointed by the Mayor, subject to confirmation by the Board of Supervisors. The term of such eleven members shall be for six years each, provided that those first appointed shall so classify themselves by lot that the term of four of said trustees shall expire on the 2nd day of January, 1931, four on the second day of January, 1933, and three on the second day of January, 1935. Thereafter appointments to said Board shall be made for the full term of six years. Vacancies on said Board shall be filled by the Mayor, subject to confirmation by the Board of Supervisors, for the unexpired term becoming vacant. In making appointments the said Board"—"appointments," mark this, "in making appointments," it is in the plural, it is not a singular appointment of the entire Board but "appointments"—"to said Board the Mayor shall give due consideration to veterans of all wars engaged in by the United States, and to such other classes of persons who may have a special interest in the purpose for which said War Memorial is to be constructed and maintained. All persons appointed to said Board shall be residents of the City and County. The members of said Board shall serve without compensation."

Now, I respectfully submit to the members of this Board that that is the measure of our power and that is also the measure of our duty in the matter. I think it has become clear to everybody, in view of the statements made by the representatives of the veterans last evening, that is would be hopeless and futile to try to find eleven members, or to find a complete Board that would be satisfactory to the veterans.

Suppose, for the sake of argument, that the Congress of the United States were to creater a new Circuit Court, and the President would be required to appoint Judges to this new Circuit Court, three judges. Can anyone argue that the Senate would have to confirm the appointment of these three judges, collectively? It is absurd even to think of it. The Senate would have to confirm the appointments of the President to this new court, which is parallel in our case to this new Board individually, for the President cannot know which of the appointees is unsatisfactory to the Senate, unless the Senate indicates, by its vote, that one of the proposed judges of this Circuit Court is not satisfactory. In the same manner our Mayor is not a mind reader, he must know which of these appointees is unsatisfactory to the Board of Supervisors. I think that that is just ordinary common sense, and that we are making ourselves ridiculous before the people of San Francisco in insisting on the confirmation of the Board of Trustees as a whole. And, besides, if we do take that position, I submit that we are recreant to our trust under that Charter amendment. Under those circumstances, Mr. Mayor, I deem it to be my duty, as a member of this Board, in order to bring this matter to a head, to invoke a rule of this Board, adopted unanimously by this Board at one of its meetings, I believe it was the meeting of January 20th, which rule reads as follows: "If any question under debate contains several points any member may have the points segregated and acted upon separately." I desire to avail myself of my rights as a member of this Board, and in the discharge of what I consider to be my duty as a member of this Board, to invoke that rule, and having invoked that rule, Mr. Mayor, I move that the confirmation—I move that the appointment of General Hunter Liggett——

SUPERVISOR HAVENNER (interrupting): A point of order, before the Supervisor proceeds with any motion on the assumption that he has exercised his right, I desire to challenge his right, if he has no objection. I do not want to interfere with the motion, but I think that I ought to be accorded the privilege of challenging your right to invoke this rule before you proceed to act under it.

SUPERVISOR ANDRIANO: Why, you cannot know what the effect of my invoking the rule is unless I proceed to make a motion in accordance with the invocation of the rule. And I therefore make a motion at this time, that the appointment, by his Honor, the Mayor, of General Hunter Liggett to the Board of Trustees be confirmed.

SUPERVISOR ROSSI: I second that motion, Mr. Mayor.

SUPERVISOR HAVENNER: Mr. Mayor.

THE MAYOR: Mr. Havenner.

SUPERVISOR HAVENNER: I intend at this time to offer, as a substitute for the whole of the motion just presented by Supervisor Andriano, another motion. And I do so for these reasons: Mr. Mayor, the Board of Supervisors has heretofore declined to confirm the identical list of nominations which is now before us. The official reason for refusing to confirm that list of nominations was a previous action of this Board, based upon its Charter authority, respectfully requesting his Honor, the Mayor, to appoint a majority of the nominees for trustees of the War Memorial who had seen service in some branch of the Military Service of the United States, in some war. In other words, we asked that a majority of the nominations be veterans. There was no other official explanation given for the previous action of this Board in declining to approve the nominations of the Mayor. I feel, therefore, that it is not fair and improper at this time to return the identical list of nominations to this Board, and demand that the Board give an additional reason, which is exactly the purpose of the procedure here now proposed, give an additional reason for declining to approve that list of nominees. So far as I am concerned, I have no personal objections to any of the individuals contained in his Honor's list of nominations. I consider, so far as my information is concerned, that they are all reputable gentlemen. I have no part—and the gentlemen who represent the veterans organizations know it, because I have told them so frankly, and they do not have any quarrel with my position—I have no part or interest in the internal discussions that have occurred in the American Legion, or any of the other veteran organizations concerning the attitude of any particular member of any one of those organizations toward the policies which they have laid down. That is their affair, they may be right, but we, as public officials, can take no cognizance of that, and they know it. I do not object individually to any man thus far proposed by the Mayor. But I do object, and I base my objection on the official action of this Board of Supervisors. I do object to his Honor's failure to comply with our respectful request, that a majority of his nominees should be veterans. Therefore, I think it eminently improper that we should be asked now to take this action and place ourselves on record individually as favoring or opposing those who make up this list of nominees. The language of that Charter amendment is, "The trustees of said War Memorial shall consist of eleven members." Now, the Mayor is not now submitting to us an individual nomination to fill a vacancy in the Board. He is now submitting to us a minority list to fill vacancies in that Board. He is submitting to us his nominations for the Board, and that Board merely consists of eleven members, and the question before the Board of Supervisors today is, shall we ratify the Mayor's recommendation for the Board of Trustees as a whole? That is the question, and any attempt to evade it is merely a technical subterfuge, and I say that without any insidious intent, but that is the exact fact. And I submit that this Board at this time should merely vote to affirm or to repudiate its previous action. We are on record already. We have not approved his Honor's list of nominations. He asks us now to consider the question, and that is about all there is to it. And, in all fairness to ourselves and in fairness to the reason which we have advanced, which is a sound public reason, the only action that we should be required to take today would be merely to affirm or to rescind our previous action. So far as I am individually concerned, if the motion made by Supervisor Andriano should prevail, and I were required today to vote individually on this list of names, all of whom I approve in their individual capacities, and in their individual reputations, I would be obliged to vote "No" on every one, giving as my reason therefor my adherence to the previous action taken by this Board, without detriment or discredit to any individual, and affirming my willingness publicly to vote for any of these gentlemen for any office for which they might be proposed, in the absence of some specific objection not heretofore presented to this Board, for any other office to which they might be nominated by his Honor, or even for the office for which they are now nominated, provided his Honor could see his way clear to comply with the request of this Board and appoint a majority of veterans on that Board of Trustees. Now, Mr. Mayor, in view of that statement, in fairness to this Board, in fairness to the individual members, because I think most of them feel as I do, we do not wish to be placed in the position of repudiating individually these gentlemen whom you have nominated. I have no objection to any one of them, but I do stand on the principle of the resolution which I presented in this Board, and which was adopted by this Board prior, Mr. Mayor, with due respect, prior to the time that you began to take an active interest in this controversy. It was not, as your Honor will remember, that action was not taken with a view to overthrowing some policy which you had publicly announced, it was taken by this Board as a result of the long delay, the long deadlock that had occurred in the private Board of Trustees over the management of this project, and we desired to end that, and we believed that the way to end it was to request that the new Board of War Memorial Trustees should contain in its membership a majority of men or women who represented the people to whom this Memorial was to be dedicated. That was our position then. It was not in the nature of a political quarrel at that time with your Honor, the Mayor. We did not consider you a party to the quarrel, we took an action which we thought was justified by the fact that the Charter amendment conferred upon this Board of Supervisors a co-responsibility with that of your Honor the Mayor. Yours is the initiative responsibility, ours is the final confirmatory responsibility, and we felt that, without any disrespect whatever, we could exercise our Charter right in advance, and request of your Honor, not that you appoint any individual because, so far as I know—I know that the Board as a whole made no individual recommendations to your Honor, I know that at none of the meetings where I was present were any individual recommendations made. We left your prerogative to you without even the suggestion that we desired to interfere with it, but we merely suggested to you that, in exercising our Charter prerogative, we would request that a majority of them be veterans. I am going to move, Mr. Mayor, if I can have a second at this time, that the rule invoked by Supervisor Andriano, rule eleven, be suspended.

SUPERVISOR MILES: I second that.

SUPERVISOR PEYSER: If you will yield just a moment, I would like to make a point of order before your motion is put. Mr. Mayor, at this time I make a point of order, that Supervisor Andriano's motion is out of order, for the following reasons: The Charter Amendment 32 reads as follows: "Creation of a Board of Trustees"—not of individuals, but, "Creation of a Board of Trustees of the War Memorial, providing for the manner of their appointment, defining their powers and duties. There shall be a Board of Trustees"—section 1, Supervisor Andriano did not read that—"There shall be a Board of Trustees of the San Francisco War Memorial, to be erected and maintained in the Civic Center in the City and County of San Francisco, which said Board shall be known as the Board of Trustees of the War Memorial," and then it goes on to say, "The trustees," meaning, the Board of Trustees. Rule 11 provides that, "If any question under debate contains several points"—"several points"—"any member may have the points segregated and acted upon separately." I do not call a man a point. There is only one thing before this Board of Supervisors today, and before I quote further I will read your Honor's submission to the Board: "I appoint, under the law directing me to do so, as Trustees of the War Memorial subject to your confirmation." Your Honor has presented to this Board of Supervisors a Board of Trustees and there are no several points before us at this time. The subject for debate is, Shall or shall not this Board of Trustees, consisting of eleven men, be approved or rejected by this Board, and I submit that my point of order is well taken, and that rule 11 is not applicable to this case. And may I say, further in explanation, that I, too, share the sentiments of Supervisor Havenner. As I said last night, I have no objection to any individual that your Honor has named. I think that they are all fine men, public spirited men, men worthy of recognition, but I do say that the members of this Board should not be placed in the predicament of having to pass upon this motion and vote "No" here. As a matter of fact the vote "No" does not mean anything personally as to them. And we well know, though our explanation may be centered in the record, that, as far as the citizens of San Francisco are concerned, our vote is "No" as to those men. I do not think it is fair to us as veterans, speaking myself as a veteran, I do not think it is fair to the individual members of this Board to confuse an issue for, after all, the issue is not any single individual, but the issue is a Board, and I object seriously to being placed in that position because I do not believe that the Charter amendment intends that provision, nor do I believe rule 11 is applicable to the situation, and I therefore ask for a ruling on my point of order.

SUPERVISOR ANDRIANO: On the point of order——

SUPERVISOR PEYSER (interrupting): I ask for a ruling on my point of order.

SUPERVISOR ANDRIANO: I desire to say a word before the ruling comes.

SUPERVISOR POWER: I merely rise with a desire to clarify the parliamentary procedure before you rule upon the point of order, and I realize debate is out of order on a point of order, but I want to call Supervisor Andriano's attention to the fact that the first procedure here should be a motion to ratify your recommendation. That has not been made. He cannot ask for a segregation of items in a motion until that motion is made. Then it is his privilege, as a member of this Board, and his right under the rules, unless they are suspended, to ask for a segregation. I leave that suggestion with you. And while I am on my feet, with your permission and the Board's I would like to ask the City Attorney as to the point raised by Supervisor Havenner, whether or not the proper action at this time before this Board, in view of the fact that the trustees before us are the same identical names as those that were rejected by the Board, and this is a continuous body notwithstanding the fact that there are six new members on it, whether or not the procedure now should be to either rescind the action, as Supervisor Havenner pointed out, or to affirm the previous action taken.

SUPERVISOR ANDRIANO: Mr. Mayor, I am willing, and I think there is merit to the suggestion of Supervisor Power, that the proper procedure would be, first, to make a motion for the confirmation of your Honor's appointments, and, secondly, to invoke the rule. I accede to his suggestion with the consent of my second.

SUPERVISOR POWER: Will you yield, will you kindly accord me the privilege of securing from the City Attorney——

SUPERVISOR ANDRIANO (interrupting): There is a point of order raised and I am acceding to the point of order, and I think there is nothing until that point of order is disposed of, there is nothing before this Board.

SUPERVISOR POWER: I made it very clear, I was merely seeking information, not any desire to debate or anything of the sort, or to delay action, I merely want that information for my own judgment.

SUPERVISOR HAVENNER: Mr. Mayor, the parliamentary situation is the question before the Board. My amendment, as a substitute to the whole to Supervisor Andriano's motion—and I yield to Supervisor Power—I made a motion to suspend the rules and I made that as an amendment to your motion, as a substitute for the whole.

SUPERVISOR ANDRIANO: I cannot comply with both of your requests, either I comply with Supervisor Power's or I comply with yours.

SUPERVISOR HAVENNER: I will be glad to comply with Supervisor Power's request and withdraw it, if you will permit him to get the answer to the question he has directed to the City Attorney.

SUPERVISOR ANDRIANO: I have no objection to his getting the information, but I do not think it is material at this particular moment.

CITY ATTORNEY O'TOOLE: Mr. Mayor, and gentlemen of the Board: I think the information called for by Supervisor Power goes to the situation as to Supervisor Havenner's motion, and my office has always taken the position, and always will, that that is a matter for your presiding officer to determine, under your rules of order and after he has ruled on the matter, you have your remedy. The City Attorney will not act as a presiding officer of this Board. You are the judges of your own rules, and the presiding officer is the judge as to whether or not the motion is in or out of order, and to rule on that question would be ruling whether Supervisor Havenner's motion was in order or out of order.

SUPERVISOR POWER: I did not ask such a question, with all due respect. I appreciate your point, but I am asking as to the legal status of the situation before us, whether or not this is properly before us as a Board, in view of the previous action this Board has already taken on this matter.

CITY ATTORNEY O'TOOLE: I will reiterate my former opinion that it is a matter for the Board to determine, not your City Attorney; it is a parliamentary and not a legal question.

SUPERVISOR HAVENNER: Mr. Mayor, I would like to develop that just a little bit before the City Attorney makes his final argument. The question, Mr. City Attorney, is a question of legal procedure, not rules of this Board. This Board has already declined to confirm, by formal action of the Board, in accordance with the Charter, declined to confirm the nominations of His Honor, the Mayor. Now, His Honor presents to us anew the same nominations. Under the intent of the Charter, under the intent of parliamentary law everywhere, is it not necessary for this Board to rescind its former action before it can consider the proposal of the Mayor?

CITY ATTORNEY O'TOOLE: That would go more to the effect of the motion than to its merits, Mr. Supervisor, and I still contend the matter is parliamentary and not legal.

SUPERVISOR PEYSER: I have made a point of order, Mr. Mayor, and I would like to have a ruling.

SUPERVISOR STANTON: Can I ask the City Attorney for an opinion? Mr. O'Toole, the fact being that this Board of Supervisors have turned down a list of names as Trustees, does not that automatically put them out of the running and a new list should be presented by the Mayor? Otherwise, in my opinion, and this is the thing that I would like to be set right on, this matter could continue on forever, the Mayor sending a list over and we rejecting the same names. Now, is it final when we reject the names, that then new names must be submitted, or can the Mayor bring back the same names to us?

CITY ATTORNEY O'TOOLE: The question is just the same as that of Supervisor Power, Mr. Supervisor.

SUPERVISOR STANTON: It is a matter as to the legality and not the procedure of this Board.

THE MAYOR: Gentlemen of the Board, I am asked——

SUPERVISOR McSHEEHY (interrupting): Just a moment, Mr. Mayor. As I understand it, Supervisor Peyser is demanding a ruling on his point of order—Supervisor Power, pardon me, I stand corrected. As I understand it, Supervisor Andriano is ready to withdraw his original motion, as suggested by Supervisor Power, and if that is consented to by the seconder, Mr. Rossi, there is nothing before the house at this time, so therefore you have no point of order to rule on, Mr. Mayor. I say this with all respect because I feel that this is going to come to what Supervisor Havenner touched on, very briefly, just in his closing, he said he was going to ask for a suspension of the rules, and, of course, I feel that motion will be properly put, at the proper time. But at this time, if Supervisor Andriano wishes to withdraw, and you agree to it, there is nothing before us, Supervisor.

SUPERVISOR ANDRIANO: I withdraw my motion.

SUPERVISOR ROSSI: I consent as the second.

THE MAYOR: Will you state your point of order again?

SUPERVISOR PEYSER: Mr. Mayor, if Supervisor Andriano withdraws his motion, there is no point of order. Did I understand you to say you withdrew your motion?

SUPERVISOR ANDRIANO: I withdrew my motion temporarily.

SUPERVISOR HAYDEN: To bring the matter to the attention of the Board in the proper legal parliamentary fashion, I now move that the recommendations made by the Mayor and in the possession of the Clerk, be formally ratified by the Board.

SUPERVISOR ROSSI: I second the motion, Mr. Mayor.

SUPERVISOR ANDRIANO: After your Honor has put the motion, I desire to speak.

THE MAYOR: It has been moved by Supervisor Hayden, seconded by Supervisor Rossi, that the nominees of the Mayor for appointment on the Board of War Memorial Trustees be confirmed. Mr. Andriano.

SUPERVISOR HAVENNER: Mr. Mayor.

THE MAYOR: Mr. Andriano has the floor.

SUPERVISOR HAVENNER: I desire to move an amendment.

SUPERVISOR ANDRIANO: I have the floor, and, consequently, I am entitled to speak first.

THE MAYOR: You have the floor.

SUPERVISOR ANDRIANO: At this time I desire to invoke rule number 11, passed unanimously by our Board, reading as follows: "If any question under debate contains several points any member may have the points segregated and acted upon separately." And I submit, anticipating the point of order that will be raised, that it is a very specious argument to say that points are not meant. Whatever is under debate, whether they be men, or motions, or subjects, is a "point," and there are eleven questions involved in this confirmation, and I therefore insist upon my right to invoke rule 11, that the names submitted be voted upon separately.

SUPERVISOR PEYSER: Mr. Mayor, a point of order: Mr. Mayor, at this time I make the point of order that Supervisor Andriano's motion is out of order, on the grounds that we have before us the consideration of a Board of Trustees. We have not before us the consideration of any individuals. In your Honor's own submission to this Board, your Honor has submitted a Board of Trustees, and I further submit that there are no several points before this Board at this time, and that the main question is, whether or not the names comprising a Board, as submitted by your Honor, are to be ratified or not. And I ask for a ruling.

SUPERVISOR ANDRIANO: I just want to call the Supervisor's attention to the fact that I made no motion, no motion is required, I am just simply standing upon my right as a member of this Board, to invoke rule eleven.

SUPERVISOR HAVENNER: Mr. Mayor, I now move, as a substitute for the whole, that this Board again reaffirm its action previously taken on the list of nominees submitted by his Honor, the Mayor.

SUPERVISOR MILES: I second the motion.

SUPERVISOR POWER: I second the motion.

SUPERVISOR PEYSER: I second the motion.

SUPERVISOR ANDRIANO: I rise to a point of order, Mr. Mayor, that the motion is not in order, that it is not a reaffirmance of the action taken by this Board. Your Honor has a perfect right to submit the same list, particularly in view of the fact that four members of this Board who voted to reject your appointments have not been returned to office, and that there are now five new members on this Board——

SUPERVISOR POWER (interrupting): Six.

SUPERVISOR ANDRIANO: Six, so that I submit that the motion made by Supervisor Havenner is out of order.

SUPERVISOR HAVENNER: With all due respect to the Supervisor, I cannot see any logic in that objection at all. I realize that there are new members on this Board, I am merely calling upon them now, by my motion as a substitute for the whole, to affirm the action taken by the Board of Supervisors prior to this time.

THE MAYOR: Anticipating these various points of order and these motions which have just been put, and acting upon the best legal advice I could receive since I heard about this rule this morning, I rule that Mr. Peyser's point of order is not well taken, and I rule that Mr. Havenner's motion is out of order, and that rule number 11 is before the Board, and that all you can possibly do—— (Laughter)

THE MAYOR: Now, I am going to tell you again, there is going to be respect in this legislative body, and continued respect in this legislative body, and no further outbursts such as occurred last night will hereafter again occur in these legislative chambers, and the Police Officers are directed to do their duty.

SUPERVISOR HAVENNER: Mr. Mayor, with all due respect, I appeal from the ruling of the Chair.

THE MAYOR: Gentlemen, an appeal has been taken from the decision of the Chair: Shall the decision of the Chair be sustained? Call the roll, Mr. Clerk.

SUPERVISOR SHANNON: A point of order, Mr. Mayor, the appeal has not been seconded.

THE MAYOR: The point of order is well taken.

SUPERVISOR PEYSER: I will second it.

SUPERVISOR SHANNON: Mr. Mayor, I have the floor. I had the floor before it was seconded.

SUPERVISOR PEYSER: I seconded the appeal.

SUPERVISOR SHANNON: After I arose—just a minute—I think I can clear this up. I realize that what Mr. Andriano is endeavoring to do is with a desire to effect a saving of time, but I want to point out to the Supervisor that, in his endeavor to save time, he is only going to waste time. All of the members of the Board agree that this Board of Trustees, as individuals, are entirely acceptable to the members of the Board. If we are called upon to vote upon them individually, I will not do as Mr. Havenner has said he will do and vote "No" on each one, I will vote "Aye" on each one. But when it comes to the ratification of the Board of Trustees that you have appointed. So therefore, Mr. Andriano, speaking through the Chair, if I vote "Aye" on each individual and then when it comes to the ratification of the Board, and you do not get your ten votes, what has the motion of Mr. Andriano accomplished? I think you might just as well withdraw your motion.

SUPERVISOR McSHEEHY: Mr. Chairman, there is such a word as consistency. Now one must be consistent. We are here today meeting, we have here perhaps four or five hundred people. All right. But we are representing a City of 700,000, and we have to give an accounting of our stewardship. Now, we have to be consistent, and a man that will vote aye for eleven men cannot consistently vote no.

SUPERVISOR SHANNON: Mr. Mayor, we have seen the same Supervisor go through the budget and vote aye on individual items in the budget, and when it comes to the budget and the tax rate, he would vote no. Now, what are you going to do with a man like that? And, Mr. Mayor, that same Supervisor that voted consistently throughout the budget on items, when Mr. McLaren was the Chairman, and voted against the School bonds, voted no when it came to the matter as a whole. And that is the very point I make that when you vote aye on the individual items, you can vote no, and when it comes to your Board, as a Board, and that is what we are voting on, the Board of Trustees, the "No" vote is the vote that counts on the Board of Trustees, and not the vote on the individual names.

SUPERVISOR McSHEEHY: Mr. Chairman, I would like to correct the Supervisor, and he is the man that I admire his wonderful memory, many a time I have complimented him on it, but there has never been a budget that I have voted no that there were not numbers and numbers of items that I voted no on. I have been consistent in reference to my vote on the budget. I have tried to be, and I will be consistent as a member of this Board of Supervisors. I have voted no alone perhaps more than any other member of this Board, but I have been consistent and I will continue to be consistent.

SUPERVISOR HAVENNER: Your Honor has ruled my motion out of order. I appeal from the ruling of the Chair.

THE MAYOR: Mr. Havenner, please repeat your motion.

(The motion of Supervisor Havenner's is read by the reporter:

"SUPERVISOR HAVENNER: Mr. Mayor, I now move, as a substitute for the whole, that this Board again reaffirm its action previously taken on the list of nominees submitted by his Honor, the Mayor.")

SUPERVISOR McSHEEHY: May I ask a question of information: Will it take a majority of those present in reference to an appeal to decide an appeal, as outlined by Supervisor Havenner? Or, will it take a majority of the members of the Board of Supervisors?

THE MAYOR: Well, it not appearing in the new rules of the Board, I do not know what the rules committee intend to do about it.

SUPERVISOR SHANNON: We are operating under Roberts' Rules of Order, Mr. Mayor, and an appeal from the decision of the Chair requires a majority vote and in a tie vote, the Chair is sustained. A majority vote.

SUPERVISOR McGOVERN: Of those present.

THE MAYOR: An appeal has been taken from the decision of the Chair on the motion made by Supervisor Havenner. Shall the decision of the Chair be sustained?

SUPERVISOR ANDRIANO: Mr. Chairman, I submit to your Honor the point of order that the appeal does not lie. The Supervisor is seeking to do by indirection what he cannot do directly. It is his right, as he sought to do before, to have the rules suspended. But I submit to your Honor that the only purpose of this appeal is to defeat my right, as a member of this Board, to invoke a particular rule of this Board, and the only way that that can be done is by suspending the rule, and that takes twelve votes. If the Supervisor desires to test this question and test it squarely he, being a parliamentarian, knows that I am right when I say that this appeal is not in good faith, that it is merely seeking to defeat my right as a Supervisor to stand upon the rules of this Board. I therefore submit to your Honor that the appeal does not lie and is out of order.

SUPERVISOR HAVENNER: Mr. Mayor, an appeal from a decision of the Chair always lies. There is no question about that. And the Supervisor has very cleverly and ingeniously twisted his argument to make it appear that I am not proceeding in good faith when, by a mere technicality, consideration of my original appeal was defeated because another Supervisor took the floor so quickly that there could not be a second. Now, that is the exact situation. There are seconds and plenty around here, and the Supervisor knows it, and another Supervisor not intending, I say not intending to defeat my appeal, took the floor, and thereupon it was ruled that my appeal was out of order because it had not been seconded. Now, if there be good faith, I appeal to the Supervisor to allow my appeal to be put to this Board. It has not been voted on, it has not been defeated fairly. Give it a chance. I am proceeding in good faith. I ask that the question on appeal be put to the Board.

SUPERVISOR McSHEEHY: Mr. Chairman, may I ask Supervisor Hayden, I have often addressed him as the Dean of the Board: During his twenty years as a Supervisor, have you ever experienced an appeal from a ruling of his Honor, the Mayor, being taken before?

SUPERVISOR HAYDEN: An appeal from the decision of the Chair?

SUPERVISOR McSHEEHY: Yes.

SUPERVISOR HAYDEN: Oh, yes.

SUPERVISOR McSHEEHY: I am talking of the Mayor?

SUPERVISOR HAYDEN: From the Mayor?

SUPERVISOR McSHEEHY: Yes.

SUPERVISOR HAYDEN: Oh, yes.

SUPERVISOR McSHEEHY: During the twelve years that I have

been a member of this Board, this is the first—and I would like anyone to call my attention to the fact—according to my memory, of an
appeal being taken from your decision as Presiding Officer.

THE MAYOR: That is all right, Mr. McSheehy. Let me tell you
something: I am acting upon legal advice right now. If the Board
wants to go contrary to the legal advice given me in the ruling that
I have just made, why, do so.

SUPERVISOR PEYSER: Question.

SUPERVISOR McSHEEHY: Just a moment. I am standing on my
feet, with all due respect, and the privilege was accorded to others.
May I simply say this, members of the Board: I have great respect
for Supervisor Havenner, we have been associated together now for
four years, and I guess we have been about as close together as any
two members of this Board. I have got great respect for him, and
above all things, in his ideals, but I am rather surprised, Supervisor,
today under a condition of this kind, for you to bring forward a
technical motion of this kind and place this entire matter in the
Board in a situation where a mere majority will decide whether a
man is within his rights when he asks for the segregation of a motion.
Now, I knew this matter was coming up, I came down here with
Roberts' Rules of Order, and I came down with another book on
parliamentary law that I happened to have at home. I am ready to
read both to the Board. Supervisor Andriano is only asking for his
legal rights as a constituted member of this Board, when he asks for
the segregation of the motion, and you have dexterously. and strate-
getically placed it in such a position now that you are asking a small
majority of this Board to override the ruling of the Mayor, which
will ostracize Supervisor Andriano from placing his motion properly
before this Board, and I am rather surprised at you, knowing you
the way I do.

THE MAYOR: The question is, shall the decision of the Chair
be sustained. I tell you, I am acting upon legal advice in the decision
that I rendered. Please call the roll, Mr. Clerk. A vote "aye" will
sustain the Chair, a vote "no" will decide against the Chair, or in
favor of the appeal from the decision, of a legal decision of the Chair.

THE CLERK: Roll call.

Ayes: Andriano, Hayden, McSheehy, Rossi.

Noes: Canepa, Havenner, McGovern, Miles, Peyser, Power, Roncovieri.

SUPERVISOR SHANNON (interrupting): I cannot explain my
vote, but I am really not conversant with the parliamentary situation.
I would like to know what Mr. Havenner's motion was, his amendment was.

SUPERVISOR HAVENNER: If I may explain, the parliamentary
situation is my appeal from the decision of the Chair in ruling my
substitute motion out of order.

SUPERVISOR SHANNON: And your substitute motion was what?

SUPERVISOR HAVENNER: That the Board reaffirm its previous
action on this list of nominees.

(Roll call continued:)

Ayes: Shannon, Suhr, Toner. Noes: Spaulding, Stanton.

THE CLERK: Nine noes, seven ayes, two absent.

SUPERVISOR ANDRIANO: Mr. Mayor.

SUPERVISOR HAVENNER: Are you discussing the motion now?

SUPERVISOR ANDRIANO: I will yield the floor to Mr. Havenner.

SUPERVISOR HAVENNER: I merely ask for a vote on my substitute motion for the whole. I will ask the reporter to read my motion.

(The reporter reads Supervisor Havenner's motion as follows: "Mr.
Mayor, I now move, as a substitute for the whole, that this Board
again reaffirm its action previously taken on the list of nominees submitted by his Honor, the Mayor.")

SUPERVISOR ANDRIANO: Mr. Mayor, we are going ring around the rosy, but I again invoke rule number eleven of our Board, unanimously adopted by this Board, and demand, Supervisor, that we vote separately upon the nominees contained in that list of names submitted by your Honor.

SUPERVISOR HAVENNER: Mr. Mayor, I make the point of order, the question is not now the confirmation or disapproval of the individuals nominated by his Honor, the Mayor, but whether this Board shall reaffirm the action which it previously took upon that list of nominees, and there can be no segregation of that question, it is indivisible.

SUPERVISOR ANDRIANO: Mr. Mayor, before you rule on the point of order, let me call your Honor's attention to the fact that whether you call it confirmation or not, I had the right, when it first came up, to invoke this rule. I saw fit not to invoke it then. I invoke it now, and I do not believe that any Supervisor, by any parliamentary legerdemain, can deny me my right to invoke the rules of this Board.

THE MAYOR: Your point of order is well taken, acting on legal advice.

SUPERVISOR HAVENNER: Mr. Mayor, I appeal from the ruling of the Chair.

SUPERVISOR PEYSER: Second.

THE MAYOR: An appeal has been taken from the decision of the Chair on granting to Mr. Andriano the right to invoke at this time rule number eleven, which has been adopted unanimously by this Board. The question is, shall the Chair be sustained?

SUPERVISOR POWER: Mr. Mayor, I would like to ask that the Clerk at this time furnish to us, especially the new members, the record showing the action that the Board previously had taken, so that I can guide myself on voting aye or no on sustaining the Chair. I have a copy before me, it is rather an unusual proceeding, I see that the previous action was taken on a motion to confirm your Trustees, that it lost by a vote of 12 to 5 and one excused from voting, and then Supervisor Andriano changed his vote from aye to no, and moved reconsideration. What I want to get at is just the exact parliamentary procedure before us. I did not get as far as finding out whether that reconsideration had been acted upon.

SUPERVISOR ANDRIANO: On the appeal may I call my colleagues' attention to this fact: That a motion to reaffirm brings back the entire motion originally affirmed, before the Board, and it is a right of every member of this Board to reaffirm the whole or any part of that original motion before the Board, and since I may see fit to reaffirm part and reject another part, because it is divisible, the original motion, I submit that I was entirely within my right in asking for a division.

SUPERVISOR HAVENNER: Mr. Mayor, the final previous action taken by this Board was a refusal to reconsider its vote taken prior thereto, whereby the nominations of his Honor, the Mayor, were not approved. My motion in effect asks this Board again to refuse to reconsider.

SUPERVISOR ANDRIANO: Granted, but does not the motion to reconsider bring back the original motion?

SUPERVISOR HAVENNER: Not at all. Are you going to claim that you would have had the right, under your motion to reconsider, to call for a division?

SUPERVISOR ANDRIANO: No, but you are the one who is making a motion to reconsider, or making a motion to reaffirm, which is synonymous with reconsider, and I will submit that Roberts Rules of Order states that a motion to reconsider brings back the entire motion before this Board.

SUPERVISOR HAVENNER: No, my motion is not to reconsider, but not to consider.

THE MAYOR: The question is on the appeal from the decision of the Chair made by Supervisor Havenner.

SUPERVISOR POWER: There is a good deal involved here. If the entire subject matter is before us, why, of course, I know how I am going to vote on your ruling, but if, as Supervisor Havenner says, that his motion does not bring back the entire situation as it· was presented to the Board before, why, then, I have to guide myself accordingly. Now, I would like to have from you what you consider the motion of Supervisor Havenner has brought to our picture, or brought to us, in so far as the parliamentary situation is concerned.

THE MAYOR: My view of the picture is that Supervisor Andriano is in perfect order, that Mr. Havenner's motion is out of order because Mr. Andriano has a right, as every member of this Board has, to invoke any rule that this Board has adopted, and I am ruling upon the rules of this Board. They are either good now or they never will be any good.

SUPERVISOR STANTON: Mr. Mayor, I think in a case of this kind there is considerable fairness that must be taken into consideration. This Board of Supervisors, it is true, before the last election, passed an ordinance or resolution, wherein they stated that they would not ratify any Board of Trustees unless a majority of them were ex-Service men. We took that matter up with you in your office and felt that that was sort of settled. I do not know of a member of the Board of Supervisors, Mr. Mayor, that has asked you individually to put any individual on the Board of Trustees. I think every member of the Board of Supervisors has said that the Trustees individually are a lot of fine fellows and have not wanted to do anything that would in any way reflect. But there has been considerable controversy, and we sat here all night and listened to your message, we listened to the war veterans last night wherein they have found considerable fault with the Trustees. They are asking and we are asking that the resolution passed by the Board of Supervisors be lived up to by you, and that you appoint a majority of war veterans, not suggesting a single name to you. Supervisor Andriano, not willing to get up himself and say that he will vote for each and every one of them separately, but insisting on some members of the Board of Supervisors voting against people possibly that they have never spoken to. And that is the position that I am in. Members of the Board of Trustees I have never spoken to, and therefore could have nothing against them. But I do not feel that I should be put in a position to get up here and vote against each one of them individually. It seems to me, if the Supervisor wants to make any statement as to his vote, that he should let us vote as we see fit. If we want to do it collectively, merely bringing the matter back to you, calling to your attention that we passed such a resolution that there should be a majority of war veterans, I want to act accordingly. That is merely the motion, and now the matter of jamming each and every Supervisor and making them vote against people that he does not want to vote against, I do not think it is fair on your part. It is merely a matter of trying to jam some other people in an unfair way.

THE MAYOR: Now, it is evidently an attempt to jam something against the Mayor. You say that you made a pledge before the last election. I did not approve that pledge because I kept my faith with the people of San Francisco. I never made a pre-election pledge in all my life. And I would not relish sitting down amongst the Board of Supervisors today and telling the people of this City they are so bound up on the outside that they cannot represent the interests of the people when they rise on their feet, and say that every man nominated by the Mayor of San Francisco is an honorable citizen, but outside political influence keeps them from voting for them.

SUPERVISOR STANTON: Mr. Mayor, that is not a fact. It was no political promise, and it was a long time before election that the veterans came in here and we gave them our word on the pledge. We told them, you can have a pledge if you want. We told them, by action of this Board, almost unanimously, that we would not ratify the list, or any list, not knowing whom you might appoint, Mr. Mayor, unless they were a majority of veterans. We had nobody in view, at least I had not and have not today, but merely feeling that it was a War Memorial, that the money was collected, the money was voted for the Memorial, as such, and wanting to have those whom the Memorial was for satisfied. That is my only idea.

THE MAYOR: Let the Mayor again say, that the Board, unanimously, says that every name submitted by the Mayor is worthy of confirmation by the Board. Let the Mayor say that he had the Supervisors in his office and every single name that is before this Board today, with the exception of one, was approved by this Board. Let me say that Colonel George Filmer——

SUPERVISOR POWER (interrupting): Let me interrupt, please, I do not mean to be discourteous, but not the new Board as at present composed.

THE MAYOR: I wanted you to say that so that you won't fall into the trap laid by Mr. Havenner, that the old Board is the same Board as is constituted today.

SUPERVISOR POWER: Don't worry about me falling into any trap, I am plenty able to take care of myself on parliamentary situations.

THE MAYOR: Now, just let it be said that the Mayor tried to get six veterans on that Board, and the Mayor named to you six veterans, the one that he could not get was Colonel George Filmer, and let the Mayor remind you that a Labor leader was suggested by Mr. Roncovieri to be put on the Board. And the Mayor failing in getting Mr. George Filmer, all of which is of record here, appointed Mr. James W. Mullen, for the reasons expressed last night. Now, this Board is putting itself in the position of trapping itself, that outside political influence, which they cannot shake off, compels them to decline the nominations of men whom they say are the finest in San Francisco. Let me say, there never was any more boss ridden body than there is today of the Supervisors who cannot act for the people of San Francisco because they are tied up by outside influence and cannot vote for the people of San Francisco.

SUPERVISOR PEYSER: Mr. Mayor, I rise to discuss the situation, and also to a matter of personal privilege. I, unfortunately, am not as wise in politics as my colleague, Mr. Power, and unwittingly I would have fallen into the trap your Honor has so carefully laid for a new member of the Board. I, for one, will say that I was not prepared, when I came to this Board, to look for traps. I am looking at the issues, fairly and squarely. I am not politically ridden by anybody, and I want that firmly known. And I say to you that my opinion today is based upon a careful perusal of the record and history, as your Honor has submitted it, and if your Honor's inference is that because I believe six members of that Board should be veterans, if your Honor's inference is that because I disagree with your Honor in the interpretation of the Charter, that I am politically ridden, I inform your Honor at this time that he is mistaken. Now, just a moment. And I say this with all sincerity, and not for the purpose of applause, but there seems to be too much of this trapping on this Board of Supervisors. And I say, here we have an issue whether or not this Board shall be confirmed. The Board was turned down at the last vote of this Board of Supervisors. Your Honor has not seen fit to change the nominees, but to come before this Board by a technical rule of procedure, which I say is out of order, the attempt to jam a new man on this Board by a political trick.

THE MAYOR: How am I trying to jam a new man by a political trick?

SUPERVISOR PEYSER: I will explain to you, I explained it last night and I will explain it again. You have submitted eleven names only. You have not given this Board a choice of any names. You have said to this Board, "Either you take these men or you take no one," and you have gone further and insisted, through your representatives, that we vote individually. Now, if we vote individually, if your Honor please, I call your respectful attention to the fact that nothing can result except the fact that we must accept five veterans on that Board. I personally have nothing against them, I have stated it last night, I state it again today, but I am confirmed to the principle that the composition of that Board is not right, in my opinion. And I certainly have a right to my opinion as a representative of the people. I also am in favor of the Opera House, possibly just as much solicitous of that as those groups who would appear to be so here today. I believe it is a fine thing for San Francisco. But I do say that this Board should have an opportunity, and the individual men should have an opportunity of expressing their opinion on the issue, and not circumventing it and trying to arrive at a conclusion by subterfuge, and it is only a subterfuge when your Honor knows that these men here sit as a body, and I stand here as an individual and am not opposed to the individuals. The issue is, whether or not your Honor should abide by or respect, I will put it that way, the wishes of the men who stood before you as representatives of the people. If your Honor does not wish to submit that sort of a list, then your Honor could submit to this Board a group of fifteen men, any that your Honor pleases, there is no suggestion made as to names or who they shall be, and then let us vote individually and select eleven men. But to come before this Board and put eleven names before us, with no option, when a vote "No" to the outside world and those who are not within the confines of this Chamber, means a reflection upon them, I think it is unfair and dastardly to put any man up to that test because it is not a fact, and that is not the issue. The issue is as to the composition of this Board, and I now call your Honor's attention to Charter Amendment 32, which provides that there shall be a Board of Trustees, I call your Honor's attention further to the fact that the motion made last time, before I was a member of this Board, was that Supervisor Hayden moved that the group be ratified, so that Supervisor Havenner's motion here to reaffirm that act is the act of denying the group and not the individual, and I submit upon that basis that your Honor has no right, as far as I am concerned, to infer, by any premise, that we are politically ridden because of the opinion we express here today.

THE MAYOR: Now, let me tell you, Mr. Peyser: You said last night that it was a tough thing for the Mayor to put you up against, a jam.

SUPERVISOR PEYSER: No, I did not say that, Mr. Mayor, I said it is unfair to put us to a vote which will not express the real issue before us, and I insist upon that still now.

THE MAYOR: But you have, as your duty as a Supervisor, to decide which one of those eleven or more are unsatisfactory to you and to this Board. If the Board were to continue the position that it takes, the Board of years would never confirm eleven Trustees. Each one of the eleven the Mayor sends you is not satisfactory, by your vote. I have told you I tried to appoint eleven, six of whom were veterans. I was asked to put a Labor man on when I had to take George Filmer off. The Board was in my Chambers and discussed every single name. I want to know which one of the eleven that accepted by invitation, and have been confirmed and approved by the Regents of the University of California, I want to know from this Board which one or more are not satisfactory so I can fill that place with a veteran.

SUPERVISOR PEYSER: Then your position is that you are not going to give me, as a member of this Board, or the others as members of this Board, the right to vote as to what the composition of that Board should be. And before I go further I would like to ask your Honor, if it is not a fact that Colonel Filmer—that Jesse Colman was put on in place of Colonel Filmer? This is just a question of information.

THE MAYOR: Well, it may have been possible at the time that Mr. Roncovieri asked me to appoint a Labor man, I am not quite clear about that, but I am quite willing to put a veteran on, if I have a vacancy there, but you have not any right to ask the Mayor to turn down an honorable man and ask him to withdraw for the purpose of the Supervisors avoiding the issue. You have not any right to go and ask me to ask a man who has already been accepted to withdraw. You have not any right to do that. You have a right to vote seriatim. Your rule number eleven says, upon the advice of the City Attorney and upon the advice of Theodore Roche this morning, and upon the advice of Supervisor Andriano, you have a right to sustain your rules and vote on those names singly, and it is not fair to the Mayor to evade that issue, and I tell you that your rules are either good or they are no good from now on, and number eleven is the rule that is at issue, and simply because you may have some political strength in here for political purposes, to defeat eleven fine names, because you refuse to vote "No" on every one of them, because you are afraid to. You said so.

SUPERVISOR PEYSER: No, I did not say so, Mr. Mayor.

THE MAYOR: Then, vote.

SUPERVISOR PEYSER: Just a minute, Mr. Mayor, any imputation as to politics is uncalled for from you. It would seem, from the stand you take here, there seems to be some politics in it, too.

THE MAYOR: There is no politics in it, I have submitted eleven names.

SUPERVISOR PEYSER: Just because I express my opinion you accuse me of politics.

THE MAYOR: You said and you admit they are all eleven fine men.

SUPERVISOR PEYSER: My objection is as to the composition of the Board.

THE MAYOR: How is the Mayor going to know what you want as to the composition of the Board if you do not vote on it? Will every single name on that Board be acceptable to you if another veteran is put on?

SUPERVISOR PEYSER: Yes.

THE MAYOR: Every single name?

SUPERVISOR PEYSER: A majority of veterans, yes.

SUPERVISOR HAVENNER: Any ten of the eleven will be.

SUPERVISOR ROSSI: I would like to seek some information. As I understand the motion as made by Supervisor Havenner, we are voting upon a dead issue, and that is reaffirming the action of this Board taken sometime last year. Now, in the event that that motion carries, what becomes of the recommendation that is before us today?

SUPERVISOR RONCOVIERI: What becomes of what?

SUPERVISOR ROSSI: What becomes of the recommendation that is before us today?

SUPERVISOR RONCOVIERI: What recommendation?

SUPERVISOR HAVENNER: It will be filed.

SUPERVISOR ROSSI: Then there is an attempt to deprive the members of this Board of their right to vote in accordance with our rule.

SUPERVISOR HAVENNER: No, if you vote down my motion——

SUPERVISOR ROSSI (interrupting): If the effect of your motion will be that it will kill the subject matter before the Board today, it will file the recommendation made by his Honor the Mayor at this time.

SUPERVISOR HAVENNER: It will be tantamount to the same action that we took before, which nobody questioned.

SUPERVISOR ROSSI: That is a dead issue.

.SUPERVISOR HAVENNER: Mr. Mayor, as a question of personal privilege, I too must resent the statement that because of its action in this matter this Board is politically ridden or boss ridden. If that statement be true, of course, it applies to me, Mr. Mayor, because I was the author of both resolutions that led up to the action of the Board, long before, Mr. Mayor, this particular question arose. I was the author of a resolution presented here prior to the submission of the bond issue for the War Memorial bonds, providing that this Board of Supervisors pledge itself to appropriate no money for the construction of the War Memorial project out of the bond issue until such time as the official plans for that project had been approved by a majority of the duly accredited representatives of the war veterans' societies of San Francisco. That was taken two and a half, nearly three years ago, that action, and it was taken because at that time the representatives of the veteran societies of San Francisco came before this Board and warned us that they believed, if these bonds were approved by the people, the private Board of Trustees, which up to that time had assumed absolute dictatorship over the whole project, would ignore the wishes of the veterans, and this Board went further and, through its constituted campaign committee, authorized certain amendments in the statements to the people, to make it clear that we intended to carry out the War Memorial project in its aspect as a definite constructive project for the housing of the various veteran organizations. And then, Mr. Mayor, some time last year, after the Charter amendment providing for the creation of a Board of War Memorial Trustees had been ratified by the Legislature, and prior to any of this discussion on the part of your Honor, I presented another resolution in keeping with the one I had presented before, respectfully requesting your Honor to appoint a majority of these eleven Trustees who should be veterans of some branch of the military service. Mr. Mayor, my only consideration throughout these three years in dealing with this matter has been a consideration of personal conviction, and if I am boss ridden, I am ridden by my own convictions, and if that be boss ridden, Mr. Mayor, I am going to be boss ridden as long as I remain in public office. And I want to say now, that the only attempt to influence my judgment on these questions has not come from the side with which I happen to agree. They have not come to me and asked me to vote this way, or that way, or the other way. But representatives of the other side have come to me and asked me whether I could not reconsider my stand. And I have told them that I could not, that I was committed by a record of conviction, and that no matter how long I stayed on this Board, I would not repudiate the stand which I have already taken. Now, Mr. Mayor, I think it is unfair to make the statement that there is any politics or bossism in this situation. I personally must resent it; it is not true so far as I am concerned.

SUPERVISOR ANDRIANO: Question.

SUPERVISOR RONCOVIERI: Mr. Mayor, I too most emphatically repudiate the statement you have made, in so far as it concerns me. When we met in your office, before you appointed anyone, it was suggested to you that you should consider the veterans; in fact, the very Charter amendment speaks of that. We had previously, before meeting you in your office and discussing this matter, adopted this resolution. I will take the trouble to read this. I want the new members to hear it. "Whereas, by resolution unanimously adopted on June 6, 1927, the Board of Supervisors is committed to the policy of withholding appropriations from funds resulting from the sale of War

Memorial bonds until the official plans for the War Memorial have been approved by the majority of the duly constituted representatives of war veteran organizations; and

"Whereas, by virtue of that resolution, the Board of Supervisors have justly recognized as paramount the rights of the ex-service men and women of San Francisco, it being the deeds of such men, living as well as dead, that the Memorial is intended to commemorate; and

"Whereas, Charter Amendment No. 32, as approved by the people, provides for the appointment of a Board of Trustees to administer all matters pertaining to that War Memorial and states"—quoted from the Charter—"that the Mayor, in making appointments, shall give due consideration to veterans of all wars in which the United States has engaged; and

"Whereas, Charter Amendment No. 32 invests in the Board of Supervisors the duty of confirming the appointments of all the members of the Board of Trustees selected by the Mayor; now, therefore be it

"Resolved, That the Board of Supervisors respectfully urge and recommend to his Honor the Mayor to appoint a majority of the members of the Board of War Memorial Trustees from that portion of the citizenry of San Francisco who have been in service with the Army, Navy or Marine Corps in time of war; and be it further

"Resolved, That the advice and counsel of the war veteran organizations, through the medium of the properly constituted representatives"—Mr Gallagher was right the other day, only he said it in his usual characteristic way—"Further Resolved, that the advice and counsel of the war veteran organizations, through the medium of the properly constituted representatives, be sought before said appointments are made, it being the opinion of this Board of Supervisors that every class or group of the people of San Francisco, with the confidence inspired by service in time of war, may look to such men for purposeful loyalty and unselfish devotion to San Francisco in time of peace." Adopted by the Board of Supervisors, December 3, 1928. Ayes: Supervisors Gallagher, Havenner, Kent, McGovern, Marks, Powers, Roncovieri, Schmidt, Stanton, Suhr, Todd, 11. Noes: Supervisors Andriano, Colman, Hayden, McSheehy, Shannon, Toner, 6. Absent: Supervisor Deasy.

Now, Mr. Mayor, I am sure, for one, that my fingers were not crossed when I voted for that. I am sure, so help me God, that nobody had spoken to me about this. It was my conviction that it was the proper thing to do. And that was about a year or so or more before you appointed your Board. So today, in voting against your recommendation, which I will do, I am not voting under compulsion or suggestion from a living soul; nobody has spoken to me. Therefore, I resent very deeply the remark of "political influence," and I think I speak for every member of the Board who voted in favor of this resolution. Now, we were told last night, after an investigation by the authorized representatives of the veterans, that wherever a War Memorial has been built, the entire Board of Trustees is made up of veterans. Now, when I stated to you that a labor representative should be on that Board, it was in your office, in the presence of others, when we first met to consult over the appointments. And I had no idea that you would at least not put six members of the veterans on this Board. When I said that to you I thought, well, you will pick out from the great ranks of labor one who has served his country. Surely, it cannot be said that in the ranks of labor there is no one who has served this country. Why, they were the bone and sinue that went to the war, and among them you will find outstanding men in the ranks of labor who could satisfy the conditions of this resolution. We did not take you by surprise. We gave you this a long time in advance. We called on you in your office; we reiterated the contents of this resolution to you.

SUPERVISOR STANTON: What is the date of it?

SUPERVISOR RONCOVIERI: This is dated and was adopted December 3, 1928. We gave you plenty of time. We played a gentlemen's game with you, Mr. Mayor, and you one day, out of a clear sky, after several weeks of delay, came in and said, "Here is my list." Now you say, "Take it or leave it."

THE MAYOR: No, I do not say that at all.

SUPERVISOR RONCOVIERI: Well, you do not say it, but you are acting it, which is worse, Mr. Mayor.

THE MAYOR: No, I do not.

SUPERVISOR RONCOVIERI: You simply say, "Take what I give you or leave it." We have already rejected the list as a whole, with no intent to disparage the character of any individual whom you have named on that list; no intent to reflect in any way upon their integrity or their honor; but we have said as a group, as Supervisor Peyser has said, they are unsatisfactory because they do not contain a majority of veterans. It seems to me that you could easily have done that, and everything would go on merrily. I have studied this question very, very carefully, particularly since the other night that we spent here with you, and from remarks made last night, as I see this situation, my colleagues on the Board, it is simply this: Much money has been wasted; thousands, hundreds of thousands of dollars, over $300,000 has been borrowed when you had money in bank; interest has been paid. The financial report is merely a little sketchy report taken from the books, unsigned by the certified public accountants. It means but very little. Now, beneath all this lies this: The veterans demand, and rightfully, that their building shall be built according to certain lines, and costing approximately $1,500,000 or $2,000,000. The gentlemen who favor the opera house feel that if the veterans gain the control, six votes on that board, that possibly the veterans may take of the $5,000,000 too much for their building and not leave enough for the opera house. And when you study this question, that is all there is to it: one side does not trust the other. The veterans themselves would gladly say that "we approve this list," if they knew positively that they would have a sufficient amount to give them what they should have and what they demand, say, a $2,000,000 building. I do not know the exact amount; I won't be bound by $2,000,000. But if they knew positively that they were going to be treated, architecturally, in the right way, they probably would approve it. And I believe that the people on the other side who want the opera house would be equally satisfied if they knew that six veterans on this Board would vote for a proper opera house costing $3,000,000 or possibly $3,500,000. It all comes back to what I said yesterday. Errors have been committed, not intentionally, perhaps. I am sure not intentionally. I feel certain of that—regarding the architectural plans. Very loosely a plan is drawn for $8,200,000, and we were told by Mr. McSheehy, who was on that Board officially, that there are 24 complete detailed plans from which contractors could proceed to build. That is not the customary way of doing business. The customary way is to demand red lead pencil sketches; work out sketches until you find that you can build the building within the amount of money that you have. Those men knew that they had but $5,000,000. They proceeded to make an $8,200,000 plan. This was all wrong. Then a second time they make a second set of plans running into $7,250,000. Another second mistake after the first. Now you will have a third set of plans. The architects admit, over their own signatures, that these figures are too high. Of course, they are too high, and they know it. We have not got $7,250,000. They know that. Now they say, "In case these figures are too high, in view of the available funds the alternative would seem to redraw the plans with a modified program as to the requirements both of the veterans and the opera house, and with the accommodations strictly limited to the funds allowed." Why, they should have known that in the beginning. That is signed, Arthur Brown, Jr., and G. L. Lansburgh, architects. That is their own statement. They made plans calling for the expenditure of $8,200,000, they made plans calling for the expenditure of $7,250,000, and then they tell you, as a third alternative, they can make the plans within the amount available.

SUPERVISOR ROSSI: A point of information, Mr. Mayor. Is a point of order in order when there is a point of order already decided by your Honor at this time?

SUPERVISOR RONCOVIERI: Let me get this off my chest.

THE MAYOR: He has talked over five minutes; he is out of order.

SUPERVISOR RONCOVIERI: Well, Mr. Mayor, you speak about "political influence". I will say this: I think that your political influence and your political whip is cracking over some of these Supervisors; that is my opinion.

SUPERVISOR STANTON: Mr. Mayor, we very patiently listened to you the other night from 11 o'clock until 8 o'clock in the morning without a complaint. And we have not commented on the length of your report. The Supervisor now rises to talk on the report that you took all night to make, and somebody gets up and says that the five-minute limit should be held on him, and I do not think that you ought to rule——

SUPERVISOR ROSSI (interrupting): I did not make that point, Mr. Mayor. I know that there is a point of order to be decided by yourself, and I would like to know whether that point of order has been decided. Supervisor Roncovieri was not speaking to that.

THE MAYOR: There is an appeal.

SUPERVISOR STANTON: I did not hear what you said, but I did hear the Mayor say that he has talked over five minutes and he is out of order, and I did not think that was fair after we have been sitting here for possibly 20 or 30 hours listening without taking part in the discussion at all.

THE MAYOR: Why shouldn't you? This is the first time a report of the history of the War Memorial has ever been prepared. It is about time the people of San Francisco had a real history of the War Memorial. It is about time that you did stay up and listen to the report of a matter that has been going on for 13 years. I just gave you that in printed form so that anybody who wants to read it and know what has transpired can do so. It is all facts.

SUPERVISOR STANTON: That is very true, and we have been very patient with you, but at the same time no member of the Board, after all that has been said, should be held to five minutes. He is talking to the subject that is before the house.

THE MAYOR: No, he got into that by talking about the architects and one thing and another. I say, he convicted himself of political influence by the fact that he says he is rejecting all the names submitted by the Mayor, and yet he is now condemning, on grounds of extravagance and incompetency, the very men whom he heretofore in the afternoon said he would endorse if one change was made. Why be afraid of telling Mr. Kingsbury that you are against him; why be afraid of telling Mr. George Hearst that you are against him; why be afraid of telling Mr. George Cameron that you are against him; why be afraid of telling General Hunter Liggett that you are against him; why be afraid of telling James I. Herz that you are against him; why be afraid of telling Frank L. Belgrano that you are against him; why be afraid of telling Robert I. Bentley that you are against him; why be afraid? That is where I say the political issue is involved, because you are not brave enough to come up and vote "No," but you want to turn them all down as a whole, for the purpose of thinking that you are hiding under a declination to vote for the whole of them when, in fact, you are voting against every one of them.

SUPERVISOR RONCOVIERI: I want to speak to a question of personal privilege: You say I am not brave. All right, I am going to prove my bravery. I say it is downright cowardice——

THE MAYOR (interrupting): On your part.

SUPERVISOR RONCOVIERI: On your part, that you do not dare to take one of those men off and substitute another. The shoe is on the other foot. You dare not take Mr. Kingsbury off, or anyone else off; you want to pass the buck; that is downright cowardice on your part. Take one man off and put on a veteran and we are all right.

THE MAYOR: And every name is satisfactory to you; every nominee?

SUPERVISOR McGOVERN: Yes.

THE MAYOR: Is every name——

SUPERVISOR RONCOVIERI (interrupting): You bring in a majority of veterans as you were asked courteously to do two years ago, in 1928.

THE MAYOR: Why, you just put me on in December, 1928, and I commenced action that you could not even start.

SUPERVISOR RONCOVIERI: We told you then——

THE MAYOR (interrupting): Let me tell you one thing more: Early in August, upon the motion of Mr. McSheehy, seconded by another member of the Board, this Board unanimously passed a resolution that the Mayor be demanded to forthwith name the eleven trustees. I came over here from my office, surprised that such a resolution had been passed, telling you that if you insisted upon the eleven names being nominated, I would bring it in the following week. Did I not do that?

SUPERVISOR McSHEEHY: Mr. Mayor.

THE MAYOR: And we had three meetings in the Mayor's office, and every name on this list was approved by the Board of Supervisors.

SUPERVISOR McSHEEHY: Mr. Mayor, you have recognized me some time back, and I simply will say this to the members of the Board: we have reached an impasse here today.

SUPERVISOR SHANNON: What is the parliamentary situation?

THE MAYOR: Trying to get a ruling on the appeal from the decision of the Chair that Mr. Havenner's motion was out of order.

SUPERVISOR McSHEEHY: I am out of order, Supervisor; we have all been out of order. I recognize the fact that I am out of order, but every speaker that you have allowed—and you have allowed them all the privilege to express themselves to some degree, and now may I simply say this to you and to the members of the Board: I was asked a direct question, just before we assembled here today, why I did vote last night No in reference to adjournment. I said I would like to see some results. I would like to see that work started. I stated here last night, "I will stay here tonight and tomorrow night and every night until you start that work." Now, I happen to be in the building business and I know of thousands of men in that line that are walking our streets, and a great many could be put to work over there. Now, we have reached an impasse here this afternoon, a positive impasse; a condition has been created here in a way that I am afraid we will come to no results whatsoever. Now, we have here rules; we have Roberts Rules of Order and our own rules, and we have agreed to those rules unanimously. And one member of this Board has asked that one rule be complied with, and through a twist or a juggling of conditions you have been voted down in your ruling. A condition is before you again, and I am afraid you will be voted down again. Then why are we staying here, and how long are we going to continue to stay here and create this impasse? If we are going to create it forever, all right. Now, we have a right, as members of this Board, and our rules prescribe those rights, and I am rather surprised—I do not want to say a word now against my friend Franck Havenner, whom I have been so closely associated with, but I am rather surprised at him again here this afternoon in invoking a condition, creating a condition that is creating an impasse, because I have such a high opinion of him. He realizes our condition. Now, I say to the members of this Board: we have to go on record. I do not wish to place any member of this Board in a jam. I have no desire to. There is no member of this Board that I hold any animosity to, but let me say this, and I speak somewhat to those who were re-elected with me last year, that the old Board was charged continually with procrastinating and not doing anything. Now, what are we doing? We are attempting to pick up a motion that was made months ago and carry it here today, and we are not allowing that motion to be properly presented. And I ask that it be segregated, and one member has asked that, and a condition is created in which the Mayor will be voted down again. And I do not know how long we are going to stay here, but I personally will stay here tomorrow and the next day and the day after, because I want to see something started over there to give men work here in San Francisco.

SUPERVISOR McGOVERN: Mr. Mayor, I think you had the crux of the thing almost answered in Supervisor Roncovieri's argument with you. You asked Supervisor Roncovieri, I believe, that if you could by any way, manner or means not remove one name, but if you could influence some one of the members or the names that you have submitted to this Board to withdraw, and substitute, in place of one of those names, a member of the veterans, whether we would vote for it or not. I will answer for my vote, "Yes," if you could get six veterans there. I am in favor of all of the members that you have submitted here at the present time. But I feel that the veterans should have a majority of the Trustees in conducting the affairs of the War Memorial, and if you should or could, in any way, manner or form, find some one of the members out of the names you have submitted who would withdraw, and that you could put a member of the Veterans on there in place of that name, I am for you.

THE MAYOR: Now, Mr. McGovern, there is nobody more anxious than I am to see that work going. That is the reason I have kept going on this thing for so long. I have never yet been able to find out if any one of those members of the eleven were unsatisfactory to the Board. I am told today, as I have been in the past, that every name is satisfactory, but the complexion is not right on account of there being five veterans, one labor man and five former members of the Board of Trustees, who handled the funds for eight years. Did the statements made last night by Mr. Glensor, Mr. Burns and Mr. Sapiro influence the members of this Board when they said they opposed every single name of the eleven? General Hunter Liggett was too old and that Frank L. Belgrano was the only name that they would stand for. Do I understand today now that those statements will be disregarded, and if the Mayor makes an appointment so that there will be six veterans, which he wants to do, that they will then be approved by the Board of Supervisors?

SUPERVISOR McGOVERN: Answering for myself, yes.

THE MAYOR: Do I hear that from all the members of the Board?

SUPERVISOR HAVENNER: The position of the Board is that there should be a majority of veterans on that Board of Trustees, yes, and if the nomination of your Honor, the sixth veteran, is satisfactory to the Board, so far as I am concerned, yes.

SUPERVISOR McGOVERN: And I am speaking for myself, too, yes.

SUPERVISOR SUHR: You will get it from me.

THE MAYOR: Mr. Roncovieri.

SUPERVISOR RONCOVIERI: You name them first, and then I will tell you afterwards.

THE MAYOR: That is just the point.

SUPERVISOR RONCOVIERI: If you had done that in the first place, we would not be here today.

SUPERVISOR ANDRIANO: Let us put the question, Mr. Mayor; let us get through.

SUPERVISOR POWER: I say, without being discourteous to you, or any other member of the Board, at this time debate is out of order; an appear from the decision of the Chair has been made, and an appeal from a decision of the Chair is not debatable.

THE MAYOR: Call the roll, Mr. Clerk.

SUPERVISOR HAVENNER: Will the Clerk state the question, please?

THE CLERK: Supervisor Havenner, seconded by Supervisor Miles, moved that the previous action of the Board be reaffirmed, whereupon the Mayor declared it out of order, and then Supervisor Havenner, seconded by Supervisor Peyser, appealed from the decision of the Chair declaring that out of order.

SUPERVISOR HAVENNER: The question is: shall the ruling of the Chair be sustained?

SUPERVISOR POWER: Mr. Mayor, I wish to say regarding my vote on this, whether to sustain the Chair or not, it has no bearing upon my vote on the main question when it is put.

THE CLERK: (Roll call.)

Ayes: Supervisors Andriano, Hayden, McSheehy, Rossi, Suhr and Toner. Noes: Supervisors Canepa, Havenner, McGovern, Miles, Peyser, Power, Roncovieri, Shannon, Spaulding and Stanton.

Absent: Supervisors Colman and Gallagher.

THE CLERK: Ten noes, six ayes, two absent.

THE MAYOR: Lost.

SUPERVISOR SHANNON: Question.

SUPERVISOR HAVENNER: State the question.

THE MAYOR: The question is that the nominees of the Mayor be turned down by the Board.

SUPERVISOR SHANNON: No, that is not the question.

THE MAYOR: What is the question?

THE CLERK: That the previous action of the Board be reaffirmed.

THE MAYOR: Well, that is the same thing.

SUPERVISOR POWER: With the consent of the mover of the motion and his second, I would ask the privilege of offering a substitute motion: That the Trustees submitted by you be returned with a recommendation from this Board that you comply with the wishes, which you have pretty well ascertained today, of the members of this Board regarding an additional veteran.

SUPERVISOR McGOVERN: Second that.

SUPERVISOR RONCOVIERI: Second that; that is good.

THE MAYOR: Call the Roll, Mr. Clerk.

THE CLERK: (Roll call.)

SUPERVISOR ANDRIANO——

SUPERVISOR ANDRIANO (interrupting): Just a minute. I would like to know if the other motion has been withdrawn?

SUPERVISOR HAVENNER: No; he has made an amendment to it.

SUPERVISOR ANDRIANO: I would like to offer now a substitute for the whole, Mr. Mayor, and in order that it may be clear, I am going to read the motion:

"Whereas, in accordance with the provisions of the Charter of the City and County of San Francisco, his Honor, Mayor Rolph, Jr., subject to confirmation by this Board, has appointed eleven citizens and residents of San Francisco as and to constitute the Board of Trustees of the War Memorial, and has requested this Board to confirm such appointments; and

"Whereas, this Board has heretofore refused to confirm said appointments to said Board of Trustees of the War Memorial, but on the contrary has rejected them; and

"Whereas, in refusing to confirm and in rejecting said appointments this Board has acted upon said appointments collectively and has not voted to confirm or reject any individual appointments; and

"Whereas, in view of the action of this Board in refusing to confirm and in rejecting said appointments as a whole, it is impossible for the Mayor to become informed as to whether or not any of said appointments or appointees are satisfactory to this Board; now therefore be it

"Resolved, That this Board proceed to consider the names of said appointees individually and vote to confirm or reject each of said appointments separately."

SUPERVISOR McSHEEHY: I will second that motion, Mr. Mayor.

THE MAYOR: The motion is before the house.

SUPERVISOR ANDRIANO: And I wish to reserve the right to speak on the motion.

SUPERVISOR PEYSER: Mr. Mayor, it is really an unfortunate situation that the real issue in this case is being continually confused. I pay my respects to Supervisor Andriano for the manner in which he has stated that motion. Now, the situation is not that we have refused to confirm any one of them. Let us face the real issue before us, and what is it? And let us not put it in the words of parliamentary law, or anything else. The issue today is, shall there be six veterans on that Board, or shall there not be, and the question whether the Mayor can find out who is rejected and who is not is not the issue. We all say that they are fine appointments, but we do not believe that the duty has been carried out to put six veterans on the Board, and we can continually proceed to motion after motion and substitution for the whole, and it will not change the situation, by innuendo or circumvention, to confuse the issue. There is no question here about the caliber of men on that Board, but we certainly have a right, and I, as a representative of the people, have a right to say whether or not I believe that the resolution of this Board of Supervisors should be carried out, to-wit: A majority of the members of the Board of Trustees shall be veterans. That is the issue. Let us not confuse it; let us not circumvent around all sorts of legal procedure; let us face the issue, and if those who accuse us of being politically boss ridden will have the stamina to face the issue and let this Board vote as to whether or not the majority shall be veterans, the question will soon be solved. Now, let us have the real issue: Shall there be six veterans on the Board or not? Let us vote on that question, and the Mayor, I presume, will be guided by that procedure.

SUPERVISOR ANDRIANO: I desire to answer the remarks of Supervisor Peyser because they were specifically directed to me. In the first place, I desire to cast no reflection upon any member of this Board concerning politics. I know nothing about politics, do not care a fig about politics, but, however, I have some idea of my duty as a Supervisor. And, without accusing any member of this Board, I respectfully submit to my colleagues on the Board that they had no right to adopt the resolution before the Mayor made his appointments. And we are not the judges as to who should go on that Board of Trustees, that is to say, whether a majority of one group or another group should go on the Board of Trustees. The people of San Francisco have spoken by passing a Charter amendment. There is not a word in that Charter amendment as to how many veterans there shall be. The Charter amendment simply says that they shall be given "due representation," just as it says that the interests or the groups that contributed to the opera house and to the art museum should be given due representation. Suppose that the groups representing the art museum and the opera house had come to us and asked that a majority of them be on the Board of Trustees. We would have been derelict in our duty if we had said to them, "Yes, we will not put our approval upon the Board of Trustees unless there is a majority of

opera men or art museum men." Suppose that the Chamber of Com.
merce or the Downtown Association had come to us and said, "We
would like to have a majority of our members on that Board of Trus.
tees." We certainly would have been recreant to our trust if we had
promised them, in advance, that we were going to give them a ma.
jority. That is the point that I make: that this Board had no right
and was recreant to its trust as public officials in pledging itself, be.
forehand, that it would not approve the list submitted by the Mayor
unless a majority of any particular group was on that Board. I sub.
mit that as a plain proposition of legislation, I submit that as a legal
proposition, that the members of this Board had no right, and when
Supervisor Roncovieri said, "We warned the Mayor beforehand," the
Mayor can well retort, "You had no right to warn me," just as the
Congress of the United States has no right to tell the President of
the United States, who has the appointing power, that certain ap.
pointees shall belong to a certain party, or that a majority of a cer.
tain group shall belong to a certain faction or a certain party.

SUPERVISOR POWER: But they do.

SUPERVISOR ANDRIANO: They may advise the President out of
court, or out of the chambers of the Congress, and they do——

SUPERVISOR STANTON (interrupting): They send the name
right in.

SUPERVISOR ANDRIANO: They do not pass a resolution in Congress, because they have a higher idea of their function, of their duty
as public officials, than we seem to have on this Board of Supervisors.
Secondly, it has been stated by practically every member of this Board
time and again, that there is no objection to any single member of
this present Board of Trustees; that they are all respectable, honorable, competent men, with the possible exception of Supervisor Roncovieri, who questions their ability. Now, it seems to me that it is
impossible to withhold the conclusion that, if we recognize the fact
that they are competent men, honest men, public-spirited men, and
yet say that we will not accept them as a group, it is rather hard,
without going to the extreme of saying that political considerations
are involved; it is rather hard to say that you are acting for the best
interests, not of a group, not of a party, but for the best interests
of the entire people of San Francisco. If you say that they are all
satisfactory, they are all competent, are not you stultifying yourself?
"Individually they are O. K., but collectively I reject them." And I
say, answering Supervisor Shannon, that we can vote aye on every
single name and then refuse to approve the Board as a whole. I say
that our approval of the Board as a whole would be an idle act, because if we approve of them all individually, a court would hold that
the entire Board has been approved. So now, Mr. Mayor, let us proceed in the manner that the people of San Francisco expect us to
proceed, in the manner that they have expressed their will in the
Charter amendment. The Charter amendment says the Mayor shall
make the appointments, the Board of Supervisors shall confirm those
appointments. I repeat what I said before, that the duty of the Board
of Supervisors, the power of the Board of Supervisors to act as legis-
lators on this question did not begin until the Mayor submitted the
list to us. We might have seen the Mayor; we might have counseled
with the Mayor to see that he would give a certain group a larger
representation, but as a Board of Supervisors we had no legal right
to commit ourselves until our power as a Board to act upon that list
of appointees was started. Now, Mr. Mayor, I submit that the procedure in this matter pending before us is entirely regular. You
were within your rights in ignoring that abuse of power on the part
of the Board of Supervisors in committing itself before the time came
for the Board of Supervisors to act; you were entirely within your
rights in ignoring that committment, because that committment, in my
humble opinion, and I am sincere in what I say, was contrary to the

express language of the Charter amendment, which represents the will of the people of San Francisco. You have submitted this list; the Board saw fit to reject it the first time. You have submitted again to a new Board this list of nominees. I say, there is only one way the Mayor can know what is in our minds, and that is by voting upon them individually. Supervisor Roncovieri has stated that he will not commit himself now beforehand; he will wait until tomorrow to act. Why didn't he use that discretion last year when this resolution was before him in connection with the naming of these veterans on the Board, and I am not arguing against the veterans; personally, I would like to see them have the entire eleven; but it is a question of principle which is before us. It is a question, I fear, that unless we Board of Supervisors come down to our senses and act according to law, the courts of this City and County will have to bring us to our senses. So how can we know? Let's be reasonable. The veterans last year— I am sure they won't deny this—stated they were satisfied with the entire membership with the exception of two; those two were Major Kendrick and Supervisor Colman. Those were the only two whom they designated by name and stated to us that they weren't satisfied; that they were not satisfactory to them. The others they said were acceptable to them. Now they come to us and tell us they are all objectionable with the exception of one and possibly of two—Frank Belgrano and General Hunter Liggett. They tell us that they are opposed to any member of the old Board of Trustees going on the new Board. They tell us that some of these nominees, because of the fact that they have been generous and magnanimous, should not be considered; and they insinuate that they are in fact opposed to them and tell us plainly that they are not acceptable to them. How are we going to satisfy them? Not by going half way with them, but by going all the way. How is the Mayor to know when Supervisor Roncovieri and others here have refused to tell him. They tell us if he puts only one more Legion man on the Board, then they will approve the list. I submit, in all frankness, that the only way, let us go through the list, and let us accept or reject them, and then the Mayor will know what to do.

Mr. Havenner is within his rights in rejecting every single one and making the statement that he believes a majority of veterans should be on the list. He is within his rights. The time to act is now, not last year when this question was not before us. Not two years ago before the Mayor ever thought of appointing the Trustees. We must have some sound procedure upon which to proceed in all matters, otherwise we shall be forever wrangling and never get anywhere.

SUPERVISOR PEYSER: I did not intend to say anything further at this time, but I cannot refrain, in view of the real legal argument which Supervisor Andriano has propounded here, to call his attention to a few facts of legal significance. In March, 1927, the members of the War Memorial Committee were advised by City Attorney John J. O'Toole that he had eliminated from the resolution for the $4,000,000 bond issue all direct mention of an art museum and opera house in order to make sure that the bond issue might conform with the statutes of California. Why was that done? To make sure that it would conform with law, and then they went out and the bond issue was advertised and campaigned on that basis, and I am satisfied with the legal phase of that part of it. Now, coming down to the action of the Board of Supervisors. The people of San Francisco voted for the War Memorial and this Board, whether wisely or unwisely, legally or illegally—and I believe, if I am correct, that his Honor was present at the time—passed this resolution stating that a majority of veterans should be appointed to this Board——

THE MAYOR (interrupting): I didn't pass it.

SUPERVISOR PEYSER: I didn't say that; I said you were sitting in the Board——

THE MAYOR: I didn't, it came over to me and I let it go through, I don't think I was even in the Board at the time.

SUPERVISOR PEYSER: I see. Then, coming down to the question of electing or rejecting these members by this Board, Supervisor Andriano knows as well as I do, or any other attorney, that in all cases where nothing has ever been done, or there is no statute which provides for it, that precedent governs. We have the common law in England for such cases, and common law in some states in this country, and finally in California we have a statute on our books to provide for cases where there is no statute covering. What is the resolution which confronts us with the building of the War Memorial? What precedent have we for running a War Memorial? We have the precedent of cities all over the United States and of cities and towns in California.

SUPERVISOR ANDRIANO: If I may, through the chair, would you yield to a question, Mr. Peyser?

SUPERVISOR PEYSER: Yes, sir.

SUPERVISOR ANDRIANO: Do you know whether those cities act according to the same charter amendment we have here in San Francisco?

SUPERVISOR PEYSER: It provides that due consideration shall be given to veterans, and when it comes down to a question of construing "due consideration" then, of course, we have to look to precedent. What is the "due consideration" given to veterans in other places? Due consideration has been the giving to them of a majority on every Board of this kind in practically every city, and therefore I, for one, am perfectly willing to be guided by that precedent.

SUPERVISOR POWER: Question.

SUPERVISOR HAVENNER: Question. State the question.

THE CHAIRMAN: What is the question?

THE CLERK: The question is on Supervisor Andriano's second of Supervisor McSheehy's motion, moving a substitute, which he read, the resolved portion of which being that this Board proceed to consider the names of said appointees individually and vote to confirm or reject each of said appointees separately.

THE MAYOR: Call the roll.

THE CLERK (roll call):

Ayes—Supervisors Andriano, Hayden, McSheehy, Power, Rossi, Suhr, Toner—7.

Noes—Supervisors Canepa, Havenner, McGovern, Miles, Peyser, Roncovieri, Shannon, Spaulding, Stanton—9.

Absent—Supervisors Colman, Gallagher—2.

THE CLERK: Nine noes and seven ayes.

SUPERVISOR HAVENNER: Call the roll on Supervisor Power's motion.

THE MAYOR: What is the motion?

THE CLERK: Supervisor Power's motion that the nominations be returned to the Mayor.

SUPERVISOR POWER: With the recommendation that the Mayor give due consideration to the request made and name at least another veteran, that another veteran be added to the list.

THE MAYOR: Call the roll.

THE CLERK (roll call):

Ayes—Supervisors Canepa, Havenner, Hayden, McGovern, Miles, Peyser, Power, Roncovieri, Rossi, Shannon, Spaulding, Stanton, Suhr, Toner—14.

Noes—Supervisors Andriano, McSheehy—2.

Absent—Supervisors Colman, Gallagher—2.

THE CLERK: Fourteen ayes, two noes and two absent.

THE MAYOR: The ayes have it and it is so ordered.

SUPERVISOR HAVENNER: I move we adjourn.

THE MAYOR: Wait a minute; the Board has not adjourned yet. I want to now read into the record the questions asked me last night.

SUPERVISOR ANDRIANO: I wish, your Honor, to tender at this time my resignation as chairman of the Rules Committee.

THE MAYOR: .Well, we are all very sorry to hear of your resignation, but it is a matter for the Board entirely.

SUPERVISOR McSHEEHY: May I say, I hope you will not do that, we need you, need you badly, need your advice, and I hope you will reconsider that resignation for at least. 24 hours. I say that as a member of the Rules Committee, and I say it in all sincerity.

SUPERVISOR HAVENNER:. There was no second to the motion.

THE MAYOR: I can readily appreciate Supervisor Andriano's feeling about the matter of being chairman of the Rules Committee when those rules have been voted down today, and having the advice of the City Attorney, and if one rule is no good, the others are no good. However, that is a matter for Mr. Andriano entirely, and it is entirely up to the Board and not to myself.

SUPERVISOR POWER: I move that the resignation be considered at a later date.

SUPERVISOR McSHEEHY: He doesn't press it.

THE MAYOR: Let me ask the Board, before I proceed with this reading into the record, because it may become necessary later, do I understand that if the Mayor can find a way of. honorably changing his nominees so that one more veteran will be added to the list, thus making eleven, that this Board will confirm the entire eleven?

SUPERVISOR McSHEEHY: Call the roll on that, if you want.

SUPERVISOR POWER: On what?

SUPERVISOR McSHEEHY: I will make it as a motion, if you wish, your Honor.

SUPERVISOR HAYDEN: Make a motion and I will second it.

THE MAYOR: The Mayor is in a very embarrassing position. The Mayor has selected eleven men whom all of you say are honorable men in this community and worthy of appointment as members of the War Memorial Trustees. The Mayor from the beginning would like to have put on all the veterans that he could. The Mayor is following a principle in this matter. The nominees when appointed must meet with the approval of the Regents of the University of California. I am going to read into the record this afternoon that trust agreement. If consideration is given to the statements made last night by Mr. Glensor and Mr. Burns and Mr. Sapiro, those names will not be confirmed by the Regents of the University of California. The Mayor is trying to find out from you which one of those eleven you wish removed and the Mayor will put a veteran in his place. You share this responsibility with me, because you put in that charter amendment that the names submitted by the Mayor need your confirmation. You are equally responsible with me. You should have, which you didn't, indicated to the Mayor which ones you wanted taken off so that the Mayor could put a veteran on in place of them. Now, you ask me to take off a gentleman whom you say is honorable, and put on a veteran; and I, therefore, must go and say to that gentleman, "I must ask you that I be permitted to excuse you from the honor I conferred upon you in asking you to accept that nomination." Again, acceptance carries with it the approval of the entire eleven. I am confronted with a lot of resignations. I am confronted with this agreement from the Regents of the University of California, and I am confronted with law suits for the bringing of suits to prevent the use of money which was given for the building of the Opera House specifically. Your action doesn't help the situation at all, and if you want to be helpful— you could be helpful—you could say to me, and you could be helpful, you could say to me, "Mayor, if you succeed in honorably getting one of those non-veterans or former War Trustee or somebody else off your Board and you nominate an acceptable veteran, we will sustain your entire eleven," and we will be on our way. Will you do that?

SUPERVISOR HAVENNER: That has been my position all the way through. I have taken the position that if the majority of nominations against whom there could be no specific and competent objection with respect to his qualifications for the office, that I would vote to approve a Board of Trustees consisting of a majority of veterans. I would like to suggest to your Honor, and I would like to amplify that to the extent I would not be bound to vote for some man previously connected with this project against whom specific objection might be made. Outside of that, any man representing some veteran organization and whose qualifications were not subject to any competent impugnment would make the entire Board satisfactory as far as I am concerned.

SUPERVISOR PEYSER: Your Honor, I am most desirous of cooperating with your Honor, and I will say that, for myself, if a man is put on there who is truly representative of the veteran organizations I also would vote for all of your appointees with the exception of one whom I am now considering on the basis of a charge made against him here. I am frank to say as to that one I am not entirely determined as yet, I am still considering.

THE MAYOR: Mr. Toner.

SUPERVISOR TONER: I agree with what my associates, Mr. Havenner and Mr. Peyser, have said; I will.

THE MAYOR: Supervisor Spaulding.

SUPERVISOR SPAULDING: I will.

THE MAYOR: Supervisor Roncovieri.

SUPERVISOR RONCOVIERI: I agree with those also.

THE MAYOR: Supervisor McSheehy.

SUPERVISOR McSHEEHY: I agree, I was trying to put a motion to that effect.

· THE MAYOR: Supervisor Rossi.

SUPERVISOR ROSSI: I certainly will, Mr. Mayor.

THE MAYOR: Supervisor Power.

SUPERVISOR POWER: I agree and supplement my recommendation that the name of a veteran be put on in place of that of Mr. Mullen.

THE MAYOR: Supervisor Canepa.

SUPERVISOR CANEPA: Your Honor, my only real objection was that there wasn't a majority of veterans appointed on the Board of Trustees, and if it is possible for the Mayor to appoint an active representative of the veterans it will be entirely satisfactory to me.

THE MAYOR: Supervisor Andriano.

SUPERVISOR ANDRIANO: Having accepted your recommendation heretofore, I think you are justified in assuming that I will accept any future recommendations that you may see fit to make, but my position is this: As a member of the Board of Supervisors I have no right in the Board of Supervisors to express beforehand what I will do when the names are submitted to us as a Board. I reserve my right, always, to speak at the proper time when my authority to speak comes in play.

THE MAYOR: I think you will find from the names I have submitted, and the encomiums of praise for the men I have submitted as nominees heretofore, apparently there will be no objection to them. Supervisor Shannon.

SUPERVISOR SHANNON: The conditions as stated by Supervisor Havenner cover my position.

THE MAYOR: Supervisor Miles.

SUPERVISOR MILES: I do not care to pledge myself at this time.

THE MAYOR: Now, you see that one vote prevents me from asking somebody to retire, because I have not the assurance of the Board of Supervisors unanimously that in the going off of one and putting a good veteran on in his place the entire list of names will be confirmed. I think you owe me that. I think you have to help me out in the situation I am in. There would have been six veterans if the question had not been raised as to this representative of labor who was appointed—I have nothing against the veterans; they have honored me more than any man in the United States has been honored, but I am confronted, and so are you, with this trust agreement, confronted with the $2,000,000 private subscriptions, or thereabouts. So much has been said about these fine, outstanding citizens that I am afraid some of them may refuse to serve. I would like to reply to Mr. Sapiro that we need $50,000 subscriptions; we need men who would put a zoo in the Park; we need men who would put up $25,000 and $50,000 subscriptions. Yet we do appreciate your $2 subscription; we do appreciate Mr. Glensor's $2 subscription; we do appreciate every subscription, whether it is for $50,000 or for half a dollar, or the widow's mite, but with 50,000 veterans and $2 apiece, that would be only $100,000, and we need this $2,000,000 plus the $4,000,000 bond issue. Another thing, please don't let it be lost sight of, that we have not been able to sell the bonds on a basis of 4½ per cent a year. I need your help to go and be released from an honorable request which you entrusted me with, and I think you, Mr. Miles, will agree with that.

SUPERVISOR MILES: I withdraw my previous statement and take the same position as Mr. Havenner and Mr. Peyser.

SUPERVISOR HAVENNER: I move, your Honor, that the privilege of the floor be granted to Mr. Sapiro.

THE MAYOR: Mr. Sapiro has the floor.

MR. MILTON SAPIRO: I want to say for the record——

SUPERVISOR HAYDEN (interrupting): I agree, your Honor.

MR. SAPIRO (continuing): I just want to state this for the Mayor, inasmuch as you refer again to the amount of the subscriptions, that if the amount of the subscriptions by the veteran organizations of San Francisco is to be the basis, that if it had not been that those veterans offered their bodies to the service of this country, something that is priceless, there would be no need for the War Memorial, and the men who have money in this country would have no need for the money; this would have been a defeated country and not a victorious country, and we are tired of being reminded of the money given for this cause.

THE MAYOR: Supervisor Stanton.

SUPERVISOR STANTON: I was outside just now, but I understand you said you would put six veterans on as members of this Board. Now, I am the president of the San Francisco Labor Council, and in connection with labor I never remember of them demanding anything of the veterans——

THE MAYOR (interrupting): But you were present.

SUPERVISOR STANTON: But we made no demands whatever for representation on this Board.

THE MAYOR: I did it.

SUPERVISOR STANTON: It was not a demand of labor.

THE MAYOR: Let me put this in the record. I have never yet referred to the subscriptions or amounts thereof, nor have I ever talked about subscriptions of the veterans. I have done nothing in the entire record of the history of the War Memorial but recognize the veterans and plead their cause, but I will not surrender to dishonesty in the repudiation of names signed to a document. Names which have been repudiated any more than I would stand for the repudiation of the name on an endorsement of a note or a signing of a contract, because when a man's name is once signed to it, it is supposed to be good, and I will never surrender nor capitulate to dishonesty——

SUPERVISOR PEYSER (interrupting): Through the Chair, I would like to ask the privilege of the floor for Mr. Sapiro.

MR. SAPIRO: If you mean anything personal, my name was not signed to those plans, and if my signature were on those plans, Mr.

Mayor, I would make the same statement. We made Mr. John Drum, when he made use of the term "repudiating the plans," and the record will show, we made him withdraw those words, because he finally was man enough to acknowledge that the plans had never been repudiated, but the Trustees after we had approved the plans changed the plans thereafter without any approval from the veterans, and you know that from the record. If you dare to intimate that anyone has been dishonest in this matter, it is dishonest to make that statement.

THE MAYOR: I want to tell you those names were signed to those plans——

MR. SAPIRO (interrupting): I have never repudiated those names, and you don't say the truth when you say the veterans repudiated those plans, because the Trustees, without notification to a person, changed those plans. What do you call that, honest or dishonest, trickery or not? Mr. Mayor, you stated that you stand for the veterans.

THE MAYOR: Yes, sir, I do.

MR. SAPIRO: Then don't take the attitude of calling them on the things for which they should not be called and not calling them on anything else.

THE MAYOR: On the mere protest, ten feet in the hallways were taken off in order to meet your requirements and in order to cut down the cost of the buildings in order that we might build these buildings according to the amount of money we had. Those names repudiate this on the ten-foot cut——

MR. SAPIRO (interrupting): Oh, no, they don't; we never repudiated the plans.

SUPERVISOR POWER: The privilege of the floor is requested for Mr. Wiedenfeld.

MR. WIEDENFELD: Mr. Mayor, honorable members of the Board of Supervisors of the City of San Francisco. The Mayor made the statement the other night that the veterans unanimously approved those plans. I have been a member of the American Legion since its inception, and a member of the Plans Committee of the American Legion, and not because any change has ever been made by the veterans did I act as I did, but because those plans were never given to the veterans and the veterans were never given a fair deal. I refused then to sign those plans and will forever until they are given a fair deal, and they are not being given it on that.

THE MAYOR: I didn't know you were even a member of the Board; I didn't know of your activity on the Board. I have never seen you at any of the meetings, neither here or in my chambers, nor have you been a member of the committee of three members from the veteran organizations, three members from the Board of Supervisors and three members from the Trustees. I wil say that if your name is not on this endorsement of those plans you are not included in the remarks that I have made, and therefore there is no need of your getting excited.

MR. WIEDENFELD: You said that it was unanimous, and I just wanted to invite your attention to the fact that it was not unanimous. I was present on November 20th in his office, and likewise it is referred to in his own report that Mr. Wiedenfeld and Mr. Gerlach did not approve those plans.

THE MAYOR: I stand upon the report.

SUPERVISOR HAVENNER: I move the privilege of the floor to Mr. Burns.

THE CHAIRMAN: Mr. Burns.

MR. JAMES B. BURNS: May I ask if his Honor would repeat the statement which he made previously, as to honesty and dishonesty, as to the names on that plan?

THE MAYOR: Yes, sir, I say that I will not surrender to dishonesty.

MR. BURNS: Just what do you mean in referring to those names in that connection?

THE MAYOR: I mean that the repudiating of those plans for the trifling excuse given is dishonest. Not dishonest in money, but dishonest in purpose.

MR. BURNS: There are many ways in which dishonesty can be manifested, no question about that, but, Mr. Mayor, I have read the record relative to exactly what went on in the open meeting at which Mr. Drum presided, and you have apparently decided to disregard the facts in that connection entirely. You do not refer at all to the 33,000 feet of basement space which the Trustees held up in front of us as satisfying the demands of all of the veterans and giving them the necessary space.

THE MAYOR: The 33,000 feet of basement space?

MR. BURNS: The location of the pillars was entirely changed.

THE CHAIRMAN: The beams and girders that hold up the building are to be the same as in the City Hall, but it is space that can be used, no doubt. I don't know, I haven't seen it, but it is space that is occupiable, the same as the location of part of the Recorder's office, the Fire Department, and other departments in this building. I was never present at any meeting where these plans were approved.

MR. BURNS: I did, and at the time those plans were approved that basement space was usable, but by the actions of the Trustees subsequently they changed those plans to such an extent, by putting in new pillars entirely, as to make the space wholly unusable for the veterans' purposes, and for which we had approved the plans.

THE MAYOR: You do not propose to have the building built, I assume from what you say, in such a manner that it would not meet the tests of the engineer and structural steel men? Or you would not have a building built that would not withstand an earthquake?

MR. BURNS: Then why did the Board of Trustees submit to us plans for our approval if those plans did not meet with the structural requirements of the engineers?

THE MAYOR: I don't know. You signed them.

MR. BURNS: All right, but there was no representation made to us at that time that they did not meet with the structural requirements.

THE MAYOR: I don't know. I assume those signatures were good, and so did everybody else.

MR. BURNS: They were good; they are still good.

SUPERVISOR RONCOVIERI: I ask the privilege of the floor for Mr. Gerlach.

THE MAYOR: Mr. Gerlach.

MR. ALVIN GERLACH: I was also a member of that committee of the American Legion that refused to sign the plans. Mr. Wiedenfeld and myself took the stand that it was wholly improper, from the standpoint of the American Legion, to approve the plans. We had a very stormy session, and the plans were finally approved by fourteen members of the committee. I think something should be said in regard to our reasons for not signing. The real reason why the American Legion changed its attitude towards those plans they had signed is this: I understand that the War Memorial Trustees got an acoustical engineer out from Chicago, who looked over the plans and said that he could not approve of them as they were drawn, that they would necessitate a change in the building which cut down the size of the building and which effected a savings of approximately $400,000, or approximately that sum. We had had a great deal of argument with the Trustees from the very beginning, on account of the building. We felt, at least I personally felt, and I think that Mr. Wiedenfeld felt the same way about it, that it was an insult to the veterans under which the circumstances, and under the conditions under which the people of San Francisco had voted $4,000,000 for this War Memorial project, to lavish the money on an opera house building, and to build a building there with a

large chunk out of it on Franklin street and on the McAllister street
side. We felt entitled to a complete building, as it was our project.
That was one of the main objections to the plans. When we found there
was to be a savings of several hundred thousand dollars on account
of the change in plans we felt that that money should go on the veterans' building, and that we should at least have a completed building.
When we were told by the Trustees that they had gone over the plans
again and found that the Opera House was going to cost more money
than they had at first figured on, and that they would have to have that
$400,000 in addition on the Opera House, then I think that the majority
of the committee came to the conclusion that they had not been dealt
fairly with by the War Memorial Trustees, and I think that that was
very largely responsible for their decision in refusing to sign any
more plans. Had those plans been drawn, or had the project been
completed in accordance with those plans which we signed, or which
were signed, we would not be here today and the buildings would be
half way up, but the War Memorial Trustees changed those plans, and
when those changes were made without our approval we refused to
approve any more plans.

SUPERVISOR HAYDEN: I ask the privilege of the floor for Mr.
Hotchner.

THE MAYOR: Mr. Hotchner:

MR. HAROLD HOTCHNER: I happened to be the chairman of the
Plans Committee, and my name is signed on those plans. Why dishonesty is brought up at this time with reference to those plans is
beyond my understanding. To begin with, our names stand. If you
will build the buildings as shown in the plans which we approved, and
under the conditions as outlined in the letter accompanying our approval, which stated certain things which were to be agreed upon, our
approval of those plans still stand. But even at that, our names stand
good for what we signed. Why charge dishonesty with the signatures
on there? I personally take offense at that statement, and my name
is on there and I am chairman of the Plans Committee.

SUPERVISOR PEYSER: I would ask the privilege of the floor for
Mr. French.

THE MAYOR: Mr. French.

MR. LEON FRENCH: Mr. Mayor, members of the Board of Supervisors, my name is also on those plans, and it is just as good today as
the day it was put on there. I certainly resent the imputation of dishonesty, and I wish to state my reasons. It happened that when that
set of plans was presented for approval by the War Memorial Trustees
to the committee, of which I have been a member since its creation,
I moved the adoption of that set of plans and I signed it, and my signature is just as good today as the day I put it on there. Subsequently
the War Memorial Trustees submitted to the American Legion War
Memorial Committee a second set of plans, conforming not to that set
of plans we had approved, but dissimilar therefrom. And I happened
to have moved the resolution that was adopted with regard to that
second set of plans, and it returned those plans with language about
like this: "We return herewith, unapproved, the set of plans you have
submitted under such and such a date, for the reasons we have ratified
and heretofore approved a set of plans for the Veterans' Building."
There is the action, and find the dishonesty in it if you can.

THE MAYOR: Let me say this to you. How was it that the members of the committee, composed of three members of the veterans'
organizations, three members of the Board of Supervisors themselves,
and the three members of the Trustees, and the Mayor, couldn't get
anywhere in the Mayor's office in the conferences we held over there?
Because we couldn't get anywhere on the plans.

MR. FRENCH: Our agreement stands today as it did the day we put
our names on the plans.

MR. HOTCHNER: If those buildings are built according to the
plans signed at that time, and in accordance with the letter accom-

panying them at that time, our signatures are just as good today as they were at the time they were signed.

THE MAYOR: You say you were cut out of space in the basement in that building because the structural iron engineers recommended that the building would not be safe unless further beams were put on.

MR. HOTCHNER: We were never so notified, Mr. Mayor.

THE MAYOR: How can you say you would proceed with those plans and that your signature stands as good on those if you are told the building is structurally weak?

MR. HOTCHNER: We have never been told that.

THE MAYOR: It has just been discussed here that the basement space was taken away from you. I will ask Mr. Wiedenfeld.

MR. WIEDENFELD: I think I can answer. When our recommendation went back to the Board—that is, the recommendation of those who signed the plans—they were told, and I think Mr. Wagstaff mentioned it, that if he would say that they would be able to eliminate—I think my statement is correct—it was three out of four, or at least two out of every four of the columns from the basement and changed them to the floor above, to the first floor, increasing the bearing strength of the steel structure to carry the load, and at the same time removing the columns and making the basement usable, on such a statement our approval was given to those plans. All of those changes were discussed, and that had not been brought out heretofore this evening, and after those changes were made their own architects agreed that it could be done. Then even after that the Board of War Memorial Trustees sent out to the concrete foundation men of San Francisco and called for bids to construct the foundation, not on those plans and changes they had agreed to, but on the original plans, with all of the columns still in the basement. What is that if it is not dishonesty? That is why the veterans are not willing to accept those plans as changed and modified without their knowledge.

THE MAYOR: I am sorry to see that it is getting so late and that some of the Supervisors are asking to be excused, because I would like to continue this argument here. All of the questions as to the objections to the excavations, the removal of the Locomobile building and the cancelling of the lease of the Standard Oil Company of the lot which they had, and which they are willing to take back and fill in, why those criticisms are made, because those things were done immediately following your approval of these plans.

MR. GLENSOR: Are you propounding a question to which you want an answer?

THE MAYOR: Yes, I want to be enlightened.

MR. GLENSOR: The answer is so plain from what has been said it seems to require very little language to express it. If, immediately following the approval of those plans they saw fit to proceed with the work, they should have stuck by those plans which were approved and not changed to a basis upon which we could not willingly allow them to proceed. Now, you asked a question just a minute ago——

THE MAYOR (interrupting): May I continue the argument with you? Why should you object to the making of plans that would make the building earthquake-proof?

MR. GLENSOR: That has never been brought up to us at all.

THE MAYOR: I am asking you the question.

MR. GLENSOR: That has never been brought up to us; we don't know yet that would.

THE MAYOR: Haven't you stated, all of you today, that all that was done, they took away the basement space because the new engineer said it was not structurally strong enough.

MR. GLENSOR: You said that; we didn't.

THE MAYOR: I didn't say it. I didn't know anything about it until you brought it up.

SUPERVISOR HAYDEN: You haven't called upon me yet. You have not taken a ballot of the Board. I don't think we are going to get anywhere by any further argument, either within or without the Board, as to the details of construction, and so forth. I think that is a matter to be ironed out when the Board of Trustees is finally selected and confirmed by this Board.

I don't think in the beginning when this Board of Supervisors recommended the Mayor that a majority of the personnel of the Trustees should be veterans that it was any good test, for the reason that the Charter amendment itself left the making of the appointments, in making appointments to the said Board, the Mayor was to give due consideration to the veterans—all veterans who had participated in any wars engaged in by the United States. I felt under that power vested in the Mayor that the Mayor exercised due consideration as to the number of veterans he thought necessary to handle the affairs of the War Memorial—as soon as I get Supervisor Roncovieri's attention here—consequently at that time, Mr. Mayor, I voted against the Havenner resolution. In the meantime you selected the eleven members of the Board of Trustees, and on that eleven Trustees you named five veterans, Mr. Mayor. That, of course, brought about a great deal of satisfaction on the part of the veterans and there were numerous meetings held in the Board which got nowhere. I think that the proper and best solution, Mr. Mayor, is the motion of Supervisor Power, for which I voted, which left to you the opportunity to try to induce some member of the Board of Trustees who is not a veteran to resign and that you then in his place nominate one more veteran, making a majority of veterans on the committee, or six in all. Mr. Mayor, in the interests of harmony, I think that is a move in the right direction. Personally, each and every member you recommended to the Board was entirely satisfactory to me, and I have in the past voted to confirm them, and I have voted today to confirm your recommendations, and I think after a ballot of the Board it seems to be the unanimous consensus of the Board that if you can induce some non-veteran on the Board to resign and appoint a veteran, that it will be in the best interests of all concerned.

THE MAYOR: I am going to try to do so, but I believe I should complete the ballot of the Board——

SUPERVISOR HAYDEN (interrupting): I believe you have made that ballot.

THE MAYOR: Yes, I have, but Mr. Sapiro asked for the privilege of the floor and brought forth this argument. Now there are three questions left that Mr. Glensor asked me through the press to answer, and I am prepared to answer them with documentary proof, and some of the proof in connection with the questions asked about the plans and the approval of the plans.

SUPERVISOR HAYDEN: Mr. Mayor, I think if you will defer any further references to plans or any further reference to construction and will follow the suggestion of the motion by Mr. Power, which is concurred in almost unanimously, and make an attempt to name the six veterans, I think you are then on the way to an harmonious solution of this question.

THE MAYOR: I hope so.

SUPERVISOR HAYDEN: If you bring in such a recommendation to the Board you can depend upon the Board for confirmation.

SUPERVISOR PEYSER: I rise to ask the privilege of the floor for Mr. Foley, whose signature appears there on the plans. I have not permitted myself, because there is one man still in doubt in my own mind——

SUPERVISOR SHANNON: I move we adjourn.

SUPERVISOR POWER: Before adjourning, would it be in order to ask you how soon you think you could resubmit the names to us?

THE MAYOR: I would. I don't know, but I would like to submit them tonight, I am so anxious to get this thing under way.

SUPERVISOR POWER: Can you by Monday?

THE MAYOR: It is a very delicate subject. I will see what I can do. Mr. Foley, you have the floor.

MR. FOLEY: My name is Foley, and my name is signed to the plans, and of course it is generally understood that when a person is present and he is called dishonest, and he fails to deny such a statement, there is always a possibility of the inference that he may be dishonest. Whether it be dishonesty of purpose or dishonesty of money, to my mind, both are equally mean. If we went into this project with dishonesty of purpose, it was just as bad as though we went in and took money from those properties. To my mind it is inconceivable that twelve or thirteen of my comrades should all have had a wrong idea about what occurred at that time. I do want to take the floor and state what some of my comrades might state who may not have an opportunity to do so direct; there are so many here. But I am sure they would state the same thing I intend to say and would subscribe to what has already been said by the other comrades. I want to say that in addition to the changes which were made after we signed the plans, we asked the Board if they had enough money to equip completely the veterans building as contemplated, and they told us that they did not have enough money to equip it completely. And we sent out to D. N. & E. Walters and got an estimate on what it would cost to complete and equip the building as it should be, and then we took the question up with Mr. Kendrick, whom we supposed was representing us upon the Board of Trustees, and upon whose representations we relied solely when we signed the plans, and he assured us that it would all be taken care of. In addition to that, other changes were represented to us, and an acoustical engineer by the name of ———————— came out here from Chicago and after examining the plans he said that for acoustical purposes five hundred feet would have to be taken out of that opera house, and that meant a saving of approximately $400,000, which we said in all fairness that that money should go towards the completion of the veterans' building. Those changes were all made after we had signed those plans. I will say, as others have said who signed those plans, and I know that those others who signed and have not had an opportunity to speak here tonight would say the same thing: that we will stand by those signatures, every one of us, if you will finish those buildings in accordance with the plans which we approved. Those plans only cover the exterior and don't purport to cover the interior, and we are perfectly willing now to go ahead and consent to the completion of the building under those plans.

SUPERVISOR MILES: I move we adjourn.

(The motion was seconded by several voices.)

THE MAYOR: I must say one word to Mr. Foley. My experience and the experience of the three members of the Board of Supervisors at all of the meetings which have taken place, I must say that you have asked a number of questions, brought up a number of things in connection with these plans which I knew nothing about; the plans were put into the hands of the War Memorial Trustees. If the Mayor has done you any injustice from the information brought to your attention, and the statements made to him, he will gladly apologize to you.

SUPERVISOR HAYDEN: Move we adjourn.

(The motion was seconded by several voices.)

THE MAYOR: If there is no objection it is so ordered.

(Adjournment.)

J. S. DUNNIGAN, Clerk.

MONDAY, MARCH 3, 1930, 2 P. M.

In Board of Supervisors, San Francisco, Monday, March 3, 1930, 2 p. m.

The Board of Supervisors met in regular session.

CALLING THE ROLL.

The roll was called and the following Supervisors were noted present:

Supervisors Andriano, Canepa, Gallagher, Havenner, Hayden, McGovern, McSheehy, Miles, Peyser, Power, Roncovieri, Rossi, Spaulding, Stanton, Suhr—15.

Absent—Supervisors Colman, Shannon, Toner—3.

Quorum present.

His Honor Mayor Rolph presiding.

APPROVAL OF JOURNAL.

The Journal of Proceedings of the previous meeting was laid over for approval until next meeting.

ROLL CALL FOR PETITIONS AND COMMUNICATIONS.

Discontinuance of S. P. Service on Ocean View Line.

The following was read by the Clerk:

Communication from City Attorney in re application of Southern Pacific Company to discontinue the operation of passenger trains on its so-called Ocean View Line between San Francisco and San Bruno, which application will be heard before the Railroad Commission on Wednesday, March 5, 1930, and advising that, in view of the small number of passengers carried on this route, they see no serious objections to the discontinuance of the service, declaring, however, that it is a matter for the Board to determine and stating that he will be guided by any instructions which he receives.

Referred to the Public Utilities Committee.

In Re Submission by Mayor James Rolph, Jr., of Nominees for War Memorial Trustees.

THE MAYOR: Can we take up the matter of the appointment of the War Memorial Trustees?

SUPERVISOR ROSSI: Yes.

THE MAYOR: Mr. Clerk, what have you on the War Memorial?

Letters from Mayor's Office.

THE CLERK: From the Mayor's office, under date of March 1, 1930:

San Francisco, March 1, 1930.

Honorable Board of Supervisors, City Hall, San Francisco, California.

Gentlemen: I attach hereto for your information letter of declination from the Hon. Herbert Fleishhacker for nomination as a War Memorial Trustee.

Very respectfully,

JAMES ROLPH, Jr., Mayor.

February 27, 1930.

Hon. James Rolph, Mayor of San Francisco, San Francisco, California.

Dear Mr. Mayor: Current newspaper reports suggest an organized opposition in the Board of Supervisors to your nominees for War Memorial Trustees.

It is most unfortunate that actual work on this splendid memorial has been so long delayed. Further and unnecessary delay can only reflect discredit on San Francisco and its patriotic people. The War

Memorial means more to San Francisco than either the whim, personal pride or ambitions of any individual or organization. I respectfully request that you withdraw my name from the list of your nominees. This request is made with the hope that in my stead you may name some citizen who shall be acceptable to the Board of Supervisors.

I am leaving for the East tonight, to be absent, probably, a month. I sincerely hope that before I return this unfortunate controversy may be terminated by the confirmation of Trustees, and that for the honor of San Francisco work upon the Memorial may proceed immediately.

Yours very truly,
HERBERT FLEISHHACKER.

Read and *ordered spread in Journal.*

Appointment of War Memorial Trustees.

The following was read by the Clerk:

February 28, 1930.

Honorable Board of Supervisors, City Hall, San Francisco, California.

Gentlemen: I nominate, for appointment, under the law authorizing and directing me to do so, as Trustees of the War Memorial, subject to your confirmation:

General Hunter Liggett, United States Army, retired, veteran of all wars.

Frank N. Belgrano, former State Commander, American Legion.

Sergeant-Major James I. Herz, 363d Infantry (San Francisco's Own), 91st Division.

Major Charles H. Kendrick, World War veteran.

Lieutenant Richard Montgomery Tobin, World War navy veteran, C. C. Thomas Post, one of the organizers of the American Legion.

Kenneth R. Kingsbury, president Standard Oil Company of California.

Robert I. Bentley, president California Packing Corporation, president Musical Association of San Francisco.

George Cameron, publisher San Francisco Chronicle.

George Hearst, publisher San Francisco Examiner.

James W. Mullen, publisher of the Labor Clarion.

Colonel Jesse C. Colman, Supervisor, World War veteran.

Respectfully submitted,
JAMES ROLPH, Jr., Mayor.

THE MAYOR: What is the pleasure of the Board?

Motion.

SUPERVISOR HAYDEN: I move that the nominations of Trustees to the War Memorial Board, as named by the Mayor, be confirmed by this Board.

SUPERVISOR McSHEEHY: I will second that motion.

SUPERVISOR ROSSI: I will second that motion.

THE MAYOR: Are you ready for the question?

SUPERVISOR GALLAGHER: Well, I would like to ask Supervisor Hayden, the mover of the motion, and the Chair a question: I would like to know, through some of you, if this is being done in legal fashion so that it will be binding? As I understand the situation, Mr. Mayor, you submitted a list of names which were rejected by the Board, in accordance with the powers granted under the charter amendment, and that action stands as the action of the Board. You have now resubmitted a list of names with one taken from the old list, and a new name added, and in order that you might protect the rights of the City, and be sure, I would ask if this is being presented in a legal way? I favor the motion, but I want to be sure, Mr. Mayor, that we are not, unconsciously or unknowingly, running into possible legal complications after the long trail we have gone over. I would ask you to get advice on that to be sure.

THE MAYOR: I have asked legal advice continuously on every move I have made in this matter.

SUPERVISOR GALLAGHER: And this point, too?

THE MAYOR: This follows the precedent of the two former nominations I made, which the Board both voted down. I am proceeding according to the Charter amendment and according to law.

SUPERVISOR GALLAGHER: You are sure, according to law?

THE MAYOR: Yes. Mr. Andriano, I ask you if you do not feel that this matter is strictly in accordance with law, the City Attorney not being here?

SUPERVISOR SHANNON: I would like to ask that the City Attorney be sent for. I have another matter that I am going to ask him about. Will the Sergeant-at-Arms kindly ask the City Attorney to be present? I have conferred with him on other matters, not in connection with this matter. I am not asking for the City Attorney in connection with this matter, Mr. Mayor.

*   *   *   *   *   *

THE MAYOR (the City Attorney having reached the room): I have just, Mr. City Attorney, sent in, in writing, the nominations of eleven citizens, all of whom reside in San Francisco, six of whom are veterans of the wars of our country, and the Board is ready to act on the nominations sent in to them for approval. Mr. Gallagher has asked the Mayor if he is sure that these appointments are all in order, and if elected, would be legally authorized to proceed, with the Board's confirmation.

SUPERVISOR HAYDEN: Mr. Mayor, it would be well to give the City Attorney the formal procedure.

THE MAYOR: Will you read the nominations, Mr. Clerk?

SUPERVISOR GALLAGHER: I might clear it up by a question. Would you want me to ask it?

THE MAYOR: Your question, as I understand it, and which I anticipated, was that Mr. Kendrick is serving as a member of the City Planning Commission.

SUPERVISOR GALLAGHER: No.

THE MAYOR: Well, I will say, for the members of the Board, I hold in my hand the resignation of Mr. Kendrick, dated March 1st. "My dear Mayor: I hereby tender you my resignation as a member of the City Planning Commission of San Francisco, this resignation to be effective at your convenience. Very truly yours, Charles H. Kendrick."

SUPERVISOR GALLAGHER: That was not my idea. My idea is this and I can ask the question: The Mayor has submitted a list of nominees or directors of the War Memorial Board. Said list was rejected by the Board by legislative action. Does the Board have to rescind its former action on the submission of a new list? Can a list, changed in one name, be submitted under the amendment, without any other legislative action except approval or disapproval?

CITY ATTORNEY O'TOOLE: If I get your question, Mr. Gallagher, you mean that, if the Mayor, having submitted ten names that were acted upon before and one additional——

SUPERVISOR GALLAGHER (interrupting): No, perhaps I will put it a different way. If the Board, having acted under the Charter amendment, and rejected the Mayor's nominees, if he then submits a revised list, or the same list of nominees, do we have to rescind any former action or can we proceed on the approval or disapproval of these nominees, as if they came in in the first instance?

CITY ATTORNEY O'TOOLE: I think you may proceed just as if they came in in the first instance, because the rejection of the names was as a whole, that is, the eleven names were rejected. Now, it might be that eleven were rejected because there was one particular name among the eleven which might have been objectionable to the Board of Supervisors. Now, the Mayor has withdrawn one name and substituted a new one.   Therefore, you are voting upon a different body, and the former action of the Board would have nothing to do with the rejection or approval of the present names.

THE MAYOR: Call the roll, Mr. Clerk.

SUPERVISOR POWER: Mr. Mayor, answering your question last Monday, I placed a qualification on my vote on this subject matter, and my statement was that, if you changed the name of Mr. James W. Mullen and substituted a veteran for it, I would vote "yes". I am going to withdraw any objection I had to the list and vote for your recommendations and forget any difficulty with Mr. Mullen, in order to expedite the building of the War Memorial.

THE MAYOR: I thank you. Proceed, Mr. Clerk.

Motion *carried* by following vote:

Ayes—Supervisors Andriano, Canepa, Gallagher, Havenner, Hayden, McSheehy, Miles, Peyser, Power, Roncovieri, Rossi, Shannon, Spaulding, Stanton, Suhr and Toner—16.

Absent—Supervisors Colman and McGovern—2.

THE CLERK: Sixteen ayes, two absent.

THE MAYOR: I wish to thank the members of the Board and I wish to thank the veterans. I again say, I approached this matter with malice towards none and charity to all, and with the desire, which I know is the desire of the people of this City, to proceed with that work. I hope the veteran organizations will throw their wholehearted support behind this Board. It has the fullest and unanimous approval of the Board of Supervisors, and I hope that nothing but harmony in the future will prevail, and that the War Memorial and the group of buildings will proceed as rapidly as possible. Supervisor Havenner said this morning that this was a memorable day and a momentous occasion in the history of San Francisco. In the rotunda of the City Hall this morning at half past ten checks of the City were passed and a deed received for all the properties of the Spring Valley Water Company, and the City now owns the water works and distributing system heretofore held by the Spring Valley Water Company. It was a great event and new history in the life of San Francisco. I hope the veterans will feel that this, too, is a great event in the life of San Francisco, and if, in my duty as Mayor in trying to arrive at a Board of eleven Trustees, if I have said anything in any way that has offended any of them, if I have done anything that has displeased them, I apologize. I want to see this work go ahead, and we all want to see it go ahead, and this particular day, the 3rd of March, with these two big events behind us, the one completed and the other going forward, will be probably one of the most historic days in the life of our City. Tonight the City gives a reception in the rotunda of the City Hall and all the offices will be illuminated, the building will be illuminated, the City orchestra will play music and the 454 clerks and employees of the Spring Valley Water Company are coming into the fold and the payroll of the City and County of San Francisco. Every officer and every official has been invited, and this is just to show that spirit of good will towards the 454 new employees and to show them, as I said this morning, that this corporation of San Francisco has a heart. And I hope the members of the Board of Supervisors and their families will be able to come tonight. All the officers have been invited and these 454 are coming with their families and with their friends. Has any member of the Board anything to add, except Mr. Havenner may want to remind every one of the ceremonies to take place the 9th of March next, of which he is chairman.

Motion.

SUPERVISOR ANDRIANO: At this time I desire to make a motion, Mr. Mayor. That the Board of Supervisors tender a vote of commendation and thanks to his Honor the Mayor for the happy solution which he has found to the War Memorial controversy, and for the excellent appointments which he has made to the War Memorial Board of Trustees.

SUPERVISOR McSHEEHY: I second that motion.

SUPERVISOR HAYDEN: Mr. Mayor, in seconding that motion, I am very glad that the Supervisor made the motion, because it is in consonance with the thoughts running through our minds at this time, because I realize that, during the long career of your Honor, and during all that time I have sat here with you, I never knew of a problem which has confronted the Board and the Mayor which was so embarrassing and so vexatious, and I think, under the Supervisors, your amicable solution in bringing about harmony between the veterans and the Board of Supervisors is one for congratulation. We cannot help but commend the veterans, Mr. Mayor, in asserting their rights, and while they were determined, I think they were honest in their convictions. You realize that in taking the recommendation of this Board, through Supervisor Power's motion, and you very promptly brought into the Board a list of nominations that has been unanimously received by this Board. I must say, Mr. Mayor, this is a very happy solution for the Board and yourself, for the veterans and for the whole people of San Francisco, and now the dirt will fly, and in time we hope to see a war monument there, erected to the memory of the man who made the supreme sacrifice for our country. It will be a monument not only to them, but it will be a monument to the Board of Supervisors.

THE MAYOR: Mr. Andriano, will you put your motion?

SUPERVISOR ANDRIANO: I have made a motion that the Board of Supervisors tender to his Honor the Mayor, and make a rising vote of commendation and thanks, for the happy solution which he has found to the War Memorial controversy, and for the excellent appointments which he has made to the War Memorial Board of Trustees. All those in favor of the resolution or motion kindly stand up.

Motion *carried* by rising vote, as follows:

Ayes—Supervisors Andriano, Canepa, Gallagher, Havenner, Hayden, McSheehy, Miles, Peyser, Power, Roncovieri, Rossi, Shannon, Spaulding, Stanton, Suhr, Toner—16.

Absent—Supervisors Colman, McGovern—2.

THE MAYOR: Thank you, members of the Board and my fellowcitizens. Mr. Havenner.

SUPERVISOR HAVENNER: Mr. Mayor, I want in this connection to express my personal gratification at the solution of this problem, and I think that it would be appropriate to express my personal regret that it should have been necessary, in order to solve this problem and to clear the way for progressive work on this great project, for Mr. Fleishhacker to have been the single individual who offered himself as a sacrifice for the good of the City. I am sure that, on the part of my colleagues, and I think I speak for all of them, there was no objection whatever to the name of Mr. Fleishhacker. We would have been glad to vote for him had his name been included in this list. And I think that he should be particularly commended for the spirit of sacrifice that he displayed in this connection.

SUPERVISOR POWER: I want to concur in that statement, most cordially.

THE MAYOR: It has been moved by Mr. Havenner, seconded by Mr. Power, that the thanks of the Board be extended to Mr. Herbert Fleishhacker for what he has done, and the regrets also that he found it necessary, from a patriotic purpose, to ask not to be renominated. All in favor will please say Aye. (Ayes.) Contrary, No. (No response.) The ayes have it and it is unanimously carried.

In re Confirmation of Board of Trustees.

MAYOR'S OFFICE

San Francisco   San Francisco, Cal.

The City and County of San Francisco, State of California, to All to Whom These Presents Shall Come, Greeting:

With the confirmation of the Honorable Board of Supervisors of the City and County of San Francisco and reposing special confidence in the fidelity and ability of General Hunter Liggett, Frank N. Belgrano, James I. Herz, Charles H. Kendrick, Richard Montgomery Tobin, Kenneth R. Kingsbury, Robert I. Bentley, George Cameron, George Hearst, James W. Mullen, Jesse C. Colman, I do, by these presents, by virtue of the authority vested in me by the Charter of the City and County of San Francisco, appoint them members of the Board of Trustees of the War Memorial of San Francisco, they to hold said office from and after the 3rd day of March, 1930, for the term to be decided by lot, in accordance with the following provisions of Section 3, Article XIV-D, of the Charter of the City and County of San Francisco:

"The terms of said eleven members shall be for six years each; provided, that those first appointed shall so classify themselves by lot that the term of four of said Trustees shall expire on the 2nd day of January, 1931; four on the 2nd day of January, 1933, and three on the 2nd day of January, 1935. Thereafter appointments to said Board shall be for the full term of six years. Vacancies on said Board shall be filled by the Mayor, subject to confirmation by the Board of Supervisors, for the unexpired term becoming vacant."

In testimony whereof, I have signed my name and have caused the seal of my office to be affixed hereto this 3rd day of March, 1930.

(Seal)   JAMES ROLPH, JR., Mayor.

Attest: EDWARD RAINEY, Executive Secretary to the Mayor.

Preliminary Plans of the Veteran and Museum Building of the War Memorial Group.

The Mayor filed the following with the Clerk of the Board of Supervisors:

Photostatic copy of blue-print showing preliminary plans of the Veteran and Museum Building of the War Memorial group, dated February 21, 1928, and endorsed by the following:

JAMES B. BURNS, Chairman.
A. DON DUNCAN.
GEORGE H. CABANISS, Jr.
HAROLD HOTCHNER.
DR. PETER THEODORE ANGEL.
EARLE J. HARRIS.
LEON FRENCH.
LOY PERKINS CERKEL.
CHAS. KENDRICK.
JAMES B. BURNS.
ALLISON E. SCHOFIELD.
EDWARD SCHARY.
THOS. M. FOLEY.
WILLIAM D. FLINN.
F. H. AINSWORTH.

Report of Rules Committee.

The following was presented and read by the Clerk:

San Francisco, March 3, 1930.

To the Board of Supervisors of the City and County of San Francisco.

Gentlemen: The Committee on Rules, to which was referred "Definition of duties of Public Buildings and Lands Committee and Streets Committee," reports as follows:

Public Buildings and Lands—Include in the "exception for land purchases" "and lands for streets, roads and boulevards."

In duties of the Streets and Tunnels Committee change the word "recommend" to "make," so that sentence will read, "and to make all necessary purchases of lands for roads, streets and boulevard purposes."

The committee recommends for approval amendment to Rule 18, providing that Supervisors may speak "ten" minutes instead of "five" on any question and shall have "ten" minutes instead of "five" to open and "ten" minutes to close.

Respectfully submitted,

SYLVESTER ANDRIANO,
JEFFERSON E. PEYSER,
JAS. B. McSHEEHY,
WARREN SHANNON,
J. EMMET HAYDEN,
Rules Committee.

SPECIAL ORDER—2:30 P. M.

Action Deferred.

The following matter was taken up and, on motion, *laid over one week*:

Amendment to Food Terminal Ordinance.

Bill No. 8208, Ordinance No. ——— (New Series), as follows:

Amending Ordinance No. 8140 (New Series), providing that wholesale food terminals, warehouses, freight yards and ferry terminals shall not be constructed or established, erected or constructed within a certain district in the City and County of San Francisco, and establishing the boundaries of said district, and providing for penalties for the violation of the provisions hereof, by including in said prohibited structures and callings airplane landings and hydroplane landings, and the landing of passengers from airplanes or hydroplanes.

Be it ordained by the People of the City and County of San Francisco as follows:

That Ordinance No. 8140, the title of which is hereinbefore recited, is hereby amended to read as follows:

Section 1. No wholesale food terminal, warehouse, freight yard, or ferry terminal, or airplane landing or hydroplane landing, or any building or structure to be used as a wholesale food terminal, warehouse, freight yard, ferry terminal, airplane landing or hydroplane landing, shall be constructed, erected or established within the territory bounded on the north by the waters of San Francisco Bay, on the east by the westerly line of Van Ness avenue, on the south by Jackson street, and on the west by the westerly line of Lyon street, nor shall any structure for any of the purposes above mentioned be constructed or erected, projecting into the waters of the bay from the land included in the above described district.

Section 2. No building permit shall be issued or granted by the Board of Public Works for the erection, construction or alteration of any building, or structure, contrary to the provisions of this ordinance, and any permit so issued or granted shall be void.

Section 3. No certificate of occupancy shall be issued or granted by the Board of Health authorizing or permitting any person, firm or corporation to occupy or use any building or structure in place within the above bounded district for or as a wholesale food terminal, warehouse, freight yard or ferry terminal.

Section 4. Any person, firm or corporation violating any of the provisions of this ordinance shall be guilty of a misdemeanor, and upon the conviction thereof shall be punishable by a fine not to exceed $500.00 or by imprisonment in the County Jail not to exceed six months, or by both such fine and imprisonment. And any person, firm or corporation violating any of the provisions of this ordinance shall be deemed guilty of a separate offense for each and every day during any portion of which any violation of this ordinance is committed, permitted or continued by such person, firm or corporation.

SPECIAL ORDER—2:30 P. M.

Rereferred.

The following matter was, on motion, ordered *rereferred to the Street Lighting Committee*:

Hyde Street Lighting.

Under the 30-day rule Supervisor Gallagher calls up out of the Lighting Committee, to which it had been previously, on September 23, 1929, referred, the following entitled bill and ordinance, to-wit:

Bill No. ——————, Ordinance No. —————— (New Series), as follows:

Ordering the improvement of Hyde street from Market street to California street by the furnishing and installing of an ornamental street lighting system, approving and adopting specifications therefor, and providing for the payment thereof by installments and outlining the district to be assessed for said improvement.

Mr. F. C. Brewster, secretary of the Fifty Vara Improvement Club, was granted the privilege of the floor and heard on the foregoing subject.

SALE OF CITY LANDS—3 P. M.

At the appointed hour the following matter was taken up and bids called for by his Honor the Mayor, but there were no offers made and the matter was *rereferred to the Buildings and Lands Committee*:

Bids or offers to be received at the chambers of the Board of Supervisors, second floor in the City Hall, City and County of San Francisco, State of California, at the hour of 3 o'clock p. m., on Monday, March 3, 1930, for the sale of the following described parcel of land owned and held by the City and County of San Francisco, a municipal corporation. Said parcel of land is situated in the City and County of San Francisco, State of California, and more particularly described as follows, to-wit:

Commencing at a point on the northerly line of Sutter street, distant thereon 137 feet 6 inches westerly from the westerly line of Gough street, running thence northerly 137 feet 6 inches; thence at right angles westerly 68 feet 9 inches; thence at right angles northerly 137 feet 6 inches to the southerly line of Bush street; thence at right angles westerly along said southerly line of Bush street 68 feet 9 inches; thence at right angles southerly 275 feet to the northerly line of Sutter street; thence at right angles easterly along said northerly line of Sutter street 137 feet 6 inches to the point of commencement; being a portion of Block 673 (W. A. 158).

Said parcel of land will be sold on the above-mentioned date at public auction, duly authorized by the said ordinance, to the person making the highest cash bid therefor, such sale, however, to be subject to confirmation by the Board of Supervisors, in accordance with law. A deposit in the sum of ten (10) per cent of the amount bid will be required of the successful bidder before the sale can be made.

SPECIAL ORDER—3:30 P. M.

Senator Thomas Maloney and Felton Taylor, Federal Census officials for the San Francisco district, appeared in response to an invitation of the Board of Supervisors. Senator Maloney explained at length the importance of the work they were about to inaugurate, with respect to its effects on San Francisco.

Hearing of Objections of Property Owners Against Closing Rhode Island Street.

Hearing of objections of property owners against the closing of Rhode Island street as described in Resolution of Intention No. 31892 (New Series), as follows:

Portion of Rhode Island street to be closed:

Beginning at the point of intersection of the northerly line of Army street and the westerly line of Rhode Island street and running thence northerly along said westerly line 373.00 feet; thence at right angles easterly 80 feet to the easterly line of Rhode Island street; thence at right angles southerly along said easterly line 373.00 feet to said northerly line of Army street; thence westerly thereon 80 feet to the point of beginning.

Referred to Streets Committee.

The foregoing matter was taken up, the names of protestants were read by the Clerk, and the subject-matter *referred to the Streets Committee for hearing.*

UNFINISHED BUSINESS.

Final Passage.

The following resolutions, heretofore passed for printing, were taken up and *finally passed* by the following vote:

Authorizations.

On recommendation of Finance Committee.

Resolution No. 32115 (New Series), as follows:

Resolved, That the following amounts be and the same are hereby authorized to be expended out of the hereinafter mentioned funds in payment to the following named claimants, to-wit:

Library Fund.

(1) American Building Maintenance Co., janitor service for public libraries (claim dated Jan. 31, 1930)..............$ 828.00

(2) Maundrell & Bowen, painting for public libraries (claim dated Jan. 31, 1930) 960.36

(3) Maundrell & Bowen, painting of public library (claim dated Jan. 31, 1930) 560.25

(4) J. H. Keefe Co., painting main public library (claim dated Jan. 31, 1930) 740.00

(5) C. E. Gordon, painting of public library (claim dated Jan. 31, 1930) 730.00

(6) Foster & Futernick Co., rebinding library books (claim dated Jan. 31, 1930) 2,718.00

(7) G. E. Stechert & Co., library books (claim dated Jan. 31, 1930) 1,451.91

(8) Sather Book Shop, library books (claim dated Jan. 31, 1930) 614.95

(9) San Francisco News Co., library books (claim dated Jan. 31, 1930) 1,690.02

M. H. de Young Memorial Museum—Appropriation 58.

(10) P. H. Enright, fourth payment, heating and ventilating the M. H. de Young Memorial Museum (claim dated Feb. 14, 1930) ....$ 1,290.90

Park Fund.

(11) C. J. Holzmueller, furnishing and installing 4500 lamps and sockets for Christmas trees, Panhandle of Golden Gate Park (claim dated Feb. 14, 1930) ....$ 3,000.00

(12)　Joel W. Kaufman, chairman Finance Committee, Christmas Fete Committee, decorations of Christmas tree, public park decorations, etc., Christmas celebration (claim dated Feb. 14, 1930) ....　5,000.00

(13)　The Turner Company, labor and material, installing heating system in Park Lodge (claim dated Feb. 14, 1930)．　586.50

(14)　Berringer & Russell, alfalfa, etc., for parks (claim dated Feb. 14, 1930) ....　724.38

Hetch Hetchy Construction Fund, Bond Issue 1928.

(15)　Coos Bay Lumber Co., lumber (claim dated Feb. 4, 1930) ....$ 1,012.65

(16)　Del Monte Meat Co., meat (claim dated Feb. 4, 1930).　1,175.34

(17)　Ingersoll-Rand Co. of California, machinery parts (claim dated Feb. 4, 1930) ....　555.15

(18)　Department Public Health (San Francisco Hospital), hospital service rendered Hetch Hetchy employees, July 1 to Dec. 31, 1929 (claim dated Feb. 4, 1930).............　992.50

(19)　Santa Fe Lumber Co., lumber (claim dated Feb. 4, 1930) . . . .　1,091.83

(20)　Coos Bay Lumber Co., lumber (claim dated Feb. 6, 1930) ....　2,159.52

(21)　Ingersoll-Rand Co. of California, machinery parts (claim dated Feb. 6, 1930)..........................　2,271.50

(22)　Montague Pipe & Steel Co., pipe (claim dated Feb. 6, 1930) ....　1,882.35

(23)　Santa Fe Lumber Co., lumber (claim dated Feb. 6, 1930)　601.40

(24)　Santa Cruz Portland Cement Co., cement (claim dated Feb. 6, 1930)..　2,008.00

Municipal Railway Fund.

(25)　American Brake Shoe & Foundry Co. of California, brake shoes (claim dated Feb. 5, 1930)...................$　810.19

(26)　Department of Public Works (Bureau of Street Repair), asphalt repairs to Municipal Railway right of way (claim dated Feb. 5, 1930).............................　859.80

(27)　Dunham, Carrigan & Hayden Co., bolts and spikes (claim dated Feb. 7, 1930) ....　1,223.00

(28)　San Francisco City Employees' Retirement System, for employees pensions, etc. (claim dated Feb. 3, 1930).......　752.85

General Fund, 1929-1930.

(29)　Pacific Gas & Electric Co., street lighting during January (claim dated Feb. 17, 1930).........................$66,662.67

(30)　County Road Fund, reimbursement of expenditures in connection with the covering of main sewers during December (claim dated Feb. 3, 1930)......................　1,133.10

(31)　Board of Park Commissioners, reimbursement for account of beautification of Civic Center (claim dated Feb. 14, 1930) ....　4,640.56

(32)　Clinton-Stephenson Construction Co., Ltd., sixth payment, repairs to Palace of Fine Arts building (claim dated Feb. 14, 1930)..　857.25

(33)　Eureka Benevolent Society, maintenance of minors (claim dated Feb. 7, 1930) ....　2,975.92

(34)　Little Children's Aid, maintenance of minors (claim dated Feb. 7, 1930) ....　11,675.50

(35)　Children's Agency, maintenance of minors (claim dated Feb. 7, 1930) ....　30,931.87

(36)　St. Vincent's School, maintenance of minors (claim dated Feb. 7, 1930) ....　1,171.56

(37)　Albertinum Orphanage, maintenance of minors (claim dated Feb. 7, 1930) ....　713.81

(38) Roman Catholic Orphanage, maintenance of minors (claim dated Feb. 7, 1930) 2,015.90

(39) Neal, Stratford & Kerr, printing for Police Department (claim dated Feb. 10, 1930) 646.50

(40) American LaFrance & Foamite Co., Fire Department apparatus parts (claim dated Jan. 31, 1930) 1,122.20

(41) Enterprise Foundry Co., grate and section bars, Fire Department (claim dated Jan. 31, 1930) 516.60

(42) Graham Fuel & Drayage Co., coal, etc., Fire Department (claim dated Jan. 31, 1930) 1,072.48

(43) Pacific Gas & Electric Co., gas and electricity, Fire Department (claim dated Jan. 31, 1930) 2,601.23

(44) Spring Valley Water Co., water furnished Fire Department, and installation of hydrants (claim dated Jan. 31, 1930) 2,053.29

(45) The Texas Co., gasoline and oil, Fire Department (claim dated Jan. 31, 1930) 1,221.63

(46) Union Oil Co. of California, fuel oil, Fire Department (claim dated Jan. 31, 1930) 712.64

(47) Joseph Hagan & Sons, burial of indigent dead (claim dated Feb. 13, 1930)..................................... 869.00

(48) H. F. Dugan Company, surgical supplies for San Francisco Hospital (claim dated Jan. 31, 1930)............... 789.11

(49) Kahn & Co., X-ray films for San Francisco Hospital (claim dated Jan. 31, 1930) 1,019.52

(50) Sussman, Wormser & Co., groceries, San Francisco Hospital (claim dated Jan. 31, 1930) 1,527.00

(51) Scatena-Galli Fruit Co., groceries and produce, San Francisco Hospital (claim dated Jan. 31, 1930).......... 1,194.87

(52) Spring Valley Water Co., water service, San Francisco Hospital (claim dated Jan. 31, 1930).................... 1,761.43

(53) Mangrum-Holbrook Co., dishes for San Francisco Hospital (claim dated Jan. 31, 1930) 2,062.00

(54) Sherry Bros. Inc., butter for Laguna Honda Home (claim dated Jan. 31, 1930)............................ 2,036.21

(55) Baumgarten Bros., meat for Laguna Honda Home (claim dated Jan. 31, 1930) 1,018.48

(56) California Meat Co., meat, Laguna Honda Home (claim dated Jan. 31, 1930) 2,651.70

(57) Dairy Dale, San Francisco Dairy Co., milk for Laguna Honda Home (claim dated Jan. 31, 1930)................ 2,324.60

(58) Del Monte Meat Co., meat for Laguna Honda Home (claim dated Jan. 31, 1930) 3,242.66

(59) J. T. Freitas Co., eggs for Laguna Honda Home (claim dated Jan. 31, 1930) 1,575.00

(60) Healy & Donaldson, tobacco for Laguna Honda Home (claim dated Jan. 31, 1930) 987.60

(61) Richfield Oil Co., fuel oil for Laguna Honda Home (claim dated Jan. 31, 1930) 1,882.72

(62) Schweitzer & Co., meat for Laguna Honda Home (claim dated Jan. 31, 1930) 1,051.49

(63) Sherry Bros. Inc., butter for Laguna Honda Home (claim dated Jan. 31, 1930) 1,547.10

(64) Spring Valley Water Co., water furnished Laguna Honda Home (claim dated Jan. 31, 1930) 1,153.32

(65) John J. Dailey, legal services rendered the City Attorney, month of February, 1930 .... 850.00

Ayes—Supervisors Andriano, Canepa, Gallagher, Havenner, Hayden, McGovern, McSheehy, Miles, Peyser, Power, Roncovieri, Rossi, Spaulding, Stanton, Suhr—15.

Absent—Supervisors Colman, Shannon, Toner—3.

Authorizations.

Also, Resolution No. 32116 (New Series), as follows:

Resolved, That the following amounts be and the same are hereby authorized to be expended out of the hereinafter mentioned funds in payment to the following named claimants, to-wit:

1928 *Hetch Hetchy Water Bonds.*

(1) Coos Bay Lumber Co., lumber (claim dated Feb. 7, 1930).$ 2,003.44

(2) Del Monte Meat Co., meat (claim dated Feb. 7, 1930).... 1,156.50

(3) Ingersoll-Rand Co. of California, nine Drifter complete and machinery parts (claim dated Feb. 7, 1930)........... 4,116.20

(4) Pacific Coast Steel Corporation, steel (claim dated Feb. 7, 1930) 1,239.44

(5) Santa Cruz Portland Cement Co., cement (claim dated Feb. 7, 1930) 526.00

(6) Sherry Bros. Inc., eggs (claim dated Feb. 7, 1930)....... 619.50

(7) United States Rubber Co., rubber coats and boots (claim dated Feb. 7, 1930) 770.40

(8) Worthington Machinery Corporation of California, Ltd., six pumps and parts (claim dated Feb. 6, 1930)........... 1,033.25

(9) Cement Gun Co., Inc., one cement gun equipped (claim dated Feb. 10, 1930) 1,640.21

(10) Consolidated Mills Co., Inc., lumber (claim dated Feb. 10, 1930) 552.41

(11) Coos Bay Lumber Co., lumber (claim dated Feb. 10, 1930) 1,499.58

(12) Haas Brothers, groceries (claim dated Feb. 10, 1930)... 559.72

(13) State Compensation Insurance Fund, premium on insurance covering Hetch Hetchy employments (claim dated Feb. 10, 1930) 6,924.35

(14) Santa Cruz Portland Cement Co., cement (claim dated Feb. 10, 1930) 1,578.00

Robinson Bequest Interest Fund.

(15) James Rolph Jr., Mayor, for relief of destitute women and children (claim dated Feb. 17, 1930).................$ 1,260.00

Playground Fund.

(16) C. F. Weber & Co., portable bleachers for playgrounds (claim dated Feb. 19, 1930) ....$ 526.10

Municipal Railway Fund.

(17) Pacific Gas and Electric Co., electricity furnished Municipal Railways, month of January, 1930 (claim dated Feb. 10, 1930) $43,899.00

(18) San Francisco City Employees' Retirement System, to match contributions from Municipal Railway employees, month of January, 1930 (claim dated Feb. 7, 1930)........ 7,967.18

Special School Tax.

(19) D. A. Pancoast, for "Von Duprin" type panic bolts furnished various schools (claim dated Feb. 8, 1930)........$ 4,210.22

(20) Park Commissioners, care of school grounds for month of January (claim dated Feb. 7, 1930)................... 1,383.33

(21) J. H. McCallum, lumber for schools (claim dated Feb. 11, 1930) 667.96

(22) Meyer Bros., final payment, general construction of addition to Sunshine School (claim dated Feb. 11, 1930)....... 4,272.23

(23) Samuel Lightner Hyman and A. Appleton, final payment for architectural services rendered for account of Second Unit of the South Side (Balboa) High School (claim dated Feb. 11, 1930) 3,446.20

(24) W. H. Crim, eighth payment, architectural services for Park-Presidio Junior High School (claim dated Feb. 19, 1930) 1,271.26

(25) Edward F. Dowd, first and final payment, electrical fixtures for Marina Elementary School (claim dated Feb. 19, 1930) 734.00

County Road Fund.

(26) Spring Valley Water Co., water for concrete work, reconstruction of streets (claim dated Feb. 8, 1930)............$ 1,067.16

(27) Eclipse Lime & Cement Co., cement for street reconstruction (claim dated Feb. 13, 1930)........................ 881.76

(28) Board of Public Works, Budget Item 461, reimbursement for repairs to equipment used in street reconstruction (claim dated Feb. 17, 1930) 1,351.75

(29) Board of Public Works, Budget Item 524, reimbursement for redressing of curbs used in street reconstruction (claim dated Feb. 7, 1930) 505.00

(30) Board of Public Works, Budget Item 524, reimbursement for redressing of curbs used in street reconstruction (claim dated Feb. 7, 1930) 998.12

(31) Board of Public Works, Budget Item 524, reimbursement for redressing of curbs used in street reconstruction (claim dated Feb. 7, 1930) 826.25

(32) Board of Public Works, Budget Item 521, reimbursement for asphalt-labor used in street reconstruction work (claim dated Feb. 7, 1930) 1,480.80

General Fund, 1929-1930.

(33) Neal, Stratford & Kerr, field books for Assessor (claim dated Feb. 18, 1930) ....$ 544.00

(34) Berringer & Russell, hay, etc., Police Department (claim dated Feb. 17, 1930) 1,241.23

(35) Glaser Bros.-Judell Co., tobacco furnished County Jail (claim dated Feb. 14, 1930) 666.93

(36) Old Homestead Bakery, bread furnished County Jails (claim dated Feb. 14, 1930) 840.79

(37) H. F. Dugan Co., hospital supplies, San Francisco Hospital (claim dated Jan. 31, 1930)....................... 785.85

(38) Kahn & Co., X-ray films, San Francisco Hospital (claim dated Jan. 31, 1930) 1,324.80

(39) Old Homestead Bakery, bread for San Francisco Hospital (claim dated Jan. 31, 1930) 1,119.36

(40) San Francisco International Fish Co., fish for San Francisco Hospital (claim dated Jan. 31, 1930)............... 649.36

(41) J. T. Freitas Co., Inc., eggs, San Francisco Hospital (claim dated Jan. 31, 1930) 2,470.72

(42) San Francisco Dairy Co., milk, San Francisco Hospital (claim dated Jan. 31, 1930) 4,453.04

(43) Fred L. Hilmer Co., butter, San Francisco Hospital (claim dated January 31, 1930) 2,238.95

(44) Troy Laundry Machinery Co., laundry extractor, furnished and installed in San Francisco Hospital (claim dated Jan. 31, 1930) 1,288.50

(45) Richfield Oil Co., fuel oil furnished San Francisco Hospital (claim dated Jan. 31, 1930) 2,399.68

(46) Schweitzer & Co., meat, San Francisco Hospital (claim dated Jan. 31, 1930) 1,662.78

(47) Del Monte Meat Co., meat for San Francisco Hospital (claim dated Jan. 31, 1930) 811.70

(48) California Meat Co., meat for San Francisco Hospital (claim dated January 31, 1930) 2,657.86

(49) Western Meat Co., meat for San Francisco Hospital
(claim dated Jan. 31, 1930) 765.71
(50) Mangrum-Holbrook Co., crockery for Laguna Honda
Home (claim dated Jan. 31, 1930) 796.27
(51) Pacific Gas & Electric Co., electricity furnished Tubercular Preventorium (claim dated Feb. 20, 1930)........... 611.80
(52) Edw. Barry Co., real estate rolls furnished Assessor
(claim dated Feb. 18, 1930) 1,136.25
(53) M. J. Lynch, second payment, furnishing and erecting
street signs (claim dated Feb. 19, 1930) 3,590.00
(54) Pacific Gas & Electric Co., lighting public buildings
(claim dated Feb. 17, 1930) 6,540.15
(55) County Road Fund, reimbursement of expenditures in
connection with covering of main sewers (claim dated Feb.
13, 1930) 935.99
(56) Spring Valley Water Co., water furnished public buildings (claim dated Feb. 13, 1930) 2,058.08
(57) Gurley-Lord Tire Co., seven pairs Gruss Air Springs for
street cleaning trucks (claim dated Feb. 13, 1930)......... 1,354.50

Special School Tax.

(56) Fred Medart Mfg. Co., gymnasium equipment for Balboa
High School (claim dated Feb. 18, 1930)...................$ 877.50
(57) Meyer Bros., acceptance payment, general construction
of Geary Street School (claim dated Feb. 21, 1930)........ 32,036.75

Ayes—Supervisors Andriano, Canepa, Gallagher, Havenner, Hayden, McGovern, McSheehy, Miles, Peyser, Power, Roncovieri, Rossi, Spaulding, Stanton, Suhr—15.

Absent—Supervisors Colman, Shannon, Toner—3.

Appropriation From Urgent Necessity, Additional Emergency Supplies by the Board of Health.

Also, Resolution No. 32117 (New Series), as follows:

Resolved, That the sum of $7,000 be and the same is hereby set aside, appropriated and authorized to be expended out of Urgent Necessity, Budget Item No. 24, Fiscal Year 1929-1930, for additional and emergency supplies by the Board of Health under the direction of the Superintendent of the Relief Home.

Ayes—Supervisors Andriano, Canepa, Gallagher, Havenner, Hayden, McGovern, McSheehy, Miles, Peyser, Power, Roncovieri, Rossi, Spaulding, Stanton, Suhr—15.

Absent—Supervisors Colman, Shannon, Toner—3.

Appropriations for Construction of Ward Building "F," Relief Home Tract.

Also, Resolution No. 32118 (New Series), as follows:

Resolved, That the following amounts be and the same are hereby set aside, appropriated and authorized to be expended out of Hospital Bond Construction Fund, Issue 1929, for the construction of Ward Building "F," Relief Home Tract, to-wit:

(1) General construction (Spivock & Spivock contract).... $95,900.00
(2) Electrical work (Knut Smith contract)................ 2,137.00
(3) Plumbing and gasfitting work (Scott Co. contract)..... 11,537.00
(4) Mechanical equipment (Scott Co. contract)............ 8,160.00
(5) Architectural fees 4,274.42
(6) Extras, incidentals and inspection.................... 10,000.00

Total $132,008.42

Ayes—Supervisors Andriano, Canepa, Gallagher, Havenner, Hayden,

McGovern, McSheehy, Miles, Peyser, Power, Roncovieri, Rossi, Spaulding, Stanton, Suhr—15.
Absent—Supervisors Colman, Shannon, Toner—3.

Appropriations Out of County Road Fund, Various Improvements.

Also, Resolution No. 32119 (New Series), as follows:

Resolved, That the following amounts be and the same are hereby
set aside, appropriated and authorized to be expended out of County
Road Fund for the following purposes, to-wit:

(1) For the improving of Chestnut street from a line 220
feet easterly from Grant avenue to the easterly line of
Kearny street, and Kearny street from Chestnut street to
to a line 79½ feet southerly from Chestnut street, at City
property $3,400.00
(2) For the improvement of the intersection of Burnside
avenue and Bosworth street, City's liability, and the con-
struction of walls and stairs. 1,850.00
(3) For the improvement of Division street between Bryant
and Florida streets, Treat avenue between Florida and Alameda streets, and Alameda street between Harrison street
and Treat avenue; assessment against City property used
as Corporation Yard 3,379.26
(4) For the reconstruction of Tehama street westerly from
Second street 3,000.00
(5) For the reconstruction of Clementina street easterly
from Third street. 700.00
(6) For the resurfacing of Castro street between Seven-
teenth and Nineteenth streets. 2,305.00

Ayes—Supervisors Andriano, Canepa, Gallagher, Havenner, Hayden,
McGovern, McSheehy, Miles, Peyser, Power, Roncovieri, Rossi, Spauld-
ing, Stanton, Suhr—-15.
Absent—Supervisors Colman, Shannon, Toner—3.

Appropriations Out of County Road Fund for Street Improvements.

Also, Resolution No. 32120 (New Series), as follows:

Resolved, That the following amounts be and the same are hereby
set aside, appropriated and authorized to be expended out of the
County Road Fund for the improvement of the following streets, to-wit:

Grand View avenue conform. $1,984.13
Havelock street, Edna to Circular. 1,557.50
Josiah and Ridge lane. 962.05

Ayes—Supervisors Andriano, Canepa, Gallagher, Havenner, Hayden,
McGovern, McSheehy, Miles, Peyser, Power, Roncovieri, Rossi, Spauld-
ing, Stanton, Suhr—15.
Absent—Supervisors Colman, Shannon, Toner—3.

Appropriations, Work in Front of City Property.

Also, Resolution No. 32121 (New Series), as follows:

Resolved, That the following amounts be and the same are hereby
set aside, appropriated and authorized to be expended out of "Work
in Front of City Property," Budget Item 34, for the following street
work at City property, to-wit:

(1) Thirty-first avenue, Kirkham to Lawton streets and
crossing $3,397.00
(2) Short street, Market to Yukon streets. 773.11

Ayes—Supervisors Andriano, Canepa, Gallagher, Havenner, Hayden,
McGovern, McSheehy, Miles, Peyser, Power, Roncovieri, Rossi, Spauld-
ing, Stanton, Suhr—15.
Absent—Supervisors Colman, Shannon, Toner—ა.

Appropriation for Construction Due to Boulevard Construction.

Also, Resolution No. 32122 (New Series), as follows:

Resolved, That the sum of $1,045 be and the same is hereby set aside, appropriated and authorized to be expended out of Boulevard Bond Issue Construction Fund for the improvement of Le Conte avenue at crossing of Lane street ($857), and reconstruction of Lane street and San Bruno avenue ($188), necessitated by the construction of the Bay Shore boulevard.

Ayes—Supervisors Andriano, Canepa, Gallagher, Havenner, Hayden, McGovern, McSheehy, Miles, Peyser, Power, Roncovieri, Rossi, Spaulding, Stanton, Suhr—15.

Absent—Supervisors Colman, Shannon, Toner—3.

Appropriations for Building Repairs and Painting Traffic Signs, Etc.

Also, Resolution No. 32123 (New Series), as follows:

Resolved, That the following amounts be and the same are hereby set aside, appropriated and authorized to be expended out of the hereinafter mentioned funds for the following purposes, to-wit:

Repairs to Public Buildings, Budget Item No. 53.

(1) For the replacing of nineteen flanged control valves on fresh water supply piping from tanks on roof of Hall of Justice $678.00

Traffic Signals, Etc., Budget Item No. 57.

(2) For the painting of traffic signs, lines and curbs during month of February, 1930................................. 700.00

Ayes—Supervisors Andriano, Canepa, Gallagher, Havenner, Hayden, McGovern, McSheehy, Miles, Peyser, Power, Roncovieri, Rossi, Spaulding, Stanton, Suhr—15.

Absent—Supervisors Colman, Shannon, Toner—3.

Reimbursement of Board of Public Works for the Painting of Traffic Signs, Etc.

Also, Resolution No. 32124 (New Series), as follows:

Resolved, That the sum of $941.20 be and the same is hereby set aside and appropriated out of "Traffic Signals," Budget Item No. 57, to the credit of "Reimbursements," Budget Item No. 442, Board of Public Works, being reimbursement for labor and materials furnished and used in the painting of traffic signs, lines and curbing during the month of December, 1929.

Ayes—Supervisors Andriano, Canepa, Gallagher, Havenner, Hayden, McGovern, McSheehy, Miles, Peyser, Power, Roncovieri, Rossi, Spaulding, Stanton, Suhr—15.

Absent—Supervisors Colman, Shannon, Toner—3.

Appropriations for Repairs to County Jail No. 1.

Also, Resolution No. 32125 (New Series), as follows:

Resolved, That the following amounts be and the same are hereby set aside and appropriated out of "Maintenance, Subsistence and Equipment," office of the Sheriff, Budget Item No. 269, to the credit of Budget Item No. 442, Board of Public Works, and authorized to be expended for the following purposes, to-wit:

(1) For the painting of the south wing at County Jail No. 1.$ 1,960.00
(2) For changing eighteen windows in County Jail No. 1 to pivot type windows..................................... 695.00

Ayes—Supervisors Andriano, Canepa, Gallagher, Havenner, Hayden, McGovern, McSheehy, Miles, Peyser, Power, Roncovieri, Rossi. Spaulding, Stanton, Suhr—15.

Absent—Supervisors Colman, Shannon, Toner—3.

Condemnation of Land Required for Opening Ord Court.

Also, Resolution No. 32126 (New Series), as follows:

Resolved, By the Board of Supervisors of the City and County of San Francisco, that public interest and necessity require the acquisition by the City and County of San Francisco, a municipal corporation, of the following properties, situated in the City and County of San Francisco, State of California, more particularly described as follows, to-wit:

Parcel 1: Beginning at the southwesterly corner of Lot 37 of Lyon & Hoag's Subdivision No 2 of Ashbury Terrace, as per map thereof recorded in Map Book "G," pages 89 and 90, records of the City and County of San Francisco; thence northwesterly along the southwesterly line of Lot 36 of above mentioned map 19.028 feet; thence northeasterly on a curve to the right whose tangent deflects 89 deg. 14 min. 19 sec. from the preceding course, radius 23 feet, central angle 46 deg. 38 min. 48 sec., a distance of 18.725 feet to the westerly line of said Lot 37; thence southwesterly along the westerly line of said Lot 37 20.684 feet to the southwesterly corner of said Lot 37 and the point of beginning.

Being a portion of Lot 36 of above mentioned map.

Parcel 2: Beginning at the southeasterly corner of Lot 39 of Lyon & Hoag's Subdivision No 2 of Ashbury Terrace, as per map thereof recorded in Map Book "G," pages 89 and 90, records of the City and County of San Francisco; thence northwesterly along the southwesterly line of Lots 39 and 38 of above mentioned map, 60 feet to the southeasterly corner of Lot 37 of above mentioned map; thence at right angles northeasterly along the northeasterly line of said Lot 37 17.50 feet; thence at right angles southeasterly along a line parallel with and distant 17.50 feet at right angles northeasterly from the southwesterly line of said Lots 38 and 39 60 feet to the southeasterly line of Lot 12 of Block 13, Flint Tract Homestead Association, as per map thereof recorded in Map Book 1, page 148, records of the City and County of San Francisco; thence at right angles southwesterly along said line of said Lot 12 and along the southeasterly line of said Lot 39 17.50 feet to the southeasterly corner of said Lot 39 and the point of beginning.

Being portions of Lots 38 and 39 of the aforesaid Ashbury Terrace and a portion of Lot 12, Block 13, Flint Tract, as mentioned above.

Parcel 3: Beginning at the southeasterly corner of Lot B of Lyon & Hoag's Subdivision No. 2 of Ashbury Terrace, as per map thereof recorded in Map Book "G," pages 89 and 90, records of the City and County of San Francisco; thence northwesterly along the southwesterly line of Lots B and A of above mentioned map 50 feet to the southeasterly line of Lot 39 of aforenamed map; thence at right angles northeasterly along said line of Lot 39 and along the southeasterly line of Lot 12, Block 13, Flint Tract Homestead Association, as per map thereof recorded in Map Book 1, page 148, records of the City and County of San Francisco, 17.50 feet; thence at right angles southeasterly along a line parallel with and distant 17.50 feet at right angles northeasterly from the southwesterly line of said Lots A and B 50 feet to the southeasterly line of Lot 14 of the above mentioned Flint Tract; thence at right angles southwesterly along said line of said Lot 14 and along the southeasterly line of above mentioned Lot B 17.50 feet to the southeasterly corner of said Lot B and the point of beginning.

Being all of Lots A and B of the aforesaid Ashbury Terrace and portions of Lots 13 and 14, Block 13, of the Flint Tract, as mentioned above.

Parcel 4: Beginning at the southeasterly corner of Lot F of Lyon & Hoag's Subdivision No 2 of Ashbury Terrace, as per map thereof recorded in Map Book "G," pages 89 and 90, records of the City and County of San Francisco; thence northwesterly along the southwesterly line of said Lot F 25 feet to the southeasterly line of Lot E of the above mentioned **map**; thence at right angles northeasterly along the southeasterly line of said Lot E and along the southeasterly line of Lot 17, Block 13, Flint Tract Homestead Association, as per map thereof recorded in Map Book 1, page 148, records of the City and County of San Francisco, 17.50 feet; thence at right angles southeasterly along a line parallel with and distant 17.50 feet at right angles northeasterly from the southwesterly line of said Lot F 25 feet to the southeasterly line of Lot 18, Block 13, of the above mentioned Flint Tract; thence at right angles southwesterly along said line of Lot 18 and along the southeasterly line of the aforesaid Lot F 17.50 feet to the southeasterly corner of Lot F and the point of beginning.

Being all of Lot F of the aforesaid Ashbury Terrace and a portion of Lot 18, Block 13, Flint Tract, as above mentioned.

Parcel 5: Beginning at the southeasterly corner of Lot J of Lyon & Hoag's Subdivision No. 2 of Ashbury Terrace, as per map thereof recorded in Map Book "G," pages 89 and 90, records of the City and County of San Francisco; thence northwesterly along the southwesterly line of said Lot J 25 feet to the southeasterly line of Lot I of aforesaid map; thence at right angles northeasterly along said line of said Lot I and along the southeasterly line of Lot 21, Block 13, Flint Tract Homestead Association, as per map thereof recorded in Map Book 1, page 148, records of the City and County of San Francisco, 17.50 feet; thence at right angles southeasterly along a line parallel with and distant 17.50 feet northeasterly from the southwesterly line of aforesaid Lot J 10.883 feet; thence easterly on a curve to the left, tangent to the preceding course, radius 136.868 feet, central angle 5 deg. 55 min. 12 sec., a distance of 14.142 feet to the southeasterly line of Lot 22, Block 13, of said aforesaid Flint Tract; thence southwesterly along said line of said Lot 22 and along the southeasterly line of aforementioned Lot J 18.23 feet to the southeasterly corner of aforesaid Lot J and the point of beginning.

Being all of Lot J of aforesaid Ashbury Terrace and a portion of Lot 22, Block 13, Flint Tract, as above mentioned. Be it

Further Resolved, That said properties are suitable, adaptable, necessary and required for the public use of said City and County of San Francisco, to-wit: For the opening, widening, construction and maintenance of Ord court. It is necessary that a fee simple title be taken for such use.

The City Attorney is hereby ordered and directed to commence proceedings in eminent domain against the owners of said parcels of land, and of any and all interests therein or claims thereto, for the condemnation thereof for the public use of the City and County of San Francisco, as aforesaid.

Ayes—Supervisors Andriano, Canepa, Gallagher, Havenner, Hayden, McGovern, McSheehy, Miles, Peyser, Power, Roncovieri, Rossi, Spaulding, Stanton, Suhr—15.

Absent—Supervisors Colman, Shannon, Toner—3.

Board of Public Works to Prepare Plans, Etc., Receive Bids and Award of Contract for 60,000 Lane Markers.

Also, Bill No. 8186, Ordinance No. 8692 (New Series), as follows:

Authorizing and directing the Board of Public Works to prepare plans and specifications, receive bids and award contract for installing approximately 60,000 pedestrian lane markers, 1000 traffic turning buttons, removing and installing 500 traffic turning buttons, installing 1000 plain safety zone buttons, installing 200 reflector type safety zone buttons, replacing approximately 400 reflector type safety zone buttons with buttons containing whole reflectors, hauling buttons to Corporation Yard and replacing broken reflectors with new ones.

Be it ordained by the People of the City and County of San Francisco as follows:

Section 1. The Board of Public Works is hereby authorized and directed to prepare plans and specifications, receive bids and award contract for installing approximately 60,000 pedestrian lane markers, 1000 traffic turning buttons, removing and installing 500 traffic turning buttons, installing 1000 plain safety zone buttons, installing 200 reflector type safety zone buttons, replacing approximately 400 reflector type safety zone buttons with buttons containing whole reflectors, hauling buttons to Corporation Yard and replacing broken reflectors with new ones.

Section 2. This ordinance shall take effect immediately.

Ayes—Supervisors Andriano, Canepa, Gallagher, Havenner, Hayden, McGovern, McSheehy, Miles, Peyser, Power, Roncovieri, Rossi, Spaulding, Stanton, Suhr—15.

Absent—Supervisors Colman, Shannon, Toner—3.

Payments for Property, County Road Fund.

Also, Resolution No. 32127 (New Series), as follows:

Resolved, That the following amounts be and the same are hereby set aside and appropriated out of County Road Fund, and authorized in payment to the following named persons; being payments for properties required for the following purposes, to-wit:

(1) To W. O. Smith and Irma E. Smith and California Pacific Title and Trust Company, for portions of Lots 7 and 8 in Block 2712 (87 ft. x 60 ft. irregular), as per the Assessor's Block Books, and required for the widening of Corbett avenue, approved by Resolution No. 32063, New Series (claim dated Feb. 10, 1930)............................ $5,125.00

(2) To Charles Monestier and Title Insurance & Guaranty Co., for all of Lot 14 in Block 2659, as per the Assessor's Block Books, and required for the extension of Market street, approved by Resolution No. 32064, New Series (claim dated Jan. 29, 1930).................................... 725.00

Ayes—Supervisors Andriano, Canepa, Gallagher, Havenner, Hayden, McGovern, McSheehy, Miles, Peyser, Power, Roncovieri, Rossi, Spaulding, Stanton, Suhr—15.

Absent—Supervisors Colman, Shannon, Toner—3.

Appropriation for Cancer Treatment by Board of Health.

Also, Resolution No. 32128 (New Series), as follows:

Resolved, That the sum of $20,000 be and the same is hereby set aside, appropriated and authorized to be expended out of "Urgent Necessity," Budget Item No. 24, for expenses of cancer treatment by the Department of Public Health.

Ayes—Supervisors Andriano, Canepa, Gallagher, Havenner, Hayden, McGovern, McSheehy, Miles, Peyser, Power, Roncovieri, Rossi, Spaulding, Stanton, Suhr—15.

Absent—Supervisors Colman, Shannon, Toner—3.

Appropriation for Employment of Bricklayer and Hodcarrier, Department of Public Works.

Also, Resolution No. 32129 (New Series), as follows:

Resolved, That the sum of $2,500 be and the same is hereby set aside and appropriated out of County Road Fund to the credit of the Department of Public Works, for the employment of additional hod carrier and bricklayer in the Sewer Repair Division for the balance of the present fiscal year. (Request of Board of Public Works, Resolution No. 109358.)

(To credit of Budget Item 559, $1,375.)
(To credit of Budget Item 560, $1,125.)

Ayes—Supervisors Andriano, Canepa, Gallagher, Havenner, Hayden,

McGovern, McSheehy, Miles, Peyser, Power, Roncovieri, Rossi, Spaulding, Stanton, Suhr—15.

Absent—Supervisors Colman, Shannon, Toner—3.

Appropriations for Repairs to County Jail No. 1.

Also, Resolution No. 32130 (New Series), as follows:

Resolved, That the sum of $3,770 be and the same is hereby set aside and appropriated out of "Maintenance, Subsistence and Equipment," Budget Item, No. 269, Sheriff's Department, to the credit of Department of Public Works, Budget Item No. 442, for the reconstruction of the floors in Federal wing and felony wing, County Jail No. 1. (Request of Sheriff, dated February 12, 1930.)

Ayes—Supervisors Andriano, Canepa, Gallagher, Havenner, Hayden, McGovern, McSheehy, Miles, Peyser, Power, Roncovieri, Rossi, Spaulding, Stanton, Suhr—15.

Absent—Supervisors Colman, Shannon, Toner—3.

Appropriation for Construction in Office of the Treasurer.

Also, Resolution No. 32131 (New Series), as follows:

Resolved, That the sum of $1,110 be and the same is hereby set aside, appropriated and authorized to be expended out of "City Hall Repairs and Painting," Budget Item No. 54, for construction of wood and glass partition and the removing and reinstalling, with necessary additions, one steel and glass booth, to new location, in office of the Treasurer, City Hall.

Ayes—Supervisors Andriano, Canepa, Gallagher, Havenner, Hayden, McGovern, McSheehy, Miles, Peyser, Power, Roncovieri, Rossi, Spaulding, Stanton, Suhr—15.

Absent—Supervisors Colman, Shannon, Toner—3.

Appropriations.

Also, Resolution No. 32132 (New Series), as follows:

Resolved, That the following amounts be and the same are hereby set aside, appropriated and authorized to be expended out of Boulevard Bond Fund, Issue 1927, for the following constructions, to-wit:

(1) For the improvement of the Great Highway, lower road, from Ulloa street to Lincoln way, including engineering, inspection and extras, per contract awarded Federal Construction Company $123,000

(2) For construction of public comfort stations at the Great Highway and Judah street, and at the Great Highway and Taraval street, including engineering, inspection and extras, per contract awarded Clinton-Stephenson Construction Company 60,000

Ayes—Supervisors Andriano, Canepa, Gallagher, Havenner, Hayden, McGovern, McSheehy, Miles, Peyser, Power, Roncovieri, Rossi, Spaulding, Stanton, Suhr—15.

Absent—Supervisors Colman, Shannon, Toner—3.

Reimbursing Board of Public Works for Gilding Iron Work, City Hall.

Also, Resolution No. 32133 (New Series), as follows:

Resolved, That the sum of $988.67 be and the same is hereby set aside and appropriated out of "City Hall Repairs and Painting," Budget Item No. 54, to the credit of Department of Public Works, Budget Item No. 442; being reimbursement for expenditure in the gilding of ornamental iron work of the City Hall.

Ayes—Supervisors Andriano, Canepa, Gallagher, Havenner, Hayden,

McGovern, McSheehy, Miles, Peyser, Power, Roncovieri, Rossi, Spaulding, Stanton, Suhr—15.

Absent—Supervisors Colman, Shannon, Toner—3.

Plans, Etc., Gridiron, Canopy, Electrical Equipment for Stage for Civic Auditorium.

Also, Bill No. 8195, Ordinance No. 8693 (New Series), as follows:

Ordering the preparation of plans and specifications for the construction of a gridiron, canopy, and the installation of electrical equipment for the stage of the Civic Auditorium; authorizing and directing the Board of Public Works to enter into contract for said construction, and permitting progressive payments to be made during the progress of said work.

Be it ordained by the people of the City and County of San Francisco as follows:

Section 1. The Board of Public Works is hereby authorized, instructed and empowered to prepare plans and specifications for the gridiron, canopy, and the installation of electrical equipment for the stage of the Civic Auditorium, and to enter into contract for the construction of said gridiron, canopy, and the installation of electrical equipment for the stage of the Civic Auditorium, in accordance with the plans and specifications so prepared.

Section 2. The said Board of Public Works is hereby authorized and permitted to incorporate in the contract for the construction of said gridiron, canopy, and the installation of electrical equipment for the stage of the Civic Auditorium conditions that progressive payments shall be made in the manner set forth in said specifications and as provided by Section 21, Chapter I, Article VI, of the Charter.

Section 3. This ordinance shall take effect immediately.

Ayes—Supervisors Andriano, Canepa, Gallagher, Havenner, Hayden, McGovern, McSheehy, Miles, Peyser, Power, Roncovieri, Rossi, Spaulding, Stanton, Suhr—15.

Absent—Supervisors Colman, Shannon, Toner—3.

Appropriation, $55,000, County Road Fund, for Property Between Clay and Merchant Streets, Adjoining The Embarcadero.

Also, Resolution No. 32134 (New Series), as follows:

Resolved, That the sum of $55,000 be and the same is hereby set aside, appropriated and authorized to be expended out of County Road Fund for the purchase of property between Clay and Merchant streets, adjoining The Embarcadero.

Ayes—Supervisors Andriano, Canepa, Gallagher, Havenner, Hayden, McGovern, McSheehy, Miles, Peyser, Power, Roncovieri, Rossi, Spaulding, Stanton, Suhr—15.

Absent—Supervisors Colman, Shannon, Toner—3.

Boiler Permits.

On recommendation of Fire Committee.

Resolution No. 32135 (New Series), as follows:

Resolved, That the following revocable permits be and are hereby granted:

Boilers.

Lesters, Limited, 609 Mission street, 15-horsepower.

Gilt Edge Creamery, 2498 Fillmore street, 10-horsepower.

The rights granted under this resolution shall be exercised within six months, otherwise said permit shall become null and void.

Ayes—Supervisors Andriano, Canepa, Gallagher, Havenner, Hayden, McGovern, McSheehy, Miles, Peyser, Power, Roncovieri, Rossi, Spaulding, Stanton, Suhr—15.

Absent—Supervisors Colman, Shannon, Toner—3.

Oil Tanks.

Also, Resolution No. 32136 (New Series), as follows:

Resolved, That the following revocable permits are hereby granted:

Oil Tanks.

Enterprise Foundry Co., southwest side Fremont street, 150 feet southeast of Folsom street, 1500 gallons capacity.

A. Germarro, 503 Cabrillo street, 1500 gallons capacity.

H. O. Lindeman, west side Nineteenth avenue, 225 feet north of California street, 1500 gallons capacity.

Mary Scheffer, 493 Eddy street, 1500 gallons capacity.

O. Mueller, 1535 Sacramento street, 1500 gallons capacity.

P. Bellegarde, 1627 Clay street, 1500 gallons capacity.

M. Solomon, southeast corner of La Playa and Balboa street, 1500 gallons capacity.

The rights granted under this resolution shall be exercised within six months, otherwise said permit shall become null and void.

Ayes—Supervisors Andriano, Canepa, Gallagher, Havenner, Hayden, McGovern, McSheehy, Miles, Peyser, Power, Roncovieri, Rossi, Spaulding, Stanton, Suhr—15.

Absent—Supervisors Colman, Shannon, Toner—3.

Action Deferred.

The following resolution was, on motion, *laid over one week*:

Laundry Permits.

Resolution No. —————— (New Series), as follows:

Resolved, That the following revocable permits be and are hereby granted:

Laundries.

Eloise Aiso, 1089 Pine street.

John Batsere, 976 Pine street.

Anna Biscay, 992 Sutter street.

Ruth Clausen, 94 Seventh street.

Mrs. V. J. Laurent, 447 Ellis street.

J. Nongue, 707 O'Farrell street.

Mme. P. Pomme, 1147 McAllister street.

Marie Sabacca, 808 Post street.

Mme. J. Saffores, 841 Powell street.

Mrs. A. Termello, 41 Franklin street.

Louise Vannucci and Gloria Cheader, 405 O'Farrell street.

The rights granted under this resolution shall be exercised within six months, otherwise said permits shall become null and void.

Blanket protest filed by Mr. Alford, Board of Trade, Laundry Industry.

Final Passage.

The following matters, heretofore passed for printing, were taken up and *finally passed* by the following vote:

Public Garage Transfer, D. C. Parker and John Boido, 1737 Jackson Street.

On recommendation of Fire Committee.

Resolution No. 32138 (New Series), as follows:

Resolved, That D. C. Parker and John Boido be and are hereby granted permission, revocable at will of the Board of Supervisors, to have transferred to them public garage permit heretofore granted E. S. Allen by Resolution 28325 (New Series) for premises at 1737 Jackson street.

The rights granted under this resolution shall be exercised within six months, otherwise said permit shall become null and void.

Ayes—Supervisors Andriano, Canepa, Gallagher, Havenner, Hayden,

McGovern, McSheehy, Miles, Peyser, Power, Roncovieri, Rossi, Spaulding, Stanton, Suhr—15.

Absent—Supervisors Colman, Shannon, Toner—3.

Public Garage Transfer, Foote & Sarin, 1301 Pierce Street.

Also, Resolution No. 32139 (New Series), as follows:

Resolved, That Foote & Sarin be and are hereby granted permission, revocable at will of the Board of Supervisors, to have transferred to them public garage permit heretofore granted Geo. D. Guenley by Resolution No. 26214 (New Series) for premises at 1301 Pierce street.

The rights granted under this resolution shall be exercised within six months, otherwise said permit shall become null and void.

Ayes—Supervisors Andriano, Canepa, Gallagher, Havenner, Hayden, McGovern, McSheehy, Miles, Peyser, Power, Roncovieri, Rossi, Spaulding, Stanton, Suhr—15.

Absent—Supervisors Colman, Shannon, Toner—3.

Automobile Supply Station Transfer, W. W. Stone and A. E. Walsh, Southwest Corner of Cabrillo Street and Forty-seventh Avenue.

Also, Resolution No. 32140 (New Series), as follows:

Resolved, That W. W. Stone and A. E. Walsh be and are hereby granted permission, revocable at will of the Board of Supervisors, to have transferred to them automobile supply station permit heretofore granted H. Heskins by Resolution No. 31976 (New Series) for premises at southwest corner of Cabrillo street and Forty-seventh avenue.

The rights granted under this permit shall be exercised within six months, otherwise said permit shall become null and void.

Ayes—Supervisors Andriano, Canepa, Gallagher, Havenner, Hayden, McGovern, McSheehy, Miles, Peyser, Power, Roncovieri, Rossi, Spaulding, Stanton, Suhr—15.

Absent—Supervisors Colman, Shannon, Toner—3.

Automobile Supply Station, George Bepler, Southeast Corner of Seventeenth and Connecticut Streets.

Also, Resolution No. 32141 (New Series), as follows:

Resolved, That Geo. Bepler be and is hereby granted permission, revocable at will of the Board of Supervisors, to maintain and operate an automobile supply station on the southeast corner of Sevententh and Connecticut streets.

The rights granted under this resolution shall be exercised within six months, otherwise said permit shall become null and void.

Ayes—Supervisors Andriano, Canepa, Gallagher, Havenner, Hayden, McGovern, McSheehy, Miles, Peyser, Power, Roncovieri, Rossi, Spaulding, Stanton, Suhr—15.

Absent—Supervisors Colman, Shannon, Toner—3.

Commercial Garage Permit, Gilmore Oil Company, Ltd., North Side of Eighteenth Street, 70 Feet East of Third Street.

Also, Resolution No. 32142 (New Series), as follows:

Resolved, That the Gilmore Oil Company, Ltd., be and is hereby granted permission, revocable at will of the Board of Supervisors, to maintain and operate a commercial garage on the north side of Eighteenth street, 70 feet east of Third street.

The rights granted under this resolution shall be exercised within six months, otherwise said permit shall become null and void.

Ayes—Supervisors Andriano, Canepa, Gallagher, Havenner, Hayden, McGovern, McSheehy, Miles, Peyser, Power, Roncovieri, Rossi, Spaulding, Stanton, Suhr—15.

Absent—Supervisors Colman, Shannon, Toner—3.

Automobile Supply Station, Gilmore Oil Company, Ltd., Northeast Corner of Eighteenth and Third Streets.

Also, Resolution No. 32143 (New Series), as follows:

Resolved, That the Gilmore Oil Company, Ltd., be and is hereby granted permission, revocable at will of the Board of Supervisors, to maintain and operate an automobile supply station at premises on the northeast corner of Eighteenth and Third streets.

The rights granted under this resolution shall be exercised within six months, otherwise said permit shall become null and void.

Ayes—Supervisors Andriano, Canepa, Gallagher, Havenner, Hayden, McGovern, McSheehy, Miles, Peyser, Power, Roncovieri, Rossi, Spaulding, Stanton, Suhr—15.

Absent—Supervisors Colman, Shannon, Toner—3.

Changing Grades on Mt. Vernon Avenue Between Alemany Boulevard and Cayuga Avenue.

On recommendation of Streets Committee.

Bill No. 8188, Ordinance No. 8694 (New Series), as follows:

Changing and reestablishing the official grades on Mt. Vernon avenue between the easterly line of Alemany boulevard produced and the westerly line of Cayuga avenue.

Ayes—Supervisors Andriano, Canepa, Gallagher, Havenner, Hayden, McGovern, McSheehy, Miles, Peyser, Power, Roncovieri, Rossi, Spaulding, Stanton, Suhr—15.

Absent—Supervisors Colman, Shannon, Toner—3.

Changing Grades on Nineteenth Street Between San Bruno and Potrero Avenues and on Utah Street Between Eighteenth and Twentieth Streets.

Also, Bill No. 8189, Ordinance No. 8695 (New Series), as follows:

Changing and reestablishing the official grades on Nineteenth street between San Bruno and Potrero avenues and on Utah street between the northerly line of Eighteenth street and Twentieth street.

Ayes—Supervisors Andriano, Canepa, Gallagher, Havenner, Hayden, McGovern, McSheehy, Miles, Peyser, Power, Roncovieri, Rossi, Spaulding, Stanton, Suhr—15.

Absent—Supervisors Colman, Shannon, Toner—3.

Changing Grades on Alta Street, 150 and 303 Feet Easterly From Montgomery Street.

Also, Bill No. 8190, Ordinance No. 8696 (New Series), as follows:

Changing and reestablishing the official grades on Alta street between lines respectively 150 feet and 303 feet easterly from Montgomery street.

Whereas, the Board of Supervisors, on the written recommendation of the Board of Public Works, did, on the 6th day of December, 1929, by Resolution No. 31716 (New Series), declare its intention to change and reestablish the grades on Alta street between lines respectively 150 feet and 303 feet easterly from Montgomery street.

Whereas, said resolution was so published for ten days, and the Board of Public Works, within ten days after the first publication of said resolution of intention, caused notices of the passage of said resolution to be conspicuously posted along all streets specified in the resolution, in the manner and as provided by law; and

Whereas, more than forty days has elapsed since the first publication of said resolution of intention; therefore,

Be it ordained by the People of the City and County of San Francisco as follows:

Section 1. The grades on the following named streets at the points hereinafter named, and at the elevations above city base as hereinafter stated, are hereby changed and established as follows:

Alta Street.

6 feet southerly from the northerly line of, 150 feet easterly from Montgomery street, 175.83 feet. (The same being the present official grade.)

6 feet northerly from the southerly line of, 150 feet easterly from Montgomery street, 175.83 feet. (The same being the present official grade.)

175 feet easterly from Montgomery street, 174.15 feet.
200 feet easterly from Montgomery street, 171.99 feet.
225 feet easterly from Montgomery street, 168.86 feet.
(Vertical curve passing through the last three described points.)
303 feet easterly from Montgomery street, 156.80 feet.

On Alta street between lines respectively 150 feet and 303 feet easterly from Montgomery street, changed and established to conform to true gradients between the grade elevations above given therefor.

Section 2. This ordinance shall take effect immediately.

Ayes—Supervisors Andriano, Canepa, Gallagher. Havenner, Hayden, McGovern, McSheehy, Miles, Peyser, Power, Roncovieri, Rossi, Spaulding, Stanton, Suhr—15.

Absent—Supervisors Colman, Shannon, Toner—3.

Changing Grades on Oakdale Avenue Between Earl and Keith Streets and on Fitch, Griffith, Hawes, Ingalls and Jennings Streets Between Newcomb and Palou Avenues.

Also, Bill No. 8191, Ordinance No. 8697 (New Series), as follows:

Changing and reestablishing the official grades on Oakdale avenue between Earl and Keith streets, and on Fitch, Griffith, Hawes, Ingalls and Jennings streets between Newcomb and Palou avenues.

Ayes—Supervisors Andriano, Canepa, Gallagher, Havenner, Hayden, McGovern, McSheehy, Miles, Peyser, Power, Roncovieri, Rossi, Spaulding, Stanton, Suhr—15.

Absent—Supervisors Colman, Shannon, Toner—3.

Width of Sidewalks on Quint Street Between Oakdale and Palou Avenues.

Also, Bill No. 8192, Ordinance No. 8698 (New Series), as follows:

Amending Ordinance No. 1061, entitled "Regulating the Width of Sidewalks," approved December 18, 1903, by adding thereto a new section to be numbered ten hundred and eighty-nine.

Be it ordained by the People of the City and County of San Francisco as follows:

Section 1. Ordinance No. 1061, entitled "Regulating the Width of Sidewalks," approved December 18, 1903, be and is hereby amended in accordance with the communication of the Board of Public Works, filed in this office January 21, 1930, by adding thereto a new section to be numbered ten hundred and eighty-nine, to read as follows:

Section 1089. The width of sidewalks on Quint street between Oakdale avenue and Palou avenue shall be ten (10) feet.

Ayes—Supervisors Andriano, Canepa, Gallagher, Havenner, Hayden. McGovern, McSheehy, Miles, Peyser, Power, Roncovieri, Rossi, Spaulding, Stanton, Suhr—15.

Absent—Supervisors Colman, Shannon, Toner—3.

Establishing Grades on Ledyard Street.

Also, Bill No. 8193, Ordinance No. 8699 (New Series), as follows:

Establishing grades on Ledyard street between Silver avenue and a line parallel with and 707.50 feet southerly therefrom.

Be it ordained by the People of the City and County of San Francisco as follows:

Section 1. The grades on Ledyard street between Silver avenue and a line parallel with and 707.50 feet southerly therefrom are hereby established at points hereinafter named, and at heights above city base as hereinafter stated, in accordance with recommendation of the Board of Public Works, filed February 3, 1930:

Ledyard Street.

Westerly line of, at Silver avenue, 83.50 feet. (The same being the present official grade.)

Easterly line of, at Silver avenue, 85.00 feet.

183.50 feet southerly from Silver avenue, 88.50 feet.

707.50 feet southerly from Silver avenue, 78.00 feet.

On Ledyard street between Silver avenue and a line parallel with and 707.50 feet southerly therefrom be established to conform to true gradients between the grade elevations above given therefor.

Section 2. This ordinance shall take effect immediately.

Ayes—Supervisors Andriano, Canepa, Gallagher, Havenner, Hayden, McGovern, McSheehy, Miles, Peyser, Power, Roncovieri, Rossi, Spaulding, Stanton, Suhr—15.

Absent—Supervisors Colman, Shannon, Toner—3.

Establishing Grades on Niagara Avenue Between Alemany Boulevard and Cayuga Avenue.

Also, Bill No. 8194, Ordinance No. 8700 (New Series), as follows:

Establishing grades on Niagara avenue between Alemany boulevard and Cayuga avenue.

Be it ordained by the People of the City and County of San Francisco as follows:

Section 1. The grades on Niagara avenue between Alemany boulevard and Cayuga avenue are hereby established in accordance with recommendation of the Board of Public Works, filed February 3, 1930.

Ayes—Supervisors Andriano, Canepa, Gallagher, Havenner, Hayden, McGovern, McSheehy, Miles, Peyser, Power, Roncovieri, Rossi, Spaulding, Stanton, Suhr—15.

Absent—Supervisors Colman, Shannon, Toner—3.

PRESENTATION OF BILLS AND ACCOUNTS.

Your Finance Committee, having examined miscellaneous demands not required by law to be passed to print, and amounting to $59,608.49, recommends same be allowed and ordered paid.

Approved by the following vote:

Ayes—Supervisors Andriano, Canepa, Gallagher, Havenner, Hayden, McGovern, McSheehy, Miles, Peyser, Power, Roncovieri, Rossi, Spaulding, Stanton, Suhr—15.

Absent—Supervisors Colman, Shannon, Toner—3.

NEW BUSINESS.

Passed for Printing.

The following matters were *passed for printing*:

Authorizations.

On recommendation of Finance Committee.

Also, Resolution No. ————— (New Series), as follows:

Resolved, That the following amounts be and the same are hereby authorized to be expended out of the hereinafter mentioned funds in payment to the following named claimants, to-wit:

Park Fund.

(1) Julius L. Girod, one orang outang, for park purposes (claim dated Feb. 28, 1930)...........................$ 625.20

(2) Pacific Gas & Electric Company, gas and electric service for parks (claim dated Feb. 28, 1930).................   1,233.66
(3) Spring Valley Water Company, water for parks (claim dated Feb. 28, 1930)......................................   935.16
(4) Berringer & Russell, hay, etc., for parks (claim dated Feb. 28, 1930) 525.64

M. H. deYoung Memorial Museum Fund.

(5) Thomas Skelly, plumbing work for M. H. deYoung Memorial Museum, third payment (claim dated Feb. 28, 1930).$ 508.08

Hetch Hetchy Construction Fund, Bond Issue 1928.

(6) Bald Eagle Meat Market, meat and fish (claim dated Feb. 14, 1930) 648.14
(7) Best Steel Casting Co, castings (claim dated Feb. 14, (1930) 767.56
(8) San Francisco City Employees' Retirement System, to match contributions from Hetch Hetchy employees (claim dated Feb. 17, 1930) 649.12
(9) Allan St. John Bowie and California Pacific Title & Trust Company, for Lots 17 to 34, inclusive, in Block 2899, as per the Assessor's Block Books, as per acceptance of offer by Resolution No. 32010, New Series; and required for reservoir purposes (claim dated Feb. 19, 1930).......   2,000.00
(10) Dr. Paul E. Dolan, medical services rendered Hetchy Hetchy employees (claim dated Feb. 19, 1930)............   1,157.00
(11) The Giant Powder Company, Consolidated, explosives (claim dated Feb. 19, 1930)...........................   2,645.30
(12) W. Haslam, Hetch Hetchy truck rental (claim dated Feb. 19, 1930) 795.48
(13) M. D. Jones, Hetch Hetchy truck rental (claim dated Feb. 19, 1930) 2.028.78
(14) St. Paul's Hospital, Livermore, hospital service rendered Hetch Hetchy employees (claim dated Feb. 19, 1930) 669.25
(15) Christenson Lumber Company, lumber (claim dated Feb. 21, 1930) 683.21
(16) Coos Bay Lumber Company, lumber (claim dated Feb. 19, 1930) 504.50
(17) Del Monte Meat Company, meat (claim dated Feb. 20, 1930) 1,810.31
(18) Delbert Hansen, Hetch Hetchy truck hire (claim dated Feb. 23, 1930) 1,638.71
(19) Ingersoll-Rand Company of California, machinery parts (claim dated Feb. 21, 1930)...........................   1,007.38
(20) Ingersoll-Rand Company of California, machinery parts (claim dated Feb. 19, 1930) 785.06
(21) Owen-Oregon Lumber Company, lumber (claim dated Feb. 19, 1930) 604.64
(22) Pacific Coast Aggregates, Inc., concrete mix, sand and gravel (claim dated Feb. 20, 1930) 520.00
(23) Pacific Coast Steel Corporation, steel (claim dated Feb. 21, 1930) 2,357.71
(24) Santa Fe Lumber Company, lumber (claim dated Feb. 21, 1930) 1,068.02
(25) Santa Cruz Portland Cement Company, cement (claim dated Feb. 21, 1930) 1,578.00
(26) Utah Fuel Company, coal (claim dated Feb. 19, 1930)..   711.88
(27) Western Butchers' Supply Company, one 1½-ton refrigerator plant installed (claim dated Feb. 21, 1930)........   1,115.00
(28) Baker, Hamilton & Pacific Company, hoist and hardware (claim dated Feb. 24, 1930)......................   737.82

(29) Challenge Cream and Butter Association, canned milk
(claim dated Feb. 24, 1930)......................... 581.25

(30) J H Creighton, truck hire (claim dated Feb. 24, 1930). 1,206.21

(31) Coos Bay Lumber Company, lumber (claim dated Feb. 25, 1930) 3,185.27

(32) Del Monte Meat Company, meat (claim dated Feb. 25, 1930) 716.12

(33) Edison Storage Battery Supply Company, Edison cells and batteries (claim dated Feb. 24, 1930)................ 23,962.72

(34) J. E. French Company, one Dodge Bros. sedan (claim dated Feb. 24, 1930) 900.00

(35) R. M. Gardiner Lumber Company, lumber (claim dated Feb. 24, 1930) 547.56

(36) The Giant Powder Company, Consolidated, explosives (claim dated Feb. 24, 1930).......................... 3,977.81

(37) Haas Bros., groceries (claim dated Feb. 25, 1930)..... 748.75

(38) Hercules Powder Company, Inc., explosives (claim dated Feb. 24, 1930) 2,657.44

(39) William L. Hughson Company, one Ford truck (claim dated Feb. 24, 1930) 729.40

(40) Delbert Hansen, truck hire (claim dated Feb. 25, 1930). 676.60

(41) Ingersoll Rand Company of California, pump, drifters and machinery parts (claim dated Feb. 24, 1930)......... 2,578.30

(42) The Charles Nelson Company, wood wedges (claim dated Feb. 24, 1930) 640.00

(43) Alfred Pereira & Bros., hauling (claim dated Feb. 24, 1930) 1,737.14

(44) Pope & Talbot, lumber (claim dated Feb. 24, 1930)..... 744.35

(45) Santa Cruz Portland Cement Company, cement (claim dated Feb. 25, 1930) 4,638.00

(46) Sherry Bros., Inc., eggs (claim dated Feb. 24, 1930)... 501.60

(47) Western Pipe and Steel Company, steel pipe (claim dated Feb. 24, 1930) 3,763.30

(48) Wilsey-Bennett Company, butter and eggs (claim dated Feb. 24, 1930) 619.05

Hetch Hetchy Power Operative Fund.

(49) Depreciation Fund, Hetch Hetchy Power Operative, reserve for depreciation, as per Charter requirement (claim dated Feb. 19, 1930) $14,583.00

(50) State Compensation Insurance Fund, premium covering Hetch Hetchy employments (claim dated Feb. 19, 1930).. 821.71

Aquarium—Appropriation 56.

(51) California Academy of Sciences, maintenance of Steinhart Aquarium, month of February (claim dated March 3, 1930)...$ 3,783.42

Installation Fund—Department of Electricity.

(52) Robert A. Smith, Inc., one Chevrolet sedan for Department of Electricity (claim dated Jan. 31, 1930)..........$ 674.00

Boulevard Bond Issue Construction Fund.

(53) San Francisco City Employees' Retirement System, to match contributions from employments on boulevard construction (claim dated Feb. 19, 1930)...................$ 512.06

Municipal Railway Fund.

(54) Marie L. Fazackerley, in settlement for any damage sustained by reason of accident April 18, 1929, at Van Ness avenue and Clay street (claim dated Feb. 19, 1930)$ 640.00

(55) American Brake Shoe and Foundry Company of California, car brake shoes (claim dated Feb. 25, 1930)..... 2,273.95

(56) The Texas Company, gasoline furnished (claim dated
Feb. 25, 1930).. 1,929.98

County Road Fund.

(57) San Francisco City Employees' Retirement System, to
match contributions from employments engaged on County
Road Fund construction (claim dated Feb. 19, 1930).....$ 1,318.93
(58) Equitable Asphalt Maintenance Company, resurfacing
of streets (claim dated Feb. 21, 1930)................. 519.32
(59) Pacific Coast Aggregates, Inc., sand and gravel for
street reconstruction (claim dated Feb. 25, 1930)........ 2,727.08
(60) Standard Oil Company of California, asphalt for street
reconstruction (claim dated Feb. 25, 1930).............. 2,436.24

Special School Tax.

(61) San Francisco City Employees' Retirement System, to
match contributions of employments paid out of Special
School Tax Fund (claim dated Feb. 19, 1930)...........$ 1,049.89
(62) MacDonald & Kahn, final payment, general construction of viewing stand at South Side (Balboa) High School
(claim dated Feb. 26, 1930).......................... 13,628.25
(63) Alta Electric Company, fifth payment, electrical work
for Roosevelt Junior High School (claim dated Feb. 26,
1930) 2,311.62
(64) Alta Electric Company, final payment, electrical work
for Geary Street School (claim dated Feb. 25, 1930)..... 2,175.90
(65) Scott Company, final payment on mechanical equipment for Geary Street School (claim dated Feb. 25, 1930) 2,699.65
(66) E. P. Finigan, gymnasium equipment for Balboa High
School (claim dated Feb. 25, 1930)................... 3,867.30

General Fund, 1929-1930.

(67) Listenwalter & Gough, wire, zincs, carbons, etc., for
Department of Electricity (claim dated Jan. 31, 1930)...$ 1,449.57
(68) Maggini Motor Car Company, three Ford touring autos
for Police Department (claim dated Feb. 24, 1930)....... 1,395.00
(69) Frank J. Reilly, ninth payment, general construction
of addition to M. H. deYoung Memorial Museum (claim
dated Feb. 28, 1930)................................. 15,041.25
(70) Preston School of Industry, maintenance of minors
(claim dated Feb. 25, 1930).......................... 700.00
(71) The B. F. Sturtevant Company, Inc., of California, two
steel plate exhaust fans with motors (claim dated Feb. 20,
1930) 726.00
(72) James Rolph, Jr., for personal services and other than
personal services, months of January and February, 1930
(claim dated March 3, 1930).......................... 1,464.16
(73) L. M. Wilbor, M. D., for payment of room allowances
to San Francisco Hospital employees, month of March
(claim dated Feb. 28, 1930).......................... 3,000.00
(74) San Francisco Society for the Prevention of Cruelty
to Animals, for the impounding, feeding, etc., of animals
(claim dated March 3, 1930).......................... 1,500.00
(75) Spring Valley Water Company, water furnished Fire
Department hydrants (claim dated Feb. 28, 1930)........ 15,597.20

Boulevard Bond Issue Construction Fund.

(76) The Magnavox Company, 5000 cast aluminum pedestrian lane markers (claim dated Feb. 25, 1930).........$ 647.50

Consolidated Street Assessment Fund.

(77) Chas L. Harney, for improvement of Oakwood street
from present termination to Nineteenth street (claim
dated Feb. 19, 1930)................................$ 1,775.00

Payment for Properties Required for Boulevard Purposes.

Also, Resolution No. ———— (New Series), as follows:

Resolved, That the following amounts be and the same are hereby set aside and appropriated out of Boulevard Bond Issue Construction Fund, 1927, and authorized in payment to the hereinafter named persons; being payments for properties required for boulevard purposes, to-wit:

(1) To Thomas P. Coyle, for all of Lot 2 in Block 2313, as per the Assessor's Block Books of the City and County, and required for the opening of Sunset boulevard; approved by Resolution No. ————, New Series (claim dated Jan. 15, 1930) $17,017.00

(2) To John Murphy and Nellie T. Murphy and City Title Insurance Company, for all of Lot 1 in Block 2365, as per the Assessor's Block Books of the City and County, and required for the opening of the Sunset boulevard; approved by Resolution No. ————, New Series (claim dated Jan. 15, 1930) 2,750.00

Appropriation for Construction of Fifteenth Street Sewer, Section A, Harrison Street to Howard Street.

Also, Resolution No. ———— (New Series), as follows:

Resolved, That the following amounts be and the same are hereby set aside, appropriated and authorized to be expended out of the 1929 Sewer Bond Construction Fund, for the construction of the Fifteenth street sewer, Section "A," from Harrison to Howard streets, to-wit:

(1) For construction of sewer, per award to Louis J Cohn..$59,334.00

(2) For extras and contingencies........................ 5,900.00

(3) For engineering and inspection...................... 4,766.00

Appropriation for Construction of Film Vault at San Francisco Hospital.

Also, Resolution No. ———— (New Series), as follows:

Resolved, That the following amounts be and the same are hereby set aside, appropriated and authorized to be expended out of "Urgent Necessity," Budget Item No. 24, for the construction of film vault on the roof of the San Francisco Hospital, to-wit:

(1) For general construction, per award to Frank J. Reilly..$ 9,581.00

(2) For extras, incidentals and inspection................. 1,500.00

Total $11,081.00

Appropriations, Painting Curbs, Etc., and Work Fronting City Property.

Also, Resolution No. ———— (New Series), as follows:

Resolved, That the following amounts be and the same are hereby set aside, appropriated and authorized to be expended out of the hereinafter mentioned accounts of the General Fund, for the following purposes, to-wit:

Traffic Signals, Etc.—Budget Item 57.

(1) For the cost of painting traffic lines and curbs, for month of March, 1930 ....$ 1,400.00

Street Work in Front of City Property—Budget Item 34.

(2) For the cost of the improvement of the crossing of Twenty-fourth avenue and Rivera street, assessable to the City..$ 1,372.50

Bernal Cut Construction Fund, Bond Issue 1927.

(3) For cost of painting traffic lines and direction arrows, Bernal Cut .. ..$ 505.00

Appropriation for the Improvement of Clayton Street at Market Street.

Also, Resolution No. ————— (New Series), as follows:

Resolved, That the sum of $8,000 be and the same is hereby set aside, appropriated and authorized to be expended out of County Road Fund for the improvement of Clayton street at Market street, per contract awarded, and including possible extras, engineering and inspection.

Appropriations for Street Reconstruction.

Also, Resolution No. ————— (New Series), as follows:

Resolved, That the following amounts be and the same are hereby set aside, appropriated and authorized to be expended out of County Road Fund for the following street reconstruction and improvements, to-wit:

(1) For the cost of improving Waterville street, from Silver avenue to Augusta street, and of Silver avenue, from Waterville street to Elmira street, and at intersections; City's portion ....$ 600.00

(2) For the cost of widening Irving street between Eighteenth and Nineteenth avenues, by the reduction of sidewalks, at City property...................................   624.00

(3) For the improvement of Castro street between Twenty-ninth and Thirtieth streets, City's liability..............   4,230.00

(4) For cost of reconstruction of dangerous corners on Chenery street at southeast corner of Diamond street, southeast corner of Randall street, and on west side of Chenery street opposite Natick street and opposite Charles street, including inspection............................   1,300.00

(5) For cost of resurfacing of Jones street between Filbert and Greenwich streets, and reconstructing curbs.........   1,400.00

(6) For cost of improving and constructing a road from the northerly line of the Marina to the Saint Francis Yacht Club 1,200.00

(7) For cost of resurfacing of Drum street between California and Sacramento streets.........................   900.00

Adopted.

The following matters were *adopted*:

On recommendation of Finance Committee.

Appropriations for Street Improvements.

Resolution No. 32137 (New Series), as follows:

Resolved, That the following amounts be and the same are hereby set aside, appropriated and authorized to be expended out of **County** Road Fund for the following purposes, to-wit:

(1) For the cost of cleaning and surfacing existing brick pavement on Pacific avenue between Lyon and Walnut streets with cement grout................................$ 400.00

(2) For the cost of construction of wall, to a height of about five feet above existing pavement, on the westerly line of Green street at the crossing of Taylor street, and the resetting of a Spring Valley water hydrant..........   450.00

(3) For the cost of construction of traffic guard fences between existing curbs at the westerly line of Broderick street and at northeast line of Buena Vista avenue with warning reflectors..   150.00

Ayes—Supervisors Andriano, Canepa, Gallagher, Havenner, Hayden, McGovern, McSheehy, Miles, Peyser, Power, Roncovieri, Rossi, Spaulding, Stanton, Suhr—15.

Absent—Supervisors Colman, Shannon, Toner—3

Appropriations for Carpentry Work, Etc., Assessor's Office and Mission Police Station.

Also, Resolution No. 32144 (New Series), as follows:

Resolved, That the following amounts be and the same are hereby set aside, appropriated and authorized to be expended out of the hereinafter mentioned accounts of the General Fund, for the following purposes, to-wit:

Repairs to Public Buildings—Budget Item 53.

(1) For cost of electric wiring the Mission Police Station..$ 300.00

City Hall Repairs—Budget Item No. 54.

(2) For cutting down counter, moving files, removing section of case, and installing shelving and gate, office of the Assessor ....$ 400.00

Ayes—Supervisors Andriano, Canepa, Gallagher, Havenner. Hayden, McGovern, McSheehy, Miles, Peyser, Power, Roncovieri, Rossi. Spaulding, Stanton, Suhr—15.

Absent—Supervisors Colman, Shannon, Toner—3.

Interdepartmental Transfer of $500, Fire Department.

Also, Resolution No. 32145 (New Series), as follows:

Resolved, That the sum of $500 be and the same is hereby set aside out of "Maintenance," Appropriation 41B, to the credit of "Stationery," Appropriation 41D, Fire Department.

Ayes—Supervisors Andriano. Canepa, Gallagher, Havenner. Hayden. McGovern, McSheehy, Miles. Peyser. Power, Roncovieri. Rossi. Spaulding, Stanton, Suhr—15.

Absent—Supervisors Colman, Shannon. Toner—3.

Appropriation, $275, for Wiring and Fixtures, Women's Jail.

Also, Resolution No. 32146 (New Series), as follows:

Resolved, That the sum of $275 be and the same is hereby set aside out of "Maintenance," Budget Item 269, Sheriff's Department, to the credit of Department of Public Works, Budget Item 442, for the furnishing and installing of necessary wiring and fixtures in the Women's Jail.

Ayes—Supervisors Andriano, Canepa, Gallagher, Havenner. Hayden, McGovern, McSheehy, Miles, Peyser. Power. Roncovieri, Rossi. Spaulding, Stanton, Suhr—15.

Absent—Supervisors Colman, Shannon. Toner—3.

Passed for Printing.

The following matters were *passed for printing*:

San Francisco Water Department Revolving Fund.

On recommendation of Finance Committee.

Also, Resolution No. ————— (New Series), as follows:

Resolved, That the sum of $20,000 be and the same is hereby set aside as a Revolving Fund out of "Water Revenue Fund" as provided by Section 13 of Ordinance No. 8691 (New Series).

Oil Tanks.

On recommendation of Fire Committee.

Also, Resolution No. ————— (New Series). as follows:

Resolved, That the following revocable permits be and are hereby granted:

Oil Tanks.

L. Widman, 1763 Golden Gate avenue, 1500 gallons capacity.

C. S. Hoffman, southeast corner of O'Farrell and Franklin streets, 1500 gallons capacity.

Nathan Rothman, 629 Golden Gate avenue, 1500 gallons capacity.

George Gibbs, south side of Ellis street, 87 feet west of Larkin street, 1500 gallons capacity.

A. E. Pessano, 3011 Van Ness avenue, 1500 gallons capacity.

The rights granted under this resolution shall be exercised within six months, otherwise said permits shall become null and void.

Garage Permit Transfer, Floyd W. Hanchett, 730-742 Ellis Street.

Also, Resolution No. ————— (New Series), as follows:

Resolved, That Floyd W. Hanchett be and is hereby granted permission, revocable at will of the Board of Supervisors, to have transferred to him public garage permit heretofore granted to William Niemann by Resolution No. 29821 (New Series) for premises at 730-742 Ellis street.

The rights granted under this resolution shall be exercised within six months, otherwise said permit shall become null and void.

Supply Station Permit Transfer, J. H. Seelye, Northwest Corner California and Steiner Streets.

Also, Resolution No. ————— (New Series), as follows:

Resolved, That J. H. Seelye be and is hereby granted permission, revocable at will of the Board of Supervisors, to have transferred to him automobile supply station permit formerly granted to the Associated Oil Company by Resolution No. 31394 (New Series) for premises at northwest corner of California and Steiner streets.

The rights granted under this resolution shall be exercised within six months, otherwise said permit shall become null and void.

Amending Section 102A of Ordinance No. 1008 (New Series), Relating to Hardwood Floors.

On recommendation of Public Buildings and Lands Committee.

Bill No. 8196, Ordinance No. ————— (New Series), as follows:

Amending Ordinance No. 7347 (New Series), entitled "Amending Ordinance No. 1008 (New Series), known as 'The Building Law' of the City and County of San Francisco, approved December 22, 1909, by adding a new section thereto and to be numbered Section 102-A, relating to hardwood floors."

Be it ordained by the People of the City and County of San Francisco as follows:

Section 1. Ordinance No. 7347 (New Series), entitled "Amending Ordinance No. 1008 (New Series), known as 'the Building Law' of the City and County of San Francisco, approved December 22, 1909, by adding a new section thereto, and to be numbered Section 102-A, relating to hardwood floors," is hereby amended as follows:

Hardwood Floors.

Section 102-A. Hardwood floors shall be laid upon a sub-flooring of at least merchantable T and G pine flooring or pine boards not more than six (6) inches in width, and not less than seven-eighths (⅞) of an inch in thickness, surface one side and edge, and laid as tightly as possible, and to be double nailed on each floor joist to obtain a smooth and even surface. These conditions shall apply to hardwood floor construction in all types of buildings.

Section 2. This ordinance shall take effect immediately.

Adopted.

The following matters were *adopted*:

Purchase of Additional Site for James Lick School, Situate Twenty-fifth and Noe Streets.

On recommendation of Public Buildings and Lands Committee.

Resolution No. 32147 (New Series), as follows:

Whereas, an offer has been received from Wm. J. Robinson to convey to the City and County of San Francisco certain land and improvements on the southerly line of Twenty-fifth street, distant 240 feet westerly from Noe street, required for school purposes; and

Whereas, the price at which said parcel of land is offered is the reasonable value thereof; therefore, be it

Resolved, That the offer of the said owner to convey to the City and County of San Francisco a good and sufficient fee simple title to the following described land, free of all encumbrances, for the sum of $5,250 be and the same is hereby accepted, the said land being described as follows, to-wit:

Commencing at a point on the southerly line of Twenty-fifth street, distant thereon 240 feet westerly from the westerly line of Noe street, running thence westerly along the said southerly line of Twenty-fifth street 28 feet; thence at a right angle southerly 114 feet; thence at a right angle easterly 28 feet; thence at a right angle northerly 114 feet to the southerly line of Twenty-fifth street and point of commencement. Being a portion of Horner's Addition Block 163, also known as Lot 33, Block No. 6547, on Assessor's Map Book.

The City Attorney is hereby directed to examine the title to said land, and, if the same is found to be vested in the aforesaid owner, free of all encumbrances, and that the taxes up to and including the current fiscal year are paid, and that the so-called McEnerney title has been procured or sufficient money reserved for the purpose of procuring the same, to report the result of his examination to the Board of Supervisors, and also to cause a good and sufficient deed for said land to be executed and delivered to the City and County upon payment of the agreed purchase price as aforesaid. And the said deed to said land is hereby accepted.

Ayes—Supervisors Andriano, Canepa, Gallagher, Havenner, Hayden, McGovern, McSheehy, Miles, Peyser, Power, Roncovieri, Rossi, Spaulding, Stanton, Suhr—15.

Absent—Supervisors Colman, Shannon, Toner—3.

Transfer of Taxicab Permits.

On recommendation of Police Committee.

Resolution No. 32148 (New Series), as follows:

Resolved, That the transfer of the following taxicab permits be and the same are hereby authorized subject to the regulations of the Police Commission:

From E. W. Guibbiny and J. O. Luke to Floyd W. Hanchett, ten cabs;

From Edward Rowland to Floyd W. Hanchett, fifty cabs;

From William Drury to Louis E. Hendricks, one cab;

From William J. Rossi to Louis Mora, one cab.

Ayes—Supervisors Andriano, Canepa, Gallagher, Havenner, Hayden, McGovern, McSheehy, Miles, Peyser, Power, Roncovieri, Rossi, Spaulding, Stanton, Suhr—15.

Absent—Supervisors Colman, Shannon, Toner—3.

Approval of Taxicab Stand Permits.

Also, Resolution No. 32149 (New Series), as follows:

Resolved, That the following taxicab stand permits be and they are hereby approved:

Yellow Cab Company, 1001 California Street, one cab.

Ayes—Supervisors Andriano, Canepa, Gallagher, Havenner, Hayden,

McGovern, McSheehy, Miles, Peyser, Power, Roncovieri, Rossi, Spaulding, Stanton, Suhr—15.

Absent—Supervisors Colman, Shannon, Toner—3.

Masquerade Ball Permit, Unione Sportiva Italiana Virtus, 415 Broadway, Sunday, March 2, 1930.

Also, Resolution No. 32150 (New Series), as follows:

Resolved, That Unione Sportiva Italiana Virtus be and it is hereby granted permission to conduct a masquerade ball, Sunday, March 2, 1930, at 415 Broadway.

Ayes—Supervisors Andriano, Canepa, Gallagher, Havenner, Hayden, McGovern, McSheehy, Miles, Peyser, Power, Roncovieri, Rossi, Spaulding, Stanton, Suhr—15.

Absent—Supervisors Colman, Shannon, Toner—3.

Extension of Time to Complete the Improvement of Belle Avenue Between St. Charles and Chester Avenues, Etc.

On recommendation of Streets Committee.

Resolution No. 32151 (New Series), as follows:

Resolved, That the Fay Improvement Company is hereby granted an extension of ninety days' time from and after March 10, 1930, within which to complete the improvement of Belle avenue between St. Charles and Chester avenues, and Chester avenue between Belle and Palmetto avenues, under public contract.

This extension of time is granted upon the recommendation of the Board of Public Works for the reason that the contractor has been delayed by traffic conditions.

Ayes—Supervisors Andriano, Canepa, Gallagher, Havenner, Hayden, McGovern, McSheehy, Miles, Peyser, Power, Roncovieri, Rossi, Spaulding, Stanton, Suhr—15.

Absent—Supervisors Colman, Shannon, Toner—3.

Extension of Time to Complete Improvement of Quintara Street Between Fifteenth and Sixteenth Avenues.

Also, Resolution No. 32152 (New Series), as follows:

Resolved, That California Construction Company is hereby granted an extension of thirty days' time from and after February 17, 1930, within which to complete the improvement of Quintara street between Fifteenth and Sixteenth avenues under public contract. This extension of time is granted upon the recommendation of the Board of Public Works for the reason that the work is completed, and this first extension is granted in order that the contractor may be protected during the period of acceptance and issuance of assessment.

Ayes—Supervisors Andriano, Canepa, Gallagher, Havenner, Hayden, McGovern, McSheehy, Miles, Peyser, Power, Roncovieri, Rossi, Spaulding, Stanton, Suhr—15.

Absent—Supervisors Colman, Shannon, Toner—3.

Closing and Abandoning Certain Portion of Seneca Avenue Lying Southeasterly From Otsego Avenue.

Also, Resolution No. 32153 (New Series), as follows:

Closing and abandoning a certain portion of Seneca avenue lying southeasterly from Otsego avenue as hereinafter described.

Whereas, this Board has, by Resolution No. 31958 (New Series), declared its intention to close up and abandon that certain portion of Seneca avenue lying southeasterly from Otsego avenue; and

Whereas, proper notice of said resolution and of said proposed closing and abandoning of that certain portion of Seneca avenue as described in Resolution of Intention No. 31958 (New Series) was duly given by the Board of Public Works of said City and County of San

Francisco by publication in the manner provided by the Charter of the City and County of San Francisco; and

Whereas, more than ten days have elapsed after the expiration of the publication of said notice, and no objections to the closing of said portion of Seneca avenue were made or delivered to the Clerk of this Board within said period of ten (10) days or at all; and

Whereas, it is the opinion of this Board that the public interest and convenience will be conserved by the closing and abandonment of said portion of Seneca avenue; and

Whereas, in and by said Resolution No. 31958 (New Series) this Board did declare that the damages, costs and expenses of closing said portion of said street are nominal and no assessment district is necessary to be formed for the purpose of paying the damages, costs and expenses thereof, the Board of Supervisors hereby declares and determines that the whole damage, cost and expense of closing said street shall be paid out of the revenues of the City and County of San Francisco;

Resolved, That said closing and abandonment of that portion of Seneca avenue as described in Resolution of Intention No. 31958 (New Series) be and the same is hereby ordered, and that said portion of Seneca avenue be and the same is hereby closed and abandoned as a public street. The said portion of Seneca avenue hereinabove referred to is more particularly described as follows, to-wit:

Beginning at the point of intersection of the southeasterly line of Otsego avenue and the northeasterly line of Seneca avenue; thence southerly on a curve to the left, tangent to said line of Otsego avenue, radius 80.102 feet, central angle 48 deg. 30 min. 27 sec., a distance of 67.816 feet to the southwesterly line of Seneca avenue; thence deflecting 41 deg. 29 min. 33 sec. to the left from the tangent to the preceding curve, and running southwesterly along the southwesterly line of Seneca avenue 157.967 feet to the southeasterly termination of Seneca avenue; thence deflecting 77 deg. 46 min. 30 sec. to the left and running northeasterly along said southeasterly termination 61.392 feet to the northeasterly line of Seneca avenue; thence northwesterly along the northeasterly line of Seneca avenue 198 feet to the said line of Otsego avenue and the point of beginning.

Be it Further Resolved, That the Clerk of this Board transmit a certified copy of this resolution to the Board of Public Works and that the Board of Public Works be instructed to proceed thereafter as required by law and the Charter of the City and County of San Francisco, and the Clerk of the Board is hereby directed to advertise this resolution in the official newspaper as required by law.

Ayes—Supervisors Andriano, Canepa, Gallagher, Havenner, Hayden, McGovern, McSheehy, Miles, Peyser, Power, Roncovieri, Rossi, Spaulding, Stanton, Suhr—15.

Absent—Supervisors Colman, Shannon, Toner—3.

Extension of Time to Complete Improvement of Swiss Avenue.

Also, Resolution No. 32154 (New Series), as follows:

Resolved, That M. Bertolino is hereby granted an extension of thirty days' time from February 9, 1930, within which to complete the improvement of the uncompleted portions of Swiss avenue between Surrey and Sussex streets under public contract. This extension of time is granted upon the recommendation of the Board of Public Works for the reason that the work is completed and this extension is necessary to keep contract alive until acceptance and issuance of the assessment.

Ayes—Supervisors Andriano, Canepa, Gallagher, Havenner, Hayden, McGovern, McSheehy, Miles, Peyser, Power, Roncovieri, Rossi, Spaulding, Stanton, Suhr—15.

Absent—Supervisors Colman, Shannon, Toner—3.

Extension of Time to Complete Improvement of Victoria Street Between Randolph and Sargents Streets.

Also, Resolution No. 32155 (New Series), as follows:

Resolved, That M. Bertolino is hereby granted an extension of thirty days' time from February 6, 1930, within which to complete the improvement of Victoria street between Randolph and Sargents streets under public contract. The work is completed and this extension is necessary to keep contract alive until acceptance and issuance of the assessment.

Ayes—Supervisors Andriano, Canepa, Gallagher, Havenner, Hayden, McGovern, McSheehy, Miles, Peyser, Power, Roncovieri, Rossi, Spaulding, Stanton, Suhr—15.

Absent—Supervisors Colman, Shannon, Toner—3.

Extension of Time to Complete Improvement of Junipero Serra Boulevard.

Also, Resolution No. 32156 (New Series), as follows:

Resolved, That Eaton & Smith be granted an extension of sixty days' time from and after January 27, 1930, within which to complete the improvement of Junipero Serra boulevard from Sloat boulevard to the County line under public contract. This extension of time is granted upon the recommendation of the Board of Public Works for the reason that the contractor has been delayed by the nonarrival of special track work for street railway reconstruction and by weather conditions. The work is now progressing satisfactorily.

Ayes—Supervisors Andriano, Canepa, Gallagher, Havenner, Hayden, McGovern, McSheehy, Miles, Peyser, Power, Roncovieri, Rossi, Spaulding, Stanton, Suhr—15.

Absent—Supervisors Colman, Shannon, Toner—3.

Passed for Printing.

The following matters were *passed for printing*:

Fixing Sidewalk Widths on Goettingen Street.

On recommendation of Streets Committee.

Bill No. 8197, Ordinance No. ——— (New Series), as follows:

Amending Ordinance No. 1061 entitled "Regulating the Width of Sidewalks," approved December 18, 1903, by amending Section Three Hundred and Ninety-seven thereof.

Be it ordained by the People of the City and County of San Francisco as follows:

Section 1. Ordinance No. 1061 entitled "Regulating the Width of Sidewalks," approved December 18, 1903, be and is hereby amended in accordance with the communication of the Board of Public Works, filed in this office Feb. 20, 1930, by amending Section Three Hundred and Ninety-seven thereof, to read as follows:

Section 397. The width of sidewalks on Goettingen street between Silver avenue and Dwight street shall be ten (10) feet.

The width of sidewalks on Goettingen street between Dwight street and Olmstead street shall be as shown on that certain map entitled "Map of Goettingen Street Between Dwight Street and Olmstead Street" showing the location of street and curb lines and the width of sidewalks.

The width of sidewalks on Goettingen street, the westerly side of, between Olmstead street and Mansell street shall be twenty (20) feet.

The width of sidewalks on Goettingen street, the easterly side of, between Olmstead street and Mansell street shall be ten (10) feet.

The width of sidewalks on Goettingen street, the westerly side of, between Ward street and Harkness street shall be twenty (20) feet.

The width of sidewalks on Goettingen street, the easterly side of, between Ward street and Harkness street shall be ten (10) feet.

The width of sidewalks on Goettingen street between Harkness street and its southerly termination shall be ten (10) feet.

Section 2. Any expense caused by the above change of walk widths shall be borne by the property owners.

Section 3. This ordinance shall take effect and be in force from and after its passage.

Ordering the Improvement of Intersection of Brighton and Lakeview Avenues and Southerly One-half of Lakeview Avenue From West Line of Brighton Avenue, Etc.

Also, Bill No. 8198, Ordinance No. ———— (New Series), as follows:

Ordering the performance of certain street work to be done in the City and County of San Francisco, approving and adopting specifications therefor.

Be it ordained by the People of the City and County of San Francisco as follows:

Section 1. The Board of Public Works, in written communication filed in the office of the Clerk of the Board of Supervisors on February 13, 1930, having recommended the ordering of the following street work, the same is hereby ordered to be done in the City and County of San Francisco in conformity with the provisions of the Street Improvement Ordinance of 1918 of said City and County of San Francisco, said work to be performed under the direction of the Board of Public Works, and to be done in accordance with the specifications prepared therefor by said Board of Public Works, and on file in its office, which said plans and specifications are hereby approved and adopted.

That said Board of Supervisors, pursuant to the provisions of Part II of the said Street Improvement Ordinance of 1918 of said City and County of San Francisco, does hereby determine and declare that the assessment to be imposed for the said contemplated improvements, respectively, may be paid in ten installments; that the period of time after the time of the payment of the first installment when each of the succeeding installments must be paid is to be one year from the time of the payment of the preceding installment, and that the rate of interest to be charged on all deferred payments shall be seven per centum per annum.

The improvement of the intersection of Brighton and Lakeview avenues, and of the southerly one-half of Lakeview avenue from the westerly line of Brighton avenue produced to a line parallel with and 25 feet easterly from the easterly line of Brighton avenue, by the construction of armored concrete curbs; by the construction of one-course concrete sidewalks on the angular corners thereof; by the construction of brick catchbasins with 10-inch vitrified clay pipe culvert; by the construction of a 12-inch vitrified clay pipe sewer along the center line of Brighton avenue between the center and the northerly lines of Lakeview avenue; by the construction of vitrified clay pipe side sewers; and by the construction of an asphaltic concrete pavement, consisting of a light traffic concrete foundation and a 1½-inch asphaltic concrete wearing surface, on the roadway thereof.

Section 2. This ordinance shall take effect immediately.

Ordering the Improvement of Harrison Street Between First and Essex Streets, Etc.

Also, Bill No. 8199, Ordinance No. ———— (New Series), as follows:

Ordering the performance of certain street work to be done in the City and County of San Francisco, approving and adopting specifications therefor.

Be it ordained by the People of the City and County of San Francisco as follows:

Section 1. The Board of Public Works, in written communication filed in the office of the Clerk of the Board of Supervisors February 13, 1930, having recommended the ordering of the following street work, the same is hereby ordered to be done in the City and County of San Francisco in conformity with the provisions of the Street Improvement Ordinance of 1918 of said City and County of San Francisco, said work to be performed under the direction of the Board of Public Works, and to be done in accordance with the speci fications prepared therefor by said Board of Public Works, and on file in its office, which said plans and specifications are hereby approved and adopted.

That said Board of Supervisors, pursuant to the provisions of Part II of the said Street Improvement Ordinance of 1918 of said City and County of San Francisco, does hereby determine and declare that the assessment to be imposed for the said contemplated improve- ments, respectively, may be paid in ten installments; that the period of time after the time of the payment of the first installment when each of the succeeding installments must be paid is to be one year from the time of the payment of the preceding installment, and that the rate of interest to be charged on all deferred payments shall be seven per centum per annum.

The improvement of Harrison street between First street and the easterly line of Essex street produced southerly, including the intersec- tion of Harrison street and Rincon street, and excepting that portion required by law to be paved by the railroad company having tracks thereon, by resetting the existing granite curbs; by the construction of granite curbs where not already constructed; by the construction of side sewers, where not already constructed; by the construction of 2-course concrete sidewalks on the angular corners of the intersection of Rincon street; and by the construction of an asphaltic concrete pavement, consisting of a 2-inch asphaltic concrete wearing surface and a 6-inch Class "F" concrete base, on the roadway thereof.

Section 2. This ordinance shall take effect immediately.

Ordering the Construction of Sidewalks on San Jose Avenue and Other Streets.

Also, Bill No. 8200, Ordinance No. ———— (New Series), as follows:

Ordering the performance of certain street work to be done in the City and County of San Francisco, approving and adopting specifi- cations therefor.

Be it ordained by the People of the City and County of San Fran- cisco as follows:

Section 1. The Board of Public Works, in written communication filed in the office of the Clerk of the Board of Supervisors February 13, 1930, having recommended the ordering of the following street work, the same is hereby ordered to be done in the City and County of San Francisco in conformity with the provisions of the Street Improvement Ordinance of 1918 of said City and County of San Francisco, said work to be performed under the direction of the Board of Public Works, and to be done in accordance with the speci- fications prepared therefor by said Board of Public Works, and on file in its office, which said plans and specifications are hereby approved and adopted.

That said Board of Supervisors, pursuant to the provisions of Part II of the said Street Improvement Ordinance of 1918 of said City and County of San Francisco, does hereby determine and declare that the assessment to be imposed for the said contemplated improve. ments, respectively, may be paid in three installments; that the period of time after the time of the payment of the first installment when each of the succeeding installments must be paid is to be one year from the time of the payment of the preceding installment, and that the rate of interest to be charged on all deferred payments shall be seven per centum per annum.

The improvement of San Jose avenue (south one-half) between Theresa and Gorham streets; San Jose avenue (south one-half) between Cotter street and Capistrano avenue; Tingley street between San Jose avenue and a point 545.47 feet south; Tingley street between Mission street and Alemany boulevard; Silver avenue between Mission street and Alemany boulevard; Admiral avenue between Mission street and Alemany boulevard; Castle Manor avenue between Mission street and Camellia avenue; Camellia avenue between Admiral avenue and Silver avenue, by the construction of artificial stone sidewalks, six feet in width, where artificial stone or bituminous rock sidewalks, six feet or more in width, have not already been constructed.

Section 2. This ordinance shall take effect immediately.

Ordering the Improvement of Quint Street, Etc.

Also, Bill No. 8201, Ordinance No. ———— (New Series), as follows:

Ordering the performance of certain street work to be done in the City and County of San Francisco, approving and adopting specifications therefor.

Be it ordained by the People of the City and County of San Francisco as follows:

Section 1. The Board of Public Works, in written communication filed in the office of the Clerk of the Board of Supervisors February 13, 1930, having recommended the ordering of the following street work, the same is hereby ordered to be done in the City and County of San Francisco in conformity with the provisions of the Street Improvement Ordinance of 1918 of said City and County of San Francisco, said work to be performed under the direction of the Board of Public Works, and to be done in accordance with the specifications prepared therefor by said Board of Public Works, and on file in its office, which said plans and specifications are hereby approved and adopted.

That said Board of Supervisors, pursuant to the provisions of Part II of the said Street Improvement Ordinance of 1918 of said City and County of San Francisco, does hereby determine and declare that the assessment to be imposed for the said contemplated improvements, respectively, may be paid in twenty installments; that the period of time after the time of the payment of the first installment when each of the succeeding installments must be paid is to be six months from the time of the payment of the preceding installment, and that the rate of interest to be charged on all deferred payments shall be seven per centum per annum.

The improvement of Quint street between Carroll avenue and the existing pavement westerly therefrom, where not already so improved, by the construction of concrete curbs, and by the construction of an asphaltic concrete pavement, consisting of a 6-inch concrete foundation and a 1½-inch asphaltic wearing surface, on the roadway thereof.

And the improvement of the crossing of Quint street and Carroll avenue by grading to official line and grade; by the construction of an 8-inch vitrified clay pipe sewer between the center and the northerly lines of Quint street; by the construction of brick catchbasins with 10-inch vitrified clay pipe culverts; by the construction of concrete curbs and artificial stone sidewalks on the angular corners, and by the construction of an asphaltic concrete pavement, consisting of a 6-inch concrete foundation and a 1½-inch asphaltic concrete wearing surface, on the roadway thereof.

Section 2. This ordinance shall take effect immediately.

Ordering the Improvement of Bright Street Between Randolph and Sargent Streets.

Also, Bill No. 8202, Ordinance No. ———— (New Series), as follows:

Ordering the performance of certain street work to be done in the City and County of San Francisco, approving and adopting specifications therefor.

Be it ordained by the People of the City and County of San Francisco as follows:

Section 1. The Board of Public Works, in written communication filed in the office of the Clerk of the Board of Supervisors February 13, 1930, having recommended the ordering of the following street work, the same is hereby ordered to be done in the City and County of San Francisco in conformity with the provisions of the Street Improvement Ordinance of 1918 of said City and County of San Francisco, said work to be performed under the direction of the Board of Public Works, and to be done in accordance with the specifications prepared therefor by said Board of Public Works, and on file in its office, which said plans and specifications are hereby approved and adopted.

That said Board of Supervisors, pursuant to the provisions of Part II of the said Street Improvement Ordinance of 1918 of said City and County of San Francisco, does hereby determine and declare that the assessment to be imposed for the said contemplated improvements, respectively, may be paid in twenty installments; that the period of time after the time of the payment of the first installment when each of the succeeding installments must be paid is to be six months from the time of the payment of the preceding installment, and that the rate of interest to be charged on all deferred payments shall be seven per centum per annum.

The improvement of Bright street between Randolph and Sargent streets, where not already so improved, by the construction of armored concrete curbs; by the construction of side sewers, and by the construction of a concrete pavement on the roadway thereof.

Section 2. This ordinance shall take effect immediately.

Adopted.

The following resolution was *adopted*:

Closing Portion of Junipero Serra Boulevard Lying Northerly From Ocean Avenue.

On recommendation of Streets Committee.

Resolution No. 32157 (New Series), as follows:

Closing and abandoning all that portion of Junipero Serra boulevard lying northerly from Ocean avenue.

Whereas, this Board has, by Resolution No. 31809 (New Series), declared its intention to close up and abandon all that portion of Junipero Serra boulevard lying northerly from Ocean avenue;

Whereas, proper notice of said resolution and of said proposed closing and abandonment of all that portion of Junipero Serra boulevard as described in Resolution of Intention No. 31809 (New Series) was duly given by the Board of Public Works of said City and County of San Francisco by publication in the manner provided by the Charter of the City and County of San Francisco;

Whereas, more than ten days have elapsed after the expiration of the publication of said notice, and no objections to the closing of said portion of Junipero Serra boulevard were made or delivered to the Clerk of this Board within said period of ten (10) days or at all.

Whereas, it is the opinion of this Board that the public interests and convenience will be conserved by the closing and abandonment of said portion of Junipero Serra boulevard;

Whereas, in and by said Resolution No. 31809 (New Series) this

Board did declare that the damages, costs and expenses of closing said portion of said street are nominal and no assessment district is necessary to be formed for the purpose of paying the damages, costs and expenses thereof, the Board of Supervisors hereby declares and determines that the whole damage, cost and expense of closing said street shall be paid out of the revenues of the City and County of San Francisco;

Resolved, That said closing and abandonment of a portion of Junipero Serra boulevard, as described in Resolution of Intention No. 31809 (New Series), be and the same is hereby ordered, and that said portion of Junipero Serra boulevard be and the same is hereby closed and abandoned as a public street. The said portion of Junipero Serra boulevard hereinabove referred to is more particularly described as follows, to-wit:

Commencing at the point of intersection of the easterly line of Junipero Serra boulevard and the southwesterly line of Ocean avenue, and running thence northwesterly along said southwesterly line 70.151 feet to the center line of the proposed Junipero Serra boulevard; thence deflecting to the right 62 deg. 59 min. 30 sec. and running northerly along said center line 120 feet to the true point of beginning; thence continuing northerly along said center line 64 feet to the southerly line of that parcel of Junipero Serra boulevard closed by Resolution No. 31026 of the Board of Supervisors, adopted June 17, 1929; thence at right angles easterly along said last-mentioned southerly line 32.50 feet; thence at right angles southerly parallel with and distant 32.50 feet at right angles easterly from the aforementioned center line 64 feet; thence at right angles westerly 32.50 feet to the true point of beginning; being a portion of Junipero Serra boulevard. Be it

Further Resolved, That the Clerk of this Board transmit a certified copy of this resolution to the Board of Public Works and that the Board of Public Works be instructed to proceed thereafter as required by law and the Charter of the City and County of San Francisco; and the Clerk of this Board is hereby directed to advertise this resolution in the official newspaper as required by law.

Ayes—Supervisors Andriano, Canepa, Gallagher, Havenner, Hayden, McGovern, McSheehy, Miles, Peyser, Power, Roncovieri, Rossi, Spaulding, Stanton, Suhr—15.

Absent—Supervisors Colman, Shannon, Toner—3.

Passed for Printing.

The following matters were *passed for printing*:

Condemnation of Land Required for Montcalm Street.

On recommendation of Streets Committee:

Resolution No. ————— (New Series), as follows:

Resolved, By the Board of Supervisors of the City and County of San Francisco, that public interest and necessity require the acquisition by the City and County of San Francisco, a municipal corporation, of the following properties, situated in the City and County of San Francisco, State of California, more particularly described as follows, to-wit:

Parcel 1. Commencing at the point of intersection of the northeasterly line of Franconia street and the southeasterly line of Montcalm street, and running thence northeasterly along said southeasterly line 70 feet to the southwesterly line of the property now or formerly owned by Fred W. zur Lowen; thence at right angles southeasterly along said southwesterly line 3.739 feet to the proposed southeasterly line of Montcalm street; thence southwesterly along said proposed southeasterly line on a curve to the right, tangent to a line deflected 67 deg. 41 min. 40 sec. to the right from the preceding course, radius 129.759 feet, central angle 31 deg. 30 min. 27 sec., a distance of 71.356

feet to the northeasterly line of Franconia street; thence northwesterly along said northeasterly line 11.779 feet to the southeasterly line of Montcalm street and the point of commencement.

Being a portion of Gift Map No 3, as per map thereof recorded in Map Book 2A and B, page 15, records of the City and County of San Francisco.

Parcel 2. Commencing at the point of intersection of the northwesterly line of Montcalm street and the easterly line of Peralta avenue, and running thence northerly along said easterly line 2.354 feet; thence easterly on a curve to the left, tangent to a line deflected 90 deg. 00 min. 00 sec. to the right from said easterly line of Peralta avenue, radius 24 feet, central angle 24 deg. 24 min. 00 sec., a distance of 10.221 feet to its point of tangency with said northwesterly line of Montcalm street; thence southwesterly along said northwesterly line 10.887 feet to the easterly line of Peralta avenue and the point of commencement.

Being a portion of Lot 1466 of Gift Map No. 3, as per map thereof recorded in Map Book 2A and B, page 15, records of the City and County of San Francisco. Be it

Further Resolved, That said property is suitable, adaptable, necessary and required for the public use of said City and County of San Francisco, to-wit: For the opening, widening, construction and maintenance of Montcalm street from its point of intersection with Macedonia street in a westerly direction to the point of interesection with Peralta avenue. It is necessary that a fee simple title be taken for such use.

The City Attorney is hereby ordered and directed to commence proceedings in eminent domain against the owners of said parcels of land, and of any and all interests therein or claims thereto, for the condemnation thereof for the public use of the City and County of San Francisco, as aforesaid.

Ordering the Improvement of Corbett Avenue, From Clayton Street to Twenty-fourth Street, Etc., City to Assume Portion of the Cost Thereof.

Also, Bill No. 8203, Ordinance No. ——— (New Series), as follows:

Ordering the performance of certain street work to be done in the City and County of San Francisco, approving and adopting specifications therefor.

Be it ordained by the People of the City and County of San Francisco as follows:

Section 1. The Board of Public Works, in written communication filed in the office of the Clerk of the Board of Supervisors, February 26, 1930, having recommended the ordering of the following street work, the same is hereby ordered to be done in the City and County of San Francisco in conformity with the provisions of the Street Improvement Ordinance of 1918 of said City and County of San Francisco, said work to be performed under the direction of the Board of Public Works, and to be done in accordance with the specifications prepared therefor by said Board of Public Works, and on file in its office, which said plans and specifications are hereby approved and adopted.

That said Board of Supervisors, pursuant to the provisions of Part II of the said Street Improvement Ordinance of 1918 of said City and County of San Francisco, does hereby determine and declare that the assessment to be imposed for the said contemplated improvements, re spectively, may be paid in twenty installments; that the period of time after the time of the payment of the first installment when each of the succeeding installments must be paid is to be six months from the time of the payment of the preceding installment, and that the rate of interest to be charged on all deferred payments shall be seven per centum per annum.

The improvement of Corbett avenue from Clayton street to Twenty-fourth street, including all intervening crossings and intersections and the necessary conform and approach work on streets adjacent thereto, by grading to official line and subgrade and by the construction of the following:

Class "B" 2500-pound concrete in retaining walls, stairs, balustrades and sidewalk curtain walls; bar reinforcing steel; vitrified clay pipe sewers; vitrified clay pipe side sewers; vitrified clay pipe Y or T branches; brick manholes complete; brick catch basins complete; reset brick catch basin; vitrified clay pipe culvert; armored concrete curb; concrete curb reset; redwood headers; asphalt-concrete pavement consisting of a 2-inch asphaltic concrete wearing surface and a 6-inch Class "F" concrete base; asphaltic concrete wearing surface; wire mesh reinforcement for concrete base; concrete sidewalk (2 course); black pipe conduit; wood bulkhead; wood stairway reconstruction; painted traffic lines; painted "Slow" signs; post-mounted "Slow" signs; pedestrian lane markers; traffic turning buttons.

Section 2. This ordinance shall take effect immediately.

Ordering the Improvement of Twentieth Avenue, South of the South Line of Irving Street, by Removal of Sand, Etc.

Also, Bill No. 8204, Ordinance No. ———— (New Series), as follows:

Ordering the performance of certain street work to be done in the City and County of San Francisco, approving and adopting specifications therefor.

Be it ordained by the People of the City and County of San Francisco as follows:

Section 1. The Board of Public Works in written communication filed in the office of the Clerk of the Board of Supervisors February 13, 1930, having recommended the ordering of the following street work, the same is hereby ordered to be done in the City and County of San Francisco in conformity with the provisions of the Street Improvement Ordinance of 1918 of said City and County of San Francisco, said work to be performed under the direction of the Board of Public Works, and to be done in accordance with the specifications prepared therefor by said Board of Public Works, and on file in its office, which said plans and specifications are hereby approved and adopted.

That said Board of Supervisors, pursuant to the provisions of Part II of the said Street Improvement Ordinance of 1918 of said City and County of San Francisco, does hereby determine and declare that the assessment to be imposed for the said contemplated improvements, respectively, may be paid in three installments; that the period of time after the time of the payment of the first installment when each of the succeeding installments must be paid is to be one year from the time of the payment of the preceding installment, and that the rate of interest to be charged on all deferred payments shall be seven per centum per annum.

The improvement of the west one-half of Twentieth avenue from a line parallel with and 75 feet south of the south line of Irving street to a line parallel with and 125 feet south of the south line of Irving street by the removal of sand from the roadway and sidewalk area and the construction of a bulkhead.

Bidder is to name price per lineal foot of a 2-foot bulkhead for this work.

Section 2. This ordinance shall take effect immediately.

Adopted.

The following resolutions were *adopted*:

Mayor to Sell Improvements for Alemany Boulevard Opening.

On recommendation of Streets Committee.

Resolution No. 32158 (New Series), as follows:

Resolved, That the Mayor be and he is hereby authorized and directed to sell at public auction, after at least five (5) days of published notice, the following described personal property owned by the City and County of San Francisco, to-wit:

Dwelling house and appurtenances situated on that certain piece or parcel of land required for the opening of Alemany boulevard, and known as 232 Sickles avenue.

The terms of sale shall be cash upon delivery of bill of sale, said dwelling house and appurtenances to be removed by the purchasers within thirty (30) days of purchase thereof.

The proceeds derived from said sale shall be deposited to the credit of Boulevard Bond Issue Fund.

Ayes—Supervisors Andriano, Canepa, Gallagher, Havenner, Hayden, McGovern, McSheehy, Miles, Peyser, Power, Roncovieri, Rossi, Spaulding, Stanton, Suhr—15.

Absent—Supervisors Colman, Shannon, Toner—3.

Loading Zones.

On recommendation of Traffic and Safety Committee.

Resolution No. 32159 (New Series), as follows:

Resolved, That the following list of loading zones, of the lengths specified, be established in front of or near the following adresses, in accordance with the provisions of Section 36 of Ordinance No. 7691 (New Series), as amended:

458 Columbus avenue, 27 feet—Buon Gusto Sausage Factory; 2 elevators.

230-242 Gough street, 18 feet—Ruby's Rest; Tobey Radio Shop; Temple Tailor.

10 Hickory street, 27 feet—J. S. Godean Co., morgue entrance.

746 Jones street, 27 feet—Belgravia Apartments; trades' entrance; one oil intake.

701 Pacific street, 18 feet—Pow Lang Co. Market.

135 Post street, 27 feet—Carlisle Stationery Co.

625 Powell street, 27 feet—625 Powell Apartments; one oil intake; trades' entrance.

535 Stockton street, 18 feet—535 Stockton Apartments; one oil intake.

645 Taylor street, 18 feet—Sussex Hotel; one oil intake.

907-911 Washington street, 18 feet—Home Dyeing and Cleaning Co.

1049 Bay street, 36 feet—Galileo High School entrance.

1095 Bay street, 18 feet—Galileo High School cafeteria.

1136 Francisco street, 36 feet—Galileo High School main entrance.

1180 Francisco street, 18 feet—Galileo High School stage entrance.

40 Fremont street, 18 feet—Bryer & Son, wholesale dry goods.

820 Jones street, 18 feet—820 Jones Apartments.

210 Larch street, 18 feet—P. J. Kelly Garage.

215 Larch street, 27 feet—Russell Mfg. Co.

147 Market street, 27 feet—California Seed Company.

2901 Polk street, 18 feet—Galileo High School.

81 Steuart street, 27 feet—Kellogg's Express Teminal.

618 Van Ness avenue, 18 feet—McKean Bros. Tire Company.

117-119 Waverly place, 18 feet—Chinese Times Pub. Co.

Ayes—Supervisors Andriano, Canepa, Gallagher, Havenner, Hayden, McGovern, McSheehy, Miles, Peyser, Power, Roncovieri, Rossi. Spaulding, Stanton, Suhr—15.

Absent—Supervisors Colman, Shannon, Toner—3.

Rescinding and Reestablishing Loading Zones.

Also, Resolution No. 32160 (New Series), as follows:

Resolved, That the following loading zones, of the lengths specified, be rescinded and reestablished, as specified herein, in front of or near the following addresses, in accordance with the provisions of Section No. 36 of Ordinance No. 7691 (New Series), as amended:

400 Brannan street, 27 feet (rescinded)—Dr. A. C. Armstrong Industrial Clinic.

163 Market street, 27 feet (rescinded)—Sunset Hotel and small stores.

610 Van Ness avenue, 27 feet, new length 18 feet—Triangle Tire Co.

595 Sutter street, 18 feet, new length 27 feet—Women's Club (Francisca Club).

Ayes—Supervisors Andriano, Canepa, Gallagher, Havenner, Hayden, McGovern, McSheehy, Miles, Peyser, Power, Roncovieri, Rossi, Spaulding, Stanton, Suhr—15.

Absent—Supervisors Colman, Shannon, Toner—3.

Passenger Loading Zones.

Also, Resolution No. 32161 (New Series), as follows:

Resolved, That the following list of passenger loading zones, of the lengths specified, be established in front of or near the following addresses, in accordance with the provisions of Section No. 36 of Ordinance No. 7691 (New Series), as amended:

930 Fillmore street, 18 feet—New Fillmore Hotel.

1549 Market street, 18 feet—El Patio Dance Hall, passenger entrance.

835 O'Farrell street, 18 feet—Hotel Iroquois.

259 Post street, 27 feet—Ransohoff's Dry Goods Co.

340 Stockton street, 18 feet—Wiltshire Hotel, passenger entrance.

400 Brannan street, 27 feet—Dr. A. C. Armstrong Industrial Clinic.

421 Ellis street, 18 feet—St. George Hotel.

2191 Sutter street, 36 feet—Iceland Ice Rink.

Ayes—Supervisors Andriano, Canepa, Gallagher, Havenner, Hayden, McGovern, McSheehy, Miles, Peyser, Power, Roncovieri, Rossi, Spaulding, Stanton, Suhr—15.

Absent—Supervisors Colman, Shannon, Toner—3.

Award of Contract, Dry Goods and Wearing Apparel.

On recommendation of Supplies Committee.

Also, Resolution No. 32162 (New Series), as follows:

Resolved, That award of contract be hereby made for furnishing dry goods and wearing apparel, on bids submitted January 20, 1930 (Proposal No. 545), and tabulation thereof on file in the Bureau of Supplies, which is by this reference made a part hereof; said matter having heretofore received full consideration in an open public meeting of the Supplies Committee of the Board of Supervisors and the awards herein approved by it, same are now made to the following, viz.:

Bid No. 8—Levi Strauss & Co.
Bid No. 9—Walton N. Moore Dry Goods Co.
Bid No. 10—Johnson & Johnson.
Bid No. 11—Eloesser-Heynemann Co.
Bid No. 12—Philadelphia Shoe Co.
Bid No. 13—Carl Munter & Co.
Bid No. 14—White Duck Clothing Mfg. Co.
Bid No. 18—Greenebaum, Weil & Michels.
Bid No. 19—D. N. & E. Walter & Co.
Bid No. 20—Goldstone Bros., Inc.
Bid No. 21—Buckingham & Hecht.
Bid No. 22—Lazare-Klein Co.

Bid No. 23—J. B. Crowley, Inc.

Bid No. 24—E. Friedlander & Sons.

Note—All above awards are made to the lowest bidder, except when award is made in consideration of deliveries or on account of the quality as determined or recommended by the Purchaser of Supplies.

Resolved, That no bonds be required.

Resolved, That all other bids submitted thereon be rejected.

Ayes—Supervisors Andriano, Canepa, Gallagher, Havenner, Hayden, McGovern, McSheehy, Miles, Peyser, Power, Roncovieri, Rossi, Spaulding, Stanton, Suhr—15.

Absent—Supervisors Colman, Shannon, Toner—3.

Award of Contract, Foodstuffs.

Also, Resolution No. 32163 (New Series), as follows:

Resolved, That award of contract be hereby made for furnishing foodstuffs during the four months' term, viz., March, April, May and June, 1930, on bids submitted February 3, 1930 (Proposal No. 552), and tabulation thereof on file in the Bureau of Supplies which is by this reference made a part hereof; said matter having heretofore received full consideration in an open public meeting of the Supplies Committee of the Board of Supervisors and the awards herein approved by it, same are now made to the following, viz.:

Bid No. 1—Schweitzer & Co., Inc.; bond $500.

Bid No. 2—Cudahy Bros. Co.; bond $100.

Bid No. 3—F. E. Booth Co., Inc.; bond $300.

Bid No. 4—Western States Grocery Co.; bond $100.

Bid No. 5—S. Paladini, Inc.; bond $200.

Bid No. 6—Western Meat Co.; bond $500.

Bid No. 7—M. J. B. Co.; no bond.

Bid No. 8—H. J. Heinz Corporation; no bond.

Bid No. 9—Baumgarten Bros.; bond $500.

Bid No. 10—Fred L. Hilmer Co.; bond $1,000.

Bid No. 11—Swift & Co.; no bond.

Bid No. 12—Challenge Cream & Butter Assn.; no bond.

Bid No. 13—S. Gumpert Co., Inc.; no bond.

Bid No. 14—Haas Bros.; no bond.

Bid No. 15—Virden Packing Co., Est. 109; no bond.

Bid No. 16—Smith, Lynden & Co.; no bond.

Bid No. 22—Del Monte Meat Co., Inc.; bond $1,000.

Bid No. 23—O'Brien, Spotorno, Mitchell & Compagno Bros.; no bond.

Bid No. 24—H. E. Teller Co.; no bond.

Bid No. 25—A. Lombard & Co.; bond $100.

Bid No. 27—Jones-Thierbach Co.; bond $100.

Bid No. 29—St. Charles Market; bond $100.

Bid No. 31—South San Francisco Pkg. & Provision Co.; bond $100.

Bid No. 32—California Meat Co.; bond $1,000.

Bid No. 36—Roth, Winter & Walsh; bond $100.

Bid No. 37—Sherry Bros., Inc.; no bond.

Note—All above awards are made to the lowest bidder, except when award is made in consideration of deliveries or on account of the quality as determined by such tests as required or recommended by the Purchaser of Supplies.

Resolved, That all other bids submitted thereon be rejected.

Ayes—Supervisors Andriano, Canepa, Gallagher, Havenner, Hayden, McGovern, McSheehy, Miles, Peyser, Power, Roncovieri, Rossi, Spaulding, Stanton, Suhr—15.

Absent—Supervisors Colman, Shannon, Toner—3.

Mayor Retires.

At 4:15 p. m. His Honor the Mayor was excused and Supervisor Rossi was elected to preside.

ROLL CALL FOR THE INTRODUCTION OF RESOLUTIONS, BILLS AND COMMUNICATIONS NOT CONSIDERED OR REPORTED UPON BY A COMMITTEE.

Mirrors in Elevators.

Supervisor Toner presented a measure providing for the installation of mirrors in City Hall elevators.

Referred to Building Committee.

Reception to Ogden Mills in the Matter of the Purchase of Mills Field.

The following was presented and read by the Clerk:

Resolution No. 32165 (New Series) as follows:

Whereas, Ogden Mills will arrive in San Francisco on or about the 12th day of March, 1930; and

Whereas, his stay in San Francisco is for the purpose of negotiating with the City and County of San Francisco relative to the purchase of Mills Field for a municipal airport, and property thereto adjacent; now therefore be it

Resolved, That the following committee, consisting of the Joint Airport and Aeronautics and Public Welfare and Publicity Committees, and the Finance Committee, act as a reception committee for Ogden Mills, and make all necessary arrangements therefor, and that the Airport and Aeronautics Committee and the Finance Committee be, and they are hereby authorized to negotiate with said Ogden Mills, relative to the purchase of Mills Field and all matters pertaining thereto, and that said Committee so appointed report its recommendations to said Board of Supervisors.

Adopted by the following vote:

Ayes—Supervisors Andriano, Canepa, Gallagher, Havenner, Hayden, McSheehy, Miles, Peyser, Power, Roncovieri, Rossi, Shannon, Spaulding, Stanton, Suhr, Toner—16.

Absent—Supervisors Colman, McGovern—2.

Transfer of Budget Items.

Supervisor Rossi presented:

Resolution No. 32164 (New Series), as follows:

Resolved, That the following amounts be and the same are hereby credited to Budget Item No. 1020, from the hereinafter designated Budget Items, to-wit:

From Budget Item No. 40, the sum of.....................$23,884.20
From Budget Item No. 50, the sum of..................... 2,956.30

$26,840.50

Adopted by the following vote:

Ayes—Supervisors Andriano, Canepa, Gallagher, Havenner, Hayden, McSheehy, Miles, Peyser, Power, Roncovieri, Rossi, Shannon, Spaulding, Stanton, Suhr, Toner—16.

Absent—Supervisors Colman, McGovern—2.

(*The Clerk explained that the foregoing was for the purpose of covering over-drafts in Publicity and Advertising.*)

Passed for Printing.

The following matter was *passed for printing.*

Appropriating $25,000 for Improvement of Sharpe's Park.

On motion of Supervisor Rossi:

Resolution No. ———— (New Series), as follows:

Resolved, That the sum of $25,000 be and the same is hereby set aside, appropriated and authorized to be expended out of General

Fund, 1929-1930, for construction and improvements at Sharpe Park, San Mateo County, California.

St. Patrick's Day Celebration.

Supervisor Gallagher presented:

Communication from St. Patrick's Day Committee inviting the Board of Supervisors to participate in the St. Patrick's Day celebration, March 17, 1930.

Supervisors Toner, Andriano and Rossi were delegated to represent the Board of Supervisors.

Ventilation of Chambers.

Supervisor Power moved that the Public Buildings and Lands Committee take steps to properly ventilate the chambers of the Board.

Supervisor Shannon, Chairman of the Committee, declared the matter would be given consideration at meeting of the Committee this week.

Repealing Resolution No. 31023 (New Series), Appraisal Bureau.

Supervisor Rossi presented:

Resolved, That Resolution No. 31023 (New Series), authorizing the Finance Committee to employ a superintendent, experts and assistants, and to purchase supplies, in connection with the appraisal of taxable real property, be and the same is hereby repealed.

Opinion of City Attorney.

A communication from the City Attorney relative to the delegation of powers of the Board of Supervisors to Committees of the Board was read by the Clerk and ordered *filed.*

Supervisor Havenner, seconded by Supervisor Shannon, moved to lay over one week in order that this matter may be put in proper legal form.

Supervisor Gallagher moved as a substitute that the subject-matter of the Stafford Appraisal Bureau and the creation of employment there be made the subject of a Special Order of Business for 4 p. m. *Accepted.*

Whereupon Supervisor Power moved that the subject-matter go over one week and be made a Special Order for 4 p. m.

Motion *carried.*

Whereupon Supervisor Havenner presented:

Resolution No. ———— (New Series), as follows:

Resolved, That for the purpose of appraising all taxable property subject to assessment within the City and County of San Francisco to the end that said assessment of said property may be equalized and the same made to conform to the true value of said property and that the Board of Supervisors, sitting as a Board of Equalization, may be fully advised as to the true value of said property, the Board of Supervisors hereby authorizes the employment of John F. Barry for a period of two weeks at a salary of $300 per month out of Item No. 76 of the Budget of the fiscal year 1929-1930.

Referred to the Finance Committee.

Report of Finance Committee on Appraisal Bureau.

March 3, 1930.

The following was presented by Supervisor Rossi and on his motion copies of same *ordered sent to each member of the Board:*

On June 29, 1926, the Board of Supervisors adopted Resolution No. 25878 (New Series), which reads as follows:

"RESOLUTION NO. 25878, NEW SERIES (Board of Supervisors, June 29, 1926.)

"Whereas, for the purpose of making a scientific appraisal of the taxable real property of the City and County in order that the Board of Supervisors may perform the duties imposed by law upon said Board as a board of equalization, it is essential to create an advisory com-·mittee, including experts in valuation matters;

"Resolved, That the following persons are hereby designated as such committee: Andrew J. Gallagher, Paul Scharrenberg, Philip Paschel, B. A. Banker, M. H. Gates, Henry Boyen, Paul A. Sinsheimer, the same to act in conjunction with the Finance Committee of this Board and with the Assessor, the entire number to constitute the Advisory Committee of the Board of Equalization; and be it further

"Resolved, That said committee be empowered to hold public hearings for the purpose of ascertaining the true values of real property subject to taxation and to report the result of its investigation to the Assessor and to the Board of Equalization on or before July 1, 1927."

(Adopted by the Board of Supervisors, June 28, 1926.)

The Board of Supervisors on July 6, 1926, adopted Resolution No. 25897 (New Series), which reads as follows:

"Authorizing for the purpose of appraising all taxable real property subject to assessment within the City and County of San Francisco to the end that said assessment of said property for the fiscal year 1927-28 and for subsequent years may be equalized and the same may conform to the true value of said property and that the Board of Supervisors, sitting as a Board of Equalization, may be fully advised as to the true value of said property, the Finance Committee of this Board to employ a superintendent and such other experts and assistants and to purchase such supplies as may be necessary to carry out the purpose herein expressed, the cost of the same to be paid from Budget Item No. 62, 1926-27."

(Adopted July 6, 1926, by the Board of Supervisors.)

On May 25, 1926, when the Budget for the fiscal year 1926-27 was under consideration, the Board of Supervisors had approved Budget Item Number 62, which was the initial appropriation to cover the cost of the appraisal authorized in the above quoted Resolutions of the Board.

Acting under the authority conferred upon them by Resolution No. 25897 (New Series), the Finance Committee employed as superintendent for the appraisal work then in contemplation one James G. Stafford.

On June 27, 1927, James G. Stafford transmitted, through the Advisory Committee to the Board of Equalization, his final report in connection with the land appraisal.

The communication of Superintendent James G. Stafford contains the following paragraph:

"The record of this appraisal in detail is contained in forty-four bound volumes of summary sheets in typewritten form, one for each block area of the City and County of San Francisco, the volume numbers and the block numbers included in each volume coinciding with the arrangement of the tax assessment roll of 1927."

At 12 o'clock noon of July 5, 1927, the Assessor delivered to the Clerk of the Board of Supervisors the Assessment Roll for the year 1927, and on July 5, 1927, at 2 p. m., the Board of Supervisors convened as a Board of Equalization, re-convened on July 11, 1927, and re-convened again on July 18, 1927, all of which is established by Journals of the Board, Volume 22, Numbers 27, 28 and 29, respectively.

During its session as a Board of Equalization 87 applications were received for the reduction or correction of assessments.

It is to be specifically noted that the Board of Supervisors had before it the Land Appraisal Reports supplied by Superintendent James G. Stafford, compiled (according to the Resolutions authorizing same) "In order that the Board of Supervisors may perform the duties imposed by law upon said Board as a Board of Equalization."

It is to be further noted that the Board of Supervisors during the period of two weeks between July 5 and July 18 held but three meetings as a Board of Equalization.

The Journals of the Board of Equalization indicate that a total of 87 applications for the reduction or correction of assessments were filed in the three sessions that were held. Thirteen (13) of these applications covered land and seventy-four (74) covered buildings.

Of the eighty-seven applications that were received certain were referred to the Assessor and certain others were taken under advisement by the Board of Equalization.

The Assessor rendered a report on all matters referred to him. Supervisor McSheehy moved that the Assessor's report on all matters referred to him be approved. Supervisor McSheehy moved that all matters taken under advisement be denied.

The land appraisal rendered by Superintendent James G. Stafford on June 27, 1927, was not made use of by the Board of Supervisors sitting as a Board of Equalization.

On January 16, 1928, the Board of Supervisors had before it, as No. 8 on the Calendar, a resolution appropriating from the General Fund the sum of $29,960. The stenographic transcript of that meeting indicates that $24,960 was to cover the salary of additional clerks at the rate of $160 per month, and that $5,000 was to cover cost of non-personal service, including additional equipment, accessories, etc.

The then Chairman of the Finance Committee—Supervisor Havenner—stated:

"The figures have been completed and the appraisement has been transmitted to him" (Assessor) "and he says that before he can decide whether he can make any use of it it will be necessary for his own department to check the accuracy of the appraisement and the accuracy of the values as they have been computed. That, of course, entails a lot of clerical work in his office, in addition to the field check which his appraisers will make on the valuation. . . . He wants to go over the basis of valuations to satisfy himself as to their reasonableness. Then he wants to have this clerical force make a check of the computations to see whether the values based on the front-foot valuations—as I understand his method—it will be to go through the whole system and satisfy himself of the accuracy of the front-foot valuations put on the various blocks in San Francisco. Having satisfied himself as to those values, and made any such corrections as he may desire to make, he will then want to make a general check of the computations of all values based on these front-foot valuations."

The appropriation was approved by the Board of Supervisors on January 16, 1928, and the Assessor undertook the task of rechecking the land appraisal.

The Budget of the City and County of San Francisco for the fiscal year 1927-28, Bill No. 8045, Order No. 7558, contained an appropriation of $125,000, listed as Budget Item No. 66, and set forth as follows:

"For the purpose of continuing and completing the appraising of all taxable property subject to assessment within the City and County of San Francisco to the end that said assessment of said property for the fiscal year 1928-29, and for subsequent years, may be equalized and the same may conform to the true value of said property and that the Board of Supervisors, sitting as a Board of Equalization, may be fully advised as to the true value of said property."

The item of $125,000, as above set forth, was provided in order that an appraisal could be made of the improvements on the land that had been appraised the year previously. In this connection it is to be borne in mind that there are, in round numbers, 130,000 structures in San Francisco subject to taxation.

Whereas the land appraisal was conducted through the medium of employing James G. Stafford as a municipal employee with the title of Superintendent, the building appraisal was conducted under a different method. The City and County entered into a contract with James G. Stafford and Associates, Incorporated. Of this corporation James G. Stafford was managing director and H. A. Mason was secretary. James G. Stafford and Associates, Incorporated, began the task of appraising the taxable improvements of the City and County of San Francisco in October of 1927. Their obligations under the contract were completed some time prior to June of 1928 and there was filed with the Board of Supervisors, prior to June 1, 1928, a report, together with all supporting data.

In the Assessor's Annual Report, as required by Section 9, Article 16, of the Charter, rendered on July 9, 1928, the Assessor stated:

"*Appraisals—(a) Land; (b) Buildings.*

In equalization sessions this year the Board will have for its guidance the valuation surveys made during 1927 and 1928 of the land and of the buildings in San Francisco by a non-elective agency of the Board of Equalization. These surveys were not made for the Assessor's office, nor were they made by the Assessor's office. They were made, as the proceedings of the Board will indicate, to provide a chart of values for the assistance of the Board in their equalization proceedings.

(a) Land Appraisal.

This report was completed prior to July 1, 1927. On January 16, 1928, the Board of Supervisors appropriated necessary funds in order that the Assessor's office might recheck the land valuation report. The work of rechecking has progressed steadily and sufficient headway has been made to permit expression of an opinion as to the general merit of the report. Without attempting to submit a detailed analysis, I will say that the land appraisal figures have been of assistance to the Assessor's office in determining the relationship between indicated front-foot "sales value" and the assessed valuations. It would, however, in my judgment, be contrary to the best interests of San Francisco for the Assessor to adopt the standards of value this appraisal reflects.

"It is my belief that the Board of Supervisors, particularly in their equalization deliberations, can reach a clearer understanding of the land assessment problems by a careful study and analysis of the land valuation report. The Assessor's office has derived a genuine benefit by following that course.

(b) Building Appraisal.

"The building appraisal report has not as yet been made public. I have no means of determining its merit. During the time that the building appraisal was in progress I extended to the building valuation engineers who were in charge of the work every possible cooperation. The calibre of the valuation technicians under whose direction the building appraisal was conducted is such that, from all indications, the Board of Equalization should, in my opinion, have a valuable chart of values to be used in their deliberations this year.

General Comment in Connection With the Appraisals.

"As a general comment in connection with these appraisals: if they are to be of permanent worth in equalization proceedings they must be kept current. Land values are constantly changing, and construction costs have been known to fluctuate as much as twenty per cent in a single year. The Board will undoubtedly give consideration to the problem of securing prompt and continuing reflection in these appraisals of this constant shift of values. In view of the fact that these appraisals are intended as a check against assessed valuations it would be highly improper for the Assessor's office to undertake the task of maintaining these appraisals on a current value basis—but if the work is not done the worth of these appraisals will be short lived."

The first Monday of July of 1928, which was July 2, at 12 o'clock noon, the Assessor delivered to the Clerk of the Board of Supervisors the Assessment Roll for the year 1928.

The Board of Supervisors did not meet on the first Monday in July as a Board of Equalization. On the second Monday in July—July 9— the Board convened as a Board of Equalization, and reconvened on July 12th, 13th and 16th.

Applications for the reduction or correction of assessments, to the total of 258, were filed with the Board of Equalization during their 1928 sessions. Of these, certain matters were referred to the Assessor and certain matters were taken under advisement by the Board of Equalization.

Of the total applications for reduction or correction of assessments, seventy (70) were referred to the Assessor and one hundred and eighty-eight (188) were taken under advisement.

Of the seventy (70) referred to the Assessor, the Assessor recommended reduction in the case of fifty-one (51) applications and recommended denial of nineteen (19) applications.

On motion of Supervisor McSheehy the Assessor's report on these seventy (70) cases was approved. Of the one hundred and eighty-eight (188) cases taken under advisement, Supervisor McSheehy moved a reduction in fifty-five (55) cases, and in his report recommending this reduction Supervisor McSheehy stated:

"These reductions are entirely made on the Stafford appraisement, based on a 50 per cent valuation."

The total amount of these fifty-five (55) reductions was $87,675.

From the foregoing it will be seen that whereas, during the equalization sessions of 1927 and 1928, a total of three hundred and forty-five (345) applications for the reduction or correction of assessments were filed with the Board of Equalization, the land and building appraisals, created "in order that the Board of Supervisors may perform the duties imposed by law upon said Board as a Board of Equalization," were used in only fifty-five (55) cases. Expressed in percentage, the land and building appraisals were utilized in only 15 per cent of the cases coming within the purview of the Board of Equalization.

In the official transcript of the proceedings of the Board of Equalization of Monday, July 16, Supervisor Havenner proposed as an amendment to an amendment, which, being accepted by the mover and seconder of the original amendment, was, under ruling of the chair, regarded as an amendment to the original amendment, to this effect:

"That the Assessor be requested by this Board of Supervisors to establish all of the assessments on the present assessment roll on a basis of uniformity with relation to a true value appraisal."

This motion was carried by a unanimous vote of the Board of Supervisors.

Clipping from San Francisco Examiner, Tuesday, July 17, 1928:

"BOARD OK.'S REAPPRAISAL BY STAFFORD. $285.365 CUT FROM WOLDEN'S ASSESSMENT ROLL AS SUPERVISORS REDUCE VALUE ON BUILDINGS.

After two years of preparation the James G. Stafford reappraisal of San Francisco property was accepted as the basic standard of valuation yesterday by the Board of Supervisors.

Sitting as the Board of Equalization, the Supervisors debated for three hours over the principles of assessment laid down in Stafford's report. At the end of the debate the board voted:

1. To reduce the assessed valuations of seventy-five pieces of property to a figure which would represent 50 per cent of the 'market value' placed on the properties in Stafford's report.

2. To request Assessor Russell L. Wolden to establish the entire assessment roll on 'a basis of uniformity'; that is, upon a basis which would give every piece of property an assessed valuation equal to 50 per cent of the 'market value' or 'sales value' as shown in Stafford's report.

Precedent Broken.

The Board broke a precedent of many years' standing when it reduced the assessments on the seventy-five properties. The practice has been to give protesting property owners a hearing and, in cases where their protests had merit, to 'refer' the case to the Assessor for adjustment. The Assessor's adjustments of these referred protests have always been approved by the Board.

Yesterday, however. the Board took seventy-five cases out of Assessor Woiden's hands entirely and referred fifty additional protests to him for adjustment. In ordering reductions on the seventy-five protests the Board slashed a total of $285,365 from the assessment roll as compiled by Wolden, and paved the way for additional reductions in referring fifty additional cases.

Assessor Wolden, in his annual statement, emphasized the fact that his assessed valuations are 'not based on the theory that valuations should represent definite and fixed percentage of the sales value.'

Theory Accepted.

The Board, nevertheless, indicated its determination to accept this theory, as laid down in Stafford's report. Here is the way it works out in two actual instances as decided yesterday:

1. The Woman's Club Building, Post and Mason streets, was assessed by Wolden at $600,000. In the Stafford appraisal the 'sales or market value' of the building was set at $878,000. Half of this 'sales value' is $439,000. The Board reduced the assessment to this figure, a reduction of $161,000.

2. A small building was assessed at $30,000 by Wolden. In the Stafford appraisal it was given a sales value of $56,000. The Board reduced the assessment to half this, or $28,000, a cut of $2,000 in taxable valuation.

Supervisor James B. McSheehy led the fight for acceptance of the Stafford theory, declaring that it has cost the City $210,000 in preparation, and eventually will lead to absolute uniformity in making assessments. It was pointed out that the Board of Equalization has the power to force the Assessor to accept this standard, as Wolden cannot appeal from the Board's decisions.

Preliminary Step.

'Our action in reducing these assessments today is a notice to the public that assessments are to be put on an equitable and uniform basis,' McSheehy declared. 'This is only a preliminary step, however, in bringing about a condition of uniformity. At present there is a wide variation in assessments. Some property is assessed too high. Much is assessed at only 10 per cent of its sales value. Under this plan it can all be brought up to a 50 per cent standard.'

Wolden declared last night that the whole aim of his department is to make assessments on an equitable and uniform basis.

The situation following the equalization proceedings of the 1927 and 1928 period was simply this: The Board of Supervisors did not utilize the land report at all, and had used the building report in only a minor sense.

The Assessor had been given practically $30,000 to check the land report submitted by Superintendent James G. Stafford, and had reported officially to the Board of Supervisors that in his judgment it would be contrary to the best interests of San Francisco to adopt the standards of value the land appraisal reflected.

The record of the land appraisal in detail, to quote from the letter of James G. Stafford when he submitted it, was 'contained in forty-four bound volumes of summary sheets in typewritten form.'

In the background of the typewritten summaries were 131 unit land value maps of the entire area of the City and County showing the appraised street frontage values as finally established by the members of the staff working under the direction of Superintendent James G. Stafford.

The Assessor's examination of the summary sheets and of the 131 appraisal maps revealed, as reported to the Board of Supervisors on June 17, 1929, over 13,000 errors. These errors, as reported to the Board of Supervisors and as the official transcript of the meeting of June 17, 1929, will show, were classified as follows:

1. Faulty dimensions in lots as appraised, 7707. That is to say that the Assessor, in making a general check of the computation of all values based on the front foot valuations, found that the value placed on 7707 parcels of land did not conform with the front foot value, because faulty dimensions were used by the staff of the Bureau of Appraisal in making their calculations.

2. Errors in valuation.

That is to say, apparent transposition of figures were discovered in the number of 4062.

3. Unit front foot values were omitted entirely on various streets in 523 cases.

4. Inconsistent valuations.

That is to say, absolute variance from values shown on adjoining sectional maps were discovered in 503 cases.

5. Failure to define limitations on valuations as listed on various blocks were discovered in 496 cases.

To summarize the Assessor's findings: Of the 131 unit land value maps submitted covering the entire area of the City and County of San Francisco 107, or 81 per cent, showed material errors.

Nothing is of record as to the accuracy of the building appraisal because no check has ever been attempted on that appraisal.

It is to be remembered, however, that more than 125,000 buildings were appraised at a gross cost under the contract of $125,000. Nothing is known as to the profit realized by James G. Stafford and Associates, Incorporated, in making the appraisal of the buildings, but it is to be assumed that some sort of a profit was made, and, therefore, it is thoroughly evident that the 130,000 taxable structures in San Francisco were appraised at an average of considerable less than one dollar ($1.00) per structure.

At 12 o'clock noon on the first Monday in July, 1929, the Assessor delivered to the Clerk of the Board of Supervisors the Assessment Roll for the year 1929.

The Supervisors did not meet as a Board of Equalization on the first Monday in July of 1929, but they did convene as such a Board on July 8, and reconvened on July 12, and finally adjourned on July 15th. It is to be noted, therefore, that the Supervisors held but three sessions as an equalizing body during 1929.

Application for the reduction or correction of assessments, totaling 243, were filed with the Board of Supervisors during their 1929 session as an equalizing body. Forty-one (41) of these applications covered applications for reduction or correction of land assessments and two hundred and two (202) applications for the reduction or correction of building assessments.

The Board of Supervisors, sitting as a Board of Equalization, established a precedent in the handling of these applications. Whereas in the past it had been their practice either to refer them to the Assessor, or to take them under advisement, in 1929 they referred every application to an Advisory Group, which was composed of the Assessor and his staff, Mr. Joseph Phillips of the Right of Way Department and two (2) experts employed under Mr. Phillips on a per diem basis.

At the conclusion of the equalization session the Assessor rendered a report recommending reductions in the case of five (5) applications covering land and one hundred and six (106) in the case of applications covering improvements. The proceedings of the 1929 Board of Equalization would seem to have been conducted along more logical lines than any of the proceedings previously had, but it is to be noted that despite the fact that the land appraisal report and the building appraisal report, that had been compiled "in order that the Board of Supervisors might perform the duties imposed by law upon said Board as a board of equalization," it was necessary to engage further expert advice, and it does not appear from the record that the expert advice thus engaged was guided in whole or in part by either the land appraisal report or the building appraisal report.

From all the information that we can gather, this advisory group conferred with the Assessor, and with his deputies, personally examined the properties under reference, again conferred with the Assessor and his deputies, and then approved and concurred in the recommendations made by the Assessor, both in the cases of reduction and denial of the applications under consideration, and the Journals of the Proceedings of the Board of Supervisors, Number 29, Volume 24, page 1431, definitely establish the fact that the recommendations of the Assessor were approved and concurred in by the experts engaged for this particular work.

Neither the Journal of the Proceedings of the Board of Supervisors, nor the official transcript of the meetings of the Board, indicate that either the land appraisal or building appraisal were used.

As a matter of fact, the transcript of the meeting of July 8th contains the following statement by one of the Supervisors:

"Let us find out if we have done anything wise in making the investment of some $250,000 to get this appraisal and let some of the members of the Board who have been most ardent in having the Stafford appraisal made defend their position."

It is to be remembered that in 1928, on motion, the Assessor had been requested to establish all assessments on a fixed percentage of the true value.

In the 1929 session Supervisor Shannon, in case after case, and in instance after instance, attempted to induce the Board of Supervisors to themselves follow the course which they had recommended to the Assessor; that is to say, basing assessed valuations at 50 per cent of the land appraisal or the building appraisal, and in each case the Board of Supervisors declined to follow such a course. The transcript of that proceeding of July 8th established that every effort made by Supervisor Shannon to make use of these appraisals in connection with applications for reduction or correction of assessments that were before the Board failed of even a second.

It is thoroughly evident that the Board of Supervisors, sitting as a Board of Equalization, have never made any use of these appraisals, despite the fact that the purpose of making the appraisals as set forth in the original resolution was "that the Board of Supervisors might perform the duties imposed by law upon said Board as a Board of Equalization."

There is no need at this time to question whether the purpose of these appraisals was equalization, or whether hhe purpose was an encroachment upon the duties of the Assessor. It is equally useless to argue that the real purpose of these appraisals is to provide the general public with a chart of true values. It is to be considered, however, that if it is intended to establish as an official record of the Board of Supervisors a chart of true values, then it is incumbent upon the Board of Supervisors to adopt those true values when sitting as a Board of Equalization. That this is true cannot be denied.

Section 3673 of the Political Code definitely empowers the Board of Supervisors to increase or lower any assessment so as to equalize the assessment of property contained in said roll and "make the assessment conform to the true value of such property in money."

Certainly with such a provision on the statute books of the State since 1880, no one can deny that if the Board of Supervisors of a county accept a certain chart of values as indicative of the true value, and further, if the Board of Supervisors themselves have, at a considerable expense, authorized the appraisal of property for the specific purpose of providing themselves with a chart of true values for use during their equalization deliberations, they must make use of such a chart of values.

The Board of Supervisors cannot urge that the time granted to them under Section 3672 of the Political Code is insufficient. That section states that the Board shall continue in session for the purpose of equalization from time to time until the business of equalization is disposed of, but not later than the third Monday in July, but Section 3885 of the Political Code, as well as countless decisions of the courts, definitely establishes that no act relating to assessment or correction of taxes is illegal because the same was not completed within the time required by law, and in no less than four (4) cases the court has ruled that this section is applicable to proceedings before the Board of Supervisors sitting as a Board of Equalization.

The courts have also ruled that if the Board of Supervisors have knowledge that certain property is under-assessed and fail to increase that assessment the entire assessment roll may be invalidated.

It cannot be denied that the Board of Supervisors of a county are at a considerable disadvantage in undertaking equalization of assessed valuations. Their handicap is due in part, at least, to the fact that the provisions of the Constitution and of the codes under which they function were enacted at a time when the entire taxation structure of the state was different than it is today. Section 3672 of the Political Code was enacted in 1891 and Section 3673 was enacted in 1880. It may be that the equalization responsibility of county supervisors can never be discharged until the basic provisions of the Constitution and the codes are changed; that they have not been discharged by the application or usage of the land appraisal or the building appraisal is self-evident.

The Assessor's office makes every year some 280,000 individual assessments.

The average number of applications for reduction or correction of assessments filed with the Board of Supervisors as a Board of Equalization is 200.

At irregular intervals certain members of the Board of Supervisors insist that there are gross inequalities in the assessment roll. That may or may not be true, but it is of record with this Board of Supervisors that the Assessor, with a limited staff of valuation men—five (5) in his land department and three (3) in his building department—is steadily and continuously revising and readjusting assessed valuations all over San Francisco.

The annual report of the Assessor for the year 1929, as filed with this Board of Supervisors, on July 1, 1929, definitely establishes that the 1929 assessment roll reflected over 30,000 valuation revisions of the tax burden of the community.

San Francisco County is no different than any other county in the State of California, in so far as vesting the responsibility for equalization of the assessments with a Board of Supervisors. Each county board in the state struggles with the same problem.

For many years the state revenues were raised by a direct levy against the counties of the state, based on the assessment roll of each particular county, and it was therefore a practice of county assessors, in what they believed to be the protection of the interests of the tax-payers of the various counties, to place a lower ratio of assessed valuation on property. In 1911 that method of raising state funds was done away with but the 1928 California State Tax Commission in their report filed with the Governor on March 5th, 1929, said:

"The ever present possibility of a state direct tax appears to be a factor in holding county assessments down. A sudden reduction in assessed valuations, following a state levy, would be difficult to explain." We faced the possibility of a return of the so-called ad valorem basis last year; we may face the same thing one year from now and for that reason the *assessed valuations of each county do not in any sense reflect a consistent relation with alleged true valuations.*

Conclusion.

First: That the assessed valuations of each county in the state in nowise reflect a consistent relation with alleged true valuations.

Second: That at a cost to the taxpayers of something in excess of $225,000, appraisals of the taxable real property of the City and County of San Francisco were made in order that the Board of Supervisors might, in accordance with the provisions of the codes, correct any inequalities that may exist in the assessments of the City and County.

Third: That these appraisals were completed and delivered to the Board of Supervisors of San Francisco.

Fourth: That the Board of Supervisors of San Francisco have never utilized these appraisals in the manner set forth in the resolution authorizing the appraisals.

Fifth: That the appraisals of the land were made in 1926-27.

Sixth: That the appraisals of the buildings were made in 1927-28.

Seventh: That in the period that has elapsed since the making of either or both of these appraisals activity in the real estate market has been appreciably diminished throughout the United States, and in San Francisco to such an extent that the appraisals no longer reflect the true value.

Eighth: That the valuation fixing authority on property for purposes of taxation is conferred by the Constitution, the Codes, and the decisions of the courts, specifically upon the Assessor.

Ninth: That the Assessor cannot, under the provisions of the Constitution, the Codes and the decisions of the courts, delegate that valuation fixing authority to anyone.

Tenth: That the history of other American cities definitely and conclusively establishes that interference with assessing officials is detrimental to the public welfare.

Recommendation.

1. That all existing books, records, data of the land appraisal and of the building appraisal be delivered to the Clerk of the Board of Supervisors with instruction that they are public records and subject to public inspection.

2. That the Resolution (No. 31,023) of this Board of Supervisors, adopted June 17th, 1929, be rescinded.

Relating to Use of Registrar's Office to Secure Signatures for Amendment for Permanent Registration.

The following was read by the Clerk:

Communication from San Francisco Labor Council, complaining of alleged improper and illegal use of the Registrar's office in securing signatures to petitions for amendment of state law to bring about permanent registration.

Supervisor Power moved that the Clerk notify the Registrar that the Board of Supervisors is not in accord with the practise complained of.

So ordered.

ADJOURNMENT.

There being no further business, the Board, at the hour of 6 p. m., adjourned.

J. S. DUNNIGAN,
Clerk.

Approved by the Board of Supervisors April 14, 1930.

Pursuant to Resolution No. 3402 (New Series) of the Board of Supervisors of the City and County of San Francisco, I, John S. Dunnigan, hereby certify that the foregoing are true and correct copies of the Journals of Proceedings of said Board of the dates thereon stated and approved as recited.

JOHN S. DUNNIGAN,
Clerk of the Board of Supervisors.
City and County of San Francisco.

Monday, March 10, 1930

urnal of Proceedings
Board of Supervisors

City and County of San Francisco

The Recorder Printing and Publishing Company
337 Bush Street, S. F.

JOURNAL OF PROCEEDINGS
BOARD OF SUPERVISORS

MONDAY, MARCH 10, 1930, 2 P. M.

In Board of Supervisors, San Francisco, Monday, March 10, 1930, 2 p. m.

CALLING THE ROLL.

The roll was called and the following Supervisors were noted present:

Supervisors Andriano, Canepa, Gallagher, Havenner, Hayden, McGovern, McSheehy, Miles, Peyser, Power, Roncovieri, Rossi, Spaulding, Stanton, Suhr, Toner—16.

Absent—Supervisors Colman, Shannon—2   .

Quorum present.

His Honor Mayor Rolph presiding.

APPROVAL OF JOURNAL.

The Journal of Proceedings of the meeting of February 3, 1930, was considered read and approved.

ROLL CALL FOR PETITIONS AND COMMUNICATIONS.

His Honor the Mayor announced that he had just come from a meeting of the unemployed in front of the City Hall, where he had listened to the demands of a committee representing the workers.

Meeting of Unemployed.

The following was presented and read by the Clerk:

San Francisco, Cal., March 8, 1930.

Honorable Board of Supervisors, City Hall, San Francisco, California.

Gentlemen: I have just received a transcript of the remarks made at the meeting with the unemployed on Thursday, March 6, 1930, and I hereby transmit same to you for your information and attention. You will note from the transcript that a demand was made that they be permitted to present their grievances to you for redress, and I assured them that they would be given that privilege on Monday at 2 p. m.

I will be glad to confer with any and all members of your honorable Board on the subject if you will do me the honor of dropping in before 2 o'clock Monday afternoon.

Very respectfully,
JAMES ROLPH, Jr., Mayor.

Death of Francesca Leavy, Mother of Purchaser of Supplies.

The following was presented and read by the Clerk:

Resolution No. 32196 (New Series), as follows:

Whereas, Francesca Leavy, mother of Leonard S. Leavy, Purchaser of Supplies, died recently; and

Whereas, Francesca Leavy lived a life of excellent example of all the virtues that make for a good family and a good citizen; be it, therefore,

Resolved, That the Board of Supervisors extend sincere sympathy and condolence to the bereaved family of the late Francesca Leavy; and be it

Further Resolved, That the Board adjourn today out of respect to the memory of the late deceased, and that a copy of this resolution be spread on the minutes of the Board and another copy be sent Leonard S. Leavy, Purchaser of Supplies.

Adopted unanimously by rising vote.

Clerk to Advertise Sale of Boulevard and Sewer Bonds.

Supervisor Rossi presented:

Resolution No. 32197 (New Series), as follows:

Resolved, That the Clerk of the Board of Supervisors be directed to advertise that on the 31st day of March, 1930, the Board of Supervisors will receive sealed proposals for the purchase of the following bonds of the City and County of San Francisco:

$2,286,000.00 Boulevard Bonds, 4½ per cent, issue of November 1, 1927, comprising: 126 $1,000.00 bonds, maturing 1935; 135 $1,000.00 bonds, maturing each year, 1936 to 1951, inclusive.

$1,020,000.00 Sewer Bonds, 4½ per cent, issue of January 1, 1929, comprising: 60 $1,000.00 bonds, maturing each year, 1939 to 1955, inclusive.

The Finance Committee shall fix the terms and conditions of sale.

Adopted by the following vote:

Ayes—Supervisors Andriano, Canepa, Gallagher, Havenner, Hayden, McGovern, McSheehy, Miles, Peyser, Power, Roncovieri, Rossi, Spaulding, Stanton, Suhr, Toner—16.

Absent—Supervisors Colman, Shannon—2.

Supervisor Toner requested reference of matters relating to Health Board to the Public Health Committee.

Leave of Absence, Alfred Ehrman, Fire Commissioner.

The following was presented and read by the Clerk:

San Francisco, Cal., March 7, 1930.

Honorable Board of Supervisors, City Hall, San Francisco, California.

Gentlemen: Application has been made to me by the Hon. Alfred Ehrman, Fire Commissioner, for leave of absence, with permission to leave the State, for a period of thirty days, beginning March 30, 1930. I respectfully request that your honorable Board concur with me in granting this leave.

Respectfully submitted,

JAMES ROLPH, Jr., Mayor.

Whereupon, the following resolution was presented and *adopted:*

Resolution No. 32192 (New Series), as follows:

Resolved, That, in accordance with the recommendation of his Honor the Mayor, Honorable Alfred Ehrman, Fire Commissioner, is hereby granted a leave of absence for a period of thirty days, commencing March 30, 1930, with permission to leave the State.

Ayes—Supervisors Andriano, Canepa, Gallagher, Havenner, Hayden, McGovern, McSheehy, Miles, Peyser, Power, Roncovieri, Rossi, Spaulding, Stanton, Suhr—15.

Absent—Supervisors Colman, Shannon, Toner—3.

Appointment of War Memorial Trustees.

The following was read and *ordered spread in the Journal*:

San Francisco, Cal., March 6, 1930.

Honorable Board of Supervisors, City Hall, San Francisco, California.

Gentlemen: Attached hereto is a duplicate of the appointment of the eleven War Memorial Trustees approved by your honorable Board on Monday, March 3, 1930.

Respectfully submitted,

JAMES ROLPH, Jr., Mayor.

Mayor's Office.

The City and County of San Francisco, State of California.

To All to Whom These Presents Shall Come—Greeting:

With the confirmation of the honorable Board of Supervisors of the City and County of San Francisco, and reposing special confidence in the fidelity and ability of General Hunter Liggett, Frank N. Belgrano, James I. Herz, Charles H. Kendrick, Richard Montgomery Tobin, Kenneth R. Kingsbury, Robert I. Bentley, George Cameron, George Hearst, James W. Mullen and Jesse C. Colman,

I do, by these presents, by virtue of the authority vested in me by the Charter of the City and County of San Francisco, appoint them members of the Board of Trustees of the War Memorial of San Francisco, they to hold said office from and after the 3rd day of March, 1930, for the term to be decided by lot, in accordance with the following provisions of Section 3, Article XIV-D, of the Charter of the City and County of San Francisco:

"The terms of said eleven members shall be for six years each; provided, that those first appointed shall so classify themselves by lot that the term of four of said Trustees shall expire on the 2nd day of January, 1931; four on the 2nd day of January, 1933, and three on the 2nd day of January, 1935. Thereafter appointments to said Board shall be for the full term of six years. Vacancies on said Board shall be filled by the Mayor, subject to confirmation by the Board of Supervisors, for the unexpired term becoming vacant."

In testimony whereof, I have signed my name and have caused the seal of my office to be affixed hereto this 3rd day of March, 1930.

(Seal)   JAMES ROLPH, Jr., Mayor.

Attest: EDWARD RAINEY,

Executive Secretary to the Mayor.

Relative to Appointment of Eight Welfare Investigators.

Communication, from his Honor James Rolph, Jr., recommending that provision be made for eight welfare investigators, at a salary of $150 per month each, to investigate and report on applications for pensions for needy aged persons, as provided by State law, said investigators to be assigned to the County Welfare Board.

Referred to Finance Committee.

Official Advertising.

San Francisco Chronicle, for each insertion in 6-point, .085 cents per one-column line. Certified check on Anglo London and Paris Bank, $1,000.

Delinquent Tax List.

1. Henry F. Budde, publisher "National Industrial Review." For each line of Delinquent Real Estate or Personal Property (6-point solid, not less than 12 ems), .044 cents.

2. Twin Peaks Sentinel. For each line of Delinquent Real Estate or Personal Property (6-point, not less than 12 ems), .04 cents.

3. Eureka District News. For each line of Delinquent Real Estate or Personal Property (6-point, not less than 12 ems), .06 cents.

Referred to Public Welfare and Publicity Committee.

Passed for Printing.

The following matter was *passed for printing*:

SPECIAL ORDER—2:30 P. M.
Amendment to Food Terminal Ordinance.

Bill No. 8208, Ordinance No. ———— (New Series), as follows:

Amending Ordinance No. 8140 (New Series), providing that wholesale food terminals, warehouses, freight yards and ferry terminals shall not be constructed or established, erected or constructed within a certain district in the City and County of San Francisco, and establishing the boundaries of said district, and providing for penalties for the violation of the provisions hereof, by including in said prohibited structures and callings airplane landings and hydroplane landings, and the landing of passengers from airplanes or hydroplanes.

Be it ordained by the People of the City and County of San Francisco as follows:

That Ordinance No. 8140, the title of which is hereinbefore recited, is hereby amended to read as follows:

Section 1. No wholesale food terminal, warehouse, freight yard, or ferry terminal, or airplane landing or hydroplane landing, or any building or structure to be used as a wholesale food terminal, warehouse, freight yard, ferry terminal, airplane landing or hydroplane landing, shall be constructed, erected or established within the territory bounded on the north by the waters of San Francisco Bay, on the east by the westerly line of Van Ness avenue, on the south by Jackson street, and on the west by the westerly line of Lyon street, nor shall any structure for any of the purposes above mentioned be constructed or erected, projecting into the waters of the bay from the land included in the above described district.

Section 2. No building permit shall be issued or granted by the Board of Public Works for the erection, construction or alteration of any building, or structure, contrary to the provisions of this ordinance, and any permit so issued or granted shall be void.

Section 3. No certificate of occupancy shall be issued or granted by the Board of Health authorizing or permitting any person, firm or corporation to occupy or use any building or structure in place within the above bounded district for or as a wholesale food terminal, warehouse, freight yard or ferry terminal.

Section 4. Any person, firm or corporation violating any of the provisions of this ordinance shall be guilty of a misdemeanor, and upon the conviction thereof shall be punishable by a fine not to exceed $500.00 or by imprisonment in the County Jail not to exceed six months, or by both such fine and imprisonment. And any person, firm or corporation violating any of the provisions of this ordinance shall be deemed guilty of a separate offense for each and every day during any portion of which any violation of this ordinance is committed, permitted or continued by such person, firm or corporation.

Ayes—Supervisors Andriano, Canepa, Gallagher, Havenner, Hayden, McGovern, Miles, Peyser, Power, Roncovieri, Rossi, Spaulding, Stanton, Suhr—14.

No—Supervisor McSheehy—1.

Absent—Supervisors Colman, Shannon, Toner—3.

HEARING OF APPEAL—3 P. M.
Action Deferred.

On motion of Supervisor Rossi, the following matter was *laid over four weeks;* no permits to be granted for structures in the meantime:

Rezoning Marina Boulevard.

Hearing of appeal of property owners from the decision of the City Planning Commission placing property on both sides of Marina boulevard between Buchanan street and Webster street, as described in Resolution No. 175 of the City Planning Commission, in the First Residential District, where not already so zoned.

PRESENTATION OF PROPOSALS.

Class-Room Supplies and Paper for School Department.

Sealed proposals were received and opened between the hours of 2 and 3 p. m. this date, for furnishing class-room supplies and paper for School Department, and *referred to the Supplies Committee.*

Publishing Delinquent Tax List.

Sealed proposals were received from publishers of daily or weekly newspapers, at 3 o'clock p. m., for the printing, publishing and distributing of the delinquent tax list, index of delinquent real estate taxpayers, and printing the sales list and other matters incidental thereto, for the fiscal year 1929-1930, in strict accordance with the Charter and the specifications, a copy of which may be had at the office of the Clerk of the Board of Supervisors.

The right to reject any or all proposals is reserved.

Referred to Supplies Committee.

Official Advertising.

Sealed proposals were received at 3 o'clock p. m. for the publishing of the official advertising for the year commencing April 1, 1930, as required by the Charter, and subject to the conditions and specifications, which, together with forms of proposals, may be obtained at the office of the Clerk of said Board.

The right to reject any or all proposals is reserved.

Referred to Supplies Committee.

SPECIAL ORDER—4 P. M.

Action Deferred.

On motion of Supervisor Havenner, the following matters were *made a Special Order for 2:30 p. m. next Monday:*

Appraisal Bureau.

On motion of Supervisor Power:

Consideration of the subject-matter of the discontinuance of the Appraisal Bureau of the Board of Equalization was *made a Special Order for 4 p. m. this day.*

Repealing Resolution No. 31023 (New Series), Appraisal Bureau.

Supervisor Rossi presented:

Resolution No. ———— (New Series), as follows:

Resolved, That Resolution No. 31023 (New Series), authorizing the Finance Committee to employ a superintendent, experts and assistants, and to purchase supplies, in connection with the appraisal of taxable real property, be and the same is hereby repealed.

UNFINISHED BUSINESS.

Final Passage.

The following matters, heretofore passed for printing, were taken up and *finally passed* by the following vote:

Authorizations.

On recommendation of Finance Committee.

Resolution No. 32166 (New Series), as follows:

Resolved, That the following amounts be and the same are hereby

authorized to be expended out of the hereinafter mentioned funds in payment to the following named claimants, to-wit:

Park Fund.

(1) Julius L. Girod, one orang outang, for park purposes (claim dated Feb. 28, 1930)...........................$ 625.20

(2) Pacific Gas & Electric Company, gas and electric service for parks (claim dated Feb. 28, 1930)................... 1,233.66

(3) Spring Valley Water Company, water for parks (claim dated Feb. 28, 1930)...................................... 935.16

(4) Berringer & Russell, hay, etc., for parks (claim dated Feb. 28, 1930) 525.64

M. H. deYoung Memorial Museum Fund.

(5) Thomas Skelly, plumbing work for M. H. deYoung Memorial Museum, third payment (claim dated Feb. 28, 1930).$ 508.08

Hetch Hetchy Construction Fund, Bond Issue 1928.

(6) Bald Eagle Meat Market, meat and fish (claim dated Feb. 14, 1930) 648.14

(7) Best Steel Casting Co, castings (claim dated Feb. 14, (1930) 767.56

(8) San Francisco City Employees' Retirement System, to match contributions from Hetch Hetchy employees (claim dated Feb. 17, 1930) 649.12

(9) Allan St. John Bowie and California Pacific Title & Trust Company, for Lots 17 to 34, inclusive, in Block 2899, as per the Assessor's Block Books, as per acceptance of offer by Resolution No. 32010, New Series; and required for reservoir purposes (claim dated Feb. 19, 1930)........ 2,000.00

(10) Dr. Paul E. Dolan, medical services rendered Hetchy Hetchy employees (claim dated Feb. 19, 1930)............ 1,157.00

(11) The Giant Powder Company, Consolidated, explosives (claim dated Feb. 19, 1930)............................ 2,645.30

(12) W. Haslam, Hetch Hetchy truck rental (claim dated Feb. 19, 1930) 795.48

(13) M. D. Jones, Hetch Hetchy truck rental (claim dated Feb. 19, 1930) 2.028.78

(14) St. Paul's Hospital, Livermore, hospital service rendered Hetch Hetchy employees (claim dated Feb. 19, 1930) 669.25

(15) Christenson Lumber Company, lumber (claim dated Feb. 21, 1930) 683.21

(16) Coos Bay Lumber Company, lumber (claim dated Feb. 19, 1930) 504.50

(17) Del Monte Meat Company, meat (claim dated Feb. 20, 1930) 1,810.31

(18) Delbert Hansen, Hetch Hetchy truck hire (claim dated Feb. 23, 1930) 1,638.71

(19) Ingersoll-Rand Company of California, machinery parts (claim dated Feb. 21, 1930)............................. 1,007.38

(20) Ingersoll-Rand Company of California, machinery parts (claim dated Feb. 19, 1930) 785.06

(21) Owen-Oregon Lumber Company, lumber (claim dated Feb. 19, 1930) 604.64

(22) Pacific Coast Aggregates, Inc., concrete mix, sand and gravel (claim dated Feb. 20, 1930) 520.00

(23) Pacific Coast Steel Corporation, steel (claim dated Feb. 21, 1930) 2,357.71

(24) Santa Fe Lumber Company, lumber (claim dated Feb. 21, 1930) 1,068.02

(25) Santa Cruz Portland Cement Company, cement (claim dated Feb. 21, 1930) 1,578.00

(26) Utah Fuel Company, coal (claim dated Feb. 19, 1930).. 711.88
(27) Western Butchers' Supply Company, one 1½-ton refrigerator plant installed (claim dated Feb. 21, 1930)........ 1,115.00
(28) Baker, Hamilton & Pacific Company, hoist and hardware (claim dated Feb. 24, 1930)...................... 737.82
(29) Challenge Cream and Butter Association, canned milk (claim dated Feb. 24, 1930)......................... 581.25
(30) J H Creighton, truck hire (claim dated Feb. 24, 1930). 1,206.21
(31) Coos Bay Lumber Company, lumber (claim dated Feb. 25, 1930) 3,185.27
(32) Del Monte Meat Company, meat (claim dated Feb. 25, 1930) 716.12
(33) Edison Storage Battery Supply Company, Edison cells and batteries (claim dated Feb. 24, 1930)................ 23,962.72
(34) J. E. French Company, one Dodge Bros. sedan (claim dated Feb. 24, 1930) 900.00
(35) R. M. Gardiner Lumber Company, lumber (claim dated Feb. 24, 1930) 547.56
(36) The Giant Powder Company, Consolidated, explosives (claim dated Feb. 24, 1930)........................... 3,977.81
(37) Haas Bros., groceries (claim dated Feb. 25, 1930)..... 748.75
(38) Hercules Powder Company, Inc., explosives (claim dated Feb. 24, 1930) 2,657.44
(39) William L. Hughson Company, one Ford truck (claim dated Feb. 24, 1930) 729.40
(40) Delbert Hansen, truck hire (claim dated Feb. 25, 1930). 676.60
(41) Ingersoll Rand Company of California, pump, drifters and machinery parts (claim dated Feb. 24, 1930)......... 2,578.30
(42) The Charles Nelson Company, wood wedges (claim dated Feb. 24, 1930) 640.00
(43) Alfred Pereira & Bros., hauling (claim dated Feb. 24, 1930) 1,737.14
(44) Pope & Talbot, lumber (claim dated Feb. 24, 1930)..... 744.35
(45) Santa Cruz Portland Cement Company, cement (claim dated Feb. 25, 1930) 4,638.00
(46) Sherry Bros., Inc., eggs (claim dated Feb. 24, 1930)... 501.60
(47) Western Pipe and Steel Company, steel pipe (claim dated Feb. 24, 1930) 3,763.30
(48) Wilsey-Bennett Company, butter and eggs (claim dated Feb. 24, 1930) 619.05

Hetch Hetchy Power Operative Fund.

(49) Depreciation Fund, Hetch Hetchy Power Operative, reserve for depreciation, as per Charter requirement (claim dated Feb. 19, 1930) $14,583.00
(50) State Compensation Insurance Fund, premium covering Hetch Hetchy employments (claim dated Feb. 19, 1930).. 821.71

Aquarium—Appropriation 56.

(51) California Academy of Sciences, maintenance of Steinhart Aquarium, month of February (claim dated March 3, 1930)...$ 3,783.42

Installation Fund—Department of Electricity.

(52) Robert A. Smith, Inc., one Chevrolet sedan for Department of Electricity (claim dated Jan. 31, 1930).........$ 674.00

Boulevard Bond Issue Construction Fund.

(53) San Francisco City Employees' Retirement System, to match contributions from employments on boulevard construction (claim dated Feb. 19, 1930)...................$ 512.06

Municipal Railway Fund.

(54) Marie L. Fazackerley, in settlement for any damage
sustained by reason of accident April 18, 1929, at Van
Ness avenue and Clay street (claim dated Feb. 19, 1930)$ 640.00
(55) American Brake Shoe and Foundry Company of California, car brake shoes (claim dated Feb. 25, 1930).....   2,273.95
(56) The Texas Company, gasoline furnished (claim dated
Feb. 25, 1930)...   1,929.98

County Road Fund.

(57) San Francisco City Employees' Retirement System, to
match contributions from employments engaged on County
Road Fund construction (claim dated Feb. 19, 1930).....$ 1,318.93
(58) Equitable Asphalt Maintenance Company, resurfacing
of streets (claim dated Feb. 21, 1930)...................   519.32
(59) Pacific Coast Aggregates, Inc., sand and gravel for
street reconstruction (claim dated Feb. 25, 1930)........   2,727.08
(60) Standard Oil Company of California, asphalt for street
reconstruction (claim dated Feb. 25, 1930)..............   2,436.24

Special School Tax.

(61) San Francisco City Employees' Retirement System, to
match contributions of employments paid out of Special
School Tax Fund (claim dated Feb. 19, 1930)...........$ 1,049.89
(62) MacDonald & Kahn, final payment, general construction of viewing stand at South Side (Balboa) High School
(claim dated Feb. 26, 1930)............................ 13,628.25
(63) Alta Electric Company, fifth payment, electrical work
for Roosevelt Junior High School (claim dated Feb. 26,
1930) 2,311.62
(64) Alta Electric Company, final payment, electrical work
for Geary Street School (claim dated Feb. 25, 1930).....   2,175.90
(65) Scott Company, final payment on mechanical equipment for Geary Street School (claim dated Feb. 25, 1930)   2,699.65
(66) E. P. Finigan, gymnasium equipment for Balboa High
School (claim dated Feb. 25, 1930).....................   3,867.30

General Fund, 1929-1930.

(67) Listenwalter & Gough, wire, zincs, carbons, etc., for
Department of Electricity (claim dated Jan. 31, 1930)...$ 1,449.57
(68) Maggini Motor Car Company, three Ford touring autos
for Police Department (claim dated Feb. 24, 1930).......   1,395.00
(69) Frank J. Reilly, ninth payment, general construction
of addition to M. H. deYoung Memorial Museum (claim
dated Feb. 28, 1930)................................... 15,041.25
(70) Preston School of Industry, maintenance of minors
(claim dated Feb. 25, 1930)............................   700.00
(71) The L. F. Sturtevant Company, Inc., of California, two
steel plate exhaust fans with motors (claim dated Feb. 20,
1930) 726.00
(72) James Rolph, Jr., for personal services and other than
personal services, months of January and February, 1930
'claim dated March 3, 1930)............................   1,464.16
(73) L. M. Wilbor, M. D., for payment of room allowances
to San Francisco Hospital employees, month of March
(claim dated Feb. 28, 1930)............................   3,000.00
(74) San Francisco Society for the Prevention of Cruelty
to Animals, for the impounding, feeding, etc., of animals
(claim dated March 3, 1930)............................   1,500.00
(75) Spring Valley Water Company, water furnished Fire
Department hydrants (claim dated Feb. 28, 1930)........ 15,597.20

Boulevard Bond Issue Construction Fund.

(76) The Magnavox Company, 5000 cast aluminum pedestrian lane markers (claim dated Feb. 20, 1930)..........$ 647.50

Consolidated Street Assessment Fund.

(77) Chas L. Harney, for improvement of Oakwood street from present termination to Nineteenth street (claim dated Feb. 19, 1930)....................................$ 1,775.00

Ayes—Supervisors Andriano, Canepa, Gallagher, Havenner, Hayden, McGovern, McSheehy, Miles, Peyser, Power, Roncovieri, Rossi, Spaulding, Stanton, Suhr, Toner—16.

Absent—Supervisors Colman, Shannon—2.

Payment for Properties Required for Boulevard Purposes.

Also, Resolution No. 32167 (New Series), as follows:

Resolved, That the following amounts be and the same are hereby set aside and appropriated out of Boulevard Bond Issue Construction Fund, 1927, and authorized in payment to the hereinafter named persons; being payments for properties required for boulevard purposes, to-wit:

(1) To Thomas P. Coyle, for all of Lot 2 in Block 2313, as per the Assessor's Block Books of the City and County, and required for the opening of Sunset boulevard; approved by Resolution No. ———, New Series (claim dated Jan. 15, 1930) $17,017.00

(2) To John Murphy and Nellie T. Murphy and City Title Insurance Company, for all of Lot 1 in Block 2365, as per the Assessor's Block Books of the City and County, and required for the opening of the Sunset boulevard; approved by Resolution No. ———, New Series (claim dated Jan. 15, 1930) 2,750.00

Ayes—Supervisors Andriano, Canepa, Gallagher, Havenner, Hayden, McGovern, McSheehy, Miles, Peyser, Power, Roncovieri, Rossi, Spaulding, Stanton, Suhr, Toner—16.

Absent—Supervisors Colman, Shannon—2.

Appropriation for Construction of Fifteenth Street Sewer, Section A, Harrison Street to Howard Street.

Also, Resolution No. 32168 (New Series), as follows:

Resolved, That the following amounts be and the same are hereby set aside, appropriated and authorized to be expended out of the 1929 Sewer Bond Construction Fund, for the construction of the Fifteenth street sewer, Section "A," from Harrison to Howard streets, to-wit:

(1) For construction of sewer, per award to Louis J Cohn..$59,334.00
(2) For extras and contingencies........................ 5,900.00
(3) For engineering and inspection...................... 4,766.00

Ayes—Supervisors Andriano, Canepa, Gallagher, Havenner, Hayden, McGovern, McSheehy, Miles, Peyser, Power, Roncovieri, Rossi, Spaulding, Stanton, Suhr, Toner—16.

Absent—Supervisors Colman, Shannon—2.

Appropriation for Construction of Film Vault at San Francisco Hospital.

Also, Resolution No. 32169 (New Series), as follows:

Resolved, That the following amounts be and the same are hereby set aside, appropriated and authorized to be expended out of "Urgent Necessity," Budget Item No. 24, for the construction of film vault on the roof of the San Francisco Hospital, to-wit:

(1) For general construction, per award to Frank J. Reilly..$ 9,581.00
(2) For extras, incidentals and inspection................. 1,500.00

Total $11,081.00

Ayes—Supervisors Andriano, Canepa, Gallagher, Havenner, Hayden,

McGovern, McSheehy, Miles, Peyser, Power, Roncovieri, Rossi, Spanlding, Stanton, Suhr, Toner—16.

Absent—Supervisors Colman, Shannon—2.

Appropriations, Painting Curbs, Etc., and Work Fronting City Property.

Also, Resolution No. 32170 (New Series), as follows:

Resolved, That the following amounts be and the same are hereby set aside, appropriated and authorized to be expended out of the hereinafter mentioned accounts of the General Fund, for the following purposes, to-wit:

Traffic Signals, Etc.—Budget Item 57.

(1) For the cost of painting traffic lines and curbs, for month of March, 1930 ....$ 1,400.00

Street Work in Front of City Property—Budget Item 34.

(2) For the cost of the improvement of the crossing of Twenty-fourth avenue and Rivera street, assessable to the City..$ 1,372.50

Bernal Cut Construction Fund, Bond Issue 1927.

(3) For cost of painting traffic lines and direction arrows, Bernal Cut .. ..$ 505.00

Ayes—Supervisors Andriano, Canepa, Gallagher, Havenner, Hayden, McGovern, McSheehy, Miles, Peyser, Power, Roncovieri, Rossi, Spaulding, Stanton, Suhr, Toner—16.

Absent—Supervisors Colman, Shannon—2.

Appropriation for the Improvement of Clayton Street at Market Street.

Also, Resolution No. 32171 (New Series), as follows:

Resolved, That the sum of $8,000 be and the same is hereby set aside, appropriated and authorized to be expended out of County Road Fund for the improvement of Clayton street at Market street, per contract awarded, and including possible extras, engineering and inspection.

Ayes—Supervisors Andriano, Canepa, Gallagher, Havenner, Hayden, McGovern, McSheehy, Miles, Peyser, Power, Roncovieri, Rossi, Spaulding, Stanton, Suhr, Toner—16.

Absent—Supervisors Colman, Shannon—2.

Appropriations for Street Reconstruction.

Also, Resolution No. 32172 (New Series), as follows:

Resolved, That the following amounts be and the same are hereby set aside, appropriated and authorized to be expended out of County Road Fund for the following street reconstruction and improvements, to-wit:

(1) For the cost of improving Waterville street, from Silver avenue to Augusta street, and of Silver avenue, from Waterville street to Elmira street, and at intersections; City's portion ....$ 600.00

(2) For the cost of widening Irving street between Eighteenth and Nineteenth avenues, by the reduction of sidewalks, at City property................................   624.00

(3) For the improvement of Castro street between Twenty-ninth and Thirtieth streets, City's liability............. 4,230.00

(4) For cost of reconstruction of dangerous corners on Chenery street at southeast corner of Diamond street, southeast corner of Randall street, and on west side of Chenery street opposite Natick street and opposite Charles street, including inspection........................... 1,300.00

(5) For cost of resurfacing of Jones street between Filbert and Greenwich streets, and reconstructing curbs......... 1,400.00

(6) For cost of improving and constructing a road from the northerly line of the Marina to the Saint Francis Yacht Club 1,200.00

(7) For cost of resurfacing of Drum street between California and Sacramento streets......................... 900.00

Ayes—Supervisors Andriano, Canepa, Gallagher, Havenner, Hayden, McGovern, McSheehy, Miles, Peyser, Power, Roncovieri, Rossi, Spaulding, Stanton, Suhr, Toner—16.

Absent—Supervisors Colman, Shannon—2.

San Francisco Water Department Revolving Fund.

Also, Resolution No. 32173 (New Series), as follows:

Resolved, That the sum of $20,000 be and the same is hereby set aside as a Revolving Fund out of "Water Revenue Fund" as provided by Section 13 of Ordinance No. 8691 (New Series).

Ayes—Supervisors Andriano, Canepa, Gallagher, Havenner, Hayden, McGovern, McSheehy, Miles, Peyser, Power, Roncovieri, Rossi, Spaulding, Stanton, Suhr, Toner—16.

Absent—Supervisors Colman, Shannon—2.

Appropriation, $25,000, Improvements at Sharpe Park.

Also, Resolution No. 32174 (New Series), as follows:

Resolved, That the sum of $25,000 be and the same is hereby set aside, appropriated and authorized to be expended out of General Fund, 1929-1930, for construction and improvements at Sharpe Park, San Mateo County, California.

Ayes—Supervisors Andriano, Canepa, Gallagher, Havenner, Hayden, McGovern, McSheehy, Miles, Peyser, Power, Roncovieri, Rossi, Spaulding, Stanton, Suhr, Toner—16.

Absent—Supervisors Colman, Shannon—2.

Appropriations, $26,615, Improvements at Mills Airport.

Also, Resolution No. 32175 (New Series), as follows:

Resolved, That the following amounts be and the same are hereby set aside, appropriated and authorized to be expended out of "Municipal Airport," Budget Item No. 50, for the following construction and improvements at Mills Field Municipal Airport, to-wit:

(1) For construction of 25-foot wide waterbound macadam roadway from south bridge to existing fence between Hangar No. 4 and ditch, about 1000 feet, with fences, drains, highway guards, bridge improvements, and waterbound macadam roadway between the highway pavement and south bridge..$10,600.00

(2) For construction of waterbound macadam roadway between the hangars and the highway guard along the ditch from south side of Hangar No. 4 to north line of Hangar No. 1, with relocation of fire hydrant at northwest corner of Hangar No. 1 .... 8,500.00

(3) For construction of waterbound macadam roadway between north line of Hangar No. 1 to south line of garage, and between ditch and fence between Administration Building and Hangar No. 1, with drain, inlets, panel gates relocated, and rocking entrance between entrance bridge and highway bridge 6,500.00

(4) Installation of outside control to doors of Hangars Nos. 2, 3 and 4... 135.00

(5) Relocation of obstruction lights between Hangar No. 4 and south end of field...................................... 600.00

(6) Stock pile of 80 cubic yards of crushed rock............. 180.00

(7) Lettering on Hangars Nos. 2, 3 and 4.................. 100.00

Total $26,615.00

Ayes—Supervisors Andriano, Canepa, Gallagher, Havenner, Hayden,

McGovern, McSheehy, Miles, Peyser, Power, Roncovieri, Rossi, Spaulding, Stanton, Suhr, Toner—16.
Absent—Supervisors Colman, Shannon—2.

Appropriation, $1,800, Reconstruction of Evans Avenue Between Third and Newhall Streets.

Also, Resolution No. 32176 (New Series), as follows:

Resolved, That the sum of $1,800 be and the same is hereby set aside, appropriated and authorized to be expended out of County Road Fund for the reconstruction of northerly side oᴌ Evans avenue between Third and Newhall streets.

Ayes—Supervisors Andriano, Canepa, Gallagher, Havenner, Hayden, McGovern, McSheehy, Miles, Peyser, Power, Roncovieri, Rossi, Spaulding, Stanton, Suhr, Toner—-16.
Absent—Supervisors Colman, Shannon—2.

Oil Tanks.

On recommendation of Fire Committee.

Resolution No. 32177 (New Series), as follows:

Resolved, That the following revocable permits be and are hereby granted:

Oil Tanks.

L. Widman, 1763 Golden Gate avenue, 1500 gallons capacity.
C. S. Hoffman, southeast corner of O'Farrell and Franklin streets, 1500 gallons capacity.
Nathan Rothman, 629 Golden Gate avenue, 1500 gallons capacity.
George Gibbs, south side of Ellis street, 87 feet west of Larkin street, 1500 gallons capacity.
A. E. Pessano, 3011 Van Ness avenue, 1500 gallons capacity.
The rights granted under this resolution shall be exercised within six months, otherwise said permits shall become null and void.

Ayes—Supervisors Andriano, Canepa, Gallagher, Havenner, Hayden, McGovern, McSheehy, Miles, Peyser, Power, Roncovieri, Rossi, Spaulding, Stanton, Suhr, Toner—16.
Absent—Supervisors Colman, Shannon—2.

Garage Permit Transfer, Floyd W. Hanchett, 730-742 Ellis Street.

Also, Resolution No. 32178 (New Series), as follows:

Resolved, That Floyd W. Hanchett be and is hereby granted permission, revocable at will of the Board of Supervisors, to have transferred to him public garage permit heretofore granted to William Niemann by Resolution No. 29821 (New Series) for premises at 730-742 Ellis street.
The rights granted under this resolution shall be exercised within six months, otherwise said permit shall become null and void.

Ayes—Supervisors Andriano, Canepa, Gallagher, Havenner, Hayden, McGovern, McSheehy, Miles, Peyser, Power, Roncovieri, Rossi, Spaulding, Stanton, Suhr, Toner—16.
Absent—Supervisors Colman, Shannon—2.

Supply Station Permit Transfer, J. H. Seelye, Northwest Corner California and Steiner Streets.

Also, Resolution No. 32179 (New Series), as follows:

Resolved, That J. H. Seelye be and is hereby granted permission, revocable at will of the Board of Supervisors, to have transferred to him automobile supply station permit formerly granted to the Associated Oil Company by Resolution No. 31394 (New Series) for premises at northwest corner of California and Steiner streets.
The rights granted under this resolution shall be exercised within six months, otherwise said permit shall become null and void.

Ayes—Supervisors Andriano, Canepa, Gallagher, Havenner, Hayden,

McGovern, McSheehy, Miles, Peyser, Power, Roncovieri, Rossi, Spaulding, Stanton, Suhr, Toner—16·

Absent—Supervisors Colman, Shannon—2·

Automobile Supply Station Permit, George Gaspar, Northwest Corner Cortland and San Bruno Avenues.

Also, Resolution No. 32180 (New Series), as follows:

Resolved, That George Gaspar be and is hereby granted permission, revocable at will of the Board of Supervisors, to maintain and operate an automobile supply station on premises at the northwest corner of Cortland and San Bruno avenues.

The rights granted under this resolution shall be exercised within six months, otherwise said permit shall become null and void.

Ayes—Supervisors Andriano, Canepa, Havenner, Hayden, McGovern, McSheehy, Miles, Peyser, Power, Roncovieri, Rossi, Spaulding, Suhr, Toner—14·

Noes—Supervisors Gallagher, Stanton—2·

Absent—Supervisors Colman, Shannon—2·

Laundry Permits.

Also, Resolution No. 32181 (New Series), as follows:

Resolved, That the following revocable permits be and are hereby granted:

Laundries.

Eloise Aiso, 1089 Pine street.

John Batsere, 976 Pine street.

Anna Biscay, 992 Sutter street.

Ruth Clausen, 94 Seventh street.

Mrs. V. J. Laurent, 447 Ellis street.

J. Nougue, 707 O'Farrell street.

Marie Sabacca, 808 Post street.

Louise Vannucci and Gloria Cheader, 405 O'Farrell street.

The rights granted under this resolution shall be exercised within six months, otherwise said permits shall become null and void.

Blanket protest filed by Mr. Alford, Board of Trade, Laundry Industry.

Ayes—Supervisors Andriano, Canepa, Gallagher, Havenner, Hayden, McGovern, McSheehy, Miles, Peyser, Power, Roncovieri, Rossi, Spaulding, Stanton, Suhr—15·

Absent—Supervisors Colman, Shannon, Toner—3·

Amending Section 102A of Ordinance No. 1008 (New Series), Relating to Hardwood Floors.

On recommendation of Public Buildings and Lands Committee.

Bill No. 8196, Ordinance No. 8701 (Ne Series), as follows:

Amending Ordinance No. 7347 (New Series), entitled "Amending Ordinance No. 1008 (New Series), known as 'The Building Law' of the City and County of San Francisco, approved December 22, 1909, by adding a new section thereto and to be numbered Section 102-A, relating to hardwood floors."

Be it ordained by the People of the City and County of San Francisco as follows:

Section 1. Ordinance No. 7347 (New Series), entitled "Amending Ordinance No. 1008 (New Series), known as 'the Building Law' of the City and County of San Francisco, approved December 22, 1909, by adding a new section thereto, and to be numbered Section 102-A, relating to hardwood floors," is hereby amended as follows:

Hardwood Floors.

Section 102-A. Hardwood floors shall be laid upon a sub-flooring of at least merchantable T and G pine flooring or pine boards not more than six (6) inches in width, and not less than seven-eighths

(⅞) of an inch in thickness, surface one side and edge, and laid as tightly as possible, and to be double nailed on each floor joist to obtain a smooth and even surface. These conditions shall apply to hardwood floor construction in all types of buildings.

Section 2. This ordinance shall take effect immediately.

Ayes—Supervisors Andriano, Canepa, Gallagher, Havenner, Hayden, McGovern, McSheehy, Miles, Peyser, Power, Roncovieri, Rossi, Spaulding, Stanton, Suhr—15.

Absent—Supervisors Colman, Shannon, Toner—3.

Fixing Sidewalk Widths on Goettingen Street.

On recommendation of Streets Committee.

Bill No. 8197, Ordinance No. 8702 (New Series), as follows:

Amending Ordinance No. 1061 entitled "Regulating the Width of Sidewalks," approved December 18, 1903, by amending Section Three Hundred and Ninety-seven thereof.

Be it ordained by the People of the City and County of San Francisco as follows:

Section 1. Ordinance No. 1061 entitled "Regulating the Width of Sidewalks," approved December 18, 1903, be and is hereby amended in accordance with the communication of the Board of Public Works, filed in this office Feb. 20, 1930, by amending Section Three Hundred and Ninety-seven thereof, to read as follows:

Section 397. The width of sidewalks on Goettingen street between Silver avenue and Dwight street shall be ten (10) feet.

The width of sidewalks on Goettingen street between Dwight street and Olmstead street shall be as shown on that certain map entitled "Map of Goettingen Street Between Dwight Street and Olmstead Street" showing the location of street and curb lines and the width of sidewalks.

The width of sidewalks on Goettingen street, the westerly side of, between Olmstead street and Mansell street shall be twenty (20) feet.

The width of sidewalks on Goettingen street, the easterly side of, between Olmstead street and Mansell street shall be ten (10) feet.

The width of sidewalks on Goettingen street, the westerly side of, between Ward street and Harkness street shall be twenty (20) feet.

The width of sidewalks on Goettingen street, the easterly side of, between Ward street and Harkness street shall be ten (10) feet.

The width of sidewalks on Goettingen street between Harkness street and its southerly termination shall be ten (10) feet.

Section 2. Any expense caused by the above change of walk widths shall be borne by the property owners.

Section 3. This ordinance shall take effect and be in force from and after its passage.

Ayes—Supervisors Andriano, Canepa, Gallagher, Havenner, Hayden, McGovern, McSheehy, Miles, Peyser, Power, Roncovieri, Rossi, Spaulding, Stanton, Suhr—15.

Absent—Supervisors Colman, Shannon, Toner—3.

Ordering the Improvement of Intersection of Brighton and Lakeview Avenues and Southerly One-half of Lakeview Avenue From West Line of Brighton Avenue, Etc.

Also, Bill No. 8198, Ordinance No. 8703 (New Series), as follows:

Ordering the performance of certain street work to be done in the City and County of San Francisco, approving and adopting specifications therefor.

Be it ordained by the People of the City and County of San Francisco as follows:

Section 1. The Board of Public Works, in written communication filed in the office of the Clerk of the Board of Supervisors on February 13, 1930, having recommended the ordering of the following street work, the same is hereby ordered to be done in the City and County of San Francisco in conformity with the provisions of the Street Improvement Ordinance of 1918 of said City and County of San Francisco, said work to be performed under the direction of the Board of Public Works, and to be done in accordance with the specifications prepared therefor by said Board of Public Works, and on file in its office, which said plans and specifications are hereby approved and adopted.

That said Board of Supervisors, pursuant to the provisions of Part II of the said Street Improvement Ordinance of 1918 of said City and County of San Francisco, does hereby determine and declare that the assessment to be imposed for the said contemplated improvements, respectively, may be paid in ten installments; that the period of time after the time of the payment of the first installment when each of the succeeding installments must be paid is to be one year from the time of the payment of the preceding installment, and that the rate of interest to be charged on all deferred payments shall be seven per centum per annum.

The improvement of the intersection of Brighton and Lakeview avenues, and of the southerly one-half of Lakeview avenue from the westerly line of Brighton avenue produced to a line parallel with and 25 feet easterly from the easterly line of Brighton avenue, by the construction of armored concrete curbs; by the construction of one-course concrete sidewalks on the angular corners thereof; by the construction of brick catchbasins with 10-inch vitrified clay pipe culvert; by the construction of a 12-inch vitrified clay pipe sewer along the center line of Brighton avenue between the center and the northerly lines of Lakeview avenue; by the construction of vitrified clay pipe side sewers; and by the construction of an asphaltic concrete pavement, consisting of a light traffic concrete foundation and a 1½-inch asphaltic concrete wearing surface, on the roadway thereof.

Section 2. This ordinance shall take effect immediately.

Ayes—Supervisors Andriano, Canepa, Gallagher, Havenner, Hayden, McGovern, McSheehy, Miles, Peyser, Power, Roncovieri, Rossi, Spaulding, Stanton, Suhr—15.

Absent—Supervisors Colman, Shannon, Toner—3.

Ordering the Improvement of Harrison Street Between First and Essex Streets, Etc.

Also, Bill No. 8199, Ordinance No. 8704 (New Series), as follows:

Ordering the performance of certain street work to be done in the City and County of San Francisco, approving and adopting specifications therefor.

Be it ordained by the People of the City and County of San Francisco as follows:

Section 1. The Board of Public Works, in written communication filed in the office of the Clerk of the Board of Supervisors February 13, 1930, having recommended the ordering of the following street work, the same is hereby ordered to be done in the City and County of San Francisco in conformity with the provisions of the Street Improvement Ordinance of 1918 of said City and County of San Francisco, said work to be performed under the direction of the Board of Public Works, and to be done in accordance with the specifications prepared therefor by said Board of Public Works, and on file in its office, which said plans and specifications are hereby approved and adopted.

That said Board of Supervisors, pursuant to the provisions of Part II of the said Street Improvement Ordinance of 1918 of said City and County of San Francisco, does hereby determine and declare that the assessment to be imposed for the said contemplated improvements, respectively, may be paid in ten installments; that the period of time after the time of the payment of the first installment when each of the succeeding installments must be paid is to be one year from the time of the payment of the preceding installment, and that the rate of interest to be charged on all deferred payments shall be seven per centum per annum.

The improvement of Harrison street between First street and the easterly line of Essex street produced southerly, including the intersection of Harrison street and Rincon street, and excepting that portion required by law to be paved by the railroad company having tracks thereon, by resetting the existing granite curbs; by the construction of granite curbs where not already constructed; by the construction of side sewers, where not already constructed; by the construction of 2-course concrete sidewalks on the angular corners of the intersection of Rincon street; and by the construction of an asphaltic concrete pavement, consisting of a 2-inch asphaltic concrete wearing surface and a 6-inch Class "F" concrete base, on the roadway thereof.

Section 2. This ordinance shall take effect immediately.

Ayes—Supervisors Andriano, Canepa, Gallagher, Havenner, Hayden, McGovern, McSheehy, Miles, Peyser, Power, Roncovieri, Rossi, Spaulding, Stanton, Suhr—15.

Absent—Supervisors Colman, Shannon, Toner—3.

Ordering the Construction of Sidewalks on San Jose Avenue and Other Streets.

Also, Bill No. 8200, Ordinance No. 8705 (New Series, as follows:

Ordering the performance of certain street work to be done in the City and County of San Francisco, approving and adopting specifications therefor.

Be it ordained by the People of the City and County of San Francisco as follows:

Section 1. The Board of Public Works, in written communication filed in the office of the Clerk of the Board of Supervisors February 13, 1930, having recommended the ordering of the following street work, the same is hereby ordered to be done in the City and County of San Francisco in conformity with the provisions of the Street Improvement Ordinance of 1918 of said City and County of San Francisco, said work to be performed under the direction of the Board of Public Works, and to be done in accordance with the specifications prepared therefor by said Board of Public Works, and on file in its office, which said plans and specifications are hereby approved and adopted.

That said Board of Supervisors, pursuant to the provisions of Part II of the said Street Improvement Ordinance of 1918 of said City and County of San Francisco, does hereby determine and declare that the assessment to be imposed for the said contemplated improvements, respectively, may be paid in three installments; that the period of time after the time of the payment of the first installment when each of the succeeding installments must be paid is to be one year from the time of the payment of the preceding installment, and that the rate of interest to be charged on all deferred payments shall be seven per centum per annum.

The improvement of San Jose avenue (south one-half) between Theresa and Gorham streets; San Jose avenue (south one-half) between Cotter street and Capistrano avenue; Tingley street between San Jose avenue and a point 545.47 feet south; Tingley street between Mission street and Alemany boulevard; Silver avenue between Mission street and Alemany boulevard; Admiral avenue between Mission street and Alemany boulevard; Castle Manor avenue between Mission street and Camellia avenue; Camellia avenue between Admiral avenue and Silver avenue, by the construction of artificial stone sidewalks, six feet in width, where artificial stone or bituminous rock sidewalks, six feet or more in width, have not already been constructed.

Section 2. This ordinance shall take effect immediately.

Ayes—Supervisors Andriano, Canepa, Gallagher, Havenner, Hayden,

McGovern, McSheehy, Miles, Peyser, Power, Roncovieri, Rossi, Spaulding, Stanton, Suhr—15.

Absent—Supervisors Colman, Shannon, Toner—3.

Ordering the Improvement of Quint Street, Etc.

Also, Bill No. 8201, Ordinance No. 8706 (New Series), as follows:

Ordering the performance of certain street work to be done in the City and County of San Francisco, approving and adopting specifications therefor.

. Be it ordained by the People of the City and County of San Francisco as follows:

Section 1. The Board of Public Works, in written communication filed in the office of the Clerk of the Board of Supervisors February 13, 1930, having recommended the ordering of the following street work, the same is hereby ordered to be done in the City and County of San Francisco in conformity with the provisions of the Street Improvement Ordinance of 1918 of said City and County of San Francisco, said work to be performed under the direction of the Board of Public Works, and to be done in accordance with the specifications prepared therefor by said Board of Public Works, and on file in its office, which said plans and specifications are hereby approved and adopted.

That said Board of Supervisors, pursuant to the provisions of Part II of the said Street Improvement Ordinance of 1918 of said City and County of San Francisco, does hereby determine and declare that the assessment to be imposed for the said contemplated improvements, respectively, may be paid in twenty installments; that the period of time after the time of the payment of the first installment when each of the succeeding installments must be paid is to be six months from the time of the payment of the preceding installment, and that the rate of interest to be charged on all deferred payments shall be seven per centum per annum.

The improvement of Quint street between Carroll avenue and the existing pavement westerly therefrom, where not already so improved, by the construction of concrete curbs, and by the construction of an asphaltic concrete pavement, consisting of a 6-inch concrete foundation and a 1½-inch asphaltic wearing surface, on the roadway thereof.

And the improvement of the crossing of Quint street and Carroll avenue by grading to official line and grade; by the construction of an 8-inch vitrified clay pipe sewer between the center and the northerly lines of Quint street; by the construction of brick catchbasins with 10-inch vitrified clay pipe culverts; by the construction of concrete curbs and artificial stone sidewalks on the angular corners, and by the construction of an asphaltic concrete pavement, consisting of a 6-inch concrete foundation and a 1½-inch asphaltic concrete wearing surface, on the roadway thereof.

Section 2. This ordinance shall take effect immediately.

Ayes—Supervisors Andriano, Canepa, Gallagher, Havenner, Hayden, McGovern, McSheehy, Miles, Peyser, Power, Roncovieri, Rossi, Spaulding, Stanton, Suhr—15.

Absent—Supervisors Colman, Shannon, Toner—3.

Ordering the Improvement of Bright Street Between Randolph and Sargent Streets.

Also, Bill No. 8202, Ordinance No. 8707 (New Series), as follows:

Ordering the performance of certain street work to be done in the City and County of San Francisco, approving and adopting specifications therefor.

Be it ordained by the People of the City and County of San Francisco as follows:

Section 1. The Board of Public Works, in written communication filed in the office of the Clerk of the Board of Supervisors February

13, 1930, having recommended the ordering of the following street work, the same is hereby ordered to be done in the City and County of San Francisco in conformity with the provisions of the Street Improvement Ordinance of 1918 of said City and County of San Francisco, said work to be performed under the direction of the Board of Public Works, and to be done in accordance with the specifications prepared therefor by said Board of Public Works, and on file in its office, which said plans and specifications are hereby approved and adopted.

That said Board of Supervisors, pursuant to the provisions of Part II of the said Street Improvement Ordinance of 1918 of said City and County of San Francisco, does hereby determine and declare that the assessment to be imposed for the said contemplated improvements, respectively, may be paid in twenty installments; that the period of time after the time of the payment of the first installment when each of the succeeding installments must be paid is to be six months from the time of the payment of the preceding installment, and that the rate of interest to be charged on all deferred payments shall be seven per centum per annum.

The improvement of Bright street between Randolph and Sargent streets, where not already so improved, by the construction of armored concrete curbs; by the construction of side sewers, and by the construction of a concrete pavement on the roadway thereof.

Section 2. This ordinance shall take effect immediately.

Ayes—Supervisors Andriano, Canepa, Gallagher, Havenner, Hayden, McGovern, McSheehy, Miles, Peyser, Power, Roncovieri, Rossi, Spaulding, Stanton, Suhr—15.

Absent—Supervisors Colman, Shannon, Toner—3.

Condemnation of Land Required for Montcalm Street.

Also, Resolution No. 32182 (New Series), as follows:

Resolved, By the Board of Supervisors of the City and County of San Francisco, that public interest and necessity require the acquisition by the City and County of San Francisco, a municipal corporation, of the following properties, situated in the City and County of San Francisco, State of California, more particularly described as follows, to-wit:

Parcel 1. Commencing at the point of intersection of the northeasterly line of Franconia street and the southeasterly line of Montcalm street, and running thence northeasterly along said southeasterly line 70 feet to the southwesterly line of the property now or formerly owned by Fred W. zur Lowen; thence at right angles southeasterly along said southwesterly line 3.739 feet to the proposed southeasterly line of Montcalm street; thence southwesterly along said proposed southeasterly line on a curve to the right, tangent to a line deflected 67 deg. 41 min. 40 sec. to the right from the preceding course, radius 129.759 feet, central angle 31 deg. 30 min. 27 sec., a distance of 71.356 feet to the northeasterly line of Franconia street; thence northwesterly along said northeasterly line 11.779 feet to the southeasterly line of Montcalm street and the point of commencement.

Being a portion of Gift Map No 3, as per man thereof recorded in Map Book 2A and B, page 15, records of the City and County of San Francisco.

Parcel 2. Commencing at the point of intersection of the northwesterly line of Montcalm street and the easterly line of Peralta avenue, and running thence northerly along said easterly line 2.354 feet; thence easterly on a curve to the left, tangent to a line deflected 90 deg. 00 min. 00 sec. to the right from said easterly line of Peralta avenue, radius 24 feet, central angle 24 deg. 24 min. 00 sec., a distance of 10.221 feet to its point of tangency with said northwesterly line of Montcalm street; thence southwesterly along said northwesterly line

10.887 feet to the easterly line of Peralta avenue and the point of commencement.

Being a portion of Lot 1466 of Gift Map No. 3, as per map thereof recorded in Map Book 2A and B, page 15, records of the City and County of San Francisco. Be it

Further Resolved, That said property is suitable, adaptable, necessary and required for the public use of said City and County of San Francisco, to-wit: For the opening, widening, construction and maintenance of Montcalm street from its point of intersection with Macedonia street in a westerly direction to the point of interesection with Peralta avenue. It is necessary that a fee simple title be taken for such use.

The City Attorney is hereby ordered and directed to commence proceedings in eminent domain against the owners of said parcels of land, and of any and all interests therein or claims thereto, for the condemnation thereof for the public use of the City and County of San Francisco, as aforesaid.

Ayes—Supervisors Andriano, Canepa, Gallagher, Havenner, Hayden, McGovern, McSheehy, Miles, Peyser, Power, Roncovieri, Rossi, Spaulding, Stanton, Suhr—15.

Absent—Supervisors Colman, Shannon, Toner—3.

Ordering the Improvement of Corbett Avenue, From Clayton Street to Twenty-fourth Street, Etc., City to Assume Portion of the Cost Thereof.

Also, Bill No. 8203, Ordinance No. 8708 (New Series), as follows:

Ordering the performance of certain street work to be done in the City and County of San Francisco, approving and adopting specifications therefor.

Be it ordained by the People of the City and County of San Francisco as follows:

Section 1. The Board of Public Works, in written communication filed in the office of the Clerk of the Board of Supervisors, February 26, 1930, having recommended the ordering of the following street work, the same is hereby ordered to be done in the City and County of San Francisco in conformity with the provisions of the Street Improvement Ordinance of 1918 of said City and County of San Francisco, said work to be performed under the direction of the Board of Public Works, and to be done in accordance with the specifications prepared therefor by said Board of Public Works, and on file in its office, which said plans and specifications are hereby approved and adopted.

That said Board of Supervisors, pursuant to the provisions of Part II of the said Street Improvement Ordinance of 1918 of said City and County of San Francisco, does hereby determine and declare that the assessment to be imposed for the said contemplated improvements, respectively, may be paid in twenty installments; that the period of time after the time of the payment of the first installment when each of the succeeding installments must be paid is to be six months from the time of the payment of the preceding installment, and that the rate of interest to be charged on all deferred payments shall be seven per centum per annum.

The improvement of Corbett avenue from Clayton street to Twenty-fourth street, including all intervening crossings and intersections and the necessary conform and approach work on streets adjacent thereto, by grading to official line and subgrade and by the construction of the following:

Class "B" 2500-pound concrete in retaining walls, stairs, balustrades and sidewalk curtain walls; bar reinforcing steel; vitrified clay pipe sewers; vitrified clay pipe side sewers; vitrified clay pipe Y or T branches; brick manholes complete; brick catch basins complete; reset brick catch basin; vitrified clay pipe culvert; armored concrete curb; concrete curb reset; redwood headers; asphalt-concrete pavement consisting of a 2-inch asphaltic concrete wearing surface and a 6-inch Class "F" concrete base; asphaltic concrete wearing surface; wire mesh reinforcement for concrete base; concrete sidewalk (2 course); black pipe conduit; wood bulkhead; wood stairway reconstruction; painted traffic lines; painted "Slow" signs; post-mounted "Slow" signs; pedestrian lane markers; traffic turning buttons.

Section 2. This ordinance shall take effect immediately.

Ayes—Supervisors Andriano, Canepa, Gallagher, Havenner, Hayden, McGovern, McSheehy, Miles, Peyser, Power, Roncovieri, Rossi, Spaulding, Stanton, Suhr—15.

Absent—Supervisors Colman, Shannon, Toner—3.

Ordering the Improvement of Twentieth Avenue, South of the South Line of Irving Street, by Removal of Sand, Etc.

Also, Bill No. 8204, Ordinance No. 8709 (New Series), as follows:

Ordering the performance of certain street work to be done in the City and County of San Francisco, approving and adopting specifications therefor.

Be it ordained by the People of the City and County of San Francisco as follows:

Section 1. The Board of Public Works in written communication filed in the office of the Clerk of the Board of Supervisors February 13, 1930, having recommended the ordering of the following street work, the same is hereby ordered to be done in the City and County of San Francisco in conformity with the provisions of the Street Improvement Ordinance of 1918 of said City and County of San Francisco, said work to be performed under the direction of the Board of Public Works, and to be done in accordance with the specifications prepared therefor by said Board of Public Works, and on file in its office, which said plans and specifications are hereby approved and adopted.

That said Board of Supervisors, pursuant to the provisions of Part II of the said Street Improvement Ordinance of 1918 of said City and County of San Francisco, does hereby determine and declare that the assessment to be imposed for the said contemplated improvements, respectively, may be paid in three installments; that the period of time after the time of the payment of the first installment when each of the succeeding installments must be paid is to be one year from the time of the payment of the preceding installment, and that the rate of interest to be charged on all deferred payments shall be seven per centum per annum.

The improvement of the west one-half of Twentieth avenue from a line parallel with and 75 feet south of the south line of Irving street to a line parallel with and 125 feet south of the south line of Irving street by the removal of sand from the roadway and sidewalk area and the construction of a bulkhead.

Bidder is to name price per lineal foot of a 2-foot bulkhead for this work.

Section 2. This ordinance shall take effect immediately.

Ayes—Supervisors Andriano, Canepa, Gallagher, Havenner, Hayden, McGovern, McSheehy, Miles, Peyser, Power, Roncovieri, Rossi, Spaulding, Stanton, Suhr—15.

Absent—Supervisors Colman, Shannon, Toner—3.

PRESENTATION OF BILLS AND ACCOUNTS.

Your Finance Committee, having examined miscellaneous demands not required by law to be passed to print, and amounting to $67,138.84, recommends same be allowed and ordered paid.

Approved by the following vote:

Ayes—Supervisors Andriano, Canepa, Gallagher, Havenner, Hayden,

McGovern, McSheehy, Miles, Peyser, Power, Roncovieri, Rossi, Spaulding, Stanton, Suhr—15.

Absent—Supervisors Colman, Shannon, Toner—3.

NEW BUSINESS.

Passed for Printing.

The following matters were *passed for printing*:

Authorizations.

On recommendation of Finance Committee.

Resolution No. ———— (New Series), as follows:

Resolved, That the following amounts be and the same are hereby authorized to be expended out of the hereinafter mentioned funds in payment to the following named claimants, to-wit:

Bernal Cut Construction Fund.

(1) MacDonald & Kahn, Inc., thirteenth payment, improvement of Bernal Cut (claim dated March 5, 1930) $25,500.00

Boulevard Bond Issue Construction Fund.

(2) Municipal Construction Company, improvement of Key avenue from Bay Shore boulevard to existing pavement (claim dated March 5, 1930) ....$ 986.00

(3) Eaton & Smith, ninth payment, improvement of Junipero Serra boulevard from Sloat boulevard to county line (claim dated March 5, 1930) 14,100.00

(4) Hanrahan Company, second payment, improvement of Alemany boulevard, section D-1, Sickles to Orizaba avenues (claim dated March 5, 1930) 10,200.00

County Road Fund.

(5) J. O'Shea, Inc., teams furnished for account of street reconstruction (claim dated Feb. 26, 1930).................$ 660.00

(6) Henry Cowell Lime & Cement Company, cement for street reconstruction (claim dated Feb. 27, 1930) 677.50

(7) The Texas Company, gasoline furnished for account of street reconstruction (claim dated Feb. 26, 1930).......... 784.03

(8) Louis J. Cohn, paving and street reconstruction, Harrison and Alameda streets, Treat avenue at Alameda and at Florida streets, Division street between Bryant and Florida streets, etc. (claim dated March 4, 1930)................. 3,379.26

(9) E. J. & M. J. Treacy, improvement of Havelock street between Edna street and Circular avenue (claim dated March 4, 1930) 1,557.50

(10) Municipal Construction Company, improvement of Josiah avenue and Ridge lane (claim dated March 4, 1930)..... 962.05

(11) Bode Gravel Company, gravel for street reconstruction (claim dated Feb. 28, 1930) 1,466.60

(12) Pacific Coast Aggregates, Inc., gravel for street reconstruction (claim dated March 4, 1930) 607.51

Municipal Railway Fund.

(13) Market Street Railway Company, repairs to crossing and paving, Market and First streets (claim dated Feb. 27, 1930) ....$ 700.58

1928 Hetch Hetchy Construction Fund.

(14) J. H. Creighton, truck hire (claim dated Feb. 28, 1930)..$ 2,143.57

(15) Consolidated Mills Company, Inc. (First National Bank of Eugene, Oregon, assignee), for lumber furnished (claim dated Feb. 27, 1930) 1,100.78

(16) Del Monte Meat Company, meat furnished (claim dated Feb. 28, 1930) 927.97

(17) Gunite Construction Company, one cement gun (claim
dated Feb. 28, 1930) 800.00

(18) The A. T. Herr Supply Company, 50 Koppel mine cars
(claim dated Feb. 27, 1930) 3,477.54

(19) Owen-Oregon Lumber Company (claim dated Feb. 27,
1930) 607.64

(20) Pioneer Rubber Mills, hose (claim dated Feb. 27, 1930) 804.69

(21) Santa Cruz Portland Cement Company, cement (claim
dated Feb. 27, 1930) 1,052.00

(22) Soule Steel Company, steel and iron (claim dated Feb.
28, 1930) 899.00

(23) Wilsey-Bennett Company, butter, etc. (claim dated Feb.
27, 1930) 731.30

(24) Chain Belt Company, chain belt (claim dated March 3,
1930) 819.36

(25) A. S. Cameron Steam Pump Works, pump parts (claim
dated March 3, 1930) 617.70

(26) Commercial Shearing & Stamping Company, 1040 Tunel
Liner plates, bolts, angle splice bars, etc. (claim dated
March 1, 1930) 6,906.89

(27) Del Monte Meat Company, meat (claim dated March 3,
1930) 703.04

(28) Grier & Mead, six storage battery locomotives, batteries
with containers (claim dated March 3, 1930)............. 8,750.00

(29) Ingersoll-Rand Company of California, machinery parts
(claim dated March 1, 1930) 807.87

(30) Owen-Oregon Lumber Company, lumber (claim dated
March 3, 1930) 607.64

(31) Pacific Coast Steel Corporation, reinforcing steel (claim
dated March 3, 1930) 2,379.80

(32) Pioneer Rubber Mills, hose and couplings (claim dated
March 1, 1930) 1,159.67

(33) Santa Cruz Portland Cement Company (claim dated
March 3, 1930) 4,044.00

(34) Western Butchers' Supply Company, refrigerating plant
(claim dated March 1, 1930) 1,201.00

(35) Wilsey-Bennett Company, butter, eggs, etc. (claim dated
March 3, 1930) 874.54

1929 *Sewer Bond Construction Fund.*

(36) Clinton Construction Company, first payment, construction of Alemany boulevard storm drain (claim dated March
5, 1930) ....$ 7,500.00

Hetch Hetchy Power Operative Fund.

(37) Hetch Hetchy Construction Fund, 1928, for materials,
supplies and equipment furnished and services rendered for
month of January, 1930 (claim dated Feb. 27, 1930).......$ 5,862.25

Special School Tax.

(38) James W. Reid, final payment for architectural services
for Marina Elementary School (claim dated March 4, 1930).$ 1,539.17

(39) Alta Electric Company, seventh payment, electrical work
for Park-Presidio Junior High School (claim dated March 4,
1930) 2,179.69

(40) Meyer Bros., seventh payment, general construction of
Park-Presidio Junior High School (claim dated March 4,
1930) 31,180.23

(41) Scott Company, seventh payment, mechanical equipment
for Park-Presidio Junior High School (claim dated March
4, 1930) 13,118.25

(42) Scott Company, sixth payment, plumbing and gasfitting
for Park-Presidio Junior High School (claim dated March
4, 1930) 2,808.53

(43) Jacks & Irvine, ninth payment, general construction of
Roosevelt Junior High School (claim dated March 4, 1930) 26,565.97
(44) Larsen & Larsen, third payment, brick work, etc., for
Roosevelt Junior High School (claim dated March 4, 1930). 17,908.88
(45) Scott Co., seventh payment, mechanical equipment of
Roosevelt Junior High School (claim dated March 4, 1930).. 5,007.38
(46) Scott Co., seventh payment, plumbing and gas-fitting
for Roosevelt Junior High School (claim dated March 4,
1930) 1,804.80

Auditorium Fund.

(47) Concert Management Arthur Judson, Inc., for services
of Giovanni Martinelli, tenor soloist, concert of March 29,
1930 (claim dated March 7, 1930)........................$ 2,000.00

General Fund, 1929-1930.

(48) Associated Charities, widows' pensions (claim dated
March 7, 1930) ....$ 8,134.10
(49) Eureka Benevolent Society, widows' pensions (claim
dated March 7, 1930) 921.42
(50) Little Children's Aid, widows' pensions (claim dated
March 7, 1930) 6,248.31
(51) Sonoma State Home, maintenance of feeble-minded,
month of December, 1929 (claim dated Feb. 17, 1930).... 10,300.00
(52) Sonoma State Home, maintenance of feeble-minded,
month of January, 1930 (claim dated Feb. 17, 1930)...... 10,080.00
(53) Duncan Matheson, Treasurer, for settlement with State
of California, for account of maintenance of narcotics at
various institutions, period May to November, 1929 (claim
dated Dec. 31, 1929).................................... 10,175.00
(54) San Francisco Chronicle, official advertising, Board of
Public Works (claim dated March 4, 1930)............... 574.98
(55) San Francisco Chronicle, official advertising, Board of
Supervisors (claim dated March 10, 1930).............. 2,187.43
(56) Spring Valley Water Co., rental of Harding Park, July
1, 1929, to March 3, 1930 (claim dated Feb. 21, 1930).... 4,041.67
(57) The Texas Co., gasoline furnished Police Department
(claim dated Feb. 28, 1930)........................... 1,243.06
(58) California Construction Co., improvement of City's portion of Short street between Market and Yukon streets
(claim dated March 4, 1930).......................... 773.11
(59) Chas. L. Harney, improvement of Thirty-first avenue
between Kirkham and Lawton streets, and crossing of
Thirty-first avenue and Lawton street (claim dated March
4, 1930) 3,397.00
(60) E. J. and M. J. Treacy, grading, paving, etc., on Twenty-
sixth street between York and Hampshire streets (claim
dated March 4, 1930) 1,930.00
(61) Richfield Oil Co. of California, fuel oil furnished Hall
of Justice and Civic Center Power House (claim dated Feb.
26, 1930) 1,897.16
(62) Healey & Donaldson, tobacco furnished Laguna Honda
Home (claim dated March 6, 1930)...................... 1,811.16
(63) Sussman, Wormser Co., sugar for Laguna Honda Home
(claim dated March 6, 1930)........................... 2,505.75
(64) H. E. Teller Co., coffee for Laguna Honda Home (claim
dated March 6, 1930)................................. 626.25

Payment for School Lands.

Also, Resolution No. ————— (New Series), as follows:

Resolved, That the sum of $5,250 be and the same is hereby set aside,
appropriated and authorized to be expended out of School Lands Fund,
and authorized in payment to Wm. J. Robinson; being payment for
land and improvements required for school purposes, and situate,

commencing at a point on the southerly line of Twenty-fifth street, distant thereon 240 feet westerly from the westerly line of Noe street, running thence westerly along the southerly line of Twenty-fifth street 28 feet; thence at a right angle southerly 114 feet; thence at a right angle easterly 28 feet; thence at a right angle northerly 114 feet; as per acceptance of offer by Resolution No. 32147 (New Series). (Claim dated March 10, 1930.)

Fixing Compensation of Attorneys for San Francisco Water Department at $12,000 Per Year.

Also, Resolution No. ———— (New Series), as follows:

Whereas, the Board of Public Works of the City and County of San Francisco having made request upon the City Attorney that, pursuant to Section 10 of Ordinance No. 8691 (New Series), he appoint and detail an attorney to render legal service to the San Francisco Water Department, and said City Attorney having so detailed an attorney to render such service, and the compensation of said attorney so detailed having been approved by said Board of Public Works at the sum of $12,000 per annum, payable in equal monthly installments; now, therefore, be it

Resolved, That the compensation of said attorney so detailed by said City Attorney be and the same is hereby fixed at the sum of $12,000 per annum, payable in equal monthly installments from the revenues of said Water Department as an operating expense thereof.

Adopted.

The following resolutions were *adopted*:

Treasurer to Pay Demands of San Francisco Water Department From General Fund Until Revenues Are Sufficient to Reimburse Same.

On recommendation of Finance Committee.

Resolution No. 32183 (New Series), as follows:

Whereas, the City and County of San Francisco has taken over and is operating the properties of the Spring Valley Water Company; and

Whereas, the moneys due for water furnished to consumers subsequent to March 3, 1930, will not be available for the purpose of paying the running expenses of the San Francisco Water Department until after April 1, 1930, and it is necessary that the employees of said department should be paid bi-monthly and other current expenses thereof should be cared for as they become due; now, therefore, be it

Resolved, That the Treasurer of the City and County of San Francisco be and he is hereby directed to pay from the General Fund of the City and County of San Francsico all demands of the San Francisco Water Department, properly approved, until the revenues of said department are sufficient to meet the same, and when said revenues are sufficient, to credit the General Fund with all amounts so disbursed.

Ayes—Supervisors Andriano, Canepa, Gallagher, Havenner, Hayden, McGovern, McSheehy, Miles, Peyser, Power, Roncovieri, Rossi, Spaulding, Stanton, Suhr—15.

Absent—Supervisors Colman, Shannon, Toner—3.

Rescinding Appropriations Heretofore Made Out of County Road Fund.

Also, Resolution No. 32184 (New Series), as follows:

Resolved, That so much of Resolution No. 31078 (New Series) as sets aside, appropriates and authorizes the expending out of County Road Fund (1) resurfacing of Berry street, Fourth street to Seventh street, $19,100, and (2) reconstruction of Fourth street, Mission street to Townsend street, $16,000, be and the same is hereby rescinded and repealed.

Ayes—Supervisors Andriano, Canepa, Gallagher, Havenner, Hayden, McGovern, McSheehy, Miles, Peyser, Power, Roncovieri, Rossi, Spaulding, Stanton, Suhr—15.

Absent—Supervisors Colman, Shannon, Toner—3.

Passed for Printing.

The following matters were *passed for printing*:

Appropriation, $26,000, for Improvement of Portola Drive, From Twenty-fourth Street to Fowler Avenue, Out of County Road Fund.

On recommendation of Finance Committee.

Resolution No. ———— (New Series), as follows:

Resolved, That the following amount be and the same is hereby set aside, appropriated and authorized to be expended out of the County Road Fund for the following purposes, to-wit:

The improvement of Portola drive, from Twenty-fourth street to Fowler avenue, $26,000.

Appropriation for Improvement of Broadway, Westerly From Van Ness Avenue.

Also, Resolution No. ———— (New Series), as follows:

Resolved, That the sum of $9,100 be and the same is hereby set aside, appropriated and authorized to be expended out of County Road Fund for the improvement of Broadway, westerly from Van Ness avenue.

Appropriation for Employments, Traffic Bureau.

Also, Resolution No. ———— (New Series), as follows:

Resolved, That the sum of $1,635 be and the same is hereby set aside, appropriated and authorized to be expended out of "Traffic Signals," etc., Budget Item No. 57, for employments and expense of the Traffic Bureau for the month of March, 1930.

Adopted.

The following resolutions were *adopted*:

Reimbursing Board of Public Works for Painting of Traffic Signs, Etc.

On recommendation of Finance Committee.

Resolution No. 32185 (New Series), as follows:

Resolved, That the following amounts be and the same are hereby set aside and appropriated out of "Traffic Signals," etc., to the credit of the Board of Public Works, Budget Item 442; being reimbursement for the cost of painting traffic signs, lines, curbs, etc., during January, 1930, to-wit:

For labor performed, the sum of............................$409.50
For material furnished...................................... 337.50

Ayes—Supervisors Andriano, Canepa, Gallagher, Havenner, Hayden, McGovern, McSheehy, Miles, Peyser, Power, Roncovieri, Rossi, Spaulding, Stanton, Suhr—15.

Absent—Supervisors Colman, Shannon, Toner—3.

Appropriation for Street Decorations, Celebration of March 17.

Also, Resolution No. 32186 (New Series), as follows:

Resolved, That the sum of $465 be and the same is hereby set aside, appropriated and authorized to be expended out of Publicity and Advertising, Appropriation 54, for the decorating of Market street in connection with the celebration of St. Patrick's Day, March 17, 1930; for the publicity and advertising of San Francisco.

Ayes—Supervisors Andriano, Canepa, Gallagher, Havenner, Hayden, McGovern, McSheehy, Miles, Peyser, Power, Roncovieri, Rossi, Spaulding, Stanton, Suhr—15.

Absent—Supervisors Colman, Shannon, Toner—3.

Transferring of Amount, $1,250, Bureau of Supplies.

Also, Resolution No. 32187 (New Series), as follows:

Resolved, That the sum of $1,250 be and the same is hereby set aside out of Appropriation 3-C, to the credit of Appropriation 3-D, Bureau of Supplies.

(Request of Purchaser of Supplies, dated March 6, 1930.)

Ayes—Supervisors Andriano, Canepa, Gallagher, Havenner, Hayden, McGovern, McSheehy, Miles, Peyser, Power, Roncovieri, Rossi, Spaulding, Stanton, Suhr—15.

Absent—Supervisors Colman, Shannon, Toner—3.

Accepting Offer to Sell Land Required for Sunset Boulevard.

Also, Resolution No. 32188 (New Series), as follows:

Resolved, That the offers of sale made by the following named persons to sell to the City and County of San Francisco the following described land, required for the Sunset boulevard, for the sums set forth opposite their respective names, be accepted:

Thomas P. Coyle, $17,017—All of Lot 2, Block 2313, as per the Assessor's Block Books of the City and County of San Francisco.

John Murphy and Nellie T. Murphy, $2,750—All of Lot 1, Block 2365, as per the Assessor's Block Books of the City and County of San Francisco.

And the City Attorney is hereby authorized to examine the title to said property, and, if the same is found satisfactory, to accept, on behalf of the City, deeds conveying said property to the City, free and clear of all encumbrances, and to record said deeds, together with copy of the resolution, in the office of the Recorder of the City and County of San Francisco.

Ayes—Supervisors Andriano, Canepa, Gallagher, Havenner, Hayden, McGovern, McSheehy, Miles, Peyser, Power, Roncovieri, Rossi, Spaulding, Stanton, Suhr—15.

Absent—Supervisors Colman, Shannon, Toner—3.

Passed for Printing.

The following matters were *passed for printing*:

Automobile Supply Station, Frank Franchini, South Side of Twenty-fourth Street, 50 Feet West of Vicksburg Street.

On recommendation of Fire Committee.

Resolution No. ———— (New Series), as follows:

Resolved, That Frank Franchini be and is hereby granted permission, revocable at will of the Board of Supervisors, to maintain and operate an automobile supply station on the south side of Twenty-fourth street, 50 feet west of Vicksburg street.

The rights granted under this resolution shall be exercised within six months, otherwise said permit shall become null and void.

Automobile Supply Station, Wm. McDonald, Southeast Corner of Steiner and Eddy Streets.

Also, Resolution No. ———— (New Series), as follows:

Resolved, That Wm. McDonald be and is hereby granted permission, revocable at will of the Board of Supervisors, to maintain and operate an automobile supply station at the southeast corner of Steiner and Eddy streets.

The rights granted under this resolution shall be exercised within six months, otherwise said permit shall become null and void.

Adopted.

The following resolution was *adopted*:

Denying Public Garage, John B. DeMaria, Columbus Avenue, Mason and Lombard Streets.

On recommendation of Fire Committee.

Resolution No. 32189 (New Series), as follows:

Resolved, That, in the exercise of the sound and reasonable discretion of the Board of Supervisors, permission is hereby denied John B. DeMaria to maintain and operate a public garage at premises located at Columbus avenue, Mason and Lombard streets.

Ayes—Supervisors Andriano, Canepa, Gallagher, Havenner, McGovern, McSheehy, Miles, Peyser, Power, Rossi, Spaulding, Stanton, Suhr—13.

Absent—Supervisors Colman, Hayden, Roncovieri, Shannon, Toner—5.

Passed for Printing.

The following resolution was *passed for printing*:

Laundry Permit.

On recommendation of Fire Committee.

Resolution No. ———— (New Series), as follows:

Resolved, That the following revocable permit be and is hereby granted:

Laundry.

Julie Pouquette, 722 Bush street.

The rights granted under this resolution shall be exercised within six months, otherwise said permit shall become null and void.

Adopted.

The following resolution was *adopteil*:

Street Lights.

On recommendation of Lighting Committee.

Resolution No. 32190 (New Series), as follows:

Resolved, That the Pacific Gas and Electric Company be and it is hereby authorized and requested to remove and install street lights as follows:

Remove 250 M. R.

Downey street between Frederick and Ashbury streets (3).

Northwest corner Oneida and Delano avenue.

Buchanan street between Sutter and Post streets.

Roosevelt way (4).

Install 250 C. P. O. B.

Front of 232 Kenwood way.

Remove 400 M. R.

Northeast corner Washington and Laguna streets.

Southwest corner Washington and Gough streets.

Northeast and southwest corners Washington and Octavia streets.

North and south sides Washington street, Gough to Laguna streets.

Oak street between Van Ness avenue and Gough street (5).

Rhode Island street between Twenty-fifth and Twenty-sixth streets.

Thirty-second avenue between Taraval and Ulloa streets (1).

Thirty-fourth avenue between Taraval and Ulloa streets (1).

Seventeenth street between Mission and Valencia streets (2).

North and south sides Fell street between Divisadero and Scott streets.

Judah street and Funston avenue.

Funston avenue between Judah and Kirkham streets.

Roosevelt way (7).

East and west sides Shotwell street between Twenty-fourth and Twenty-fifth streets.

Corner Twenty-fifth and Shotwell streets.

Southwest corner Twenty-sixth avenue and Santiago street.

Change 400 M. R.

Sanchez and Twenty-fifth streets.

Twenty-fifth street, east of Noe street.

Install 400 C. P. O. B.

East and west sides Twenty-sixth avenue between Taraval and Santiago streets.

Southwest corner Twenty-sixth avenue between Taraval and Santiago streets.

North and south sides Fell street between Scott and Divisadero streets.

Missouri street, front of No. 514.

East side Missouri street. second pole north of Twenty-second street.

Downey street between Frederick and Ashbury streets (3).

Corner Adam and Eve streets.

Buchanan street between Sutter and Post streets.

North and south sides Oak street between Van Ness avenue and Franklin and Gough streets.

Northeast and southwest corners Franklin and Oak streets and Oak and Gough streets.

Eighteenth street between San Carlos and Lexington avenue.

East and west sides Shotwell street between Twenty-fourth and Twenty-fifth streets.

Northwest and southeast corners Twenty-fifth and Shotwell streets.

West side Rhode Island street between Twenty-fifth and Twenty-sixth streets.

East side Rhode Island street, opposite No. 1482.

East and west sides Thirty-second and Thirty-fourth avenues between Taraval and Ulloa streets.

Crescent avenue between Mission and Leese streets.

Newman street between Bennington and Andover streets.

North and south sides Seventeenth street between Mission and Valencia streets.

Seventeenth street and Hoff avenue.

Baltimore way between Naylor and South Hill boulevard.

North and south sides Fell street between Divisadero and Scott streets.

Northwest corner Oneida and Delano avenue.

Tioga street near Alpha street.

Girard street between Harkness and Ward streets.

Brussell street between Harkness and Ward streets.

Goettingen street between Harkness and Ward streets.

East side Sanchez street, south of Twenty-fifth street.

South side Twenty-fifth street, west of Sanchez street.

Northeast and southwest corners Judah street and Funston avenue.

East and west sides Funston avenue between Judah and Kirkham streets.

Tennessee street between Twenty-first and Twenty-second streets.

Morse and Rolph streets.

Bright street between Randolph and Sargent streets.

Buchanan street between Sutter and Post streets.

Roosevelt way as per map (29).

Change M. R. to C. P. O. B.

Third street between Townsend and Channel streets.

Remove Gas.

West side Third street, first and second south of Townsend street.
South side Townsend street, first west of Third street.

Install 600 C. P. O. B.

East and west sides Third street between King and Berry streets.
West side Third street between Berry and Channel streets.

Install 400 C. P. Type "C."

Southwest corner Washington and Gough streets.
Northeast corner Washington and Laguna streets.
Northeast and southwest corners Washington and Octavia streets.
North and south sides Washington street between Gough and Laguna
streets.

Ayes—Supervisors Andriano, Canepa, Gallagher, Havenner, Hayden,
McGovern, McSheehy, Miles, Peyser, Power, Roncovieri, Rossi, Spaulding, Stanton, Suhr—15.

Absent—Supervisors Colman, Shannon, Toner—3.

Passed for Printing.

The following matters were *passed for printing*:

Establishing Underground District, Third Street, From East Line of Townsend Street to Channel, Approximately 942 Feet.

On recommendation of Lighting Committee.

Bill No. 8205, Ordinance No. ———— (New Series), as follows:

Amending Order No. 214 (Second Series), entitled "Providing for placing wires and conduits underground in the City and County of San Francisco," by adding a new section, to be known as Section 1-ll.

Be it ordained by the People of the City and County of San Francisco as follows:

Section 1-ll. An additional district to those heretofore described within which it shall be unlawful to maintain poles and overhead wires after July 31, 1930, is hereby designated, to-wit:

Underground District No. 46. Third street, from the east line of Townsend street to Channel, approximately 942 feet.

Establishing Underground District, Webster Street, From the South Side of Union Street to the North Side of Green Street, Approximately 275 Feet.

Also, Bill No. 8206, Ordinance No. ———— (New Series), as follows:

Amending Order No. 214 (Second Series), entitled "Providing for placing wires and conduits underground in the City and County of San Francisco," by adding a new section, to be known as Section 1-mm.

Be it ordained by the People of the City and County of San Francisco as follows:

Section 1-mm. An additional district to those heretofore described, within which it shall be unlawful to maintain poles and overhead wires after September 1, 1930, is hereby designated, to-wit:

Underground District No. 47. Webster street, from the south side of Union street to the north side of Green street, approximately 275 feet.

Amending License Ordinance to Facilitate Collection of Delinquent Taxes and Abandoning Exemption Clauses.

On recommendation of Police Committee.

Bill No. 8207, Ordinance No. ———— (New Series), as follows:

Amending Section 2 of Ordinance No. 5132, as amended by Ordinance No. 8464 (New Series), entitled "Imposing license taxes on certain businesses, callings, trades or employments within the City and County of San Francisco."

Be it ordained by the People of the City and County of San Francisco as follows:

Section 1. Section 2 of Ordinance No. 5132 (New Series), the title of which is recited above, is hereby amended to read as follows:

License Payable in Advance—Where Payable—Penalty for Non-Payment.

Section 2. On and after April 1, 1930, all license taxes, unless, by ordinance, specifically provided otherwise, shall be due and payable quarterly in advance, and fall due on the first day of October, the first day of January, the first day of April and the first day of July in each calendar year, depending upon the particular quarter in which a licensee begins business. In all cases of licenses on new business collectible at periods other than the months of October, January, April and July, the Tax Collector shall pro rate on a monthly basis the amount of license fee due for any given quarter.

Whenever a license tax is imposed by ordinance it shall be unlawful to do or perform the act or to carry on the business, trade, profession or calling for which a license is required, or to own, keep or use the article or thing, for the owning, keeping or using of which a license is required, unless such license be first procured.

All licenses are payable, when due, at the office of the Tax Collector, in the City Hall, and if not paid within thirty (30) days after the same become due, the Tax Collector shall add 10 per cent to the amount of the license as a penalty for non-payment. If the license is not paid within sixty days after the same becomes due, the Tax Collector shall add 15 per cent to the amount of the license as a penalty for non-payment. If the license is not paid within ninety. (90) days after the same becomes due, the Tax Collector shall add twenty-five per cent to the amount of the license as a penalty for non-payment. Provided, however, when a licensee has failed for a period of six months or more to pay a license fee, and has allowed the license to become delinquent for this or a longer period, the Tax Collector shall, in such instances, impose a penalty of fifty per cent on the total amount of license delinquent, and shall turn over a complete list of such licensees to the Chief of Police for arrest and prosecution under the provisions of this ordinance. Nothing shall permit the exemption of the penalties mentioned in this section.

Section 2. This ordinance shall take effect immediately.

Adopted.

The following resolution was *adopted*:

Authorizing the Mayor to Apply to the United States Land Office, Secretary of the Interior et al., for Permission to Hold and Occupy Certain Lands of the Public Domain Necessary for the Protection of the Waters of Moccasin Reregulating Reservoir.

On recommendation of Public Utilities Committee.

Resolution No. 32191 (New Series), as follows:

Whereas, for the successful consummation of the policy of the City and County of San Francisco of developing and completing a municipal water supply, with the Hetch Hetchy Valley, Lake Eleanor and the waters of the Tuolumne River and its tributaries in Tuolumne County, California, as the source for obtaining said water supply, it is necessary to secure certain lands of the public domain for the protection of the waters of Moccasin reregulating reservoir from contamination; said lands being in addition to other lands heretofore granted to said City and County for the same purpose; and

Whereas, the City Engineer has recommended the amendment of the location of the protective area described as Parcel 1 in Resolution No. 25883 (New Series) of this Board, so as to extend the limits of said protective area; now, therefore, be it

Resolved, That the hereinafter described locations be and the same are hereby adopted by the City and County of San Francisco as the definite locations of said lands necessary for the extension of said protective area, said locations constituting an amendment of the location of the protective area described in Resolution No. 25883 (New Series), hereinabove referred to, in that the locations hereinafter described are added to said protective area.

The Mayor of the City and County is hereby authorized to apply to the United States Land Office, the Secretary of the Interior, and any other departments of government, on behalf of the City and County, for permission to hold and occupy said lands of the public domain as necessary for the protection of the waters of said reservoir from contamination. Said application shall be made under the Act of Congress approved on the 19th day of December, 1913, entitled: "An Act granting to the City and County of San Francisco certain rights of way in, over and through certain public lands, the Yosemite National Park, and Stanislaus National Forest, and certain lands in the Yosemite National Park, the Stanislaus National Forest, and the public lands in the State of California, and for other purposes," in order that the City and County may obtain the benefits of said Act.

The City Engineer is authorized and directed to prepare all the necessary surveys, maps and field notes for said application.

The City Attorney is authorized and directed to appear before the United States Land Office, the Secretary of the Interior, or any other department of government, for and on behalf of the City and County, in the matter of this application.

Following is a description of the definite locations of the lands necessary for the protection of the waters of said reservoir from contamination, all located in Townships 1 and 2 South, Range 15 East, M. D. B. and M., Tuolumne County, California:

Parcel 1: A portion of the San Juan mining claim and mill site, located in the southwest quarter of the southeast quarter of Section 27, Township 1 South, Range 15 East. Containing 4.4 acres.

Parcel 2: The southeast quarter, the north half of the southwest quarter, the southwest quarter of the northwest quarter, the west half of the southeast quarter of the northwest quarter, the southeast quarter of the southeast quarter of the northwest quarter, and the south half of the southwest quarter of the northeast quarter of Section 34, Township 1 South, Range 15 East. Containing 330 acres.

Parcel 3: Lots 3 and 4 and the southeast quarter of the northwest quarter of Section 2, Township 2 South, Range 15 East. Containing 139.80 acres.

Parcel 4: Lots 13 and 14 and the south half of Lots 15 and 16 of Section 26, and Lots 3 and 19 of Section 35, Township 1 South, Range 15 East. Containing 153.70 acres.

Parcel 5: Lots 16, 17 and 18 of Section 35, Township 1 South, Range 15 East. Containing 21.14 acres.

Parcel 6: That certain tract of land in Section 35, Township 1 South, Range 15 East, shown and designated as the Little Comstock mill site, a portion of Mineral Survey No. 3557, on the records of the United States Surveyor-General for California. Containing 5 acres.

Said Parcels 1, 2, 3, 4, 5 and 6 contain an aggregate area of 654.04 acres.

Ayes—Supervisors Andriano, Canepa, Gallagher, Havenner, Hayden, McGovern, McSheehy, Miles, Peyser, Power, Roncovieri, Rossi, Spaulding, Stanton, Suhr—15.

Absent—Supervisors Colman, Shannon, Toner—3.

Motion of Supervisor Power to Expunge from Record Remarks Relative to Shooting Affair in San Mateo County.

Supervisor Andriano: I desire to explain my vote that in voting against the motion to expunge from the record I do not wish to be understood as in any way approving what Supervisor Havenner has done. That is a matter between himself and his conscience, but I believe that it is the constitutional right of the members to bring any matter that they see fit, and which is in order, before the Board, and that matter cannot be expunged from the record by a vote of the members of the Board. For that reason I will vote against it.

Supervisor Gallagher: Mr. Chairman, because I regard the ruling of the Chair as extremely dangerous, as unprecedented, and attacking the sacred rights of the public and the members, and, without regard to the subject-matter here involved, at this time I wish to vote "No" on this expunging.

Supervisor McSheehy: My vote requires an explanation, so the record will show that it simply means this: That I intend to vote "No" simply because you are depriving the Supervisor of his constitutional rights. We live in a country that we all admire, and only because our rights are respected' at all times. And we here today as a legislative body are depriving one of our members of his constitutional rights in reference to this particular matter, and for that reason I am voting "No."

Motion *carried* by the following vote:

Ayes—Supervisors Canepa, Havenner, Hayden, McGovern, Miles, Peyser, Power, Roncovieri, Rossi, Spaulding, Stanton, Suhr, Toner—13.

Noes—Supervisors Andriano, Gallagher, McSheehy—3.

Absent—Supervisors Colman, Shannon—2.

Passed for Printing.

The following resolution was *passed for printing*:

Appropriation, $6,000, Purchase of "The Dough Boy" Monument, Memorial Grove.

On motion of Supervisor Rossi:

Resolution No. ———— (New Series), as follows:

Resolved, That the City and County of San Francisco enter into a contract with the Grove of Memory Association, Native Daughters of the Golden West and Native Sons of the Golden West, a corporation, for the erection, for and on behalf of the City and County of San Francisco, of a monument known as "The Dough Boy," which said monument shall, with the permission of the Board of Park Commissioners, be erected in the Grove of Memory in Golden Gate Park, at such place therein as said Board shall direct, and which said monument shall be erected in memory of the members of the United States Military Forces who gave up their lives in the World War; be it

Further Resolved, That the cost of said monument shall not exceed the sum of six thousand ($6,000) dollars, which said sum shall be payable when said monument shall be completed and erected to the satisfaction of the Board of Park Commissioners and the Board of Supervisors; be it

Further Resolved, That the Mayor and the Clerk of the Board of Supervisors be and they are hereby authorized and directed to execute the aforesaid agreement, for and on behalf of the City, and to agree upon the terms thereof pursuant to the provisions of this resolution; and be it

Further Resolved, That the sum of six thousand ($6,000) dollars be and the same is hereby appropriated from Budget Item No. 73, Account No. 1091, 1929-30 Budget, and authorized to be paid to said Grove of Memory Association, Native Daughters of the Golden West and Native Sons of the Golden West for the erection of said monument.

Passed for Printing.

The following resolution was *passed for printing*:

Blasting Permit, Lang Realty Company, Mt. Davidson.

Resolution No. ———— (New Series), as follows:

Resolved, That the Lang Realty Company be and is hereby granted permission, revocable at will of the Board of Supervisors, to explode blasts on private property situate on Mt. Davidson, west of Twin Peaks, adjoining Mt. Davidson Park; provided said permitee shall execute and file a good and sufficient bond in the sum of $5,000, as fixed by the Board of Public Works and approved by his Honor the Mayor, in accordance with Ordinance No. 1204; provided, also, that said blasts shall be exploded only between the hours of 7 a. m. and 6 p. m., and that the work of blasting shall be performed to the satisfaction of the Board of Public Works; and that if any of the conditions of this resolution be violated by said Lang Realty Company, then the privileges and all the rights accruing thereunder shall immediately become null and void.

Street Car Advertising, San Francisco Baseball Clubs.

Resolution No. 32193 (New Series), as follows:

Resolved, That the San Francisco Baseball Club and the Mission Baseball Club be and they are hereby granted permits to advertise on the outside of the street cars of the Market Street Railroad Company (provided said cars when used for said advertising purposes are not used to carry passengers) the playing of baseball games to be held in San Francisco for the period covering the baseball season.

. *Adopted* by the following vote:

Ayes—Suervisors Andriano, Canepa, Gallagher, Havenner, Hayden, McGovern, McSheehy, Miles, Peyser, Power, Roncovieri, Rossi, Spaulding, Stanton, Suhr, Toner—16.

Absent—Supervisors Colman, Shannon—2.

Mayor to Appoint Citizens' Reception Committee, Army Air Corps Maneuvers at Mills Field.

Supervisor Spaulding presented:

Resolution No. 32194 (New Series), as follows:

Whereas, San Francisco Municipal Airport may be selected for the greatest assemblage of American army aviation forces ever assembled in one place; and

Whereas, the presence of this assembly of war planes and the spectacular maneuvers to be staged here will attract thousands of visitors to this city from all over the Pacific Coast; and

Whereas, all these advantages are open to San Francisco if it takes aggressive steps at once to bring the army air forces here; therefore, be it

Resolved, That this Board request Mayor Rolph to appoint a citizens' committee, with authority to invite the Army Air Corps to San Francisco and prepare a fittingly hospitable reception for the officers and men, and to advertise the event, to the end that residents of near-by cities may be acquainted with the spectacle to take place in San Francisco.

Adopted by the following vote:

Ayes—Supervisors Andriano, Canepa, Gallagher, Havenner, Hayden, McGovern, McSheehy, Miles, Power, Roncovieri, Rossi, Spaulding, Stanton, Suhr—14.

Absent—Supervisors Colman, Peyser, Shannon, Toner—4.

Appropriation for Army Air Maneuvers.

Supervisor Spaulding presented:

Resolution No. 32195 (New Series), as follows:

Whereas, great benefit and thousands of visitors to the City may be derived from the proper exploitation of the army air maneuvers which may be held over San Francisco; and

Whereas, it is necessary that this event be widely advertised as a tourist attraction; therefore, be it

Resolved, That the Finance Committee appropriate sufficient funds to defray expenses of San Francisco's part in the army air maneuvers.

Adopted by the following vote:

Ayes—Supervisors Andriano, Canepa, Gallagher, Havenner, Hayden, McGovern, McSheehy, Miles, Power, Roncovieri, Rossi, Spaulding, Stanton, Suhr—14.

Absent—Supervisors Colman, Peyser, Shannon, Toner—4.

Report of Health Committee on Garbage Disposal.

The following was presented by Supervisor McSheehy, copies ordered sent to each member, and the subject-matter made a *Special Order for 3 p. m. next Monday:*

To the Honorable Mayor and the Board of Supervisors of the City and County of San Francisco—Gentlemen:

Your Public Health Committee respectfully submits the following report, which is the third report filed by said Committee on the question of garbage disposal:

We are annexing the two former reports presented by this committee to the Board for the purpose of refreshing the memory of the members who were on the Board when these reports were submitted and further to acquaint the new members of what has been done by the Health Committee prior to their taking office.

Whereas, on the election held November 5, 1928, by a vote of 45,570 for and 39,291 against, the electors determined upon incineration as the method of disposing of San Francisco garbage and rubbish; and

Whereas, in order to carry out said policy as so declared and expressed, it is necessary that an incinerator be constructed in the City and County of San Francisco for the purpose of incinerating the garbage and rubbish collected therein; and

Whereas, there is urgent necessity that said incinerator should be constructed without further delay; therefore, be it

Financed Publicly.

Resolved, That the Finance Committee of this Board be instructed, in making up the budget for the year 1930-1931, to allot sufficient moneys in said budget for the purchase of a block of land contiguous to the present incinerator now located at Fifteenth and De Haro streets and erect thereon an incinerator of the most modern type that will burn 800 tons of garbage and rubbish in twenty-four hours.

Financed Privately.

Resolved, That the Board of Supervisors of the City and County of San Francisco does hereby declare that an incinerator should be financed by private capital under the following conditions:

(a) That said incinerator should be constructed at or near the site of the present incinerator at Fifteenth and De Haro streets, either upon the property belonging to the City or upon privately owned property to be purchased by person, firm or corporation financing said incinerator, and if constructed upon property now owned or hereafter acquired by the City, that a reasonable rental should be paid for the use of said property by the person, firm or corporation financing and operating said incinerator.

(b) That said incinerator should have a capacity of incinerating eight hundred tons of garbage and rubbish per 24-hour day in the most up-to-date and economical manner, and without necessitating the segregation of the wet from the dry garbage by the householders of the City and County.

(c) That the person, firm or corporation financing and operating said incinerator shall be given the exclusive privilege, for a period of at least twenty-five years, of incinerating all garbage and rubbish collected in the City and County of San Francisco, with the exception of that character of garbage commonly known as "swill," which may be collected from hotels, restaurants and other similar places.

(d) That the person, firm or corporation financing and operating said incinerator shall agree with the City and County that said City and County may acquire and take over said incinerator and all of the equipment thereof and the land upon which the same is situated, if said land is not already owned by the City, at any time during the period of twenty-five years mentioned in the last paragraph, at the cost thereof less a reasonable amount for depreciation on said incinerator and equipment figured as of the date on which the same may be taken over by the City. If the amount to be paid for said incinerator and said property cannot be agreed upon between the owner thereof and the City, the same amount shall be fixed by arbitration, the owner of said incinerator and the City to each appoint one arbiter, and the two so appointed to choose a third, and the price fixed for said incinerator and said land shall be the price at which the City may acquire the same. If said incinerator is not taken over by the City before the expiration of the term during which the financer of said incinerator has been given the privilege of incinerating the garbage and rubbish collected in the City and County of San Francisco, said incinerator shall at that time revert without cost to the City and County of San Francisco and shall be the property of said City and County.

Be It Resolved, That the person, firm or corporation given the exclusive franchise or privilege of financing or operating said incinerator, be required to furnish a bond in such amount as this Board may require, guaranteeing that said incinerator will be constructed according to accepted specifications, and that said person, firm or corporation operating the same will perform its contract with said City and County of San Francisco for the full term thereof or until said incinerator is taken over by said City and County.

Further Resolved, That the Board of Supervisors select the type of incinerator to be constructed and that the Board of Public Works have supervision of said construction. We feel that although private capital may finance this plant, nevertheless, we view it as a quasi public utility from the fact that the plant will eventually revert to the City or may be purchased by the City at any time after completion; hence we recommend that all possible safeguards be thrown about it.

Type of Incinerator.

We recommend that any incinerator constructed have the following fundamental requirements, as we deem the same necessary for a suitable incinerator:

1. An incinerator must have good general formation and architectural design, good working conditions, and require a minimum amount of labor.

2. The plant must destroy rubbish and garbage in a sanitary and inoffensive manner, with complete destruction at minimum cost. If an incinerator is insanitary and offensive it fails in its principles and is a total loss. For that reason the initial cost is not altogether the determining factor.

3. The furnace of the incinerator must preferably be of brick type, thus giving better radiation.

4. The plant must be such that there will be no interference or delay in the collection of refuse or in delivering it to the plant. The cheapest plant to operate and keep in repair is one which has a uniform, regulated operation. Mechanical feed and automatic hoppers are therefore essential.

5. The incinerator must be equipped with shaker grates, the latter preventing clinkers. Clinkers are the bane of most incinerators. The

shaker grates should operate over an ash pit with a special drop for
cans and non-combustible substances.

6. A single-cell furnace fails of efficiency for want of mutual assistance; for that reason a four-cell furnace is preferable, and the committee recommends it, as we feel that the mutual assistance type is
of great help in the complete destruction of garbage.

7. The baffle wall is another important requirement of the good
incinerator. The baffle wall increases the efficiency of a furnace by
changing the direction of the flow of the gases, which breaks stratification, thus greatly increasing the distances the gases must travel, so
that those gases are retained for a longer period. Great additional
heat is utilized by the retention of the gas.

Whereas, your committee has found the type of incinerator built
by the Superior Incinerator Company for the city of Chicago in 1928
to embody the above-described qualifications, and a model for modern
refuse burners. We attach the accompanying specifications provided
through the courtesy of the city engineer of Chicago, L. Gayton. These
are the major specifications for the incinerator which we recommend
for San Francisco. We recommend the Superior type of incinerator,
or its equal.

Resolved, That whether the City constructs the incinerator itself,
or permits it to be privately financed, that a plant embodying the
above-mentioned features be adhered to, for the reason that the features mentioned are absolutely necessary from both a sanitary and an
economical standpoint.

Resolved, That the Board of Public Works be directed to have plans
and specifications made from the attached specifications and call for
bids for an incinerator that will burn 800 tons of garbage or rubbish
in twenty-four hours and award contract for said incinerator. We
further recommend that the person, firm or corporation financing said
incinerator shall have the exclusive privilege of incinerating the
garbage and rubbish in San Francisco upon the terms and conditions
hereinbefore set forth, for a period of not more than twenty-five years,
at a cost not to exceed one dollar per ton.- In case the plant is privately financed, we recommend that the name of the company awarded
the contract for the erection of an incinerator be required to provide
a bond in a sufficient sum to guarantee specific performance of contract; and we further recommend that the name of the company
awarded the contract to build this incinerator be embodied in the
franchise, permit or agreement, and that said incinerator be built by
said company.

MINORITY RESOLUTION ON SUBJECT OF INCINERATOR.

The following was also presented, copies ordered sent to members
and subject matter made Special Order of Business for 3 p. m. next
Monday.

Whereas, the electors of the City and County of San Francisco did,
at the general election held on the 5th day of November, 1929, express
and declare as their policy that the garbage collected in the City and
County of San Francisco should be disposed of by incineration; and

Whereas, in order to carry out said policy as so declared and expressed it is necessary that an incinerator be constructed in the City
and County of San Francisco for the purpose of incinerating the garbage collected therein; and

Whereas, there is urgent necessity that said incinerator should be
constructed without further delay; and

Whereas, the limit of taxation fixed by the Charter of the City and
County of San Francisco will not permit the levying of a sufficient
amount of tax to defray the cost of the construction of said incinerator; and

Whereas, it is the sense of the Board of Supervisors that, in view
of the large bond issue that must be submitted to the people during the

year 1930 for the purpose of acquiring the properties of the Pacific Gas and Electric Company and Great Western Power Company heretofore evaluated by the State Railroad Commission of California, that no additional bond issues should be submitted for approval until after said bond issues for the acquisition of the properties of said Pacific Gas and Electric Company and Great Western Power Company are disposed of; now, therefore, be it

Resolved, That the Board of Supervisors of the City and County of San Francisco does hereby declare that an incinerator should be constructed by private capital under the following conditions:

(a) That said incinerator should be constructed at or near the site of the present incinerator at Fifteenth and De Haro streets, either upon the property belonging to the City or upon privately owned property, and if constructed upon property now owned or hereafter acquired by the City that a reasonable rental should be paid by the person, firm or corporation erecting and operating said incinerator.

(b) That said incinerator should have a capacity of incinerating at least eight hundred tons of garbage per day in the most up-to-date and economical manner, and without necessitating the segregation of the wet from the dry garbage by the householders of the City and County, and without any discharge of odor or undue amount of smoke, and with the least possible amount of unconsumed material remaining after said incineration.

(c) That the person, firm or corporation constructing or operating said incinerator shall agree with the City and County that in return for an exclusive franchise to incinerate the garbage of the City and County for a period of 25 years that said garbage will be incinerated at a price not to exceed $1.00 per ton, and said City and County may acquire and take over said incinerator and all of the equipment thereof and the land upon which the same is situated, if said land is not already owned by the City, at the cost thereof less a reasonable amount for depreciation on said incinerator and equipment figured as of the date on which the same may be taken over by the City, and that if the amount to be paid for said incinerator and equipment and said property cannot be agreed upon between the owner thereof and the City, the said amount shall be fixed by arbitration, the owner of said incinerator and the City to each appoint one arbiter, and the two so appointed to choose a third, and the price fixed by two of said three arbiters for said incinerator and said land shall be the price at which the City may acquire the same, and that if said incinerator is not taken over by the City before the expiration of the term of 25 years for which the constructor of said incinerator has been given the privilege of incinerating the garbage collected in the City and County of San Francisco that said incinerator and all its equipment, and the land on which the same is situated, shall revert to and become the property of the City and County at the expiration of said term of 25 years without charge or payment of any kind.

(d) That the person, firm or corporation erecting said incinerator shall be given the exclusive privilege, for a period of at least twenty-five years, of incinerating all garbage collected in the City and County of San Francisco, with the exception of that character of garbage commonly known as "swill," which may be collected from hotels, restaurants and other similar places, provided that said swill must also be incinerated if circumstances require the disposition of the same by incineration.

(e) That the person, firm or corporation given the privilege of erecting said incinerator, shall file with the Board of Supervisors a bond, in such sum as the Board of Supervisors shall direct, for the completion of said incinerator in accordance with the plans and specifications submitted therefor, as well as an additional bond that said incinerator will properly incinerate all garbage under the provisions contained in any agreement for the construction thereof, and that said person, firm or corporation constructing said incinerator will, when given the exclusive privilege of incinerating the garbage collected in the City and County of San Francisco, perform his contract with said City and County for the full term thereof or until said incinerator is taken over by said City and County; be it

Further Resolved, That any and all persons offering to construct said incinerator shall present to the Board of Supervisors with any offer to construct the same, full and complete plans and specifications showing the construction of the same in detail, and the character and kind of material used in and about said construction, and shall, in addition thereto, specify the price or charge which shall be made for the incineration of said garbage, but in no case in excess of $1 per ton; and be it

Further Resolved, That, for the purpose of carrying out and making effective the terms of this resolution, the Board of Public Works, through the City Engineer, be directed to forthwith report to this Board the most feasible site at or near the site of the present inciner-ator, which may be found available for the construction and mainte-nance of said incinerator, and the approximate cost at which said site may be obtained, if the same is not already owned by the City, and that upon a site for said incinerator being agreed upon by this Board, that the said Board of Public Works, through the City Engi-neer, be directed to make suitable borings and investigations to ascer-tain if said site is suitable for the purpose mentioned; and be it

Further Resolved, That, upon a suitable site being determined for the construction of said incinerator, this Board enact suitable legislation calling for the receipt of proposals for the construction of said incinerator and for the incineration of the garbage collected in the City and County, and authorizing and entering into a contract with the person, firm or corporation who will construct said incin-crator, according to the plans and specifications deemed most bene-ficial to the City by the City Engineer and such engineering experts and specialists in garbage incineration as he may select as consultants, and who will agree to incinerate the garbage collected in said City and County at the least possible cost, not exceeding $1 per ton, and with the greatest return for the privilege of so doing, said privilege to exist for a period of not longer than twenty-five years. That the least amount to be paid to the City and County for the privilege of in-cinerating said garbage shall be three per cent. of the annual net receipts of said incinerator.

Mayor Authorized to Take Official Cognizance of the Death of Notable Persons, Arrival of Distinguished Visitors, Etc.

Supervisor Gallagher moved that the chairman of the Finance Com-mittee be authorized to appoint committees during Board meetings on notice of death of notable persons, arrival of distinguished visitors or any occasion calling for official recognition.

Motion *carried.*

St. Patrick's Day Celebration.

Supervisor Gallagher, on behalf of the St. Patrick's Day Celebration Committee, thanked the Board for the Market street decorations and music and requested that a committee of the Board be appointed to participate in the parade and represent the City government on Sun-day, March 16, 1930, leaving the Civic Center at 9:30, thence to Sacred Heart Church, where high mass will be celebrated.

Supervisors Rossi, Toner and Roncovieri were appointed to attend.

ADJOURNMENT.

There being no further business, the Board at 6:30 p. m. adjourned.

J. S. DUNNIGAN, Clerk.

Approved by the Board of Supervisors April 21, 1930.

Pursuant to Resolution No. 3402 (New Series) of the Board of Supervisors of the City and County of San Francisco, I, John S. Dunnigan, ereby certify that the foregoing are true and correct copies of the ournals of Proceedings of said Board of the dates thereon stated and pproved as recited.

JOHN S. DUNNIGAN,
Clerk of the Board of Supervisors.
City and County of San Francisco.

Vol. 25—New Series No. 12

Monday, March 17, 1930

Journal of Proceedings
Board of Supervisors

City and County of San Francisco

The Recorder Printing and Publishing Company
337 Bush Street, S. F.

JOURNAL OF PROCEEDINGS
BOARD OF SUPERVISORS

MONDAY, MARCH 17, 1930, 2 P. M.

In Board of Supervisors, San Francisco, Monday, March 17, 1930, 2 p. m.

CALLING THE ROLL.

The roll was called and the following Supervisors were noted present:

Supervisors Andriano, Canepa, Colman, Havenner, Hayden, McSheehy, Miles, Peyser, Roncovieri, Rossi, Stanton, Suhr, Toner—13.

Absent—Supervisors Shannon, Spaulding—2.

Supervisor Gallagher noted present at 2:15 p. m., at No. 7 on Calendar.

Supervisor McGovern noted present at 2:25 p. m., at No. 7 on Calendar.

Supervisor Power noted present at 2:15 p. m., at No. 7 on Calendar.

Quorum present.

His Honor Mayor Rolph presiding.

APPROVAL OF JOURNAL.

The Journal of Proceedings of the previous meeting was laid over for approval until next meeting.

ROLL CALL FOR PETITIONS AND COMMUNICATIONS.

Appropriations for Memorial Grove.

March 14, 1930.

The Board of Supervisors, Supervisors' Chambers, City Hall.

Gentlemen: Referring to an article appearing in the press on Tuesday, March 11, 1930, concerning the appropriation of $6,000 to the organization known as "The Native Sons and Daughters" for the provision of a doughboy statue in Memory Grove, Golden Gate Park.

While San Francisco Chapter No. 1, Gold Star Mothers of America, rejoices in any improvements thru which San Francisco may honor her hero dead, we deeply deplore and object to any drawing on the fund of $10,000 allotted for the nourishment of 700 trees now planted in Heroes' Grove, Golden Gate Park.

This same Chapter earnestly protests the action of the Board of Supervisors in this matter. Since 1919 Mrs. Leah H. Davis, now Past President, has labored indefatigably for funds to complete this grove. In 1928 an appropriation of $30,000 was set aside by this City for this project, in payments of $10,000 each of three consecutive issues.

Possibly an error has been made in conflicting Heroes' Grove with Memory Grove.

Therefore, be it

Resolved, That San Francisco Chapter No. 1 of the Gold Star Mothers of America does hereby respectfully request a hearing on this matter at an early date; and be it

Further Resolved, That copies of this resolution be forwarded to the Mayor and the Board of Supervisors of San Francisco and to the Park Commissioners.

EMILY ANDREWS,
President.

MAY F. BRUKER,
Recording Secretary.

(Mrs. Leda H. Davis, Past President, was heard at length on foregoing matter.)

Supervisor Andriano moved that the following be made part of the
record. No objection. *So ordered.*

In re Incinerator Proposals.

March 4, 1930.

Hon. J. M. Toner, M. D., Chairman Health Committee, Board of Supervisors, San Francisco, California.

Dear Sir: The San Francisco Bureau of Governmental Research
understands, from reports in the press, that the Health Committee has
three proposals under consideration relative to the problem of garbage
disposal: (1) whether the City shall finance and build (and perhaps
operate) a municipal incinerator; (2) whether the construction and
operation of an incinerator by private interests shall be recommended;
and (3) whether an appropriation of $25,000 to the Bureau of Engi-
neering shall be recommended to defray the cost of preparing plans
and specifications for a new incinerator pending determination of the
question of public or private financing, construction and operation.

The Bureau has been engaged for the past two years in a study of
local garbage problems, with particular reference to collection. It has
accumulated a considerable amount of data and information on this
phase of the subject, and, incidentally, various data on the subject of
garbage and refuse disposal. The facts, conclusions and recommendations derived from this study will be made public at the earliest possible date in the form of a report to the Board of Public Health.

At this time the Bureau wishes to submit to you such excerpts from
this forthcoming report as deal with the question of garbage and refuse
disposal, now pending before your committee, with the thought that
these may be helpful. They are as follows:

A new incinerator is an admitted necessity. The incinerator now
being used has been condemned for a number of years as being a
nuisance and as being inadequate. An injunction, held in abeyance
pending the development of plans by the City for the construction of
a new incinerator, will ultimately compel its abandonment.

At the November, 1929, election the vote of the people on the various
questions of refuse collection and disposal policy (1) opposed municipal collection of garbage and refuse, (2) established incineration as
the disposal policy to be followed by the City, (3) rejected fill-and-cover
as an alternative disposal method, and (4) opposed both private construction and public construction of an incinerator, the effect of this
conflicting vote being to leave the matter open for determination by
the Board of Supervisors.

The cost of a new incinerator, including land, is estimated as
$1,000,000. With the impracticability or impossibility of appropriating
such a sum in the 1930-31 budget (equivalent to an added tax rate of
about 12 cents per $100), and the practical certainty, as evidenced by
the November vote, that a bond issue for such purpose would fail to
secure the necessary two-thirds vote, it is considered by the Bureau
that the immediate solution of the disposal problem involves the construction and operation of an incinerator by private interests under
a long-time franchise or contract, under which the City will be given
the right to acquire and operate the plant at any time.

The two phases of refuse collection and disposal are closely allied;
therefore, the efficiency and economy of operation in each is dependent
to a certain degree on the methods used in both. It is our opinion
that unless the collectors—who, from the standpoint of health and
sanitation, should be required to enter into a single contract with the
City for refuse and garbage collection—can develop proposals, acceptable to the City, for such private construction and operation of an
incinerator, such private operation will constitute a source of unending friction between the individual collectors, the private operator of
the incinerator, and the City. Under an incinerator contract with

someone other than the refuse collectors the City would undoubtedly be required to assume the obligation of seeing that all refuse collected is delivered to the incinerator, particularly combustible refuse, which would be in conflict with the present salvaging practices of the scavengers and would embroil the City, as the regulating agency, in unending regulatory difficulties.

The 1927 garbage ordinance, among other things, fixed $1 per ton as the maximum rate that may be charged for the incineration of refuse. Incinerator revenues derived from the charge of $1 per ton paid by the scavengers according to tonnage of refuse delivered by each, amounts to approximately $180,000 per year. Labor charges for incineration operation and disposal of residue after incineration approximate $147,000, and other costs of operation and maintenance, $30,000, leaving a surplus of about $3,000. The present incinerator operating costs are, therefore, practically $1 per ton. This plant, however, designed for a capacity of 400 tons per 16-hour day, handles 600 tons daily, incinerating only about 60 per cent of the total refuse, leaving about 40 per cent as excess residue to be hauled away and used for fill.

In the event of the construction of a new incinerator by private capital the disposal cost will probably have to be increased if the initial cost approximates $1,000,000. The present rate of $1.00 per ton may be inadequate to cover maintenance and operating costs for the complete combustion of materials. In addition, interest and amortization charges will probably amount to 8 to 10 per cent a year on the initial cost of a new plant—a fixed charge of, say, $100,000 per year for a million-dollar plant.

Modern incinerators have been and are being operated at or near the $1 per ton figure; however, these figures, as far as is known, do not include overhead or capital charges, and usually apply to incinerators located in small communities or in cities requiring segregation, where only the combustible rubbish is incinerated. In Toronto, Canada, where ashes and incombustibles are segregated and the kitchen refuse is wrapped, the labor and maintenance cost for incineration in a recently constructed Sterling incinerator was $1.12 per ton in 1928. The total cost of this plant was $550,100, and the total tonnage handled in 1928 was 80,471 tons, which would make the capital charges about 70 cents per ton. This, added to the $1.12 per ton for labor and maintenance, gives a total cost of $1.82 per ton for disposal. A modern plant at Buffalo, N. Y., is operating at a cost of $1.61 per ton, not including capital charges. Here, also, the incombustibles are segregated and the wet garbage is wrapped.

These figures indicate that the disposal costs for a new plant, including interest and amortization charges, may be considerably more than the $1 per ton now charged. With mixed garbage having a high moisture content, as is the case in San Francisco, the difficulty and the cost of incineration is considerably increased.

If the $1 per ton disposal charge, specified as a maximum by the 1927 ordinance, is inadequate, (1) an increased rate must be paid voluntarily by the collectors, or (2) a subsidy from the City would be necessary to make up the difference, or (3) the $1 maximum specified by initiative ordinance must be changed, requiring vote of the people on the amendment or repeal of the 1927 initiative ordinance.

If the latter course is followed and a new ordinance drafted the Bureau feels that the City should place both the collection and the disposal of refuse on a contract basis, preferably with the same contractor, until such time as the City may find it necessary or desirable to undertake both collection and disposal as municipal functions.

The proposal to appropriate $25,000 to the Bureau of Engineering to defray the cost of preparing plans and specifications for a new incinerator, pending determination of the question of public or private financing, construction and operation, seems premature at this time in view of the probability that the plant will be privately constructed. In lieu thereof the compilation by the City Engineer of a "schedule of minimum requirements" for incinerator construction and operation' for San Francisco would act as a bar to undesirable or experimental types of plant, would establish a minimum basis for bidders in the preparation of their own plans and specifications, and would seem to be all that the City requires at the present time. Such a schedule would tend to limit the field, as far as the type of plant is concerned, to incinerators of reliable construction, and yet allow sufficient individuality of design to provide competitive bidding. The later selection and approval of the plans and specifications representing the type of plant best adapted to San Francisco's needs should be in charge of the City Engineer, and an appropriation for such purpose might be required when bids are received.

Respectfully submitted,

SAN FRANCISCO BUREAU· OF GOVERNMENTAL RESEARCH.
By WM. H. NANRY, Director.

Report of Joint Committee on Streets and Street Lighting in re Lighting Standards.

Supervisor Power presented the following:

March 17, 1930.

Honorable Board of Supervisors, City and County of San Francisco, City Hall.

Gentlemen: Your Committee on Streets and Street Lighting begs leave to report that it has acted favorably upon the following motion offered by Supervisor Gallagher at its meeting on the 14th instant, to-wit: That the street-lighting specifications be rereferred to the City Engineer with the request that he draw designs for double and single bracket concrete standards, centrifugally spun; a design for a cast-iron standard in two pieces; a bronze standard; a combination bronze and concrete standard; an all-steel standard, and a standard of the taper tube type, single and double design.

Respectfully submitted,

JAMES E. POWER,
VICTOR J. CANEPA,
ANDREW J. GALLAGHER,
Joint Committee on Streets and Street Lighting.

City Engineer to Draw Designs for Lighting Standards.

Supervisor Power presented:

Resolution No. 32234 (New Series), as follows:

Resolved, That the street-lighting specifications be rereferred to the City Engineer, with the request that he draw designs for the following types: Double and single bracket concrete standards, centrifugally spun; a design for a cast-iron standard in two pieces; a bronze standard; a combination bronze and concrete standard; an all-steel standard, and a standard of the taper tube type, single and double design.

Adopted by the following vote:

Ayes—Supervisors Canepa, Gallagher, Hayden, McSheehy, Miles, Peyser, Power, Roncovieri, Rossi, Suhr, Toner—11.

Noes—Supervisors Andriano, McGovern, Stanton—3.

Absent—Supervisors Colman, Havenner, Shannon, Spaulding—4.

Reduction in Lighting Rate.

Supervisor Stanton presented:

Communication, from the Pacific Gas and Electric Company, calling attention to its voluntary reduction in certain classes of street-lighting rates.

Referred to Lighting Committee.

UNFINISHED BUSINESS.

Final Passage.

The following matters. heretofore passed for printing, were taken up and *finally passed* by the following vote:

Authorizations.

On recommendation of Finance Committee.

Resolution No. 32198 (New Series), as follows:

Resolved, That the following amounts be and the same are hereby authorized to be expended out of the hereinafter mentioned funds in payment to the following named claimants, to-wit:

Bernal Cut Construction Fund.

(1) MacDonald & Kahn, Inc., thirteenth payment, improvement of Bernal Cut (claim dated March 5, 1930).........$25,500.00

Boulevard Bond Issue Construction Fund.

(2) Municipal Construction Company, improvement of Key avenue from Bay Shore boulevard to existing pavement (claim dated March 5, 1930) ....$ 986.00

(3) Eaton & Smith, ninth payment, improvement of Junipero Serra boulevard from Sloat boulevard to county line (claim dated March 5, 1930) 14,100.00

(4) Hanrahan Company, second payment, improvement of Alemany boulevard, section D-1, Sickles to Orizaba avenues (claim dated March 5, 1930) 10,200.00

County Road Fund.

(5) J. O'Shea, Inc., teams furnished for account of street reconstruction (claim dated Feb. 26, 1930).................$ 660.00

(6) Henry Cowell Lime & Cement Company, cement for street reconstruction (claim dated Feb. 27, 1930) 677.50

(7) The Texas Company, gasoline furnished for account of street reconstruction (claim dated Feb. 26, 1930).......... 784.03

(8) Louis J. Cohn, paving and street reconstruction, Harrison and Alameda streets, Treat avenue at Alameda and at Florida streets, Division street between Bryant and Florida streets, etc. (claim dated March 4, 1930)................. 3,379.26

(9) E. J. & M. J. Treacy, improvement of Havelock street between Edna street and Circular avenue (claim dated March 4, 1930) 1,557.50

(10) Municipal Construction Company, improvement of Josiah avenue and Ridge lane (claim dated March 4, 1930)..... 962.05

(11) Bode Gravel Company, gravel for street reconstruction (claim dated Feb. 28, 1930) 1,466.60

(12) Pacific Coast Aggregates, Inc., gravel for street reconstruction (claim dated March 4, 1930) 607.51

Municipal Railway Fund.

(13) Market Street Railway Company, repairs to crossing and paving, Market and First streets (claim dated Feb. 27, 1930) ....$ 700.58

1928 Hetch Hetchy Construction Fund.

(14) J. H. Creighton, truck hire (claim dated Feb. 28, 1930) . $ 2,143.57

(15) Consolidated Mills Company, Inc. (First National Bank of Eugene, Oregon, assignee), for lumber furnished (claim dated Feb. 27, 1930) 1,100.78

(16) Del Monte Meat Company, meat furnished (claim dated Feb. 28, 1930) 927.97

(17) Gunite Construction Company, one cement gun (claim dated Feb. 28, 1930) 800.00

(18) The A. T. Herr Supply Company, 50 Koppel mine cars (claim dated Feb. 27, 1930) 3,477.54

(19) Owen-Oregon Lumber Company (claim dated Feb. 27, 1930) 607.64

(20) Pioneer Rubber Mills, hose (claim dated Feb. 27, 1930)   804.69
(21) Santa Cruz Portland Cement Company, cement (claim
dated Feb. 27, 1930) 1,052.00
(22) Soule Steel Company, steel and iron (claim dated Feb.
28, 1930) 899.00
(23) Wilsey-Bennett Company, butter, etc. (claim dated Feb.
27, 1930) 731.30
(24) Chain Belt Company, chain belt (claim dated March 3,
1930) 819.36
(25) A. S. Cameron Steam Pump Works, pump parts (claim
dated March 3, 1930) 617.70
(26) Commercial Shearing & Stamping Company, 1040 Tunel
Liner plates, bolts, angle splice bars, etc. (claim dated
March 1, 1930) 6,906.89
(27) Del Monte Meat Company, meat (claim dated March 3,
1930) 703.04
(28) Grier & Mead, six storage battery locomotives, batteries
with containers (claim dated March 3, 1930)............. 8,750.00
(29) Ingersoll-Rand Company of California, machinery parts
(claim dated March 1, 1930) 807.87
(30) Owen-Oregon Lumber Company, lumber (claim dated
March 3, 1930) 607.64
(31) Pacific Coast Steel Corporation, reinforcing steel (claim
dated March 3, 1930) 2,379.80
(32) Pioneer Rubber Mills, hose and couplings (claim dated
March 1, 1930) 1,159.67
(33) Santa Cruz Portland Cement Company (claim dated
March 3, 1930) 4,044.00
(34) Western Butchers' Supply Company, refrigerating plant
(claim dated March 1, 1930) 1,201.00
(35) Wilsey-Bennett Company, butter, eggs, etc. (claim dated
March 3, 1930) 874.54

1929 *Sewer Bond Construction Fund.*

(36) Clinton Construction Company, first payment, construction of Alemany boulevard storm drain (claim dated March
5, 1930) ....$ 7,500.00

Hetch Hetchy Power Operative Fund.

(37) Hetch Hetchy Construction Fund, 1928, for materials,
supplies and equipment furnished and services rendered for
month of January, 1930 (claim dated Feb. 27, 1930).......$ 5,862.25

Special School Tax.

(38) James W. Reid, final payment for architectural services
for Marina Elementary School (claim dated March 4, 1930).$ 1,539.17
(39) Alta Electric Company, seventh payment, electrical work
for Park-Presidio Junior High School (claim dated March 4,
1930) 2,179.69
(40) Meyer Bros., seventh payment, general construction of
Park-Presidio Junior High School (claim dated March 4,
1930) 31,180.23
(41) Scott Company, seventh payment, mechanical equipment
for Park-Presidio Junior High School (claim dated March
4, 1930) 13,118.25
(42) Scott Company, sixth payment, plumbing and gasfitting
for Park-Presidio Junior High School (claim dated March
4, 1930) 2,808.53
(43) Jacks & Irvine, ninth payment, general construction of
Roosevelt Junior High School (claim dated March 4, 1930) 26,565.97
(44) Larsen & Larsen, third payment, brick work, etc., for
Roosevelt Junior High School (claim dated March 4, 1930). 17,908.88
(45) Scott Co., seventh payment, mechanical equipment of

Roosevelt Junior High School (claim dated March 4, 1930).. 5,007.38

(46) Scott Co., seventh payment, plumbing and gas-fitting for Roosevelt Junior High School (claim dated March 4, 1930) 1,804.80

Auditorium Fund.

(47) Concert Management Arthur Judson, Inc., for services of Giovanni Martinelli, tenor soloist, concert of March 29, 1930 (claim dated March 7, 1930)........................$ 2,000.00

General Fund, 1929-1930.

(48) Associated Charities, widows' pensions (claim dated March 7, 1930) ....$ 8,134.10

(49) Eureka Benevolent Society, widows' pensions (claim dated March 7, 1930) 921.42

(50) Little Children's Aid, widows' pensions (claim dated March 7, 1930) 6,248.31

(51) Sonoma State Home, maintenance of feeble-minded, month of December, 1929 (claim dated Feb. 17, 1930).... 10,300.00

(52) Sonoma State Home, maintenance of feeble-minded, month of January, 1930 (claim dated Feb. 17, 1930)...... 10,080.00

(53) Duncan Matheson, Treasurer, for settlement with State of California, for account of maintenance of narcotics at various institutions, period May to November, 1929 (claim dated Dec. 31, 1929)................................. 10,175.00

(54) San Francisco Chronicle, official advertising, Board of Public Works (claim dated March 4, 1930)............... 574.98

(55) San Francisco Chronicle, official advertising, Board of Supervisors (claim dated March 10, 1930)............. 2,187.43

(56) Spring Valley Water Co., rental of Harding Park, July 1, 1929, to March 3, 1930 (claim dated Feb. 21, 1930).... 4,041.67

(57) The Texas Co., gasoline furnished Police Department (claim dated Feb. 28, 1930)........................... 1,243.06

(58) California Construction Co., improvement of City's portion of Short street between Market and Yukon streets (claim dated March 4, 1930)........................... 773.11

(59) Chas. L. Harney, improvement of Thirty-first avenue between Kirkham and Lawton streets, and crossing of Thirty-first avenue and Lawton street (claim dated March 4, 1930) 3,397.00

(60) E. J. and M. J. Treacy, grading, paving, etc., on Twenty-sixth street between York and Hampshire streets (claim dated March 4, 1930) 1,930.00

(61) Richfield Oil Co. of California, fuel oil furnished Hall of Justice and Civic Center Power House (claim dated Feb. 26, 1930) 1,897.16

(62) Healey & Donaldson, tobacco furnished Laguna Honda Home (claim dated March 6, 1930)...................... 1,811.16

(63) Sussman, Wormser Co., sugar for Laguna Honda Home (claim dated March 6, 1930).......................... 2,505.75

(64) H. E. Teller Co., coffee for Laguna Honda Home (claim dated March 6, 1930)............................... 626.25

Ayes—Supervisors Andriano, Canepa, Colman, Gallagher, Havenner, Hayden, McGovern, McSheehy, Miles, Peyser, Power, Roncovieri, Rossi, Stanton, Suhr, Toner—16.

Absent—Supervisors Shannon, Spaulding—2.

Payment for School Lands.

Also, Resolution No. 32199 (New Series), as follows:

Resolved, That the sum of $5,250 be and the same is hereby set aside, appropriated and authorized to be expended out of School Lands Fund, and authorized in payment to Wm. J. Robinson; being payment for land and improvements required for school purposes, and situate, commencing at a point on the southerly line of Twenty-fifth street, distant thereon 240 feet westerly from the westerly line of Noe street, running thence westerly along the southerly line of Twenty-fifth street 28 feet; thence at a right angle southerly 114 feet; thence at a right angle easterly 28 feet; thence at a right angle northerly 114 feet; as per acceptance of offer by Resolution No. 32147 (New Series). (Claim dated March 10, 1930.)

Ayes—Supervisors Andriano, Canepa, Colman, Gallagher, Havenner, Hayden, McGovern, McSheehy, Miles, Peyser, Power, Roncovieri, Rossi, Stanton, Suhr, Toner—16.

Absent—Supervisors Shannon, Spaulding—2.

Fixing Compensation of Attorneys for San Francisco Water Department at $12,000 Per Year.

Also, Resolution No. 32200 (New Series), as follows:

Whereas, the Board of Public Works of the City and County of San Francisco having made request upon the City Attorney that, pursuant to Section 10 of Ordinance No. 8691 (New Series), he appoint and detail an attorney to render legal service to the San Francisco Water Department, and said City Attorney having so detailed an attorney to render such service, and the compensation of said attorney so detailed having been approved by said Board of Public Works at the sum of $12,000 per annum, payable in equal monthly installments; now, therefore, be it

Resolved, That the compensation of said attorney so detailed by said City Attorney be and the same is hereby fixed at the sum of $12,000 per annum, payable in equal monthly installments from the revenues of said Water Department as an operating expense thereof.

Ayes—Supervisors Andriano, Canepa, Colman, Gallagher, Havenner, Hayden, McGovern, McSheehy, Miles, Peyser, Power, Roncovieri, Rossi, Stanton, Suhr, Toner—16.

Absent—Supervisors Shannon, Spaulding—2.

Appropriation, $26,000, for Improvement of Portola Drive, From Twenty-fourth Street to Fowler Avenue, Out of County Road Fund.

Also, Resolution No. 32201 (New Series), as follows:

Resolved, That the following amount be and the same is hereby set aside, appropriated and authorized to be expended out of the County Road Fund for the following purposes, to-wit:

The improvement of Portola drive, from Twenty-fourth street to Fowler avenue, $26,000.

Ayes—Supervisors Andriano, Canepa, Colman, Gallagher, Havenner, Hayden, McGovern, McSheehy, Miles, Peyser, Power, Roncovieri, Rossi, Stanton, Suhr, Toner—16.

Absent—Supervisors Shannon, Spaulding—2.

Appropriation for Improvement of Broadway, Westerly From Van Ness Avenue.

Also, Resolution No. 32202 (New Series), as follows:

Resolved, That the sum of $9,100 be and the same is hereby set aside, appropriated and authorized to be expended out of County Road Fund for the improvement of Broadway, westerly from Van Ness avenue.

Ayes—Supervisors Andriano, Canepa, Colman, Gallagher, Havenner, Hayden, McGovern, McSheehy, Miles, Peyser, Power, Roncovieri, Rossi, Stanton, Suhr, Toner—16.

Absent—Supervisors Shannon, Spaulding—2.

Appropriation for Employments, Traffic Bureau.

Also, Resolution No. 32203 (New Series), as follows:

Resolved, That the sum of $1,635 be and the same is hereby set aside, appropriated and authorized to be expended out of "Traffic Signals," etc., Budget Item No. 57, for employments and expense of the Traffic Bureau for the month of March, 1930.

Ayes—Supervisors Andriano, Canepa, Colman, Gallagher, Havenner, Hayden, McGovern, McSheehy, Miles, Peyser, Power, Roncovieri, Rossi, Stanton, Suhr, Toner—16.

Absent—Supervisors Shannon, Spaulding—2.

Appropriation, $6,000, Purchase of "The Dough Boy" Monument, Memorial Grove.

Also, Resolution No. 32204 (New Series), as follows:

Resolved, That the City and County of San Francisco enter into a contract with the Grove of Memory Association, Native Daughters of the Golden West and Native Sons of the Golden West, a corporation, for the erection, for and on behalf of the City and County of San Francisco, of a monument known as "The Dough Boy," which said monument shall, with the permission of the Board of Park Commissioners, be erected in the Grove of Memory in Golden Gate Park, at such place therein as said Board shall direct, and which said monument shall be erected in memory of the members of the United States Military Forces who gave up their lives in the World War; be it

Further Resolved, That the cost of said monument shall not exceed the sum of six thousand ($6,000) dollars, which said sum shall be payable when said monument shall be completed and erected to the satisfaction of the Board of Park Commissioners and the Board of Supervisors; be it

Further Resolved, That the Mayor and the Clerk of the Board of Supervisors be and they are hereby authorized and directed to execute the aforesaid agreement, for and on behalf of the City, and to agree upon the terms thereof pursuant to the provisions of this resolution; and be it

Further Resolved, That the sum of six thousand ($6,000) dollars be and the same is hereby appropriated from Budget Item No. 73, Account No. 1091, 1929-30 Budget, and authorized to be paid to said Grove of Memory Association, Native Daughters of the Golden West and Native Sons of the Golden West for the erection of said monument.

Ayes—Supervisors Andriano, Canepa, Colman, Gallagher, Havenner, Hayden, McGovern, McSheehy, Miles, Peyser, Power, Roncovieri, Rossi, Stanton, Suhr, Toner—16.

Absent—Supervisors Shannon, Spaulding—2.

Amendment to Food Terminal Ordinance.

On recommendation of Education, Parks and Playgrounds Committee.

Bill No. 8208, Ordinance No. 8710 (New Series), as follows:

Amending Ordinance No. 8140 (New Series), providing that wholesale food terminals, warehouses, freight yards and ferry terminals shall not be constructed or established, erected or constructed within a certain district in the City and County of San Francisco, and establishing the boundaries of said district, and providing for penalties for the violation of the provisions hereof, by including in said prohibited structures and callings airplane landings and hydroplane landings, and the landing of passengers from airplanes or hydroplanes.

Be it ordained by the People of the City and County of San Francisco as follows:

That Ordinance No. 8140, the title of which is hereinbefore recited, is hereby amended to read as follows:

Section 1. No wholesale food terminal, warehouse, freight yard, or ferry terminal, or airplane landing or hydroplane landing, or any building or structure to be used as a wholesale food terminal, warehouse, freight yard, ferry terminal, airplane landing or hydroplane landing, shall be constructed, erected or established within the territory bounded on the north by the waters of San Francisco Bay, on the east by the westerly line of Van Ness avenue, on the south by Jackson street, and on the west by the westerly line of Lyon street, nor shall any structure for any of the purposes above mentioned be constructed or erected, projecting into the waters of the bay from the land included in the above described district.

Section 2. No building permit shall be issued or granted by the Board of Public Works for the erection, construction or alteration of any building, or structure, contrary to the provisions of this ordinance, and any permit so issued or granted shall be void.

Section 3. No certificate of occupancy shall be issued or granted by the Board of Health authorizing or permitting any person, firm or corporation to occupy or use any building or structure in place within the above bounded district for or as a wholesale food terminal, warehouse, freight yard or ferry terminal.

Section 4. Any person, firm or corporation violating any of the provisions of this ordinance shall be guilty of a misdemeanor, and upon the conviction thereof shall be punishable by a fine not to exceed $500.00 or by imprisonment in the County Jail not to exceed six months, or by both such fine and imprisonment. And any person, firm or corporation violating any of the provisions of this ordinance shall be deemed guilty of a separate offense for each and every day during any portion of which any violation of this ordinance is committed, permitted or continued by such person, firm or corporation.

Ayes—Supervisors Andriano, Canepa, Colman, Gallagher, Havenner, Hayden, McGovern, McSheehy, Miles, Peyser, Power, Roncovieri, Rossi, Stanton, Suhr, Toner—16.

Absent—Supervisors Shannon, Spaulding—2.

Automobile Supply Station, Frank Franchini, South Side of Twenty-fourth Street, 50 Feet West of Vicksburg Street.

On recommendation of Fire Committee.

Resolution No. 32205 (New Series), as follows:

Resolved, That Frank Franchini be and is hereby granted permission, revocable at will of the Board of Supervisors, to maintain and operate an automobile supply station on the south side of Twenty-fourth street, 50 feet west of Vicksburg street.

The rights granted under this resolution shall be exercised within six months, otherwise said permit shall become null and void.

Ayes—Supervisors Andriano, Canepa, Colman, Gallagher, Havenner, Hayden, McGovern, McSheehy, Miles, Peyser, Power, Roncovieri, Rossi, Stanton, Suhr, Toner—16.

Absent—Supervisors Shannon, Spaulding—2.

Automobile Supply Station, Wm. McDonald, Southeast Corner of Steiner and Eddy Streets.

Also, Resolution No. 32206 (New Series), as follows:

Resolved, That Wm. McDonald be and is hereby granted permission, revocable at will of the Board of Supervisors, to maintain and operate an automobile supply station at the southeast corner of Steiner and Eddy streets.

The rights granted under this resolution shall be exercised within six months, otherwise said permit shall become null and void.

Ayes—Supervisors Andriano, Canepa, Colman, Gallagher, Havenner, Hayden, McGovern, McSheehy, Miles, Peyser, Power, Roncovieri, Rossi, Stanton, Suhr, Toner—16.

Absent—Supervisors Shannon, Spaulding—2.

Laundry Permit.

Also, Resolution No. 32207 (New Series), as follows:

Resolved, That the following revocable permit be and is hereby granted:

Laundry.

Julie Pouquette, 722 Bush street.

The rights granted under this resolution shall be exercised within six months, otherwise said permit shall become null and void.

Ayes—Supervisors Andriano, Canepa, Colman, Gallagher, Havenner, Hayden, McGovern, McSheehy, Miles, Peyser, Power, Roncovieri, Rossi, Stanton, Suhr, Toner—16.

Absent—Supervisors Shannon, Spaulding—2.

Blasting Permit, Lang Realty Company, Mt. Davidson.

Also, Resolution No. 32208 (New Series), as follows:

Resolved, That the Lang Realty Company be and is hereby granted permission, revocable at will of the Board of Supervisors, to explode blasts on private property situate on Mt. Davidson, west of Twin Peaks, adjoining Mt. Davidson Park; provided said permitee shall execute and file a good and sufficient bond in the sum of $5,000, as fixed by the Board of Public Works and approved by his Honor the Mayor, in accordance with Ordinance No. 1204; provided, also, that said blasts shall be exploded only between the hours of 7 a. m. and 6 p. m., and that the work of blasting shall be performed to the satisfaction of the Board of Public Works; and that if any of the conditions of this resolution be violated by said Lang Realty Company, then the privileges and all the rights accruing thereunder shall immediately become null and void.

Ayes—Supervisors Andriano, Canepa, Colman, Gallagher, Havenner, Hayden, McGovern, McSheehy, Miles, Peyser, Power, Roncovieri, Rossi, Stanton, Suhr, Toner—16.

Absent—Supervisors Shannon, Spaulding—2.

Establishing Underground District, Third Street, From East Line of Townsend Street to Channel, Approximately 942 Feet.

On recommendation of Lighting Committee.

Bill No. 8205, Ordinance No. 8711 (New Series), as follows:

Amending Order No. 214 (Second Series), entitled "Providing for placing wires and conduits underground in the City and County of San Francisco," by adding a new section, to be known as Section 1-ll.

Be it ordained by the People of the City and County of San Francisco as follows:

Section 1-ll. An additional district to those heretofore described within which it shall be unlawful to maintain poles and overhead wires after July 31, 1930, is hereby designated, to-wit:

Underground District No. 46. Third street, from the east line of Townsend street to Channel, approximately 942 feet.

Ayes—Supervisors Andriano, Canepa, Colman, Gallagher, Havenner, Hayden, McGovern, McSheehy, Miles, Peyser, Power, Roncovieri, Rossi, Stanton, Suhr, Toner—16.

Absent—Supervisors Shannon, Spaulding—2.

Establishing Underground District, Webster Street, From the South Side of Union Street to the North Side of Green Street, Approximately 275 Feet.

Also, Bill No. 8206, Ordinance No. 8712 (New Series), as follows:

Amending Order No. 214 (Second Series), entitled "Providing for placing wires and conduits underground in the City and County of San Francisco," by adding a new section, to be known as Section 1-mm.

Be it ordained by the People of the City and County of San Francisco as follows:

Section 1-mm. An additional district to those heretofore described, within which it shall be unlawful to maintain poles and overhead wires after September 1, 1930, is hereby designated, to-wit:

Underground District No. 47. Webster street, from the south side of Union street to the north side of Green street, approximately 275 feet.

Ayes—Supervisors Andriano, Canepa, Colman, Gallagher, Havenner, Hayden, McGovern, McSheehy, Miles, Peyser, Power, Roncovieri, Rossi, Stanton, Suhr, Toner—16.

Absent—Supervisors Shannon, Spaulding—2.

Amending License Ordinance to Facilitate Collection of Delinquent Taxes and Abandoning Exemption Clauses.

On recommendation of Police Committee.

Bill No. 8207, Ordinance No. 8713 (New Series), as follows:

Amending Section 2 of Ordinance No. 5132, as amended by Ordinance No. 8464 (New Series), entitled "Imposing license taxes on certain businesses, callings, trades or employments within the City and County of San Francisco."

Be it ordained by the People of the City and County of San Francisco as follows:

Section 1. Section 2 of Ordinance No. 5132 (New Series), the title of which is recited above, is hereby amended to read as follows:

License Payable in Advance—Where Payable—Penalty for Non-Payment.

Section 2. On and after April 1, 1930, all license taxes, unless, by ordinance, specifically provided otherwise, shall be due and payable quarterly in advance, and fall due on the first day of October, the first day of January, the first day of April and the first day of July in each calendar year, depending upon the particular quarter in which a licensee begins business. In all cases of licenses on new business collectible at periods other than the months of October, January, April and July, the Tax Collector shall pro rate on a monthly basis the amount of license fee due for any given quarter.

Whenever a license tax is imposed by ordinance it shall be unlawful to do or perform the act or to carry on the business, trade, profession or calling for which a license is required, or to own, keep or use the article or thing, for the owning, keeping or using of which a license is required, unless such license be first procured.

All licenses are payable, when due, at the office of the Tax Collector, in the City Hall, and if not paid within thirty (30) days after the same become due, the Tax Collector shall add 10 per cent to the amount of the license as a penalty for non-payment. If the license is not paid within sixty days after the same becomes due, the Tax Collector shall add 15 per cent to the amount of the license as a penalty for non-payment. If the license is not paid within ninety (90) days after the same becomes due, the Tax Collector shall add twenty-five per cent to the amount of the license as a penalty for non-payment. Provided, however, when a licensee has failed for a period of six months or more to pay a license fee, and has allowed the license to become delinquent for this or a longer period, the Tax Collector shall, in such instances, impose a penalty of fifty per cent on the total amount of license delinquent, and shall turn over a complete list of such licensees to the Chief of Police for arrest and prosecution under the provisions of this ordinance. Nothing shall permit the exemption of the penalties mentioned in this section.

Section 2. This ordinance shall take effect immediately.

Ayes—Supervisors Andriano, Canepa, Colman, Gallagher, Havenner, Hayden, McGovern, McSheehy, Miles, Peyser, Power, Roncovieri, Rossi, Stanton, Suhr, Toner—16.

Absent—Supervisors Shannon, Spaulding—2.

PRESENTATION OF BILLS AND ACCOUNTS.

Your Finance Committee, having examined miscellaneous demands not required by law to be passed to print, and amounting to $54,487.61, recommends same be allowed and ordered paid.

Approved by the following vote:

Ayes—Supervisors Andriano, Canepa, Colman, Gallagher, Havenner, Hayden, McGovern, McSheehy, Miles, Peyser, Power, Roncovieri, Rossi, Stanton, Suhr, Toner—16.

Absent—Supervisors Shannon, Spaulding—2.

NEW BUSINESS.

Passed for Printing.

The following matters were *passed for printing*:

Authorizations.

On recommendation of Finance Committee.

Resolution No. ———— (New Series) as follows:

Resolved, That the following amounts be and the same are hereby authorized to be expended out of the hereinafter mentioned funds in payment to the following named claimants, to-wit:

Library Fund.

(1) Foster & Futernick Company, binding Public Library books (claim dated Feb. 28, 1930) ....$ 1,375.10

(2) American Building Maintenance Company, janitor service for Public Libraries (claim dated Feb. 28, 1930) 810.00

(3) Technical Book Company, library books (claim dated Feb. 28, 1930) 845.16

(4) G. E. Stechert & Co., library books (claim dated Feb. 28, 1930) 2,376.35

(5) Sather Gate Book Shop, library books (claim dated Feb. 28, 1930) 1,546.42

(6) San Francisco News Company, library books (claim dated Feb. 28, 1930) 1,277.45

California Palace Legion of Honor—Appropriation 59

(7) Felix F. Schoenstein & Sons, furnishing electric heaters, wiring and circuits, and installing telephone system connecting all organ chambers (claim dated March 14, 1930).. 2,140.20

M. H. De Young Museum—Appropriation 58.

(8) P. J. Enright, heating and ventilating M. H. de Young Memorial Museum, fifth payment (claim dated March 14, 1930) ....$ 569.81

1929 *Hospital Bond Construction Fund.*

(9) John Reid, Jr., final payment, architectural services, Ward building "F," for Relief Home (claim dated March 12, 1930) ....$ 4,238.42

1928 *Hetch Hetchy Construction Fund.*

(10) Best Steel Casting Company, castings furnished Hetch Hetchy Water Construction (claim dated March 8, 1930)..$ 1,694.56

(11) Boiler Tank & Pipe Company, tunnel forms (claim dated March 10, 1930) 1,261.86

(12) Coos Bay Lumber Company, lumber (claim dated March 10, 1930) 3,515.33

(13) Del Monte Meat Company, meats (claim dated March 8, 1930) 1,289.28

(14) Ingersoll-Rand Company of California, machinery and pump parts (claim dated March 10, 1930)................. 3,359.91

(15) The Charles Nelson Company, lumber (claim dated March 10, 1930) 660.00

(16) Owen-Oregon Lumber Company, lumber (claim dated March 10, 1930) 600.86

(17) Pacific Coast Aggregates, Inc., concrete sand (claim dated March 8, 1930) 821.28

(18) Pacific Coast Steel Corporation, steel (claim dated March 10, 1930) 2,452.01

(19) Santa Cruz Portland Cement Company, cement (claim dated March 10, 1930) 2,630.00

(20) Shell Oil Company, gasoline and oils (claim dated March 8, 1930) 560.17

(21) United States Rubber Company, rubber boots, etc. (claim dated March 10, 1930) 1,815.50

(22) Western Pipe & Steel Company, riveted pipe (claim dated March 10, 1930) 1,881.65

Park Fund.

(23) Railway Express Agency, express charges on shipments (claim dated March 14, 1930) ....$ 693.65

Municipal Railway Fund.

(24) Pacific Gas & Electric Company, gas and electricity furnished Municipal Railway, for February (claim dated March 11, 1930) $40,026.11

(25) San Francisco City Employees Retirement System, to match contributions from Municipal Railway employees (claim dated March 7, 1930) 1,487.26

(26) San Francisco City Employees Retirement System, to match contributions from Municipal Railway employees (claim dated March 10, 1930) 7,149.19

(27) Panama Lamp & Commercial Company, electric lamps (claim dated March 10, 1930) 831.60

Boulevard Bonds.

(28) Eaton & Smith, tenth payment, improvement of 19th avenue extension from Sloat boulevard to Worcester avenue (claim dated March 12, 1930) $11,000.00

County Road Fund.

(29) Federal Construction Company, extra work in connection with improvement of Grand View avenue (claim dated March 10, 1930) ....$ 1,914.13

(30) Department of Public Works (Appropriation 33-B), reimbursement for asphalt labor used on street reconstruction work during February, 1930 (claim dated March 10, 1930). 2,937.48

Special School Tax.

(31) American Studios, gridiron and stage equipment for Galileo High School (claim dated March 11, 1930)........$ 3,481.00

(32) Park Commissioners, reimbursement for care of school grounds (claim dated March 11, 1930).................... 1,466.67

(33) D. A. Pancoast Company, "Van Duprin" type panic bolts, etc., for school buildings (claim dated March 11, 1930).... 888.90

(34) Miller & Pflueger, third payment, architectural services on Roosevelt Junior High School (claim dated March 12, 1930) 606.25

(35) W. H. Crim, ninth payment, architectural services on Park-Presidio Junior High School (claim dated March 12, 1930) 1,182.88

(36) San Francisco City Employees Retirement System, to match contributions from employees paid from Special School Tax (claim dated March 12, 1930) 886.88

Auditorium Fund.

(37) Musical Association of San Francisco, services of Sym-

phony Orchestra, concert of March 29, 1930 (claim dated
March 14, 1930) ....$ 2,000.00

The Water Revenue Fund.

(38) Revolving Fund, San Francisco Water Department, for
payments as provided by Section 13, Ordinance No. 8691
(New Series) (claim dated March 3, 1930).................$20,000.00

General Fund, 1929-1930.

(39) Joseph Hagan & Sons, burial of indigent dead (claim
dated March 13, 1930).....................................$ 851.00

(40) Herbert F. Dugan, drug sundries, San Francisco Hospital
(claim dated Feb. 28, 1930)...............................   1,826.06

(41) Sussman, Wormser & Co., groceries, San Francisco Hospital (claim dated Feb. 28, 1930).........................   3,079.90

(42) Fred L. Hilmer Co., butter, San Francisco Hospital
(claim dated Feb. 28, 1930)...............................   2,071.79

(43) San Francisco Dairy Co., milk, San Francisco Hospital
(claim dated Feb. 28, 1930)...............................   4,286.39

(44) C. Nauman & Co., produce, San Francisco Hospital (claim
dated Feb. 28, 1930)......................................   828.50

(45) L. Lagomarsino & Co., produce, San Francisco Hospital
(claim dated Feb. 28, 1930)...............................   996.24

(46) Eames Company, 100 sets bed casters, expansion adapters,
San Francisco Hospital (claim dated Feb. 28, 1930)........   520.00

(47) Richfield Oil Company, fuel oil, San Francisco Hospital
(claim dated Feb. 28, 1930)...............................   1,898.35

(48) Addressograph Company, partial payment on addressograph machinery, Department of Elections (claim dated
March 13, 1930)...   7,000.00

(49) Board of Park Commissioners, reimbursement for account of improvements to Palace of Fine Arts (claim dated
March 14, 1930)...   714.95

(50) Standard Gypsum Company, casting plaster, etc., for
the Palace of Fine Arts (claim dated March 14, 1930)......   810.50

(51) Clinton-Stephenson Construction Company, final payment, repairs to Palace of Fine Arts (claim dated March 14,
1930) 9,945.92

(52) William J. Quinn, police contingent expense for March
(claim dated March 10, 1930)..............................   750.00

(53) Wm. L. Hughson, one Ford touring auto for Police Department (claim dated March 10, 1930).....................   542.21

(54) St. Vincent's School, maintenance of minors (claim dated
March 10, 1930) 1,171.18

(55) Roman Catholic Orphanage, maintenance of minors
(claim dated March 10, 1930)..............................   1,938.13

(56) Albertinum Orphanage, maintenance of minors (claim
dated March 10, 1930).....................................   689.20

(57) Little Children's Aid, maintenance of minors (claim
dated March 10, 1930)..................................... 12,279.39

(58) Eureka Benevolent Society, maintenance of minors
(claim dated March 10, 1930)..............................   3,239.22

(59) Children's Agency, maintenance of minors (claim dated
March 12, 1930) 30,810.57

(60) Market Street Railway Company, eighth payment for
property at Frederick and Willard streets, Arguello boulevard and Golden Gate Park, per Ordinance No. 5830, New
Series (claim dated March 17, 1930).......................   7,750.00

(61) The Recorder Printing and Publishing Company, printing of Superior Court Calendars for February (claim dated
March 17, 1930)...   515.00

(62) The Recorder Printing and Publishing Company, printing of Supervisors' Calendar, Journal, etc. (claim dated
March 17, 1930)...   1,278.12

(63) Pacific Gas and Electric Company, street lighting, month
of February (claim dated March 17, 1930)................ 61,082.02

(64) Sonoma State Home, maintenance of feeble-minded
(claim dated March 17, 1930)......................... 10,500.00

(65) A. P. Jacobs, rental of premises No. 333 Kearny street,
March 3 to April 3, 1930 (claim dated March 17, 1930)...... 1,120.75

(66) National Surety Company, depository bond in favor of
Duncan Matheson, Treasurer, in amount of $1,000,000 for
funds on deposit in Bank of America, New York (claim dated
March 6, 1930).. 1,000.00

(67) National Surety Company, depository bond in favor of
Duncan Matheson, Treasurer, in amount of $250,000, for
funds on deposit in Bank of America, New York (claim
dated March 6, 1930)................................. 1,250.00

(68) The Mercury Press, 512 copies Street Railway Transportation Requirements of San Francisco (claim dated March 11,
1930) 1,000.00

(69) Department of Public Works, Bureau of Building Repair,
reimbursement for amount of painting material purchased
for account of traffic painting (claim dated March 10, 1930).   585.40

(70) The Texas Company, gasoline furnished for account of
street cleaning (claim dated March 10, 1930).............   512.85

(71) Spring Valley Water Company, water furnished public
buildings, February (claim dated March 10, 1930)........ 1,938.73

(72) Pacific Gas and Electric Company, lighting public buildings (claim dated March 11, 1930)...................... 5,327.19

(73 Pacific Gas and Electric Company, gas and electricity
furnished Fire Department (claim dated Feb. 28, 1930)..... 2,201.95

(74) Seagrave Corporation, Fire Department apparatus parts
(claim dated Feb. 28, 1930)........................... 1,068.85

(75) The Spring Valley Water Co., water for fire houses, installing hydrants and high-pressure water system (claim
dated Feb. 28, 1930)................................. 1,757.78

(76) Standard Oil Company of California, fuel oil, etc., for
Fire Department (claim dated Feb. 28, 1930)............   630.78

(77) The Texas Company, gasoline, etc., for Fire Department
(claim dated Feb. 28, 1930)........................... 1,219.36

Appropriation for Dredging Opposite the Baker Street and Pierce Street Sewer Outfalls.

Also, Resolution No. ———— (New Series), as follows:

Resolved, That the sum of $2,500 be and the same is hereby set aside,
appropriated and authorized to be expended out of "Extension and Reconstruction of Sewers," Budget Item 37, for the cost of dredging opposite the Baker street and Pierce street sewer outfalls.

Appropriations Out of County Road Fund.

Also, Resolution No. ———— (New Series), as follows:

Resolved, That the following amounts be and the same are hereby
set aside, appropriated and authorized to be expended out of County
Road Fund for the following purposes, to-wit:

(1) For portion of the cost of the improvement of Sanchez
street between Twenty-first and Hill streets, including the
crossings of Twenty-first and Hill streets with Sanchez
streets $4,500.00

(2) For the cost of widening the roadway of Fair avenue between Mission and Coleridge streets, by reducing the sidewalk from 10 to 7 feet, removal of existing basalt blocks,
repaving with concrete and performing the necessary conform work at Mission and Coleridge streets............. 2,400.00

Adopted.

The following resolution was *adopted*:

Appropriations Out of County Road Fund for Various Roadway Improvements.

On recommendation of Finance Committee.

Resolution No. 32209 (New Series), as follows:

Resolved, That the following amounts be and the same are hereby set aside, appropriated and authorized to be expended out of County Road Fund for the following purposes, to-wit:

(1) For the construction of temporary roadway on Twenty-fifth avenue southerly from Vicente street 400 feet, to be of rock, about 12 feet in width and 10 inches in depth......$ 250.00

(2) For construction of red rock macadam pavement, 20 feet in width and 120 feet long, with necessary 2 by 8-inch redwood headers, each side, on Marin street from easterly line of the Southern Pacific right of way to a line 120 feet easterly therefrom 200.00

(3) For cost of repairing pipe rail fence at Twenty-fifth and Collingwood streets, Sanchez street, south of Twentieth street, Cumberland and Sanchez streets, Sanchez street from Nineteenth to Cumberland streets, Liberty street from Church to Sanchez streets, Church street from Eighteenth to Nineteenth streets and Seventeenth street, west of Castro street 354.00

Ayes—Supervisors Andriano, Canepa, Colman, Gallagher, Havenner, Hayden, McGovern, McSheehy, Miles, Peyser, Power, Roncovieri, Rossi, Stanton, Suhr, Toner—16.

Absent—Supervisors Shannon, Spaulding—2.

Accepting Percentages of Receipts, Market Street Railway Company.

Also, Resolution No. 32210 (New Series), as follows:

Resolved, That the statements heretofore filed by the Market Street Railway Company showing gross receipts from passenger fares for the month of January, 1930, upon which percentages in the following amounts are due the City and County be and the same are hereby accepted, to-wit:

Parkside—Twentieth avenue, etc..................$521.74
Gough street 38.74
Parnassus avenue, etc............................. 243.99

Further Resolved, That the Market Street Railway Company is hereby directed to deposit with the Treasurer of the City and County the hereinabove mentioned sums, the same to be placed to the credit of the General Fund.

Ayes—Supervisors Andriano, Canepa, Colman, Gallagher, Havenner, Hayden, McGovern, McSheehy, Miles, Peyser, Power, Roncovieri, Rossi, Stanton, Suhr, Toner—16.

Absent—Supervisors Shannon, Spaulding—2.

Passed for Printing.

The following bill was *passed for printing*:

Creating Positions of Eight Welfare Investigators at a Salary of $150 Per Month Each.

On recommendation of Finance Committee.

Bill No. 8209, Ordinance No. ——— (New Series), as follows:

Creating the positions of eight welfare investigators in the County Welfare Department heretofore created by Ordinance No. 8542 (New Series), authorizing the appointment of said eight welfare investigators and fixing their compensation at $150 per month.

Be it ordained by the People of the City and County of San Francisco as follows:

Section 1. The positions of eight welfare investigators in the County Welfare Department heretofore created by Ordinance No. 8542 (New Series) are hereby created, and the appointment of said eight welfare investigators at $150 per month each by the Board of Supervisors is hereby authorized.

Section 2. This ordinance shall take effect immediately.

Adopted.

The following resolutions were *adopted*:

Accepting Offer to Sell Land for Sunset Boulevard.

On recommendation of Finance Committee.

Resolution No. 32211 (New Series), as follows:

Resolved, That the offer of sale made by the following named persons to sell to the City and County of San Francisco the following described land, required for the Sunset boulevard, for the sum set forth opposite their names, be accepted:

James F. Farrell and Mary Farrell, $3,000—All of Lot 41, Block 2389, as per the Assessor's Block Books of the City and County of San Francisco.

And the City Attorney is hereby authorized to examine the title to said property, and if the same is found satisfactory, to accept, on behalf of the City, deed conveying said property to the City, free and clear of all encumbrances, and to record said deed, together with a copy of this resolution, in the office of the Recorder of the City and County of San Francisco.

Ayes—Supervisors Andriano, Canepa, Colman, Gallagher, Havenner, Hayden, McGovern, McSheehy, Miles, Peyser, Power, Roncovieri, Rossi, Stanton, Suhr, Toner—16.

Absent—Supervisors Shannon, Spaulding—2.

Accepting Offer to Sell Land for Widening San Jose Avenue.

Also, Resolution No. 32212 (New Series), as follows:

Resolved, That the offer of sale made by the following named owners to sell to the City and County of San Francisco the following described land, required for the widening of San Jose avenue as an approach to Alemany boulevard, for the sum set forth opposite their names, be accepted:

Theresa Bootz and Henrietta Welch, $6,000.

Parcel 1: The southeasterly portion of Lot 1, in Block 7158, as per the Assessor's Block Books of the City and County of San Francisco.

Parcel "A": The northwesterly portion of Lot 1, in Block 7158, as per the Assessor's Block Books of the City and County of San Francisco.

And the City Attorney is hereby authorized to examine the title to said property, and, if the same is found satisfactory, to accept, on behalf of the City, a deed conveying said property to the City, free and clear of all encumbrances, and to record said deed, together with a copy of this resolution, in the office of the Recorder of the City and County of San Francisco.

Be it further

Resolved, That in order to facilitate the possible exchange or sale of said Parcel "A," purchased from said Theresa Bootz and Henrietta Welch, the deed to said Parcel "A" be taken in the name of the Title Insurance and Guaranty Company for the City and County of San Francisco, and under the direction of said City and County of San Francisco.

Ayes—Supervisors Andriano, Canepa, Colman, Gallagher, Havenner, Hayden, McGovern, McSheehy, Miles, Peyser, Power, Roncovieri, Rossi, Stanton, Suhr, Toner—16.

Absent—Supervisors Shannon, Spaulding—2.

Accepting Offer to Sell Land Required in Connection With Construction, Etc., of Hetch Hetchy Aqueduct.

Also, Resolution No. 32213 (New Series), as follows:

Resolved, That the offer of sale made by the following named persons to sell to the City and County of San Francisco the following described land, situated in the County of San Joaquin, State of California, required in connection with the construction, maintenance and operation of the Hetch Hetchy aqueduct, for the sum set forth opposite their names, be accepted:

John F. Flynn and Owen Flynn, $300—A portion of the northeast quarter of Section 34, Township 3 South, Range 4 East, M. D. B. and M., containing 3.6 acres.

(As per detailed description and written offer on file.)

And the City Attorney is hereby authorized to examine the title to said land, and, if the same is found in satisfactory condition, to accept, on behalf of the City and County of San Francisco, a deed conveying said land to said City and County, free and clear of all encumbrances, and to record said deed, together with copy of this resolution, in the office of the County Recorder of San Joaquin County, California.

Ayes—Supervisors Andriano, Canepa, Colman, Gallagher, Havenner, Hayden, McGovern, McSheehy, Miles, Peyser, Power, Roncovieri, Rossi, Stanton, Suhr, Toner—16.

Absent—Supervisors Shannon, Spaulding—2.

Accepting Offer to Sell Land Required for Bay Shore Boulevard.

Also, Resolution No. 32214 (New Series), as follows:

Resolved, That the offer of sale made by the following owners to sell to the City and County of San Francisco the following described lands, required for the opening of Bay Shore boulevard, for the sum set forth opposite their names, be accepted:

John Landers and Augusta Landers, $1,488.50—Lot 20, Block 5477, as per the Assessor's Block Books of the City and County of San Francisco.

(As per written offer on file.)

The City Attorney is hereby authorized to examine the title to said property, and, if the same is found in satisfactory condition, to accept, on behalf of the City, a deed conveying said property to the City, free and clear of all encumbrances, and to record said deed, together with copy of this resolution, in the office of the Recorder of the City and Countyof San Francisco.

Ayes—Supervisors Andriano, Canepa, Colman, Gallagher, Havenner, Hayden, McGovern, McSheehy, Miles, Peyser, Power, Roncovieri, Rossi, Stanton, Suhr, Toner—16.

Absent—Supervisors Shannon, Spaulding—2.

Passed for Printing.

The following matters were *passed for printing*:

Oil Tanks and Boilers.

On recommendation of Fire Committee.

Resolution No. ————— (New Series), as follows:

Resolved, That the following revocable permits be and are hereby granted:

Oil Tanks.

N. George Wienholz, southwest corner of Broderick and O'Farrell streets, 1500 gallons capacity.

F. Tocker, 825 De Haro street, 1500 gallons capacity.

C. Peterson Co., south side of O'Farrell street, 150 feet west of Leavenworth street, 1500 gallons capacity.

G. Poy, north side of McAllister street, 65 feet west of Webster street, 1500 gallons capacity.

Edward Jose, east side of Gough street, 120 feet north of Jackson street, 1500 gallons capacity.

American Engraving and Colorplate Company, west side of Zeno place, 180 feet south of Folsom street, 1500 gallons capacity.

Gardner Dailey, 3747 Jackson street, 750 gallons capacity.

Andrew D. Himmelman, 41 Octavia street, 1500 gallons capacity.

Boilers.

G. F. Thomas Dyeing and Cleaning Works, 859 Fourteenth street, 10 horsepower.

The rights granted under this resolution shall be exercised within six months, otherwise said permits shall become null and void.

Transfer Public Garage Permit, Haran & Woods, North Side of Clement Street, 57 Feet 6 Inches East of Twenty-first Avenue.

Also, Resolution No. ———— (New Series), as follows:

Resolved, That Haran & Woods be and are hereby granted permission, revocable at will of the Board of Supervisors, to have transferred to them public garage permit heretofore granted Frederick W. Schmidt, by Resolution No. 28406 (New Series), for premises north side of Clement street, 57 feet 6 inches east of Twenty-first avenue.

The rights granted under this resolution shall be exercised within six months, otherwise said permit shall become null and void.

Approving Types of Lighting Standard for Boulevards.

On recommendation of Joint Committee on Streets and Street Lighting.

Resolution No. ———— (New Series), as follows:

Whereas, the question of the type of lighting standard for boulevards has been awaiting a decision by the Board of Supervisors for many months; and

Whereas, it is advisable to make a decision on this important matter; now, therefore, be it

Resolved, That it be declared the policy of the Board of Supervisors that both the concrete and the metal type of standards be contracted for on the basis of one third of the total purchased be of concrete and two-thirds be of the metal type.

Motion.

Supervisor Stanton moved that the resolution be amended by striking out the word "concrete" and inserting in lieu thereof the words "cast iron."

Supervisor Colman moved as an amendment to the amendment that it be the policy of the Board to purchase concrete centrifugally spun poles for the boulevards.

Amendment to the amendment *lost* by the following vote:

Ayes—Supervisors Andriano, Colman, Havenner, Miles, Peyser—5.

Noes—Supervisors Canepa, Gallagher, Hayden, McGovern, McSheehy, Power, Roncovieri, Rossi, Stanton, Suhr, Toner—11.

Absent—Supervisors Shannon, Spaulding—2.

Whereupon, the roll was called on Supervisor Stanton's amendment and the same was *defeated* by the following vote:

Ayes—Supervisors McGovern, Stanton—2.

Noes—Supervisors Andriano, Canepa, Colman, Gallagher, Havenner, Hayden, McSheehy, Miles, Peyser, Power, Roncovieri, Rossi, Suhr, Toner—14.

Absent—Supervisors Shannon, Spaulding—2.

Supervisor Colman thereupon moved to amend the original resolution, providing for a 50-50 selection of concrete and metal standards.

The amendment was *defeated* by the following vote:

Ayes—Supervisors Andriano, Colman, Havenner, Hayden, Miles, Peyser, Rossi, Suhr—8.

Noes—Supervisors Canepa, Gallagher, McGovern, McSheehy, Power, Roncovieri, Stanton, Toner—8.

Absent—Supervisors Shannon, Spaulding—2.

Resolution Adopted.

Whereupon, the roll was càlled on Supervisor Power's resolution and the same was *adopted* by the following vote:

Resolution No. 32232 (New Series), as follows:

Whereas, the question of the type of lighting standard for boulevards has been awaiting a decision by the Board of Supervisors for many months; and

Whereas, it is advisable to make a decision on this important matter; now, therefore, be it

Resolved, That it be declared the policy of the Board of Supervisors that both the concrete and the metal type of standards be contracted for on the basis of one-third of the total purchased be of concrete and two-thirds be of the metal type.

Ayes—Supervisors Canepa, Gallagher, Havenner, Hayden, McSheehy, Miles, Peyser, Power, Roncovieri, Rossi, Suhr, Toner—12.

Noes—Supervisors Andriano, Colman, McGovern, Stanton—4 .

Absent—Supervisors Shannon, Spaulding—2.

Adopted.

The following resolution was *adopted*:

Extension of Time to Complete Improvement of Rivoli Street by Construction of Sidewalks.

On recommendation of Streets Committee.

Resolution No. 32215 (New Series), as follows:

Resolved, That M. Bertolino is hereby granted an extension of ninety days' time from and after March 11, 1930, within which to complete the improvement of Rivoli street, 125 feet easterly from Cole street, etc., by the construction of sidewalks.

This extension of time is granted upon the recommendation of the Board of Public Works for the reason that the work is completed and this extension is granted to cover the time necessary for the issuance of the assessment.

Ayes—Supervisors Andriano, Canepa, Colman, Gallagher, Havenner, Hayden, McGovern, McSheehy, Miles, Peyser, Power, Roncovieri, Rossi, Stanton, Suhr, Toner—16.'

Absent—Supervisors Shannon, Spaulding—2.

Passed for Printing.

The following bill was *passed for printing*:

Ordering the Improvement of Lobos Street.

On recommendation of Streets Committee.

Bill No. 8210, Ordinance No. ————— (New Series), as follows:

Ordering the performance of certain street work to be done in the City and County of San Francisco, approving and adopting specifications therefor.

Be it ordained by the People of the City and County of San Francisco as follows:

Section 1. The Board of Public Works in written communication filed in the office of the Clerk of the Board of Supervisors February 10, 1930, having recommended the ordering of the following street work, the same is hereby ordered to be done in the City and County of San Francisco in conformity with the provisions of the Street Improvement Ordinance of 1918 of said City and County of San Francisco, said work to be performed under the direction of the Board of Public Works, and to be done in accordance with the specifications prepared therefor by said Board of Public Works, and on file in its office, which said plans and specifications are hereby approved and adopted.

That said Board of Supervisors, pursuant to the provisions of Part II of the said Street Improvement Ordinance of 1918 of said City and County of San Francisco, does hereby determine and declare that the assessment to be imposed for the said contemplated improvements, respectively, may be paid in twenty installments; that the period of time after the time of the payment of the first installment when each of the succeeding installments must be paid is to be six months from the time of the payment of the preceding installment, and that the rate of interest to be charged on all deferred payments shall be seven per centum per annum.

The improvement of the southerly one-half of Lobos street from a line parallel with and 275 feet easterly from Plymouth avenue to a line parallel with and 400 feet easterly from Plymouth avenue, by the construction of armored concrete curbs; by the construction of a 6-inch ironstone pipe side sewer and by the construction of an asphaltic concrete pavement, consisting of a 6-inch concrete foundation and a one and one-half inch asphaltic concrete wearing surface on the roadway thereof.

Section 2. This ordinance shall take effect immediately.

Adopted.

The following resolutions were *adopted*:

Change of Name of Academy Street to Arlington Street.

On recommendation of Streets Committee.

Resolution No. 32216 (New Series), as follows:

Whereas, the Board of Public Works did, by Resolution No. 109640 (Second Series), adopted February 26, 1930, recommend to the Board of Supervisors that the name of Academy street, located on the west line of Bernal Cut between Charles and Fairmount streets be changed to Arlington street; now, therefore, be it

Resolved, That the name of Academy street, located on the west line of Bernal Cut between Charles and Fairmount streets be and is hereby changed to Arlington street.

Ayes—Supervisors Andriano, Canepa, Colman, Gallagher, Havenner, Hayden, McGovern, McSheehy, Miles, Peyser, Power, Roncovieri, Rossi, Stanton, Suhr, Toner—16.

Absent—Supervisors Shannon, Spaulding—2.

Extension of Time to Complete Improvement of Douglass Street Between Army and Twenty-eighth Streets.

Also, Resolution No. 32217 (New Series), as follows:

Resolved, That California Construction Company is hereby granted an extension of ninety days' time from and after March 8, 1930, within which to complete the improvement of Douglass street between Army and Twenty-eighth streets under public contract. This extension of time is granted upon the recommendation of the Board of Public Works for the reason that the contractor has been delayed by the rains.

Ayes—Supervisors Andriano, Canepa, Colman, Gallagher, Havenner, Hayden, McGovern, McSheehy, Miles, Peyser, Power, Roncovieri, Rossi, Stanton, Suhr, Toner—16.

Absent—Supervisors Shannon, Spaulding—2.

Accepting Deed From Julie Verdier et al. to Land for Opening Bay Shore Boulevard.

Also, Resolution No. 32218 (New Series), as follows:

Resolved, That the deed from Julie Verdier and Adrien Verdier to City and County of San Francisco, a municipal corporation, conveying unto said City and County of San Francisco a portion of Lots 10 and 11, Block 5466, as per the Assessor's Block Books of the City and

County of San Francisco, in connection with the acquisition of land required for the opening of Bay Shore boulevard be and the same is hereby accepted.

The City Attorney is hereby authorized to record said deed, together with copy of this resolution, in the office of the Recorder of the City and County of San Francisco.

Ayes—Supervisors Andriano, Canepa, Colman, Gallagher, Havenner, Hayden, McGovern, McSheehy, Miles, Peyser, Power, Roncovieri, Rossi, Stanton, Suhr, Toner—16.

Absent—Supervisors Shannon, Spaulding—2.

Approval of Grade Map of Castro Street Between Twenty-ninth and Thirtieth Streets, Etc.

Also, Resolution No. 32219 (New Series), as follows:

Whereas, the Board of Public Works did, by Resolution No. 101944 (Second Series), approve a map showing the proposed change and establishment of official grades on Castro street between Twenty-ninth street and the southerly line of Thirtieth street and on Thirtieth street between a line parallel with Noe street and 379 feet westerly therefrom; now, therefore, be it

Resolved, That the map showing the proposed change and establishment of official grades on Castro street between Twenty-ninth street and the southerly line of Thirtieth street and on Thirtieth street between a line parallel with Noe street and 379 feet westerly therefrom be and the same is hereby approved.

Ayes—Supervisors Andriano, Canepa, Colman, Gallagher, Havenner, Hayden, McGovern, McSheehy, Miles, Peyser, Power, Roncovieri, Rossi, Stanton, Suhr, Toner—16.

Absent—Supervisors Shannon, Spaulding—2.

Approving Grade Map of Portion of Glen Park.

Also, Resolution No. 32220 (New Series), as follows:

Whereas, the Board of Public Works did, by Resolution No. 107866 (Second Series), approve a map entitled "Grade map of a portion of Glen Park," showing the establishment of grades on Diamond street between Moffitt and Berkeley streets and on other streets; now, therefore, be it

Resolved, That the map entitled "Grade map of a portion of Glen Park," showing the establishment of grades on Diamond street between Moffitt and Berkeley streets and on other streets be and the same is hereby approved.

Ayes—Supervisors Andriano, Canepa, Colman, Gallagher, Havenner, Hayden, McGovern, McSheehy, Miles, Peyser, Power, Roncovieri, Rossi, Stanton, Suhr, Toner—16.

Absent—Supervisors Shannon, Spaulding—2.

Extension of Time to Complete Improvement of Josiah Avenue Between Lakeview and Summit Avenues.

Also, Resolution No. 32221 (New Series), as follows:

Resolved, That M. Bertolino is hereby granted the following extensions of time to complete street work under public contracts, viz.:

(1) Ninety days' time from and after March 11, 1930, to complete the improvement of Josiah avenue between Lakeview and Summit avenues.

This extension of time is granted upon the recommendation of the Board of Public Works for the reason that the grading has been completed.

(2) Ninety days' time from and after November 26, 1929, within which to complete the construction of sidewalks on Santiago street between Fourteenth and Fifteenth avenues.

This extension of time is granted upon the recommendation of the Board of Public Works for the reason that the work has been completed. This extension is granted in order that contractor may be protected during period of acceptance and the issuance of assessment.

Ayes—Supervisors Andriano, Canepa, Colman, Gallagher, Havenner, Hayden, McGovern, McSheehy, Miles, Peyser, Power, Roncovieri, Rossi, Stanton, Suhr, Toner—16.

Absent—Supervisors Shannon, Spaulding—2.

Accepting Offer of Fernando Nelson & Sons to Sell Lands for the Widening of Corbett Avenue.

Also, Resolution No. 32222 (New Series), as follows:

Resolved, That the offer of sale made by the following named owner to sell to the City and County of San Francisco the following described land, required for the widening of Corbett avenue, for the sum set forth opposite its name, be accepted:

Fernando Nelson & Sons—$1.00.

Parcel 1: Portions of Lots 3 and 4, in Block 2719, as shown on the map of Twin Peaks Terrace.

Parcel 2: Portions of Lots 8 and 9, in Block 2719, as shown on the map of Twin Peaks Terrace.

Parcel 3: Portions of Lots 10 and 12, in Block 2719, as shown on the map of Twin Peaks Terrace.

Parcel 4: Portions of Lots 19 to 23, both inclusive, in Block 2719, as shown on the map of Twin Peaks Terrace.

Parcel 5: Portions of Lots 13 to 17, both inclusive, in Block 2718, as shown on the map of Twin Peaks Terrace.

Parcel 6: Portions of Lots 13 and 14, in Block 2718, as shown on map entitled "Map of Twin Peaks Terrace."

Parcel 7: Portion of Lot 9, in Block 2745, as shown on the map of Twin Peaks Terrace. (All as per detailed description and written offer on file.)

As a further consideration it is understood that said Fernando Nelson & Sons is to receive a deed from the City and County of San Francisco to the following described parcels of land now portions of Corbett avenue and Graystone terrace, which said portions are to be closed and abandoned in accordance with the provisions of the Act of May 1, 1911:

Parcel A: That portion of Corbett avenue shown upon the Map of Twin Peaks Terrace, filed July 30, 1915, in Book "H" of Maps, pages 29, 30 and 31, in the office of the Recorder of the City and County of San Francisco, State of California, described as follows:

Beginning at a point on the westerly line of Corbett avenue, distant thereon 20.602 feet southerly from the second angle point on said westerly line of Corbett avenue, southeasterly from the southerly line of Clayton street as shown on the map above referred to, said angle point being on the easterly line of Lot 10, in Block 2719, as shown on said map; thence southerly along the said westerly line of Corbett avenue 111.803 feet to an angle thereon; thence deflecting to the left 55 deg. and running southeasterly along the southwesterly line of Corbett avenue 52.057 feet to an angle thereon; thence deflecting 55 deg. to the left and running northeasterly along the southeasterly line of said Corbett avenue 76.01 feet; thence westerly, northwesterly and northerly along the arc of a curve to the right, the tangent of which at the last-named point deflects 155 deg. 07 min. 43 sec. to the left from the preceding course, said curve having a radius of 125 feet, central angle 81 deg. 03 min. 11 sec., a distance of 176.83 feet to the point of beginning.

Parcel B: That portion of Corbett avenue as shown on the map of Twin Peaks Terrace, filed July 30, 1915, in Book "H" of Maps, pages 29, 30 and 31, in the office of the Recorder of the City and County of San Francisco, State of California, described as follows:

Beginning at a point on the westerly line of Corbett avenue, distant thereon 7.640 feet northerly from the second angle point in said westerly line which is southeasterly of the southerly line of Clayton street, said angle point being in the easterly line of Lot 10, in Block 2719, as shown on the map above referred to; running thence southerly along said westerly line of Corbett avenue 7.640 feet to the angle point above referred to; thence deflecting 8 deg. 52 min. to the left and continuing southerly along said westerly line of Corbett avenue 2.834 feet; thence northerly along the arc of a curve to the right tangent to a line deflecting 175 deg. 55 min. 28 sec. to the left from the preceding course at the last-named point, said curve having a radius of 125 feet and a central angle of 4 deg. 47 min. 28 sec., a distance of 10.453 feet to the point of beginning.

Parcel C: That portion of Graystone terrace (formerly Fout avenue), as shown on the map of Twin Peaks Terrace, filed July 30, 1915, in Book "H" of Maps, pages 29, 30 and 31, in the office of the Recorder of the City and County of San Francisco, State of California, described as follows:

Beginning at a point on the southwesterly line of Graystone terrace (formerly Fout avenue), distant thereon 1.412 feet northwesterly from its intersection with the westerly line of Corbett avenue; running thence northwesterly along said southwesterly line of Graystone terrace 339.627 feet to the southeasterly line of Copper alley; thence deflecting to the right 83 deg. 41 min. 24 sec. and running northeasterly along the southeasterly line of Copper alley extended in a northeasterly direction 1.754 feet to the intersection with the extension south 48 deg. 51 min. 09 sec. east of that portion of the southwesterly line of Graystone terrace lying immediately northwest of Copper alley; thence deflecting 86 deg. 17 min. 39 sec. to the right and running south 48 deg. 51 min. 09 sec. east along the said southeasterly extension of the southwesterly line of Graystone terrace 203.843 feet; thence continuing southeasterly along the arc of a curve to the right, tangent to the preceding course, having a radius of 134.27 feet and a central angle of 34 deg. 20 min. 52 sec. a distance of 80.492 feet; thence southerly tangent to the preceding course 66.297 feet to the point of beginning.

Parcel D: Beginning at a point on the westerly line of Corbett avenue, distant thereon 57.511 feet southerly from the southeasterly line of Copper alley, and running thence southerly along said westerly line 38.649 feet to an angle point therein; thence deflecting to the left 7 deg. 03 min. 41 sec. and continuing southerly along said westerly line 7.585 feet to the proposed westerly line of Corbett avenue; thence deflecting to the left 174 deg. 05 min. 41 sec. and running northerly along said proposed westerly line 46.186 feet to the westerly line of Corbett avenue and the point of beginning.

Being a portion of Corbett avenue.

And the City Attorney is hereby authorized to examine the title to said property, and if the same is found satisfactory to accept, on behalf of the City and County of San Francisco, deed conveying said property to said City and County, free and clear of all encumbrances, and to record said deed, together with a copy of this resolution, in the office of the Recorder of the City and County of San Francisco.

And immediately after the closing and abandonment of said portions of Corbett avenue and Graystone terrace, hereinabove described as Parcels A, B, C and D, the Mayor and the Clerk of the Board of Supervisors, in the name of the City and County of San Francisco, are hereby authorized and directed to execute a deed conveying said Parcels A, B, C and D to said Fernando Nelson & Sons.

Ayes—Supervisors Andriano, Canepa, Colman, Gallagher, Havenner, Hayden, McGovern, McSheehy, Miles, Peyser, Power, Roncovieri, Rossi, Stanton, Suhr, Toner—16.

Absent—Supervisors Shannon, Spaulding—2.

Approval of Map of Oakwood Street.

Also, Resolution No. 32223 (New Series), as follows:

Whereas, the Board of Public Works did, by Resolution No. 109761 (Second Series), approve a map showing the extension of Oakwood street through to Nineteenth street; now, therefore, be it

Resolved, That the map showing the extension of Oakwood street through to Nineteenth street be and the same is hereby approved.

Ayes—Supervisors Andriano, Canepa, Colman, Gallagher, Havenner, Hayden, McGovern, McSheehy, Miles, Peyser, Power, Roncovieri, Rossi, Stanton, Suhr, Toner—16.

Absent—Supervisors Shannon, Spaulding—2.

Authorizing the Mayor to Sell at Public Auction Dwelling House at No. 232 Sickles Avenue.

Also, Resolution No. 32224 (New Series), as follows:

Resolved, That the Mayor be and he is hereby authorized and directed to sell at public auction, after at least five (5) days of published notice, the following described personal property, owned by the City and County of San Francisco, to-wit:

Dwelling house and appurtenances, situated on that certain piece or parcel of land required for the opening of Alemany boulevard, and known as 232 Sickles avenue.

The terms of sale shall be cash upon delivery of bill of sale, said dwelling house and appurtenances to be removed by the purchasers within thirty (30) days of purchase thereof.

The proceeds derived from said sale shall be deposited to the credit of Boulevard Bond Issue Fund.

Ayes—Supervisors Andriano, Canepa, Colman, Gallagher, Havenner, Hayden, McGovern, McSheehy, Miles, Peyser, Power, Roncovieri, Rossi, Stanton, Suhr, Toner—16.

Absent—Supervisors Shannon, Spaulding—2.

Passed for Printing.

The following matters were *passed for printing*:

Establishing Grades on Cayuga Avenue and on Seneca Avenue.

On recommendation of Streets Committee.

Bill No. 8211, Ordinance No. ———— (New Series), as follows:

Establishing grades on Cayuga avenue and on Seneca avenue as hereinafter described.

Be it ordained by the People of the City and County of San Francisco as follows:

Section 1. The grades on Cayuga avenue and on Seneca avenue are hereby established at points hereinafter named and at heights above city base as hereinafter stated. in accordance with recommendation of the Board of Public Works, filed March 11, 1930:

Cayuga Avenue.

Oneida avenue, intersection, 145.00 feet. (The same being the present official grade.)

215 feet southwesterly from Oneida avenue, 146.37 feet.

At the southwesterly end of the first curve southwesterly from Oneida avenue, 148.29 feet.

Northwesterly curb line of, 19.49 feet northeasterly from the easterly end of the curb return to Seneca avenue, 149.44 feet.

Northwesterly curb line of, 20.51 feet westerly from the easterly end of the curb return to Seneca avenue, 149.54 feet.

Northwesterly curb line of, 17.18 feet southerly from the northerly end of the curb return to Seneca avenue, 149.51 feet.

Northwesterly curb line of, 16.09 feet northeasterly from the westerly end of the curb return to Seneca avenue, 149.64 feet.

Southeasterly curb line of, 13.95 feet northwesterly from the southeasterly curb return to Seneca avenue, 149.30 feet.

Seneca Avenue.

12 feet southwesterly from the northeasterly line of, at Alemany boulevard northwesterly line, 177.79 feet.

12 feet northeasterly from the southwesterly line of, at Alemany boulevard northwesterly line, 178.60.

11 feet northwesterly from Bannock street produced, 176.53 feet.

Northeasterly curb line of, 6.56 feet northwesterly from the southeasterly end of the curb return to Cayuga avenue, 149.72 feet.

Southwesterly curb line of, 36.05 feet southeasterly from the southeasterly end of the curb return to Cayuga avenue, 149.80 feet.

Southwesterly curb line of, 13.95 feet northwesterly from the southeasterly end of the curb return to Cayuga avenue, 149.30 feet.

Southwesterly curb line of, 17.18 feet southerly from the northerly end of the curb return to Cayuga avenue, 149.51 feet.

Northeasterly curb line of, 20.51 feet westerly from the easterly end of the curb return to Cayuga avenue, 149.54 feet.

Northeasterly curb line of, 17.36 feet northwesterly from the westerly end of the curb return to Cayuga avenue, 149.65 feet.

Northeasterly curb line of, 53.83 feet northeasterly from the southwesterly end of the curb return to Otsego avenue, 150.76 feet.

Northeasterly line of, produced southeasterly at Otsego avenue, 151.00 feet. (The same being the present official grade.)

15 feet southwesterly from the northeasterly line of, at Otsego avenue northwesterly line, 151.00 feet. (The same being the present official grade.)

Southwesterly curb line of, 124.08 feet southeasterly from the beginning of the curve easterly from Delano avenue, 151.00 feet.

On Cayuga avenue between Oneida avenue produced and the southwesterly line of Seneca avenue, and on Seneca avenue between Alemany boulevard and the northwesterly line of Otsego avenue produced, be established to conform to true gradients between the grade elevations above given therefor.

Section 2. This ordinance shall take effect immediately.

Width of Sidewalks on Kirkwood Avenue.

Also, Bill No. 8212, Ordinance No. ———— (New Series), as follows:

Amending Ordinance No. 1061, entitled "Regulating the Width of Sidewalks," approved December 18, 1903, by amending Section Five Hundred and Sixty thereof.

Be it ordained by the People of the City and County of San Francisco as follows:

Section 1. Ordinance No. 1061, entitled "Regulating the Width of Sidewalks," approved December 18, 1903, be and is hereby amended in accordance with the communication of the Board of Public Works, filed in this office March 11, 1930, by amending Section Five Hundred and Sixty thereof, to read as follows:

Section 560. The width of sidewalks on Kirkwood avenue between Islais street and Mendell street shall be fifteen (15) feet.

The width of sidewalks on Kirkwood avenue between Mendell street and Lane street shall be twenty-two (22) feet and six (6) inches.

The width of sidewalks on Kirkwood avenue between Lane street and Water Front street shall be fifteen (15) feet.

Section 2. Any expense caused by the above change of walk widths shall be borne by the property owners.

Section 3. This ordinance shall take effect and be in force from and after its passage.

Width of Sidewalks on Cayuga Avenue and on Seneca Avenue.

Also, Bill No. 8213, Ordinance No. ———— (New Series), as follows:

Amending Ordinance No. 1061, entitled "Regulating the Width of Sidewalks," approved December 18, 1903, by adding thereto new sections, to be numbered ten hundred and ninety and ten hundred and ninety-one.

Be it ordained by the People of the City and County of San Francisco as follows:

Section 1. Ordinance No. 1061, entitled "Regulating the Width of Sidewalks," approved December 18, 1903, be and is hereby amended, in accordance with the communication of the Board of Public Works, filed in this office March 3, 1930, by adding thereto new sections, to be numbered ten hundred and ninety and ten hundred and ninety-one, to read as follows:

Section 1090. The width of sidewalks on Cayuga avenue between Oneida avenue and Seneca avenue shall be as shown on that certain map entitled "Map of Cayuga avenue between Oneida avenue and Seneca avenue," showing the location of street and curb lines and the width of sidewalks.

Section 1091. The width of sidewalks on Seneca avenue between Otsego avenue and Alemany boulevard shall be as shown on that certain map entitled "Map of Seneca avenue between Otsego avenue and Alemany boulevard," showing the location of street and curb lines and the width of sidewalks.

Section 2. Any expense caused by the above change of walk widths shall be borne by the property owners.

Section 3. This ordinance shall take effect and be in force from and after its passage.

Repealing That Portion of Ordinance No. 8652 (New Series), Ordering the Improvement of Portions of Thirty-fourth, Thirty-seventh and Forty-eighth Avenues by the Removal of Sand and the Construction of Bulkheads.

Also, Bill No. 8214, Ordinance No. ———— (New Series), as follows:

Repealing that portion of Ordinance No. 8652 (New Series) in so far as it relates to the improvement of certain portions of Thirty-fourth avenue, Thirty-seventh avenue and Forty-eighth avenue, by the removal of sand and the construction of bulkheads.

Be it ordained by the People of the City and County of San Francisco as follows:

Section 1. Ordinance No. 8652 (New Series), in so far as it relates to the improvement of certain portions of Thirty-fourth avenue, Thirty-seventh avenue and Forty-eighth avenue, by the removal of sand and the construction of bulkheads, is hereby repealed.

Section 2. This ordinance shall take effect immediately.

Full Acceptance of Roadway of Certain Streets.

Also, Bill No. 8215, Ordinance No. ———— (New Series), as follows:

Providing for full acceptance of the roadway of Alameda street between Treat avenue and Harrison street, Division street between Bryant and Florida streets, Delano avenue between Geneva and Niagara avenues, Madison street between Silliman and Felton streets, Naples street between Amázon and Geneva avenues, Naples street between Geneva avenue and Rolph street and between Rolph and Munich streets, Ripley street between Folsom and Alabama streets, Twenty-sixth street between York and Hampshire streets, Twentieth street between Sanchez and Noe streets, Treat avenue between Florida and Alabama streets, crossing of Division and Florida streets, intersection of Treat avenue, Alabama street and Alameda street, intersection of Delano and Seminola avenues, crossing of Madison and Silliman streets, crossing of Naples street and Geneva avenue, crossing of Naples and Rolph streets, intersections of Naples and Athens streets, Naples and Seville streets and Brunswick street and Naples and Munich streets, intersection of Ripley and Harrison streets, crossing of Twentieth and Sanchez streets, crossing of Delano and Niagara avenues.

Be it ordained by the People of the City and County of San Francisco as follows:

Section 1. The roadways of the following named streets, including the curbs on both sides thereof, having been constructed to the satisfaction of the Board of Public Works and of the Board of Supervisors, are hereby fully accepted by the City and County of San Francisco (except those portions required by law to be kept in order by the railroad company having tracks thereon), in accordance with the provisions of Section 23, Chapter 2, Article VI of the Charter, said roadways having been paved with asphaltic concrete and concrete and curbs laid thereon, and are in good condition throughout, and have sewers, gas and water mains laid therein, to-wit: Alameda street between Treat avenue and Harrison street, Division street between Bryant and Florida streets, Delano avenue between Geneva and Niagara avenues, Madison street between Silliman and Felton streets, Naples street between Amazon and Geneva avenues, Naples street between Geneva avenue and Rolph street and between Rolph and Munich streets, Ripley street between Folsom and Alabama streets, Twenty-sixth street between York and Hampshire streets, Twentieth street between Sanchez and Noe streets, Treat avenue between Florida and Alabama streets, crossing of Division and Florida streets, intersection of Treat avenue, Alabama street and Alameda street, intersection of Delano and Seminola avenues, crossing of Madison and Silliman streets, crossing of Naples street and Geneva avenue, crossing of Naples and Rolph streets, intersections of Naples and Athens streets, Naples and Seville streets and Brunswick street and Naples and Munich streets, intersection of Ripley and Harrison streets, crossing of Twentieth and Sanchez streets, crossing of Delano and Niagara avenues.

Section 2. This ordinance shall take effect immediately.

Conditional Acceptance of Roadway of Certain Streets.

Also, Bill No. 8216, Ordinance No. ———— (New Series), as follows:

Providing for conditional acceptance of the roadways of Donner avenue between Phelps street and the westerly line of Hudson Garden Tract; Evans avenue between Marin and Napoleon streets; Hollister street between Hawes and Griffith streets; Keith street between Wallace and Yosemite avenues; Lakeview avenue between Plymouth and Capitol avenues, including the intersections of Lakeview and Granada avenues and Lakeview and Miramar avenues, and between Capitol and Jules avenues, including the intersection of Faxon avenue; Rodeo avenue between Teddy avenue and Brussels street and the intersection of Rodeo avenue and Somerset street; Rankin street between Davidson and Evans avenues between Islais street and Custer avenue; Twenty-eighth avenue between Noriega and Ortega streets; Thirty-eighth avenue between Rivera and Santiago streets; Forty-fourth avenue between Lawton and Moraga streets; Forty-fifth avenue between Moraga and Noriega streets; Kirkham street between Thirty-first and Thirty-second avenues; Santiago street between Forty-seventh and Forty-eighth avenues; Wallace street between Third and Keith streets; Yosemite avenue between Third and Keith streets; crossing of Keith street and Yosemite avenue; crossing of Wallace and Keith streets; crossing of Palou avenue and Griffith street; crossing of Madison and Felton streets.

Be it ordained by the People of the City and County of San Francisco as follows:

Section 1. The roadways of the following named streets, including the curbs on both sides thereof, having been constructed to the satisfaction of the Board of Public Works and of the Board of Supervisors, are hereby conditionally accepted by the City and County of San Francisco (except those portions required by law to be kept in order by the railroad company having tracks thereon), in accordance with the provisions of Section 23, Chapter 2, Article VI, of the Charter, said roadways having been paved with asphaltic concrete and curbs laid thereon, and are in good condition throughout; sewers and gas mains have been laid therein; no water mains have been laid therein, to-wit:

Donner avenue between Phelps street and the westerly line of Hudson Garden Tract; Evans avenue between Marin and Napoleon streets; Hollister street between Hawes and Griffith streets; Keith street between Wallace and Yosemite avenues; Lakeview avenue between Plymouth and Capitol avenues, including the intersections of Lakeview and Granada avenues and Lakeview and Miramar avenues, and between Capitol and Jules avenues, including the intersection of Faxon avenue; Rodeo avenue between Teddy avenue and Brussels street and the intersection of Rodeo avenue and Somerst street; Rankin street between Davidson and Evans avenues between Islais street and Custer avenue; Twenty-eighth avenue between Noriega and Ortega streets; Thirty-eighth avenue between Rivera and Santiago streets; Forty-fourth avenue between Lawton and Moraga streets; Forty-fifth avenue between Moraga and Noriega streets; Kirkham street between Thirty-first and Thirty-second avenues; Santiago street between Forty-seventh and Forty-eighth avenues; Wallace avenue between Third and Keith streets; Yosemite avenue between Third and Keith streets; crossing of Keith street and Yosemite avenue; crossing of Wallace avenue and Keith street; crossing of Palou avenue and Griffith street; crossing of Madison and Felton streets.

Section 2. This ordinance shall take effect immediately.

Conditional Acceptance of Roadway of Certain Streets.

Also, Bill No. 8217, Ordinance No. ———— (New Series), as follows:

Providing for the conditional acceptance of the roadways of Key avenue between Keith street and Bay Shore boulevard; Lawton street between Seventeenth and Eighteenth avenues; Ramsell street between Randolph street and its southerly termination; Twentieth street between Mississippi street and Pennsylvania avenue; Victoria street between Sargent and Randolph streets; Vernon street between Randolph street and a line 479 feet southerly from Randolph street; Valley street between Castro street and Diamond street; Wisconsin street between Nineteenth and Twentieth streets; Quintara street between Fifteenth and Sixteenth avenues.

Be it ordained by the People of the City and County of San Francisco as follows:

Section 1. The roadways of the following named streets, including the curbs on both sides thereof, having been constructed to the satisfaction of the Board of Public Works and of the Board of Supervisors, are hereby conditionally accepted by the City and County of San Francisco (except those portions required by law to be kept in order by the railroad company having tracks thereon), in accordance with the provisions of Section 23, Chapter 2, Article VI, of the Charter, said roadways having been paved with concrete and curbs laid thereon, and are in good condition throughout; sewers and gas mains have been laid therein; no water mains have been laid therein:

Key avenue between Keith street and Bay Shore boulevard; Lawton street between Seventeenth and Eighteenth avenues; Ramsell street between Randolph street and its southerly termination; Twentieth street between Mississippi street and Pennsylvania avenue; Victoria street between Sargent and Randolph streets; Vernon street between Randolph street and a line 479 feet southerly from Randolph street; Valley street between Castro street and Diamond street; Wisconsin street between Nineteenth and Twentieth street; Quintara street between Fifteenth and Sixteenth avenues.

Section 2. This ordinance shall take effect immediately.

Adopted.

The following resolutions were *adopted*:

Rescinding and Reestablishing Loading Zones.

On recommendation of Traffic and Safety Committee.

Resolution No. 32225 (New Series), as follows:

Resolved, That the following loading zones, of the lengths specified, be rescinded and reestablished as specified herein, in front of or near the following addresses, in accordance with the provisions of Section No. 36 of Ordinance No. 7691 (New Series), as amended:

157-161 Ellis street, 36 feet, new length 18 feet—Hotel St. Clair; Hotel Willard; 2 elevators.

125 O'Farrell street, 72 feet (rescinded)—Orpheum Theater.

680 Sansome street, 27 feet, new length 45 feet—U. S. Appraisers' Building; Coast Guard.

406 Montgomery street, 27 feet (rescinded)—Kohl Building.

9 City Hall avenue, 9 feet, new length 18 feet—Book Concern Building; Bender-Moss Company.

885 Market street, 18 feet, new length 27 feet—C. H. Baker Shoe Co.

Ayes—Supervisors Andriano, Canepa, Colman, Gallagher, Havenner, Hayden, McGovern, McSheehy, Miles, Peyser, Power, Roncovieri, Rossi, Stanton, Suhr, Toner—16.

Absent—Supervisors Shannon, Spaulding—2.

Establishing Passenger Loading Zones.

Also, Resolution No. 32226 (New Series), as follows:

Resolved, That the following list of passenger loading zones, of the lengths specified, be established in front of or near the following addresses, in accordance with the provisions of Section No. 36 of Ordinance No. 7691 (New Series), as amended:

4450 Geary street, 27 feet—McAvoy & O'Hara Funeral Parlors.

246 McAllister street, 18 feet—Hotel Glenburn.

147 O'Farrell street, 45 feet—Columbia Theater.

290 Sutter street, 18 feet—Davis-Schonwasser Co.

406 Montgomery street, 27 feet—Kohl Building.

2465 Mission street, 36 feet—Majestic Theater.

Ayes—Supervisors Andriano, Canepa, Colman, Gallagher, Havenner, Hayden, McGovern, McSheehy, Miles, Peyser, Power, Roncovieri, Rossi, Stanton, Suhr, Toner—16.

Absent—Supervisors Shannon, Spaulding—2.

Establishing Loading Zones.

Also, Resolution No. 32227 (New Series), as follows:

Resolved, That the following list of loading zones, of the lengths specified, be established in front of or near the following addresses, in accordance with the provisions of Section 36 of Ordinance No. 7691 (New Series), as amended:

1200 California street, 18 feet—Hillcrest Apartments.

85 Columbia Square street, 18 feet—Tittle Electric Fixture Co.

308 Eleventh street, 27 feet—Animated Products Co.; F & T Coffee Shop.

161 Ellis street, 18 feet—Hotel Willard.

1234 Golden Gate avenue, 36 feet—Dial Radio Shop.

276 Sutter street, 27 feet—To facilitate loading of street car passengers.

275-289 Turk street, 36 feet—King Edward Apartments; Eagle Print Co.; Padre Apartments; in four stores.

371-381 Turk street, 36 feet—Chaumont Apartments; Kipling Apartments; one oil intake; west end of block.

572 Valencia street, 27 feet—Stedd Whse. Tobacco Co.

1550 Bryant street, 36 feet—Rainier Brewing Co.

310 Fourth street, 27 feet—Coast Machinery Co.

735 Frederick street, 36 feet—Polytechnic High School Cafeteria.

168 Kissling street, 36 feet—Golden Gate Iron Works.

3000-3004 Sixteenth street, 27 feet—Anglo California Trust Co.

1031-1035 Valencia street, 27 feet—Winn's Cottage Cheese Factory.

126 Fifth street, 27 feet—Chronicle Building.

Ayes—Supervisors Andriano, Canepa, Colman, Gallagher, Havenner, Hayden, McGovern, McSheehy, Miles, Peyser, Power, Roncovieri, Rossi, Stanton, Suhr, Toner—16.

Absent—Supervisors Shannon, Spaulding—2.

Award of Contract for Official Advertising, April 1, 1930, to April 1, 1931, to The Chronicle.

On recommendation of Supplies Committee.

Resolution No. 32228 (New Series), as follows:

Resolved, That the contract for doing official advertising for the City and County of San Francisco for one year, from April 1, 1930, to and including April 1, 1931, in a daily newspaper in the City and County of San Francisco which has a bona fide daily circulation of at least 8000 copies and has been in existence at the time of letting such contract for at least two years, and to deliver daily to the office of the Board of Supervisors, and to any other office or department of the City and County authorized to advertise, as many copies of the "official newspaper," not to exceed one hundred and fifty, as may be directed by the Clerk of the Board of Supervisors, and must also deliver, as directed by said Clerk, at least ten, and not to exceed one hundred and twenty-five copies of slips of all orders, ordinances, resolutions or notices published by order of the Board of Supervisors, or by any other department or officer of the municipal government authorized or permitted to advertise in said "official newspaper," also deliver at least one hundred copies of all resolutions, orders, ordinances or notices published by order of any of the officers or departments of the City and County (other than the Board of Supervisors), to such office or department causing said publication, in strict accordance with the specifications and the advertisement inviting proposals thereon, is hereby awarded to The Chronicle Publishing Company, the lowest responsible bidder, to be published in the San Francisco Chronicle, which is hereby designated as the "official newspaper," at the price bid therefor, viz:

For each insertion in six-point type, per one column line, eight and five-tenths cents (.08 5/10) per line, provided the sureties on its bond, which is hereby fixed at ten thousand (10,000) dollars, are satisfactory to his Honor the Mayor, who is hereby authorized to enter into said contract.

The San Francisco Chronicle newspaper is hereby declared and designated to be the "official newspaper" of the City and County for one year, from April 1, 1930, to and including April 1, 1931.

Ayes—Supervisors Andriano, Canepa, Colman, Gallagher, Havenner, Hayden, McGovern, McSheehy, Miles, Peyser, Power, Roncovieri, Rossi, Stanton, Suhr, Toner—16.

Absent—Supervisors Shannon, Spaulding—2.

Fixing Rates for Advertising in Official Newspaper to Be Collected by the Clerk of the Board, April 1, 1930, to April 1, 1931.

Also, Resolution No. 32229 (New Series), as follows:

Resolved, That the Clerk of the Board of Supervisors be and he is

hereby authorized and directed to collect the following rates for advertising for publications made in the official newspaper from April 1,
1930, to April 1, 1931, to-wit:

For proposal notices inviting bids, resolutions of award of contract,
bills and ordinances granting franchises, ten (10) cents per line.

For resolutions granting extension of time to complete contract, the
sum of three dollars and fifty cents shall be paid to cover the cost of
advertising.

For resolutions granting permits for engines and boilers and oil
storage, the sum of five dollars shall be paid to cover the cost of advertising.

For resolutions granting permits for blasting, dyeing and cleaning
works, garages, automobile supply stations, parking stations, furnaces,
hospitals, gas works, laundries, medical colleges, planing mills and
woodworking establishments, stables and undertaking establishments,
or for masked balls, or for any other permit which requires license
fee in connection therewith, the sum of ten dollars shall be paid to
cover the cost of advertising.

Resolved, That all sums of money so collected shall be immediately
paid into the Treasury by said Clerk, as provided by Chapter III,
Article III, of the Charter, and the Treasurer of this City and County
is hereby directed to issue to the Clerk of the Board of Supervisors
his receipt for the money so collected and paid to said Treasurer.

Resolved, That the above rates of advertising, so far as they are
applicable, shall be collected by all officers, offices and departments of
this City and County.

Ayes—Supervisors Andriano, Canepa, Colman, Gallagher, Havenner,
Hayden, McGovern, McSheehy, Miles, Peyser, Power, Roncovieri, Rossi,
Stanton, Suhr, Toner—16.

Absent—Supervisors Shannon, Spaulding—2.

Award of Contract for Publishing Delinquent Tax List, 1929-1930, to Twin Peaks Sentinel.

Also, Resolution No. 32230 (New Series), as follows:

Resolved, That the contract for publishing the Delinquent Tax List,
Index of Delinquent Real Estate Taxpayers and Sales List and other
matters incidental thereto, for the fiscal year 1929-1930, is hereby
awarded to the Twin Peaks Sentinel at the price bid therefor, viz.:

Four (4) cents per line (the same being the lowest bid submitted),
in accordance with the specifications therefor and according to law,
and the Mayor is hereby authorized to enter into such contract upon
the filing of a good and sufficient bond in the sum of five thousand
($5000) dollars, conditioned upon the faithful performance of such
contract.

All other bids are hereby rejected.

Ayes—Supervisors Andriano, Canepa, Colman, Gallagher, Havenner,
Hayden, McGovern, McSheehy, Miles, Peyser, Power, Roncovieri, Rossi,
Stanton, Suhr, Toner—16.

Absent—Supervisors Shannon, Spaulding—2.

SPECIAL ORDER—3 P. M.

The following matters were taken up:

Report of Health Committee on Garbage Disposal.

To the Honorable Mayor and the Board of Supervisors of the City
and County of San Francisco—Gentlemen:

Your Public Health Committee respectfully submits the following
report, which is the third report filed by said Committee on the question of garbage disposal:

We are annexing the two former reports presented by this committee to the Board for the purpose of refreshing the memory of the

members who were on the Board when these reports were submitted and further to acquaint the new members of what has been done by the Health Committee prior to their taking office.

Whereas, on the election held November 5, 1928, by a vote of 45,570 for and 39,291 against, the electors determined upon incineration as the method of disposing of San Francisco garbage and rubbish; and

Whereas, in order to carry out said policy as so declared and expressed, it is necessary that an incinerator be constructed in the City and County of San Francisco for the purpose of incinerating the garbage and rubbish collected therein; and

Whereas, there is urgent necessity that said incinerator should be constructed without further delay; therefore, be it

Financed Publicly.

Resolved, That the Finance Committee of this Board be instructed, in making up the budget for the year 1930-1931, to allot sufficient moneys in said budget for the purchase of a block of land contiguous to the present incinerator now located at Fifteenth and De Haro streets and erect thereon an incinerator of the most modern type that will burn 800 tons of garbage and rubbish in twenty-four hours.

Financed Privately.

Resolved, That the Board of Supervisors of the City and County of San Francisco does hereby declare that an incinerator should be financed by private capital under the following conditions:

(a) That said incinerator should be constructed at or near the site of the present incinerator at Fifteenth and De Haro streets, either upon the property belonging to the City or upon privately owned property to be purchased by person, firm or corporation financing said incinerator, and if constructed upon property now owned or hereafter acquired by the City, that a reasonable rental should be paid for the use of said property by the person, firm or corporation financing and operating said incinerator.

(b) That said incinerator should have a capacity of incinerating eight hundred tons of garbage and rubbish per 24-hour day in the most up-to-date and economical manner, and without necessitating the segregation of the wet from the dry garbage by the householders of the City and County.

(c) That the person, firm or corporation financing and operating said incinerator shall be given the exclusive privilege, for a period of at least twenty-five years, of incinerating all garbage and rubbish collected in the City and County of San Francisco, with the exception of that character of garbage commonly known as "swill," which may be collected from hotels, restaurants and other similar places.

(d) That the person, firm or corporation financing and operating said incinerator shall agree with the City and County that said City and County may acquire and take over said incinerator and all of the equipment thereof and the land upon which the same is situated, if said land is not already owned by the City, at any time during the period of twenty-five years mentioned in the last paragraph, at the cost thereof less a reasonable amount for depreciation on said incinerator and equipment figured as of the date on which the same may be taken over by the City. If the amount to be paid for said incinerator and said property cannot be agreed upon between the owner thereof and the City, the same amount shall be fixed by arbitration, the owner of said incinerator and the City to each appoint one arbiter, and the two so appointed to choose a third, and the price fixed for said incinerator and said land shall be the price at which the City may acquire the same. If said incinerator is not taken over by the City before the expiration of the term during which the financer of said incinerator has been given the privilege of incinerating the garbage and rubbish collected in the City and County of San Francisco, said incinerator shall at that time revert without cost to the

City and County of San Francisco and shall be the property of said City and County.

Be It Resolved, That the person, firm or corporation given the exclusive franchise or privilege of financing or operating said incinerator, be required to furnish a bond in such amount as this Board may require, guaranteeing that said incinerator will be constructed according to accepted specifications, and that said person, firm or corporation operating the same will perform its contract with said City and County of San Francisco for the full term thereof or until said incinerator is taken over by said City and County.

Further Resolved, That the Board of Supervisors select the type of incinerator to be constructed and that the Board of Public Works have supervision of said construction. We feel that although private capital may finance this plant, nevertheless, we view it as a quasi public utility from the fact that the plant will eventually revert to the City or may be purchased by the City at any time after completion; hence we recommend that all possible safeguards be thrown about it.

Type of Incinerator.

We recommend that any incinerator constructed have the following fundamental requirements, as we deem the same necessary for a suitable incinerator:

1. An incinerator must have good general formation and architectural design, good working conditions, and require a minimum amount of labor.

2. The plant must destroy rubbish and garbage in a sanitary and inoffensive manner, with complete destruction at minimum cost. If an incinerator is insanitary and offensive it fails in its principles and is a total loss. For that reason the initial cost is not altogether the determining factor.

3. The furnace of the incinerator must preferably be of brick type, thus giving better radiation.

4. The plant must be such that there will be no interference or delay in the collection of refuse or in delivering it to the plant. The cheapest plant to operate and keep in repair is one which has a uniform, regulated operation. Mechanical feed and automatic hoppers are therefore essential.

5. The incinerator must be equipped with shaker grates, the latter preventing clinkers. Clinkers are the bane of most incinerators. The shaker grates should operate over an ash pit with a special drop for cans and non-combustible substances.

6. A single-cell furnace fails of efficiency for want of mutual assistance; for that reason a four-cell furnace is preferable, and the committee recommends it, as we feel that the mutual assistance type is of great help in the complete destruction of garbage.

7. The baffle wall is another important requirement of the good incinerator. The baffle wall increases the efficiency of a furnace by changing the direction of the flow of the gases, which breaks stratification, thus greatly increasing the distances the gases must travel, so that those gases are retained for a longer period. Great additional heat is utilized by the retention of the gas.

Whereas, your committee has found the type of incinerator built by the Superior Incinerator Company for the city of Chicago in 1928 to embody the above-described qualifications, and a model for modern refuse burners. We attach the accompanying specifications provided through the courtesy of the city engineer of Chicago, L. Gayton. These are the major specifications for the incinerator which we recommend for San Francisco. We recommend the Superior type of incinerator, or its equal.

Resolved, That whether the City constructs the incinerator itself, or permits it to be privately financed, that a plant embodying the above-mentioned features be adhered to, for the reason that the fea-

tures mentioned are absolutely necessary from both a sanitary and an
economical standpoint.

Resolved, That the Board of Public Works be directed to have plans
and specifications made from the attached specifications and call for
bids for an incinerator that will burn 800 tons of garbage or rubbish
in twenty-four hours and award contract for said incinerator. We
further recommend that the person, firm or corporation financing said
incinerator shall have the exclusive privilege of incinerating the
garbage and rubbish in San Francisco upon the terms and conditions
hereinbefore set forth, for a period of not more than twenty-five years,
at a cost not to exceed one dollar per ton. In case the plant is privately financed, we recommend that the name of the company awarded
the contract for the erection of an incinerator be required to provide
a bond in a sufficient sum to guarantee specific performance of contract; and we further recommend that the name of the company
awarded the contract to build this incinerator be embodied in the
franchise, permit or agreement, and that said incinerator be built by
said company.

Minority Resolution on Subject of Incinerator.

Presented by Supervisor Roncovieri:

Whereas, the electors of the City and County of San Francisco did,
at the general election held on the 5th day of November, 1929, express
and declare as their policy that the garbage collected in the City and
County of San Francisco should be disposed of by incineration; and

Whereas, in order to carry out said policy as so declared and expressed it is necessary that an incinerator be constructed in the City
and County of San Francisco for the purpose of incinerating the garbage collected therein; and

Whereas, there is urgent necessity that said incinerator should be
constructed without further delay; and

Whereas, the limit of taxation fixed by the Charter of the City and
County of San Francisco will not permit the levying of a sufficient
amount of tax to defray the cost of the construction of said incinerator; and

Whereas, it is the sense of the Board of Supervisors that, in view
of the large bond issue that must be submitted to the people during the
year 1930 for the purpose of acquiring the properties of the Pacific
Gas and Electric Company and Great Western Power Company heretofore evaluated by the State Railroad Commission of California, that no
additional bond issues should be submitted for approval until after said
bond issues for the acquisition of the properties of said Pacific Gas and
Electric Company and Great Western Power Company are disposed of;
now, therefore, be it

Resolved, That the Board of Supervisors of the City and County of
San Francisco does hereby declare that an incinerator should be constructed by private capital under the following conditions:

(a) That said incinerator should be constructed at or near the site
of the present incinerator at Fifteenth and De Haro streets, either
upon the property belonging to the City or upon privately owned property, and if constructed upon property now owned or hereafter acquired
by the City that a reasonable rental should be paid by the person,
firm or corporation erecting and operating said incinerator.

(b) That said incinerator should have a capacity of incinerating at
least eight hundred tons of garbage per day in the most up-to-date and
economical manner, and without necessitating the segregation of the
wet from the dry garbage by the householders of the City and County,
and without any discharge of odor or undue amount of smoke, and
with the least possible amount of unconsumed material remaining after
said incineration.

(c) That the person, firm or corporation constructing or operating
said incinerator shall agree with the City and County that in return

for an exclusive franchise to incinerate the garbage of the City and County for a period of 25 years that said garbage will be incinerated at a price not to exceed $1.00 per ton, and said City and County may acquire and take over said incinerator and all of the equipment thereof and the land upon which the same is situated, if said land is not already owned by the City, at the cost thereeof less a reasonable amount for depreciation on said incinerator and equipment figured as of the date on which the same may be taken over by the City, and that if the amount to be paid for said incinerator and equipment and said property cannot be agreed upon between the owner thereof and the City, the said amount shall be fixed by arbitration, the owner of said incinerator and the City to each appoint one arbiter, and the two so appointed to choose a third, and the price fixed by two of said three arbiters for said incinerator and said land shall be the price at which the City may acquire the same, and that if said incinerator is not taken over by the City before the expiration of the term of 25 years for which the constructor of said incinerator has been given the privilege of incinerating the garbage collected in the City and County of San Francisco that said incinerator and all its equipment, and the land on which the same is situated, shall revert to and become the property of the City and County at the expiration of said term of 25 years without charge or payment of any kind.

(d) That the person, firm or corporation erecting said incinerator shall be given the exclusive privilege, for a period of at least twenty-five years, of incinerating all garbage collected in the City and County of San Francisco, with the exception of that character of garbage commouly known as "swill," which may be collected from hotels, restaurants and other similar places, provided that said swill must also be incinerated if circumstances require the disposition of the same by incineration.

(e) That the person, firm or corporation given the privilege of erecting said incinerator, shall file with the Board of Supervisors a bond, in such sum as the Board of Supervisors shall direct, for the completion of said incinerator in accordance with the plans and specifications submitted therefor, as well as an additional bond that said incinerator will properly incinerate all garbage under the provisions contained in any agreement for the construction thereof, and that said person, firm or corporation constructing said incinerator will, when given the exclusive privilege of incinerating the garbage collected in the City and County of San Francisco, perform his contract with said City and County for the full term thereof or until said incinerator is taken over by said City and County; be it

Further Resolved, That any and all persons offering to construct said incinerator shall present to the Board of Supervisors with any offer to construct the same, full and complete plans and specifications showing the construction of the same in detail, and the character and kind of material used in and about said construction, and shall, in addition thereto, specify the price or charge which shall be made for the incineration of said garbage, but in no case in excess of $1 per ton; and be it

Further Resolved, That, for the purpose of carrying out and making effective the terms of this resolution, the Board of Public Works, through the City Engineer, be directed to forthwith report to this Board the most feasible site at or near the site of the present incinerator, which may be found available for the construction and maintenance of said incinerator, and the approximate cost at which said site may be obtained, if the same is not already owned by the City, and that upon a site for said incinerator being agreed upon by this Board, that the said Board of Public Works, through the City Engineer, be directed to make suitable borings and investigations to ascertain if said site is suitable for the purpose mentioned; and be it

Further Resolved, That, upon a suitable site being determined for the construction of said incinerator, this Board enact suitable legislation calling for the receipt of proposals for the construction of said incinerator and for the incineration of the garbage collected in the City and County, and authorizing and entering into a contract with the person, firm or corporation who will construct said incinerator, according to the plans and specifications deemed most beneficial to the City by the City Engineer and such engineering experts and specialists in garbage incineration as he may select as consultants, and who will agree to incinerate the garbage collected in said City and County at the least possible cost, not exceeding $1 per ton, and with the greatest return for the privilege of so doing, said privilege to exist for a period of not longer than twenty-five years. That the least amount to be paid to the City and County for the privilege of incinerating said garbage shall be three per cent. of the annual net receipts of said incinerator.

Garbage Incineration.

The following resolution was submitted by Supervisor Roncovieri as a corollary to the minority resolution heretofore presented to the Board:

Whereas, on November 5, 1929, the electors of the City and County of San Francisco approved the policy of incineration of the City's garbage; and

Whereas, the City has no plans or specifications for an incinerator; and

Whereas, the City Engineer has requested that the Board of Supervisors appropriate $25,000 to enable him to prepare general plans and specifications for an incinerator, and for the additional purpose of making necessary tests for piling foundations on the land upon which such incinerator will be constructed; now, therefore, be it

Resolved, That the Board of Supervisors hereby officially adopts the policy of incineration of the garbage of this City and County; and be it

Further Resolved, That in order to expedite the construction of the incinerator the sum of $25,000 be and is hereby appropriated for the use of the City Engineer, Hon. M. M. O'Shaughnessy, for the following purposes, and for such other purposes as he may deem necessary in connection with the construction of said incinerator: Firstly, to make complete engineering studies, and employ such specialist engineers as he may deem necessary to assist him as consultants and advisors in the preparation of general plans and specifications that will secure for the City the benefits of competitive open bidding within a group of selected types of incinerators that will give San Francisco the best, the most efficient and the most up-to-date incinerator; and, secondly, to select the most feasible site at or near the present incinerator at Fifteenth and De Haro streets, and to make an appraisal thereof; and, thirdly, to make such borings and other foundation piling tests on the site selected as he may deem necessary, as advance preparation for the building of the incinerator thereon.

Withdrawn.

The foregoing resolution was subsequently withdrawn in favor of the following resolution presented by Supervisor Rossi:

Resolution No. 32231 (New Series), as follows:

Whereas, the electors of the City and County of San Francisco did, at the general election held on the 5th day of November, 1929, express and declare as their policy that the garbage collected in the City and County of San Francisco should be disposed of by incineration; and

Whereas, in order to carry out said policy as so declared and expressed it is necessary that an incinerator be constructed in the City and County of San Francisco for the purpose of incinerating the garbage collected therein; and

Whereas, there is urgent necessity that said incinerator should be constructed without further unnecessary delay; and

Whereas, in order to conserve time, the existing plant being absolutely obsolete, and in view of the fact that plans and specifications are necessary, irrespective of the method of financing; and

Whereas, the City Engineer was authorized by Resolution No. 31004 (New Series) of the Board of Supervisors, approved June 13, 1929, to make a study and report upon the proper type of incinerator for San Francisco; and

Whereas, such report was made by the City Engineer to the Board of Supervisors in August, 1929, carrying definite recommendations as to the method of procedure; now, therefore, be it

Resolved, That the Board of Supervisors of the City and County of San Francisco make an appropriation and authorize the City Engineer to prepare plans and specifications immediately for the proper type of incinerator, including the preparation of foundation data calling for test pit observations, test borings and test piling, on such site or sites as are found to be available for an incinerator at or near the site of the present incinerator, at Fifteenth and De Haro streets; and be it

Further Resolved, That such plans and specifications cover the type of foundation, the type of building, the approaches thereto, the general arrangement of furnaces in the building, such furnaces to be in accord with requirements set up in recommendation for refuse incineration by the City Engineer, dated August 12, 1929, the method of handling incoming and outgoing materials, and all essential requirements for obtaining an efficient modern incinerator; and be it now

Further Resolved, That the Board of Supervisors does make an appropriation of $25,000 to provide for cost of obtaining foundation data and preparing plans and specifications, and does authorize the City Engineer to proceed with the work of preparing plans and specifications; and be it now

Further Resolved, That, upon presentation of plans and specifications to the Board of Supervisors and the approval thereof by said Board, thereupon said Board of Supervisors will authorize the receipt of bids for the construction of a plant privately built in conformity with such plans and specifications, with the understanding that all bids submitted shall contain a recapture clause whereby the City and County of San Francisco may take over the plant after a term of years at a stipulated price.

Supervisor Power asked for a separation of the resolution and reference of the $25,000 appropriation part of the resolution to the Finance Committee.

There being no objection, it was *so ordered*.

Supervisor McSheehy moved as an amendment the following: After the first "Whereas," insert "Resolved, That the Finance Committee of this Board be requested, in making up the Budget of this year (1930-1931), to allocate sufficient money in said Budget for the purchase of a block of land contiguous to the present incinerator, now loated at Fifteenth and De Haro streets, and erect thereon an incinerator of the most modern type, that will burn 800 tons of garbage a day at a cost not to exceed one dollar per ton.

Referred to Finance Committee on point of order raised by Supervisor Andriano.

Supervisor Havenner moved to amend the final paragraph, after the words, "thereupon said Board of Supervisors shall take the necessary legal steps to submit a bond issue," after the word "thereupon," "Said Board shall take the necessary legal steps to submit a bond issue, representing the estimated cost of said incinerator, to the voters of San Francisco at the general election in November, 1930."

Amendment *lost* by the following vote:

Aye—Supervisor Havenner—1.

Noes—Supervisors Andriano, Canepa, Colman, Gallagher, Hayden, McGovern, McSheehy, Miles, Peyser, Power, Roncovieri, Rossi, Stanton, Suhr, Toner—15.

Absent—Supervisors Shannon, Spaulding—2.

McSheehy Amendment Defeated.

Whereupon, a roll call was had on Supervisor McSheehy's amendment, heretofore referred to the Finance Committee, and the same was *defeated* by the following vote:

Ayes—Supervisors McSheehy, Miles—2.

Noes—Supervisors Andriano, Canepa, Colman, Gallagher, Havenner, Hayden, McGovern, Peyser, Power, Roncovieri, Rossi, Stanton, Suhr, Toner—14.

Absent—Supervisors Shannon, Spaulding—2.

Adopted.

Whereupon, the roll was called on the original resolution, presented by Supervisor Rossi, amended by reducing appropriation from $25,000 to $10,000, and the same was *adopted* by the following vote:

Resolution No. 32231 (New Series), as follows:

Whereas, the electors of the City and County of San Francisco did, at the general election held on the 5th day of November, 1929, express and declare as their policy that the garbage collected in the City and County of San Francisco should be disposed of by incineration; and

Whereas, in order to carry out said policy as so declared and expressed, it is necessary that an incinerator be constructed in the City and County of San Francisco for the purpose of incinerating the garbage collected therein; and

Whereas, there is urgent necessity that said incinerator should be constructed without further unnecessary delay; and

Whereas, in order to conserve time, the existing plant being absolutely obsolete, and in view of the fact that plans and specifications are necessary, irrespective of the method of financing; and

Whereas, the City Engineer was authorized, by Resolution No. 31004 (New Series) of the Board of Supervisors, approved June 13, 1929, to make a study and report upon the proper type of incinerator for San Francisco; and

Whereas, such report was made by the City Engineer to the Board of Supervisors in August, 1929, carrying definite recommendations as to the method of procedure; now, therefore, be it

Resolved, That the Board of Supervisors of the City and County of San Francisco make an appropriation and authorize the City Engineer to prepare plans and specifications immediately for the proper type of incinerator, including the preparation of foundation data, calling for test pit observations, test borings and test piling, on such site or sites as are found to be available for an incinerator, at or near the site of the present incinerator, at Fifteenth and De Haro streets; and be it

Further Resolved, That such plans and specifications cover the type of foundation, the type of building, the approaches thereto, the general arrangement of furnaces in the building, such furnaces to be in accord with requirements set up in recommendation for refuse incineration by the City Engineer, dated August 12, 1929, the method of handling incoming and outgoing materials, and all essential requirements for obtaining an efficient modern incinerator; and be it now

Further Resolved, That the Board of Supervisors does make an appropriation of $10,000 to provide for cost of obtaining foundation data and preparing plans and specifications, and does authorize the City Engineer to proceed with the work of preparing plans and specifications; and be it

Further Resolved, That upon presentation of plans and specifications to the Board of Supervisors and the approval thereof by said Board, thereupon said Board of Supervisors will authorize the receipt of bids for the construction of a plant privately built in conformity with such plans and specifications, with the understanding that all bids submitted shall contain a recapture clause whereby the City and County of San Francisco may take over the plant after a term of years at a stipulated price.

Ayes—Supervisors Andriano, Canepa, Colman, Gallagher, Havenner, Hayden, McGovern, McSheehy, Miles, Peyser, Power, Roncovieri, Rossi, Stanton, Suhr, Toner—16.

Absent—Supervisors Shannon, Spaulding—2.

Passed for Printing.

The following resolutions were *passed for printing*:

Appropriation, $10,000, Foundation Data, Plans, Etc., Garbage Incinerator.

On motion of Supervisor Rossi:

Resolution No. ————— (New Series), as follows:

Resolved, That the sum of $10,000 be and the same is hereby set aside, appropriated and authorized to be expended out of the General Fund, Fiscal Year 1929-1930, for the expense of obtaining foundation data and preparing plans and specifications by the City Engineer for a garbage incinerator.

Appropriation, $10,000, Publicity and Educational Purposes, Population Enumeration.

On motion of Supervisor Rossi:

Resolution No. ————— (New Series), as follows:

Resolved, That the sum of ten thousand ($10,000) dollars be and the same is hereby set aside, appropriated and authorized to be expended out of "Urgent Necessity," Budget Item No. 24, Fiscal Year 1929-1930, for publicity and educational purposes in connection with the enumeration of the population of the City and County of San Francisco.

ROLL CALL FOR THE INTRODUCTION OF RESOLUTIONS, BILLS AND COMMUNICATIONS NOT CONSIDERED OR REPORTED UPON BY A COMMITTEE.

Passed for Printing.

The following resolution was *passed for printing*:

Automobile Supply Station Permit, J. L. Hanley, Northeast Corner Worcester Avenue and Junipero Serra Boulevard.

Resolution No. ————— (New Series), as follows:

Resolved, That J. L. Hanley be and is hereby granted permission, revocable at will of the Board of Supervisors, to maintain and operate an automobile supply station at premises on the northeast corner of Worcester avenue and Junipero Serra boulevard.

The rights granted under this resolution shall be exercised within six months, otherwise said permit shall become null and void.

City Attorney to Consider Provisions of Political Code as to Functions of the Board of Equalization.

Supervisor Havenner moved that the City Attorney be requested, in consultation with the Assessor, to make a study of the provisions of the Political Code which define and prescribe the duties of the Board of Supervisors sitting as a Board of Equalization, and to report back to this Board such amendments and additions to the present statutes as, in his judgment, might make functions of the Board of Supervisors practically operative.

Referred to Judiciary Committee.

Citizens' Committee, Census Enumeration.

Supervisor Gallagher presented:

Resolution No. 32233 (New Series), as follows:

Whereas, it is of vital importance to San Francisco that a correct enumeration of the population be made, and it is the desire of the municipality to cooperate in every manner possible toward an accurate census as provided by Federal statute;

Resolved, That his Honor the Mayor be authorized and requested to appoint a Citizens Committee to consist of representatives of civic, fraternal, religious, commercial and labor organizations to cooperate in an educational and publicity campaign to inform the residents of their duty to respond to census enumerators.

The Board of Supervisors and the several departments of the city government are also authori ed to participate in this cooperation.

Adopted by the following ·te:

Ayes—Supervisors Andria ю, Canepa, Colman, Gallagher, Havenner, Hayden, McGovern, McSheehy, Miles, Peyser, Power, Roncovieri, Rossi, Stanton, Suhr, Toner—16.

Absent—Supervisors Shannon, Spaulding—2.

ADJOURNMENT.

There being no further business, the Board at the hour of 6:45 p. m. adjourned.

J. S. DUNNIGAN, Clerk.

Approved by the Board of Supervisors May 5, 1930.

Pursuant to Resolution No. 3402 (New Series) of the Board of Supervisors of the City and County of San Francisco, I, John S. Dunnigan, hereby certify that the foregoing are true and correct copies of the Journals of Proceedings of said Board of the dates thereon stated and approved as recited.

JOHN S. DUNNIGAN,
Clerk of the Board of Supervisors.
City and County of San Francisco.

25—New Series   No. 13

Monday, March 24, 1930

urnal of Proceedings
Board of Supervisors

City and County of San Francisco

The Recorder Printing and Publishing Company
337 Bush Street, S. F.

OURNAL OF PROCEEDINGS
BOARD OF SUPERVISORS

MONDAY, MARCH 24, 1930, 10 A. M.

In Board of Supervisors, San Francisco, Monday, March 24, 1930, 10 a. m.

The Board of Supervisors met in regular session.

CALLING THE ROLL.

The roll was called and the following Supervisors were noted present:

Supervisors Andriano, Canepa, Colman, Gallagher, Havenner, Hayden, McGovern, McSheehy, Miles, Peyser, Power, Roncovieri, Rossi, Shannon, Spaulding, Stanton—16.

Absent—Supervisors Suhr, Toner—2.

Quorum present.

His Honor Mayor Rolph presiding.

APPROVAL OF JOURNAL.

The Journal of Proceedings of the meeting of February 10, 1930, was considered read and approved.

PRESENTATION OF PROPOSALS.

Annual Supplies.

Sealed proposals were received and opened between the hours of 2 and 3 p. m. on Monday, March 24, 1930, for furnishing supplies in the following classes, viz.:

Class 1—Milk, ice cream and groceries.

Class 3—Enameled wares, aluminum ware, tinware, japanned and galvanized wares and kitchen utensils.

Class 5—Fuel and gasoline.

Class 6—Boiler compounds and fire brick.

Class 8—Lubricants.

Class 10—Household supplies and cordage.

Class 14—Photographic and blue printing supplies.

Class 15—Drugs, medicines, chemicals, hospital appliances and surgical instruments.

Class 16—Street and sewer material.

Class 17—Drafting and engineers' supplies.

Class 18—Incandescent electric lamps.

Referred to Supplies Committee.

Action Deferred.

The following matter, on motion of Supervisor Power, *was laid over one week:*

Hearing of Appeal, Henry Cowell Lime & Cement Company.

Hearing of appeal of Henry Cowell Lime & Cement Company from the action and decision of the Board of Public Works in overruling the protest of Henry Cowell Lime & Cement Company against the improvement of the north half of Commercial street from the west line of The Embarcadero to a line at right angles with Commercial street and 125 feet 6¼ inches west of the west line of The Embarcadero, by the construction of full width artificial stone sidewalks, where sidewalks are not now to official grade, and the construction of a retaining wall to support this sidewalk, as set forth in Resolution of Intention No. 96689 (Second Series).

Leave of Absence Granted Mayor Rolph and Supervisor Rossi Appointed Acting Mayor.

The following resolution was presented and *adopted*:

Resolution No. 32255 (New Series), as follows:

Resolved, That his Honor Mayor James Rolph, Jr., be and he is hereby granted a leave of absence for a period of ten days, commencing March 27, 1930, with permission to leave the State; and be it

Further Resolved, That, during the absence of his Honor the Mayor, Supervisor Angelo J. Rossi be and is hereby appointed Acting Mayor.

Adopted by the following vote:

Ayes—Supervisors Andriano, Canepa, Colman, Gallagher, Havenner, Hayden, McGovern, McSheehy, Miles, Peyser, Power, Roncovieri, Rossi, Shannon, Spaulding, Stanton—16.

Absent—Supervisors Suhr, Toner—2.

UNFINISHED BUSINESS.

Final Passage.

The following matters, heretofore passed for printing, were taken up and *finally passed* by the following vote:

Authorizations.

On recommendation of Finance Committee.

Resolution No. 32235 (New Series), as follows:

Resolved, That the following amounts be and the same are hereby authorized to be expended out of the hereinafter mentioned funds in payment to the following named claimants, to-wit:

Library Fund.

(1) Foster & Futernick Company, binding Public Library books (claim dated Feb. 28, 1930) ....$ 1,375.10

(2) American Building Maintenance Company, janitor service for Public Libraries (claim dated Feb. 28, 1930).......... 810.00

(3) Technical Book Company, library books (claim dated Feb. 28, 1930) 845.16

(4) G. E. Stechert & Co., library books (claim dated Feb. 28, 1930) 2,376.35

(5) Sather Gate Book Shop, library books (claim dated Feb. 28, 1930) 1,546.42

(6) San Francisco News Company, library books (claim dated Feb. 28, 1930) 1,277.45

California Palace Legion of Honor—Appropriation 59

(7) Felix F. Schoenstein & Sons, furnishing electric heaters, wiring and circuits, and installing telephone system connecting all organ chambers (claim dated March 14, 1930)..$ 2,140.20

M. H. De Young Museum—Appropriation 58.

(8) P. J. Enright, heating and ventilating M. H. de Young Memorial Museum, fifth payment (claim dated March 14, 1930) ....$ 569.81

1929 Hospital Bond Construction Fund.

(9) John Reid, Jr., final payment, architectural services, Ward building "F," for Relief Home (claim dated March 12, 1930) ....$ 4,238.42

1928 Hetch Hetchy Construction Fund.

(10) Best Steel Casting Company, castings furnished Hetch Hetchy Water Construction (claim dated March 8, 1930)..$ 1,694.56

(11) Boiler Tank & Pipe Company, tunnel forms (claim dated
March 10, 1930) 1,261.86
(12) Coos Bay Lumber Company, lumber (claim dated March
10, 1930) 3,515.33
(13) Del Monte Meat Company, meats (claim dated March
8, 1930) ....•.......................... 1,289.28
(14) Ingersoll-Rand Company of California, machinery and
pump parts (claim dated March 10, 1930)................ 3,359.91
(15) The Charles Nelson Company, lumber (claim dated March
10, 1930) 660.00
(16) Owen-Oregon Lumber Company, lumber (claim dated
March 10, 1930) 600.86
(17) Pacific Coast Aggregates, Inc., concrete sand (claim
dated March 8, 1930) 821.28
(18) Pacific Coast Steel Corporation, steel (claim dated March
10, 1930) 2,452.01
(19) Santa Cruz Portland Cement Company, cement (claim
dated March 10, 1930) 2,630.00
(20) Shell Oil Company, gasoline and oils (claim dated March
8, 1930) 560.17
(21) United States Rubber Company, rubber boots, etc. (claim
dated March 10, 1930) 1,815.50
(22) Western Pipe & Steel Company, riveted pipe (claim
dated March 10, 1930) 1,881.65

Park Fund.

(23) Railway Express Agency, express charges on shipments
(claim dated March 14, 1930) ....$ 693.65

Municipal Railway Fund.

(24) Pacific Gas & Electric Company, gas and electricity furnished Municipal Railway, for February (claim dated
March 11, 1930) $40,026.11
(25) San Francisco City Employees Retirement System, to
match contributions from Municipal Railway employees
(claim dated March 7, 1930) 1,487.26
(26) San Francisco City Employees Retirement System, to
match contributions from Municipal Railway employees
(claim dated March 10, 1930) 7,149.19
(27) Panama Lamp & Commercial Company, electric lamps
(claim dated March 10, 1930) 831.60

Boulevard Bonds.

(28) Eaton & Smith, tenth payment, improvement of 19th
avenue extension from Sloat boulevard to Worcester avenue
(claim dated March 12, 1930) $11,000.00

County Road Fund.

(29) Federal Construction Company, extra work in connection with improvement of Grand View avenue (claim dated
March 10, 1930) ....$ 1,914.13
(30) Department of Public Works (Appropriation 33-B), reimbursement for asphalt labor used on street reconstruction
work during February, 1930 (claim dated March 10, 1930). 2,937.48

Special School Tax.

(31) American Studios, gridiron and stage equipment for
Galileo High School (claim dated March 11, 1930)........$ 3,481.00
(32) Park Commissioners, reimbursement for care of school
grounds (claim dated March 11, 1930).................... 1,466.67
(33) D. A. Pancoast Company, "Van Duprin" type panic bolts,
etc., for school buildings (claim dated March 11, 1930).... 888.90
(34) Miller & Pflueger, third payment, architectural services
on Roosevelt Junior High School (claim dated March 12,
1930) 606.25

(35) W. H. Crim, ninth payment, architectural services on
Park-Presidio Junior High School (claim dated March 12,
1930) 1,182.88
(36) San Francisco City Employees Retirement System, to
match contributions from employees paid from Special
School Tax (claim dated March 12, 1930) ..:............. 886.88

Auditorium Fund.

(37) Musical Association of San Francisco, services of Symphony Orchestra, concert of March 29, 1930 (claim dated
March 14, 1930) ....$ 2,000.00

The Water Revenue Fund.

(38) Revolving Fund, San Francisco Water Department, for
payments as provided by Section 13, Ordinance No. 8691
(New Series) (claim dated March 3, 1930)................$20,000.00

General Fund, 1929-1930.

(39) Joseph Hagan & Sons, burial of indigent dead (claim
dated March 13, 1930)..................................$ 851.00
(40) Herbert F. Dugan, drug sundries, San Francisco Hospital
(claim dated Feb. 28, 1930)............................. 1,826.06
(41) Sussman, Wormser & Co., groceries, San Francisco Hospital (claim dated Feb. 28, 1930)....................... 3,079.90
(42) Fred L. Hilmer Co., butter, San Francisco Hospital
(claim dated Feb. 28, 1930)............................. 2,071.79
(43) San Francisco Dairy Co., milk, San Francisco Hospital
(claim dated Feb. 28, 1930)............................. 4,286.39
(44) C. Nauman & Co., produce, San Francisco Hospital (claim
dated Feb. 28, 1930)...................................   828.50
(45) L. Lagomarsino & Co., produce, San Francisco Hospital
(claim dated Feb. 28, 1930).............................   996.24
(46) Eames Company, 100 sets bed casters, expansion adapters,
San Francisco Hospital (claim dated Feb. 28, 1930)........   520.00
(47) Richfield Oil Company, fuel oil, San Francisco Hospital
(claim dated Feb. 28, 1930)............................. 1,898.35
(48) Addressograph Company, partial payment on addressograph machinery, Department of Elections (claim dated
March 13, 1930).. 7,000.00
(49) Board of Park Commissioners, reimbursement for account of improvements to Palace of Fine Arts (claim dated
March 14, 1930)..   714.95
(50) Standard Gypsum Company, casting plaster, etc., for
the Palace of Fine Arts (claim dated March 14, 1930)......   810.50
(51) Clinton-Stephenson Construction Company, final payment, repairs to Palace of Fine Arts (claim dated March 14,
1930) 9,945.92
(52) William J. Quinn, police contingent expense for March
(claim dated March 10, 1930)...........................   750.00
(53) Wm. L. Hughson, one Ford touring auto for Police Department (claim dated March 10, 1930)..................   542.21
(54) St. Vincent's School, maintenance of minors (claim dated
March 10, 1930) 1,171.18
(55) Roman Catholic Orphanage, maintenance of minors
(claim dated March 10, 1930)........................... 1,938.13
(56) Albertinum Orphanage, maintenance of minors (claim
dated March 10, 1930)..................................   689.20
(57) Little Children's Aid, maintenance of minors (claim
dated March 10, 1930)..................................12,279.39
(58) Eureka Benevolent Society, maintenance of minors
(claim dated March 10, 1930)........................... 3,239.22
(59) Children's Agency, maintenance of minors (claim dated
March 12, 1930) 30,810.57
(60) Market Street Railway Company, eighth payment for

property at Frederick and Willard streets, Arguello boulevard and Golden Gate Park, per Ordinance No. 5830, New Series (claim dated March 17, 1930)..................... 7,750.00

(61) The Recorder Printing and Publishing Company, printing of Superior Court Calendars for February (claim dated March 17, 1930).. 515.00

(62) The Recorder Printing and Publishing Company, printing of Supervisors' Calendar, Journal, etc. (claim dated March 17, 1930).. 1,278.12

(63) Pacific Gas and Electric Company, street lighting, month of February (claim dated March 17, 1930)................ 61,082.02

(64) Sonoma State Home, maintenance of feeble-minded (claim dated March 17, 1930).......................... 10,500.00

(65) A. P. Jacobs, rental of premises No. 333 Kearny street, March 3 to April 3, 1930 (claim dated March 17, 1930)...... 1,120.75

(66) National Surety Company, depository bond in favor of Duncan Matheson, Treasurer, in amount of $1,000,000 for funds on deposit in Bank of America, New York (claim dated March 6, 1930)... 1,000.00

(67) National Surety Company, depository bond in favor of Duncan Matheson, Treasurer, in amount of $250,000, for funds on deposit in Bank of America, New York (claim dated March 6, 1930).................................... 1,250.00

(68) The Mercury Press, 512 copies Street Railway Transportation Requirements of San Francisco (claim dated March 11, 1930) 1,000.00

(69) Department of Public Works, Bureau of Building Repair, reimbursement for amount of painting material purchased for account of traffic painting (claim dated March 10, 1930). 585.40

(70) The Texas Company, gasoline furnished for account of street cleaning (claim dated March 10, 1930)............. 512.85

(71) Spring Valley Water Company, water furnished public buildings, February (claim dated March 10, 1930)........ 1,938.73

(72) Pacific Gas and Electric Company, lighting public buildings (claim dated March 11, 1930)...................... 5,327.19

(73 Pacific Gas and Electric Company, gas and electricity furnished Fire Department (claim dated Feb. 28, 1930)..... 2,201.95

(74) Seagrave Corporation, Fire Department apparatus parts (claim dated Feb. 28, 1930)........................... 1,068.85

(75) The Spring Valley Water Co., water for fire houses, installing hydrants and high-pressure water system (claim dated Feb. 28, 1930).................................... 1,757.78

(76) Standard Oil Company of California, fuel oil, etc., for Fire Department (claim dated Feb. 28, 1930)............. 630.78

(77) The Texas Company, gasoline, etc., for Fire Department (claim dated Feb. 28, 1930).......................... 1,219.36

Ayes—Supervisors Andriano, Canepa, Colman, Gallagher, Havenner, Hayden, McGovern, McSheehy, Miles, Peyser, Power, Roncovieri, Rossi, Shannon, Spaulding, Stanton—16.

Absent—Supervisors Suhr, Toner—2.

Appropriation for Dredging Opposite the Baker Street and Pierce Street Sewer Outfalls.

Also, Resolution No. 32236 (New Series), as follows:

Resolved, That the sum of $2,500 be and the same is hereby set aside, appropriated and authorized to be expended out of "Extension and Reconstruction of Sewers," Budget Item 37, for the cost of dredging opposite the Baker street and Pierce street sewer outfalls.

Ayes—Supervisors Andriano, Canepa, Colman, Gallagher, Havenner, Hayden, McGovern, McSheehy, Miles, Peyser, Power, Roncovieri, Rossi, Shannon, Spaulding, Stanton—16.

Absent—Supervisors Suhr, Toner—2.

Appropriations Out of County Road Fund.

Also, Resolution No. 32237 (New Series), as follows:

Resolved, That the following amounts be and the same are hereby set aside, appropriated and authorized to be expended out of County Road Fund for the following purposes, to-wit:

(1) For portion of the cost of the improvement of Sanchez street between Twenty-first and Hill streets, including the crossings of Twenty-first and Hill streets with Sanchez streets $4,500.00

(2) For the cost of widening the roadway of Fair avenue between Mission and Coleridge streets, by reducing the sidewalk from 10 to 7 feet, removal of existing basalt blocks, repaving with concrete and performing the necessary conform work at Mission and Coleridge streets............. 2,400.00

Ayes—Supervisors Andriano, Canepa, Colman, Gallagher, Havenner, Hayden, McGovern, McSheehy, Miles, Peyser, Power, Roncovieri, Rossi, Shannon, Spaulding, Stanton—16.

Absent—Supervisors Suhr, Toner—2.

Creating Positions of Eight Welfare Investigators at a Salary of $150 Per Month Each.

Also, Bill No. 8209, Ordinance No. 8714 (New Series), as follows:

Creating the positions of eight welfare investigators in the County Welfare Department heretofore created by Ordinance No. 8542 (New Series), authorizing the appointment of said eight welfare investigators and fixing their compensation at $150 per month.

Be it ordained by the People of the City and County of San Francisco as follows:

Section 1. The positions of eight welfare investigators in the County Welfare Department heretofore created by Ordinance No. 8542 (New Series) are hereby created, and the appointment of said eight welfare investigators at $150 per month each by the Board of Supervisors is hereby authorized.

Section 2. This ordinance shall take effect immediately.

Ayes—Supervisors Andriano, Canepa, Colman, Gallagher, Havenner, Hayden, McGovern, McSheehy, Miles, Peyser, Power, Roncovieri, Rossi, Shannon, Spaulding, Stanton—16.

Absent—Supervisors Suhr, Toner—2.

Appropriation, $10,000, Foundation Data, Plans, Etc., Garbage Incinerator.

Also, Resolution No. 32238 (New Series), as follows:

Resolved, That the sum of $10,000 be and the same is hereby set aside, appropriated and authorized to be expended out of the General Fund, Fiscal Year 1929-1930, for the expense of obtaining foundation data and preparing plans and specifications by the City Engineer for a garbage incinerator.

Ayes—Supervisors Andriano, Canepa, Colman, Gallagher, Havenner, Hayden, McGovern, McSheehy, Miles, Peyser, Power, Roncovieri, Rossi, Shannon, Spaulding, Stanton—16.

Absent—Supervisors Suhr, Toner—2.

Appropriation, $10,000, Publicity and Educational Purposes, Population Enumeration.

Also, Resolution No. 32239 (New Series), as follows:

Resolved, That the sum of ten thousand ($10,000) dollars be and the same is hereby set aside, appropriated and authorized to be expended out of "Urgent Necessity," Budget Item No. 24, Fiscal Year 1929-1930, for publicity and educational purposes in connection with the enumeration of the population of the City and County of San Francisco.

Ayes—Supervisors Andriano, Canepa, Colman, Gallagher, Havenner, Hayden, McGovern, McSheehy, Miles, Peyser, Power, Roncovieri, Rossi, Shannon, Spaulding, Stanton—16.

Absent—Supervisors Suhr, Toner—2.

Oil Tanks and Boilers.

On recommendation of Fire Committee.

Resolution No. 32240 (New Series), as follows:

Resolved, That the following revocable permits be and are hereby granted:

Oil Tanks.

N. George Wienholz, southwest corner of Broderick and O'Farrell streets, 1500 gallons capacity.

F. Tocker, 825 De Haro street, 1500 gallons capacity.

C. Peterson Co., south side of O'Farrell street, 150 feet west of Leavenworth street, 1500 gallons capacity.

G. Poy, north side of McAllister street, 65 feet west of Webster street, 1500 gallons capacity.

Edward Jose, east side of Gough street, 120 feet north of Jackson street, 1500 gallons capacity.

American Engraving and Colorplate Company, west side of Zeno place, 180 feet south of Folsom street, 1500 gallons capacity.

Gardner Dailey, 3747 Jackson street, 750 gallons capacity.

Andrew D. Himmelman, 41 Octavia street, 1500 gallons capacity.

Boilers.

G. F. Thomas Dyeing and Cleaning Works, 859 Fourteenth street, 10 horsepower.

The rights granted under this resolution shall be exercised within six months, otherwise said permits shall become null and void.

Ayes—Supervisors Andriano, Canepa, Colman, Gallagher, Havenner, Hayden, McGovern, McSheehy, Miles, Peyser, Power, Roncovieri, Rossi, Shannon, Spaulding, Stanton—16.

Absent—Supervisors Suhr, Toner—2.

Transfer Public Garage Permit, Haran & Woods, North Side of Clement Street, 57 Feet 6 Inches East of Twenty-first Avenue.

Also, Resolution No. 32241 (New Series), as follows:

Resolved, That Haran & Woods be and are hereby granted permission, revocable at will of the Board of Supervisors, to have transferred to them public garage permit heretofore granted Frederick W. Schmidt, by Resolution No. 28406 (New Series), for premises north side of Clement street, 57 feet 6 inches east of Twenty-first avenue.

The rights granted under this resolution shall be exercised within six months, otherwise said permit shall become null and void.

Ayes—Supervisors Andriano, Canepa, Colman, Gallagher, Havenner, Hayden, McGovern, McSheehy, Miles, Peyser, Power, Roncovieri, Rossi, Shannon, Spaulding, Stanton—16.

Absent—Supervisors Suhr, Toner—2.

Automobile Supply Station Permit, J. L. Hanley, Northeast Corner Worcester Avenue and Junipero Serra Boulevard.

Also, Resolution No. 32242 (New Series), as follows:

Resolved, That J. L. Hanley be and is hereby granted permission, revocable at will of the Board of Supervisors, to maintain and operate an automobile supply station at premises on the northeast corner of Worcester avenue and Junipero Serra boulevard.

The rights granted under this resolution shall be exercised within six months, otherwise said permit shall become null and void.

Ayes—Supervisors Andriano, Canepa, Colman, Gallagher, Havenner,

Hayden, McGovern, McSheehy, Miles, Peyser, Power, Roncovieri, Rossi, Shannon, Spaulding, Stanton—16.

Absent—Supervisors Suhr, Toner—2.

Ordering the Improvement of Lobos Street.

On recommendation of Streets Committee.

Bill No. 8210, Ordinance No. 8715 (New Series), as follows:

Ordering the performance of certain street work to be done in the City and County of San Francisco, approving and adopting specifications therefor.

Be it ordained by the People of the City and County of San Francisco as follows:

Section 1. The Board of Public Works in written communication filed in the office of the Clerk of the Board of Supervisors February 10, 1930, having recommended the ordering of the following street work, the same is hereby ordered to be done in the City and County of San Francisco in conformity with the provisions of the Street Improvement Ordinance of 1918 of said City and County of San Francisco, said work to be performed under the direction of the Board of Public Works, and to be done in accordance with the specifications prepared therefor by said Board of Public Works, and on file in its office, which said plans and specifications are hereby approved and adopted.

That said Board of Supervisors, pursuant to the provisions of Part II of the said Street Improvement Ordinance of 1918 of said City and County of San Francisco, does hereby determine and declare that the assessment to be imposed for the said contemplated improvements, respectively, may be paid in twenty installments; that the period of time after the time of the payment of the first installment when each of the succeeding installments must be paid is to be six months from the time of the payment of the preceding installment, and that the rate of interest to be charged on all deferred payments shall be seven per centum per annum.

The improvement of the southerly one-half of Lobos street from a line parallel with and 275 feet easterly from Plymouth avenue to a line parallel with and 400 feet easterly from Plymouth avenue, by the construction of armored concrete curbs; by the construction of a 6-inch ironstone pipe side sewer and by the construction of an asphaltic concrete pavement, consisting of a 6-inch concrete foundation and a one and one-half inch asphaltic concrete wearing surface on the roadway thereof.

Section 2. This ordinance shall take effect immediately.

Ayes—Supervisors Andriano, Canepa, Colman, Gallagher, Havenner, Hayden, McGovern, McSheehy, Miles, Peyser, Power, Roncovieri, Rossi, Shannon, Spaulding, Stanton—16.

Absent—Supervisors Suhr, Toner—2.

Establishing Grades on Cayuga Avenue and on Seneca Avenue.

Also, Bill No. 8211, Ordinance No. 8716 (New Series), as follows:

Establishing grades on Cayuga avenue and on Seneca avenue as hereinafter described.

Be it ordained by the People of the City and County of San Francisco as follows:

Section 1. The grades on Cayuga avenue and on Seneca avenue are hereby established at points hereinafter named and at heights above city base as hereinafter stated. in accordance with recommendation of the Board of Public Works, filed March 11, 1930:

Cayuga Avenue.

Oneida avenue, intersection, 145.00 feet. (The same being the present official grade.)

215 feet southwesterly from Oneida avenue, 146.37 feet.

At the southwesterly end of the first curve southwesterly from
Oneida avenue, 148.29 feet.

Northwesterly curb line of, 19.49 feet northeasterly from the easterly end of the curb return to Seneca avenue, 149.44 feet.

Northwesterly curb line of, 20.51 feet westerly from the easterly end
of the curb return to Seneca avenue, 149.54 feet.

Northwesterly curb line of, 17.18 feet southerly from the northerly
end of the curb return to Seneca avenue, 149.51 feet.

Northwesterly curb line of, 16.09 feet northeasterly from the westerly end of the curb return to Seneca avenue, 149.64 feet.

Southeasterly curb line of, 13.95 feet northwesterly from the southeasterly curb return to Seneca avenue, 149.30 feet.

Seneca Avenue.

12 feet southwesterly from the northeasterly line of, at Alemany
boulevard northwesterly line, 177.79 feet.

12 feet northeasterly from the southwesterly line of, at Alemany
boulevard northwesterly line, 178.60.

11 feet northwesterly from Bannock street produced, 176.53 feet.

Northeasterly curb line of, 6.56 feet northwesterly from the southeasterly end of the curb return to Cayuga avenue, 149.72 feet.

Southwesterly curb line of, 36.05 feet southeasterly from the southeasterly end of the curb return to Cayuga avenue, 149.80 feet.

Southwesterly curb line of, 13.95 feet northwesterly from the southeasterly end of the curb return to Cayuga avenue, 149.30 feet.

Southwesterly curb line of, 17.18 feet southerly from the northerly
end of the curb return to Cayuga avenue, 149.51 feet.

Northeasterly curb line of, 20.51 feet westerly from the easterly end
of the curb return to Cayuga avenue, 149.54 feet.

Northeasterly curb line of, 17.26 feet northwesterly from the westerly end of the curb return to Cayuga avenue, 149.65 feet.

Northeasterly curb line of, 53.83 feet northeasterly from the southwesterly end of the curb return to Otsego avenue, 150.76 feet.

Northeasterly line of, produced southeasterly at Otsego avenue,
151.00 feet. (The same being the present official grade.)

15 feet southwesterly from the northeasterly line of, at Otsego avenue northwesterly line, 151.00 feet. (The same being the present official
grade.)

Southwesterly curb line of, 124.08 feet southeasterly from the beginning of the curve easterly from Delano avenue, 151.00 feet.

On Cayuga avenue between Oneida avenue produced and the southwesterly line of Seneca avenue, and on Seneca avenue between
Alemany boulevard and the northwesterly line of Otsego avenue
produced, be established to conform to true gradients between the grade
elevations above given therefor.

Section 2. This ordinance shall take effect immediately.

Ayes—Supervisors Andriano, Canepa, Colman, Gallagher, Havenner,
Hayden, McGovern, McSheehy, Miles, Peyser, Power, Roncovieri, Rossi,
Shannon, Spaulding, Stanton—16.

Absent—Supervisors Suhr, Toner—2.

Width of Sidewalks on Kirkwood Avenue.

Also, Bill No. 8212, Ordinance No. 8717 (New Series), as follows:

Amending Ordinance No. 1061, entitled "Regulating the Width of
Sidewalks," approved December 18, 1903, by amending Section Five
Hundred and Sixty thereof.

Be it ordained by the People of the City and County of San Francisco as follows:

Section 1. Ordinance No. 1061, entitled "Regulating the Width of
Sidewalks," approved December 18, 1903, be and is hereby amended
in accordance with the communication of the Board of Public Works.

filed in this office March 11, 1930, by amending Section Five Hundred and Sixty thereof, to read as follows:

Section 560. The width of sidewalks on Kirkwood avenue between Islais street and Mendell street shall be fifteen (15) feet.

The width of sidewalks on Kirkwood avenue between Mendell street and Lane street shall be twenty-two (22) feet and six (6) inches.

The width of sidewalks on Kirkwood avenue between Lane street and Water Front street shall be fifteen (15) feet.

Section 2. Any expense caused by the above change of walk widths shall be borne by the property owners.

Section 3. This ordinance shall take effect and be in force from and after its passage.

Ayes—Supervisors Andriano, Canepa, Colman, Gallagher, Havenner, Hayden, McGovern, McSheehy, Miles, Peyser, Power, Roncovieri, Rossi, Shannon, Spaulding, Stanton—16.

Absent—Supervisors Suhr, Toner—2.

Width of Sidewalks on Cayuga Avenue and on Seneca Avenue.

Also, Bill No. 8213, Ordinance No. 8718 (New Series), as follows:

Amending Ordinance No. 1061, entitled "Regulating the Width of Sidewalks," approved December 18, 1903, by adding thereto new sections, to be numbered ten hundred and ninety and ten hundred and ninety-one.

Be it ordained by the People of the City and County of San Francisco as follows:

Section 1. Ordinance No. 1061, entitled "Regulating the Width of Sidewalks,", approved December 18, 1903, be and is hereby amended, in accordance with the communication of the Board of Public Works, filed in this office March 3, 1930, by adding thereto new sections, to be numbered ten hundred and ninety and ten hundred and ninety-one, to read as follows:

Section 1090. The width of sidewalks on Cayuga avenue between Oneida avenue and Seneca avenue shall be as shown on that certain map entitled "Map of Cayuga avenue between Oneida avenue and Seneca avenue," showing the location of street and curb lines and the width of sidewalks.

Section 1091. The width of sidewalks on Seneca avenue between Otsego avenue and Alemany boulevard shall be as shown on that certain map entitled "Map of Seneca avenue between Otsego avenue and Alemany boulevard," showing the location of street and curb lines and the width of sidewalks.

Section 2. Any expense caused by the above change of walk widths shall be borne by the property owners.

Section 3. This ordinance shall take effect and be in force from and after its passage.

Ayes—Supervisors Andriano, Canepa, Colman, Gallagher, Havenner, Hayden, McGovern, McSheehy, Miles, Peyser, Power, Roncovieri, Rossi, Shannon, Spaulding, Stanton—16.

Absent—Supervisors Suhr, Toner—2.

Repealing That Portion of Ordinance No. 8652 (New Series), Ordering the Improvement of Portions of Thirty-fourth, Thirty-seventh and Forty-eighth Avenues by the Removal of Sand and the Construction of Bulkheads.

Also, Bill No. 8214, Ordinance No. 8719 (New Series), as follows:

Repealing that portion of Ordinance No. 8652 (New Series) in so far as it relates to the improvement of certain portions of Thirty-fourth avenue, Thirty-seventh avenue and Forty-eighth avenue, by the removal of sand and the construction of bulkheads.

Be it ordained by the People of the City and County of San Francisco as follows:

Section 1. Ordinance No. 8652 (New Series), in so far as it relates to the improvement of certain portions of Thirty-fourth avenue, Thirty-seventh avenue and Forty-eighth avenue, by the removal of sand and the construction of bulkheads, is hereby repealed.

Section 2. This ordinance shall take effect immediately.

Ayes—Supervisors Andriano, Canepa, Colman, Gallagher, Havenner, Hayden, McGovern, McSheehy, Miles, Peyser, Power, Roncovieri, Rossi, Shannon, Spaulding, Stanton—16.

Absent—Supervisors Suhr, Toner—2.

Full Acceptance of Roadway of Certain Streets.

Also, Bill No. 8215, Ordinance No. 8720 (New Series), as follows:

Providing for full acceptance of the roadway of Alameda street between Treat avenue and Harrison street, Division street between Bryant and Florida streets, Delano avenue between Geneva and Niagara avenues, Madison street between Silliman and Felton streets, Naples street between Amazon and Geneva avenues, Naples street between Geneva avenue and Rolph street and between Rolph and Munich streets, Ripley street between Folsom and Alabama streets, Twenty-sixth street between York and Hampshire streets, Twentieth street between Sanchez and Noe streets, Treat avenue between Florida and Alabama streets, crossing of Division and Florida streets, intersection of Treat avenue, Alabama street and Alameda street, intersection of Delano and Seminola avenues, crossing of Madison and Silliman streets, crossing of Naples street and Geneva avenue, crossing of Naples and Rolph streets, intersections of Naples and Athens streets, Naples and Seville streets and Brunswick street and Naples and Munich streets, intersection of Ripley and Harrison streets, crossing of Twentieth and Sanchez streets, crossing of Delano and Niagara avenues.

Be it ordained by the People of the City and County of San Francisco as follows:

Section 1. The roadways of the following named streets, including the curbs on both sides thereof, having been constructed to the satisfaction of the Board of Public Works and of the Board of Supervisors, are hereby fully accepted by the City and County of San Francisco (except those portions required by law to be kept in order by the railroad company having tracks thereon), in accordance with the provisions of Section 23, Chapter 2, Article VI of the Charter, said roadways having been paved with asphaltic concrete and concrete and curbs laid thereon, and are in good condition throughout, and have sewers, gas and water mains laid therein, to-wit: Alameda street between Treat avenue and Harrison street, Division street between Bryant and Florida streets, Delano avenue between Geneva and Niagara avenues, Madison street between Silliman and Felton streets, Naples street between Amazon and Geneva avenues, Naples street between Geneva avenue and Rolph street and between Rolph and Munich streets, Ripley street between Folsom and Alabama streets, Twenty-sixth street between York and Hampshire streets, Twentieth street between Sanchez and Noe streets, Treat avenue between Florida and Alabama streets, crossing of Division and Florida streets, intersection of Treat avenue, Alabama street and Alameda street, intersection of Delano and Seminola avenues, crossing of Madison and Silliman streets, crossing of Naples street and Geneva avenue, crossing of Naples and Rolph streets, intersections of Naples and Athens streets, Naples and Seville streets and Brunswick street and Naples and Munich streets, intersection of Ripley and Harrison streets, crossing of Twentieth and Sanchez streets, crossing of Delano and Niagara avenues.

Section 2. This ordinance shall take effect immediately.

Ayes—Supervisors Andriano, Canepa, Colman, Gallagher, Havenner, Hayden, McGovern, McSheehy, Miles, Peyser, Power, Roncovieri, Rossi, Shannon, Spaulding, Stanton—16.

Absent—Supervisors Suhr, Toner—2.

Conditional Acceptance of Roadway of Certain Streets.

Also, Bill No. 8216, Ordinance No. 8721 (New Series), as follows:

Providing for conditional acceptance of the roadways of Donner avenue between Phelps street and the westerly line of Hudson Garden Tract; Evans avenue between Marin and Napoleon streets; Hollister street between Hawes and Griffith streets; Keith street between Wallace and Yosemite avenues; Lakeview avenue between Plymouth and Capitol avenues, including the intersections of Lakeview and Granada avenues and Lakeview and Miramar avenues, and between Capitol and Jules avenues, including the intersection of Faxon avenue; Rodeo avenue between Teddy avenue and Brussels street and the intersection of Rodeo avenue and Somerset street; Rankin street between Davidson and Evans avenues between Islais street and Custer avenue; Twenty-eighth avenue between Noriega and Ortega streets; Thirty-eighth avenue between Rivera and Santiago streets; Forty-fourth avenue between Lawton and Moraga streets; Forty-fifth avenue between Moraga and Noriega streets; Kirkham street between Thirty-first and Thirty-second avenues; Santiago street between Forty-seventh and Forty-eighth avenues; Wallace street between Third and Keith streets; Yosemite avenue between Third and Keith streets; crossing of Keith street and Yosemite avenue; crossing of Wallace and Keith streets; crossing of Palou avenue and Griffith street; crossing of Madison and Felton streets.

Be it ordained by the People of the City and County of San Francisco as follows:

Section 1. The roadways of the following named streets, including the curbs on both sides thereof, having been constructed to the satisfaction of the Board of Public Works and of the Board of Supervisors, are hereby conditionally accepted by the City and County of San Francisco (except those portions required by law to be kept in order by the railroad company having tracks thereon), in accordance with the provisions of Section 23, Chapter 2, Article VI, of the Charter, said roadways having been paved with asphaltic concrete and curbs laid thereon, and are in good condition throughout; sewers and gas mains have been laid therein; no water mains have been laid therein, to-wit:

Donner avenue between Phelps street and the westerly line of Hudson Garden Tract; Evans avenue between Marin and Napoleon streets; Hollister street between Hawes and Griffith streets; Keith street between Wallace and Yosemite avenues; Lakeview avenue between Plymouth and Capitol avenues, including the intersections of Lakeview and Granada avenues and Lakeview and Miramar avenues, and between Capitol and Jules avenues, including the intersection of Faxon avenue; Rodeo avenue between Teddy avenue and Brussels street and the intersection of Rodeo avenue and Somerst street; Rankin street between Davidson and Evans avenues between Islais street and Custer avenue; Twenty-eighth avenue between Noriega and Ortega streets; Thirty-eighth avenue between Rivera and Santiago streets; Forty-fourth avenue between Lawton and Moraga streets; Forty-fifth avenue between Moraga and Noriega streets; Kirkham street between Thirty-first and Thirty-second avenues; Santiago street between Forty-seventh and Forty-eighth avenues; Wallace avenue between Third and Keith streets; Yosemite avenue between Third and Keith streets; crossing of Keith street and Yosemite avenue; crossing of Wallace avenue and Keith street; crossing of Palou avenue and Griffith street; crossing of Madison and Felton streets.

Section 2. This ordinance shall take effect immediately.

Ayes—Supervisors Andriano, Canepa, Colman, Gallagher, Havenner, Hayden, McGovern, McSheehy, Miles, Peyser, Power, Roncovieri, Rossi, Shannon, Spaulding, Stanton—16.

Absent—Supervisors Suhr, Toner—2.

Conditional Acceptance of Roadway of Certain Streets.

Also, Bill No. 8217, Ordinance No. 8722 (New Series), as follows:

Providing for the conditional acceptance of the roadways of Key avenue between Keith street and Bay Shore boulevard; Lawton street between Seventeenth and Eighteenth avenues; Ramsell street between Randolph street and its southerly termination; Twentieth street between Mississippi street and Pennsylvania avenue; Victoria street between Sargent and Randolph streets; Vernon street between Randolph street and a line 479 feet southerly from Randolph street; Valley street between Castro street and Diamond street; Wisconsin street between Nineteenth and Twentieth streets; Quintara street between Fifteenth and Sixteenth avenues.

Be it ordained by the People of the City and County of San Francisco as follows:

Section 1. The roadways of the following named streets, including the curbs on both sides thereof, having been constructed to the satisfaction of the Board of Public Works and of the Board of Supervisors, are hereby conditionally accepted by the City and County of San Francisco (except those portions required by law to be kept in order by the railroad company having tracks thereon), in accordance with the provisions of Section 23, Chapter 2, Article VI, of the Charter, said roadways having been paved with concrete and curbs laid thereon, and are in good condition throughout; sewers and gas mains have been laid therein; no water mains have been laid therein:

Key avenue between Keith street and Bay Shore boulevard; Lawton street between Seventeenth and Eighteenth avenues; Ramsell street between Randolph street and its southerly termination; Twentieth street between Mississippi street and Pennsylvania avenue; Victoria street between Sargent and Randolph streets; Vernon street between Randolph street and a line 479 feet southerly from Randolph street; Valley street between Castro street and Diamond street; Wisconsin street between Nineteenth and Twentieth street; Quintara street between Fifteenth and Sixteenth avenues.

Section 2. This ordinance shall take effect immediately.

Ayes—Supervisors Andriano, Canepa, Colman, Gallagher, Havenner, Hayden, McGovern, McSheehy, Miles, Peyser, Power, Roncovieri, Rossi, Shannon, Spaulding, Stanton—16.

Absent—Supervisors Suhr, Toner—2.

PRESENTATION OF BILLS AND ACCOUNTS.

Your Finance Committee, having examined miscellaneous demands not required by law to be passed to print, and amounting to $76,797.96, recommends same be allowed and ordered paid.

Approved by the following vote:

Ayes—Supervisors Andriano, Canepa, Colman, Gallagher, Havenner, Hayden, McGovern, McSheehy, Miles, Peyser, Power, Roncovieri, Rossi, Shannon, Spaulding, Stanton—16.

Absent—Supervisors Suhr, Toner—2.

NEW BUSINESS.

Passed for Printing.

The following matters were *passed for printing*:

Authorizations.

On recommendation of Finance Committee.

Resolution No. ———— (New Series) as follows:

Resolved, That the following amounts be and the same are hereby authorized to be expended out of the hereinafter mentioned funds in payment to the following named claimants, to-wit:

Auditorium Fund.

(1) Pacific Gas & Electric Company, gas and electric service
furnished Civic Auditorium, month of February (claim
dated March 15, 1930) ....$ 1,164.96

Park Fund.

(2) Berringer & Russell, hay, etc., for parks (claim dated
March 21, 1930) ....$ 668.74
(3) Golden State Milk Products Company, ice cream for parks
(claim dated March 21, 1930) 1,506.00
(4) Langendorf United Bakeries, Inc., bread, etc., for parks
(claim dated March 31, 1930) 520.90
(5) San Francisco Dairy Company, milk for parks (claim
dated March 21, 1930) 514.56
(6) Sherry Bros., Inc., butter and eggs for parks (claim dated
March 21, 1930) 520.77

Municipal Railway Fund.

(7) Ray Crosse and May Crosse, in full settlement for account
of damages and personal injuries sustained December 11,
1928 (claim dated March 14, 1930) ....$ 1,000.00
(8) Meyer Rosenberg, first payment for reconstruction of
Taraval street tracks of Municipal Railways (claim dated
March 15, 1930) 9,150.00

Boulevard Bonds.

(9) Louis J. Cohn, final payment for improvement Bay Shore
boulevard, Potrero to Silver avenues (claim dated March
19, 1930) ....$ 2,987.34

County Road Fund.

(10) Santa Cruz Portland Cement Company, cement for street
reconstruction (claim dated March 12, 1930)............$ 826.17
(11) San Francisco City Employees' Retirement System, to
match contributions from employees engaged on street reconstruction (claim dated March 12, 1930).............. 1,487.58

Hetch Hetchy Construction Fund, Bond Issue 1928.

(12) Del Monte Meat Company, meat (claim dated March 17,
1930) ....$ 606.25
(13) Dr. Paul E. Dolan, medical services rendered Hetch
Hetchy employees during February (claim dated March 14,
1930) 1,256.75
(14) A. Levy & J. Zentner Co., fruit and produce (claim dated
March 17, 1930) 562.81
(15) Pacific Coast Aggregates, Inc., sand (claim dated March
17, 1930) 816.25
(16) San Francisco City Employees' Retirement System, to
match contributions from Hetch Hetchy employees (claim
dated March 15, 1930) 591.32
(17) United States Rubber Company, rubber boots and coats
(claim dated March 15, 1930) 1,003.82

Hetch Hetchy Power Operative Fund.

(18) Depreciation Fund, Hetch Hetchy power operations, as
reserve depreciation, per Charter requirement (claim dated
March 14, 1930) $14,584.00
(19) Pope & Talbot, lumber (claim dated March 14, 1930)....   578.25
(20) Santa Cruz Portland Cement Company, cement (claim
dated March 14, 1930) 570.50

Special School Tax.

(21) Oscar Aaron, final payment, plumbing work for Geary
Street School (claim dated March 19, 1930).............$ 2,092.87

County Road Fund.

(22) Fay Improvement Company, eighth payment, improvement of Portola drive from 24th street to Fowler avenue claim dated March 19, 1930) $23,400.00

General Fund, 1929-1930

(23) Hanni & Girerd, repairs to Police Department autos (claim dated March 17, 1930) ....$ 591.45

(24) Berringer & Russell, hay, etc., for Police Department (claim dated March 17, 1930) 1,217.84

(25) Old Homestead Bakery, bread for County Jails (claim dated March 14, 1930) 810.29

(26) Greenebaum, Weil & Michaels, men's clothing, County Jails (claim dated March 14, 1930)...................... 899.31

(27) N. Randall Ellis, engineering service rendered telephone rate litigation (claim dated March 13, 1930).............. 750.00

(28) Reid Bros., bandages, etc, for Emergency Hospitals (claim dated Feb. 28, 1930)............................ 917.80

(29) Old Homestead Bakery, bread for San Francisco Hospital (claim dated Feb. 28, 1930)...................... 1,060.11

(30) Western Meat Company, meats for San Francisco Hospital (claim dated Feb. 28, 1930)...................... 830.27

(31) Del Monte Meat Company, meats for San Francisco Hospital (claim dated Feb. 28, 1930)...................... 1,412.36

(32) San Francisco International Fish Company, fish for San Francisco Hospital (claim dated Feb. 28, 1930).......... 561.20

(33) Schweitzer & Co., meats for San Francisco Hospital (claim dated Feb. 28, 1930)............................ 803.03

(34) J. T. Freitas Co., eggs, San Francisco Hospital (claim dated Feb. 28, 1930).................................. 1,985.81

(35) Scatena-Galli Fruit Company, fruit and produce, San Francisco Hospital (claim dated Feb. 28, 1930).......... 1,086.00

(36) Spring Valley Water Company, water for hospitals (claim dated March 13, 1930).......................... 1,568.05

(37) Baumgarten Bros., meats for Laguna Honda Home (claim dated Feb. 28, 1930)............................ 1,209.04

(38) California Meat Company, meat for Laguna Honda Home (claim dated Feb. 28, 1930)...................... 1,806.13

(39) Dairy Dale San Francisco Dairy Company, milk for Laguna Honda Home (claim dated Feb. 28, 1930)........ 2,127.60

(40) Del Monte Meat Company, meat for Laguna Honda Home (claim dated Feb. 28, 1930)...................... 3,686.89

(41) J. T. Freitas Co., Inc., eggs for Laguna Honda Home (claim dated Feb. 28, 1930)............................ 1,617.88

(42) C. Nauman & Co., produce for Laguna Honda Home (claim dated Feb. 28, 1930)............................ 1,155.67

(43) Richfield Oil Company, fuel oil for Laguna Honda Home (claim dated Feb. 28, 1930)...................... 1,544.03

(44) Sherry Bros., butter for Laguna Honda Home (claim dated Feb. 28, 1930).................................. 1,806.86

(45) Spring Valley Water Company, water furnished Laguna Honda Home (claim dated March 13, 1930).............. 961.94

(46) Monarch Flour Company, flour for Laguna Honda Home (claim dated Feb. 28, 1930).......................... 1,322.25

(47) Associated Charities, relief for unemployed (claim dated Feb. 28, 1930).................................. 6,534.19

(48) Frank J. Reilly, tenth payment, construction of addition to M. H. De Young Memorial Museum (claim dated March 21, 1930) 5,957.35

(49) California Printing Company, printing of building zone ordinance and maps (claim dated March 19, 1930)........ 884.60

Spring Valley Water Bonds.

(50) Gilmartin Company, Inc., printing of Spring Valley
Water Company deed (claim dated March 18, 1930).......$ 813.55

Payments for Properties Required for Boulevards.

Also, Resolution No. ————— (New Series), as follows:

Resolved, That the following amounts be and the same are hereby
set aside and appropriated out of Boulevard Bond Fund, Issue 1927,
and authorized in payment to the hereinafter named persons; being
payments for properties required for boulevard purposes, to-wit:

(1) James F. Farrell and Mary Farrell and California Pacific
Title and Trust Company, for all of Lot 41 in Block 2369, as
per the Assessor's Block Books of the City and County of
San Francisco, and required for the opening of the Sunset
boulevard; as per acceptance of offer by Resolution No.
32211, New Series (claim dated March 5, 1930)...........$ 3,000.00

(2) James Landers and Augusta Landers and Title Insurance
and Guaranty Co., for Lot 20 in Block 5477, as per the Assessor's Block Books of the City and County of San Francisco, and required for the opening of the Bay Shore boulevard; as per acceptance of offer by Resolution No. 32214,
New Series (claim dated March 11, 1930)...............   1,488.50

(3) Theresa Bootz and Henrietta Welch and Title Insurance and Guaranty Co., for Lot 1 in Block 7158, as per the
Assessor's Block Books of the City and County of San Francisco, and required for the widening of San Jose avenue as
an approach to Alemany boulevard; as per acceptance of
offer by Resolution No. 32212, New Series (claim dated
March 11, 1930) 6,000.00

Payments for Lands Required for Playgrounds.

Also, Resolution No. ————— (New Series), as follows:

Resolved, That the following amounts be and the same are hereby
set aside and appropriated out of Playground Fund, and authorized in
payment to the hereinafter named persons; being payments for lands
required for playground purposes, to-wit:

(1) To S. Szemanski and Sophie Szemanski, for Lot No. 21 of
Block 4164, as per the Assessor's Block Books of the City
and County of San Francisco; required for playground purposes (claim dated March 13, 1930).....................$ 1,250.00

(2) To Johannes Nelsen and Valborg Nelsen, for Lot No. 20
of Block 4164, as per the Assessor's Block Books of the City
and County of San Francisco; required for playground purposes (claim dated March 17, 1930).....................   1,250.00

Adopted.

The following matters were *adopted*:

**Additional Appropriation, $167.50, for Printing City Engineer's
Report on Street Railway Requirements in San Francisco.**

On recommendation of Finance Committee.

Resolution No. 32243 (New Series), as follows:

Resolved, That the sum of $167.50 be and the same is hereby set
aside, appropriated and authorized to be expended out of Appropriation 3-C (Printing, etc., Bureau of Supplies), for printing of City Engineer's report on street railway transportation requirements of San
Francisco.

Ayes—Supervisors Andriano, Canepa, Colman, Gallagher, Havenner,
Hayden, McGovern, McSheehy, Miles, Peyser, Power, Roncovieri, Rossi,
Shannon, Spaulding, Stanton—16.

Absent—Supervisors Suhr, Toner—2.

Appropriating $2,500 Towards Completion of the City's Accounting System.

Also, Resolution No. 32241 (New Series), as follows:

Resolved, That the sum of $2,500 be and the same is hereby set aside, appropriated and authorized to be expended out of the General Fund for the expense, during balance of the fiscal year, of continuing toward the completion of the City's accounting system.

Ayes—Supervisors Andriano, Canepa, Colman, Gallagher, Havenner, Hayden, McGovern, McSheehy, Miles, Peyser, Power, Roncovieri, Rossi, Shannon, Spaulding, Stanton—16.

Absent—Supervisors Suhr, Toner—2.

Passed for Printing.

The following matters were *passed for printing*:

Appropriations for Traffic Beacons and Line-Painting Machine.

On recommendation of Finance Committee.

Resolution No. ————— (New Series), as follows:

Resolved, That the following amounts be and the same are hereby set aside, appropriated and authorized to be expended out of "Traffic Signals," etc., Budget Item No. 57, for the following purposes, to-wit:

(1) For the purchase of one "Simmons" Spray Traffic Line
Painting Machine, to be used in marking new and existing
highways within the City and County of San Francisco....$ 527.60

(2) For the cost of installing beacons on safety zones at
southeasterly side of Valencia and Mission streets, and at
the intersections of Market street with Gough street, Laguna street, Geary street and Van Ness avenue, including
conduits, wiring, etc...................................   1,000.00

Appropriation for Assistant Superintendent of Street Cleaning.

Also, Resolution No. ————— (New Series), as follows:

Resolved, That the sum of $800 be and the same is hereby set aside, appropriated and authorized to be expended out of County Road Fund for the employment of an assistant superintendent of Street Cleaning, beginning March 1, 1930, at $200 per month.

Adopted.

The following resolution was *adopted*:

City Attorney to Dismiss Condemnation Proceedings.

On recommendation of Public Health Committee.

Resolution No. 32244 (New Series), as follows:

Whereas, the Board of Supervisors of the City and County of San Francisco, by resolution, has determined to abandon the eminent domain proceedings hereinafter mentioned; now, therefore, be it

Resolved, That the City Attorney be and he is hereby authorized and directed to dismiss that certain action in eminent domain proceedings pending in the Superior Court of the State of California, in and for the City and County of San Francisco, entitled "City and County of San Francisco v. George P. Moran et al.," numbered 215536 on the files of the Clerk of said Court, in so far as it relates to the following named defendants: Mary A. McConaghy, John McConaghy, D. Zelinsky & Sons, Inc., a corporation, and Neal McConaghy, and in so far as it affects the lands described as Parcels 5 and 5-A in Paragraph IX of the complaint on file.

Ayes—Supervisors Andriano, Canepa, Colman, Gallagher, Havenner, Hayden, McGovern, McSheehy, Miles, Peyser, Power, Roncovieri, Rossi, Shannon, Spaulding, Stanton—16.

Absent—Supervisors Suhr, Toner—2.

Passed for Printing.

The following matters were *passed for printing*:

Parking Station, J. D. Campbell, North Side Turk Street, West of Jones Street.

On recommendation of Fire Committee.

Resolution No. ———— (New Series), as follows:

Resolved, That J. D. Campbell be and is hereby granted permission, revocable at will of the Board of Supervisors, to maintain and operate an automobile parking station on premises north side of Turk street, 152 feet 8 inches west of Jones street.

The rights granted under this resolution shall be exercised within six months, otherwise said permit shall become null and void.

Public Garage Permit, R. A. Duclos, South Side of O'Farrell Street, 150 Feet West of Leavenworth Street.

Also, Resolution No. ———— (New Series), as follows:

Resolved, That R. A. Duclos be and is hereby granted permission, revocable at will of the Board of Supervisors, to maintain and operate a public garage under the Alexander Hamilton Hotel on the south side of O'Farrell street, 150 feet west of Leavenworth street.

The rights granted under this resolution shall be exercised within six months, otherwise said permit shall become null and void.

Public Garage Permit, Clyde E. Rausch, 945 Post Street.

Also, Resolution No. ———— (New Series), as follows:

Resolved, That Clyde E Rausch be and is hereby granted permission, revocable at will of the Board of Supervisors, to maintain and operate a public garage at 945 Post street.

The rights granted under this resolution shall be exercised within six months, otherwise said permit shall become null and void.

Public Garage Permit, Louis Noce, 2470 California Street.

Also, Resolution No. ———— (New Series), as follows:

Resolved, That Louis Noce be and is hereby granted permission, revocable at will of the Board of Supervisors, to maintain and operate a public garage at premises 2470 California street.

The rights granted under this resolution shall be exercised within six months, otherwise said permit shall become null and void.

Automobile Supply Station Permit, A. L. Campbell, Southwest Corner Ninth and Folsom Streets.

Also, Resolution No. ———— (New Series), as follows:

Resolved, That A. L. Campbell be and is hereby granted permission, revocable at will of the Board of Supervisors, to maintain and operate an automobile supply station on the southwest corner of Ninth and Folsom streets.

The rights granted under this resolution shall be exercised within six months, otherwise said permit shall become null and void.

Referred.

The following bill was, on motion, *referred to the Police Committee*:

Amendments to Taxicab Ordinance, Relative to Fees, Etc.

Bill No. 8218, Ordinance No. ———— (New Series), as follows:

Amending Subdivision (b) of Section 1, Section 3, Section 6, and Subdivision (c) of Section 7 of Ordinance No. 8637 (New Series), entitled "Providing for the issuance of certificates of public convenience and necessity in connection with the issuance of licenses for the operation of taxicabs, as defined in Ordinance No. 6979 (New Series), and providing for the issuance of certificates of public convenience and necessity in connection with the operation of sightseeing buses as said buses are defined in Ordinance No. 5118 (New Series), and providing a penalty for any violation thereof."

Be it ordained by the People of the City and County of San Francisco as follows:

Section 1. Subdivision (b) of Section 1, Section 3, Section 6, and Subdivision (c) of Section 7 of Ordinance No. 8637 (New Series), the title of which is recited above, are hereby amended to read as follows:

Section 1. That no license shall be issued for the operation of any taxicab, as the same is defined in Ordinance No. 6979 (New Series), unless and until the Board of Supervisors of the City and County of San Francisco shall, by resolution, declare that public convenience and necessity require the proposed taxicab service for which application for a license is made;

Provided, that such declaration of public convenience and necessity shall not be necessary:

(a) For the licensing of the same number of taxicabs licensed for operation by the applicant under the same name and colors on the day upon which this ordinance shall take effect, or the renewal of the same number of licenses annually thereafter; or

(b) For the renewal of licenses to the applicant for the number of taxicabs of the applicant for which the said Board of Supervisors shall have, at any time prior to the date of application for such renewal, made a declaration of public convenience and necessity.

Every person, firm or corporation holding a license authorizing the operation of a taxicab under and pursuant to the provisions of Ordinance No. 6979 (New Series) of this City and County shall, on or before the 1st day of April, 1930, file with the Clerk of this Board of Supervisors an affidavit setting forth the number of taxicabs which it is then licensed to operate, and shall describe the colors on the same.

Section 3. Any applicant for a license to operate a taxicab in accordance with the terms of Ordinance No. 6979 (New Series) shall make proper application to this Board of Supervisors for its declaration of the public convenience and necessity, on blanks to be furnished by the Clerk of said Board of Supervisors, and immediately upon the filing of such an application said Clerk shall cause a notice to be published in the official newspaper of the City of San Francisco, which said notice shall set forth the fact that said application has been filed for a license to operate a taxicab or taxicab business the name of the applicant, kind of equipment and number of vehicles to be operated. Said notice is to be published for three successive days. On filing the application the applicant shall pay to the Clerk the sum of fifteen ($15) dollars for one vehicle and one ($1) dollar for each additional vehicle for which a certificate of public convenience and necessity is desired to cover the cost and expenses of advertising the notice of application and the resolution granting the permit. All holders of existing licenses for the operation of taxicabs shall thereupon be entitled to file any complaints in protest that said holders may see fit at the time of the holding of the investigation and hearing. The Board of Supervisors shall consider all of the complaints and protests and in conducting its hearing shall have the right to call such witnesses as it may see fit. In all of such hearings the burden of proof shall be upon the applicant to establish, by clear, cogent and convincing evidence, which shall satisfy the said Board of Supervisors beyond a reasonable doubt, that public convenience and necessity require such operation of the vehicle or vehicles for which the said application has been made, and that such application in all other respects should be granted.

Section 6. All persons, firms or corporations within the purview of this ordinance shall regularly and daily operate his or its licensed taxicab business during each day of the licensed year to the extent reasonably necessary to meet the public demand for such taxicab service. Upon abandonment of such taxicab business for a period of ten (10) consecutive days by an owner or operator, the Board of Supervisors shall, upon hearing, after five (5) days' notice to the said applicant, thereupon direct the Police Commission of the City and County of San Francisco to revoke its said license, which it may have granted to said applicant in accordance with the terms and provisions of the aforesaid Ordinance No. 6979 (New Series), and said license shall be revoked. Such permits as are herein granted shall be transferable upon written application to said Board of Supervisors and the payment of the fee required of new applicants, and consent having been so obtained from said Board of Supervisors, and any and all such certificates of public necessity and convenience and all rights herein granted may be rescinded and ordered revoked for cause, and said Police Commission shall, upon notification of said action by said Board of Supervisors, revoke any and all such permits.

Section 7. No person, firm or corporation, after six (6) months from date of passage of this ordinance, shall operate any motor vehicle, as herein defined, unless and until such person, firm or corporation shall

(a) File with the Board of Supervisors a sworn statement showing the ability of said person, firm or corporation to pay all damages which may result from any and all accidents due to the negligent use or operation of such vehicle, and in the event such showing is unsatisfactory said Board may compel said person, firm or corporation to

(b) File with the said Board security, indemnity or bond guaranteeing the payment by said person, firm or corporation of all such damages; or

(c) Insure to a reasonable amount said person's, firm's or corporation's liability to pay such damages.

Said person, firm or corporation shall, not later than the first week in July of each year, and as often as said Board of Supervisors shall direct, file, in writing, upon a form prescribed by said Board of Supervisors, financial statement or statements of such insurance or indemnity or bonds or security held or secured by said person, firm or corporation and pay to said Clerk the sum of five ($5) dollars to cover the costs and expenses of examining said statements.

Failure to make satisfactory proof of ability to so respond in damages shall be deemed cause for cancellation of any and all permits so to operate.

Section 2. This ordinance shall take effect immediately.

Adopted.

The following resolutions were *adopted*:

Transfer of Rights, Title, Etc., Granted to United States District Engineer by Secretary of War, to Golden Gate Bridge and Highway District.

On recommendation of Public Utilities Committee.

Resolution No. 32245 (New Series), as follows:

Whereas, under date of March 20, 1924, application was made through the United States District Engineer for approval of the plans of a bridge to be constructed across the Golden Gate, San Francisco Bay, in behalf of the City and County of San Francisco and the County of Marin, two political subdivisions of the State of California; and

Whereas, said application did receive full consideration by the War Department, and on the 20th day of December, 1924, John W. Weeks, Secretary of War, did issue a certain document approving the plans submitted at said hearing upon certain conditions therein named, and directing that said counties proceed with such plans and submit applications for definite permits necessary before actual construction commence; and

Whereas, in proceeding with said plans the City and County of San Francisco and the County of Marin did elect to form, with the counties of Del Norte, Sonoma and portions of the counties of Mendocino and Napa, a certain political subdivision of the State of California, for the express object and purpose of carrying out the plans theretofore formulated by said City and County of San Francisco and the County of Marin, for constructing said bridge across the Golden Gate; and

Whereas, the directions of the said Secretary of War with respect to preparing detailed plans of the bridge are being carried out by said Golden Gate Bridge and Highway District in furtherance and pursuance of the original plan to bridge the Golden Gate, referred to in said communication of said John W. Weeks, Secretary of War, dated November 20, 1924; now, therefore, be it

Resolved, By the Board of Supervisors of the City and County of San Francisco, the legislative body of said City and County of San Francisco, that all rights, titles, privileges, or licenses which said City and County was granted under the said applictaion to the United States District Engineer by the said communication of the said John W. Weeks, Secretary of War, be and the same are hereby transferred, granted and assigned by the said City and County of San Francisco to the Golden Gate Bridge and Highway District, a political subdivision of the State of California, as the successor in interest of the City and County of San Francisco in the said plans and project of the constructing of a bridge across the Golden Gate, and the said Golden Gate Bridge and Highway District is hereby designated as the successor in interest of the City and County of San Francisco, and the agency which it has selected for the purpose of further carrying out and advancing the said plans and securing the approval and permits mentioned in the said communication of said John W. Weeks, Secretary of War, dated December 20, 1924.

Ayes—Supervisors Andriano, Canepa, Colman, Gallagher, Havenner, Hayden, McGovern, McSheehy, Miles, Peyser, Power, Roncovieri, Rossi, Shannon, Spaulding, Stanton—16.

Absent—Supervisors Suhr, Toner—2.

Stipulation From Spring Valley Water Company Dismissing Proceedings Before Railroad Commission Regarding Increase of Water Rates.

Also, Resolution No. 32246 (New Series), as follows:

Whereas, there are certain proceedings pending before the California Railroad Commission, instituted in the name of the City and County, for decrease in water rates charged by the Spring Valley Water Company, and proceedings instituted in the name of the Spring Valley Water Company for increase in rates; and

Whereas, the City and County of San Francisco has acquired the operative properties of the Spring Valley Water Company; now, therefore, be it

Resolved, That the City Attorney is hereby authorized and directed to obtain a stipulation from the Spring Valley Water Company dismissing its proceedings before the Railroad Commission and that the City Attorney file a dismissal of the proceedings instituted by the City and County of San Francisco, whereby the Spring Valley Water Company seeks increase of water rates and the City seeks decrease of water rates charged by the said Spring Valley Water Company.

Ayes—Supervisors Andriano, Canepa, Colman, Gallagher, Havenner,
Hayden, McGovern, McSheehy, Miles, Peyser, Power, Roncovieri, Rossi,
Shannon, Spaulding, Stanton—16.
Absent—Supervisors Suhr, Toner—2.

Passed for Printing.

The following bill was *passed for printing*:

Regulating the Powers and Defining the Duties of the Board of Public Works in Entering Into Contracts for the Use and Occupation of Lands Under the Control of San Francisco Water Department.

On recommendation of Public Utilities Committee.

Bill No. 8219, Ordinance No. ———— (New Series), as follows:

Regulating the powers and defining the duties of the Board of Public
Works in entering into contracts for the use and occupation of lands
under the control of San Francisco Water Department.

Be it ordained by the People of the City and County of San Francisco as follows:

Section 1. The Board of Public Works is hereby granted power to
enter into contracts with persons, firms and corporations for the use
and occupation of lands now under the control of the San Francisco
Water Department, which use and occupation are not incompatible
with the conduct of supplying water to the inhabitants of the City
and County of San Francisco and in other localities where water may
be supplied by said department.

Section 2. Contracts for the use and occupation of any of said
properties shall be entered into only upon the recommendations in
writing made by the head of the Water Department to the Board of
Public Works, which recommendations shall set forth a general description of the lands to be occupied, the purposes for which they are
to be occupied and the consideration which should be charged for such
occupation and how and when said consideration shall be paid. Upon
receiving said report the Board of Public Works shall in open meeting
give consideration to the same, and if the said Board shall determine
that it will be for the benefit and best interests of the said Water Department that said contracts be entered into, and that the consideration
to be received for said occupation is fair and reasonable and the best
consideration obtainable therefor and that the proposed use of said
property will not interfere with the use of said property by the City
for the purposes for which it was acquired, the said Board of Public
Works may enter into contracts for the use and occupation of such
property upon the terms recommended by the head of the Water
Department.

Section 3. The consideration to be paid under contracts described
herein may be for cash, interest in crops or other valuable consideration, and no contract shall be entered into for a period longer than
three years. All revenues from all contracts shall be credited to San
Francisco Water Department.

Section 4. All contracts for the use and occupation of lands shall
first be approved on their face as to terms and conditions by the head
of the Water Department and approved as to form by the City Attorney
or attorney for the Water Department.

Section 5. This ordinance shall take effect and be in force from and
after the date of its passage.

Adopted.

The following Resolutions were *adopted*:

Establishing Loading Zones.

On recommendation of Traffic and Safety Committee.

Resolution No. 32247 (New Series), as follows:

Resolved, That the following list of loading zones, of the lengths
specified, be established in front of or near the following addresses,

in accordance with the provisions of Section 36 of Ordinance No. 7691 (New Series) as amended:

639 Front street, 18 feet—American Box Co., 1 elevator.

160 Jackson street, 27 feet—Bertrand Seed Co.

801 Jones street, 18 feet—Pleasanton Hotel Apts.

316 Mission street, 18 feet—S. Levey Whse. Mdse. Co., 1 elevator.

1081-1095 Mission street, 45 feet—Dept. of Public Health, Central Office.

1338 Mission street, 27 feet—Security Storage Co., Calif. Plumbing Sup. Co.

1179 McAllister street, 36 feet—Std. Floor Covering Co., Milton Market, 4 stores.

134 Sacramento street, 27 feet—Tidemann & McMorran Grocery Co., 1 elevator.

10 Spear street, 36 feet—Rothschild Gen. Mdse. Co.

3288 Twenty-fourth street, 27 feet—Rossi Drug Co., Std. Express, Liberty Hat Co., 1 elevator.

Ayes—Supervisors Andriano, Canepa, Colman, Gallagher, Havenner, Hayden, McGovern, McSheehy, Miles, Peyser, Power, Roncovieri, Rossi, Shannon, Spaulding, Stanton—16.

Absent—Supervisors Suhr, Toner—2.

Establishing Passenger Loading Zones.

Also, Resolution No. 32248 (New Series), as follows:

Resolved, That the following list of passenger loading zones, of the lengths specified, be established in front of or near the following addresses, in accordance with the provisions of Section No. 36 of Ordinance No. 7691 (New Series) as amended:

1250 Jones street, 18 feet—Clay-Jones Apts.

Ayes—Supervisors Andriano, Canepa, Colman, Gallagher, Havenner, Hayden, McGovern, McSheehy, Miles, Peyser, Power, Roncovieri, Rossi, Shannon, Spaulding, Stanton—16.

Absent—Supervisors Suhr, Toner—2.

Rescinding and Reestablishing Loading Zones.

Also, Resolution No. 32249 (New Series), as follows:

Resolved, That the following loading zone, of the length specified, be rescinded and reestablished as specified herein, in front of or near the following address, in accordance with the provisions of Section No. 36 of Ordinance No. 7691 (New Series) as amended:

2554 Mission street, existing length, 36 feet; new length, 18 feet—Hales Mission Store.

Ayes—Supervisors Andriano, Canepa, Colman, Gallagher, Havenner, Hayden, McGovern, McSheehy, Miles, Peyser, Power, Roncovieri, Rossi, Shannon, Spaulding, Stanton—16.

Absent—Supervisors Suhr, Toner—2.

Disposal of Board of Health Junk.

On recommendation of Supplies Committee.

Resolution No. 32250 (New Series), as follows:

Resolved, That whenever upon the survey and representations of the superintendents of the respective institutions under the jurisdiction of the Board of Health, and the petition of the Health Officer, when, as and if approved by the Purchaser of Supplies, that certain personal property is unfit and unnecessary for the use of the City and County, viz.: Junk enameled steel utensils having no salvage value, that the same may then be considered as condemned and the Department of Public Health is hereby authorized to dispose of same by carting it to a public dump.

Ayes—Supervisors Andriano, Canepa, Colman, Gallagher, Havenner, Hayden, McGovern, McSheehy, Miles, Peyser, Power, Roncovieri, Rossi, Shannon, Spaulding, Stanton—16.

Absent—Supervisors Suhr, Toner—2.

ROLL CALL FOR THE INTRODUCTION OF RESOLUTIONS, BILLS AND COMMUNICATIONS NOT CONSIDERED OR REPORTED UPON BY A COMMITTEE.

Passed for Printing.

The following matters were *passed for printing*:

Stable Permit.

On motion of Supervisor McSheehy:

Resolution No. ———— (New Series), as follows:

Resolved, That George Neary be and is hereby granted permission, revocable at will of the Board of Supervisors, to maintain and operate private stable for six horses on the east line of Forty-eighth avenue, 250 feet south of Ortega street.

The rights granted under this permit shall be exercised within six months, otherwise said permit shall become null and void.

Passed for Printing.

The following resolution was *passed for printing*:

Transfer of Automobile Supply Station Permit.

On motion of Supervisor Canepa:

Resolution No. ———— (New Series), as follows:

Resolved, That the Shell Oil Company be and is hereby granted permission, revocable at will of the Board of Supervisors, to have transferred to it automobile supply station permit heretofore granted Paul Arata by Resolution No. 31550 (New Series) for premises at southeast corner of San Jose and Ocean avenues.

The rights granted under this resolution shall be exercised within six months, otherwise said permit shall become null and void.

Board Endorses St. Francis Community Church Drive.

Supervisor Havenner presented:

Resolution No. 32251 (New Series), as follows:

Whereas, the St. Francis Community Church, Episcopal, completed about a year ago, stands as a splendid example of Spanish Mission architecture; and

Whereas, said beautiful structure stands as a symbol for the best and highest ideals of life; and

Whereas, there is about to be started a campaign drive for $50,000 with which to complete the several units of the group not yet finished; now, therefore, be it

Resolved, That the Board of Supervisors of the City and County of San Francisco endorses the effort of the pastor and parishioners of St. Francis Community Church, Episcopal, to raise the money required to complete their plan of buildings; and be it

Further Resolved, That a copy of this resolution be spread upon the minutes of this Board and that a copy be sent to the pastor of St. Francis Community Church, Episcopal.

Adopted by the following vote:

Ayes—Supervisors Andriano, Canepa, Colman, Gallagher, Havenner, Hayden, McGovern, McSheehy, Miles, Peyser, Power, Roncovieri, Rossi, Shannon, Spaulding, Stanton—16.

Absent—Supervisors Suhr, Toner—2.

Better Homes and Clean-Up Week.

Supervisor Peyser presented:

Resolution No. 32252 (New Series), as follows:

Whereas, April 27 to May 3, 1930, inclusive, has been dedicated to Better Homes and Clean-Up Week"; and

Whereas, much can be done to beautify our city and to render it more sanitary and attractive as a place of abode; now, therefore, be it

Resolved, That his Honor the Mayor be and is hereby authorized to issue a proclamation declaring April 27 to May 3, 1930, inclusive, "Better Homes and Clean-Up Week" and to appoint a Citizens' Committee to cooperate in this movement for the beautifying of our city.

Adopted by the following vote:

Ayes—Supervisors Andriano, Canepa, Colman, Gallagher, Havenner, Hayden, McGovern, McSheehy, Miles, Peyser, Power, Roncovieri, Rossi, Shannon, Spaulding, Stanton—16.

Absent—Supervisors Suhr, Toner—2.

Presented by Supervisor Power:

Closing and Abandoning Certain Portions of City Hall Avenue.

Resolution No. 32253 (New Series), as follows:

Whereas, this Board has, by Resolution No. 10054 (New Series), declared its intention to close up and abandon certain portions of City Hall avenue; and

Whereas, proper notice of said resolution and of said proposed closing and abandoning of certain portions of City Hall avenue, as described in Resolution of Intention No. 10054 (New Series), was duly given by the Board of Public Works of the City and County of San Francisco by publication in the manner provided by the Charter of the City and County of San Francisco; and

Whereas, more than ten days have elapsed after the expiration of the publication of said notice, and no objections to the closing of said portions of City Hall avenue were made or delivered to the Clerk of this Board within said period of ten (10) days, or at all; and

Whereas, it is the opinion of this Board that the public interest and convenience will be conserved by the closing and abandonment of certain portions of City Hall avenue as hereinafter more particularly described; and

Whereas, in and by said Resolution No. 10054 (New Series) this Board did declare that the damages, costs and expenses of closing said portions of City Hall avenue are nominal and no assessment district is necessary to be formed for the purpose of paying the damages, costs and expenses thereof, the Board of Supervisors hereby declares and determines that the whole damage, cost and expense of closing certain portions of City Hall avenue, as hereinafter more particularly described, shall be paid out of the revenues of the City and County of San Francisco; now, therefore, be it

Resolved, That the closing and abandonment of certain portions of City Hall avenue, as hereinafter more particularly described, be and the same is hereby ordered, and that these certain portions of City Hall avenue be and the same are hereby closed and abandoned as an open public street. That certain portions of City Hall avenue hereinabove referred to are more particularly described as follows, to-wit:

Parcel 1. Beginning at a point formed by the intersection of the northerly line of Grove street with the northwesterly line of City Hall avenue; thence northeasterly along the northwesterly line of City Hall avenue to a point formed by the intersection of the northwesterly line of City Hall avenue with a line parallel with and distant 80 feet at right angles southerly from the center line of Fulton street (if extended and produced; thence easterly along said parallel line to a point formed by the intersection of said parallel line with the westerly line of Hyde street (if extended and produced); thence southerly along the westerly line of Hyde street (if extended and producd) to a point formed by the intersection of the westerly line of Hyde street (if extended and produced) with the southeasterly line of City Hall avenue; thence southwesterly along the southeasterly line of City Hall avenue to a point formed by the intersection of the northerly line of Grove street (if extended and produced) with the southeasterly line of City Hall avenue; thence westerly along the northerly line of Grove street (if extended and produced) to a point formed by the intersection of the northerly line of Grove street with the northwesterly line of City Hall avenue and the point of beginning.

Parcel 2. Beginning at a point formed by the intersection of the westerly line of Leavenworth street with the northwesterly line of City Hall avenue; thence southerly along the westerly line of Leavenworth street (if extended and produced) to a point on the southeasterly line of City Hall avenue; thence southwesterly along the southeasterly line of City Hall avenue to a point formed by the intersection of a line parallel with and distant 80 feet at right angles northerly from the center line of Fulton street (if extended and produced) with the southeasterly line of City Hall avenue; thence westerly along said parallel line to a point on the northwesterly line of City Hall avenue; thence northeasterly along the northwesterly line of City Hall avenue to a point formed by the intersection of the northwesterly line of City Hall avenue with the westerly line of Leavenworth street and the point of beginning. Be it

Further Resolved, That the Clerk of this Board transmit a certified copy of this resolution to the Board of Public Works, and that the Board of Public Works be instructed to proceed thereafter as required by law and the Charter of the City and County of San Francisco; and the Clerk of this Board is hereby directed to advertise this resolution in the official newspaper as required by law.

Adopted by the following vote:

Ayes—Supervisors Andriano, Canepa, Colman, Gallagher, Havenner, Hayden, McGovern, McSheehy, Miles, Peyser, Power, Roncovieri, Rossi, Shannon, Spaulding, Stanton—16.

Absent—Supervisors Suhr, Toner—2.

Referred.

The following was presented by Supervisor Shannon and *referred to the Public Buildings and Lands Committee:*

Condemnation of Land on Ocean Avenue, West of Mission Street, Emergency Hospital.

Resolution No. ———— (New Series), as follows:

Resolved, by the Board of Supervisors of the City and County of San Francisco, that public interest and necessity require the acquisition by the City and County of San Francisco, a municipal corporation, of the following property situated in the City and County of San Francisco, State of California, more particularly described as follows, to-wit:

Commencing at a point on the northerly line of Ocean avenue, distant westerly thereon 443.533 feet from the northwesterly line of Mission street, said point of commencement being the most easterly corner of that certain parcel of land designated Parcel 2, conveyed to the City and County of San Francisco by William B. McKinnon by deed recorded June 12, 1928, in Volume 1688, at page 58, Official Records of said City and County; thence westerly, northwesterly and northerly along the northeasterly line of the property so conveyed, being a curve to the right tangent to said northerly line of Ocean avenue at the point of commencement, radius 50 feet, central angle 106 degrees 26 minutes 08 seconds, an arc distance of 98.883 feet; thence continuing northerly along the easterly line of the property so conveyed, tangent to the preceding course, 33.206 feet; thence continuing northerly along said easterly line of the property so conveyed, and along the westerly line of the land deeded to said William B. McKinnon by the City and County of San Francisco, and recorded July 17, 1928, in Volume 1694, at page 328, Official Records of said City and County, being the arc of a curve to the right, tangent to the preceding course, radius 450 feet, central angle 11 minutes 43 seconds, an arc distance of 88.582 feet to the southwesterly line of Lot 18 of Wm. A. Lange's Subdivision of Block 1 of the Academy Tract, as per map thereof recorded in Map Book E and F, at page 68, Records of the City and County of San Francisco; thence southeasterly along the southwesterly line of said Lot 18, 72.63 feet to the westerly line of Lot 19 of said Wm. A. Lange's Subdivision of said Block 1; thence southerly, along the westerly line of said Lot 19, 135.71 feet to the northerly line of Ocean avenue; thence deflecting 78 degrees 26 minutes 50 seconds to the right and running westerly along said northerly line of Ocean avenue 24.55 feet, more or less, to the point of commencement.

Be it Further Resolved, That said property is suitable, adaptable, necessary and required for the public use of said City and County of San Francisco. It is necessary that a fee simple title be taken for such use.

The City Attorney is hereby ordered and directed to commence proceedings in eminent domain against the owners of said parcel of land and of any and all interest therein or claims thereto, for the condemnation thereof for the public use of the City and County of San Francisco, as aforesaid.

Passed for Printing.

The following resolution was *passed for printing*:

Appropriation, $10,000, Out of Budget Item 50, "Municipal Airport Fund," for Maneuvers at Mills Field, April 19 and 20, 1930.

Supervisor Spaulding presented from Finance and Airport Committees:

Resolution No. ———— (New Series), as follows:

Whereas, Mills Field has been chosen by General W. E. Gilmore, Chief of the Air Department of the United States Army, as the base for the United States Air Maneuvers, which will take place April 19 and 20, 1930; and

Whereas, the entire United States Army air fleet, embracing over 200 fighting craft of all kinds (being the largest assemblage of fighting planes ever assembled in the world), will assemble at Mills Field on these dates; and

Whereas, these air maneuvers will attract the attention of people from all over the United States to Mills Field and San Francisco; now, therefore, be it

Resolved, That the sum of $10,000 be and the same is hereby set aside, appropriated and authorized to be expended out of "Municipal Airport Fund," Budget Item No. 50, fiscal year 1929-1930, for general expenses in connection with these maneuvers, including necessary permanent and temporary improvements for Mills Field.

Mayor Retires.

At 3:30 p. m. Mayor Rolph and visitors retired and Supervisor Rossi was elected to preside.

Passed for Printing.

The following bill was *passed for printing*:

Granting to United States Government Site for Federal Building in Civic Center.

On motion of Supervisor Shannon:

Bill No. 8220, Ordinance No. ———— (New Series), as follows:

Agreeing to grant to the United States of America a site situate in the Civic Center of the City and County of San Francisco for the erection thereon of a Federal office building, and determining the con ditions under which said grant shall be made and the size of said site, and authorizing the Mayor of the City and County of San Francisco and the Clerk of the Board of Supervisors thereof to execute and deliver to the United States of America a deed conveying to the United States of America the hereinafter described real property as a site for the erection thereon of a Federal office building, and providing for the conveyance of additional land for said site, all pursuant to the provisions of Section 10a of Chapter II, Article II, of the Charter of the City and County of San Francisco.

Be it ordained by the People of the City and County of San Francisco as follows:

Section 1. That whereas, Section 10a of Chapter II, Article II, of the Charter of the City and County of San Francisco, authorizes the Board of Supervisors to cause to be conveyed to the United States of America, by a good and sufficient deed, and without monetary consideration, a site on the northeast corner of Hyde and Fulton streets, in the Civic Center in the City and County of San Francisco, which said site shall be used by the said United States of America for the erection thereon of a Federal office building.

Section 2. And whereas, the hereinafter described real property is situate on the northeast corner of Fulton and Hyde streets, in said Civic Center, and is unoccupied by any building or structure belonging to the City and County of San Francisco, and the United States of America has agreed to erect and maintain thereon a Federal office building, provided said property be transferred to the United States of America without any monetary consideration.

Section 3. The Board of Supervisors of the City and County of San Francisco hereby determines that the size and the site of said lands to be conveyed to the said United States of America for said Federal office building should be as hereinafter set forth.

Section 4. That the City and County of San Francisco does hereby offer to the United States of America the hereinafter described real property for the erection and maintenance thereon by the United States of America of a Federal office building, and does hereby agree to grant to the United States of America, without any monetary consideration, the hereinafter described real property, upon condition that the said United States of America shall cause to be erected and maintained thereon a Federal office building, which said building shall conform in general type of architecture and construction to the other buildings contained in the Civic Center.

Section 5. That the Mayor of the City and County of San Francisco and the Clerk of the Board of Supervisors be and they are hereby authorized, empowered and directed to make, execute and deliver to the United States of America a good and sufficient deed conveying to said United States of America the hereinafter described real property for the purposes herein set forth, which conveyance shall be made when the said Mayor is given satisfactory proof that the building to be erected and maintained thereon shall, in its general type of architecture and construction, conform to the other buildings at present erected in the Civic Center.

Section 6. That the site to be conveyed to said United States of America, in conformity with this ordinance, is described as follows, to-wit:

Commencing at the point of intersection of the southerly line of McAllister street with the easterly line of Hyde street produced southerly; thence southerly along said easterly line 207.375 feet; thence southeasterly on a curve to the right, tangent to a line deflected 90 deg. to the left from the preceding course, radius 42 feet, central angle 61 deg. 33 min. 58 sec., a distance of 45.128 feet to a point distant 229.375 feet at right angles southerly from the southerly line of McAllister street;

thence easterly parallel with the southerly line of McAllister street and 229.375 feet at right angles southerly therefrom, a distance of 375.568 feet to the westerly line of Leavenworth street produced southerly; thence at right angles northerly along said westerly line 229.375 feet to the southerly line of McAllister street; thence at right angles westerly along the southerly line of McAllister street 412.50 feet to the easterly line of Hyde street produced southerly, and point of commencement.

Saving and excepting therefrom the following described parcel of land:

All those portions of Lots Nos. 22 and 24, according to map entitled "Map of Yerba Buena Park, Park avenue and City Hall avenue, showing subdivision of property to be sold under Act of the Legislature, approved April 4, 1870," filed in the office of the County Recorder of the City and County of San Francisco, State of California, March 18, 1871, and recorded in Map Book E and F, page 38, embraced within the above description.

Section 7. That upon the City and County of San Francisco acquiring title to the real property hereinbefore excepted from the conveyance to be made pursuant to this ordinance, that the Mayor of the City and County of San Francisco and the Clerk of the Board of Supervisors be authorized to execute to the United States of America an additional deed conveying said excepted property to said United States of America for the purposes and upon the conditions herein contained.

Section 8. This ordinance shall become effective immediately upon its passage.

SPECIAL ORDER—2:30 P. M.

The matter of the discontinuance of the Appraisal Bureau of the Board of Equalization, made a Special Order of Business for 2:30 p. m. this day, was taken up.

Recommendation Disapproving Employment of John F. Barry.

San Francisco, March 14, 1930.

To the Honorable, the Board of Supervisors, City and County of San Francisco.

Gentlemen: Your Finance Committee had under consideration resolution presented by Supervisor Havenner, providing for the employment of John F. Barry for two weeks in connection with the appraising of all taxable real property subject to assessment with the City County of San Francisco, and recommends that it be disapproved.

Respectfully submitted,
ANGELO J. ROSSI,
J. EMMET HAYDEN,
JAMES E. POWER,
Finance Committee.

Discontinuation of Appraisal Bureau.

Supervisor Power presented the following resolution and moved its adoption:

Resolution No. 32254 (New Series), as follows:

Resolved, That Resolution No. 31023 (New Series), authorizing the Finance Committee to employ a superintendent, experts and assistants, and to purchase supplies in connection with the appraisal of taxable real property, be and the same is hereby repealed.

Providing for the Creation of a Department of Appraisal and Valuation.

Presented by Supervisor Havenner to correct procedure and legalize former action, the validity of which is questioned:

Bill No. ————, Ordinance No. ———— (New Series), as follows:

Providing for the creation of a Department of Appraisal and Evaluation, defining the powers of said department and prescribing its duties,
and providing for its employees, and for their qualifications, and how
they shall be appointed.

Be it ordained by the People of the City and County of San Francisco as follows:

Section 1. There is hereby created a Department of Appraisal and
Evaluation, which shall be under the jurisdiction of the Board of
Supervisors, and the employees of said department shall be deemed
to be employees of the Board of Supervisors.

Section 2. That the duties of said department shall be:

(a) To advise the Board of Supervisors sitting as a County Board
of Equalization, and to furnish data to said Board of Equalization to
enable said Board to equalize the assessment of all taxable property
in the City and County, to the end that the taxation of said property
may be in proportion to its value.

(b) To advise the Board of Supervisors as to the true and fair
value of any and all property and the improvements thereon, which
said Board may desire to purchase for public purpose.

(c) To give to any officer, department or bureau of the City and
County, all data relative to the value of any property in the City and
County of San Francisco.

(d) As the same are accumulated, compiled, colated or made up,
to maintain such maps, records, books and files as may be necessary
to ascertain at any time when called upon, the true and correct value
of property in the City and County of San Francisco.

(e) To consummate under the direction of the Board of Supervisors, when directed to do so, and at the price fixed by said Board,
the purchase of any property required by the City and County for
public purposes, when the same is to be acquired by purchase.

Section 3. Said department shall be constituted as follows: The
chief right of way agent of the Right of Way Department at present
being maintained in connection with the Bureau of Engineering in
the Board of Public Works, and three persons who at the date of their
appointment to said department are experts in the appraisal of real
property and the improvements thereon in the City and County of San
Francisco.

Section 4. That said department shall from time to time, and whenever required to do so, furnish to the Board of Supervisors, as well
as to any other official, department or bureau of the City and County
of San Francisco, their opinion as to the value of any and all property in the City and County of San Francisco, together with all data
upon which said opinion is based, and said department or the members thereof may be called upon to give testimony in court as to the
value of any property which is the subject of eminent domain proceedings brought on behalf of the City and County.

Section 5. That the members of said department mentioned in Section 3 hereof shall be required to give such time to the affairs of said
department as the Board of Supervisors shall deem necessary.

Section 6. That there shall be a secretary of said department, who
shall have charge of all the records, maps, books, files and data of
said department, and who is hereby charged with the duty of properly
indexing, entering and maintaining all data collected or presented by
the members of said department, and in addition to said secretary
there shall be such additional employees as may from time to time
be deemed necessary for the conduct and maintenance of said department, and in addition thereto there shall be a civil engineer detailed
to said dpartment by the Board of Public Works.

Section 7. The Board of Public Works is hereby directed to detail
to said department a civil engineer, to the end that in the valuation
of property to be acquired for public purposes, the said department
of this Board may be advised as to the adaptability of property for
the purposes for which it is to be acquired.

Section 8. That the members of said department, and all the employees thereof, shall be appointed, by resolution of the Board of Supervisors, and the compensation of the members of said department and its employees shall be fixed by said Board, save and except that the salary of the engineer detailed to said department shall be fixed by the Board of Public Works and paid as the Board of Supervisors shall direct.

Section 9. This ordinance shall take effect immediately upon its passage.

Referred to Finance Committee.

(Supervisor McSheehy asked that he be notified of Finance Committee meeting when above matter is considered and that copy be sent to all members, and that they be invited to attend.)

City Attorney to Study and Report on Provisions of Political Code as to Duties of Board of Equalization.

Supervisor Havenner moved that the City Attorney be requested, in consultation with the Assessor, to make a study of the provisions of the Political Code which define and prescribe the duties of the Board of Supervisors sitting as a Board of Equalization, to report back to this Board such amendments and additions to the present statutes as in his judgment might make functions of the Board of Supervisors practically operative.

Referred to Judiciary Committee.

Motion.

Whereupon, Supervisor Power renewed his motion to adopt resolution discontinuing Appraisal Bureau and repealing Resolution No. 31023 (New Series), authorizing the Finance Committee to employ a superintendent, etc.

Supervisor Havenner moved, as an amendment, that action be deferred until his bill is reported, so that there will be no break in the continuity of procedure as regards creation of Appraisal Bureau.

Supervisor Gallagher, seconded by Supervisor Havenner, moved to postpone three weeks.

Motion *lost* by the following vote:

Ayes—Supervisors Canepa, Colman, Gallagher, Havenner, McGovern, McSheehy, Roncovieri—7.

Noes—Supervisors Andriano, Hayden, Miles, Peyser, Power, Rossi, Shannon, Spaulding, Stanton—9.

Absent—Supervisors Suhr, Toner—2.

Adopted.

Whereupon, the roll was called and the resolution *adopted* as follows, to-wit:

Resolution No. 32254 (New Series), as follows:

Resolved, That Resolution No. 31023 (New Series), authorizing the Finance Committee to employ a superintendent, experts and assistants, and to purchase supplies, in connection with the appraisal of taxable real property, be and the same is hereby repealed.

Ayes—Supervisors Andriano, Canepa, Colman, Gallagher, Hayden, McGovern, Miles, Peyser, Power, Rossi, Shannon, Spaulding, Stanton —13.

Noes—Supervisors Havenner, McSheehy, Roncovieri—3.

Absent—Supervisors Suhr, Toner—2.

Garbage Incinerator.

The following was presented and read by the Clerk:

Communication, from Mrs. Edwin R. Sheldon, president San Francisco Center of the California League of Women Voters, expressing its condemnation of the action taken at the meeting the Board of

Supervisors on March 17, 1930, with respect to the inauguration of a plan for the incineration of garbage in San Francisco.

Ordered *filed*.

Police Department Commended.

Supervisor Shannon moved that this Board extend a vote of thanks to the members of the San Francisco Police Department for the prompt manner in which they handled a situation in these chambers today that otherwise might have resulted in a very serious condition, and further moved that a copy of this resolution be sent to the Board of Police Commissioners.

Letter of Thanks.

2215 Wyoming Avenue,
March 17, 1930.

Mr. J. S. Dunnigan, Clerk, City and County of San Francisco, San Francisco, Calif.

Dear Sir: I beg to acknowledge your kind letter of condolence, and ask that you convey to the Board of Supervisors of the City and County of San Francisco, and the people of San Francisco, my sincere gratitude for your eloquent expression of appreciation of my late husband, and sympathy for myself.

Very sincerely yours,
(Signed)   HELEN H. TAFT.

March 24, 1930—*Read and filed*

Invitation to Attend Formal Opening, Sommer & Kaufman Building.

Communication, from Sommer & Kaufman, calling attention to completion of their new building on Market street between Ellis and Powell, and inviting attendance at formal opening, Thursday evening, March 27.

Read and invitation accepted, notices to be sent to members.

Yacht Harbor Survey.

Supervisor Gallagher requested report on the Yacht Harbor survey.

Report on Lumber Delivered to Hetch Hetchy Requested.

Supervisor Gallagher moved that the Clerk be directed to request the Board of Public Works to file with this Board, at the earliest possible date, the names of the bidders, locations of deliveries and prices of all lumber delivered to Hetch Hetchy construction project during the period of the last two years.

So ordered.

Visiting Delegation.

David W. Hoan, Mayor of Milwaukee, and his wife, together with a visiting delegation of officials and newspaper men, were presented to the members of the Board of Supervisors by his Honor Mayor Rolph.

The visitors expressed their gratification with their reception and their delight in the hospitality and attractions of the City of San Francisco.

Supervisor Hayden responded on behalf of the Board of Supervisors.

Street Paving Matters.

Supervisor Stanton, seconded by Supervisor Spaulding, moved that Streets Committee investigate and report on street paving contracts in view of certain statements in recent newspaper reports and, and request City Engineer to be present at next meeting.

So ordered.

ADJOURNMENT.

There being no further business the Board of Supervisors at the hour of 5 p. m. adjourned.

J. S. DUNNIGAN, Clerk.

Approved by the Board of Supervisors May 5, 1930.

Pursuant to Resolution No. 3402 (New Series) of the Board of Supervisors of the City and County of San Francisco, I, John S. Dunnigan, hereby certify that the foregoing are true and correct copies of the Journals of Proceedings of said Board of the dates thereon stated and approved as recited.

JOHN S. DUNNIGAN,
Clerk of the Board of Supervisors.
City and County of San Francisco.

l. 25—New Series   No. 14

Monday, March 31, 1930

ournal of Proceedings
Board of Supervisors

City and County of San Francisco

The Recorder Printing and Publishing Company
337 Bush Street, S. F.

JOURNAL OF PROCEEDINGS
BOARD OF SUPERVISORS

In Board of Supervisors, San Francisco, Monday, March 31, 1930, p. m.

The Board of Supervisors met in regular session.

CALLING THE ROLL.

The roll was called and the following Supervisors were noted present:

Supervisors Andriano, Canepa, Colman, Gallagher, Havenner, Haylen, McGovern, McSheehy, Miles, Peyser, Power, Roncovieri, Rossi, Shannon, Spaulding, Stanton, Suhr, Toner.

Quorum present.

His Honor Mayor Rolph presiding.

APPROVAL OF JOURNAL.

The Journal of Proceedings of the previous meeting was laid over for approval until next meeting.

Proceedings in Relation to Resolution of Eulogy and Condolence on the Death of Doctor Jacob Nieto.

SUPERVISOR PEYSER: Mr. Mayor.

THE MAYOR: Mr. Peyser.

SUPERVISOR PEYSER: Mr. Mayor and members of the Board, since our last meeting San Francisco has suffered the loss of one of its great citizens. On March 26 of this year, last Friday, Rabbi Jacob Nieto passed on. Rabbi Jacob Nieto was identified with San Francisco for nearly four-score years. Being a rabbi, in his activities he naturally ministered to the Jewish community of San Francisco and as such was a great and able leader. He was very profound in his knowledge and had goodness in his heart. But, in addition to his ecclesiastical duties, Rabbi Nieto concerned himself with the citizenry of San Francisco and the upbuilding of this community, and during all his years he spent many hours and much of his time to help San Francisco become a prosperous and glorious city. He was one who was determined in his convictions, he was one who believed that truth should prevail, and when he did so believe he left no stone unturned to see that truth came out on top. I say that, in the loss of Doctor Nieto, not only does the Jewry of San Francisco but also the community as a whole suffer an irreparable loss. He had a heart of gold, his wisdom was great and he had a soul for humanity. And therefore, Mr. Mayor, I will ask that in respect to his memory, when the Board of Supervisors adjourn it does so out of respect to Rabbi Nieto, and I am also offering at this time a resolution which I ask that the Board adopt.

SUPERVISOR GALLAGHER: I desire to second the motion and also the resolution.

THE MAYOR: Please read the resolution, Mr. Clerk.

THE CLERK (reading):

"Whereas, Rabbi Nieto died on March 26, 1930; and

"Whereas, the said Rabbi Jacob Nieto was identified with the civic life of our community for nearly forty years; and

"Whereas, his activities were always directed toward the betterment of humanity and the upbuilding of our city; and

"Whereas, by his passing San Francisco suffers an irreparable loss; now, therefore, be it

"Resolved, That when this Board adjourns, it does so out of respect to the memory of said Rabbi Jacob Nieto, and that the Clerk be directed, on behalf of the Board of Supervisors, to extend to the bereaved family and relatives the deep sympathy and the sincere condolences of the Board of Supervisors."

SUPERVISOR GALLAGHER: Mr. Mayor, I ask for the privilege of seconding the resolution by Mr. Peyser and the motion that he made. And I would like to humbly testify, if I could, to what we who are not of the faith of Doctor Nieto thought of him and how we regarded him. I can remember many years ago when a very lowly set of people, in very humble circumstances, and considered by some of not much importance as far as things in this world go, were in a very bitter struggle for better conditions for themselves and the labor world, and I remember well how, sacrificing even the friendship of people who were very close to him because of the opinions he held, and because of the assistance he gave them, Doctor Nieto came to their rescue to such a degree that he pulled a victory from sheer defeat. Among those of the Catholic faith he was more than highly regarded because of his works and because of his willingness to go anywhere at any time in any good cause, and to speak and to work for any cause that to him seemed worth while.

I had the honor on several occasions of having him act as my sponsor, and the cheering, whole-hearted, straightforward manner in which he met one on requests of the kind of which I speak was a very encouraging factor. And I re-echo and would reiterate and emphasize, if I could, the statements made by Mr. Peyser. The loss of Doctor Nieto is a great loss to this community because his type is very rare. A man of the cloth, with great influence and with power to be heard, and a potent factor in whatever affairs he desired to take part in, he was so outspoken that it was refreshing, because it was so rare. And I am sure that while his own people and those close to him in his own faith mourn him greatly, I can say, speaking particularly if I may for those of us that knew him of another faith, that we mourn him also. I may say that to the cause of the Irish he was also a friend. That may seem singular, but he was. He was forever ready to say what was on his mind relative to the rights and wrongs of Ireland and her people. And they, I am sure, feel a little sadder in heart and know that a loss has occurred in the death of Doctor Nieto.

SUPERVISOR HAYDEN: Mr. Chairman, I attended the services yesterday in memory of the late Doctor Jacob Nieto. I was very much impressed by the beautiful eulogy rendered by Mr. Aaron Sapiro of New York City. Mr. Sapiro was a San Francisco boy, raised in the Jewish Orphanage of this city, and Doctor Nieto, realizing that he had wonderful talent as a boy, undertook to take him in hand and provide an education for him, which is now reflected in the man who is a leader among the Jewish people of this nation and a leader in any community where he may be.

While we of the Board of Supervisors join with Supervisor Peyser in paying this tribute with respect to the memory of the late Doctor Nieto, there is present here today a gentleman, a distinguished citizen and a former member of the Board of Supervisors, one of his own faith and a leader among Jewish people of the city, and I personally, Mr. Mayor, through you and the Board, would like to call on ex-Supervisor Milton Marks to say a few words by way of eulogium to the memory of Doctor Nieto.

SUPERVISOR PEYSER: Second the motion.

THE MAYOR: Mr. Marks.

MR. MILTON MARKS: Mr. Mayor and gentlemen of the Board of

Supervisors: It is a difficult thing for me to appraise the value of the services of a religious leader whose period of activity in San Francisco is more extended than my entire life. But I do know that what the Board of Supervisors says today in this resolution is an expression of the point of view of the city which this Board represents. And while it is not quite accurate to say that Doctor Nieto served the city for four-score years, it is correct to say that for thirty-seven years of his life he gave devoted attention to the needs and the causes and the aspirations, not only of the people of his religion, but to that of the people of all creeds. I believe the most beautiful tribute that could have been paid a man, outside of the eloquent tribute that was paid to him yesterday by Aaron Sapiro, was the actual physical presence in the temple, crowded to capacity, of the people of all creeds and all religions and of all classes of life.

Gentlemen of the Board, I believe it can be said of him that he was a pastor in the real sense; that he ministered carefully and intimately to the personal needs of the members of his flock. He did this with a loving kindness and with an understanding of them which gave him strength. I believe that we do not easily lose religious leaders of whatever creed, that we do not easily see them go from us without feeling that there is a void in the community, and I know that I speak for this Board and echo the sentiment of this Board when I say that thirty-seven years of useful service to the community and useful service to the city has been ended with the termination of the career of a leader beloved by all.

SUPERVISOR HAVENNER: Mr. Mayor, I, too, desire to make my tribute, very humbly and reverently, to the memory of Doctor Nieto. When the history of San Francisco is written, Mr. Mayor, the name of Doctor Jacob Nieto must occupy a prominent part in the annals of the recent life of our city. He was one of the great humanitarians in the national life of America, in his generation. What Supervisor Gallagher has said concerning his readiness and his important work in behalf of those who were struggling for better condition of life, for the things that go to make up the human aspect of our civilization, cannot be emphasized too much. He participated in every humanitarian movement of labor in our city and in our State in recent years. The people who believe, as most of us do, that the most important function of government is to minister to the happiness of human beings will remember him always with a devoted and kindly affection.

SUPERVISOR ROSSI: Mr. Mayor and members of the Board of Supervisors: It was my honor as Acting Mayor to represent you at the funeral services of our beloved fellow-citizen. The passing of Doctor Nieto was a very sad moment in the life of San Francisco. Doctor Nieto was not alone a very brilliant man; he was broadminded, kindly and sympathetic; he always worked for the welfare and the good of others, and, above all, he was democratic. He was a civic leader. Whenever San Francisco called upon its citizenry to hedp in any cause for the common good, Doctor Nieto was always in the forefront. In his passing San Francisco has suffered an irreparable loss, and in deepest sorrow we join our fellow-citizens in expressing our sympathy to his bereaved family.

SUPERVISOR COLMAN: Mr. Mayor, may I also have the privilege of saying a word of eulogy? I am proud, indeed, to belong to the faith of Doctor Nieto, and proud, also, of the fact of a close personal friendship with him extending over years. He was a real lover of humanity. When joy came to the members of his congregation, he rejoiced with them; when sorrow came, he shared in their sorrow. He was a helpful, kindly man, with a good word for everyone, and it must have been his creed that if he could not say a good word he said nothing. We can ill afford to lose a man combining such wonderful traits and who, in addition to his ecclesiastical duties, found time to earnestly support every worthy activity for the good of his city, State and nation.

· THE MAYOR: Gentlemen of the Board and my fellow-citizens: It was a great shock to me, as it was to all the people of this city who knew, in lifetime, the Reverend Jacob Nieto, when the news came that he had passed away. Seldom do we give much thought, as we go along through life, to how soon one of our closest friends or even one of those in our own home might pass away, and seldom do we realize how the older ones of us are growing older day by day, and when we find men like Reverend Jacob Nieto, going along every day, and each day becoming older, as each and every one of us are becoming older, and we know how our circle of friends is being diminished, and we know only too late that what we might have said to them when in life, they were taken away before we could say it. In the midst of life we are in death. And the Reverend Jacob Nieto, a good, courteous, God-fearing, courageous, influential man in this city has been laid away in the sleep of eternity. I knew Doctor Jacob Nieto long before I was ever honored with the office of Mayor of this city. I knew him when I was engaged in business life and in the activities of the semi-public organizations of this city, and he was just the same then as he has been all the years that we have known him in our public life. I have seen him in all kinds of weather—fair weather, rough weather, stormy weather—but he was the same genial, approachable, noble gentleman all the time. I have been with him on platforms where he has spoken in the interests and for the helpfulness of all creeds. I have been in his synagogue and I have naturally been close to him as Mayor all these nearly twenty years. And his loss and his death has created a great void here in the life of San Francisco. I never heard a man deliver more beautiful tributes over the biers of his departed members of his congregation and his Jewish friends and neighbors than were delivered by Doctor Jacob Nieto. They came as words from the heart, words from the mind, studied to fit every occasion. And I remember once, at the services of a dearly beloved woman that he loved and she loved him; she, left a widow, brought up a family, a brood of five children without the help of a husband, and I shall never forget the beautiful tribute he paid her, which was typical of God's service, when he said that she reminded him of the little bantam hen that had her little brood of five children and the great hawk flew down from the skies to gobble up her little brood, but the little bantam hen hovered over her little brood, kept them away from the hawk until somebody came along and did away with the hawk. It was a beautiful tribute, and you can see, from the lesson of that tribute from the mind of that man, the human side of him and the noble character that he was.

Over in the war the Jewish rabbi, if he was present when a Protestant boy or a Catholic boy passed away, the Jewish rabbi performed the last touch, the service of the Almighty. And Jacob Nieto, no matter what the creed or what the religion, was always there to do his bit. I, as Mayor, pay tribute to his memory today. I regret that circumstances were such that at the last minute when I heard of his death I had to leave this city because of the serious illness of Mr. Joseph J. Tynan, but I did not go without telephoning Mr. Gus Lachman, who, I think, was the closet friend of his in life, and it was Gus Lachman's mother that he spoke of as the little bantam hen that raised that Lachman family. And I expressed my sorrow to him and through him to Mrs. Nieto, and appointed a substitute to take my place at the funeral services.

I think the Board has done a noble thing. I congratulate you, Mr. Peyser, for bringing in a well-worded and well-prepared tribute to his memory, and the resolution before the Board is now that, when this Board adjourns, that it adjourns out of respect to the memory of a good, faithful, honorable, outstanding God's nobleman in our midst who has passed away. All in favor of the resolution will please rise. (All members of the Board rise.)

THE MAYOR: It is so ordered.

SUPERVISOR GALLAGHER: Mr. Mayor, to complete the proceedings, I would ask Mr. Peyser to consent that I may make a motion in addition, that the resolution be suitably engrossed and it be signed by yourself and the members of the Board and sent to the family, and that the Clerk be instructed to procure for the family a copy of the stenographic record of what has been said here at this time, to be presented with the engrossed resolution.

SUPERVISOR PEYSER: Second the motion.

THE MAYOR: All in favor please say aye. (Ayes.) The ayes have it and it is so ordered and unanimously carried.

ROLL CALL FOR PETITIONS.

Communication from the National Aeronautic Association, declaring that the action of the Board of Supervisors in deciding to acquire the entire Mills acreage of eleven hundred (1100) acres for airport development to be highly commendatory, and trusting that nothing will interfere to affect the legality of such a transaction, because of its importance in the development of San Francisco's industry and commerce.

Read and ordered *filed*.

Letter of Thanks, Police Department.

Communication from Wm. J. Quinn, Chief of Police, acknowledging receipt of resolution of the Board of Supervisors adopted last Monday commendatory of the action of the Police Department in the matter of the recent "Red" demonstration, and expressing the appreciation of the department for same.

Read and ordered *filed*.

Lumber on Hetch Hetchy Project.

In response to a motion of Supervisor Gallagher, made at last meeting, the following was presented:

Communication from the Board of Public Works transmitting photostat copies of tabulation of lumber bids received on Hetch Hetchy project, and copy of letter of City Engineer of March 28th explanatory thereof.

Read and ordered *filed*.

Mayor's Veto, Resolution No. 32231 (New Series), Declaration of Policy, Garbage Incinerator.

The following was presented, read, and *laid over one week*:

March 27, 1930.

Honorable Board of Supervisors, City Hall, San Francisco, California.

Gentlemen: Acting upon the opinion of the Hon. John J. O'Toole, City Attorney, dated March 27, 1930, I hereby return to you, without my approval, Resolution No. 32231, adopted by your honorable Board March 17, 1930. A copy of the City Attorney's opinion is attached hereto.

Respectfully submitted,
JAMES ROLPH, Jr., Mayor.

(Enclosures: Opinion of City Attorney and original copy of Resolution No. 32231 (New Series) of the Board of Supervisors.)

PRESENTATION OF PROPOSALS.

Sale of Bonds.

Sealed bids for the purchase of certain bonds of the City of San Francisco, State of California, were received by the Board of Supervisors up to the hour of 3 o'clock p. m. on Monday, March 31, 1930, and opened by said Board at said time.

The bonds offered are described as follows:

Two million two hundred and eighty-six thousand dollars Boulevard Bonds, four and one-half per cent, issue of November 1, 1927, comprising 126 $1,000 bonds maturing 1935; 135 $1,000 bonds maturing each year, 1936 to 1951, inclusive.

One million twenty thousand dollars Sewer Bonds, four and one-half per cent, issue of January 1, 1929, comprising 60 $1,000 bonds maturing each year, 1939 to 1955, inclusive.

The said described bonds bear interest at the rate of four and one-half per centum per annum, payable semi-annually, and shall not be sold at a price less than the par value thereof, together with accrued interest thereon at date of delivery.

Bidders may bid for the whole or any part of the bonds here offered, and when a less amount of the whole amount offered is bid on, the bidder shall state the year or years of maturity thereof.

The bonds offered are tax exempt, State and Federal.

Delivery of the bonds to the purchaser will be made within ten days from the date of award, or within such time thereafter as may be agreed upon by the purchaser and Finance Committee of the Board of Supervisors.

All proposals for the purchase of such bonds shall be accompanied by a deposit of five per cent of the amount bid, in lawful money of the United States, or by a deposit of a certified check payable to J. S. Dunnigan, Clerk of the Board of Supervisors of the City and County, for a like sum, provided that no deposit need exceed the sum of $10,000, and that no deposit need be given by the State of California, which money or check shall be forfeited by the bidder in case he fails to accept and pay for the bonds bid for by him if his bid is accepted.

The approval of Thomson, Wood & Hoffman, attorneys, New York, as to the legality of these bonds is on file in the Clerk's office.

This notice is given pursuant to the direction of a resolution of the Board of Supervisors adopted March 10, 1930.

Bids.

The following bids were received and *referred to the Finance Committee:*

Bid No. 1—R. H. Moulton & Company, syndicate agents, $3,316,389. (R. H. Moulton & Co.; Harris Trust & Savings Bank, Chicago; Bankers Company, New York; Continental-Illinois Company, Chicago; Security-First National Company of Los Angeles; American Securities Company; Anglo-California Trust Company.)

Bid No. 2—Heller, Bruce & Co., $3,339,391. (Joint bid of Lehman Bros., Kountze Bros., Wells Fargo Bank and Union Trust Company, Graham, Parsons & Co., Dean, Witter & Co., Emanuel & Co., Mississippi Valley Co., Inc., Wells-Dickey Company, Bosworth, Chanute, Laughridge & Co., Stern Bros. & Co., Heller, Bruce & Co.)

Bid No. 3—The National City Co., by Stewart Krieger, $3,306,000. (First Old Colony Corp., Kean, Taylor & Co., Wallace & Co., Wm. Cavalier & Co., E. R. Gundelfinger, Inc.; plus premium, $14,513.24.)

Bid No. 4—Anglo London Paris Company, $3,334,729. (Anglo London Paris Company; First National Bank, New York; National Bankitaly Company; First Detroit Company, Inc.; Eldredge Company.)

Bid No. 5—America Investment Company, $3,313,240.14.

Steel Pipe.

Sealed proposals were received and opened between the hours of 2 and 3 p. m. this date for furnishing steel pipe and *referred to Supplies Committee.*

Cast-Iron Pipe.

Sealed proposals were received and opened between the hours of 2 ,d 3 p. m. this date for furnishing cast-iron pipe for San Francisco .ater Department and *referred to Supplies Committee.*

Car Wheels.

'Sealed proposals were received and opened between the hours of 2 ;d 3 p. m. this date for furnishing car wheels and *referred to the| upplies Committee.*

Action Deferred.

The following matter was *laid over one week*:

Hearing of Appeal, Henry Cowell Lime and Cement Company.

Hearing of appeal of Henry Cowell Lime & Cement Company from 1e action and decision of the Board of Public Works in overruling 1e protest of Henry Cowell Lime & Cement Company against the nprovement of the north half of Commercial street from the west line f The Embarcadero to a line at right angles with Commercial street nd 125 feet 6¾ inches west of the west line of The Embarcadero, by 1e construction of full width artificial stone sidewalks, where side-walks are not now to official grade, and the construction of a retaining rall to support this sidewalk, as set forth in Resolution of Intention Jo. 96689 (Second Series).

UNFINISHED BUSINESS.

Final Passage.

The following matters, heretofore passed for printing, were taken \p and *finally passed* by the following vote:

Authorizations.

On recommendation of Finance Committee.

Resolution No. 32257 (New Series), as follows:

Resolved, That the following amounts be and the same are hereby authorized to be expended out of the hereinafter mentioned funds in >ayment to the following named claimants, to-wit:

Auditorium Fund.

(1) Pacific Gas & Electric Company, gas and electric service furnished Civic Auditorium, month of February (claim dated March 15, 1930) ....\$ 1,164.96

Park Fund.

(2) Berringer & Russell, hay, etc., for parks (claim dated March 21, 1930) ....\$ 668.74

(3) Golden State Milk Products Company, ice cream for parks (claim dated March 21, 1930) 1,506.00

(4) Langendorf United Bakeries, Inc., bread, etc., for parks (claim dated March 31, 1930) 520.90

(5) San Francisco Dairy Company, milk for parks (claim dated March 21, 1930) 514.56

(6) Sherry Bros., Inc., butter and eggs for parks (claim dated March 21, 1930) 520.77

Municipal Railway Fund.

(7) Ray Crosse and May Crosse, in full settlement for account of damages and personal injuries sustained December 11, 1928 (claim dated March 14, 1930) ....\$ 1,000.00

(8) Meyer Rosenberg, first payment for reconstruction of Taravai street tracks of Municipal Railways (claim dated March 15, 1930) 9,150.00

Boulevard Bonds.

(9) Louis J. Cohn, final payment for improvement Bay Shore boulevard, Potrero to Silver avenues (claim dated March 19, 1930) ....$ 2,987.3

County Road Fund.

(10) Santa Cruz Portland Cement Company, cement for street reconstruction (claim dated March 12, 1930)..............$ 826.1?

(11) San Francisco City Employees' Retirement System, to match contributions from employees engaged on street reconstruction (claim dated March 12, 1930)...............   1,487.5?

Hetch Hetchy Construction Fund, Bond Issue 1928.

(12) Del Monte Meat Company, meat (claim dated March 17, 1930) .. ..$ 606.2?

(13) Dr. Paul E. Dolan, medical services rendered Hetch Hetchy employees during February (claim dated March 14, 1930) ....   1,256.7?

(14) A. Levy & J. Zentner Co., fruit and produce (claim dated March 17, 1930) 562.81

(15) Pacific Coast Aggregates, Inc., sand (claim dated March 17, 1930) 816.25

(16) San Francisco City Employees' Retirement System, to match contributions from Hetch Hetchy employees (claim dated March 15, 1930) 591.32

(17) United States Rubber Company, rubber boots and coats (claim dated March 15, 1930) 1,003.82

Hetch Hetchy Power Operative Fund.

(18) Depreciation Fund, Hetch Hetchy power operations, as reserve depreciation, per Charter requirement (claim dated March 14, 1930) $14,584.00

(19) Pope & Talbot, lumber (claim dated March 14, 1930)....   578.25

(20) Santa Cruz Portland Cement Company, cement (claim dated March 14, 1930) 570.50

Special School Tax.

(21) Oscar Aaron, final payment, plumbing work for Geary Street School (claim dated March 19, 1930)..............$ 2,092.87

County Road Fund.

(22) Fay Improvement Company, eighth payment, improvement of Portola drive from 24th street to Fowler avenue claim dated March 19, 1930) $23,400.00

General Fund, 1929-1930

(23) Hanni & Girerd, repairs to Police Department autos (claim dated March 17, 1930) ....$ 591.45

(24) Berringer & Russell, hay, etc., for Police Department (claim dated March 17, 1930) 1,217.84

(25) Old Homestead Bakery, bread for County Jails (claim dated March 14, 1930) 810.29

(26) Greenebaum, Weil & Michaels, men's clothing, County Jails (claim dated March 14, 1930).....................   899.31

(27) N. Randall Ellis, engineering service rendered telephone rate litigation (claim dated March 13, 1930)..............   750.00

(28) Reid Bros., bandages, etc, for Emergency Hospitals (claim dated Feb. 28, 1930)............................   917.80

(29) Old Homestead Bakery, bread for San Francisco Hospital (claim dated Feb. 28, 1930)......................   1,060.11

(30) Western Meat Company, meats for San Francisco Hospital (claim dated Feb. 28, 1930)......................   830.27

(31) Del Monte Meat Company, meats for San Francisco Hospital (claim dated Feb. 28, 1930)........................   1,412.36

(32) San Francisco International Fish Company, fish for San Francisco Hospital (claim dated Feb. 28, 1930) 561.20

(33) Schweitzer & Co., meats for San Francisco Hospital (claim dated Feb. 28, 1930) 803.03

(34) J. T. Freitas Co., eggs, San Francisco Hospital (claim dated Feb. 28, 1930) 1,985.81

(35) Scatena-Galli Fruit Company, fruit and produce, San Francisco Hospital (claim dated Feb. 28, 1930) 1,086.00

(36) Spring Valley Water Company, water for hospitals (claim dated March 13, 1930) 1,568.05

(37) Baumgarten Bros., meats for Laguna Honda Home (claim dated Feb. 28, 1930) 1,209.04

(38) California Meat Company, meat for Laguna Honda Home (claim dated Feb. 28, 1930) 1,806.13

(39) Dairy Dale San Francisco Dairy Company, milk for Laguna Honda Home (claim dated Feb. 28, 1930) 2,127.60

(40) Del Monte Meat Company, meat for Laguna Honda Home (claim dated Feb. 28, 1930) 3,686.89

(41) J. T. Freitas Co., Inc., eggs for Laguna Honda Home (claim dated Feb. 28, 1930) 1,617.88

(42) C. Nauman & Co., produce for Laguna Honda Home (claim dated Feb. 28, 1930) 1,155.67

(43) Richfield Oil Company, fuel oil for Laguna Honda Home (claim dated Feb. 28, 1930) 1,544.03

(44) Sherry Bros., butter for Laguna Honda Home (claim dated Feb. 28, 1930) 1,806.86

(45) Spring Valley Water Company, water furnished Laguna Honda Home (claim dated March 13, 1930) 961.94

(46) Monarch Flour Company, flour for Laguna Honda Home (claim dated Feb. 28, 1930) 1,322.25

(47) Associated Charities, relief for unemployed (claim dated Feb. 28, 1930) 6,534.19

(48) Frank J. Reilly, tenth payment, construction of addition to M. H. De Young Memorial Museum (claim dated March 21, 1930) 5,957.35

(49) California Printing Company, printing of building zone ordinance and maps (claim dated March 19, 1930) 884.60

Spring Valley Water Bonds.

(50) Gilmartin Company, Inc., printing of Spring Valley Water Company deed (claim dated March 18, 1930) ....$ 813.55

Ayes—Supervisors Andriano, Canepa, Colman, Gallagher, Havenner, Hayden, McGovern, McSheehy, Miles, Peyser, Power, Roncovieri, Rossi, Shannon, Spaulding, Suhr, Toner—17.

Absent—Supervisor Stanton—1.

Payments for Properties Required for Boulevards.

Also, Resolution No. 32258 (New Series), as follows:

Resolved, That the following amounts be and the same are hereby set aside and appropriated out of Boulevard Bond Fund, Issue 1927, and authorized in payment to the hereinafter named persons; being payments for properties required for boulevard purposes, to-wit:

(1) James F. Farrell and Mary Farrell and California Pacific Title and Trust Company, for all of Lot 41 in Block 2369, as per the Assessor's Block Books of the City and County of San Francisco, and required for the opening of the Sunset boulevard; as per acceptance of offer by Resolution No. 32211, New Series (claim dated March 5, 1930) ....$ 3,000.00

(2) James Landers and Augusta Landers and Title Insurance and Guaranty Co., for Lot 20 in Block 5477, as per the Assessor's Block Books of the City and County of San Fran-

cisco, and required for the opening of the Bay Shore boulevard; as per acceptance of offer by Resolution No. 32214,
New Series (claim dated March 11, 1930).............. 1,488.50
(3) Theresa Bootz and Henrietta Welch and Title Insurance and Guaranty Co., for Lot 1 in Block 7158, as per the
Assessor's Block Books of the City and County of San Francisco, and required for the widening of San Jose avenue as
an approach to Alemany boulevard; as per acceptance of
offer by Resolution No. 32212, New Series (claim dated
March 11, 1930) 6,000.00

Ayes—Supervisors Andriano, Canepa, Colman, Gallagher, Havenner,
Hayden, McGovern, McSheehy, Miles, Peyser, Power, Roncovieri, Rossi,
Shannon, Spaulding, Suhr, Toner—17.
Absent—Supervisor Stanton—1.

Payments for Lands Required for Playgrounds.

Also, Resolution No. 32259 (New Series), as follows:

Resolved, That the following amounts be and the same are hereby
set aside and appropriated out of Playground Fund, and authorized in
payment to the hereinafter named persons; being payments for lands
required for playground purposes, to-wit:
(1) To S. Szemanski and Sophie Szemanski, for Lot No. 21 of
Block 4164, as per the Assessor's Block Books of the City
and County of San Francisco; required for playground purposes (claim dated March 13, 1930)...................$ 1,250.00
(2) To Johannes Nelsen and Valborg Nelsen, for Lot No. 20
of Block 4164, as per the Assessor's Block Books of the City
and County of San Francisco; required for playground purposes (claim dated March 17, 1930)...................... 1,250.00

Ayes—Supervisors Andriano, Canepa, Colman, Gallagher, Havenner,
Hayden, McGovern, McSheehy, Miles, Peyser, Power, Roncovieri, Rossi,
Shannon, Spaulding, Suhr, Toner—17.
Absent—Supervisor Stanton—1.

Appropriating $2,500 Towards Completion of the City's Account-
ing System.

Also, Resolution No. 32260 (New Series), as follows:

Resolved, That the sum of $2,500 be and the same is hereby set aside,
appropriated and authorized to be expended out of the General Fund
for the expense, during balance of the fiscal year, of continuing toward
the completion of the City's accounting system.

Ayes—Supervisors Andriano, Canepa, Colman, Gallagher, Havenner,
Hayden, McGovern, McSheehy, Miles, Peyser, Power, Roncovieri, Rossi,
Shannon, Spaulding, Suhr, Toner—17.
Absent—Supervisor Stanton—1.

Appropriations for Traffic Beacons and Line-Painting Machine.

Also, Resolution No. 32261 (New Series), as follows:

Resolved, That the following amounts be and the same are hereby
set aside, appropriated and authorized to be expended out of "Traffic
Signals," etc., Budget Item No. 57, for the following purposes, to-wit:
(1) For the purchase of one "Simmons" Spray Traffic Line
Painting Machine, to be used in marking new and existing
highways within the City and County of San Francisco....$ 527.60
(2) For the cost of installing beacons on safety zones at
southeasterly side of Valencia and Mission streets, and at
the intersections of Market street with Gough street, Laguna street, Geary street and Van Ness avenue, including
conduits, wiring, etc................................... 1,000.00

Ayes—Supervisors Andriano, Canepa, Colman, Gallagher, Havenner,

Hayden, McGovern, McSheehy, Miles, Peyser, Power, Roncovieri, Rossi, Shannon, Spaulding, Suhr, Toner—17.

Absent—Supervisor Stanton—1.

Appropriation for Assistant Superintendent of Street Cleaning.

Also, Resolution No. 32262 (New Series), as follows:

Resolved, That the sum of $800 be and the same is hereby set aside, appropriated and authorized to be expended out of County Road Fund for the employment of an assistant superintendent of Street Cleaning, beginning March 1, 1930, at $200 per month.

Ayes—Supervisors Andriano, Canepa, Colman, Gallagher, Havenner, Hayden, McGovern, McSheehy, Miles, Peyser, Power, Roncovieri, Rossi, Shannon, Spaulding, Suhr, Toner—17.

Absent—Supervisor Stanton—1.

Appropriation, $10,000, Out of Budget Item 50, "Municipal Airport Fund," for Maneuvers at Mills Field, April 19 and 20, 1930.

Also, Resolution No. 32263 (New Series), as follows:

Whereas, Mills Field has been chosen by General W. E. Gilmore, Chief of the Air Department of the United States Army, as the base for the United States Air Maneuvers, which will take place April 19 and 20, 1930; and

Whereas, the entire United States Army air fleet, embracing over 200 fighting craft of all kinds (being the largest assemblage of fighting planes ever assembled in the world), will assemble at Mills Field on these dates; and

Whereas, these air maneuvers will attract the attention of people from all over the United States to Mills Field and San Francisco; now, therefore, be it

Resolved, That the sum of $10,000 be and the same is hereby set aside, appropriated and authorized to be expended out of "Municipal Airport Fund," Budget Item No. 50, fiscal year 1929-1930, for general expenses in connection with these maneuvers, including necessary permanent and temporary improvements for Mills Field.

Ayes—Supervisors Andriano, Canepa, Colman, Gallagher, Havenner, Hayden, McGovern, McSheehy, Miles, Peyser, Power, Roncovieri, Rossi, Shannon, Spaulding, Suhr, Toner—17.

Absent—Supervisor Stanton—1.

Granting to United States Government Site for Federal Building in Civic Center.

Bill No. 8220, Ordinance No. 8723 (New Series), as follows:

Agreeing to grant to the United States of America a site situate in the Civic Center of the City and County of San Francisco for the erection thereon of a Federal office building, and determining the conditions under which said grant shall be made and the size of said site, and authorizing the Mayor of the City and County of San Francisco and the Clerk of the Board of Supervisors thereof to execute and deliver to the United States of America a deed conveying to the United States of America the hereinafter described real property as a site for the erection thereon of a Federal office building, and providing for the conveyance of additional land for said site, all pursuant to the provisions of Section 10a of Chapter II, Article II, of the Charter of the City and County of San Francisco.

Be it ordained by the People of the City and County of San Francisco as follows:

Section 1. That whereas, Section 10a of Chapter II, Article II, of the Charter of the City and County of San Francisco, authorizes the Board of Supervisors to cause to be conveyed to the United States

of America, by a good and sufficient deed, and without monetary consideration, a site on the northeast corner of Hyde and Fulton streets,
in the Civic Center in the City and County of San Francisco, which
said site shall be used by the said United States of America for the
erection thereon of a Federal office building.

Section 2. And whereas, the hereinafter described real property is
situate on the northeast corner of Fulton and Hyde streets, in said
Civic Center, and is unoccupied by any building or structure belonging to the City and County of San Francisco, and the United States
of America has agreed to erect and maintain thereon a Federal office
building, provided said property be transferred to the United States of
America without any monetary consideration.

Section 3. The Board of Supervisors of the City and County of San
Francisco hereby determines that the size and the site of said lands
to be conveyed to the said United States of America for said Federal
office building should be as hereinafter set forth.

Section 4. That the City and County of San Francisco does hereby
offer to the United States of America the hereinafter described real
property for the erection and maintenance thereon by the United
States of America of a Federal office building, and does hereby agree
to grant to the United States of America, without any monetary consideration, the hereinafter described real property, upon condition
that the said United States of America shall cause to be erected and
maintained thereon a Federal office building, which said building shall
conform in general type of architecture and construction to the other
buildings contained in the Civic Center.

Section 5. That the Mayor of the City and County of San Francisco
and the Clerk of the Board of Supervisors be and they are hereby
authorized, empowered and directed to make, execute and deliver to
the United States of America a good and sufficient deed conveying
to said United States of America the hereinafter described real property for the purposes herein set forth, which conveyance shall be
made when the said Mayor is given satisfactory proof that the building to be erected and maintained thereon shall, in its general type
of architecture and construction, conform to the other buildings at
present erected in the Civic Center.

Section 6. That the site to be conveyed to said United States of
America, in conformity with this ordinance, is described as follows,
to-wit:

Commencing at the point of intersection of the southerly line of Mc-
Allister street with the easterly line of Hyde street produced southerly;
thence southerly along said easterly line 207.375 feet; thence southeasterly on a curve to the right, tangent to a line deflected 90 deg. to
the left from the preceding course, radius 42 feet, central angle 61 deg.
33 min. 58 sec., a distance of 45.128 feet to a point distant 229.375 feet
at right angles southerly from the southerly line of McAllister street;
thence easterly parallel with the southerly line of McAllister street
and 229.375 feet at right angles southerly therefrom, a distance of
375.568 feet to the westerly line of Leavenworth street produced southerly; thence at right angles northerly along said westerly line 229.375
feet to the southerly line of McAllister street; thence at right angles
westerly along the southerly line of McAllister street 412.50 feet to
the easterly line of Hyde street produced southerly, and point of commencement.

Saving and excepting therefrom the following described parcel of
land:

All those portions of Lots Nos. 22 and 24, according to map entitled
"Map of Yerba Buena Park, Park avenue and City Hall avenue, showing subdivision of property to be sold under Act of the Legislature,
approved April 4, 1870," filed in the office of the County Recorder of
the City and County of San Francisco, State of California, March 18,

871, and recorded in Map Book E and F, page 38, embraced within the above description.

Section 7. That upon the City and County of San Francisco acquiring title to the real property hereinbefore excepted from the conveyance to be made pursuant to this ordinance, that the Mayor of the City and County of San Francisco and the Clerk of the Board of Supervisors be authorized to execute to the United States of America an additional deed conveying said excepted property to said United States of America for the purposes and upon the conditions herein contained.

Section 8. This ordinance shall become effective immediately upon its passage.

Ayes—Supervisors Andriano, Canepa, Colman, Gallagher, Havenner, Hayden, McGovern, McSheehy, Miles, Peyser, Power, Roncovieri, Rossi, Shannon, Spaulding, Suhr, Toner—17.

Absent—Supervisor Stanton—1.

Parking Station, J. D. Campbell, North Side Turk Street, West of Jones Street.

On recommendation of Fire Committee.

Resolution No. 32264 (New Series), as follows:

Resolved, That J. D. Campbell be and is hereby granted permission, revocable at will of the Board of Supervisors, to maintain and operate an automobile parking station on premises north side of Turk street, 152 feet 8 inches west of Jones street.

The rights granted under this resolution shall be exercised within six months, otherwise said permit shall become null and void.

Ayes—Supervisors Andriano, Canepa, Colman, Gallagher, Havenner, Hayden, McGovern, McSheehy, Miles, Peyser, Power, Roncovieri, Rossi, Shannon, Spaulding, Suhr, Toner—17.

Absent—Supervisor Stanton—1.

Public Garage Permit, R. A. Duclos, South Side of O'Farrell Street, 150 Feet West of Leavenworth Street.

Also, Resolution No. 32265 (New Series), as follows:

Resolved, That R. A. Duclos be and is hereby granted permission, revocable at will of the Board of Supervisors, to maintain and operate a public garage under the Alexander Hamilton Hotel on the south side of O'Farrell street, 150 feet west of Leavenworth street.

The rights granted under this resolution shall be exercised within six months, otherwise said permit shall become null and void.

Ayes—Supervisors Andriano, Canepa, Colman, Gallagher, Havenner, Hayden, McGovern, McSheehy, Miles, Peyser, Power, Roncovieri, Rossi, Shannon, Spaulding, Suhr, Toner—17.

Absent—Supervisor Stanton—1.

Public Garage Permit, Clyde E. Rausch, 945 Post Street.

Also, Resolution No. 32266 (New Series), as follows:

Resolved, That Clyde E Rausch be and is hereby granted permission, revocable at will of the Board of Supervisors, to maintain and operate a public garage at 945 Post street.

The rights granted under this resolution shall be exercised within six months, otherwise said permit shall become null and void.

Ayes—Supervisors Andriano, Canepa, Colman, Gallagher, Havenner, Hayden, McGovern, McSheehy, Miles, Peyser, Power, Roncovieri, Rossi, Shannon, Spaulding, Suhr, Toner—17.

Absent—Supervisor Stanton—1.

Public Garage Permit, Louis Noce, 2470 California Street.

Also, Resolution No. 32267 (New Series), as follows:

Resolved, That Louis Noce be and is hereby granted permission, revocable at will of the Board of Supervisors, to maintain and operate a public garage at premises 2470 California street.

The rights granted under this resolution shall be exercised within six months, otherwise said permit shall become null and void.

Ayes—Supervisors Andriano, Canepa, Colman, Gallagher, Havenner, Hayden, McGovern, McSheehy, Miles, Peyser, Power, Roncovieri, Rossi, Shannon, Spaulding, Suhr, Toner—17.

Absent—Supervisor Stanton—1.

Automobile Supply Station Permit, A. L. Campbell, Southwest Corner Ninth and Folsom Streets.

Also, Resolution No. 32268 (New Series), as follows:

Resolved, That A. L. Campbell be and is hereby granted permission, revocable at will of the Board of Supervisors, to maintain and operate an automobile supply station on the southwest corner of Ninth and Folsom streets.

The rights granted under this resolution shall be exercised within six months, otherwise said permit shall become null and void.

Ayes—Supervisors Andriano, Canepa, Colman, Gallagher, Havenner, Hayden, McGovern, McSheehy, Miles, Peyser, Power, Roncovieri, Rossi, Shannon, Spaulding, Suhr, Toner—17.

Absent—Supervisor Stanton—1.

Transfer of Automobile Supply Station Permit.

Also, Resolution No. 32269 (New Series), as follows:

Resolved, That the Shell Oil Company be and is hereby granted permission, revocable at will of the Board of Supervisors, to have transferred to it automobile supply station permit heretofore granted Paul Arata by Resolution No. 31550 (New Series) for premises at southeast corner of San Jose and Ocean avenues.

The rights granted under this resolution shall be exercised within six months, otherwise said permit shall become null and void.

Ayes—Supervisors Andriano, Canepa, Colman, Gallagher, Havenner, Hayden, McGovern, McSheehy, Miles, Peyser, Power, Roncovieri, Rossi, Shannon, Spaulding, Suhr, Toner—17.

Absent—Supervisor Stanton—1.

Action Deferred.

The following resolution was *laid over one week*, hearing to be had in Health Committee:

Permit for Private Stable, George Neary, East Line Forty-eighth Avenue, 250 Feet South of Ortega Street.

Resolution No. ——————— (New Series), as follows:

Resolved, That George Neary be and is hereby granted permission, revocable at will of the Board of Supervisors, to maintain and operate private stable for six horses on the east line of Forty-eighth avenue, 250 feet south of Ortega street.

The rights granted under this resolution shall be exercised within six months, otherwise said permit shall become null and void.

Several protests filed since passage to print.

Final Passage.

The following bill, heretofore passed for printing, was taken up and *finally passed* by the following vote:

Regulating the Powers and Defining the Duties of the Board of Public Works in Entering Into Contracts for the Use and Occupation of Lands Under the Control of San Francisco Water Department.

On recommendation of Public Utilities Committee.

Bill No. 8219, Ordinance No. 8724 (New Series), as follows:

Regulating the powers and defining the duties of the Board of Public Works in entering into contracts for the use and occupation of lands under the control of San Francisco Water Department.

Be it ordained by the People of the City and County of San Francisco as follows:

Section 1. The Board of Public Works is hereby granted power to enter into contracts with persons, firms and corporations for the use and occupation of lands now under the control of the San Francisco Water Department, which use and occupation are not incompatible with the conduct of supplying water to the inhabitants of the City and County of San Francisco and in other localities where water may be supplied by said department.

Section 2. Contracts for the use and occupation of any of said properties shall be entered into only upon the recommendations in writing made by the head of the Water Department to the Board of Public Works, which recommendations shall set forth a general description of the lands to be occupied, the purposes for which they are to be occupied and the consideration which should be charged for such occupation and how and when said consideration shall be paid. Upon receiving said report the Board of Public Works shall in open meeting give consideration to the same, and if the said Board shall determine that it will be for the benefit and best interests of the said Water Department that said contracts be entered into, and that the consideration to be received for said occupation is fair and reasonable and the best consideration obtainable therefor and that the proposed use of said property will not interfere with the use of said property by the City for the purposes for which it was acquired, the said Board of Public Works may enter into contracts for the use and occupation of such property upon the terms recommended by the head of the Water Department.

Section 3. The consideration to be paid under contracts described herein may be for cash, interest in crops or other valuable consideration, and no contract shall be entered into for a period longer than three years. All revenues from all contracts shall be credited to San Francisco Water Department.

Section 4. All contracts for the use and occupation of lands shall first be approved on their face as to terms and conditions by the head of the Water Department and approved as to form by the City Attorney or attorney for the Water Department.

Section 5. This ordinance shall take effect and be in force from and after the date of its passage.

Ayes—Supervisors Andriano, Canepa, Colman, Gallagher, Havenner, Hayden, McGovern, McSheehy, Miles, Peyser, Power, Roncovieri, Rossi, Shannon, Spaulding, Stanton, Suhr, Toner—18.

PRESENTATION OF BILLS AND ACCOUNTS.

Your Finance Committee, having examined miscellaneous demands not required by law to be passed to print, and amounting to $70,934.42 recommends same be allowed and ordered paid.

Approved by the following vote:

Ayes—Supervisors Andriano, Canepa, Colman, Gallagher, Havenner,

Hayden. McGovern, McSheehy, Miles, Peyser, Power, Roncovieri, Rossi Shannon, Spaulding, Stanton, Suhr, Toner—18.

Urgent Necessity

Citizens' Census Committee expenses ....$ 1,377.65

Ayes—Supervisors Andriano, Canepa, Colman, Gallagher, Havenner, Hayden, McGovern, McSheehy, Miles, Peyser, Power, Roncovieri, Rossi, Shannon, Spaulding, Stanton, Suhr, Toner—18.

NEW BUSINESS.

Passed for Printing.

The following matters were *passed for printing*:

Authorizations.

On recommendation of Finance Committee.

Resolution No. ———— (New Series), as follows:

Resolved, That the following amounts be and the same are hereby authorized to be expended out of the hereinafter mentioned accounts in payment to the following named claimants, to-wit:

Hetch Hetchy Construction Fund, Bond Issue 1928.

(1) Coos Bay Lumber Co., lumber (claim dated Mar. 18, 1930) ....$ 1,052.76

(2) Santa Cruz Portland Cement Co., cement (claim dated Mar. 18, 1930) 5,260.00

(3) W. H. Worden Co., steel hoisting cable (claim dated Mar. 18, 1930) 663.24

(4) J. H. Creighton, hauling (claim dated Mar. 20, 1930).... 1,735.50

(5) Coos Bay Lumber Co., lumber (claim dated Mar. 20, 1930) 4,239.30

(6) Coos Bay Lumber Co., lumber (claim dated Mar. 21, 1930) 3,171.54

(7) Consolidated Mills Co. Inc., lumber (claim dated Mar. 20, 1930) 522.76

(8) Del Monte Meat Co., meat (claim dated Mar. 20, 1930).. 857.25

(9) Edison Storage Battery Supply Co., Edison cells (claim dated Mar. 21, 1930) 12,329.08

(10) Delbert Hansen, truck hire (claim dated Mar. 20, 1930) 1,778.67

(11) Owen-Oregon Lumber Co., lumber (claim dated Mar. 21, 1930) 1,215.28

(12) Pacific Coast Aggregates, Inc., sand and gravel (claim dated Mar. 20, 1930) 938.27

(13) The Charles Nelson Co., wood wedges (claim dated Mar. 20, 1930) 640.00

(14) Pioneer Rubber Mills, digger belts (claim dated Mar. 20, 1930) 764.86

(15) Wilsey Bennett Co., foodstuffs (claim dated Mar. 21, 1930) 1,409.42

(16) Byron Jackson Co., one 4-stage multiplex pump, complete, and parts (claim dated Mar. 21, 1930).............. 3.309.80

(17) J. H. Creighton, truck hire (claim dated Mar. 21, 1930) 924.39

(18) Coos Bay Lumber Co., lumber (claim dated Mar. 20, 1930) 5,190.33

(19) Consolidated Mills Co., Inc., lumber (claim dated Mar. 20, 1930) 648.00

(20) Garfield & Co., one Plymouth 5-ton gear-driven locomotive (claim dated Mar. 20, 1930) 2,237.00

(21) Grier & Mead, one Cuff Compressor complete, 42 Koppel cars, etc. (claim dated Mar. 21, 1930).................... 6,700.00

(22) Ingersoll-Rand Co. of Calif., one centrifugal pump and machine parts (claim dated Mar. 20, 1930).............. 1,509.02

(23) Maydwell & Hartzell, all-rubber lamp cord (claim dated Mar. 21, 1930) 901.26

24) Myers-Whaley Co., Inc., conveyor belts, chains, etc. (claim dated Mar. 21, 1930) 1,248.78

25) Owen-Oregon Lumber Co., lumber (claim dated Mar. 20, 1930) 2,417.00

26) Pioneer Rubber Mills, hose, belts, etc. (claim dated Mar. 21, 1930) 1,186.20

27) Santa Cruz Portland Cement Co., cement (claim dated Mar. 21, 1930) 3,538.00

28) Santa Fe Lumber Co, lumber (claim dated Mar. 21, 1930) 1,172.24

29) State Compensation Insurance Fund, premium on insurance covering Hetch Hetchy employments (claim dated Mar. 21, 1930) 8,344.12

Municipal Railway Fund

30) Remensperger Bros., one Ford sedan for Municipal Railways (claim dated Mar. 20, 1930)....................$ 664.25

Special School Tax

31) Ashley, Evers & Hayes, final payment, architectural servces for Geary St. School (claim dated Mar. 24, 1930).$ 1,556.93

Hetch Hetchy Power Operative Fund

32) Hales & Symons, Inc., asbestos shingles, etc. (claim dated Mar. 24, 1930) ....$ 1,098.71

33) Hetch Hetchy Construction Fund, materials, supplies, equipment and services rendered Hetch Hetchy Power Operative Fund during February, 1930 (claim dated Mar. 24, 1930) ....$ 6,271.64

County Road Fund

34) Calaveras Cement Co., cement for street reconstruction (claim dated Mar. 20, 1930) ....$ 1,394.63

35) Henry Cowell Lime & Cement Co, cement for street reconstruction (claim dated Mar. 20, 1930)............... 542.00

36) Granfield, Farrar & Carlin, sand furnished for street reconstruction (claim dated Mar. 20, 1930)............... 641.25

37) Standard Oil Co. of California, asphalt for street reconstruction (claim dated Mar. 20, 1930)................. 2,430.31

38) Pacific Portland Cement Co, cement for street reconstruction (claim dated Mar. 24, 1930).................. 638.01

39) Stores & Yards, Dept. of Public Works, reimbursement for repairs to equipment, month of February (claim dated Mar. 20, 1930) 1,149.44

Spring Valley Water Bonds

40) Lester, Herrick & Herrick and William Dolge & Co., professional services in making examination of accounts of Spring Valley Water Co. (claim dated Mar. 22, 1930)..$ 992.50

Publicity and Advertising—Appropriation 54

41) California State Chamber of Commerce, maintenance of Map of San Francisco exhibiting its resources, and distribution of data, months of December, January and February (claim dated Mar. 31, 1930) ....$ 1,500

Park Fund

42) N. Clark & Sons, furnishing and laying tile, convenience station, Golden Gate Park (claim dated Mar. 28, 1930).....$ 615.00

43) Pacific Gas & Electric Co., gas and electric service for parks (claim dated Mar. 28, 1930)...................... 1,273.79

44) Spring Valley Water Co., water furnished parks during February (claim dated Mar. 28, 1930)................... 1,156.49

General Fund—1929-1930

45) San Francisco Chronicle, official advertising, Board of Supervisors (claim dated Mar. 31, 1930).................$ 1,781.29

(46) Market Street Railway Co., refund of second installment
of taxes paid on property at Frederick and Willard streets,
under purchase by the city; per agreement dated Mar. 12,
1923 (claim dated Mar. 31, 1930)........................ 1,329.75
(47) Flynn & Collins, Inc., Ford coupe for Dept. Public Works
(claim dated Mar. 17, 1930) 636.10
(48) Photostat Corporation, photostat paper for Bureau of
Engineering (claim dated Mar. 17, 1930)................ 526.80
(49) Richfield Oil Co. of California, fuel oil for Civic Center
Power House (claim dated Mar. 17, 1930)................ 953.47
(50) County Road Fund, reimbursement for expenditures
made for account of covering of main sewers (claim dated
Mar. 30, 1930) 615.09
(51) Healy-Tibbitts Construction Co., payment in full for construction of Mariposa street outfall sewer (claim dated
Mar. 26, 1930) 2,854.00
(52) T. M. Gallagher, construction of sidewalks at James
Rolph Playground (claim dated Mar. 26, 1930).......... 670.00
(53) Board of State Harbor Commissioners, dredging mud at
foot of Baker street, and on Pierce street, for sewer outfalls
(claim dated Mar. 26, 1930) 2,250.00
(54) Annie M. Curley, Industrial Accident Commission award
for account of injuries sustained in line of duty as assistant Probation Officer (claim dated Mar. 24, 1930)...... 533.09
(55) General Electric X-Ray Corporation, X-ray films for San
Francisco Hospital (claim dated Mar. 27, 1930) 4,379.63
(56) California Meat Co., meat for S. F. Hospital (claim
dated Mar. 27, 1930) 2,439.52
(57) Associated Charities, unemployment relief (claim dated
Mar. 27, 1930) 7,965.81
(58) Pacific Gas & Electric Co., gas and electric service,
Laguna Honda Home (claim dated Mar. 27, 1930)....... 508.76
(59) Buckingham & Hecht, shoes for Laguna Honda Home
(claim dated Mar. 27, 1930) 625.25
(60) A. Levy & J. Zentner Co., potatoes for Laguna Honda
Home (claim dated Mar. 27, 1930) 1,018.80
(61) Levi Strauss & Co., cotton goods for Laguna Honda
Home (claim dated Mar. 27, 1930) 969.17
(62) L. M. Wilbor, M. D., Supt. of San Francisco Hospital,
for room allowances to hospital employees (claim dated
Mar. 27, 1930) 3,000.00
(63) W. L. Hughson Co., Ford sedan for Juvenile Court
(claim dated Mar. 24, 1930) 567.35

Appropriations, Boulevard and Sewer Bond Funds.

Also, Resolution No. ———— (New Series), as follows:

Resolved, That there be and is hereby set aside, appropriated and
authorized to be expended the sum of $30,000 out of Sewer Bond Fund,
and the sum of $20,000 out of Boulevard Bond Fund for the expense of
preparing plans and specifications and making studies of boulevards
and sewers during the next six months.

(Board of Public Works Resolution No. 109840, Second Series).

Adopted.

The following resolutions were *adopted:*

City Attorney to Compromise Damage Claim of Minnie L. Mor-tenson, Municipal Car Accident.

On recommendation of Finance Committee.

Resolution No. 32270 (New Series), as follows:

Whereas, Minnie L. Mortenson sustained severe injuries while a
passenger on Municipal car "D" line on or about October 13, 1929; and

Whereas, City Attorney John J. O'Toole has this day recommended a compromise and settlement of the claim of said Minnie P. Mortenson; now, therefore, be it

Resolved, That the City Attorney be and he is hereby authorized and empowered to compromise and settle said claim for the sum of three thousand ($3,000) dollars.

Ayes—Supervisors Andriano, Canepa, Colman, Gallagher, Havenner, Hayden, McGovern, McSheehy, Miles, Peyser, Power, Roncovieri, Rossi, Shannon, Spaulding, Stanton, Suhr, Toner—18.

Acceptance of Offer to Sell Land, Somerset and Silliman Streets.

Also, Resolution No. 32271 (New Series), as follows:

Resolved, That the City and County of San Francisco accept title to that certain lot, tract or parcel of land situate, lying and being in the City and County of San Francisco, State of California, bounded and described as follows, to-wit:

Beginning at a point formed by the intersection of the southwesterly line of Somerset street with the southeasterly line of Silliman street, and running thence southwesterly along the southeasterly line of Silliman street 120 feet; thence at a right angle southeasterly 400 feet to the northwesterly line of Felton street; thence northeasterly along the northwesterly line of Felton street 120 feet to the southwesterly line of Somerset street; thence northwesterly along the southwesterly line of Somerset street 400 feet to the point of beginning.

Being the northeasterly one-half of Block No. 28, University Mound Survey, as per map thereof recorded May 1, 1863, in Book 2 "A" and "B" of Maps, page 43, in the office of the Recorder of the City and County of San Francisco, State of California.

That the City Attorney be and is hereby directed to accept a deed to said property and upon the receipt of same to forthwith record same in the office of the Recorder of the City and County of San Francisco.

Ayes—Supervisors Andriano, Canepa, Colman, Gallagher, Havenner, Hayden, McGovern, McSheehy, Miles, Peyser, Power, Roncovieri, Rossi, Shannon, Spaulding, Stanton, Suhr, Toner—18.

Auditor to Cancel Erroneous Assessment.

Also, Resolution No. 32272 (New Series), as follows:

Whereas, the Assessor has reported that the property of Frank I. Ingersoll was erroneously assessed and sold to the State on June 29, 1929, Sale No. 2313, and recommends that said assessment and sale be cancelled, and the City Attorney having consented thereto; therefore, be it

Resolved, That the Auditor be directed to cancel said assessment and sale as provided in Sections 3804 and 3805 of the Political Code.

Ayes—Supervisors Andriano, Canepa, Colman, Gallagher, Havenner, Hayden, McGovern, McSheehy, Miles, Peyser, Power, Roncovieri, Rossi, Shannon, Spaulding, Stanton, Suhr, Toner—18.

Accepting Offer of Sale of Land Required for Widening of Chenery Street.

Also, Resolution No. 32273 (New Series), as follows:

Resolved, That the offer of sale made by the following named persons to sell to the City and County of San Francisco the following described land, required for the widening of Chenery street, opposite Randall street, for the sum set forth opposite their names, be accepted:

Frank and Josephine Cusimano, $82—Portion of Lot 1, Block 6663, as per the Assessor's Block Books of the City and County of San Francisco. (As per detailed description and written offer on file.)

And the City Attorney is hereby authorized to examine the title to said property, and, if the same is found satisfactory, to accept, on behalf of the City, deed conveying said property to the City, free and clear of all encumbrances, and to record said deed, together with a copy of this resolution, in the office of the Recorder of the City and County of San Francisco, State of California.

Ayes—Supervisors Andriano, Canepa, Colman, Gallagher, Havenner, Hayden, McGovern, McSheehy, Miles, Peyser, Power, Roncovieri, Rossi, Shannon, Spaulding, Stanton, Suhr, Toner—18.

Accepting Offer of Sale of Land for Alemany Boulevard.

Also, Resolution No. 32274 (New Series), as follows:

Resolved, That the offer of sale made by the following named owner to sell to the City and County of San Francisco the following described land, required for the opening of Alemany boulevard, for the sum set forth opposite his name, be accepted:

Sidney F. Warren, $200—Portion of Lot 33, Block 7140, as per the Assessor's Block Books of the City and County of San Francisco. (As per detailed description and written offer on file.)

And the City Attorney is hereby authorized to examine the title to said property, and, if the same is found satisfactory, to accept, on behalf of the City, a deed conveying said property to the City, free and clear of all encumbrances, and to record said deed, together with a copy of this resolution, in the office of the Recorder of the City and County of San Francisco.

Ayes—Supervisors Andriano, Canepa, Colman, Gallagher, Havenner, Hayden, McGovern, McSheehy, Miles, Peyser, Power, Roncovieri, Rossi. Shannon, Spaulding, Stanton, Suhr, Toner—18.

Accepting Offer of Sale of Land for Bay Shore Boulevard.

Also, Resolution No. 32275 (New Series), as follows:

Resolved, That the offers of sale made by the following named owners to sell to the City and County of San Francisco the following described lands, required for the opening of Bay Shore boulevard, for the sums set forth opposite their names, be accepted:

E. A. Hughes, $1,850—All of Lot 20, Block 5477, as per the Assessor's Block Books of the City and County of San Francisco.

Lucius L. Solomons, $210—Portion of Lot 25, Block 5560, as per the Assessor's Block Books of the City and County of San Francisco. (As per detailed description and written offer on file.)

The City Attorney is hereby authorized to examine the title to said property, and, if the same is found in satisfactory condition, to accept, on behalf of the City, deeds conveying said property to the City, free and clear of all encumbrances, and to record said deeds, together with a copy of this resolution, in the office of the Recorder of the City and County of San Francisco.

Ayes—Supervisors Andriano, Canepa, Colman, Gallagher, Havenner. Hayden, McGovern, McSheehy, Miles, Peyser, Power, Roncovieri, Rossi. Shannon, Spaulding, Stanton, Suhr, Toner—18.

Accepting Offer to Release City and County of San Francisco From All Claims of Damages Caused by Construction of Bay Shore Boulevard.

Also, Resolution No. 32276 (New Series), as follows:

Whereas, the following owner of property adjacent to the proposed Bay Shore boulevard has offered to release the City and County of San Francisco, its contractors or agents, from all claim or claims of damages to his property or the buildings thereon caused by the grading and construction of the proposed Bay Shore boulevard to the proposed official grade and the grading and construction of adjacent streets to said proposed Bay Shore boulevard; and

Whereas, the City Attorney has recommended the acceptance of the said offer as per the following terms, viz.:

F. J. Varni, $532.50—Lot 14, Block 5375, as per the Assessor's Block Books of the City and County of San Francisco, and also known as No. 150 Boutwell street.

Resolved, That the said offer be accepted and the City Attorney is hereby authorized to close negotiations and superintend the payment of said specified amount to the above mentioned person upon receipt of the proper release.

Ayes—Supervisors Andriano, Canepa, Colman, Gallagher, Havenner, Hayden, McGovern, McSheehy, Miles, Peyser, Power, Roncovieri, Rossi, Shannon, Spaulding, Stanton, Suhr, Toner—18.

Accepting Offer to Release City From All Claims of Damages by Construction of Bay Shore Boulevard.

Also, Resolution No. 32277 (New Series), as follows:

Whereas, the following owner of property adjacent to the proposed Bay Shore boulevard has offered to release the City and County of San Francisco, its contractors or agents, from all claim or claims of damages to her property or the buildings thereon caused by the grading and construction of the proposed Bay Shore boulevard to the proposed official grade and the grading and construction of adjacent streets to said proposed Bay Shore boulevard; and

Whereas, the City Attorney has recommended the acceptance of the said offer as per the following terms, viz.:

Maria A. Montes, $400—Lots 26 and 27, Block 5465, as per the Assessor's Block Books of the City and County of San Francisco, and also known as No. 99 Wheat street.

Resolved, That the said offer be accepted and the City Attorney is hereby authorized to close negotiations and superintend the payment of said specified amount to the above named person upon receipt of the proper release.

Ayes—Supervisors Andriano, Canepa, Colman, Gallagher, Havenner, Hayden, McGovern, McSheehy, Miles, Peyser, Power, Roncovieri, Rossi, Shannon, Spaulding, Stanton, Suhr, Toner—18.

Accepting Offer to Release City From Damages, Opening of Bay Shore Boulevard.

Also, Resolution No. 32278 (New Series), as follows:

Whereas, the following owners of property adjacent to the proposed Bay Shore boulevard have offered to release the City and County of San Francisco, its contractors or agents, from all claim or claims of damages to their property or the buildings thereon caused by the grading and construction of the proposed Bay Shore boulevard to the proposed official grade and the grading and construction of adjacent streets to said proposed Bay Shore boluevard; and

Whereas, the City Attorney has recommended the acceptance of the said offers as per the following terms, viz.:

G. W. Laine and Minnie Laine, $1,402—Lots 15 and 16, Block 5471, as per the Assessor's Block Books of the City and County of San Francisco, and also known as No. 3321 Lane street.

Ida Seaborg, $150—Lots 8 and 9, Block 5479, as per the Assessor's Block Books of the City and County of San Francisco, and also known as No. 1035 Meade avenue.

Resolved, That the said offers be accepted and the City Attorney is hereby authorized and directed to close negotiations and superintend the payment of said specified amounts to the above mentioned persons upon receipt of the proper releases.

Ayes—Supervisors Andriano, Canepa, Colman, Gallagher, Havenner, Hayden, McGovern, McSheehy, Miles, Peyser, Power, Roncovieri, Rossi, Shannon, Spaulding, Stanton, Suhr, Toner—18.

Accepting Offer to Release City and County of San Francisco From All Claims of Damages Caused by Bernal Cut.

Also, Resolution No. 32279 (New Series), as follows:

Whereas, the following owners of property adjacent to the proposed Bernal Cut have offered to release the City and County of San Francisco, its contractors or agents, from all claim or claims of damage to their property, or the buildings thereon, caused by the grading and construction of the proposed Bernal Cut to the proposed official grade and the grading and construction of adjacent streets to said proposed Bernal Cut; and

Whereas, the City Attorney has recommended the acceptance of the said offer, as per the following terms, viz.:

Thomas Walsh and Katherine Walsh, $628—Lot 19, Block 6662, as per the Assessor's Block Books of the City and County of San Francisco, also known as No. 77 Randall street.

Resolved, That the said offer be accepted and the City Attorney is hereby authorized and directed to close negotiations and superintend the payment of said specified amount to the above-mentioned persons upon receipt of the proper release.

Ayes—Supervisors Andriano, Canepa, Colman, Gallagher, Havenner, Hayden, McGovern, McSheehy, Miles, Peyser, Power, Roncovieri, Rossi, Shannon, Spaulding, Stanton, Suhr, Toner—18.

Appropriations, County Road Fund.

Also, Resolution No. 32280 (New Series), as follows:

Resolved, That the following amounts be and the same are hereby set aside, appropriated and authorized to be expended out of County Road Fund for the following purposes, to-wit:

(1) For cost of performing conform work at the intersection of Josiah and Lake View avenues, in connection with improvement of unfinished portion of Josiah avenue from Lake View avenue southerly............................$ 225.00
(2) For cost of construction of sidewalks on the south side of Market street between Danvers street and Mono street...   270.00
(3) For cost of construction of 100 feet of concrete curb from Twin Peaks boulevard southwesterly from Crown Terrace..   100.00

Ayes—Supervisors Andriano, Canepa, Colman, Gallagher, Havenner, Hayden, McGovern, McSheehy, Miles, Peyser, Power, Roncovieri, Rossi, Shannon, Spaulding, Stanton, Suhr, Toner—18.

Passed for Printing.

The following resolutions were *passed for printing*:

Appropriation Out of County Road Fund to Joint Highway District No. 9, for Construction of the San Francisco-San Mateo-Santa Cruz Shore Line Highway.

On recommendation of Finance Committee.

Resolution No. ————— (New Series), as follows:

Resolved, That the sum of $35,000 be and the same is hereby set aside and appropriated out of County Road Fund, and authorized in payment to Joint Highway District No. 9, being San Francisco's contribution toward the construction of first unit of the San Francisco-San Mateo-Santa Cruz Shore Line Highway.

Appropriations Out of County Road Fund, Various Purposes.

Also, Resolution No. ————— (New Series), as follows:

Resolved, That the following amounts be and the same are hereby set aside, appropriated and authorized to be expended out of the County Road Fund for the following purposes, to-wit:

(1) For the improvement of the Stockton Street Tunnel by waterproofing, painting, lighting and miscellaneous repairs, per contract awarded to Conrad B. Sovig..............$12,972.00

(2) For installation by the Department of Electricity of Traffic signals at the intersection of Sloat boulevard and Nineteenth avenue—four signal heads, one control box and cable 934.00

(3) For removal of sand from roadway and sidewalk area on Thirty-eighth and Thirty-fourth avenues between Judah and Kirkham streets 2,583.90

(4) For cost of widening and surfacing to a width of 15 feet, with red rock water bound macadam surface, the existing road on Alabama street south of Ripley street, through private property to connect with Bernal Heights boulevard at Esmeralda avenue 600.00

Adopted.

The following resolution was *adopted*:

Board of Public Works Interdepartmental Reimbursements.

On recommendation of Finance Committee.

Resolution No. 32281 (New Series), as follows:

Resolved, That the following amounts be and the same are hereby set aside out of the hereinafter mentioned Budget Items, Department of Public Works, to the credit of "Stores and Yards," Budget Item 461, Department of Public Works; being reimbursements for expenditures in connection with repairs to equipment for the various Bureaus, to-wit:

Street Cleaning. Budget Item 552.........................$ 533.93
Sewer Repair, Budget Item 565 .... 388.00
Auto Maintenance, Budget Item 577 .... 84.25
Bureau of Engineering, Budget Item 504 .... 35.12
Building Repair, Budget Item 446 .... 7.44
Stores and Yards, Budget Item 469 .... 15.75

Ayes—Supervisors Andriano, Canepa, Colman, Gallagher, Havenner, Hayden. McGovern, McSheehy, Miles, Peyser, Power, Roncovieri, Rossi, Shannon. Spaulding, Stanton, Suhr, Toner—18.

Passed for Printing.

The following matter was *passed for printing*:

Appropriations Out of County Road Fund for Street Reconstruction by Board of Public Works.

On recommendation of Finance Committee.

Resolution No. ————— (New Series), as follows:

Resolved, That the following amounts be and the same are hereby set aside, appropriated and authorized to be expended out of County Road Fund for the reconstruction of the following streets by the Board of Public Works, to-wit:

(1) Octavia street between Filbert and Greenwich streets, improvement ....$ 800.00

(2) Webster street, McAllister street to Fulton street, resurfacing 800.00

(3) Twenty-seventh avenue, Geary street to Clement street, improvement of.. 2,500.00
(4) Laurel street, Clay street to Pacific avenue.............. 5,200.00
(5) Maple street, Washington street to Jackson street........ 1,800.00
(6) Pine street, Lyon street to Presidio avenue.............. 2,500.00
(7) Lyon street, Geary street to Post street................. 4,025.00
(8) Baker street, Geary street to Post street................ 1,800.00
(9) Twelfth avenue, Anza street to Balboa street............. 3,400.00
(10) Broadway, Van Ness avenue to Octavia street............ 9,160.00
(11) Lyon street, Jackson street to Pacific avenue........... 2,050.00
(12) Broderick street, Pacific avenue to Broadway.......... 2,050.00
(13) Larkin-Francisco streets ramp, including Chestnut street, Taylor street to Jones street............................ 3,500.00

Total $39,585.00

Adopted.

The following resolution was *adopted*:

Transfer of Funds, Sheriff's Department.

On recommendation of Finance Committee.

Resolution No. 32284 (New Series), as follows:

Resolved, That the sum of $1,400 be and the same is hereby set aside out of Appropriation 14-B to the credit of Appropriation 14-C, Sheriff's Department.

Ayes—Supervisors Andriano, Canepa, Colman, Gallagher, Havenner, Hayden, McGovern, McSheehy, Miles, Peyser, Power, Roncovieri, Rossi, Shannon, Spaulding, Stanton, Suhr, Toner—18.

Passed for Printing.

The following matters were *passed for printing*:

Ordering the Improvement of Alemany Boulevard, Section "C," From Ocean Avenue to San Jose Avenue.

On recommendation of Streets Committee.

Bill No. 8221, Ordinance No. ———— (New Series), as follows:

Ordering the improvement of Alemany boulevard, Section "C" from Ocean avenue to San Jose avenue, a distance of about 7800 feet with a width of 100 feet, by grading and the construction of a retaining wall and initial sewer construction. Authorizing, directing and empowering the Board of Public Works to enter into contract for said improvement in accordance with plans and specifications prepared therefor, approving said plans and specifications and authorizing progressive payments to be made during the construction of said improvement, the cost of said improvements to be borne out of Boulevard Bond Issue, 1927.

Be it ordained by the People of the City and County of San Francisco as follows:

Section 1. The Board of Public Works is hereby authorized, instructed and empowered to enter into contract for the improvement of Alemany boulevard, Section "C," a distance of 7800 feet with a width of 100 feet by grading and the construction of a retaining wall and initial sewer construction in accordance with plans and specifications prepared therefor, approving and adopting said plans and specifications.

The cost of said improvement to be borne out of funds of the Boulevard Bond Issue, 1927.

Section 2. The Board of Public Works is hereby authorized and permitted to incorporate in the contract for the improvement of said Alemany boulevard, conditions that progressive payments shall be made in the manner set forth in said specifications on file in the office of the Board of Public Works and as provided by the Charter of the City and County of San Francisco.

Section 3. This Ordinance shall take effect immediately.

Ordering the Construction of Sewer Leading From Fourteenth and Market Streets to Fifteenth and Howard Streets.

Also, Bill No. 8222, Ordinance No. ———— (New Series), as follows:

Authorizing the preparation of plans and specifications for the construction of a sewer leading from Fourteenth and Market streets to Fifteenth and Howard streets, Section B, contract No. 4; ordering the construction of said sewer in accordance with said plans and specifications prepared therefor; authorizing and directing the Board of Public Works to enter into contract for the construction of said sewer, and permitting progressive payments to be made during the course of said work, the cost of said work to be borne out of Sewer Bonds, 1929.

Be it ordained by the People of the City and County of San Francisco as follows:

Section 1. The Board of Public Works is hereby authorized, instructed and empowered to prepare plans and specifications for the construction of a sewer leading from Fourteenth and Market streets to Fifteenth and Howard streets, Section B, contract No. 4, and to enter into contract for the construction of said sewer hereinbefore specified, which is hereby ordered, in accordance with said plans and specifications prepared therefor. The cost of said sewer to be borne out of funds of the Sewer Bonds, 1929.

Section 2. The Board of Public Works is hereby authorized and permitted to incorporate in the contract for the construction of said sewer, conditions that progressive payments shall be made in the manner set forth in said specifications on file in the office of the Board of Public Works and as provided for by the Charter of the City and County of San Francisco.

Section 3. This Ordinance shall take effect immediately.

Ordering Construction of Fillmore Street Main Sewer, Section "D," Payable Sewer Bonds, 1929.

Also, Bill No. 8223, Ordinance No. ———— (New Series), as follows:

Authorizing the preparation of plans and specifications for the construction of the Fillmore street main sewer, Section "D;" ordering the construction of said sewer in accordance with said plans and specifications prepared therefor; authorizing and directing the Board of Public Works to enter into contract for the construction of said sewer, and permitting progressive payments to be made during the course of said work, the cost of said work to be borne out of Sewer Bonds, 1929.

Be it ordained by the People of the City and County of San Francisco as follows:

Section 1. The Board of Public Works is hereby authorized, instructed and empowered to prepare plans and specifications for the construction of Fillmore street main sewer, Section "D," and to enter into contract for the construction of said sewer hereinbefore specified, which is hereby ordered, in accordance with said plans and specifications prepared therefor. The cost of said sewer to be borne out of funds of the Sewer Bonds, 1929.

Section 2. The Board of Public Works is hereby authorized and permitted to incorporate in the contract for the construction of said sewer, conditions that progressive payments shall be made in the manner set forth in said specifications on file in the office of the Board of Public Works and as provided for by the Charter of the City and County of San Francisco.

Section 3. This Ordinance shall take effect immediately.

Ordering Construction of Fillmore Street Main Sewer, Section "B," Payable Sewer Bonds, 1929.

Also, Bill No. 8224, Ordinance No. ———— (New Series), as follows:

Authorizing the preparation of plans and specifications for the con-struction of the Fillmore street main sewer, Section "B,"; ordering the construction of said sewer in accordance with said plans and specifica-tions prepared therefor; authorizing and directing the Board of Public Works to enter into contract for the construction of said sewer, and permitting progressive payments to be made during the course of said work, the cost of said work to be borne out of Sewer Bonds, 1929.

Be it ordained by the People of the City and County of San Fran-cisco as follows:

Section 1. The Board of Public Works is hereby authorized, in-structed and empowered to prepare plans and specifications for the construction of Fillmore street main sewer, Section "B," and to enter into contract for the construction of said sewer hereinbefore specified, which is hereby ordered, in accordance with said plans and specifica-tions prepared therefor. The cost of said sewer to be borne out of funds of the Sewer Bonds, 1929.

Section 2. The Board of Public Works is hereby authorized and per-mitted to incorporate, in the contract for the construction of said sewer, conditions that progressive payments shall be made in the manner set forth in said specifications on file in the office of the Board of Public Works, and as provided for by the Charter of the City and County of San Francisco.

Section 3. This ordinance shall take effect immediately.

Ordering Construction of College Hill Tunnel Sewer, Section "K," of the North Point Main, Payable Sewer Bonds, 1929.

Also, Bill No. 8225, Ordinance No. ———— (New Series), as follows:

Authorizing the preparation of plans and specifications for the con-struction of the College Hill tunnel sewer (Section "K" of the North Point main); ordering the construction of said sewer in accordance with said plans and specifications prepared therefor; authorizing and directing the Board of Public Works to enter into contract for the con-struction of said sewer, and permitting progressive payments to be made during the course of said work, the cost of said work to be borne out of Sewer Bonds, 1929.

Be it ordained by the People of the City and County of San Fran-cisco as follows:

Section 1. The Board of Public Works is hereby authorized, in-structed and empowered to prepare plans and specifications for the construction of the College Hill tunnel sewer (Section "K" of the North Point main), and to enter into contract for the construction of said sewer hereinbefore specified, which is hereby ordered, in accord-ance with said plans and specifications prepared therefor. The cost of said sewer to be borne out of funds of the Sewer Bonds, 1929.

Section 2. The Board of Public Works is hereby authorized and per-mitted to incorporate, in the contract for the construction of said sewer, conditions that progressive payments shall be made in the manner set forth in said specifications on file in the office of the Board of Public Works, and as provided for by the Charter of the City and County of San Francisco.

Section 3. This ordinance shall take effect immediately.

Ordering Construction of Fillmore Street Main Sewer, Section "C," Payable Sewer Bonds, 1929.

Also, Bill No. 8226, Ordinance No. ———— (New Series), as follows:

Authorizing the preparation of plans and specifications for the con-struction of the Fillmore street main sewer, Section "C"; ordering the construction of said sewer in accordance with said plans and specifications prepared therefor; authorizing and directing the Board of Public Works to enter into contract for the construction of said sewer, and permitting progressive payments to be made during the course of said work, the cost of said work to be borne out of Sewer Bonds, 1929.

Be it ordained by the People of the City and County of San Francisco as follows:

Section 1. The Board of Public Works is hereby authorized, instructed and empowered to prepare plans and specifications for the construction of the Fillmore street main sewer, Section "C," and to enter into contract for the construction of said sewer hereinbefore specified, which is hereby ordered, in accordance with said plans and specifications prepared therefor. The cost of said sewer to be borne out of funds of the Sewer Bonds, 1929.

Section 2. The Board of Public Works is hereby authorized and permitted to incorporate, in the contract for the construction of said sewer, conditions that progressive payments shall be made in the manner set forth in said specifications on file in the office of the Board of Public Works, and as provided for by the Charter of the City and County of San Francisco.

Section 3. This ordinance shall take effect immediately.

Ordering Construction of Geary Street and Twenty-third Avenue Main Sewers, Payable Sewer Bonds, 1929.

Also, Bill No. 8227, Ordinance No. ———— (New Series), as follows:

Authorizing the preparation of plans and specifications for the construction of the Geary street and Twenty-third avenue main sewers; ordering the construction of said sewers in accordance with said plans and specifications prepared therefor; authorizing and directing the Board of Public Works to enter into contract for the construction of said sewers, and permitting progressive payments to be made during the course of said work, the cost of said work to be borne out of Sewer Bonds, 1929.

Be it ordained by the People of the City and County of San Francisco as follows:

Section 1. The Board of Public Works is hereby authorized, instructed and empowered to prepare plans and specifications for the construction of the Geary street and Twenty-third avenue main sewers, and to enter into contract for the construction of said sewers hereinbefore specified, which is hereby ordered, in accordance with said plans and specifications prepared therefor. The cost of said sewer to be borne out of funds of the Sewer Bonds, 1929.

Section 2. The Board of Public Works is hereby authorized and permitted to incorporate, in the contract for the construction of said sewer, conditions that progressive payments shall be made in the manner set forth in said specifications on file in the office of the Board of Public Works, and as provided for by the Charter of the City and County of San Francisco.

Section 3. This ordinance shall take effect immediately.

Appropriations, Various Purposes.

On recommendation of Finance Committee.

Resolution No. ———— (New Series), as follows:

Resolved, That the following amounts be and the same are hereby set aside, appropriated and authorized to be expended out of the hereinafter mentioned funds for the following purposes, to-wit:

City Hall Repairs—Budget Item 54.

(1) For expense of providing locking system for the six City Hall elevators which will prevent the bottom landing door being opened from outside of hoistway by means of a key when the elevator is away from the landing..........$ 720.00

Extension and Reconstruction of Sewers—Budget Item **37.**

(2) For cost of constructing a concrete aqueduct in Wayland
street between University and Cambridge streets.........$ 1,000.00

General Fund, 1929-1930.

(3) For payment of Sunset tunnel assessment, designated as
Assessments Nos. 6352 and G 15, on properties sold to the
City and County of San Francisco February 18, 1929, for
nonpayment of the Sunset tunnel assessment .. ..$ 588.89

Appropriations, Various Purposes.

Also, Resolution No. ————— (New Series), as follows:

Resolved, That the following amounts be and the same are hereby
set aside, appropriated and authorized to be expended out of the hereinafter mentioned funds for the following purposes, to-wit:

Special School Tax.

(1) For the furnishing and installing of thirteen radiator
guards in the Sunshine School .. ..$ 425.00

Repairs to Public Buildings, Etc.—Budget Item 53.

(2) For replacing tile on wall and replacing of floor, apparatus room, Fire Department Engine House No. 45........$ 483.00

Extension and Reconstruction of Sewers—Budget Item 37.

(3) To the credit of "Tearing Up Streets Fund," to cover cost,
additional to amount paid by property owners, for side
sewer installations in Nineteenth street between Tennesssee
and Third streets; Sutter street between Kearny and Montgomery streets, and in Francisco street between Leavenworth and Hyde streets .. ..$ 256.00
(Per resolution of Board of Public Works, No. 109888, Second Series.)

(4) For cost of lowering and constructing new main sewer in
Faith street between Holladay avenue and Brewster street.$ 225.00

Adopted.

The following resolution was adopted:

**Endorsing Assembly Constitutional Amendment No. 21, and Author-
izing the Mayor to Appoint a Special Committee to Cooperate
With the Other Counties in Obtaining the Approval of Said
Amendment by the People.**

On recommendation of Finance Committee.

Resolution No. 32283 (New Series), as follows:

Whereas, in the year 1911 the State of California put into operation
a tax system which can be generally classified as a dual tax system,
which said system practically segregates the sources of revenue for
State purposes from the sources of revenue for county and municipal
purposes;

And whereas, the operation of said tax system has demonstrated
that a great number of inequities exist in said system which have
resulted, and unless corrected will result, in an unfair discrimination
against various counties of the State;

And whereas, for the purpose of remedying said inequities to at
least some extent, the forty-eighth session of the Legislature of the
State of California ordered submitted to the electors of the State a
certain amendment to the Constitution of the State of California, designated as Assembly Constitutional Amendment No. 21;

And whereas, said amendment provides for the reimbursement to
the various counties and cities and counties of the State for loss in
revenue sustained by said counties and cities and counties by the with-

drawal of the property taxed for State purposes pursuant to certain provisions of the Constitution of the State;

And whereas, the City and County of San Francisco, together with thirty-seven other counties in the State of California, will greatly benefit by the approval of said constitutional amendment, by reason of the large amount of operative properties which are not subject to taxation for local purposes in the City and County of San Francisco and in said other counties; now, therefore, be it

Resolved, That the Board of Supervisors of the City and County of San Francisco does hereby record itself as being in favor of the adoption and approval of said Assembly Constitutional Amendment No. 21, which shall be voted upon by the people at the general State election to be held during the month of November of the present year, and said Board hereby pledges itself to use all lawful and honorable means to obtain the approval of said amendment; and be it

Further Resolved, That the Mayor of the City and County of San Francisco is hereby authorized to appoint a special committee of such number as he shall see fit, to cooperate with the other counties in the State in obtaining the approval of said amendment by the people, and to present to the electors of the City and County of San Francisco the benefits which will accrue to said City and County by said approval.

Ayes—Supervisors Andriano, Canepa, Colman, Gallagher, Havenner, Hayden, McGovern, McSheehy, Miles, Peyser, Power, Roncovieri, Rossi, Shannon, Spaulding, Stanton, Suhr, Toner—18.

Passed for Printing.

The following matters were *passed for printing*:

Oil Tanks and Boilers.

On recommendation of Fire Committee.

Resolution No. ———— (New Series), as follows:

Resolved, That the following revocable permits be and are hereby granted:

Oil Tanks.

The Roman Catholic Archbishop of San Francisco, northeast corner of Eighteenth avenue and Vicente street, 1500 gallons capacity.

R. W. Murray, 1818 Fifteenth street, 1500 gallons capacity.

A. R. McDowell, 1100 Cabrillo street, 1500 gallons capacity.

Mrs. A. Swett, 170 San Anselmo avenue, 1500 gallons capacity.

John Milonas, 1335 Eighteenth street, 1500 gallons capacity.

J. Kipnis, 5607 California street, 1500 gallons capacity.

Mrs. Emma Ingham, 4430 California street, 1500 gallons capacity.

Boilers.

Ocean Shore Iron Works, 318 Divisadero street, 10-horsepower.

The rights granted under this resolution shall be exercised within six months, otherwise said permit shall become null and void.

Automobile Supply Station Permit, Standard Oil Company, North-east Corner Fell and Gough Streets.

Also, Resolution No. ———— (New Series), as follows:

Resolved, That the Standard Oil Company of California be and is hereby granted permission, revocable at will of the Board of Supervisors, to maintain and operate an automobile supply station at the northeast corner of Fell and Gough streets.

The rights granted under this resolution shall be exercised within six months, otherwise said permit shall become null and void.

Adopted.

The following resolutions were *adopted*:

Street Lights.

On recommendation of Lighting Committee.

Resolution No. 32284 (New Series), as follows:

Resolved, That the Pacific Gas and Electric Company be and it is hereby authorized and requested to remove and install street lights as follows:

Remove 400 M. R.

Nineteenth and Twentieth streets between Valencia and Mission streets.

Twenty-eighth avenue between Irving and Judah streets.

Vallejo street between Scott and Divisadero streets.

Army street between Dolores and Sanchez streets (4).

Eighth street between Folsom and Harrison streets (2).

Lenox way between Taraval and Ulloa streets (2).

Wawona street between Taraval and Ulloa streets (2).

Twenty-fifth avenue between Clement and California streets.

Seventeenth avenue between Taraval and Vicente streets (4).

Thirty-third avenue between Balboa and Cabrillo streets.

Ninth avenue between Judah and Kirkham streets.

Thirty-first avenue between Balboa and Cabrillo streets.

Delta and Sunnydale avenue.

Thirty-first avenue between Irving and Judah streets.

Remove 250 M. R.

Twenty-seventh street between Dolores and Church streets.

Install Type "C" 400 C. P.

North side of Ulloa street, west of Rockaway avenue (end of Church).

Install Type "C" 300-Watt.

Southwest corner Fourth and Howard streets.

Install 600 C. P. O. B.

North side Bush street, east of Divisadero street (front of Christian Church).

Install 400 C. P. O. B.

East and west sides Twenty-fifth avenue between Clement and California streets.

Retiro way between Casa way and Fillmore street (2).

Eighth street between Folsom and Harrison streets (3).

West side San Carlos street between Twentieth and Twenty-first streets.

North and south sides Vallejo street between Scott and Divisadero streets.

Front of No. 334 La Grande avenue.

East and west sides Twenty-eighth avenue between Irving and Judah streets.

De Haro street between Twenty-third and Twenty-fourth streets.

East side Wawona street, south of Taraval street.

East side Wawona street, north of Ulloa street.

West side Wawona street between Taraval and Ulloa streets.

East and west sides Seventeenth avenue between Taraval and Ulloa streets.

Northeast and southwest corners Seventeenth avenue and Ulloa street.

Northwest and southeast corners Seventeenth avenue and Vicente street.

East side Seventeenth avenue, north of Vicente street.

York street between Twenty-sixth and Army streets.

East and west sides Ninth avenue between Judah and Kirkham streets.

Thirty-eighth avenue between Judah and Kirkham streets.

East and west sides Thirty-first avenue between Balboa and Cabrillo streets.

Northeast corner Delta and Sunnydale avenue.

Josiah avenue between Summit and Lakeview avenues.

North and south sides Twenty-seventh street between Dolores and Church streets.

East and west sides Thirty-third avenue between Balboa and Cabrillo streets.

Thirty-eighth avenue between Judah and Kirkham streets.

Thirty-first avenue between Irving and Judah streets.

North and south sides Army street between Dolores and Sanchez streets.

East side Cecilia avenue, north of Santiago street.

Parsons street between McAllister and Fulton streets.

Nineteenth and Twentieth streets between Valencia and Lexington streets and Lexington and San Carlos and San Carlos and Mission streets.

Utah street between Twenty-third and Twenty-fourth streets.

Twenty-ninth street between Noe and Castro streets.

Twenty-ninth street between Castro and Diamond streets.

Twenty-ninth street between Noe and Diamond streets.

East and west sides Lenox way between Ulloa and Taraval streets (3).

Morse and Rolph streets.

Alabama street between Precita and Army streets.

Change M. R. to O. B.

Sycamore and San Carlos streets.

Sycamore and Lexington streets.

Sycamore street between Valencia and Lexington streets.

Sixteenth avenue between Noriega and Ortega streets.

Install 250 C. P. O. B.

Cypress alley north of Twenty-sixth street.

Ruth street between Mission street and Watson place.

Watson place and Ruth street.

Osage alley between Twenty-fourth and Twenty-fifth streets.

Ayes—Supervisors Andriano, Canepa, Colman, Gallagher, Havenner, Hayden, McGovern, McSheehy, Miles, Peyser, Power, Roncovieri, Rossi, Shannon, Spaulding, Stanton, Suhr, Toner—18.

Purchase of Land for School Purposes, Twenty-fifth Street, Easterly From Castro Street (Lick School).

On recommendation of Public Buildings and Lands Committee.

Resolution No. 32285 (New Series), as follows:

Whereas, an offer has been received from Marguretha Drewes to convey to the City and County of San Francisco certain land and improvements on the southerly line of Twenty-fifth street, distant 155 feet easterly from Castro street, required for school purposes; and

Whereas, the price at which said parcel of land is offered is the reasonable value thereof; therefore, be it

Resolved, That the offer so said owner to convey to the City and County of San Francisco a good and sufficient fee simple title to the following described land, free of all encumbrances, for the sum of $13,000, be and the same is hereby accepted, the said lands being described as follows, to-wit:

Commencing at a point on the southerly line of Twenty-fifth street, distant thereon 155 feet easterly from the easterly line of Castro street, running thence easterly along said southerly line of Twenty-fifth street 30 feet; thence at a right angle southerly 114 feet; thence at a right angle westerly 30 feet; thence at a right angle northerly 114 feet to the southerly line of Twenty-fifth street and point of commencement. Being a portion of Horner's Addition Block **163**, **also** known as Block 6547 on Assessor's Map Book.

The City Attorney is hereby directed to examine the title to said land, and, if the same is found to be vested in the aforesaid owner, free of all encumbrances, and that the taxes up to and including the current fiscal year are paid, and that the so-called McEnerney title has been procured or sufficient money reserved for the purpose of procuring the same, to report the result of his examination to the Board of Supervisors, and also to cause a good and sufficient deed for said land to be executed and delivered to the City and County upon payment of the agreed purchase price as aforesaid. And the said deed to said land is hereby accepted.

Ayes—Supervisors Andriano, Canepa, Colman, Gallagher, Havenner, Hayden, McGovern, McSheehy, Miles, Peyser, Power, Roncovieri, Rossi, Shannon, Spaulding, Stanton, Suhr, Toner—18.

Purchase of Land for School Purposes, West Line Thirty-eighth Avenue, North of Ulloa street.

Also, Resolution No. 32286 (New Series), as follows:

Whereas, an offer has been received from Mary Schott to convey to the City and County of San Francisco certain land and improvements on the westerly line of Thirty-eighth avenue, distant 250 feet northerly from Ulloa street, required for school purposes; and

Whereas, the price at which said parcel of land is offered is the reasonable value thereof; therefore, be it

Resolved, That the offer of the said owner to convey to the City and County of San Francisco a good and sufficient fee simple title to the following described land, free of all encumbrances, for the sum of $1,000, be and the same is hereby accepted, the said lands being described as follows, to-wit:

Commencing at a point on the westerly line of Thirty-eighth avenue, distant thereon 250 feet northerly from the northerly line of Ulloa street, running thence northerly along said westerly line of Thirty-eighth avenue 25 feet; thence at a right angle westerly 120 feet; thence at a right angle southerly 25 feet; thence at a right angle easterly 120 feet to the westerly line of Thirty-eighth avenue and point of commencement. Being a portion of O. L. Block 1159, also known as Block 2387 on Assessor's Map Book.

The City Attorney is hereby directed to examine the title to said land, and, if the same is found to be vested in the aforesaid owner, free of all encumbrances, and that the taxes up to and including the current fiscal year are paid, and that the so-called McEnerney title has been procured or sufficient money reserved for the purpose of procuring the same, to report the result of his examination to the Board of Supervisors, and also to cause a good and sufficient deed for said land to be executed and delivered to the City and County upon payment of the agreed purchase price as aforesaid. And the said deed to said land is hereby accepted.

Ayes—Supervisors Andriano, Canepa, Colman, Gallagher, Havenner, Hayden, McGovern, McSheehy, Miles, Peyser, Power, Roncovieri, Rossi, Shannon, Spaulding, Stanton, Suhr, Toner—18.

Purchase of Land for School Purposes, Northerly Line of Ulloa Street, Westerly From Thirty-eighth Avenue.

Also, Resolution No. 32287 (New Series), as follows:

Whereas, an offer has been received from Charles T. McNamara to convey to the City and County of San Francisco certain land on the northerly line of Ulloa street, distant 57 feet 6 inches westerly from Thirty-eighth avenue, required for school purposes; and

Whereas, the price at which said parcel of land is offered is the reasonable value thereof; therefore, be it

Resolved, That the offer of the said owner to convey to the City and County of San Francisco a good and sufficient fee simple title to the following described land, free of all encumbrances, for the sum of $3,000, be and the same is hereby accepted, the said lands being described as follows, to-wit:

Commencing at a point on the northerly line of Ulloa street, distant thereon 57 feet 6 inches westerly from the westerly line of Thirty-eighth avenue, running thence westerly along said northerly line of Thirty-eighth avenue 50 feet; thence at a right angle northerly 100 feet; thence at a right angle easterly 50 feet; thence at a right angle southerly 100 feet to the northerly line of Ulloa street and point of commencement. Being a portion of O. L. Block No. 1159, also known as Block 2387 on Assessor's Map Book.

The City Attorney is hereby directed to examine the title to said land, and, if the same is found to be vested in the aforesaid owner, free of all encumbrances, and that the taxes up to and including the current fiscal year are paid, and that the so-called McEnerney title has been procured or sufficient money reserved for the purpose of procuring the same, to report the result of his examination to the Board of Supervisors, and also to cause a good and sufficient deed for said land to be executed and delivered to the City and County upon payment of the agreed purchase price as aforesaid. And the said deed to said land is hereby accepted.

Ayes—Supervisors Andriano, Canepa, Colman, Gallagher, Havenner, Hayden, McGovern, McSheehy, Miles, Peyser, Power, Roncovieri, Rossi, Shannon, Spaulding, Stanton, Suhr, Toner—18.

Purchase of Land for School Purposes, Situated at North Line of Lawton Street, From Thirtieth Avenue to Thirty-first Avenue.

Also, Resolution No. 32288 (New Series), as follows:

Whereas, an offer has been received from Henry J. Kissel and Hugh J. Doyle to convey to the City and County of San Francisco certain land on the north line of Lawton street from Thirtieth to Thirty-first avenue, required for school purposes; and

Whereas, the price at which said parcel of land is offered is the reasonable value thereof; therefore, be it

Resolved, That the offer of the said owner to convey to the City and County of San Francisco a good and sufficient fee simple title to the following described land, free of all encumbrances, for the sum of $20,000, be and the same is hereby accepted, the said lands being described as follows, to-wit:

Commencing at a point formed by the intersection of the northerly line of Lawton street with the westerly line of Thirtieth avenue, running thence westerly along said northerly line of Lawton street 240 feet to the easterly line of Thirty-first avenue; thence at a right angle northerly along the easterly line of Thirty-first avenue 100 feet; thence at a right angle easterly 240 feet to the westerly line of Thirtieth avenue; thence at a right angle southerly along the westerly line of Thirtieth avenue 100 feet to the northerly line of Lawton street and point of commencement. Being a portion of O. L. Block 798, also known as Block 1876 on Assessor's Map Book.

The City Attorney is hereby directed to examine the title to said land, and, if the same is found to be vested in the aforesaid owners, free of all encumbrances, and that the taxes up to and including the current fiscal year are paid, and that the so-called McEnerney title has been procured or sufficient money reserved for the purpose of procuring the same, to report the result of his examination to the

Board of Supervisors, and also to cause a good and sufficient deed for said land to be executed and delivered to the City and County upon payment of the agreed purchase price as aforesaid. And the said deed to said land is hereby accepted.

Ayes—Supervisors Andriano, Canepa, Colman, Gallagher, Havenner, Hayden, McGovern, McSheehy, Miles, Peyser, Power, Roncovieri, Rossi, Shannon, Spaulding, Stanton, Suhr, Toner—18.

Passed for Printing.

The following resolution was *passed for printing*:

Condemnation of Land on Ocean Avenue, West of Mission Street, Emergency Hospital.

On recommendation of Public Buildings and Lands Committee.

Resolution No. ————— (New Series), as follows:

Resolved, by the Board of Supervisors of the City and County of San Francisco, that public interest and necessity require the acquisition by the City and County of San Francisco, a municipal corporation, of the following property, situated in the City and County of San Francisco, State of California, more particularly described as follows, to-wit:

Commencing at a point on the northerly line of Ocean avenue, distant westerly thereon 443.533 feet from the northwesterly line of Mission street, said point of commencement being the most easterly corner of that certain parcel of land designated Parcel 2, conveyed to the City and County of San Francisco by William B. McKinnon by deed recorded June 12, 1928, in Volume 1688, at page 58, Official Records of said City and County; thence westerly, northwesterly and northerly along the northeasterly line of the property so conveyed, being a curve to the right tangent to said northerly line of Ocean avenue at the point of commencement, radius 50 feet, central angle 106 degrees 26 minutes 08 seconds, an arc distance of 98.883 feet; thence continuing northerly along the easterly line of the property so conveyed, tangent to the preceding course, 33.206 feet; thence continuing northerly along said easterly line of the property so conveyed, and along the westerly line of the land deeded to said William B. McKinnon by the iCty and County of San Francisco, and recorded July 17, 1928, in Volume 1694, at page 328, Official Records of said City and County, being the arc of a curve to the right, tangent to the preceding course, radius 450 feet, central angle 11 degrees 16 minutes 43 seconds, an arc distance of 88.582 feet to the southwesterly line of Lot 18 of Wm. A. Lange's Subdivision of Block 1 of th Academy Tract, as per map thereof recorded in Map Book E and F, at page 68, Records of the City and County of San Francisco; thence southeasterly along the southwesterly line of said Lot 18, 72.63 feet to the westerly line of Lot 19 of said Wm. A. Lange's Subdivision of said Block 1; thence southerly, along the westerly line of said Lot 19, 135.71 feet to the northerly line of Ocean avenue; thence deflecting 78 degrees 26 minutes 50 seconds to the right and running westerly along said northerly line of Ocean avenue 24.55 feet, more or less, to the point of commencement.

Be it Further Resolved, That said property is suitable, adaptable, necessary and required for the public use of said City and County of San Francisco. It is necessary that a fee simple title be taken for such use.

The City Attorney is hereby ordered and directed to commence proceedings in eminent domain against the owners of said parcel of land and of any and all interest therein or claims thereto, for the condemnation thereof for the public use of the City and County of San Francisco, as aforesaid.

Adopted.

The following resolutions were *adopted*:

Circus Permit, Al G. Barnes' Wild Animal Shows, Bryant and Sixteenth Streets, April 24, 25, 26 and 27, 1930, Inclusive.

On recommendation of Police Committee.

Resolution No. 32289 (New Series), as follows:

Resolved, That Al G. Barnes' Wild Animal Shows be and they are hereby granted permission to conduct an open-air exhibition at Bryant and Sixteenth streets from April 24 to 27, 1930, inclusive.

Ayes—Supervisors Andriano, Canepa, Colman, Gallagher, Havenner, Hayden, McGovern, McSheehy, Miles, Peyser, Power, Roncovieri, Rossi, Shannon, Spaulding, Stanton, Suhr, Toner—18.

Cancellation of Taxicab Stand Permits.

Also, Resolution No. 32290 (New Series), as follows:

Resolved, That the following taxicab stand permits be and they are hereby cancelled:

Red Top Cab Company, 2539 Mission street.

Yellow Cab Company, 3086 Twenty-fourth street, 3660 Fillmore street and 1205 Larkin street.

Ayes—Supervisors Andriano, Canepa, Colman, Gallagher, Havenner, Hayden, McGovern, McSheehy, Miles, Peyser, Power, Roncovieri, Rossi, Shannon, Spaulding, Stanton, Suhr, Toner—18.

Referred.

The following matters were *referred to the Police Committee*:

Transfer of Taxicab Stand Permits.

Resolution No. ———— (New Series), as follows:

Resolved, That the following one-cab stand permits be and they are hereby transferred:

From De Luxe Cab Company to Green Top Cabs, Ltd., 651 Kearny street and 701 Hyde street.

From California Cab Company to Green Top Cabs, Ltd., 415 Leavenworth street, 804 Larkin street, 99 Jones street and 1698 Fifteenth street.

Approval of Taxicab Stand Permits.

Also, Resolution No. ———— (New Series), as follows:

Resolved, That the following one-cab stand permits be and they are hereby granted:

White and Blue Cab Company, 165 Eddy street and 560 Polk street.

Green Top Cabs, Ltd., 760 Broadway, 1455 Divisadero street, 2002 Divisadero street, 1607 Ellis street, 361 Hyde street, 1000 Jackson street, 1103 Leavenworth street, 745 Lincoln way, 734 Lombard street, 3740 Mission street, 901 Montgomery street, 294 Noe street, 460 Polk street, 294 Second avenue, 159 Sixth street, 706 Stanyan street, 3000 Steiner street and 495 Thirtieth avenue.

Passed for Printing.

The following bill was *passed for printing*:

Auctioneers' Ordinance Amendment.

On recommendation of Police Committee.

Bill No. 8228, Ordinance No. ———— (New Series), as follows:

Amending Sections 4 and 5 of Ordinance No. 6803 (New Series), entitled "Regulating the calling of auctioneers and sale of property by auction and prescribing a penalty for a violation thereof, and repealing Ordinance No. 2366 (New Series)."

Be it ordained by the People of the City and County of San Francisco as follows:

Section 1. Sections 4 and 5 of Ordinance No. 6803 (New Series), the title of which is recited above, are hereby amended to read as follows:

Section 4. The provisions of Section 2 shall not apply to any bona fide sale of a stock of merchandise by public auction where the owner thereof or the creditors of the owner are engaged in the legitimate closing out of the business of such owner and such sale is held upon the premises where the business of the owner had been carried on for not less than one year immediately preceding; provided, however, that no public auction conducted under the provisions of this section shall continue for a period longer than thirty days at any one time.

Section 5. In all cases where a public auction sale is held under the provisions of Section 4, the owner or the creditors of the owner must take an inventory of the stock of merchandise on the premises, which is to be sold at said public auction, and must submit said inventory to the Chief of Police at least 24 hours prior to the commencement of the auction sale. The inventory required by this section must show each item of merchandise contained in the stock to be offered for sale in the premises by public auction, and the said owner or creditor of the owner must take and subscribe an oath, to be attached to the inventory, that the said inventory contains a true and itemized account of all the property to be sold at said public auction, and that the same is a bona fide closing out of the business of such owner and that the owner intends to retire from said business. No property or merchandise shall be sold under the provisions of Section 4 except those itemized and shown in the inventory provided for herein.

Section 2. This ordinance shall take effect immediately.

Action Deferred.

The following matter was *laid over one week*:

Amending the Regulation of Contractors, and Owners of Restaurants, Cafeterias, or Soft Drink Parlors.

Bill No. 8229, Ordinance No. ———— (New Series), as follows:

Amending Sections 32 and 65 of Ordinance No. 5132 (New Series), entitled "Imposing license taxes on certain businesses, callings, trades or employments within the City and County of San Francisco."

Be it ordained by the People of the City and County of San Francisco as follows:

Section 1. Sections 32 and 65 of Ordinance No. 5132 (New Series), the title of which is recited above, are hereby amended to read as follows:

Section 32. (a) Every person, firm or corporation engaged in the occupation of and doing business as a contractor, sub-contractor, or as a builder, or engaged in the construction or repair of any building, street, sidewalk, sewer, engineering structure, or any engineering operation, or advertising himself as engaged in or superintending building construction, sewer construction, plumbing construction, street construction, or general construction, where the cost or value of the job or the bid tendered exceeds five hundred dollars, shall pay a license fee of twelve and fifty one-hundredths ($12.50) dollars per quarter.

(b) Every person, firm or corporation so engaged or advertising himself as so engaged in any business or job described as above, where the value or cost of the job or bid tendered is less than five hundred dollars, shall pay a license fee of five ($5) dollars per quarter.

(c) Every person, firm or corporation engaged in the business of sign or general painting (except automobile painters) shall pay a license fee of twelve and fifty one-hundredths ($12.50) dollars per quarter.

(d) Master electricians and master fixture electricians, as described under the provisions of Section 49 of this ordinance, shall pay the license fee provided for in Section 49, and shall thereby be exempt from the license fees imposed in Section 32 of this ordinance.

Section 65. Owners, agents, managers, or keepers of restaurants, cafeterias, or places of refreshment, or persons engaged as caterers, or persons conducting soft drink places, shall pay a license as follows:

Those whose gross receipts are less than three hundred dollars per quarter shall pay a license fee of five ($5) dollars per quarter.

Those whose gross receipts are more than three hundred dollars and less than ten thousand dollars per quarter shall pay a license fee of ten ($10) dollars per quarter, and for every additional two thousand dollars, or fraction thereof, gross receipts per quarter, one ($1) dollar per quarter.

Section 2. This ordinance shall take effect immediately.

Passed for Printing.

The following matters were *passed for printing*:

Ordering the Improvement of Phelps Street Between Jerrold Avenue and Evans Avenue, Etc.

On recommendation of Streets Committee.

Bill No. 8230, Ordinance No. ———— (New Series), as follows:

Ordering the performance of certain street work to be done in the City and County of San Francisco, approving and adopting specifications therefor.

Be it ordained by the People of the City and County of San Francisco as follows:

Section 1. The Board of Public Works in written communication filed in the office of the Clerk of the Board of Supervisors March 12, 1930, having recommended the ordering of the following street work, the same is hereby ordered to be done in the City and County of San Francisco in conformity with the provisions of the Street Improvement Ordinance of 1918 of said City and County of San Francisco, said work to be performed under the direction of the Board of Public Works, and to be done in accordance with the specifications prepared therefor by said Board of Public Works, and on file in its office, which said plans and specifications are hereby approved and adopted.

That said Board of Supervisors, pursuant to the provisions of Part II of the said Street Improvement Ordinance of 1918 of said City and County of San Francisco, does hereby determine and declare that the assessment to be imposed for the said contemplated improvements, respectively, may be paid in twenty installments; that the period of time after the time of the payment of the first installment when each of the succeeding installments must be paid is to be six months from the time of the payment of the preceding installment, and that the rate of interest to be charged on all deferred payments shall be seven per centum per annum.

The improvement of Phelps street between Jerrold avenue and Evans avenue, including the crossings of Phelps street and Innes avenue, Phelps street and Hudson avenue, Phelps street and Galvez avenue, and Phelps street and Fairfax avenue, by grading to official line and grade.

Section 2. This ordinance shall take effect immediately.

Ordering Improvement of Utah Street, From Eighteenth Street to Nineteenth Street, and of Nineteenth Street, From Utah Street to San Bruno Avenue.

Also, Bill No. 8231, Ordinance No. ———— (New Series), as follows:

Ordering the performance of certain street work to be done in the City and County of San Francisco, approving and adopting specifications therefor.

Be it ordained by the People of the City and County of San Francisco as follows:

Section 1. The Board of Public Works, in written communication filed in the office of the Clerk of the Board of Supervisors March 12, 1930, having recommended the ordering of the following street work, the same is hereby ordered to be done in the City and County of San Francisco in conformity with the provisions of the Street Improvement Ordinance of 1918 of said City and County of San Francisco, said work to be performed under the direction of the Board of Public Works, and to be done in accordance with the specifications prepared therefor by said Board of Public Works, and on file in its office, which said plans and specifications are hereby approved and adopted.

That said Board of Supervisors, pursuant to the provision of Part II of the said Street Improvement Ordinance of 1918 of said City and County of San Francisco, does hereby determine and declare that the assessment to be imposed for the said contemplated improvements, respectively, may be paid in twenty installments; that the period of time after the time of the payment of the first installment when each of the succeeding installments must be paid is to be six months from the time of the payment of the preceding installment, and that the rate of interest to be charged on all deferred payments shall be seven per centum per annum.

The improvement of Utah street, from Eighteenth street to Nineteenth street, and of Nineteenth street, from Utah street to San Bruno avenue, by grading to official line and subgrade, and by the construction of the following: Class "B," 2500-pound concrete in retaining walls, stairs, balustrades and gutters; bar reinforcing steel. Class "E," 6-inch concrete pavement; asphaltic concrete wearing surface (conform pavement); concrete sidewalk (2-course); armored concrete curb; concrete curb reset; cement mortar gutters; pipe rail fence (2 pipes and concrete posts); traffic warning reflectors; vitrified clay pipe sewers; vitrified clay pipe side sewers; vitrified clay pipe "Y" or "T" branches; vitrified clay pipe culverts; brick manholes, complete; brick drop manhole, complete; brick catchbasins, complete; reset brick catchbasin; conversion of standard brick manhole to drop manhole; storm water inlet.

Section 2. This ordinance shall take effect immediately.

Releasing, Cancelling and Annulling Contract Awarded A. G. Raisch for Improvement of Kirkham Street Between Sixteenth and Seventeenth Avenues.

Also, Bill No. 8232, Ordinance No. ———— (New Series), as follows:

Releasing, cancelling and annulling that certain contract made and entered into by and between A. G. Raisch and the Board of Public Works for the improvement of Kirkham street between Sixteenth and Seventeenth avenues and repealing Ordinnace No. 8672 (New Series).

Be it ordained by the People of the City and County of San Francisco as follows:

Section 1. That certain contract entered into by and between A. G. Raisch and the Board of Public Works, awarded by Resolution No. 109495 (Second Series), for the improvement of Kirkham street between Sixteenth and Seventeenth avenues, is hereby cancelled and annulled and A. G. Raisch is hereby released from said contract for the reasons specified in Resolution No. 109811 (Second Series).

Section 2. Ordinance No. 8672 (New Series), ordering the improvement of Kirkham street between Sixteenth and Seventeenth avenues, is hereby repealed.

Section 3. This ordinance shall take effect immediately.

Adopted.

The following resolutions were *adopted*:

Extension of Time to Complete Improvement of Alemany Boulevard.

On recommendation of Streets Committee.

Resolution No. 32291 (New Series), as follows:

Resolved, That Hanrahan Company is hereby granted an extension of ninety days' time from and after March 15, 1930, within which to complete the improvement of Alemany boulevard, Section D-1, Sickles avenue to Orizaba avenue, Contract 10.

This extension is granted upon the recommendation of the Board of Public Works for the reason that the contractor was unable to proceed with the work for almost one year after award of contract while condemnation suits against the property required for the right of way were being settled. Weather conditions, and also failure of the public utility corporations to remove their facilities, have further delayed the completion of the work. Work now progressing satisfactorily.

Ayes—Supervisors Andriano, Canepa, Colman, Gallagher, Havenner, Hayden, McGovern, McSheehy, Miles, Peyser, Power, Roncovieri, Rossi, Shannon, Spaulding, Stanton, Suhr, Toner—18.

Extension of Time to Complete Improvement of Faxon Avenue Between Thrift and Montana Streets.

Also, Resolution No. 32292 (New Series), as follows:

Resolved, That E. J. Treacy be granted an extension of sixty days' time from and after March 11, 1930, within which to complete the improvement of Faxon avenue between Thrift and Montana streets, where not already improved.

This extension is granted upon the recommendation of the Board of Public Works for the reason that the work has been completed; this extension is granted in order that the contractor may be protected during the period of acceptance and issuance of assessment.

Ayes—Supervisors Andriano, Canepa, Colman, Gallagher, Havenner, Hayden, McGovern, McSheehy, Miles, Peyser, Power, Roncovieri, Rossi, Shannon, Spaulding, Stanton, Suhr, Toner—18.

Extension of Time to Complete Improvement of Crossing, Sargent and Victoria Streets.

Also, Resolution No. 32293 (New Series), as follows:

Resolved, That the Municipal Construction Company is hereby granted an extension of sixty days' time from and after March 12, 1930, within which to complete the improvement of the crossing of Sargent and Victoria streets.

This extension is granted upon the recommendation of the Board of Public Works for the reason that the grading has been completed, and it is desirable that the work on the two adjacent streets, which is now being performed, be completed in order that the material may be hauled to the above mentioned crossing, thus allowing the work to proceed satisfactorily.

Ayes—Supervisors Andriano, Canepa, Colman, Gallagher, Havenner, Hayden, McGovern, McSheehy, Miles, Peyser, Power, Roncovieri, Rossi, Shannon, Spaulding, Stanton, Suhr, Toner—18.

Dedicating Certain Portions of Corbett Avenue and Graystone Terrace.

Also, Resolution No. 32305 (New Series), as follows:

Whereas, that certain deed, executed March 1, 1930, by and between Fernando Nelson & Sons, a corporation, and the City and County of

San Francisco, has been accepted by Resolution No. 32222 (New Series) of the Board of Supervisors; now, therefore, be it

Resolved, That portions of the lands covered by said deed, as hereinafter more particularly described, be and they are hereby set apart
and dedicated as an open public street, to be known as Corbett avenue, to-wit:

Parcels 1, 2, 3, 6 and 7 of above-mentioned deed.

Portions of Parcel 4 of above-mentioned deed, more particularly described as follows, to-wit:

Part of Lots 19 to 23, both inclusive, in Block 2719, as shown on
the map of Twin Peaks Terrace, filed July 30, 1915, in Book "H" of
Maps, pages 29, 30 and 31, in the office of the Recorder of the City and
County of San Francisco, State of California, described as follows:

Beginning at the point of intersection of the southerly line of Corbett avenue with the northwesterly line of Iron alley, as shown on the
map above referred to, running thence westerly along the said southerly line of Corbett avenue 9.725 feet to an angle point thereon; thence
deflecting 20 deg. 28 min. 15 sec. to the left and running southwesterly
along the southeasterly line of Corbett avenue 82.569 feet to an angle
point on the said southeasterly line of Corbett avenue; thence deflecting 19 deg. 04 min. 46 sec. to the left and continuing southwesterly
along the southeasterly line of Corbett avenue 84.615 feet; thence
northeasterly along the arc of a curve to the left, tangent to a line
deflecting 155 deg. 07 min. 43 sec. to the left from the preceding course
at the last named point, said curve having a radius of 125 feet and
a central angle of 19 deg. 15 min. 54 sec., a distance of 42.03 feet;
thence continuing northeasterly tangent to the preceding course 93.958
feet; thence continuing northeasterly along the arc of a curve to the
right, tangent to the preceding course, with a radius of 75 feet, central
angle 29 deg. 33 min. 16 sec., a distance of 38.687 feet to the said northwesterly line of Iron alley at a point distant southwesterly thereon
0.520 feet from the point of beginning; thence deflecting 72 deg. 39
min. 26 sec. to the left from the tangent to the preceding course at the
last named point and running northeasterly along said line of Iron
alley 0.520 feet to the southerly line of Corbett avenue and the point
of beginning.

Portion of Parcel 5 of above-mentioned deed, more particularly described as follows, to-wit:

That portion of Lots 15 to 17, both inclusive, of Block 2718, as shown
on the map of Twin Peaks Terrace, filed July 30, 1915, in Book "H"
of Maps, pages 29, 30 and 31, in the office of the Recorder of the City
and County of San Francisco, State of California, described as follows:

Beginning at the easterly termination of the curve of 10-foot radius
at the intersection of the northeasterly line of Graystone Terrace (formerly Fout avenue) and the westerly line of Corbett avenue, said
point of beginning being a point on the westerly line of Corbett avenue, running thence northerly along said westerly line of Corbett
avenue 67.71 feet to an angle point therein; thence deflecting 9 deg.
04 min. 55 sec. to the left and continuing northerly along said westerly
line of Corbett avenue 91.972 feet; thence deflecting 174 deg. 05 min.
41 sec. to the left and running southerly 167.576 feet to its intersection with the above-mentioned curve of 10-foot radius; thence northeasterly and northerly along the arc of a curve to the left, tangent to
a line deflecting 115 deg. 18 min. 23 sec. to the left from the preceding
course at the last named point, said curve having a radius of 10
feet, central angle 61 deg. 31 min. 01 sec., a distance of 10.737 feet to
the westerly line of Corbett avenue and the point of beginning.

Ayes—Supervisors Andriano, Canepa, Colman, Gallagher, Havenner,
Hayden, McGovern, McSheehy, Miles, Peyser, Power, Roncovieri, Rossi,
Shannon, Spaulding, Stanton, Suhr, Toner —18.

Passed for Printing.

The following matters were *passed for printing*:

Widths of Sidewalks, Valley Street.

Bill No. 8233, Ordinance No. ———— (New Series), as follows:

Amending Ordinance No. 1061, entitled "Regulating the Width of Sidewalks," approved December 18, 1903, by amending Section one hundred and sixty-eight thereof.

Be it ordained by the People of the City and County of San Francisco as follows:

Section 1. Ordinance No. 1061, entitled "Regulating the Width of Sidewalks," approved December 18, 1903, be and is hereby amended in accordance with the communication of the Board of Public Works filed in this office March 20, 1930, by amending Section one hundred and sixty-eight thereof to read as follows:

Section 168. The width of sidewalks on Valley street between Burnham street and Diamond street shall be twelve (12) feet.

The width of sidewalks on Valley street between Diamond street and Castro street shall be as shown on that certain map entitled "Map of Valley street between Diamond street and Castro street," showing the location of street and curb lines and the width of sidewalks.

The width of sidewalks on Valley street, the northerly side of, between Castro street and Noe street, shall be ten (10) feet.

The width of sidewalks on Valley street, the southerly side of, between Castro street and Noe street, shall be twenty-four (24) feet.

The width of sidewalks on Valley street between Noe street and San Jose avenue shall be twelve (12) feet.

Section 2. Any expense caused by the above change of walk widths shall be borne by the property owners.

Section 3. This ordinance shall take effect and be in force from and after its passage.

Widths of Sidewalks on Fair Avenue.

Also, Bill No. 8234, Ordinance No. ———— (New Series), as follows:

Amending Ordinance No. 1061, entitled "Regulating the Width of Sidewalks," approved December 18, 1903, by adding thereto a new section, to be numbered ten hundred and ninety-two.

Be it ordained by the People of the City and County of San Francisco as follows:

Section 1. Ordinance No. 1061, entitled "Regulating the Width of Sidewalks," approved December 18, 1903, be and is hereby amended in accordance with the communication of the Board of Public Works filed in this office March 24, 1930, by adding thereto a new section, to be numbered ten hundred and ninety-two, to read as follows:

Section 1092. The width of sidewalks on Fair avenue between Mission street and Coleridge street shall be seven (7) feet.

Section 2. Any expense caused by the above change of walk widths shall be borne by the property owners.

Section 3. This ordinance shall take effect and be in force from and after its passage.

Rereferred.

The following matter was *rereferred to the Streets Committee*:

Intention to Close Portion of Blackstone Court Lying Westerly From Franklin Street.

Resolution No. ———— (New Series), as follows:

Resolved, That the public interest requires that the certain following described portion of Blackstone court, lying westerly from Franklin street, be closed and abandoned; and be it

Further Resolved, That it is the intention of the Board of Supervisors to close and abandon all that portion of Blackstone court more particularly described as follows, to-wit:

All of Blackstone court lying between its westerly termination and the westerly line of Franklin street.

Said closing and abandonment of said Blackstone court shall be done and made in the manner and in accordance with the provisions of Section 2, Chapter 3, of Article VI of the Charter of the City and County of San Francisco, as amended, and the sections of said chapter and article following Section 2; and be it

Further Resolved, That the damage, cost and expense of said closing and abandonment be paid out of the revenue of the City and County of San Francisco.

And the Clerk of this Board is hereby directed to transmit to the Board of Public Works a certified copy of this resolution, and the Board of Public Works is hereby directed to give notice of said contemplated closing and abandonment of said Blackstone court in the manner provided by law, and to cause notice to be published in the official newspaper as required by law.

Adopted.

The following resolutions were *adopted*:

Granting Permission to W. H. Trowbridge to Lay a Two-Inch Pipe From Lombard Street and Columbus Avenue Across Lombard Street to Crystal Palace Salt Water Baths.

On recommendation of Streets Committee.

Resolution No. 32294 (New Series), as follows:

Resolved, That W. H. Trowbridge is hereby granted permission, revocable at will of the Board of Supervisors, to lay a two-inch pipe for conveying water from a well in the Entella Hotel, located at Lombard and Columbus avenue, across Lombard street to the Crystal Palace Salt Water Baths.

Provided, said two-inch pipe shall be laid to the satisfaction and under the supervision of the Board of Public Works.

Provided, W. H. Trowbridge shall pave and keep in repair, to the satisfaction of the Board of Public Works, the roadway for a space of two feet over said two-inch pipe.

Ayes—Supervisors Andriano, Canepa, Colman, Gallagher, Havenner, Hayden, McGovern, McSheehy, Miles, Peyser, Power, Roncovieri, Rossi, Shannon, Spaulding, Stanton, Suhr, Toner—18.

Award of Contract, Manufactured Furniture for School Department.

On recommendation of Supplies Committee.

Resolution No. 32295 (New Series), as follows:

Resolved, That award of contract be hereby made for furnishing manufactured furniture for School Department on bids submitted February 3, 1930 (Proposal No. 550), as follows, viz.:

Item
No.

1—16 biology tables, $79.40 each; R. Brandlein & Co.

2—140 bookkeeping tables, $19 each; Haas Wood and Ivory Works.

3—275 Cafeteria tables, round, diameter 36 inches, $7.85 each; Braas & Kuhn Co.

4—10 comptometer tables, $22.50 each; Haas Wood and Ivory Works.

5—60 designing tables, $2.70 each; The Woodcraft Company.

6—210 freehand drawing tables, $3.65 each; The Woodcraft Company.

7—1 lecture table, $89; Empire Planing Mill.

8—100 lunch-room tables, $9.31 each; R. Brandlein & Co.

9—200 lunch-room benches, $4.26 each; R. Brandlein & Co.

.0—50 library tables, $24.50 each; Empire Planing Mill.
.1—120 mechanical drawing tables, $20.50 each; Empire Planing Mill.
.2—25 sewing tables, $4.80 each; The Woodcraft Company.
.3—225 teachers' tables, $8.80 each; R. Brandlein & Co.
.4—150 dictionary stands, $2.60 each; The Woodcraft Company.
.5—500 easels, $3.20 each; The Woodcraft Company.
.6—50 gymnasium stools, $3.10 each; Empire Planing Mill.
.7—50 library card cases, $1.50 each; The Woodcraft Company.
.8—6 library book trucks, $21 each; Home Manufacturing Company.
.9—12 teachers' cabinets (storage), $25 each; Empire Planing Mill.
20—12 teachers' cabinets (wardrobe), $25 each; Empire Planing Mill.
21—100 work benches, $7.40 each; R. Brandlein & Co.

Resolved, That bonds for faithful performance of contract be required as follows, viz.: R. Brandlein & Co., $1,000; Haas Wood and Ivory Works, $500; Braas & Kuhn Co., $500; The Woodcraft Company, $800; Empire Planing Mill. $1,000; Home Manufacturing Company, none.

Note: All above awards are made to the lowest bidder except when award is made in consideration of deliveries or on account of the quality as determined by such tests as required or recommended by the Purchaser of Supplies.

Resolved, That all other bids submitted thereon be rejected.

Ayes—Supervisors Andriano, Canepa, Colman, Gallagher, Havenner, Hayden, McGovern, McSheehy, Miles, Peyser, Power, Roncovieri, Rossi, Shannon, Spaulding, Stanton, Suhr, Toner—18.

Rescinding and Reestablishing Loading Zones.

On recommendation of Traffic and Safety Committee.

Resolution No. 32296 (New Series), as follows:

Resolved, That the following loading zones, of the lengths specified, be rescinded and reestablished as specified herein, in front of or near the following addresses, in accordance with the provisions of Section No. 36 of Ordinance No. 7691 (New Series), as amended:

210 Ellis street, 27 feet, rescinded—Hotel Larne, 2 elevators, small stores.

818-822 Mission street, 36 feet, rescinded—Gille Show Print; National Piano Co; California Hat Co.; Western Rotogravure Co.

616-620 Sutter street, 36 feet to 27 feet, reestablished—Y. W. C. A.; 1 elevator and oil supply.

Ayes—Supervisors Andriano, Canepa, Colman, Gallagher, Havenner, Hayden, McGovern, McSheehy, Miles, Peyser, Power, Roncovieri, Rossi, Shannon, Spaulding, Stanton, Suhr, Toner—18.

Establishing Passenger Loading Zones.

Also, Resolution No. 32297 (New Series), as follows:

Resolved, That the following list of passenger loading zones, of the lengths specified, be established in front of or near the following addresses, in accordance with the provisions of Section No. 36 of Ordinance No. 7691 (New Series), as amended:

210 Ellis street, 18 feet—Hotel Larne passenger entrance.
3281—Sixteenth street, 18 feet—St. Matthew's Lutheran Church.

Ayes—Supervisors Andriano, Canepa, Colman, Gallagher, Havenner, Hayden, McGovern, McSheehy, Miles, Peyser, Power, Roncovieri, Rossi, Shannon, Spaulding, Stanton, Suhr, Toner—18.

Establishing Loading Zones.

Also, Resolution No. 32298 (New Series), as follows:

Resolved, That the following list of loading zones, of the lengths specified, be established in front of or near the following addresses,

in accordance with the provisions of Section 36 of Ordinance No. 76!
(New Series), as amended:

210 Ellis street, 18 feet—Hotel Larne; 2 elevators.
873-875 Folsom street, 18 feet—Western Nipple Works.
805 Montgomery street, 18 feet—Challenge Butter Co.

Ayes—Supervisors Andriano, Canepa, Colman, Gallagher, Havennen
Hayden, McGovern, McSheehy, Miles, Peyser, Power, Roncovieri, Ross,
Shannon, Spaulding, Stanton, Suhr, Toner—18.

ROLL CALL FOR THE INTRODUCTION OF RESOLUTIONS, BILLS AND COMMUNICATIONS NOT CONSIDERED OI REPORTED UPON BY A COMMITTEE.

Passed for Printing.

The following matters were *passed for printing*:

Appropriation for Construction of Gridiron and Canopy, Civic Auditorium.

Resolution No. ————— (New Series), as follows:

Resolved, That the sum of $44,625 be and the same is hereby set
aside, appropriated and authorized to be expended out of the General
Fund, 1929-1930, for the construction of the gridiron and canopy for
the stage of the Civic Auditorium, per award of contract to J. L.
Stuart, Manufacturing Co., and including possible extras, incidentals
and inspection.

Board of Public Works to Prepare Plans, Etc., Incinerator.

On recommendation of Finance and Health Committees.

Bill No. ————, Ordinance No. ————— (New Series), as follows:
Calling upon and directing the Board of Public Works to prepare
and furnish to the Board of Supervisors plans and estimates for an
incinerator and directing that said Board of Public Works make certain preliminary borings, observations and investigations in order to
determine the adaptability of certain sites for the construction thereon
of an incinerator.

That whereas, for the purpose of carrying out of the policy, as expressed by the people of the City and County of San Francisco, relative to the disposition of garbage, it is necessary that an incinerator
be constructed in the City and County of San Francisco without further or unnecessary delay;

Section 2. That the Board of Public Works be and it is hereby
directed to prepare and furnish, through the City Engineer, plans and
specifications for an incinerator of sufficient size, and of such type and
character, as will incinerate each twenty-four hours all of the garbage
and refuse collected in the City and County. Said plans and specifications shall include all foundation data necessary for the construction of said incinerator and show specifically the nature and arrangement of chimney, furnaces and approaches in, on or to said incinerator.

Sec. 3. That said Board of Public Works be and it is hereby further
directed to make, through the City Engineer, test pit observations,
test boring and test piling on such site or sites as may be available
for such incinerator at or near the present incinerator at Fifteenth
and De Haro streets, and to report to the board the result of said
observations and tests.

Sec. 4. That the cost of the work herein directed to be performed
shall be defrayed from the moneys heretofore appropriated by Resolution No. 32238 (New Series), heretofore adopted by the Board of Supervisors.

Sec. 5. That it is the intention of the Board of Supervisors that
when the aforesaid plans and specifications are approved by said
Board to accept bids for the construction of said incinerator in conformity therewith, and to grant to the person, firm or corporation who

ill make the most advantageous offer to the City for the construction hd operation of said incinerator, the exclusive privilege of incin-'ating the garbage and refuse collected in the City for a period of venty-five years, with the right of the City to recapture the same at a agreed price.

Sec. 6. This ordinance shall become effective immediately on its ssage.

Referred to Finance and Health Committees jointly.

Adopted.

The following resolution was *adopted*:

Acquisition of Land for Mills Airport.

Resolution No. 32299 (New Series), as follows:

Whereas, a joint committee composed of the members of the Finance Committee and the Airport Committee of the Board of Supervisors ave, pursuant to authority given by the Board of Supervisors, nego-iated with Ogden L. Mills relative to the acquisition of a suitable mount of property for the maintenance by the City and County of San Francisco of an airport in San Mateo County; and

Whereas, said Ogden L. Mills has intimated that the Mills Estate Company, of which he is a representative, would dispose of approxi-nately eleven hundred and twenty acres of land, including and adja-tent to the present Mills Field Airport, at a price of one million and fty thousand ($1,050,000) dollars, agreeing that the City might take uch portions of said property each year for a period of ten years as night be mutually agreed upon between the representatives of the Mills Estate Company and the representatives of the City and County of San Francisco; now, therefore, be it

Resolved, That the Board of Supervisors of the City and County of San Francisco deem it advisable that at the present time an airport of suffi-:ient size to take care of the present as well as the future needs of the City should be acquired and that the said eleven hundred and twenty acres owned by the said Mills Estate Company is in all respects suitable for the maintenance of said airport and by its acquisition the City has the further advantage of obtaining the benefit of all the improvements heretofore constructed by the City on Mills Field, which have cost approximately five hundred thousand ($500,000) dollars; and be it

Further Resolved, That the Finance Committee and the Airport Committee of this Board, together with the City Engineer and the City Attorney, be and they are hereby authorized to offer to said Ogden L. Mills the sum of one million and fifty thousand ($1,050,000) dol-lars for approximately eleven hundred and twenty acres of land, in-cluding and adjacent to the present Mills Field Airport, the said land to be acquired in such portions as may be hereafter mutually agreed upon between the City and the said Mills Estate Company and over a period not to exceed ten years and that said purchase price herein-before authorized to be without interest; and be it

Further Resolved, That the said committee be and it is hereby directed, upon the acceptance of said offer by said Ogden L. Mills, to present to this Board for its approval an agreement between the City and the said Mills Estate Company providing for the acquisition of said land upon the terms and conditions herein set forth.

Adopted by the following vote:

Ayes—Supervisors Andriano, Canepa, Colman, Gallagher, Havenner, Hayden, McGovern, McSheehy, Miles, Peyser, Power, Roncovieri, Rossi, Shannon, Spaulding, Stanton, Suhr, Toner—18.

Accepting Offer to Sell Land, Widening Clayton Street.

Resolution No. 32300 (New Series), as follows:

Resolved, That the offer of sale made by the following named owner to sell to the City and County of San Francisco the following described

land, required for the widening of Clayton street at Market street, to
the sum set forth opposite her name, be accepted:

Anna F. Holmberg, $2,000—All of Lot 12a of Block 2704, as per
Assessor's Block Books of the City and County of San Francisco, Stat
of California. (As per written offer on file.)

And the City Attorney is hereby authorized to examine the title
to said property, and if the same is found satisfactory, to accept, on
behalf of the City, a deed conveying said property to the City, free
and clear of all encumbrances and to record said deed, together with
a copy of this resolution, in the office of the Recorder of the City and
County of San Francisco.

Adopted by the following vote:

Ayes—Supervisors Andriano, Canepa, Colman, Gallagher, Havenner,
Hayden, McGovern, McSheehy, Miles, Peyser, Power, Roncovieri, Rossi
Shannon, Spaulding, Stanton, Suhr, Toner—18.

Intention to Close Portion of Bancroft Avenue.

Resolution No. 32301 (New Series), as follows:

Resolved, That the public interest requires that all that portion of
Bancroft avenue in the City and County of San Francisco lying between the easterly line of Phelps street and the westerly boundary
of the property described in the decree of the Superior Court of the
State of California, in and for the City and County of San Francisco, made and entered in an action entitled "The Bank of California.
National Association, as executor of the last will and testament of
Frank H. Gardiner, deceased, vs. All Persons, etc.," No. 39632, recorded
in the office of the Recorder of the City and County of San Francisco,
in Volume 1912 of Official Records, at page 171, on the 19th day of
September, 1929, and the property described in that certain deed from
The Bank of California, National Association, as executor of the last
will and testament of Frank H. Gardiner, deceased, to M. H. Cameron,
which said deed was recorded in the office of the Recorder of the City
and County of San Francisco in Book 1559 of Official Records, at
page 5, said boundary line being a line running from a point on the
southwesterly line of Bancroft avenue fifty-four (54) feet six (6)
inches from the southeasterly line of Phelps street north fifteen (15)
degrees twenty-nine (29) minutes thirty-eight (38) seconds east to a
point on the northeasterly line of Bancroft avenue twenty-five (25) feet
three (3) inches from the southeasterly line of Phelps street, be closed
and abandoned. Be it

Further Resolved, That it is the intention of the Board of Supervisors to close and abandon all that portion of Bancroft avenue lying
between the easterly line of Phelps street and the westerly boundary
of the property described in the decree of the Superior Court of the
State of California, in and for the City and County of San Francisco,
made and entered in an action entitled "The Bank of California, National Association, as executor of the last will and testament of Frank
H. Gardiner, deceased, vs. All Persons, etc.," No. 39632, recorded in
the office of the Recorder of the City and County of San Francisco in
Volume 1912 of Official Records, at page 171, on the 19th day of September, 1929, and the property described in that certain deed from
The Bank of California, National Association, as executor of the last
will and testament of Frank H. Gardiner, deceased, to M. H. Cameron,
which said deed was recorded in the office of the Recorder of the City
and County of San Francisco in Book 1559 of Official Records, at page
5, said boundary line being a line running from a point on the southwesterly line of Bancroft avenue fifty-four (54) feet six (6) inches
from the southeasterly line of Phelps street north fifteen (15) degrees
twenty-nine (29) minutes thirty-eight (38) seconds east to a point on
the northeasterly line of Bancroft avenue twenty-five (25) feet three
(3) inches from the southeasterly line of Phelps street.

Said closing up and abandonment of said portion of Bancroft avenue above described shall be done and made in the manner and in accordance with the provisions of Section 2, Chapter 3 of Article 6 of the Charter as amended, and the sections of said chapter and article following Section 2. Be it

Further Resolved, That the damage, cost and expense of said closing and abandonment of said portion of Bancroft avenue as above described be paid out of the revenue of the City and County of San Francisco.

And the Clerk is hereby directed to transmit to the Board of Public Works a certified copy of this resolution, and the Board of Public Works is hereby directed to give notice of said contemplated closing and abandonment of said street in the manner provided by law, and to cause notice to be published in the San Francisco Chronicle, as required by law.

Adopted by the following vote:

Ayes—Supervisors Andriano, Canepa, Gallagher, Havenner, Hayden, McGovern, McSheehy, Miles, Power, Roncovieri, Rossi, Shannon, Spaulding, Stanton, Suhr, Toner—16.

Absent—Supervisors Colman, Peyser—2.

Celebration of Construction of Sunset Boulevard.

Supervisor Power presented:

Resolution No. 32302 (New Series), as follows:

Whereas, publicity has been given to a proposed celebration in connection with the beginning of construction work on the Sunset boulevard; and

Whereas, the proposed date for the celebration is tentatively set for early in April; and

Whereas, it will be impossible to begin any construction work on the Sunset boulevard until after the bonds are delivered and the necessary ordinances are passed by this Board and bids called for and received, which will delay actual work for a period of at least ninety days; and

Whereas, the information on this matter has been conveyed to the residents of the Sunset District by publicity agents; therefore, be it

Resolved, That the residents of the Sunset District be and they are hereby advised of the facts as recited in the preamble of this resolution; and be it

Further Resolved, That the Streets Committee of this Board be instructed to notify, through the press, the residents and property owners of the Sunset District, that they will be given ample notice of the commencement of work on the boulevard, so that they may plan for any celebration they wish.

Adopted by the following vote:

Ayes—Supervisors Andriano, Canepa, Gallagher, Havenner, Hayden, McGovern, McSheehy, Miles, Power, Roncovieri, Rossi, Shannon, Spaulding, Stanton, Suhr, Toner—16.

Absent—Supervisors Colman, Peyser—2.

Citizens' Reception Committee. University of Southern California Band.

Resolution No. 32303 (New Series), as follows:

Resolved, That his Honor the Mayor be and is hereby requested to appoint a citizens' committee to greet the University of Southern California (Trojan) Band, which will arrive in San Francisco April 15, 1930, to give a concert under the auspices of the Optimist Club.

Adopted by the following vote:

Ayes—Supervisors Andriano, Canepa, Gallagher, Havenner, Hayden, McGovern, McSheehy, Miles, Power, Roncovieri, Rossi, Shannon, Spaulding, Stanton, Suhr, Toner—16.

Absent—Supervisors Colman, Peyser—2.

Regimental Colors 347th Artillery.

Supervisor Spaulding presented:

Resolution No. 32304 (New Series), as follows:

Whereas, the colors of the famous 363d Infantry Regiment are on display in the rotunda of the City Hall; and

Whereas, it is desirable and appropriate that the regimental colors and standard of the 347th Field Artillery (91st Division), another San Francisco fighting unit of the World War, which are now in Sacramento, be returned to San Francisco and be placed permanently in the City Hall with the colors of the 363d Infantry; now, therefore, be it

Resolved, That his Excellency Governor C. C. Young be and he is hereby requested to turn over the regimental colors and standard of the 347th Field Artillery to the Mayor and Board of Supervisors of the City and County of San Francisco.

Adopted by the following vote:

Ayes—Supervisors Andriano, Canepa, Gallagher, Havenner, Hayden, McGovern, McSheehy, Miles, Power, Roncovieri, Rossi, Shannon, Spaulding, Stanton, Suhr, Toner—16.

Absent—Supervisors Colman, Peyser—2.

Extension of Municipal Railway to Sloat Boulevard.
Supervisor Power presented:

Resolution No. ————— (New Series), as follows:

Whereas, if the present terminus at Forty-eighth avenue and Taravai street of the Municipal Railway, known as the "Taravai Line," were extended to Sloat boulevard at a point near the Fleishhacker Playground, it would probably greatly improve the income of said line; now, therefore, be it

Resolved, That the Board of Public Works be and they are hereby requested to furnish to the Board of Supervisors an estimate of the cost of extending this line of the Municipal Railway to Sloat boulevard, and they are also requested to make a survey of the possible increase in receipts provided said extension were made.

Referred to Public Utilities Committee.

Finance Committee to Appropriate $5,000 for Manufacturing and Distribution Census.

Supervisor Gallagher presented:

Resolved, That the Finance Committee is requested to recommend the sum of five thousand dollars for the purpose of assisting in the taking of a manufacturing and distribution census under the auspices of the United States Government.

Referred to Finance and Industrial Development Committee.

Street Paving Matters.

Relative to newspaper reports of alleged irregularities in street paving matters, City Engineer M. M. O'Shaughnessy and Assistant City Engineer Clyde Healy were heard at length.

Motion.

Supervisor Stanton moved (a) that the Streets Committee investigate these different matters, and (b) that the Board of Public Works furnish the committee with a list of all extras done on streets and boulevards in the City of San Francisco in the last four years, and the number of yards of private property that has been filled in, the names of the property owners and the amounts of money that were paid for that work.

Supervisor Gallagher asked for a segregation of the motion.

So *ordered.*

Whereupon, the roll was called on the question "That the Streets Committee investigate these different matters," and the same *carried* by the following vote:

Ayes—Supervisors Canepa, Havenner, McGovern, McSheehy, Miles, Peyser, Power, Roncovieri, Rossi, Shannon, Spaulding, Stanton—12.

Noes—Supervisors Andriano, Colman, Gallagher, Hayden, Suhr, Toner—6.

Thereupon, the roll was called on the latter part of the motion, "That the Board of Public Works furnish the committee with a list of all extras done on streets and boulevards in the City of San Francisco in the last four years, and the number of yards of private property that has been filled in, the names of the property owners and the amounts of money that were paid for that work," and the same carried by the following vote:

Ayes—Supervisors Canepa, Gallagher, Havenner, Hayden, McGovern, McSheehy, Miles, Peyser, Power, Roncovieri, Rossi, Shannon, Spaulding—16.

Noes—Supervisors Andriano, Colman—2.

Thereupon, the roll was called on the motion as a whole, and the same *carried* by the following vote:

Ayes—Supervisors Canepa, Havenner, McGovern, McSheehy, Miles, Peyser, Power, Roncovieri, Rossi, Shannon, Spaulding, Stanton, Toner—13.

Noes—Supervisors Andriano, Colman, Gallagher, Hayden, Suhr—5.

Air Maneuvers at Sacramento.

Supervisor McSheehy moved that the Mayor be authorized to appoint a committee to go to Sacramento to attend United States army air maneuvers.

Supervisor Spaulding announced that Major Gilmore of the United States army would transport officials by plane, leaving from Mills Field.

The Mayor appointed members of the Airport Committee, Supervisors McSheehy and Toner.

Referred.

Supervisor Gallagher presented two bills sent to him, one for $65 and another for $35, being for official celebration greeting the "Malolo" and Golden Gate bridge celebration.

Referred to Public Welfare Committee.

ADJOURNMENT.

There being no further business, the Board at 6:55 p. m. adjourned.

J. S. DUNNIGAN, Clerk.

Approved by the Board of Supervisors May 5, 1930.

Pursuant to Resolution No. 3402 (New Series) of the Board of Supervisors of the City and County of San Francisco, I, John S. Dunnigan, hereby certify that the foregoing is a true and correct copy of the Journal of Proceedings of said Board of the date thereon stated and approved as recited.

JOHN S. DUNNIGAN,
Clerk of the Board of Supervisors.
City and County of San Francisco.

Monday, April 7, 1930

·rnal of Proceedings
Board of Supervisors

City and County of San Francisco

Recorder Printing and Publishing Company
337 Bush Street, S. F.

Lightning Source UK Ltd.
Milton Keynes UK
UKHW012017201118
332601UK00013B/2090/P

9 780332 769172